DICKENSON SERIES ON CONTEMPORARY THOUGHT IN ACCOUNTING
John W. Buckley, Editor

CONTEMPORARY STUDIES IN THE EVOLUTION OF ACCOUNTING THOUGHT
Michael Chatfield

CONTEMPORARY THOUGHT ON FEDERAL INCOME TAXATION
Charles J. Gaa

CONTEMPORARY ACCOUNTING AND ITS ENVIRONMENT
John W. Buckley

CONTEMPORARY ACCOUNTING AND THE COMPUTER
Leonard W. Hein

CONTEMPORARY COST ACCOUNTING AND CONTROL
George J. Benston

CONTEMPORARY AUDITING
Wayne S. Boutell

CONTEMPORARY THOUGHT IN ACCOUNTING AND ORGANIZATIONAL CONTROL
K. Fred Skousen
Belverd E. Needles, Jr.

forthcoming:

CONTEMPORARY ACCOUNTING THEORY
Eldon S. Hendriksen
Bruce P. Budge

ACCOUNTING

an information systems approach

John W. Buckley
University of California, Los Angeles

Kevin M. Lightner
California State University, San Diego

Dickenson Publishing Company, Inc.
Encino, California, and Belmont, California

ISBN-0-8221-0097-5

Library of Congress Catalog Card Number: 72-93646

Printed in the United States of America

Printing (last digit): 9 8 7 6 5 4 3 2 1

Cover and interior designed by Jill Casty

To those teachers who set us on the academic path and to our students, past and present, from whom we have learned so much, we dedicate this volume.

ACKNOWLEDGMENTS

The authors express their sincere appreciation to the many persons who assisted them on this project, and to the authors and publishers who have generously granted permission for the use of illustrative materials. Specific credit is cited in these instances throughout the text. In addition, we would like to note that the many questions taken or adapted from the CPA examinations, which appear at the ends of chapters, are copyrighted by the American Institute of Certified Public Accountants, Inc. and are used with their permission. Also, the tables of logarithms in Appendix C are from Thomas Marshall Simpson, Zareh M. Pirenian, Bolling H. Crenshaw, and John Riner, *Mathematics of Finance,* Fourth Edition © 1969, pp. 441–457, reprinted by permission of Prentice-Hall, Inc., Englewood Cliffs, New Jersey.

Our particular thanks go to Richard A. Samuelson, Belverd Needles, Jr., Alan P. Johnson, John J. Willingham, Robert W. Koehler, Leonard W. Hein, and Clayton Tidyman for offering constructive comments on the manuscript at various stages.

We are especially grateful to Joseph V. Nash, John Czerniewicz, and Hungfu Chiang for specific assistance on certain chapters. Marlene Buckley and Sharon Douglas were particularly helpful to us in editing and revising the manuscript. The editing and production of the text was ably carried out by Jane Johnson and Elaine Linden.

J.W.B.
K.M.L.

contents

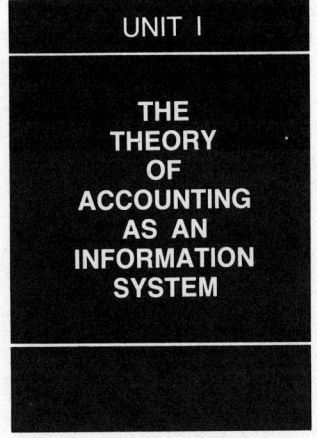

CHAPTER

4 THE STRUCTURE OF ACCOUNTING 85

CHAPTER

5 INCOME MEASUREMENT 120

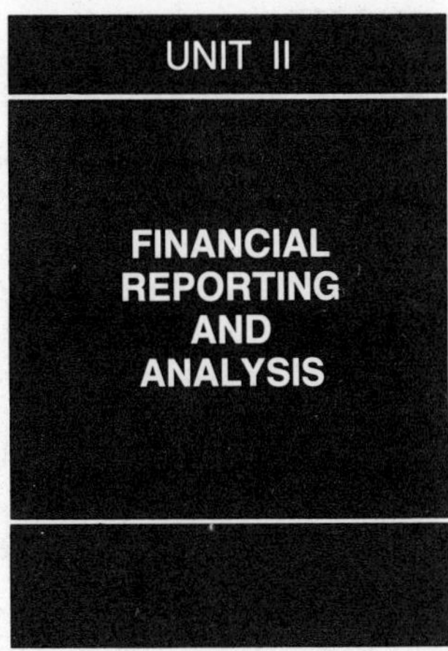

CHAPTER

6 FINANCIAL STATEMENTS AND CONVENTIONS 158

CHAPTER 7 FINANCIAL STATEMENT ANALYSIS 236

CHAPTER 8 PRICE-LEVEL ACCOUNTING AND REPORTING 299

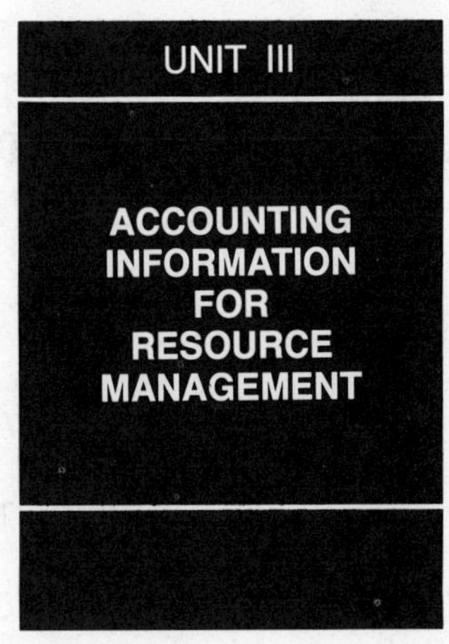
UNIT III
ACCOUNTING INFORMATION FOR RESOURCE MANAGEMENT

CHAPTER 11 CREDIT MANAGEMENT 429

CHAPTER 12 INVENTORY MANAGEMENT 474

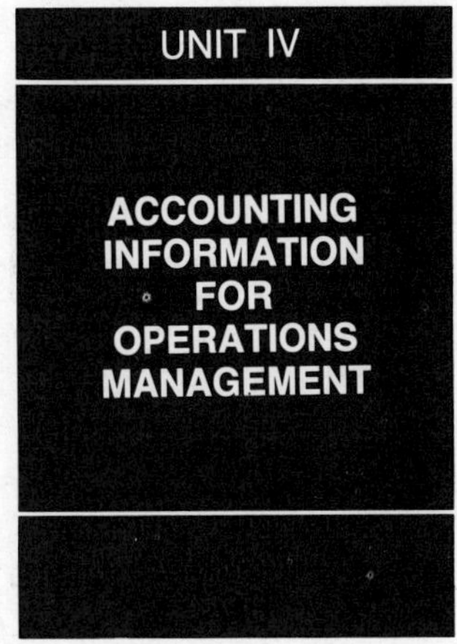
UNIT IV
ACCOUNTING
INFORMATION
FOR
OPERATIONS
MANAGEMENT

CHAPTER 15 ACCOUNTING INFORMATION FOR MARKETING MANAGEMENT 613

CHAPTER 16 ACCOUNTING INFORMATION FOR PERSONNEL AND ADMINISTRATIVE OPERATIONS 662

UNIT V
ACCOUNTING INFORMATION FOR CONTROL

CHAPTER

19 COST ACCOUNTING SYSTEMS 800

CHAPTER

20 STANDARD COSTS AND VARIANCE ANALYSIS 853

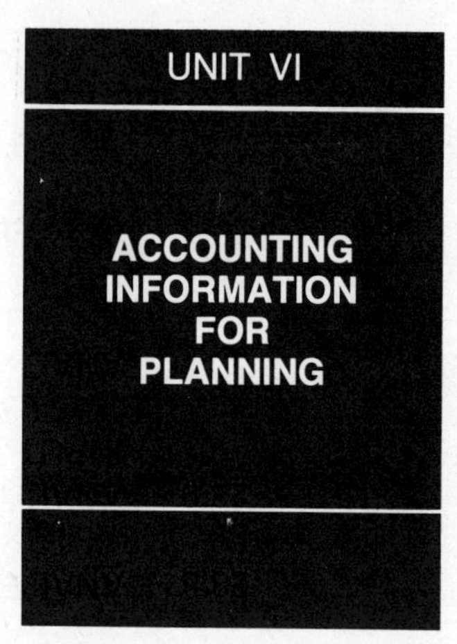
UNIT VI
ACCOUNTING INFORMATION FOR PLANNING

CHAPTER 22 FORECASTING 952

CHAPTER 23 OPERATIONAL BUDGETING 993

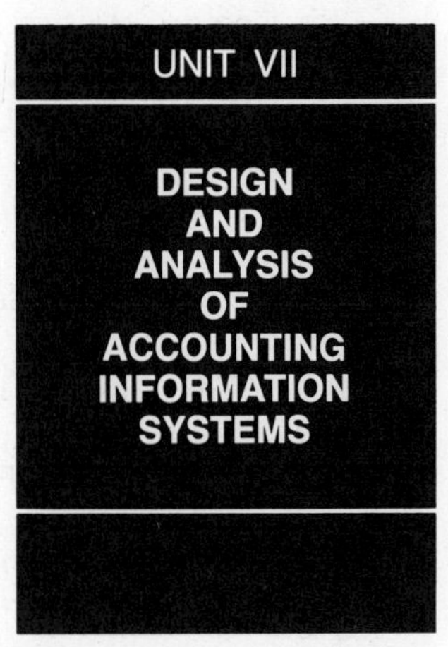
UNIT VII
DESIGN AND ANALYSIS OF ACCOUNTING INFORMATION SYSTEMS

CHAPTER

27 FINANCIAL AND OPERATIONAL AUDITING 1171

PREFACE

This book is an introduction to accounting as an *art* and as a *science*. The art of accounting refers to those traditional principles and practices which have evolved through the ages in a manner analogous to the common law. The collective art of accounting—which has been labeled facetiously as "the sacred cows of accounting"—has been the main thrust of most introductions to the field, but in most instances these materials are unaccompanied by historical perspective or linkage. In part, our text adheres to this tradition. It acknowledges that the social behavior of man—particularly when incorporated within some unique organization such as a profession—always has and undoubtedly always will be in measure ritualistic.

The aspiring accountant must master the art of accounting. This ability is needed not only for membership in the accounting profession, but as a medium for communication with other accountants. In common with all professions, the art of accounting includes a unique vocabulary, uniques rules of evidence and inference, ethical codes, and other norms and artifacts of professionalism.

The art of accounting, as with all viable ritualism, is not impervious to change. In fact it must change in order to survive. The art of accounting is in a constant state of evolution.

While the art of accounting provides the exclusivity which is essential to professionalism, it also tends to dogma and insularity. If these tendencies remain unchallenged they will in time reduce accounting from a socially meaningful activity to a relic of historic interest only. A viable profession must find the proper balance between its art and science, and this balance should be present in its educational literature. Art speaks to those qualities which make a profession unique, while science inquires into issues of relevance.

The task of science is to seek the meaning of things. The inquiry may be of an historic nature: "What were the conditions which gave rise to a particular belief or practice?" The inquiry may be of contemporary importance: "What do the users of accounting services expect in the way of information, benefits, or controls?" Or the inquiry may be directed toward the future: "What demands will society place upon accounting services in the next decade?"

From an educator's point of view the learning process incident to the art of accounting is relatively well defined. It consists of mastering a vocabulary and a set of rules, i.e., the "common law of accounting." It consists of analyzing and solving problems for which traditional formats are available. It consists of developing professional judgment by being apprenticed to more experienced accountants.

By contrast, developing the scientific acumen of the student accountant is not an easy task. To attempt to do so in a text is even more difficult. But we believe that a worthwhile attempt has been made in this book. The objective here is to develop in students of accounting analytic skills which look beyond traditional formats for better solutions to old problems and the ability to diagnose new problems; to develop a healthy skepticism in the student such that he will not take things at face value but search constantly for meaning; to inculcate within the student the belief that a profession is valueless unless the services it renders to its users are valuable. We believe that student accountants should not only be accommodating to change but able to initiate orderly development.

The scientific validity of accounting arises from its role as an information system. The term *information system* as used in this text should not be confused with computers. Computers are data processors of significant ability and are part of the arsenal of resources available to the accountant in developing and managing his information system. "Information systems" connotes a formalized approach to the design and management of information flows. This focus suggests that the validity of accounting rests upon its relevance as an information system which is geared to the utility of its users. An important consideration of information systems is the value of information. Implicit is a cost-benefit model which urges that we constantly seek for the means to provide better information at lower cost.

Accounting: An Information Systems Approach is a comprehensive and fairly demanding introduction to accounting. It integrates financial and management accounting within the framework of information systems. Its format can be described by the titles assigned to the major divisions of the book:

I. THE THEORY OF ACCOUNTING AS AN INFORMATION SYSTEM
II. FINANCIAL REPORTING AND ANALYSIS
III. ACCOUNTING INFORMATION FOR RESOURCE MANAGEMENT
IV. ACCOUNTING INFORMATION FOR OPERATIONS MANAGEMENT
V. ACCOUNTING INFORMATION FOR CONTROL
VI. ACCOUNTING INFORMATION FOR PLANNING
VII. DESIGN AND ANALYSIS OF ACCOUNTING INFORMATION SYSTEMS

While this book incorporates more quantitative analysis than most introductory texts, the level of presentation has been held within the range of abilities of most contemporary accounting professors and students. In the typical instance alternative nonmathematical solutions accompany the quantitative treatment.

The authors hope that instructors and students in accounting will find this approach to be stimulating and relevant to the needs of our times.

John W. Buckley, Los Angeles
Kevin M. Lightner, San Diego

UNIT I

THE THEORY OF ACCOUNTING AS AN INFORMATION SYSTEM

The key words in the title of this text are "accounting," "information," and "systems." *Accounting* is an activity which identifies, collects, processes, reports, and analyzes economic data. *Information* is useful data, and a *system* is a network of resources geared to a particular purpose, in this case the transformation of data into information.

In Unit I we establish the framework for accounting as an information system. As such we focus on its importance in identifying, collecting, processing, reporting, and analyzing useful data in a controlled manner.

The notion of useful data means that the accounting system has utility only in satisfying needs—it has no inherent value. These needs may be personal, as exemplified by a checkbook register which gives us a running balance of our bank account; or they may be organizational, as when a business firm wishes to know its profit from operations for a specific period of time.

In this text we will concentrate on the accounting information system as it relates to organizations. Our view of an organization contains the following characteristics:

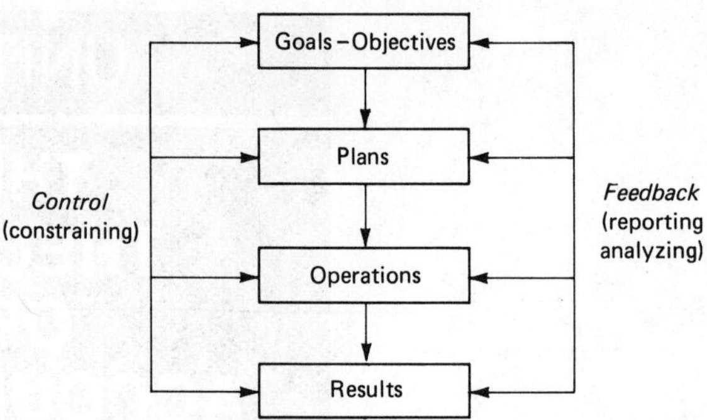

An organization has certain *goals* or *objectives.* An objective of most business organizations is to maximize profit; not-for-profit organizations seek to optimize cost-effectiveness. *Plans* are developed to meet these goals. These plans include long-range and short-range forecasting and budgeting. *Operations* commence in accordance with the plans, and the *results* of operations are summarized periodically.

Control is viewed as a continuous constraint on the system. It is a necessary and useful constraint in that it promotes conformance of plans and operations to the objectives. Controls take many forms—they include policies and procedures, mechanical devices, or stratified positions of authority.

Feedback is also a continuous activity. It reports conformance or variation from planned operations. It reports on the relevance of controls to operations. Feedback is distinguished from control. The fact that a control device is measuring a deviation does not mean that this fact is being reported; such reporting is a function of feedback. Also, a process may be over- or under-controlled, or controls may not be working that should be working. It is a function of feedback to bring these matters to the timely attention of those who can take corrective action. Finally, feedback supplies information on the results of operations for comparison with the original goals of the organization. It also informs outside parties as to the progress of the firm. These reports not only indicate whether or not the objectives have been reached, but they diagnose probable causes for variations.

We view the organization as a *goal-seeker,* with realistically defined needs, whose methods for achievement are rational. This view enables us to employ a systematic methodology in defining the needs of an organization and in designing systems to provide information in a time and manner conducive to the optimum deployment of resources. The methodology we have chosen for this purpose is called *the systems approach.* This approach makes it possible for us to formalize the study of organizations and their information systems. It is allied to model-building in that we abstract the organization from its environment. From unlimited data in the organization's environment, we extract data that is pertinent to its own needs. This data most often requires processing or "transforming" before it becomes useful for decision making purposes.

There are costs attached to converting data into information, and it follows that we must constantly make trade-offs between the value of information and the cost of obtaining it. The timeliness of information is another important consideration; each bit of information has relevance to a fleeting need and becomes less valuable or useful if it is not available at that strategic moment.

Most organizations have a number of information systems; when these are combined functionally into one system we refer to it as an *integrated* system. One of the most important information systems in a modern organization is the accounting system, which is also one of the oldest systems. Until recently, however, accounting has been considered more of an art than a science. Its practices are steeped in tradition, and its principles have evolved from practice in a manner reminiscent of common law. It has surrounded itself with a mysterious aura, including jargon, as a form of protectionism; and more often than not in the past, executive decisions have been constrained by what the accounting system *does* provide in the way of information as contrasted with what it could or *should* provide if it were responsive to the organization's needs.

The thrust of contemporary accounting education and practice views accounting as a viable information system that meets the needs of its users, both those internal and external to the firm. In Unit I we build the case for accounting as an information system, in conformance with general systems and information theory. In later units we show how the accounting system provides information relevant to resource management and planning and control.

CHAPTER

1

SYSTEMS AND INFORMATION SYSTEMS

1.1 ACCOUNTING IS AN INFORMATION SYSTEM

Accounting is an information system. Its purpose is to provide economic data to a variety of decision makers according to their needs and entitlement to the information. The sub-functions of accounting include data collection, processing and control, summarization, distribution, and interpretation.

The users of accounting data can be partitioned into two broad groups: (1) external and (2) internal. External users include stockholders, investors generally, creditors, governmental agencies, customers and vendors, competitors, labor unions, and the public interest at large. Internal users comprise managers who require different information depending on their level in an organization or on the particular function they perform.

Accounting is an information system, so the learning of accounting should begin with an introduction to "systems" and "information systems" because the

Portions of chapter 1 appeared in John W. Buckley, "Goal-Process-System Interaction in Management," *Business Horizons*, December 1971, pp. 81–92. The common material is reproduced with the permission of the editor, *Business Horizons.*

accounting system conforms in principle to these larger systems, and because systems concepts and terminology are increasingly finding their way into accounting literature and practice. With this foundation students in accounting will be able to draw inferences from systems in general to the accounting system in particular, and *vice versa*.

1.2 THE NEED FOR CLARITY IN DEFINING SYSTEMS

"Systems" is one of the most ubiquitous words in our vocabulary. We were introduced to this term at an early age. We learned of "school systems," the "solar system," and other elementary systems. Our systems vocabulary grew as our education progressed. We learned of "physiological systems," "transportation systems," "political systems," "the systems approach," "planning and control systems," and a host of other systems concepts. Clearly then, the term "systems" has wide application.

Unfortunately, the meaning of "systems" is shrouded in ambiguity. Ask for a succinct definition of the word, and you will be surprised to find how vague are the answers. Those with more exposure to systems theory couch their ambiguity in expressions such as "interconnected networks of interrelated entities," leaving themselves and their listeners with a vague uneasiness as to the meaning of the word.

This ambiguity leads to much abuse of systems concepts and hinders our efforts to design, operate, and evaluate systems. But the notion of a system is so basic and so potentially useful that we should try to clarify it. We should distinguish at once between two broad uses of the word "systems" as it is employed in:

1. General systems theory.
2. Operating systems theory.

1.3 GENERAL SYSTEMS THEORY

General systems theory refers to a *way* or *approach* by which to observe and solve problems. Because of its emphasis on the *way* in which one tackles problems, it is often referred to as "the systems approach," or more viscerally, as "organized common sense."

The systems approach insists on the broadest possible understanding of a problem, involves exploring all feasible alternatives, and selects the best solution through rational means.

To illustrate the systems approach, consider the problem of meeting the demand for more electricity.[1] A search for feasible alternatives begins. Long-range solutions provide more flexibility in that they allow us to consider alternatives which may not be feasible at present. If the need is immediate, our search is bounded by the existing state of technology.

---

[1] The June 12, 1972, issues of *Time* and *Newsweek* contain feature articles on the growing electricity crisis. Also see Barry Commer, *The Closing Circle* (New York: Alfred A. Knopf, Inc., 1971), and Paul R. and Anne H. Ehrlich, *Population Resources Environment: Issues in Human Ecology* (San Francisco: W. H. Freeman & Co., 1970).

There are basically three means for generating electrical power at present: (1) hydroelectricity, (2) the use of hydrocarbons such as coal, gas, or oil, and (3) nuclear power. Feasibility involves technological, economic, and social considerations. There are pros and cons to each alternative. While hydroelectric power plants produce "clean" electricity at relatively low cost, there is an insufficient number of suitable sites for dams and the distance to major user areas is too great. A new social cost has been added recently in the destruction of scenic river beds. Conventional power plants using coal or oil produce smog and other contaminants, and they are inefficient in converting hydrocarbons into electric power. Nuclear plants are more efficient, but the problem of thermal pollution and the fear of accidents weigh heavily on the negative scale.

In the language of general systems theory, every alternative has a cost-benefit relationship. Thus, it is not practical to think of zero-cost solutions, but rather to seek the option which has the lowest relative cost and highest benefit. (This may involve a combination of alternatives.) In our example, a decision *not to pollute the air* may necessitate a decision *to pollute the water.* Final decisions of this type are often made in the social arena.

Suppose that perfect data are available which lead us to favor nuclear plants for techno-economic reasons. While our problem may appear to be solved in quantitative terms, the systems approach requires that we go further, for even good theoretic solutions may fail for want of public acceptance. The systems approach requires that we ask for public opinion. If it is favorable, implementation can proceed. But if it is opposed, it becomes necessary either to change public opinion or to choose a less optimal strategy.

In those instances where the best solution involves a technology which has no operating history, the systems approach calls for testing under real-world conditions. These simulations provide decision makers with positive instead of theoretical data and reduce the risks of choosing and implementing faulty solutions.

This discussion points to some fundamentals of general systems theory: (1) it consists of a *structured* approach to problem-solving; (2) its *methodology is explicit,* which means that there are guidelines to problem-solving; (3) the *boundaries* of a problem are identified; (4) all feasible solutions are measured in terms of *cost-benefit;* and (5) the *best solution,* in the light of technical, economic, and social considerations, is adopted.

1.4 OPERATING SYSTEMS THEORY

We have defined "systems" in the context of general systems theory as a scientific approach to problem-solving. But "systems" has another meaning. When we speak of a transportation system, an accounting system, or a weapons delivery system, we think of a system not as a methodology or approach, but rather as a functioning medium through which things get accomplished.

We can obtain a better understanding of "systems" in the operational sense of the term by placing it in a context with two other concepts with which it is closely related. These related terms are "goal" and "process," which together with "system" form a cohesive theoretic structure which we will refer to as a *GPS Complex* (Exhibit 1-1).

EXHIBIT 1-1 GPS COMPLEX

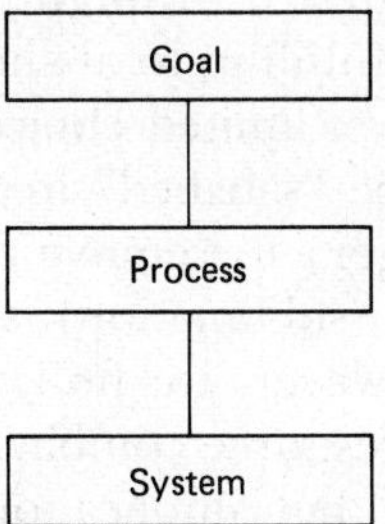

A *goal* is an objective—some desired attainment. A *process* is a set of activities or a strategy by which we attain goals. The *system* comprises the resources needed to perform the strategy.

EXHIBIT 1-2 DEFINITION OF GPS TERMS

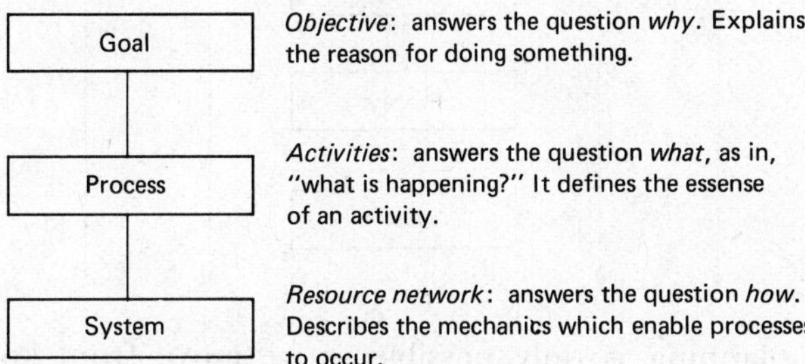

The logic of the GPS Complex can be illustrated by an example from physiology (Exhibit 1-3).

EXHIBIT 1-3 AN EXAMPLE FROM PHYSIOLOGY

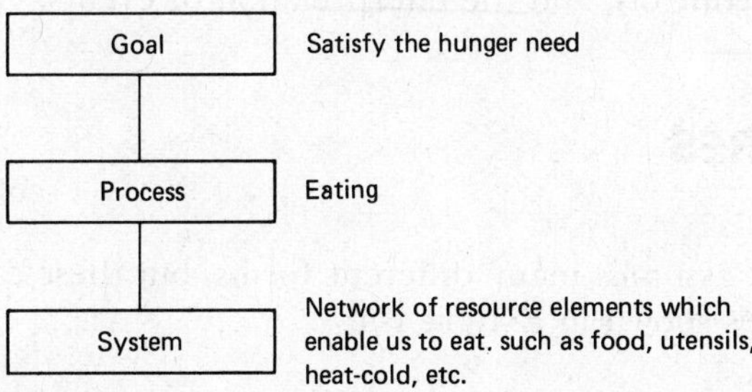

We observe that goals cannot be reached without processes, and that processes cannot take place without systems.[2]

[2]Robert N. Anthony, *Planning and Control Systems: A Framework for Analysis* (Cambridge, Mass.: Harvard University Press, 1965), p. 5, distinguishes between *processes* and *systems* in these words:

> In brief, a system facilitates a process; it is the means by which processes occur. The distinction is similar to that between anatomy and physiology. Anatomy deals with structure—what it is; whereas physiology deals with process—how it functions. The digestive system facilitates the process of digestion.

Another observation is appropriate at this point. As decision makers our options increase as we move downward through the GPS Complex. Having asserted a goal, we have no option but to fulfill it, to abandon it, or to modify it in favor of a new goal. However, given a goal, a limited choice as to processes exists. In our example, the hunger need could be "satisfied" in a limited number of ways. An alternative to eating would be surgery to remove the hunger-inducing impulses, or a process by which mental control (sublimation) is exercised over the physical urge. Moving to the systems level, however, we find that alternatives are numerous, as illustrated by the many possible resource combinations by which to assuage hunger.

The GPS Complex has other implications for management planning and control, as shown in Exhibit 1-4.

EXHIBIT 1-4 MANAGEMENT FLOWS THROUGH THE GPS COMPLEX

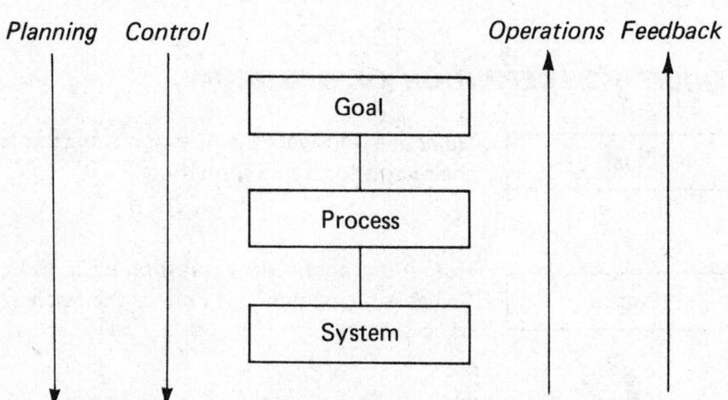

Effective planning is only possible as we move from known goals to the *definition* of processes and the *design* of systems. Hence the flow is downward through the GPS Complex. Similarly, controls flow from goals. Their purpose is to assure that activities conform to plans.

Operations, on the other hand, commence at the systems level, generating an activity flow which culminates in results (achieved goals). Feedback also originates at the systems level in the form of reports on the level of activity, on exceptions, on the functioning of controls, and the interpretation of events.

1.5 GPS STRUCTURES

The GPS Complex assumes many different forms, but these can be grouped under the three basic types shown in Exhibit 1-5.

TYPE A STRUCTURE

In *Type A* each element is related exclusively to the other elements. For example, to meet the goal of telling time, we have the timekeeping process, and the system element is a watch. Unless the watch also serves some other objective, such as adornment, its sole function is to enable us to tell time through the process of timekeeping. Compared with *Types B* and *C*, Type A is a relatively easy structure to design and operate. Cost-benefit analysis is aided in that there are no shared systems costs or process benefits.

In the language of set theory, in the Type A structure the elements G, P, and S occupy contiguous areas (Exhibit 1-6).

EXHIBIT 1-5 GPS STRUCTURES

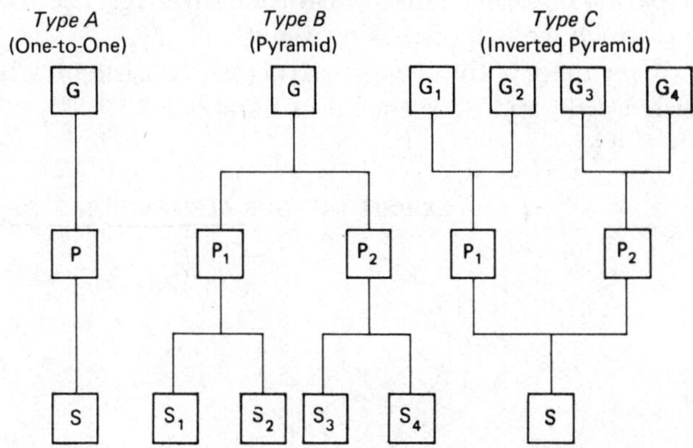

EXHIBIT 1-6 GPS ELEMENTS IN TYPE A STRUCTURE

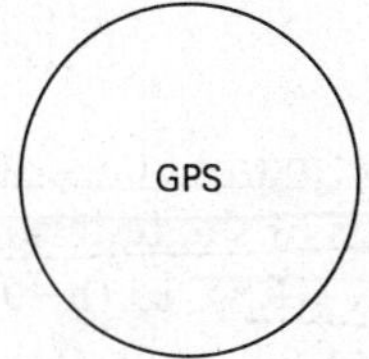

TYPE B STRUCTURE

In *Type B* the whole focus of the structure is on a single, very important (and usually complex) goal. The task of getting man to the moon and back serves as a ready example. A goal like this requires several processes and many systems. Each process and system is a *necessary* but not a *sufficient* factor in reaching the goal. Processes have to combine with other processes, and systems with other systems, in order to reach the objective. Hence we have an interdependency among processes and among systems.

The "pyramid" is characterized by its sensitivity. As in the marble games we play, removal of one supporting element leads to the collapse of the whole structure. Also, it is difficult to add new elements after the initial design without destroying its symmetry. Major modifications call for redesign of the structure as a whole.

Managing a pyramid requires a holistic approach. Each part must be viewed in terms of its impact on the whole. Because of the sensitive interdependencies between the elements of a pyramid, network techniques, such as PERT (see p. 42) are useful management tools.

The singular advantage of the pyramid is that all energy is directed toward one goal. This has both behavioral and economic implications. The behavioral implication is that employees in a pyramid have a discernable goal (motivator) and can measure their contribution towards its attainment. From an economic viewpoint, it is relatively easy to calculate the final cost of achieving a goal in that there are no shared costs at the goal level.

The pyramid is typical of most projects and is often found in initiate organizations. The latter often begin with a single major purpose but transform progressively into the inverted pyramid form. This transformation gives rise to behavioral and economic problems which we will discuss presently.

In terms of set theory, the Type B structure consists of a hierarchy of importance in the order G, P, and S, as shown in Exhibit 1-7.

EXHIBIT 1-7 GPS ELEMENTS IN TYPE B STRUCTURE

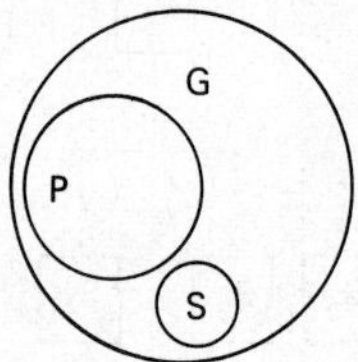

TYPE C STRUCTURE

In the "inverted pyramid" we have many goals, fewer processes, and one large system. For example, the multiple goals of the federal government are financed through one large revenue-collection system (IRS). In the *Type C* structure a goal is a *necessary* but not a *sufficient* reason for having the underlying process, and similarly a process is a *necessary* but not a *sufficient* reason for the existence of the system. In other words, a system serves a number of processes, and a process serves a number of goals.

The inverted pyramid is characterized by its insensitivity and impersonality. If we remove a goal we cannot remove the underlying elements because they serve other goals as well. Removing goals in the inverted pyramid gives rise to redundancy (unused capacity) with its attendant economic costs. On the other hand if we keep adding goals we increasingly strain (overload) the underlying processes and systems. Because there is no direct linkage between goals and the supporting elements, there is a tendency to think in terms of goals without concern for their impact on the process-system elements.

The inverted pyramid is typical of large organizations and is obvious particularly in the structure of government.

We referred earlier to the behavioral and economic problems which are inherent in the inverted pyramid. The economic problem is posed by the difficulty of tracing costs. Since process and system costs are shared among many goals, it is difficult to know the cost of reaching a particular goal. At best we have to rely on fairly arbitrary allocation devices for partitioning costs among goals.

The behavioral problem arises from the intrinsic impersonality of the inverted pyramid. Employees, who form part of the systems network (i.e., "human resources"), have difficulty in relating to multiple goals, some of which are in conflict with each other. Lacking a strong goal-identification, survival of the system becomes a goal in its own right.

We mentioned the typical transformation of pyramids into inverted pyramids. A scenario of this metamorphosis might run as follows. A single, visible goal gives way to many goals, which become more obscure and meaningless. Employees are progressively isolated from the goals of the organization. Altruistic motivation gives way to self-interest—it becomes each man for himself. Performance becomes competitive rather than complementary. Self-interest progresses into fear and insecurity with pronounced efforts to achieve insularity and invulnerability per the organization itself. Efforts toward change are viewed as personal threats. In lieu of extra-organization (social) goals, the major goal becomes one of sustaining the system and making it as impervious to attack as possible. Lacking social motivation, the organization progressively fails.

Another example is investment behavior. A new firm appeals to investors on the basis of social goals—it intends to provide goods or services which will have social (and hence economic) appeal. COMSAT (Commercial Satellite Corporation) is a case in point. There were many years of active trading in COMSAT stock before it launched its first satellite. In cases of which COMSAT is typical, there is no history of earnings. Generally, the financial statements reveal minimal collateral in the event of failure. What then are investors buying? Simply stated, they are sharing a dream—they believe in the basic purpose of the firm. When an organization inverts, however, investors too lack knowledge or association with its goals. The stock market now pulses on earnings and other internal data rather than on exogenous factors. Somewhere in the process of changing its GPS structure, the dream is lost.

Since many of our major organizations are of the inverted pyramid form, we need to study and inderstand them if we are to prevent the organization senility which now appears inevitable.

A set theory view of the inverted pyramid would show S as occupying the area of most importance, then P and G in that order, as shown in Exhibit 1-8.

EXHIBIT 1-8 GPS ELEMENTS IN TYPE C STRUCTURE

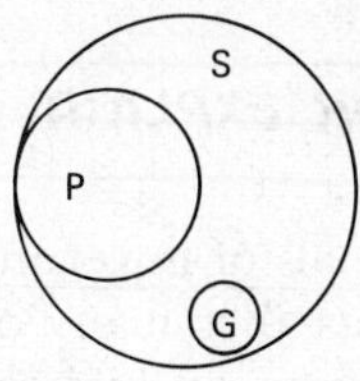

Our analysis continues by examining the elements of the GPS Complex in more detail.

1.6 GOALS

Each of the GPS Complex elements has properties which bear on the function of management. Some attributes of *goals* are:

1. They are assertive.
2. They are neutral.
3. They may be explicit or implicit.
4. They may be compatible or incompatible.
5. They may be operational or non-operational.

We will discuss these matters in turn.

GOALS ARE ASSERTIVE

Goals are stated objectives. I can assert a goal; you can assert a goal. What makes some goals more important than others is based in part on *who* makes the assertion and on the willingness of others to accept *his* goal. Rank, the art of persuasion, access to media, and many other factors improve one's position to assert goals on behalf of others.

GOALS ARE NEUTRAL

Goals are not intrinsically "right" or "wrong." What makes some goals good and others bad is determined by existing social values. Hence a "good" goal at one time may be a "bad" goal at some other time if the value set has changed in the interval. For example, in 1960 President John F. Kennedy asserted a goal "to send man to the moon and back within the decade." In the social climate of 1960 this was viewed by most of us as a "good" goal. The same goal articulated in the 1970s might have far less acceptance.

This fact makes it necessary for goal-setters to tap the social mainstream constantly if they are to set forth goals which will lead to general acceptance. Unfortunately this need is frustrated by the increasing insularity of higher offices.

GOALS MAY BE IMPLICIT OR EXPLICIT

Ask the question, "what are the goals of government?" The confusion which attends the answer is indicative of the fact that many of our large organizations function without explicit goals, by which we mean higher level or external goals as opposed to internal goals, such as improving efficiency or earnings. Yet each system at work is producing results (which we will call *achieved goals*), so that failure to enunciate goals does not imply their nonexistence. Where goals are not explicit, we can deduce them by observing the system at work. This is a poor substitute for explicit goals in that the ability and resources of observers differ widely, leading to very different conclusions as to the goals in question. The story of the four blind men and the elephant comes to mind. Each concluded it was a different creature because he was able to feel only a small part of the elephant's body. Making goals explicit raises the level of argument to the goals themselves, and to variances between goals and actual results, rather than to powers of observation.

GOALS MAY BE COMPATIBLE OR INCOMPATIBLE

Goals must be compatible with the supporting processes and systems if we are to have achievement. We noted that any system at work produces results (*achieved goals*). Therefore if a new goal is incompatible with the existing substructure, and if no changes are made in the substructure, the old results will continue in force and the new goals will become empty promises.

Simply to state a goal in the context of an incompatible substructure and expect achievement is an idle wish. Many of these process-system structures are deeply entrenched, so that knowledge of their limitations to change is advisable before setting objectives. It is, perhaps, the failure to recognize incompatibility and entrenchment which leads many office-seekers to overstate their intentions.

Goals are "impossible" to reach where the needed processes cannot be defined and/or the needed systems cannot be implemented. Goals are "impractical" where the cost of changing the substructure exceeds the derived benefit.

GOALS MAY BE OPERATIONAL OR NON-OPERATIONAL

An *operational* goal lends itself to measurement, a *non-operational* goal is purely subjective. An operational goal provides a basis for monitoring progress and achievement. Operational goals need not be quantitative in nature. To agree to meet a friend at a certain time and place is an operational goal because you either did or did not meet.[3] On the other hand, a goal such as "to improve employee morale" is non-operational, because what constitutes "morale" is uncertain in the first place. Many important goals are subjective or non-operational. For this reason we should seek ways to make them operational, rather than abandon them. Improving morale is a case in point. If you ask an executive why he believes morale has improved, he will likely cite an increase in productivity, a decrease in turnover, and other objective indices to support his claim. If these are in fact the means by which morale is measured, then we can formalize these indices as part of the goal itself. Indirect measures for subjective goals are termed *surrogates*.[4] Surrogates for morale might include:

Productivity
Turnover
Absenteeism
Formal complaints

Only indices which are capable of objective measurement can be used as surrogates. Also, there must be agreement that certain surrogates will be accepted as the means for operationalizing a goal.

[3]Where operational goals are not quantified we are limited to a yes-no outcome.

[4]A more intensive treatment of the relationship between principals and surrogates is provided by S. I. Hayakawa, *Language in Thought and Action*, 2nd ed. (New York: Harcourt, Brace & World, Inc., 1964), chapter 2; and Yuji Ijiri, *The Foundations of Accounting Measurement* (Englewood Cliffs, N.J.: Prentice-Hall, Inc., 1967), pp. 1-31.

For purposes of measurement, it is necessary to go one step beyond identifying surrogates. They are unlikely to be of equal importance vis-à-vis a goal. Hence we must weight them in the order of their perceived importance to a goal:

	productivity	40%
	turnover	30%
	absenteeism	20%
	formal complaints	10%
=	morale	100%

The above weighting implies that a change in productivity has four times the significance on the issue of morale than does a change in the number of formal complaints.

Complex goals such as "improving morale" usually require several surrogates. If only one surrogate were needed it should, of course, replace the goal as being a more useful statement of purpose. On the other hand, it is not necessary to exhaust the universe of surrogates. Once we have accounted for a high percentage of the goal activity through the weighting of surrogates, the rest can be ignored as being statistically insignificant.[5]

Operational goals provide us with a number of benefits. In terms of motivation, employees will have a clear picture of what is expected of them and what indices will be used to measure goal-attainment. From a measurement viewpoint, operational goals force us to clarify our objectives, and this in turn facilitates evaluation in that we know the extent to which we have met our objectives.

1.7 PROCESSES

A *process* is a set of activities pertinent to a goal or result. Processes can be thought of as transformations: food is digested, persons are transported, presidents are elected, raw material is converted into products, and so forth. As noted in these examples, processes move things from one state of nature to another.

EXHIBIT 1-9 FINITE PROCESS

Begins |————————————| Ends

Some processes are *finite* (terminal) and can be represented by a straight line (Exhibit 1-9). Examples are the processes of life, production of a product, a collegiate education, or electing a president.

Other processes are *repetitive* and can be represented by a circle (Exhibit 1-10). The function of a repetitive process is to maintain a level of activity. The heart function and circulation are examples in physiology; the weekly payroll is an example in finance. There are processes within processes and we can depict these process rela-

[5]This observation is germaine to many data collection problems. For example, in obtaining credit information it may not be necessary to exhaust the possible pool of information, but rather to collect data on the most significant surrogates for the complex principals of "character" and "capacity."

tionships as networks. A network of the major life processes is illustrated in Exhibit 1-11.

EXHIBIT 1-10 REPETITIVE PROCESS

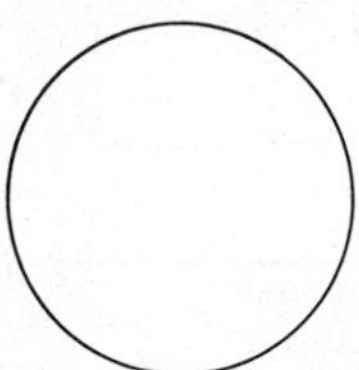

EXHIBIT 1-11 NETWORK OF MAJOR LIFE PROCESSES[6]

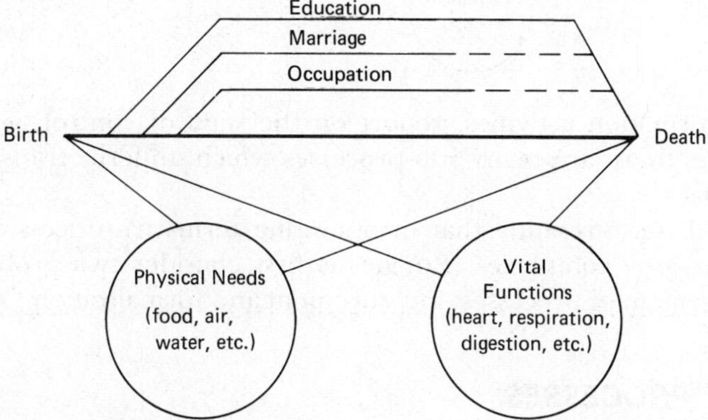

In all process networks there is one *macro-process.* In our example it is the life process, beginning with birth and ending with death.

Our observations lead us to believe that all macro-processes are *finite* (in the absence of proof as to eternity or perpetual motion). Hence all repetitive processes exist in support of one or more finite processes. The objective of a repetitive process is to maintain a cycle of activity in favor of some larger finite process. There is no aggregation or procession of events in repetitive processes. A repetitive process can be said to succeed or fail on the basis of its ability to maintain a desired level of activity.

It follows that break-down in a repetitive process has consequence to some larger finite process; and conversely, ending a finite process also ends its supporting repetitive functions.

THE ORGANIZATION TRI-PROCESS

Organizations have three major process elements, as depicted in Exhibit 1-12. We refer to this structure as a *tri-process complex.*

The macro-process transforms inputs into outputs. Input-output varies in terms of the function of the organization. Schools transform unskilled persons into skilled ones; manufacturers convert raw materials into products; accountants produce financial statements out of raw data.

Control ensures that results conform to plans. The purpose of feedback is to

[6]The systems which facilitate these processes come to mind quite readily: cardio-vascular, respiratory, nervous, digestive, endocrine, educational, socioeconomic, etc.

EXHIBIT 1-12 THE TRI-PROCESS COMPLEX IN ORGANIZATIONS

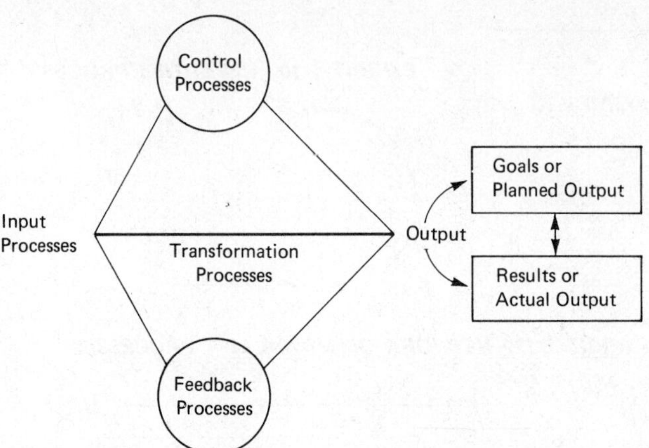

monitor transformation activities, report on the state of control, and interpret results. Of course, there are many sub-processes which underlie transformation, control, and feedback.

We shall see presently that in operating terms tri-process complexes have counterpart *tri-system* complexes. But let us first consider two problems associated with the management of processes: measurement and formalization.

MEASURING PROCESSES

We have discussed the problem of measuring goals. Processes also pose problems of measurement. The problem is that there is infinite gradation within processes. For example, we age constantly, not once a year on our birthday. The problem of infinite gradation is resolved through *scaling* (Exhibit 1-13).

EXHIBIT 1-13 SCALING PROCESSES

EXHIBIT 1-14 QUANTITATIVE SCALES

PROCESS	SCALE(S)
Time	years, months, days, hours, minutes, seconds
Speed	miles per hour
Life	years of age
Education	grades, classes
Business acitivity	fiscal periods

Scales may be quantitative in nature (Exhibit 1-14). Or scales may be qualitative, as in constructing a house (Exhibit 1-15).

EXHIBIT 1-15 QUALITATIVE SCALES

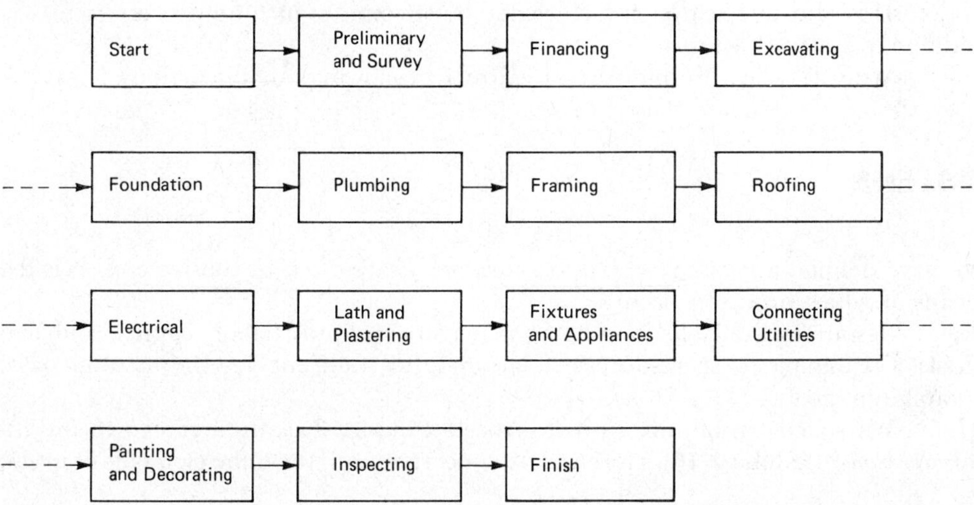

With qualitative scaling, persons must be thoroughly familiar with the process in order to monitor progress. For someone knowledgeable in house construction, a report to the effect that "we are at the plumbing stage" would be meaningful process information.

Scales can be refined. For example, we now refer to computer speeds in nanoseconds.[7] Refining scales conforms to a general rule of economics in that an optimal scale exists at the point where the marginal benefits of refinement exceed marginal costs to the widest extent. This rule places a practical limit on the degree to which we refine scales.

Defining processes is absolutely essential if we are to make efficiency judgments. We will return to this point later.

FORMALIZING PROCESSES

Processes may be formal or informal. We formalize processes through such media as maps, blueprints, flow charts, descriptions, instructions, guides, organization charts, and manuals. Informal processes are communicated through skill exchanges, work experiences, verbal instructions, and observation. Some fairly complex processes take place without formalization. Persons thoroughly familiar with the process of construction, for example, can build a house without blueprints.

While systems management has made great strides in the past decade, the management of processes is not yet off home base. Many complex processes in organizations, not the least being decision processes, are now uncharted. This paucity of formalized processes is the root cause of much mismanagement.

Many informal processes could be formalized if we made the effort. Some

[7]One-billionth of a second, or 10^{-9} second.

processes which have previously been held to be too complex to formalize are yielding to advanced techniques such as decision modeling, simulation, and dynamic programming.

We can expect to see great advances in formalizing processes in the years ahead. Perhaps in time we will even have process specialists. The reason for this prognosis is that our search for efficiency must come to include process factors in addition to systems factors.

We will return to the issue of efficiency following our discussion of systems.

1.8 SYSTEMS

We have defined a *system* as a resource network geared to a purposive end. It is the means by which processes occur.

Resources available to systems managers comprise labor, capital, and materials. Combining these resources in meaningful ways enables the attainment of organization goals.

We stated earlier that the tri-process complex has an alter ego in the *tri-systems complex* (Exhibit 1-16). Here we are concerned with the same elements of input,

EXHIBIT 1-16 THE TRI-SYSTEM COMPLEX IN ORGANIZATIONS

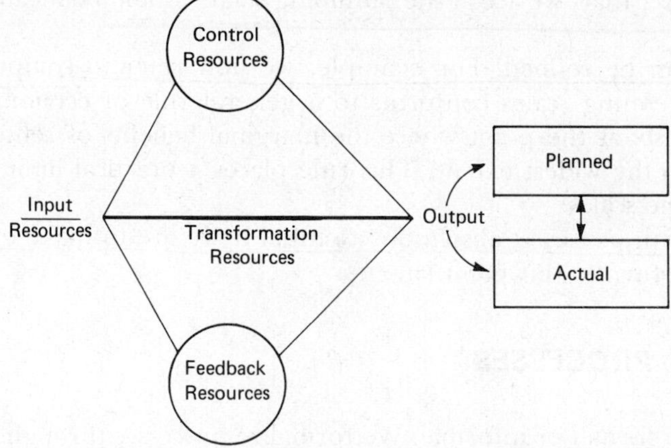

output, feedback, and transformation; but our viewpoint is different. The difference is that in process terms we are concerned with the essence of the activity, while from a systems perspective we are concerned with the mix of resources required to make the process operational. *What* takes place in the context of operations defines its processes—*how* those operations occur defines its systems.

Consider accounting as an operating system. Its purpose is to facilitate the decision making processes of users. The input is raw data. This data is admitted to the accounting system, is transformed, and exits the system in the form of financial reports (Exhibit 1-17).

On the one hand the system faces an environment of unlimited data, while on the other it faces unlimited user wants. No system can cope with these conditions.

EXHIBIT 1-17 AN OPERATING SYSTEM FOR ACCOUNTING

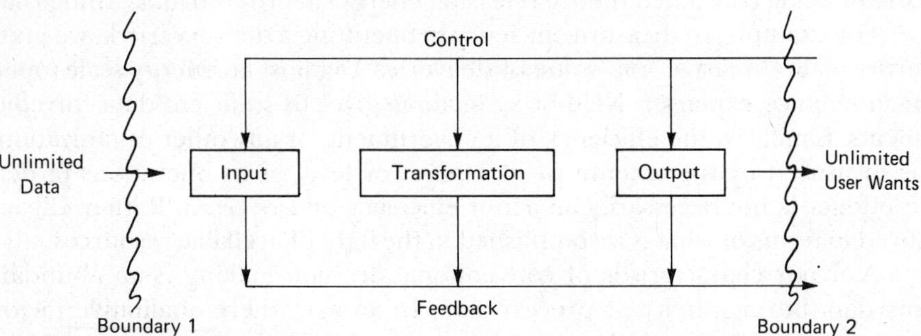

Accordingly, each system has its limitations as denoted by boundaries 1 and 2. Boundary 1 serves as a screen in that only a portion of the data in the environment is admitted to the system. Boundary 2 serves as a screen in that various users get certain information based on their needs, their entitlement to the information, and the constraints (including costs) of providing it. Without boundaries we have no system. The nature of these boundaries also distinguishes one system from another.

The admission of data to the accounting system is not random; that is, we do not take every *n*th item in a newspaper, for example, and admit it to the system. Rather, well-defined input rules are present which promote a rational screening. It follows that there are transformation, control, feedback, and output rules and procedures.

Systems too can be formalized through design and engineering processes. Many of the devices by which processes are formalized, as detailed earlier, are used in formalizing systems. Again the difference is substantive—a system is concerned with *what* is being formalized. In the case of processes we are defining the nature of operations, while in formalizing systems we are designing the utilization of resource elements.

The need for a distinction between processes and systems is clarified as we turn to the issue of efficiency.

1.9 EFFICIENCY

The ultimate objective in management is to reach goals in the most efficient way. Making efficiency judgments requires both *process* and *systems* data. For example, the most efficient water delivery project is the one which delivers

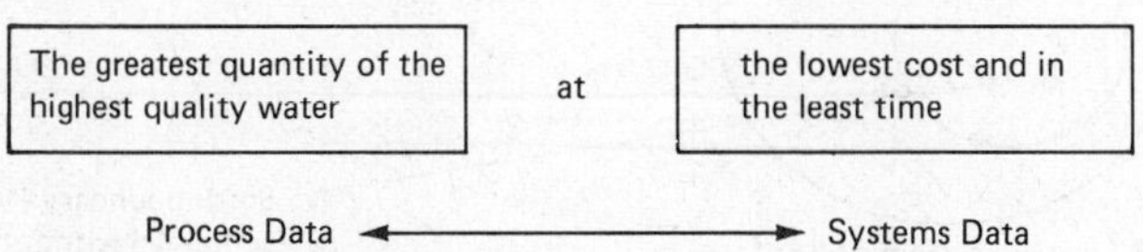

Process data is of a qualitative nature, while systems data is generally expressed in terms of cost or time-cost. A process can be said to yield *activity* data, while a system gives us *energy* data. The notion of activity stems from the fact that something

is happening in a process, while the concept of energy arises from the fact that resources are being consumed (hence releasing energy) in order to make things happen.

For example, to measure efficiency in operating a delivery truck, we juxtapose an activity scale ("mileage" or "value of deliveries") against an energy scale (operating and maintenance expense). Neither scale alone gives us sufficient data for efficiency judgments. Similarly, the efficiency of a government, or any other organization, cannot be measured by the amount of its budget or level of its operations (a decrease in the budget is not necessarily an act of efficiency or *vice versa*). Rather efficiency is measured in terms of what is accomplished in the light of available resources.

A major characteristic of conventional decision making is an abundance of systems data but a scarcity of process data. In an age where qualitative factors are reaching parity with economic concerns, the need to define and measure processes emerges as a major challenge.

1.10 BASIC SYSTEMS CONCEPTS

In our discussion of *general systems theory* ("the systems approach") and of *operating systems,* you have encountered some important concepts.

BOUNDARIES

You have learned that systems have *boundaries.* Without a boundary we would have no system. These boundaries are important because they tell us about the limitations or constraints of a system—what it *should be able* to do and what it *should not be able* to do. Boundaries also distinguish one system from another.

SYSTEMS AND SUB-SYSTEMS

If the boundaries of one system are a sub-set of the boundaries of another system, the smaller system is a *sub-system* of the larger one (Exhibit 1-18).

EXHIBIT 1-18 A SYSTEM AND SUB-SYSTEM

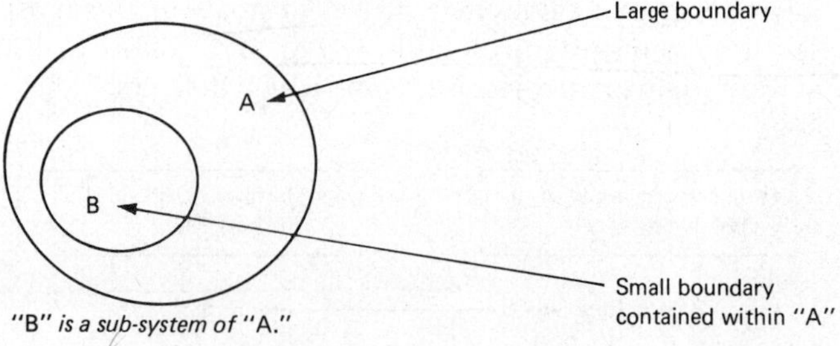

"B" *is a sub-system of* "A."

The relationship of the accounting system to the macroeconomic system can be represented as shown in Exhibit 1-19.

In other instances the boundary of one system may overlap with the boundary of some other system (Exhibit 1-20). For example, part of the information needed for payroll purposes (a sub-system of accounting) may be the same as is needed for personnel management purposes (a sub-system of management information systems); hence, there is some degree of interdependency between these systems.

EXHIBIT 1-19 SYSTEM WITHIN SYSTEM: FROM MACROECONOMICS TO ACCOUNTING

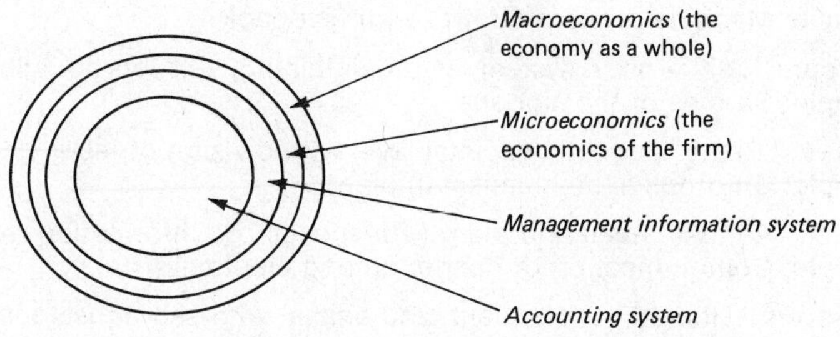

EXHIBIT 1-20 PARTIALLY INTERDEPENDENT SYSTEMS

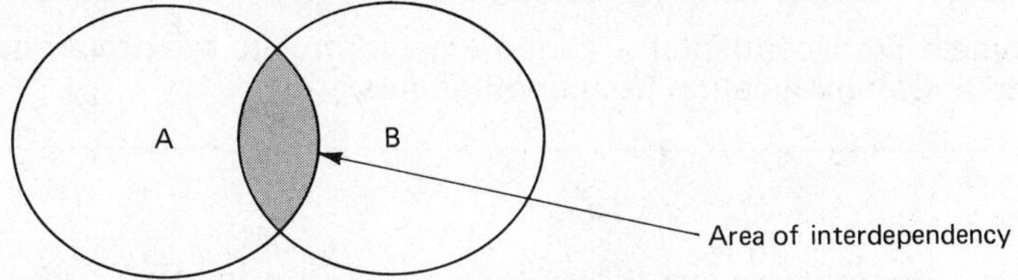

CLASSIFICATION OF SYSTEMS

Students who have taken elementary zoology are familiar with the conventional taxonomy in that field (Exhibit 1-21).

EXHIBIT 1-21 TAXONOMY IN THE BIOLOGICAL SCIENCES

CLASSIFICATION	EXAMPLE
Phylum	Chordata
Class	Aves
Order	Anseriformes
Family	Anatidae
Genus	Branta
Species	Canadensis
Scientific name	Branta Canadensis
Common name	Canada Goose

Efforts to construct a taxonomy of systems are just beginning. Kenneth Boulding has suggested the following classification (Exhibit 1-22).[8]

[8] "General Systems Theory—The Skeleton of Science," *Management Science* 2 (1956): 197–208. Reprinted with permission.

EXHIBIT 1-22 BOULDING'S HIERARCHY OF SYSTEMS

Phase one: "Frameworks"—static structures
Example: Electron configuration around an atomic nucleus.

Phase two: "Clockworks"—dynamic structures, equilibrium cases
Example: The motion of a pendulum.

Phase three: "Cybernetics"—control and communication
Example: Machine process control with feedback.

Phase four: "Cell"—open system, self-maintaining, self-reproduction
Example: Studies of the amoeba.

Phase five: "Plant"—genetic-societal level with division of labor
Example: Chlorophyll mechanism in plants.

Phase six: "Animal"—cell and plant with specialized information receptors
Example: Communication of danger among elephants.

Phase seven: "Human"—cell, plant, and animal with self-consciousness
Example: Study of allergies?

Phase eight: "Social organizations"—congregations of humans
Example: Individual behavior on committees.

Phase nine: "Transcendental"—cannot now formulate the proper questions
Example: Communication from another galaxy?

In terms of this schema there are sub-systems of accounting that conform to each of phases one through eight, while the accounting system itself belongs in phase eight because it stresses communications between social organizations and institutions.

THE BOUNDARIES OF A SYSTEM

A system is defined by its boundaries. The boundaries tell us what a system can do and what a system cannot do. We referred to these boundaries earlier.

Because no system can cope with all of the resources in the environment or

EXHIBIT 1-23 BOUNDARY AS CIRCUMSCRIBING A SYSTEM

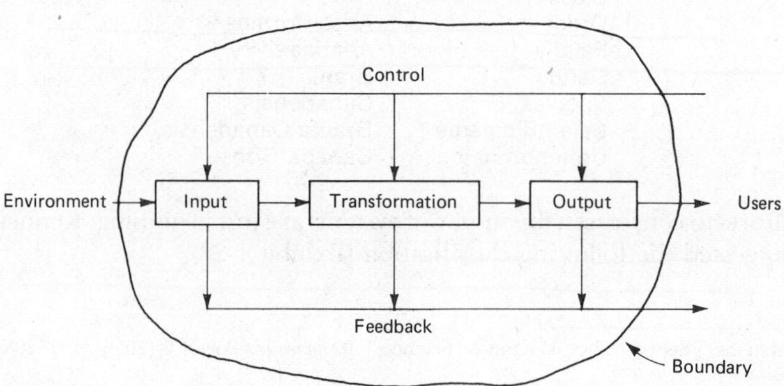

cater to all possible users, boundaries or operating parameters become necessary. Boundary 1 in Exhibit 1-17 separates the system from its environment, which is to say that the system only intends to admit into its process a fraction of environmental resources. Boundary 2 discriminates among user needs, which is to say that the system intends only to satisfy a specific fraction of users' needs.

It is acceptable to show the boundary as circumscribing a system (Exhibit 1-23), and in our discussion of *closed* and *open* systems, you will see that it is useful to think of a boundary in this sense.

CLOSED AND OPEN SYSTEMS

Exhibit 1-24 depicts a *closed* system. Compare it to Exhibit 1-25, which illustrates an *open* system.

EXHIBIT 1-24 A CLOSED SYSTEM

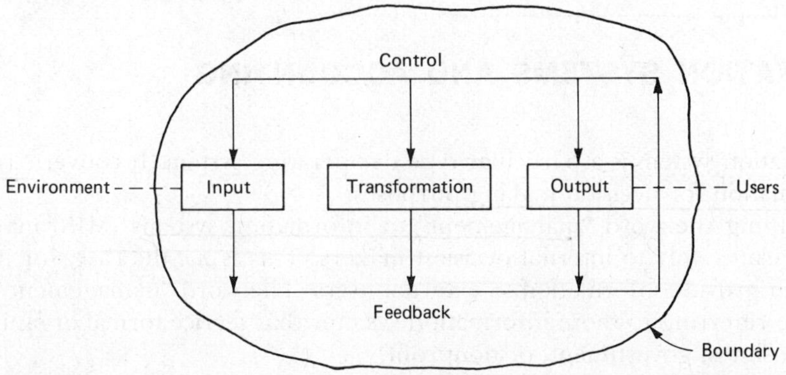

Observe that in a *closed* system, feedback does not cross the boundary but connects directly with control. In a closed system, feedback acts upon control without external intervention. An example is a heating system governed by a thermostat. A sensing device transmits information (feedback) to a control mechanism, which instructs the activity to either increase (produce more heat) or decrease (produce less heat). Having set the desired temperature on the control device, the user need not intervene further in the operation of the system.

In an *open* system, of which accounting is an example, feedback is furnished to a user who may or may not take action to change controls or activities. Feedback does not necessarily elicit a response. Another feature of an open system is that the user, in deciding whether or not to take action, is influenced by stimuli from sources outside the system. For example, information concerning a competitor may influence him to make changes, or legal requirements may make it necessary for him to alter his activities or controls.

The manager of an open system should be distinguished from other users in that he can be thought of as being an integral part of the feedback-control loop (Exhibit 1-25).

While other users may influence controls and activities in the long run, the manager has a particular responsibility for seeing that the system operates effectively.

EXHIBIT 1-25 MANAGER AS PART OF FEEDBACK-CONTROL LOOP

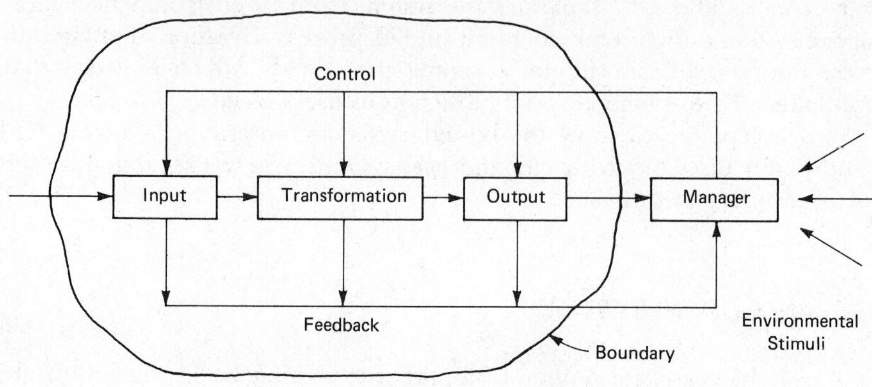

Some users of financial reports may be satisfied with the "annual report" once each year, but other managers require more frequent information, perhaps on a daily basis or less, in order to control their enterprises effectively.

1.11 INFORMATION SYSTEMS AND ACCOUNTING

An information system is a particular type of operating system. It converts raw data into information for decision making purposes.

Adding the word "management" to information systems (MIS) may imply that MIS relates only to internal decision makers. This is *not* the case, for it is also designed to provide information to external users. The word "management" means that we are referring to those information systems that service formal organizations, whether business, government, or nonprofit.

The propositions underlying MIS are:

1. A *business* is a set of problems or decision needs that require solution.
2. *Management* is the process of assigning problems to the most qualified person.
3. The *most qualified person* is the one who consistently can make the best decisions on the basis of the least costly information.
4. *Information* is the value of data to a decision maker.
5. The *purpose of MIS* is to furnish decision makers with information.

Most MIS have several sub-systems, of which the accounting system is generally the largest and most pervasive. The accounting system can be viewed as the hub of MIS, as shown in Exhibit 1-26.

The accounting system plays a principal role in managing the flow of economic data in organizations and among them. It is the only system through which both managers and external users get a picture of the organization as a total entity. It ties together the other sub-systems.

The formal products of the accounting system are the financial statements. They provide users with operating statistics through the *income statement,* including net income or loss for a specific period of time; and with resource statistics through

EXHIBIT 1-26 ACCOUNTING AS THE HUB OF MIS

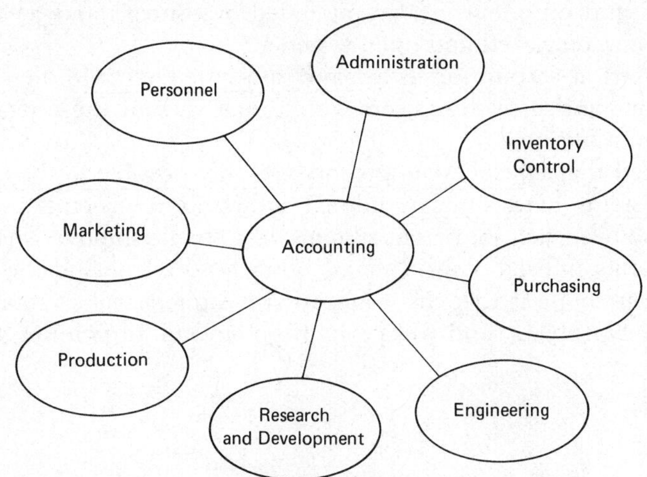

the *balance sheet,* so that users can evaluate the firm's assets (resources), liabilities (claims against resources), and equity position (net resources accruing to the owners of the business), as of a particular date.

In addition to the formal outputs of the accounting system, a stream of information and many reports are generated for internal management purposes and for specific external needs, such as credit reporting or compliance with government regulations.

Accounting is an information system. Accordingly this text will follow the basic framework set forth in this chapter in structuring the material that follows. For example, each function we discuss is assumed to be purposive, i.e., there is a good reason for doing it. We will talk about accounting inputs, the transformation of accounting data, and output. We will discuss general and specific controls relating to accounting activity, and we will illustrate the functions of feedback.

1.12 SUMMARY

This chapter provides a foundation for accounting as an information system. "The systems approach" was discussed as a useful way in which to view events or solve problems. It involves a broad approach to problem-solving in which various alternatives are considered in arriving at the best solution. It also stresses the importance of testing public acceptance before implementing even good ideas.

"Systems" also has an operating meaning. A theory of operating systems recognizes the important interplay between goals, processes, and systems (GPS). These elements can be arranged in various ways to form complexes that have important relevance to the management of organizations. The basic complexes are (1) one-to-one, (2) the pyramid, and (3) the inverted pyramid. The nature and measurement problems attending goals, processes, and systems was discussed in detail.

Some basic concepts underlying all systems theory include boundaries, systems and sub-systems, classification norms, and the operating elements of input, transformation, and output which are attended by controls and feedback. We also distinguished between closed and open systems.

We looked at accounting as a major sub-system of MIS, tieing together the other sub-systems and providing users with a total view of the financial operations and resources of a business.

We noted that efficiency judgments are only possible in the context of both process and systems data. Our traditional information structures, particularly in accounting, have been rich sources of systems data but are impoverished as to process data. We view this imbalance as a major obstacle to advancing the technology of management. Our hope is that this conceptual treatment will serve at least to highlight a significant problem, and will perhaps go beyond, in pointing to more useful frameworks.

CHAPTER 1 REFERENCES AND ADDITIONAL READINGS

Anthony, Robert N. *Planning and Control Systems: A Framework for Analysis.* Boston: Harvard University Press, 1965.

Blumenthal, Sherman C. *Management Information Systems: A Framework for Planning and Development.* Englewood Cliffs, N.J.: Prentice-Hall, Inc., 1969.

Brightman, Richard W. *Information Systems for Modern Management.* New York: The Macmillan Company, 1971.

Buckley, Walter. *Sociology and Modern Systems Theory.* Englewood Cliffs, N.J.: Prentice-Hall, Inc., 1967.

Ditri, Arnold E.; Shaw, John C.; and Atkins, William. *Managing the EDP Function.* New York: McGraw-Hill Book Company, 1971.

Emery, James C. *Organizational Planning and Control Systems: Theory and Technology.* New York: The Macmillan Company, 1969.

Emshoff, James R., and Sisson, Roger L. *Design and Use of Computer Simulation Models.* New York: The Macmillan Company, 1970.

Glans, Thomas B. et al. *Management Systems.* New York: Holt, Rinehart & Winston, Inc., 1968.

Head, Robert V. *Real-time Business Systems.* New York: Holt, Rinehart & Winston, Inc., 1964.

Heany, Donald F. *Development of Information Systems.* New York: The Ronald Press Company, 1968.

Ijiri, Yuji, *Management Goals and Accounting for Control.* Amsterdam: North-Holland Publishing Company, 1965.

Ijiri, Yuji. *The Foundations of Accounting Measurement.* Englewood Cliffs, N.J.: Prentice-Hall, Inc., 1967.

Johnson, Richard A.; Kast, Fremont E.; and Rosenzweig, James E. *The Theory and Management of Systems.* New York: McGraw-Hill Book Company, 1963.

Langefors, Borje. *Theoretical Analysis of Information Systems.* Lund, Sweden: Studentlitteratur, 1968.

McMillan, Claude, and Gonzalez, Richard F. *Systems Analysis: A Computer Approach to Decision Models.* Homewood, Ill.: Richard D. Irwin, Inc., 1968.

Malcolm, Donald G., and Rowe, Alan J., eds. *Management Control Systems.* New York: John Wiley & Sons, Inc., 1960.

Rappaport, Alfred, ed. *Information for Decision Making.* Englewood Cliffs, N.J.: Prentice-Hall, Inc., 1970.

Sackman, Harold. *Computers, Systems Science, and Evolving Society.* New York: John Wiley & Sons, Inc., 1967.

Schoderbek, Peter P., ed. *Management Systems.* New York: John Wiley & Sons, Inc., 1967.

Shannon, Claude E., and Weaver, Warren. *The Mathematical Theory of Communication.* Urbana, Ill.: University of Illinois Press, 1964.

Simon, Herbert A. *The New Science of Management Decision.* New York: Harper & Row, 1960.

Zani, William M. "Blueprint for MIS." *Harvard Business Review,* November–December 1970, pp. 95 ff.

CHAPTER 1 QUESTIONS, PROBLEMS, AND CASES

1- 1. Distinguish *the systems approach* from an *operating system.*

1- 2. "In a *finite* process there is infinite gradation between beginning and end." "The problem of infinite gradation is solved through scaling." How? Distinguish between quantitative and qualitative scaling.

1- 3. Identify and explain the four fundamental features of "the systems approach."

1- 4. Distinguish between *process* and *system.*

1- 5. "Many good process theories have failed because of two common problems." What are they?

1- 6. A tri-system complex contains a control loop and a feedback loop. What are the purposes of each?

1- 7. How are processes measured?

1- 8. Illustrate the importance of boundaries in designing a system.

1- 9. "In a more general sense a process can be said to yield *activity* data, while a system produces *energy* data." Explain the meaning of this statement.

1-10. Distinguish between *feedback* and *control.*

1-11. Indicate whether the following systems are open or closed, and briefly explain why:
(a) Respiratory system (in humans)
(b) Automobile assembly line
(c) Oil refining
(d) Payroll computation and distribution
(e) Student registration
(f) Simulated supermarket queue
(g) Tape controlled drill press
(h) Manufacture of transistors
(i) Mining gold
(j) Airplane and pilot

1-12. "The manager of an open system should be distinguished from other users." How and why?

1-13. "A major weakness of traditional information systems has been the abundance of *energy* data as opposed to little or no *activity* data." Evaluate this statement.

1-14. What is needed in order to make efficiency judgments?

1-15. What are the chief advantages and disadvantages of "pyramid" and "inverted pyramid" GPS structures?

1-16. Identify the basic elements of an operating system:

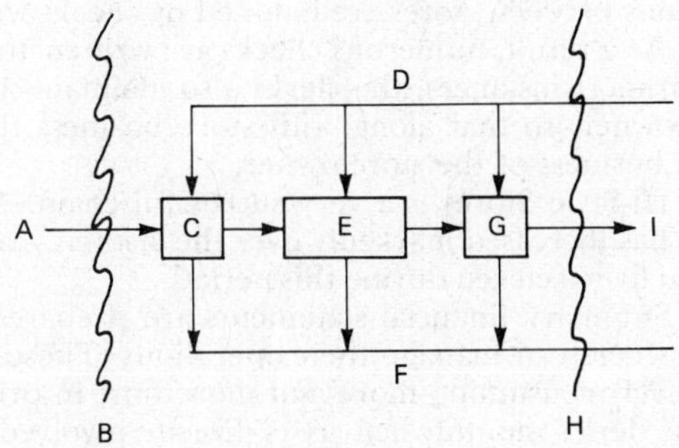

Is the system depicted open or closed? How is one or the other distinguished?

1-17. Suppose you are a credit manager. The complex goal is to determine whether an applicant is a good credit risk. Identify and weight the surrogates you would use to reach your goal. How can you prove that your model works?

1-18. ***SYSTEMS APPROACH*** The Rouflex Company is a large land developer. Recently, it negotiated a contract for the development of a vast swamp basin into a recreational park area. The swamp is damp to muddy during the summer months and usually under three inches of water the rest of the year. The area is not a particularly rainy spot, but due to the surrounding mountains, it gets a large amount of run-off water. Essentially, the swamp area is a drainage basin.

Because of water conditions, the swamp is an ideal spawning ground for numerous varieties of bird life. The nutriments produced by relatively stagnant water have produced large quantities of algae and other water prone plant and animal life. As a result, a well nourished ecological chain has developed that supports a large bird population—some varieties of which are found only in this location. If the area changed drastically, some rare species might disappear.

Illustrate how the systems approach can be applied to the solution of this problem.

1-19. ***GPS COMPLEXES*** Mr. Stock, the supervisor of Unit A, receives a special weekly cost break-down on each type of subassembly produced in his department. This report is very detailed and requires a great deal of back-up data gathering and summarization. Much of the data, however, comes from sources common to the data requirements of routine reports.

At the first of the year, Mr. Stock retires. The new supervisor operates under a different management style, and hence, considers the detailed cost analysis to be worthless. Although the report is still prepared, the new manager never uses it. He has, however, requested a special weekly report on labor time efficiency and quality control. Although such a report has been promised, no data sources are available as yet for this purpose.

What GPS Complex is at work in this situation, and what goal attributes are involved? Explain your conclusions.

1-20. ***SYSTEMS APPROACH*** Hi-Style Stores Inc., a retail appliance chain, has engaged your firm to redesign its accounting system. The chain, operating since 1936, is a loose conglomeration of individually owned stores. For instance, one owner may own five stores, another seven, and so on. There are nine owners and fifty-seven stores. The accounting for all stores is centralized in a main office in San Francisco. Each store, however, retains its individual identity, and records are maintained on a per store basis. Only purchasing is truly centralized. One clerk may handle from two to six stores, depending on the volume of sales. A store's records are individually maintained and any transactions between stores are handled by checks written on that store's bank account. As a result, numerous checks are written and merely routed between clerks. In most instances, the clerks also maintain the personal bank account of each owner, so that along with store business they also must handle the personal business of the store owner.

Hi-Style Stores is a very successful chain. As a result, the volume of business has increased markedly over the last ten years. The number of clerks rose from five to eleven during this period.

Summary financial statements are prepared monthly for each store so that owners can manage their operations. These statements, however, are progressively consuming more and more time in preparation. In fact, at least 30% of a clerk's monthly activity is directly involved with statement formulation.

Your preliminary analysis shows that much of the financial statement data is not used by an owner, and some information is repeated in different locations on the statements. The owners do not keep close watch on their centralized accounting operations and are not aware of their growing problem. The accounting supervisor has indicated that his staff would have to increase by at least five clerks if the statements are to be on time. This way each clerk would be handling fewer stores.

Apply the systems approach and attempt to find a solution. What design changes would you recommend?

1-21. ***GOALS*** Hyatt Company's goal is to be "profitable." Suppose the operating results for the last four years show:

	Income
19x1	240,000
19x2	248,000
19x3	260,000
19x4	283,000

Is Hyatt Company meeting its goal?

What if the Dearett Company, the most profitable in the industry, shows the following results:

	Income
19x1	490,000
19x2	515,000
19x3	525,000
19x4	537,000

Considering this new data, is Hyatt Company meeting its goal?

What if each company shows the following asset bases:

	Hyatt Co. Assets	Dearett Co. Assets
19x1	3,428,500	12,250,000
19x2	3,648,000	13,200,000
19x3	3,710,000	13,200,000
19x4	4,162,000	13,425,000

What evaluation can now be made concerning Hyatt's success in meeting its goal? With all the available information, what are the surrogates for measuring "profitability" of the Hyatt Company?

1-22. ***GOALS*** The Tri-State Bank has fifty-two branch offices in the state of New York. Two years ago the bank instituted a management training program for aspiring young executives. The purpose of the program was to educate the trainee about each facet of banking operations (i.e., construction loans, mortgages, estate planning, demand deposits, etc.).

The progress of each participant was measured by written exams (graded A, B, C, D, or F) and by written evaluations of program supervisors.

One day, in the cafeteria, a trainee was overheard saying, "All I care about is getting the highest grade on the next exam."

Discuss the significance of the trainee's statement as it relates to the use of surrogates for operationalizing goals.

CHAPTER

CONCEPTUAL FOUNDATIONS FOR ACCOUNTING AS AN INFORMATION SYSTEM

2.1 THE ROLE OF THEORY

A large body of formal theory underlies the concept of accounting as an information system. We can touch only on some of the more significant concepts in this chapter. Theory is useful for two purposes: (1) it enables us to distill the essence of real-world events and formulate general statements which can then be applied to all similar events, and (2) it enables us to conceive of new real-world relationships. The former approach is referred to as *inductive* theorizing, while the latter is called *deductive* theorizing.

To illustrate these types of theory you will recall that Newton formulated the Law of Gravity from the real-world observation of falling objects. This is an example of inductive theory. Einstein on the other hand assumed a relationship between matter and energy expressed by the famous equation $E = MC^2$. before it could be observed in real world events.[1] The success of nuclear fission proved that Einstein's theory was correct. Einstein's theory was deductive.

Both forms of theory are used in information and systems analysis. Using

[1]That is, energy = mass × the square of the speed of light.

the deductive method, an analyst may assume that certain information is useful to decision makers. Subsequent analysis may prove or disprove his theory. Alternatively, he can analyze the information needs of users in advance and then proceed to furnish them with the information that his inquiry shows to be effective. This procedure utilizes the inductive approach.

Inductive theory which describes real-world events is called *descriptive* theory. Theory which states that events *should* occur in a certain way is called *prescriptive* or *normative* theory. Normative theory is a branch of deductive theory, but it differs from the latter in that it theorizes in terms of the ideal outcome.

2.2 DECISION THEORY

Decision theory is the cornerstone of information and systems analysis. It is partly *descriptive* in nature in that it is based on some generalized observations of decision makers at work, and it is partly *normative* in that it prescribes an ideal framework for problem-solving.

A basic decision model is shown in Exhibit 2-1.

EXHIBIT 2-1 BASIC DECISION MODEL

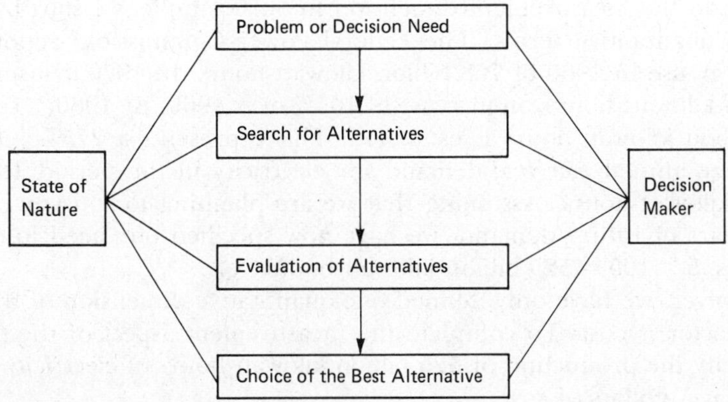

The objective of the decision is to solve some problem, which is often referred to as a "decision need." Once the problem is defined, the decision maker searches for possible alternatives. There are almost always various solutions to a given problem. Next, the alternatives should be evaluated on the basis of their cost-benefit, and the best alternative should then be chosen. In all of these matters, the decision maker works against certain handicaps. These handicaps in sum are referred to as the *state of nature.* Among some obvious limitations are the following:

1. Inability to define the problem accurately.
2. Inability to recognize all possible solutions.
3. Inability to assess the true costs and benefits of each alternative.
4. Inability to choose the alternative which appears to be best on the basis of analysis.
5. The personal limitations of the decision maker, such as his intelligence or per-

ceptiveness. These personal attributes are often referred to collectively as *the bounded rationality* of the decision maker.

Consider the application of this decision model to the problem of meeting the demand for more electricity as discussed in chapter 1. The decision need or goal is to meet the increased demand for electricity. The search for feasible alternatives ensues. In our example the alternatives were (1) hydroelectricity, (2) conventional power plants utilizing coal, gas, or oil, and (3) nuclear power plants.

These alternatives are evaluated in terms of their cost-benefit, and the best alternative is selected. The state of nature imposes limitations on an optimal solution; in this case, in the form of social values.

2.3 MEASUREMENT THEORY

The problem we have just cited has been posed in non-measurement terms. Actually, we cannot solve problems of this type if measurement is absent. To state this point in the extreme case, there is no solution to an electrical demand which is infinite in size. Also, in most cases we are modifying an existing state of the world, such as increasing the present supply of electricity. The costs and benefits associated with these changes are called *marginal costs* and *benefits.*

To add the measurement dimension to our example, we start by specifying the need in quantitative terms. The Federal Power Commission[2] reported a total electric energy use in 1960 of 763 billion kilowatt-hours. In 1970, consumption was 1,564 billion kilowatt-hours, an increase of 105% over 1960. By 1980, a consumption of 2,866 billion kilowatt-hours is estimated. This represents a 275% increase over 1960. Average annual *marginal* demand for electricity in the period 1960–1980 is 105 billion kilowatt-hours. Assuming that we are planning to construct facilities to meet five years of future demand, we have now specified our need in quantitative terms, that is, $5 \times 105 = 525$ billion kilowatt-hours.

However, we have only defined one quantitative dimension of the problem. The other factor is cost. To complete the measurement aspect of the problem we need to specify the production of 525 billion kilowatt-hours of electricity over a five-year period at X dollars of cost.

Having specified the objective in these terms, each alternative is now evaluated by this standard. While not all aspects of a problem can be reduced to measurable form, such as the beauty of a scenic river bed, certainly the technical considerations should be handled in this way.

OPERATIONALIZING GOALS

We noted in chapter 1 that operational goals are stated in measurement terms. Where the goal—such as "morale"—does not lend itself to measurement, surrogates are found to stand in place of the subjective goal.

If we are unable to operationalize a goal, it follows that we cannot assess the cost-benefit of alternatives required to reach that goal.

[2]Federal Power Commission, Release no. 11,830, January 30, 1962.

MEASUREMENT SCALES

Measurement is defined as the assignment of numerals to events or objects according to a standard or scale. Stevens has developed the most widely used classification of measurement scales (Exhibit 2-2).[3]

The *nominal* scale simply assigns numbers as labels to identify objects. The number has no other meaning and bears no relationship to other numbers. The number "16," which identifies the quarterback on the football team, is a case in point.

The *ordinal* scale is used to rank-order objects. It does not tell the magnitude of the objects or the differences in magnitudes between the objects. An example is the ranking of the ten largest urban population areas in the world:[4]

1. Tokyo 14,770,277
2. New York 14,114,927
3. Buenos Aires........................ 8,408,930
4. Paris 8,196,746
5. London 7,948,270
6. Osaka.................................. 7,781,000
7. Moscow 7,061,000
8. Shanghai 6,977,000
9. Los Angeles 6,488,791
10. Chicago.............................. 5,959,213

The ordinal ranking, as we have said, ignores the magnitude of the object (the population figures are not included in an ordinal ranking) and the distance between objects on the scale. Notice how small the difference is between items 1 and 2 and how large the difference is between 2 and 3, but an ordinal ranking would not provide this type of information.

The *interval* scale extends measurement to the magnitudes of numbers. It gives significance to magnitude by determining the equality of intervals or differences. The mean population of the ten largest urban population areas above is 8,770,615. The standard deviation in the above population is 3,082,207.[5] Using the mean as the midpoint of our interval scale, we can show the size of these population areas in relation to each other:

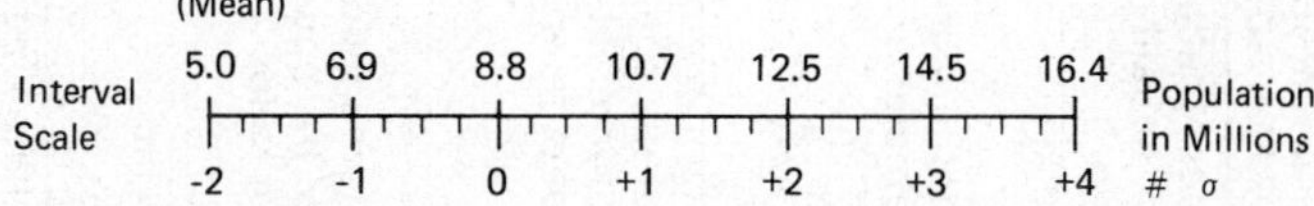

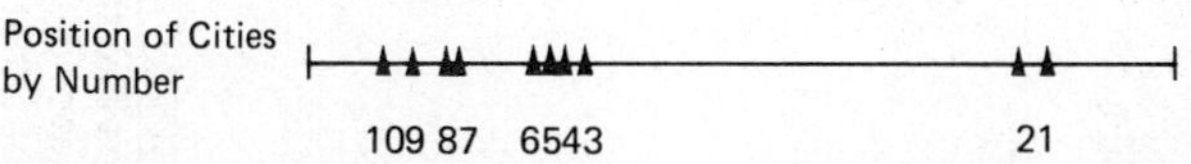

[3] S. S. Stevens, "Measurement and Man," *Science* 127, no. 3295 (February 1958): 383–89.

[4] Based on census within the period 1960–1970.

[5] Using the formula for ungrouped data

$$s = \sqrt{\frac{\Sigma(X - \bar{X})^2}{N - 1}}$$

where s = standard deviation, X = population figure for each city, $\bar{X}$ = the mean of the population figures, and N = the number of observations—in this case, 10.

EXHIBIT 2-2 A CLASSIFICATION OF SCALES OF MEASUREMENT

SCALE	BASIC EMPIRICAL OPERATIONS	MATHEMATICAL GROUP STRUCTURE	PERMISSIBLE STATISTICS (INVARIANTIVE)	TYPICAL EXAMPLES
Nominal	Determination of equality	Permutation group $x' = f(x)$ where $f(x)$ means any one-to-one substitution	Number of cases Mode "Information" measures Contingency correlation	"Numbering" of football players Assignment of type or model numbers to classes
Ordinal	Determination of greater or less	Isotonic group $x' = f(x)$ where $f(x)$ means any increasing monotonic function	Median Percentiles Order correlation (type 0: interpreted as a test of order)	Hardness of minerals Grades of leather, lumber, wool, and so forth Intelligence test raw scores
Interval	Determination of the equality of intervals or of differences	Linear or affine group $x' = ax + b$ $a > 0$	Mean Standard deviation Order correlation (type I: interpreted as r) Product moment (r)	Temperature (Fahrenheit and Celsius) Position on a line Calendar time Potential energy Intelligence test "standard scores" (?)
Ratio	Determination of the equality of ratios	Similarity group $x' = cx$ $c > 0$	Geometric mean Harmonic mean Percent variation	Length, numerosity, density, work, time intervals, and so forth Temperature (Kelvin) Loudness (sones) Brightness (brils)

The rules and the resulting kinds of scales are tabulated above. The basic operations needed to create a given scale are all those listed in the second column, down to and including the operation listed opposite the scale. The third column gives the mathematical transformations that leave the scale form invariant. Any number x on a scale can be replaced by another number x' where x' is the function of x listed in column 2. The fourth column lists, cumulatively downward, examples of statistics that show invariance under the transformations of column 3 (the mode, however, is invariant only for discrete variables).

SOURCE: Stevens, "Measurement and Man," as adapted by Richard Mattesich, *Accounting and Analytical Methods* (Homewood, Ill.: Richard D. Irwin, Inc., 1964), p. 69. Reprinted with permission.

This refinement in measurement adds considerably to our decision making ability. Buenos Aires (as number 3) does not bear the same relationship to New York (number 2) as the latter does to Tokyo. New York could become number 1 by adding 655,351 to its population, but to replace New York as number 2, Buenos Aires would have to add 5,705,998 to its population!

The *ratio* scale is the most complex of all. As stated in Exhibit 2-2, it determines the equality of ratios. Consider a simple example. A store reports profits of \$5,000, \$10,000, and \$90,000 in 1972, 1973, and 1974 respectively. The store's profits increased by two times from 1972 to 1973, and by nine times between 1973 and 1974. The mean of these two numbers, reflecting "average growth per year," is $(2+9)/2 = 5.5$ times. If we are only given the profit figure for 1972, applying this multiple would suggest the following profit figures for 1973 and 1974:

Given 1972 profit = \$ 5,000
We deduce 1973 profit = \$ 27,500 (\$ 5,000 × 5.5)
We deduce 1974 profit = \$151,250 (\$27,500 × 5.5)

The mean of the ratios 2 and 9 has lead to very erroneous conclusions. A more appropriate statistic for getting an average measure of ratios is the *geometric mean.*[6] Using a conventional table of common logarithms, we compute the geometric mean as follows:

$$\log 2 = 0.30103$$
$$\log 9 = 0.95424$$
$$\sum_{i=1}^{n} \log x_i = 1.25527$$

Hence

$$\log G = \frac{1.25527}{2}$$

Antilog

$$= .62763$$

$$G = 4.2426$$

Substituting the multiplier 4.2426 in the previous example, we now get these estimates for 1973 and 1974 profits:

Given 1972 profit = \$ 5,000
We deduce 1973 profit = \$21,213 (\$ 5,000 × 4.2426)
We deduce 1974 profit = \$90,000 (\$21,213 × 4.2426)

[6]The geometric mean is the *n*th root of the product *X*, that is,

$$G = \sqrt[n]{x_1 \cdot x_2 \cdot x_3 \cdot \cdot \cdot x_n}$$

It can be obtained more readily through the use of logarithms, that is,

$$\log G = \frac{\sum_{i=1}^{n} \log x_i}{n}$$

While the estimate for 1973 is not perfect, the 1974 estimate is precisely on target. Obviously, the *geometric* mean is a more appropriate scale of the ratios among numbers than the *arithmetic* mean, especially where there is great disproportion among the ratios.

Returning to the ten largest urban areas, the arithmetic mean of ratios between each city is 1.122. The geometric mean (as computed above) for the cities is 1.106. If we start with the population of Chicago and work progressively to an estimation of the population of Tokyo, these ratios will yield the following results (in millions):

Cities in Reverse Order	Actual	Arithmetic Mean Estimate	Arithmetic Mean Difference	Geometric Mean Estimate	Geometric Mean Difference
		(*X* 1.12)		(*G* 1.106)	
10. Chicago	6.0	6.0	—	6.0	—
9. Los Angeles	6.5	6.7	+ .2	6.6	+ .1
8. Shanghai	7.0	7.5	+ .5	7.3	+ .3
7. Moscow	7.1	8.4	+ 1.3	8.1	+ 1.0
6. Osaka	7.8	9.4	+ 1.6	8.9	+ 1.1
5. London	7.9	10.5	+ 2.6	9.9	+ 2.0
4. Paris	8.2	11.8	+ 3.6	11.0	+ 2.8
3. Buenos Aires	8.4	13.2	+ 4.8	12.1	+ 3.7
2. New York	14.1	14.8	+ .7	13.4	− .7
1. Tokyo	14.8	16.6	+ 1.8	14.8	0
Net differences			+17.1		+10.3
Differences in final estimate			+ 1.8		0

The concept of the ratio scale enables us to determine whether different ratio measures applied to numerical data yield the same results. We can then choose the ratio measure which is most appropriate to the data in question.

The various statistical operations that can be performed on these scales are shown in Exhibit 2-3.

THE CERTAINTY OF MEASUREMENT

You will recall that measurement consists of assigning numerals to events or objects in accordance with some scale or standard. We have already discussed briefly the importance of scales. We extend this analysis by examining the level of certainty which attaches to the numerals we assign.

Imperfections of Measurement

We have long thought of measurement as being absolute. Bill is six feet tall; the balance in our checking account is precisely $123.58; I arrive at work at 8:00 A.M. each morning, and so forth. It may be unsettling to discover that no measurement is absolute. There is no such thing as perfect measurement for a number of reasons.

Measurement will always be imperfect because *no scale we use is perfect.* In

EXHIBIT 2-3 EXAMPLES OF STATISTICAL MEASURES APPLICABLE TO MEASUREMENTS MADE ON THE VARIOUS CLASSES OF SCALES

Classes of Scales / *Statistical Operations*	*Nominal*	*Ordinal*	*Interval*	*Ratio*
Measures of Location	Mode	Median	Mean	Geometric Mean; Harmonic Mean
Dispersion	Information (*H*)	Percentiles	Standard Average Deviation	Percent Variation
Association or Correlation	Information Transmitted (*T*); Contingency Correlation	Rank-Order Correlation	Product-Moment Correlation; Correlation Ratio	All of these
Significance Tests	Chi Square Test	Sign Test; Run Test	Critical Ratio Test; *t* Test; *f* Test	All of these

SOURCE: Mattesich, *Accounting and Analytical Methods,* p. 70. Used with permission.

fact, all scales are arbitrary. Why do some people measure distance in feet and others in meters, or weights in ounces as opposed to grams? Tradition has it that the "yard" was based on the distance between the nose and fingertip of King Henry VIII. Every existing scale has numerous alternatives, including "better ones" in almost every instance. For example, in measuring human aging, why don't we use one of these alternatives in place of "years of age": (1) psychological age, (2) physical condition age, or (3) a combination of (1) and (2)?

The choice of a scale is based on tradition and utility. Occasionally we witness changes in scales, as illustrated recently by the conversion of British money to the decimal system, which will be followed by the conversion of other measures to the metric system.[7] The changing of established scales is not only very costly, but it also requires changes in personal customs and habits.

But even with a "perfect" scale, there would be problems in measurement.

[7]Similar action is under consideration in the United States. In 1968 President Johnson signed into law the Metric Study Bill, which authorized the secretary of commerce to make a full-scale inquiry of conversion to the metric system. Legislation was being considered by Congress in 1972, as this book went to press. A study committee was proposed to plan for conversion.

Test this point by asking a group of people to measure the same object, such as the length of a room or a table, using the same ruler or yardstick. You must stipulate that they measure the object as accurately as possible, say within one-sixteenth of an inch. You will undoubtedly receive a series of different figures, and if the group was large enough the results would tend to be distributed in the pattern of the normal bell-shaped curve. Measurement will always be imperfect because *our abilities to use the same scale differ markedly.*

If we proceed on the assumption that we do have a valid scale and know how to use it properly, a further problem remains. The things we are trying to measure have different properties. Determining the length of an object such as a table, assessing the distance at which it is safe to follow the automobile ahead of us, or predicting the temperature tomorrow—all these illustrate how measurement becomes more difficult as we confront more complex problems.

Certainty, Risk, and Uncertainty

In measurement theory we divide these problems into three broad categories: *certainty, risk,* and *uncertainty.*

Problems of *certainty* are those which we can measure with 100% assurance. *Uncertainty* cannot be measured at all. With this type of problem we have 0% assurance. Problems of *risk* occupy the area between these extremes. They can be measured with an assurance which is higher than 0% but less than 100%.

We can restate these rules in the language of probabilities. The measurement of certainty is $p = 1$ (it has a probability of 1 or 100%). With problems of uncertainty, $p = 0$. Problems of risk have a probability range expressed as $0 < p < 1$. We are saying that the probability that an event will occur is greater than zero ($0 < p$) but less than 100% ($p < 1$).

Problems of certainty are described as *deterministic.* Problems of risk are said to be *probabilistic.* If we report that net profit for a given year is $1,000,000, we are stating a deterministic measure. We tend to apply deterministic measures to many problems of risk. In fact, net profit is seldom known with certainty. To state profit in probabilistic terms we would say that "we are 95% *confident* that profit for the period is plus or minus $10,000 of being $1,000,000." A more convenient way to make this statement would be "profit is $1,000,000 at a confidence level of 95% within the range ±$10,000."

We have added the new concept of a range. It should be apparent that when we are dealing with problems of risk, our best estimate ($1,000,000) may be either too high or too low. Probabilistic data should be attended by *both* of these numbers. To illustrate this point, consider the difference in the following statements:

1. Profit is $1,000,000 at a confidence level of 95%, within the range ± $10,000.
2. Profit is $1,000,000 at a confidence level of 95%, within the range ± $100,000.

Even though the confidence level is the same in both statements, the range is quite different. Statement 1 says that the actual profit figure lies between the values $990,000 and $1,010,000 with 95% confidence. Statement 2 says that the profit figure at the same confidence level is between the values $900,000 and $1,100,000.

With probabilistic measures there is a trade-off between the confidence level and the range (or reliability) estimate. For example, with statement 1 above, we could raise the confidence level by increasing the range. If we broadened the range to ± $100,000, the confidence level might be 99%. Conversely, with statement 2 we would have to lower the confidence level if we wished to narrow the range to ± $10,000. In fact, to achieve this more restricted range the confidence level might drop to as low as 80%. For this reason it is important to use both of these numbers in reporting probabilistic data.

A long-standing criticism of accounting has been its reliance on deterministic models in financial reporting. Even where accountants do use probabilistic models at present—as they do for estimating receivables—this information is not furnished to investors via the financial statements. C. West Churchman elaborates on this criticism:[8]

> . . . two other aspects of costs that are definitely relevant to policy formation and are definitely lacking in accounting systems. Few (I'd be inclined to say "No") costs are known with certainty. The errors in cost figures (or return figures) are clearly important in decisions of management. They are important in deciding how much effort to put into the task of gathering cost information and transmitting it. The errors are also important in understanding the risks entailed in decisions. Yet company data-processing systems do not generate information about the errors of estimated costs, and in this respect, again, we lack a sound basis for verifying managerial decisions based on costs.

Rules for Determining Probability

The probability of an event is determined by the formula $p(E) = O/C$, by which we mean that the probability that an event (E) will occur is determined by:

$$\frac{\text{Number of Possible Outcomes}}{\text{Total Number of Cases}}$$

For example, the probability that heads will appear on one flip of the coin is 50% or .5, because only one outcome is possible (either heads or tails), while the total number of cases (heads and tails) is two. We can state this outcome formally as $p(H) = .5$. It follows that $p(T) = .5$ as well. Because each toss of the coin is *independent,* these odds do not change regardless of the number of attempts.

Similarly, the probability that the number six will appear on one throw of the die is $p(\#6) = 1/6$ or $16\frac{2}{3}\%$. The probability that I will cut an ace from one shuffle of a deck of cards is $p(A) = 4/52$ or 7.7%, as there are fifty-two cards and four aces in a deck. If we don't add the ace back into the deck, the probability of drawing an ace as the next card is $p(A) = 3/51$ or 5.9%, as there are now only fifty-one cards and three aces left in the deck.

While we cannot expand further on probabilities in this book, the following rules may be of value:

RULE 1: The entire probability range including problems of certainty, uncertainty, and risk is given as:

$$0 \leq p(E) \leq 1$$

[8] C. West Churchman, *Prediction and Optimal Decision: Philosophical Issues of a Science of Values* (Englewood Cliffs, N.J.: Prentice-Hall, Inc., 1961), p. 65.

RULE 2: Problems of risk cover the range:

$$0 < p(\text{E}) < 1$$

RULE 3: The probability that an event will occur is determined by:

$$p(\text{E}) = \frac{O}{C} \quad \text{or} \quad \frac{\text{Number of Possible Outcomes}}{\text{Total Number of Cases}}$$

RULE 4: The probability that an event will *not* occur is:

$$1 - p(\text{E})$$

RULE 5: Events are said to be *mutually exclusive* where one outcome precludes the other. For example, the appearance of heads on the toss of a coin eliminates tails as the outcome.

RULE 6: *Addition.* If two events, X and Y, are mutually exclusive, the probability *either* will occur is:

$$p(\text{X or Y}) = p(\text{X}) + p(\text{Y})$$

Example: Of a total of fifty marbles, four are red (X) and six are blue (Y). What is the probability of drawing either a red or a blue marble?

$$p(\text{X or Y}) = \frac{4}{50} + \frac{6}{50} = \frac{10}{50} = .2 \text{ or } 20\%$$

RULE 7: *Multiplication.* If two events, X and Y, are independent, the probability that both events will occur is:

$$p(\text{X and Y}) = p(\text{X}) \times p(\text{Y})$$

Example: There is a 30% chance that Mr. Brown (X) will be elected mayor on November 5. There is a 50% chance that it will rain (Y) on November 5. What is the probability that Mr. Brown will be elected on a rainy day?

$$p(\text{X and Y}) = .30 \times .50 = .15$$

RULE 8: *Addition, where the events are not mutually exclusive.* Where X and Y are not mutually exclusive, the probability either X or Y will occur is determined by the formula:

$$p(\text{X or Y}) = p(\text{X}) + p(\text{Y}) - p(\text{X and Y})$$

Example: There are four aces (X) and thirteen spades (Y) in a deck of cards. What is the probability that I will draw either an ace (X) or a spade (Y)?

$$p(\text{X}) = \frac{4}{52}$$

$$p(\text{Y}) = \frac{13}{52}$$

$$p(\text{X and Y}) = \frac{4}{52} \times \frac{13}{52} = \frac{52}{2704} = \frac{1}{52} \quad \text{(See Rule 7)}$$

therefore:

$$p(\text{X or Y}) = \frac{4}{52} + \frac{13}{52} - \frac{1}{52} = \frac{16}{52}$$

X and Y are not independent in this example, since one card is the ace of spades. The probability of drawing an ace of spades is 1/52 and this number must be subtracted from the probability of drawing an ace or a spade.

RULE 9: *Multiplication, where events are not independent.* Where X and Y are not independent, the probability that event X will occur given Y is:

$$p(\text{X}/\text{Y}) = \frac{p(\text{X} \cap \text{Y})}{p(\text{Y})}$$

or that Y will occur given X is:

$$p(\text{Y}/\text{X}) = \frac{p(\text{Y} \cap \text{X})}{p(\text{X})}$$

where, $\cap$ = intercept, X/Y means that X is conditional on Y, and vice versa for Y/X. We refer to this type of problem as one of *conditional probability.* As the name suggests, one event precedes the other and hence the second outcome is conditional upon the first.

Example: There is an 80% chance that I will go to the baseball game on Friday night (X). There is a 10% chance that I will meet Harold at the game (Y) provided I go. What is the probability that I will meet Harold at the game?

$$\begin{aligned} p(\text{Y} \cap \text{X}) &= p(\text{X}) \times p(\text{Y}/\text{X}) \\ &= .8 \times .1 \\ &= .08 \end{aligned}$$

2.4 COMPLEX DECISIONS

DECISION NETWORKS

We have limited our discussion thus far to single decisions. It is readily apparent, however, that decisions are often dependent on other decisions. A variety of dependencies among decisions (or activities) are defined in Exhibit 2-4.

EXHIBIT 2-4 TYPES OF DEPENDENT DECISIONS OR ACTIVITIES

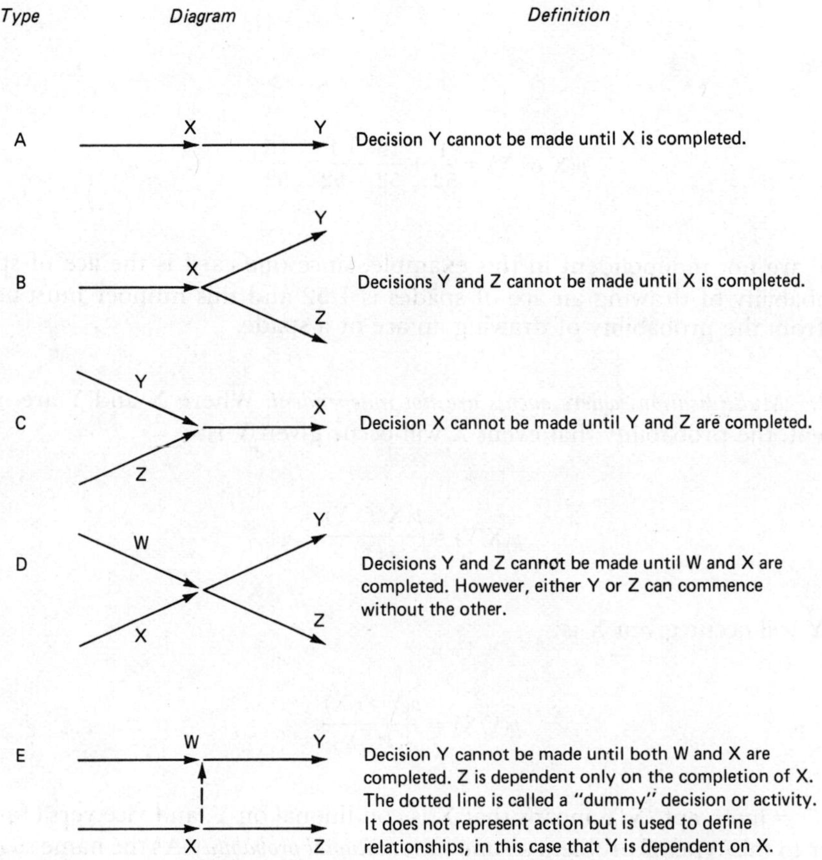

Type
Diagram
Definition
A
X
Y
Decision Y cannot be made until X is completed.
B
X
Y
Z
Decisions Y and Z cannot be made until X is completed.
C
Y
Z
X
Decision X cannot be made until Y and Z are completed.
D
W
X
Y
Z
Decisions Y and Z cannot be made until W and X are completed. However, either Y or Z can commence without the other.
E
W
Y
X
Z
Decision Y cannot be made until both W and X are completed. Z is dependent only on the completion of X. The dotted line is called a "dummy" decision or activity. It does not represent action but is used to define relationships, in this case that Y is dependent on X.

These dependent decisions or activities form *networks*. The basic building block of networks are *events* and *activities*. The event represents the culmination of the activity. In the case of decisions, the *lines* represent decision processes while the *node* (circle) refers to the decision itself.

EXHIBIT 2-5 NETWORK COMPONENTS

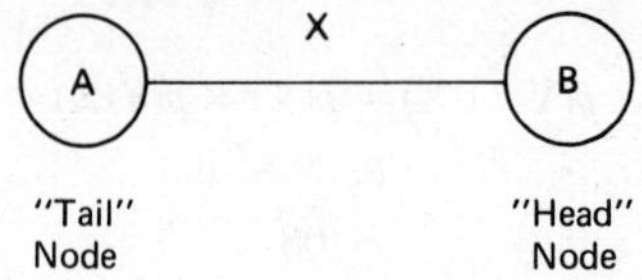

In Exhibit 2-5, activity X connects events A and B. Note that A is called the "tail" node, while B is called the "head" node.

Exhibit 2-6 represents a "six-event" construction project.

EXHIBIT 2-6 SIX-EVENT NETWORK

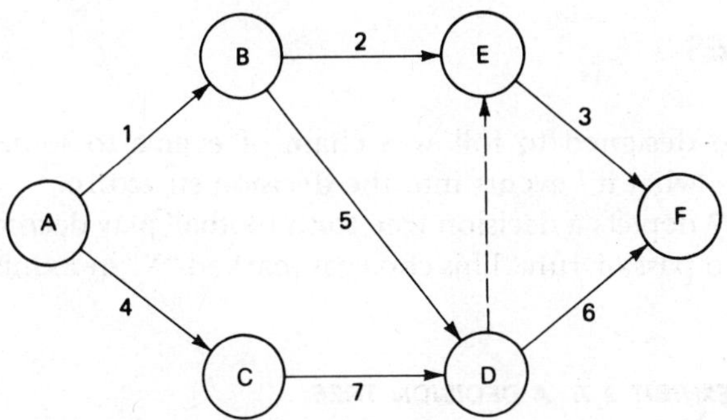

The number of days to complete each activity is indicated. For example, activity A-B requires one day; activity E-F requires three days; and so forth.

If you think of Exhibit 2-6 as a road map, and you wish to get from Town A to Town F, there are *five* alternative routes or *paths:*

		Distance	Slack
Path 1:	A-B-E-F	1 + 2 + 3 = 6	11
Path 2:	A-B-D-E-F	1 + 5 + 0 + 3 = 9	8
Path 3:	A-B-D-F	1 + 5 + 6 = 12	5
Path 4:	A-C-D-E-F	4 + 7 + 0 + 3 = 14	3
Path 5:	A-C-D-F	4 + 7 + 6 = 17	0

If your objective is to minimize travel time, you would take path 1. In network problems, however, we do not have this choice. All paths are being traveled simultaneously and no one can reach F before anyone else. For example, we cannot leave E until the D-E group has arrived. In problems of this type our concern shifts from the shortest path to the *longest* one, which is called the *critical path.* It is critical because it determines the overall length of the project. The critical path in Exhibit 2-6 is path 5, as it requires seventeen days. We can reduce the overall length of the project by supervising this path more critically than the others.

The differences between the critical path and all other paths are referred to as *slack.* Path 4 has three days of slack, path 3 has five days of slack, path 2 has eight days of slack, and path 1 has eleven days of slack. Slack measures the extent to which we can be inefficient in these given activities without lengthening the overall project.

Formal systems of network analysis are known as PERT (program evaluation and review technique) and CPM (critical path method). Activities can be measured in units of time, money, or both. These network systems have proved of great value in controlling major projects, including the design and installation of management information systems.

DECISION TREES

Decision trees are designed to follow a chain of events to some final outcome. It allows us to bring "what if" events into the decision structure.

Exhibit 2-7 depicts a decision tree for a football play decision. On a given play we have a choice to pass or run. This choice is marked "X" in Exhibit 2-7. If we decide

EXHIBIT 2-7 A DECISION TREE

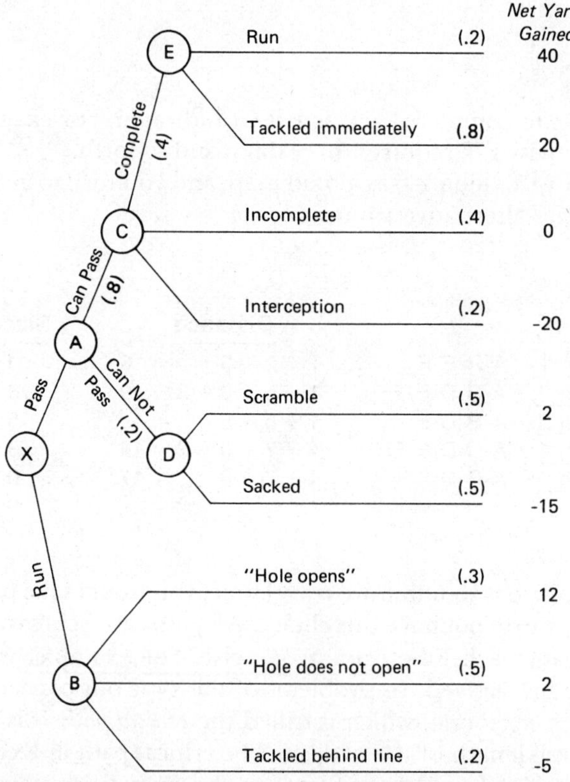

to pass (select option A) there are a number of various outcomes. There are also various outcomes if we select option B. All of these outcomes, identified by the lines which exit circles A through E, are called "chance events." In this decision tree there is only one decision, X, which is to *pass* or *run*. All events thereafter are based on chance.

The probabilities that these events will occur are shown in brackets. For example, if we decide to pass there is an 80% (.8) chance that we can pass and a 20% (.2) chance that we will be unable to pass. Notice that these two factors total 100% (1), which accounts for all of the possible outcomes of A. The possible outcomes of all other events also add to 1.

To complete the decision table we need an estimate of the final outcome for each chance event. In this example we are concerned with "net yards gained." Notice that if we can pass, several things can happen: (1) we can complete the pass, (2) the pass will fall incomplete, and (3) the pass will be intercepted. Probabilities of .4, .4, and .2 (for a total of 1) have been assigned to these outcomes. If we complete the pass (E), we have two possible outcomes. The receiver can run further with the ball *or* he is tackled immediately.

With decision trees we calculate the "expected value" of each outcome, working from the branches of the tree back to the base decision. The solution to this problem is shown in Exhibit 2-8. Having caught the ball at E, the expected value of running further is $.2 \times 40 = 8$ yards. The expected value of being tackled immediately is

EXHIBIT 2-8 EXPECTED VALUE OF CHANCE EVENTS

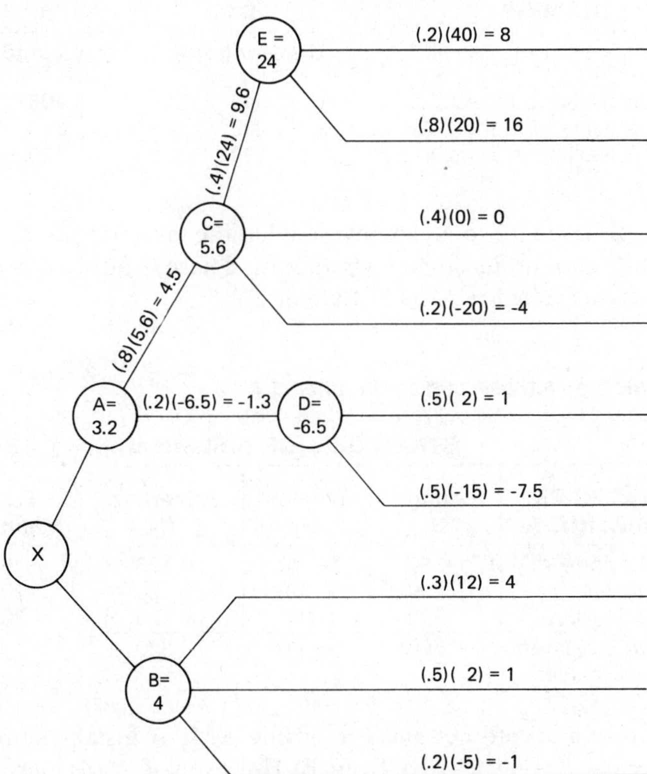

$.8 \times 20 = 16$ yards. As these are mutually exclusive outcomes, we add them according to Rule 6 to obtain the expected value of E, which is 24 yards. This outcome, in turn, is combined with the other possible results of C to yield an expected value of C of 5.6 yards, and so forth back to A and B. Given all of the probable outcomes of decision X, our choice should be option B in that it is likely to yield 4 yards instead of 3.2 for option A.

DECISION STRATEGIES

A *strategy* is a decision process which takes into account the actions of others. This type of decision making is often referred to as *game theory* in that it recognizes that others react to our decisions, and if we can anticipate their reaction we are more likely to make the right decision. Decision strategy is based on the general principle that one person's gain is another person's loss.

As an example we will use two airlines (A and B) which are considering three *independent* strategies for increasing their share of passenger traffic. The three strategies are: (1) install a lounge, (2) have movies in flight, and (3) advertise in *Time* magazine. The probable trade-offs are computed as follows:

STRATEGY	If A does, but B does not, A will gain from B (Passengers)	If B does, but A does not, B will gain from A (Passengers)
1. Install a lounge	340	400
2. Movies in flight	200	260
3. Advertise in *Time*	100	120

Because B has more capital to invest, it has the most to gain from all strategies. Airline A can only gain under limited conditions. These conditions become apparent if we prepare a *payoff table* for A, as in Exhibit 2-9.

EXHIBIT 2-9 PAYOFF TABLE FOR AIRLINE A

	STRATEGIES OF AIRLINE B			
STRATEGIES OF AIRLINE A	**Lounge B_1**	**Movies B_2**	**Advertise B_3**	**Row Minimum**
A_1 Lounge	− 60	+ 80	+220	− 60*
A_2 Movies	−200	− 60	+ 80	−200
A_3 Advertise	−300	−160	− 20	−300
Column Maximum	− 60*	+ 80	+220	

*Minimax solution.

The plusses indicate net gains to airline A. If A installs lounges and B advertises, A will gain 220 passengers from B. However, if A decides to spend its resources on advertising while B installs lounges, A will lose 300 passengers. Given this analysis, A has no choice but to install lounges if B does. While A will still lose 60 passengers, it would lose many more if it selected one of the other strategies.

The best solution to this type of problem is called *minimax* in that it consists of selecting the minimum figure in each row, the maximum figure in each column, and choosing figures which are *equal and represent the best outcome* for A. Of course if A learns that B has already committed its budget for advertising, A can benefit from B's error by installing lounges and attracting 220 passengers from B.

2.5 BEHAVIOR AND ORGANIZATION THEORY

Decisions are made by people. Information systems function through the actions of people. For these reasons, decision theory which ignores the human factor is incomplete. Again, there is a vast literature on the behavior of people in organizations, and we can only scratch the surface of this important topic. The accountant needs to develop an interest in behavioral science and organization theory if he is to interact effectively with other persons in the organization. On the one hand he needs to be responsive to the needs of others, but he must also exercise leadership over his staff and motivate them to higher levels of achievement. The persons with whom he deals in the organization range from top executives to supervisors and foremen. The way in which he interacts with these various types of people must differ depending on their personality traits and other factors.

TRADITIONAL AND CONTEMPORARY THEORY

Broadly speaking, there are two distinct schools of organization theory: (1) the traditional, and (2) the contemporary. These schools differ widely as to the role of goals, motivation, leadership style, and type of management information system required. The contrasts are sketched in Exhibit 2-10:

EXHIBIT 2-10 TRADITIONAL VERSUS CONTEMPORARY ORGANIZATION THEORY

GOALS

Traditional	Contemporary
1. There is a single goal, which is to maximize profit.	1. There are many goals of a social, economic, and personal nature.
2. The single profit goal can be divided into sub-goals, such as departmental budgets, and assigned to various parts of the organization.	2. The complexity of many goals makes division extremely difficult. Rather, it can be expected that groups will form around various goals, similar to political parties. This viewpoint stresses that people are likely to ascribe to different goals.
3. Goals can be added together to form bigger goals.	3. Goals are not additive in that they are often in conflict with each other. Compromises, trade-offs, and persuasion lead to the selection of some goals versus others.

EXHIBIT 2-10 (CONTINUED)

Traditional	**Contemporary**
4. Everyone works together to achieve the common purpose.	4. Persons are working toward different objectives within the same organization.

MOTIVATION

Traditional	**Contemporary**
1. There is one major motivation—economic reward. Greater pay achieves greater output.	1. There are many motivators at work in addition to economic reward.
2. Work is basically unpleasant to people. Economic reward makes it palatable.	2. Work can be made pleasant and enjoyable. The solution to unpleasant work is "job enrichment" rather than merely an increase in economic reward.
3. People are basically inefficient and wasteful.	3. People are basically efficient. Often organizational rules and procedures turn people into inefficient and wasteful creatures. The search for causes of inefficiency shifts from people to the institution.

LEADERSHIP STYLE

Traditional	**Contemporary**
1. The climate is one of *authority*—people must know "who is boss." People can be made to listen and obey.	1. The climate is one of *persuasion.* The leader convinces people of the value of his objectives.
2. Increased supervision produces increased output.	2. People are basically self-motivated. While they respond favorably to leadership, they resent exploitation. The wrong type of supervision will lower rather than increase output.
3. The art of management consists of manipulating the reward structure. Paying higher wages to more efficient workers will induce the others to greater efforts.	3. The art of management consists of knowing the individual as a person and applying a variety of motivators as may be needed in his particular circumstances. Greater economic reward is not the most effective motivator, as mentioned above.

EXHIBIT 2-10 (CONTINUED)

ROLE OF THE MANAGEMENT INFORMATION SYSTEM

Traditional	Contemporary
1. Supply data which is needed to maximize profit. (The accounting system has performed this role historically.)	1. Supply data as to all major goals and objectives of the organization.
2. Only economic data is required.	2. A variety of socioeconomic data is required.
3. Only cost data is needed for control purposes.	3. Decisions can only be made where we have information as to costs and benefits. Both types of data are needed.
4. As we are dealing primarily with quantitative, financial information, uniformity in reporting is desirable.	4. Information is needed for different purposes. The need is for diversity rather than uniformity.

Traditional theory is evidenced strongly in economics and scientific management. Much of economics builds upon the concepts of profit maximization and financial reward as being the critical motivator. The work of the Gilbreths,[9] Taylor,[10] and other *scientific management theorists* focused on mechanistic aspects of productivity. Their tool in trade was time and motion studies. This quantitative approach to organization theory is evident in the more recent works of Von Neumann,[11] Hitch,[12] and Schlaifer.[13]

Contemporary organization theory has its roots in psychology. What is known today as "behavioral science" is the application of psychology to formal organizations—how people behave in work environments. One of the earliest specialists in this field was Max Weber.[14]

IMPORTANT CONTEMPORARY THEORIES

Contemporary organization theory is dominant presently, and we will focus briefly on three important theories: (1) types of motivation, (2) levels of motivation, and (3) leadership style.

[9]The Gilbreths are best known for their book, *Cheaper by the Dozen.* The more serious work is by Lillian Gilbreth, *The Psychology of Management* (New York: The Macmillan Company, 1914).

[10]Frederick W. Taylor, *The Principles of Scientific Management* (New York: Harper & Row, 1911).

[11]John Von Neumann, "The General and Logical Theory of Automata," *Cerebral Mechanisms in Behavior* (New York: John Wiley & Sons, Inc., 1951); and with Oskar Morgenstern, *Theory of Games and Economic Behavior* (Princeton, N.J.: Princeton University Press, 1944).

[12]Charles J. Hitch, *Decision Making for Defense* (Berkeley: University of California Press, 1966).

[13]Robert D. Schlaifer, *Analysis of Decisions Under Uncertainty* (New York: McGraw-Hill Book Company, 1967).

[14]Max Weber, *The Theory of Social and Economic Organizations* (London: Oxford University Press, 1947).

EXHIBIT 2-11 FACTORS AFFECTING WORK ATTITUDES

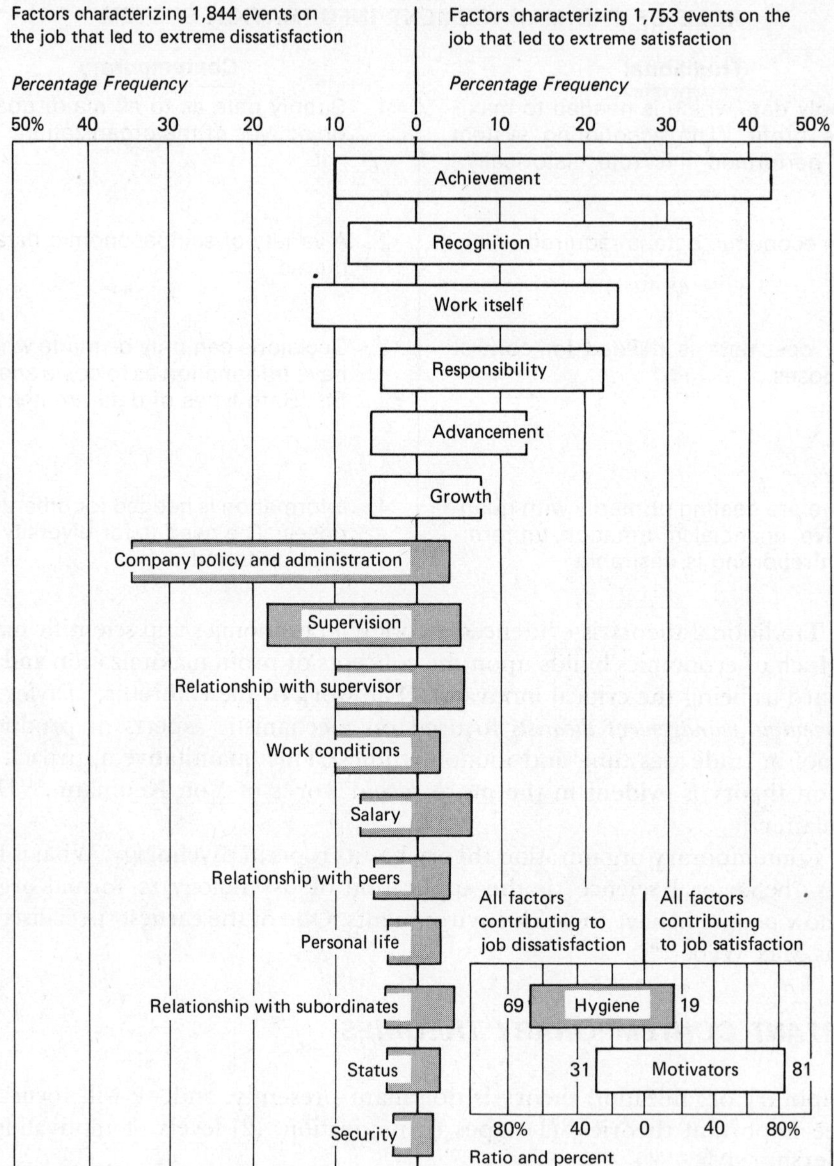

SOURCE: Frederick Herzberg, "How Do You Motivate Employees?" p. 57. Used with permission.

Frederick Herzberg has studied the interesting question of why persons may lack motivation even though pay and other working conditions are outstanding.[15] This investigation led him to distinguish between *hygiene factors* and *motivators.* Stated simply, hygiene factors can prevent people from being unhappy but they do not con-

[15]Frederick Herzberg, "One More Time: How Do You Motivate Employees?" *Harvard Business Review,* January-February 1968, p. 53; and "Job Enrichment Pays Off," *Harvard Business Review,* March–April 1969, p. 61.

tribute much to happiness in the work environment. On the other hand, motivators contribute to happiness (they constitute what is called "job enrichment"), but they cannot prevent unhappiness in the absence of hygiene factors. Hygiene factors include items such as pay, physical environment, working hours, titles, supervisory relationships, and authority over subordinates. Motivators include such items as achievement, recognition, meaningful work, advancement, and personal growth. A summary of Herzberg's analysis on the effectiveness of these factors is contained in Exhibit 2-11.

The psychologist A. H. Maslow has linked *needs* and *motivation*.[16] He has demonstrated that as certain needs are satisfied, new motivators are required to make progress beyond that point. This work has led to the development of a "need pyramid" or hierarchy, as shown in Exhibit 2-12.

EXHIBIT 2-12 MASLOW'S NEED HIERARCHY

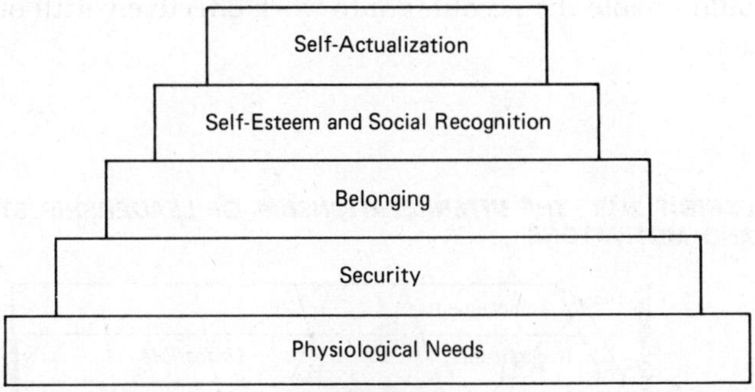

Self-Actualization

Self-Esteem and Social Recognition

Belonging

Security

Physiological Needs

Our most basic needs are physiological: rest, food, and freedom from illness. Economic motivation is strongest at this level. As these basic needs are met, safety and security become important. Working conditions, seniority, pension plans, and other fringe benefits play an important motivational role at this level and account for the drive toward unionization.

After security needs are satisfied, factors such as affiliation and need for love and companionship come into play. These needs can be met by providing adequate opportunity for socializing. Teams, organized sports, conferences, and similar strategies are employed for this purpose. Next there is the need for self-esteem and recognition. The focus shifts to individual attention because each person achieves self-esteem and looks for recognition as an individual. The highest level is self-actualization. Motivation at this level arises primarily from *within* the individual. He is capable of setting goals for himself and achieving them. External motivation is much less important to a person who has fulfilled all of the lower level needs.

Rensis Likert[17] has devoted much study to leadership styles. He has recognized four major types of leadership: (1) exploitive, (2) benevolent authority, (3) consultative, and (4) participative. The *exploitive* leader views people as machines and has little concern for their higher level needs. He appeals to basic physical and economic security; he uses fear, threats, punishments, and occasional rewards to achieve his objectives. The *benevolent authoritative* leader assumes a "fatherly" attitude toward his employees. He identifies organizational goals as being his own. By pleasing him,

[16] A. H. Maslow, *Motivation and Personality* (New York: Harper & Row, 1954).

[17] Rensis Likert, *New Patterns of Management* (New York: McGraw-Hill Book Company, 1961), pp. 223–33.

employees are achieving the organization's goals as well. Loyalty is supreme. Rewards are viewed as personal favors and evidence that employees have pleased the boss. *Consultative* leadership inquires as to employee opinion, but "decisions are still made at the top after weighing the advice." In terms of Maslow's hierarchy, this type of leadership could furnish motivators through the "belonging" level. The *participative* leader is the most progressive. He attempts to synthesize employee opinion and act in the interests of the majority. Employees participate in decision making. This type of leadership permits motivators at the top level of self-actualization to be brought into play.

The interrelationship among these three theories is illustrated in Exhibit 2-13. Notice that the leadership style determines how far we can progress toward need satisfaction through the use of higher level motivators.

Finally, Herzberg and others[18] have studied human factors of managers at various levels in the organization as summarized in Exhibit 2-14. A knowledge of these factors should enable the accountant to work effectively with others at all levels in the organization.

EXHIBIT 2-13 THE INTERRELATIONSHIP OF LEADERSHIP STYLES, NEEDS, AND MOTIVATORS

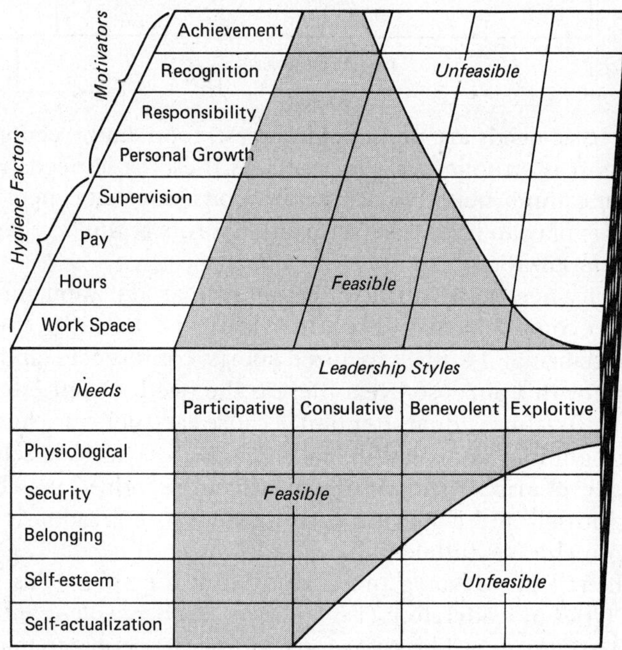

[18]Frederick Herzberg, Bernard Mausner, and Barbara Block Synderman, *The Motivation to Work* (New York: John Wiley & Sons, Inc., 1959).

EXHIBIT 2-14 HUMAN FACTORS AT VARIOUS ORGANIZATIONAL LEVELS

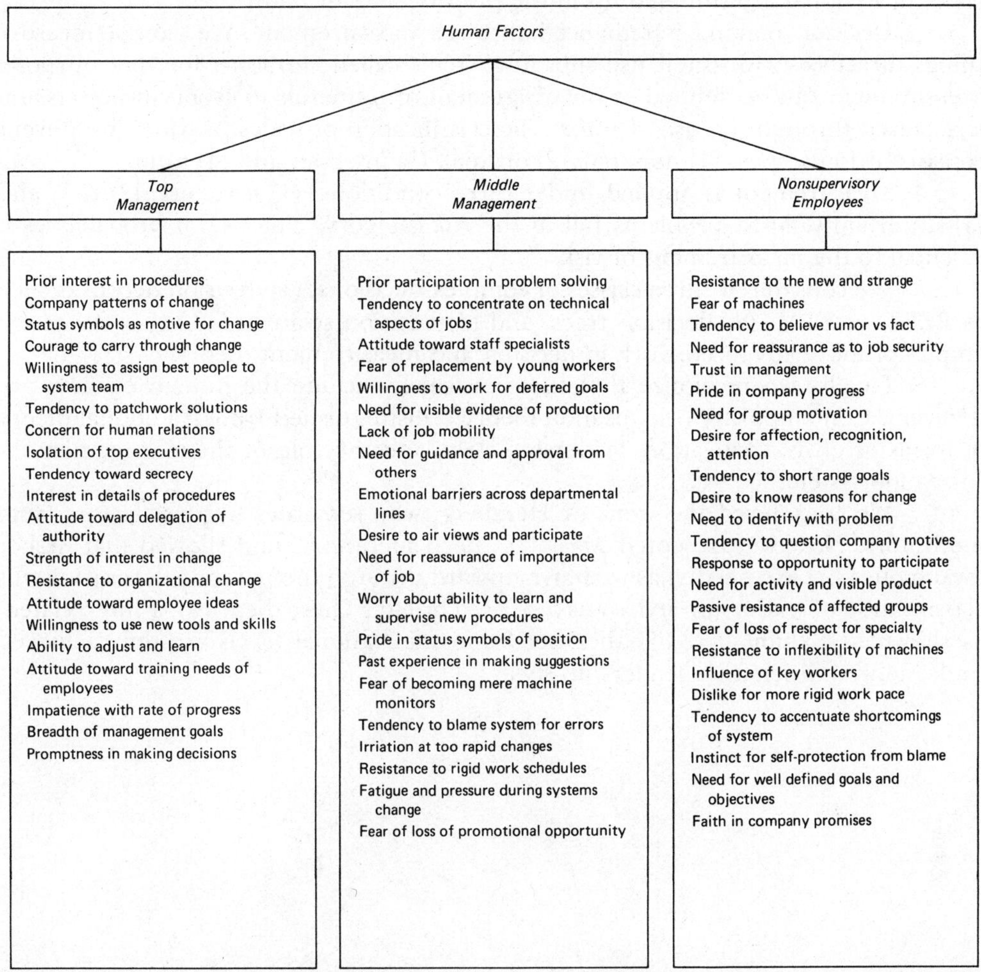

SOURCE: James B. Bower and J. Bruce Sefert, "Human Factors in Systems Design," *Management Services,* November–December 1965, p. 92. Copyright 1965 by the American Institute of Certified Public Accountants, Inc. Used with permission.

2.6 SUMMARY

We have considered some of the conceptual foundations for accounting as an information system in this chapter. We began by stressing the importance of theory in designing and operating information systems. A basic decision model is shown in Exhibit 2-1. According to this model, a decision maker can identify a problem and then undertake a systematic search for the best solution. The handicaps he experiences in so doing are summed up in the phrase "state of nature."

Decision making is enhanced through measurement. We cannot measure things directly, so we often use substitute items called *surrogates* for that purpose. Measurement can be defined as the assignment of numerals to events or objects and is achieved through the use of *scales*. The classification of scales provided by Stevens consists of four types: (1) nominal, (2) ordinal, (3) interval, and (4) ratio.

Measurement is applied under three conditions: (1) certainty, (2) risk, and (3) uncertainty. Most problems fall in the *risk* category. The use of probabilities is essential to the measurement of risk.

We considered three classes of complex decisions: (1) decision networks such as PERT or CPM, (2) decision trees, and (3) decision strategies. They serve as examples of more advanced work in decision and measurement theory.

Finally, we recognize that theories which exclude the human element are deficient. Contemporary organization theory is distinguished from traditional theory in terms of goals, motivation, leadership style, and the role of the management information system.

We considered the work of Herzberg, who separates hygiene factors from motivators. Next we presented Maslow's "need hierarchy" and showed that higher level motivators are needed as we move upward through the pyramid. Rensis Likert's classification of leadership styles was discussed briefly. These theories are interrelated, as shown in Exhibit 2-13. Higher need and motivational levels are only achieved under more participative leadership styles.

CHAPTER 2 REFERENCES AND ADDITIONAL READINGS

Boulding, Kenneth E. "General Systems Theory—The Skeleton of Science." *Management Science*, April 1956, pp. 197–208.

Bross, Irwin D. F. *Design for Decision*. New York: The Macmillan Company, 1961.

Buckley, John W. "Goal-Process-System Interaction in Management." *Business Horizons*, December 1971, pp. 81–92.

Churchman, C. West. *The Systems Approach*. New York: Dell Publishing Company, 1968, pp. 1–78: "What is a System?"

Mockler, Robert J. "The Systems Approach to Business Organization and Decision Making." *California Management Review*, Spring 1968, pp. 53–58.

Murdick, Robert G., and Ross, Joel E. *Information Systems for Modern Management*. Englewood Cliffs, N.J.: Prentice-Hall, Inc., 1971, pp. 31–86: "Development of Management and Organization Theory," and pp. 67–102: "Modern Organization Theory: Behavioral Aspects."

Shaffer, L. R.; Ritter, J. B.; and Meyer, W. L. *The Critical Path Method*. New York: McGraw-Hill Book Company, 1965.

Williams, J. D. *The Compleat Strategyst*. New York: McGraw-Hill Book Company, 1954.

CHAPTER 2 QUESTIONS, PROBLEMS, AND CASES

2- 1. Distinguish between *inductive* and *deductive* theory. Which is being applied in the following instances?
   (a) Two objects of different weight are dropped from the Leaning Tower of Pisa to determine which one hits the ground first.
   (b) In *The Twentieth Century,* a book published in 1883, Albert Robida predicted that pictures could be transmitted through air waves.

2- 2. Complete the basic decision model below;

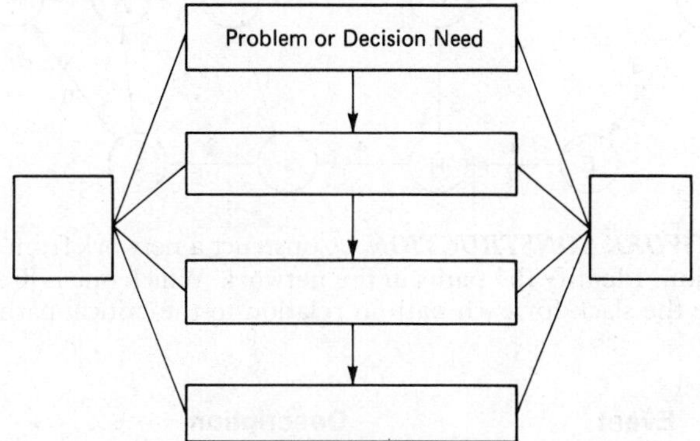

2- 3. There is frequent current reference to *cost-benefit.* Define this expression in relation to the electrical demand problem discussed in chapter 2.

2- 4. The objective of credit management is to assess *capacity* to repay the debt and the *character* of the debtor. How would you measure such abstract concepts?

2- 5. Define measurement. Give examples of measurement scales. Where do measurement scales come from?

2- 6. Stevens has defined four types of measurement scales: (a) nominal, (b) ordinal, (c) interval, and (d) ratio. Give an example of each.

2- 7. "A long-standing criticism of accounting has been its reliance on deterministic models in financial reporting." Why is reliance on a deterministic model subject to criticism?

2- 8. Discuss the differences between traditional and contemporary organization theory as to: (a) goals, (b) motivation, (c) leadership style, and (d) role of the management information system.

2- 9. Why is leadership style important in terms of need satisfaction and type of motivation applied?

2-10. ***PROBABILISTIC MEASURES*** Solve these probability problems using the rules in chapter 2:
   (a) You are a boy in search of a date. The girls are identified only by number. Actually there are three blonds and four brunettes. What is the probability that you will choose a blond? A brunette?
   (b) There is a 15% chance that it will rain on April 30. There is a 50% chance that April 30 will be selected for a school outing to the beach. What are the odds of a rainy day at the beach?
   (c) There is an 80% probability that you will drive along Pearblossom Highway on Saturday evening, and there is a 10% probability that you will see

a deer crossing the highway. What is the probability of seeing a deer crossing the highway on Saturday evening?

(d) What is the probability of drawing a queen *or* a heart from the first draw of a deck of cards?

2-11. ***NETWORK ANALYSIS*** Identify the paths in the following network. Which one is the critical path? Why is it called the critical path? Compute the slack of all other paths in relation to the critical path. (Number the paths 1, 2, . . . from the shortest to the longest.) Units are in days.

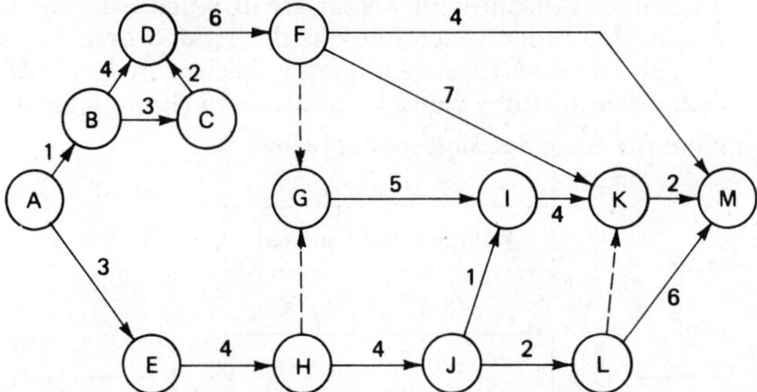

2-12. ***NETWORK CONSTRUCTION*** Construct a network from the following information. Identify the paths in the network. Which one is the critical path? Compute the slack for each path in relation to the critical path.

Event	Description	Minutes
A	The alarm rings	
B	Get out of bed	5
C	Fill the tub with water	6
D	Brush teeth while tub is filling	1
E	Shave while tub is filling	3
F	Put eggs on to boil while tub is filling	1
G	Wait for water to cool down, tub too hot	3
H	Reduce heat to "warm" on eggs	1
I	Bathe & dry	5
J	Make coffee	8
K	Dress	5
L	Toast bread	3
M	Bring in newspaper	2
N	Have breakfast and read paper	6
O	Clear table	2
P	Lock house and leave for work	

How can we reduce the critical path and get to sleep a little later?

2-13. ***DECISION TREE*** Compute the expected values of the chance events in the following decision tree, and determine which decisions to make on the basis of the information provided. The problem deals with introducing a new product to the market. The final outcomes are in millions of dollars in sales.

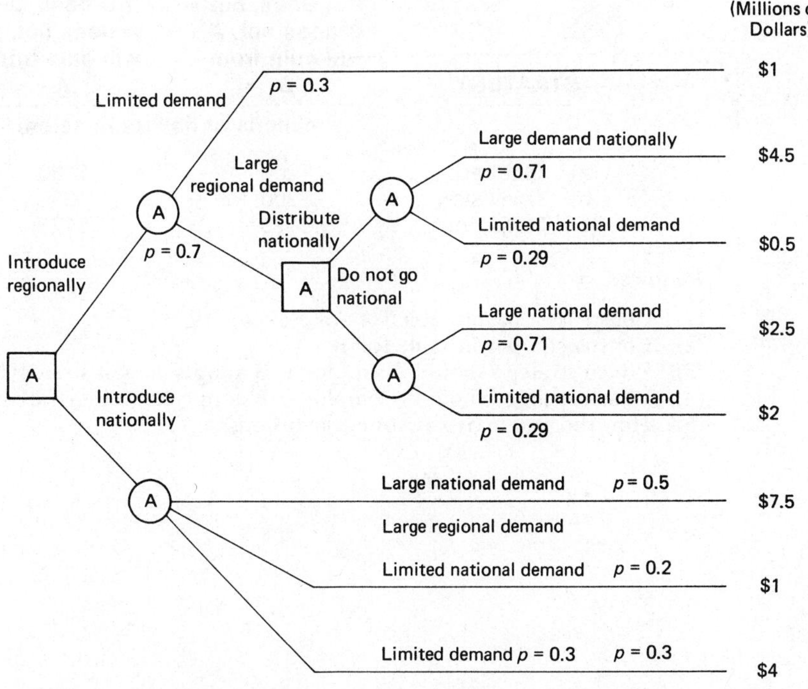

2-14. ***DECISION TREE*** Construct and solve a decision tree problem given this information. The basic decision is whether to manufacture or import a given item. Our calculations are based on selling 10,000 items. The items will sell for $100 each and our analysis at present indicates that it would cost $40 per item if we import and $41 per item if we manufacture. However, we have been urged to take various possible future events into consideration. We are furnished with these estimates:

(a) There is a 20% probability that the government will impose a 10% tax on imports, effective immediately.
(b) If the government imposes the tax, there is a 70% probability that we will bear the full burden of the tax.
(c) There is a 40% probability that transportation costs on imports will increase by $1.50 per item.
(d) There is a 40% probability that the foreign supplier will increase his price by 5% on the last 5,000 items.
(e) If we manufacture there is a 10% chance that labor costs will increase by 10% for the last 5,000 items. Labor costs are at present $20 an item.
(f) If we manufacture there is a 40% probability that raw material costs will increase for the last 8,000 items from $10 to $12 an item.
(g) There is a 50% probability that there will be no cost increases during the period.

2-15. ***PAYOFF TABLE*** Company A has $100,000 to spend on increased advertising. It is considering one of three strategies: (a) billboards, (b) television, or (c) magazines. Its competitor is company B. Analysts for company A provide you with the following data:

STRATEGY	If A does, but B does not, A will gain from B	If B does, but A does not, B will gain from A
	(millions of dollars in sales)	
(a) Billboards	$200	$180
(b) Television	$300	$350
(c) Magazines	$170	$175

Required:

(1) Construct a payoff table for A.
(2) Construct a payoff table for B.
(3) Which strategy should A employ if B adopts its best strategy?
(4) Which strategy should A employ if B adopts its worst strategy?
(5) How did you arrive at your conclusions?

CHAPTER

3

ACCOUNTING AS AN INFORMATION SYSTEM

3.1 ACCOUNTING AS AN INFORMATION SYSTEM

The accounting function in organizations conforms in theory to an information system. We view it as having the characteristics shown in Exhibit 3-1.

EXHIBIT 3-1 THE ACCOUNTING INFORMATION SYSTEM

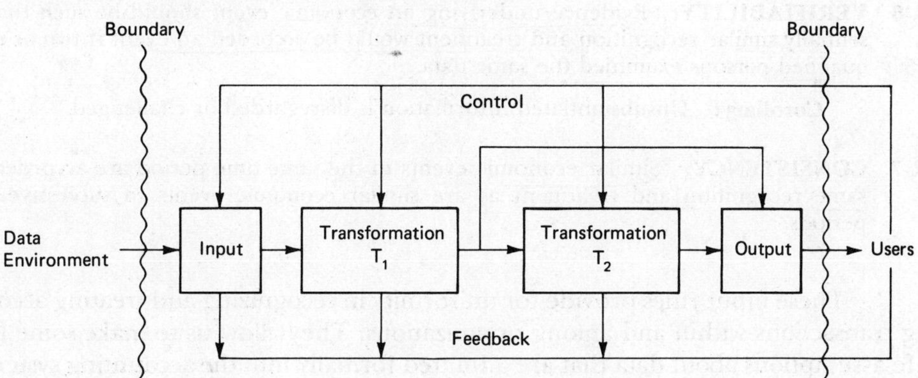

From unlimited data in the environment, the accounting system admits particular data. This data undergoes processing or transformation, and periodically exits the system in the form of financial statements and reports.

3.2 INPUT

THEORY

Referring to Exhibit 3-1, let us consider input into the accounting information system. From a vast amount of known or obtainable data in the environment, only a discrete fraction is admitted into the system. The selection of data is not random. It is accomplished within a framework of carefully defined rules which we identify as (IR-Input Rule):

IR-1 ENTITY: The system serves a particular organization or entity, and admits data relating only to that entity.

Corollary: Data not relating to the entity is disregarded.

IR-2 ECONOMIC EVENTS: The system admits information regarding economic events or transactions generated by past, present, or future exchanges.

Corollary: Noneconomic and hypothetical events are disregarded.

IR-3 QUANTIFICATION: The system admits information which has numbers assigned to it. (Money is the most common but not the only form of quantitative measurement.)

Corollary: Non-quantifiable information is disregarded.

IR-4 RELEVANCE: The system admits information that is known or is assumed to meet the needs of actual or potential users.

Corollary: Information known or assumed to be irrelevant to the needs of actual or potential users is disregarded.

IR-5 NEUTRALITY: The system admits information that is objective and free from bias.

Corollary: Information in the system can be deemed to be neutral unless there is evidence to the contrary.

IR-6 VERIFIABILITY: Evidence underlying an economic event should be such that essentially similar recognition and treatment would be accorded an event if two or more qualified persons examined the same data.

Corollary: Unsubstantiated information is disregarded or challenged.

IR-7 CONSISTENCY: Similar economic events in the same time period are accorded the same recognition and treatment as are similar economic events in successive time periods.

These input rules provide for uniformity in recognizing and treating accounting transactions within and among organizations. They allow us to make some fairly safe assumptions about data that are admitted formally into the accounting system, as well as to know the type of information which is excluded. Accordingly, we can assume that the data admitted is pertinent to a particular organization or entity. For example, when a sale is reported, we can assume that *our* organization made the sale. We can also assume that the sale is an accomplished economic event—it is not contingent nor hypothetical. We can assume that the sale involved consideration or value, and that the money-number assigned to the event was an actual exchange price. The system recognizes the sales transaction because the event is relevant to the needs of the organization. We can assume, unless there is evidence to the contrary, that the transaction was accomplished at arm's-length in the competitive marketplace, and that it occurred in the manner and time period reported. Supporting the transaction is evidence in the form of a contract of sale, invoice, or similar document. The recognition and nature of the treatment given to this sales event conforms with the treatment given to similar sales events, in the same period and in past periods, unless there is a notice of a change in method.

Some further comments on the nature of accounting evidence may be helpful. The fundamental evidence for an accounting event is a *written* record which is referred to as a "transaction document." This is true even in computerized systems. At what point does the accounting system recognize a sale? Suppose a willing buyer and seller agree to price and terms by telephone and their conversation is recorded with the knowledge and consent of both parties. Would the accounting system recognize a sale on the basis of this evidence? No! It would not respond to the event until there was a signed contract of sale or an exchange of cash for a sales receipt. In this example there could be a *legal* sale where there is not an *accounting* sale. Accounting evidence should not be confused with legal evidence.

In the future we may expect departures from the steadfast rule of written documents providing the sole evidence for accounting events.

CONTROL

There are a number of controls operative at the input stage of the system. One control is to pre-number transaction documents such as checks and sales receipts so that we can account for each one. Another control is to separate duties; that is, to have more than one person involved in handling a transaction. This control recognizes that it is difficult for two or more persons to agree to practice dishonesty. Another control is the structure of the accounting system itself; it requires conformance with internal operating controls before a transaction is recognized. These controls can be detrimental where an archaic system thwarts the efforts of the firm to obtain required information. It points to the need for periodic review of the system itself to see that it does meet the current needs of the organization. Still another control is to have different levels of persons in the organization authorized to approve transactions of different magnitudes, such as purchase orders and disbursements.

All of these and other input controls are the product of systems design in accordance with an organization's objectives, policies, and procedures.

FEEDBACK

Feedback reports on the functioning of the system and its controls. It brings problems to the attention of management, and it periodically reviews and reports on nonproblem areas as well. This is important because grey areas of marginal inefficiency are often more harmful to an organization in the long run than are problems which are acute and cognizable.

Some of the specific input concerns are whether the controls are in effect all of the time; whether over-control or under-control is present; or whether the controls which are present are those which were planned for that particular situation. Another useful feedback is a detailed report on transactions which are rejected by the system at the input stage. This type of report is sometimes referred to as an "exception report." Analyzing the reasons for input errors, usually in clerical and keypunch operations, is helpful in improving efficiency. These *control* reports, *exception* reports, as well as *comparative* reports and *interpretive* reports, are usual feedback devices at all stages of the system.

3.3 TRANSFORMATION$_1$ ("JOURNALIZING")

THEORY

In Exhibit 3-1 we pictured the accounting information system as having two transformation stages, which we have labeled T_1 and T_2. The function of transformation is to take raw data and "convert" it into meaningful information.

T_1 is the process of *journalizing.* In manual accounting systems, a specific accounting record or book called a *journal* is used for this purpose (Exhibit 3-2).

EXHIBIT 3-2 THE JOURNAL

1970		Description	Post-Ref.	Debit	Credit
Jan	1	Cash	11110	10,000	
		Capital account	31120		10,000
		To record capital			
	2	Equipment	12410	5,000	
		Accounts payable	21110		5,000

In computerized accounting systems the journal as a specific book or record is dispensed with, but the journalizing function is retained by determining a cause-and-effect relationship for every accounting event. We can examine this function by considering the rules of accounting which relate to the T_1 process (T_1R=Transformation$_1$ Rule):

T_1R-1 ELEMENTS: Each event must be traceable to a known or determinable element of the accounting system. These elements are called "accounts."

Corollary: An event which does not affect a known or determinable account is rejected at T_1.

T_1R-2 DUALITY: Each event has a cause-and-effect relationship on the elements or accounts of the system. Two accounts are affected by each event. (Duality is achieved by the "debit-credit" convention.)

Corollary: An event which does not affect any two known or determinable accounts is rejected at T_1.

T_1R-3 CONSISTENCY: Essentially, similar recognition and assignment of an event to the accounts would be made if two or more qualified persons examined the same data.

Corollary: An event essentially similar to a precedent event which is not assigned to the accounts in the same way is rejected or challenged at T_1.

These rules tell us that the function of "journalizing" is (1) to identify the accounts which are affected by an accounting event, and (2) to establish the *duality* or cause-and-effect relationship of each event.

The *account* is the basic building block of the accounting system. It provides a means for identifying and labeling the types of events that we wish to have the system recognize. It is the smallest unit or center in the system to which we trace and in which we aggregate economic events.

The structure of the accounting system, as detailed in chapter 4, is based on a theory of equality between total resources and equities, or:

RESOURCES = EQUITIES
(Assets) =(Liabilities + Owners' Equity)

This state of equality is referred to as "balance," and the *balance sheet* is a periodic report which shows the status of all assets and equities of an organization at a certain point in time. Total assets *always* equal total equities. This state of equality between opposing categories in the system is a highly useful notion, for it enables us to distinguish the origins of the claims against resources.

To illustrate the function of T_1, let us suppose that a cash sale in the amount of $100 has reached the input stage, and that the event meets all of the input rules of the system. For input purposes the event can be stated simply as "Cash Sale $100." There is no duality at this point. However, the known accounts affected by this event are "Cash" and "Sales," and duality is achieved by the following T_1 instructions:

Increase (Debit): Cash	$100	
Increase (Credit): Sales		$100

The nature of the transaction itself tells us that both cash and sales have been increased by $100, and the above instruction makes it possible for us to record the dual aspect of the event.

CONTROL

The principal control at T_1 is the Chart of Accounts.[1] This "chart" contains a list of all accounts that have been approved for a particular accounting system. EDP (Electronic

[1] An illustrative Chart of Accounts is contained in Appendix A.

Data Processing) requires that numbers as well as titles be assigned to accounts.[2] The Chart of Accounts serves as a control in that it limits the number of accounts to which we can assign events; it provides for uniformity in labeling events; and it rejects transactions that cannot be assigned to an approved account, or which have been given an erroneous name or number. These unusual events require special handling.

Other controls at T_1 include the designation of certain persons to make the assignment of events to accounts; batch control and other balancing methods to ensure an equality between debit and credit entries; as well as numerical control of documents and transactions.

A special operating control is needed with EDP to determine whether or not to complete a particular "run" based on the number and significance of transactions that are rejected at T_1.

FEEDBACK

Feedback at T_1, and at other phases of the system, may be periodic or continuous. Periodic feedback reports on the adequacy of the Chart of Accounts to handle current transactions, on consistency in treating similar events, and on the effectiveness of account coding. As mentioned earlier, feedback of a comparative and interpretive nature is useful, as well as feedback on the control system and on exceptions.

As shown in Exhibit 3-1, T_1 may generate output directly. An example is a subsidiary journal, which is used to issue cash receipt and disbursement reports.

3.4 TRANSFORMATION$_2$ ("POSTING")

THEORY

In a manual accounting system, the T_2 process is referred to as *posting*. Journal entries are recorded in *accounts* in a book called a *ledger*. The ledger is simply a set of all accounts. The essential aspects of an account are illustrated by the "T-account" format, shown in Exhibit 3-3.

The ledger as a specific book is dispensed with in EDP systems, although various printout records take its place; and the term "posting" is no longer used. However, the function of the ledger is retained, which is to sort and aggregate data in accordance with the following rules (T_2R = Transformation$_2$ Rule):

T_2R-1 SORTING: Economic data is recorded in the accounts, as designated by journal entries.

Corollary: Data improperly designated to an account of the system is rejected at T_2.

T_2R-2 AGGREGATION: Data is aggregated in the accounts—similar data in the same account. Positive aggregation increases the balance of an account, while negative aggregation decreases the balance of an account.

[2] Principles and methods of account coding are discussed in Appendix E.

Corollary: Transposition of positive or negative aggregation produces imbalance in the system.

EXHIBIT 3-3 T-ACCOUNT FORMAT

DEBIT				CREDIT			
Date	**Notation**	**Ref.**	**Amount**	**Date**	**Notation**	**Ref.**	**Amount**

The T_2 process is analogous to the function of a post office – it sorts incoming events into their respective boxes ("accounts") according to a given address. The T_2 process is more formal, however, in that it records the events in the date order in which they occur; it records a journal and/or document number on each event in order to trace its origin; and it records both outgoing and incoming events to the same address.

Perhaps a better example is a bank. Banks have a separate account for each depositor. Each event regarding a certain account is recorded on the date in which the bank processes the transaction; a deposit or check reference number is assigned to each event; both outgoing (payments) and incoming (deposits) events are recorded; and a running monetary balance is maintained for each depositor. Positive aggregations (deposits) increase, while negative aggregations (checks issued) decrease, the balance of the account.

CONTROL

Our control at T_2 is to monitor the process of aggregation. Because each event has a dual impact on the accounts, a summary of balances in all of the accounts at any point in time should give us the same debit and credit totals. This summarization of accounts is referred to as a *trial balance* (Exhibit 3-4).

Again, the Chart of Accounts serves as a control at T_2 in that it limits the number of and identifies the ledger accounts which comprise the trial balance.

FEEDBACK

Feedback at T_2 is similar to that at T_1. It reports on the adequacy of the Chart of Accounts and on the effectiveness of account coding. Also there is feedback on events rejected at T_2, as well as to causes of imbalance in the trial balance.

EXHIBIT 3-4

THE UCLAN COMPANY
TRIAL BALANCE
DECEMBER 31, 19–

ACCOUNT* NUMBER	ACCOUNT	DEBIT	CREDIT
11100	Cash	$ 20,800	
11200	Accounts receivable	39,700	
11300	Allowance for doubtful accounts		$ 800
11500	Marketable securities	38,700	
11600	Inventory	49,000	
11800	Investments	2,800	
12100	Land	10,000	
12200	Buildings	70,000	
12300	Accumulated depreciation–buildings		30,000
12400	Equipment	29,000	
12500	Accumulated depreciation–equipment		11,600
13000	Intangible assets	600	
21100	Accounts payable		11,200
21200	Accrued expenses payable (salaries and wages)		14,800
21650	Bonds payable		20,000
31100	Capital stock		34,600
31210	Retained earnings		88,900
31230	Dividends paid	17,800	
41100	Sales		304,900
41140	Sales returns & allowances	3,400	
41210	Interest income		2,600
41300	Cost of goods sold	99,500	
60000–70000	Selling, administrative and general expenses	137,600	
80020	Interest expense	500	
	Totals	$519,400	$519,400

*Account numbers throughout the text are assigned in accordance with the Chart of Accounts in Appendix A.

3.5 OUTPUT

THEORY

An accounting information system furnishes a wide variety of reports or outputs. These range from formal financial statements intended for persons external to the firm to specialized reports for internal management purposes. As noted, this output falls into two broad classes: (1) *external* and (2) *internal.*

External users of accounting reports include stockholder-investors, creditors-lenders, customers-borrowers, labor, and government (including the Internal Revenue Service [IRS], the Securities and Exchange Commission [SEC], and other regulatory agencies). More will be said in later chapters regarding the nature and use of accounting reports.

The formal outputs of the accounting information system are "the financial statements." These consist of: (1) the *balance sheet or statement of financial position,* (2) the *income statement,* (3) the *statement of retained earnings*[3], and (4) the *statement of changes in financial position.* The financial statements include their related footnotes and the auditors' opinion, but they exclude remarks of officers of the organization and other statements, statistics, and projections, even though these items generally are included in *annual reports.* The financial statements are designed primarily for external users, but they are of value to management as well.

Rules relating to the output of the financial statements are (OR = Output Rule):

OR-1 **ENTITY:** The financial statements are those of a particular organization or entity.

Corollary: Accounting data pertaining to other entities or persons (including owners) is excluded.

OR-2 **TIME PERIODS (MATCHING):** Accounting events occur during (or can be assigned to specifiable) periods of time.

Corollary: Events which cannot be assigned to specifiable periods of time are excluded.

OR-3 **GOING CONCERN:** The entity is deemed to have an indefinite future life.

Corollary: Where there is evidence that the entity has a limited life, its financial statements should be stated in terms of liquidation rather than going concern.

OR-4 **CONSISTENCY:** Methods used in accounting for a given entity should be appropriate for the measurement of its financial position and activities; (1) they should be applied consistently to similar accounting events; and (2) they should be followed consistently from period to period.

Corollary: A change in method should be brought explicitly to the attention of readers and users of financial statements.

OR-5 **TENTATIVENESS:** Financial position and operating results for relatively short periods of time are tentative whenever partition or approximation of accounting data as to past, present, or future periods is required.

Corollary: The appearance of "absoluteness" as to partition or approximation of data should be avoided where tentativeness is present.

OR-6 **DISCLOSURE:** The financial statements should disclose that which is necessary to avoid making them misleading within the context of generally accepted accounting rules and procedures.

Corollary: Disclosure as to rules and procedures is as fundamental to making statements not misleading to users as is the disclosure of the accounting data itself.

OR-7 **EXCHANGE PRICE:** Financial position and the results of operations are stated in terms of prices (values) generated by past, present, or future exchanges which have actually taken place or are expected to.

Corollary: Hypothetical, arbitrary, and sentimental values are excluded.

[3]The statement of retained earnings is used to show changes in the earned capital of corporations; a *statement of capital* is used to show changes in the capital position of owners who do business in partnerships or proprietorships.

OR-8 **STABLE MONEY UNIT:** Financial statements are based on the assumption that a stable purchasing power of the monetary unit exists.

Corollary: Financial statements based on data adjusted to some index of purchasing power should clearly indicate the manner of adjustment and its effect on the statements as compared with unadjusted data.

OR-9 **NEUTRALITY:** General purpose financial statements are unbiased with respect to any identifiable class of user.

Corollary: Financial statements intended for a particular class of user should indicate their bias.

OR-10 **ORDERED CLASSES:** Financial statements classify accounts into conventionally ordered classes between and within the respective statements.

Corollary: Financial statements that do not classify accounts into conventionally ordered classes are not considered acceptable in form.

DISCUSSION OF OUTPUT RULES

Entity

As with input data, we can assume that the financial statements refer to a specific *entity,* which is viewed as being distinct from other entities and from its owners. The entity of a corporation is a legal fact in addition to being an accounting rule. The corporation is viewed at law as being an artificial being with all of the rights and privileges of any other person. Among these rights is private property ownership. Stockholders, therefore, do not have claim to any specific assets of the corporation. What they do have is a residual (after creditors) interest in proceeds from the sale of corporate assets in the event of dissolution; or they have dividends, voting rights, and increases in the value of their shares if the firm is successful. For partnerships, and even for the smallest proprietorship, it makes good business sense to separate personal money matters from those of the business.

Time Periods (Matching)

The *time period* rule reminds us that the business process is essentially a continuing one. An entity does not literally cease operations at the end of a year and reopen again. A continuing time horizon represents infinity for measurement purposes and, as we know, it is impossible to measure infinity. The rule of periodicity makes it possible for us to mark off discrete time intervals in order to measure and compare interperiod performance. The standard time interval for financial reporting is a twelve-month period known as a *fiscal year.* The fiscal year may coincide with the calendar year; it may be any arbitrary twelve-month period, such as the July 1–June 30 period used by government; or it could be a *natural business year,* in which case the fiscal year would date with the typical low-point in business activity. There is only one set of financial statements per fiscal period—the year-end statements or *annual report.* Monthly, quarterly, or other *interim* financial statements may be issued, but these do not have the status of the financial statements, nor do they give rise to a new accounting cycle.

The periodicity rule makes it possible for us to compare interperiod data. Accordingly, the sales of year 1 (y_1) can be compared with those of year 2 (y_2). If it were not for this rule, sales would simply aggregate over an extended period into a meaningless mass of data.

From the time period rule we can deduce the practice of *accrual* accounting and the related concept of *matching*. According to the matching concept, transactions which are time-related are assigned to their proper time periods. For example, if first and last months' rents are collected, the first month's rent is an earned revenue in reporting for the current month, but the last month's rent does not belong to the revenue of this month. Hence, it is treated as "deferred" or "unearned income" and appears in the financial statements as a "liability" until it is "earned," that is, until it is assigned to revenue in the month to which it belongs.

A second aspect of the matching concept is to assign activity-related transactions to the activity to which they belong. For example, suppose we purchase two used automobiles for resale—a Volkswagen and a Cadillac. These vehicles enter merchandise inventory at the time of purchase as shown by the following entry:

Merchandise inventory...............	$2,200	
Cash		$2,200

Notation: Purchase of two used automobiles. A Volkswagen for $800, and a Cadillac for $1,400.

At the time we sell one of these vehicles (say the Cadillac, for $1,600 cash), we match its sale with the cost of the Cadillac, and not with the cost of the Volkswagen. The following entries accomplish our objective:

1. Recording the event at selling price:

Cash............................	$1,600	
Sales		$1,600

Notation: Sale of Cadillac at selling price.

2. Recording the event at cost price:

Cost of Sales................	$1,400	
Merchandise inventory		$1,400

Notation: Sale of Cadillac at cost price.

If this is the only transaction for the period, our income statement would be simply:

INCOME STATEMENT

Sales	$1,600
Cost of sales.................	1,400
Net income....................	$ 200

If we matched the sale of the Cadillac with the cost of the Volkswagen, we would report an *incorrect* net income of $800. The inventory value on our balance sheet would be misstated by showing an item in stock worth $1,400 (the cost of the Cadillac) instead of $800 (the cost of the Volkswagen).

Going Concern

The *going-concern* rule leads to a different classification and valuation of accounts than would be needed if we assumed (or knew) that the business would not continue. Facing liquidation, we would arrange assets in the order in which they could be sold for cash in the short-run market. Land might be easier to sell than merchandise inventory, and our ranking would show this fact. Equities would be ranked in the priority of their legal claims—long-term mortgages would precede accounts payable because of the secured nature of the indebtedness. The money values assigned to assets and equities under liquidation would differ substantially from going-concern values. Because the going-concern rules imply the realization of invested capital in future time periods, it cautions users to examine the data in terms of probabilities rather than certainties.

Consistency

The *consistency* rule places a burden on management to call the user's attention to any change in any accounting method that has a material effect on the data being reported. In the absence of notice, the user can assume that no material change has been made. By reporting on an exception basis, this consistency rule makes it unnecessary to restate the multitude of accounting methods and procedures that are used each time the financial statements are issued.

The consistency rule prevents a lot of possible data manipulation. Accounting practice allows for many alternative methods and procedures. For example, there are a number of inventory valuation and depreciation methods. Exhibit 3-5 shows how two oil companies with the same gross revenue can arrive at substantially different net incomes through the use of alternative methods.

If the same methods are used consistently from period to period, net differences over the long term will be minimized. But undisciplined changes can lead to much data distortion.

The consistency rule does not outlaw change. To do so would be to block progress. It allows for change, but requires that the user's attention be drawn to a change and to its effect on the data being presented.

Tentativeness

The *tentativeness* rule stresses the need for distinguishing absolute or complete events from those which are partial or approximate. A *cash sale* is a complete transaction; a *credit sale* is not a complete transaction, so reporting income at the point of making a credit sale is a tentative assignment and assumes cash realization at a future date.

Because of the tentative nature of credit sales, a fraction of the sales amount, based on experience and statistical methods, is placed in an "allowance for doubtful accounts" to which bad debt losses are charged when they materialize. There are many forms of partitioning and approximation of data in accounting reports; these reports do not distinguish tentative from complete events. The tentativeness rule requires that accounting reports should not give an appearance of absoluteness where this is not the case, and it cautions users of reports to be aware of the extent of implicit tentativeness in particular accounts and in the statements as a whole.

Disclosure

The *disclosure* rule seeks to prevent the issuance of misleading accounting reports. From this rule we deduce the related concept of *materiality,* which calls for a level of disclosure based on the significance of the event or data. If a manager, for example, were given the following statement of expenses, his attention would be drawn quite naturally to the marked item:

STATEMENT OF EXPENSES

	Salaries	$5,000
	Rent	1,000
	Telephone	30
→	Miscellaneous expenses	2,000
		$8,030

With respect to the statement as a whole, and to the other accounts, the miscellaneous expense item of $2,000 is obviously out of line. As the name of the account implies, the $2,000 consists of an unknown number of small events, each of which is considered insignificant. But when added together, the sum of these events is very material in its context. Since we have recognized an object-class expense of $30 for "telephone," any other object-class accounts totaling $30 or more that are now buried in the miscellaneous expense account should be extracted and shown separately. There are no hard and fast rules for materiality, but guidelines are used by many organizations and by auditors.

Because of the concise nature of the financial statements, additional information in the form of explanatory footnotes is usually required in order to make the statements not misleading. These footnotes are part of the disclosure process. It follows that they should not be ambiguous or written at a level of "jargonese" that makes it difficult for intended users to get the full story.

The rule of disclosure does not require that an organization give out every bit of information it possesses. Like many other rules, it has a special frame of reference —in this case the body of *generally accepted accounting principles* (rules and procedures) —to which it relates. Full disclosure means that all material events and relationships are shown and explained as called for by the accepted body of rules and procedures. Because these rules and procedures interrelate with the financial data that is disclosed, an understanding of these rules is as meaningful to the interpretation of financial statements as the data itself.

EXHIBIT 3-5 DIFFERENCE IN REPORTED NET INCOME THROUGH THE USE OF ALTERNATIVE ACCOUNTING METHODS BY OIL COMPANY A AND OIL COMPANY B

NET INCOME OF COMPANY B DIFFERS BECAUSE OF:

	Company A	Use of Stock Options for Incentive	Use of Straight-Line Depreciation	Capitalization and Amortization of IDC	Capitalization and Amortization of Nonproductive Exploration	Use of Pay-As-You-Go Basis for Pensions	Flow-Through of Investment Credit	No Provision for Deferred Taxes	Including Loss Carry-Forward in Year Realized	Effect of Acquisition by Pooling-of-Interest	Company B
	Col. 1	Col. 2	Col. 3	Col. 4	Col. 5	Col. 6	Col. 7	Col. 8	Col. 9	Col. 10	Col. 11
Oil and gas sales	$4,000,000										$4,000,000
Production expenses	800,000										800,000
General and Administrative	400,000										400,000
Officers' compensation—											
Base salaries	100,000										100,000
Cash bonuses	40,000	$(40,000)									0
Depreciation and depletion	400,000		$(100,000)								300,000
Intangible development costs	500,000			$(500,000)							0
Amortization of IDC	0			100,000							100,000
Nonproductive exploration	200,000				$(200,000)						0
Amortization of nonproductive exploration	0				40,000						40,000
Pensions	50,000					$(40,000)					10,000
	$2,490,000										$1,750,000
Income before taxes	$1,510,000										$2,250,000

Income taxes—											
Currently payable	500,000	20,000				20,000					540,000
Deferral of investment credit	30,000						$(30,000)				0
Deferred provision	0		50,000	200,000	80,000			$(280,000)			50,000
Reduction from operating loss carry-forward	0								$(100,000)		(100,000)
Total tax provision	$ 530,000										$ 490,000
Operating income	$ 980,000										$1,760,000
Amortization of excess cost created from acquisition by purchase	65,000									$(65,000)	0
Net income	$ 915,000	$ 20,000	$ 50,000	$ 200,000	$ 80,000	$ 20,000	$ 30,000	$ 280,000	$ 100,000	$ 65,000	$1,760,000
Per share earnings on 915,000 shares	$ 1.00										$ 1.92
Market value per share based on 15 times earnings	$15.00										$28.80

SOURCE: R. L. Sikora, Arthur Anderson & Co., "Controversial and Confusing Aspects of Financial Reporting" (Address before the Denver Society of Security Analysts. Denver, Colorado, November 16, 1965). Reprinted with permission.

Exchange Price

It should not be difficult to understand why a rule is needed to govern the values that are assigned to accounts. If such a rule did not exist a firm could assign values on very flimsy grounds. For example, the value assigned to a building could be what the president "thought" it was worth. (We know from our own experience that one person's valuation of his property does not necessarily mean that it is worth that much to someone else.) And other values, such as the "worth" of a certain individual to an organization, could be used to increase reported assets. Little credence would be given to a financial reporting system that permitted a free reign in assigning values.

The *exchange* price rule brings order to the scene by requiring two things: (1) that values be based on exchange prices, and (2) that the exchanges be actual or expected. The building mentioned above was purchased (or constructed) by the firm and the cost was an actual exchange price. Thereafter, according to this rule, the building carries this value, adjusted for depreciation, and not some other figure based on what the president "thinks" that it is worth. Similarly, the "worth" of the individual to the organization does not involve an actual or expected exchange price, so this value is excluded from the statements.

From the exchange price rule we can deduce the concept of *objectivity*. This concept leads us to prefer values based on objective rather than subjective evidence, and requires that the evidence be verifiable.

Stable Money Unit

Currency has both a *face value* and a *purchasing power value*. The United States bill featuring a portrait of George Washington has a face value of $1. This relationship is constant. What a bill of $1 will actually purchase in goods and services at a particular time is another question. It is common knowledge that in a period of rising prices (inflation) $1 will buy less, and in a period of falling prices (recession) $1 will buy more. This quality of money is known as purchasing power.

Purchasing power changes constantly, and there are problems as well as considerable subjectivity associated with measuring general and specific price-level fluctuations and using these measurements to adjust data in the financial statements. For these reasons, the *stable money unit* rule calls for using the face value of currency in financial reporting. Changes in purchasing power which occur after an accounting event has been recognized are not used to modify the event. This means that the financial statements represent dollars of many different purchasing powers, each one keyed to a transaction at a particular price-level.

The stable money unit rule applies to financial transactions generally and is not restricted to the accounting system. Customarily when we borrow an amount—say $1,000—we agree to repay that amount plus a possible interest charge. If we repay the loan a year later when the purchasing power of the dollar has declined—say by 4%—we still repay $1,000. Ignoring interest, the 4% decline in purchasing power represents a *gain* to the borrower of $40.

Neutrality

Financial statements serve the needs of many users, including investors, vendors, customers, financial institutions, labor, and government. The *neutrality* rule requires that the financial statements be unbiased with respect to any identifiable class of user. This rule does not prevent issuing special-purpose statements for a particular user, but it requires that the statements clearly indicate their restricted use.

Ordered Classes

The *ordered classes* rule makes it necessary to organize the data in financial statements in terms of conventional standards. This rule promotes uniformity in financial reporting and requires that data be organized in a manner that facilitates understanding and analysis.

3.6 LIMITATIONS OF OUTPUT RULES

These rules are important to a proper understanding and interpretation of financial statements. They provide for uniformity in external reporting, making it possible to compare one company's financial statements with those of others; and they provide for consistency in reporting on a company's financial position and results of operations from one accounting period to another.

Some limitations are necessary in order to have this uniformity. For example, actual cost is used instead of current value even though the actual exchange price (cost) may not represent real value in a specific case. Land, which may have appreciated in value substantially over a period of years, is still carried at cost. The reason for using cost is because it is an *actual* (known or *objective*) value—while the alternatives all have varying degrees of subjectivity.

Consider the possible alternative methods for valuing a building:

1. Cost: The actual price paid for the building. "Book value" is a cost-based concept. It is the actual price paid, less accumulated depreciation.
2. Appraisal Values:
   a. Replacement: Value of the building based on what it would cost currently to build it. This value is usually computed by multiplying the square footage of a building by a current cost of construction index for that type and quality of building.
   b. Capitalization: An expression of value based on the earning power of the building. This value is computed by dividing a given interest rate into the net rent or earnings (or savings) of the building:

   $$\frac{\text{Net Income}}{\text{Interest Rate}} = \text{Value}$$

   For example, a building with a net income of $100,000, using a .08% interest rate, would have a capitalized value of $1,250,000.

c. Comparables: A value of the building based on an appraiser's comparing it with buildings of a similar type, use, and location that have recently been sold.

3. Assessed Value: A value based on county assessment for property tax purposes. The assessed value is usually a legal fraction of the market value of the property as determined by government appraisers. The value of property can be obtained by dividing the assessed value by the prescribed tax-assessment ratio:

$$\frac{\text{Assessed Value}}{\text{Tax-Assessment Ratio}} = \text{Value}$$

For example, in California, the legal tax-assessment ratio is 25% of market value. Hence a building with a $200,000 assessed value has an indicated market value of $800,000.

4. Market Value: While the purpose of the appraisal and assessment methods is to arrive at market value, this value is theoretically defined as the amount that a willing buyer and seller, in an arm's-length transaction, would accept as an exchange price.

Subjectivity in the alternatives to cost are apparent: (1) The replacement method relies on physical measurements, indexes, and other variables such as type and quality, which allow for a wide range of judgment. (2) The capitalization method requires a somewhat arbitrary interest rate and assumes a future level of earnings, either of which may be subject to speculation; and, of course, different firms would likely choose different interest rates in similar situations. (3) The comparables method has a number of subjective variables, such as the basis and nature of the comparable sales transactions, financing terms, and difficulty in defining a true comparable. (4) The assessment method uses any or all of the above methods, but it is subject to political and other considerations. A property in one location may be assessed quite differently from other properties in the same or other tax area(s). A comparison of assessed values and actual sales in many instances has proved the unreliability of this method for approximating current value. (5) The market value method has little practical use because of failure to comprehend why a property does not change hands in the presence of a willing buyer and seller.

The search for alternatives to historical cost as the basis for valuation is gaining greater impetus in the accounting literature. We discuss these alternatives in chapter 5.

Another major limitation is the use of the stable money unit rule. This rule assumes that the purchasing power of the monetary unit is constant over time, even though there is ample evidence to the contrary. Statistics in an annual report might show sales now (y_{10}) compared with sales ten years ago (y_1) as follows:

	y_1	y_{10}
Sales	$100,000	$180,000

There may or may not have been a "real" increase in sales of $80,000. If the purchasing power of the dollar is the same at both points in time, the $80,000 would be a "real" increase. Indexes are used to measure the purchase power of money, and an index is needed to interpret the above data:

	y_1	y_{10}
Sales	$100,000	$180,000
Index	100	160

There are now two ways to place y_1 and y_{10} sales into the same money-value context:

Use y_1 as a base and restate y_{10} sales in terms of y_1 money value. Y_1 becomes a constant and y_{10}, as with all periods subsequent to y_1, would be adjusted backwards (to the y_1 base index). This is the "constant dollar" method, and the adjusted y_{10} sales would be referred to as "y_{10} constant dollar sales in terms of y_1."

	y_1	y_{10}	Difference
Unadjusted sales	$100,000	$180,000	+$80,000
Index	100	160	–
Adjustment	–	$180,000 $\left(\frac{100}{160}\right)$	–
Adjusted sales	$100,000	$112,500	+$12,500

Use y_{10} as a base and restate y_1 in terms of P_{10} money value. Y_{10} becomes a constant. (Y_{11} will become the constant next year, and so forth). This is the "current dollar" method, as all prior periods are restated in comparison with the current period. In this case, y_1 sales would be referred to as "y_1 current dollar sales in terms of y_{10}."

	y_1	y_{10}	Difference
Unadjusted sales	$100,000	$180,000	+$80,000
Index	100	160	–
Adjustment	$100,000 $\left(\frac{160}{100}\right)$	–	–
Adjusted sales	$160,000	$180,000	+$20,000

The real growth in sales is $12,500, computed on a constant dollar basis, and $20,000, computed on a current dollar basis. As price-level changes may have a significant effect on financial data, users of financial statements should take this factor into account in evaluating performance and plans. This subject is discussed further in chapter 8.

Some remaining limitations of these accounting rules can be treated in less detail:

1. Only quantitative data is reported. Non-quantitative but highly important factors, such as quality of management, customer goodwill, or political or social relationships, are not explicit values in financial statements.
2. Forecasts, budgets, and other planning data are excluded from the financial statements, even though this data may provide a better clue to the future than historical data in many instances.
3. The financial statements do not articulate with prior budgets and plans, nor do they show what might have been achieved had full potential been realized or certain actions taken.

There is much advanced research in accounting that has as its goal the measurement and reporting of data that has hitherto been considered subjective or intangible. We can expect that some of these rules will change as the new methods are tested and gain significant acceptance in practice.

3.7 CONTROL

The principal control of output is the audit. *Internal audits* are performed by persons within the organization, while *independent audits* are performed by persons external to the firm, principally by *certified public accountants* (CPAs).[4] The right to practice public accounting is regulated by state law.

A control aspect of the internal audit is to assure that organization procedures are being applied consistently in the generation of accounting reports. A control purpose of the independent audit is to see that "generally accepted accounting principles" have been applied consistently in the generation of the financial statements. These principles include the rules discussed previously as well as the body of acceptable accounting procedures, such as those relating to inventory costing or depreciation.

The audit contains many control features, which are referred to collectively as "generally accepted auditing standards."[5] One such control is the *cut-off*, whereby allocation of events to their proper time periods is assured. Other major controls include observation of the physical count of inventory, and confirmation of accounts receivable.

3.8 FEEDBACK

Feedback at the output stage conforms with the basic types described earlier. There is feedback on the control systems: on its design, implementation, and effectiveness. There is feedback as to exceptional items and treatments. For example, the *independent auditor* provides an "opinion" as to whether or not the financial statements "fairly represent" the results of operations and financial position in accordance with generally accepted accounting principles, applied on a basis consistent with that of the preceding year. There is often comparative feedback in the form of data for a number of preceding years; and there is interpretive feedback in the form of footnotes and other remarks.

3.9 SUMMARY

The accounting information system from Exhibit 3-1 can now be expanded to include rules, controls, and feedback details. This elaborated form of the system is contained

[4] See *Accounting Principles Board Statement No. 4, Basic Concepts and Accounting Principles Underlying Financial Statements of Business Enterprises* (New York: American Institute of Certified Public Accountants, October 1970).

[5] The auditing standards of CPAs are set forth in *Auditing Standards and Procedures, Statement No. 33* (New York: American Institute of Certified Public Accountants, 1963).

EXHIBIT 3-6 THE ACCOUNTING INFORMATION SYSTEM DETAILED

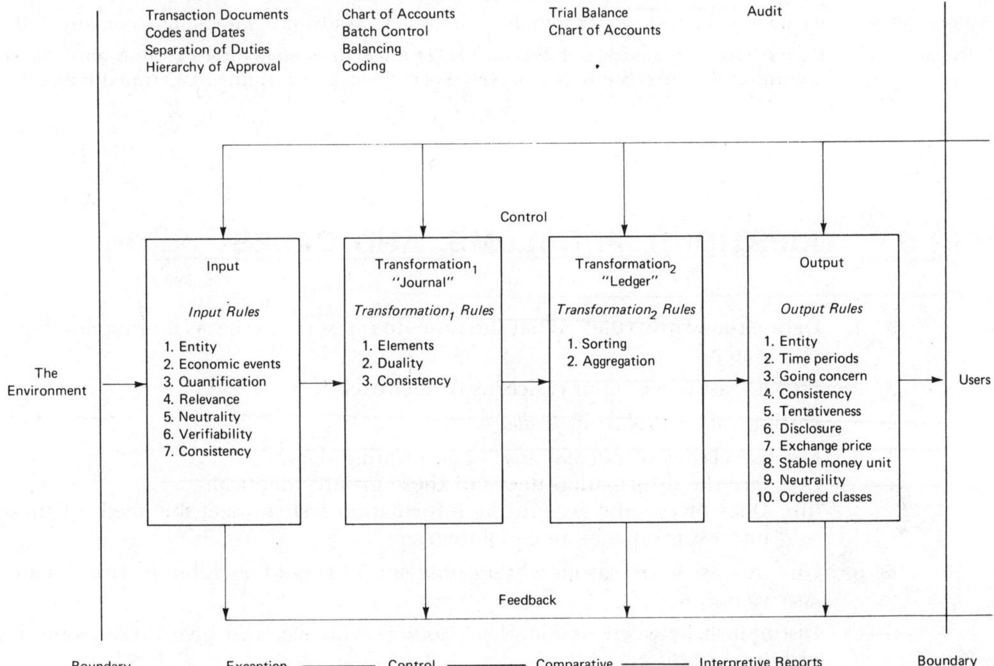

in Exhibit 3-6. It provides an excellent review of major characteristics of the formal financial accounting process. Information relative to a given entity and relevant to the needs of users (particularly *external* users) is extracted from the environment in compliance with a conventional set of rules, is processed or transformed in accordance with other rules, and exits the system in the form of financial statements which are prepared in accordance with output rules. Ensuring conformance to the rules and safeguarding against mishandling the data is the function of the control system. Feedback provides reports on exceptions, on the functioning of controls, and data relative to the performance of other business enterprises.

CHAPTER 3 REFERENCES AND ADDITIONAL READINGS

Buckley, John W. *Contemporary Accounting and Its Environment.* Belmont, Calif.: Dickenson Publishing Company, 1969.

Chambers, Raymond J. *Accounting, Evaluation, and Economic Behavior.* Englewood Cliffs, N.J.: Prentice-Hall, Inc., 1966.

Committee to Prepare a Statement of Basic Accounting Theory. *A Statement of Basic Accounting Theory.* Sarasota, Fla.: American Accounting Association, 1966.

Hendriksen, Eldon S. *Accounting Theory.* Rev. ed. Homewood, Ill.: Richard D. Irwin, Inc., 1970.

Ijiri, Yuji. *The Foundations of Accounting Measurement: A Mathematical, Economic, and Behavioral Inquiry.* Englewood Cliffs, N.J.: Prentice-Hall, Inc., 1967.

McNeill, Eugene I. *Financial Accounting: A Decision Information System.* Pacific Palisades, Calif.: Goodyear Publishing Company, 1970.

Moonitz, Maurice. *The Basic Postulates of Accounting.* Accounting Research Study No. 1. New York: American Institute of Certified Public Accountants, 1961.

Salmonson, R. F. *Basic Financial Accounting Theory.* Belmont, Calif.: Wadsworth Publishing Company, 1969.

Sprouse, Robert T., and Moonitz, Maurice. *A Tentative Set of Broad Accounting Principles for Business Enterprises.* Accounting Research Study No. 3. New York: American Institute of Certified Public Accountants, 1962.

CHAPTER 3 QUESTIONS, PROBLEMS, AND CASES

3- 1. Define the word "rule." What purpose does it serve in the accounting information system?

3- 2. List at least three input concerns of feedback.

3- 3. Distinguish *control* from *feedback.*

3- 4. List five classes of *external users* of accounting data:
   (a) Are the information needs of these groups identical?
   (b) Does or can the accounting information system meet the needs of these interest groups in an equal degree?

3- 5. Give at least four reasons why *internal* output should be different from that of *external* output.

3- 6. Distinguish between *legal* and *accounting* evidence, and give three examples of how they differ.

3- 7. How do the following controls work? Give an example of each:
   (a) Numbering and coding
   (b) Hierarchy of authority
   (c) The Chart of Accounts
   (d) Balancing

3- 8. Distinguish *feedback* from *output.*

3- 9. Give an example of each of the following types of feedback:
   (a) Exception reporting
   (b) Control reporting
   (c) Comparative reporting
   (d) Interpretive reporting

3-10. What are some alternative values to cost, and why have these alternatives not received ready acceptance by the accounting profession?

3-11. "The structure of the accounting system is based on a theory of equality between total resources and equities." Explain what is meant by this statement. Explain how the theory operates.

3-12. Distinguish between a *functional* and an *object-class* account, and give three examples of each.

3-13. What is the primary function of the *journal* and the *ledger?*

3-14. "The principal control at T_1 is the Chart of Accounts." Explain.

3-15. "The T_2 process is analogous to the function of a post office." Explain the analogy.

3-16. "Feedback at T_2 is similar to that at T_1." How is it similar?

3-17. Distinguish between a *fiscal year, calendar year,* and *natural business year.*"

3-18. What is the difference in status between *interim* and *annual* reports?

3-19. What output rule enables us to compare interperiod data? Explain how.

3-20. Explain the meaning or implication of the following terms and concepts:
   (a) Matching concept

(b) Deferral
(c) Liquidity preference of accounts
(d) Materiality
(e) Objective evidence
(f) Face value
(g) Purchasing power value

3-21. What are the requirements imposed by the consistency output rule? To what extent is change not allowed?

3-22. "A credit sale is not a complete transaction." Explain the meaning of this statement.

3-23. How are changes in purchasing power handled in financial statements? What output rule governs what must be done? What problems are posed by the enforcing of this output rule?

3-24. Distinguish between the control purposes of the internal audit and that of the independent audit.

3-25. Describe the feedback in operation at a system's output stage.

3-26. Identify the basic elements of an accounting system:

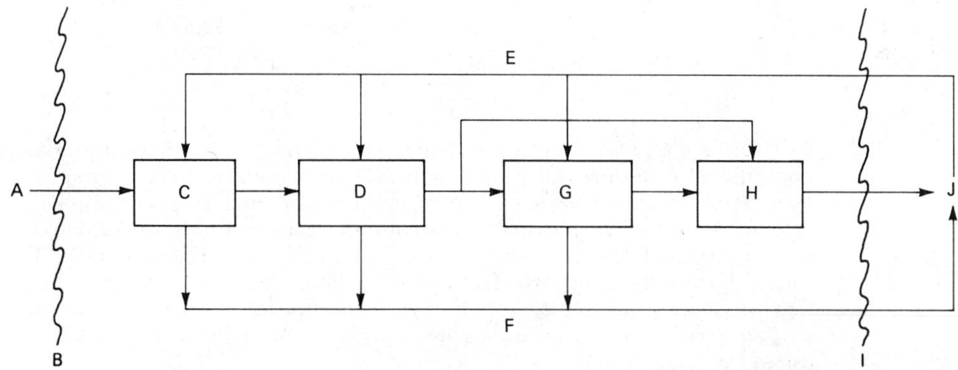

3-27. The Reflex Corporation changed its method of calculating the expiration (depreciation) of operating assets. As a result, its income for the year increased markedly. What output rule (or rules) are applicable in this situation, and what action (or actions) must be implemented?

3-28. A metal shredding machine has a market value of $40,000. Its original cost was $58,000. Since the machine was bought, however, the general price-level has increased 4% a year. What output rule (or rules) are involved in this situation, and what action (or actions) must be contemplated?

3-29. "General purpose financial statements are unbiased with respect to any identifiable class of user." What output rule is expressed by this statement? Are general purpose statements biased to any particular class of user? If so, what class? If a particular class is favored, how are the financial statements affected?

3-30. ***OBJECTIVE MEASUREMENT*** Accountants acknowledge that financial statements reporting the results of operations for relatively short periods of time, say one year, are tentative whenever allocations between past, present, and future periods are required. On the other hand the "objectivity" postulate leads to the logical deduction that changes in assets and liabilities, and the related effects (if any) on revenues, expenses, retained earnings, and the like, should not be given formal recognition in the accounts earlier than the point of time at which they can be measured in objective terms. Can this apparent conflict be resolved? Discuss.

(Adapted from the CPA exam.)

3-31. ***OUTPUT RULES*** The Albrict Company has issued its financial statements for 1974. The financial statements are presented in standard format and were prepared in accordance with generally accepted accounting principles.

The company produces bicycle parts and sells almost its entire output to one buyer – the Logan Bicycle Company. The company, however, has been involved in a dispute with the Logan Company over the payment of approximately $50,000 for goods bought over the first four months of the year. The buyer claimed that 40% of the goods were defective and, thus, computed an allowance of $20,000. After examining the goods, however, the Albrict Company claimed the damage resulted from the buyer's conveyor system. The buyer, on the other hand, claimed the goods were received in defective condition. The legal outcome is still pending at the end of 1974.

What output rule (or rules) are involved in this dispute, and what are the resulting implications?

3-32. ***PRICE-LEVEL ADJUSTMENT*** Interpret the following data by computing the "real" increase or decrease in operating expenses under:

(a) The constant dollar method.
(b) The current dollar method.

	Year 1	**Year 5**
Operating expenses	$848,000	$1,100,000
Index	125	160

3-33. ***CURRENT COSTS*** Financial statements are tools for the communication of quantifiable economic information to readers who use them as one of the factors in making a variety of management and investment decisions and judgments. To fulfill this function, accounting data should be quantifiable and should also be relevant to the kinds of judgments and decisions made. They should be verifiable and free from personal bias. There are many who believe that for some purposes current cost is a more useful measure than historical cost and recommend that dual statements be prepared showing both historical and current costs.

(a) Discuss the ways in which historical costs and current costs conform to the standards of verifiability and freedom from bias.
(b) Describe briefly how the current cost of the following assets might be determined:
    (1) Inventory
    (2) Investments in marketable securities
    (3) Equipment and machinery
    (4) Natural resources
    (5) Goodwill

(From the CPA exam.)

3-34. ***INPUT RULES*** Which of the following information is acceptable for entry into the accounting information system of Marfax Corporation? For the items rejected, indicate which *input rules* are not satisfied.

(a) Marfax Corporation purchases $1,000 of inventory.
(b) The Tri-Flow Company files a $1,000,000 suit against the Marfax Corporation for patent infringement.
(c) The president of Marfax Corporation retires.
(d) A five-year-old machine used in Marfax Corporation operations is thought to be worth $30,000. A new and similar machine, however, has a cost of $26,000.
(e) The Marfax Corporation employees have been granted a 5% increase in salary.
(f) The company just completed the installation of a new $80,000 factory lighting system.

(g) The supervisor of Department 12 just left on a vacation to Hawaii.
(h) Mr. Lockwood, a company vice-president, took home $15 worth of company supplies to use for his personal business.
(i) The company janitor was awarded a $200 stereo phonograph set upon retirement as a token of appreciation for forty years of company service.
(j) The company cafeteria is overcharging by an average of 10%. The employees have threatened a boycott. The cafeteria, however, is the only eating establishment within ten miles.

3-35. ***JOURNALIZING*** Which of the following accounting events can be journalized (transaction T_1)? For all positive responses indicate the possible accounts affected; for all negative responses indicate which transformation rules are not met.
(a) Inventory is purchased for $100 cash.
(b) Owners invest $10,000 in the business.
(c) Employees invest $5,000 in services.
(d) Company obtains a bank loan of $20,000.
(e) A company-owned building now has a market value of $40,000.
(f) An owner has withdrawn $200 for his personal use.
(g) The company received $100,000 in cash as a settlement on a recent lawsuit.
(h) A building worth $30,000 was destroyed by fire.
(i) A 10% price reduction has increased customer goodwill.
(j) Sales are budgeted at $800,000.

3-36. ***TRIAL BALANCE*** Mr. Jansen has just completed a trial balance of his company's accounts. During the year, however, the bookkeeper made the following errors:
(a) A $500 cash purchase of inventory was not recorded.
(b) The debit balance of $45,700 in accounts receivable was recorded in the trial balance as a debit of $47,500.
(c) A $560 cash receipt from a customer on account was recorded as a credit of $500 to accounts receivable and a credit of $500 to cash.
(d) A $2,000 withdrawal by the owner was recorded as a debit to salary expense and a credit to cash.
(e) A $700 cash revenue was recorded only as a credit in service sales.
(f) An equipment purchase on account was recorded as a debit of $20,000 to equipment and a credit of $2,000 to accounts payable.
(g) A $500 payment on account was recorded twice (both debit and credit).

What effect do these errors (individually) have on the outcome of the analysis? Are trial balance totals unequal? If so, what is the amount of the difference and which of the trial balance totals, debit or credit, is the larger?

3-37. ***VALUATION*** Consider the following data for a building owned by the Joseph Thompson Investment Corporation:
(a) A 15,000 sq. ft. building was purchased on January 30, 1968, for $100,-000.
(b) Mr. Lyle has indicated a willingness to take the building in trade for an undeveloped real estate worth $150,000.
(c) Cost of Construction Index is now $14 a square foot.
(d) Rental income from the building is $10,500 annually.
(e) The building has an assessed value of $45,500.
(f) The tax-assessment ratio is 35%.
(g) Interest rate for borrowing is 8%.
(h) A similar 15,000 sq. ft. building was sold this year for $110,000.

Required:

(1) Compute the building value under each of the following alternatives:
  a. Replacement value
  b. Comparable value
  c. Cost
  d. Assessed value
  e. Market value
  f. Capitalization value

(2) Discuss the subjectiveness of each valuation method.

3-38. ***VALUATION*** A small but growing road-building contractor would like to bid on a contract to rebuild and surface 10.6 miles of road. The job is considerably larger than any he has attempted in the past and, if he wins the contract, he estimates that he will need a $100,000 line of credit for working capital.

The contractor's most recent statement of financial position shows that he has a net worth of $170,000, of which $110,000 represents the book value of road-building equipment. Most of the equipment was acquired a few years ago at a bankruptcy sale. The equipment has a current fair value several times as great as book value.

The contractor knows that his bank will not give him a $100,000 line of credit on the basis of a position statement which shows his net worth at $170,000. He wants to adjust his accounting records to show the current fair value of the equipment and to prepare a revised position statement.

Required:

(a) List the factors that, alone or in combination, may have caused the difference between the book value and the current fair value of the equipment.

(b) The current fair value of fixed assets may be estimated by using one of the following methods:
  (1) Reproduction cost
  (2) Replacement cost
  (3) Capitalization of earnings

  Describe each of the three methods of estimating the current fair value of fixed assets and discuss the possible limitations of each.

(c) Discuss the propriety of adjusting the accounting records to show the fair value of the equipment and preparing a revised position statement. Suggest a possible alternative approach. Your answer should take into consideration the factors that may have caused the difference between the book value and the current fair value of the equipment.

(From the CPA exam.)

CHAPTER

THE STRUCTURE OF ACCOUNTING

4.1 THE NEED FOR ACCOUNTING

Accounting is a necessary accoutrement of economic man. This was true of economic man in antiquity, and it is true of economic man today. The sophistication of accounting will change in response to the complexity of economic activity, but there is a surprising consistency in the basic need for accounting in economic societies.

Consider some of the decisions which we face as individuals: (1) How much income will I receive in a given period? (2) What payments will be necessary? (3) Are these amounts larger or smaller than in some other period? (4) If income exceeds payments, what will I do with the balance? (5) If income is insufficient to meet the payments, how do I make ends meet? (6) What were the sources and amounts of income for the year—and to whom and in what amounts were payments made? (7) Am I wealthier or poorer at the end of the year?

As individuals, we resolve these questions through primitive records and reports. However, enlarge the number and scope of this type of question manyfold, multiply the number of decision makers who interact with a single accounting information system, and you can begin to understand both the purpose and complexity of accounting in more advanced economic settings. Record-keeping and reporting at this level must be systematized and managed by experts.

4.2 PRIMITIVE ACCOUNTING

Primitive accounting is not limited to any historical period. In fact, it bears no relationship to chronology. As noted, most of our personal accounting needs are met through primitive accounting systems consisting of checkbooks, rudimentary budgets, and financial summaries and reports in the form of tax returns.

These elemental needs—including tax assessment and reporting—are present in any society which incorporates commercial activity, although the tools of accounting may vary widely. The civilizations of the Mesopotamian Valley from 4500 B.C. to 500 B.C. maintained accounting records on clay tablets. Zenon papyri was the accounting medium used in Ptolemaic Egypt in the third century B.C. Accounting among the Incas in ancient Peru anteceded their ability to write. The accounting system in this instance consisted of a *quipu* or braided rope, of which different colored strands referred to various types of property, while the number of knots in each strand represented the quantity of that property owned. In medieval England a fairly elaborate accounting and tax system was maintained on narrow hazelwood sticks, eight to nine inches long, which were notched to represent money amounts. The "tally stick" as a medium of accounting endured in England for 700 years—from the ninth to the sixteenth century.

Primitive accounting represents an incomplete system of accounting. Only critical events are recorded. The scope and complexity of economic activity that can be covered adequately by primitive accounting is necessarily limited.

4.3 SINGLE-ENTRY ACCOUNTING

Single-entry accounting is more advanced, being more formal and complete than primitive accounting. Books of account such as a daybook, cash record, and ledger are maintained. But single-entry accounting lacks the duality feature of double-entry accounting; i.e., there is only one dimension to each accounting event. If you take your checkbook (using it as a daybook and cash record), and set up a ledger consisting of such accounts as rent, utilities, automobile payments, etc., you would have a single-entry accounting system.

4.4 DOUBLE-ENTRY ACCOUNTING

What we have shown in part is that accounting is utilitarian. It arises in response to needs. As economic needs become more complex, a more complex accounting structure is needed. Double-entry accounting evolved in response to the needs of multiple ownership in a single business entity. Primitive and single-entry accounting could not show the interests of several owners in a common undertaking.

The need for an improved system of accounting became acute in mercantile Italy, where several persons would join to finance voyages by merchant ships. They would contribute capital to provision a ship, pay its crew, and purchase merchandise in foreign lands. Upon the ship's return, the merchandise would be sold and the proceeds distributed to the several owners in proportion to their effort and investment. These joint ventures converted in time into ongoing multiple-owner businesses.

While the true inventor of double-entry accounting is unknown, Luca Pacioli is generally credited with this attainment because in 1494 he published the first text on the subject, entitled *Summa de Arithmetica, Geometria, Proportioni et Proportionalita.* The debit-credit structure of accounting laid down in 1494 has survived intact to our times. It is the foundation of modern accounting and is accommodative of the cost-benefit models which underlie current decision theory.

What Pacioli proposed was that each accounting event has a *cause-and-effect relationship*. The "account" was structured in accordance with this concept of duality (Exhibit 4-1).

EXHIBIT 4-1 DEBIT-CREDIT STRUCTURE OF AN ACCOUNT

Debit	Credit

Suppose that three persons each contribute $1,000 in cash for the type of joint venture we discuss above. Double-entry accounting would recognize that the business had a total of $3,000 in cash and that this sum derives from three owners:

EXHIBIT 4-2 A JOINT VENTURE

ASSETS (Debit-balance accounts)		EQUITIES (Credit-balance accounts)	
Cash	$3,000	Owner A	$1,000
		Owner B	1,000
		Owner C	1,000
Total	$3,000	Total	$3,000

The T_1 or journal entry to record the above transaction would be:

Debit: Cash		$3,000	
Credit:	Owner A		$1,000
	Owner B		1,000
	Owner C		1,000

Notation: To record the contribution of owners to the joint venture.

You will notice that the balance sheet in Exhibit 4-2 is of the same basic structure as the account, with assets representing *debit*-type accounts and equities representing *credit*-type accounts.

4.5 THE ACCOUNTING EQUATION

The duality concept requires equality between debits and credits at all times. This relationship is known as the *accounting equation:*

ASSETS = EQUITIES

Assets are *resources* which a firm owns, such as cash, inventory, or plant and equipment. Equities represent the *interest* of parties in those resources. There are two principal types of equity-holders: creditors and owners. Creditors' equity is termed *liabilities,* while owners' equity is referred to in several ways: (1) as "owners' or stockholders' equity," (2) as "capital," or (3) as "net worth." The first term is preferred.

The accounting equation can be expanded to reflect the two classes of equity-holders.

ASSETS = LIABILITIES + OWNERS' EQUITY

This expansion is useful for legal reasons, as creditors have a prior claim on the assets of a business in the event of liquidation. But it is also useful from an analytic point of view, in order to ascertain the extent to which a business is *leveraged,* i.e., the proportion of capital furnished by creditors as opposed to owners.

A balance sheet presented in *the account form* adheres to the above equation. A balance sheet in *the report form* varies the equation to emphasize the residual equity of owners:

ASSETS − LIABILITIES = OWNERS' EQUITY

4.6 CASH ACCOUNTING[1]

In a cash accounting system, events are only recorded when a cash exchange has taken place. For example, if a sale is made on credit terms, the sales event is only recorded when payment is received. Similarly, purchases and other obligations are only recognized when payment has been made.

4.7 ACCRUAL ACCOUNTING

Accrual accounting recognizes events which meet two conditions: (1) the effort which gives rise to a transaction is complete, and (2) an obligation to pay is in hand. In the credit sales example, the sale would be recognized when the buyer has received the

[1] Cash accounting is quite limited in application, hence we will concentrate our attention on accrual accounting throughout this text.

merchandise (no further effort on the part of the seller is required to make the merchandise salable), and the seller has received a commitment on the part of the buyer to pay for the merchandise. An invoice signed by the buyer is usually sufficient evidence of the obligation to pay.

Under the concept of accrual accounting, purchase orders are not recorded formally in the accounts because condition (1) has not been met. While the purchase order is an obligation to pay, the vendor has not undertaken his share of the effort to complete the transaction.

4.8 THE ACCOUNT

The *account* is the basic construct of accounting, as mentioned earlier. There are two types of accounts: (1) *real* and (2) *nominal.*

The balance sheet consists of real accounts, while the income statement consists of nominal accounts. Real accounts are continuous accounts. The balance in the account at the end of one accounting period is carried forward to the next period. We can illustrate the behavior of a real account graphically in Exhibit 4-3.

EXHIBIT 4-3 BEHAVIOR OF A REAL ACCOUNT

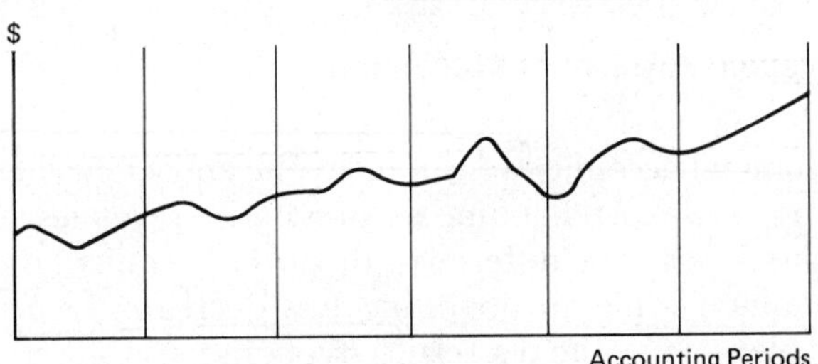

For example, the cash account is a real account. The balance in this account fluctuates continuously as deposits and payments are made. The balance existing at the end of an accounting period is measured and reported, but activity in the account continues.

Nominal accounts are periodic accounts. The balances in these accounts at the end of an accounting period are *closed,* which means they are transferred to owners' equity. The behavior of a nominal account is depicted in Exhibit 4-4.

EXHIBIT 4-4 BEHAVIOR OF A NOMINAL ACCOUNT

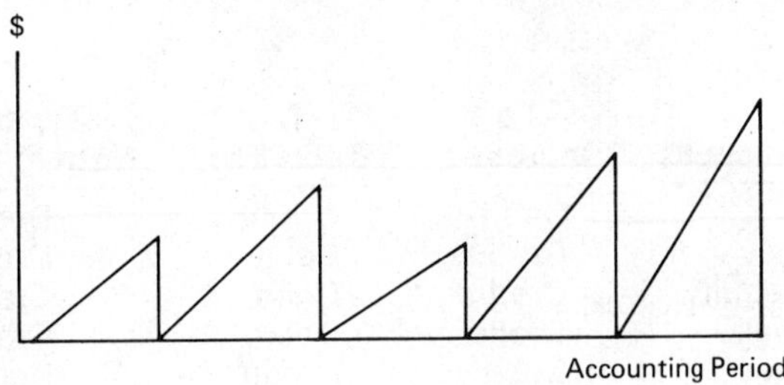

For example, the sales account is a nominal account. In fact, there is a different sales account for every period. The 1970 sales account increases during the year as sales are made. At the end of the year the account is closed to owners' equity through the closing statement. A new account is started for 1971 sales. If nominal accounts did not behave in this manner, the sales account would just continue to grow to a point where it would be a meaningless mass of data. Comparison of sales for different accounting periods would be impossible.

Nominal accounts are, in fact, control accounts pertinent to operating transactions which affect owners' equity, i.e., revenue and expense accounts. The accounting equation can be expanded to include nominal accounts:

$$\text{ASSETS} = \text{LIABILITIES} + \text{OWNERS' INVESTMENT} + \text{REVENUES} - \text{EXPENSES}$$

Nominal accounts as represented in the income statement are not essential mathematically to accounting. That is to say, every accounting transaction has an impact on the balance sheet and can be accommodated within its framework. For example, if we had no nominal accounts, how would we record a rent payment in the amount of $100? Because we have no rent expense account, the entry would be made directly to balance sheet accounts:

Debit (Decrease): Owners' equity................$100
    Credit (Decrease): Cash........................ $100

Notation: Payment of $100 in rent.

By using nominal accounts we can delay the entry to owners' equity until the end of an accounting period. At that time we summarize revenues and expenses in the income statement and post the difference to owners' equity. An operating profit increases owners' equity, while an operating loss decreases owners' equity. By this procedure we are able to show the net results of operations for a given period of time.

The other reason for having nominal accounts is for control purposes. If all operating transactions were recorded directly to owners' equity, it would be impossible to classify revenues and expenses such as rent expense, salaries, etc.

4.9 DEBIT-CREDIT RULES

We have noticed that the accounting system comprises five types of accounts: (1) assets, (2) liabilities, (3) owners' equity, (4) revenues (and gains), and (5) expenses (and losses). The debit-credit rules pertaining to these types of accounts are summarized as follows:

Type of Account	To Increase	To Decrease	Typical or Normal Balance
Assets	Debit	Credit	Debit
Liabilities	Credit	Debit	Credit
Owners' equity:	Credit	Debit	Credit
Revenues	Credit	Debit	Credit
Expenses	Debit	Credit	Debit

You will notice reference to a "typical or normal balance." It is possible to have a balance which is not typical for a particular account. For example, cash is typically a debit-balance account. If we overdraw our cash account, it will show a credit balance. In this event cash has become a liability. Instead of the bank owing us money, we now owe the bank money.

4.10 THE PROCESS-STRUCTURE OF ACCOUNTING

In chapter 3 we provided a foundation for accounting as an information system—an operating system in which data is input, transformed, and output. In Exhibit 4-5 we elaborate on the mechanics of this structure.

EXHIBIT 4-5 THE PROCESS-STRUCTURE OF THE ACCOUNTING INFORMATION SYSTEM

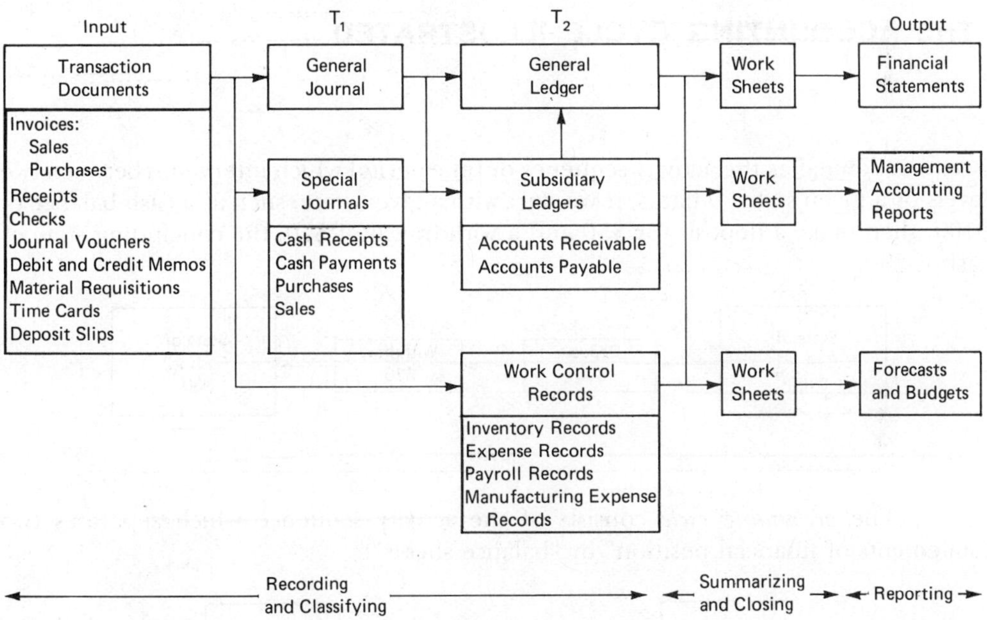

The recording process begins with *transaction documents.* There are various documents designed to capture accounting *events.* A *sales invoice* indicates that a credit sale has been made. A *credit memo* records the fact that a customer has returned some merchandise and wishes to have his account credited. Instead of waiting for us to issue a credit memo, he may furnish us with a *debit memo* at the time he returns the merchandise. This document serves as the basis for crediting his account, while on the other hand recognizing that we have added to our inventory. In most instances these transaction documents are pre-numbered so that we can account for all of them.

Journals are used to establish the duality of accounting events and to classify similar events into common categories. Special journals are used to facilitate the classification of many similar type entries. Only the totals in these journals are posted to the ledger accounts. We will discuss these special journals in later chapters.

Ledgers are used to extend the classification process. Again, to avoid many entries into the general ledger and to promote division of labor, subsidiary ledgers are kept for such specialized accounts as receivables and payables. The general ledger in these instances contains only one account (called a *control account*) for all accounts receivable or accounts payable to which the total of the subsidiary ledger is posted at the end of an accounting period.

In addition to formal ledgers, most firms maintain a series of work control records. This data does not enter into the formal accounting process, but it is used for management accounting reports and for forecasting and budgeting purposes. The primary reason for this type of record is to allow the manager of an activity to maintain accounting control.

Periodically the information contained in the ledger is summarized into reports. When this occurs in relation to the financial statements, it is called the *closing process*.

4.11 THE ACCOUNTING CYCLE ILLUSTRATED

A *cycle* is defined as the activity sequence or time period which intervenes between two levels of a given state.[2] That is, if we start with a given state, such as a cash balance of $100, then make a deposit for $50 and a withdrawal of $70, the concluding state of cash is $80:

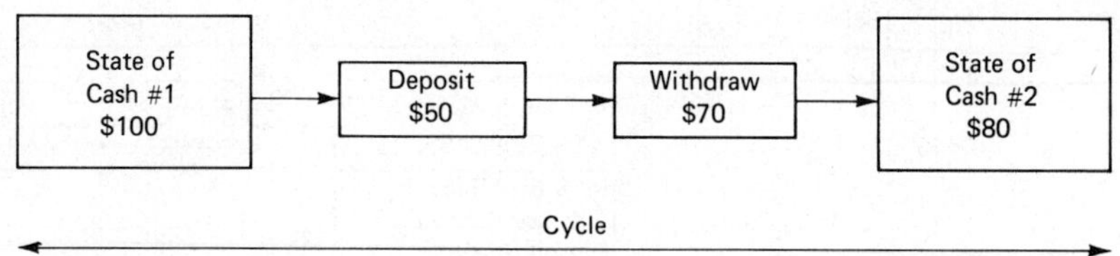

The *accounting cycle* consists of the activity sequence which separates two "statements of financial position" or "balance sheets":[3]

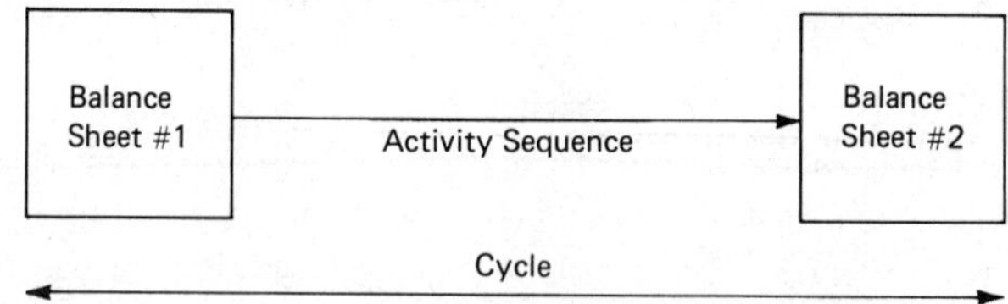

The following example illustrates the accounting cycle. We begin with a balance sheet dated January 1, 1973. It reflects the assets, liabilities, and owner's equity position of Mr. David Jensen as of that date.

[2] Cycles are often measured by the time period involved in completing the activity sequence, hence we can speak of thirty-day or one-year cycles.

[3] "Statement of financial position" and "balance sheet" are synonymous. While the former is more expressive of the purpose of the statement, "balance sheet" is the most commonly used title for this document. Accordingly, we will use "balance sheet" consistently in this text.

A. *Balance Sheet Position #1:*

EXHIBIT 4-6

THE JENSEN COMPANY
BALANCE SHEET
JANUARY 1, 1973

ASSETS		LIABILITIES	
Current Assets:		**Current Liabilities:**	
Cash	$ 2,000	Accounts payable	$ 6,400
Inventory	13,000	Current portion of notes payable	1,200
	15,000		7,600
Long-Lived Assets:		**Long-Term Liabilities:**	
Furniture & equipment	5,000	Notes payable	2,400
		Total liabilities	$10,000
		OWNER'S EQUITY	
		Jensen, Capital	$10,000
Total assets	$20,000	Total equities	$20,000

Notes:

1. *Current assets* refer to those assets which will convert into cash within the normal operating cycle of the business[4] or one year, whichever is longer. We assume that The Jensen Company has a normal operating cycle of one year or less, and hence uses the one-year rule. It is expected, therefore, that the items in inventory as of January 1, 1973, will be sold before the end of the year.
2. *Current liabilities* refer to payments which are due within the same time period as defined by the current assets. This includes the payments on the notes payable which fall due in 1973.
3. *Notes Payable* covers the furniture and equipment. The sales contract calls for payments of $118 a month for 36 months. The total of $4,248 consists of $3,600 in principal and $648 in interest. Only the principal portion of the debt is reflected in the balance sheet. Of the total principal portion, $1,200 refers to the principal payments of $100 a month during 1973. This is shown as a current liability. Principal payments due in 1974 and 1975 are shown as a long-term liability.

B. *Input:* The Jensen Company engaged in the following transactions during the month of January, 1973. (These transactions or *events* comprise the input to the accounting system.)

1. Issued a check for $1,000, which covered rent of $500 each for the months of January and December, 1973.

[4]The *normal operating cycle* is defined by the time-period involved in moving from one cash position to another through the normal course of business. A whiskey manufacturer has a long operating cycle as it takes many years to complete the process. A bakery, on the other hand, has a very short operating cycle as measured by the length of the process from acquiring ingredients to selling the bakery products.

2. Made sales of $15,000, of which $13,000 was for cash and $2,000 was on credit terms of thirty days.
3. Incurred the following cash expenditures in addition to the rent payment:
   a. Utilities bill for the month of January, $100.
   b. Fire and comprehensive liability insurance premiums for $1,080 covering the three-year period from January 1, 1973 to December 31, 1975.
   c. Salaries of $2,000 to Jensen and his employees.
   d. Advertising invoices for January, totaling $500.
   e. Telephone bill for $100, applicable to the month of January.
   f. Office stationery and supplies for $600.
4. Purchased $9,000 of inventory from vendors on account.
5. Made cash payments to vendors in January of $7,000.
6. David Jensen withdrew $1,000 for his personal use in addition to his salary in 3(c) above.
7. A $118 check was drawn in favor of the holder of the note payable, representing $100 in principal and $18 in interest due for the month of January, 1973.

C. *First Transformation* (T_1): The above transactions are journalized as follows:

		Debit	Credit
1.	Debit: Rent expense	$ 1,000	
	Credit: Cash		$ 1,000
	Notation: Rent of $500 each for the months of January and December, 1973.		
2.	Debit: Cash............................	$13,000	
	Accounts receivable.......	2,000	
	Credit: Sales.......................		$15,000
	Notation: Sales for the month of January, 1973.		
3a.	Debit: Utilities expense	$ 100	
	Credit: Cash		$ 100
	Notation: Utilities bill for the month of January, 1973.		
3b.	Debit: Insurance expense...........	$ 1,080	
	Credit: Cash		$ 1,080
	Notation: Insurance premiums for the 36-month period from January 1, 1973 to December 31, 1975.		
3c.	Debit: Salaries expense	$ 2,000	
	Credit: Cash		$ 2,000
	Notation: Salaries for Mr. Jensen and employees for the month of January, 1973.		
3d.	Debit: Advertising expense..........	$ 500	
	Credit: Cash		$ 500
	Notation: Advertising expenses for the month of January, 1973.		

		Debit	Credit
3e.	Debit: Telephone expense..........$	100	
	Credit: Cash		$ 100
	Notation: Telephone bill for the month of January, 1973.		
3f.	Debit: Office expense.................$	600	
	Credit: Cash		$ 600
	Notation: Purchase of office stationery and supplies for the month of January, 1973.		
4.	Debit: Inventory.........................$	9,000	
	Credit: Accounts payable		$ 9,000
	Notation: Purchase of merchandise inventory on credit.		
5.	Debit: Accounts payable ....$	7,000	
	Credit: Cash		$ 7,000
	Notation: Payments on account.		
6.	Debit: Jensen—Drawings account.................................$	1,000	
	Credit: Cash		$ 1,000
	Notation: David Jensen withdrew $1,000 for personal use.		
7.	Debit: Notes payable................$	100	
	Interest expense	18	
	Credit: Cash		$ 118
	Notation: Payment on note for the month of January, 1973.		

D. *Second Transformation* (T_2): The journal items are now "posted" to the ledger accounts:

BALANCE SHEET ACCOUNTS

Cash

	Debit		Credit
Bal.	2,000	(1)	$ 1,000
(2)	13,000	(3a)	100
		(3b)	1,080
		(3c)	2,000
		(3d)	500
		(3e)	100
		(3f)	600
		(5)	7,000
		(6)	1,000
		(7)	118
	$15,000		$13,498
Bal.	$1,502		

Accounts Receivable

	Debit	Credit
(2)	$ 2,000	

Inventory

	Debit	Credit
Bal.	$13,000	
(4)	9,000	
Bal.	$22,000	

Furniture & Equipment

	Debit		Credit
Bal.	$ 5,000		

Notes Payable

	Debit		Credit
(7)	$ 100	Bal.	$ 3,600
		Bal.	$ 3,500

Accounts Payable

	Debit		Credit
(5)	$ 7,000	Bal.	$ 6,400
		(4)	9,000
	$ 7,000		$15,400
		Bal.	$ 8,400

Jensen – Capital

	Debit		Credit
		Bal.	$10,000

Jensen – Drawings

	Debit		Credit
(6)	$ 1,000		

INCOME STATEMENT ACCOUNTS

Sales

	Debit		Credit
		(2)	$15,000

Advertising Expenses

	Debit		Credit
(3d)	$ 500		

Rent Expense

	Debit		Credit
(1)	$ 1,000		

Telephone Expense

	Debit		Credit
(3e)	$ 100		

Utilities Expense

	Debit		Credit
(3a)	$ 100		

Office Expense

	Debit		Credit
(3f)	$ 600		

Insurance Expense

	Debit		Credit
(3b)	$ 1,080		

Interest Expense

	Debit		Credit
(7)	$ 18		

Salaries Expense

	Debit		Credit
(3c)	$ 2,000		

E. *Summarize Ledger Accounts:* The ledger accounts can now be summarized into a *preliminary trial balance:*

EXHIBIT 4-7

THE JENSEN COMPANY
PRELIMINARY TRIAL BALANCE
JANUARY 31, 1973

ACCOUNT	DEBIT	CREDIT
Cash	$ 1,502	
Accounts receivable	2,000	
Inventory	22,000	
Furniture & equipment	5,000	
Accounts payable		$ 8,400
Notes payable		3,500
Jensen – Capital account		10,000
Jensen – Drawings account	1,000	
Sales		15,000
Rent expense	1,000	
Utilities expense	100	
Insurance expense	1,080	
Salaries expense	2,000	
Advertising expense	500	
Telephone expense	100	
Office expense	600	
Interest expense	18	
Totals	$36,900	$36,900

This trial balance is preliminary because it does not reflect the proper *matching* between revenues and expenses, as discussed in chapter 3. For example, insurance expense for the month of January should be

$$\frac{\$1{,}080}{36} = \$30$$

as the premium extends over thirty-six months. Similarly, while we have recorded sales, we have not computed the cost of goods sold, i.e., the cost of the inventory that was sold during the month of January.

F. *Make Adjustments:* The following adjustments are necessary to achieve the proper matching of revenues and expenses:

8. Distinguish between prepaid rent (an asset) and rent expense. December rent, in the amount of $500, is prepaid. January rent for $500 is an expense for the month of January.
9. Distinguish between prepaid insurance and insurance expense. The amounts are $1,050 and $30 respectively.
10. Ascertain whether office stationery and supplies are still on hand at the end of January. Assume that supplies on hand represent $500 of the original payment

of $600. Accordingly, $500 should be reflected as an asset and $100 as office expense.

11. An actual (or "physical") count of merchandise inventory on hand at the end of January totals $12,000. As total inventory on hand was $22,000, it indicates that inventory valued at $10,000 was sold during the period.
12. Record depreciation on furniture and equipment for the month of January, 1973. For this purpose we assume that the asset account is depreciated in equal monthly amounts over ten years. The depreciation for January is

$$\frac{\$5000}{120} = \$42 \text{ (approx.)}$$

G. T_1 *Transformation of Adjustments:* These adjustments are journalized as follows:

	Debit	Credit
8. Debit: Prepaid rent	$ 500	
Credit: Rent expense		$ 500
Notation: To record prepaid portion of rent applicable to December, 1973.		
9. Debit: Prepaid insurance	$ 1,050	
Credit: Insurance expense		$ 1,050
Notation: To record insurance premiums applicable to future periods.		
10. Debit: Office supplies	$ 500	
Credit: Office expense		$ 500
Notation: To record office supplies on hand as of January 31, 1973.		
11. Debit: Cost of goods sold	$10,000	
Credit: Inventory		$10,000
Notation: To record inventory sold in January, 1973.		
12. Debit: Depreciation expense	$ 42	
Credit: Accumulated depreciation		$ 42
Notation: To record depreciation on furniture and equipment for January, 1973.		

Actually, there is no need to formalize these T_1 transactions for interim statement purposes, in that the adjustments differ from month to month. Year-end adjustments are recorded formally as shown above.

We should note that it is also correct to make original entries of this type to balance sheet accounts and make periodic adjustments to expense accounts. For example, we could have recorded the payment of insurance premiums in the first instance as follows:

Debit: Prepaid insurance	$1,080	
Credit: Cash		$1,080

and made this adjustment at the end of January:

Debit: Insurance expense	$ 30	
Credit: Prepaid insurance		$ 30

Notation: Record insurance premium applicable to the month of January, 1973.

H. *T_2 Transformation of Adjustments:* The journal entries relating to adjustments are posted to the accounts. Again, this is not done for interim statements but only for year-end adjustments. Although this is an interim closing, we post these entries for illustrative purposes. Only the accounts affected are shown below:

BALANCE SHEET ACCOUNTS

Prepaid Insurance

	Debit		Credit
(9)	$ 1,050		

Prepaid Rent

	Debit		Credit
(8)	$ 500		

Office Supplies

	Debit		Credit
(10)	$ 500		

Inventory

	Debit		Credit
Bal.	$13,000	(11)	$10,000
(4)	9,000		
	$22,000		$10,000
Bal.	$12,000		

Accumulated Depreciation

	Debit		Credit
		(12)	$ 42

INCOME STATEMENT ACCOUNTS

Rent Expense

	Debit		Credit
(1)	$ 1,000	(8)	$500
Bal.	$ 500		

Insurance Expense

	Debit		Credit
(3b)	$ 1,080	(9)	$1,050
Bal.	$ 30		

Office Expense

	Debit		Credit
(3f)	$ 600	(10)	$500
Bal.	$ 100		

Cost of Goods Sold

	Debit		Credit
(11)	$10,000		

Depreciation Expense

	Debit		Credit
(12)	$ 42		

I. *Adjusted Trial Balance:* We now have an adjusted trial balance which does reflect the proper matching of revenues and expenses:

EXHIBIT 4-8

THE JENSEN COMPANY
ADJUSTED TRIAL BALANCE
JANUARY 31, 1973

ACCOUNT	DEBIT	CREDIT
Cash	$ 1,502	
Accounts receivable	2,000	
Inventory	12,000	
Office supplies	500	
Prepaid rent	500	
Prepaid insurance	1,050	
Furniture & equipment	5,000	
Accumulated depreciation on furniture & equipment		$ 42
Accounts payable		8,400
Notes payable		3,500
Jensen—Capital account		10,000
Jensen—Drawings account	1,000	
Sales		15,000
Cost of goods sold	10,000	
Rent expense	500	
Utilities expense	100	
Insurance expense	30	
Salaries expense	2,000	
Advertising expense	500	
Telephone expense	100	
Office expense	100	
Interest expense	18	
Depreciation expense	42	
Totals	$36,942	$36,942

J. *The Worksheet Approach to Making Adjustments:* A convenient method for making adjustments and extending dollar amounts to the proper statements is to use a worksheet, as illustrated in Exhibit 4-9.

EXHIBIT 4-9

THE JENSEN COMPANY
WORKSHEET
JANUARY 31, 1973

	PRELIMINARY TRIAL BALANCE		ADJUSTMENTS		ADJUSTED TRIAL BALANCE		INCOME STATEMENT		BALANCE SHEET	
ACCOUNTS	Debit	Credit	Debit	Credit	Debit	Credit	Debit	Credit	Debit	Credit
Cash	1,502				1,502				1,502	
Accounts receivable	2,000				2,000				2,000	
Inventory	22,000			(11) 10,000	12,000				12,000	
Furniture & equipment	5,000				5,000				5,000	
Accounts payable		8,400				8,400				8,400
Notes payable		3,500				3,500				3,500
Jensen—Capital		10,000				10,000				10,000
Jensen—Drawings	1,000				1,000				1,000	
Sales		15,000				15,000		15,000		
Rent expense	1,000			(8) 500	500		500			
Utilities expense	100				100		100			
Insurance expense	1,080			(9) 1,050	30		30			
Salaries expense	2,000				2,000		2,000			
Advertising expense	500				500		500			
Telephone expense	100				100		100			
Office expense	600			(10) 500	100		100			
Interest expense	18				18		18			
	36,900	36,900								
Office supplies			500 (10)		500				500	
Prepaid rent			500 (8)		500				500	
Prepaid insurance			1,050 (9)		1,050				1,050	
Accumulated depreciation				(12) 42		42				42
Depreciation expense			42 (12)		42		42			
Cost of goods sold			10,000 (11)		10,000		10,000			
			12,092	12,092	36,942	36,942	13,390	15,000		
Net income							1,610			1,610
							15,000	15,000	23,552	23,552

K. *Closing Income Statement Accounts:* Each year the income statement accounts are closed by means of this compound journal entry:

	Debit	Credit
Debit: Sales	$15,000	
Credit: Cost of goods sold		$10,000
Rent expense		500
Insurance expense		30
Utilities expense		100
Salaries expense		2,000
Advertising expense		500
Telephone expense		100
Office expense		100
Interest expense		18
Depreciation expense		42
Jensen – Capital		1,610

Notation: Close income statement accounts to owner's equity.

Since our example involves interim statements, there should be no closing of the income statement accounts. The above example is used to *illustrate* year-end closing. The closing entry simply reverses the debit-credit relationship of the income statement, and the journal entry is balanced by the amount of income or loss for the period. The effect of the closing entry is to reduce the income statement accounts to zero and transfer the income of the period to owner's equity.

L. *Prepare Formal Statements:* The income statement, statement of changes in capital, and balance sheet can now be prepared from the worksheet information in Exhibit 4-9.

EXHIBIT 4-10

THE JENSEN COMPANY
INCOME STATEMENT
FOR THE MONTH OF JANUARY, 1973

Sales		$15,000
Cost of goods sold		10,000
Gross profit		5,000
Administrative expenses:		
Rent expense	$ 500	
Insurance expense	30	
Utilities expense	100	
Salaries expense	2,000	
Advertising expense	500	
Telephone expense	100	
Office expense	100	
Interest expense	18	
Depreciation expense	42	3,390
Net income		$ 1,610

EXHIBIT 4-11

THE JENSEN COMPANY
STATEMENT OF CHANGES IN CAPITAL
FOR THE MONTH OF JANUARY, 1973

Capital account, January 1, 1973	$10,000
Add: Net income for January	1,610
	11,610
Less: Drawings during January	1,000
Capital account, January 31, 1973	$10,610

EXHIBIT 4-12

THE JENSEN COMPANY
BALANCE SHEET
JANUARY 31, 1973

ASSETS			LIABILITIES	
Current:			**Current:**	
Cash		$ 1,502	Accounts payable	$ 8,400
Accounts receivable		2,000	Current portion of	
Inventory		12,000	long-term debt	1,100
Prepaid expenses		1,330		9,500
		16,832	**Long-Term Liabilities:**	
Long-Lived Assets:			Notes payable	2,400
Furniture & equip.	$5,000		Total liabilities	11,900
Less: Accumulated				
depreciation	42	4,958	**OWNER'S EQUITY**	
Deferred charges		720	Jensen, Capital	10,610
Total assets		$22,510	Total equities	$22,510

(The item in deferred charges is $720 of insurance premiums covering 1974 and 1975.)

The cycle we have just completed is depicted in Exhibit 4-13.

By means of the accounting cycle we can measure changes in owners' equity between two time periods. In the example, Jensen's equity has increased by $610 in addition to his salary and the $1,000 he withdrew from the business for his personal use.

EXHIBIT 4-13 THE ACCOUNTING CYCLE EXPANDED

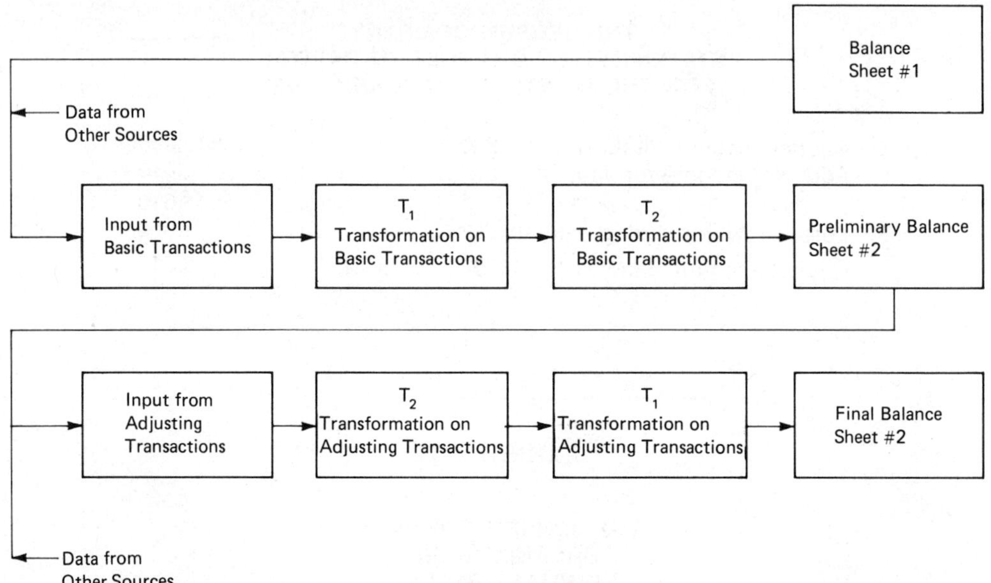

4.12 MANAGEMENT ACCOUNTING

What we have described so far is the *financial* output of the accounting information system. These formal statements are of use primarily to individuals outside the firm; investors, stockholders, and the government. By its nature, the financial accounting system is of limited utility to those within the organization. These individuals (managers) require rather different information.

The requirements of *management* accounting as well as those of *financial* accounting must be taken into account in designing the *total* accounting information system.

As a total information source, the periodic financial statements have many shortcomings from a management viewpoint: (1) they fail to measure progress toward enterprise objectives; (2) they orient to the past rather than the future; (3) they present data for the firm as a whole, which may not be what is required for the good management of its individual parts; (4) there is a critical time-lag in feedback; and (5) adherence to generally accepted accounting principles makes the data less useful to certain decisions. Exhibit 4-14 summarizes a number of the important differences between financial and managerial accounting.

These differences should not lead us to conclude that the two accounting systems are fundamentally opposed. On the contrary, they complement each other. Each system has its place. Each satisfies the information needs of its particular users.

EXHIBIT 4-14 FINANCIAL VERSUS MANAGERIAL ACCOUNTING SYSTEMS

CHARACTERISTIC	FINANCIAL ACCOUNTING SYSTEM	MANAGEMENT ACCOUNTING SYSTEM
1. Purpose	To record and report actual accounting transactions in accordance with generally accepted accounting principles	To furnish economic data for decision making
2. Scope	The fiscal record	Environment and all operating data
3. User-orientation	External	Internal
4. Time-orientation	Past	Present and future
5. Methodology	Generally accepted accounting principles and methods	Operations management principles and techniques
6. Precision	Ostensibly absolute	Relative
7. Realization	Actual	Potential
8. Necessity	Legally required	Operationally required
9. Incidence	Periodic	Periodic and as needed
10. Catalyst	Tradition	Executive action

CLASSIFICATION OF INFORMATION

Having developed the structure of an information system, let us consider the form and content of the information itself.

Each piece of managerial information has its own cost-benefit ratio. We would certainly be unwise to generate and transmit data that is redundant or trivial, yet that is precisely what happens in many firms. Computerized data processing can generate vast quantities of information—more than can be utilized effectively in many instances.

By use of the cost-benefit ratio, we may choose among alternative information structures and classes of information. Exhibit 4-15 shows a break-down of the major information classes. (The percentages are hypothetical.)

EXHIBIT 4-15 MAJOR INFORMATION CLASSES

ENTITY CLASSES	PAST %	PRESENT %	FUTURE %	TOTAL %
Socioeconomic	2	3	5	10
Competition:				
Select	4	10	6	20
Industry	2	5	3	10
Internal (self)	10	30	20	60
Total	18	48	34	100

Each of the *entity* classes in Exhibit 4-15 includes seven major *functional* classes:

Financial
Personnel/Labor
Law and Government
Market
Production
Logistics
Research and Development

Combining the entity and functional classes results in the three-dimensional information structure shown in Exhibit 4-16. Note that data must be considered as falling *mainly* into one or the other of the functional classes. As we pointed out below, the data will sometimes overlap into two or more classes. This overlap must be recognized as a source of possible confusion within the information system.

EXHIBIT 4-16 THREE-DIMENSIONAL INFORMATION STRUCTURE

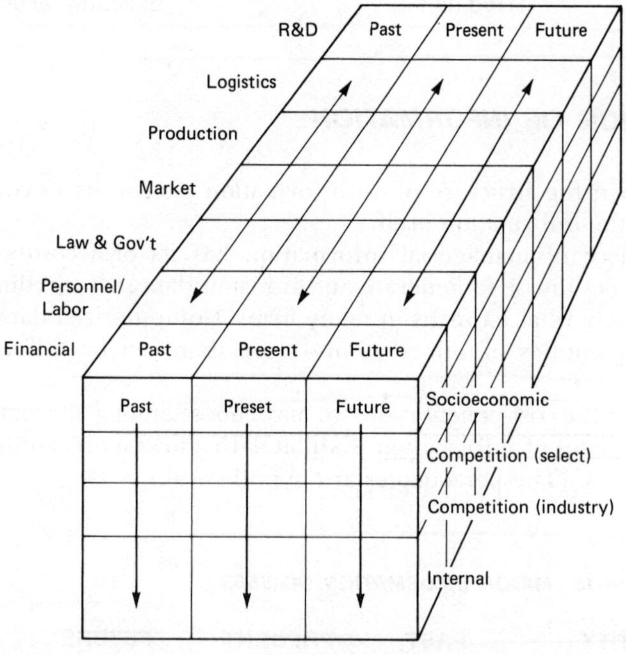

Let us consider the functional classes in more detail.

Financial: Includes data on cash and other financial resources, income and expenses, the money market, credit, and so on. Financial data is the largest functional class, and probably accounts for 50% or more of total management information. This information comes mainly from the accounting system.

Personnel/Labor: Includes data on employee induction, utilization, and turnover, as well as education and training, the labor market, skill inventories, union and labor negotiations, and other people-related activities. Note that there is considerable overlap with financial information in the area of payroll and timekeeping.

Law and Government: Comprises information on tax and business law and government regulations in areas such as stock registration, import-export, and product safety. This information class overlaps the personnel/labor category especially in the field of state and federal labor and minimum wage laws and fair employment regulations.

Market: Information is of two general types: survey and feedback. Market survey, or *demographic analysis,* involves collection of data to determine population characteristics such as age, sex, income group, consumption patterns, and educational level. Other survey information includes data on competitors and related industries.

Feedback data, as the name implies, involves data on product acceptance and public reaction to advertising.

Production: Includes inventory, efficiency, work flow, schedules, and other manufacturing-related data. Internally, production data goes hand-in-hand with personnel/labor and financial information. Externally, it is tied to market data.

Logistics: In many cases it can be considered to be a sub-set of production information. In some organizations, however, logistics is the responsibility of a separate group. It involves the management of the location of objects and the movement of machinery, products, manpower, and facilities from place to place. The inventory function (counting and locating) may be part of the logistics effort.

Research and Development: This function is an integral part of every progressive firm. Information is required to assess its competitiveness, effectiveness, and direction. This category includes product testing. For many firms, especially those involved with government contracts, the development and testing of a product may cost more in material and man-hours than the delivered product itself. Clearly, personnel/labor, production, logistics, and financial information are all involved in the research and development data class.

ORGANIZATION AND INFORMATION

The information model just discussed represents the entire body of management information. Individuals in different positions in the firm have different need portions of the whole; probably no one could use the entire 126 ($6 \times 7 \times 3$) categories of data available. We must, therefore, construct a model of a functional organization to assign available data on the basis of actual need.

Even in a perfect information setting, different persons confronted with identical data will make different decisions. To avoid irreconcilable viewpoints, it is necessary to assign specific decision roles to specific people. The result is an *organization,* and the decision roles are implicitly depicted in an organization chart, as in Exhibit 4-17.

The main function of the chart is to depict lines of responsibility. For example, the accounting department head reports to the financial vice-president, who in turn reports to the president. The flow of information follows essentially the same channels, as discussed earlier, while the "chain of command" flows in the opposite direction.

Each position in the management hierarchy acts as a filter as well as an information transmission/reception station. We refer to this process of filtering and summarizing as *conditioning* the information. An important feature of the conditioned information is the "exception" principle; that is, the disclosure of material departures from plan. The practice of highlighting unusual events gives rise to what is known as the "management by exception" principle.

EXHIBIT 4-17 AN ORGANIZATION CHART

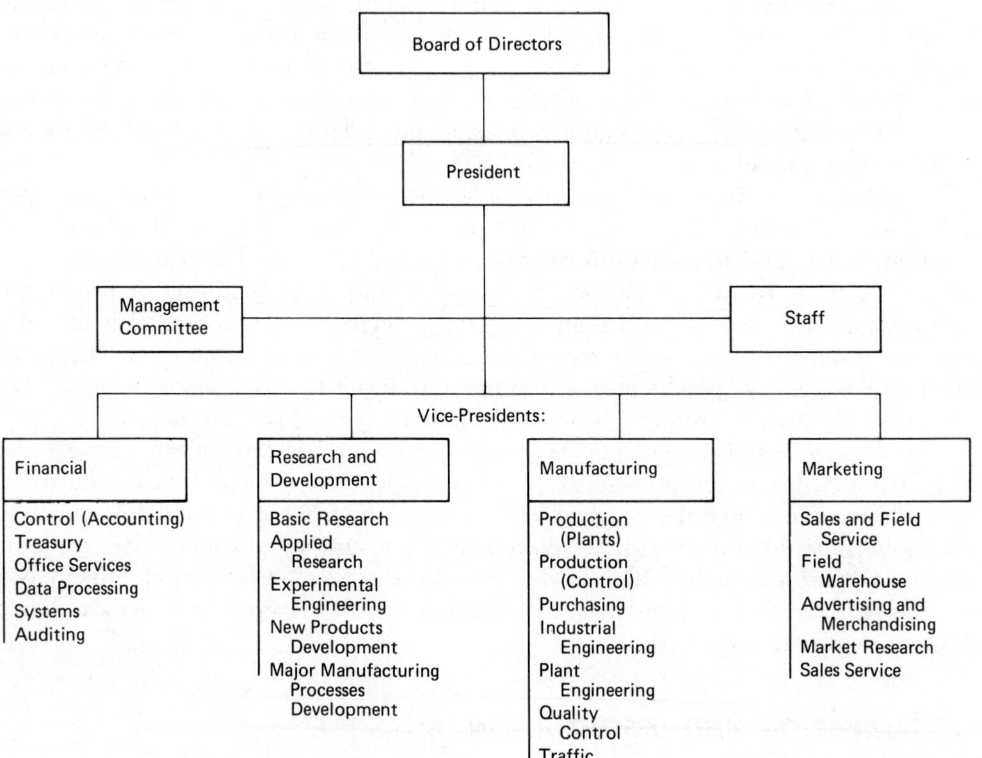

Exhibit 4-18 shows the trend of information conditioning plotted against positions in the management hierarchy. Note the vertical axis at the right, "timeliness."

EXHIBIT 4-18 THE INFORMATION CONDITIONING PYRAMID

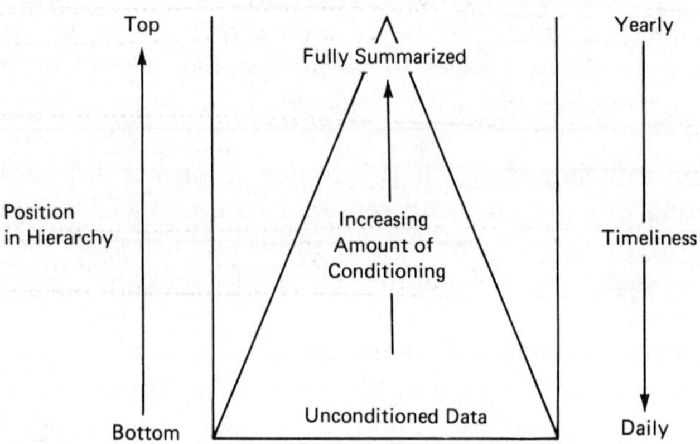

At the lowest levels, decisions must be made day by day or oftener. Information that is absolutely current is required at the operating level. At the top of the pyramid most decisions are with respect to long-range goals, so the information need not be updated so often. The point is that while the accounting department head may require daily reports, the financial vice-president needs data weekly, and a monthly report on the same information may be most suitable to the president's needs.

We may express this concept in a slightly different way. Consider the "information continuum" diagram in Exhibit 4-19. Note that while the absolute *amount* of information remains unchanged as we move upwards in the hierarchy, the *content* changes radically.

EXHIBIT 4-19 THE INFORMATION CONTINUUM

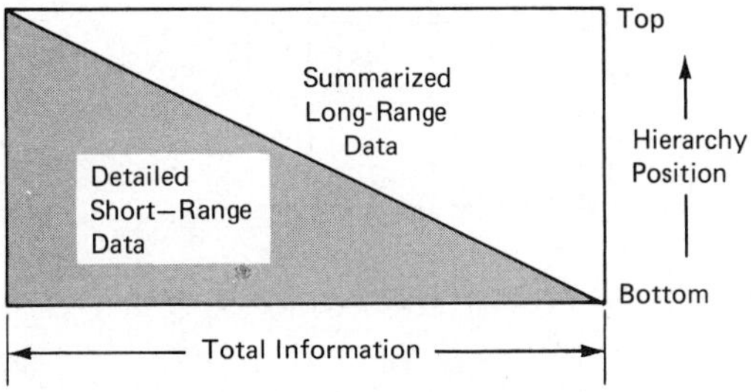

MANAGEMENT AND THE ACCOUNTING INFORMATION SYSTEM

We have discussed the general requirements for information with respect to needs, structure, and flow. Let us now examine specifically the requirements for an accounting information system; that is, an information system providing *financial* data to management.

An organization reaches its objectives through the utilization of *resources*. In the accounting information system, we are concerned primarily with quantifiable resource management; resources whose utilization we can measure in terms of effort expended (cost) and reward obtained (benefit). Resource options constitute the *alternatives* we spoke of previously.

The information system should be structured to provide data for different organizational needs. For example, those concerned with financial management problems will deal most closely with a particular "slice" of the total information system depicted in Exhibit 4-16. This slice appears in Exhibit 4-20.

It is obvious from the discussion so far that the accounting system must supply internal data for internal management use. In managing resources, the firm draws upon and contributes to its external environment as illustrated by the diagram in Exhibit 4-21. For this reason, the system should augment its internal data with environmental data.

The accounting information system is concerned with the internal and external aspects of six major resources:

Capital
Credit

Cash
People
Physical substances
Intangible factors, such as personality and motivation of employees

EXHIBIT 4-20 THE FINANCIAL INFORMATION "SLICE"

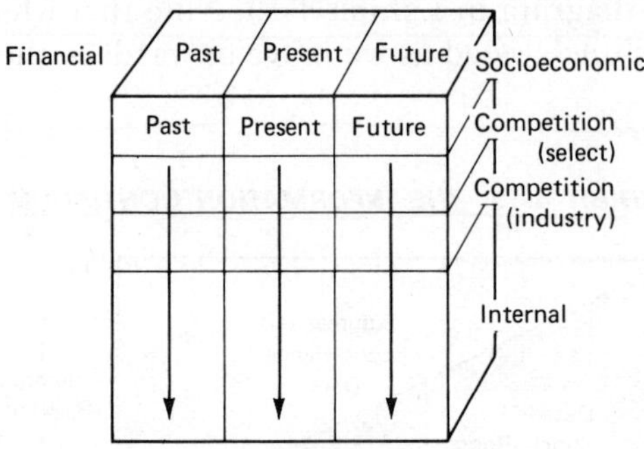

EXHIBIT 4-21 RESOURCE INTERACTION OF THE FIRM

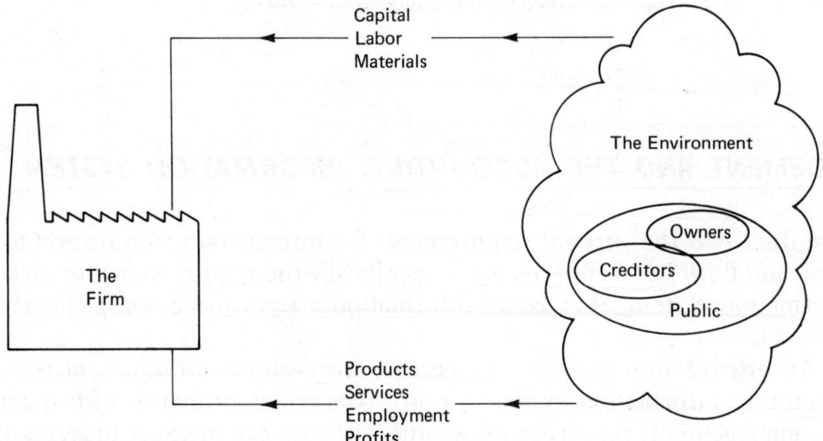

For the purposes of the information system, these resources are defined as follows:

Capital is long-term financing provided by owners and creditors. By "long-term" we mean that no repayment is required within the *normal operational cycle* in the case of creditors, or at any time other than through dissolution in the case of owners. Creditors' capital is usually referred to as *long-term liability*, and consists of such items as mortgages, bonds, and debentures. Owners' and creditors' capital are placed in the same category in that they both provide for the *capitalization* of the firm. Because no imminent repayment is necessary, these funds can be used to finance facilities (land, buildings, furniture, and equipment) and provide a reserve for current operations, which we refer to as *working capital*.

Considerable information is needed to manage capital resources. For example, information is needed regarding alternative forms, sources, and terms of capital financing; ratio of owner/creditor capital; and the valuation of owners' equity.

Credit allows for the purchase of goods and services on a delayed-payment basis. In accounting terminology, credit sets up what is known as an *accounts payable* where we are the *debtor,* and an *accounts receivable* where we are the *creditor.* Credit should be payable or receivable within the normal operating cycle to be classified as such.

Information is needed for the management of credit resources. For example, to whom we extend credit, and in what amounts, is a common information need. Information is needed regarding credit ratings and terms, and on collection and payment efficiency. Having accurate information on the cost of credit is essential to pricing and purchasing.

Cash is an important resource of the firm, as it is the ultimate medium of exchange. This resource must be guarded most carefully against fraud and embezzlement. Information is needed on long-range and short-range sources and uses of cash, and on the function of cash controls. It is important to know in what form cash is or should be held; that is, in a checking account, savings, marketable securities, or long-term investments. It is essential to know the cash conversion cycle of such assets as accounts receivable and inventory, and to monitor the changing purchasing power of cash.

People are accounted for imperfectly as a resource. The accounting system does not as yet place a value on a particular person or skill other than through the graduated wage and salary structure. Nevertheless, the cost of human resources is a major component of total operating expenses and a major factor in pricing saleable goods and services.

Managers need considerable information from the accounting system in order to optimize the use of human resources. Information regarding actual and comparative wage and salary structures and on fringe benefits is needed. Information and control of chargeable time is essential. Tracing specific effort to a particular job or product is needed for pricing, in addition to a variety of information required for labor negotiations. Firms working on government contracts are confronted with stringent requirements regarding man-hour accounting documentation and methods.

Physical Substances can be classified into two major groups: (1) those which are held for sale in the normal course of business, and (2) those which house and support the operations of the firm. The first category is termed *merchandise inventory* and comprises ready-made goods which are held for retail sale, or manufactured goods which are held for wholesale and/or retail sale. The second category is termed *long-lived assets* and consists of the facilities of the firm; that is, such things as land, buildings, furniture, fixtures, and equipment.

Necessary information on merchandise inventory includes knowing where, when, and how much to purchase or sell; how to store and move merchandise most efficiently; payoff on advertising; and a host of other detail.

In managing *facilities,* we need to know where to locate them; whether we should lease or buy; where, when, and what to buy and sell; and how to allocate the cost of facilities to time periods and products.

Intangible factors are difficult to measure within the current state of the art in accounting. To some extent, however, these factors are captured indirectly in the accounting numbers. For example, motivation levels should be reflected in increased output and cost efficiencies. Imaginative leadership may reveal itself in active research and development, updated product lines, and low turnover among employees. The problem at present is that while these intangible factors do impact on accounting numbers, critical delays may be involved. Negative or positive utilization of intangible resources may be at work for some time before the financial statements record the fact. For this reason the search for more adequate measures of intangible resources should be accelerated.

We can flow chart the elements within the resource management cycle (Exhibit 4-22). It is understood that the accounting information system furnishes data for each step. Obviously, an efficient and accurate financial information system is needed for optimal resource management.

EXHIBIT 4-22 THE RESOURCE MANAGEMENT CYCLE

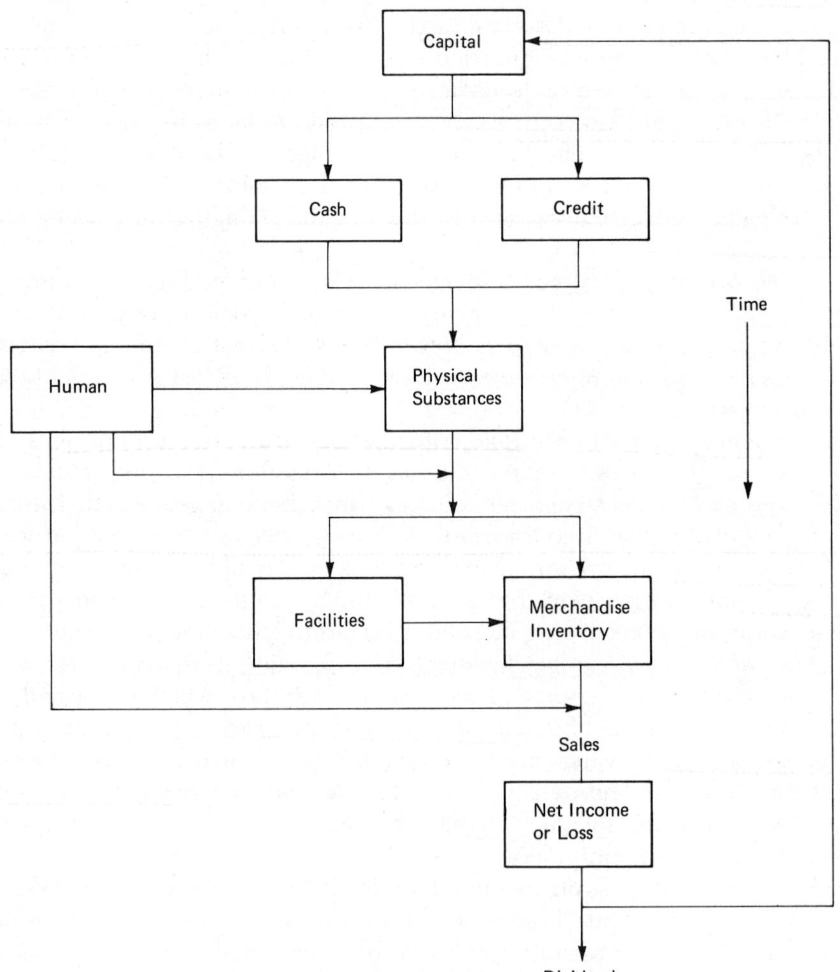

4.13 SUMMARY

While double-entry accounting dates from the time of Pacioli, there have been progressive developments through the years—all in response to changing user needs. The emergence of stockholders who play no role in the management of the enterprise has given rise to the institution of financial reporting as we know it. The financial statements are designed for this purpose.

Similarly, the increasing complexity in operations has led to the emergence of cost and management accounting. The need for planning has led to forecasts and budgets. The needs of specialized types of institutions, such as governments, have prompted the development of specialized accounting systems such as "fund accounting."

The *financial* accounting system serves particularly the external user, with a secondary benefit to management; the *managerial* accounting system is essentially directed towards internal users, with limited relevance to outside users.

In the design and operation of these systems, it is important to understand the decision making process and the needs and expectations of users. The objective in systems design is to optimize the right type of information for its intended use. This requires a knowledge of the organization and the various decision roles that it represents.

An efficient accounting information system is one that combines financial and management data. While the outputs may differ, economy and coordination can be achieved if input and transformation of both types (or modifications of one type) of data are managed in one integrative and interactive system.

CHAPTER 4 REFERENCES AND ADDITIONAL READINGS

Albers, H. H. *Principles of Management.* New York: John Wiley & Sons, Inc., 1969.

Alexis, Marcus, and Wilson, Charles Z. *Organizational Decision Making.* Englewood Cliffs, N.J.: Prentice-Hall, Inc., 1967.

Anthony, Robert N. *Planning and Control Systems: A Framework for Analysis.* Cambridge, Mass.: Harvard University Press, 1965.

Burns, Thomas J., and Hendrickson, Harvey S., eds. "The Accounting Model and Financial Statements." In *The Accounting Primer: An Introduction to Financial Accounting.* New York: McGraw-Hill Book Company, 1972.

Carey, John L. "The Origins of Modern Financial Reporting." *The Journal of Accountancy,* September 1969, pp. 35–48.

Chatfield, Michael. *Contemporary Studies in the Evolution of Accounting Thought.* Belmont, Calif.: Dickenson Publishing Company, 1968.

Fisch, G. G. *Organization for Profit.* New York: McGraw-Hill Book Company, 1964.

Frishkoff, Paul E. "Capitalism and the Development of Bookkeeping: A Reconsideration." *The International Journal of Accounting Education and Research,* Spring 1970, pp. 29–37.

Hare, Van Court Jr. *Systems Analysis: A Diagnostic Approach.* New York: Harcourt, Brace & World, Inc., 1967.

Heany, Donald F. *Development of Information Systems.* New York: The Ronald Press Company, 1968.

Ijiri, Yuji. *Management Goals and Accounting for Control.* Chicago: Rand McNally & Company, 1965.

Johnson, Richard A.; Kast, Fremont E.; and Rosenzweig, James E. *The Theory and Management of Systems.* McGraw-Hill Book Company, 1967.

Littleton, A. C., and Yamey, B. S. *Studies in the History of Accounting.* Homewood, Ill.: Richard D. Irwin, Inc., 1956.

Luoma, Gary A. *Accounting Information in Managerial Decision-Making for Small and Medium Manufacturers.* Research Monograph No. 2. New York: National Association of Accountants, 1967.

Parker, R. H. "Accounting History: A Selected Bibliography." *Abacus,* September 1965, pp. 62–84.

Schrader, William J.; Malcom, Robert E.; and Willingham, John J. *Financial Accounting.* Homewood, Ill.: Richard D. Irwin, Inc., 1970, pp. 3–130.

Sollenberger, Harold M. *Major Changes Caused by the Implementation of a Management Information System.* Research Monograph No. 4. New York: National Association of Accountants, 1968.

Toan, Arthur B. Jr. *Using Information to Manage.* New York: The Ronald Press Company, 1968.

CHAPTER 4 QUESTIONS, PROBLEMS, AND CASES

4- 1. Distinguish among the following systems of accounting:
(a) Primitive
(b) Single-entry
(c) Double-entry

4- 2. Who is credited with the invention of double-entry accounting?

4- 3. What inadequacy of single-entry accounting prompted the development of double-entry accounting? What business activity in mercantile Italy provided the impetus?

4- 4. Give an example of where an accounting system was, in effect, prior to a society's ability to write.

4- 5. What is a "tally stick"?

4- 6. Give three examples of how output needs have brought about changes in the structure of the accounting system.

4- 7. Explain the difference between an *organization chart* and an *information flow chart.*

4- 8. Operationalize the following objectives:
(a) Improve quality
(b) Improve the "image" of the firm
(c) Beat the competition
(d) Keep the customer happy
(e) Improve the social concern of the firm
(f) Select a good credit risk

4- 9. Expand the *accounting equation* to include nominal accounts.

4-10. "Nominal accounts as represented in the income statement are not mathematically essential to accounting." Explain the meaning of this statement. Show the journal entry to record a sale of $3,000 assuming (a) there are nominal accounts, and (b) there are no nominal accounts.

4-11. Referring to Exhibit 4-16, define what you believe to be the proper sphere of the accounting information system. What system or systems would furnish the remaining information?

4-12. "Output requirements govern the type of accounting system that is designed." What is meant by this statement?

4-13. From a management viewpoint, what are the chief shortcomings of periodic financial statements?

4-14. Decision making, as a complex psycho-physiological process, contains some assumptions about the decision maker. What are they?

4-15. "The essential purpose of an enterprise is to optimize resource management in the social interest." Comment on this statement.

4-16. Explain what is meant by a *decision hierarchy.*

4-17. "Important objectives are seldom achieved through a single decision." Explain what is meant by this statement.

4-18. What would you say of an organization where the top echelon concerned itself primarily with detailed, short-range information?

4-19. Give five reasons why the financial accounting information system serves an imperfect internal role.

4-20. Identify the following accounts as being either *real* or *nominal:*

	Real	Nominal
Cash		
Salaries expense		
Sales...		
Owner's investment		
Accounts receivable...................		
Plant & equipment.....................		
Manufacturing expense.............		
Income tax expense...................		
Dividends paid		

4-21. Identify five major *functional* information classes, and describe each.

4-22. Cite five generalized rules of a well-run organization.

4-23. What are the six major resources of an accounting information system? Define each. Flow chart the interaction of these resources.

4-24. Identify the elements of an organization as a system:

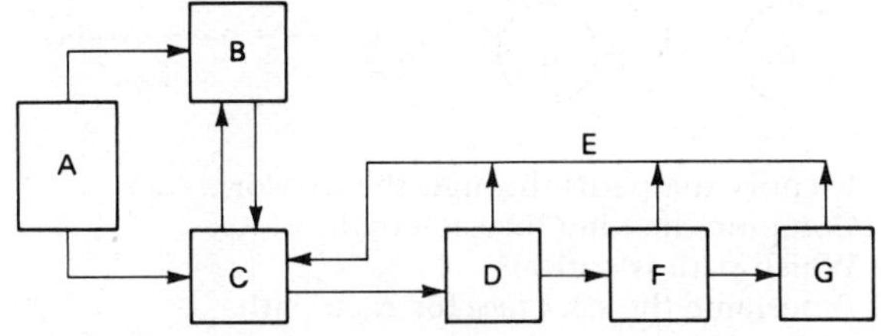

4-25. Complete the debit-credit rule table below:

Type of Account	To Increase	To Decrease	Typical or Normal Balance
Assets			
Liabilities			
Owners' equity			
Investment			
Revenues			
Expenses			

4-26. Explain the meaning or implication of the following terms or phrases:
(a) Leverage
(b) Closing process
(c) Transaction document
(d) Credit memo
(e) Debit memo
(f) Special journals
(g) Subsidiary ledgers
(h) Work control records
(i) Effectiveness ratio
(j) Organization chart
(k) Conditioning of information
(l) Information continuum
(m) Cost-benefit ratio
(n) Capitalization

4-27. ***BALANCE SHEET*** Suppose a business is just starting and only two transactions are significant:

(a) Mr. Koth and Mr. Sutter each contribute $5,000 to get the business started.

(b) The business purchases a $20,000 machine on credit.

Prepare a balance sheet in (1) account form and (2) in report form.

4-28. ***NETWORK ANALYSIS*** (See chapter 2.) Consider the following network model, with a starting point A and a goal at event L:

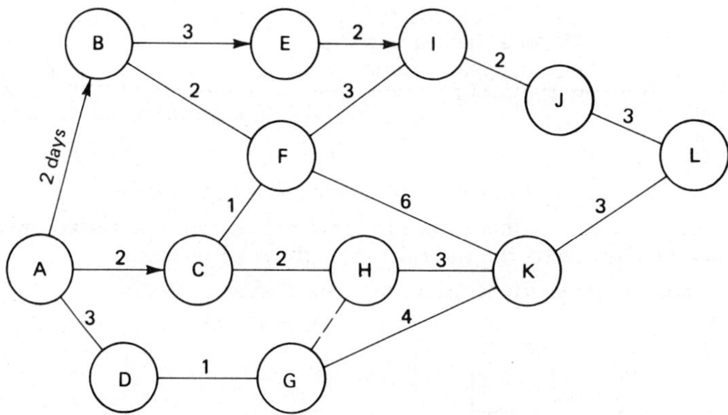

(a) Identify the paths through the network.
(b) Compute the time for each path.
(c) Which path is critical?
(d) Determine the *slack time* for each path.

4-29. ***JOURNAL ENTRIES*** Give the journal entry to record each of the following transactions:

(a) Mr. Hyatt withdraws $200 from the business.
(b) A bill of $800 for machine repairs is paid.
(c) Mr. Noto lends the business $4,000.
(d) Inventory costing $200 is sold for $240.
(e) A $10,000 machine is bought for credit.

4-30. ***FINANCIAL VERSUS MANAGERIAL ACCOUNTING SYSTEMS*** For both a financial accounting system and a management accounting system, describe each of the following characteristics:

Characteristic	Financial Accounting System	Management Accounting System
1. Purpose		
2. Scope		
3. User-orientation		
4. Time-orientation		
5. Methodology		
6. Precision		
7. Realization		
8. Necessity		
9. Incidence		
10. Catalyst		

4-31. ***ACCOUNTING EQUATION*** The following information is available for the Syverson Company:

	Jan. 1, 19x1	Dec. 31, 19x1
Cash	$10,500	$ 9,500
Other assets	50,000	45,000
Liabilities	26,000	23,000

If there are no investments and no withdrawals by the owner during 19*x*1, what is the income or loss for 19*x*1?

4-32. ***ACCOUNTING EQUATION*** Hanson's capital account balance at the end of an accounting period was $3,200. During the period Hanson invested $1,770 and withdrew $670. His income statement showed a profit of $500. What was Hanson's capital account balance at the beginning of the period?

4-33. ***BALANCE SHEET RELATIONSHIPS*** How much will capital increase or decrease if:
(a) Assets increase by $1,000 and liabilities increase by $500?
(b) Assets increase by $700 and liabilities decrease by $300?
(c) Assets increase by $500 and liabilities increase by $1,000?
(d) Assets decrease by $2,000 and liabilities decrease by $1,200?
(e) Assets decrease by $600 and liabilities increase by $800?

4-34. ***THE ACCOUNTING CYCLE***

ANDERSON COMPANY
BALANCE SHEET
JANUARY 1, 1973

ASSETS		LIABILITIES	
Current Assets:		**Current Liabilities:**	
Cash	$ 3,000	Accounts payable	$ 6,000
Accounts receivable	5,000	Current portion of notes payable	1,000
Inventory	17,000		
Long-Lived Assets:		**Long-Term Liabilities:**	
Furniture and equipment	8,000	Notes payable	4,000
		OWNERS' EQUITY	
		Anderson capital	22,000
Total Assets	$33,000	Total equities	$33,000

Given: 1973 transactions

(a) Sales of $210,000 included credit sales of $200,000 and cash sales of $10,000.
(b) Inventory of $96,000 purchased on credit.
(c) $202,000 in accounts receivable collected.
(d) Paid $99,000 on account.
(e) Paid the following operating expenses:

Salaries ($18,000 Mr. Anderson, $84,600 employees)	$102,600
Rent	2,400
Utilities	800
Supplies	200

(f) Purchased a new cash register in January for $1,500 with ⅓ down and the balance to be paid in two equal yearly installments beginning January, 1974, interest free.

(g) Paid cash $500 for a fire insurance policy. (Post total to prepaid expense account.)

(h) Mr. Anderson paid $5,000 from his personal account for a truck and registered it in the company name.

(i) Interest of $600 and the current portion of notes payable was paid.

Required:

(1) Journalize the transactions for 1973.
(2) Post the transactions to ledger accounts.
(3) Prepare the preliminary trial balance.

Given: December, 1973, adjusting entries

(j) Physical inventory at the end of the period was valued at $6,000.

(k) $50 in accounts receivable were "written off" during the year and all remaining accounts appear to be "good."

(l) Mr. Anderson decides to withdraw from capital the amount paid as his salary during the year.

(m) At the end of December, four years remain on the five-year fire insurance policy.

(n) Interest on the note payable is 6% per annum. Capitalize the prepaid portion of interest paid.

(o) Depreciation charges for furniture and equipment is $950; for the truck, $1,000.

(p) Current portion of the note payable of $1,000.

Required:

(4) Journalize the adjusting entries.
(5) Post them to the ledger accounts.
(6) Prepare adjusted trial balance.
(7) Prepare formal financial statements: income statement, statement of changes in capital, and balance sheet.
(8) Close the income statement accounts. (Prepare journal entry and post to the accounts.)

4-35. ***THE WORKSHEET*** Refer to Precision Mechanics worksheet on page 119.

Adjusting Entries:

(a) Salaries earned but not paid as of December 31, 1973, amount to $2,000.

(b) Depreciation expense for 1973 is $3,000.

(c) A physical inventory taken as of December 31, 1973, indicates actual value of inventory to be $25,500. (Assume the difference was error in recording perpetual inventory transactions resulting in understated cost of goods sold.)

(d) Organization costs are being amortized over five years at the rate of $1,000 per year.

(e) Office supply transactions are as follows:

Physical inventory 12/31/72	$1,000
Purchases during year	500
Physical inventory 12/31/73	700

(f) Of the rent paid, $500 represents the last month's rent on a five-year lease.

Required:

(1) Complete the worksheet.
(2) Prepare formal financial statements: income statement, statement of changes in retained earnings, and balance sheet.

PRECISION MECHANICS
TRIAL BALANCE
DECEMBER 31, 1973

ACCOUNTS	PRELIMINARY TRIAL BALANCE		ADJUSTMENTS		ADJUSTED TRIAL BALANCE		INCOME STATEMENT		BALANCE SHEET	
	Debit	Credit	Debit	Credit	Debit	Credit	Debit	Credit	Debit	Credit
Cash	10,000									
Accounts receivable	13,000									
Inventory	27,000									
Prepaid expenses	4,000									
Office supplies	1,000									
Furniture and equip.	38,000									
Acc. dep. furn. & equip.		9,000								
Unamort. org. costs	3,000									
Accounts payable		12,000								
Capital stock at par		50,000								
Retained earnings		3,300								
Sales		273,400								
Cost of goods sold	175,000									
Salary expense	48,000									
Advertising expense	11,000									
Rent	6,500									
Auto expense	5,000									
Telephone & telegraph	3,000									
Utility expense	2,000									
Office supply exp.	500									
Insurance	400									
Miscellaneous	300									
	$347,700	$347,700								
Depreciation exp.										
Organization exp.										
Accrued Salary exp.										
Deferred exp.										

CHAPTER

5

INCOME MEASUREMENT

5.1 PURPOSE OF INCOME MEASUREMENT

The purpose of income measurement is to assess the effectiveness of *operations* as they relate to the goal(s) of an enterprise. More specifically, income measurement is used to: (1) compute return on investment, (2) evaluate the performance of persons in organizations, (3) serve as a motivator for improved performance, (4) measure changes in the "well-offness" of an enterprise, (5) report on operating effectiveness for external and internal purposes, (6) facilitate the comparison of inter-firm effectiveness, and (7) meet the information needs of regulatory and taxing agencies.

Fisher, the noted economist, has identified three types of income:[1]

1. *Psychic* or enjoyment income, consisting of agreeable sensations and experiences.
2. *Real* income as measured by what money will buy, i.e., in terms of purchasing power or effectiveness.
3. *Money* income, consisting of the money available for purchasing.

[1] Irving Fisher, *The Theory of Interest* (New York: The Macmillan Company, 1930), pp. 10–11.

The term "income" in accounting is restricted generally to the third type—*money* income. Traditionally, the accounting system has measured only this type of income for financial reporting purposes. But efforts are being made to extend income measurement to category (2) for financial reporting purposes, as illustrated by the progress toward price-level accounting (chapter 8). This external effort toward measuring *real* income is matched by the increasing emphasis that is being given to cost-effectiveness in internal management (chapters 3 and 4).

5.2 MEASUREMENT AND ACCOUNTING

That accountants need to measure income illustrates that accounting is a measurement discipline. The fact that the phenomena which accountants attempt to measure are of a complex socio-physical nature creates problems and opportunities. The problems include the illusive search for "perfect" measurements and frustration because progress toward better measurement appears at times to be painstakingly slow. But *because* accountants confront complex measurement problems, the field offers an ever-present challenge to the researcher or theorist whose motivation lies in extending the frontiers of a discipline. Professor Ackoff has said that "measurement, perhaps more than any other research activity, has been the principal stimulus of progress in both pure and applied science."[2]

We have noted in chapter 2 that *measurement* is the assignment of numerals to events or objects according to some rule or standard. The assignment of numerals to economic transactions is the principal function of accounting. In most cases these numerals are in the form of money values. The aggregation of these values is used to measure the *wealth* and *income* of businesses and individuals. From these assessments of wealth and income, policy makers control the distribution of economic resources through taxation and other means. It is obviously very important that close attention be paid to *how* accounting numbers are generated if we seek to optimize social controls.

5.3 WEALTH AND INCOME

Wealth is owners' equity at any particular point in time. It is computed similarly for individuals and businesses. If you were asked to assess your personal wealth, you would undoubtedly proceed as follows:

I own assets of $X value
− I owe debts totaling $Y
= I am worth $X − $Y

You will notice this procedure as being identical to the format of the *accounting equation* discussed in chapter 4; that is,

$$A = L - OE$$
$$A - L = OE$$

[2]Russell L. Ackoff, *Scientific Method* (New York: John Wiley & Sons, Inc., 1962), pp. 215–16.

There would be a difference between your wealth as you measure it and as it would be measured according to present accounting rules. Specifically, you would value your assets at what they are worth today, while the accounting rules insist that you value them in terms of what it cost you to acquire them. *Historical cost* currently is the basis for assigning money values in accounting, as stated in chapter 3. We observed that the reason historical cost is so tenacious is due to its greater objectivity. Later in this chapter we will note that the choice of a measuring *standard* is not limited to *historical cost* versus *current market value.* Improving the standard by which we assign values to assets and liabilities will require better measures of wealth.

Income is the difference between *wealth* positions at two points in time, adjusted by investments or withdrawals by the owner during that time period. Income for David Jensen in chapter 4, for the month of January, 1973, was:

His wealth or capital as of January 31, 1973	$10,610
His wealth or capital as of January 1, 1973	10,000
Net increase in wealth	610
Adjusted for:	
Salary earned (say, $1,000)	1,000
Cash withdrawn from the business	1,000
Income for January, 1973	$ 2,610

Because income is defined as the difference between wealth positions, it follows that the values which are used to assess wealth are also determinants of income.

In this chapter we discuss current income measurement in accounting, which is followed by a brief discussion of some alternative procedures. First, however, we attend to the special problem of measuring *periodic* income.

5.4 PERMANENT VERSUS PERIODIC INCOME

Some special problems attach to the measurement of business income. First, there is the problem of obtaining *any one number* that will measure a phenomenon as complex as organizational effectiveness. In chapter 1 we indicated that complex principles require several surrogates. We also mentioned that "efficiency" cannot be measured by energy (resource consumption) data only. While the income statement does juxtapose input (cost of goods + expenses) against output (sales), it does not measure all types of input (consumption of human resources, for example) nor does it measure all types of output (goodwill, employee morale, etc.).

Second, as we mention in chapter 17, income can not be measured entirely until we have completed an investment life-cycle. For example, suppose we invest $1,000 in common stock consisting of 100 shares of $10 each. We receive dividends of 5%, or $50 a year for five years. At the end of five years we sell the stock for $15 a share for a total of $1,500. Ignoring discounting (Appendix B), our total income is:

Dividends: 5 × $50	= $250
Appreciation in value	= 500
Total	$750

Because of the convention that income can only be recognized when it is realized—that is, when an exchange transaction has actually taken place—the appreciation in the value of the stock throughout the five-year period is ignored until the point of conversion. Also there is no assurance that any appreciation will be realized until an actual exchange has taken place. If we knew that appreciation was occurring at a constant rate (non-compounded) over the period, the "economic" income per annum would be:

		Y_1	Y_2	Y_3	Y_4	Y_5	Total
Economic Income:	Dividends	$ 50	50	50	50	50	$250
	Appreciation	100	100	100	100	100	500
	Total	$150	150	150	150	150	$750

whereas "accounting" income per annum is:

		Y_1	Y_2	Y_3	Y_4	Y_5	Total
Accounting Income:	Dividends	$50	50	50	50	50	$250
	Appreciation	—	—	—	—	500	500
	Total	$50	50	50	50	550	$750

Life-cycle income from an investment is called *permanent income.* Unfortunately, most investors (and other users) are unable to wait for the end of the life-cycle of businesses in order to compute proper income. Instead, estimates of permanent income are made in each accounting period. These annual estimates are called *periodic income* measures.

5.5 CONVENTIONAL INCOME MEASUREMENT

THE ACCOUNTANT'S DEFINITION OF INCOME

The accountant's concept of income is based on the principle of *cost assumption.* Here income is defined as the difference between revenues earned and expenses incurred in producing those revenues. As mentioned previously, appreciation or "gains" are not recognized as income for accounting purposes until such gains are *realized. Realization* means that assets (generally cash or the right to receive cash) have been received in exchange for an asset owned by the entity. The exchange price of an event constitutes its value for accounting purposes. Income can be realized under the accrual method of accounting at the time when a transaction is effected rather than when cash payment is made, as stated previously.

Revenue is difficult to define, for it includes sales, non-operating income, and extraordinary gains. The most appropriate definition would be along the lines that "revenue is the sum of transactions which increase retained earnings."

The accountant distinguishes between "cost" and "expense." *Cost* represents the outlay of cash, equities, or services required to purchase assets and pay for business expenses. If these outlays (or expenditures) benefit future operating periods, they appear in the balance sheet as assets. Assets, other than cash, can be thought of as "unexpired costs." Outlays which contribute to revenues of the period are termed *expenses,* and appear in the income statement. They are also called "expired costs." The expression *cost of goods sold* implies "expired cost of goods sold" or "expired costs of acquiring inventory." Similarly, depreciation is an expired cost of acquiring a physical asset.

The distinction between cost and expense is generally dispensed with in the management accounting literature, and we follow that practice in this text, especially in the material following chapter 13, i.e., beginning with production operations in chapter 14.

THE INCOME STATEMENT

The financial document that is used currently to measure income is *the income statement.* It is also referred to as "the statement of income," "the operating statement," or less frequently as "the profit and loss statement."

An income statement may be constructed in one of several formats.

Single-Step Income Statement

An income statement prepared on this basis makes no provision for intermediate income measurement. Total expenses are deducted from total revenues without recognizing gross profit or non-operating income and expenses as separate categories:

	Revenues
−	Expenses
=	Net Income

Multi-Step Income Statement

An income statement prepared on this basis does provide for intermediate income measurement, i.e., *gross profit, net operating income,* and *net income.* It also distinguishes between operating and non-operating income and expenses:

	Sales or Operating Revenue
−	Cost of Goods Sold
=	Gross Profit
−	Selling Expenses
−	Administrative Expenses
=	Net Operating Income
+	Non-Operating Income
−	Non-Operating Expenses
=	Net Income

Current Operating Versus All-Inclusive Income Statement

In the treatment of (1) extraordinary gains and losses, and/or (2) charges and credits arising from adjusting items relating to the income of prior periods, the *all-inclusive income statement* includes these items. The *current operating statement* excludes them, in which case they appear instead in the *statement of retained earnings* (Exhibit 5-1).

EXHIBIT 5-1 CURRENT OPERATING VERSUS ALL-INCLUSIVE INCOME STATEMENT

CURRENT OPERATING	**ALL-INCLUSIVE**
Income Statement	**Income Statement**
Net Operating Income —as shown above	Net Operating Income —as shown above
+ Non-Operating Income	+ Non-Operating Income
− Non-Operating Expenses	− Non-Operating Expenses
	+ Extraordinary Gains
	− Extraordinary Losses
	+ Credits—Prior Periods
	− Charges—Prior Periods
= Net Income	= Net Income
Statement of Retained Earnings	**Statement of Retained Earnings**
Retained Earnings— beginning of year	Retained Earnings— beginning of year
+ Net Income—as shown above	+ Net Income—as shown above
+ Extraordinary Gains	
− Extraordinary Losses	
+ Credits—Prior Periods	
− Charges—Prior Periods	
− Dividends/Drawings	− Dividends/Drawings
= Retained Earnings—end of year	= Retained Earnings—end of year

NON-OPERATING INCOME AND EXPENSES

Some revenues flow into an entity which are not related directly to its principal business activity; examples are interest income on investments, rental income from subleasing, or royalties from inventions. Such revenues are termed *non-operating,* that is, they are incidental to the operating mainstream of the firm. Similarly, unrelated expenses are classified as non-operating. *Interest expense* is a primary example.

Although non-operating income and expenses occur with regularity, it is held that a clearer picture of operating performance can be obtained by classifying these items separately in the income statement.

EXTRAORDINARY GAINS AND LOSSES

Extraordinary gains and losses are items of material value that result from unusual and generally unpredictable events, such as gain or loss on the sale of long-lived assets, or losses by fire, earthquake, or theft. The treatment of extraordinary items in income measurement has been the subject of intensive debate among accountants, as discussed below.

CURRENT OPERATING VERSUS ALL-INCLUSIVE STATEMENTS

One school of thought holds that extraordinary items should not be included in the income statement. In their view, the income statement should show only the results of a firm's operations on a regular, normal basis. Extraordinary items distort operating performance if they are used to adjust net income. For example, a low net income based on a poor operating record could be improved by selling a long-lived asset at a profit, misleading the reader into believing that operating performance is better than it really is. Or conversely, an uninsured loss could detract from an otherwise good operating record. The primary argument in favor of an income statement that is free of extraordinary items (called a *current operating statement,* as mentioned previously) is that users of financial statements prefer a net income figure that is not distorted by unusual (extraordinary) events. Instead, the theorists believe these items should be included in the *statement of retained earnings.*

Other authorities believe that all events of a period should be contained in the income statement, whether they are "ordinary" or "extraordinary." The basis for this view is that a firm's financial well-being—as measured by its ability to reward investors or expand—is affected by unusual events in addition to current operations. By including such items in the income statement, these persons believe that the income statement is less susceptible to manipulation, as illustrated by a possible tendency to classify events as extraordinary in borderline cases in an effort to improve the profit picture. Thus, if the determination of extraordinary items is left to management's discretion, as with the current operating statement method, the exclusion of certain important items from income analysis could result. Placing this information in the statement of retained earnings decreases its visibility and importance, according to these theorists. Proponents of this type of statement (called an *all-inclusive income statement*) advocate the disclosure of all extraordinary items in the income statement, thus relying on the judgment of the user(s) of the statement to make his own determination as to the relevance or importance of the data.

The all-inclusive income statement method has received the support of the Accounting Principles Board (APB) of the American Institute of Certified Public Accountants (AICPA) in their *Opinion No. 9.* The judgment of the Board was that the income statement should include all events which take place during an accounting period with the exception of items that properly belong to prior periods, such as the refund on a prior year's income tax. According to *APB Opinion No. 9,* extraordinary items should be separated from, and reported after, net operating income, giving full disclosure as to the nature and amounts of such items.

THE STATEMENT OF RETAINED EARNINGS (OR "CHANGES IN CAPITAL")

The document which links the income statement and balance sheet is the *statement of retained earnings* (for corporations) or the *statement of changes in capital* (for partnerships and proprietorships). The basic format of these statements is illustrated in Exhibit 5-2.

The difference in these statements is that the statement of changes in capital deals with changes in all of the owners' equity accounts, while the statement of re-

EXHIBIT 5-2 BASIC FORMAT FOR STATEMENT OF CHANGES IN CAPITAL OR RETAINED EARNINGS

I STATEMENT OF CHANGES IN CAPITAL (Proprietorships & Partnerships)		II STATEMENT OF RETAINED EARNINGS (Corporations)	
Capital, beginning of period	$	Retained earnings, beginning of period	$
		Add: Net income	
Add: Additional capital		Total retained earnings available	$
Net income		Less: Dividends paid	
Total capital available	$		
Less: Capital withdrawn by owners		Retained earnings, end of period	$
Capital, end of period	$		

tained earnings deals only with changes in *earned capital,* i.e., retained earnings. It does not show changes in contributed or paid-in capital, such as the issue of additional stock.

In addition to the items shown in Exhibit 5-2, certain entries pertaining to prior periods may be included in the statement of retained earnings, provided they meet the criteria set forth in *APB Opinion No. 9:*

1. The item must be material in amount.
2. It must be directly related to business activities of a particular prior period(s).
3. It must not be attributable to a subsequent event, i.e., an event which occurred after the preparation of the financial statements.
4. It must be determined by persons other than management.
5. It must be a final determination of an item—not an estimate.

Adjustments that meet these criteria are rare in financial accounting, but the APB does give examples, such as settlements relating to prior period income taxes, renegotiation proceedings, or settlements arising from litigations.

5.6 INCOME VERSUS CASH FLOW

Most organizations maintain their accounts under the *accrual* method of accounting, which gives rise to a difference in timing between income and cash flow, as illustrated in Exhibit 5-3.

Because of the timing difference between income and cash flow, it is important to stress that the income statement is not a *cash flow* statement, and that where accounts are maintained under the accrual method of accounting, it is necessary to plan and measure cash flow as distinct from planning and measuring income.

Where sales, purchases, and operating expenses are relatively stable over time, the income statement may approximate cash flow with the exception of *depreciation* (which is not a cash outlay but is an expense) and *principal payments* on the amortization of debt (which is a cash outlay but not an expense). In these instances it is acceptable practice to *convert* income to cash flow as shown in Exhibit 5-4.

EXHIBIT 5-3 TIMING DIFFERENCES BETWEEN INCOME AND CASH FLOW

	UNDER ACCRUAL ACCOUNTING	
EXAMPLES	**Cash Flow Precedes Income Flow**	**Income Flow Precedes Cash Flow**
Revenue		
Rent is paid in advance	X	
A credit sale		X
Expenses		
Depreciation on an asset	X	
Goods sold are purchased on account		X
Wages are earned but unpaid		X
Rent is prepaid	X	
A stock of supplies is purchased for cash	X	

EXHIBIT 5-4 ADJUSTING INCOME TO CASH FLOW

ADD-BACK DEPRECIATION

(Without Income Tax)

Revenue		$100,000
Operating expenses (excluding depreciation)	$70,000	
Depreciation	20,000	(90,000)
Net income		$ 10,000
Add-back depreciation		20,000
Principal payments on debt		⟨15,000⟩
Cash flow		$ 15,000

5.7 INCOME PLANNING UNDER THE CONVENTIONAL MODEL

We have discussed the nature and purposes of income measurement. These topics are largely historical. The objective is to record and measure past events, and in some cases, current events.

To manage any business activity efficiently and assure its continuity, knowledge of the past is only a part of the managerial process. The proper focus of management should be *forward* in order to plan for future events. The primary accounting documents which embody future plans are *budgets* and *pro forma* statements.

BUDGETS AND PRO FORMA STATEMENTS

Budgets and *pro forma* statements can be distinguished in that budgets deal with planned or functional areas or segments of a firm, while *pro forma* statements are projected financial statements (usually income statements and/or balance sheets) based on the outcome of planned, probable, or hypothetical operations or events, coupled with the use of specific accounting and tax strategies.

Comprehensive budgeting involves the assembly of a number of subsidiary budgets into a master financial plan (Exhibit 5-5).

EXHIBIT 5-5 COMPREHENSIVE BUDGETING

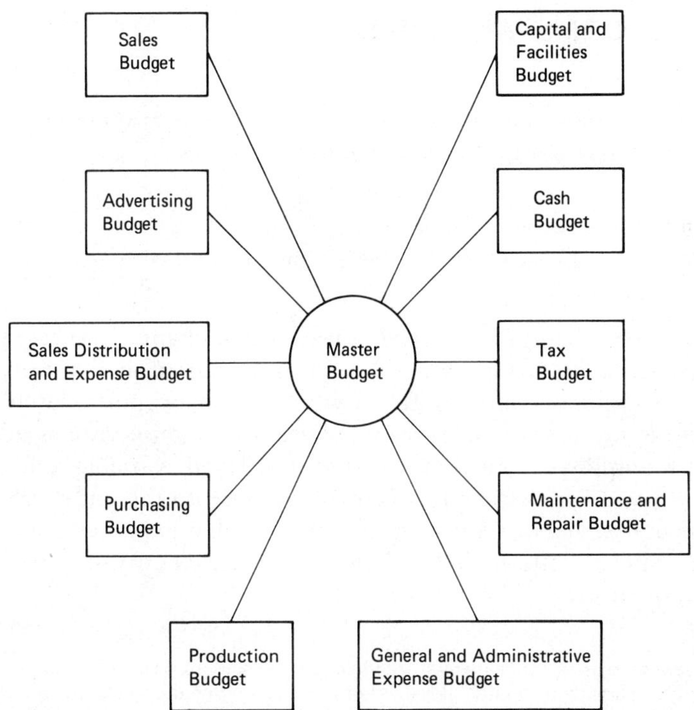

Annual budgets are often apportioned to monthly intervals or less, and the budget for one time period may differ from that of other periods depending upon expected levels of activity. Similarly, budgets for various levels of activity can be formulated in advance (*flexible budgets*) so that an alternate plan is available in the event that the actual activity level differs from the original plan.

Budgets often serve as control devices requiring approval of expenditures against an available budget provision.

Pro forma statements are financial statements that reflect expected outcomes under certain assumptions:

1 If Companies X and Y are considering a merger, *pro forma* statements could be drawn up to show how XY's income statement and balance sheet would appear after the merger.

2 If Company X is considering the addition of a new plant or product line, *pro forma* statements would show the impact of the expansion in terms of X's income statement and balance sheet.
3 If Company X is making a substantial change in the selling price of its product, *pro forma* income statements will indicate sales activity and income at current or at some projected volume.
4 If operations for the next year proceed according to plan, *pro forma* statements projected for the end of period will reflect the results of operations in terms of income and financial position.

Chapters 22 and 23 deal further with forecasts and budgets.

5.8 MARGINAL INCOME ANALYSIS

Certain expenses in most enterprises are fixed. That is, they do not vary in relation to changes in activity levels under certain conditions:[3]

1. During the one-year period, and
2. Where the change in activity level is within the normal operating range.

On the other hand there are expenses which change in direct proportion to changes in activity level (*variable expenses*), such as the cost of similar units of inventory. A third class of expenses varies with activity, but not proportionately (*semi-variable expenses*), such as the cost of supervision where a new supervisor is added for, say, every ten new employees. Further treatment of fixed, variable, and semi-variable expenses is reserved for chapter 18. We proceed here on the understanding that it is possible to recognize fixed, semi-variable, and variable expenses and to decompose semi-variable expenses into their fixed and variable elements so as to have two categories instead of three:

[3] These assumptions regarding *fixed* expenses are important because in terms of assumption 1, all expenses are fixed in the very short run, such as the need to meet an end-of-the-week payroll; and conversely all expenses are variable in the very long run. In terms of assumption 2, changes in fixed expenses will occur if there is a very substantial reduction or increase in the level of activity. Hence, fixed expenses are defined for a relevant or normal activity range:

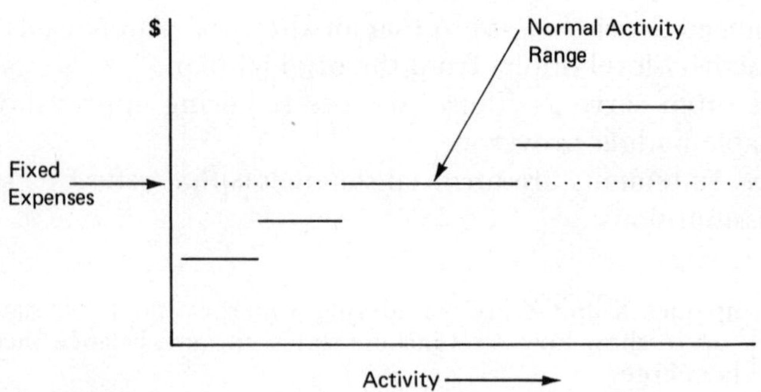

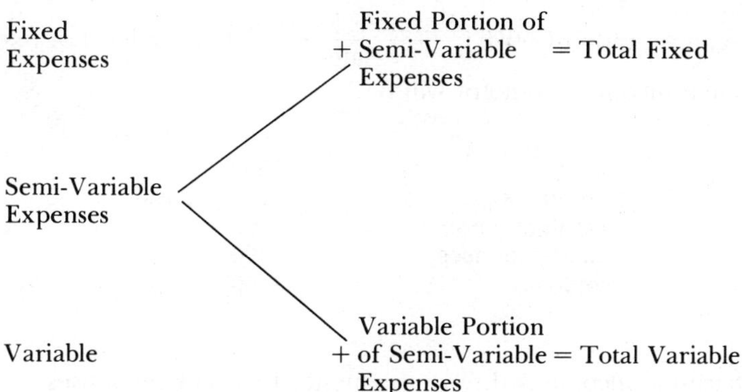

We assume further that the variable expenses are directly related to number of units sold.[4] If the variable expense portion of one unit sold is 40¢ and we sell ten items, then total variable expense for the ten items is $4.

An income statement that has these relationships as its foundations is referred to as a *marginal income statement* and has the following format:

EXHIBIT 5-6 MARGINAL INCOME STATEMENT FORMAT

Sales	$1,000	
Variable expenses	⟨ 500⟩	(50%)
Marginal income	500	
Fixed expenses	⟨ 400⟩	
Net income	$ 100	

If in the above example we double the number of units sold, without changing our basic relationships, the new statement will be as follows:

Sales	$2,000	
Variable expenses	⟨ 1,000⟩	(50%)
Marginal income	1,000	
Fixed expenses	⟨ 400⟩	
Net income	$ 600	

Observe that when sales double, variable expenses change in direct proportion to sales. But fixed expenses do not change, hence, the resulting net income is not twice but six times the former figure. If sales decline by half, without altering

[4] Variability, as we shall see later, may relate to many activity scales. Car rental based on mileage is a variable expense because of the direct relationship between miles and rental charge. Some examples of different activity scales are:

Expense	Activity Scale
Electricity	KWH per meter reading
Water	Gallons per meter reading
Direct materials	No. of units manufactured
Direct labor	No. of units manufactured

the variable expense ratio of 50% $\left(\frac{\text{Variable Expense}}{\text{Sales}}\right)$ or the level of fixed expenses, the new marginal income statement will be:

Sales	$500	
Variable expenses	⟨ 250 ⟩	(50%)
Marginal income	250	
Fixed expenses	⟨ 400 ⟩	
Net loss	($150)	

Notice that marginal income is the complement of variable expenses.

We examine these relationships further in chapter 18.

5.9 ALTERNATIVE INCOME STATEMENTS

The conventional income statement that is used currently in financial reporting, and which we discussed in section 5.5, is based on the principle of cost assumption or absorption. Accordingly, it is referred to as the *absorption* method of income measurement.

Two alternatives are discussed widely in the literature: (1) direct costing, and (2) the marginal income approach. We introduced the latter in section 5.8 and will return to it in later chapters.

A different net income figure would result from the application of these alternative income statement models, as illustrated in Exhibit 5-7. *Direct* income measurement differs from absorption in that the fixed expenses associated with purchasing or manufacturing inventory during a given period are subtracted from sales in the period in which the expenses are incurred, rather than being absorbed in inventory and entering the income statement only when the inventory is sold. In other words, fixed expenses of purchasing or manufacturing inventory are treated as "period" rather than as "product" costs (see Exhibit 18-8 of chapter 18).

If inventory is increasing in relation to sales, direct income measurement would result in a *lower* net income than under absorption costing, and *vice versa.* This is because under absorption costing these fixed expenses would enter into inventory rather than cost of goods sold.

Marginal income measurement differs from absorption in two respects: (1) general and administrative expenses are broken down into their fixed and variable components, which are then treated as period and product costs respectively; and (2) the fixed expenses of purchasing or manufacturing inventory for the period are treated as deductions from marginal income rather than sales.

In periods in which inventory is growing in relation to sales, the marginal method will show a greater net income figure *if* variable general and administrative expenses exceed the fixed expenses of purchasing or manufacturing inventory, and *vice versa.*

For convenience, let us designate all cost of goods items as "manufacturing"

EXHIBIT 5-7 ABSORPTION, DIRECT, AND MARGINAL INCOME MEASUREMENT

ABSORPTION

Sales
Less: Total cost of goods sold during the period
= Gross Profit
Less: Total general and administrative expenses incurred during the period
= Net Income

DIRECT

Sales
Less: Fixed expenses associated with purchasing or manufacturing inventory during the period
Less: Variable costs of goods sold during the period
= Gross Profit by Direct Costing
Less: Total general and administrative expenses incurred during the period
= Net Income

MARGINAL

Sales
Less: Variable costs of goods sold during the period
Less: Variable general and administrative expenses incurred during the period
= Marginal Income
Less: Fixed expenses associated with purchasing or manufacturing inventory during the period
Less: Fixed general and administrative expenses incurred during the period
= Net Income

costs. The distinction among the three income measurement methods in terms of period and product costs can be summarized as follows:

	Absorption	**Direct**	**Marginal**
Sales	same	same	same
Fixed manufacturing	product	period	period
Variable manufacturing	product	product	product
Fixed G & A	period	period	period
Variable G & A	period	period	product

Income measurement would differ according to these general rules:

If inventory is increasing in relation to sales:

direct income $<$ absorption income
direct income $<$ marginal net income
absorption income $\lessgtr$ marginal net income if variable G & A $\lessgtr$ fixed manufacturing

If inventory is decreasing in relation to sales:

direct income $>$ absorption income
direct income $>$ marginal net income
absorption income $\lessgtr$ marginal net income if variable G & A $\gtrless$ fixed manufacturing

Only absorption income measurement is permitted in financial reporting at present, although direct and marginal statements are used extensively for internal management purposes.

5.10 CONTROLS ASSOCIATED WITH CONVENTIONAL INCOME MEASUREMENT

Stewardship and management controls are applicable to income measurement.

STEWARDSHIP CONTROLS

The objective of stewardship controls is to safeguard assets. Proper records provide evidence that transactions have been handled correctly. With respect to income, stewardship controls include the following requirements:

1. That income measurement should reflect fairly the results of operations. This means that non-operating and extraordinary items should be distinguished from operating ones.

2. That there has been an appropriate application of income measurement rules and regulations for the following reporting purposes:

a. *For financial statement reporting:* This requires that income has been determined in accordance with generally accepted accounting principles applied on a consistent basis from year to year.

b. *For tax reporting:* This requires that all items of income and all deductions have been reported and treated in accordance with the provisions of the Internal Revenue Code (1954) as amended and amplified by IRS regulations and judicial decisions.

As we discussed previously, income reported for tax purposes often differs from financial net income. As such, separate reports are needed for tax purposes.

c. *For reporting to regulatory agencies:* Companies that are subject to the jurisdiction of regulatory agencies such as the Interstate Commerce Commission, the Public Utilities Commissions, and similar agencies are required to submit statements of income prepared in accordance with rules set forth by those agencies. The methods of reporting income for regulated industries may differ markedly from generally accepted accounting principles. Separate records may have to be maintained to generate the required information.

3. That the timing of accounting transactions accord with the requirement that stewardship controls entail the fair measurement and reporting of operations. For example, income measurement requires that a correct "cut-off" of transactions be made. *Cut-off* refers to assigning transactions to the period to which they belong. For example, if a company's reporting year ends December 31, only sales made through that date should be allocated to that period. If any January sales were to be included, income would be distorted. Similarly, all purchases made through December 31 should be used in determining income. If December purchases are not recorded until January, income for the period ending December 31 would be overstated.

Proper cut-off of transactions is one phase of the matching concept discussed earlier. As we said, cut-off assigns transactions to appropriate *time periods.* Matching of costs and expenses with revenues can be *time-related* or *activity-related.* The time-related aspect is implemented through a proper cut-off of transactions. On the other hand, matching of revenues and costs may be activity-related. Some costs cannot be matched against revenues in the period the cost is incurred or accrues. The matching concept requires that revenues and applicable costs be considered together. Thus, even though direct (manufacturing) labor costs are incurred in one year, these costs are associated with a product and are not charged to income until that product is sold. Generally such activity-related costs are held in inventory and matched against subsequent sales.

4. An objective of stewardship controls is the *integrity* of the accounting system. This entails the following specific points:

a. *Propriety:* This means that all *proper* transactions have been included in the determination of income and all *improper* transactions have been excluded. For example, travel and entertainment expenses may be proper deductions from income; however, if such expenses were incurred for nonbusiness reasons (personal expenses of executives), these transactions should be excluded from income determination.

b. *Evidence:* The integrity of the accounts is supported by sufficient evidence. Physical evidence such as invoices, paid checks, and other vouchers support transactions entered into accounting records.

MANAGEMENT CONTROLS

Management controls go beyond ensuring the integrity of the accounts; their objective is the control of sales and expenses with a view toward increasing income. Management controls of income and expenses rely upon (1) a network of authorities, and (2) budgetary control.

Authority

Any system of controls requires a network of authority. This is a *framework* of *delegated responsibility.* Various individuals in an organization are assigned the task of approving transactions. For example, a salesman generally initiates sales orders; however, a credit manager has the authority to approve a customer's credit standing before an order is filled. With respect to disbursements, a plant manager may have the authority to spend specified amounts on plant equipment. Any request for plant equipment in excess of such an amount may require approval from a committee or board of directors.

Such networks of authority aid in controlling income and expense by requiring that transactions pass through one or more checkpoints.

Budgetary Controls

Budgetary controls constitute the most useful tool for management control of income and expense. The existence of a good budgeting program includes the following points:

1. Definitive operating plans have been formulized and recorded.
2. Standards of performance have been set.
3. Comparison of budgeted and actual amounts is made regularly and significant differences are analyzed for cause.

Budgets may be based on one premise (operating level), or they may be flexible. Flexible budgets are formalized financial plans which take into account various possible levels of operations. Flexible budgets allow management to appraise the effects of new conditions and institute new policies in response to changing conditions.[5]

The network of authority discussed above is used extensively in a sound system of budgetary control. All expenditures above a specified amount may require *approval against budgeted amounts* before a commitment is made. Initiation of new products, research and development projects, advertising campaigns, and other commitments usually require approval against budgeted amounts before any action can be taken.

The approval procedure has the following steps:

1. Request for expenditure is made to the proper authority level.
2. The current level of expenditures is determined and compared to the budget to see whether the current request can be accommodated.
3. If the request will cause actual amounts to exceed budgeted amounts, then either
   a. The request is denied, or
   b. An additional budget appropriation is made to cover the request.
4. If the request is in line with the budgeted amounts, the request is approved.

Budgetary controls are often implemented through the use of *quotas*. The quota system is frequently used in controlling sales. Each salesman (or sales unit) is assigned a sales quota as a part of the budgetary process. The quota specifies expected sales activity and may be used not only as a control device, but also to *motivate* sales activity. Sales bonuses are often granted on the basis of achieved activity above quota.

Expense quotas are often used to control expenses such as travel expenses. A company may compute air fare, hotel costs, and meals in advance and use this amount as a reimburseable limit. For control purposes, quotas focus attention on the difference between planned sales or expenses and actual amounts. Significant differences either above or below quota signal the need for investigation.

5.11 FEEDBACK ASSOCIATED WITH CONVENTIONAL INCOME MEASUREMENT

Feedback on income measurement provides information about past earnings, and in some cases, on the current state of affairs (real-time reporting systems). Feedback is related either to financial reporting or internal reporting.

[5]Flexible budgeting is discussed further in chapter 23.

EXTERNAL FEEDBACK

The basic financial document for reporting income is the income statement discussed earlier. We have also previously discussed the two most common reporting forms: single-step and multi-step income statements. The single-step format for reporting to shareholders in an annual report is used more frequently than the multi-step statement.[6]

There are certain items which should be disclosed on the income statement, such as sales, costs of sales, selling expenses, general and administrative expenses, income taxes, and extraordinary items. However, there is a question of how much detail should be shown for information or competitive reasons. Arguments are currently heard in connection with disclosures by conglomerates and other diversified companies. Diversified companies have operations in widely different fields and there is a growing interest in requiring such companies to disclose their income and expense by activity line, so that an investor can appraise the contribution of each major corporate activity.

Other items requiring disclosure include depreciation. A footnote should indicate the method employed in computing depreciation, as well as the lives selected for major asset groups. If revenue includes foreign operations, a footnote should indicate the method of evaluating sales in foreign currencies.

A more important form of external feedback includes comparative data on other companies, particularly competitors in the same industry. The disclosure requirements of financial reporting are aimed at achieving a degree of uniformity such that comparisons are possible, at least within industries. This objective is enunciated in *APB Statement No. 4* as follows:[7]

> The most important of the other conditions is that, ideally, differences between enterprises' financial statements should arise from basic differences in the enterprises themselves or from the nature of their transactions and not merely from differences in financial accounting practices and procedures. One of the most important unsolved problems at present, therefore, is the general acceptance of alternative accounting practices under circumstances which themselves do not appear to be sufficiently different to justify different practices.

5.12 SOME ALTERNATIVE MODELS FOR MEASURING BUSINESS INCOME

We have discussed the conventional model for measuring business income—past, present, and future. But other alternatives are being discussed vigorously in the literature, and students in accounting should be briefed on the essence of some of the more widely discussed alternatives.

[6]The American Institution of Certified Public Accountants, in its annual publication, *Accounting Trends and Techniques,* reported in 1966 that 375 firms out of its sample of 600 firms used the single-step income statement in their annual report. The other 225 used the multi-step statement.

[7]*Accounting Principles Board Statement No. 4* (New York: American Institute of Certified Public Accountants, 1970), pp. 39–40.

CAPITAL MAINTENANCE MODEL FOR MEASURING INCOME

Adam Smith first defined income as the amount that can be consumed without invading capital.[8] J. R. Hicks expanded on this concept by defining income as the amount that a person can consume during a period and be as "well off" at the end of a period as he was at the beginning.[9] This concept requires that some value be assigned to capital, because income is defined as the difference between capital positions. Income for a period would be measured as follows under the Hicksian definition:

$$I_e = (\Sigma A_{t+1} - \Sigma D_{t+1}) - (\Sigma A_t - \Sigma D_t)$$

where

I_e = economic income for period $t + 1$.
A = operating assets at their current worth.
D = debt, measured in money value that is required for settlement.

Accordingly, if the net assets of a firm were $100,000 at the beginning of a year and $150,000 at the end of a year, income for the period would be $50,000, assuming no capital transactions such as sale of stock or payment of dividends. Of course, in measuring income in this manner, the result will vary depending on the type of value-system used. Several options are possible:

1. Input Values:
   a. *Historical Cost:* If assets and liabilities were valued on the basis of historical cost, the income measurement would be the same as under the conventional model where the all-inclusive statement is used. The income figure would have to be adjusted for dividends paid and for capital transactions.
   b. *Current Cost:* When current input values are used, income is the same as under historical cost, except that holding gains (unrealized gains and losses) are included in income without the need for an actual exchange.
2. Output Values:
   a. *Current Cash Equivalent:*[10] Under this concept assets would be valued at what they could be sold for in cash at the point of valuation, and liabilities would be valued at a current cash amount that they could be settled for at the point of valuation. The problem with this method is in obtaining a realistic value where the sale of assets and the settlement of debt is an assumption rather than a reality.
   b. *Market Valuation:* One version of market valuation calls for current market values, in a manner similar to current cash equivalents, to be assigned to assets and liabilities; although it does not presume that all exchanges will be for cash. It suffers from the same defect mentioned with reference to current cash equivalents.

[8]Adam Smith, *The Wealth of Nations* (New York: Random House, 1937). The original title was *An Inquiry into the Nature and Causes of the Wealth of Nations* (London, 1776).

[9]J. R. Hicks, *Value and Capital,* 2nd ed. (Oxford: Clarendon Press, 1946), p. 172.

[10]Raymond J. Chambers, *Accounting Evaluation and Economic Behavior* (Englewood Cliffs, N.J.: Prentice-Hall, Inc., 1966), p. 92.

> A second version avoids the conventional financial statements altogether. It proposes that the value of the firm can be obtained by multiplying the number of shares outstanding by the quoted market price per share. The difference in this value at different points would represent income for the intervening period(s). The difficulty with this approach is that the market price of a share does not contemplate the sale of all shares at once, in addition to the other fickle characteristics of stock market prices.

The difficulty in getting general agreement on an appropriate valuation technique has prevented the practical measurement of business income on the basis of capital maintenance.

"CAPITALIZING INCOME" OR "THE PERMANENT CAPITAL" CONCEPT

This concept places a value on capital equal to the sum of all expected future cash distributions by the firm to its stockholders, including a final amount to be paid upon the liquidation of the firm. This concept can be applied under either *deterministic* (certainty) or *probabilistic* (risk) assumptions. In either case we need information as to three variables: (1) cash distributions for each year, (2) the number of years remaining, and (3) an interest rate to be used for discounting the future money streams to present value (Appendix B). The formula for this purpose is:

$$P_o = R_1(1+i)^{-1} + R_2(1+i)^{-2} + \ldots + R_n(1+i)^{-n} \qquad (1)$$

or

$$P_0 = \sum_{t=1}^{n} \frac{R_t}{(1+i)^t} \qquad (2)$$

where

P_0 = the capitalized (present) value of future cash streams at time 0.
R_t = the cash distribution expected in period t.
i = an interest rate (discount factor).
n = the number of expected years of life.

Income for the first year can be computed by the formula:

$$I_1 = P_1 - P_0 + R_1 \qquad (3)$$

where the value of P_1 is as follows:

$$P_1 = \sum_{t=2}^{n} \frac{R_t}{(1+i)^{t-1}} \qquad (4)$$

Let us return to our former example (p. 122), where we invest $1,000 in stock (or a business venture) and where we receive cash distributions of $50 each year for five years plus an additional (liquidation) sum of $1,500 at the end of the fifth year. These cash sums can be arrayed as follows:

	Y_1	Y_2	Y_3	Y_4	Y_5
Cash Distributions	$50	$50	$50	$50	$1,550

If the discount rate is 6%, the capitalized value of future earnings at the beginning of year 1 would be $1,331.10, while at the beginning of year 2 the capitalized value for the remaining period would be $1,361.25.[11] Net income (loss) for Y_1 is computed as follows:

Cash distributed at the end of year 1	$ 50.00
Capitalized value at the beginning of year 2................	1,361.25
Total value of the firm at the end of year 1	1,411.25
Less: Capitalized value at the beginning of year 1..........	1,331.10
Income for year one	$ 80.15

Income under this concept of measurement for the five years of the investment would be:

	Capitalized Value beginning of	Difference	Add Cash Distribution	Total Income
Y_1	$1,331.10	$30.15	$ 50.00	$ 80.15
Y_2	1,361.25	32.00	50.00	82.00
Y_3	1,393.25	33.40	50.00	83.40
Y_4	1,426.65	35.00	50.00	85.00
Y_5	1,461.65	(1,461.65)	1,550.00	88.35
Y_6	0		Total	$418.90

Where probabilities are used, the periodic cash payments in the future are estimated. For example, if in year 1 the subjective estimate of the dividend is $60 with a .6 probability and $35 with a .4 probability, the estimate would be $50:

$$\begin{aligned} \$60 \times .6 &= \$36 \\ 35 \times .4 &= \underline{\ 14} \\ & \ \ \underline{\underline{\$50}} \end{aligned}$$

[11] As illustrated in Appendix B, these present value problems can be solved quite readily through the use of tables (in this case Table B-2). The present value factors at 6% applicable to this problem are used to discount the future cash receipts:

	Beginning of Year 1	Beginning of Year 2
Y_1 (hence)	$ 50 × .943 = $ 47.15	$ 50 × .943 = $ 47.15
Y_2	50 × .890 = 44.50	50 × .890 = 44.50
Y_3	50 × .840 = 42.00	50 × .840 = 42.00
Y_4	50 × .792 = 39.60	1,550 × .792 = 1,227.60
Y_5	1,550 × .747 = 1,157.85	
	Total = $1,331.10	Total = $1,361.25

We would then proceed as formerly.

The obvious drawback of the capitalization approach is that it assumes knowledge as to future cash distributions.

THE VALUE-ADDED CONCEPT OF INCOME[12]

The term *value-added* refers to the price that a firm receives for its goods and services less the cost of obtaining the goods and services.[13] This concept can be expanded to an income model in which all employees, owners, creditors, and government (through taxation) are viewed as beneficiaries of business income. Financial statements under this assumption have been envisaged by Prince:

EXHIBIT 5-8 A TOTAL-VALUE STATEMENT

THEORETICAL FORMULA

Total Utility Received = Total Utility Expended

or

Total Income Received = Total Income Expended

OPERATIONAL FORMULA

(Money Value of Aggregate Inputs of Goods and Services, the Non-Money Value of the Goals of Survival, Status, Power, Prestige, and Other Psychological and Sociological Elements, State of Expectations, Tastes and Preferences, Level of Technology, Innovations, Population)*. . . ./Market Structure/Legal Structure/Religious Structure/Governmental System/ Banking System/Community System/Education System/	(Money Value of Aggregate Outputs of Goods and Services, the Non-Money Value of the Goals of Survival, Status, Power, Prestige, and Other Psychological and Sociological Elements, State of Expectations, Tastes and Preferences, Level of Technology, Innovations, Population)*. . . ./Market Structure/ Legal Structure/ Religious Structure/ Governmental System/ BankingSystem/ Community System/ Education System/

*All items within the parentheses are endogenous (internal) factors; the others, separated by virgules, are all exogenous (external) factors.

SOURCE: Thomas R. Prince, *Extension of the Boundaries of Accounting Theory* (Cincinnati: South-Western Publishing Company, 1963), p. 79. Reprinted with permission of the publisher.

Considerable advancement in measurement theory is needed before we can achieve the total value concept advanced by Prince, but it does illustrate the opportunities for improving income measurement which lie ahead.

[12]See Waino W. Suojanen, "Accounting Theory and the Large Corporation," *The Accounting Review* XXIX (July 1954): 391–98.

[13]The value-added approach to taxation is discussed in chapter 21.

5.13 SUMMARY

Income measurement is the principal means for gauging the success of business operations. Because of the importance of income measurement to such issues as dividend policy, market price of stock, personnel and labor relations, income taxation, credit, business expansion or contraction, and broad social policy, it is a central concern of accounting information systems and the theorists who design them. Accordingly, a critical objective of accounting is to obtain an income measurement figure that is most nearly indicative of the actual operating effectiveness of an enterprise.

Income is measured conventionally by the income statement. The underlying theory at present is one of *cost assumption.* Under this assumption, income is defined as the difference between revenues generated in a period less the costs and expenses associated with producing those revenues. The conventional model includes estimations of future incomes (forecasts, budgets, and *pro forma* income statements) and provides for certain analytic operations (marginal income analysis).

Alternative models for income measurement have been proposed. The more important ones have been discussed briefly in this chapter: (1) capital maintenance, (2) capitalization, and (3) value-added.

CHAPTER 5 REFERENCES AND ADDITIONAL READINGS

MEASUREMENT

Ackoff, Russell L. *Scientific Method.* New York: John Wiley & Sons, Inc., 1962.

Churchman, C. West. *Prediction and Optimal Decision: Philosophical Issues of a Science of Values.* Englewood Cliffs, N.J.: Prentice-Hall, Inc., 1961.

Russell, Bertrand. *Introduction to Mathematical Philosophy.* New York: The Macmillan Company, 1920.

Silsbee, F. B. "Measure for Measure: Some Problems and Paradoxes of Precision." *Journal of the Washington Academy of Science,* series 2 (1951): 213.

Stevens, S. S. "Measurement, Psychophysics, and Utility." In *Measurement,* edited by C. West Churchman and Philburn Ratoosh. New York: John Wiley & Sons, Inc., 1959, p. 25.

Stevens, S. S. "Measurement and Man." *Science* 127, no. 3295 (February 1958): 383–89.

Whitehead, A. N. *Science and the Modern World,* New York: The Macmillan Company, 1925; Pelican Mentor, 1948.

MEASUREMENT IN ACCOUNTING

Anton, Hector. "Some Aspects of Measurement and Accounting." *Journal of Accounting Research,* Spring 1964, pp. 1–9.

Ijiri, Yuji. "Axioms and Structures of Conventional Accounting Measurement." *The Accounting Review,* January 1965, pp. 26–53.

Ijiri, Yuji, and Jaedicke, Robert K. "Reliability and Objectivity of Accounting Measurements." *The Accounting Review,* July 1966, pp. 474–83.

Mattesich, Richard. *Accounting and Analytical Methods.* Homewood, Ill.: Richard D. Irwin, Inc., 1964.

MEASURING BUSINESS INCOME UNDER THE CONVENTIONAL MODEL

Alexander, Sidney S. "Income Measurement in a Dynamic Economy." Five Monographs of Business Income. New York: Study Group on Business Income of the American Institute of Accountants, July 1, 1950. Reprinted in W. T. Baxter and Sidney Davidson. *Studies in Accounting Theory.* Homewood, Ill.: Richard D. Irwin, Inc., 1962, pp. 126–200.

Bedford, Norton M. *Income Determination Theory: An Accounting Framework.* Reading, Mass.: Addison-Wesley Publishing Company, 1965.

Bierman, Harold Jr., and Davidson, Sidney. "The Income Concept—Value Increment or Earnings Predictor." *The Accounting Review* XLIV (April 1969): 239–46.

Hendriksen, Eldon. *Accounting Theory.* 2nd ed. Homewood, Ill.: Richard D. Irwin, Inc., 1970, pp. 124–58.

Vatter, William J., "Income Models, Book Yield, and the Rate of Return." *The Accounting Review* XLI (October 1966): 681–98.

Wise, T. A. "Those Uncertain Actuaries." *Fortune,* December 1965, p. 154, and January 1966, p. 164.

ALTERNATIVE MODELS OF INCOME MEASUREMENT

Bierman, Harold Jr., and Davidson, Sidney. "The Income Concept—Value Increment or Earnings Predictor." *The Accounting Review,* April 1969, pp. 239–46.

Chambers, R. J. *Accounting Evaluation and Economic Behavior.* Englewood Cliffs, N.J.: Prentice-Hall, Inc. 1966.

Chambers, R. J. "Measures and Values." *The Accounting Review,* April 1968, pp. 239–47.

Edwards, Edgar O., and Bell, Philip W. *The Theory and Measurement of Business Income.* Berkeley: University of California Press, 1961.

Fisher, Irving. *The Nature of Capital and Income.* London: Macmillan & Co., Ltd., 1906.

Hicks, J. R. *Value and Capital.* 2nd ed. Oxford: Clarendon Press, 1946.

Penman, Stephen H. "What Net Asset Value?—An Extension of a Familiar Debate." *The Accounting Review,* April 1970, pp. 333–46.

Prince, Thomas R. *Extension of the Boundaries of Accounting Theory.* Cincinnati: South-Western Publishing Company, 1963.

Shwayder, Keith. "A Critique of Economic Income as an Accounting Concept." *Abacus,* August 1967, pp. 23–35.

Sterling, Robert R. *Theory of Measurement of Enterprise Income.* Lawrence, Kansas: University of Kansas Press, 1970.

CHAPTER 5 QUESTIONS, PROBLEMS, AND CASES

5- 1. List and discuss several objectives of income measurement.

5- 2. Define or explain the use of the following terms or phrases:
- (a) Appreciation
- (b) Principle of cost assumption
- (c) Realization
- (d) Revenue
- (e) Costs
- (f) Expenses
- (g) Extraordinary gains and losses
- (h) Flexible budget

5- 3. What are the possible alternative formats for the construction of an income statement? Explain each format.

5- 4. Distinguish between a *current operating* and an *all-inclusive* income statement by identifying those items included or excluded from the *income statement* and from the *statement of retained earnings.* Give the arguments used in support of each method. Which method has received the support of the APB?

5- 5. "Some revenues flow into an entity which are not related directly to its principle business activity." Identify the descriptive term given to these revenues, and give some examples of such revenues.

5- 6. How would income measurement differ under *direct* costing as opposed to *absorption* costing?

5- 7. "*Pro forma* statements are financial statements that reflect expected outcome under certain assumptions." What are four such assumptions?

5- 8. *Opinion No. 9* of the Accounting Principles Board ruled that the income statement should include all events which take place during an accounting period, with the exception of prior period adjustments. These adjustments are included in the statement of retained earnings. What are the five criteria that determine whether an item is a prior period adjustment? Give some examples of items that can meet such criteria.

5- 9. "The fact that the phenomena which accountants attempt to measure are of a complex socio-physical nature creates problems and opportunities." Identify and discuss several of these problems.

5-10. What is the basic difference between a statement of changes in capital and a statement of retained earnings?

5-11. Under what operational circumstances is it acceptable practice to convert income to cash flow?

5-12. Explain briefly how income measurement would be affected under the proposed alternatives:
(a) Capital maintenance
(b) Capitalization
(c) Value-added

5-13. Distinguish between *real* and *money* income.

5-14. What are five uses of the conventional model of income measurement?

5-15. Distinguish between *permanent* and *periodic* income.

5-16. What types of expenses are found in the category of general and administrative expenses? Give some examples.

5-17. What assumption underlies the conventional model of income measurement?

5-18. Distinguish between *budgets* and *pro forma statements.*

5-19. Distinguish between the following expenses by defining and giving example of each:
(a) Fixed
(b) Variable
(c) Semi-variable

5-20. "Because variable expenses generally can be traced directly to their respective projects or departments, the marginal income figure is a more valid measure of operating efficiency than is net income." Explain the meaning of this statement.

5-21. Contrast income measurement under *absorption, direct,* and *marginal* costing.

5-22. What are the requirements of stewardship controls over income?

5-23. "Income measurement requires that a correct cut-off of transactions be made." What does *cut-off* mean?

5-24. Matching of costs and expenses with revenues can be *time-related* or *activity-related.* Explain the distinction.

5-25. The following terms are related to stewardship controls that are concerned with *integrity* of the accounting system. Explain the meaning and use of each term as it relates to the integrity of the system.

(a) Propriety
(b) Evidence
(c) Realization
(d) Objectivity
(e) Conservatism

5-26. Explain and give examples of the management controls that rely upon "a network of authorities and approvals." What are the steps of an approval procedure employing budgetary control?

5-27. What are the three aspects of a good budgeting program for management control of income and expenses?

5-28. Explain the use of *quotas* as a budgetary device for controling and motivating activity.

5-29. Under the capital maintenance model for measuring income, the net assets of a firm must be valued at the beginning and end of a period. Explain the following methods for making such valuation.
(a) Historical cost
(b) Current cost
(c) Current cash equivalent
(d) Market valuation

5-30. Distinguish among *operating, non-operating,* and *extraordinary* items.

5-31. ***ADJUSTING INCOME TO CASH FLOWS*** Assuming sales and operating expenses are relatively stable over time, convert the following income statement to a cash flow statement (prepare a schedule). The operating expenses include depreciation of $2,600 and interest expense of $700. The principle payment for the period is $3,300 and the income tax rate is 40%.

Revenue	$53,500
Operating expenses	41,100
Net income from operations	12,400
Income tax (40%)	4,960
Net income	$ 7,440

5-32. ***MARGINAL INCOME ANALYSIS*** The Coulter Company's marginal income statement for 19*x*1 is:

Sales	$870,000
Variable expenses	391,500
Marginal income	478,500
Fixed expenses	350,000
Net income	$128,500

Required: Consider each situation individually.

(a) If the sales for 19*x*2 are expected to be 20% higher than 19*x*1, what is the expected income in 19*x*2?
(b) If the desired net income for 19*x*2 is $200,000, what sales revenue is needed?
(c) If the fixed expenses increase by $100,000 and variable expenses decrease 15%, what sales level is needed to maintain the same net income of $128,500?
(d) If the desired net income for 19*x*2 is 18% of sales, what sales level must be achieved?

5-33. ***MATCHING CONCEPT*** After the presentation of your report on the examination of the financial statements to the board of directors of the Savage Publishing Company, one of the new directors says he is surprised the income statement assumes that an equal proportion of the revenue is earned with the publication of every issue of the company's magazine. He feels that the "crucial event" in the process of earning revenue in the magazine business is the cash sale of the subscription. He says that he does not understand why—other than for the smoothing of income—most of the revenue cannot be "realized" in the period of the sale.

Required:

(a) List the various accepted methods for recognizing revenue in the accounts and explain when the methods are appropriate. Do not limit your listing to the methods for the recognition of revenue in magazine publishing.

(b) Discuss the propriety of timing the recognition of revenue in the Savage Publishing Company's accounts with:
 (1) the cash sale of the magazine subscription.
 (2) the publication of the magazine every month.
 (3) both events, by recognizing a portion of the revenue with cash sale of the magazine subscription and a portion of the revenue with the publication of the magazine every month.

(From the CPA exam.)

5-34. ***INCOME MEASUREMENT—ALTERNATIVE METHODS*** The Aim Company, a farm corporation, produced the following in its first year of operations:

	Selling Price Per Bushel
9,000 bushels of wheat	$2.40
6,000 bushels of oats	1.40

During the year it sold two-thirds of the grain produced and collected three-fourths of the selling price on the grain sold; the balance is to be collected in equal amounts during each of the two following years. Additional data for the first year:

Wealth at beginning of year 1	$100,000	
Wealth at end of year 1	115,000	
Depreciation on productive plant and equipment	3,000	
Other production costs (cash)	4,500	
Miscellaneous administrative costs (cash)	3,600	
Grain storage costs	-0-	
Selling and delivery costs (incurred and paid at time of sale)—per bushel		.10
Additional stockholder investments during year 1	-0-	
Dividends paid to stockholders during year 1	10,000	
Income taxes	-0-	

The Aim Company is enthusiastic about the accountant's concept of matching costs and revenues; it wishes to carry the idea to the extreme and to match with revenues not only all direct costs but also all indirect costs such as those for administration.

Required:

(a) If revenues were recognized when production is complete (i.e., inventory is carried at net selling price), compute the income with the company's matching objective for the first year.

(b) If revenue were recognized on the sales basis, compute the income in accordance with the company's matching objective for the first year.

(c) If revenue were recognized on the cash-collection basis, compute the income in accordance with the company's matching objective for the first year.

(d) Recently the company's president was introduced to a noted British economist who convinced him that the accountant's accrual approach to measuring income in fact was merely a partial accrual, and that full accrual would require consideration of changes in "wealth" which was defined as "the present value of expected net future receipts." Following this it was suggested that a full accrual income for a period would be determined to be the amount that could be spent during a period while leaving wealth unchanged. Compute the income for the first year using the economist's approach.

(Adapted from the CPA exam.)

5-35. ***CONTRIBUTION TO PROFIT—MARGINAL INCOME ANALYSIS*** The Markey Corporation has four main product lines: A, B, C, and D. The sales and operating costs of each are as follows:

	A	B	C	D
Selling price per unit	$14.00	$16.50	$10.00	$ 8.00
No. of units sold	32,000	31,000	65,000	95,000
Variable cost per unit	$ 8.20	$10.00	$ 7.80	$ 6.20
Fixed expense allocated	$150,000.00	$150,000.00	$150,000.00	$150,000.00

(a) Prepare a marginal income statement by product line. Which product line has the highest contribution to profit?

(b) Suppose the company is contemplating adding a new product, E, to its present lines. The potential sales are 100,000 units and the variable cost per unit is $7.40. In addition, it will be necessary to increase plant capacity, thus increasing fixed costs by $42,000. Should product E be produced and sold by the Markey Corporation if it can be sold for $9 per unit? How is the company profit affected?

(c) Assuming the same sales level, unit selling prices, and variable costs as given, should the product line with the least contribution to profit be dropped and product E added? In this instance the plant capacity would not have to be increased.

5-36. ***REALIZATION*** Much of accounting is concerned with the determination of income and the valuation of assets through the application of accounting principles and conventions. An example of the latter is the realization convention, which controls the timing of revenue recognition; its influence is said to pervade both the income statement and the balance sheet.

Required:

(a) Explain the accounting concept of income.

(b) Discuss the realization convention and its significance to the process of periodic income determination.

(c) Discuss the effect of the realization convention on the valuation of assets for balance sheet purposes.

(From the CPA exam.)

5-37. ***CAPITALIZING INCOME*** Suppose Mr. Kelly invests in 20,000 shares at $10 each of Lungsdorf Company's common stock. Mr. Kelly expects to receive the following cash dividends for the next four years:

Year 1	$18,000
Year 2	20,000
Year 3	22,000
Year 4	23,000

At the end of the four years Mr. Kelly expects the market value per share of common stock to be $16.

Required:

(a) Using the permanent capital concept, compute the income for each of the four years using a discount rate of 8% (refer to Appendix B for present value factors). Contrast with conventional income measurement.

(b) Suppose each year's dividends are given as several probable values:

YEAR							
1		2		3		4	
Dividend	Prob.	Dividend	Prob.	Dividend	Prob.	Dividend	Prob.
$17,500	.7	$18,500	.4	$18,500	.4	$19,000	.4
19,000	.3	20,000	.4	22,000	.5	24,000	.5
		25,000	.2	26,000	.1	26,000	.1

What is the income for each of the four years using the permanent capital concept and a discount rate of 8%?

5-38. ***PROFIT ANALYSIS BY SALES TERRITORIES*** In recent years distribution expenses of the Avey Company have increased more than other expenditures. For more effective control the company plans to provide each local manager with an income statement for his territory showing monthly and year-to-date amounts for the current and the previous year. Each sales office is supervised by a local manager; sales orders are forwarded to the main office and filled from a central warehouse; billing and collections are also centrally processed. Expenses are first classified by function and then allocated to each territory in the following ways:

Function	Basis
Sales salaries	Actual
Other selling expenses	Relative sales dollars
Warehousing	Relative sales dollars
Packing and shipping	Weight of package
Billing and collections	Number of billings
General administration	Equally

Required:

(a) (1) Explain responsibility accounting and the classification of revenues and expenses under this concept.

(2) What are the objectives of profit analysis by sales territories in income statements?

(b) (1) Discuss the effectiveness of Avey Company's comparative income statements by sales territories as a tool for planning and control. Include in your answer additional factors that should be considered and changes that might be desirable for effective planning by management and evaluation of the local sales managers.

(2) Compare the degree of control that can be achieved over production costs and distribution costs and explain why the degree of control differs.

(3) Criticize Avey Company's allocation and/or inclusion of:
a. Warehousing expense
b. Other selling expenses
c. General administration expense

(From the CPA exam.)

5-39. ***DIRECT COSTING VERSUS ABSORPTION COSTING*** The Pute Company reported the following operating results for 19*x*1:

Sales:	62,000 units at $8 per unit
Production:	66,400 units
Variable production cost per unit:	
Material	$2.50
Labor	1.90
Overhead	1.00
	$5.40

Fixed production costs (fixed overhead): $59,760
Selling & administrative expenses:
Variable costs per unit: $.80
Fixed: $32,000
Beginning inventory: None
No work-in-process beginning and ending

Required:

(a) Prepare an income statement for 19*x*1 using:
(1) The direct costing method
(2) The absorption costing method

(b) Assume there is a beginning inventory of 5,000 units and the cost breakdown per unit is as follows:

Variable $5.40
Fixed .85

Prepare an income statement assuming FIFO inventory procedure and income is computed using:
(1) Direct costing
(2) Absorption costing

(c) Same as (b), except LIFO is used.

5-40. ***ABSORPTION, DIRECT AND MARGINAL COSTING*** The following annual flexible budget has been prepared for use in making decisions relating to product X.

	100,000 Units	150,000 Units	200,000 Units
Sales volume	$800,000	$1,200,000	$1,600,000
Manufacturing costs:			
Variable	300,000	450,000	600,000
Fixed	200,000	200,000	200,000
	500,000	650,000	800,000
Selling and other expenses:			
Variable	200,000	300,000	400,000
Fixed	160,000	160,000	160,000
	360,000	460,000	560,000
Income (or loss)	$(60,000)	$ 90,000	$ 240,000

The 200,000 unit budget has been adopted and will be used for allocating fixed manufacturing costs to units of product X; at the end of the first six months the following information is available:

Production completed	120,000 Units
Sales	60,000 Units

All fixed costs are budgeted and incurred uniformly throughout the year and all costs incurred coincide with the budget. Variable selling and other expenses are incurred on the basis of units sold.

Over- and under-applied fixed manufacturing costs are deferred until year-end. Annual sales have the following seasonal pattern:

	Portion of Annual Sales
First quarter	10%
Second quarter	20
Third quarter	30
Fourth quarter	40
	100%

(a) What is the amount of fixed factory costs applied to product during the first six months under absorption costing?

(b) Assuming that 90,000 units of product X were sold during the first six months and that this is to be used as a basis, what is the revised budget estimate for the total number of units to be sold during this year?

(Adapted from the CPA exam.)

(c) Following the format on p. 133, prepare income statements for the first six months under the absorption, direct, and marginal methods.

UNIT II

FINANCIAL REPORTING AND ANALYSIS

The wide public ownership of business enterprises has necessitated the institution of financial reporting. In 1964, 18 million Americans owned some common stock. In 1970, stockholders numbered 31 million. A large corporation such as American Telephone & Telegraph boasts about 2,500,000 stockholders, with no single shareholder owning more than 1% of the total capital stock. Berle and Means[1] have commented on the growing separation between ownership and control in the early 1930s, and the trend continues. Recent studies indicate that management as a group owns an average of only 3% of its company's outstanding stock. A person holding as little as one-fifth of a company's stock can often achieve effective control.

These stockholders are active. Between 8 and 16 million shares trade hands on a typical day on the national stock exchanges. While on the one hand the capriciousness of stockholders is well known—as illustrated by the way in which political events can trigger market activity—the entire system depends upon financial reporting as its basic foundation. The accountant is in the hub of this activity. It is the accounting profession which determines the format, principles, and values expressed in financial statements. Accountants are employed by business firms to generate the

[1]A. A. Berle, Jr. and Gardner C. Means, *The Modern Corporation and Private Property* (New York: Commerce Clearing House, 1932).

data needed for financial reporting. Independent accountants or "auditors" inspect the financial records of business firms to determine compliance with "generally accepted accounting principles." Then accountants assist investors in interpreting financial statements.

The student of accounting should be thoroughly familiar with the institution of financial reporting. The process can be described briefly as follows:

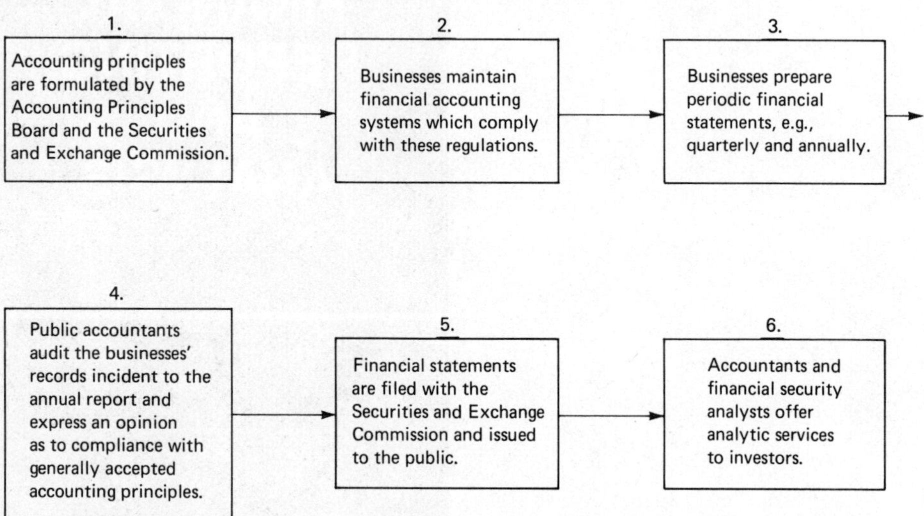

The Accounting Principles Board (APB) has been the policy-making body most closely associated with the formulating of accounting principles and auditing standards since 1959.

What is known as "generally accepted accounting principles" consists primarily of fifty-one *Accounting Research Bulletins*[2] issued by the predecessor policy group to the APB (that is, The Committee on Accounting Procedure [1939–1959]), and *Opinions* of the APB since 1959. In addition, established practices among certified public accountants may be considered "generally accepted accounting principles," as stated below. The Council of the American Institute of CPAs issued a Special Bulletin in October 1964, on this subject. The essential passages are:[3]

> The Council of the Institute, at its meeting October 2, 1964, unanimously adopted recommendations that members should see to it that departures from Opinions of the Accounting Principles Board (as well as effective Accounting Research Bulletins issued by the former Committee on Accounting Procedure) are disclosed, either in footnotes to financial statements or in the audit reports of members in their capacity as independent auditors.
>
> * * *
>
> "Generally accepted accounting principles" are those principles which have substantial authoritative support.

---

[2] *Accounting Research and Terminology Bulletins* (New York: American Institute of Certified Public Accountants, 1961).

[3] As cited in the Report of the Study on Establishment of Accounting Principles, *Establishing Financial Accounting Standards* (New York: American Institute of Certified Public Accountants, March 1972), pp. 41–42. Copyright 1964 by the American Institute of Certified Public Accountants, Inc. Reprinted with permission.

* * *

Opinions of the Accounting Principles Board constitute "substantial authoritative support."

"Substantial authoritative support" can exist for accounting principles that differ from Opinions of the Accounting Principles Board.

* * *

If an accounting principle that differs materially in its effect from one accepted in an Opinion of the Accounting Principles Board is applied in financial statements, the reporting member must decide whether the principle has substantial authoritative support and is applicable in the circumstances.

If he concludes that it does not, he would either qualify his opinion, disclaim an opinion, or give an adverse opinion as appropriate. . . .

If he concludes that it does have substantial authoritative support:

(1) he would give an unqualified opinion and

(2) disclose the fact of departure from the opinion in a separate paragraph in his report or see that it is disclosed in a footnote to the financial statements and, where practicable, its effects on the financial statements.

As of the date of writing, the APB has issued the following *Opinions* and *Statements* and was actively working on additional opinions, as noted below:

A. *APB Opinions*[4]

APB *OPINION*		ACCOUNTING RESEARCH STUDY		APB ACTIVE AGENDA DATES		
No.	Title	No.	Date	Committee appointed	First substantively discussed	Opinion published
1	*New Depreciation Guidelines and Rules*	—	—		10/1962	11/1962
2	*Accounting for the "Investment Credit"*	—	—		10/1961	12/1962
3	*The Statement of Source and Application of Funds*	2	1961		6/1962	10/1963
4	*Amending APB Opinion No. 2*	—	—		3/1964	3/1964
5	*Reporting of Leases in Financial Statements of Lessee*	4	1962	mid-1962	10/1962	9/1964
6	*Status of Accounting Research Bulletins*	—	—	11/1964	11/1964	10/1965
7	*Accounting for Leases in Financial Statements of Lessor*	4	1962	11/1964	1/1965	5/1966
8	*Accounting for the Cost of Pension Plans*	8	1965	6/1965	2/1966	11/1966
9	*Reporting the Results of Operations*	—	—	9/1965	12/1965	12/1966
10	*Omnibus Opinion—1966*	—	—	12/1965	4/1966	12/1966
11	*Accounting for Income Taxes*	9	1966	12/1965	2/1966	12/1967
12	*Omnibus Opinion—1967*	—	—	1/1967	3/1967	12/1967

[4]Ibid., pp. 99–100.

APB OPINION No.	Title	ACCOUNTING RESEARCH STUDY No.	Date	APB ACTIVE AGENDA DATES Committee appointed	First substantively discussed	Opinion published
13	*Amending Paragraph 6 of APB Opinion No. 9, Application to Commercial Banks*	—	—	1/1967	9/1968	3/1969
14	*Accounting for Convertible Debt and Debt Issued with Stock Purchase Warrants*	—	—	8/1967	10/1967	3/1969
15	*Earnings per Share*	—	—	8/1967	10/1967	5/1969
16	*Business Combinations*	5	1963	9/1968	1/1969	8/1970
17	*Intangible Assets*	10	1968	9/1968	1/1969	8/1970
18	*The Equity Method of Accounting for Investments in Common Stock*	—	—	7/1968	3/1969	3/1971
19	*Reporting Changes in Financial Position*	2	1961	11/1969	10/1970	3/1971
20	*Accounting Changes*	—	—	3/1967	1/1968	7/1971
21	*Interest on Receivables and Payables*	—	—	11/1969	9/1970	8/1971

B. *APB Statements*

No. 1 *Statement of Accounting Principles Board re Accounting Research Studies No. 1 and 3*, 1962.
No. 2 *Disclosure of Supplemental Financial Information by Diversified Companies*, 1967.
No. 3 *Financial Statements Restated for General Price-Level Changes*, 1969.
No. 4 *Basic Concepts and Accounting Principles Underlying Financial Statements of Business Enterprises*, 1970.

C. *APB Calendar as of January 1, 1972*[5]

TOPIC	ACCOUNTING RESEARCH STUDY Actual	Planned	APB COMMITTEE APPOINTED
Translating foreign operations		1972	10/1971
Part 1—U.S. devaluation			
Part 2—general project			
Income taxes—special areas			5/1969
Accounting policy			10/1968
Stock compensation			1/1971
Marketable securities			5/1969
Retirement of debt			9/1969

[5]Ibid., p. 102.

TOPIC	ACCOUNTING RESEARCH STUDY Actual	ACCOUNTING RESEARCH STUDY Planned	APB COMMITTEE APPOINTED
Amending *APB Opinions Nos.* 5 and 7			2/1967
Extractive industries	1969		mid-1968
Part 1—oil and gas industry			
Part 2—minerals			
Noncash transactions			11/1969
Interim financial reporting			1/1968
Diversified companies			9/1966
Components of an enterprise			6/1965
Capitalization of interest			10/1971
Opinion No. 9—extraordinary items			12/1971
Self-insurance provisions			12/1971

In addition to the above, the AICPA Institute's Accounting Research Division has published eleven Accounting Research Studies to date:

D. *Accounting Research Studies*

No. 1 Maurice Moonitz, *The Basic Postulates of Accounting,* 1961.

No. 2 Perry Mason, *Cash Flow Analysis and the Funds Statement,* 1961.

No. 3 Robert T. Sprouse and Maurice Moonitz, *A Tentative Set of Broad Accounting Principles for Business Enterprises,* 1962.

No. 4 John H. Myers, *Reporting of Leases in Financial Statements,* 1962.

No. 5 Arthur R. Wyatt, *A Critical Study of Accounting for Business Combinations,* 1963.

No. 6 Staff of the Accounting Research Division, *Reporting the Financial Effects of Price-Level Changes,* 1963.

No. 7 Paul Grady, *Inventory of Generally Accepted Accounting Principles for Business Enterprises,* 1965.

No. 8 Ernest L. Hicks, *Accounting for the Cost of Pension Plans,* 1965.

No. 9 Homer A. Black, *Interperiod Allocation of Corporate Income Taxes,* 1966.

No. 10 George R. Catlett and Norman O. Olson, *Accounting for Goodwill,* 1968.

No. 11 Robert E. Field, *Financial Reporting in the Extractive Industries,* 1969.

No. 12 Leonard Lorensen, *Reporting Foreign Operations of U.S. Companies in U.S. Dollars,* 1972.

A significant change in setting accounting policy was under way at the date of writing. The report of the Study on Establishment of Accounting Principles—known as the "Wheat Report" because Mr. Francis M. Wheat chaired the study—had just been published and adopted. It recommended the following policy structure:[6]

[6] Ibid., p. 103.

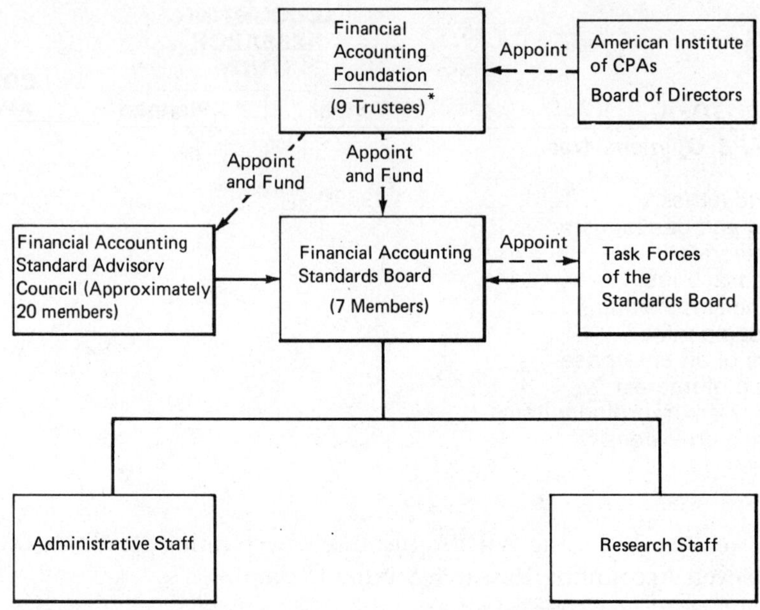

*Four of the nine trustees will be appointed from lists of nominees submitted respectively by the Financial Executives Institute, National Association of Accountants, Financial Analysts Federation, and the American Accounting Association.

The principle features of the proposal are to broaden participation in the policy-making structure and to separate the policy group organizationally from the jurisdiction of any particular accounting group. The purpose of the latter is, of course, to increase the objectivity of policy-making.

The role of governmental agencies in accounting policy cannot be minimized. The *Securities and Exchange Act of 1934* empowered the Securities and Exchange Commission (SEC) "to prescribe the form and content of financial statements filed by reporting companies, and to specify the methods to be followed in their preparation."[7] However, in carrying out its functions over the years, the SEC has sought to work closely with the accounting profession in setting accounting policy. In reporting to a congressional committee in 1964, the SEC stated:[8]

> Much improvement in financial reporting practices has occurred since the enactment of the first Federal securities law in 1933. The Commission believes that its policy of working with and supporting the accounting profession in the development of accounting principles has directly influenced this progress and is the best means of assuring continuing improvement of accounting practices.

The Wheat Commission report advocates a continuation of this close liaison between governmental and private policy-making as being in the best interests of a creative system of financial reporting.

[7] Ibid., p. 48. Under the Securities Exchange Act of 1934, all nonexempt companies with over $1,000,000 of assets and 500 shareholders of record must file periodic reports, including financial statements, with the SEC.

[8] Statement of the SEC to the Subcommittee on Commerce and Finance of the Committee on Interstate and Foreign Commerce, House of Representatives, February 19, 1964.

Various governmental agencies play a role in specifying accounting principles and procedures for enterprises under their jurisdiction. The Federal Communications Commission (FCC) and Civil Aeronautics Board (CAB) have permitted firms in their jurisdiction to follow "generally accepted accounting principles" in lieu of establishing separate policy. Separate policy does exist, however, for firms under the jurisdiction of Interstate Commerce Commission (ICC)[9] and the Public Utilities Commission (PUC).

The Internal Revenue Service (IRS) administers the tax code which requires reporting specific to tax requirements, and the General Accounting Office (GAO), through its Cost Accounting Standards Board, is empowered to specify accounting rules and procedures for firms which benefit from federal government contracts.

In this unit we discuss the institution of financial reporting with specific focus on formal financial statements. Chapter 6 deals with financial accounting statements and conventions. Chapter 7 is concerned with understanding and interpreting these statements. Chapter 8 concerns the important subject of price-level changes (fluctuations in the purchasing power of the money unit) and the impact of these changes on financial reporting.

[9]Although the ICC relaxed this requirement in 1962 and has since permitted its firms to choose between ICC rules and "generally accepted accounting principles."

CHAPTER

6

FINANCIAL STATEMENTS AND CONVENTIONS

6.1 FINANCIAL REPORTING

The output of the accounting information system benefits many users, or more specifically many user classes. We have recognized the two broad categories of internal and external users. Throughout the text we present examples of internal reporting. In this chapter we will concentrate on external reporting, and rapidly narrow in on the principal form of external reporting, i.e., the *financial statements*.

External reporting is not limited to the financial statements, which are generally part of a larger document known as the *annual report*.[1] For example, one form of external reporting is to the Internal Revenue Service in relation to income taxation. Data generated for tax purposes may differ from data compiled in the financial statements. There are two primary reasons for differences between tax and financial reporting:

1. Theoretical:
   Income tax regulations favor a *cash* basis of accounting, while the *accrual* basis is preferred via accounting theory.

[1] Excerpts from an annual report are contained in the appendix to this chapter.

Example: It is September, 19*x*1. We rent an apartment for $100 per month on the basis of a one-year lease. We require first and last month's rent at the beginning of the lease period.

a. *Tax Treatment:* Income tax regulations insist that we report $200 as income in year 19*x*1. This is consistent with cash-basis accounting (Sec. 61; 1.61–8).[2]
b. *Accrual Accounting Treatment:* Only September 19*x*1 rent is taken into income in that year. The other $100 is carried as "prepaid rent" (a liability) until September 19*x*2, when the amount is transferred to income.

If we followed tax law for financial reporting purposes, we would report thirteen months of income in 19*x*1 and only eleven months in 19*x*2. The accrual method is more descriptive of events than the cash method; hence it is favored in financial reporting.

2. Pragmatic:

Tax laws often allow for options in accounting treatment. For example, the tax code permits several methods of depreciation, several methods for pricing inventory, and so forth. In many instances a "liberalized" treatment is intended to act as an incentive toward particular types of economic activity. The 1969 Tax Reform Act encouraged the construction of low-rental housing by manipulating accounting for depreciation and capital gains. In 1962 the "investment tax credit" was used as an incentive to modernize plant and equipment.

In instances where optional methods are allowed, it is appropriate and proper for firms to use the most advantageous method for tax purposes and a more conservative method for financial reporting. In fact we might question the wisdom of a management that failed to maximize its income tax prerogatives.

For these reasons we can look forward to continuing and proper differences between tax and financial reporting. In fact, liberating financial reporting from the pragmatic restrictions of tax law permits accountants to innovate in financial reporting without the threat of illegality.

Bankers are a special class of external user. The information that credit loan officers need to make loan decisions is different in nature and purpose from the information contained in the financial statements. In this case the primary concern is loan repayment. In the first instance, repayment is expected out of operations, which necessitates a forecast extending over the period of the loan. If operations fail, expectation for repayment shifts to the assets of the firm. Here the emphasis is on liquidity. The extent to which assets are saleable and uncommitted to the payment of other liabilities is a key factor in a loan decision.

There are even various vehicles for reporting to the investing public. For example, a corporation seeking the public issue of its stock must make thorough disclosure in its *prospectus*.[3] This document contains a considerable amount of data furnished by the accounting information system. Corporations are also required to furnish the Securities and Exchange Commission (a governmental agency which acts in behalf of investors) with financial data (on Form 10-K) that is more encompassing than data in the financial statements. In addition, most firms issue financial data regarding expected future performance, backlog, and other matters of interest to investors which are not an official part of the financial statements.

We conclude that financial statements are only one form of financial reporting to external users. This form of reporting can be thought of as the official or *formal*

[2]Tax law is quite inconsistent, which makes a theoretical structure difficult. For example, while prepaid rent "received" by a landlord is income in the year of receipt, "advance" rent payments by a tenant can only be deducted as a business expense in the period to which they relate.

[3]For an example of a prospectus, see the appendix to this chapter.

output of the financial accounting system. It is formal in the sense that this output is regulated closely, including the requirement of an audit of the records underlying the statements by a certified public accountant.

6.2 PURPOSE OF FINANCIAL REPORTING

Reynolds Girdler has referred to annual reports as the "18,000,000 Books Nobody Reads." He asserts that the financial statements are too technical and complex to be understood by the average investor.[4] This raises the question as to the purpose of financial reporting. Certainly, if the only purpose of the financial statements is to give investors the information they need to make rational choices, then it can be said that it fails in several respects:

1. Timing: investment decisions are made continuously, while the financial statements are issued periodically. Interim reports are generally issued on a quarterly basis, while the annual report is, of course, issued once a year.
2. Time-Orientation: investors are primarily concerned with future events—the financial statements describe essentially past events.
3. Context: data in isolation of its context is meaningless. Investors need to know how a given company is performing vis-à-vis its competitors. The financial statements do not compare a company against industry performance.
4. Communication: investors know little about the techniques or dialect of accounting. They desire communication at their level of understanding. The financial statements cater to a trained and technical audience.

Progress toward better communication with the investing public should certainly be a continuing objective of financial reporting. But whether the financial statements can ever provide investors with all the information they need—when they need it—is doubtful. As stated in chapter 1, no system can afford to give every user all of the information he *needs*, let alone *wants*. There is a cost-benefit constraint in financial reporting that makes it impossible to furnish real-time information at the present state of the art. In addition, the financial statements are geared to the behavior of the conservative, long-range investor; not to the speculator. With this primary user in mind, frequent reporting is less critical.

As to the time-orientation issue, firms are reluctant to issue detailed budgets and projections, even though these are available for internal purposes. The reasons for hesitancy are obvious. First, management wishes to avoid accountability for failure to meet projections which were uncertain at the start. More specifically, they fear that litigation will arise out of unfulfilled expectations on the part of investors. Second, information as to future events is often highly confidential, and publicizing plans and expectations could injure rather than promote a firm's performance. Management asserts that it is in the interest of their stockholders *not* to disclose projections and plans. The issue of time-orientation is not technical but pragmatic. The fears mentioned above need to be mitigated if progress is to be made in this direction.[5]

[4] Reynolds Girdler, "18,000,000 Books Nobody Reads," *Saturday Review*, April 13, 1963.

[5] We should point out that progress is being made toward including forecast information in annual reports. The financial statements of Commonwealth Edison Company, for example (which are part of the appendix

On the question of context, advocates of financial reporting insist that it is not feasible for a firm to compare its performance with that of specific competitors or with the industry at large. Again the issue is not a technical one—we have the ability to make such comparisons. Rather the issue is one of *ethics.* Business ethics in this regard is not unlike the ethics of medicine, where it is deemed inappropriate for one medical practitioner to compare his skills or performance against those of his colleagues. Implied in this ethic is an assumption about the rationality of users of these services, i.e., an informal communication will develop that distinguishes good practitioners (or firms) from poor ones. In any case there is some question as to whether a relaxation of this ethic will be productive or counter-productive. In those areas of social behavior where this ethic is absent we notice that a commitment to truth is replaced by contrivances intended to deceive the user into believing that the subject entity is far superior to its peers.

What of communications? Advocates of the current mode of financial reporting make no apology for the format or contents of their statements. They insist correctly that investors in the United States are better informed than their counterparts in any other country. They point to the steady improvement in financial reporting in the United States over the past twenty to thirty years, and promise continued steady progress in the future. As to the communications level, they take pride in the fact that they are producing a sophisticated and technical product. To "water it down" to the suggested level of understanding, they assert, is an unreasoned request. An analogous demand would be for the legal and medical professions to translate their lexicons into the vernacular. Much would be lost in the translation. A layman's vocabulary is simply too confined to encompass the terminology of a highly specialized technology. How would nuclear physics, the mathematics of communication, aerospace engineering, and many other technical fields translate into the vernacular? Volumes would be needed instead of pages, without any guarantee that understanding would improve.

Accounting is a technology of remarkable sophistication. How would phrases such as "sum-of-the-years'-digits depreciation," "serial maturity of a bond," or "the equity interest of minority stockholders in the net assets of the company," translate into the vernacular? The standard dictionary for accountants[6]—which is by no means a complete lexicon—comprises some 2,600 entries covering over 500 pages of printed text. A good portion of this information would be needed to understand even one set of corporate financial statements.

In part the burden for improving communications falls upon the user. Does he not have some responsibility for gaining a working knowledge of the language of accounting? He accepts this responsibility in many other facets of life. An automobile manufacturer produces a technical product. He assumes that persons who purchase an automobile know how to drive (a "working knowledge"). For matters beyond a basic level of understanding they call upon the assistance of experts—mechanics.

---

to this chapter), contain a five-year forecast. There is active discussion at the policy level of requiring forecast information in financial reports in the United States. In this connection it is of interest to note that this practice is already a requirement in the United Kingdom.

See John J. Willingham, Charles E. Smith, and Martin E. Taylor, "Should the CPA's Opinion be Extended to Include Forecasts?" *The Financial Executive,* September 1970, pp. 80–89; also, Institute of Chartered Accountants in England and Wales, *Accountants' Reports on Profit Forecasts,* July 1969; and Eldon S. Hendriksen, "Disclosure—Insights into Requirements in the United Kingdom," *The International Journal of Accounting,* Spring 1969, pp. 21–32.

[6]Eric L. Kohler, *A Dictionary for Accountants* (Englewood Cliffs, N.J.: Prentice-Hall, Inc., 1963).

What are the alternatives to this approach? Either to cease making automobiles because they are too technical; to create a nontechnical (but also nonfunctional) product such as bicycles, which can be understood by more users; or to educate the masses as to technology of automobiles. None of these alternatives appears to improve upon the conventional approach.

Let us return to accounting. The accounting product is of necessity a technical one. Users should obtain a working knowledge in accounting by reading books or taking courses. In more complex matters they should refer to experts: professional accountants and/or financial security analysts.

All of these comments refer to *one* purpose of financial reporting, which is to give investors the information they need to make rational choices.

Another important function is served by the institution of financial reporting, which in some respects has nothing to do with the formal output of financial statements. We can refer to this purpose as one of establishing a *credibility climate* such that investors or other constituencies have confidence in the basic integrity of the financial reporting of organizations.[7] This confidence stems from the fact that rules and regulations of accounting processes and reports are promulgated and enforced. The fact that firms must open their financial records to independent, trained observers leads to a general level of confidence as to the reliability of accounting data.

The audit of fiscal records and statements is referred to as "the attest function."[8] All companies which trade their stock on the public exchanges are required by law to submit to annual audits. Many additional organizations, including not-for-profit ones such as governments and hospital and school districts, now require the attest function as a means for giving their governing boards and constituencies improved assurance as to the functioning and reliability of their accounting systems and controls.

This concept of a credibility climate is important in financial reporting. Without it the most elaborate accounting reports would be viewed with skepticism. If public confidence in financial reporting deteriorates, the former concerns of timing, time-orientation, context, and communications will be of secondary importance. Credibility at the present level of reporting is necessary if further progress is to be meaningful.

Users are able to and do ask for interpretations of technical matters in financial reports; but clarification is meaningless if the underlying data is inaccurate.

In the discussion that follows we will deal first—and principally—with current financial reporting statements and norms. In the latter part of the chapter we will discuss several efforts that are being made to improve financial reporting.

6.3 CURRENT FINANCIAL REPORTING

The formal output of the accounting information system is the financial statements, which comprise four interdependent documents: (1) balance sheet; (2) income statement; (3) statement of retained earnings; and (4) statement of changes in financial

[7]See John W. Buckley, "Accounting Principles and the Social Ethic," *The Financial Executive*, October 1971, pp. 32–47.

[8]For a more intensive treatment of "the attest function" please read chapter 27 on financial and operational audits.

position. The statement of changes in financial position is now required in financial reporting.[9]

The financial statements are most often incorporated into annual reports, yet we must distinguish between these documents. The "attest function" referred to previously is limited to the financial statements and to their related footnotes. Independent verification of the remaining contents of the annual report should not be assumed. The annual report, exclusive of the financial statements, typically contains this type of information:

1. Financial summaries, e.g., income and balance sheet data for the preceding ten years or so.
2. Backlog, i.e., unfilled orders for the company's products.
3. Descriptions of the firm's products and services.
4. Statements as to new products and/or the nature of research and development that the company is engaged in.
5. Executive keynotes: indicating the arrival, promotion, or departure of key personnel.

This information is unquestionably of interest to stockholders and other users; and there has been a consistent trend in the United States of improving the quality of annual reports.

The financial statements are issued only once a year. *Interim* statements may be issued monthly or quarterly, but they do not carry the authority of the financial statements nor are the interim reports the object of audit and attestation. What interim statements lack in authority, however, is compensated for by their utility, for they do provide investors with more frequent reports on a company's progress.

6.4 THE BALANCE SHEET

Exhibit 6-1 contains an illustrative balance sheet. The purpose of this statement is to depict the financial position of a firm as of a specific date. Because the title "statement of financial position" is more descriptive of the function of this document, its use in lieu of "balance sheet" has been recommended strongly in the accounting literature. However, "balance sheet," after an early decline, is showing a strong resurgence in the battle of titles.[10] A representative sample shows that "balance sheet" is preferred in

[9]See *Accounting Principles Board Opinion No. 19, Reporting Changes in Financial Position* (New York: American Institute of Certified Public Accountants, March 1971).

[10]G. Edward Phillips and Ronald M. Copeland, *Financial Statements: Problems from Current Practice* (Englewood Cliffs, N.J.: Prentice-Hall, Inc., 1969), p. 3, shows a trend away from and then back to "balance sheet" as the preferred title of this statement:

Balance sheet title:	**1946**	**1960**	**1966**
Balance sheet	578	456	489
Financial position	12	103	81
Financial condition	6	35	27
Other captions	4	6	3
Total in representative sample	600	600	600

practice by a ratio of four to one against all competitors. For this reason we will adhere to this conventional title in this text.

Some salient comments on the balance sheet follow. They are keyed to Exhibit 6-1 to facilitate reference:

EXHIBIT 6-1

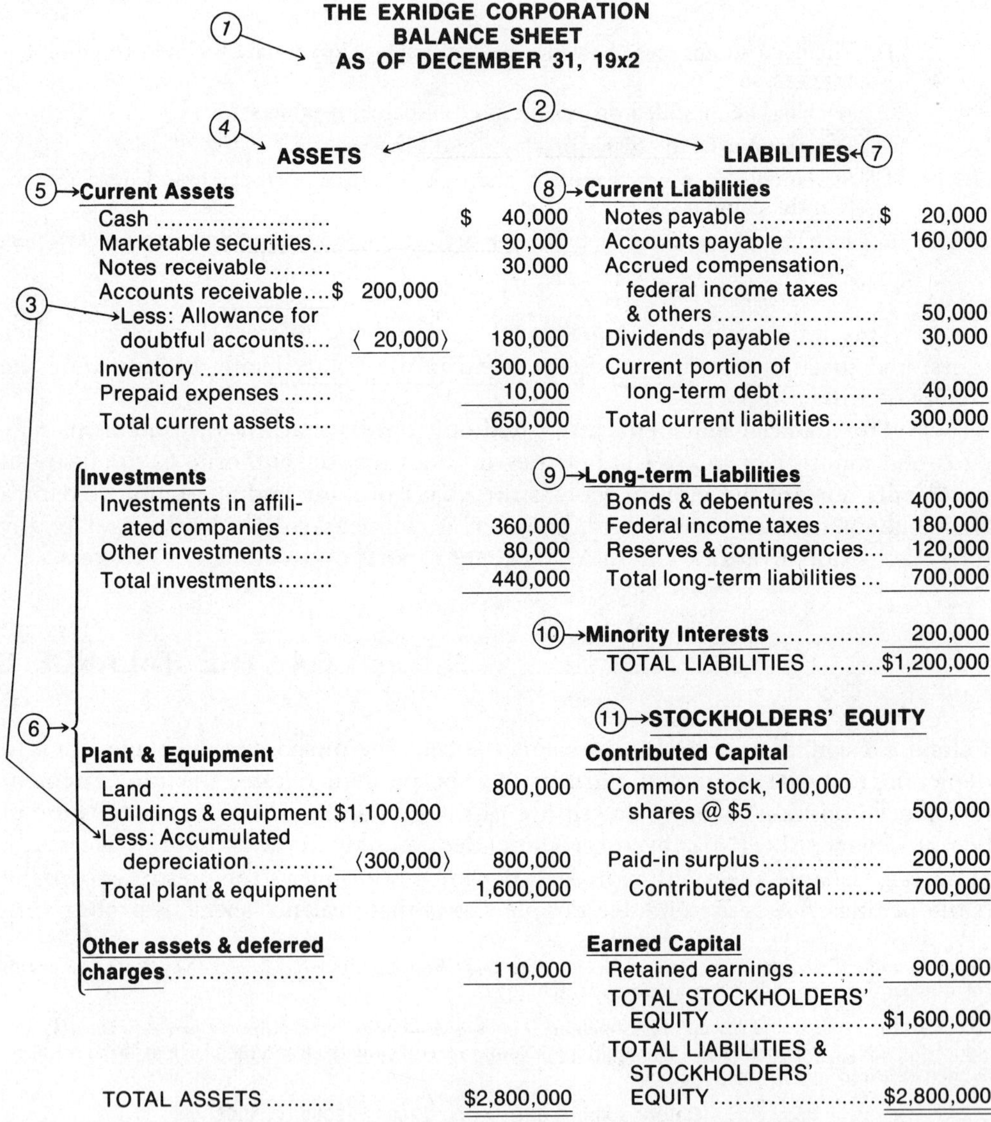

THE EXRIDGE CORPORATION
BALANCE SHEET
AS OF DECEMBER 31, 19x2 (1)

(2)

(4) **ASSETS**

(5) **Current Assets**		
Cash		$ 40,000
Marketable securities		90,000
Notes receivable		30,000
Accounts receivable	$ 200,000	
(3) Less: Allowance for doubtful accounts	⟨ 20,000⟩	180,000
Inventory		300,000
Prepaid expenses		10,000
Total current assets		650,000
(6) **Investments**		
Investments in affiliated companies		360,000
Other investments		80,000
Total investments		440,000
Plant & Equipment		
Land		800,000
Buildings & equipment	$1,100,000	
Less: Accumulated depreciation	⟨300,000⟩	800,000
Total plant & equipment		1,600,000
Other assets & deferred charges		110,000
TOTAL ASSETS		$2,800,000

LIABILITIES (7)

(8) **Current Liabilities**	
Notes payable	$ 20,000
Accounts payable	160,000
Accrued compensation, federal income taxes & others	50,000
Dividends payable	30,000
Current portion of long-term debt	40,000
Total current liabilities	300,000
(9) **Long-term Liabilities**	
Bonds & debentures	400,000
Federal income taxes	180,000
Reserves & contingencies	120,000
Total long-term liabilities	700,000
(10) **Minority Interests**	200,000
TOTAL LIABILITIES	$1,200,000
(11) **STOCKHOLDERS' EQUITY**	
Contributed Capital	
Common stock, 100,000 shares @ $5	500,000
Paid-in surplus	200,000
Contributed capital	700,000
Earned Capital	
Retained earnings	900,000
TOTAL STOCKHOLDERS' EQUITY	$1,600,000
TOTAL LIABILITIES & STOCKHOLDERS' EQUITY	$2,800,000

1. *Date:* The statement relates to a specific day. It does not cover a period of time, as does the income statement. In the financial statements the date is the end of the fiscal period, which may be based on a calendar year, a natural business year, or any arbitrary twelve-month period. Recognition of a specific date is necessary, because the condition of accounts described in the balance sheet is

only true at a specific moment in time. For example, Exridge Corporation is reported to have $40,000 in cash. This is the cash balance on December 31, 19*x*2—not on some other date.

Great care is taken to ensure a proper accounting on the date of the balance sheet. A cut-off is made in the various accounts to separate items that occur after the specified date. Where the audit of accounts follows the date of the balance sheet, which is customary, a careful reconstruction of items is undertaken to *deduce* the proper amount of the account on the closing day of business. For example, in auditing the cash account, deposits and withdrawals made after the closing date are adjusted in order to arrive at the actual cash balance pertinent to the balance sheet date.

2. *Format:* Exhibit 6-1 depicts an account format of the balance sheet, for which the equation is:

$$\text{Assets} = \text{Liabilities} + \text{Owners' Equity}$$

A less-used alternative is the report format, for which the equation is:

$$\text{Assets} - \text{Liabilities} = \text{Owners' Equity}$$

The account format conforms to the basic construct in accounting:

$$\text{Debits} = \text{Credits}$$

Accordingly all asset accounts are "natural debit-balance" accounts, while all equities are "natural credit-balance" accounts.

All credit-balance accounts in the balance sheet are *equity* accounts, with liabilities representing creditors' equity, and the interest of stockholders representing owners' equity.

An axiom of accounting is that debits = credits at all times. The term "balance sheet" relates to the equality of debits and credits.

3. *Contra-accounts:* There are exceptions to the rule that all natural debit or credit accounts are listed under assets or equities respectively. Two examples are noted in Exhibit 6-1. Allowance for doubtful accounts is a natural credit-balance account, but it is offset against accounts receivable. This account is intended to cover delinquencies in receivables, and hence it is appropriate to show it in conjunction with accounts receivable.

The other example is accumulated depreciation. It is customary to carry depreciable assets at their full acquisition cost until the point of their disposition. The depreciation of these assets is "accumulated" in the offset account. The difference between cost and accumulated depreciation is referred to as *book value.*

This type of account is called a *contra-account.* The use of offsets is strictly limited to those contra-accounts that provide additional information. It would be improper, for example, to offset accounts payable against accounts receivable, as this would result in less information.

4. *Assets:* Assets are things of value, i.e., resources. More specifically they represent only those resources that can be measured objectively. Executive talent, customer goodwill, and many other resources of undeniable value are excluded in current financial reporting because of the lack of objective measurement.

5. *Current assets:* Current assets are distinguished from long-lived assets by the criterion of *liquidity,* by which we mean "approximation to cash." The presumption is that current assets will convert to cash (or cash equivalents such as "marketable securities") within the *normal operating cycle* of the firm or *one year* from the balance sheet date, whichever is longer.
   a. *Normal operating cycle:* The normal operating cycle is the period of time that it takes to move from one cash position to another through the normal course of business, as depicted below:

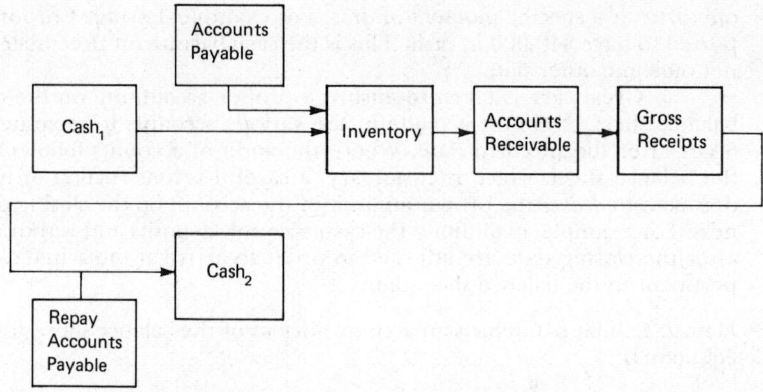

Some businesses, such as bakeries, have very short operating cycles. The manufacturer of a first-rate whisky may have an operating cycle of eight years or more. Where the normal operating cycle is less than one year, the one-year rule applies. Where it is more than one year, the natural cycle becomes the criterion for classifying current assets. It is acceptable for the whisky manufacturer to classify as inventory those costs incurred in making whiskey that will only be sold many years hence in the normal course of business.

b. *Current asset rule in interim reports:* The liquidity rule of one year is the next twelve-month period from the balance sheet date. This holds true for interim statements as well. If the fiscal year is January 1 to December 31, and we are issuing an interim report after one month (on January 31), the "current period" extends to January 31 twelve months hence. It overrides the year-end date of December 31. If this were not the case, the current period would differ from month to month—at January 31 we would have an eleven-month period, at February 28 a ten-month period, and so on until at November 30 we would have a one-month period. A fluctuating current period would make interim comparisons difficult.

c. *Classification of current asset accounts:* Within the current asset section, accounts are classified in a descending order of liquidity. Marketable securities, which represents investments that can readily be converted into cash, is listed immediately under cash.

Notes receivable precedes accounts receivable because of superior negotiability. Notes receivable is listed first even though the due date of the notes may exceed the collection period of receivables. In most instances a note can be *discounted* readily into cash. Cash can also be raised on receivables through *factoring,* but with less certainty.

All receivables represent amounts due to the firm—usually from customers.

The allowance for doubtful accounts is created to cover that portion of receivables that in time prove to be uncollectible.

Inventory is listed next. Accounts receivable represents a money claim. Inventory has not yet been sold, hence there is no money claim as yet. For this reason "accounts receivable" is accorded the higher rank in terms of liquidity.

Inventory represents the merchandise that a firm intends to sell in the normal course of business. It includes raw material, work-in-process, as well as finished goods in manufacturing enterprises.

Prepaid expenses represents money outlays for resources that will be consumed within the normal operating cycle. For example, if we pay first and last month's rent in January 19*x*2, the portion pertaining to December 19*x*2 is *prepaid*. The accounting treatment of this event can be illustrated by the following T_1 journal entries:

Entry in January:

Increase (Debit) Rent expense........................	$200	
Prepaid expense	200	
Decrease (Credit) Cash..............................		$400

Notation: First and last month's rent expense. January rent charged to expense, December rent deferred as a prepaid expense.

Entry in December:

Increase (Debit) Rent expense........................	$200	
Decrease (Credit) Prepaid expense		$200

Notation: Transfer of prepaid rent for the month of December 19x2 to rent expense.

If the prepaid item is not "consumed" within the next normal operating cycle, it is treated as a deferred charge under (6) and not as a prepaid expense.

Office and other supplies are a common source of prepaid expenses. Supply inventories are not considered part of merchandise inventory because there is no intention to sell these supplies for profit in the normal course of business.

6. *Long-lived assets:* Long-lived or fixed assets describe those resources that will benefit more than one accounting period, i.e., they are not liquidated within the normal operating cycle or one year, whichever is longer.

The term "long-lived" or "fixed" assets may not appear on the balance sheet, but it refers implicitly (if not explicitly) to all categories of resources other than current assets.

a. *Investments:* Investments in affiliated companies should be distinguished from regular investments. The nature of investments may or may not be different from marketable securities, i.e., they may be blue-chip securities which have immediate convertibility into cash, or they may be held in less liquid forms such as real estate, long-term government bonds, and so forth. In the former instance, the distinction between investments and marketable securities is decided, not on the nature of the security, but rather on the intentions of the holder. If the firm intends to liquidate the security within the normal operating cycle, it should be classified as a marketable security; but if the intention is to hold the investment for a period longer than the normal operating cycle, it should be classified as an investment.

   Real estate held for purposes of investment, which is not used in the normal operations of the business, is properly classified as an investment and not as plant and equipment.

   Some investments represent funds that are held for specific purposes. For example, some investments may be linked to pension and retirement funds. This type of investment is called "restricted"—it should not be viewed as a source of operating cash even in the long term.

b. *Plant and equipment:* These assets are employed in the normal course of business, but they benefit several accounting periods.

   The order of ranking is in terms of longevity. Land has the longest life, so it is listed first, followed by buildings, equipment and machinery, furniture and fixtures, etc.

Land does not depreciate in value, hence for tax and accounting purposes no depreciation is permitted. Other items within plant and equipment do depreciate. As stated earlier, the convention is to show plant and equipment at cost, offset by an accumulated depreciation account in which the annual depreciation charges "accumulate."

The value of plant and equipment *net* of accumulated depreciation is referred to as "book value."

c. *Other assets and deferred charges:* We have defined *deferred charges* as prepaid items that will not be consumed in operations during the accounting period.

The major component of other assets is intangible costs. Intangible assets have no physical existence. Their value is based on the rights and benefits that ownership confers upon the owners.

The most common intangible assets encountered in financial reporting are:

Patents & copyrights:	They represent the costs of obtaining protection to produce unique products without the fear of infringement.
Organization costs:	The setup costs of organizing a business. These costs benefit many future accounting periods.
Goodwill:	This asset is recognized only in a sales-purchase transaction. It represents the excess in price paid to acquire a business over the value of all other assets purchased. Ostensibly, the difference in value is attributable to location, satisfied customers, and other intangible factors.

7. *Liabilities:* Liabilities represent the claims of creditors against the resources of the firm. They can also be viewed as sources for obtaining assets other than from owners. The former definition is legalistic, the latter is operational.
8. *Current liabilities:* These are liabilities that call for settlement within the normal operating cycle, most generally defined as one year from the balance sheet date.

a. *Notes and accounts payable:* All payables represent amounts due to creditors by the firm. Notes and accounts payable are obligations most generally arising from the purchase (on credit) of goods and services in the normal course of business; although a note payable arising from a short-term money loan is not uncommon.

b. *Accrued items:* These are liabilities arising out of operations which have been recognized as claims against current income but which have yet to be paid.

For example, employees may have performed services for which they have not been paid as of the date of the balance sheet. Nonetheless, income is charged for the cost of services and a corresponding liability is recognized by means of this journal entry:

Increase (Debit) Wages expense	$500	
Increase (Credit) Accrued wages payable		$500

Notation: Recognizing obligation for services rendered but as yet unpaid.

The entry upon paying the employee is:

Decrease (Debit) Accrued wages payable	$500	
Decrease (Credit) Cash		$500

Notation: Payment of accrued wages payable.

Similarly, income taxes are computed as of the date of the balance sheet, but are actually paid at some future date. However, income taxes are charged to income for the period and accrued as a liability in the manner shown above.

At year-end it is also customary to declare dividends. Again, the declaration of dividends precedes payment. Dividend expense is charged in the statement of retained earnings for the period and a corresponding liability is recognized. This liability is liquidated in the identical manner shown above.

c. *Current portion of long-term debt:* That portion of a long-term liability which calls for payment within one year of the balance sheet date is shown as a current liability.

9. *Long-term liabilities:* These liabilities have a due date beyond one year. They form, together with stockholders' equity, the *capital structure* of the firm.
   a. *Bonds and debentures:* These are long-term debt securities offered for public subscription. They generally carry a fixed interest rate, and may be sold at a premium or discount depending upon the state of financial conditions at the time of the offering.
   b. *Reserve for federal income taxes:* Financial accounting often differs from tax reporting, as mentioned earlier. Federal income tax computed for tax purposes may be lower than the tax computation based on financial income. Actual tax paid is determined by the former computation. The tax difference is often in the nature of a temporary advantage or credit which will reverse in some future period. Hence, the difference in tax is credited to a reserve account to provide for periods of tax reversal.
   c. *Reserves and contingencies:* This category of liability includes such items as reserves for employee pension funds (often offset by the investments mentioned previously). It may include reserves to cover defects under guarantees and warranties. In insurance companies, a reserve is set aside for probable claims based on actuarial analysis.

10. *Minority interests:* A company may not own 100% of the outstanding shares of its affiliates or subsidiaries. This item—minority interests—represents that portion of the equity interest in a subsidiary which is owned by third parties.

    This item is classified alternatively under stockholders' equity—but as a distinct item.

11. *Stockholders' equity:* Stockholders are said to have a "residual" equity in the assets of a business. The claims of creditors have preference in the event of liquidation.
    a. *Contributed capital:* This portion of stockholders' equity results from the sale of stock. It is customary to show the sale of stock at "par" or "stated value" as a separate item, which is then adjusted by any surplus or discount that is realized upon the issue of the stock.
    b. *Retained earnings:* This form of capital results from operations. It represents accumulated net income after dividends. The separation of contributed capital and retained earnings is required by law, except under some reorganization provisions.

6.5 FINANCIAL STATEMENT CONVENTIONS

In chapter 3 we discussed the output rules of financial reporting in considerable detail. These rules are reiterated here in summary form for purposes of emphasizing the assumptions underlying the financial statements. While these assumptions have relevance to each of the four statements comprising the financial statements, they are most pertinent to the balance sheet, hence we summarize them at this point:

OR-1 **ENTITY:** Financial statements are those of a particular entity; in this case the Exridge Corporation.

OR-2 **TIME PERIODS (MATCHING):** Accounting events have been assigned to their proper time periods in terms of the matching convention.

OR-3 **GOING CONCERN:**[11] Exridge Corporation is not in danger of liquidation; hence its financial statements are prepared on the assumption that it will continue to remain in business over the foreseeable future.

OR-4 **CONSISTENCY:** Accounting methods used in this period are consistent with those used in the preceding period. Consistency also implies that the accounting methods employed are in accordance with generally accepted accounting principles. Variances in interperiod consistency or from pronouncements of the Accounting Principles Board (its *Opinions*) must be disclosed either in footnotes to the financial statements or in the auditor's opinion.

OR-5 **TENTATIVENESS:** Figures in the financial statements should be viewed as being accurate within some probability range rather than as "absolute" amounts.

OR-6 **DISCLOSURE:** Given the current conventions of accounting, the financial statements contain and present information that is designed to illuminate and not confuse or mislead the knowledgeable reader.

OR-7 **EXCHANGE PRICE:** Actual exchange price ("historical cost") is the current generally accepted method for recording values.

OR-8 **STABLE MONEY UNIT:** Financial data in the statements is *not* adjusted for changes in the purchasing power of the money unit.

OR-9 **NEUTRALITY:** Financial statements are issued to all users in the public sector without bias in favor of any specific user class.

OR-10 **ORDERED CLASSES:** Financial data in the statements is organized along accustomed lines in order to promote uniformity and comparability in financial reporting.

These assumptions are not stated explicitly in the financial statements, so the utility of the statements is enhanced by having a thorough knowledge of the ground rules under which they are issued.

6.6 BALANCE SHEET VALUATION NORMS

Some specific valuation norms in the balance sheet should be noted:

Asset	Valuation Norm
Marketable securities.......	Lower of cost or market
Inventory, other than LIFO	Lower of cost or market

[11] The de facto going concern horizon appears to be one year, although in theory there is the assumption of an indefinite future life.

Investments	Lower of cost or market[12]
Plant & equipment	Cost adjusted for depreciation
Intangible assets	Cost less amortization
Equities	
Liabilities	Known or estimated cost of settlement
Capital stock	Proceeds from issue at par, adjusted for premium or discount

You will notice that "cost" is the basis of valuation, except in those instances where market value is less than cost.

6.7 THE INCOME STATEMENT

The purpose of an income statement is to show the results of operations for a specific period of time. An illustrative income statement for the Exridge Corporation is shown in Exhibit 6-2.

EXHIBIT 6-2

THE EXRIDGE CORPORATION
(1)→INCOME STATEMENT
(2)→FOR THE YEAR ENDED, DECEMBER 31, 19x2

(3)→Net sales		$3,000,000
(4)→Cost of goods sold		1,880,000
(5) Gross profit		1,120,000
(6)→Selling expenses	$250,000	
(7)→Administrative expenses	400,000	
(8)→Depreciation of plant & equipment	150,000	800,000
(9)→Net operating income		320,000
(10)→Non-operating items—net expense	(20,000)	
(11)→Extraordinary gains & losses—net gain	200,000	180,000
Net income before federal income taxes		500,000
(12)→Federal income taxes:		
Current	90,000	
Deferred	100,000	190,000
Net income before minority interests		310,000
(13)→Minority interests		15,000
(14)→Net income		$ 295,000
(15)→Earnings per share		$2.95
(15)→Earnings per share—fully diluted or *pro forma*		2.87

An interpretation of the income statement, keyed to the above items, follows:

[12] *Accounting Principles Board Opinion No. 18, The Equity Method of Accounting for Investments in Common Stock* (New York: American Institute of Certified Public Accountants, March 1971), calls for accounting for the common stock of subsidiaries under the *equity* rather than the *cost* method. Most *advanced* accounting textbooks discuss this subject in depth.

1. *Title:* "Income statement" is the preferred title as shown by the following summary:[13]

INCOME STATEMENT TITLE

	1966	1955	1946
Income statement	389	361	317
Statement of earnings	178	135	10
Profit and loss statement	2	56	236
Statement of operations	26	30	10
Miscellaneous terms	5	16	20
No income statement	–	2	7
Total	600	600	600

2. *Period:* The income statement covers a specific period of time, i.e., the annual fiscal period. Interim income statements may be prepared monthly or quarterly.
3. *Net sales:* Sales are revenues which arise from normal activities of the firm.

   Revenue is a generic term that includes (1) sales, (2) non-operating income, and (3) extraordinary gains. It can be defined as "credits to earned capital during an accounting period."

   Net sales means that gross sales have been adjusted for the following items: *discounts,* and *returns & allowances.*
4. *Cost of goods sold:* This item reflects the costs of purchasing or manufacturing the goods that were sold during the annual operating period. The expression "cost of sales" is sometimes used instead of "cost of goods sold."

   Cost of goods sold may be computed directly, or it can be *deduced* by means of an inventory count:

DEDUCING COST OF GOODS SOLD

Inventory as of January 1, 19x2	$ 480,000
Purchases during the year	1,700,000
Total available	2,180,000
Less: Inventory as of December 31, 19x2	300,000
Cost of goods sold	$1,880,000

   Cost of goods sold is deduced in those instances where inventory consists of numerous small items, as in a supermarket. In such circumstances it is impractical to keep an itemized record of the cost of goods sold.
5. *Gross profit:* The gross profit or "gross margin" computation enables us to ascertain whether or not we have a basically healthy relationship between the cost and the selling price of our products.
6. *Selling expenses:* The cost of marketing products is associated with administrative expenses. This category includes such expenses as advertising, salaries and commissions to sales personnel, and delivery expenses.
7. *Administrative expenses:* This category includes such items as officers' and office salaries and wages, office supplies, and other general and administrative expenses such as telecommunications, utilities, and rent.
8. *Depreciation:* Depreciation of plant and equipment is often shown as a separate item of expense. Alternatively it may be included in cost of goods sold, selling expenses, and administrative expenses as follows:

[13] Philips and Copeland, *Financial Statements,* p. 3.

	Type of Depreciation
a. Cost of goods sold	Depreciation related to manufacturing plant and equipment or to the physical assets of the purchasing department.
b. Selling expenses	Depreciation of stores, counters, and equipment.
c. Administrative expenses	Depreciation of general offices including buildings, furniture, fixtures, and equipment.

Showing depreciation as a separate item facilitates price-level adjustments, as illustrated in chapter 8.

9. *Net operating income:* Net operating income is the difference between gross profit and total operating expenses (selling + administration). This figure shows the results of operations in the *normal* course of business.

10. *Non-operating items:* These items occur regularly but are not directly related to the normal activity of the firm.

    For example, if a manufacturing firm rents some excess space, such rental income would be classified as non-operating income. For a firm whose business is renting space, rent income would constitute its sales.

    Financing costs such as interest are usually considered non-operating.

    There are non-operating *income* and *expenses,* e.g., interest income and expense. It is customary to "net" these items in the income statement. In Exhibit 6-2 non-operating expenses exceed income by $20,000.

11. *Extraordinary items:* These items do not occur regularly. They are of a significant amount. Their occurrence is generally unpredictable. They are not related to the normal activity of the firm.

    Again we may have extraordinary gains and/or losses.

    An example of an extraordinary gain is where we sell a long-lived asset in excess of its book value.

    Examples of extraordinary losses include sale of long-lived assets at less than their book value, or uninsured portions of casualty losses such as theft, fire, earthquake, or flood.

    In Exhibit 6-2 gains exceed losses by $200,000.

    Extraordinary items generally fall under capital gains and losses income tax treatment. The capital gains tax rate is 50% of a taxpayer's regular tax rate, with a ceiling of 25%. Extraordinary items should be reflected on the income statement net of their applicable income tax.

12. *Federal income taxes:* Federal income taxes as computed on the tax return for the period totaled $90,000. Different methods of accounting were used for financial reporting than were used for income tax purposes. *If* income taxes had been paid on the basis of the $500,000 reported in the income statement (Exhibit 6-2), the figure would have been $190,000. The difference of $100,000 is recorded as a long-term liability in the balance sheet. (See Exhibit 6-1. This account had a balance of $80,000 from previous years.)

13. *Minority interests:* In note 10 to the balance sheet we observed that the Exridge Corporation did not own 100% of the stock of its subsidiaries. The consolidated income statement in Exhibit 6-2 includes the total income and expenses of the subsidiaries as well as that of the parent company. It is customary to consolidate on these terms where the parent company owns 50% or more of subsidiaries' stock.

    However, not all of the subsidiaries' net income belongs to the Exridge Corporation; $15,000 is deducted in arriving at net income. This amount represents that portion of net income after tax which belongs to the subsidiaries' minority stockholders.

14. *Net income:* This is the final income figure. It is sometimes referred to as "net income after tax." This amount of \$295,000 is available for distribution to stockholders in the form of dividends, or it can be "retained" in the business as earned capital. Most commonly a portion of net income is paid in dividends and a portion retained as earned capital.
15. *Earnings per share:* Earnings per share (EPS) is computed as follows:

$$\frac{\text{Net Income ("after tax")}}{\text{Number of Common Shares Outstanding}}$$

In Exhibit 6-1 (the balance sheet) we noted that 100,000 shares of common stock were outstanding; hence:

$$\frac{\$295{,}000}{100{,}000} = \$2.95 \text{ per share}$$

Firms may issue bonds or debentures that are "convertible," which means that the holder has the option of trading his bonds or debentures for common stock. Of the bonds and debentures listed in Exhibit 6-1, some contain this convertible provision. If all these bonds are converted, we would have, say, 105,000 shares outstanding; hence:

$$\frac{\$295{,}000 + \$6{,}000}{100{,}000 + 5{,}000} = \$2.87 \text{ per share, "fully diluted"}$$

The term *pro forma* earnings per share is also used.

There are, say, 1,000 convertible bonds × \$100 each = \$100,000, which bear a 6% interest rate. The conversion price is \$20, so

$$\frac{\$100{,}000}{\$20} = 5{,}000 \text{ shares upon conversion}$$

Upon conversion, \$6,000 can be deducted from non-operating expense. On a *pro forma* basis, then, we would have \$301,000 in income divided by 105,000 shares of common stock.

6.8 THE STATEMENT OF RETAINED EARNINGS

The statement of retained earnings details the changes which have occurred in earned capital during the same time period pertinent to the other statements. This statement consists of the four items, as illustrated in Exhibit 6-3.

EXHIBIT 6-3

THE EXRIDGE CORPORATION
(1)→STATEMENT OF RETAINED EARNINGS
(2)→FOR THE YEAR ENDED, DECEMBER 31, 19x2

(3)→Retained earnings as of January 1, 19x2	\$700,000
(4)→Add: Net income	295,000
	995,000
(5)→Less: Dividends declared and paid	95,000
(6)→Retained earnings as of December 31, 19x2	\$900,000

APB Opinion No. 9 allows the inclusion of other data in the statement of retained earnings in rare instances.[14]

For our purposes we will limit the statement of retained earnings to the items shown in Exhibit 6-3. Appropriate comments keyed to Exhibit 6-3 follow:

1. *Title:* "Statement of retained earnings" shows the changes in *earned* as opposed to *contributed* capital of corporations.

   The analogous document for proprietorships and partnerships is termed a *statement of changes in capital.* In these instances transactions involving total owners' equity are included, e.g., additional capital paid in or withdrawn by the proprietor or partner(s). The corporate statement of retained earnings only accounts for changes in earned capital.

   These formats are compared below:

EXHIBIT 6-4 BASIC FORMAT FOR STATEMENT OF CHANGES IN CAPITAL OR RETAINED EARNINGS

I STATEMENT OF CHANGES IN CAPITAL (Proprietorships & Partnerships)		II STATEMENT OF RETAINED EARNINGS (Corporations)	
Capital, beginning of period	$	Retained earnings, beginning of period	$
Add: Additional capital contributed......................		Add: Net income	
Net income......................		Total retained earnings available...........................	$
Total capital available	$	Less: Dividends paid............	
Less: Capital withdrawn by owners........................			
Capital, end of period	$	Retained earnings, end of period	$

[14]*Accounting Principles Board Opinion No. 9* (New York: American Institute of Certified Public Accountants, December 1966), p. 113:

Par. 18: With respect to prior period adjustments, the Board has concluded that those rare items which relate directly to the operations of a specific prior period or periods, which are material and which qualify under the criteria described in paragraphs 23 and 25 below should, in single period statements, be reflected as adjustments of the opening balance of retained earnings. . . .

Par. 23: Adjustments . . . are limited to . . . (items) which (a) can be specifically identified with and directly related to the business activities of particular prior periods, and (b) are not attributable to economic events occurring subsequent to the date of the financial statements for the prior period, and (c) depend primarily on determinations by persons other than management and (d) were not susceptible of reasonable estimation prior to such determination. . . .

Par. 25: A change in the application of accounting principles may create a situation in which retroactive application is appropriate. . . . Examples are changes in the basis of preparing consolidated financial statements or in the basis of carrying investments in subsidiaries (e.g., from cost to the equity method).

2. *Period:* The same time periods as discussed before pertain. Interim statements of retained earnings are not common.
3. *Beginning balance:* This figure is obtained from the balance sheet dated December 31, 19*x*1. The retained earnings balance at the end of one period becomes the beginning balance in the next period.
4. *Net income:* Net income after tax is transferred to this statement from the income statement. We note that it includes non-operating and extraordinary items.
5. *Dividends declared and paid:* This item may refer to "dividends paid," "dividends declared," or "dividends declared and paid." Where a dividend is declared but not paid, the item is included in the statement of retained earnings and a corresponding liability is created, as illustrated in note 8b to the balance sheet.

   The reference "dividends declared and paid" implies that quarterly dividends were paid during the year; and that a year-end dividend has been declared but not yet paid.
6. *Ending balance:* This figure represents the cumulative retained earnings as of the end of the period. It agrees with the related entry in the balance sheet (Exhibit 6-1).

6.9 COMPARATIVE FINANCIAL STATEMENTS

Most financial statements are in *comparative* form, which means that they cover a two-year period.[15] Let us assemble the financial statements of the Exridge Corporation for the current period, 19*x*2, and show the comparative data for 19*x*1.

Comparative statements aid in understanding the function of the *funds statement.* They also provide clues as to a firm's progress. They can be misleading where major changes have occurred, such as mergers and acquisitions.

Even a cursory examination of these comparative financial statements reveals that operations in 19*x*2 were not as profitable as 19*x*1. Although sales increased to $3,000,000 from $2,700,000, net operating income declined from $410,000 to $320,-000. The reason net income for 19*x*2 exceeded 19*x*1 was due to the extraordinary gain. This illustrates the importance of separating non-operating and extraordinary items from operating data.

[15]Philips and Copeland, *Financial Statements,* p. 4, indicate the extent to which comparative statements are used in financial reporting:

	1966	1955	1946
All statements in comparative form	543	379	164
Some statements in comparative form	51	89	92
No statements in comparative form	6	132	344
Representative sample	600	600	600

EXHIBIT 6-5

THE EXRIDGE CORPORATION BALANCE SHEET AS OF DECEMBER 31, 19x2

ASSETS

	19x2	19x1
Current Assets		
Cash	$ 40,000	$ 30,000
Marketable securities	90,000	95,000
Notes receivable	30,000	50,000
Accounts receivable (net)	180,000	150,000
Inventory	300,000	400,000
Prepaid expenses	10,000	15,000
Total current assets	650,000	740,000
Investments		
In affiliates	360,000	360,000
Other investments	80,000	50,000
	440,000	410,000
Plant & Equipment		
Land	800,000	700,000
Buildings & equipment	1,100,000	900,000
Less: Accum. depr.	(300,000)	(200,000)
	1,600,000	1,400,000
Other Assets and Deferred Charges	110,000	100,000
Total assets	$2,800,000	$2,650,000

LIABILITIES

	19x2	19x1
Current Liabilities		
Notes payable	$ 20,000	$ 130,000
Accounts payable	160,000	200,000
Accrued expenses	50,000	40,000
Dividends payable	30,000	20,000
Current portion of debt	40,000	40,000
Total current liabilities	300,000	430,000
Long-term Liabilities		
Bonds & debentures	400,000	440,000
Federal income taxes	180,000	80,000
Reserves & contingencies	120,000	100,000
Total L-t liabilities	700,000	620,000
Minority Interests*	200,000	200,000
Total liabilities	1,200,000	1,250,000

STOCKHOLDERS' EQUITY

	19x2	19x1
Contributed Capital		
Common stock, 100,000 @ $5	500,000	500,000
Paid-in surplus	200,000	200,000
	700,000	700,000
Earned Capital		
Retained earnings	900,000	700,000
Total stockholders' equity	1,600,000	1,400,000
Total liabilities & equity	$2,800,000	$2,650,000

*Minority interest has not increased because of the accounting method of consolidation, and because it is assumed that the subsidiary company paid 100% of its earnings in 19x2 as dividends. The consolidation of financial statements and computation of minority interest are covered in advanced accounting courses.

EXHIBIT 6-6

THE EXRIDGE CORPORATION
INCOME STATEMENT
FOR THE YEAR ENDED, DECEMBER 31, 19x2

	19x2	19x1
Net sales	$3,000,000	$2,700,000
Cost of goods sold	1,880,000	1,590,000
Gross profit	1,120,000	1,110,000
Operating expenses		
Selling	250,000	220,000
General & administrative	400,000	360,000
Depreciation of plant & equipment	150,000	120,000
Total	800,000	700,000
Net operating income	$ 320,000	$ 410,000
Non-operating items—net expense	(20,000)	(30,000)
Extraordinary gain, net of applicable tax	200,000	—
Total	180,000	(30,000)
Net income before federal income taxes	500,000	380,000
Federal income taxes		
Current	90,000	80,000
Deferred	100,000	80,000
Total	190,000	160,000
Net income before minority interests	310,000	220,000
Net income attributable to minority interests	15,000	12,000
Net income	$ 295,000	$ 208,000
(1) Earnings per share before extraordinary items	$ .95	$ 2.08
(1) Earnings per share on extraordinary items	2.00	—
(1) Earnings per share on net income	$ 2.95	$ 2.08
(2) *Pro forma* earnings per share	2.87	2.04

Notes:

1. *Opinion No. 9*, p. 119, states: "It is the Board's opinion that the reporting of per share data should disclose amounts for (a) income before extraordinary items, (b) extraordinary items, if any (less applicable income tax), and (c) net income—the total of (a) and (b)."

   This rule is illustrated in Exhibit 6-6. Net income is adjusted ("gains" are subtracted, "losses" are added) by extraordinary items (net of applicable tax):

EPS Before Extraordinary Items:	19x2		19x1	
Net Income	$295,000		$208,000	(1)
Extraordinary items	200,000	Gain	0	(2)
Net Income before E.I.	95,000		208,000	(3)

   (3) is divided by number of shares of common stock outstanding to obtain EPS before extraordinary items:

	19x2	19x1
$\frac{\$95{,}000}{100{,}000} =$	$ .95	
$\frac{\$208{,}000}{100{,}000} =$		$2.08

EPS is then computed on extraordinary items alone:

	19x2	19x1
$\frac{\$200{,}000}{100{,}000} =$	$2.00	
$\frac{0}{100{,}000} =$		0

The above are added to yield EPS on Net Income:

	19x2	19x1
	$2.95	$2.08

This should agree with EPS computed the basis of Net Income:

	19x2	19x1
$\frac{\$295{,}000}{100{,}000} =$	$2.95	
$\frac{\$208{,}000}{100{,}000} =$		$2.08

Note that only extraordinary (not non-operating) items are involved.

Number of shares outstanding did not change between 19*x*1 and 19*x*2.

The break-down of EPS on net income can also be done on a *pro forma* basis.

2. *Pro forma* EPS is computed as follows:

	19x2	19x1
$\frac{\$208{,}000 + \$6{,}000}{100{,}000 + 5{,}000} =$		$2.04
$\frac{\$295{,}000 + \$6{,}000}{100{,}000 + 5{,}000} =$	$2.87	

See note 15 to Exhibit 6-2.

We assume that conversion is at $20 in 19*x*1 and in 19*x*2.

EXHIBIT 6-7

THE EXRIDGE CORPORATION
STATEMENT OF RETAINED EARNINGS
FOR THE YEAR ENDED, DECEMBER 31, 19x2

	19x2	19x1
Retained earnings, January 1	$700,000	$572,000
Add: Net income	295,000	208,000
	995,000	780,000
Less: Dividends declared & paid	95,000	80,000
Retained earnings, December 31	$900,000	$700,000

6.10 THE STATEMENT OF CHANGES IN FINANCIAL POSITION

This statement has been commonly known as "the funds statement." The term *funds* in accounting has at least four different meanings: (1) cash; (2) cash or investments set aside for a specific purpose, e.g., a pension fund; (3) working capital; and (4) all financial resources.[16] When we use the term in the context of the statement of changes in financial position we refer to working capital.

Working capital is the excess of current assets over current liabilities. Referring to Exhibit 6-5, we can compute the working capital of the Exridge Corporation for 19*x*1 and 19*x*2 quite readily:

	19x2	19x1
Current assets	$650,000	$740,000
Current liabilities	300,000	430,000
Working capital	$350,000	$310,000
Increase 19*x*2 over 19*x*1	$ 40,000	

Why is working capital important? It is important because it represents the only discretionary funds that management has for making short-term decisions:

Total assets or resources
Less: Long-lived assets, which by definition are not available for short-term decisions.
= Current assets
Less: Current liabilities, which represent commitments against current resources.
= Working capital

[16] While statements of change in financial position in published annual reports predominantly utilize the working capital concept, the Accounting Principles Board in *Opinion No. 3* prefers "a concept broader than that of working capital . . . [which] will include the financial aspects of all significant transactions, e.g., non-fund transactions such as the acquisition of property through the issue of securities."

In *Accounting Principles Board Opinion No. 19, Reporting Changes in Financial Position* (New York: American Institute of Certified Public Accountants, March 1971), the term "statement of changes in financial position" is suggested in lieu of the commonly held title "funds statement." In part the change in title stresses the need to include in the statement changes among non-working capital accounts; for example, where an increase in a long-term liability, such as a mortgage, gives rise to plant and equipment (e.g., a building), without directly affecting working capital.

Example: A secretary wants a new typewriter. Can we afford it? The answer comes from examining working capital position – not the cash balance. The fact that we have sufficient cash to pay for it does not mean that we can *afford* the typewriter.

SOURCES AND USES OF WORKING CAPITAL

The statement of changes in financial position is often referred to as a statement of "sources and uses of working capital." How do we obtain and utilize working capital? To illustrate the derivation of sources and uses of working capital consider a balance sheet as having four parts, as in Exhibit 6-8.

EXHIBIT 6-8

Working Capital	Long-Term Liabilities
Long-Lived Assets	Owners' Equity

There are no current liabilities in our balance sheet because they have been subtracted from current assets in arriving at working capital.

Alternative sources of working capital are (1) sale of fixed assets; (2) increase in long-term debt; and (3) increase in owners' equity. We arrive at this conclusion by considering each alternative source (or use) as belonging to a mutually exclusive set with working capital. For example, if we only have two accounts, working capital and long-lived assets, and we wish to increase working capital, what happens to long-lived assets? They decrease. If we only have working capital and long-term debt, working capital is increased by increasing long-term debt because of the debit-credit convention in accounting.

Alternative uses of working capital are (1) purchase of fixed assets; (2) decrease in long-term debt; and (3) decrease in owners' equity. We can show these relationships (Exhibit 6-9) by elaborating on Exhibit 6-8.

EXHIBIT 6-9

U	S			U	S
–	+	Working Capital	Long-Term Liabilities	–	+
+	–	Long-Lived Assets	Owners' Equity	–	+

(S = Sources; U = Uses)

Owners' equity, as we have already observed, has two parts: contributed and earned capital. We distinguish between these forms of equity in funds analysis (Exhibit 6-10).

EXHIBIT 6-10

U	S			U	S
–	+	Working Capital	Long-Term Liabilities	–	+
+	–	Long-Lived Assets	Owners' Equity		
			(a) Contributed capital	–	+
			(b) Operating income	–	+
			(c) Operating expenses or loss	+	–

We can summarize by diagramming the sources and uses of funds, as shown in Exhibit 6-11.

EXHIBIT 6-11

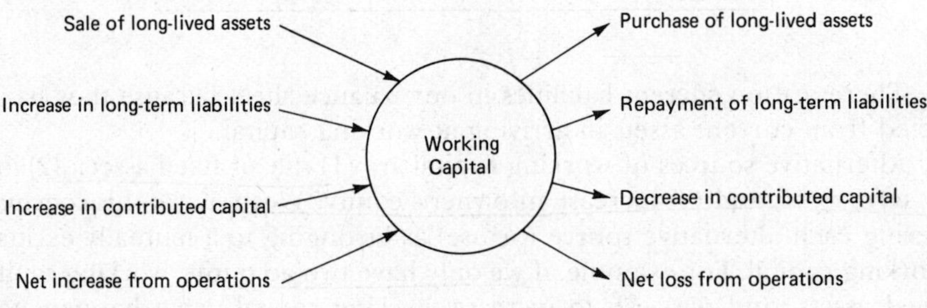

THE CONCEPT OF POOLED RESOURCES

The concept of *pooled resources* is basic as well as pervasive in accounting, and it underscores the need for the statement of changes in financial position.

To illustrate this concept, let us assume that Mr. Alpha contributes $1,000 in cash to begin a business. At this point in time a balance sheet would yield this information.

ALPHA COMPANY
BALANCE SHEET

Cash..................	$1,000	Owner's equity..................	$1,000

It is not difficult to see the relationship between the cash contributed to the business and Mr. Alpha's equity. At this point Mr. Alpha accepts a partner, Mr. Beta, who also contributes $1,000 in cash. A balance sheet at this point would reflect the entrance of Mr. Beta into the business:

ALPHA-BETA COMPANY
BALANCE SHEET

Cash	$2,000	Owners' equity:	
		Mr. Alpha	$1,000
		Mr. Beta	1,000
Total	$2,000	Total	$2,000

We can readily see the relationship between the $2,000 in cash and the $1,000 of equity for each partner. But as soon as we diversify further this apparent relationship becomes blurred. Assume now that Alpha-Beta Company purchases $1,200 in inventory for cash.

ALPHA-BETA COMPANY
BALANCE SHEET

Cash	$ 800	Owners' equity	
Inventory	1,200	Mr. Alpha	1,000
		Mr. Beta	1,000
Total	$2,000	Total	$2,000

Now, who owns the cash and who owns the inventory? We can highlight the problem by assuming that the inventory is destroyed in an uninsured loss. Mr. Beta may feel that since Mr. Alpha invested first, $1,000 of the loss belongs to Mr. Alpha. In fact, they are each said to have an "equity interest" in the net assets of the company, which now total $800. If the partners share on a 50:50 basis they will each receive $400 upon dissolution of the company at the point of the loss, even though they each contributed $1,000. They could have an equity interest of some other ratio, in which case the remaining assets would be distributed in terms of the agreed-upon ratio.

Here are some further examples to illustrate the pervasiveness of the concept of pooled resources. In each case we have inflow and outflow from a pool (Exhibit 6-12).

EXHIBIT 6-12

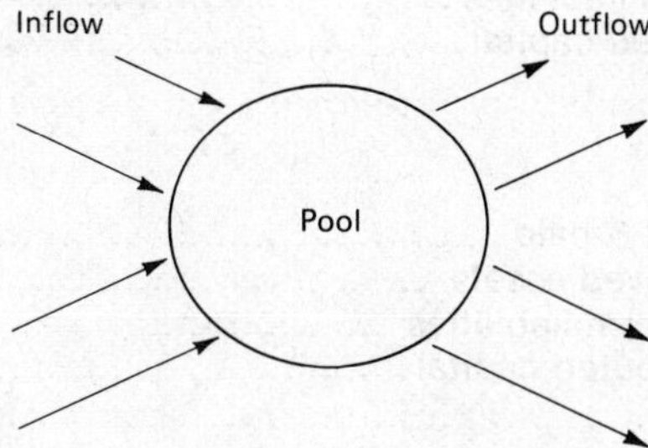

Examples:

1. Stockholders contribute cash to a business, but they cannot trace their individual contributions to any particular use.
2. Many of us have checking or savings accounts. Our deposits enter a pool from which various investments are made. We cannot trace our particular deposit to any specific investment.
3. The taxes we pay enter governmental pools or treasuries from which various disbursements are made. We cannot trace our particular tax dollar to any specific outlay.

In similar manner the sources of working capital enter a pool from which various dispositions are made. It is impossible to trace a particular source to a particular use.

Over the years the most embarrassing questions at annual stockholders' meetings have been of this type:

1. Where did profits go?
2. Why were dividends not larger in view of the profits made?
3. How was it possible to distribute dividends in the face of a loss?
4. What happened to the proceeds from the sale of stock?
5. What happened to the proceeds from the sale of fixed assets?
6. How did the company manage to retire long-term debt in advance of schedule?
7. What became of the proceeds of the bond issue?

The questions seem reasonable, but directors have been unable to answer them. In fact, they could not answer them because of the concept of pooled resources. The statement of changes in financial position provides the answer to all of these questions simultaneously (Exhibit 6-13).

EXHIBIT 6-13

THE EXRIDGE CORPORATION
(1)→**STATEMENT OF CHANGES IN FINANCIAL POSITION**
(2)→**FOR THE YEAR ENDED, DECEMBER 31, 19x2**

(3)→**SOURCES**		
(4)→Operations—(5) Net income before extraordinary items	$ 95,000	
(6)→Gain on sale of long-lived assets	200,000	
Net income	295,000	
(7)→Add-back depreciation	150,000	$ 445,000
(8)→Sale of long-lived assets (at book value)		500,000
(9)→Increase in long-term liabilities		80,000
(10)→Increase in contributed capital		0
Total sources		1,025,000
(11)→**USES**		
Dividends declared & paid	95,000	
(12)→Purchase of long-lived assets	890,000	
(13)→Decrease in long-term liabilities	0	
(13)→Decrease in contributed capital	0	
Total uses		985,000
Net increase in working capital		$ 40,000

The answers to the questions on p. 184 now become apparent. The sources of working capital entered a pool and from the pool various disbursements were made, as indicated by the uses.

Explanatory notes on the statement of changes in financial position contained in Exhibit 6-13 follow:

1. *Title:* The statement has had a variety of titles prior to the issuance of *Accounting Principles Board Opinion No. 19* (in March 1971), as noted below. Significant adherence to the title "statement of changes in financial position," as used in this text, can be expected for financial periods ending on or after December 31, 1971:

	1966[17]
Source and application of:	
Funds	193
Working capital	15
Source and use of:	
Funds	74
Working capital	13
Source and disposition of:	
Funds	44
Working capital	21
Changes in working capital	42
Analysis or summary of changes in working capital	20
Working capital	24
Funds statements	24
Other titles	33
No funds statement	97
Total	600

2. *Date:* The statement covers changes in working capital during the same time period as the other statements.
3. *Sources:* We have said before that there are four major sources of working capital. These are listed in the statement in Exhibit 6-13, even though one of them—increase in contributed capital—was inactive during 19*x*2. In financial reporting inactive sources and uses are *not* shown in the statement of changes in financial position.
4. *Operations:* If operations result in a net income, we have a *source* of working capital. If they result in a loss we have a *use* of working capital. If a net loss is offset by gains and depreciation resulting in a positive net balance, it is customary to include operations as a source:

Operations—Net loss	(———)	
Depreciation	———	
Total		———

5. *Net income:* Net income should be separated from extraordinary items. We recognized this separation in computing earnings per share in Exhibit 6-6.
6. *Gain on sale of long-lived assets:* Any extraordinary gains or losses are recognized at this point. In our example we have a gain of $200,000 in 19*x*2, which we will say resulted from selling long-lived assets in excess of their book value.

[17]Philips and Copeland, *Financial Statements,* p. 121.

Let us assume that the Exridge Corporation sold building and equipment during 19x2 as follows:

1. Cost of building & equipment	$550,000
2. Accumulated depreciation on assets that were sold	⟨50,000⟩
3. Book value of assets that were sold	500,000
4. They were sold for cash	700,000
5. Gain on sale was (4 − 3)	$200,000

The journal entry at the point of sale would be:

Increase (Debit) Cash	$700,000	
Decrease (Debit) Accumulated depreciation	50,000	
	$750,000	
Decrease (Credit) Building & equipment		$550,000
Increase (Credit) Gain on sale of building & equipment		200,000
		$750,000

The gain is the only item in the above entry that appears in the income statement.

7. *Depreciation:* Listing depreciation as a "source" of working capital may suggest that *it is* a source. Depreciation *is not* a source of working capital; neither is it a use.

If depreciation were the only operating expense during the period, earned capital would be reduced by the amount of depreciation. Depreciation has no effect on the working capital accounts (current assets and current liabilities). We do not receive cash by reason of depreciation; nor receivables; nor inventory. We do not owe anything by virtue of depreciation, nor does it give rise to a liability.

Depreciation is neutral with respect to working capital. Why then do we include it as a source in the statement?

You will notice from the income statement (Exhibit 6-6) that depreciation in the amount of $150,000 is listed as an operating expense in 19x2. All other items in the income statement affect working capital—except depreciation.

Sales increase working capital. Cost of goods sold decreases working capital, as do selling and administrative expenses. It is acceptable to show these detailed elements of the income statement as sources and uses; but this is unnecessary, as the statement of changes in financial position is shown in the context of an income statement. We can always examine the income statement for the derivations of net income.

Because depreciation was *deducted* in arriving at net income, it is restored in the statement; hence the word "add-back." It was treated as a use of funds in the income statement, which is appropriate for measuring the results of operations.

We could, of course, show net income of $445,000 ($295,000 + $150,000), but this would only confuse the reader. He has noted the income figure from the income statement, and would question the use of a different figure in the statement of changes in financial position. In order to have these statements articulate with each other, the add-back technique is used.

8. *Sale of long-lived assets:* We have shown the "gain" on sale of long-lived assets as an element of operations. This should be done in order to have the net income

figure in the statement of changes in financial position agree with the net income figure in the income statement.

Proceeds from the sale of long-lived assets were actually $700,000. As we have recognized $200,000 of this amount in income, the other $500,000 is shown as a conversion at book value.

9. *Increase in long-term liabilities:* Because the balance sheet provides details as to long-term liability accounts, we need only refer to them as a class of items in the funds statement. We note that long-term liabilities as a group increased by $80,000 during the year. This is a source of working capital. Any increase in minority interests would also be treated as a source.
10. *Increase in contributed capital:* As noted before, this item would not be shown in an actual statment of changes in financial position because it was inactive during 19*x*2. Any increase in contributed capital (Exhibit 6-5) during the period would represent a source of working capital.
11. *Uses:* There are also four uses of working capital. Dividends represent a decrease in earned capital – hence it is a use of working capital.
12. *Purchase of long-lived assets:* Sales and purchases of long-lived assets are shown separately as sources and uses. Purchases are not offset against sales. This is true of the other categories as well.

    In note 6 we were told that assets costing $550,000 were sold during the period. This item is added to the difference in the buildings and equipment amounts for 19*x*1 and 19*x*2 to compute the amount of the assets purchased during 19*x*2:

Building & equipment account 19*x*2	$1,100,000
Building & equipment account 19*x*1	⟨900,000⟩
Net increase	200,000
Add: cost of building & equipment sold during 19*x*2	550,000
Total building & equipment purchased during 19*x*2	750,000

In addition, other long-lived assets were purchased:

Building & equipment (above)	$ 750,000
Land	100,000
Investments	30,000
Other assets & deferred charges	10,000
Total	$ 890,000

13. *Other uses:* These items would not be shown on an actual funds statement because they were inactive during 19*x*2.
14. *Net increase in working capital:* This figure agrees with our prior computation on p. 180, indicating that we have accounted for all sources and uses.

6.11 THE EVOLUTION OF FINANCIAL REPORTING

We have discussed current financial reporting conventions to this point. We have demonstrated that financial reporting is not static. The required use of the statement of changes in financial position is an example of the evolutionary trends in financial reporting.

There are several other trends which will play an increasing role in future financial reporting. We discuss a few of the more significant ones here.

LEASES

Accounting Principles Board Opinion No. 5, issued in 1964, made it a requirement that (1) leases which are clearly in substance installment purchases of property be treated as purchases, and (2) leases which are not in substance purchases be *disclosed* rather than *capitalized* in the financial statements. The disclosure can be made in the body of the statement or in the accompanying footnotes.

Prior to *APB Opinion No. 5,* disclosure of information pertaining to leases in financial statements was not commonplace. Trends in the disclosure of lease information are affirmed by the following statistics:[18]

LONG-TERM LEASES: DISCLOSURE BY LESSORS

	1966
Information disclosed by lessors:	
Types of property	40
Annual or aggregate rental amount	13
Expiration date or terms of leases	3
Renewal or purchase option	3
Other information	11
Total	70
Number of companies:	
Setting forth details	45
Not setting forth details	21
Not indicating leases	534
	600
Accounting method for lease-related assets:	
Financing method:	
In current or other assets as receivable	3
Residual value in property section	7
Operating method, in property section	2
Method not identified or inferred	12
Total number of items with balance sheet disclosure	24

[18] Philips and Copeland, *Financial Statements,* p. 72.

LONG-TERM LEASES: DISCLOSURE BY LESSEES

	1966	1960	1951
Information disclosed by lessees:			
Annual or aggregate rental amount	177	148	61
Schedule of rentals by period of years	44	N/C	N/C
Types of property	142	N/C	N/C
Expiration date or term of leases	132	115	26
Minimum rent or basis for calculating rent	125	N/C	N/C
Renewal or purchase option	65	15	13
Number of leases	45	60	37
Sell-leaseback feature	14	22	3
Other information	19	N/C	N/C
Total	763	360	140
Number of companies:			
Setting forth details	265	117	61
Not setting forth details	48	105	139
Not indicating leases	287	378	400
	600	600	600

N/C—Not compiled.

PRICE-LEVEL

We mentioned earlier that financial statements are prepared on an assumption of stable purchasing power. In 1963 the American Institute of Certified Public Accountants published its research study on price-level changes.[19] Progress is being made toward reporting the effects of price-level changes in financial statements. Following the publication of the research study in 1963, the board has more recently recommended that firms *supplement* their conventional financial statements with price-level adjusted data. We anticipate a trend in the disclosure of price-level adjusted financial data, leading in time to required disclosure. This subject is dealt with more extensively in chapter 8.

ACCOUNTING FOR HUMAN RESOURCES

Attempts are even being made to account for and report on human resources in financial statements—at present in the form of supplemental information. The financial statements of R. G. Barry Corporation, contained in the appendix to this chapter, are illustrative of this trend.

Years may pass before accounting for human resources is an integral part of financial reporting. But many of the ingredients of financial reporting that we now take for granted had such humble beginnings. A few firms appear willing to give more information than is required. As the utility of the new information is proven, more firms subscribe to the disclosure. Ultimately the demand for such information is strong enough to prompt action by regulatory bodies.

[19]*Reporting the Financial Effects of Price-Level Changes,* Accounting Research Study No. 6 (New York: American Institute of Certified Public Accountants, 1963).

CURRENT VALUES

We can also expect a trend toward valuing assets on a basis other than historical cost. Current values are already permitted in purchasing a business, but as yet it is not permissible to restate the value of assets other than through the purchase of another firm.

Price-level accounting requires a restatement of the value of assets, but it only takes into account the change in value that results from variations in purchasing power. It does not take into account appreciation or depreciation in value due to other factors, such as appreciation in the value of land resulting from increasing demand.

It is expected that price-level accounting will point to the need for full adjustment to current values.

FORECAST DATA[20]

The inclusion of forecast data in annual reports is an issue which is steadily gaining acceptance within professional circles. At the time of this writing, the SEC was holding public hearings on the subject. Professional groups such as the FEI (Financial Executives Institute), AICPA, NAA (National Association of Accountants), and others have given intensive study to this matter. The United Kingdom and several other countries have moved in this direction and their experiences have been followed with close interest in the United States.

The role of the CPA-auditor in this area is being defined more in terms of attesting to the *assumptions* and *methodology* underlying forecasts rather than verification of the data itself.

For an example of published forecast data in the form of *pro forma,* see the Commonwealth Edison Company's *Financial Review, 1971,* in the appendix to this chapter.

These innovative trends indicate that financial reporting is a viable and responsive institution. Those who have a strong interest in improving the quality of financial reports can do something about it. We may lament the pace at which change occurs, but even the pace can be accelerated if sufficient effort is made. Changes in financial reporting appear to be most responsive to empirical efforts and not to armchair theorizing.

6.12 SUMMARY

We have discussed current and future financial reporting conventions. We were concerned in this chapter with the formal outputs of the accounting information system, i.e., the financial statements.

[20]See John J. Willingham, Charles E. Smith, and Martin E. Taylor, "Should the CPA's Opinion Be Extended to Include Forecasts," *The Financial Executive,* September 1970, pp. 80–89. Also, the Institute of Chartered Accountants in England and Wales, *Accountants' Reports on Profit Forecasts,* July 1969; and Eldon S. Hendriksen, "Disclosure – Insights into Requirements in the United Kingdom," *The International Journal of Accountancy,* Spring 1969, pp. 21–32.

The financial statements comprise four interdependent documents: (1) the balance sheet, (2) the income statement, (3) the statement of retained earnings, and (4) the statement of changes in financial position. We discussed the purpose and content of these statements in considerable detail. The purpose of the balance sheet is to portray the financial position of a firm on a specific date. The purpose of the income statement is to show the results of operations during a period of time (usually one year). The statement of retained earnings details the changes in earned capital during the same period of time; and the statement indicates the sources and uses of working capital during the period.

We noted that financial reporting is a viable and responsive institution. Some major trends that will affect financial reporting in the future were discussed briefly: (1) reporting leases, (2) price-level adjustments, (3) accounting for human resources, (4) current value accounting, and (5) the inclusion of forecast information in financial statements.

CHAPTER 6 REFERENCES AND ADDITIONAL READINGS

American Institute of Certified Public Accountants. Refer to Accounting Principles Board *Opinions* and *Statements*, as well as the *Accounting Research Studies* listed in the Unit II introduction.

Backer, Morton. *Financial Reporting for Security Investment and Credit Decisions.* Research Studies in Management Reporting No. 3. New York: National Association of Accountants, 1970.

Ball, Ray, and Brown, Philip. "Portfolio Theory and Accounting." *Journal of Accounting Research,* Autumn 1969, pp. 300–320.

Beaver, William H.; Kettler, Paul; and Scholes, Myron. "The Association Between Market Determined and Accounting Determined Risk Measures." *The Accounting Review,* October 1970, pp. 654–82.

Benston, George J. "Published Corporate Accounting Data and Stock Prices." *Empirical Research in Accounting: Selected Studies 1967,* supplement to the *Journal of Accounting Research,* pp. 1–54.

———. "The Value of the SEC's Accounting Disclosure Requirements." *The Accounting Review,* July 1969, pp. 515–32.

Bevis, Herman W. *Corporate Financial Reporting in a Competitive Environment.* New York: Columbia University Press, 1965.

Block, Frank E. "A Security Analyst Looks at Accounting." *The Financial Executive,* November 1971, pp. 22–24.

Block, Max. "Improving the Credibility of Financial Statements." *The CPA Journal,* January 1972, pp. 51–61.

Bollom, William J., and Weygandt, Jerry J. "An Examination of Some Interim Reporting Theories for a Seasonal Business." *The Accounting Review,* January 1972, pp. 75–84.

Brenner, Vincent C. "Are Annual Reports Being Read?" *National Public Accountant,* November 1971, pp. 16–21.

Brenner, Vincent C. "Financial Statement Users' Views of the Desirability of Reporting Current Cost Information." *Journal of Accounting Research,* Autumn 1970, pp. 159–66.

Burton, John C. "Symposium on Ethics in Corporate Financial Reporting." *Journal of Accountancy,* January 1972, pp. 46–50.

Carey, John L. *The Rise of the Accounting Profession.* Volume I (1896–1936); Volume II (1937–1969). New York: American Institute of Certified Public Accountants, 1969 and 1970.

Chambers, Raymond J. *Accounting Evaluation and Economic Behavior.* Englewood Cliffs, N. J.: Prentice-Hall, Inc., 1966.

Committee to Prepare a Statement of Basic Accounting Theory. *A Statement of Basic Accounting Theory.* Sarasota, Fla.: American Accounting Association, 1966.

Curley, Anthony J. "Conglomerate Earnings Per Share: Real and Transitory Growth." *The Accounting Review*, July 1971, pp. 519–28.

Deinzer, Harvey T. *Development of Accounting Thought.* New York: Holt, Rinehart & Winston, Inc., 1965.

Hendriksen, Eldon S. *Accounting Theory.* Rev. ed. Homewood, Ill.: Richard D. Irwin, Inc., 1970.

Jones, Donald P. "Management Freedom in Annual Reports." *The Financial Executive*, August 1971, pp. 23–26.

Kellog, Howard L., and Poloway, Morton. *Accountants SEC Practice Manual.* Chicago: Commerce Clearing House, 1971.

Lev, Baruch. "The Informational Approach to Aggregation in Financial Statements." *Journal of Accounting Research*, Spring 1970, pp. 78–94.

Newton, James E. "SEC Rules for Revelation." *The Financial Executive*, October 1971, pp. 28–31.

Niederhoffer, Victor. "The Predictive Content of First-Quarter Earnings Reports." *The Journal of Business*, January 1970, pp. 60–62.

Pacter, Paul. "Applying APB Opinion No. 18—Equity Method." *The Journal of Accountancy*, September 1971, pp. 54–67.

Palomba, Giuseppe. *A Mathematical Interpretation of the Balance Sheet.* New York: Augustus M. Kelly, Publishers, 1968.

Parker, James E. "New Rules for Determining Earnings Per Share." *Financial Analysts Journal*, February 1970, pp. 49–53.

Philips, G. Edward, and Copeland, Ronald M. *Financial Statements: Problems from Current Practice.* Englewood Cliffs, N. J.: Prentice-Hall, Inc., 1969.

Rappaport, Alfred, and Lerner, Eugene M. "Public Reporting by Diversified Companies." *Financial Analysts Journal*, January-February 1970, pp. 54–64.

Ross, Howard. *Financial Statements: A Crusade for Current Values.* Toronto: Pitman Publishing Company, 1969.

Schoenfeld, Hanns-Martin. "New German Regulations for the Publication of Financial Statements." *International Journal of Accounting*, Spring 1970, pp. 69–88.

Smith, James E., and Smith, Nora P. "Readability: A Measure of the Performance of the Communication Function in Financial Reporting." *The Accounting Review*, July 1971, pp. 552–61.

Sterling, Robert R. "The Going Concern: An Examination." *Accounting Review*, July 1968, pp. 481–502.

______. "Elements of Pure Accounting Theory." *Accounting Review*, January 1967, pp. 62–73.

______. "Conservatism: The Fundamental Principle of Valuation in Traditional Accounting." *Abacus*, December 1967, pp. 109–132.

Taft, Robert W. "The Greening of the Red Herring Prospectus." *The Financial Executive*, November 1971, pp. 73–76.

Thomas, Eliot B. *Federal Securities Act Handbook.* Philadelphia: Committee on Continuing Legal Education of the American Law Institute and American Bar Association, 1969.

Toan, Arthur B. Jr. "Does Accountancy's View of Human Behavior Meet Today's Needs?" *The Price Waterhouse Review.* Summer-Autumn 1971, pp. 12–19.

CHAPTER 6 QUESTIONS, PROBLEMS, AND CASES

6- 1. List and discuss the chief criticisms of financial reporting in the United States. Propose solutions.

6- 2. "Data generated for tax purposes may differ from data compiled in the financial statements." What are the primary reasons for this difference?

6- 3. Since bank loan decisions are predicated upon the ability of the borrower to repay, what financial information is most valuable to the lender?

6- 4. Identify and state the purpose of the four documents that comprise the financial statements.

6- 5. Discuss the *normal operating cycle* concept and contrast it with the concept of a fiscal or financial year.

6- 6. "If the only purpose of the financial statements is to give investors the information they need to make rational choices, then it can be said that it fails in several respects." What are these shortcomings?

6- 7. Should firms issue detailed budgets and projections as external information? Explain.

6- 8. "No system can afford to give every user all the information he *needs,* let alone wants." Comment on this statement.

6- 9. Give the meaning or implication of each term or phrase:
(a) Prospectus
(b) Formal output statements
(c) Business ethics
(d) Credibility climate
(e) Attest function
(f) Production function
(g) Convertible bonds
(h) Prior period adjustment

6-10. List and define ten output rules governing financial statements.

6-11. Distinguish *operating, non-operating,* and *extraordinary* items as contained in an income statement.

6-12. What is meant by the term "*pro forma* earnings per share"?

6-13. What burden for improving the communications level of financial reporting belongs to the user and what burden belongs to the accountant?

6-14. Why is it so important to establish a credibility climate in financial reporting?

6-15. What is *working capital* and why is it important?

6-16. Explain the concept of *pooled resources.*

6-17. Identify some innovative trends in financial reporting.

6-18. Besides the financial statements, what information does the annual report typically contain? Is this information verified by independent auditors? Why?

6-19. "What interim statements lack in authority is compensated for by their utility." Explain the meaning of this statement.

6-20. Depict the normal operating cycle by completing the following diagram:

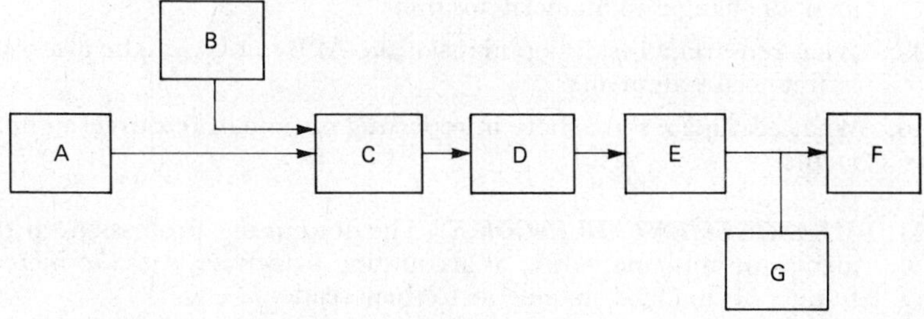

6-21. Explain the current asset rule in interim reports.

6-22. Within the current asset section of the balance sheet, how is the order of accounts determined?

6-23. Are supplies and merchandise inventory both prepaid expenses? Explain.

6-24. Distinguish between investments and marketable securities. Is liquidity a major consideration? Why?

6-25. Discuss the nature and purpose of *contra-accounts.*

6-26. How is the rank order of plant and equipment accounts determined? Why do you suppose this particular order has developed?

6-27. Give the meaning or implication of each balance sheet term or phrase:

(a) Cut-off
(b) Contra-accounts
(c) Liquidity
(d) Deferred charge
(e) Restricted investment
(f) Book value
(g) Accruals
(h) Minority interest
(i) Contributed capital

6-28. Explain the nature of *intangible assets.* List and define three intangible assets commonly encountered in financial reporting.

6-29. Give both the legal and operational definition of a liability.

6-30. Distinguish between a *deferred charge* and a *prepaid expense.*

6-31. "Stockholders are said to have a *residual equity* in the assets of a business." Explain the meaning of this statement.

6-32. "The utility of the financial statements is enhanced by having a thorough knowledge of the ground rules under which they are issued." What are the ground rules, and why do they increase utility?

6-33. Discuss the role of *conservatism* in the application of valuation norms for balance sheet accounts.

6-34. What is the computational difference between primary earnings per share, earnings per share on extraordinary items, and fully diluted earnings per share?

6-35. What type of depreciation can be included in:
(a) Cost of goods sold
(b) Selling expenses
(c) Administrative expenses

6-36. What is the opinion of the Accounting Principles Board concerning the reflection of prior period adjustments in the statement of retained earnings? What criteria determines the propriety of an adjustment?

6-37. "Depreciation is not a source of working capital." Explain its appearance on the statement of changes in financial position as a *source.*

6-38. Why not show net income exclusive of depreciation as a net figure on the statement of changes in financial position?

6-39. What requirements did opinions of the APB impose on the disclosure of leases in financial statements?

6-40. What advantages are there in reporting of human resources in financial statements?

6-41. ***MEASUREMENT OF INCOME*** The accounting profession, in the development and implementation of accounting principles, seeks to increase the usefulness of financial statements to their readers.

Required:

(a) An authoritative accounting body recommended including in net income all items of profit and loss recognized in the period except prior period adjustments and capital transactions involving equity accounts, with extraordinary items shown separately as an element of net income of the period.
(1) List the *advantages* of the recommendation.
(2) List the *disadvantages* of the recommendation.

(b) The recommendation specified in requirement (a) above is based on the premise that capital transactions should be distinguished from income.
(1) Why should capital transactions be distinguished from income?

(2) In what way does the income expected to be generated by an asset relate to its acquisition cost and valuation in financial statements? Discuss.

(From the CPA exam.)

6-42. ***INCOME STATEMENT*** Prepare an income statement from the following data:

Selling expenses are 10% of sales. General expenses are 15% of sales and also equal 25% of the cost of goods sold. Merchandise inventory at the end of the year is $52,000; this is 30% greater than the beginning inventory. Income before income taxes for the year is $60,000. The income tax rate is 22% on the first $25,000 of net income, and 50% on income in excess of $25,000.

6-43. ***JOURNAL ENTRIES*** Assume the Johnston Company prepares financial statements on December 31, 19*x*1. Give journal entries to record the following:

(a) Factory employees are paid $3,500 every two weeks (fourteen days). The next payday is January 3, 19*x*2.
(b) $1,200 of supplies were used this year.
(c) This year the Johnston Company's income tax is computed as $22,700.
(d) The Rider Company was bought for $85,000. The fair market value of the business, however, was only $67,000 at the date of purchase.
(e) The Johnston Company declared a cash dividend of $8,000.
(f) The Johnston Company paid a cash dividend of $8,000.
(g) Federal income tax computed for tax purposes is $22,700. The computation based on financial income, however, is $31,200.

6-44. ***SOURCE AND USE OF FUNDS*** Suppose the entry to record the sale of equipment is:

(Debit)	Cash	34,000	
(Debit)	Accumulated depreciation	32,600	
(Debit)	Loss on sale of equipment	3,400	
(Credit)	Equipment		70,000

What information from this sale appears on the statement of source and application of funds, and how is it shown?

6-45. ***DEFERRALS*** Assume that during 19*x*1 the Sommerhill Clothing Store had the following transactions:

July 28—Paid $4,780 for a three-year insurance coverage beginning on September 1, 19*x*1.

Sept. 30—Collected $1,200 from a tennant who is leasing a portion of the company's warehouse. The rent was for the six months beginning October 1, 19*x*1.

Excluding cash, give the *account* and the *amount* that would appear on the financial statements prepared on Dec. 31, 19*x*1. Do not prepare financial statements.

6-46. ***INCOME STATEMENT*** Given the following information, construct an income statement including the computation of earnings per share (before and after extraordinary items and fully diluted):

General and administrative expenses	$ 60,000
Federal income tax for tax purposes	10,800
Federal income tax on financial income	21,000

Depreciation of plant and equipment	28,000
Merchandise inventory, Jan. 1, 19x1	110,000
Merchandise inventory, Dec. 31, 19x1	98,200
Sales discount	4,800
Net income of minority interests	10,000
Extraordinary gains (net of tax)	84,000
Non-operating expenses	8,400
Purchases	326,100
Sales returns and allowances	16,000
Extraordinary losses (net of tax)	4,000
Non-operating income	14,600
Selling expenses	92,000
Gross sales	584,000

Additional Information:
25,000 common shares outstanding.
500 convertible bonds at $100 each with an interest rate of 5%. Conversion price of shares is $40.

6-47. ***SOURCES AND USES OF WORKING CAPITAL*** Describe the following as either sources or uses of working capital:

(a) Sold $40,000 of operating assets.
(b) Sold $8,000 of inventory.
(c) Paid off a $1,000 short-term note.
(d) Net income was $52,000.
(e) Paid dividends of $40,000 to stockholders.
(f) Sold $100,000 in common stock.
(g) Purchased inventory of $12,000.
(h) Assumed a $140,000 mortgage for a new building.
(i) Invested in marketable securities.
(j) Received $60,000 from a successful lawsuit.
(k) Minority interest increased by $5,000.

6-48. ***EARNINGS PER SHARE*** Suppose the following information is available:

Net Income $483,000
Earnings per Share $3.22
Pro Forma Earnings per Share $3.18
5.9% convertible bonds, convertible at $30 per share

Required:

Compute the dollar amount of convertible bonds.

6-49. ***INCOME STATEMENT*** Supply the missing figures:

Sales	150		200	189
Selling expenses		10	13	12
Total operating expenses	45			
Merchandise inventory, Jan. 1	10		25	32
Cost of goods sold		87		
Administrative expenses	20	18		15
Gross profit on sales	60			86
Merchandise inventory, Dec. 31		33	11	
Net income from operations		25	31	
Purchases	95	100	97	
Goods available for sale				127

Note: *Each column is an individual problem*—work each column separately.

6-50. ***STATEMENT OF CHANGES IN FINANCIAL POSITION*** The balance sheets of the Griffin Company provided the information shown below:

	Dec. 31, 1969	Dec. 31, 1970
Cash	$ 4,000	$ 13,000
Accounts receivable	9,000	10,000
Inventory	7,000	5,000
Permanent investments	2,000	2,000
Plant	30,000	30,000
Equipment	20,000	22,000
Land	10,000	20,000
Patents	8,000	7,000
Goodwill	1,000	0
	$91,000	$109,000
Allowance for deprec.—plant	$ 7,000	$ 10,000
Allowance for deprec.—equip	10,000	8,000
Accounts payable	8,000	7,000
Accrued wages	1,000	0
Long-term notes payable	10,000	13,000
Capital stock	50,000	60,000
Retained earnings	5,000	11,000
	$91,000	$109,000

Additional data:

(a) Net income for the year, $7,000.
(b) Depreciation on plant for the year, $3,000.
(c) Depreciation on equipment for the year, $2,000.
(d) Amortization of patents for the year, $1,000.
(e) At the end of the year sold equipment costing $8,000 for $3,000 cash. The equipment was 50% depreciated.
(f) Purchased land costing $10,000; paid $2,000 cash; gave long-term note for the balance.
(g) Paid $5,000 on long-term notes.
(h) Sold $10,000 capital stock at par.
(i) Wrote off goodwill.
(j) Purchased equipment costing $10,000; paid one-half in cash, balance due in twelve months.

Required:

Prepare a statement of changes in financial position.

6-51. ***BALANCE SHEET*** John Tuffy is the sole proprietor of Tuffy's Soup Company. The soup company is an established business founded over thirty years ago by Mr. Tuffy himself. Lately, Mr. Tuffy has experienced a cash flow problem. Because of a very low cash balance, he has applied for an $8,000 loan from the Green Dollar State Bank.

As part of the loan application, the bank requires its applicants to submit a balance sheet. Mr. Tuffy, however, has never maintained formal business records; instead he records any significant activity in a notebook diary. With your assistance Mr. Tuffy is hoping to construct the necessary financial statement. From the notebook and Mr. Tuffy's memory you obtain the following information about assets and liabilities:

Assets

Cash in the cash register	$ 75
Owed to the Soup Company by customers	3,700
Mr. Tuffy's personal bank account	840

Tuffy Soup Company's bank account	500
Cost of ingredients in inventory on hand	14,300
Mr. Tuffy's personal residence	38,000
Soup preparation premises used in the business	41,000
Office furniture owned by the business	3,200
Municipal bonds owned by Mrs. Tuffy	4,000

Liabilities

Owed to creditors of Tuffy's Soup Company	$ 9,000
Mr. Tuffy's outstanding personal bills	1,500
Salaries owed to employees	1,450
Mortgage due in 1978 on the Soup Company's premises	11,000

Mr. Tuffy invested $15,000 when the business was first established over thirty years ago. Because of the Soup Company's success, no further funds have been invested since the company was founded, except for Mr. Tuffy's recent investment in cash of $800 needed to meet the company's current obligations.

Required:

Prepare a balance sheet for the Tuffy Soup Company.

6-52. ***PREPARATION OF FINANCIAL STATEMENT DATA*** Consider the following account balances of the Zeebee Service Company at the close of its fiscal year on December 31, 19*x*1:

Accounts payable	$ 16,000
Accounts receivable	22,400
Accumulated depreciation – equipment	26,400
Advertising (prepaid)	1,500
Cash	9,000
Depreciation expense	4,800
Insurance expense	1,200
Notes payable	26,000
Prepaid insurance	1,400
Salaries expense	52,000
Salaries payable	7,800
Sales	162,000
Store & office equipment	51,000
Supplies	8,000
Supplies used	43,500
Utilities expense	6,000

Required:

Using the account balance information, calculate:

(a) The trial balance total at December 31, 19*x*1.
(b) Working capital.
(c) The end-total (balancing figure) as it would appear on the balance sheet for the Zeebee Service Company as of December 31, 19*x*1.
(d) Capital at December 31, 19*x*1.
(e) Income from operations.

6-53. ***STATEMENT OF CHANGES IN FINANCIAL POSITION*** The net changes in the balance sheet accounts of Gilmore Company for the year 19*x*1 are shown below:

	Debit	Credit
Investments		$25,000
Land	$ 3,200	
Buildings	35,000	
Machinery	6,000	
Office equipment		1,500
Allowance for depreciation:		
Buildings		2,000
Machinery		900
Office equipment	600	
Discount on bonds	2,000	
Bonds payable		40,000
Capital stock—preferred	10,000	
Capital stock—common		10,000
Paid-in capital		5,000
Retained earnings		9,800
Working capital	37,400	
	$94,200	$94,200

Additional information:

(a) Cash dividends of $18,000 were declared December 15, 19*x*1, payable January 15, 19*x*2.
(b) The investments were sold for $27,500.
(c) A building which cost $45,000 and had a depreciated basis of $40,500 was sold for $50,000.
(d) The following entry was made to record an exchange of an old machine for a new one:

Machinery	$13,000	
Allowance for depreciation—machinery	5,000	
Machinery		$ 7,000
Cash		11,000

(e) A fully depreciated office machine which cost $15,000 was written off.
(f) Preferred stock of $10,000 par value was redeemed for $10,200.
(g) The company sold 1,000 shares of its common stock (par value $10) on June 15, 19*x*1, for $15 a share. There were 13,240 shares outstanding on December 31, 19*x*1.

Required: Prepare a statement of changes in financial position.

(Adapted from the CPA exam.)

APPENDIX TO CHAPTER 6

PROSPECTUS

1,335,690 SHARES

TIME INCORPORATED

COMMON STOCK

Par Value $1 Per Share

OFFERED AS SET FORTH HEREIN UNDER
"STOCK OPTION PLANS"
TO CERTAIN KEY EMPLOYEES OF
TIME INCORPORATED AND ITS SUBSIDIARIES

The shares of Common Stock to which this Prospectus relates have been listed (subject to notice of issuance as to unissued shares) on the New York Stock Exchange.

Some or all of the 1,335,690 shares of Common Stock to which this Prospectus relates, acquired or to be acquired upon exercise of the options referred to herein, may from time to time be sold on the New York Stock Exchange at prices then prevailing on such Exchange without the payment of any underwriting commissions or discounts other than brokers' fees normally paid in connection with normal brokers' transactions effected on such exchange. No part of the proceeds of such resales will be received by the Company. The Company understands that the Securities and Exchange Commission may take the view (such optionees not so conceding) that some or all of the optionees making resales may be underwriters within the meaning of the Securities Act of 1933 with respect to such resales. This Prospectus is made applicable to any such resale.

The closing price for the Common Stock on the New York Stock Exchange on April 26, 1972, was $55¼ per share.

THESE SECURITIES HAVE NOT BEEN APPROVED OR DISAPPROVED BY THE SECURITIES AND EXCHANGE COMMISSION NOR HAS THE COMMISSION PASSED UPON THE ACCURACY OR ADEQUACY OF THIS PROSPECTUS. ANY REPRESENTATION TO THE CONTRARY IS A CRIMINAL OFFENSE.

This Prospectus does not constitute an offer to sell securities in any State to any person to whom it is unlawful to make such offer in such State.

No person has been authorized by the Company to give any information or to make any representations other than as contained in this Prospectus in connection with the offer contained in this Prospectus and, if given or made, such information or representations must not be relied upon.

Neither delivery of this Prospectus nor any sale made hereunder shall, under any circumstances, create any implication that there has been no change in the affairs of the Company since the date hereof. If any such change occurs which is material, this Prospectus will be amended or supplemented prior to such delivery or sale.

STOCK OPTION PLANS*

Old Plans

The Company's** original "Restricted Stock Option Plan for Key Employees of Time Incorporated and Its Subsidiaries" was ratified by the stockholders of the Company on April 19, 1956, and amendments thereto were similarly ratified on April 18, 1957. It expired by its terms on December 31, 1958. The Company's second such stock option plan was ratified by the stockholders on April 20, 1961, and expired on December 31, 1962. The Company's third such stock option plan was ratified by the stockholders on April 18, 1963, and expired on December 31, 1965. In addition, on April 11, 1960, the

The date of this Prospectus is April 28, 1972.

Company's subsidiary, Eastex Incorporated, granted restricted stock options to five key employees of Eastex to purchase an aggregate of 19,500 shares of Common Stock of the Company. The aforementioned stock option plans and the options granted by Eastex are herein together called the Old Plans. All options granted under the Old Plans have been exercised or have terminated.

1967 Plan

On April 20, 1967, the stockholders approved a "Qualified Stock Option Plan for Key Employees of Time Incorporated and Its Subsidiaries" (herein called the 1967 Plan), and such 1967 Plan terminated in accordance with its terms on December 31, 1969.

The purchase price of the Common Stock under each option granted under the 1967 Plan is not less than 100% of the fair market value of the stock on the date of grant. Such fair market value was determined by the Board of Directors at not less than the mean of the high and low prices of the Common Stock on the New York Stock Exchange on the day on which the option was granted.

The term of each such option is five years from the date of grant, subject to earlier termination if the optionee dies or leaves the service of the Company. The options are nontransferable except by will or the laws of descent and distribution. Each option provides that the optionee agrees to remain in the employ of the Company, or at its election one of its subsidiaries, for at least two years from the date of grant. In all cases of termination of employment (otherwise than by reason of death or in violation of the optionee's employment agreement), the optionee may exercise his option, to the extent exercisable at the date of termination, within a period of three months after such termination, but not after five years from the date of grant. Upon the death of the optionee, his option, to the extent exercisable at the date of his death, may be exercised by his legatee, personal representative or distributee within a period of one year after his death, but not after five years from the date of grant.

The options contain provisions for the adjustment of the number and class of shares covered thereby and the option price contained therein in the event of changes in the outstanding shares of Common Stock by reason of stock dividends, split ups, recapitalizations, mergers, consolidations, combinations or exchanges of shares and the like. Each such option granted by the Company is exercisable (cumulatively to the extent not previously exercised) at the rate of one-fifth of the aggregate number of shares covered thereby for each successive six months' period following the date of grant. Directors of the Company, as such, were not eligible to receive options. As required by the Internal Revenue Code of 1954, as amended, an option granted under the 1967 Plan, although otherwise exercisable, may not be exercised if the optionee has "outstanding" (as defined in such Code) another previously issued qualified or restricted stock option with a higher option price.

New Plan

A new "1969 Qualified Stock Option Plan for Key Employees of Time Incorporated and Its Subsidiaries" (herein called the New Plan) was adopted by the Board of Directors on October 16,

---

* This Prospectus is applicable to (i) the 924,990 shares of Common Stock of the Company which have heretofore been issued upon the exercise of options granted under the Old Plans, (ii) the 85,700 shares which may be issued upon the exercise of options granted under the 1967 Plan and (iii) the 325,000 shares which may be issued upon the exercise of options which have been and may be granted under the New Plan or which have heretofore been issued upon the exercise of options granted thereunder. This Prospectus is made applicable to said 1,335,690 shares after the issuance thereof for the reason that it might be deemed that some of the persons who have acquired or shall acquire shares upon the exercise of such options either (a) have purchased or may purchase such shares from the Company with a view to distribution or (b) are or will be "directly or indirectly controlling or controlled by the issuer" within the meaning of Section 2(11) of the Securities Act of 1933, as amended, and might effectuate sales of such shares under circumstances requiring the delivery of the shares to be preceded by a Prospectus.

** Except where the context indicates otherwise, "the Company" means Time Incorporated and/or one or more or all of its subsidiaries. The principal executive office of Time Incorporated is located at Time & Life Building, Rockefeller Center, New York, N. Y. 10020 (Tel. No. 212-586-1212).

1969, and was approved by the stockholders of the Company on April 16, 1970. The purpose of the New Plan is to provide an additional incentive to such key employees to continue in the employ of the Company or its subsidiaries and to give them a greater interest as stockholders in the continued and increasing success of the Company.

325,000 shares of the Company's authorized but unissued Common Stock were reserved for issuance upon exercise of options granted under the New Plan. The New Plan is administered by the Board of Directors (or by a committee of at least three members thereof, each of whom shall be ineligible to participate in the New Plan) which may grant options only to regular salaried employees (including officers) of the Company and its subsidiaries, except that Messrs. Roy E. Larsen and James A. Linen are expressly excluded from receiving any options under the New Plan. Directors of the Company, as such, are not eligible to receive options. In determining the employees to whom, and the time or times at which, options shall be granted under the New Plan, the Board of Directors may take into account the nature of the services rendered by the respective employees, their present and potential contributions to the Company's success and such other factors as the Board in its discretion shall deem relevant.

The purchase price specified in each option must be at least 100% of the fair market value of the Common Stock on the date of grant. Such fair market value is determined by the Board of Directors at not less than the mean of the high and low prices of the Common Stock on the New York Stock Exchange on the day on which the option is granted.

The term of each option is determined by the Board of Directors but may not be more than five years from the date of grant, subject to earlier termination if the optionee dies or leaves the service of the Company. Options are not transferable except by will or the laws of descent and distribution. Each employee receiving an option must agree to remain in the employ of the Company or one of its subsidiaries for at least two years from the date of grant. In all cases of termination of employment (otherwise than by reason of death or in violation of the optionee's employment agreement), the optionee may exercise his option, to the extent exercisable at the date of termination, within a period of three months after such termination, but not after five years from the date of grant. Upon the death of the optionee, his option, to the extent exercisable at the date of his death, may be exercised by his legatee, personal representative or distributee within a period of one year after his death, but not after five years from the date of grant.

The options may contain such provisions as the Board of Directors shall determine to be appropriate for the adjustment of the number and class of shares covered thereby and the option price contained therein in the event of changes in the outstanding shares of Common Stock by reason of stock dividends, split ups, recapitalizations, mergers, consolidations, combinations or exchanges of shares and the like; and, in the event of any such change in the outstanding Common Stock of the Company, the aggregate number and class of shares of Common Stock available under the New Plan and the maximum number of shares which may be granted to any individual shall be appropriately adjusted by the Board of Directors. Except as provided above, no eligible employee may receive options under the New Plan covering in excess of 10,000 shares. As required by the Internal Revenue Code of 1954, as amended, an option granted under the New Plan, although otherwise exercisable, may not be exercised if the optionee has "outstanding" (as defined in such Code) another previously issued qualified or restricted stock option with a higher option price. An option granted under the New Plan may be exercisable in whole at any time or in part from time to time as the Board of Directors may determine. Each option presently outstanding under the New Plan is exercisable (cumulatively to the extent not previously exercised) at the rate of one-fifth of the aggregate numbers of shares covered thereby for each successive six months' period following the date of grant.

Unless theretofore terminated by the Board of Directors, the New Plan will terminate on December 31, 1973. Subject to certain limitations set forth therein, the Board of Directors may make such modifications of the New Plan as it may deem advisable. No termination or modification of the New Plan may, without the consent of an optionee, adversely affect his rights under an option theretofore granted him.

Summary

As of March 1, 1972, there were outstanding options granted under the New Plan to purchase 202,550 shares of Common Stock at $48.50 per share, 250 shares at $40.75 per share, 1,500 shares at

$33.50 per share and 76,500 shares at $52.57 per share, such options to expire on October 16, 1974, December 18, 1974, August 20, 1975, and July 15, 1976, respectively. Of such options (i) options to purchase 10,000 shares and 3,000 shares at $48.50 per share were held by James R. Shepley, a Director and the President of the Company, and by Henry Luce III, a Director and Vice President of the Company, respectively, (ii) options to purchase 10,000 shares at $52.57 per share were held by each of Andrew Heiskell, a Director and Chairman of the Board of the Company, and Hedley Donovan, a Director and Editor-in-Chief of the Company, and (iii) options to purchase a total of 69,500 shares at $48.50 per share, 250 shares at $40.75 per share, 1,500 shares at $33.50 per share and 27,500 shares at $52.57 per share were held by all directors and officers of the Company as a group (27 people).

As of March 1, 1972, there were outstanding options granted under the 1967 Plan to purchase a total of 85,700 shares of Common Stock at various prices averaging $94.92 per share, such options to expire on various dates from July 20, 1972, to December 18, 1974. Of such options, options to purchase a total of 18,000 shares at an average purchase price per share of $83.03 were held by all directors and officers of the Company as a group (15 people).

All such options are "qualified stock options" as defined in Section 422 of the Internal Revenue Code of 1954, as amended.

The closing price for the Common Stock on the New York Stock Exchange on March 1, 1972, was $62¾ per share.

During the life of the options described in this Prospectus, the optionees would realize a profit if they were to exercise their options and thereafter sell shares acquired thereby at a time when the market value of the Common Stock was higher than their option prices. The proportionate interest in the Company of persons owning Common Stock at the time of such exercise would be reduced. This factor could (the Company not so conceding) affect the ability of the Company to obtain additional capital by selling Common Stock to the public, should it ever desire to do so.

Counsel for the Company have advised that under the Internal Revenue Code of 1954, as amended, if shares of Common Stock of the Company are issued to the original holder of an option granted under the New Plan or the 1967 Plan upon his timely exercise of that option, then, if the option price is not less than 100% of the fair market value of the stock at the time of granting the option, if the holder meets the eligibility requirements of such Code, if no disposition of shares acquired upon the exercise of such options occurs within three years after such shares are transferred to the original holder and if at all times from the date of the granting of the option to a date three months before the date of exercise of such option the optionee has been an employee of the Company or a subsidiary, (i) no income will be realized by such holder at the time of the grant of the option or the transfer of the shares to him; (ii) when he sells such shares, any amount realized by him in excess of the option price will be taxed to him as a long-term capital gain and any loss sustained by him will be a long-term capital loss; and (iii) no deduction will be allowable to the Company for federal income tax purposes in connection with the grant or exercise of the option. Such counsel have also advised that, in the case of the exercise after December 31, 1969, of options granted under the New Plan or the 1967 Plan, the difference between the option price and the fair market value of such shares at the time of such exercise will constitute an "item of tax preference" to such employee, which, depending on his particular tax position (1) may be subject to tax at a 10% rate, and (2) may reduce the amount of his earned income, if any, eligible for the maximum tax on earned income which became fully effective in 1972.

CONSOLIDATED STATEMENT OF INCOME

The following statement of the Company and subsidiaries has been examined by Ernst & Ernst, independent accountants, whose opinion appears elsewhere in this Prospectus. The statement should be read in conjunction with the consolidated financial statements of the Company and subsidiaries, and related notes, for the two years ended December 31, 1971, together with the report of Ernst & Ernst, all of which are contained in the Annual Report of the Company for 1971 and are incorporated in this Prospectus as set forth under the heading "Financial Statements".

	Year Ended December 31,				
	1967	1968	1969	1970	1971
Revenues (1):					
Magazine advertising	$234,631,004	$239,553,976	$246,451,777	$224,067,987	$216,293,251
Circulation, books, paper products, broadcasting, and other sources	259,220,467	300,439,992	338,180,229	379,175,974	390,514,494
	493,851,471	539,993,968	584,632,006	603,243,961	606,807,745
Costs and Expenses (1):					
Editorial, production, manufacturing and distribution	314,230,442	352,782,767	382,963,764	391,058,404	380,300,060
Selling, administrative and general	126,978,847	136,196,028	162,736,517	176,294,226(2)	185,678,770
	441,209,289	488,978,795	545,700,281	567,352,630	565,978,830
Operating Income	52,642,182	51,015,173	38,931,725	35,891,331	40,828,915
Other Income:					
Interest	2,423,858	2,714,440	2,673,712	2,376,406	3,405,312
Dividends	2,058,949	2,357,202	2,726,592	2,959,356	2,232,244
Net gains from sales of securities	—	113,269	—	685,219(3)	600
Other	1,734,940	1,286,801	1,833,703	1,883,417	2,300,442
	6,217,747	6,471,712	7,234,007	7,904,398	7,938,598
	58,859,929	57,486,885	46,165,732	43,795,729	48,767,513
Other Deductions:					
Interest on long-term debt	5,387,762	6,968,027	7,448,891	6,933,242	6,656,008
Other (including minority interests in net income of subsidiaries)	2,462,281(4)	1,332,543	631,896	2,498,629(4)	2,264,749(4)
Loss (Income) from discontinued operations (1)	2,124,362	558,136	237,370	(252,336)	—
	9,974,405	8,858,706	8,318,157	9,179,535	8,920,757
Income Before Income Taxes and Extraordinary Items	48,885,524	48,628,179	37,847,575	34,616,194	39,846,756
Income Taxes (5):					
Federal and foreign taxes	19,252,615	20,591,803	16,856,295	10,149,232	14,444,030
Deferred federal taxes	(1,528,004)	966,973	633,730	4,400,768	2,805,970
	17,724,611	21,558,776	17,490,025	14,550,000	17,250,000
Income Before Extraordinary Items	31,160,913	27,069,403	20,357,550	20,066,194	22,596,756
Extraordinary items, net of federal income taxes (6)	—	5,030,978	3,558,102	560,830	667,745
Net Income	$ 31,160,913	$ 32,100,381	$ 23,915,652	$ 20,627,024	$ 23,264,501
Amounts per share of Common Stock (7):					
Income before extraordinary items	$4.36	$3.76	$2.81	$2.76	$3.11
Extraordinary items, net of federal income taxes	—	.70	.49	.08	.09
Net income	4.36	4.46	3.30	2.84	3.20
Dividends paid	2.30	2.30	2.30	1.90	1.90

NOTES TO CONSOLIDATED STATEMENT OF INCOME

(1) The Company has discontinued the publication of Life International and the selling activities of Family Publication Services, Inc., effective December 31, 1970, and the publication of Life En Espanol effective December 31, 1969. Revenues and costs and expenses have been restated and the operating loss or income of the discontinued businesses has been reclassified to other deductions as follows:

	Year Ended December 31,			
	1967	1968	1969	1970
Revenues	$25,778,000	$27,818,000	$33,857,000	$29,374,000
Costs and expenses	27,902,000	28,376,000	34,094,000	29,122,000
Loss (income)	$ 2,124,000	$ 558,000	$ 237,000	($ 252,000)

(2) During 1970 the Company changed its accounting policy to capitalize the promotion costs of book and record series and to amortize such costs, previously expensed as incurred, over a 12-month period. In 1970 this change increased net income by approximately $200,000. 1969 and prior years have not been restated because the effect on net income was not material.

(3) In 1970 the Company realized capital gains of approximately $1,300,000 from the sale of securities, mainly from the sale of its holdings of stock of C. T. Land and Building Corp., T. C. Industrial Park, Inc., Editorial Abril, S.A. and a portion of its holding of stock of Itek Corporation. Offsetting these gains were realized losses on the sale of its holding of stock in Producciones Argentinas de Television, S.A.C.I. of approximately $400,000 and losses on the sale of other marketable securities.

(4) Includes in 1967 provisions for losses on investments of $2,244,173, less net gains of $328,844 from sales of securities, and in 1970 and 1971 includes $1,138,095 and $783,757, respectively, interest expense on the Company's revolving line of credit.

(5) The full amounts of the investment credit for the years 1967, 1968, 1969, 1970 and 1971, approximately $3,467,000, $650,000, $680,000, $135,000 and $92,000, respectively, have been applied as a reduction of federal income tax expense.

(6) See Notes to Financial Statements for the above-mentioned Annual Report of the Company for 1971 and 1970. In 1968 extraordinary items, all net of federal income taxes aggregating $1,341,000, were a gain of $2,758,000 from the sale of Itek Corporation common stock, a gain of $1,481,000 from the sale of three parcels of real estate, a loss of $1,610,000 from the sale of marketable securities, a gain of $3,124,000 realized by Little, Brown and Company from the sale of its investment in the common stock of Grosset & Dunlap, Inc., and a provision of $722,000 for possible losses on other investments. In 1969 extraordinary items, all net of federal income tax credits of $190,025, were a gain of $3,877,000 from the sale of the Chicago Time & Life Building, a gain of $1,518,000 from the sale of CATV systems and certain other property, a provision for loss of $987,000 from the termination of Life En Espanol, and a provision of $850,000 for possible losses on other investments.

(7) Based on the average number of shares outstanding during each respective year. Stock options have not been included in the computation of earnings per share because they have a dilution factor of less than three percent.

Although total revenues increased in each of the years 1967 through 1970, operating income declined in each such year due primarily to increased costs for magazine printing, paper and distribution. Results in 1967 reflected substantial start up costs for major expansions at Eastex Incorporated and St. Francisville Paper Company (see "Certain Recent Developments") and development costs of a new subsidiary, Selling-Areas Marketing, Inc. High costs have characterized the production of magazine paper at St. Francisville Paper Company since such expansion. Results in 1969 and 1970 were affected by the cost of printing and distributing LIFE to former subscribers to the Saturday Evening Post without receiving any circulation revenues, pursuant to an agreement with The Curtis Publishing Company. 1,300,000 and 700,000 subscriptions were substituted pursuant to this agreement in 1969 and 1970, respectively. Substantial postal rate increases occurred in 1968, 1969, 1970 and 1971.

See "Certain Recent Developments" for information with respect to the sale by the Company of its over-the-air broadcasting properties.

OPINION OF INDEPENDENT ACCOUNTANTS

Board of Directors
Time Incorporated
New York, N. Y.

We have examined the consolidated statement of income of Time Incorporated and subsidiaries for the five years ended December 31, 1971, included in this Prospectus. Our examination was made in accordance with generally accepted auditing standards, and accordingly included such tests of the accounting records and other auditing procedures as we consider necessary in the circumstances.

In our opinion, the accompanying consolidated statement of income presents fairly the consolidated results of the operations of Time Incorporated and subsidiaries for the five years ended December 31, 1971, in conformity with generally accepted accounting principles, applied on a consistent basis.

ERNST & ERNST

New York, N. Y.
February 17, 1972.

MARKET PRICES

The following table shows the reported high and low sales prices of the Company's Common Stock on the New York Stock Exchange for each of the years 1967 through 1971 and for the period from January 1, 1972, through April 26, 1972:

	High	Low
1967	115	88⅝
1968	109⅞	86⅛
1969	100⅜	36⅜
1970	45	25½
1971	62¾	40⅝
1972 (January 1 through April 26)	64¾	53½

CERTAIN RECENT DEVELOPMENTS

The Company's wholly owned subsidiary, Eastex Incorporated, completed expansions of its pulp and paperboard mill in December 1967 and late 1970, at costs of approximately $43,000,000 and $2,100,000, respectively.

In late 1967, St. Francisville Paper Company, 50% of the stock of which is owned by the Company, completed a major expansion of its machine coated paper mill at a cost of approximately $36,000,000.

In August 1968, the Company acquired Little Brown and Company (Inc.), a publisher of general and juvenile trade books, legal and medical books and college textbooks, in exchange for 170,000 shares of Common Stock of the Company.

The Company entered the newspaper publishing business with the acquisitions in May 1969 of Pioneer Publishing Company and in September 1969 of Lloyd Hollister Inc. for cash. These two companies were subsequently merged to form Pioneer Press, Inc., which now publishes 18 weekly newspapers reaching approximately 100,000 subscribers in the Chicago suburbs. Eight papers formerly published by Pioneer were sold during 1971.

Also during 1969, a films division was established after the acquisition, for 13,500 shares of Common Stock of the Company, of Peter M. Robeck & Company, Inc., a film distributor. Also during 1969 the Company acquired for cash two relatively small book clubs, The Book Find Club and Seven Arts Books Society, and the Company's subsidiary New York Graphic Society Ltd. acquired Alva Museum Replicas, Inc., a producer of sculpture replicas.

The Company's foreign language magazine, Life En Español, was discontinued at the end of 1969, and the English language international editions of Life were discontinued at the end of 1970.

In late 1970, the Company sold Rayburn Country, a land development subsidiary, and approximately 25,500 acres of the Company's adjacent timberland in East Texas for $6,352,000, leaving the aggregate timberland holdings of the Company at approximately 585,000 acres.

Family Publications Service, Inc., a wholly owned subsidiary which was engaged in the sale of magazine subscriptions door-to-door on the paid-during-service or installment basis, ceased the sale of new subscriptions early in 1971. It is currently engaged only in collecting receivables due in respect of prior sales.

Effective March 8, 1971, the Company and McGraw-Hill, Inc., entered into a definitive agreement providing for the sale of the Company's over-the-air television broadcasting properties to McGraw-Hill for an aggregate consideration of approximately $69.3 million which is subject to certain adjustments which will not materially affect the gain realized on the sale. These properties had aggregate net tangible assets of approximately $8.4 million at December 31, 1971. This amount does not include an allocation of the approximately $17.8 million of Excess of Purchase Prices over Net Tangible Assets associated with the original purchases by the Company of the over-the-air television and radio broadcasting properties. Although no final determination has been made, the Company anticipates that most of this $17.8 million would be allocable to the television properties. Under the contract, McGraw-Hill would pay approximately

30% in cash at closing, and the balance in 7½% negotiable unsecured senior notes maturing in eight equal annual installments. The transaction is expected to qualify for tax purposes as an installment sale with the result that federal income tax (mostly at capital gains rates) accrues only as the purchase price is received in or converted to cash. On March 13, 1972, the FCC published an order approving the sale. However, persons who originally petitioned the FCC to deny approval of the sale have filed notice requesting judicial review of the order. Accordingly the FCC order will not become final until such request is withdrawn or finally disposed of. If the FCC order does not become final on or prior to June 2, 1972, either of the Company or McGraw-Hill may terminate the agreement. In early January 1972 the first of the Company's eight radio stations was sold for $2,900,000. The sales of four more of the Company's radio stations for an aggregate of $4,850,000 were concluded in mid-February 1972. The Company has also agreed to sell its remaining three radio stations for an aggregate of $3,300,000, subject to FCC approval and certain other conditions; petitions of opposition have been filed with the FCC with respect to these sales, but the Company believes they will be approved. If the above radio and television sales were all to be consummated, the Company would no longer be engaged in the over-the-air broadcasting business in the United States. The Company's CATV interests in the United States will not be affected. The combined over-the-air broadcasting business contributed approximately 4% to consolidated revenues and 14% to consolidated income before income taxes and extraordinary items in 1971 and approximately 5% and 18%, respectively, in 1970. Even without these sources of income, the Company would not expect a substantial reduction in its net income since it would receive significant amounts of income from the above-mentioned notes and from the interim investment of the cash proceeds. In the future the Company would expect to realize both earnings and revenues as the funds were redeployed in new fields. The Company entered into these agreements believing it is an appropriate time to redeploy its resources in other fields that could be more profitable in the long run such as expansion of its investment in CATV and CATV services and investment in the emergent field of video cassettes.

The Company has a 47% interest in Sterling Communications, Inc., which operates, through a subsidiary, a CATV system in the lower half of Manhattan. To raise funds for the expansion of the Manhattan CATV system, Sterling arranged for a $13.2 million bank loan in mid-1971. The Company agreed to purchase $6 million of the loan from the bank if not paid at maturity and, as to the balance of the loan, to make such investments in Sterling as may be required to maintain Sterling's consolidated net worth at specified levels. In return for these commitments, the Company received initially warrants to purchase 300,000 shares of Sterling Common Stock, which (together with convertible notes of Sterling held by the Company) are sufficient, if exercised, to give the Company a majority interest in Sterling. Sterling has agreed with the bank to raise an aditional $6,000,000 through the sale of equity securities prior to September 30, 1972. In the absence of other purchasers, the Company has agreed to purchase these securities and may thereby further increase its percentage ownership.

DESCRIPTION OF COMMON STOCK

The Transfer Agent for the Company's Common Stock, par value $1 per share, is The Chase Manhattan Bank (National Association), One Chase Manhattan Plaza, New York, N. Y. 10015. The Registrar is Chemical Bank, 20 Pine Street, New York, N. Y. 10015.

For a full description of the Common Stock, reference is made to the Company's Restated Certificate of Incorporation as amended, a copy of which has been filed as an Exhibit to the Registration Statements. The following statements are subject to the provisions thereof and are qualified by such reference.

Dividend Rights. Subject to the restrictive covenants contained in the loan agreement relating to the Company's notes payable to a bank and credit agreements with certain banks, holders of Common Stock are entitled to such dividends as may be declared by the Board of Directors. The Company has covenanted under such loan agreement and such credit agreements not to pay any dividends on the Common Stock (except dividends payable in shares of its stock), or purchase any shares of the Common Stock, unless, after giving effect thereto, "adjusted consolidated retained income" shall equal at least 150% of the unpaid principal amount of the notes outstanding under such loan agreement and such credit agreements. As of December 31, 1971, approximately $194,000,000 of consolidated retained income was free of such restrictions. However, the credit agreements also require the Company to maintain "consolidated net current assets" of (i) 1½ times the sum of the aggregate commitments outstanding under the credit agreements plus the indebtedness outstanding under the loan agreement or (ii) $60,000,000, whichever is larger; the amount thereof, as of December 31, 1971, exceeded such requirements by approximately $90,000,000. The loan agreement contains less restrictive requirements on "consolidated net current assets".

Other Rights. In the event of dissolution or liquidation of the Company, the holders of Common Stock will share ratably in all remaining assets. The holders of Common Stock have no pre-emptive or conversion rights and there are no redemption or sinking fund rights applicable to the Common Stock. Each holder of Common Stock is entitled to one vote for each share registered in his name on the books of the Company. The outstanding shares of Common Stock, including the shares offered hereby, are fully paid and non-assessable.

PRINCIPAL HOLDER OF SECURITIES

The only person who is known by the Company to hold of record or beneficially more than 10% of its outstanding Common Stock is The Henry Luce Foundation, Inc., a charitable membership corporation, which was the record and beneficial owner of 876,069 shares of Common Stock on February 1, 1972, constituting approximately 12% of the Common Stock outstanding on that date. The members of The Henry Luce Foundation are Henry Luce III, Peter Paul Luce, Mrs. Elisabeth Luce Moore, Maurice T. Moore, Roy Larsen and Charles L. Stillman. The directors of the Foundation are Henry Luce III, Mrs. Moore, Mr. Larsen and Mr. Stillman. Henry Luce III is President of the Foundation. Messrs. Henry Luce III and Larsen are directors and officers of the Company.

LEGAL OPINION

The legality of the Common Stock offered hereby has been passed upon by Messrs. Cravath, Swaine & Moore, One Chase Manhattan Plaza, New York, N. Y. 10005, counsel for the Company.

FINANCIAL STATEMENTS

The consolidated financial statements of the Company and subsidiaries for the two years ended December 31, 1971, and related notes, together with the report of Ernst & Ernst, independent accountants, included in the Annual Report of the Company for the year 1971, are incorporated in this Prospectus by reference to pages 19 through 25, inclusive, of said Annual Report. A copy of such Annual Report will be delivered to each employee to whom this Prospectus is sent or given, unless such employee otherwise has received a copy of such Annual Report as a stockholder of the Company.

EXPERTS

The financial statements incorporated herein by reference in the preceding paragraph and the "Consolidated Statement of Income" included herein have been so incorporated or included by the Company in reliance upon the opinions of Ernst & Ernst, independent accountants, incorporated herein by reference and included herein, given upon the authority of such firm as experts in accounting and auditing.

CONSOLIDATED STATEMENT OF INCOME

Time Incorporated and Subsidiaries — The accompanying notes are an integral part of this financial statement

	Year Ended December 31, 1971	Year Ended December 31, 1970
Revenues		
Magazine advertising	$216,293,000	$224,068,000
Circulation, books, paper products, broadcasting and other sources	390,515,000	379,176,000
	606,808,000	603,244,000
Costs and Expenses		
Editorial, production, manufacturing and distribution	380,300,000	391,059,000
Selling, administrative and general	185,679,000	176,294,000
	565,979,000	567,353,000
Operating Income	40,829,000	35,891,000
Other Income	7,939,000	8,157,000
Other Deductions	8,921,000	9,432,000
Income Before Income Taxes and Extraordinary Items	39,847,000	34,616,000
Federal and Foreign Income Taxes	17,250,000	14,550,000
Income Before Extraordinary Items	22,597,000	20,066,000
Extraordinary Items, net of federal income tax credit of $2,220,000 in 1971 and expense of $54,000 in 1970	668,000	561,000
Net Income	$ 23,265,000	$ 20,627,000
Per Share of Common Stock:		
Income Before Extraordinary Items	$3.11	$2.76
Extraordinary Items, net of federal income taxes	.09	.08
Net Income	$3.20	$2.84

CONSOLIDATED BALANCE SHEET

Time Incorporated and Subsidiaries — The accompanying notes are an integral part of this financial statement

Assets	December 31, 1971	December 31, 1970
Current Assets		
Cash	$ 35,674,000	$ 33,487,000
Marketable securities — at cost:		
U.S. Government and other short-term securities (approximately market)	14,965,000	11,935,000
Preferred and common stocks — quoted market prices $29,000,000 in 1971 and $26,700,000 in 1970	27,516,000	27,293,000
Receivables, less allowances of $15,878,000 in 1971 and $18,723,000 in 1970	85,317,000	90,796,000

Accountants' Report

TO THE BOARD OF DIRECTORS AND STOCKHOLDERS OF TIME INCORPORATED

We have examined the consolidated financial statements of Time Incorporated and subsidiaries for the years ended December 31, 1971 and 1970. Our examinations were made in accordance with generally accepted auditing standards, and accordingly included such tests of the accounting records and such other auditing procedures as we considered necessary in the circumstances.

In our opinion, the accompanying balance sheets and statements of income, stockholders' equity and changes in financial position present fairly the consolidated financial position of Time Incorporated and subsidiaries at December 31, 1971 and 1970, and the consolidated results of their operations, changes in stockholders' equity and changes in financial position for the years then ended, in conformity with generally accepted accounting principles applied on a consistent basis.

Ernst & Ernst

New York, New York
February 17, 1972

Inventories — at the lower of cost or market:		
Work in process and finished goods	36,206,000	30,258,000
Paper and other materials	14,066,000	16,671,000
Prepaid expenses	22,041,000	12,969,000
Total Current Assets	235,785,000	223,409,000
Investments — at cost less allowances		
Companies 20% to 50% owned	42,787,000	44,631,000
Other	22,564,000	23,385,000
	65,351,000	68,016,000
Property and Equipment — on the basis of cost		
Buildings	62,793,000	66,598,000
Machinery and equipment	192,441,000	187,852,000
Leasehold improvements	18,429,000	17,484,000
	273,663,000	271,934,000
Less allowances for depreciation and amortization	123,797,000	111,815,000
	149,866,000	160,119,000
Timber and timberland, less depletion	22,427,000	22,677,000
Land	7,277,000	7,434,000
	179,570,000	190,230,000
Excess of Purchase Prices over Net Tangible Assets of Acquired Properties	34,182,000	33,461,000
Other Assets	29,189,000	30,500,000
Total Assets	$544,077,000	$545,616,000

Liabilities and Stockholders' Equity	December 31, 1971	December 31, 1970
Current Liabilities		
Accounts payable and accrued expenses	$ 67,819,000	$ 59,472,000
Employee compensation and profit-sharing contributions	9,225,000	8,566,000
Federal and foreign income taxes	1,201,000	1,674,000
Loans and current portion of long-term debt	4,111,000	13,142,000
Total Current Liabilities	82,356,000	82,854,000
Unearned Portion of Paid Subscriptions	82,105,000	86,822,000
Long-Term Debt	104,980,000	114,821,000
Deferred Federal Income Taxes	21,251,000	14,443,000
Other Liabilities	7,727,000	10,736,000

Stockholders' Equity		
Common Stock — $1 par value; authorized 10,000,000 shares; issued and outstanding, 7,278,000 shares in 1971 and 7,257,000 in 1970	7,278,000	7,257,000
Additional paid-in capital	17,607,000	17,474,000
Retained income	220,773,000	211,209,000
	245,658,000	235,940,000
Total Liabilities and Stockholders' Equity	$544,077,000	$545,616,000

CONSOLIDATED STATEMENT OF STOCKHOLDERS' EQUITY

Time Incorporated and Subsidiaries The accompanying notes are an integral part of this financial statement

	Year Ended December 31, 1971	Year Ended December 31, 1970
Common Stock		
Balance at beginning of year	$ 7,257,000	$ 7,257,000
Par value of shares issued to acquire Haverhill's, Inc.	18,000	
	7,275,000	
Par value of shares issued under stock option plans	3,000	
Balance at end of year	$ 7,278,000	$ 7,257,000
Additional Paid-In Capital		
Balance at beginning of year	$ 17,474,000	$ 17,474,000
Excess of proceeds over par value of Common Stock issued under stock option plans	133,000	
Balance at end of year	$ 17,607,000	$ 17,474,000
Retained Income		
Balance at beginning of year	$211,209,000	$204,371,000
Haverhill's Inc., at date of pooling	98,000	
	211,307,000	
Net Income—$3.20 a share in 1971 and $2.84 a share in 1970	23,265,000	20,627,000
	234,572,000	224,998,000
Dividends paid — $1.90 a share in 1971 and 1970	13,799,000	13,789,000
Balance at end of year	$220,773,000	$211,209,000

CONSOLIDATED STATEMENT OF CHANGES IN FINANCIAL POSITION

Time Incorporated and Subsidiaries The accompanying notes are an integral part of this financial statement

	Year Ended December 31, 1971	Year Ended December 31, 1970
Sources of Working Capital		
From operations:		
Income before extraordinary items	$22,597,000	$20,066,000
Charges to net income not affecting working capital:		
Depreciation, amortization and depletion	16,106,000	16,671,000
Deferred federal income taxes	1,493,000	4,401,000
Provisions for losses on investments		184,000
Total from Operations Excluding Extraordinary Items	40,196,000	41,322,000

	1971	1970
Extraordinary items	668,000	561,000
Charges (credits) not affecting working capital:		
Deferred federal income taxes	989,000	480,000
Provisions for losses on investments	1,303,000	
Long-term note received on sale of timberland		(5,245,000)
Total from Operations	43,156,000	37,118,000
Increase in unearned portion of paid subscriptions		1,799,000
Dispositions of property and equipment	3,576,000	7,357,000
Dispositions of investments	6,139,000	4,839,000
Decrease in other assets	1,311,000	
Increase in long-term debt	1,760,000	3,870,000
Issuance of common stock	154,000	
Miscellaneous	694,000	
	$56,790,000	$54,983,000
Application of Working Capital		
Dividends paid to stockholders	$13,799,000	$13,789,000
Purchase of property and equipment	10,025,000	13,138,000
Repayment of long-term debt	11,601,000	11,077,000
Decrease in unearned portion of paid subscriptions	4,717,000	
Additions to investments	3,774,000	2,378,000
Increase in other assets		5,067,000
Miscellaneous		4,582,000
	43,916,000	50,031,000
Increase in Working Capital	$12,874,000	$ 4,952,000
Increase (Decrease) in Working Capital, by Component		
Cash and marketable securities	$ 5,440,000	$ 501,000
Receivables	(5,479,000)	4,922,000
Inventories	3,343,000	(1,446,000)
Prepaid expense	9,072,000	(180,000)
Net Change in Current Assets	12,376,000	3,797,000
Accounts payable and accrued expenses	8,347,000	(3,793,000)
Employee compensation and profit-sharing contribution	659,000	(2,355,000)
Federal and foreign income taxes	(473,000)	(3,778,000)
Loans and current portion of long-term debt	(9,031,000)	8,771,000
Net Change in Current Liabilities	(498,000)	(1,155,000)
Increase in Working Capital	$12,874,000	$ 4,952,000

NOTES TO FINANCIAL STATEMENTS

Time Incorporated and Subsidiaries—December 31, 1971

Principles of Consolidation
The consolidated financial statements include the accounts of the Company and all subsidiaries.

On October 1, 1971, the Company acquired all the capital stock of Haverhill's, Inc., and two affiliated companies in exchange for 17,988 shares of the Company's common stock. The acquisition has been accounted for as a pooling of interests. However, the operations of Haverhill's and affiliates for periods prior to October 1, 1971, have not been included in the consolidated financial statements because they were not material.

Effective December 31, 1970, the Company discontinued the publication of Life International and the subscription selling activities of a subsidiary, Family Publications Service, Inc. Revenues and costs and expenses for 1970 have been restated by $29,374,000 and $29,122,000, respectively, to reflect the discontinuance. The 1970 operating income of these businesses, not material, has been reclassified to other income.

In 1970 the Company changed its accounting policy to capitalize—and amortize over a 12-month period—promotion costs of book and record series previously expensed as incurred. The change increased net income in 1970 by approximately $200,000.

Investments in Companies 20% to 50% Owned

The principal investments in this category are General Learning Corporation (50% owned), St. Francisville Paper Company (50% owned), Rock-Time, Inc. (45% owned) and numerous CATV companies of which the largest is Sterling Communications, Inc., in New York. The Company's equity in the net assets of these companies was approximately equal to cost, and its share of their combined net losses was not material in 1971 or 1970.

The Company's investment in Sterling Communications, Inc., at December 31, 1971, comprised a 47% equity interest at cost of $3,800,000 and loans totalling $4,700,000. During 1971 Sterling arranged a bank loan for $13,150,000 with provisions requiring the Company to purchase $6,000,000 of the loan from the bank if not paid at its five-year maturity, to support the balance of the loan, due in seven years, by making additional investments as required for Sterling to maintain specified levels of net worth and to arrange for a minimum $6,000,000 sale of equity securities by Sterling in 1972 which the Company will be required to buy in the absence of other purchasers. As a result of these commitments and other financial transactions, the Company has the right to acquire a majority of the stock of Sterling.

Stock Options

The table below shows the changes during 1971 and 1970 in options granted to key employees to purchase shares of the Company's common stock. There were 35,150 shares at December 31, 1971, and 103,100 shares at December 31, 1970, available for granting of options. Each option granted by the Company is exercisable as to one fifth of the aggregate number of shares covered by it on or after certain specified semi-annual dates subsequent to the date of grant but in no event later than five years from the date of grant. At December 31, 1971 and 1970, options for 253,440 shares and 168,500 shares, respectively, were exercisable. The option prices, which are not less than 100% of the fair market value on the dates of grant, are payable in full at the time the options are exercised.

Shares Under Option

	Price Range Per Share	Number of Shares 1971	1970
Balance at January 1	$33.50-$106.88	311,200	411,700
Options Granted–1971	$52.57	78,000	–
Options Granted–1970	$33.50	–	1,500
		389,200	413,200
Options Exercised	$48.50	(2,800)	–
Options Terminated	$40.75-$106.88	(12,400)	(102,000)
Balance at December 31	$33.50-$106.88	374,000	311,200

Retirement Plans

The Company and its subsidiaries have retirement plans covering substantially all employees, including those in foreign countries. Retirement plan expense was approximately $3,000,000 in 1971 and $2,500,000 in 1970. The Company's policy is to fund pension cost accrued and, as a result, substantially all retirement plans are fully funded.

Depreciation

Depreciation is computed generally by the straight-line method over the estimated useful lives of the assets.

Commitments and Contingent Liabilities

In February 1972 the Company sold its radio-broadcasting properties in Denver and Grand Rapids for $4,800,000. The Company has contracts to sell the remaining radio properties for $3,400,000 and its five television broadcasting properties for $69,300,000, all subject to timely approval of the Federal Communications Commission and certain other conditions.

The Company has a revolving line of credit with a group of banks for short-term borrowings of up to $25,000,000 over a period ending November 30, 1973. There was no balance outstanding at December 31, 1971. The balance outstanding at December 31, 1970, was $8,000,000.

The Company leases space in the Time & Life Building in New York City under a lease expiring in 1980 at an annual rate (including building services) of approximately $6,400,000.

At December 31, 1971, the Company had commitments and contingent liabilities in connection with investments, purchases of property and equipment, and long-term paper and printing contracts. In addition, there were pending against the Company and subsidiaries lawsuits and claims arising in the regular course of business (including lawsuits arising under the federal truth-in-lending law). In the opinion of management, recoveries, if any, by plaintiffs or claimants, that may result from all such lawsuits and claims should not be material in relation to the net worth of the Company and subsidiaries.

Other Income, Other Deductions and Extraordinary Items

Other income is comprised mainly of dividends and interest of $5,638,000 in 1971 and $5,336,000 in 1970.

Other deductions consist principally of interest expense of $7,692,000 in 1971 and $8,251,000 in 1970.

Extraordinary items in 1971, all net of federal income tax, include a capital gain of $2,457,000 from the sale of investment in QSP, Inc., a magazine subscription sales organization, a gain of $1,875,000 from the sale of radio station KOGO-AM in San Diego, and a loss of $3,625,000 incurred in conjunction with the reduction in LIFE's circulation and a subsequent centralization of its printing operations.

Extraordinary items in 1970, all net of federal income taxes, include a capital gain of $3,740,000 from the sale of Rayburn Country, a Texas-based land development subsidiary, plus surrounding timberland and provisions for a loss of $2,125,000 from the termination of Life International and a loss of $1,025,000 from the discontinuance of the subscription selling activities of Family Publications Service.

Federal and Foreign Income Taxes

Provisions for income taxes are low in relation to income before income taxes primarily due to income of low tax rate foreign subsidiaries and dividend income.

The full amount of the investment credit in 1971, which was not material, has been applied as a reduction of federal income tax expense.

Long-Term Debt	1971	1970
Time Incorporated:		
Notes payable to bank – unsecured – payable $5,600,000 on January 1, 1973 and $12,000,000 on January 1, 1974	$ 17,600,000	$ 23,200,000
Notes payable to banks (Eurodollar loans) – unsecured – payable March 31, 1974	6,000,000	6,000,000
Eastex Incorporated:		
Notes payable to bank – unsecured – payable in annual installments of $1,900,000 on January 1, 1973 through 1975, and $5,700,000 on January 1, 1976	11,400,000	13,300,000
Sinking Fund First Mortgage Bonds – maturing on July 2, 1985 – require semiannual sinking fund payments of (i) $750,000 from January 2, 1973 through July 2, 1975 and (ii) $1,650,000 from January 2, 1976 through July 2, 1985	37,500,000	39,000,000
Eastex Packaging, Incorporated – notes payable to bank – unsecured – payable in semi-annual installments of $300,000 from January 1, 1973 through January 1, 1976	2,100,000	2,700,000
Mortgage Notes on buildings owned by subsidiaries – payable in quarterly installments of $663,000 (including interest) through 1990	27,857,000	27,696,000
Other Notes Payable	2,523,000	2,925,000
	$104,980,000	$114,821,000

Restrictions: Credit agreements covering the Company's notes payable to a bank and the revolving line of credit described under Commitments and Contingent Liabilities require maintenance of minimum consolidated net current assets (as defined) and impose limits on payment of dividends. At December 31, 1971, net current assets were approximately $90,000,000 in excess of this requirement, and approximately $194,000,000 of retained income was unrestricted as to payment of dividends.

In connection with their long-term debts, Eastex and Eastex Packaging have agreed to observe restrictions with respect to payment of dividends, maintenance of working capital, prepayment of debt, incurring additional debt, etc. Payment of these debts is not guaranteed by the Company. However, until these debts are paid, the Company may not dispose of any portion of its investment in these subsidiaries without the consent of the lending institutions. Of the total net assets of these subsidiaries at December 31, 1971 approximately $69,000,000 (including $19,000,000 of net current assets) is effectively restricted to the securing of long-term debt and thus not available for distribution to the Company.

FIVE-YEAR FINANCIAL SUMMARY

Time Incorporated and Subsidiaries

	1971	1970	1969	1968	1967
Income and Dividends (millions)					
Revenues*	$606.8	$603.2	$584.6	$540.0	$493.9
Operating income*	40.8	35.9	38.9	51.0	52.6
Income before income taxes and extraordinary items	39.8	34.6	37.8	48.6	48.9
Income before extraordinary items	22.6	20.1	20.4	27.1	31.2
Extraordinary items, net of income taxes	.7	.6	3.6	5.0	
Net income	23.3	20.6	23.9	32.1	31.2
Dividends paid	13.8	13.8	16.7	16.5	16.2
Year-End Financial Condition (millions)					
Current assets	$235.8	$223.4	$219.6	$213.4	$203.1
Working capital	153.4	140.6	135.6	139.7	134.0
Total assets	544.1	545.6	545.4	514.0	485.9
Unearned portion of paid subscriptions	82.1	86.8	85.0	82.4	77.6
Long-term debt	105.0	114.8	122.0	115.1	116.7
Stockholders' equity	245.7	235.9	229.1	221.0	204.1
Amount Per Share					
Income before extraordinary items	$ 3.11	$ 2.76	$ 2.81	$ 3.76	$ 4.36
Extraordinary items, net of income taxes	.09	.08	.49	.70	
Net income	3.20	2.84	3.30	4.46	4.36
Dividends paid	1.90	1.90	2.30	2.30	2.30
Stockholders' equity	33.75	32.51	31.56	30.54	28.40

*Restated for discontinued operations for years prior to 1971 – see notes, page 24.

PHILLIPS PETROLEUM COMPANY

CONSOLIDATED BALANCE SHEETS AT DECEMBER 31

ASSETS

	1971	1970*
Current Assets:		
Cash, including time deposits	$ 187,989,000	$ 132,317,000
Short-term investments, at cost	37,126,000	4,769,000
Notes and accounts receivable—(less reserves: 1971—$7,566,000; 1970—$6,010,000)	382,745,000	410,563,000
Inventories—Note 1:		
Crude oil, petroleum products, and merchandise	259,251,000	234,513,000
Materials and supplies	36,102,000	35,690,000
Total Current Assets	903,213,000	817,852,000
Investments and Long-Term Receivables—(less reserves: 1971—$8,771,000; 1970—$7,611,000)—Notes 1 and 2	391,735,000	361,620,000
Properties, Plants, and Equipment, at cost, less reserves—Note 3	1,838,037,000	1,850,524,000
Prepaid and Deferred Charges	33,714,000	41,484,000
	$3,166,699,000	$3,071,480,000

LIABILITIES AND STOCKHOLDERS' EQUITY

	1971	1970*
Current Liabilities:		
Notes payable	$ 17,327,000	$ 32,416,000
Accounts payable	237,159,000	247,924,000
Long-term debt—due within one year	52,157,000	106,064,000
Accrued taxes	102,549,000	114,487,000
Other accruals	36,130,000	28,842,000
Total Current Liabilities	445,322,000	529,733,000
Long-Term Debt—Note 4	800,191,000	687,913,000
Deferred Credits:		
Income taxes—Note 5	62,996,000	57,246,000
Other	41,776,000	36,333,000
Total Deferred Credits	104,772,000	93,579,000
Reserve for Contingencies	60,672,000	57,433,000
Minority Interest in Consolidated Subsidiaries	6,557,000	9,938,000
Stockholders' Equity:		
Common stock, $2.50 par value—Note 6:		
Shares authorized—100,000,000		
Shares issued—(1971—76,192,076; 1970—76,126,545)	190,480,000	190,317,000
Capital in excess of par value of common stock—Note 6	437,248,000	433,312,000
Earnings employed in the business	1,160,881,000	1,125,350,000
	1,788,609,000	1,748,979,000
Less treasury stock, at cost—(1971—1,451,401 shares; 1970—2,064,552 shares)—Note 6	39,424,000	56,095,000
Total Stockholders' Equity	1,749,185,000	1,692,884,000
	$3,166,699,000	$3,071,480,000

*Restated. See Note 1.

PHILLIPS PETROLEUM COMPANY

CONSOLIDATED STATEMENTS OF INCOME AND EARNINGS EMPLOYED IN THE BUSINESS

	1971	1970*
Revenues:		
Gross operating revenues	$2,363,199,000	$2,273,100,000
Other revenues (including equity in earnings of non-consolidated companies)—Note 1	49,103,000	38,224,000
	2,412,302,000	2,311,324,000
Costs and Expenses:		
Cost of sales and services	1,615,338,000	1,541,184,000
Selling, general, and administrative expense	288,278,000	288,034,000
Depreciation, depletion, amortization, and retirements	201,268,000	198,446,000
Taxes other than income taxes**	59,675,000	57,613,000
Interest and expense on indebtedness	62,602,000	54,217,000
Provision for income taxes—Note 5	52,825,000	51,950,000
	2,279,986,000	2,191,444,000
Income Before Extraordinary Item	132,316,000	119,880,000
Provision for Estimated Losses on Foreign Assets (less applicable income tax credit of $4,000,000)	—	(8,700,000)
Net Income	132,316,000	111,180,000
Earnings Employed in the Business at Beginning of Year	1,125,350,000	1,110,434,000
	1,257,666,000	1,221,614,000
Dividends Paid ($1.30 a share)	96,785,000	96,264,000
Earnings Employed in the Business at End of Year	$1,160,881,000	$1,125,350,000
Per Share of Common Stock:		
Income before extraordinary item	$ 1.78	$ 1.62
Extraordinary item	—	(.12)
Net income	$ 1.78	$ 1.50

CONSOLIDATED STATEMENTS OF SOURCE AND APPLICATION OF FUNDS

		1971	1970*
	Income before extraordinary item	$ 132,316,000	$ 119,880,000
	Depreciation, depletion, amortization, and retirements	201,268,000	198,446,000
SOURCE	Deferred income taxes	5,750,000	(2,496,000)
	Other (including equity in undistributed earnings of non-consolidated companies)	(6,637,000)	762,000
	Funds from operations	332,697,000	316,592,000
	Long-term debt	256,950,000	10,002,000
	Property sales and retirements (including extraordinary item)	43,696,000	31,070,000
	Sales of investments	14,352,000	23,061,000
	Capital stock	20,770,000	535,000
	Other	6,510,000	2,811,000
		$ 674,975,000	$ 384,071,000
	Capital expenditures	$ 224,966,000	$ 239,369,000
	Investments and long-term receivables	37,694,000	15,560,000
APPLICATION	Reduction in long-term debt	144,672,000	109,502,000
	Cash dividends	96,785,000	96,264,000
	Increase (decrease) in working capital	169,772,000	(89,920,000)
	Other	1,086,000	13,296,000
		$ 674,975,000	$ 384,071,000
	Cash	$ 55,672,000	$ (4,641,000)
	Short-term investments	32,357,000	(45,698,000)
WORKING	Notes and accounts receivable	(27,818,000)	18,267,000
CAPITAL	Inventories	25,150,000	(2,661,000)
CHANGES	Total current assets	85,361,000	(34,733,000)
	Notes payable	(15,089,000)	11,017,000
	Accounts payable	(10,765,000)	18,252,000
	Long-term debt due within one year	(53,907,000)	30,183,000
	Accrued taxes and other accruals	(4,650,000)	(4,265,000)
	Total current liabilities	(84,411,000)	55,187,000
	Increase (decrease) in working capital	$ 169,772,000	$ (89,920,000)

*Restated. See Note 1.

**In addition, taxes of $269,000,000 in 1971 and $252,000,000 in 1970 were collected on the sale of petroleum products and paid to taxing agencies.

NOTES TO FINANCIAL STATEMENTS

NOTE 1—ACCOUNTING POLICIES

Principles of Consolidation—The consolidated statements include the accounts of companies owned more than 50%. Current assets and liabilities recorded in foreign currencies are translated into dollars at exchange rates in effect at year-end. All other foreign assets and liabilities, in general, are translated at exchange rates in effect when acquired or incurred. Exchange differences, which are not material, arising from these procedures are reflected in income.

Inventories—Crude oil and petroleum products are priced substantially at cost, which is lower than market in the aggregate, calculated mainly by the last-in, first-out method with crude oil on an annual basis and refined products, chemicals, and natural gasoline products on a monthly basis. Materials and supplies are priced at average cost or replacement cost, with allowance for condition of used material.

Investments—On January 1, 1971, the Company adopted the equity method of accounting retroactively for investments in companies owned 20% to 50%, inclusive, and in joint-venture type companies, as recommended by Accounting Principles Board Opinion No. 18. This change in accounting policy added $8,516,000 (11.4¢ a share) to 1971 net income. The 1970 financial statements have been restated to reflect this new policy and, accordingly, income before extraordinary item for that year has been increased $2,825,000 (3.8¢ a share), net income has been decreased $6,045,000 (8.2¢ a share), and earnings employed in the business at beginning of year has been increased $16,642,000 (after applicable income taxes of $3,465,000). The reduction in 1970 net income occurred because the $8,870,000 profit on sale of a security investment reflected as an extraordinary item is associated, under equity accounting, with the years in which the income was earned. Investments in other companies are carried at cost.

Depreciation—Depreciation of properties, plants, and equipment subject thereto, is determined by the group straight-line method, individual unit straight-line method, and the unit of production method, applying the method considered most appropriate for each type of property.

Depletion—Leasehold costs of producing properties and the intangible development costs of productive wells are amortized on the unit of production method based on estimated recoverable oil and gas reserves. Dry hole costs are charged against income.

Undeveloped Leases—Leasehold costs of undeveloped oil and gas properties are capitalized, and that portion of the cost applicable to properties which it is estimated will be surrendered is amortized over the estimated holding period.

Property Dispositions—When complete units of depreciable property are retired or are sold for continued use, reserves are reduced by the applicable amounts and any profit or loss is credited or charged to income. When less than complete units of depreciable property are retired or disposed of the difference between asset cost and salvage value is charged or credited to the reserve for depreciation.

Maintenance and Repairs—Minor renewals and replacements are charged against income. Major renewals and replacements are charged to property accounts.

Research and Development Expenses—Research and development expenses are charged against income as incurred.

Investment Tax Credits—Investment tax credits are applied as a reduction of the provision for income taxes in the years used.

NOTE 2—INVESTMENTS

Refer to Note 1 for a change in accounting for certain investments. The most significant of these investments is 10,326,321 shares of the common stock of Pacific Petroleums Ltd. ("Pacific"), representing 48.57% of the total shares outstanding. These securities had a carrying value of $151,069,000 and a quoted market value of $320,116,000 at December 31, 1971, which does not purport to be realizable value. At the same date, net assets of Pacific in Canadian dollars amounted to $296,071,000, which consists of current assets $29,554,000, net property, plant and equipment $382,622,000, investments $22,971,000, other assets $3,657,000, current liabilities $23,947,000, and long-term debt $118,786,000. Earnings of Pacific for 1971 in Canadian dollars were $22,084,000, exclusive of deferred income taxes of $2,200,000 on depreciable assets.

NOTE 3—PROPERTIES, PLANTS, AND EQUIPMENT

The Company's investment in properties, plants, and equipment is summarized as follows:

	December 31	
	1971	1970
Production	$1,796,344,000	$1,749,487,000
Manufacturing	1,284,637,000	1,229,673,000
Transportation	276,106,000	279,742,000
Marketing	326,519,000	337,556,000
Other	95,888,000	96,369,000
	3,779,494,000	3,692,827,000
Less depreciation, depletion, and amortization	1,941,457,000	1,842,303,000
	$1,838,037,000	$1,850,524,000

NOTE 4—LONG-TERM DEBT

Long-term debt due after one year at December 31, 1971, consists of the following:

7⅝% Debentures Due 2001	$200,000,000
6% Guaranteed Sinking Fund Debentures Due 1981	20,808,000
5½% Guaranteed Swiss Bonds due 1983	13,838,000
First Mortgage and Leasehold 3% Sinking Fund Bonds due 1973-1975	1,440,000
Notes payable to banks, insurance companies, and others:	
At 4%-5%, due 1973-1987	110,489,000
At 5⅛%-6¼%, due 1973-1991	357,563,000
At 7%-9¾%, due 1973-1984	62,072,000
Purchase obligations	33,981,000
Total	$800,191,000

Arrangements existed at year end for a subsidiary to borrow an additional $30,307,000 to finance its portion of the development of a new oil field in the North Sea. Repayments of such loans would commence in June 1973 and continue through 1981.

NOTE 5—INCOME TAXES

The provision for income taxes includes an increase of $5,750,000 in 1971 and a decrease of $2,496,000 in 1970 for deferred income taxes, and reductions of $2,838,000 in 1971 and $1,910,000 in 1970 for investment tax credits.

NOTE 6—COMMON STOCK

The Company's restricted stock option plan was terminated December 31, 1963, except for the options then outstanding. Options to purchase 151,709 shares were outstanding to 403 key employees at January 1, 1971. During the year, options for 65,639 shares were exercised for an aggregate of $1,858,000 and options for 1,260 shares were cancelled. At December 31, 1971, options expiring in 1972 and 1973 were outstanding to 257 key employees to purchase 84,810 shares at an average price of $27.55. All of these options are exercisable.

At January 1, 1971, options for 52,760 shares of treasury stock were also outstanding to 11 individuals at an average price of $26.42 a share. These options, granted in connection with the acquisition of various corporations, became exercisable in cumulative installments beginning in 1964 and expire in 1972 and 1973. During 1971, options for 1,400 shares were exercised.

Capital in excess of par value of common stock was increased during 1971 by $3,936,000 resulting from the exercise of stock options and the sale or exchange of 610,673 shares of treasury stock.

NOTE 7—COMMITMENTS AND CONTINGENT LIABILITIES

At December 31, 1971, the Company had leases expiring more than three years from that date covering bulk and service stations, tank cars, office space, and other facilities. The minimum rentals payable under these leases for each of the next five years are estimated as follows: 1972—$48,600,000; 1973—$48,600,000; 1974—$48,600,000; 1975—$47,800,000; 1976—$46,600,000. Rental income from such stations subleased and mileage income on such leased tank cars are estimated at $25,100,000 for 1972 and are not expected to differ significantly through 1976.

At December 31, 1971, the Company was contingently liable for $127,336,000 of obligations of other companies. In addition, the Company has contingent liabilities with respect to claims and commitments arising from agreements with pipeline companies in which it holds stock interests whereby it may be required to provide such companies with additional funds through advances against future charges for transportation of crude oil or petroleum products. A number of suits are also pending in various courts in which the parent company or a subsidiary appears as plaintiff or defendant, including a federal anti-trust proceeding which seeks to force divestiture of the properties acquired from Tidewater Oil Company on July 14, 1966.

While it is impossible to estimate the ultimate liability in respect to contingent liabilities, the Company is of the opinion that the aggregate amount of such liabilities for which adequate provision has not been made is not significant in relation to total consolidated assets.

NOTE 8—RETIREMENT INCOME PLANS

The parent company and its subsidiaries have retirement plans covering substantially all of their employees. These plans are being funded based on pension costs accrued as determined by actuarial studies. Charges to income for such plans were $15,495,000 for 1971 and $13,121,000 for 1970.

During the year the principal retirement plan was revised to provide additional benefits, lower employee costs, and automatic participation on a noncontributory basis for employees after one year of recognized continuous service, with optional participation on a contributory basis. These changes will result in an estimated increase in annual Company contributions of $3,200,000.

NOTE 9—FOREIGN

The balance sheets include net assets applicable to operations in foreign countries in the approximate amounts of $532,298,000 for 1971 and $490,331,000 for 1970.

REPORT OF CERTIFIED PUBLIC ACCOUNTANTS

The Board of Directors,
Phillips Petroleum Company:

We have examined the accompanying consolidated balance sheet of Phillips Petroleum Company at December 31, 1971 and the related consolidated statements of income and earnings employed in the business and source and application of funds for the year then ended. Our examination was made in accordance with generally accepted auditing standards, and accordingly included such tests of the accounting records and such other auditing procedures as we considered necessary in the circumstances. We have previously reported on the financial statements for 1970 under date of February 4, 1971. The accompanying financial statements for that year have been revised as described in Note 1.

In our opinion, the statements mentioned above present fairly the consolidated financial position of Phillips Petroleum Company at December 31, 1971 and 1970 and the consolidated results of their operations and the source and application of their consolidated funds for the years then ended, in conformity with generally accepted accounting principles applied on a consistent basis during the period, after restatement of the prior year as explained in Note 1.

ARTHUR YOUNG & COMPANY

Tulsa, Oklahoma
February 15, 1972

TEN-YEAR FINANCIAL REVIEW (dollars in millions, except per share amounts)

	1971	1970	1969	1968	1967	1966	1965	1964	1963	1962
CONSOLIDATED BALANCE SHEETS AT DECEMBER 31										
Assets										
Current assets:										
Cash and short-term investments	$ 225.1	137.1	187.4	135.4	147.1	176.2	93.9	89.7	113.4	87.2
Notes and accounts receivable, less reserves	382.8	410.6	392.3	388.3	351.5	303.2	219.4	192.6	183.2	171.8
Inventories:										
Crude oil and petroleum products	240.5	212.6	217.6	220.3	203.9	191.1	134.1	130.4	127.7	112.8
Merchandise	18.7	21.9	24.1	21.5	24.3	27.1	17.9	14.5	12.8	11.0
Materials and supplies	36.1	35.7	31.2	29.6	30.8	31.5	25.5	22.0	23.2	22.5
Total current assets	903.2	817.9	852.6	795.1	757.6	729.1	490.8	449.2	460.3	405.3
Investments and long-term receivables, less reserves	391.8	361.6	383.5	332.1	317.8	311.7	309.3	278.5	247.2	230.1
Properties, plants, and equipment, less reserves	1,838.0	1,850.5	1,846.4	1,749.9	1,709.7	1,657.9	1,208.7	1,131.1	1,084.6	1,084.5
Prepaid and deferred charges	33.7	41.5	39.9	36.4	29.6	32.4	20.3	16.4	14.2	15.4
Total assets	3,166.7	3,071.5	3,122.4	2,913.5	2,814.7	2,731.1	2,029.1	1,875.2	1,806.3	1,735.3
Liabilities and stockholders' equity										
Current liabilities:										
Notes payable	$ 17.3	32.4	21.4	27.1	45.6	56.5	—	—	—	—
Accounts payable	237.2	247.9	229.7	239.7	220.2	197.3	160.3	134.6	125.1	117.1
Long-term debt—due within one year	52.2	106.1	75.9	47.1	49.9	180.9	3.5	16.9	32.1	17.0
Accrued taxes	102.5	114.5	119.7	87.5	86.3	102.5	59.0	53.8	67.1	50.4
Other accruals	36.1	28.9	27.9	27.5	27.7	34.6	20.8	19.5	17.1	16.2
Total current liabilities	445.3	529.8	474.6	428.9	429.7	571.8	243.6	224.8	241.4	200.7
Long-term debt	800.2	687.9	787.4	655.2	690.0	660.3	333.7	260.6	201.5	223.0
Deferred income taxes	63.0	57.3	59.7	68.4	70.9	62.8	86.8	81.5	73.0	60.6
Other deferred credits	41.8	36.3	51.7	63.5	61.2	46.7	45.6	43.9	32.1	30.6
Reserve for contingencies	60.7	57.4	50.5	45.2	27.6	29.9	24.2	22.2	19.8	15.1
Minority interest in consolidated subsidiaries	6.5	9.9	21.1	15.6	15.9	11.9	—	—	—	—
Stockholders' equity:										
Common stock, $2.50 par value	190.5	190.3	190.3	189.7	179.6	173.2	172.3	172.0	172.0	172.0
Capital in excess of par value of common stock	437.2	433.3	433.3	427.4	329.2	271.9	264.2	261.6	261.0	288.1
Earnings employed in the business	1,160.9	1,125.4	1,110.4	1,076.5	1,067.9	961.1	918.2	859.0	811.8	747.3
	1,788.6	1,749.0	1,734.0	1,693.6	1,576.7	1,406.2	1,354.7	1,292.6	1,244.8	1,207.4
Less treasury stock	39.4	56.1	56.6	56.9	57.3	58.5	59.5	50.4	6.3	2.1
Total stockholders' equity	1,749.2	1,692.9	1,677.4	1,636.7	1,519.4	1,347.7	1,295.2	1,242.2	1,238.5	1,205.3
Total liabilities and stockholders' equity	3,166.7	3,071.5	3,122.4	2,913.5	2,814.7	2,731.1	2,029.1	1,875.2	1,806.3	1,735.3
Stockholders' equity per share*	$ 23.40	22.86	22.66	22.18	21.79	20.08	19.41	18.56	18.07	17.55

	1971	1970	1969	1968	1967	1966	1965	1964	1963	1962
CONSOLIDATED STATEMENTS OF PROPERTIES, PLANTS, AND EQUIPMENT										
Gross investment										
Production	$1,796.4	1,749.5	1,729.6	1,587.8	1,495.9	1,460.6	1,390.7	1,342.8	1,279.7	1,257.4
Manufacturing	1,284.6	1,229.7	1,165.1	1,112.8	1,065.2	967.6	669.9	629.5	592.1	515.5
Transportation	276.1	279.7	278.6	276.1	271.6	272.2	195.3	191.5	178.0	164.1
Marketing	326.5	337.5	329.7	323.4	346.9	347.7	188.4	168.6	167.5	147.7
Other	95.9	96.4	93.1	93.4	88.4	97.2	79.8	76.6	71.8	92.3
	3,779.5	3,692.8	3,596.1	3,393.5	3,268.0	3,145.3	2,524.1	2,409.0	2,289.1	2,177.0
Net investment										
Production	$ 756.7	743.2	745.5	651.3	598.4	593.3	600.8	557.5	529.7	564.5
Manufacturing	684.8	682.9	668.9	660.2	644.0	567.9	323.7	304.4	292.9	273.6
Transportation	125.6	135.2	142.8	146.9	150.9	161.2	101.5	103.5	96.0	87.8
Marketing	221.2	237.5	237.8	238.0	265.6	274.4	137.0	122.2	125.5	108.2
Other	49.7	51.7	51.4	53.5	50.8	61.1	45.7	43.5	40.5	50.4
	1,838.0	1,850.5	1,846.4	1,749.9	1,709.7	1,657.9	1,208.7	1,131.1	1,084.6	1,084.5

*Adjusted for two-for-one stock split in 1969.

Note—Financial data for 1970, 1969, 1968 and 1967 have been restated to reflect the adoption of equity accounting for investments (see Note 1 to financial statements).

TEN-YEAR FINANCIAL REVIEW (dollars in millions, except per share amounts)

	1971	1970	1969	1968	1967	1966	1965	1964	1963	1962
CONSOLIDATED BALANCE SHEETS AT DECEMBER 31										
Assets										
Current assets:										
Cash and short-term investments	$ 225.1	137.1	187.4	135.4	147.1	176.2	93.9	89.7	113.4	87.2
Notes and accounts receivable, less reserves	382.8	410.6	392.3	388.3	351.5	303.2	219.4	192.6	183.2	171.8
Inventories:										
Crude oil and petroleum products	240.5	212.6	217.6	220.3	203.9	191.1	134.1	130.4	127.7	112.8
Merchandise	18.7	21.9	24.1	21.5	24.3	27.1	17.9	14.5	12.8	11.0
Materials and supplies	36.1	35.7	31.2	29.6	30.8	31.5	25.5	22.0	23.2	22.5
Total current assets	903.2	817.9	852.6	795.1	757.6	729.1	490.8	449.2	460.3	405.3
Investments and long-term receivables, less reserves	391.8	361.6	383.5	332.1	317.8	311.7	309.3	278.5	247.2	230.1
Properties, plants, and equipment, less reserves	1,838.0	1,850.5	1,846.4	1,749.9	1,709.7	1,657.9	1,208.7	1,131.1	1,084.6	1,084.5
Prepaid and deferred charges	33.7	41.5	39.9	36.4	29.6	32.4	20.3	16.4	14.2	15.4
Total assets	3,166.7	3,071.5	3,122.4	2,913.5	2,814.7	2,731.1	2,029.1	1,875.2	1,806.3	1,735.3
Liabilities and stockholders' equity										
Current liabilities:										
Notes payable	$ 17.3	32.4	21.4	27.1	45.6	56.5	—	—	—	—
Accounts payable	237.2	247.9	229.7	239.7	220.2	197.3	160.3	134.6	125.1	117.1
Long-term debt—due within one year	52.2	106.1	75.9	47.1	49.9	180.9	3.5	16.9	32.1	17.0
Accrued taxes	102.5	114.5	119.7	87.5	86.3	102.5	59.0	53.8	67.1	50.4
Other accruals	36.1	28.9	27.9	27.5	27.7	34.6	20.8	19.5	17.1	16.2
Total current liabilities	445.3	529.8	474.6	428.9	429.7	571.8	243.6	224.8	241.4	200.7
Long-term debt	800.2	687.9	787.4	655.2	690.0	660.3	333.7	260.6	201.5	223.0
Deferred income taxes	63.0	57.3	59.7	68.4	70.9	62.8	86.8	81.5	73.0	60.6
Other deferred credits	41.8	36.3	51.7	63.5	61.2	46.7	45.6	43.9	32.1	30.6
Reserve for contingencies	60.7	57.4	50.5	45.2	27.6	29.9	24.2	22.2	19.8	15.1
Minority interest in consolidated subsidiaries	6.5	9.9	21.1	15.6	15.9	11.9	—	—	—	—
Stockholders' equity:										
Common stock, $2.50 par value	190.5	190.3	190.3	189.7	179.6	173.2	172.3	172.0	172.0	172.0
Capital in excess of par value of common stock	437.2	433.3	433.3	427.4	329.2	271.9	264.2	261.6	261.0	288.1
Earnings employed in the business	1,160.9	1,125.4	1,110.4	1,076.5	1,067.9	961.1	918.2	859.0	811.8	747.3
	1,788.6	1,749.0	1,734.0	1,693.6	1,576.7	1,406.2	1,354.7	1,292.6	1,244.8	1,207.4
Less treasury stock	39.4	56.1	56.6	56.9	57.3	58.5	59.5	50.4	6.3	2.1
Total stockholders' equity	1,749.2	1,692.9	1,677.4	1,636.7	1,519.4	1,347.7	1,295.2	1,242.2	1,238.5	1,205.3
Total liabilities and stockholders' equity	3,166.7	3,071.5	3,122.4	2,913.5	2,814.7	2,731.1	2,029.1	1,875.2	1,806.3	1,735.3
Stockholders' equity per share*	$ 23.40	22.86	22.66	22.18	21.79	20.08	19.41	18.56	18.07	17.55

	1971	1970	1969	1968	1967	1966	1965	1964	1963	1962
CONSOLIDATED STATEMENTS OF PROPERTIES, PLANTS, AND EQUIPMENT										
Gross investment										
Production	$1,796.4	1,749.5	1,729.6	1,587.8	1,495.9	1,460.6	1,390.7	1,342.8	1,279.7	1,257.4
Manufacturing	1,284.6	1,229.7	1,165.1	1,112.8	1,065.2	967.6	669.9	629.5	592.1	515.5
Transportation	276.1	279.7	278.6	276.1	271.6	272.2	195.3	191.5	178.0	164.1
Marketing	326.5	337.5	329.7	323.4	346.9	347.7	188.4	168.6	167.5	147.7
Other	95.9	96.4	93.1	93.4	88.4	97.2	79.8	76.6	71.8	92.3
	3,779.5	3,692.8	3,596.1	3,393.5	3,268.0	3,145.3	2,524.1	2,409.0	2,289.1	2,177.0
Net investment										
Production	$ 756.7	743.2	745.5	651.3	598.4	593.3	600.8	557.5	529.7	564.5
Manufacturing	684.8	682.9	668.9	660.2	644.0	567.9	323.7	304.4	292.9	273.6
Transportation	125.6	135.2	142.8	146.9	150.9	161.2	101.5	103.5	96.0	87.8
Marketing	221.2	237.5	237.8	238.0	265.6	274.4	137.0	122.2	125.5	108.2
Other	49.7	51.7	51.4	53.5	50.8	61.1	45.7	43.5	40.5	50.4
	1,838.0	1,850.5	1,846.4	1,749.9	1,709.7	1,657.9	1,208.7	1,131.1	1,084.6	1,084.5

*Adjusted for two-for-one stock split in 1969.

Note—Financial data for 1970, 1969, 1968 and 1967 have been restated to reflect the adoption of equity accounting for investments (see Note 1 to financial statements).

	1971	1970	1969	1968	1967	1966	1965	1964	1963	1962
REVENUES FROM CHEMICALS, FIBERS, AND FABRICATED PRODUCTS										
Plastic feedstocks and resins	$ 76.8	84.4	85.3	72.9	61.5	56.7	45.7	37.1	40.2	45.5
Rubber chemicals	84.7	73.9	71.4	71.1	60.0	62.9	59.0	58.9	58.1	68.7
Fertilizers	90.9	71.8	69.3	67.5	74.1	82.6	59.7	50.2	43.0	42.4
Fabricated products	89.3	96.3	97.1	104.9	105.8	90.5	85.7	76.5	81.7	—
Synthetic fibers	70.2	57.6	59.3	50.1	31.8	7.0	—	—	—	—
Other products	83.1	93.2	90.3	80.1	65.0	57.5	56.6	48.5	44.4	44.9
	495.0	477.2	472.7	446.6	398.2	357.2	306.7	271.2	267.4	201.5
OTHER DATA										
Shares outstanding at year end—thousands*	74,741	74,062	74,041	73,776	69,717	67,118	66,739	66,929	68,551	68,695
Number of stockholders at year end	166,012	172,979	157,052	145,665	139,670	139,224	137,739	137,589	130,324	128,882
Total payroll including employee benefits	$ 352.8	335.0	326.8	328.9	312.3	281.8	248.9	237.6	233.9	119.6
Number of employees at year end	33,280	32,208	32,660	35,359	35,724	34,667	29,873	28,298	27,816	25,648

*Adjusted for two-for-one stock split in 1969.

TEN-YEAR OPERATING REVIEW

	1971	1970	1969	1968	1967	1966	1965	1964	1963	1962
NET PRODUCTION OF LIQUID RAW MATERIALS—thousands of barrels daily										
Crude Oil										
United States										
Texas	54.9	54.6	51.8	53.7	54.4	52.8	51.5	52.6	54.4	53.7
Louisiana	24.8	29.6	28.1	29.3	28.3	24.9	18.7	14.7	12.4	10.4
Oklahoma	15.6	15.5	16.2	17.7	20.0	22.4	23.7	23.9	23.3	23.1
New Mexico	9.8	10.4	10.3	10.3	10.1	10.3	9.2	8.8	7.8	7.2
Alaska	5.5	5.6	6.9	8.9	3.9	.2	—	—	—	—
Wyoming	3.7	6.3	6.2	3.6	3.3	2.6	2.3	2.2	2.3	2.4
Utah	3.0	3.3	3.4	4.0	3.1	1.8	1.5	1.9	3.3	3.6
Other states	12.8	13.6	14.7	12.4	11.7	12.9	13.4	14.0	14.6	14.2
	130.1	138.9	137.6	139.9	134.8	127.9	120.3	118.1	118.1	114.6
Outside United States										
Canada	13.1	12.2	10.4	9.7	9.0	8.3	7.9	8.0	7.7	5.6
Latin America	20.2	21.3	22.0	26.4	34.0	36.1	34.8	30.6	33.7	34.3
Middle East	14.0	34.4	35.3	32.0	33.0	37.2	39.7	40.3	38.4	36.3
Africa	25.5	20.0	40.0	30.1	25.4	23.1	5.6	1.1	—	—
Europe	2.3	—	—	—	—	—	—	—	—	—
	75.1	87.9	107.7	98.2	101.4	104.7	88.0	80.0	79.8	76.2
Total crude oil	205.2	226.8	245.3	238.1	236.2	232.6	208.3	198.1	197.9	190.8
Natural Gas Liquids										
United States	135.4	131.8	130.3	138.7	132.1	125.2	121.4	114.2	112.0	106.3
Canada	12.8	12.9	11.2	8.9	8.9	8.4	8.0	3.9	.3	.2
Latin America	2.6	2.2	1.1	1.2	1.2	1.2	1.4	1.4	1.5	1.6
Europe	.2	.2	—	—	—	—	—	—	—	—
Total natural gas liquids	151.0	147.1	142.6	148.8	142.2	134.8	130.8	119.5	113.8	108.1
Total all liquids	356.2	373.9	387.9	386.9	378.4	367.4	339.1	317.6	311.7	298.9

Note—Operating data for 1967 through 1971 includes operating results, in proportion to the Company's stock interests, of non-consolidated companies owned 20% or more. Data prior to 1967 includes the Company's interest in such companies owned one-third or more.

	1971	1970	1969	1968	1967	1966	1965	1964	1963	1962
NET NATURAL GAS PRODUCTION— millions of cubic feet daily										
United States	1,566	1,591	1,436	1,429	1,460	1,397	1,330	1,336	1,329	1,322
Canada	179	179	155	127	116	96	87	79	69	67
Latin America	41	48	33	—	—	—	—	—	—	—
Europe	58	40	14	4	4	5	—	—	—	—
	1,844	1,858	1,638	1,560	1,580	1,498	1,417	1,415	1,398	1,389
WELL COMPLETIONS—Net										
United States—Exploratory	21	25	24	24	17	14	40	41	49	39
—Development	70	67	118	98	80	116	202	261	252	226
Outside United States—Exploratory	30	30	26	32	20	30	22	18	20	20
—Development	39	14	19	27	28	63	51	32	28	46
	160	136	187	181	145	223	315	352	349	331
OIL AND GAS WELLS—Net										
United States—Oil	6,004	6,316	6,457	6,387	6,590	6,808	6,873	6,879	6,790	6,630
—Gas and condensate	1,936	1,964	1,997	1,961	1,953	1,946	1,921	1,882	1,821	1,807
Outside United States—All wells	850	829	974	955	1,061	1,033	837	838	823	687
	8,790	9,109	9,428	9,303	9,604	9,787	9,631	9,599	9,434	9,124
NET OIL AND GAS ACREAGE—thousands of acres										
United States	5,382	5,275	4,728	4,618	4,333	4,666	4,995	5,030	5,050	5,330
Canada	6,507	6,273	5,862	4,600	3,563	3,476	2,808	2,349	2,150	1,611
Latin America	696	3,186	4,895	5,008	1,910	2,259	1,934	1,502	1,908	2,119
Europe	1,227	1,424	1,394	1,375	1,238	1,234	1,231	355	1,510	1,510
Africa	8,403	9,009	13,860	16,999	18,398	20,739	18,797	18,109	19,314	8,932
Middle East	13,852	13,852	12,762	12,787	2,102	638	638	311	311	311
Southeast Asia	38,852	47,106	57,627	40,000	—	—	—	—	—	—
Australia	6,272	7,290	9,290	10,833	16,978	26,690	24,383	19,164	22,600	29,480
	81,191	93,415	110,418	96,220	48,522	59,702	54,786	46,820	52,843	49,293
REFINERY RUNS—thousands of barrels daily										
United States—Crude oil	371	364	359	356	335	292	249	248	241	238
—Natural gas liquids	157	162	158	159	162	159	156	156	148	142
Outside United States—All liquids	77	93	88	87	68	58	38	32	30	26
	605	619	605	602	565	509	443	436	419	406
REFINERY CAPACITY—thousands of barrels daily										
United States—Crude oil	398	398	390	390	410	410	289	289	289	289
—Natural gas liquids	165	165	165	165	165	165	160	160	160	160
Outside United States—All liquids	100	100	148	147	97	119	56	46	44	44
	663	663	703	702	672	694	505	495	493	493
PETROLEUM PRODUCTS SOLD—thousands of barrels daily										
United States										
Automotive gasoline	311	314	294	279	252	222	188	183	175	175
Aviation fuels	27	35	38	36	36	25	21	25	29	32
Distillates—including kerosene	98	106	109	120	111	97	92	88	92	92
Liquefied petroleum gases	106	114	107	106	124	135	126	120	122	116
Other products	41	47	48	44	43	38	30	31	26	23
	583	616	596	585	566	517	457	447	444	438
Outside United States	141	131	132	114	83	65	41	37	27	26
Total	724	747	728	699	649	582	498	484	471	464
MARKETING OUTLETS	24,562	25,536	25,914	26,155	26,513	27,240	23,677	23,520	23,662	23,569

Note—Operating data for 1967 through 1971 includes operating results, in proportion to the Company's stock interests, of non-consolidated companies owned 20% or more. Data prior to 1967 includes the Company's interest in such companies owned one-third or more.

Uniform Forecast for Utility Analysts[1]

In January 1971 we applied to the Illinois Commerce Commission for a 10.4% rate increase. In December 1971 we received about two-thirds of our request and, if our rate case projections for 1972 are confirmed by actual operating experience, additional rate relief will be available in 1973.

	1971 (actual)	1972	1973	1974	1975	1976
Load Data—MW						
Owned Net Generating Capability—Summer Peak	**11,434**	13,243[2]	16,432	16,482	16,356	17,077
Less: Summer Limitations	**264**	284	336	336	330	324
Plus: Firm Purchases & Diversity Exchange	**750**	825	200	700	700	700
Pumped Storage Purchase	—	—	—	624	624	624
Net Capability	**11,920**	13,784	16,296	17,470	17,350	18,077
Peak Load (own system)	**10,943**	12,190	13,180	14,230	15,340	16,540
Firm Sales to Other Utilities at Time of Peak	**30**	410	60	410	100	40
Total Peak Load	**10,973**	12,600	13,240	14,640	15,440	16,580
Reserve Margin[3]	**947**	1,184	3,056	2,830	1,910	1,497
Reserve Percentage[4]	**9.3%**	10.1%	23.4%	20.3%	13.0%	9.4%
Capital Requirements (in millions)						
Plant Construction Expenditures	**$570**	$470	$390	$560	$780	$800
Nuclear Fuel Expenditures (net of amortization)	**79**	20	(11)	15	26	25
Mortgage Bond Maturities	—	—	100	176	110	100
Redemption of 9.44% Prior Preferred Stock	—	110	—	—	—	—
Debenture Sinking Fund Purchases (principal amount)	**5**	6	6	6	6	6
Capital Sources (in millions)						
Depreciation	**$114**	$132	$154	$169	$176	$188
Net Tax Deferrals from Liberalized Depreciation (normalized)	**30**	43	52	50	50	55
Investment Tax Credit (normalized) Net of Amortization	**11**	20	12	4	15	12
Employe Stock Purchase Plan	**5**	5	5	5	5	5
Sale of Downstate Properties	—	24	—	—	—	—
Planned Outside Financing[5]		130[6]	210	470	620	610
Allowance for Funds Used During Construction (in millions)						
Includes nuclear fuel	**$49**	$45	$21	$30	$55	$80
Property Retirements (in millions)	**$58**	$40	$45	$55	$60	$75

(1) The figures are for electric operations only. An updated forecast will be sent to you about twice a year. When reviewing Commonwealth, please check your files for the most recent copy.

(2) This assumes neither of the Quad-Cities units nor Zion Unit 1 will be available at the time of the 1972 peak.

(3) The 1973 and 1974 margins were planned to provide safeguards against delays in units scheduled for those years. Capacity in excess of a sound reserve margin will be made available for sale.

(4) Reserve percentage is reserve margin expressed as a percent of total peak load minus firm purchases and diversity exchanges.

(5) The timing of financing may be changed somewhat to take advantage of altered market conditions.

(6) This excludes $190 million from the sale of common stock and warrants in February 1972 and provision for refunding $140 million of commercial paper outstanding on January 1, 1972.

Highlights

(Showing % Increase or *Decrease* Compared with Prior Year)

Average Annual Increase or *Decrease* Since 1961 (1)		1971		1970		1969		1968		1967		1966		1965		1964		1963		1962		1961	
5.1%	Net income on common stock (in millions)	**$124.4**	***0.2%***	$124.6	*1.2%*	$126.1	0.5%	$125.6	0.6%	$124.8	5.7%	$118.0	8.4%	$108.8	9.0%	$ 99.8	9.0%	$ 91.6	7.0%	$ 85.6	10.5%	$ 77.5	6.9%
4.7	Earnings per common and common equivalent share (2)	**$ 2.86** (3)	***3.1***	$ 2.95	*1.7*	$ 3.00	0.3	$ 2.99	0.3	$ 2.98	5.7	$ 2.82	8.0	$ 2.61	8.8	$ 2.40	9.1	$ 2.20	6.8	$ 2.06	10.2	$ 1.87	6.9
9.0	Cash dividends paid per common share (4)	**$ 2.20**	–	$ 2.20	–	$ 2.20	–	$ 2.20	4.8	$ 2.10	5.0	$ 2.00	11.1	$ 1.80	28.6	$ 1.40	12.0	$ 1.25	13.6	$ 1.10	10.0	$ 1.00	–
	Electric operating revenues (in millions)–																						
7.2	Residential only	**$378.7**	**11.2**	$340.4	12.0	$304.0	7.9	$281.6	9.9	$256.3	4.7	$244.8	8.2	$226.2	4.9	$215.6	6.1	$203.2	4.7	$194.1	3.7	$187.1	5.8
6.5	Ultimate consumers	**$970.8**	**11.7**	$869.3	10.9	$783.6	7.6	$728.0	8.0	$674.0	4.3	$646.1	7.2	$602.4	4.7	$575.2	4.5	$550.7	4.4	$527.4	5.3	$501.0	5.0
6.5	Total	**$989.6**	**11.6**	$887.0	10.7	$801.1	7.5	$745.3	8.2	$689.1	4.6	$658.8	7.0	$615.7	5.0	$586.4	4.5	$560.9	4.0	$539.4	5.7	$510.5	4.9
	Kilowatthours sold (in millions)–																						
8.5	Residential only	**13,740**	**5.7**	12,999	9.9	11,826	9.2	10,827	12.1	9,656	5.8	9,127	11.0	8,219	6.8	7,698	8.5	7,098	7.1	6,629	6.3	6,238	7.1
7.5	Ultimate consumers	**47,634**	**4.3**	45,657	6.3	42,933	8.1	39,702	8.6	36,553	4.9	34,858	9.9	31,716	7.9	29,407	7.8	27,292	6.6	25,593	8.3	23,626	5.6
7.6	Total	**48,765**	**4.1**	46,841	5.5	44,387	7.4	41,321	9.6	37,685	5.5	35,712	9.3	32,682	8.5	30,130	8.3	27,832	6.2	26,212	8.6	24,126	5.3
1.8	Number of electric customers at end of year (in thousands)	**2,610**	**1.4**	2,575	1.4	2,539	2.2	2,484	1.5	2,446	1.5	2,410	1.8	2,368	1.9	2,323	2.0	2,278	1.8	2,239	2.0	2,195	1.7
6.5	Average residential use per customer–Kwh	**5,813**	**4.1**	5,585	7.9	5,174	6.9	4,840	10.2	4,391	4.0	4,224	8.8	3,882	4.5	3,715	6.3	3,496	4.9	3,332	4.1	3,202	4.8
1.0	Average revenue per kilowatthour	**2.01¢**	**6.9**	1.88¢	5.0	1.79¢	–	1.79¢	*1.1*	1.81¢	*1.1*	1.83¢	*2.1*	1.87¢	*3.1*	1.93¢	*3.5*	2.00¢	*2.0*	2.04¢	*2.9*	2.10¢	*0.5*

(1) Computed using the least squares method.
(2) Adjusted to reflect the 1961-64 common stock dividends and the 1961 2-for-1 common stock split.
(3) Assumes conversion of outstanding warrants issued May 3, 1971.
(4) In addition, stock dividends of 2%, 2%, 1½%, and 1% were declared in the years 1961-64 inclusive.

On December 9, 1966, Central Illinois Electric and Gas Co. ("Central") was merged into Commonwealth. n this Financial Review, the financial statements and related operating data of Commonwealth and Central prior to the merger have been restated on a combined basis in accordance with the "pooling of interests" concept of accounting, except where otherwise noted.

Electric Revenues, Kilowatthours and Customers

	1971	1970	1969	1968	1967	1966	1965	1964	1963	1962	1961
Electric Operating Revenues (in millions)											
Residential	**$378.7**	$340.4	$304.0	$281.6	$256.3	$244.8	$226.2	$215.6	$203.2	$194.1	$187.1
Small commercial and industrial	**344.9**	313.7	286.2	269.9	253.7	243.0	228.9	221.5	215.9	208.9	198.6
Large commercial and industrial (1)	**177.8**	155.3	139.4	126.5	117.4	114.5	107.5	101.2	96.4	91.8	85.4
Public authorities (1)	**63.5**	54.4	48.6	44.6	41.2	38.2	34.3	31.4	29.4	26.6	23.9
Electric railroads	**5.9**	5.5	5.4	5.4	5.4	5.6	5.5	5.5	5.8	6.0	6.0
Total revenues from ultimate consumers	**$970.8**	$869.3	$783.6	$728.0	$674.0	$646.1	$602.4	$575.2	$550.7	$527.4	$501.0
Sales for resale	**10.0**	9.4	9.8	11.2	9.7	7.4	8.3	6.2	5.4	7.4	5.1
Other revenues	**8.8**	8.3	7.7	6.1	5.4	5.3	5.0	5.0	4.8	4.6	4.4
Total	**$989.6**	$887.0	$801.1	$745.3	$689.1	$658.8	$615.7	$586.4	$560.9	$539.4	$510.5
Percent outside Chicago (ultimate consumers)	**60.8%**	59.9%	59.0%	57.7%	56.8%	55.6%	54.7%	53.7%	52.7%	51.9%	51.0%
Kilowatthours (in millions)											
Generated (net)	**48,264**	47,613	45,382	44,489	40,981	39,075	35,378	32,182	29,619	27,661	25,304
Purchased and interchanged (net)	**4,771**	3,147	2,903	472	61	(135)	283	805	877	1,049	1,320
Total electric output	**53,035**	50,760	48,285	44,961	41,042	38,940	35,661	32,987	30,496	28,710	26,624
Deduct—losses and company use	**4,270**	3,919	3,898	3,640	3,357	3,228	2,979	2,857	2,664	2,498	2,498
Total available for sale	**48,765**	46,841	44,387	41,321	37,685	35,712	32,682	30,130	27,832	26,212	24,126
Sales:											
Residential	**13,740**	12,999	11,826	10,827	9,656	9,127	8,219	7,698	7,098	6,629	6,238
Small commercial and industrial	**14,820**	14,243	13,378	12,552	11,711	11,114	10,189	9,548	8,922	8,488	7,836
Large commercial and industrial (1)	**14,652**	14,241	13,781	12,602	11,699	11,444	10,478	9,606	8,897	8,321	7,610
Public authorities (1)	**4,032**	3,774	3,563	3,336	3,097	2,787	2,447	2,187	1,999	1,751	1,543
Electric railroads	**390**	400	385	385	390	386	383	368	376	404	399
Total sales to ultimate consumers	**47,634**	45,657	42,933	39,702	36,553	34,858	31,716	29,407	27,292	25,593	23,626
Sales for resale	**1,131**	1,184	1,454	1,619	1,132	854	966	723	540	619	500
Total sales	**48,765**	46,841	44,387	41,321	37,685	35,712	32,682	30,130	27,832	26,212	24,126
Percent outside Chicago (ultimate consumers)	**61.3%**	60.4%	59.7%	58.5%	57.8%	56.5%	55.7%	54.9%	54.0%	53.3%	52.1%
Number of Electric Customers (at end of year)											
Residential	**2,379,535**	2,345,231	2,308,041	2,254,371	2,216,713	2,179,949	2,138,022	2,092,802	2,048,609	2,009,573	1,965,941
Small commercial and industrial	**220,311**	220,000	221,149	220,164	220,503	221,012	220,759	221,695	221,018	220,813	220,673
Large commercial and industrial (1)	**672**	658	665	638	615	612	596	590	589	557	543
Public authorities (1)	**9,664**	9,385	9,099	8,864	8,595	8,402	8,238	8,059	7,926	7,727	7,412
Electric railroads	**2**	2	2	2	2	2	2	2	3	3	4
Resale	**8**	6	6	6	6	7	7	7	5	5	6
Total	**2,610,192**	2,575,282	2,538,962	2,484,045	2,446,434	2,409,984	2,367,624	2,323,155	2,278,150	2,238,678	2,194,579
Increase over previous year	**34,910**	36,320	54,917	37,611	36,450	42,360	44,469	45,005	39,472	44,099	37,721
Average Revenue Per Kilowatthour											
Residential (excluding light bulb service)	**2.72¢**	2.58¢	2.53¢	2.56¢	2.61¢	2.64¢	2.70¢	2.75¢	2.82¢	2.88¢	2.95¢
Small commercial and industrial	**2.33**	2.20	2.14	2.15	2.17	2.19	2.25	2.32	2.42	2.46	2.53
Large commercial and industrial	**1.21**	1.09	1.01	1.00	1.00	1.00	1.03	1.05	1.08	1.10	1.12

(1) Figures prior to 1967 have been restated to reflect reclassification of Argonne National Laboratory from a large commercial and industrial customer to a public authority.

Financial Ratios

	1971	1970	1969	1968	1967	1966	1965	1964	1963	1962	1961
Income Account—Electric											
Percent of operating revenues—											
Operating expenses (except maintenance and depreciation)	**41.6%**	38.4%	34.6%	32.0%	31.3%	31.6%	32.1%	33.6%	32.8%	33.3%	33.6%
Maintenance expenses	**6.0**	6.2	5.9	6.2	6.2	5.9	6.9	5.6	5.4	5.6	5.7
Total operating expenses (except depreciation)	**47.6**	44.6	40.5	38.2	37.5	37.5	39.0	39.2	38.2	38.9	39.3
Depreciation (straight line)	**11.5**	12.0	12.6	12.6	12.7	12.5	12.6	12.5	12.6	11.8	11.1
Taxes (except income)	**14.4**	14.6	14.7	14.1	13.6	13.1	12.2	12.0	12.0	12.1	12.2
Investment tax credit deferred (net)	**1.1**	.5	.5	.8	.7	.5	.6	.3	.6	.3	—
Total operating expenses and taxes (except income)	**74.6**	71.7	68.3	65.7	64.5	63.6	64.4	64.0	63.4	63.1	62.6
Income taxes (including deferred)	**6.7**	9.2	11.8	13.4	13.6	14.5	14.0	14.7	15.0	15.4	16.1
Total operating expenses and taxes	**81.3**	80.9	80.1	79.1	78.1	78.1	78.4	78.7	78.4	78.5	78.7
Operating income	**18.7**	19.1	19.9	20.9	21.9	21.9	21.6	21.3	21.6	21.5	21.3
All taxes (including deferred income taxes)	**21.1**	23.8	26.5	27.5	27.2	27.6	26.2	26.7	27.0	27.5	28.3
Net income	**14.6**	15.2	16.5	17.7	19.0	18.9	18.8	18.1	17.5	17.3	17.1
Percent of average depreciable plant—											
Depreciation	**3.32**	3.30	3.31	3.30	3.29	3.27	3.21	3.16	3.14	3.01	2.85
Depreciation plus deferred income taxes and investment tax credits (net)	**4.47**	3.86	3.87	3.91	3.80	3.73	3.71	3.60	3.79	3.67	3.53
Interest on Debt—Times Earned											
Before income taxes and tax deferrals	**3.06**	3.46	4.60	5.98	7.04	8.23	8.15	7.75	7.36	7.05	7.12
Common Stock (Commonwealth only)											
Dividends paid per share—											
Cash	**$ 2.20**	$ 2.20	$ 2.20	$ 2.20	$ 2.10	$ 2.00	$ 1.80	$ 1.40	$ 1.25	$ 1.10	$ 1.00
Stock	**—**	—	—	—	—	—	—	1%	1½%	2%	2%
Dividend payout ratios—											
Cash only	**75.3%**	74.6%	73.4%	73.5%	72.1%	70.8%	70.8%	61.7%	56.9%	52.5%	49.0%
Cash and stock (1)	**75.3**	74.6	73.4	73.5	72.1	70.8	70.8	84.0	90.7	91.0	93.8
Book value per common and common equivalent share at end of year	**$23.84**	$22.65	$22.11	$21.26	$20.42	$19.55	$21.14	$20.33	$19.55	$18.82	$18.14
Market price per share (N.Y.S.E.)—											
High	**43⅞**	40½	50⅛	51½	55¼	54¾	58¼	58¾	54¼	45¾	50⅜
Low	**34½**	28⅛	36	41⅞	44¼	40⅜	51⅛	48⅛	44¼	35	34 1/16
End of year	**39¾**	38⅜	37½	48⅝	47	51⅜	53½	55⅛	49⅞	44	45⅝
Balance Sheet—December 31											
Percent mortgage debt of depreciated utility plant (2)	**45.2%**	46.5%	43.3%	41.3%	36.8%	36.3%	31.7%	32.9%	33.9%	34.4%	35.5%
Percent long-term debt of depreciated utility plant (2)	**50.0**	52.4	50.3	49.6	46.3	47.0	43.4	45.4	47.2	48.3	50.1
Percent accumulated provision for depreciation of plant and equipment—											
Completed plant	**28.9**	29.8	30.4	30.0	29.9	29.6	28.8	28.0	26.2	25.3	24.9
Total plant	**24.1**	25.7	27.1	27.9	28.1	28.0	27.6	26.8	25.7	24.4	23.5
Percent of total capitalization—(3)											
First mortgage bonds	**50.9**	51.7	48.1	44.7	40.5	39.0	34.7	35.3	36.0	36.8	37.2
Sinking fund debentures	**5.4**	6.5	7.9	9.0	10.5	11.5	13.5	14.1	14.9	15.7	16.0
Preferred and preference stocks	**11.7**	8.0	5.7	6.2	6.8	7.2	—	—	—	—	1.6
Common stock equity	**32.0**	33.8	38.3	40.1	42.2	42.3	51.8	50.6	49.1	47.5	45.2

(1) The dividend stock was priced at $45.83, $42.40, $51.60 and $54.21 per share in 1961, 1962, 1963 and 1964, respectively.
(2) Includes nuclear fuel beginning in 1970.
(3) 1961-65 Commonwealth only.

Statements of Consolidated Income (in millions) [1]

	1971	1970	1969	1968	1967	1966	1965	1964	1963	1962	1961
Electric Operating Revenues	$989.6	$887.0	$801.1	$745.3	$689.1	$658.8	$615.7	$586.4	$560.9	$539.4	$510.5
Electric Operating Expenses and Taxes:											
Fuel	$213.0	$179.0	$137.6	$123.3	$107.9	$103.7	$ 96.9	$ 91.4	$ 87.1	$ 81.7	$ 76.7
Purchased and interchanged power (net)	50.3	24.0	16.8	3.1	2.7	.9	2.2	4.8	2.8	3.6	4.1
Operation	148.1	137.5	123.3	112.1	105.3	103.7	98.8	101.1	94.2	94.3	91.0
Maintenance	59.4	55.5	47.3	46.4	42.6	38.8	42.2	32.7	30.1	30.4	28.9
Depreciation (straight line)	114.1	106.7	100.9	94.0	87.6	82.5	77.2	73.0	70.6	63.7	56.7
Taxes (except income)	142.5	129.6	117.6	104.7	93.9	86.0	75.3	70.3	67.7	65.2	62.2
Income taxes—(2)											
Federal	32.2	61.3	78.2	88.2	84.5	86.8	77.4	77.7	72.7	70.3	67.9
State	4.0	5.5	2.6	—	—	—	—	—	—	—	—
Deferred (net)	29.9	14.5	13.7	11.9	9.3	8.4	8.5	8.9	11.3	12.7	14.1
Investment tax credit deferred (net)	11.2	4.1	3.8	6.0	4.6	3.4	3.9	1.5	3.4	1.8	—
	$804.7	$717.7	$641.8	$589.7	$538.4	$514.2	$482.4	$461.4	$439.9	$423.7	$401.6
Electric Operating Income	$184.9	$169.3	$159.3	$155.6	$150.7	$144.6	$133.3	$125.0	$121.0	$115.7	$108.9
Other Income:											
Allowance for funds used during construction	$ 48.6	$ 33.8	$ 22.2	$ 12.9	$ 7.9	$ 5.4	$ 4.4	$ 4.0	$ 2.6	$ 5.0	$ 5.0
Operating income of gas and steam heating properties prior to transfer to Mid-Illinois Gas Company	—	—	—	3.7	3.9	3.1	3.0	2.4	2.1	1.7	1.3
Income from Mid-Illinois Gas Company(3)	—	2.8	2.7	—	—	—	—	—	—	—	—
Miscellaneous (net)	2.4	6.5	8.1	7.8	7.5	5.5	4.4	4.9	2.4	1.7	2.4
Income tax credits applicable to nonoperating activities (net)(2)	12.3	8.2	3.8	1.0	.1	.1	—	(.3)	(.1)	.2	(.3)
	$ 63.3	$ 51.3	$ 36.8	$ 25.4	$ 19.4	$ 14.1	$ 11.8	$ 11.0	$ 7.0	$ 8.6	$ 8.4
	$248.2	$220.6	$196.1	$181.0	$170.1	$158.7	$145.1	$136.0	$128.0	$124.3	$117.3
Deductions:											
Interest on debt	$102.0	$ 84.9	$ 61.7	$ 48.2	$ 38.5	$ 31.3	$ 29.1	$ 29.3	$ 29.5	$ 29.7	$ 28.0
Other deductions	1.4	1.3	2.1	1.0	.6	2.7	.5	.3	.4	1.4	2.2
	$103.4	$ 86.2	$ 63.8	$ 49.2	$ 39.1	$ 34.0	$ 29.6	$ 29.6	$ 29.9	$ 31.1	$ 30.2
Net Income	$144.8	$134.4	$132 3	$131.8	$131.0	$124.7	$115.5	$106.4	$ 98.1	$ 93.2	$ 87.1
Provision for Dividends on Preferred and Preference Stocks(4)	20.4	9.8	6.2	6.2	6.2	6.7	6.7	6.6	6.5	7.6	9.6
Net Income on Common Stock	$124.4	$124.6	$126.1	$125.6	$124.8	$118.0	$108.8	$ 99.8	$ 91.6	$ 85.6	$ 77.5
Earnings per Common and Common Equivalent Share(5)	$ 2.86	$ 2.95	$ 3.00	$ 2.99	$ 2.98	$ 2.82	$ 2.61	$ 2.40	$ 2.20	$ 2.06	$ 1.87

(1) Central was merged into Commonwealth on December 9, 1966. In accordance with the "pooling of interests" concept of accounting, the statements of consolidated income for 1966 and prior years include the revenues and expenses of Central for periods prior to the merger.

(2) The reduction of income taxes resulting from interest charges applicable to nonoperating activities, principally construction, is classified as Other Income.
Allowance for funds used during construction has been computed at a rate of 7% per year since January 1, 1969. Prior to that time we were using somewhat lower rates in the 6% range. The 7% rate is a conservative approximation of current overall money costs reduced by the income tax savings on the interest portion thereof. This reduction has the effect of "normalizing" these tax savings, thus avoiding overstatement of current income, a procedure consistent with our policy of normalizing other tax benefits such as accelerated depreciation. Allocations have been made to reflect the income tax savings from interest incurred on construction and other nonoperating activities. The amount of such savings is included in the Other Income section of the income statement in the caption "Income tax credits applicable to nonoperating activities (net)." The sum of the tax credits, plus the allowance for funds used during construction, approximates the amount of before-tax earnings applicable to construction activities.

(3) On December 30, 1968, Commonwealth's gas and steam heating properties were transferred to Mid-Illinois Gas Company, a newly formed wholly-owned subsidiary.
On November 30, 1970, Commonwealth distributed to common shareholders its entire ownership of common stock of Mid-Illinois Gas Company.

(4) Includes dividends accrued on Commonwealth's 4.64% and 5.25% preferred stocks redeemed in 1961 and 1962, respectively, and on Central's preferred stock redeemed prior to the merger and dividend requirements on the $1.425 convertible preferred stock substituted for Central's common stock in the merger as if such convertible preferred stock had been outstanding throughout each year.

(5) Earnings per share were computed using the weighted average number of shares of common stock and common stock equivalents outstanding. Additional shares of common stock which would be issued if all outstanding warrants were converted have been considered common stock equivalents.

The Service Annuity Systems cover all regular employes. Payments to the trust funds were equivalent to actuarial normal costs based on the aggregate cost method. The $307 million book value of the funds at December 31, 1971, approximated the actuarially computed value of vested benefits estimated at that date.

Consolidated Balance Sheets (in millions)

December 31	1971	1970	1969	1968	1967	1966	1965	1964	1963	1962	1961
Assets											
Utility Plant:											
Plant and equipment, at original cost	$4,612.6	$4,100.4	$3,714.2	$3,347.7	$3,109.2	$2,885.4	$2,714.4	$2,583.7	$2,473.9	$2,398.5	$2,295.7
Less—Accumulated provision for depreciation	1,110.7	1,053.0	1,006.8	933.1	874.8	807.7	750.1	692.2	635.0	585.5	540.0
	$3,501.9	$3,047.4	$2,707.4	$2,414.6	$2,234.4	$2,077.7	$1,964.3	$1,891.5	$1,838.9	$1,813.0	$1,755.7
Nuclear fuel, at amortized cost	193.6	114.4	70.9	36.1	6.8	5.1	6.1	5.6	6.9	7.8	8.1
	$3,695.5	$3,161.8	$2,778.3	$2,450.7	$2,241.2	$2,082.8	$1,970.4	$1,897.1	$1,845.8	$1,820.8	$1,763.8
Deposit with Mortgage Trustee	$ —	$ —	$ —	$ 25.0	$ —	$ —	$ —	$ —	$ —	$ —	$ —
Investments:											
Subsidiary companies not consolidated—Mid-Illinois Gas Company, at underlying book value	$ —	$ —	$ 18.5	$ 14.2	$ —	$ —	$ —	$ —	$ —	$ —	$ —
Other—at underlying book value	23.4	17.5	—	—	—	—	—	—	—	—	—
at cost	—	—	7.7	7.8	8.9	10.0	7.3	6.3	6.7	6.8	6.9
Other investments, at cost	2.0	1.8	1.0	1.2	8.5	3.0	3.6	4.4	4.8	.4	.2
	$ 25.4	$ 19.3	$ 27.2	$ 23.2	$ 17.4	$ 13.0	$ 10.9	$ 10.7	$ 11.5	$ 7.2	$ 7.1
Current Assets:											
Cash	$ 14.7	$ 10.0	$ 12.6	$ 7.4	$ 12.3	$ 10.1	$ 11.6	$ 11.3	$ 12.3	$ 12.7	$ 13.4
Temporary cash investments, at cost	.1	6.6	3.3	15.5	29.3	64.3	21.6	41.6	39.1	8.3	21.0
Special deposits	15.8	12.1	7.8	3.8	2.3	6.8	3.3	3.4	3.2	3.9	46.2
Receivables	88.4	86.6	72.1	60.0	57.0	52.9	46.9	42.4	40.5	37.6	39.0
Provision for uncollectible accounts	(1.5)	(1.5)	(1.5)	(1.8)	(1.8)	(1.8)	(1.9)	(1.9)	(1.8)	(1.8)	(1.8)
Preferred stock subscriptions	—	16.5	—	—	—	—	—	—	—	—	—
Coal and fuel oil, at average cost	38.6	28.5	21.3	18.7	23.5	21.3	18.7	20.4	19.2	21.3	18.5
Materials and supplies, at average cost	23.4	22.1	20.3	16.5	17.3	16.1	11.8	11.0	10.6	11.3	12.1
Prepayments	2.6	3.0	2.9	2.7	2.6	2.1	2.2	1.8	1.5	1.4	2.6
	$ 182.1	$ 183.9	$ 138.8	$ 122.8	$ 142.5	$ 171.8	$ 114.2	$ 130.0	$ 124.6	$ 94.7	$ 151.0
Deferred Charges	$ 12.9	$ 10.0	$ 3.8	$ 2.6	$ 2.4	$ 1.6	$ 1.3	$ 1.4	$ 1.3	$ 1.3	$ 1.3
	$3,915.9	$3,375.0	$2,948.1	$2,624.3	$2,403.5	$2,269.2	$2,096.8	$2,039.2	$1,983.2	$1,924.0	$1,923.2
Liabilities											
Capitalization:											
Stockholders' equity	$1,435.4	$1,189.8	$1,070.0	$1,031.8	$ 994.5	$ 956.3	$ 926.1	$ 888.6	$ 843.5	$ 799.2	$ 779.5
Long-term debt	1,849.2	1,657.0	1,362.5	1,198.8	1,034.7	977.3	852.7	859.6	867.1	875.9	879.0
Total Capitalization	$3,284.6	$2,846.8	$2,432.5	$2,230.6	$2,029.2	$1,933.6	$1,778.8	$1,748.2	$1,710.6	$1,675.1	$1,658.5
Current Liabilities:											
Notes payable	$ 140.0	$ 97.0	$ 136.1	$ 50.0	$ 50.0	$ —	$ 6.5	$ 5.0	$ 3.6	$ 3.2	$ 2.0
Accounts payable	53.1	52.3	38.6	30.3	27.9	39.2	29.8	22.1	27.2	23.6	22.0
Accrued interest	37.2	29.9	22.0	15.7	11.7	11.6	9.5	9.6	9.6	9.6	9.5
Accrued taxes	92.5	89.2	83.9	79.7	81.3	94.0	98.3	97.9	94.5	91.2	88.1
Dividends payable	29.9	26.8	24.7	24.7	24.6	21.9	22.0	19.8	15.3	13.0	11.0
Customer deposits	11.3	10.3	10.1	10.1	10.1	10.8	10.8	10.2	9.3	7.9	6.4
Other	1.3	3.4	3.4	4.7	5.1	9.8	5.7	4.1	4.2	7.0	47.7
	$ 365.3	$ 308.9	$ 318.8	$ 215.2	$ 210.7	$ 187.3	$ 182.6	$ 168.7	$ 163.7	$ 155.5	$ 186.7
Deferred Liabilities:											
Accumulated deferred income taxes	$ 194.3	$ 164.3	$ 149.9	$ 136.2	$ 126.7	$ 117.1	$ 108.2	$ 99.3	$ 90.0	$ 78.4	$ 65.4
Accumulated deferred investment tax credits being amortized over the lives of related property	43.6	32.4	28.3	24.5	19.1	14.5	11.0	6.9	5.3	1.8	—
Other	28.1	22.6	18.6	17.8	17.8	16.7	16.2	16.1	13.6	13.2	12.6
	$ 266.0	$ 219.3	$ 196.8	$ 178.5	$ 163.6	$ 148.3	$ 135.4	$ 122.3	$ 108.9	$ 93.4	$ 78.0
	$3,915.9	$3,375.0	$2,948.1	$2,624.3	$2,403.5	$2,269.2	$2,096.8	$2,039.2	$1,983.2	$1,924.0	$1,923.2

Central was merged into Commonwealth on December 9, 1966. In accordance with the "pooling of interests" concept of accounting, the 1961-65 balance sheets include the assets and liabilities of both companies.

At December 31, 1971, purchase commitments, principally related to construction, approximated $844 million.

Statement of Consolidated Capitalization (in millions)

December 31, 1971	
Stockholders' Equity:	
Common stock, $12.50 par value per share—	
Authorized 75,000,000 shares (349,050 shares reserved for Employe Stock Purchase Plan, 2,397,025 shares reserved for conversion of $1.425 convertible preferred stock and 4,171,469 shares reserved for exercise or conversion of warrants)—Outstanding 42,678,313 shares	$ 533.5
Preference stock, without par value—	
Authorized 16,000,000 shares—issuable in series—	
$1.90 series—Outstanding 4,249,549 shares	106.2
$2.00 series—Outstanding 2,000,000 shares	51.6
$1.425 convertible preferred stock, without par value—(each share convertible into 6/10ths of a common share—redeemable at $42.00 per share)—Authorized and outstanding 3,995,043 shares	127.0
Prior preferred stock, $100 par value per share—	
Authorized 1,850,000 shares—issuable in series—9.44% series—Outstanding 1,000,000 shares	100.0
Premium on common stock and other paid-in capital (1)	161.1
Capital stock and warrant expense	(4.7)
Retained earnings	360.7
Total Stockholders' Equity (2)	$1,435.4
Long-Term Debt:	
First Mortgage Bonds—	
Issued by Commonwealth—	
3%, Series L, dated August 1, 1944, due February 1, 1977	$ 180.0
3%, Series M, dated April 1, 1945, due April 1, 1985	100.0
3%, Series N, dated June 1, 1948, due June 1, 1978	50.0
3¼%, Series O, dated July 1, 1952, due July 1, 1982	40.0
3%, Series Q, dated May 1, 1954, due May 1, 1984	50.0
3½%, Series R, dated June 1, 1956, due June 1, 1986	40.0
4¼%, Series S, dated March 1, 1957, due March 1, 1987	50.0
3¾%, Series T, dated March 1, 1958, due March 1, 1988	50.0
4⅝%, Series U, dated March 1, 1960, due March 1, 1990	30.0
5¼%, Series V, dated April 1, 1966, due April 1, 1996	50.0
5¾%, Series W, dated November 1, 1966, due November 1, 1996	50.0
5¾%, Series X, dated December 1, 1966, due December 1, 1996	50.0
5⅜%, Series Y, dated April 1, 1967, due April 1, 1997	50.0
6¼%, Series Z, dated February 1, 1968, due February 1, 1998	50.0
6¾%, Series 15, dated July 1, 1968, due July 1, 1998	50.0
6⅜%, Series 16, dated October 1, 1968, due October 1, 1998	75.0
8%, Series 17, dated July 1, 1969, due July 1, 1973	100.0
7.30%, Series 18, dated April 1, 1969, due April 1, 1974	75.0
8¾%, Series 19, dated January 1, 1970, due January 1, 1975	100.0
8%, Series 20, dated April 1, 1970, due October 1, 1975	100.0
7¾%, Series 21, dated October 1, 1970, due October 1, 1976	100.0
7½%, Series 22, dated January 1, 1971, due January 1, 2001	100.0
8%, Series 23, dated August 1, 1971, due August 1, 2001	100.0
	$1,640.0
Assumed by Commonwealth as prior lien bonds in the Central merger—	
2⅞% Series, dated January 1, 1950, due January 1, 1975	$ .8
3% Series, dated February 1, 1945, due February 1, 1975	10.6
2¾% Series, dated July 1, 1947, due July 1, 1977	2.0
3½% Series, dated January 1, 1952, due January 1, 1982	4.0
3⅜% Series, dated June 1, 1955, due June 1, 1985	4.0
5% Series, dated July 1, 1960, due July 1, 1990	10.0
	$ 31.4
Total First Mortgage Bonds	$1,671.4

Statement of Consolidated Capitalization (in millions) continued

December 31, 1971	
Sinking Fund Debentures—	
3%, dated April 1, 1949, due April 1, 1999	$ 23.8
2¾%, dated October 1, 1949, due April 1, 1999	23.3
2⅞%, dated October 1, 1950, due April 1, 2001	25.9
3⅛%, dated October 1, 1954, due October 1, 2004	30.0
3⅞%, dated January 1, 1958, due January 1, 2008	32.4
4⅝%, dated January 1, 1959, due January 1, 2009	13.2
4¾%, dated December 1, 1961, due December 1, 2011	29.2
Total Sinking Fund Debentures	$ 177.8
Total Long-Term Debt	$1,849.2
Total Capitalization	$3,284.6

(1) As of December 31, 1971, 4,171,469 common stock purchase warrants were outstanding. Each warrant entitles the holder to purchase one share of common stock for $30 or to convert such warrant into common stock at a conversion rate of one share of common stock for three warrants. The option to purchase shares of common stock will expire on April 30, 1981. Thereafter, any unexercised warrants will continue to be convertible into common stock.

(2) On February 2, 1972, Commonwealth offered to its common shareholders the right to purchase 4,270,152 units at a subscription price of $45 per unit, each unit consisting of one share of common stock and one common stock purchase warrant. On February 18, 1972, Commonwealth called for redemption on March 20, 1972 the outstanding 1,000,000 shares of 9.44% Cumulative Prior Preferred Stock at $110 per share plus accrued dividends. A portion of the proceeds of the February 2, 1972 offering will be used for the redemption.

Statement of Consolidated Retained Earnings (in millions)

	1971
Balance beginning of year	$331.1
Add:	
Net income	144.8
	$475.9
Deduct:	
Cash dividends on—	
Common stock	$ 93.7
Preferred and preference stocks	21.5
	$115.2
Balance end of year	$360.7

Statement of Consolidated Premium on Common Stock and Other Paid-in Capital (in millions)

	1971
Balance beginning of year	$102.2
Add:	
Premium on issuance of common stock	3.7
Proceeds from issuance of 4,249,549 common stock purchase warrants	55.2
Balance end of year	$161.1

Statements of Consolidated Changes in Financial Position (in millions) (1)

	1971	1970	1969	1968	1967	1966	1965	1964	1963	1962	1961
Funds Provided By:											
Retained earnings—											
Net income	**$144.8**	$134.4	$132.3	$131.8	$131.0	$124.7	$115.5	$106.4	$ 98.1	$ 93.2	$ 87.1
Less—Cash dividends on stock	**115.2**	103.4	98.8	98.5	96.7	87.9	81.5	65.8	56.5	50.3	45.1
	$ 29.6	$ 31.0	$ 33.5	$ 33.3	$ 34.3	$ 36.8	$ 34.0	$ 40.6	$ 41.6	$ 42.9	$ 42.0
Add—Amounts not requiring current outlay of funds—											
Depreciation	**114.1**	106.7	100.9	95.1	88.6	83.4	77.9	73.6	71.2	64.4	57.5
Deferred income taxes and investment tax credits (net)	**41.1**	18.5	17.5	18.3	14.3	12.4	13.0	10.9	15.1	14.8	14.2
Other non-cash items (net)	**(1.2)**	(6.2)	(4.5)	(3.7)	(2.9)	(1.7)	(1.1)	(1.3)	(1.1)	(.7)	(.9)
Funds provided internally	**$183.6**	$150.0	$147.4	$143.0	$134.3	$130.9	$123.8	$123.8	$126.8	$121.4	$112.8
Sales of securities—											
First mortgage bonds and debentures	**198.9**	299.6	175.1	174.3	67.7	131.8	—	—	—	—	40.0
Capital stock and warrants	**216.1**	103.0	4.6	4.2	3.9	3.8	3.7	3.4	3.1	3.1	2.9
Changes in bank loans, commercial paper and other working capital (net)	**58.1**	(55.0)	87.7	49.1	52.7	(53.0)	29.6	(.3)	(21.8)	25.0	38.3
	$656.7	$497.6	$414.8	$370.6	$258.6	$213.5	$157.1	$126.9	$108.1	$149.5	$194.0
Funds Applied To:											
Plant construction	**$570.4**	$449.9	$396.3	$319.9	$246.9	$198.6	$152.0	$136.9	$103.1	$123.4	$151.0
Nuclear fuel (net)	**79.2**	44.0	35.1	31.1	1.5	(.7)	.1	(1.6)	.5	(1.2)	.3
Sinking fund retirements	**4.8**	2.8	6.7	7.3	7.7	6.1	5.8	6.4	7.7	2.5	3.3
Preferred stock redemptions	—	—	—	—	—	10.3	—	.—	—	26.3	42.6
Deposit with mortgage trustee	—	—	(25.0)	25.0	—	—	—	—	—	—	—
Other items (net)	**2.3**	.9	1.7	(12.7)	2.5	(.8)	(.8)	(14.8)	(3.2)	(1.5)	(3.2)
	$656.7	$497.6	$414.8	$370.6	$258.6	$213.5	$157.1	$126.9	$108.1	$149.5	$194.0

HUMAN RESOURCE ACCOUNTING

[The information presented (in the table) is provided only to illustrate the informational value of human resource accounting for more effective internal management of the business. The figures included regarding investments and amortization of human resources are unaudited and you are cautioned for purposes of evaluating the performance of this company to refer to the conventional certified accounting data further on in this report.]

During the past year work continued on the development of Barry's Human Resource Accounting System. The basic purpose of the system is to develop a method of measuring in dollar terms the changes that occur in the human resources of a business that conventional accounting does not currently consider.

BASIC CONCEPT

Management can be considered as the process of planning, organizing, leading and controlling a complex mix of resources to accomplish the objectives of the organization. Those resources, we believe, are: physical resources of the company as represented by buildings and equipment, financial resources, and human resources which consist of the people who comprise the organization and proprietary resources which consist of trademarks, patents, and company name and reputation.

In order to determine more precisely the effectiveness of management's performance it is necessary to have information about the status of investments in the acquisition, maintenance, and utilization of all resources of the company.

Without such information, it is difficult for a company to know whether profit is being generated by converting a resource into cash or conversely whether sub-optimal performance really has been generated by investments in developing the human resources which we expensed under conventional accounting practice.

DEFINITION

Human Resource Accounting is an attempt to identify, quantify, and report investments made in resources of an organization that are not presently accounted for under conventional accounting practice. Basically, it is an information-system that tells management what changes over time are occurring to the human resources of the business. It must be considered as an element of a total system of management—not as a separate "device" or "gimmick" to focus attention on human resources.

OBJECTIVES

Broadly, the Human Resource Accounting Information System is being designed to provide better answers to these kinds of questions: What is the quality of profit performance? Are sufficient human capabilities being acquired to achieve the objectives of the enterprise? Are they being developed adequately? To what degree are they being properly maintained? Are these capabilities being properly utilized by the organization?

"THE TOTAL CONCEPT"
R. G. BARRY CORPORATION AND SUBSIDIARIES
PRO-FORMA
(FINANCIAL AND HUMAN RESOURCE ACCOUNTING)

BALANCE SHEET

	1969 Financial and Human Resource	1969 Financial Only
Assets		
Total Current Assets	$10,003,628	$10,003,628
Net Property, Plant and Equipment	1,770,717	1,770,717
Excess of Purchase Price of Subsidiaries over Net Assets Acquired	1,188,704	1,188,704
Net Investments in Human Resources	986,094	–
Other Assets	106,783	106,783
	$14,055,926	$13,069,832
Liabilities and Stockholders' Equity		
Total Current Liabilities	$ 5,715,708	$ 5,715,708
Long Term Debt, Excluding Current Installments	1,935,500	1,935,500
Deferred Compensation	62,380	62,380
Deferred Federal Income Taxes as a Result of Appropriation for Human Resources	493,047	–
Stockholders' Equity:		
Capital Stock	879,116	879,116
Additional Capital in Excess of Par Value	1,736,253	1,736,253
Retained Earnings:		
Financial	2,740,875	2,740,875
Appropriation for Human Resources	493,047	–
Total Stockholders' Equity	5,849,291	5,356,244
	$14,055,926	$13,069,832

STATEMENT OF INCOME

	1969 Financial and Human Resource	1969 Financial Only
Net sales	$25,310,588	$25,310,588
Cost of sales	16,275,876	16,275,876
Gross profit	9,034,712	9,034,712
Selling, general and administrative expenses	6,737,313	6,737,313
Operating income	2,297,399	2,297,399
Other deductions, net	953,177	953,177
Income before Federal income taxes	1,344,222	1,344,222
Human Resource expenses applicable to future periods	173,569	–
Adjusted income before Federal income taxes	1,517,791	1,344,222
Federal income taxes	730,785	644,000
Net income	$ 787,006	$ 700,222

As expressed in our 1968 Annual Report, our specific objectives in development of human resource accounting are: 1) to provide Barry managers with specific feedback information on their performance in managing the organizational resources entrusted to their care so that they can make proper adjustments to their pattern of operations to correct adverse trends or further improve the condition of these resources; 2) to provide Barry managers with additional information pertaining to human resources to assist in their decision-making; and 3) to provide the organization with a more accurate accounting of its return on total resources employed, rather than just the physical resources, and to enable management to analyze how changes in the status of the resources employed affect the achievement of corporate objectives.

APPROACH

The approach used has been to account for investments in securing and developing the organization's human resources. Outlay costs for recruiting, acquiring, training, familiarizing, and developing management personnel are accumulated and capitalized. In accordance with the approach conventional accounting employs for classification of an expenditure as an asset, only those outlays which have an expected value beyond the current accounting period deserve consideration as investments. Those outlays which are likely to be consumed within a twelve-month period are properly classified as expense items. The investments in human resources are amortized over the expected useful period of the investment. The basic outlays in connection with acquiring and integrating new management people are amortized over their expected tenure with the company. Investments made for training or development are amortized over a much shorter period of time. The system now covers all management personnel at all locations of the corporation.

Research and development of the system began in late 1966 as a joint effort between the Institute for Social Research, of the University of Michigan, and R. G. Barry. Representing the Institute in the development of the system were Rensis Likert, Director of the Institute for Social Research; William C. Pyle, Director, Human Resource Accounting Research, who was responsible for much of the theoretical and conceptual work; and Lee Brummet, Professor of Accounting, of the University of Michigan Business School. For Barry, the team members were Edward Stan, Treasurer; Robert L. Woodruff, Vice President, Personnel; and Richard Burrell, Controller.

APPLICATIONS

There are many potential applications for human resource accounting. Considering outlays for human resource investments which have a useful life over a number of years would have an impact upon the current year's revenue. Recognizing investments in human resources and their useful lives, losses resulting from improper maintenance of those resources can be shown in dollar terms. Estimating the useful lives of investments also provides a basis for planning for the orderly replacement of human capabilities as they expire, supplementing conventional manpower planning. Finally, recognizing investments in human resources will allow management to calculate dollar return on investment on a more comprehensive resource base for a particular profit center.

SUMMARY

From the standpoint of management, knowledge of the human resource investments, maintenance and returns is necessary for proper decision-making and planning long-range corporate growth. As industry becomes increasingly technical, and management becomes progressively more complex, we believe conventional accounting practice will come to recognize human resource accounting in financial reporting.

At this stage, the Human Resource Accounting System at R. G. Barry is best regarded as a potentially important tool of the overall management system. It is not an end in itself, and needs continuing refinement and development.

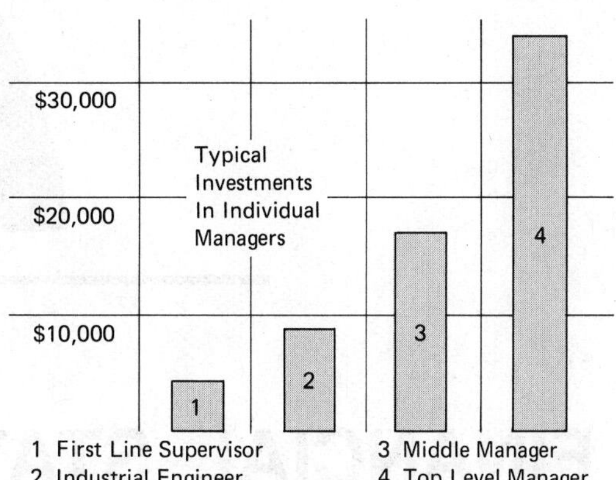

FINANCIAL STATEMENT ANALYSIS

7.1 FINANCIAL STATEMENT ANALYSIS

Financial statements in isolation of their context provide very little useful information. For example, the Exridge Corporation in the preceding chapter reported sales of \$3,000,000 in 19x2. This figure is meaningless in the abstract, but we can give it meaning in several ways:

1. We can compare sales in 19x2 with other accounts in that year.
2. We can compare sales in 19x2 with sales in prior periods.
3. We can compare Exridge's sales with those of its competitors.
4. We can compare sales in 19x2 against the budgeted or expected sales for the period.

The purpose of financial statement analysis is to give meaning to particular accounts such as sales. But we are also interested in giving meaning to sets of accounts, to the relationships between accounts and sets of accounts, as well as to the financial statements as a whole. In a synergistic sense, the financial statements as a whole represent something more than the sum of their parts. Related to the notion of *synergism* is the concept of *holism,* i.e., the understanding of detail can only be achieved within the context of an understanding of the entity as a whole. This articulation between the individual elements and the financial statements as a whole is critical, as is the relationship between a company and its economic reference group.

We mentioned four ways in which to give meaning to Exridge's sales for 19*x*2: (1) intraperiod comparison; (2) interperiod comparison; (3) inter-firm comparison; and (4) comparison vis-à-vis the budget. We discuss budgeting and variance analysis extensively in chapters 23 and 18. In this chapter our concern is with the other forms of comparison.

All of the techniques illustrated in this chapter can be used in conjunction with published financial statements. We emphasize that these techniques are crude measures of analysis. They point to possible problem areas, but further investigation is needed to narrow in on the causes of variances, to determine whether variances were controllable or not, or whether variances are likely to have impact on future operations. But even a cursory analysis of financial statements can provide much meaningful information to the trained observor. Consistent analysis from period to period is even more fruitful, as it points to significant trends and developments.

7.2 RATIO ANALYSIS

Ratio analysis[1] is used to examine the relationships between accounts and sets of accounts. Its purpose is to measure efficiency and performance. These qualities are complex principles, analogous to our discussion of measuring "morale" in chapter 1. We stated at that time that a complex principle cannot be measured directly. Instead, it is measured indirectly through recognizing appropriate surrogates. We emphasized that a complex principle requires several surrogates. For this reason no one ratio or indicator should be used to measure efficiency or performance. In the first decade of the 1900s, there was almost total reliance on the *current ratio* as being the magic clue to organizational performance. It was this idol that stimulated Alexander Wall to propose a broader basis of financial analysis in 1919.[2] From this beginning Wall went on to develop systematic financial statement analysis which became the prototype for our current practice.[3]

Today the danger is that *earnings* and its derivatives of *earnings per share* and *price-earnings ratio* are being emphasized to the exclusion of other indicators. Reliance on any single measure is inappropriate. A negative indicator in one area may be more than offset by positive indicators in other areas.

[1]Empirical tests which seek to determine whether these ratios measure what the literature has long held to be true are currently being undertaken. See William H. Beaver, "Financial Ratios as Predictors of Failure," *Empirical Research in Accounting: Selected Studies 1966,* supplement to the *Journal of Accounting Research* 4 (1966): 71–126, and Jarrod W. Wilcox, "A Gambler's Ruin Prediction of Business Failure Using Accounting Data," *Sloan Management Review,* Spring 1971, pp. 1–10. These studies challenge some traditional uses of financial ratios.

[2]Alexander Wall, "Study of Credit Barometers," *Federal Reserve Bulletin* V (March 1919): 229–43.

[3]Wall, *Analytical Credits* (Indianapolis: The Bobbs-Merrill Co., 1921); with Raymond W. Duning, *Ratio Analysis of Financial Statements* (New York: Harper & Row, 1928); with Raymond W. Duning, *Analyzing Financial Statements* (New York: American Institute of Banking, 1930); and *How to Evaluate Financial Statements* (New York: Harper & Row, 1936).

Ratio analysis has now been extended to many relationships. Exhibit 7-4 (p. 253) is a fairly comprehensive but by no means complete list of available ratios. Students confronting a wide variety of ratios are likely to be more confused than illuminated by the experience. Accordingly, we will focus on six ratio categories which we believe to be critical, and augment this detailed discussion with the ratios contained in Exhibit 7-4.

We will use the financial statements of the Exridge Corporation (Exhibits 6-5, 6-6, and 6-7) to illustrate these key ratios.

EARNING POWER

Intraperiod

Earning power measures the ability of assets to generate earnings. In 19*x*2 the Exridge Corporation has a total investment in assets of $2,800,000. In that year, these assets generated sales of $3,000,000. This relationship between total assets and sales is referred to as earning power. We measure this relationship by means of a *turnover* or multiplier ratio:

$$\text{Earning Power} = \frac{\text{Sales}}{\text{Assets}} = \frac{\$3{,}000{,}000}{\$2{,}800{,}000} = 1.07x$$

where x = turnover ratio. This is to say that assets turned over into sales 1.07 times.

This ratio can be extended to compare assets with *gross profit* and with *net income*. These ratios are referred to as *gross* and *net* earning power respectively. In 19*x*2 these ratios for the Exridge Corporation were:

$$\text{Gross Earning Power} = \frac{\text{Gross Profit}}{\text{Assets}} = \frac{\$1{,}120{,}000}{\$2{,}800{,}000} = .40x$$

$$\text{Net Earning Power} = \frac{\text{Net Income}}{\text{Assets}} = \frac{\$295{,}000}{\$2{,}800{,}000} = .105x$$

This ratio, as well as the others which we will discuss, is given more meaning as we extend our analysis to other periods and to other firms.

Interperiod

Interperiod analysis measures the effectiveness of changes in the resource base. For example, the Exridge Corporation increased its assets in 19*x*2 by $150,000 over 19*x*1. We can calculate the effectiveness of this marginal increase in assets as follows:

EARNING POWER

	19x1	Marginal Analysis	19x2
Earning power.........	$\left(\frac{\$2,700,000}{\$2,650,000}\right) = 1.02x$	$\left(\frac{\$300,000}{\$150,000}\right) = 2.00x$	$\left(\frac{\$3,000,000}{\$2,800,000}\right) = 1.07x$
Gross earning power.....................	$\left(\frac{\$1,110,000}{\$2,650,000}\right) = .42x$	$\left(\frac{\$10,000}{\$150,000}\right) = .07x$	$\left(\frac{\$1,120,000}{\$2,800,000}\right) = .40x$
Net earning power.....................	$\left(\frac{\$208,000}{\$2,650,000}\right) = .078x$	$\left(\frac{\$87,000}{\$150,000}\right) = .58x$	$\left(\frac{\$295,000}{\$2,800,000}\right) = .105x$

The analysis can be refined to focus on net *operating* income, as opposed to net income:

Net operating earning power.........	$\left(\frac{\$410,000}{\$2,650,000}\right) = .155x$	$\left(\frac{\langle\$90,000\rangle}{\$150,000}\right) = .60x$	$\left(\frac{\$320,000}{\$2,800,000}\right) = .114x$

We can now make the following observations:

1. The marginal increase in assets was highly productive as to sales. Each dollar invested in assets in 19*x*1 generated $1.02 dollars in sales. The additional investment of $300,000 in assets generated $2.00 per dollar in sales.
2. Gross earning power declined in the period 19*x*1–19*x*2, despite the very favorable earning power ratio. This decline in marginal gross profit suggests problems in purchasing and/or production.
3. Net earning power increased in 19*x*2 over 19*x*1, but this was attributable in the main to the capital gain in 19*x*2. The "net operating earning power" computation focuses more accurately on the operating picture.

The net earning power ratios are indicative of administrative performance. However, net income is influenced by gross profit, so that a major change in gross profit will carry over into net income. For this reason, it may be advisable to compute the relationship between assets and operating expenses to obtain a measure of administrative effectiveness which is not influenced by gross profit:

OPERATING EXPENSES/ASSETS

	19x1	Marginal Analysis	19x2
Operating expenses/assets	$\left(\frac{\$700,000}{\$2,650,000}\right) = .26x$	$\left(\frac{\$100,000}{\$150,000}\right) = .67x$	$\left(\frac{\$800,000}{\$2,800,000}\right) = .29x$

It is now clear that operating expenses increased on a marginal basis, exclusive of the influence of gross profit.

The interperiod analysis of earning power indicates whether marginal increases in assets are productive. Often a new investment in assets will not reach its full potential in one year. For this reason, interperiod analysis should cover several years. As published annual reports often include ten-year summaries, data for extended analysis is available. Analysis over several periods should provide insights into the effectiveness of expansion or contraction efforts.

This type of analysis refutes the objective of growth for growth's sake. It inquires into the productivity of growth. This analysis, performed from a managerial perspective, should distinguish productive from nonproductive growth. Not every organization should keep growing, and many have failed because they grew beyond their point of optimization.

Inter-Firm

Additional meaning can be given to the earning power and other ratios by comparing a firm with industry statistics, such as those contained in Exhibit 7-5.[4] Comparison may be made with the industry as a whole ("industry averages") or with a few specific competitors.

An example of the uses of inter-firm earning power analysis follows. Consider the earning power data of firms A and B—two firms in the same industry:

	Relation-ship	FIRM A			FIRM B		
		$	Earning Power Multiplier		$	Earning Power Multiplier	
			Assets	Sales		Assets	Sales
Total assets		$1,000,000			$2,000,000		
Sales	A	2,500,000	2.5x		4,000,000	2.0x	
Gross profit	B	1,250,000	1.25x	.50x	2,000,000	1.0x	.50x
Net income	C	100,000	.10x	.04x	250,000	.125x	.0625x

In crude terms, relationship A is a measure of marketing efficiency, B of purchasing or production efficiency, and C of administrative efficiency. Accordingly, we can make these comparisons between firms A and B:

Marketing function: A has a better marketing function than B.

Production function: While each firm has a cost of goods sold ratio of 50%, A is extracting more gross profit per dollar invested in assets than B. Given a larger volume of business, B should have a lower cost of goods sold ratio through the economies of scale.

Administrative function: B has the more efficient administration.

This data is useful in determining relative strengths and weaknesses, as shown above. This type of analysis also lends itself to acquisition decisions. Suppose that firm X wishes to acquire *either* firm A or B. The purchase price is not a consideration. These outcomes appear reasonable:

[4]Sources of published data relevant to financial statement analysis are cited in the references to this chapter.

	Acquisition Decision
1. Firm X has strong administration but weak marketing	X+ A
2. Firm X has weak administration but strong marketing	X + B
3. Firm X wants to show significant short-term improvements in profits per dollar invested	X + A

The first two decisions are based on complementing strong and weak areas. In decision three, short-term improvements in profits can be made readily where there is a strong marketing function. It is relatively easy to control expenses and show immediate increases in profit. Correcting a sluggish market function is a more difficult and long-range assignment.

LIQUIDITY

A theoretical profile of the earning power of the major classes of assets would be as shown in Exhibit 7-1.

EXHIBIT 7-1 EARNING POWER OF ASSETS

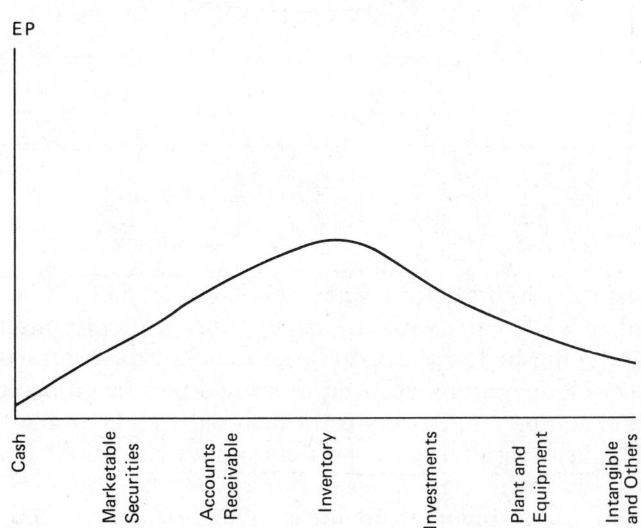

Because inventory has the highest earning power, what prevents us from holding all of our assets in the form of inventory (Exhibit 7-2)?

There is an opposite force at work—*liquidity*, i.e., the ability to pay current indebtedness and finance current operations. A liquidity profile of assets (Exhibit 7-3) is the inverse of earning power. Inventory which has the highest earning power often has the least liquidity in a financial crunch. It is this opposition of liquidity and earning power that calls for a portfolio approach to asset management.

High earning power alone does not equate with organizational strength. Consider a manufacturing firm that made a very successful product and took in

EXHIBIT 7-2 EARNING POWER OF INVENTORY

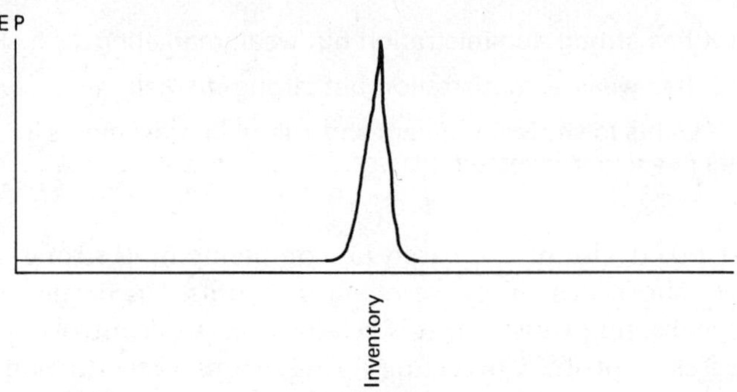

EXHIBIT 7-3 LIQUIDITY PROFILE OF ASSETS

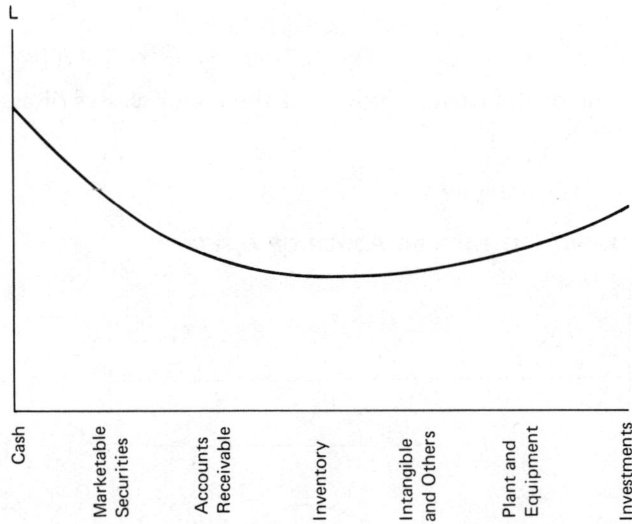

orders beyond its capacity to deliver within the contract dates. The manufacturing process required several years, with the major portion of the purchase price paid upon delivery of the finished product. In order to honor the contracts, the firm went into around-the-clock operations. It hired untrained persons; it had to acquire additional facilities and equipment. Payments for materials and labor had to be made on a current basis. The firm rapidly reached a tight money condition. There is an axiom of borrowing that says "when you don't need money, everyone is willing to loan it to you; but when you do need money, no one is willing to loan it to you." This firm was unable to raise the financing it needed to complete its contracts. It was finally forced into a merger with a cash-rich firm. A most successful marketing effort in this case led to a financial crises. The liquidity position of the firm could not support the volume of business that was generated.

There are two major liquidity ratios: (1) the *current ratio;* and (2) the *acid-test* ratio. The current ratio is a one-year test of liquidity in conformance with our definition of current assets and liabilities. It is computed by dividing current liabilities into current assets. Current ratios for the Exridge Corporation (Exhibit 6-5) for 19*x*1 and 19*x*2 are:

	19x1	19x2
Current ratio	$\left(\frac{\$740,000}{\$430,000}\right) = 1.7:1$	$\left(\frac{\$650,000}{\$300,000}\right) = 2.2:1$

This ratio is most often expressed as simply 1.7 and 2.2 respectively. An increase in this ratio is generally considered a favorable indicator.

The acid-test ratio is a more stringent measure of liquidity, relating in theory to a thirty-day period. This ratio is computed by dividing total current liabilities into a sub-set of current assets known as "quick assets":

Cash
\+ Marketable Securities
\+ Notes & Accounts Receivable
= Quick Assets

The acid-test ratios for the Exridge Corporation for years 19*x*1 and 19*x*2 are:

	19x1	19x2
Acid-test ratio..................	$\left(\frac{\$325,000}{\$430,000}\right) = .76$	$\left(\frac{\$340,000}{\$300,000}\right) = 1.1$

A rule of thumb for these ratios is 2:1 for the current ratio and 1:1 for the acid-test ratio, but industry norms vary widely as illustrated in Exhibit 7-5 (p. 258).

An acid-test ratio that is below normal suggests immediate liquidity pressure. When the ratio is above normal it may indicate an unfavorable balance between quick assets and inventory.

In common with other ratios, more meaning can be assigned to the liquidity ratios through interperiod and inter-firm analysis.

CREDIT MANAGEMENT

An inquiry into the effectiveness of credit management can be made by computing the average collection period of accounts receivable. A two-step[5] formula can be used for this purpose:

$$S_d = \frac{S}{d} \tag{1}$$

$$C_d = \frac{\left(\frac{AR_1 + AR_2}{2}\right)}{S_d} \tag{2}$$

[5]Or a one-step formula can be used: $C_d = \left[\frac{\left(\frac{AR_1 + AR_2}{2}\right)}{\left(\frac{S}{d}\right)}\right]$

where

S_d = average sales per day.
S = total sales for the period.
d = days in the period (360 days is used for annual periods).
C_d = average collection period in days.
AR = accounts receivable (AR_1 at beginning of period, AR_2 at end of period).

The average collection period for the Exridge Corporation for 19x1 and 19x2 is:[6]

	19x1	19x2
$$\left[\frac{\left(\frac{\$140{,}000 + \$150{,}000}{2}\right)}{\left(\frac{\$2{,}700{,}000}{360}\right)}\right] = \frac{\$145{,}000}{\$\ 7{,}500}$$	= 19.3 days	
$$\left[\frac{\left(\frac{\$150{,}000 + \$180{,}000}{2}\right)}{\left(\frac{\$3{,}000{,}000}{360}\right)}\right] = \frac{\$165{,}000}{\$\ 8{,}333}$$		= 19.8 days

An increase in the collection period indicates a less effective credit management function. In the example, collection was less effective in 19x2 than in 19x1.

In fact, we can compute the cost (or savings) of changes in the collection period by means of the future value of an annuity formula (see Appendix B, Table B-3). The rationale is that the daily collections can be invested and therefore a savings or cost can be computed on the basis of the opportunity earnings.

Using the above data, and providing a cost of capital of 10%, we compute the cost (or savings) by means of the formula:

$$F_n = A\left[\frac{(1+r)^n - 1}{r}\right]$$

where

F_n = the total value of future payments (collections) including accrued interest.
A = the periodic payment, in this case \$8,333.
r = the interest rate, in this case 10% or .10 per annum. Because we are planning to compute interest on a daily basis, $r = .10/360 = .000278$; which is a close approximation of the equivalent daily rate.

[6]The beginning balance in accounts receivable for 19x1 is given as being \$140,000. If this data is unavailable, the solitary figure for the period—in this case \$150,000—should be used.

n = the number of periods, in this case 9.2 days, computed as follows:

a. the collection period has increased from 19.3 to 19.8 days, or .5 days.

b. the average collection period for 19*x*1 and 19*x*2 is

$$\frac{19.3 + 19.8}{2} = 19.55 \text{ days}$$

and there are 360/19.55 = 18.41 such periods in the financial year.

c. the total number of days involved is .5 × 18.41 = 9.2 days.

hence[7]

$$F_n = \$8{,}333 \left[\frac{(1 + .000278)^{9.2} - 1}{.000278}\right]$$
$$= \$8{,}333 \left(\frac{1.00256 - 1}{.000278}\right)$$
$$= \underline{\underline{\$76{,}773}}$$

The amount $76,773 represents the total cash flow of $8,333 a day for 9.2 days at a 10% annual interest rate. It is apparent that without interest this sum would be $8,333 × 9.2 = $76,664. The difference between these amounts is the cost (in this case) of extending the credit period by .5 days; i.e., $76,773 − $76,664 = $109.

A longhand solution to the same problem would be:

$$\frac{.10(\$8{,}333) \times 9.2}{360} = \frac{\$7{,}666.36}{360} = \$21.30$$
$$\frac{.10(\$8{,}333) \times 8.2}{360} = \frac{\$6{,}833.06}{360} = 18.98$$
$$\frac{.10(\$8{,}333) \times 7.2}{360} = \frac{\$5{,}999.76}{360} = 16.67$$
$$\frac{.10(\$8{,}333) \times 6.2}{360} = \frac{\$5{,}166.46}{360} = 14.35$$
$$\frac{.10(\$8{,}333) \times 5.2}{360} = \frac{\$4{,}333.16}{360} = 12.04$$
$$\frac{.10(\$8{,}333) \times 4.2}{360} = \frac{\$3{,}499.86}{360} = 9.72$$
$$\frac{.10(\$8{,}333) \times 3.2}{360} = \frac{\$2{,}666.56}{360} = 7.41$$
$$\frac{.10(\$8{,}333) \times 2.2}{360} = \frac{\$1{,}833.26}{360} = 5.09$$
$$\frac{.10(\$8{,}333) \times 1.2}{360} = \frac{\$999.96}{360} = 2.78$$
$$\frac{.10(\$8{,}333) \times .2}{360} = \frac{\$166.66}{360} = .46$$
$$\text{Total} \quad \underline{\underline{\$108.80}}$$

[7]Logarithms can be used to solve this problem (see Appendix C). In this case log 1.000278 × 9.2 = .0001207 × 9.2 = .0011106, whose antilog is 1.00256.

While in general terms, decreases in the collection period are considered favorable, the impact of these changes on sales is required in the final analysis in order to determine whether or not the decreases in collection period are achieved at the expense of sales.

Industry norms are important in interpreting this ratio. In Exhibit 7-5 we notice that collection periods vary widely among industries, e.g., fifty-five days for precision instruments to twenty-two days for canned and dried foods.

In interpreting this ratio, the general credit picture may be important. In recessionary periods the collection period may be extended without casting reflection on the credit management function.

This ratio also needs to be interpreted for any major changes in product lines or in credit policy before reaching a judgment as to credit management performance.

INVENTORY MANAGEMENT

We note that inventory relates or "turns over" into cost of goods sold and *not* into sales:[8]

1. We make one entry when we purchase inventory:

   Increase (Debit) Inventory.................$800
   Decrease (Credit) Cash $800

   Notation: Purchase of one item of inventory for cash.

2. We make two entries when we sell the item:

   a. Increase (Debit) Cash $1,000
      Increase (Credit) Sales.............. $1,000

      Notation: Sale of item for cash.

   b. Increase (Debit) Cost of goods sold.................$800
      Decrease (Credit) Inventory......................... $800

      Notation: Recording sale of item at its cost price, and eliminating item from inventory.

Notice that inventory is decreased by an entry to cost of goods sold, while sales is offset by a cash entry.

Inventory turnover is computed by dividing average inventory for the period into cost of goods sold. This ratio for the Exridge Corporation for years 19*x*1 and 19*x*2 is:[9]

	19x1	19x2
$\left(\frac{\$1{,}590{,}000}{\$400{,}000}\right)$	$= 4.0x$	
$\left[\frac{\$1{,}880{,}000}{\left(\frac{\$400{,}000 + \$300{,}000}{2}\right)}\right]$		$= 5.4x$

[8]The exception to the rule is in those instances where inventory is carried at retail prices, as in food markets.

[9]As no beginning inventory figure is available, we use the $400,000 for 19*x*1.

An increase in this ratio is considered favorable. It means that we are carrying less inventory in relation to sales. This ratio can be extended to give us the *average holding period* for inventory by dividing the turnover ratio into the days in the period. The inventory holding periods for 19*x*1 and 19*x*2 are:

$$19x1\colon \frac{360 \text{ days}}{4} = \text{90-day average holding period}$$

$$19x2\colon \frac{360 \text{ days}}{5.4} = \text{67-day average holding period}$$

As with changes in the collection period, we can also compute the cost or savings associated with changes in the inventory holding period. An increase in the holding period means additional carrying costs, and *vice versa.*

This computation differs from the collection period example in that the inventory is constant over the period of change, while the collection amount is in the nature of a periodic payment (see chapter 17 and Appendix C for the distinction between lump sum and annuity payments).

Again, we furnish a 10% factor, but in this case it represents the cost of carrying an item in inventory for one year, expressed as a cost of acquiring that item; i.e., 10% of the cost of purchasing the item is required to carry it in stock for one year.[10]

To compute the effect of a change in the holding period, we use the future value of $1 formula shown in Table B-1, Appendix B. The above example is used to calculate the savings (in this case) of reducing the inventory holding period from ninety to sixty-seven days. Again, any benefit from reducing the inventory holding period must be examined in relation to a possible reduction in sales. The basic formula is:

$$F_n = A\ (1 + r)^n$$

where

F_n = the total value of the lump sum amount plus accrued interest in period n.

A = amount or lump sum invested now – in this case $350,000, representing the average inventory for 19*x*2.

r = the interest rate – in this case 10%, representing carrying costs ex-

[10] Thomas M. Whitin, *The Theory of Inventory Management* (Princeton, N.J.: Princeton University Press, 1957), p. 221, estimates that the average annual carrying costs as a percentage of cost of goods sold is approximately 25%, broken down as follows:

Storage facilities	0.25%
Insurance	.25
Taxes	.50
Transportation	.50
Handling and distribution	2.50
Depreciation	5.00
Interest	6.00
Obsolescence	10.00
Total	25.00%

pressed as a percentage of cost of goods sold. The equivalent daily rate is .10/360 = .000278.

n = the time period involved, computed as follows:

a. the holding period has decreased from ninety to sixty-seven days, or twenty-three days.

b. the average holding period for 19x1 and 19x2 is

$$\frac{90 + 67}{2} = 78 \text{ days}$$

and there are 360/78 = 4.62 such periods in the financial year.

c. the total number of days involved is 23 × 4.62 = 106.26.

hence

$$\begin{aligned} F_n &= \$350{,}000\ (1.000278)^{106.26} \\ &= \$350{,}000\ (1.02996) \\ &= \underline{\underline{\$360{,}486}} \end{aligned}$$

The savings is the difference between \$360,486 and \$350,000, which amounts to \$10,486.

DEBT MANAGEMENT

There are two principal debt management ratios: (1) *debt-equity,* and (2) *debt-asset.* The first measures the relationship between owners' equity (or net worth) and debt. It is computed by dividing owners' equity into total debt. This ratio for the Exridge Corporation for year 19*x*1 and 19*x*2 is:

	19x1	19x2
Debt-equity ratio:	$\left(\frac{\$1{,}250{,}000}{\$1{,}400{,}000}\right) = .89$ or 89%	$\left(\frac{\$1{,}200{,}000}{\$1{,}600{,}000}\right) = .75$ or 75%

Total debt was equal to 89% of owners' equity in 19*x*1, but this was reduced to 75% in 19*x*2—a favorable trend.

The second ratio compares total debt to total assets. This ratio is used as a collateral index. It indicates the extent to which total assets exceed total debt. The lower this ratio, the greater the cushion against creditors' losses in the event of liquidation.

This ratio for the Exridge Corporation for 19*x*1 and 19*x*2 is:

	19x1	19x2
Debt-asset ratio:	$\left(\frac{\$1{,}250{,}000}{\$2{,}650{,}000}\right) = .47$ or 47%	$\left(\frac{\$1{,}200{,}000}{\$2{,}800{,}000}\right) = .43$ or 43%

Total debt was equal to 47% of total assets in 19*x*1, but this was reduced to 43% in 19*x*2—again a favorable trend.

RETURN ON INVESTMENT

This category of ratio measures the return on owners' investment. Three principal ratios are used for this purpose: (1) *earnings per share,* (2) *price-earnings,* and (3) *yield.*

Earnings per share (EPS) is computed by dividing the number of common shares outstanding into net income for the period. This ratio is an integral part of financial reporting. Some firms may report several EPS ratios based on the following considerations:

1. Whether net income for the period includes extraordinary items.
2. Whether the firm possesses a *simple* or *complex* capital structure.[11]
3. Whether net income for the period includes corrections or changes in income reported in prior periods.

The income statement for The Exridge Corporation (Exhibit 6-6) indicates the following earnings per share data for 19*x*1 and 19*x*2:

	19x1	**19x2**
Earnings per share before extraordinary items	$2.08	$ .95
Earnings per share on extraordinary items	–	2.00
Earnings per share on net income	2.08	2.95
Pro forma (or fully diluted) earnings per share	2.04	2.87

Where extraordinary items are included in income, it is necessary to compute EPS before such items; i.e., on net operating income and EPS on extraordinary items. This detail, in the above example, points to the fact that while EPS on net income increased in 19*x*2, this result was achieved through extraordinary rather than operating transactions.

The Exridge Corporation has a *complex* capital structure, hence it is necessary to include a *pro forma* EPS computation which assumes that *all* contingent issuances of common stock have taken place at the beginning of 19*x*1 and 19*x*2 respectively. The denominator of the EPS equation in this case is said to consist of "common stock equivalents,"[12] in addition to the number of common shares outstanding.

[11] *APB Opinion No. 15* defines *simple* capital structures as those which consist of only common stock and do not include potentially dilutive convertible securities, options, warrants, or other rights which upon exercise or conversion would increase the number of common shares and hence reduce or "dilute" earnings per share. In such cases a single EPS ratio is sufficient for financial reporting under a title such as *earnings per common share.*

Complex capital structures include the items mentioned above. In such cases, two EPS ratios are necessary; the first based on outstanding common shares and those securities that are in substance equivalent to common shares, and the second is a *pro forma* presentation which reflects the dilution of earnings per share that would have occurred if *all* contingent issuances of common stock were in effect at the beginning of the period. The latter ratio is also referred to as *fully diluted earnings per share.*

[12] *APB Opinion No. 15* defines a *common stock equivalent* as a security which is not, in form, a common stock, but which usually contains provisions to enable its holder to become a common stockholder, and which,

Changes in accounting methods call for the computation of EPS before and after such changes. *APB Opinion No. 20* deals with this subject. The following extract from the 1971 Annual Report of Transamerica Corporation illustrates the inclusion of an EPS computation based on the effect of accounting changes:

	1971	Per Share	1970	Per Share
Net Operating Income	$96,384,000		$37,594,000	
Provision for income taxes	37,854,000		9,519,000	
	$58,530,000	$0.90	$28,075,000	$0.43
Net gain on investment transactions, principally sale of corporate stocks, less related income taxes	3,402,000	0.05	7,903,000	0.12
Income before additional provision for losses and effect of accounting change	$61,932,000	$0.95	$35,978,000	$0.55
Additional provision for losses on film productions, less related income taxes	—	—	27,500,000	0.43
Income before effect of accounting change	$61,932,000	$0.95	$ 8,478,000	$0.12
Cumulative effect of accounting change relating to life insurance operations, less related income taxes	—	—	34,167,000	0.54
Consolidated Net Income	$61,932,000	$0.95	$42,645,000	$0.66

When common stock is issued or repurchased during the computation period, a *weighted average* of the shares outstanding during the period is used. The weighting is accomplished by relating shares outstanding by the number of months. For example if 120,000 shares are outstanding for four months and 180,000 shares are outstanding for eight months, the number of shares that is used for computing EPS is 160,000:

$$\begin{aligned} 120{,}000 \times 4 \text{ months} &= 480{,}000 \\ 180{,}000 \times \underline{8} \text{ months} &= \underline{1{,}440{,}000} \\ \underline{12} \qquad & \underline{1{,}920{,}000}/12 = 160{,}000 \text{ shares.} \end{aligned}$$

Another measure of return on investment is the *price-earnings ratio.* This ratio is based on the current market price of a share divided by its earnings per share. Where a series of EPS figures are included in the income statement, the *pro forma* computation is used as the denominator in this equation. Assume that the market price of Exridge stock is $25 as of the balance sheet date in 19*x*1 and $32 for the comparable data in 19*x*2.[13] The respective price-earnings ratios are:

because of the terms and the circumstances under which it is issued, is in substance equivalent to common stock. Examples are convertible debt, convertible preferred stock, stock options and warrants, participating securities and two-class common stocks, and contingent shares.

[13] While the market price used in the price-earnings ratio is generally the quoted selling price as of the balance sheet date, some analysts prefer a simple average price:

$$\frac{\text{Selling Price, 1st Day of Period} + \text{Selling Price, Last Day of Period}}{2}$$

	19x1	19x2
Price-earnings ratio:	$\frac{\$25.00}{\$\ 2.08} = 12x$	$\frac{\$32.00}{\$\ 2.95} = 10.8x$

The result is often referred as the *multiplier*, i.e., Exridge stock on December 31, 19*x*2 is selling at 10.8 times EPS.

The reciprocal of the price-earnings ratio indicates the percent return on current market value. For example, a price-earnings ratio of 20*x* equates with a 5% return. Of course, not all earnings are distributed in the form of dividends, so *yield* may vary from this figure.

Yield is a measure of *actual* return on investment to the stockholder. As noted, earnings in the computation above may not be fully distributed in the form of dividends. If earnings are fully distributed, the reciprocal of the price-earnings ratio would represent yield for that period; i.e., 100/12 = 8.5% in 19*x*1, and 100/10.8 = 9.26% in 19*x*2 in the above example.

However, the Exridge Corporation paid $80,000 in dividends in 19*x*1 and $95,000 in 19*x*2. As there were 100,000 shares outstanding in each period, dividends per share were $.80 in 19*x*1 and $.95 in 19*x*2. Yield is computed by dividing dividends per share by the current selling price of the stock:

	19x1	19x2
Yield:	$\frac{\$.80}{\$25.00} = .032$ or 3.2%	$\frac{\$.95}{\$32.00} = .03$ or 3.0%

Theoretically, yield includes dividends plus increases (or minus decreases) in the market value of the stock. As these changes in value are only realized upon final sale of the stock, true yield can only be determined at the end of an investment cycle, as noted further in chapter 17. Yield quotations published by stock brokerage firms and others use the technique illustrated for the Exridge Corporation above.

SUMMARY OF RATIOS

The key ratios for the Exridge Corporation are summarized below:

Key Ratios	19x1	19x2	Comment
1. Earning Power			
1–1 Earning power	1.02*x*	1.07*x*	Improved marketing effort.
1–2 Gross earning power	.42*x*	.40*x*	Higher production costs.
1–3 Net earning power	.08*x*	.105*x*	Increase due to capital gain. Administrative expenses increased.
2. Liquidity			
2–1 Current ratio	1.7	2.2	Considerable improvement in working capital.
2–2 Acid-test ratio	.76	1.1	Considerable improvement in short-term liquidity.

Key Ratios	19x1	19x2	Comment
3. Credit Management			
3–1 Collection period	19.3 days	19.8 days	Slight decrease in collections.
4. Inventory Management			
4–1 Inventory turnover	4.0*x*	5.4*x*	Marked improvement in inventory management.
4–2 Inventory holding period	90 days	67 days	22-day reduction in average holding period.
5. Debt Management			
5–1 Debt-equity	89%	75%	Decrease in debt pressure vis-à-vis owners.
5–2 Debt-asset	47%	43%	Improved credit cushion.
6. Return on Investment			
6–1 Earnings per share			
Before extraordinary items	$2.08	$ .95	
On extraordinary items	–	2.00	
On net income	$2.08	$2.95	Increase due to capital gain in 19*x*2.
6–2 Price-earnings ratio	12*x*	10.8*x*	Less optimism in market concerning Exridge stock.
6–3 Yield	3.2%	3.0%	Decrease in yield. Yield less than industry average.

The above summary illustrates the difficulty of measuring performance on the basis of a single index. In certain aspects, Exridge showed considerable improvement in 19*x*2: e.g., in liquidity position, in inventory management, and in debt pressure. There was less effectiveness in other areas, particularly in purchasing-production and in administration. We have a better balance sheet in 19*x*2, but a poorer income statement. We can conclude that Exridge is basically healthy, but needs to pay more attention in 19*x*3 to production and administration.

EXHIBIT 7-4 SCHEDULE OF RATIOS

CATEGORY	RATIO	METHOD OF COMPUTATION	APPLIED TO EXRIDGE 19x2	NOTATION
1. EARNING POWER	1–1 Earning Power	$\frac{\text{Sales}}{\text{Total Assets}}$	$\left(\frac{\$3{,}000{,}000}{\$2{,}800{,}000}\right) = 1.07x$	Measures the ability of assets to generate sales, i.e., a test of the marketing function.
	1–2 Gross Earning Power	$\frac{\text{Gross Profit}}{\text{Total Assets}}$	$\left(\frac{\$1{,}120{,}000}{\$2{,}800{,}000}\right) = .40x$	Measures ability of assets to generate gross profit. A test of production or purchasing efficiency.
	1–3 Net Earning Power	$\frac{\text{Net Income}}{\text{Total Assets}}$	$\left(\frac{\$295{,}000}{\$2{,}800{,}000}\right) = .105x$	Measures the ability of assets to generate net income. As differentiated from above ratios, it is a measure of administrative efficiency.
2. LIQUIDITY	2–1 Current	$\frac{\text{Current Assets}}{\text{Current Liabilities}}$	$\left(\frac{\$650{,}000}{\$300{,}000}\right) = 2.2$	Measures a firm's ability to meet current debt within the normal operating cycle, i.e., one year.
	2–2 Acid-Test	$\frac{\text{Quick Assets}}{\text{Current Liabilities}}$	$\left(\frac{\$340{,}000}{\$300{,}000}\right) = 1.1$	A measure of liquidity in the immediate future term, which is generally defined as 30 days. Quick assets comprise cash, marketable securities, and receivables.
	2–3 Cash to Total Assets	$\frac{\text{Cash} + \text{Marketable Securities}}{\text{Total Assets}}$	$\left(\frac{\$130{,}000}{\$2{,}800{,}000}\right) = 4.7\%$	Percentage of assets held in the form of cash or cash equivalents.

EXHIBIT 7-4 (CONTINUED)

CATEGORY	RATIO	METHOD OF COMPUTATION	APPLIED TO EXRIDGE 19x2	NOTATION
	2–4 Cash to Sales	$\frac{\text{Cash} + \text{Marketable Securities}}{\text{Sales}}$	$\left(\frac{\$130{,}000}{\$3{,}000{,}000}\right) = 4.3\%$	Percentage of sales held in the form of cash or cash equivalents. This is a useful index in cash management.
3. CREDIT MANAGEMENT	3–1 Collection Period	$\frac{\text{Average Accounts Receivable}}{\text{Average Daily Sales}}$	$\left(\frac{\$165{,}000}{\$8{,}333}\right) = 19.8$ days	Measures the amount of average daily sales represented in the average balance of accounts receivable, i.e., average collection period.
	3–2 Receivables to Sales	$\frac{\text{Average Accounts Receivable}}{\text{Sales}}$	$\left(\frac{\$165{,}000}{\$3{,}000{,}000}\right) = 5.5\%$	Measures the relationship between uncollected debt and sales. Sales can be increased by liberal extension of credit, in which case the ratio would be high. A low ratio may indicate a tightening of credit policy.
4. INVENTORY MANAGEMENT	4–1 Inventory Turnover	$\frac{\text{Cost of Goods Sold}}{\text{Average Inventory}}$	$\left(\frac{\$1{,}880{,}000}{\$350{,}000}\right) = 5.4x$	Measures the number of times inventory is "sold out" during the period. A higher ratio indicates greater merchandising capacity, freshness and saleability of the inventory.

EXHIBIT 7-4 (CONTINUED)

CATEGORY	RATIO	METHOD OF COMPUTATION	APPLIED TO EXRIDGE 19x2	NOTATION
	4–2 Inventory Holding Period	$\frac{\text{Days in Period}}{\text{Inventory Turnover Rate}}$	$\left(\frac{360}{5.4x}\right) = 67$ days	Measures average period in which an item is held in inventory. This index is useful in determining re-order points.
	4–3 Inventory to Total Assets	$\frac{\text{Inventory}}{\text{Total Assets}}$	$\left(\frac{\$300,000}{\$2,800,000}\right) = 10.7\%$	Measures the percentage of assets held in the form of inventory. As inventory is the source of most earning power, an adequate ratio is essential. A high ratio may mean poor inventory management, or buildup for one reason or another.
5. DEBT MANAGEMENT	5–1a Debt to Equity	$\frac{\text{Total Debt}}{\text{Total Owners' Equity}}$	$\left(\frac{\$1,200,000}{\$1,600,000}\right) = .75\%$	A measure of debt pressure on owners' equity, carrying overtones of management control. A ratio of 1 would indicate that total debt = owners' equity. Owners equity is also referred to as "net worth."

EXHIBIT 7-4 (CONTINUED)

CATEGORY	RATIO	METHOD OF COMPUTATION	APPLIED TO EXRIDGE 19x2	NOTATION
	5–1b Long-Term Debt to Equity	$\frac{\text{Long-Term Debt}}{\text{Owner's Equity}}$	$\left(\frac{\$900,000}{\$1,600,000}\right) = 56\%$	As long-term debt + equity represent the "capitalization" of a firm, this ratio measures proportion of capitalization represented by long-term debt.
	5–2 Debt to Total Assets	$\frac{\text{Total Debt}}{\text{Total Assets}}$	$\left(\frac{\$1,200,000}{\$2,800,000}\right) = 43\%$	A measure of collateral support for creditors' claims in the event of liquidation.
	5–3 Long-Term Debt to Long-Lived Assets	$\frac{\text{Long-Term Debt}}{\text{Long-Lived Assets}}$	$\left(\frac{\$900,000}{\$2,150,000}\right) = 42\%$	A measure of collateral which supports long-term debt.
6. RETURN ON INVESTMENT or PROFITABILITY	6–1 Earnings Per Share	$\frac{\text{Net Income}}{\text{Average Number of Common Shares Outstanding}}$	$\left(\frac{\$295,000}{100,000}\right) = \$2.95$	Net income of the firm distributed over the number of shares outstanding.
	6–2 Price-Earnings Ratio	$\frac{\text{Market Price per Share}}{\text{Earnings per Share}}$	$\left(\frac{\$32.00}{\$2.95}\right) = 10.8x$	A measure of potential yield.
	6–3 Yield	$\frac{\text{Dividends per Share}}{\text{Market Price per Share}}$	$\left(\frac{\$.95}{\$32.00}\right) = 3.0\%$	A measure of actual yield for the period excluding gain or loss on sale.

EXHIBIT 7-4 (CONTINUED)

CATEGORY	RATIO	METHOD OF COMPUTATION	APPLIED TO EXRIDGE 19x2	NOTATION
	6–4 Net Income to Sales	$\frac{\text{Net Income}}{\text{Total Sales}}$	$\left(\frac{\$295,000}{\$3,000,000}\right) = 9.8\%$	Measures the net profit margin on sales.
	6–5 Gross Profit to Sales	$\frac{\text{Gross Profit}}{\text{Total Sales}}$	$\left(\frac{\$1,120,000}{\$3,000,000}\right) = 37.3\%$	Measures the gross profit margin on sales.
	6–6 Net Income to Owners' Equity	$\frac{\text{Net Income}}{\text{Owners' Equity}}$	$\left(\frac{\$295,000}{\$1,600,000}\right) = 18.4\%$	Measures the percentage return on owners' equity.
	6–7 Book Value Per Share	$\frac{\text{Total Owners' Equity}}{\text{Number of Shares}}$	$\left(\frac{\$1,600,000}{100,000}\right) = \$16$	The total value of owners' equity, including contributed and earned capital, distributed per share outstanding.

EXHIBIT 7-5 SELECTED FINANCIAL STATEMENT DATA AND RATIOS

	MANUFACTURERS OF—MEN'S WORK CLOTHING 12 Statements Ended on or about June 30, 1970 40 Statements Ended on or about December 31, 1970					MANUFACTURERS OF—WOMEN'S DRESSES 49 Statements Ended on or about June 30, 1970 51 Statements Ended on or about December 31, 1970				
Asset Size	**Under $250M**	**$250M & Less than $1MM**	**$1MM & Less than $10MM**	**$10MM & Less than $25MM**	**All Sizes**	**Under $250M**	**$250M & Less than $1MM**	**$1MM & Less than $10MM**	**$10MM & Less than $25MM**	**All Sizes**
Number of Statements		**13**	**31**		**52**	**19**	**37**	**40**		**100**
Assets	%	%	%	%	%	%	%	%	%	%
Cash		5.1	6.4		5.4	14.0	9.3	6.9		5.7
Marketable Securities		5.6	1.4		1.1	.0	1.9	3.3		6.1
Receivables Net		35.1	26.9		27.5	34.5	40.2	34.4		34.6
Inventory Net		27.9	44.1		45.7	28.1	31.8	34.3		33.9
All Other Current		1.2	1.2		1.4	6.7	2.5	3.1		2.7
Total Current		74.8	79.9		81.2	83.4	85.7	82.0		83.1
Fixed Assets Net		14.0	14.4		14.0	8.8	9.4	10.1		10.4
All Other Non-Current		11.2	5.6		4.8	7.9	4.9	8.0		6.5
Total		100.0	100.0		100.0	100.0	100.0	100.0		100.0
Liabilities										
Due To Banks—Short Term		7.1	8.8		9.4	5.9	12.5	11.1		8.7
Due To Trade		14.0	13.1		13.8	23.2	28.4	24.7		24.3
Income Taxes		1.4	2.4		2.4	2.5	2.8	3.2		3.4
Current Maturities LT Debt		.9	1.2		1.4	.8	.7	.9		.9
All Other Current		16.9	8.3		8.3	16.6	9.2	9.1		7.9
Total Current Debt		40.2	33.8		35.3	49.0	53.7	49.1		45.1
Non-Current Debt Unsub.		7.6	9.5		10.4	3.7	3.3	5.0		6.3
Total Unsubordinated Debt		47.7	43.4		45.7	52.7	57.0	54.0		51.4
Subordinated Debt		.0	.8		1.0	1.9	2.8	.6		.7
Tangible Net Worth		52.3	55.8		53.3	45.4	40.2	45.4		47.9
Total		100.0	100.0		100.0	100.0	100.0	100.0		100.0
Income Data										
Net Sales		100.0	100.0*		100.0*	100.0	100.0*	100.0*		100.0*
Cost Of Sales		85.9	82.2		81.5	76.6	77.0	75.8		75.2
Gross Profit		14.1	17.8		18.5	23.4	23.0	24.2		24.8
All Other Expense Net		13.4	13.3		14.0	23.3	20.7	22.3		22.3
Profit Before Taxes		.7	4.5		4.5	.1	2.3	1.9		2.5
Ratios										
		1.5	1.5		1.7	1.6	1.4	1.4		1.5
Quick		.7	1.1		1.1	.8	.9	.9		.9
		.4	.5		.6	.6	.7	.7		.7

EXHIBIT 7-5 (CONTINUED)

Asset Size Number of Statements	Under $250M	$250M & Less than $1MM 13	$1MM & Less than $10MM 31	$10MM & Less than $25MM	All Sizes 52	Under $250M 19	$250M & Less than $1MM 37	$1MM & Less than $10MM 40	$10MM & Less than $25MM	All Sizes 100
Current		2.5 1.5 1.2	3.4 2.4 1.7		3.5 2.3 1.7	2.4 1.6 1.1	2.1 1.5 1.2	2.1 1.7 1.4		2.2 1.6 1.3
Fixed/Worth		.1 .2 .3	.1 .2 .4		.1 .2 .4	.0 .1 .5	.0 .2 .5	.1 .1 .4		.1 .1 .5
Debt/Worth		.5 .8 1.8	.5 .9 1.4		.5 .9 1.4	.6 1.3 3.0	.8 2.0 3.1	.7 1.2 2.3		.7 1.3 2.8
Unsub. Debt/Capital Funds		.5 .8 1.8	.5 .9 1.2		.5 .9 1.3	.6 1.3 2.1	.8 1.8 2.7	.7 1.2 1.8		.7 1.3 2.5
Sales/Receivables		**32** 11.2 **47** 7.6 **67** 5.4	**28** 12.7 **46** 7.8 **58** 6.2		**28** 12.7 **43** 8.4 **57** 6.3	**20** 18.1 **39** 9.2 **71** 5.1	**30** 12.0 **48** 7.5 **54** 6.7	**38** 9.6 **45** 8.0 **53** 6.8		**30** 12.0 **44** 8.1 **55** 6.6
Cost Sales/Inventory		**32** 11.4 **55** 6.5 **82** 4.4	**72** 5.0 **100** 3.6 **139** 2.6		**54** 6.7 **86** 4.2 **129** 2.8	**23** 16.0 **55** 6.6 **80** 4.5	**28** 12.7 **41** 8.8 **68** 5.3	**40** 8.9 **53** 6.8 **84** 4.3		**32** 11.1 **49** 7.4 **72** 5.0
Sales/Working Capital		10.7 5.3 2.3	7.9 3.9 3.4		8.1 5.0 3.4	13.9 7.4 3.2	18.8 13.2 6.2	12.1 9.2 5.4		15.5 9.9 5.0
Sales/Worth		6.6 4.3 2.3	5.9 3.7 2.8		6.2 4.1 2.9	15.4 8.9 4.1	14.4 10.6 5.3	10.0 6.5 4.5		12.6 7.3 4.5
% Profit Bef. Taxes/Worth		31.9 13.9 3.3	22.5 14.9 4.8		24.5 15.8 4.9	11.8 4.8 8.3	31.2 18.6 4.4	33.0 15.7 3.2		32.0 14.0 2.8
% Profit Bef. Taxes/Tot. Assets		10.0 5.1 10.8	14.9 7.7 2.6		12.4 8.1 2.6	5.2 1.9 5.0	12.7 6.3 .6	13.2 6.1 1.9		12.1 4.7 .6
Net Sales Total Assets		**$20995M** **8463M**	**$226908M** **105005M**		**$372534M** **173100M**	**$9244M** **2500M**	**$75091M** **20896M**	**$297827M** **104851M**		**$510667M** **180258M**

EXHIBIT 7-5 (CONTINUED)

	MANUFACTURERS OF—DRUGS & MEDICINES 22 Statements Ended on or about June 30, 1970 27 Statements Ended on or about December 31, 1970					MANUFACTURERS OF—MEAT PACKING 46 Statements Ended on or about June 30, 1970 100 Statements Ended on or about December 31, 1970				
Asset Size	**Under $250M**	**$250M & Less than $1MM**	**$1MM & Less than $10MM**	**$10MM & Less than $25MM**	**All Sizes**	**Under $250M**	**$250M & Less than $1MM**	**$1MM & Less than $10MM**	**$10MM & Less than $25MM**	**All Sizes**
Number of Statements		**16**	**19**	**10**	**49**		**42**	**75**	**20**	**146**
Assets	%	%	%	%	%	%	%	%	%	%
Cash		5.4	7.0	7.4	7.2		8.3	8.0	6.8	7.4
Marketable Securities		1.7	1.8	3.5	2.9		.0	.6	.5	.5
Receivables Net		22.2	20.5	21.4	21.2		31.0	26.0	26.9	26.7
Inventory Net		24.1	27.4	23.2	24.5		18.4	21.4	21.7	21.4
All Other Current		1.6	2.3	1.6	1.8		1.6	1.5	1.9	1.7
Total Current		55.0	58.9	57.1	57.6		59.3	57.5	57.7	57.7
Fixed Assets Net		33.7	25.8	35.4	32.4		35.0	36.1	37.1	36.7
All Other Non-Current		11.3	15.3	7.5	10.0		5.7	6.3	5.1	5.6
Total		100.0	100.0	100.0	100.0		100.0	100.0	100.0	100.0
Liabilities										
Due To Banks—Short Term		5.6	9.1	5.8	6.8		10.5	7.5	13.8	11.2
Due To Trade		9.7	9.4	10.9	10.4		15.1	12.7	9.8	11.1
Income Taxes		2.8	4.7	3.4	3.8		2.4	2.5	.8	1.5
Current Maturities LT Debt		1.6	2.6	4.4	3.7		2.6	1.7	1.1	1.4
All Other Current		4.5	5.5	3.8	4.4		8.5	7.8	7.7	7.7
Total Current Debt		24.2	31.3	28.2	29.1		39.1	32.2	33.2	33.0
Non-Current Debt Unsub.		9.7	9.7	18.4	15.4		11.0	12.7	16.6	14.8
Total Unsubordinated Debt		33.9	41.0	46.6	44.4		50.1	44.8	49.8	47.8
Subordinated Debt		.5	.9	1.0	1.0		2.7	.8	.0	.4
Tangible Net Worth		65.5	58.0	52.4	54.6		47.2	54.4	50.2	51.7
Total		100.0	100.0	100.0	100.0		100.0	100.0	100.0	100.0
Income Data										
Net Sales		100.0	100.0	100.0	100.0		100.0*	100.0*	100.0	100.0*
Cost Of Sales		51.2	61.9	57.4	58.5		90.4	90.1	93.8	92.0
Gross Profit		48.8	38.1	42.6	41.5		9.6	9.9	6.2	8.0
All Other Expense Net		41.7	23.2	27.7	26.9		8.7	8.5	5.8	7.1
Profit Before Taxes		7.1	14.9	14.9	14.6		.9	1.4	.4	.9
Ratios										
		1.9	1.4	1.7	1.6		1.4	1.6	1.6	1.5
Quick		1.2	1.0	1.3	1.0		1.0	1.1	1.0	1.1
		.8	.6	.6	.6		.8	.7	.9	.7

EXHIBIT 7-5 (CONTINUED)

Asset Size Number of Statements	Under $250M	$250M & Less than $1MM 16	$1MM & Less than $10MM 19	$10MM & Less than $25MM 10	All Sizes 49	Under $250M	$250M & Less than $1MM 42	$1MM & Less than $10MM 75	$10MM & Less than $25MM 20	All Sizes 146
Current		3.4	2.8	2.9	3.0		2.4	2.4	3.2	2.5
		2.8	2.0	2.6	2.2		1.7	1.7	1.6	1.7
		1.8	1.2	1.3	1.2		1.1	1.3	1.2	1.2
Fixed/Worth		.3	.3	.4	.3		.4	.5	.5	.5
		.5	.5	.7	.6		.7	.7	.8	.7
		.7	.8	1.1	.9		1.2	1.0	1.3	1.0
Debt/Worth		.3	.4	.5	.4		.6	.5	.6	.5
		.5	.8	.7	.7		1.1	.9	1.2	.9
		1.1	1.5	2.1	1.4		2.0	1.8	2.7	2.0
Unsub. Debt/Capital Funds		.3	.4	.5	.4		.6	.5	.6	.5
		.5	.7	.7	.7		.9	.9	1.2	.9
		1.1	1.1	1.2	1.3		1.5	1.6	2.6	1.7
Sales/Receivables		**38** 9.5	**41** 8.8	**54** 6.7	**41** 8.8		**11** 32.8	**10** 37.0	**13** 28.6	**11** 34.0
		46 7.8	**49** 7.3	**57** 6.3	**48** 7.5		**13** 26.8	**13** 28.1	**14** 25.7	**13** 27.0
		55 6.5	**69** 5.2	**67** 5.4	**62** 5.8		**21** 17.6	**18** 20.1	**15** 23.5	**18** 19.7
Cost Sales/Inventory		**69** 5.2	**78** 4.6	**82** 4.4	**75** 4.8		**6** 58.2	**9** 40.2	**6** 60.3	**8** 45.0
		129 2.8	**144** 2.5	**171** 2.1	**144** 2.5		**13** 28.7	**13** 27.0	**14** 26.2	**13** 27.0
		171 2.1	**171** 2.1	**200** 1.8	**180** 2.0		**27** 13.3	**22** 16.5	**25** 14.7	**23** 15.7
Sales/Working Capital		8.3	7.3	5.4	8.4		38.3	42.0	48.0	41.1
		4.9	5.0	4.5	5.0		18.6	24.7	23.9	22.9
		3.3	2.9	2.5	3.2		5.6	16.4	9.8	12.2
Sales/Worth		3.4	3.3	4.8	4.3		28.8	25.1	21.0	24.7
		2.5	2.4	3.4	2.6		12.2	14.1	15.5	13.7
		1.6	1.9	2.0	1.9		5.2	8.7	9.4	8.4
% Profit Bef. Taxes/Worth		25.1	34.5	53.3	40.4		24.9	24.5	11.1	22.9
		15.2	20.1	33.7	20.5		16.3	17.1	7.2	14.4
		6.8	14.3	10.5	11.6		7.7	7.5	11.3	6.2
% Profit Bef. Taxes/Tot. Assets		16.5	18.1	28.8	18.7		12.7	14.0	7.6	12.6
		9.4	12.7	18.7	12.5		7.2	8.2	3.5	7.4
		4.3	4.7	3.7	5.1		2.1	3.5	4.3	2.7
Net Sales		**$15819M**	**$112371M**	**$249942M**	**$379052M**		**$186550M**	**$1704516M**	**$2057030M**	**$3955644M**
Total Assets		**9787M**	**75832M**	**160498M**	**246476M**		**23678M**	**222909M**	**326932M**	**574949M**

EXHIBIT 7-5 (CONTINUED)

	WHOLESALERS OF—GENERAL GROCERIES 119 Statements Ended on or about June 30, 1970 95 Statements Ended on or about December 31, 1970					WHOLESALERS OF—PETROLEUM PRODUCTS 54 Statements Ended on or about June 30, 1970 62 Statements Ended on or about December 31, 1970				
Asset Size	**Under $250M**	**$250M & Less than $1MM**	**$1MM & Less than $10MM**	**$10MM & Less than $25MM**	**All Sizes**	**Under $250M**	**$250M & Less than $1MM**	**$1MM & Less than $10MM**	**$10MM & Less than $25MM**	**All Sizes**
Number of Statements	**30**	**69**	**102**	**13**	**214**	**22**	**49**	**41**		**116**
Assets	%	%	%	%	%	%	%	%	%	%
Cash	8.2	5.7	4.6	8.0	5.9	8.4	6.9	7.4		6.2
Marketable Securities	.0	1.2	.5	.2	.4	.0	.7	.4		.7
Receivables Net	29.6	27.4	24.3	11.4	19.8	29.8	24.2	25.3		21.2
Inventory Net	39.0	41.9	43.4	39.3	41.8	15.6	13.1	14.4		11.8
All Other Current	3.3	1.6	.9	.9	1.0	2.3	1.5	1.5		1.2
Total Current	80.0	77.8	73.6	59.8	68.9	56.1	46.4	48.9		41.1
Fixed Assets Net	11.9	15.0	19.1	34.8	24.5	37.8	41.5	44.5		50.9
All Other Non-Current	8.1	7.2	7.3	5.4	6.6	6.1	12.1	6.6		8.0
Total	100.0	100.0	100.0	100.0	100.0	100.0	100.0	100.0		100.0
Liabilities										
Due To Banks—Short Term	4.4	11.5	9.6	6.4	8.5	3.8	3.7	5.5		4.3
Due To Trade	25.5	20.3	24.9	24.7	24.6	23.7	14.2	20.6		18.1
Income Taxes	1.2	1.6	1.9	2.3	2.0	2.8	2.0	3.2		2.3
Current Maturities LT Debt	2.7	1.7	1.5	2.7	2.0	4.0	4.9	3.2		4.2
All Other Current	12.2	11.5	7.1	5.7	6.9	7.4	7.7	6.5		4.9
Total Current Debt	46.0	46.7	45.0	41.8	44.0	41.7	32.4	38.9		33.9
Non-Current Debt Unsub.	7.0	8.5	11.3	25.6	16.3	13.2	20.7	15.7		16.7
Total Unsubordinated Debt	53.1	55.2	56.3	67.4	60.3	54.9	53.1	54.6		50.5
Subordinated Debt	2.0	2.7	2.2	1.9	2.1	.3	.0	1.7		.9
Tangible Net Worth	44.9	42.2	41.5	30.7	37.6	44.8	46.9	43.8		48.6
Total	100.0	100.0	100.0	100.0	100.0	100.0	100.0	100.0		100.0
Income Data										
Net Sales	100.0*	100.0*	100.0*	100.0	100.0*	100.0	100.0*	100.0*		100.0*
Cost Of Sales	78.8	85.3	91.1	88.6	89.9	80.8	79.6	83.5		80.5
Gross Profit	21.2	14.7	8.9	11.4	10.1	19.2	20.4	16.5		19.5
All Other Expense Net	20.2	13.6	7.8	9.9	8.9	16.7	18.6	12.5		16.4
Profit Before Taxes	1.0	1.1	1.0	1.5	1.2	2.5	1.8	4.0		3.1
Ratios										
	1.4	1.0	1.0	.6	1.0	1.2	1.3	1.1		1.2
Quick	.9	.7	.7	.5	.7	.9	.9	.8		.9
	.6	.5	.5	.4	.5	.7	.7	.6		.6

EXHIBIT 7-5 (CONTINUED)

Asset Size Number of Statements	Under $250M 30	$250M & Less than $1MM 69	$1MM & Less than $10MM 102	$10MM & Less than $25MM 13	All Sizes 214	Under $250M 22	$250M & Less than $1MM 49	$1MM & Less than $10MM 41	$10MM & Less than $25MM	All Sizes 116
	2.9	2.3	2.2	1.6	2.3	2.0	1.9	1.5		1.8
Current	2.0	1.8	1.6	1.5	1.6	1.3	1.4	1.2		1.3
	1.2	1.3	1.4	1.3	1.4	1.0	1.0	.9		.9
	.1	.1	.1	.6	.1	.5	.4	.6		.6
Fixed/Worth	.2	.3	.4	.8	.3	.8	.9	1.0		.9
	.6	.6	.7	1.5	.7	1.0	1.4	2.0		1.6
	.7	.8	.8	1.6	.8	.5	.7	.8		.7
Debt/Worth	1.1	1.4	1.4	1.9	1.4	1.3	1.1	1.3		1.2
	1.9	2.4	2.4	2.4	2.4	2.3	2.5	2.3		2.4
	.7	.7	.7	1.2	.7	.5	.7	.7		.7
Unsub. Debt/Capital Funds	1.0	1.2	1.3	1.9	1.3	1.6	1.1	1.3		1.2
	1.6	2.2	2.1	2.4	2.2	2.6	2.5	2.2		2.5
	16 23.2	**13** 27.7	**9** 38.8	**5** 74.4	**10** 38.0	**17** 21.6	**21** 17.6	**20** 18.4		**19** 18.8
Sales/Receivables	**25** 14.5	**24** 15.0	**15** 24.2	**8** 44.4	**17** 21.6	**26** 13.8	**28** 13.1	**27** 13.5		**27** 13.2
	32 11.3	**33** 11.0	**27** 13.6	**9** 39.1	**29** 12.3	**48** 7.5	**40** 9.1	**40** 9.0		**40** 9.0
	37 9.7	**32** 11.4	**22** 16.4	**21** 16.9	**23** 15.7	**12** 31.0	**15** 23.6	**13** 28.1		**12** 29.3
Cost Sales/Inventory	**54** 6.7	**45** 8.0	**29** 12.4	**23** 15.4	**37** 9.8	**19** 18.7	**22** 16.1	**18** 20.6		**20** 18.2
	0 .0	**61** 5.9	**43** 8.3	**32** 11.1	**55** 6.5	**61** 5.9	**40** 9.1	**28** 12.9		**36** 10.0
	14.3	19.4	31.6	37.2	26.8	35.4	20.5	22.5		22.6
Sales/Working Capital	9.4	12.1	19.2	28.4	15.5	8.8	10.0	7.3		9.0
	4.0	7.6	10.2	22.7	8.3	63.6	85.0	25.7		57.6
	18.3	16.3	23.0	26.3	20.7	22.4	10.6	9.0		11.4
Sales/Worth	11.8	10.6	16.5	17.3	13.6	9.8	6.6	7.5		7.0
	7.2	7.7	8.9	12.3	8.3	4.6	3.9	4.9		4.0
	21.2	20.7	26.2	30.2	24.6	58.8	18.8	33.0		30.4
% Profit Bef. Taxes/Worth	8.1	11.3	12.2	23.6	12.2	29.4	10.7	21.2		16.8
	.0	5.6	7.0	18.6	5.6	17.8	4.9	11.6		7.7
	11.8	7.5	8.7	11.8	8.9	15.0	7.0	12.9		12.4
% Profit Bef. Taxes/Tot. Assets	3.7	4.5	5.1	8.7	5.1	12.3	4.4	8.0		6.8
	.0	2.8	2.7	6.9	2.6	8.6	1.5	3.4		3.0
Net Sales	**$25025M**	**$181236M**	**$2159804M**	**$1322734M**	**$3688799M**	**$17583M**	**$82022M**	**$309828M**		**$471802M**
Total Assets	**4421M**	**37487M**	**331478M**	**214525M**	**587911M**	**3431M**	**27790M**	**103983M**		**193710M**

EXHIBIT 7-5 (CONTINUED)

Asset Size	RETAILERS OF—GROCERIES & MEATS 83 Statements Ended on or about June 30, 1970 104 Statements Ended on or about December 31, 1970					SERVICES—EQUIPMENT RENTAL & LEASING 60 Statements Ended on or about June 30, 1970 93 Statements Ended on or about December 31, 1970				
	Under $250M	$250M & Less than $1MM	$1MM & Less than $10MM	$10MM & Less than $25MM	All Sizes	Under $250M	$250M & Less than $1MM	$1MM & Less than $10MM	$10MM & Less than $25MM	All Sizes
Number of Statements	65	56	50	16	187	36	55	46	16	153
Assets	%	%	%	%	%	%	%	%	%	%
Cash	13.4	10.5	11.6	6.6	8.8	6.3	6.3	5.4	4.1	4.7
Marketable Securities	.9	2.1	1.2	1.9	1.6	1.4	1.3	2.9	.1	1.2
Receivables Net	5.7	9.0	5.8	7.7	7.0	16.4	18.5	32.4	39.0	34.9
Inventory Net	29.6	29.1	35.7	39.7	37.4	14.9	9.7	11.8	2.9	6.7
All Other Current	2.0	4.2	1.9	1.3	1.7	5.3	3.3	6.0	3.1	4.2
Total Current	51.6	54.9	56.2	57.2	56.6	44.4	39.2	58.5	49.2	51.7
Fixed Assets Net	37.8	33.4	37.3	38.3	37.6	41.0	52.7	31.2	35.4	35.3
All Other Non-Current	10.6	11.8	6.6	4.5	5.7	14.7	8.1	10.3	15.3	13.0
Total	100.0	100.0	100.0	100.0	100.0	100.0	100.0	100.0	100.0	100.0
Liabilities										
Due To Banks—Short Term	5.3	5.4	1.6	3.6	3.0	8.0	7.6	21.4	25.5	22.5
Due To Trade	17.5	17.8	21.8	21.4	21.3	11.3	10.4	5.5	6.0	6.2
Income Taxes	1.9	2.8	2.9	1.6	2.2	1.7	1.7	1.2	2.1	1.7
Current Maturities LT Debt	5.1	2.6	4.6	1.9	3.0	5.7	10.1	8.2	4.3	6.1
All Other Current	8.2	10.5	7.9	5.1	6.5	14.3	7.7	8.3	4.3	6.1
Total Current Debt	38.1	39.1	38.9	33.8	36.0	40.9	37.4	44.7	42.1	42.6
Non-Current Debt Unsub.	21.2	14.6	17.2	14.9	15.8	23.0	22.6	28.2	33.4	30.7
Total Unsubordinated Debt	59.3	53.7	56.1	48.6	51.8	63.9	60.1	73.0	75.5	73.3
Subordinated Debt	1.5	.8	1.6	.9	1.2	3.8	1.1	4.0	6.7	5.3
Tangible Net Worth	39.2	45.5	42.3	50.4	47.0	32.3	38.8	23.0	17.9	21.4
Total	100.0	100.0	100.0	100.0	100.0	100.0	100.0	100.0	100.0	100.0
Income Data										
Net Sales	100.0*	100.0*	100.0	100.0	100.0*	100.0*	100.0*	100.0	100.0	100.0*
Cost Of Sales	81.2	80.7	81.6	83.6	82.6					
Gross Profit	18.8	19.3	18.4	16.4	17.4					
All Other Expense Net	17.2	17.5	16.9	15.0	15.9	102.0	92.1	95.9	94.1	94.7
Profit Before Taxes	1.5	1.8	1.5	1.4	1.5	2.0	7.9	4.1	5.9	5.3

EXHIBIT 7-5 (CONTINUED)

Asset Size Number of Statements	Under $250M 65	$250M & Less than $1MM 56	$1MM & Less than $10MM 50	$10MM & Less than $25MM 16	All Sizes 187	Under $250M 36	$250M & Less than $1MM 55	$1MM & Less than $10MM 46	$10MM & Less than $25MM 16	All Sizes 153
Ratios										
	1.1	1.0	.6	.5	1.0	.9	1.0	1.2	1.6	1.1
Quick	.6	.5	.4	.4	.5	.5	.6	.7	1.0	.6
	.2	.2	.3	.3	.2	.3	.2	.3	.6	.3
	2.8	2.0	1.8	2.0	2.1	1.5	1.5	1.7	1.8	1.5
Current	1.7	1.4	1.4	1.6	1.4	1.0	.9	1.2	1.0	1.0
	1.0	1.0	1.0	1.4	1.0	.5	.3	.6	.8	.4
	.3	.3	.7	.6	.4	.3	.5	.2	.2	.3
Fixed/Worth	.8	.6	.9	.8	.8	1.2	1.3	.8	1.2	1.2
	1.7	1.0	1.4	1.1	1.3	1.7	3.4	2.9	3.5	3.0
	.5	.7	1.0	.7	.7	.9	.8	1.5	2.8	1.1
Debt/Worth	1.0	1.2	1.4	1.0	1.2	1.9	2.0	3.4	5.0	2.6
	2.9	1.7	2.5	1.4	2.2	4.7	4.7	6.0	9.1	5.7
	.4	.8	.9	.6	.6	.9	.7	1.4	2.1	.9
Unsub. Debt/Capital Funds	1.0	1.2	1.4	.9	1.2	1.8	1.7	2.9	4.0	2.4
	2.8	1.6	2.3	1.4	2.2	4.3	4.2	4.6	6.5	4.7
	7 49.2	**6** 58.0	**5** 74.3	**6** 65.0	**6** 65.0	**32** 11.4	**36** 10.0	**37** 9.7	**64** 5.6	**36** 9.9
Sales/Receivables	**19** 18.6	**14** 25.0	**7** 51.0	**8** 45.7	**10** 35.9	**64** 5.6	**61** 5.9	**60** 6.0	**360** 1.0	**67** 5.4
	0 .0	**106** 3.4	**14** 25.2	**13** 28.9	**61** 5.9	**0** .0	**300** 1.2	**450** .8	**200** .3	**450** .8
	16 22.3	**16** 22.8	**18** 19.8	**27** 13.6	**17** 21.5					
Cost Sales/Inventory	**23** 16.0	**23** 16.0	**25** 14.5	**31** 11.6	**25** 14.7					
	31 11.6	**36** 9.9	**33** 11.0	**39** 9.3	**34** 10.6					
	21.2	28.0	40.2	39.6	31.3	2.1	5.7	2.4	2.9	3.3
Sales/Working Capital	12.7	15.9	26.1	27.4	17.4	66.5	16.9	.5	.3	47.0
	69.4	2.1	78.5	20.2	1.2	4.5	1.8	4.6	5.2	2.9
	18.3	19.1	23.2	14.2	20.1	4.9	4.0	3.2	4.7	4.0
Sales/Worth	9.2	10.9	16.0	11.3	12.3	2.5	2.0	1.8	3.0	2.0
	5.7	7.7	11.0	9.7	7.9	1.4	1.1	.9	.8	1.0

EXHIBIT 7-5 (CONTINUED)

	RETAILERS OF—GROCERIES & MEATS 83 Statements Ended on or about June 30, 1970 104 Statements Ended on or about December 31, 1970					SERVICES—EQUIPMENT RENTAL & LEASING 60 Statements Ended on or about June 30, 1970 93 Statements Ended on or about December 31, 1970				
Asset Size Number of Statements	**Under $250M 65**	**$250M & Less than $1MM 56**	**$1MM & Less than $10MM 50**	**$10MM & Less than $25MM 16**	**All Sizes 187**	**Under $250M 36**	**$250M & Less than $1MM 55**	**$1MM & Less than $10MM 46**	**$10MM & Less than $25MM 16**	**All Sizes 153**
% Profit Bef. Taxes/Worth	54.8 29.1 3.7	30.5 19.0 9.7	28.1 20.4 10.7	24.5 18.1 10.2	36.5 20.7 9.2	59.4 27.1 10.6	32.8 21.4 5.3	33.5 17.2 4.7	22.1 11.2 2.8	36.7 20.0 4.9
% Profit Bef. Taxes/Tot. Assets	24.3 10.0 1.1	15.5 8.8 5.1	12.1 8.1 3.3	11.5 9.9 4.9	15.8 8.8 3.4	18.2 8.7 .0	13.0 5.3 .6	7.1 3.2 .8	3.6 2.2 .5	11.8 4.2 .8
Net Sales Total Assets	**$45852M 7400M**	**$164071M 26286M**	**$1110997M 178619M**	**$1547735M 267460M**	**$2868655M 479765M**	**$4993M 4422M**	**$30153M 30816M**	**$86083M 145172M**	**$102263M 228570M**	**$223492M 408980M**

SOURCE: *Annual Statement Studies*, 1971 Edition (Philadelphia, Pennsylvania: Robert Morris Associates, Second Printing, 1972). Copyright, Robert Morris Associates, 1971. Used with permission.

The three figures indicated for each ratio are the upper quartile, median, and lower quartile respectively, based on arraying the data in order from the strongest to the weakest.

Firms are classified according to the total dollar value of their assets, where M = thousands and MM = millions of dollars. Firms with total assets in excess of 25 m llions of dollars are not included at present in the Robert Morris Associates Statistics. See Dun & Bradstreet, *Selected Business Ratios*, for this purpose.

Disclaimer Statement

RMA cannot emphasize too strongly that their composite figures for each industry may *not* be representative of that entire industry (except by coincidence), for the following reasons:

1. The only companies with a chance of being included in their study in the first place are those for whom their submitting banks have recent figures.
2. Even from this restricted group of potentially includable companies, those which are chosen, and the total number chosen, are not determined in any random or otherwise statistically reliable manner.
3. Many companies in their study have *varied* product lines; they are "mini-conglomerates," if you will. All they can do in these cases is categorize them by their *primary* product line, and be willing to tolerate any "impurity" thereby introduced.

In a word, don't automatically consider their figures as representative norms and don't attach any more or less significance to them than is indicated by the unique aspects of the data collection.

7.3 BETA AND ALPHA FACTORS

Recognizing that a primary purpose of financial analysis is to forecast the future, there is a constant search for better predictors. A promising development in recent years is the use of *beta* (β) and *alpha* (α) factors for this purpose.[14]

The beta factor is a measure of the relationship between a company's stock and the market as a whole. It is used to predict the return on a stock or portfolio of stock in relation to the expected return on a broad based market index such as *Standard and Poors.* In that return is a determinant of stock prices. It can also be said that the beta factor measures the relationship between the price of a stock and the market average.

Beta factors are computed by the formula $\beta = \text{Cov}\,(X_1,X_2)/\text{Var}\,X_2$; that is, the covariance of the individual stock (or portfolio) in relation to the market, divided by the variance in the market, where:

X_1 = the stock or portfolio rates of return.
X_2 = the market rates of return.
Var = variance, which is the standard deviation (see p. 33n) squared.
Cov = covariance, or the expected value (E) of the product of the deviations (σ) of two random variables from their respective means (μ), or:
$\sigma_{12} = \mu_{11} = E[(X_1 - \mu_1)(X_2 - \mu_2)]$
where $\mu_1 = E(X_1)$ and $\mu_2 = E(X_2)$

The expected rate of return[15] of a given stock or portfolio $E(R_j)$ is computed by the formula:

$$E(R_j) - R_f = [E(R_m) - R_f]\beta_j \qquad (1)$$

where R_f is a risk-free rate,[16] $E(R_m)$ is the expected return on the broad market index, and β_j is a measure of the volatility of a given stock or portfolio relative to the market.

A beta factor of 1.00 means that the expected behavior of a given stock exactly parallels that of the market. Substituting a beta factor of 1.00 in the above equation and using an risk-free interest rate of .05, we notice that if the market return is .10 so is the expected return of the stock in question:

$$E(R_j) = R_f + [E(R_m) - R_f]\beta_j \qquad (2)$$
$$= .05 + (.10 - .05)1.00 \qquad (3)$$
$$= .05 + (.05)1.00 \qquad (4)$$
$$= .10 \qquad (5)$$

Expected values for other beta factors can be computed readily from this formula as illustrated below:

[14] This form of analysis is an outgrowth of the definitive work that is being done in portfolio theory. For some basic references see: F. Modigliani and M. H. Miller, "The Cost of Capital, Corporate Finance, and the Theory of Investment," *American Economic Review,* (June, 1958); Harry Markowitz, *Portfolio Selection: Efficient Diversification of Investments,* (New York: John Wiley & Sons, Inc., 1959); William F. Sharpe, *Portfolio Theory and Capital Markets,* (New York: McGraw-Hill Book Company, 1970); R. S. Hamada, "Portfolio Analysis, Market Equilibrium, and Corporation Finance," *Journal of Finance,* (March, 1969); and Michael C. Jensen, *Studies in the Theory of Capital Markets,* (New York: Praeger Publishers, 1972).

[15] Return is defined in this type of analysis as dividends plus increases (or minus decreases) in the stock prices in question.

[16] The risk-free rate of interest has characteristically been set at the 4 to 5% level.

(a) The expected market return is 10%:

Beta Factor	Computation $E(R_j) = R_f + E(R_m) - R_f$		$E(R_j)$
.2	.05+(.10–.05) .2	=	.06
.5	.05+(.10–.05) .5	=	.075
1.0	.05+(.10–.05)1.0	=	.10
1.5	.05+(.10–.05)1.5	=	.125
2.0	.05+(.10–.05)2.0	=	.15
3.0	.05+(.10–.05)3.0	=	.20
4.0	.05+(.10–.05)3.0	=	.25

(b) The expected market return is –10%:

Beta Factor	Computation		$E(R_j)$
.2	.05+(–.10–.05) .2	=	.02
.5	.05+(–.10–.05) .5	=	–.025
1.0	.05+(–.10–.05)1.0	=	–.10
1.5	.05+(–.10–.05)1.5	=	–.175
2.0	.05+(–.10–.05)2.0	=	–.25
3.0	.05+(–.10–.05)3.0	=	–.40
4.0	.05+(–.10–.05)4.0	=	–.55

A high beta corresponds with a high-risk stock and *vice versa.* A high beta stock will soar above the market when it is rising, but drop by a larger percentage than the composite index when the market falls.

Because beta factors are used for estimating, they may lead to expected (ex ante) values which may or may not be realized. This is where *alpha* enters the picture. Alpha accounts for the difference between expected and actual (ex post) values. Mathematically, alpha enters the former equation as a correction or non-equilibrium factor:

$$E(R_j) - R_f = \alpha + [E(R_m) - R_f]\beta_j \tag{6}$$

If a stock whose beta is 1.00 has a return of 6% when the market's return is 10%, the stock's alpha is, (where $A(\text{R})$ = actual return):

$$\alpha = [A(R_j) - R_f] - [E(R_m) - R_f]\beta_j \tag{7}$$

$$\alpha = (.06 - .05) - (.10 - .05)1 \tag{8}$$

$$\alpha = .01 - .05 \tag{9}$$

$$\alpha = -.04 \text{ or } -4\% \tag{10}$$

Alphas are usually stated in percentages, i.e., –4% in the above example. These beta and alpha factors have generated considerable interest among financial theorists and analysts. Several major brokerage firms, including Merrill Lynch and Oliphant & Co. perform beta consulting services for their clients. The Electronic Stock Evaluator Corporation of Long Island systematically issues beta and alpha factors. Managers of portfolios and funds are now beginning to set investment policy in terms of these factors.

Beta and alpha factors for some of the major mutual funds for the period ending March 31, 1972 were:[17]

[17] Data generated by Wiesenberger Financial Services, Inc. and reported in *Business Week,* (April 22, 1972), p. 72.

Fund	Alpha	Beta
American Express Capital	− 0.1	1.26
American Investors	−10.2	1.35
Axe-Houghton Stock	+ .2	0.81
Burnham	+ 8.5	1.20
Channing Special	+ 9.7	1.53
Chase Special Fund of Boston	+ 9.1	1.37
Dreyfus Leverage	+ 9.6	1.39
Edie Special Growth	+14.8	1.01
Enterprise	+ 4.1	1.05
Lexington Research	− 4.6	1.02
Oppenheimer	+ 4.5	1.01
Putnam Equities	+15.9	1.41
Side	− 3.2	1.40

The data reflect alpha and beta factors of the portfolios of these mutual funds. In addition each stock has its own factors. For example, Ling-Temco-Vought had a beta of 2.17, Standard Oil of New Jersey .74, ITT 1.25, and AT&T .82 for the same period.

Considerably more development and application of alpha and beta factors can be expected in the years ahead.

7.4 STANDARD RATIOS

A *standard ratio* represents a series of ratios. It results from compressing a series of ratios into one representative figure. Standard ratios are used in two ways: (1) to compress a series of past ratios into one representative ratio; or (2) to compress a series of ratios pertaining to other firms into one representative industry ratio. Comparing a firm with its own history is referred to as *horizontal* analysis, while comparing it to its industry is called *vertical* analysis (Exhibit 7-6):

EXHIBIT 7-6 HORIZONTAL AND VERTICAL ANALYSIS

	Current Ratios					
	1970	1969	1968	1967	1966	1965
Firm A	2.1					
B	1.6					
C	1.4					
Subject Firm D	2.0	2.2	2.1	2.5	2.0	1.9
E	2.3					
F	1.9					
G	3.4					
H	3.1					

To which past figure do we compare the subject firm's current ratio of 2.00 in 1970? Or in seeking an industry comparison for 1970, to which other firm do we compare firm D? By means of a horizontal standard ratio we compress the 1965–1969 ratios into one figure, and we do the same vertically for firms A through H, including D.

There are various statistical techniques for developing a standard ratio. We will discuss those that are used most frequently for this purpose: (1) mean, (2) median, (3) interquartile average, and (4) moving average.

MEAN

The *mean* is obtained by dividing the sum of the data by the number of items, i.e.,

$$\frac{\Sigma D}{n}$$

where Σ = sum, D = data; and n = number of items. Horizontal compression yields this standard ratio based on the mean:

$$\left(\frac{2.2 + 2.1 + 2.5 + 2.0 + 1.9}{5}\right) = \frac{10.7}{5} = 2.14$$

Vertical compression yields a standard ratio for the industry:

$$\left(\frac{2.1 + 1.6 + 1.4 + 2.0 + 2.3 + 1.9 + 3.4 + 3.1}{8}\right) = \frac{17.8}{8} = 2.225$$

The arithmetic mean gives equal weight to each ratio. While equal weight may be appropriate for vertical analysis, there are those who feel that more recent data on the horizontal axis should receive greater emphasis.

MEDIAN

The *median* is the middle number where a series of data is arranged in order of magnitude. Where there is no natural middle number, as in all cases where n = an even number of items, the median is defined as the mean of the two middle items. The horizontal median is:

2.5
2.2
2.1 – the median is 2.1
2.0
1.9

The vertical median is:

3.4
3.1
2.3
2.1
2.0
1.9
1.6
1.4

$$\begin{matrix}2.1\\2.0\end{matrix} = \left(\frac{2.1 + 2.0}{2}\right) = \left(\frac{4.1}{2}\right) = \text{the median is 2.05}$$

The median does not take into account the value of data other than middle number. If the distribution of data is not symmetrical, the median is not descriptive of central tendency.

INTERQUARTILE AVERAGE

The *interquartile average* is defined as the mean of the sum of the first and third quartiles. The horizontal interquartile average is:

2.5	2.5	
2.2	2.2 – Median of upper half	
2.1 – Median	2.1 2.1	$= \frac{2.2 + 2.0}{2} = 2.10$
2.0	2.0 – Median of lower	
1.9	1.9 half	

The vertical interquartile average is:

3.4	3.4	
3.1	3.1	
2.3	2.3 – Median of upper half	
2.1	2.1	
2.05 – Median	2.05 2.05	$\frac{2.3 + 1.9}{2} = 2.10$
2.0	2.0	
1.9	1.9 – Median of lower	
1.6	1.6 half	
1.4	1.4	

MOVING AVERAGE

The *moving average* is pertinent to vertical or horizontal compression. A two-unit moving average gives a 50% weight to the lastest item:

1969	1968	1967	1966	1965
2.2	2.1	2.5		

$$\frac{2.0 + 1.9}{2}$$

$$\frac{2.5 + 1.95}{2}$$

$$\frac{2.1 + 2.225}{2}$$

$$\frac{2.2 + 2.1625}{2}$$

2.18125 = two-unit moving average.

A three-unit moving average gives a 1/3 weight to the latest number, a four-unit moving average = a 25% weight to latest number, and so forth. A three-unit moving average is illustrated:

1969	1968	1967	1966	1965
2.2	2.1			

$$\frac{2.5 + 2.0 + 1.9}{3}$$

$$\frac{2.2 + 2.1 + 2.13}{3}$$

2.14 = three-unit moving average

A particular moving average should be selected on the basis of the desired weight to the most recent data. It can be seen that the moving average method will take into account *all* past data.

SUMMARY OF METHODS

A summary of standard ratios developed under the four methods is shown below:

	Vertical Standard Ratios	Horizontal Standard Ratios
Mean	2.125	2.14
Median	2.05	2.10
Interquartile average	2.10	2.10
Moving average:		
Two-unit		2.18
Three-unit		2.14
Subject ratio	2.00	

The various statistical methods yield different standard ratios. For this reason it is important to use one method consistently or to disclose a change in method. More reliable industry comparisons can be made by using the same statistical technique for horizontal compression of data which is used by the compiler of the industry statistics.

7.5 THE USE OF STANDARD RATIOS

The use of standard ratios does not preclude more specific interperiod and inter-firm comparison. The characteristics between the current period and some specific previous period may provide a more valid comparison than can be obtained through the use of a standard ratio. For example, if the current period is a recessionary one, a previous recessionary period may provide a pertinent comparison.

Similarly, comparison with some particular firms in an industry should be used to augment standard ratio analysis. Specific inter-firm comparison allows us to relate the subject firm to those of equal size (generally measured in terms of sales volume), similar products, same geographic regions, etc. In fact each firm can be thought of as having a particular profile across a series of continua as illustrated in Exhibit 7-7. A comparison between firms with relatively close profiles should be an objective of inter-firm analysis.

EXHIBIT 7-7

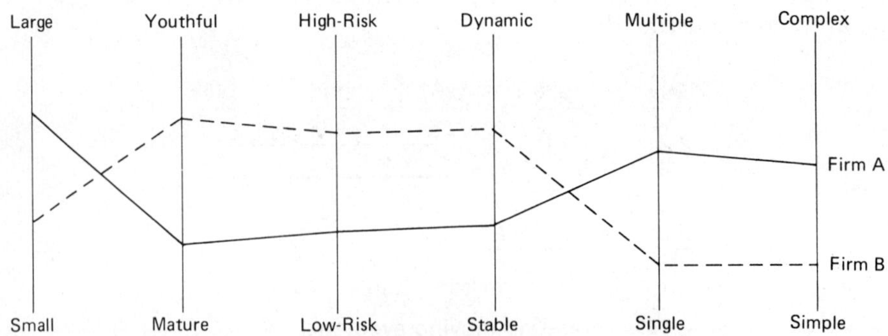

EXHIBIT 7-8 DETAILED INDUSTRY RATIOS

CURRENT RATIOS OF 24 CEMENT COMPANIES (1966)

Group		Current Ratio
1	Monolith Portland Cement Company	1.09
1	Northwestern States Portland Cement Company	1.49
3	American Cement Corporation	1.57
4	Martin-Marietta Corporation	1.73
1	O K C Corporation	1.95
2	St. Lawrence Cement Company	2.01
2	Medusa Portland Cement Company	2.04
3	Canada Cement Company, Ltd.	2.14
3	Marquette Cement Manufacturing Company	2.31
3	General Portland Cement Company	2.50
2	Alpha Portland Cement Company	2.59
2	Penn-Dixie Cement Corporation	2.70
1	Oregon Portland Cement Company	2.94
3	Lehigh Portland Cement Company	3.04
3	Ideal Cement Company	3.08
1	Louisville Cement Company	3.39
4	Lone Star Cement Corporation	3.48
1	Coplay Cement Manufacturing Company	3.98
2	Missouri Portland Cement Company	4.16
1	Whitehall Cement Manufacturing Company	4.30
1	Keystone Portland Cement Company	4.57
1	Giant Portland Cement Company	6.17
2	California Portland Cement Company	7.57
1	Nazareth Cement Company	7.71

CURRENT RATIOS OF 22 BREWING COMPANIES (1966)

Group		Current Ratio
1	Oland and Son, Ltd.	1.20
4	Schlitz (Jos.) Brewing Company	1.47
1	Grain Belt Breweries, Inc.	1.62
1	Lone Star Brewing Company	1.70
2	Rheingold Corporation	1.83
3	Pabst Brewing Company	1.87
1	Heileman (G.) Brewing Company	1.87
2	Meister Brau, Inc.	1.97
2	Associated Brewing Company	2.10
1	Pittsburgh Brewing Company	2.10
1	Burger Brewing Company	2.29
2	Labatt (John), Ltd.	2.50
1	Duquesne Brewing Company of Pittsburg	2.59
3	Falstaff Brewing Corporation	2.59
2	Molson Breweries, Ltd.	2.60
4	Anheuser-Busch, Inc.	2.61
2	Olympia Brewing Company	2.72
1	Iroquois Industries, Inc.	2.96
1	Sicks' Rainier Brewing Company	3.03
4	Canadian Breweries, Ltd.	3.39
2	General Brewing Company	4.00
2	Pearl Brewing Company	4.16

	Sales	
Group	Cement	Brewing
1	1– 49 million	1– 19 million
2	50– 99 "	20– 99 "
3	100–250 "	100–200 "
4	Over 250 "	Over 200 "

SOURCE: John N. Myer, *Financial Statement Analysis* (Englewood Cliffs, N.J.: Prentice-Hall, Inc., 1969), pp. 237–38. Used with permission.

EXHIBIT 7-9 KEY BUSINESS RATIOS FOR SELECTED INDUSTRIES, 1970

MANUFACTURING AND CONSTRUCTION

Line of Business (and number of concerns reporting)	Current assets to current debt	Net profits on net sales	Net profits on tangible net worth	Net profits on net working capital	Net sales to tangible net worth	Net sales to net working capital	Collection period	Net sales to inventory	Fixed assets to tangible net worth	Current debt to tangible net worth	Total debt to tangible net worth	Inventory to net working capital	Current debt to inventory	Funded debts to net working capital
	Times	Per cent	Per cent	Per cent	Times	Times	Days	Times	Per cent	Per cent	Per cent	Per cent	Per cent	Per cent
2871–72–79	2.86	4.53	13.77	29.57	4.04	17.62	37	12.8	29.8	28.8	69.4	35.6	90.6	17.9
Agricultural Chemicals	**1.84**	**2.05**	**8.24**	**14.00**	**2.49**	**5.35**	**59**	**8.7**	**47.5**	**52.7**	**135.0**	**89.6**	**135.3**	**118.3**
(43)	1.18	0.89	2.75	5.25	2.04	3.33	100	5.3	82.3	91.6	218.2	168.3	243.4	201.1
3722–23–29	3.43	3.73	9.16	13.59	3.37	5.94	38	8.1	36.7	23.0	51.7	59.0	68.2	27.6
Airplane Parts &	**2.42**	**1.91**	**4.46**	**5.58**	**2.35**	**4.08**	**53**	**5.2**	**56.0**	**36.9**	**78.9**	**82.6**	**100.0**	**69.0**
Accessories (68)	1.59	0.07	0.20	0.27	1.89	3.04	74	3.8	81.9	80.0	135.6	135.6	126.7	98.9
2051–52	2.94	2.85	9.98	43.54	5.73	24.22	17	41.2	57.0	16.6	38.1	33.7	134.7	23.9
Bakery Products	**1.94**	**1.22**	**5.85**	**22.02**	**4.22**	**13.20**	**22**	**30.0**	**71.6**	**29.9**	**52.6**	**60.3**	**196.8**	**63.0**
(65)	1.40	0.57	2.62	12.51	3.17	9.06	30	18.4	93.9	44.1	87.9	86.0	303.7	152.5
3312–13–15–16–17	3.31	5.81	10.54	23.42	2.92	5.56	38	7.5	31.5	14.9	38.8	72.5	57.2	31.8
Blast Furnaces, Steel Wks.	**2.40**	**3.07**	**6.18**	**13.89**	**1.96**	**4.13**	**44**	**4.9**	**59.9**	**29.7**	**66.0**	**90.5**	**77.6**	**53.5**
& Rolling Mills (71)	1.50	1.34	3.01	6.19	1.50	3.18	58	4.0	79.8	47.7	99.3	114.0	102.1	132.5
2331	2.13	3.19	23.82	28.84	11.96	16.12	33	22.6	4.4	72.5	86.7	53.3	126.3	7.8
Blouses & Waists, Wom-	**1.62**	**1.65**	**10.50**	**12.38**	**9.34**	**12.33**	**43**	**14.3**	**9.8**	**136.3**	**178.4**	**83.0**	**174.9**	**23.1**
en's & Misses' (54)	1.40	0.64	3.43	4.67	5.85	6.48	56	7.9	18.2	210.5	269.8	120.8	273.2	34.0
2731–32	4.21	6.50	13.85	19.68	3.12	4.10	53	6.9	14.1	20.7	37.9	40.6	56.8	7.2
Books: Publishing, Pub-	**2.86**	**3.92**	**8.22**	**10.60**	**2.04**	**2.86**	**65**	**3.9**	**36.0**	**43.6**	**71.7**	**63.8**	**81.0**	**24.2**
lishing & Printing (54)	1.94	1.50	3.70	4.20	1.43	2.00	100	2.9	48.5	67.6	119.8	86.6	173.8	76.3
3811 Engineering, Labo-	5.18	5.83	11.40	15.43	2.57	3.36	52	4.7	28.0	15.9	47.6	54.6	34.9	16.7
ratory & Scientific	**3.43**	**2.11**	**5.74**	**7.69**	**2.06**	**2.50**	**67**	**3.8**	**41.9**	**34.5**	**84.9**	**71.1**	**60.6**	**43.3**
Instruments (41)	2.31	(1.26)	(2.78)	(4.17)	1.78	2.16	86	2.8	61.1	65.2	136.0	90.8	81.7	70.1
3712–13	3.79	3.63	11.30	19.98	5.49	8.65	29	9.4	23.9	26.0	40.3	58.4	64.5	10.8
Passenger Car, Truck &	**2.11**	**1.95**	**7.07**	**12.21**	**3.86**	**5.60**	**47**	**6.6**	**38.4**	**54.6**	**96.6**	**95.2**	**102.5**	**19.8**
Bus Bodies (47)	1.60	0.32	2.80	5.46	2.40	3.60	56	5.1	69.1	97.0	142.4	129.2	129.1	58.7
2911	1.76	6.80	11.62	68.89	3.39	19.07	44	30.1	7.1	6.6	12.8	40.6	100.0	33.3
Petroleum Refining	**1.09**	**3.41**	**7.45**	**32.35**	**1.91**	**8.89**	**54**	**14.2**	**34.1**	**23.0**	**35.2**	**82.6**	**119.1**	**112.0**
(53)	1.00	1.74	3.62	21.59	1.36	4.70	66	9.0	79.2	62.0	120.1	204.2	184.1	262.9
3841–42–43	5.29	6.07	14.82	21.16	3.28	4.76	43	7.5	19.2	18.0	32.6	56.0	36.8	10.9
Surgical, Medical & Den-	**3.20**	**4.21**	**9.97**	**11.82**	**2.62**	**3.52**	**56**	**4.8**	**35.3**	**30.8**	**59.4**	**72.2**	**62.2**	**29.5**
tal Instruments (62)	2.11	2.20	5.53	6.26	1.89	2.68	67	3.5	51.5	53.5	91.2	98.4	98.5	63.0
3941–42–43–49	2.74	4.82	16.66	23.26	4.63	8.79	46	6.9	19.6	41.0	71.7	77.1	77.0	22.6
Toys, Amusement &	**1.89**	**1.80**	**8.08**	**9.80**	**3.74**	**5.12**	**60**	**4.7**	**39.1**	**75.1**	**122.2**	**106.2**	**119.1**	**42.3**
Sporting Goods (62)	1.35	0.53	2.16	2.92	2.28	3.30	92	3.6	65.5	132.3	176.3	165.7	147.6	61.5

EXHIBIT 7-9 (CONTINUED)

	Line of Business (and number of concerns reporting)	Current assets to current debt	Net profits on net sales	Net profits on tangible net worth	Net profits on net working capital	Net sales to tangible net worth	Net sales to net working capital	Collection period	Net sales to inventory	Fixed assets to tangible net worth	Current debt to tangible net worth	Total debt to tangible net worth	Inventory to net working capital	Current debt to inventory	Funded debts to net working capital
		Times	Per cent	Per cent	Per cent	Times	Times	Days	Times	Per cent	Per cent	Per cent	Per cent	Per cent	Per cent
WHOLESALING	5077	3.34	4.35	18.56	19.22	8.20	8.87	37	9.0	4.2	39.2	58.6	63.8	57.6	10.5
	Air Condtg. & Refrigtn.	**2.13**	**2.78**	**13.91**	**14.23**	**4.64**	**5.60**	**50**	**6.3**	**11.3**	**66.4**	**99.9**	**90.9**	**88.6**	**23.8**
	Equipt. & Supplies (53)	1.57	1.58	7.89	9.84	3.25	3.84	64	3.9	25.6	184.4	270.8	134.7	165.6	57.0
	5013	3.90	3.46	15.18	18.52	5.34	6.49	28	6.7	6.3	30.9	54.8	72.3	46.6	12.3
	Automotive Equipment	**2.62**	**2.20**	**9.21**	**11.28**	**3.92**	**4.59**	**34**	**5.1**	**13.1**	**50.4**	**90.4**	**92.6**	**65.2**	**28.1**
	(184)	1.95	1.15	4.76	5.78	2.90	3.52	45	3.9	26.9	81.0	145.8	129.0	97.4	53.2
	5095	3.07	2.00	14.24	27.66	10.97	18.91	7	15.3	10.2	30.9	59.7	69.2	62.2	21.7
	Beer, Wine & Alcoholic	**1.87**	**1.11**	**8.21**	**13.19**	**7.38**	**10.94**	**24**	**9.6**	**26.7**	**77.9**	**138.7**	**114.1**	**99.7**	**41.2**
	Beverages (88)	1.41	0.43	3.29	5.67	5.11	7.58	36	6.3	50.4	162.5	241.3	197.3	132.3	61.8
	5029	3.08	2.88	15.77	28.89	8.27	17.21	37	15.9	12.7	33.9	95.0	46.1	94.7	32.6
	Chemicals & Allied	**1.74**	**1.39**	**8.42**	**15.63**	**5.90**	**8.52**	**51**	**11.7**	**28.2**	**60.9**	**162.8**	**82.1**	**138.6**	**57.9**
	Products (49)	1.43	0.42	4.78	5.76	3.02	5.95	65	7.7	48.4	140.1	234.0	123.9	236.1	96.3
RETAILING	5969	3.95	4.49	16.13	28.27	4.91	12.27	**	17.1	20.0	21.0	55.0	45.2	54.5	19.9
	Farm & Garden	**2.23**	**2.51**	**9.12**	**16.18**	**3.36**	**6.45**	**	**9.1**	**43.9**	**46.9**	**89.8**	**75.8**	**120.7**	**53.3**
	Supply Stores (76)	1.50	1.42	4.29	7.56	2.30	4.06	**	5.7	64.1	73.4	116.4	114.9	213.3	124.2
	5712	6.33	4.38	10.10	12.34	4.37	5.58	46	6.2	3.6	19.7	52.6	34.3	50.2	8.5
	Furniture Stores (183)	**2.81**	**2.22**	**5.85**	**6.46**	**2.45**	**2.75**	**92**	**4.6**	**10.6**	**52.4**	**87.2**	**63.0**	**90.3**	**18.5**
		1.76	0.64	1.77	2.03	1.67	1.69	202	3.6	21.8	91.8	163.9	121.8	129.5	39.3
	5541	3.84	4.14	11.23	33.04	5.22	13.13	**	23.9	23.9	17.0	34.2	41.9	69.9	22.6
	Gasoline Service	**2.33**	**2.51**	**7.82**	**19.93**	**3.22**	**6.93**	**	**9.9**	**46.6**	**32.4**	**61.8**	**82.6**	**128.2**	**56.2**
	Stations (70)	1.47	1.13	4.77	10.88	1.83	4.54	**	6.1	66.4	66.5	113.3	120.8	191.9	139.7
	5411	2.35	1.71	15.47	48.19	13.51	39.52	**	22.9	38.7	34.2	64.2	85.5	67.9	27.4
	Grocery Stores (137)	**1.66**	**0.99**	**10.30**	**23.12**	**9.70**	**21.65**	**	**16.8**	**67.4**	**58.3**	**106.4**	**136.1**	**94.0**	**72.6**
		1.27	0.63	7.28	15.51	6.89	13.00	**	12.8	90.9	84.1	169.5	233.5	124.1	184.0
	5251	7.82	4.35	12.45	14.54	4.30	4.59	**	5.4	5.8	11.1	44.1	62.1	25.2	15.3
	Hardware Stores (97)	**3.81**	**2.52**	**6.94**	**8.80**	**2.59**	**3.15**	**	**3.9**	**14.7**	**25.3**	**63.0**	**82.7**	**46.0**	**31.4**
		2.19	0.98	2.83	3.76	1.71	2.24	**	3.0	35.3	74.3	113.3	113.2	76.1	66.3

SOURCE: *1970 Key Business Ratios* (New York: Dun & Bradstreet, Inc., 99 Church Street, 10007). Used with permission. The three figures are the upper quartile, median, and lower quartile respectively, where the data from the firms in a given category is ranked in order of strongest to the weakest ratio. The collection period is not computed in instances marked** due to the predominantly cash nature of the business or insufficient credit information.

Exhibit 7-8 illustrates the wide variance in industry data. Some compilers of industry statistics segment standard ratios as illustrated in Exhibits 7-5 and 7-9. Exhibit 7-9 shows standard ratios for first, second, and third quartiles, respectively.

7.6 TREND ANALYSIS

Plotting a series of ratio changes often leads to the discovery of important trends. Trends are important in that they often point to the probable course of future events. Also, the detection of unfavorable trends at an early date promotes timely remedies.

Trend analysis may be applied to any item in the financial statements or to any group of items. Presentation of data may be in tabular or graphic form.

EXHIBIT 7-10 TABULAR

	1970		1969		1968		1967 (Base)	
Net sales	$1,400,000	156%	$1,200,000	133%	$1,100,000	122%	$900,000	100%
Total operating expenses	1,340,000	158	1,110,000	131	1,030,000	121	850,000	100
Inventory	530,000	151	475,000	136	410,000	117	350,000	100
Fixed assets	280,000	112	290,000	116	240,000	96	250,000	100
Current liabilities	675,000	153	640,000	145	390,000	89	440,000	100
Net worth	1,575,000	171	1,331,000	145	912,000	99	920,000	100

EXHIBIT 7-11 GRAPHIC

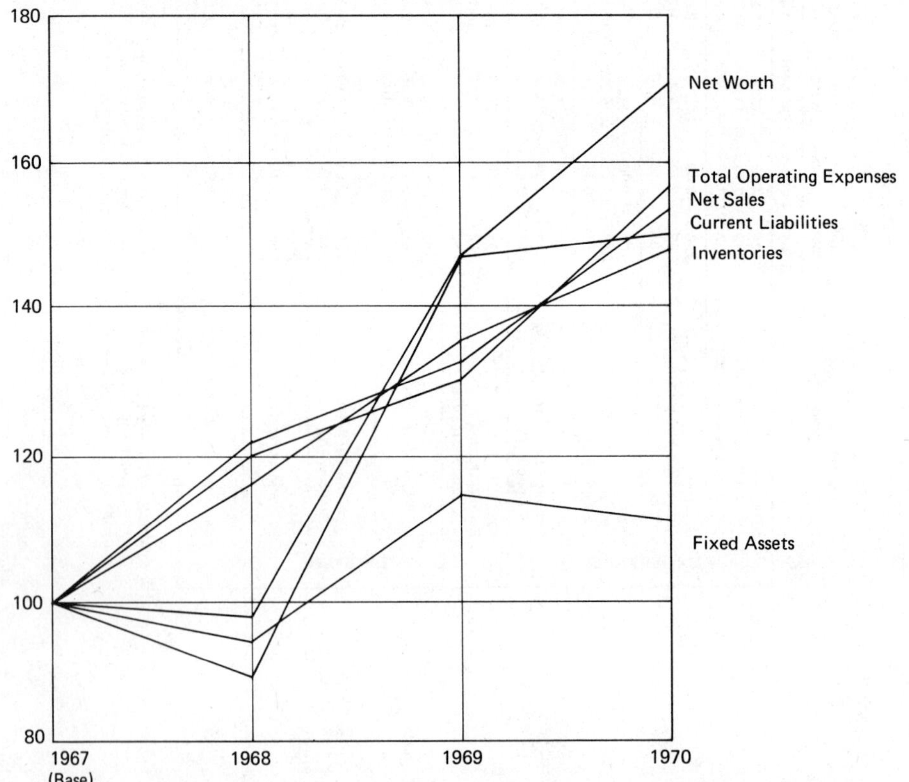

EXHIBIT 7-12 TREND IN HOTEL SALES

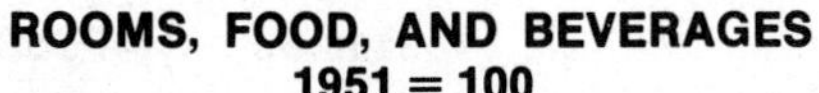
ROOMS, FOOD, AND BEVERAGES
1951 = 100

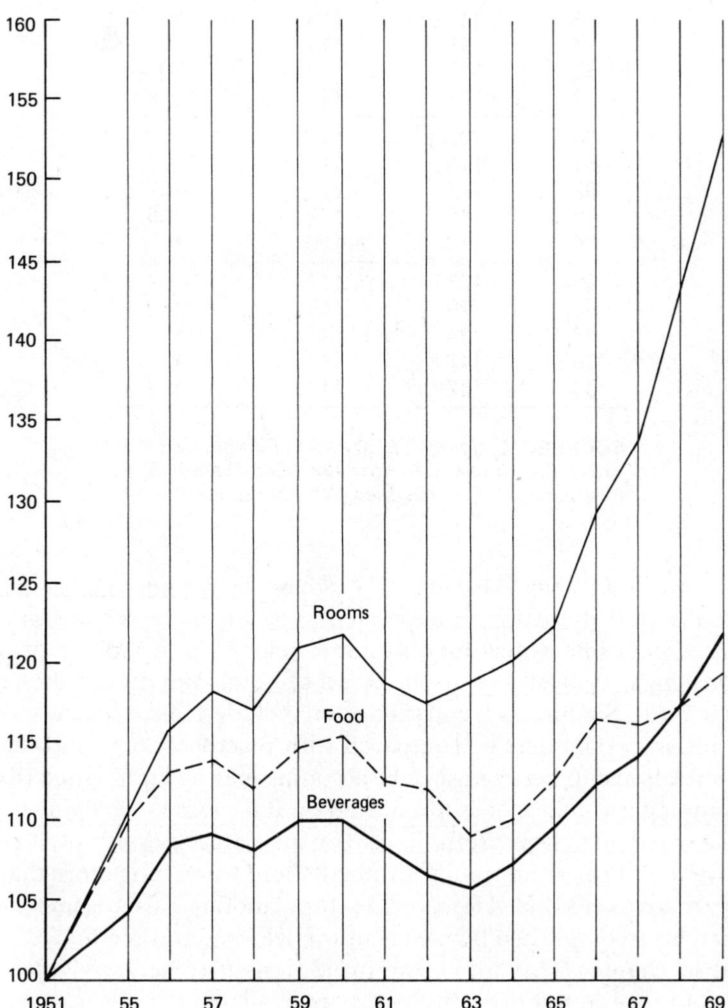

EXHIBIT 7-12 (CONTINUED)

	Rooms	**Food**	**Beverages**
1955	111	110	104
56	115	113	107
57	118	114	109
58	117	112	107
59	121	115	110
60	122	115	110
61	118	112	108
62	117	112	107
63	115	109	105
64	118	110	107
65	123	112	109
66	129	116	112
67	134	116	114
68	143	117	117
69	152	119	122

SOURCE: *Lodging Industry: 1970 Edition,* Laventhol, Krekstein, Horwath & Horwath, 1845 Walnut Street, Pliladelphia, Pa., p. 40. Used with permission.

As noted in Exhibits 7-10 and 7-11, a base year is selected for trend analysis. Data for each period thereafter is expressed as a percentage of the base year. Each display of trend data should feature only a few items. This technique draws attention to key relationships, as illustrated in the trend of hotel sales during the period 1951–1969 (Exhibit 7-12). Significant trends are often included in corporate annual reports. Internal or industry data may be compared with macroeconomic indicators (Exhibit 7-13); or the relationship between specific accounts may be highlighted (Exhibit 7-14).

A semi-logarithmic scale is often used on the *y* axis to scale down accentuated trends. While trend analysis is useful in portraying past relationships, it also has value as a predictive tool. Projecting trends is difficult, and something more than extrapolation of past trends is needed. However, extrapolation is a useful first step. A linear projection can be accomplished by means of the least squares method. This technique is illustrated in chapter 22. Curvilinear projections may be more representative of past trends, and several standard functions are available for this purpose. Extension of historical data needs to be influenced by subjective judgments regarding future events. For this reason extrapolation should not be relied upon as the only guide to the future.

7.7 NORMALIZED STATEMENT ANALYSIS

A financial statement is "normalized" by reducing it to some common denominator. One form of normalization is the *percentage composition statement.* In the income statement sales are equated with 100% for each period; every other item in the income statement is then expressed as a percentage of sales. In the balance sheet total assets and total equities are each set at 100%, with each asset and equity account described as a percentage of the total.

EXHIBIT 7-13

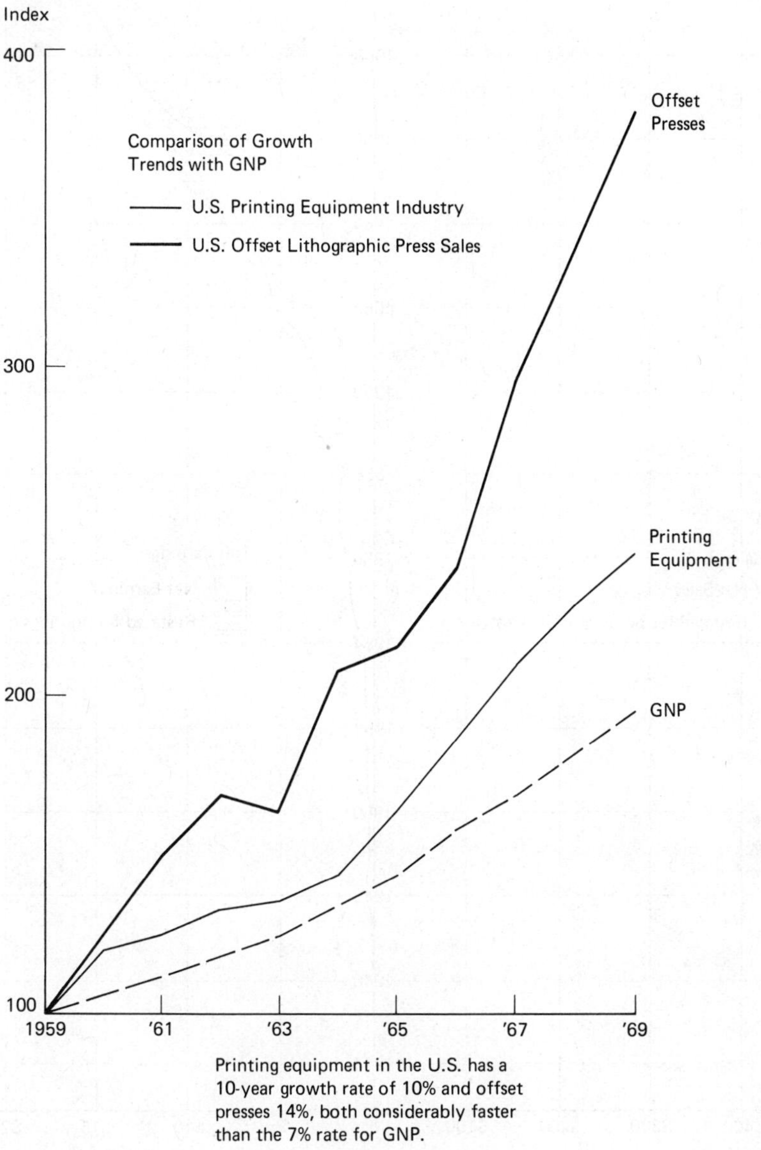

Index

400

300

200

100

Comparison of Growth Trends with GNP

—— U.S. Printing Equipment Industry

—— U.S. Offset Lithographic Press Sales

Offset Presses

Printing Equipment

GNP

1959 '61 '63 '65 '67 '69

Printing equipment in the U.S. has a 10-year growth rate of 10% and offset presses 14%, both considerably faster than the 7% rate for GNP.

SOURCE: Harris-Intertype Corporation, *1970 Annual Report,* June 30, 1970.

Percentage composition income statements for Dow Chemical Company (Exhibit 7-16) reveal important relationships that are obscured by the conventional money figures in Exhibit 7-15. Comparative balance sheets for Dow Chemical are presented in Exhibits 7-17 and 7-18.

Expressing relationships in terms of a *common dollar* is another form of normalized analysis. An example of common dollar analysis is contained in Exhibit 7-19.

EXHIBIT 7-14

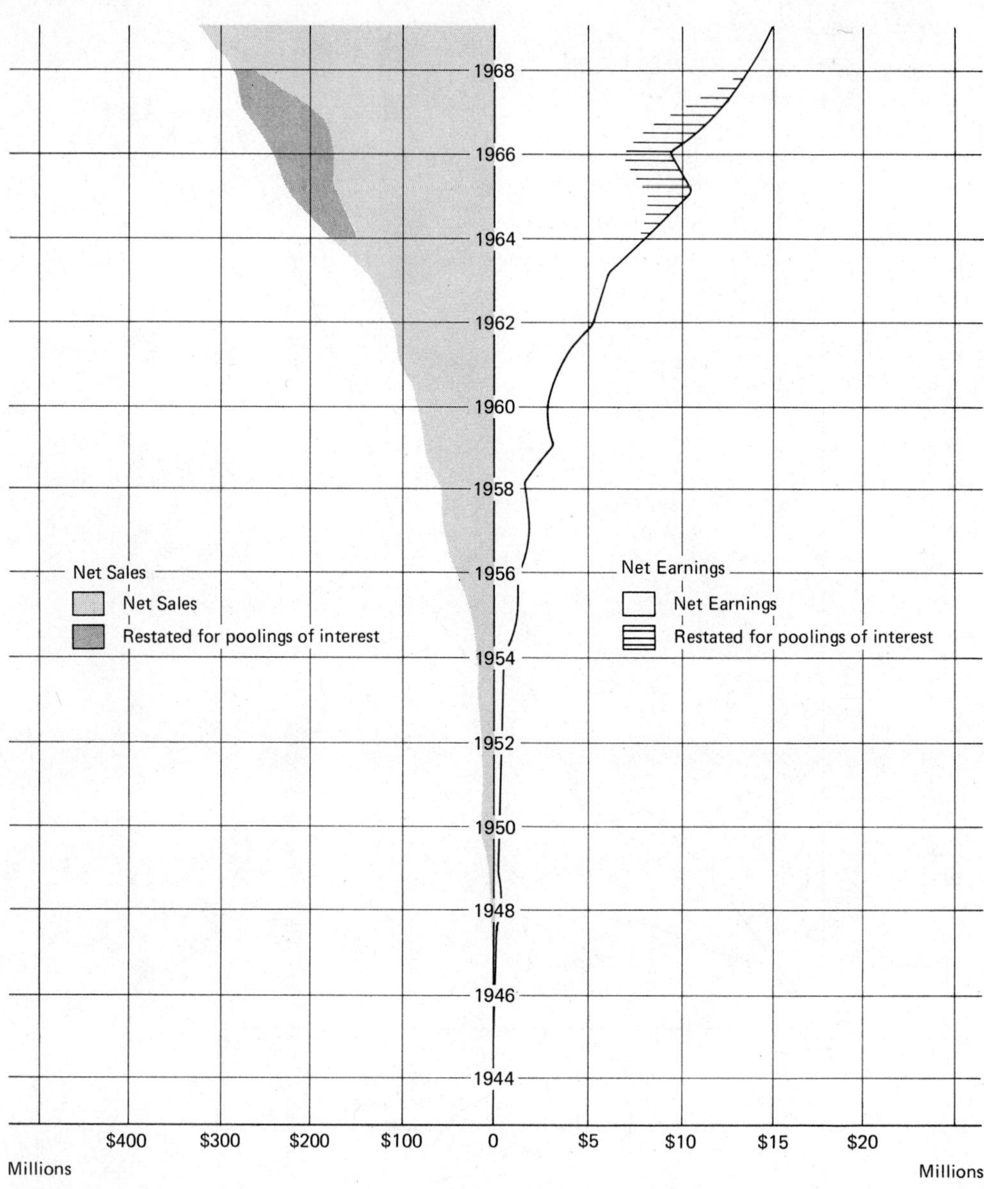

SOURCE: Purex Corporation Ltd., *1969 Annual Report,* June 30, 1969.

EXHIBIT 7-15

DOW CHEMICAL COMPANY COMPARATIVE INCOME STATEMENTS

(Dollars '000,000)

	1959	1960	1961	1962	1963	1964	1965	1966	1967	1968
Sales	$781.4	817.5	890.6	926.2	967.6	1077.5	1176.2	1309.7	1382.7	1652.5
Cost of sales	463.2	512.6	572.5	583.9	612.1	684.2	744.4	833.4	872.4	1058.8
Gross profit	318.2	304.9	318.1	342.3	355.5	393.3	431.8	476.3	510.3	593.7
Selling & admin.	91.7	114.1	115.8	117.6	119.9	139.1	139.1	149.7	156.1	214.5
Depreciation	78.4	89.8	103.2	99.6	99.6	98.9	115.8	122.8	136.2	157.2
Operating exp.	170.1	203.9	219.0	217.2	219.5	238.0	254.9	272.5	292.3	371.7
Net oper. income	148.1	101.0	99.0	125.1	136.1	155.3	176.8	203.8	218.0	222.0
Other items*	(2.6)	(6.8)	(3.5)	(6.3)	(9.2)	(8.5)	(5.2)	2.0	(.6)	(10.0)
Income tax	68.3	43.7	43.3	58.5	64.6	67.5	73.5	79.5	85.7	92.0
Net income	$ 82.4	64.1	59.2	72.9	80.7	96.3	108.5	122.3	132.9	140.0

*Includes non-operating, extraordinary items and interests of minority stockholders. ( ) = credit or positive balance.

EXHIBIT 7-16

DOW CHEMICAL COMPANY COMPARATIVE INCOME STATEMENTS

(Percentage)

	1959	1960	1961	1962	1963	1964	1965	1966	1967	1968
Sales	100.0	100.0	100.0	100.0	100.0	100.0	100.0	100.0	100.0	100.0
Cost of sales	59.3	62.7	64.3	63.0	63.3	63.5	63.3	63.6	63.1	64.1
Gross profit	40.7	37.3	35.7	37.0	36.7	36.5	36.7	36.4	36.9	35.9
Selling & admin.	11.7	14.0	13.0	12.7	12.4	12.9	11.8	11.4	11.3	13.0
Depreciation	10.0	11.0	11.6	10.7	10.3	9.2	9.8	9.4	9.9	9.5
Operating exp.	21.7	25.0	24.6	23.4	22.7	22.1	21.6	20.8	21.2	22.5
Net oper. income	19.0	12.3	11.1	13.6	14.0	14.4	15.1	15.6	15.7	13.4
Other items	(.2)	(1.0)	(.5)	(.6)	(1.0)	(.8)	(.3)	.2	.0	(.6)
Income tax	8.7	5.4	4.9	6.3	6.7	6.3	6.2	6.1	6.2	5.6
Net income	10.5	7.9	6.7	7.9	8.3	8.9	9.2	9.3	9.5	8.4

EXHIBIT 7-17

DOW CHEMICAL COMPANY COMPARATIVE BALANCE SHEETS

(Dollars '000,000)

ASSETS	1959	1960	1961	1962	1963	1964	1965	1966	1967	1968
Cash & equivalent	$ 37	40	39	43	54	104	115	127	105	142
Receivables	123	140	159	148	199	206	219	255	307	358
Inventories	156	172	162	165	167	187	183	195	216	275
Current assets	316	352	360	356	420	497	517	577	628	775
Investments	17	57	66	76	78	136	248	264	366	340
Deferred charges	5	8	11	10	11	12	8	9	16	25
Plant & equip. (net)	560	620	615	578	557	623	751	850	896	1127
Intangibles	4	3	3	2	3	3	3	5	5	45
Total assets & equities	$902	1040	1055	1022	1069	1271	1527	1705	1911	2312
EQUITIES										
Current liabilities	160	243	227	196	176	267	256	293	426	576
Long-term debt	156	146	147	127	168	240	456	553	553	726
Total debt	316	389	374	323	344	507	712	846	979	1302
Owners' equity	$586	651	681	699	725	764	815	859	932	1010

EXHIBIT 7-18

DOW CHEMICAL COMPANY COMPARATIVE BALANCE SHEETS

(Percentage)

ASSETS	1959	1960	1961	1962	1963	1964	1965	1966	1967	1968
Cash & equivalent	4.1	3.8	3.7	4.2	5.1	8.2	7.5	7.5	5.5	6.1
Receivables	13.6	13.5	15.1	14.5	18.6	16.2	14.3	14.9	16.1	15.5
Inventories	17.3	16.6	15.3	16.1	15.6	14.7	12.0	11.4	11.3	11.9
Current assets	35.0	33.9	34.1	34.8	39.3	39.1	33.8	33.8	32.9	33.5
Investments	1.9	5.5	6.2	7.4	7.3	10.8	16.2	15.5	19.2	14.7
Deferred charges	.6	.8	1.1	1.0	1.0	.9	.5	.5	.8	1.1
Plant & equip. (net)	62.1	59.5	58.3	56.6	52.1	49.0	49.3	49.9	46.9	48.8
Intangibles	.4	.3	.3	.2	.3	.2	.2	.3	.3	1.9
Total	100.0	100.0	100.0	100.0	100.0	100.0	100.0	100.0	100.0	100.0
EQUITIES										
Current liabilities	17.7	23.3	21.5	19.2	16.5	21.0	16.8	17.2	22.3	24.5
Long-term debt	17.3	14.0	14.0	12.4	15.6	19.0	29.8	32.5	28.9	31.8
Total debt	35.0	37.3	35.5	31.6	32.1	40.0	46.6	49.7	51.2	56.3
Owners' equity	65.0	62.6	64.5	68.4	67.9	60.0	53.4	50.3	48.8	43.7

EXHIBIT 7-19 THE HOTEL DOLLAR, 1969

Where it comes from

49.9¢	Room Sales
29.3¢	Food Sales
12.1¢	Beverage Sales
2.4¢	Telephone Sales
1.2¢	Store Rentals
5.1¢	Other Sources

Where it goes

36.7¢	Payroll (cash)
10.2¢	Cost of Food (net)
3.4¢	Cost of Beverage
16.0¢	Departmental Expenses
5.0¢	Administrative Expenses
2.5¢	Advertising & Promotion
3.2¢	Heat, Light & Power
3.7¢	Repairs & Maintenance
4.8¢	Municipal Taxes
7.7¢	Depreciation
3.4¢	Federal Income Tax
3.4¢	Return on Investment Equivalent to 1.51% on Fair Value of Investment

SOURCE: *Lodging Industry: 1970*, p. 18. Used with permission.

7.8 FUNDS ANALYSIS

We discussed the nature and importance of the statement of changes in financial position in chapter 6. Complete funds analysis comprises three statements, of which the statement of changes in financial position is the only one which is typically included in the annual report. The three statements are:

1. The statement of changes in financial position
2. Distribution of working capital
3. Cash flow statement

The statement of changes in financial position identifies the sources and uses of working capital during the fiscal period. The statement of distribution of working capital shows the form in which working capital is held. The cash flow statement shows the sources and uses of cash during the fiscal period.

We will use the Exridge Corporation's financial statements (Exhibits 6-5, 6-6, and 6-7) to illustrate funds analysis. In Exhibit 7-20 we repeat the statement of changes in financial position contained in Exhibit 6-13. Chapter 6 contains instructions for developing the statement of changes in financial position. The statement of

EXHIBIT 7-20

THE EXRIDGE CORPORATION
STATEMENT OF CHANGES IN FINANCIAL POSITION
FOR THE YEAR ENDED, DEC. 31, 19x2

SOURCES		
Operations—Net income before extraordinary items	$ 95,000	
Gain on sale of assets	200,000	
Net income	295,000	
Add-back depreciation	150,000	$ 445,000
Sale of long-lived assets (at book value)		500,000
Increase in long-term liabilities		80,000
Total sources		$1,025,000
USES		
Dividends declared and paid	$ 95,000	
Purchase of long-lived assets	890,000	
Total uses		985,000
Increase in working capital		$ 40,000

EXHIBIT 7-21

THE EXRIDGE CORPORATION
STATEMENT OF DISTRIBUTION OF WORKING CAPITAL
FOR THE YEAR ENDED, DEC. 31, 19x2

WORKING CAPITAL IS HELD IN THE FORM OF	19x1	19x2	Net Change
Current Assets			
Cash	$ 30,000	$ 40,000	+ 10,000
Marketable securities	95,000	90,000	− 5,000
Notes receivable	50,000	30,000	− 20,000
Accounts receivable	150,000	180,000	+ 30,000
Inventory	400,000	300,000	− 100,000
Prepaid expenses	15,000	10,000	− 5,000
Total current assets	740,000	650,000	− 90,000
Current Liabilities:			
Notes payable	130,000	20,000	+ 110,000
Accounts payable	200,000	160,000	+ 40,000
Accrued expenses	40,000	50,000	− 10,000
Dividends payable	20,000	30,000	− 10,000
Current portion of L-T debt	40,000	40,000	0
Total current liabilities	430,000	300,000	+ 130,000
Increase in working capital	$310,000	$350,000	+ 40,000

changes in financial position indicates that working capital increased by $40,000 during 19*x*2. In what form is this increase in working capital held? Is it all held in the form of cash? Inventory? Was it all used to decrease current liabilities? The purpose of the *statement of distribution of working capital* is to answer this type of question (Exhibit 7-21).

Again, there is no simple answer to the question "what did you do with the increase (or decrease) in working capital?" because of the concept of pooled resources. The above statement explains the disposition of working capital during the fiscal period. If a change in working capital was planned for a specific reason, say to increase inventory, then the above statement can be used to compare actual disposition of working capital versus the plan.

Cash is such a critical asset that it is often useful to narrow in on the sources and uses of cash during a given period. The *cash flow statement* is an elaboration of the funds statement. All sources of funds are also sources of cash; all uses of funds are also uses of cash. But there are sources and uses of cash *in addition* to the sources and uses of funds:

ADDITIONAL SOURCES OF CASH:

1. Decrease in any current asset account other than cash.
2. Increase in any current liability account.

ADDITIONAL USES OF CASH:

1. Increase in any current asset account other than cash.
2. Decrease in any current liability account.

The relationship between *funds* and *cash* can be represented by the following sets in Exhibit 7-22.

EXHIBIT 7-22 SET RELATIONSHIP: FUNDS AND CASH

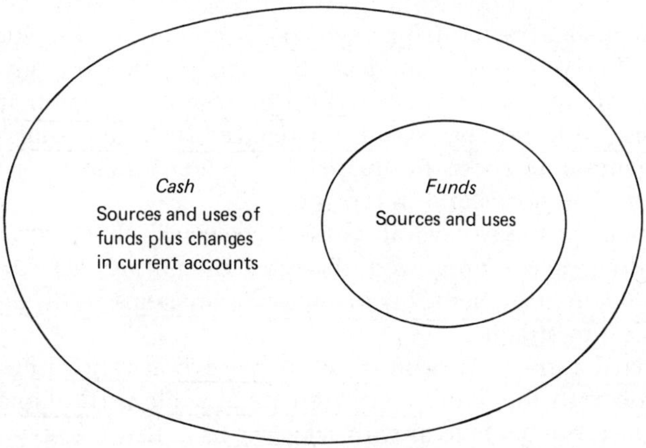

In set theory terms, cash is a larger set than funds in that is has more sources and uses. The cash flow statement for the Exridge Corporation is shown in Exhibit 7-23.

EXHIBIT 7-23

THE EXRIDGE CORPORATION
CASH FLOW STATEMENT
FOR THE YEAR ENDED, DEC. 31, 19x2

SOURCES		
Sources of funds (Exhibit 7-20)	$1,025,000	
Add: Current asset accounts which decreased (other than cash)	130,000	
Current liability accounts which increased	20,000	
Total sources of cash		$1,175,000
USES		
Uses of funds (Exhibit 7-20)	$ 985,000	
Add: Current asset accounts which increased (other than cash)	30,000	
Current liability accounts which decreased	150,000	
Total uses of cash		1,165,000
Increase in cash		$ 10,000

The net change in cash should agree with the balance sheet account. Break-down of the sources and uses of funds in the cash flow statement is unnecessary where the cash flow statement is presented in conjunction with a statement of changes in financial position. For the same reason it is unnecessary to detail changes in current accounts in the cash flow statement when this detail is contained in the statement of distribution of working capital.

7.9 SUMMARY

Financial statements abstracted from their environment provide very little meaningful information. The purpose of financial statement analysis is to give them meaning. Five principal techniques were presented in this chapter: (1) ratio analysis, (2) standard ratio analysis, (3) trend analysis, (4) normalized statement analysis, and (5) funds analysis. The general purpose of financial statement analysis is to measure performance—in absolute terms and as a trend.

It is important to use several types of ratios, as reliance on one or two ratios may be misleading. We emphasized six ratio categories: (1) earning power, (2) liquidity, (3) credit management, (4) inventory management, (5) debt management, and (6) return on investment.

A standard ratio is the compression of several ratios into one. Horizontal analysis has to do with the firm's own prior data, while vertical analysis compares a firm with its industry as a whole or with select firms in the industry. There should be consistency in the use of statistical techniques in developing standard ratios in order to have valid comparison.

As the name suggests, trend ratios are used to show the relationship between important events. In addition to being of historical significance, trends can be used as the basis for predicting future relationships; but extrapolation techniques should be tempered with sound subjective judgment.

Normalized analysis reduces data to a common denominator. In this chapter we discussed *percentage composition* and *common dollar* analysis.

We presented the statement of changes in financial position in chapter 6. Here we extended funds analysis to include the *statement of distribution of working capital* and the *cash flow statement.* The former shows the form in which changes in working capital is held, while the latter indicates the sources and uses of cash during the fiscal period.

CHAPTER 7 REFERENCES AND ADDITIONAL READINGS

MAJOR SOURCES OF STANDARD RATIOS

Annual corporate reports
Accounting Corporation of America
Dun & Bradstreet
Federal Trade Commission
Fitch Investor's Service
Financial Dymanics Inc.
Moody's Manuals
Robert Morris Associates
Securities & Exchange Commission
Standard & Poors
Trade Associations
Wall Street Journal

REFERENCES

Fraser, Ronald. "How Useful are Financial Ratios as Predictors of Corporate Behavior?" *Cost and Management* (Canada), November–December 1970, pp. 48–50.

Guthman, H. G. *Analysis of Financial Statements.* 4th ed. Englewood Cliffs, N.J.: Prentice-Hall, Inc., 1953.

Helfert, Erich A. *Techniques of Financial Analysis.* Homewood, Ill.: Richard D. Irwin, Inc., 1963.

Horrigan, James O. "A Short History of Financial Ratio Analysis." *The Accounting Review,* April 1968, pp. 284–94.

Johnson, Robert W. *Financial Management,* Boston: Allyn & Bacon, Inc., 1959.

Kennedy, R. D., and McMullen, S. Y. *Financial Statements: Form, Analysis and Interpretation.* 4th ed. Homewood, Ill.: Richard D. Irwin, Inc., 1962.

Kinney, William R. "A Note on Ratio Analysis and Geometry." *The Journal of Accountancy,* March 1969, pp. 84–86.

Mecimore, Charles D. "Classifying and Selecting Financial Ratios." *Management Accounting,* February 1968, pp. 11–17.

Mecimore, Charles D. "Some Empirical Distributions of Financial Ratios." *Management Accounting,* September 1968, pp. 13–16.

Myer, John N. *Financial Statement Analysis.* 4th ed. Englewood Cliffs, N.J.: Prentice-Hall, Inc., 1969.

Park, Colin, and Gladson, John W. *Working Capital: Flow-of-Funds Analysis for Management Planning & Control.* New York: The Macmillan Company, 1963.

Phillips, G. Edward, and Copeland, Ronald M. *Financial Statements: Problems from Current Practice.* Englewood Cliffs, N.J.: Prentice-Hall, Inc., 1969.

Ross, Howard. *Financial Statements: A Crusade for Current Values.* Toronto: Pitman Publishing Corporation, 1969.

Wall, Alexander. *Basic Financial Statement Analysis.* New York: Harper & Row, 1942.

Wall, Alexander. *How to Evaluate Financial Statements.* New York: Harper & Row, 1936.

Wall, Alexander, and Duning, R. W. *Ratio Analysis of Financial Statements.* New York: Harper & Row, 1928.

Wilcox, Jarrod W. "A Gambler's Ruin Prediction of Business Failure Using Accounting Data." *Sloan Management Review,* Spring 1971, pp. 1–10.

CHAPTER 7 QUESTIONS, PROBLEMS, AND CASES

7- 1. How do the principles of *synergism* and *holism* relate to financial statement analysis?

7- 2. List four ways in which isolated financial data can be given meaning in a contextual framework.

7- 3. The purpose of ratio analysis is to measure efficiency and performance. Explain how this is achieved.

7- 4. Name two types of *standard ratios.*

7- 5. Distinguish between a statement of changes in financial position and a distribution of working capital statement.

7- 6. What does the term *normalized statement analysis* mean?

7- 7. What are the six major ratio categories, and what are the measurement objectives of each?

7- 8. Explain the meaning or implication of the following terms or phrases:
(a) Turnover
(b) Quick assets
(c) Base year
(d) Normalizing financial statements
(e) Common dollar

7- 9. Distinguish between *intraperiod, interperiod,* and *inter-firm* earning power.

7-10. If the gross earning power declines despite a favorable earning power ratio, what problems are suggested?

7-11. Why might it be advisable to compute a ratio between assets and operating expenses? Doesn't the net earnings power ratio provide the same information?

7-12. Why should interperiod analysis cover several years (more than two)? How can this expanded analysis provide insights into the effectiveness of growth?

7-13. Explain the juxtaposition of *liquidity* and *earnings.*

7-14. What is meant by the term *pooled resources* and how does this concept relate to funds analysis?

7-15. What earning power data provides a crude estimate of:
(a) marketing efficiency
(b) production efficiency
(c) administrative efficiency

7-16. "Because inventory has the highest earning power, what prevents us from holding all of our assets in the form of inventory?"

7-17. If sales are $2,520,000 and average accounts receivable is $320,000, what is the average collection period?

7-18. Explain why inventory turns over into cost of goods sold rather than into sales.

7-19. Distinguish *horizontal* from *vertical* analysis.

7-20. Define *earning power* and distinguish it from *liquidity.* Include in your discussion a pictorial profile of each. Discuss the opposition of liquidity and earning power in asset management.

7-21. What are two ways standard ratios are used?

7-22. Cite some advantages for using trend analysis to highlight financial data.

7-23. How is a percentage composition statement prepared? What is gained from its preparation?

7-24. "In set theory terms, cash is a larger set than funds in that it has more sources and uses." What are the additional sources and uses? Pictorially show the set relationship between funds and cash.

7-25. ***IDENTIFICATION OF RATIOS*** For each of the following descriptions, name the ratio involved and the method of computation (formula):
(a) Measures the ability of assets to generate net income.
(b) A measure of liquidity in the immediate future.
(c) Measures the average period an item is held in inventory.
(d) A measure of collateral support for creditor's claims in the event of liquidation.
(e) Measures a firm's ability to meet current debt within the normal operating cycle.
(f) A measure of debt pressure on owners' equity.
(g) A measure of potential yield.

7-26. ***PRICE-EARNINGS RATIO AND YIELD*** Suppose the market price per share of Martin Sales Incorporated is $84 on Jan. 1, 19*x*1, and $102 on Dec. 31, 19*x*1. On Dec. 31 there are 55,000 common shares outstanding and $100,000 in 5% convertible bonds outstanding. The conversion price for the bonds is $105. What is the *price-earnings ratio* and the *yield* based on *pro forma* earnings and on an average market price (assume earnings = dividends), if the net income for 19*x*1 is $344,000?

7-27. ***COMPARATIVE FINANCIAL STATEMENTS*** Financial statement analysis and interpretation is an integral part of the accounting function. Comparative financial position and operating statements are commonly used tools of analysis and interpretation.

Required:

(a) Discuss the inherent limitations of single-year statements for purposes of analysis and interpretation. Include in your discussion the extent to which these limitations are overcome by the use of comparative statements.
(b) Comparative balance sheets and comparative income statements that show a firm's financial history for each of the last ten years may be misleading. Discuss the factors or conditions that might contribute to misinterpretations. Include a discussion of the additional information and supplementary data that might be included in or provided with the statements to prevent misinterpretations.

(From the CPA exam.)

7-28. ***CREDIT MANAGEMENT*** Suppose the average collection period of accounts receivable is 25 days. The beginning balance of accounts receivable is $217,000 and the ending balance is $196,500. Assuming 360 days in the annual period, what is the total sales for the period?

7-29. ***CASH FLOW STATEMENT*** Prepare a cash flow statement from the data given in problem 6-50 (chapter 6).

7-30. ***INTERPERIOD EARNING POWER ANALYSIS*** Consider the following company and industry data:

Company Data:	**19x1**	**19x2**	**19x3**
Sales	$840,000	$920,000	$1,010,000
Gross profit	378,000	377,000	394,000
Operating expenses	268,000	259,000	273,000
Net operating income	110,000	118,000	121,000
Net income	84,000	101,000	98,000
Assets	490,000	520,000	540,000

Industry Data (three-year averages):	
Earning Power Ratio	2.10
Gross Earning Power Ratio	.70
Net Earning Power Ratio	.14
Net Operating Earning Power Ratio	.28
Operating Expenses/Assets Ratio	.45

Required:

(a) Prepare a complete interperiod earning power analysis that measures the effectiveness of changes in the resource base.
(b) From the interperiod analysis, what observations can you make concerning the company's operations?
(c) Using an inter-firm analysis, what conclusions can you draw concerning the company's efficiency in:
(1) Marketing
(2) Production
(3) Administration

7-31. ***INTER-FIRM ANALYSIS*** Suppose you are considering the acquisition of company A or company B – two companies in the same industry. Your information is limited to the following data:

	Company A	**Company B**
Operating assets	$1,000,000	$2,000,000
Sales	3,000,000	5,000,000
Profit	300,000	750,000

Required:

Explain the reasons for choosing either company A or company B if:
(a) You have a strong sales force but weak administration?
(b) You wanted to show the more spectacular short-term improvement?
(c) You have strong administration but weak sales.

7-32. ***RATIO ANALYSIS*** Derr Sales Corporation's management is concerned over the corporation's current financial position and return on investment. They request your assistance in analyzing their financial statements and furnish the following statements:

DERR SALES CORPORATION
STATEMENT OF WORKING CAPITAL DEFICIT
DECEMBER 31, 19x1

Current liabilities		$223,050
Less current assets:		
Cash	$ 5,973	
Accounts receivable, net	70,952	
Inventory	113,125	190,050
Working capital deficit		$ 33,000

DERR SALES CORPORATION
INCOME STATEMENT
FOR THE YEAR ENDED DECEMBER 31, 19x1

Sales (90,500 units)	$760,200
Cost of goods sold	452,500
Gross profit	307,700
Selling and general expenses, including $22,980 depreciation	155,660
Income before taxes	152,040
Income taxes	76,020
Net income	$ 76,020

Additional Data:

Assets other than current assets consist of land, building, and equipment with a book value of $352,950 on December 31, 19*x*1.

Required:

Assuming Derr Sales Corporation operates 300 days per year, compute the following:
(a) Number of days, sales uncollected.
(b) Inventory turnover.
(c) Number of days, operations to cover the working capital deficit.
(d) Return on total assets as a product of asset turnover and the net income ratio (sometimes called profit margin).

(Adapted from the CPA exam.)

7-33. ***STANDARD RATIOS*** Consider the following earnings per share for firms A through M:

	19x1	19x2	19x3	19x4	19x5	19x6	19x7
Firm A							3.30
B							2.94
C							1.76
D							3.60
E							4.02
F							2.27
G							2.10
H	3.92	4.61	3.97	4.09	4.12	4.08	4.15
I							1.53
J							3.40
K							2.98
L							3.23
M							4.01

Required:

(a) Compute a horizontal standard ratio for firm H using:
  (1) The median.
  (2) Interquartile average.
  (3) Three-unit moving average.
(b) Compute a vertical standard ratio for the industry in 19*x*7 using:
  (1) The mean.
  (2) Interquartile average.
  (3) Four-unit moving average.

(c) For this problem, what conclusions, if any, can we draw from a comparison of the horizontal and vertical standard ratios?
(d) Compare the mean to the median as a consensus measurement.

7-34. ***RATIO ANALYSIS AND DISTRIBUTION OF WORKING CAPITAL*** Consider the following financial data of the Wyman Corporation:

Balance Sheet Accounts:	**Dec. 31 19x0**	**Dec. 31 19x1**	**Dec. 31 19x2**	**Dec. 31 19x3**
Cash on hand	$ 400	$ 400	$ 600	$ 600
Cash in Ridge City Bank	6,800	7,600	8,900	7,100
Cash in Tri-State Bank	4,300	4,000	7,800	3,200
Short-term state revenue bonds	12,800	4,300	10,900	–
Notes receivable from officers	–	9,800	2,400	–
Notes receivable–customers	–	–	15,400	19,000
Accounts receivable	20,400	28,000	17,200	18,400
Merchandise inventory	11,280	11,300	11,240	11,100
Office supplies	3,100	2,700	2,900	3,200
Prepaid subscriptions	240	300	280	310
Prepaid rent	740	770	770	780
Prepaid insurance	640	600	610	560
Equipment (net of deprec.)	40,000	39,000	32,400	31,400
Buildings (net of deprec.)	70,000	68,000	66,000	65,000
Land	15,000	15,000	15,000	15,000
Investments in affiliates	4,000	4,000	6,000	6,500
Patents	8,000	7,600	7,200	6,800
Goodwill	2,000	1,600	1,200	800
Notes payable	7,800	22,000	18,000	5,000
Accounts payable	35,800	52,790	48,770	34,910
Accrued wages	8,600	8,100	8,500	8,300
Federal income taxes payable	1,200	1,400	1,300	2,500
Notes payable–long term	12,200	2,200	26,000	26,000
Reserve for income taxes	4,300	4,800	4,200	5,100
Minority interest	20,000	20,000	23,000	24,500
Common stock (50,000 shares authorized, 30,000 issued, par value $1.20)	36,000	36,000	36,000	36,000
Pain-in capital	6,000	6,000	6,000	6,000
Retained earnings	22,000	31,680	35,030	41,440

Income Statement Summary:	**19x0**	**For Year Ended: 19x1**	**19x2**	**19x3**
Gross sales		$74,000	$76,500	$72,000
Sales discount		2,800	3,000	3,200
Purchases of inventory		43,000	45,200	38,000
Selling expenses		9,800	10,700	9,900
Administrative expenses		3,400	3,400	3,300
Depreciation on equip. & build.		3,000	2,800	2,800
Non-operating expenses				
Extraordinary gains		4,800	–	800
Extraordinary losses		–	1,200	–
Federal income taxes:				
Current		2,800	2,900	4,050
Deferred		2,100	1,700	2,150
Minority interest income		1,400	1,340	2,000

Industry Ratios (Standard ratios were compiled using an interquartile average):	19x1	19x2	19x3
Current ratio	2.1	2.1	2.2
Acid-test ratio	.9	1.0	.9
Average collection period	25.0	24.8	25.2
Inventory turnover	6.0	5.8	6.1
Earning power ratio	2.4	2.4	2.4
Gross earning power ratio	1.5	1.6	1.5
Debt-equity ratio	.54	.55	.54
Earnings per share	.60	.60	.62

Required:

(a) Calculate the following ratios for 19*x*1, 19*x*2, and 19*x*3:
   (1) Earning power
   (2) Gross earning power
   (3) Net earning power
   (4) Net operating earning power
   (5) Operating expenses/assets
   (6) Average collection period
   (7) Inventory turnover
   (8) Debt-equity
   (9) Debt-asset
   (10) Earnings per share
   (11) Current ratio
   (12) Acid-test ratio
   (13) Cash to total assets
   (14) Average holding period

(b) From the ratios calculated in part (a), evaluate the earning power and liquidity of the Wyman Corporation.

(c) Evaluate the company's efficiency or effectiveness in:
   (1) Marketing
   (2) Production
   (3) Credit management
   (4) Inventory management
   (5) Debt management

(d) Present a graphical trend analysis of:
   (1) Gross profit
   (2) Accounts receivable
   (3) Accounts payable

(e) From the financial data for the Wyman Corporation, prepare a statement of distribution of working capital for 19*x*3.

7-35. ***BALANCE SHEET PREPARATION*** Suppose the balance sheet for the end of 19*x*0, and the cash flow statement for year ended 19*x*1, are as follows:

FLINT CORPORATION
BALANCE SHEET
DECEMBER 31, 19x0

Current assets	$ 847,560	Current liabilities	$ 506,260
Long-lived assets	4,543,700	Long-term liabilities	1,870,000
		Capital	3,015,000
Total assets	$5,391,260	Total liab. & capital	$5,391,260

FLINT CORPORATION
CASH FLOW STATEMENT
FOR YEAR ENDED DECEMBER 31, 19x1

SOURCES		
Operations:		
Net income before extraordinary items	$360,800	
Loss from sale of assets	12,300	
Net income	348,500	
Add-back depreciation	210,000	$558,500
Sale of long-lived assets		186,000
Current asset accounts (other than cash) which decreased		11,000
Current liability accounts which increased		32,320
Total sources of cash		$787,820
USES		
Dividends declared and paid		160,000
Decrease in long-term liabilities		100,000
Purchase of long-lived assets		534,000
Current asset accounts (other than cash) which increased		7,800
Current liability accounts which decreased		11,700
Total uses of cash		$813,500
Decrease in cash		$ 25,680

Required:

Prepare a balance sheet for December 31, 19*x*1. Use the same summary form as last year.

7-36. ***RATIO ANALYSIS*** On the basis of the information provided, complete the following balance sheet:

BALANCE SHEET

Assets		**Equities**	
Cash	______	Accounts payable	$256,000
Receivables	______	Common stock	400,000
Inventory	______	Retained earnings	______
Fixed assets	______		
Total	______	Total	______

Data:

(a) Days in period, 300.
(b) Gross profit margin, 20%.
(c) Days sales in accounts receivables, 30 days.
(d) Inventory turnover (based on year-end inventory), 4*x*.
(e) Acid-test ratio, 0.7:1.
(f) Debt-equity ratio, 1:2.
(g) Average daily sales, $5,000.

7-37. ***COMPARATIVE FINANCIAL DATA*** Growth Products, Inc., one of your clients, requested that you review the proposed presentation of selected financial data to be included in its 1969 annual report in graphical form. The company has three divisions: a Natural Gas Division formed in 1951, a Chemical Division formed in 1958, and a Textile Division formed in 1966. Management compiled the following data from the company's financial statements:

	1967	1968	1969
Sales (in thousands):			
Natural gas	$1,000	$1,100	$1,100
Chemicals	800	900	1,000
Textiles	200	400	900
Total sales	$2,000	$2,400	$3,000
Sources of funds (in thousands):			
Net income (after extraordinary items)	$ 200	$ 290	$ 400
Add deprec., depletion, amortization	40	55	80
Total	240	345	480
Issuance of bonds payable	60	50	100
Total sources of funds	$ 300	$ 395	$ 580
Applications of funds (in thousands):			
Dividends	$ 100	$ 160	$ 330
Acquisition of plant and equipment	135	170	180
Increase in working capital	45	35	60
Other	20	30	10
Total applications of funds	$ 300	$ 395	$ 580

Required:

(a) Why is it desirable to present comparative financial statements and other historical, statistical-type summaries of financial data, including graphs and charts, for a number of periods in annual and other financial reports?

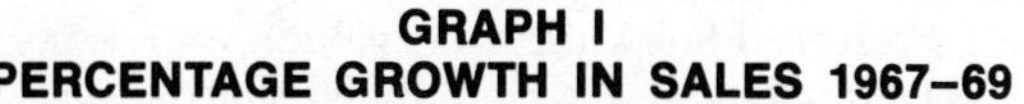

GRAPH I
PERCENTAGE GROWTH IN SALES 1967–69

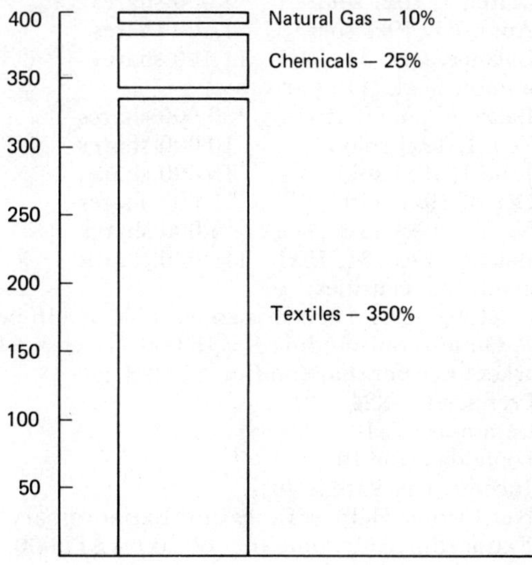

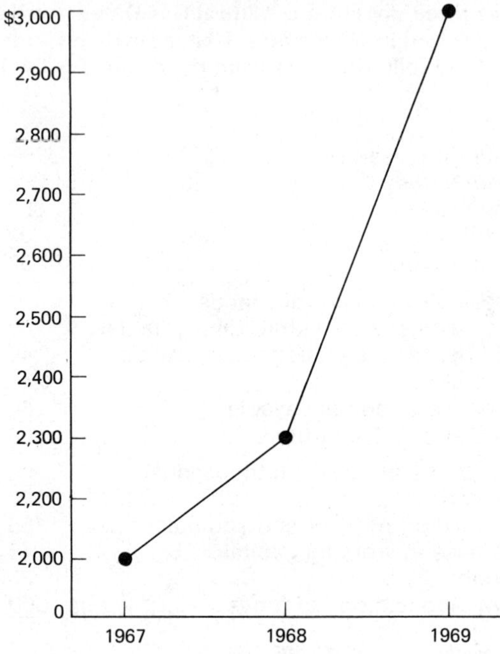

(b) Evaluate each of the following graphs prepared by Growth Products, Inc., for possible inclusion in its 1969 annual report. Recommend changes, if any, which should be made in the graphs. Consider each graph separately.

7-38. ***RETURN ON INVESTMENT*** Suppose the following information is available for the Benson Company:

(a) 6% Preferred Stock ($20 par value):

Balance, Jan. 1, 19*x*1	8,000 shares
March 1, 19*x*1 sold	2,000 shares
August 1, 19*x*1 sold	1,500 shares
Balance, Dec. 31, 19*x*1	11,500 shares

(b) Common stock ($15 par value):

Balance, Jan. 1, 19*x*1	80,000 shares
Feb. 1, 19*x*1 sold	10,000 shares
June 1, 19*x*1 sold	15,000 shares
Oct. 1, 19*x*1 sold	5,000 shares
Nov. 1, 19*x*1 sold	5,000 shares
Balance, Dec. 31, 19*x*1	115,000 shares

(c) Convertible securities:
(1) $160,000 of 4% bonds convertible at $16 per share.
(2) Options outstanding for 15,000 shares at $18 per share.

(d) Market Price per share on Dec. 31, 19*x*1:
Preferred: $24
Common: $18

(e) Income data for 19*x*1:
Income Tax Rate is 40%.
Net Income Before Taxes and Extraordinary Items = $396,000.
Extraordinary Income (net of tax) is $14,000.

GRAPH III

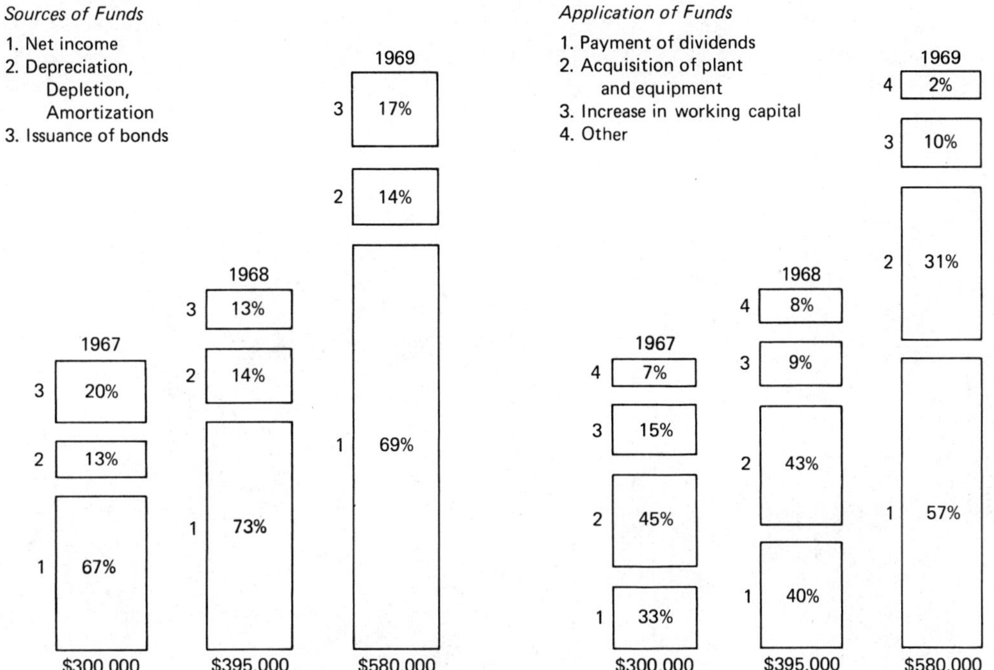

(From the CPA exam.)

(f) Cash dividends paid in 19*x*1 were:
Preferred: $25,800
Common: $210,000

Required:

(1) Compute the *weighted average* of:
 a. Common shares outstanding during 19*x*1.
 b. Preferred shares outstanding during 19*x*1.

(2) Compute the *undiluted earnings per share* based upon:
 a. Net income after tax (exclusive of extraordinary items).
 b. Extraordinary income (net of tax).
 c. Total income after tax.

(3) Compute the *diluted earnings per share* based upon:
 a. Net income after tax (exclusive of extraordinary items).
 b. Extraordinary income (net of tax).
 c. Total income after tax.

(4) Compute the *price-earnings ratio* of common shares.
(5) Compute the *return on common stock* based on current market value.
(6) Compute the *yield* based on dividends per weighted average shares for:
  a. Preferred
  b. Common

CHAPTER

8

PRICE-LEVEL ACCOUNTING AND REPORTING

8.1 PRICE-LEVELS

The term *price-level* refers to the general purchasing power of a currency, e.g., the dollar. In chapter 3 we mentioned that one of the traditional output rules in accounting is the *stable money* convention. This means that financial statements are prepared under the assumption of a stable price-level, even though the reality of changing price-levels is well known.

Suppose a firm reports the following sales for years 1959 and 1969 respectively:

	1959	1969
Sales	$100,000	$200,000

Because financial data is unadjusted for price-level changes, there is the presumption that sales actually increased by $100,000 or 100% in the ten-year period. Price-level changes are measured by indexes (Exhibit 8-1); so in order to determine the *real* increase in sales, we need price index data. We will use the *GNP Price Deflator Index* (as given in Exhibit 8-1) for this purpose:

	1959	1969
Sales........................	$100,000	$200,000
GNP Deflator Index ...	101.6	128.1

EXHIBIT 8-1 TREND OF MAJOR PRICE INDEXES IN THE UNITED STATES, 1940–1969

	WHOLESALE PRICE INDEX (1957–59 = 100)		CONSUMER PRICE INDEX* (1957–59 = 100)		GNP IMPLICIT PRICE DEFLATOR INDEX (1958 = 100)	
	Index	**% Change**	**Index**	**% Change**	**Index**	**% Change**
1940	43.0	–	48.8	–	43.9	–
1941	47.8	11.1	51.3	5.1	47.2	7.5
1942	54.0	13.0	56.8	10.7	53.0	12.3
1943	56.5	4.6	60.3	6.2	56.8	7.2
1944	56.9	.7	61.3	1.7	58.2	2.5
1945	57.9	1.8	62.7	2.3	59.7	2.6
1946	66.1	14.2	68.0	8.4	66.7	11.7
1947	81.2	22.8	77.8	14.4	74.6	11.8
1948	87.9	8.3	83.8	7.7	79.6	6.7
1949	83.5	(5.1)	83.0	.6	79.1	(.6)
1950	86.8	4.0	83.8	.9	80.2	1.4
1951	96.7	11.4	90.5	8.0	85.6	6.7
1952	94.0	(2.8)	92.5	2.2	87.5	2.2
1953	92.7	(1.4)	93.2	.8	88.3	.9
1954	92.9	.2	93.6	.6	89.6	1.5
1955	93.2	.3	93.3	(.3)	90.0	1.5
1956	96.2	3.2	94.7	1.4	94.0	3.4
1957	99.0	2.9	98.0	3.5	97.5	3.7
1958	100.4	1.4	100.7	2.7	100.0	2.6
1959	100.6	.2	101.5	.8	101.6	1.6
1960	100.7	.1	103.1	1.5	103.3	1.7
1961	100.3	(.4)	104.2	1.1	104.6	1.3
1962	100.6	.3	105.4	1.2	105.7	1.1
1963	100.3	(.3)	106.7	1.2	107.1	1.3
1964	100.5	.2	108.1	1.3	108.9	1.7
1965	102.5	.2	109.9	1.7	110.9	1.8
1966	105.9	3.3	113.1	2.9	113.9	2.7
1967	106.1	.2	116.3	2.9	117.3	3.0
1968	108.8	2.6	121.2	4.3	122.3	4.3
1969	113.0	3.9	127.7	5.4	128.1	4.7

*The Consumer Price Index is also known as the Cost of Living Index.

We can compute the *real* increase in sales in one of two ways: through (1) a *constant* adjustment, or (2) a *current* adjustment. A constant adjustment calls for a restatement of current data in terms of some base year. In this case we need to restate 1969 sales in terms of 1959 dollars:

EXHIBIT 8-2 CONSTANT DOLLAR ADJUSTMENT

	1959		1969
Sales—unadjusted	$100,000		$200,000
Index	101.6		128.1
Restate 1969	–	$\left(\frac{101.6}{128.1}\right)^*$	200,000
Sales—adjusted	$100,000		$158,626
"Real" increase in constant dollars		$58,626	

*The two index numbers can be reduced to a "conversion factor," e.g., $\frac{101.6}{128.1} = .79313$.

A current adjustment means restating previous data in terms of the current price-level. In our example, 1959 sales should be restated in terms of the 1969 price-level:

EXHIBIT 8-3 CURRENT DOLLAR ADJUSTMENT

	1959		1969
Sales—unadjusted	$100,000		$200,000
Index	101.6		128.1
Restate 1959	$100,000$\left(\frac{128.1}{101.6}\right)^*$		—
Sales—adjusted	$126,083		$200,000
"Real" increase in current dollars		$73,917	

*Again we can substitute a conversion factor: $\frac{128.1}{101.6} = 1.26083$.

The current dollar adjustment is preferred in accounting, for two reasons: (1) we are reviewing data in the current period and it is more convenient to think in terms of current dollars; and (2) a number of accounts in the financial statements, i.e., monetary assets and liabilities, are always stated in current dollars in the current period and confusion would result from restating these items in constant dollars. For example, the cash account in the current period is stated in current dollars. To restate the cash balance in terms of some previous period would confuse the issue. We will discuss monetary items in greater detail later.

Returning to our example, we note that the *stable money* rule led to a false conclusion regarding the increase of sales. Sales did not increase by $100,000 or 100%, but rather by $73,917 or 74%. We used a United States price index to adjust the sales data. If the firm reporting these sales was located in some other country, the price index for that country would be used instead. There is a wide disparity between price-level changes in various countries, as noted in Exhibit 8-4.

Assume that the firm reporting the sales is Brazilian. The price-level in Brazil changed in the period 1959 to 1969 from 100 to 2—or a compounded annual depre-

EXHIBIT 8-4 PRICE-LEVEL CHANGES IN FIFTY COUNTRIES 1959–1970

DEPRECIATION OF MONEY IN INDUSTRIALIZED COUNTRIES

	Indexes of Value of Money (1959 = 100)		Annual Rates of Depreciation		
	1964	1969	'59–'69*	'68–'69	'69–'70†
Greece	93	83	1.9%	2.3%	2.3%
Finland	79	61	4.8	2.2	2.5
Switzerland	87	74	3.0	2.5	2.5
Australia	92	78	2.4	2.8	3.1
Germany (F.R.)	89	78	2.4	2.6	3.6
Italy	80	70	3.6	2.5	3.7
Austria	85	72	3.2	3.0	3.8
Spain	79	58	5.3	2.2	3.9
Belgium	91	77	2.6	3.6	4.0
Canada	93	78	2.4	4.3	4.0
Luxembourg	93	81	2.1	2.2	4.1
Netherlands	86	67	3.8	6.9	4.1
South Africa	92	79	2.3	2.8	4.4
New Zealand	90	73	3.1	4.7	4.9
Denmark	81	59	5.1	3.2	5.2
United Kingdom	87	71	3.4	5.1	5.3
France	82	69	3.7	5.7	5.4
United States	94	79	2.2	5.1	5.7
Sweden	84	69	3.7	2.6	5.8
Turkey	82	57	5.5	4.8	6.3
Portugal	88	67	3.9	8.1	6.4
Ireland	85	68	3.8	6.9	6.6
Japan	77	60	5.0	4.9	7.5
Norway	85	71	3.3	3.0	8.6
Iceland	63	37	9.5	16.2	11.8

*Compounded annually. †Based on average of monthly data available for 1970 compared with corresponding period of 1969.

ciation in the value of the money unit of 31.4%. Expressing this price-level change in current terms, the appropriate index figures comparable to those in Exhibit 8-1 are:

	1959	1964	1969
Brazil price index[1]	100	929	4,568

[1]An approximate value for 1964 and 1969 can be obtained by computing $\frac{100}{11}(100)$ and $\frac{100}{2}(100)$ respectively. More precision is obtained by using the future value of an annuity formula in Table B-3 of Appendix B to this text, i.e.:

$$F = A\left[\frac{(1+r)^n - 1}{r}\right]$$

As the compound interest rate is 31.4%, we have

$$F = 100\left[\frac{(1.314)^5 - 1}{.314}\right]$$

and

DEPRECIATION OF MONEY IN LESS-DEVELOPED COUNTRIES

	Indexes of Value of Money (1959 = 100)		Annual Rates of Depreciation		
	1964	1969	'59–'69*	'68–'69	'69–'70†
Honduras	92	81	2.1%	2.6%	–0.4%
Thailand	94	83	1.9	2.1	1.5
Morocco	80	77	2.6	2.8	1.5
Venezuela	98	90	1.1	2.3	1.7
Dominican Rep.	86	85	1.6	1.0	1.9
El Salvador	100	96	0.4	–0.3	2.9
Guatemala	100	96	0.5	2.2	3.1
Israel	75	60	4.9	2.4	3.3
Iran	84	78	2.4	3.0	3.3
Bolivia	72	55	5.8	3.1	3.4
Ecuador	83	67	3.8	6.0	3.9
Peru	69	39	9.0	5.9	4.0
Mexico	90	77	2.5	2.8	4.0
Pakistan	87	70	3.6	3.1	4.5
China (Taiwan)	75	63	4.6	4.8	4.6
India	80	56	5.6	0.8	4.8
Colombia	56	36	9.8	9.2	8.1
Argentina	36	13	18.4	7.1	8.8
Jamaica	86	71	3.4	5.8	9.3
Philippines	67	56	5.7	2.8	10.7
Indonesia	5	‡	58.2	5.8	12.0
Korea	51	29	11.5	11.0	14.5
Brazil	11	2	31.4	18.8	17.9
Chile	35	11	19.7	23.4	23.8
Vietnam	84	20	14.9	18.0	27.2

*Compounded annually. †Based on average of monthly data available for 1970 compared with corresponding period of 1969. ‡Less than one.

SOURCE: First National City Bank, New York, *Monthly Economic Letter,* September 1970, p. 103. Used with permission.

This means that it would take NCR (new cruzeiro) 4,568 in 1969 to buy goods and services that only cost NCR 100 in 1959. The previous sales figures of 100,000 in 1959 and 200,000 in 1969 would represent a very significant loss in terms of Brazilian price-level changes:

	1959	1969
Sales—unadjusted	NCR 100,000	NCR 200,000
Index (above)	100	4,568
Restate 1959	NCR $100{,}000\left(\frac{4{,}568}{100}\right)$	–
Sales—adjusted on current basis	NCR 4,568,000	NCR 200,000
"Real" loss in current terms	NCR 4,368,000	

$$F = 100\left[\frac{(1.314)^{10} - 1}{.314}\right]$$

respectively.

At the Brazilian rate of inflation in the period 1959–69, our firm would need to report sales of NCR 4,568,000 in 1969 just to keep even with the price-level change!

We have only adjusted for sales data. Most other accounts in the financial statements also require adjustment, but conventional financial statements do not contain sufficient information[2] to permit the analyst to make a comprehensive adjustment.

The problem is complicated at the international business level. If financial statements were published for each country in which a multi-national business firm conducted operations, the analyst could make a reasonable attempt at adjusting for price-level changes, although the task would be quite onerous. But most multinational firms incorporate the financial data of their foreign subsidiaries and affiliates into one statement, which is referred to as a *consolidated* statement. The consolidation process does involve restating foreign currencies into the monetary unit of the holding company. However, the conversion is often effected at the *official* rate of exchange and not at the prevailing price-levels.

Official exchange rates are determined by governmental decree. This relationship may stay in effect many years despite a wide discrepancy in the price-levels of the respective countries. For this reason the conversion of foreign currencies by means of the official exchange rates does not accommodate the problem of price-level reporting. One exception to this rule is Canada, which in 1970 dispensed with an official value to its currency, thus permitting it to "float" in value with respect to other currencies as economic circumstances warrant.

8.2 PRICE-LEVEL REPORTING IN FINANCIAL STATEMENTS

As noted previously, a convention of financial reporting in the United States is the stable money rule. Other countries, notably the Netherlands, Italy, and Japan have for many years encouraged price-level adjusted financial statements.[3] In France, Italy, and Japan price-level adjusted statements are prepared on the basis of government *revalorization* provisions. These governments prepare annual "coefficients of revaluation" which attempt to compensate for the effects of inflation on asset values. Companies may use current or replacement cost as asset values as long as the revaluations remain within the limits of the stated coefficients.

Efforts to move toward price-level reporting in the United States have been awkward and slow, for reasons we will mention shortly, but progress is being made. In June 1969, the policy making body of the accounting profession, the Accounting Principles Board, issued its *Statement No. 3*,[4] entitled, *Financial Statements Restated for General Price-Level Changes.*" In effect this statement recommended price-level reporting in the United States under these ground rules:

[2]As we shall note later in this chapter, information as to age of each depreciable asset or asset group is needed, as are inventory ages, particularly where LIFO is used.

[3]*Reporting the Effects of Price-Level Changes*, Accounting Research Study 6 (New York: American Institute of Certified Public Accountants, 1963).

[4]*Statements* of the Accounting Principles Board are in the nature of recommendations; its *Opinions* are obligatory.

1. That price-level adjusted statements ought to supplement and not replace historical-dollar or stable money statements.
2. That assets and liabilities be separated into monetary and non-monetary categories; and that purchasing power gains and losses on monetary assets be included in price-level reporting.
3. That in consolidating foreign operations in countries where the degree of inflation or deflation is so great as to make conventional statements meaningless, the statements of those affiliates can be incorporated into the consolidated statements at the prevailing currency values in those countries without regard for the stable money rule.
4. That an index of the general price level, as opposed to specific[5] price indexes, be used in price-level reporting.
5. The Gross National Product (GNP) Implicit Price Deflator Index is the most comprehensive indicator of the general price level in the United States, and that its use is recommended in price-level reporting as opposed to the other major indexes: the Wholesale Price Index or the Consumer Price Index.

Given the recommendatory nature of *Statement No. 3,* there is some question as to its impact on practice. But at least the accounting profession has taken a positive step toward price-level reporting after debating the issue vigorously for more than two decades. In fact, Henry W. Sweeney[6] first focused on the issue in the 1920s and his book, *Stabilized Accounting,* is considered a classic in the field.

In 1951 Professor Joel Dean demonstrated that the effect of price-level adjustments on reported net income can be quite severe.[7] Adjustments were applied to all assets on the balance sheets of General Electric Co., Radio Corporation of America, and Westinghouse Electric Corp., for the years 1935 through 1948. The assets were stated in terms of their 1935 prices by deflating each major group by means of special indexes. Changes in assets for year to year were adjusted for dividends and new capital additions to arrive at "adjusted" net income. The results are contained in Exhibit 8-5.

Professor Dean pointed out, for example, that General Electric Co. in 1947 reported net income of $102.7 millions while in fact the company had a "real" loss of $8.2 millions. Professor Dean and many other proponents of price-level reporting stressed the consequences of *stable money* reporting. These consequences are exemplified by the 1947 unadjusted and adjusted income figures for General Electric Co.:

1. Net income based on the stable money rule is fictitious where price changes have actually occurred. In periods of rising prices (inflation), stable money net income is overstated. In periods of falling prices (deflation) stable money net income is understated.
2. Price-level changes have been with mankind since the days of the pharaohs. The

[5]A general price index measures the movement of all prices. This may differ from the price trend of a specific good or service. For example, the cost of construction may differ from the general price trend. A construction index is illustrative of a specific index.

[6]Henry W. Sweeney, "German Inflation Accounting," *Journal of Accountancy,* February 1928, pp. 104–116; "How Inflation Affects Balance Sheets," *The Accounting Review,* December 1934, pp. 275–99; *Stabilized Accounting* (New York: Harper & Row, 1936); and "Stabilized Depreciation," *The Accounting Review,* September 1931, pp. 165–78.

[7]Joel Dean, "Measurement of Profits for Executive Decisions," *The Accounting Review,* April 1951, pp. 185–96.

phenomenon is real and is of long standing, hence it should be dealt with as a reality of economic life and not as some taboo.

3. The general price trend in the 1900s has been one of rising prices. Under these conditions, stable money net income is overstated. The consequences of overstating income include the following:
   a. *Taxes* may be paid out of capital rather than income. Assuming a 50% tax rate, General Electric Co. presumably paid $50 million in federal income tax in 1947 when in fact it suffered a net loss on a price-level adjusted basis. As GEC had no income, the tax was paid out of owners' equity.
   b. *Dividends* may in truth represent a dilution of capital rather than a distribution of earnings. Again, we can assume that GEC paid dividends in 1947. As the company had no true income for the period, the dividends were in fact a distribution of contributed capital. Returning capital to stockholders and labeling it a "dividend" has the effect of diluting owners' equity.
   c. *Illusions* are apt to arise where net income is overstated. Labor unions and employees insist on higher wages, stockholders insist on higher dividends; and the management of the company may decide to expand operations on the basis of the improper yardstick.
4. Price-level indexes are available in the United States and in most countries of the world, so that adjustments are technically feasible.

EXHIBIT 8-5 TOTAL EARNINGS AVAILABLE FOR INTEREST AND DIVIDENDS ($1,000)

	GENERAL ELECTRIC CO.		RADIO CORPORATION OF AMERICA		WESTINGHOUSE ELECTRIC CORP.	
Year	Per Books	In Constant (1935) Dollars	Per Books	In Constant (1935) Dollars	Per Books	In Constant (1935) Dollars
1935	$ 31,020	$ 30,302	$ 5,518	$ 5,408	$ 10,802	$10,830
6	46,152	39,536	6,477	5,437	14,976	12,495
7	64,512	39,878	7,907	4,391	19,294	9,224
8	28,432	32,266	8,778	8,973	8,827	11,094
9	42,764	38,881	7,578	7,092	14,188	13,230
1940	58,539	45,630	9,253	7,437	17,709	13,441
1	60,167	32,541	10,466	5,714	21,797	8,408
2	51,637	23,660	12,094	2,010	17,912	2,567
3	50,865	30,953	16,181	5,811	25,299	11,670
4	57,544	27,764	9,747	3,576	25,701	12,024
5	58,666	22,031	11,812	5,942	28,188	10,203
6	42,385	5,604	11,216	2,485	6,896	(13,544)
7	102,681	(8,190)	19,300	(829)	51,988	(12,312)
8	201,534	58,868	24,583	5,060	53,907	2,769
Total 1935–1948	$896,898	$419,724	$160,910	$68,507	$317,484	$92,099

SOURCE: Joel Dean, "Measurement of Profits for Executive Decisions," pp. 185–96. Used with permission.

Those opposing price-level reporting have raised counter-arguments such as these:

1. The problem of measuring price-level changes is at best a very imperfect science. Much work needs to be done in improving price-level measurement before its use should be advocated in financial reporting.

2. Again on the subject of indexes, there is the question of which index to use for general price-levels; and the more stringent issue of whether or not specific indexes should be used rather than a general index.
3. Reporting price-level adjusted data in financial statements would add to the frustrations of users who are complaining of the present complexity of financial reporting.
4. A particular deficiency of general indexes is their inability to distinguish quality changes from pure price-level changes.
5. Some pseudo adjustors have come into being, such as LIFO inventory pricing and accelerated depreciation, which mitigate price-level changes.
6. Price-level reporting can not be considered apart from some broader reporting issues, particularly the question of current value reporting.

We will speak to these issues presently. But for now the proponents appear to be gaining ground, and appearance of price-level financial statements issued as supplements to conventional statements should become commonplace in the years ahead.

8.3 THE CONSTRUCTION OF INDEXES

There are three basic procedures in constructing an index: (1) identifying the universe; (2) selecting a sample; and (3) applying a formula to the sample.

The *universe* comprises all items with similar characteristics. If an index of automobile prices is the objective, then all automobiles sold during a given period constitute the universe.

A *sample* is a statistically reliable segment of a universe. There are two basic criteria for determining adequate sample size: (1) the *precision level,* or the degree to which the sample characteristics will represent the characteristics of the universe; and (2) the *confidence level,* or the probability that the sample will, in fact, represent the characteristics of the universe.

A *formula* is used to consolidate sub-components of an index class into a single index number; e.g., the Consumer Price Index resolves into one index the various food, fuel, utilities, and other indexes that comprise the representative items in the group.

Four formulae are most frequently used for this purpose: *Laspeyres, Paasche, Fisher,* and a *fixed-weight* formula which is a variation of the Laspeyres formula. The symbols used in common by these formulae are:

p = the price of a commodity or service.

q = the quantity of that commodity or service.

p_0, q_0 = the price or quantity of a commodity or service in the base period.

p_n, q_n = the price or quantity of a commodity or service in a period other than the base period.

p_a, q_a = the price or quantity of a commodity or service in some arbitrary period.

Σ = the sum of all the terms.

Laspeyres Formula: this formula uses the weights of the base period to determine the weights of the current period:

$$\text{Index} = \frac{\Sigma(p_n q_0)}{\Sigma(p_0 q_0)} \qquad (1)$$

Paasche Formula: this formula uses the weights of the current period and converts the weights of the base period to those of the current period:

$$\text{Index} = \frac{\Sigma(p_n q_n)}{\Sigma(p_0 q_n)} \qquad (2)$$

Fisher Formula: this formula is a geometric average of the Laspeyres and Paasche formulae, i.e., both base period and current quantities are used as weights:

$$\text{Index} = \sqrt{\frac{\Sigma(p_n q_0)}{\Sigma(p_0 q_0)} \times \frac{\Sigma(p_n q_n)}{\Sigma(p_0 q_n)}} \qquad (3)$$

Fixed-Weight Formula: this formula differs from the Laspeyres formula in that it uses the weights of a *fixed* period other than the base period for determining the change in the prices of fixed quantities of specific items.

$$\text{Index} = \frac{\Sigma(p_n q_a)}{\Sigma(p_0 q_a)} \qquad (4)$$

The application of these formulae is illustrated by a very simple example. We only have two commodities—meat and potatoes—and the respective quantities and prices in 1960 and 1970 are:

EXHIBIT **8-6**

		1960 (Base)		1970	
	Average (q_a)	**Quantity** (q_0)	**Price (lb)** (p_0)	**Quantity** (q_n)	**Price (lb)** (p_n)
Meat	40	100	$1.00	200	$1.50
Potatoes	160	200	.06	300	.12

	FORMULA	INDEX 1970	INDEX 1960 Base
Laspeyres	$\frac{(M\ \$1.50 \times 100) + (P\ \$.12 \times 200)}{(M\ \$1.00 \times 100) + (P\ \$.06 \times 200)} = \frac{174}{112} = 1.5536 \times 100 =$	155.4	100
Paasche	$\frac{(M\ \$1.50 \times 200) + (P\ \$.12 \times 300)}{(M\ \$1.00 \times 200) + (P\ \$.06 \times 300)} = \frac{336}{218} = 1.5413 \times 100 =$	154.1	100
Fisher	$\sqrt{\left(\frac{174}{112}\right) \times \left(\frac{336}{218}\right)} = \sqrt{1.5536 \times 1.5413} = \sqrt{2.3945} = 1.5474 \times 100 =$	154.7	100
Fixed-Weight	$\frac{(M\ \$1.50 \times 40) + (P\ \$.12 \times 160)}{(M\ \$1.00 \times 40) + (P\ \$.06 \times 160)} = \frac{79.2}{49.6} = 1.5968 \times 100 =$	159.7	100

8.4 GENERAL PRICE INDEXES IN THE UNITED STATES

There are three major indexes of general prices in the United States: (1) the Wholesale Price Index (WPI), (2) the Consumer (or Cost of Living) Price Index (CPI), and (3) the GNP Implicit Price Deflator Index (GNPI). The trend in these indexes for the period 1940–1969 is contained in Exhibit 8-1, as well as the percentage change per year. The relationship between these indexes and the sectors of the economy is sketched in Exhibit 8-7.

EXHIBIT 8-7 PRICE INDEXES VIS-À-VIS SECTORS OF THE ECONOMY

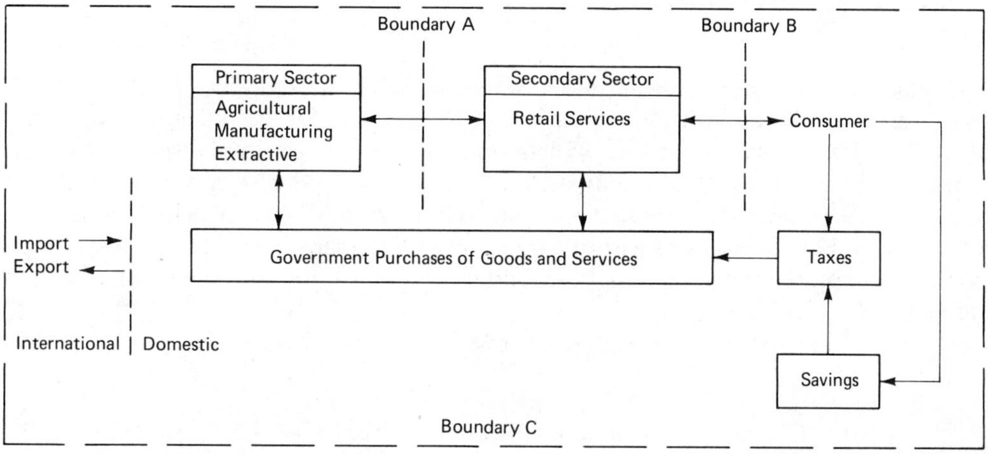

The WPI measures the movement of prices across boundary A, i.e., from the primary to the secondary sector.[8] The CPI measures changes in prices across boundary B, i.e., the prices that retailers and service organizations extract from consumers. A comparison of these indexes is useful in tracing price changes to one sector or the other. Referring to Exhibit 8-1, we notice that in the period 1958–1964 the WPI did not vary at all, while the CPI increased 7.1% in the same period.

The WPI and CPI indexes both limit their analysis to only one of the components of gross national product: (1) personal *consumption* expenditures. They measure price-level changes based on actual prices paid for goods and services in the private sector. They ignore the other three components of gross national product: (2) gross private domestic savings, (3) government purchases of goods and services, and (4) import-export trade. As import-export trade plays a relatively small role in GNP in the United States, the omission of this factor would not be critical; but savings and government expenditures are critical variables.

Consumption trends alone cannot measure the comparative "well-offness" of consumers. If persons can maintain the same standard of living in periods of rising

[8]The primary sector is essentially production, while the secondary sector is essentially service (as is government). In this connection the steady shift from production to services in the United States should be noted. In 1900, 70% of the American work force was in production of goods. By 1980, 70% of the American work force will be providing services, while only 30% will be producing goods.

prices and convert a stable ratio of annual earnings into savings, there is a real question as to the presence of inflation. The assumption of the WPI and CPI indexes is that savings will deteriorate in the face of prices which exceed wage increases.

Government purchases of goods and services at federal, state, and local levels was 22.7% of GNP in 1969 (up from 8.3% of GNP in 1929).[9] Government expenditures are such a major factor in GNP currently that no general price-level index can afford to ignore this variable.

For these reasons, the GNPI is favored by experts as being the best of the general price-indexes in the United States. However, the WPI and CPI indexes are still useful for other purposes. The principal characteristics of these major indexes are summarized below.

WHOLESALE PRICE INDEX

"Wholesale" as defined by this index refers to sales in large lots in the primary sector, i.e., the first important commercial transaction for each commodity. Steel industry sales to manufacturers which occur within the primary sector are part of the WPI. The study of economic transactions within and between defined sectors is known as *input-output* analysis. It is a comprehensive field of inquiry in its own right. The point is that transactions within a sector as well as transactions between sectors—in this case between the primary and secondary sectors—enter into the construction of indexes.

Here are some other features of the WPI in summary form:

1. *Age:* It is the oldest continuous price index in the United States, dating from 1890.
2. *Formula:* Fixed-weight.
3. *Universe:* Total of primary sector transactions in the United States.
4. *Sample size:* The sample size has been increased several times. Since 1961 the sample has covered 2,400 commodities. The sample size was 1,600 in the 1947–60 period, and 900 prior to 1947.
5. *Weights:* Effective January 1967, the weights are values of net shipments of commodities as derived from the industrial censuses of 1963 and other data. The weight formula has had one revision in its history—this occurred in January 1961.
6. *Compiler:* U.S. Department of Labor, Bureau of Labor Statistics.
7. *Frequency:* The index is updated monthly.
8. *Base period:* The current index uses as its base the average prices for the period 1957–1959.

[9] U.S. Department of Commerce, *Statistical Abstract of the United States* (published annually). The component values of GNP for 1929 and 1969 in billions of dollars were:

	1929	%	1969	%
Personal consumption	$ 77.2	74.9	$577.5	62.0
Gross private domestic investment	16.2	15.7	139.8	15.0
Net export of goods and services	1.1	1.1	1.9	.3
Government purchases of goods and services	8.5	8.3	212.2	22.7
Total GNP	$103.1	100.0	$931.4	100.0

CONSUMER PRICE INDEX

This index is referred to colloquially as the "Cost of Living Index." Neither is "Consumer Price Index" its true name, but rather "The Index of Change in Prices of Goods and Services Purchased by City Wage-Earner and Clerical-Worker Families to Maintain Their Level of Living." Its true name is more descriptive of its objective and limitations, although the search for a shorter title can be readily understood. The purpose of this index is to measure the costs incident to maintaining a standard of living by a sub-set of the consumer population: city-dwelling families who are wage earners and/or clerical workers. Other characteristics of this index are summarized as follows:

1. *Age:* The CPI dates from 1919, but is retroactive to 1913.
2. *Formula:* Fixed-weight.
3. *Universe:* City-dwelling, wage-earning families.
4. *Sample size:* The current sample (post-1964) includes approximately 400 items. Prior to 1964 the sample size was 300 items.

   The sample covers fifty-six geographic areas, including thirty-seven standard metropolitan areas. Prior to the revision in 1964 the CPI was said to be representative of the buying patterns of 64% of the urban population and 40% of the total U.S. population.[10]
5. *Weights:* The weighting is in terms of the importance of an item in the typical moderate-income family's budget; e.g., if food is 20% of a typical family's budget, then changes in the price of food will have a 20% weight in arriving at the index value.
6. *Compiler:* U.S. Department of Labor, Bureau of Labor Statistics.
7. *Frequency:* The index is updated monthly.
8. *Base period:* The current series uses as its base the average prices for the period 1957–1959.
9. *Revisions:* There have been five revisions of this index. Revisions involve (a) bringing the "market basket" of goods and services up to date, e.g., to include new products and delete obsolescent ones; (b) revising the weights; and (c) improving the sample and methodology.

   Revisions of weights:

Weights based on	Applicable over the period
1917–1919	1913–1935
1934–1936	1936–1949
1947–1949	1950–1952
–1950	1953–1963
1960–1961	1964–

An example of the weighting structure employed in the CPI index is contained in Exhibit 8-8.

[10] *Labor Law Reporter,* Union Contacts Arbitration 1 (Chicago: Commerce Clearing House, 1960), pp. 56, 100–102.

EXHIBIT 8-8 CONSUMER PRICE INDEXES—RELATIVE IMPORTANCE OF COMMODITY GROUPS AND SERVICES (PERCENT DISTRIBUTION): 1947 TO 1961

[Excludes Alaska and Hawaii. The relative importance of a component of the Consumer Price Index at any given time represents its expenditure weight multiplied by the relative price change from the weight date to a later period and the result expressed as a percentage of the total for all items. Changes in the relative importance of a component result from (*a*) major weight revisions based on comprehensive consumer expenditure surveys; (*b*) minor weight adjustments to take account of changes in the list of items priced; and (*c*) different rates of price change among the various items. In the absence of a weight revision, if prices of all items changed at the same rate, the relative importance of each item or group in the index would remain unchanged.]

Commodity Group and Services	1947–49 avg.	January 1950	December 1960	December 1961
All commodities	72.9	68.7	63.7	63.3
All services	27.1	31.3	36.3	36.7
Food	42.7	33.3	28.5	28.1
Food at home	42.7	33.3	23.6	23.1
Cereals and bakery products	5.8	3.9	3.3	3.3
Meats, poultry, and fish	13.4	10.6	6.7	6.6
Dairy products	8.3	6.1	4.0	3.9
Fruits and vegetables	8.7	7.0	4.4	4.3
Other foods at home	6.5	5.7	5.2	5.0
Food away from home:				
Restaurant meals	—	—	4.9	5.0
Housing	26.9	25.1	32.7	32.7
Rent	[1]13.5	[1]11.6	6.2	6.2
Home purchase and upkeep	—	—	12.2	12.1
Gas and electricity	1.9	2.1	2.1	2.1
Solid fuels and fuel oil	2.7	1.4	1.2	1.3
House furnishings	4.8	5.7	5.5	5.5
Household operation	4.0	4.3	5.5	5.5

Commodity Group and Services	1947–49 avg.	January 1950	December 1960	December 1961
Apparel	12.6	12.8	8.8	8.8
Men's and boys' apparel	4.4	3.7	2.8	2.8
Men's apparel	4.1	3.2	2.4	2.5
Boys' apparel	0.3	0.5	0.4	0.3
Women's and girls' apparel	4.6	5.3	3.7	3.7
Women's apparel	4.2	4.9	3.1	3.0
Girls' apparel	0.4	0.4	0.6	0.7
Footwear	3.0	2.2	1.6	1.6
Other apparel	0.2	0.5	0.7	0.7
Apparel services: Dry cleaning	0.4	1.1	(2)	(2)
Transportation	7.1	11.4	11.5	11.7
Private	4.8	7.9	9.9	10.0
Public	2.3	3.5	1.6	1.7
Medical care	3.3	5.2	5.7	5.8
Medical care services	2.9	4.4	4.9	5.1
Prescriptions and drugs	0.4	0.8	0.8	0.7
Personal care	2.5	2.4	2.3	2.3
Reading and recreation	2.8	5.8	5.4	5.5
Other goods and services	2.1	4.0	5.1	5.1

[1]Includes home upkeep. [2]Included in household operation.

SOURCE: Department of Labor, Bureau of Labor Statistics.

GROSS NATIONAL PRODUCT IMPLICIT PRICE DEFLATOR INDEX

The GNPI is a composite index which includes the WPI and CPI. Its purpose is to eliminate price-level changes from total GNP. The deflated GNP is referred to as GNP in "constant dollars" (of 1958). Through the use of deflators, GNP in one period can be compared with that of another period net of the effects of price-level changes. A summary of the principal features of the GNPI follows:

1. *Age:* Annual deflators date from 1929–1957; seasonally adjusted quarterly deflators from 1947 to the present.
2. *Formula:* Paasche type.
3. *Universe:* All economic transactions contemplated in the Gross National Product: (1) personal consumption expenditures, (2) gross private domestic investment, (3) net exports of goods and services, and (4) government purchases of goods and services.

EXHIBIT 8-9 GROSS NATIONAL PRODUCT IN CURRENT AND CONSTANT DOLLARS, 1929 TO 1969

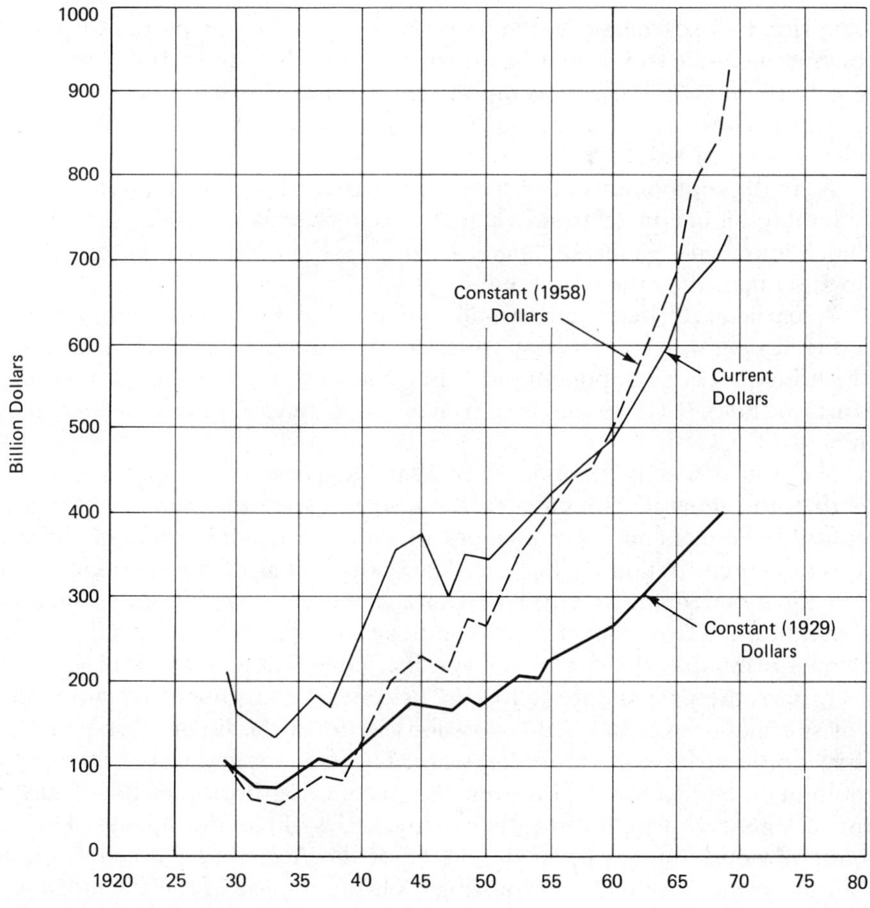

SOURCE: Department of Commerce, Office of Business Economics.

4. *Sample size:* The sample is a composite of the indexes used to compute Gross National Product, including the WPI, the CPI, the Composite Construction Index, and many others. Each index is used to deflate the portions of Gross National Product to which they apply.
5. *Weights:* There are no weights in the GNP index itself, although weights are used in constructing the underlying indexes. There is an implicit weighting per the construct of Gross National Product itself.
6. *Compiler:* U.S. Department of Commerce, Office of Business Economics.
7. *Frequency:* This index is updated quarterly on a seasonally adjusted basis.
8. *Base period:* The base period for the current series is 1958.

A comparison of Gross National Product in *current* dollars (unadjusted for price-level changes) and *constant* dollars (adjusted or "deflated" for price-level changes) is contained in Exhibit 8-9.

8.5 SPECIFIC PRICE INDEXES IN THE UNITED STATES

Specific price indexes measure the movement of prices of particular goods and services. Specific price trends may be measured formally by indexes or simply by comparing a series of catalogs. The components of the major indexes are, in fact, subindexes in their own right. Some of the major components of the WPI and CPI indexes are plotted in Exhibit 8-10.

As to the components of WPI, we notice that "processed foods and feeds" has a considerably higher price trend than the composite WPI, while "farm products" has a much lower one. Similarly, "medical care" rose much more rapidly in the period 1959 to 1969 than the other components of CPI.

A particularly important specific price trend from an accounting point of view is one dealing with construction costs. Cost of construction is not included in WPI or CPI, although it is a component index in GNPI. The relationship of the Composite Construction Index (CCI) to the price trends of the general price indexes can be seen in Exhibit 8-11.

We notice that in periods after 1948, the cost of construction rose more rapidly than the general price indexes. A construction index is important in accounting because buildings and other facilities represent a major portion of the assets of most business organizations. The price-level adjustment of depreciation is a major factor in the restatement of income. Where a cost construction index such as CCI varies significantly from general price indexes, proponents of specific price-level adjustments insist that the use of the specific index will lead to more valid results.

In fact, the proponents of specific price-level adjustments recommend that a series of specific indexes be used for various items in the financial statements, e.g., a construction cost index for buildings and facilities, catalog prices for inventories and equipment, and so forth. However, the Accounting Principles Board has moved in favor of a general price index rather than a series of specific indexes. This preference quite obviously hinges upon the desire of the Accounting Principles Board to maintain uniformity in financial reporting. Policing the use of specific indexes would be a most difficult task.

EXHIBIT 8-10 WHOLESALE AND CONSUMER PRICE INDEXES: 1955 TO 1969, SHOWING MAJOR COMPONENT PRICE TRENDS

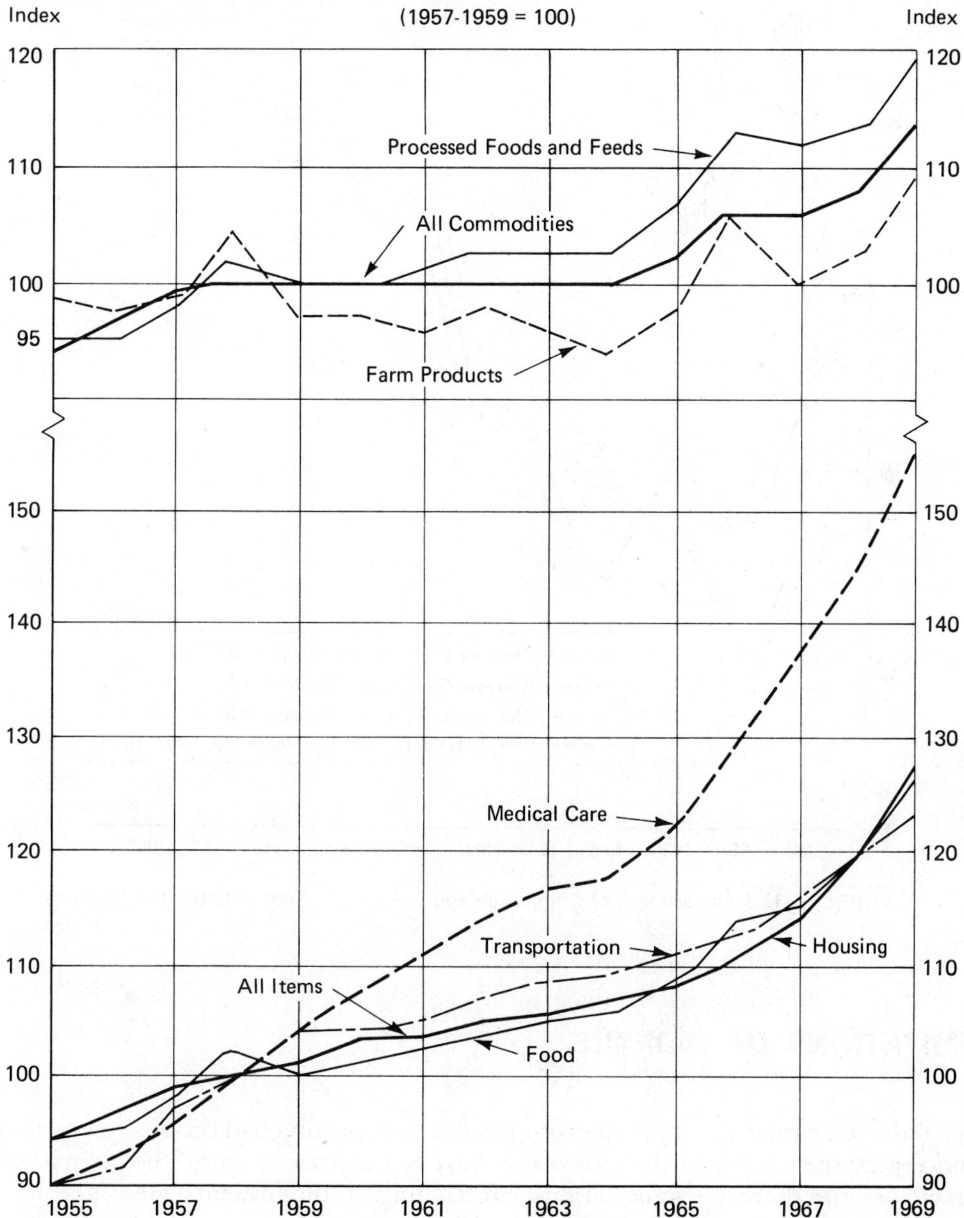

SOURCE: Chart prepared by Dept. of Commerce, Bureau of the Census. Data from Dept. of Labor, Bureau of Labor Statistics.

EXHIBIT 8-11 COMPOSITE CONSTRUCTION INDEX AND THE THREE MAJOR GENERAL PRICE INDEXES

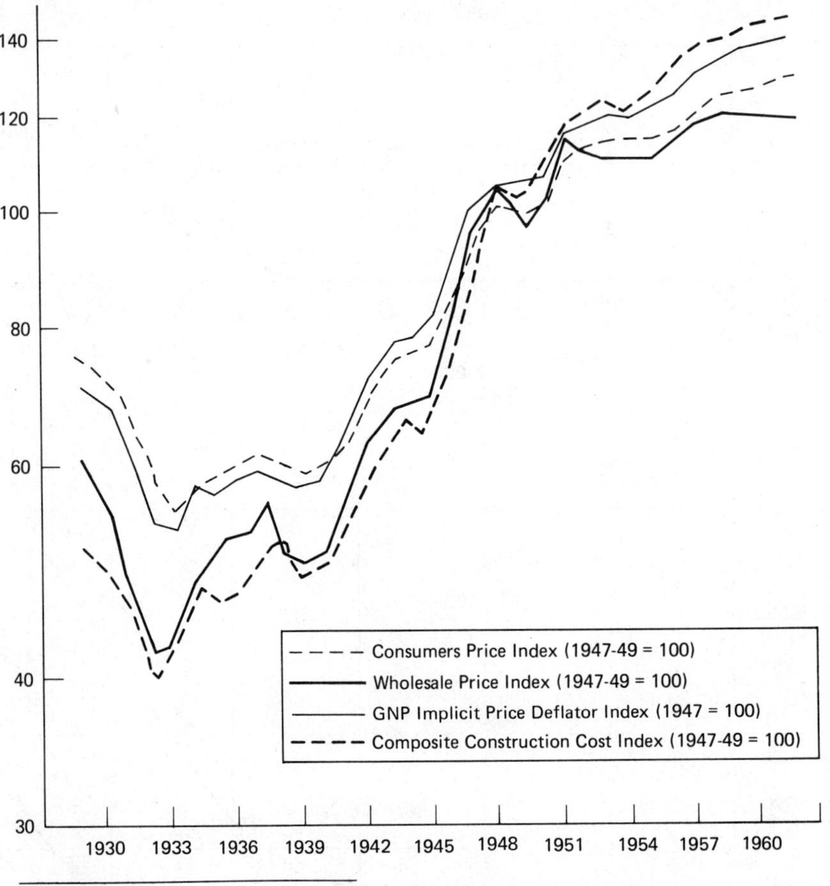

SOURCE: U.S. Department of Commerce and U.S. Department of Labor Publications.

8.6 LIMITATIONS OF INDEXES

We observed earlier that opponents to price-level reporting had serious reservations concerning the validity of the indexes we have at the present time. The point is well taken, because there are some serious shortcomings at the present state of the art in measuring price-levels. Our simple example of meat and potatoes (Exhibit 8-6) illustrated how the same basic data could lead to a number of index values based on the methodological approach that is used. The range between the index values for 1970 in Exhibit 8-6 was 6 points, i.e., from 154 to 160. We notice that the fixed-weight method is used in computing WPI and CPI, and that these indexes in turn form in part the substance of the GNP index. Yet the fixed-weight formula, as demonstrated in Exhibit 8-6, does not take into effect any change in quantities which occur after the period in which the weights are established.

There are other major limitations, including:

1. The inability of indexes to separate changes in prices stemming from product improvement as opposed to price-level changes (inflation or deflation).
2. Questions as to the validity of the statistical methods employed in sampling and weighting.
3. Inability of indexes to cope with supply and demand shifts.

We will discuss these limitations briefly in turn.

TECHNOLOGICAL VERSUS PRICE-LEVEL FACTORS

The fact that a product costs more in 1970 than it did in 1960 could be at least partly because it is a better product. For example, a 1970 automobile includes many modifications and improvements over a 1960 automobile, which if added to the 1960 model in mass production quantities would undoubtedly affect the price ratio. Similarly, the fact that medical costs have increased dramatically in recent years may be partially a function of improved medical services. Certainly the diagnostic equipment that is now present in many doctors' offices represents, in the same instance, increased cost and substantially improved service. While the compilers of national price indexes make every effort to compare products of comparable quality through subjective analysis, it is clear that at present they lack the ability to differentiate between technological and price-level factors in an objective manner.

SAMPLING AND WEIGHTING

There are numerous questions of a methodological nature, including the multiplicity of formulae which we mentioned previously. In addition there is the question of how items in the samples are selected. The approach that is used is *judgmental*—i.e., experts pick the items based on their knowledge of the economic behavior they are witnessing. Under these circumstances it is impossible to prove that the sample is representative of the universe. It is also impossible to compute sampling errors. These issues make it difficult to satisfy critics as to the validity of the resulting index numbers.

Then there is a question as to weighting. Both WPI and CPI rely on a fixed-weight methodology, and as these indexes enter into the GNP index, it also is influenced by the weights. The weights that are used in CPI are established by a survey and revised less often than once in ten years. At issue is both the construct of the weights and the frequency of their revision. The problems incident to weighting in CPI are typical of the other indexes as well.

SUPPLY AND DEMAND

The present indexes are unable to cope with the dynamics of supply and demand. It is a well-established economic principle that prices are sensitive to shifts in supply and demand. For example, the price of color television sets in the 1960s decreased sharply as the result of two factors: technological innovation in producing sets at lower cost and the tremendous increase in the supply of color television sets. We have already spoken to the technological issue, but what of the supply issue? If CPI were composed only of this item, the 1960s would have been among the greatest deflationary periods in history! This hypothesis is nonsense, of course, but it speaks to the point. How are economies of scale represented in the present indexes? Surely the distinction between the production of 6.7 million passenger cars in 1960 versus 4.3 million in 1958 should have some bearing on the prices of automobiles in those respective years.

But as quantity variances are ignored in the fixed-weight formula, these supply-and-demand factors fail to be accounted for in the national price indexes.

Notwithstanding the limitations of indexes, there is merit in price-level reporting. Certainly the indexes we have are better than none at all, and failure to make any adjustment for price-level changes can lead to very serious distortion of financial data, as we have shown previously. However, progress in price-level reporting must be accompanied by a continuing search for improved indexes.

8.7 MEASURING PRICE-LEVEL CHANGES

Price-level changes affect both income and balance sheet accounts. Let us examine these conditions separately for the moment.

INCOME ACCOUNTS

Consider the following income statement (Exhibit 8-12):

EXHIBIT 8-12

INCOME STATEMENT
FOR THE YEAR ENDED, DECEMBER 31, 1969

Sales		$100,000
Inventory, January 1, 1969	$20,000	
Purchases during 1969	60,000	
	80,000	
Inventory, December 31, 1969	10,000	
Cost of goods sold		70,000
Gross profit		30,000
General and administrative (G & A)	10,000	
Depreciation	10,000	20,000
Net income		$ 10,000

Assume that (1) sales, purchases, and G & A are uniform throughout the year; (2) that the inventory pricing method is LIFO and that all of the beginning inventory bears a 1958 cost price; and (3) that all of the depreciation is on building and equipment purchased in 1949 for $250,000, and bears a twenty-five-year life. Depreciation is by straight-line.

We will use the GNPI in Exhibit 8-1. We need four index numbers to adjust the above income statement:

1. The index for 1949 is needed for the depreciation adjustment.
2. The index for 1958 is needed for the inventory adjustment.
3. The average index for 1969 is needed for the other items.
4. The ending index for 1969 is needed for all items.

The first three index numbers are given. The fourth quarter index for 1969 is also needed but is not given in Exhibit 8-1. Let us assume that the fourth quarter figure is 130. Accordingly:

	Index	Computation to Obtain Conversion Factor	Conversion Factor
1949	79.1	130.0/ 79.1	1.6435
1958	100.0	130.0/100.0	1.3000
1969—average	128.1	130.0/128.1	1.0148
1969—4th quarter	130.0	130.0/130.0	1.0000

Notice that our adjustment is into current dollars, as illustrated in Exhibit 8-3. We can proceed to adjust the income statement for price-level changes as follows:

EXHIBIT 8-13

INCOME STATEMENT
FOR THE YEAR ENDED, DECEMBER 31, 1969

	Unadjusted	Conversion Factor	Adjusted
Sales	$100,000	1.0148	$101,480
Inventory, January 1	20,000	1.3000	26,000
Purchases	60,000	1.0148	60,888
Available	80,000		86,888
Inventory, December 31	10,000	1.3000	13,000
Cost of goods sold	70,000		73,888
Gross profit	$ 30,000		$ 27,592
Gen. & administrative	10,000	1.0148	10,148
Depreciation (see note)	10,000	1.6435	16,435
Total	20,000		26,583
Net income	$ 10,000		$ 1,009

Depreciation Note: Depreciation is adjusted by restating the original cost of the assets giving rise to depreciation in terms of current dollars, and then recomputing depreciation on the basis of the restated value by dividing the useful life into the unadjusted and adjusted cost figures, respectively.

Depreciation	$ 10,000		$ 16,435
Original cost	250,000	1.6435	410,875
Divided by estimated useful life to obtain depreciation above	25 yrs.		25 yrs.

While the conversion factor applied directly to depreciation gives us the correct figure above, this is because we have only one base price on our depreciable assets. If some of the assets date to periods other than 1949, the depreciation components would have to be adjusted individually or a weighted conversion factor would have to be developed. Assume the previous data on depreciable assets, except that $125,000 were purchased in 1949 and $125,000 in 1958. The depreciation adjustment would be:

		Unadjusted	Conversion Factor	Adjusted
	Total depreciation	$ 10,000	—	$ 14,717
(a)	Depreciation on 1949 assets	5,000	1.6435	8,217
	1949 Assets—original cost	125,000	1.6435	205,437
	Divided by useful life	25 yrs.		25 yrs.
(b)	Depreciation on 1958 assets	5,000	1.3000	6,500
	1958 Assets—original cost	125,000	1.3000	162,500
	Divided by useful life	25 yrs.		25 yrs.

You will notice from the foregoing data that the inventory and depreciation adjustments have the most significant effect on the restatement of net income. In this case the LIFO inventory carries a base price which is eleven years old. The reason the adjustment to cost of goods sold is in excess of 1.0148 is because 50% of the LIFO base stock was absorbed in 1969. If beginning and ending inventory were equal in our example, the adjustment to cost of goods sold would have been precisely 1.0148:

LIFO ADJUSTMENT

(Beginning inventory = ending inventory)

	Unadjusted	Conversion Factor	Adjusted
Inventory, January 1	$20,000	1.3000	$26,000
Purchases	60,000	1.0148	60,888
Available	80,000		86,888
Inventory, December 31	20,000	1.3000	26,000
Cost of goods sold	$60,000	1.0148	$60,888

If ending inventory was greater than beginning inventory in this example, the ending inventory would consist of mixed prices:

LIFO ADJUSTMENT

(Beginning inventory < ending inventory)

	Unadjusted	Conversion Factor	Adjusted
Inventory, January 1	$20,000	1.3000	$26,000
Purchases	60,000	1.0148	60,888
Available	80,000		86,888
Inventory, December 31	30,000	–	36,148
Cost of goods sold	$50,000	1.0148	$50,740
Computation of Ending Inventory			
Inventory with 1958 base price	20,000	1.3000	26,000
Inventory with 1969 base price	10,000	1.0148	10,148
Total	$30,000		$36,148

This specific identification of inventory base prices is necessary for adjustments in future periods. For purposes of adjusting for FIFO and weighted average, let us assume that beginning inventory is carried at a base price of 122 in each case. This approximates the index value for 1968. The conversion factor for beginning inventory is 130/122 = 1.0656.

FIFO ADJUSTMENT

	Unadjusted	Conversion Factor	Adjusted
Inventory, January 1	$20,000	1.0655	$21,312
Purchases	60,000	1.0148	60,888
Available	80,000		82,200
Inventory, December 31	30,000	1.0148	30,444
Cost of goods sold	$50,000	–	$51,756

FIFO inventory carried forward into the next period would bear the average index value for 1969. If most of the ending inventory is acquired in the fourth quarter of 1969, it could be adjusted on that basis.

WEIGHTED AVERAGE ADJUSTMENT

	Unadjusted	Conversion Factor	Adjusted
Inventory, January 1	$20,000	1.0655	$21,312
Purchases	60,000	1.0148	60,888
Available	80,000	1.0275*	82,200
Inventory, December 31	33,000	1.0275*	30,825
Cost of goods sold	$50,000	1.0275*	$51,375

$^{*}\frac{82,200}{80,000} = 1.0275$

Inventory carried forward into 1970 would bear the derived index value of 1.0275.

BALANCE SHEET ACCOUNTS

We are accustomed to the belief that profit or loss is accommodated in the income statement. This belief is upset in price-level accounting. In periods of price changes we can experience profit or loss through simply holding certain assets and liabilities. For example, in a period of rising prices, a cache of money would steadily lose value. This is a loss!

That sub-set of assets and liabilities which give rise to balance sheet profits and losses are referred to as *monetary* items. Monetary items comprise monetary assets and monetary liabilities.

A monetary item is one in which the *amount* is fixed by statute or contract and is therefore not affected by a change in the price-level. An example is *accounts receivable.* Once we have sold the merchandise, the amount of the obligation is fixed. If the credit sale was for $100, the customer will pay $100. Having settled on the amount of the obligation at point of sale, no further adjustment is made to the $100 figure for price-level changes in the period between the sale and collection. Similarly, once mortgage payments have been determined, they are not affected by subsequent price-level changes.

Monetary liabilities are subtracted from monetary assets to yield *net* monetary items. The effects of holding monetary items in changing price-levels can be summarized as follows:

IN PERIODS OF RISING PRICES:

1. A gain results from holding monetary liabilities.
2. A loss results from holding monetary assets.

IN PERIODS OF FALLING PRICES:

1. A loss results from holding monetary liabilities.
2. A gain results from holding monetary assets.

For most purposes we can consider monetary items to consist of the following:

MONETARY ASSETS:

Cash
Notes and Accounts Receivable
Investments in Bonds

MONETARY LIABILITIES:

All current and long-term liabilities with the exception of such items as deferred taxes and reserves.

A comprehensive list of monetary assets and liabilities is contained in an appendix to this chapter.

Monetary items need not be adjusted in the current year because they are already stated in current dollars. However, in preparing comparative adjusted statements, the monetary items of all prior years do require adjustment in order to achieve comparability with the current year.

The gain or loss resulting from holding monetary items is referred to as *purchasing power gain or loss.*

Purchasing power gains or losses can be computed (approximately) by means of this formula. (A non-formula approach is illustrated in the example in section 8.8.)

$$X = M_b(P_b - P_a) + M_e(P_a - P_e)$$

where

X = the purchasing power loss (gain, if negative)
M = the balance of the monetary accounts, i.e., net monetary items (positive if a debit, i.e., excess of monetary assets over monetary liabilities; negative if a credit)
P = purchasing power as measured by an index
b = beginning of period
a = average of period
e = end of period

Purchasing power gains or losses are not reported in adjusted income statements, but are disclosed as a separate item in the adjusted balance sheet, as shown in the following example.

8.8 AN ILLUSTRATION IN ADJUSTING FINANCIAL STATEMENTS FOR PRICE-LEVEL CHANGES

A company began operations on January 1, 1964. Its financial statements on December 31, 1964 and 1965 were:

COMPARATIVE INCOME STATEMENTS

	1964		1965	
Sales		$500,000		$600,000
Cost of goods sold				
Beginning inventory	$100,000		$150,000	
Purchases	300,000		350,000	
Available	$400,000		$500,000	
Less: Ending inventory	150,000	250,000	200,000	300,000
Gross profit		$250,000		$300,000
Expenses:				
Selling	$120,000		$140,000	
Administrative	95,000		105,000	
Depreciation	5,000	220,000	5,000	250,000
Net operating income		$ 30,000		$ 50,000
Income tax (50%)		15,000		25,000
Net income after tax		$ 15,000		$ 25,000

COMPARATIVE STATEMENTS OF RETAINED EARNINGS

	1964	1965
Retained earnings, Jan. 1	$----	$10,000
Add: Net income after tax	15,000	25,000
	$15,000	$35,000
Less: Dividends paid	5,000	10,000
Balance, Dec. 31	$10,000	$25,000

Notes:

1. Sales and purchases were uniform throughout the year.
2. FIFO inventory costing is used.
3. The physical assets cost $85,000 and had an estimated useful life of seventeen years.
4. Dividends were paid on December 31 of each year.

COMPARATIVE BALANCE SHEETS

	1964		1965
	Jan. 1	Dec. 31	December 31
ASSETS			
Monetary			
Cash	$ 35,000	$ 20,000	$ 15,000
Receivables	50,000	40,000	35,000
Investments (bonds)	40,000	40,000	40,000
	$125,000	$100,000	$ 90,000
Non-Monetary			
Inventory	100,000	150,000	200,000
Physical assets (net)	85,000	80,000	75,000
	185,000	230,000	275,000
Total assets	$310,000	$330,000	$365,000
LIABILITIES			
Monetary			
Current liabilities	$ 10,000	$ 20,000	$ 40,000
Long-term liabilities	30,000	30,000	30,000
	$ 40,000	$ 50,000	$ 70,000
STOCKHOLDERS' EQUITY			
Capital stock	270,000	270,000	270,000
Retained earnings	–	10,000	25,000
	270,000	280,000	295,000
Total equities	$310,000	$330,000	$365,000
Net Monetary Items	$ 85,000	$ 50,000	$ 20,000

Assume the following hypothetical index values:[11]

1963 – 4th Quarter: 100
1964 – 4th Quarter: 110 1964 – Average: 108
1965 – 4th Quarter: 120 1965 – Average: 116

The financial statements as of December 31, 1964 would be adjusted as follows:

INCOME STATEMENT
FOR THE YEAR ENDED, DECEMBER 31, 1964

	Unadjusted	Multiplier	Adjusted
Sales	$500,000	110/108	$509,260
Cost of goods sold:			
Beginning inventory	100,000	110/100	110,000
Purchases	300,000	110/108	305,560
Available	400,000		415,560
Ending inventory	150,000	110/108	152,780
Cost of goods sold	250,000		262,780
Gross profit	250,000		246,480
Expenses:			
Selling	120,000	110/108	122,220
Administrative	95,000	110/108	96,760
Depreciation	5,000	110/100	5,500
	220,000		224,480
Net income before tax	$ 30,000		$ 22,000
Income tax	15,000		15,000*
Net income after tax	$ 15,000		$ 7,000

*Under existing internal revenue laws, federal income tax cannot be computed on the basis of price-level adjusted statements, hence the tax would be $15,000 in either case. If internal revenue laws did permit tax computation on the basis of adjusted statements, the adjusted tax would be $11,000.

[11] These indexes may be applied directly as "multipliers," which is the approach that is illustrated, or they can be stated in terms of "conversion factors," as demonstrated previously. The conversion factors for 1964 and 1965 would be:

Conversion Factors

1964	1965
110/100 = 1.1000	120/100 = 1.2000
110/108 = 1.0185	120/108 = 1.1111
110/110 = 1.0000	120/110 = 1.0909
	120/116 = 1.0345
	120/120 = 1.0000

STATEMENT OF RETAINED EARNINGS
DECEMBER 31, 1964

	Unadjusted	Multiplier	Adjusted
Balance, January 1	–		–
Add: Net income	$ 15,000		$ 7,000
	15,000		7,000
Less: Dividends paid	5,000	110/110	5,000
Balance, December 31	$ 10,000		$ 2,000

BALANCE SHEET
DECEMBER 31, 1964

ASSETS	Unadjusted	Multiplier	Adjusted
Monetary			
Cash	$ 20,000	–	$ 20,000
Receivables	40,000	–	40,000
Investments (bonds)	40,000	–	40,000
	100,000		100,000
Non-Monetary			
Inventories	150,000	110/108	152,780
Physical assets (net)	80,000	110/100	88,000
	230,000		240,780
Total assets	$330,000		$340,780
LIABILITIES			
Monetary			
Current liabilities	$ 20,000	–	$ 20,000
Long-term liabilities	30,000		30,000
	50,000		50,000
STOCKHOLDERS' EQUITY			
Capital stock	270,000	110/100	297,000
Retained earnings	10,000		2,000
Purchasing power gain (or loss)	–		(8,220)*
Total stockholders' equity	280,000		290,780
Total equities	$330,000		$340,780

*Verification of the purchasing power gain or (loss) may be obtained as follows:

PURCHASING POWER GAIN OR (LOSS)
FOR 1964

	Unadjusted	Multiplier	Adjusted
Net monetary items, Jan. 1	$ 85,000	110/100	$ 93,500
Add: Sales	500,000	110/108	509,260
	585,000		602,760

	Unadjusted	Multiplier	Adjusted
Less: Purchases	300,000	110/108	305,560
Selling expenses	120,000	110/108	122,220
Administrative expenses	95,000	110/108	96,760
Income tax	15,000	110/110	15,000
Dividends paid	5,000	110/110	5,000
	535,000		544,540
Net monetary items, Dec. 31	50,000 →		58,220
			→ 50,000
Purchasing power loss			$ 8,220

The 1965 financial statements would be adjusted in a similar manner. If comparative statements are required, however, it is necessary to readjust all preceding statements (in this case 1964) in terms of 1965 prices. The comparative statements in this case are:

COMPARATIVE INCOME STATEMENTS FOR 1964 AND 1965

	Unadjusted		Multiplier		Adjusted	
	1964	1965	1964	1965	1964	1965
Sales	$500,000	$600,000	120/108	120/116	$555,560	$620,690
Cost of goods sold:						
Beginning inventory	100,000	150,000	120/100	120/108	120,000	166,670
Purchases	300,000	350,000	120/108	120/116	333,330	362,070
Available	400,000	500,000			453,330	528,740
Ending inventory	150,000	200,000	120/108	120/116	166,670	206,900
Cost of goods sold	250,000	300,000			286,660	321,840
Gross profit	$250,000	$300,000			$268,900	$298,850
Expenses:						
Selling	120,000	140,000	120/108	120/116	133,330	144,830
Administrative	95,000	105,000	120/108	120/116	105,560	108,620
Depreciation	5,000	5,000	120/100	120/100	6,000	6,000
Total	220,000	250,000			244,890	259,450
Net income before tax	$ 30,000	$ 50,000			$ 24,010	$ 39,400
Income tax	15,000	25,000	120/110	120/120	16,360	25,000
Net income	$ 15,000	$ 25,000			$ 7,650	$ 14,400

COMPARATIVE STATEMENTS OF RETAINED EARNINGS DECEMBER 31, 1964 AND 1965

	Unadjusted		Multiplier		Adjusted	
	1964	1965	1964	1965	1964	1965
Balance, January 1	$ –	$10,000			$ –	$ 2,200
Add: Net income	15,000	25,000			7,650	14,400
	15,000	35,000			7,650	16,600
Less: Dividends paid	5,000	10,000	120/110	120/120	5,450	10,000
Balance, December 31	$10,000	$25,000			$2,200	$ 6,600

COMPARATIVE BALANCE SHEETS
AS OF JANUARY 1964, DECEMBER 1964, AND DECEMBER 1965

	Unadjusted			Multiplier			Adjusted		
	Jan. 1964	Dec. 1964	Dec. 1965	Jan. 1964	Dec. 1964	Dec. 1965	Jan. 1964	Dec. 1964	Dec. 1965
ASSETS									
Monetary									
Cash	$ 35,000	$ 20,000	$ 15,000	120/100	120/110	—	$ 42,000	$ 21,820	$ 15,000
Receivables	50,000	40,000	35,000	120/100	120/110	—	60,000	43,640	35,000
Investments	40,000	40,000	40,000	120/100	120/110	—	48,000	43,640	40,000
	125,000	100,000	90,000				150,000	109,100	90,000
Non-Monetary									
Inventories	100,000	150,000	200,000	120/100	120/108	120/116	120,000	166,670	206,900
Physical assets (net)	85,000	80,000	75,000	120/100	120/100	120/100	102,000	96,000	90,000
	185,000	230,000	275,000				222,000	262,670	296,900
Total assets	$310,000	$330,000	$365,000				$372,000	$371,770	$386,900
LIABILITIES									
Monetary									
Current liabilities	10,000	20,000	40,000	120/100	120/110	—	12,000	21,820	40,000
Long-term liabilities	30,000	30,000	30,000	120/100	120/110	—	36,000	32,730	30,000
	40,000	50,000	70,000				48,000	54,550	70,000
STOCKHOLDERS' EQUITY									
Capital stock	270,000	270,000	270,000	120/100	120/100	120/100	324,000	324,000	324,000
Retained earnings	—	10,000	25,000				—	2,200	6,600
Purchasing power gain or (loss)	—	—	—				—	(8,980)	(13,700)
	270,000	280,000	295,000				324,000	317,220	316,900
Total equities	$310,000	$330,000	$365,000				$372,000	$371,770	$386,900

PURCHASING POWER GAIN OR (LOSS)
FOR 1964 AND 1965

1964		**Unadjusted**	**Multiplier**	**Adjusted**
Net Monetary assets, Jan. 1		$ 85,000	120/100	$102,000
Add: Sales		500,000	120/108	555,560
		585,000		657,560
Less:	Purchases	300,000	120/108	333,330
	Selling expenses	120,000	120/108	133,330
	Administrative expenses	95,000	120/108	105,560
	Income tax	15,000	120/110	16,360
	Dividends	5,000	120/110	5,450
		535,000		594,030
Net monetary assets, Dec. 31		$ 50,000		63,530
Adjusted net monetary assets			120/110	54,550
Purchasing power loss				$ 8,980
1965				
Net monetary assets, Jan. 1		$ 50,000	120/110	$ 54,550
Add: Sales		600,000	120/116	620,690
		650,000		675,240
Less:	Purchases	350,000	120/116	362,070
	Selling expenses	140,000	120/116	144,830
	Administrative expenses	105,000	120/116	108,620
	Income tax	25,000	120/120	25,000
	Dividends	10,000	120/120	10,000
		630,000		650,520
Net monetary assets, Dec. 31		$ 20,000		24,720
				20,000
Purchasing power loss for 1965				4,720
Add: purchasing power loss for 1964				8,980
Cumulative purchasing power loss				$ 13,700

Where comparative statements are used, you will notice that it is necessary to restate all prior years in terms of the current years. For example we have three "sales" figures for the year 1964 over a two-year period:

1964 sales unadjusted	$500,000
1964 sales adjusted for 1964 price-level changes	509,260
1964 sales adjusted to 4th quarter 1965 index	555,560

This type of adjustment is necessary where we use the *current* method. In this way we can compare 1965 sales with those of 1964 in terms of dollars of the same purchasing power.

8.9 EFFECT OF PRICE-LEVEL CHANGES ON STOCKHOLDERS' EQUITY

We will use the example in section 8.8 to illustrate the effect of price-level changes on stockholders' equity. Consider in our example that capital stock consists of 27,000 shares of common stock issued at $10 per share for a total of $270,000. Paid-in capital remains unchanged in the period 1964 through 1965. Return on stockholders' equity on a unadjusted basis is:

	Unadjusted						
	1964		1965		Total	Average	
Dividends	$ 5,000		$ 10,000		$15,000	$ 7,500	
Retained earnings	10,000		15,000		25,000	12,500	
Total	15,000	= 5.4%	25,000	= 8.4%	40,000	20,000	= 7.0%
Stockholders' equity	280,000		295,000			287,500	

The *unadjusted* book value per share is:

	1964		1965	
Stockholders' equity	$280,000	= $10.37	$295,000	= $10.93
No. of shares	27,000		27,000	

Adjusted return on stockholders' equity is:

	Adjusted to 4th Quarter 1965 Index						
	1964		1965		Total	Average	
Dividends	$ 5,450		$ 10,000		$15,450	$ 7,725	
Retained earnings	2,200		4,400		6,600	3,300	
Purchasing power loss	(8,980)		(4,720)		(13,700)	(6,850)	
Total	(1,330)	= (.4%)	9,680	= 3.1%	8,350	4,175	= 1.3%
Stockholders' equity	317,220		316,900			317,060	

The book value per share adjusted to 1965 prices is:

	1964		1965	
Stockholders' equity	$317,220	= $11.75	$316,900	= $11.74
No. of shares	27,000		27,000	

A comparison of book values can be used to compute the net gain or loss on stockholders' equity.

	Book Value per Share		
	Unadjusted	Adjusted	Net Loss
1964	$10.37	$11.75	($1.38)
1965	$10.93	$11.74	($ .81)

This is to say that despite the dividends and retained earnings, there was a net loss on investment of $.81 per share based on 1965 prices. If the market price of the shares at the end of 1965 equaled $11.74, a stockholder selling at that point would realize exactly zero on his investment for two years on the basis of price-level adjusted dollars. Of course, any increase in value over $11.74 would represent a net gain on investment, and a market price less than $11.74 would represent a loss.

ASSET PORTFOLIOS AND PRICE-LEVEL CHANGES

We mentioned earlier that the depreciation adjustment is a major factor in price-level accounting. This is because the assets underlying the depreciation may be of distant vintage. It follows then that firms with high ratios of depreciable assets are more affected by price-level changes than firms with low ratios. To make this contrast as vivid as possible, consider the composition of assets of firms A and B:

	Firm A	Firm B
Non-depreciable assets	90% or $90,000	10% or $10,000
Depreciable assets (cost)	10% or $10,000	90% or $90,000

Assume that the assets were acquired in each case in 1949. The average useful life in each case is twenty-five years, and straight-line depreciation is used. Both firms have the same net income after depreciation for the year 1969:

	Unadjusted	
	Firm A	Firm B
Net operating income before depreciation	$10,400	$13,600
Depreciation for 1969	400	3,600
Net income	$10,000	$10,000

As the adjustment to other items in the income statement is minimal, let us assume that adjusted net operating income before depreciation is the same as shown above. Depreciation is adjusted in each instance by the conversion factor $128.1/79.1 = 1.6195$ (the GNP indexes for 1969 and 1949 respectively).

	Adjusted	
	Firm A	Firm B
Net operating income before depreciation	$10,400	$13,600
Depreciation	648	5,830
Adjusted net income	$ 9,752	$ 7,770

We can conclude that firms with high ratios of depreciable assets will be more greatly affected by price-level accounting and reporting. This is descriptive of most firms in the primary sector of the economy.

8.10 SUMMARY

Price-level changes refer to changes in the purchasing power of a money unit, e.g., the dollar. Price-level changes are measured by indexes of general purchasing power, of which there are three in the United States: (1) the Wholesale Price Index, (2) the Consumer Price Index, and (3) the Gross National Product Implicit Price Deflator Index. The last of these has been recommended by the Accounting Principles Board in its *Statement No. 3* for use in adjusting financial statements for price-level purposes. *Statement No. 3,* issued in 1969, recommends that firms report price-level effects on a supplementary basis.

We discussed the construction, methodology, and limitations of measuring price changes at present, and concluded that price-level reporting does provide more meaningful data despite the shortcomings of our existing indexes.

A comprehensive illustration of price-level adjustment to financial statements was presented, as well as its effects on measuring the return on stockholders' investment.

Finally, we pointed out that price-level changes affect capital intensive industries to a much greater extent than non-capital industries.

CHAPTER 8 APPENDIX

MONETARY AND NON-MONETARY ITEMS

This appendix provides examples of monetary and non-monetary items with an explanation of the reason for classification when needed.

	Monetary	Non-monetary
ASSETS		
Cash on hand and demand bank deposits (domestic currency)	X	
Time deposits (domestic currency)	X	
Foreign currency on hand and claims to foreign currency		X
Marketable securities		
Stocks		X
Bonds	(see discussion)	
Bonds held as a short-term investment may be held for price speculation. If so, they are non-monetary. If the bonds are held primarily for the fixed income characteristic, they are monetary.		
Accounts and notes receivable	X	
Allowance for doubtful accounts and notes receivable	X	
Inventories produced under fixed price contracts accounted for at the contract price	X	
These items are in effect receivables of a fixed amount.		

	Monetary	Non-monetary
Other inventories		X
Advances to employees	X	
Prepaid insurance, taxes, advertising, rent These represent an amount of services for which expenditures have been made and which will be amortized to expense in the future. In financial statements they are substantially the same kind of item as fixed assets.		X
Prepaid interest Related to notes payable, a monetary item.	X	
Receivables under capitalized financing leases	X	
Long-term receivables	X	
Refundable deposits	X	
Advances to unconsolidated subsidiaries If there is no expectation that the advances will ever be collected, they are in effect additional investments and are non-monetary.	X	
Investments in unconsolidated subsidiaries If an investment is carried at cost, it is non-monetary. If an investment is carried on the equity basis, the statements of the subsidiary should be restated for general prive-level changes . . . and the equity method should then be applied.	(see discussion)	
Pension, sinking, and other funds Depends on composition of the fund – bonds are generally monetary and stocks non-monetary.	(see discussion)	
Investments in convertible bonds If the bond is held for price speculation or with expectation of converting into common stock the investment is non-monetary. If the bond is held for the fixed principal and interest, it is monetary.	(see discussion)	
Property, plant, and equipment		X
Allowance for depreciation		X
Cash surrender value of life insurance	X	
Advances paid on purchase contracts The items to be received are non-monetary.		X
Unamortized discount on bonds payable Related to bonds payable, a monetary item.	X	
Deferred charges for income taxes – deferred method A cost deferred as an expense of future periods is non-monetary.		X
Other deferred charges which represent costs incurred to be charged against future income		X
Patents, trademarks, licenses, formulas		X
Goodwill		X
Other intangible assets		X

LIABILITIES

	Monetary	Non-monetary
Accounts and notes payable	X	
Accrued expenses payable (salaries, wages, etc.) Similar to accounts payable, amount is fixed.	X	
Cash dividends payable	X	

	Monetary	Non-monetary
Debts payable in foreign currency		X
Refundable deposits	X	
Advances received on sales contracts The obligation will be satisfied by delivery of goods that are non-monetary.		X
Accrued losses on firm purchase commitments	X	
Bonds payable	X	
Convertible bonds payable Treated as monetary debt until converted.	X	
Obligations under capitalized leases	X	
Other long-term debt	X	
Deferred taxes—deferred method Cost savings deferred as a reduction of expenses of future periods.		X
Deferred investment credits		X
Accrued pension cost	X	
Reserve for self-insurance Although reserve for self-insurance is non-monetary, it may be stated in the same amount in both the historical-dollar and general price-level statements if the adequacy of the reserve in terms of current costs has been determined at year end for the historical-dollar statements.		X
Deferred income		X
Provision for guarantees Provision for guarantees is non-monetary because it is a liability to provide goods or services. It may be stated in the same amount in both the historical-dollar and general price-level statements if the adequacy of the provision in terms of current costs has been determined at year end for the historical-dollar statements.		X
Accrued vacation pay Accrued vacation pay is monetary if it is based on a fixed contract. It is non-monetary if it is payable based on wage or salary rates that may change after the balance sheet date.	(see discussion)	

OWNERS' EQUITY

	Monetary	Non-monetary
Minority interest		X
Preferred stock		X

Classifying preferred stock as non-monetary is based on the fact that the amount accounted for is the proceeds received when the stock was issued. The proceeds must be restated to present them in terms of the general purchasing power of the dollar at the balance sheet date.

The amount of a nonconvertible callable preferred stock should not exceed the call price in the general price-level balance sheet. The periodic change in the excess of the restated proceeds over the call price, if any, should not be included in net income, but should be added to net income to determine net income to common stockholders in the same manner as preferred dividends are deducted to determine net income to common stockholders.

A different viewpoint held by some Board members is that preferred stock is a monetary item and that general price-level gains or losses from preferred stock outstanding should be included in the computation of net income.

	Monetary	Non-monetary
Common stock		X
Additional paid-in capital		X
Retained earnings	(see discussion)	

Retained earnings is a residual and need not be classified as either monetary or non-monetary.

SOURCE: *Accounting Principles Board Statement No. 3, Financial Statements Restated for General Price-Level Changes* (New York: American Institute of Certified Public Accountants, 1969), pp. 26–30. Used with permission.

CHAPTER 8 REFERENCES AND ADDITIONAL READINGS

GENERAL PRICE INDEXES ARE PUBLISHED PERIODICALLY BY:

U.S. Department of Commerce, *Survey of Current Business*, (Quarterly).

U.S. Government Printing Office, *Economic Report of the President*, (January of each year).

U.S. Department of Labor, *Monthly Labor Review*.

U.S. Department of Commerce, *Statistical Abstract of the United States*, (Annually).

OTHER REFERENCES ARE:

Accounting Principles Board Statement No. 3, Financial Statements Restated for General Price-Level Changes. New York: American Institute of Certified Public Accountants, 1969.

Chambers, Raymond J. "A Study of a Price-Level Study." *Abacus* (Australia), December 1966, pp. 97–118.

Chambers, Raymond J. "The Price-Level Problem and Some Intellectual Grooves." *Journal of Accounting Research*, Autumn 1965, pp. 242–52.

Dickerson, Peter J. *Business Income—A Critical Analysis*. Berkeley: Institute of Business and Economic Research, University of California, 1965.

Estes, Ralph W. "An Assessment of the Usefulness of Current Cost and Price-Level Information by Financial Statement Users." *Journal of Accounting Research*, Autumn 1968, pp. 200–207.

Fieldcamp, Dale. "International Accounting in an Inflationary Economy." *The International Journal of Accounting*, Fall 1968, pp. 155–64.

Gynther, R. S. *Accounting for Price-Level Changes: Theory and Procedures*. Oxford, England: Pergamon Press, 1966.

Hakansson, Nils H. "On the Relevance of Price-Level Accounting." *Journal of Accounting Research*, Spring 1969, pp. 22–31.

Hendriksen, Eldon S. "Purchasing Power and Replacement Cost Concepts—Are They Related?" *The Accounting Review*, July 1963, pp. 483–91.

Hendriksen, Eldon S. *Accounting Theory*. Rev. ed. Homewood, Ill.: Richard D. Irwin, Inc., 1970, pp. 200–236.

Johnson, Glenn I. "The Monetary and Nonmonetary Distinction." *The Accounting Review*, October 1965, pp. 821–23.

Jones, Ralph C. *Price-Level Changes and Financial Statements: Case Studies of Four Companies*. Sarasota, Fla.: American Accounting Association, 1955.

Jones, Ralph C. *Effects of Price-Level Changes on Business Capital and Taxes*. Sarasota, Fla.: American Accounting Association, 1956.

Levy, H. "Inflation and Price-Level Accounting—The Challenge of the Seventies." *Chartered Accountant in Australia*, May 1971, pp. 9–12.

Lyons, Scott A. "Accounting for Price-Level Changes in the Replacement of Fixed Assets." *Cost and Management* (Canada), March–April 1969, pp. 43–44.

Mann, Everett J. "Inflation and Accounting in Brazil." *Journal of Accountancy,* November 1967, pp. 49–53.

Mason, Perry. *Price-Level Changes and Financial Statements: Basic Concepts and Methods.* Sarasota, Fla.: American Accounting Association, 1956.

Mathews, R. L. "Price-Level Changes and Useless Information." *Journal of Accounting Research,* Spring 1965, pp. 133–55.

Mathews, R. L. "Income, Price Changes and the Valuation Controversy in Accounting." *The Accounting Review,* July 1968, pp. 509–516.

Moonitz, Maurice. "Price-Level Accounting and Scales of Measurement." *The Accounting Review,* July 1970, pp. 465–75.

Rosenfield, Rosen. "Accounting for Inflation – A Field Test." *Journal of Accountancy,* June 1969, pp. 45–50.

Shwayder, Keith. "Expected and Unexpected Price-Level Changes." *The Accounting Review,* April 1971, pp. 306–319.

Spencer, Charles H., and Barnhisel, Thomas S. "A Decade of Price-Level Changes – The Effect on the Financial Statements of Cummins Engine Company." *The Accounting Review,* January 1965, pp. 144–53.

Staff of the Accounting Research Division. *Reporting the Financial Effects of Price-Level Changes.* Accounting Research Study No. 6. New York: American Institute of Certified Public Accountants, 1963.

Summers, Edward L., and Deskins, James W. "A Classification Scheme of Methods for Reporting Effects of Resource Price Changes." *International Journal of Accounting,* Fall 1970, pp. 101–119.

Sweeney, H. W. *Stabilized Accounting.* New York: Harper & Row, 1936.

CHAPTER 8 QUESTIONS, PROBLEMS, AND CASES

8- 1. What is meant by the term *purchasing power?*

8- 2. How are price-level changes measured?

8- 3. Distinguish *purchasing power gains and losses* from price-level adjusted *profit and loss.*

8- 4. Identify and explain the traditional output rule which contends unchanging price-levels. Who demonstrated convincingly the fallacy of this rule by adjusting the reported net incomes of General Electric, RCA, and Westinghouse for the years 1935–1948? What were his findings?

8- 5. "Conventional financial statements do not contain sufficient information to permit the analyst to make a comprehensive price-level adjustment." What particular information is missing?

8- 6. "The conversion of foreign currencies by means of the official exchange rates does not accommodate the problem of price-level reporting." Why not?

8- 7. What are *coefficients of revaluation?* How are they used?

8- 8. Distinguish between *general* and *specific* price indexes. Which are more preferable from an accounting point of view?

8- 9. Identify and discuss three limitations of general price indexes.

8-10. Indicate whether the following items are *monetary* or *non-monetary:*

	Monetary	Non-Monetary
(a) Cash in bank....................		
(b) Accounts receivable...........		
(c) Investment in stocks		
(d) Investment in bonds...........		
(e) Prepaid expenses		
(f) Accounts payable		

(g) Bonds payable..................
(h) Common stock..................
(i) Retained earnings.............

8-11. In recommending price-level reporting, what ground rules where laid by the Accounting Principles Board in its *Statement No. 3?*

8-12. "The general price trend in the 1900s has been one of rising prices. Under these conditions, stable money net income is overstated." Why is it overstated and not understated? What are the consequences of overstating income?

8-13. Explain the difference between a *constant* and a *current* adjustment. Which is preferred in adjusting financial statements?

8-14. Identify the four components of gross national product.

8-15. What is the difference between the three major general price indexes in the United States: (a) the Wholesale Price Index, (b) the Consumer Price Index, and (c) the Gross National Product Implicit Price Deflator Index.

8-16. Will all firms be equally affected by price-level changes? Explain and give examples.

8-17. What are the three basic procedures for constructing an index?

8-18. Define or explain the implications of the following terms and phrases:
(a) "Real" increase
(b) Price index
(c) Official exchange rate
(d) Precision level
(e) Confidence level
(f) Input-output analysis
(g) Composite Construction Index
(h) Monetary item
(i) Purchasing power gains or losses
(j) Multipliers

8-19. The Wholesale Price Index and the Consumer Price Index are compiled from a limited analysis. How is the analysis limited? What components of Gross National Product are ignored?

8-20. In the United States, which index is the best general price index? For what reason or reasons?

8-21. Name at least five major components of the WPI and CPI indexes. What important specific price trend is not included in WPI or CPI, but is included in GNPI? Why is this component index of GNPI important to accounting?

8-22. Give a summary description of the WPI, CPI, and GNPI indexes for each of the features listed below:
(a) Age
(b) Type of formula
(c) Universe
(d) Sample size
(e) Weight
(f) Compiler
(g) Frequency of updating
(h) Base period

8-23. "The present indexes are unable to cope with the dynamics of supply and demand." Explain the meaning of this statement.

8-24. Summarize the effects of holding monetary items in:
(a) periods of rising prices
(b) periods of falling prices

8-25. In a year after year adjustment of comparative financial data, which method—constant or current—involves more computations? Why?

8-26. "Firms with high ratios of depreciable assets are more affected by price-level changes than firms with low ratios." Why?

8-27. ***ARGUMENTS FOR AND AGAINST PRICE-LEVEL ADJUSTMENTS*** A common objective of accountants is to prepare meaningful financial statements. To attain this objective many accountants maintain that the financial statements must be adjusted for changes in price-level. Other accountants believe that financial statements should continue to be prepared on the basis of unadjusted historical cost.

Required:

(a) List arguments for adjusting financial statements for changes in price-level.
(b) List the arguments for preparing financial statements on only the basis of unadjusted historical cost.
(c) In their discussions about accounting for changes in price-levels and the methods of measuring them, uninformed individuals have frequently failed to distinguish between adjustments for changes in the price-levels of specific goods and services and adjustments for changes in the general purchasing power of the dollar. What is the distinction? Which are "price-level adjustments"? Discuss.

(From the CPA exam.)

8-28. ***PRICE-LEVEL ADJUSTMENT*** Consider the following sales data:

	19x1	19x2	19x3	19x4	19x5
Sales	$16,200	$18,400	$18,600	$19,800	$21,000
Unadjusted increase in sales	—	2,200	200	1,200	1,200
Index	98.6	100.8	102.7	102.9	104.2

Required:

(a) What is the real change in sales each year in terms of 19*x*3 dollars?
(b) What is the real change in sales each year in current dollars?

8-29. ***PRICE INDEXES*** Assume there are only three commodities. The quantities and prices of each for 1960, 1966, and 1972 are as follows:

	Fixed Period 1960		Base Period 1966		Current Period 1972	
Commodity	Quantity	Price	Quantity	Price	Quantity	Price
A	40	4.20	60	4.90	70	5.80
B	120	12.00	200	14.70	300	20.05
C	60	.86	90	1.10	80	1.85

Required:

Compute price indexes for 1960, 1966, and 1972 using a:

(a) Laspeyres formula
(b) Paasche formula
(c) Fisher formula
(d) Fixed-weight formula

8-30. ***ADJUSTMENT OF DEPRECIATION EXPENSE*** Consider the following data:
Unadjusted Depreciation Expense for 1969 = $89,000
Composition of Fixed Assets (all use straight-line deprec.):

	Date Purchased	Cost	Estimated Life
Machine 1	1952	$440,000	20 years
Machine 2	1958	560,000	16 years
Machine 3	1966	320,000	10 years

Required:

Compute the adjusted (in current dollars) depreciation expense for 1969 using the GNP indexes in Exhibit 8-1 and an ending index for 1969 of 130.0.

8-31. ***ADJUSTMENT OF INVENTORY*** Assume the following cost of goods schedule:

Inventory, Jan. 1, 1969	$ 134,500
Purchases	1,787,000
Goods available for sale	1,921,500
Inventory, Dec. 31, 1969	163,400
Cost of goods sold	$1,758,100

Required:

For each of the following questions, use the GNP indexes of Exhibit 8-1 and an ending index for 1969 of 130.0.

(a) Assuming the inventory pricing method is LIFO, and the beginning inventory consists of $24,000 at 1960 prices, $83,000 at 1964 prices, and $27,500 at 1968 prices, prepare an adjusted cost of goods sold schedule.

(b) Assuming the inventory pricing method is FIFO, prepare an adjusted cost of goods sold schedule.

(c) Assuming the inventory pricing method is weighted average, prepare an adjusted cost of goods sold schedule.

8-32. ***PRICE-LEVEL ADJUSTMENTS*** Skadden, Inc., a retailer, was organized during 1966. Skadden's management has decided to supplement its December 31, 1969, historical dollar financial statements with general price-level financial statements. The following general ledger trial balance (historical dollar) and additional information have been furnished:

SKADDEN, INC.
TRIAL BALANCE
DECEMBER 31, 1969

	Debit	Credit
Cash and receivables (net)	$ 540,000	$
Marketable securities (common stock)	400,000	
Inventory	440,000	
Equipment	650,000	
Equipment—accumulated depreciation		164,000
Accounts payable		300,000
6% First mortgage bonds, due 1987		500,000
Common stock, $10 par		1,000,000
Retained earnings, December 31, 1968	46,000	
Sales		1,900,000
Cost of sales	1,508,000	
Depreciation	65,000	
Other operating expenses and interest	215,000	
	$3,864,000	$3,864,000

(a) Monetary assets (cash and receivables) exceeded monetary liabilities (accounts payable and bonds payable) by $445,000 at December 31, 1968. The amounts of monetary items are fixed in terms of numbers of dollars regardless of changes in specific prices or in the general price-level.

(b) Purchases ($1,840,000 in 1969) and sales are made uniformly throughout the year.

(c) Depreciation is computed on a straight-line basis, with a full year's depreciation being taken in the year of acquisition and none in the year of retirement. The depreciation rate is 10% and no salvage value is anticipated. Acquisitions and retirements have been made fairly evenly over each year and the retirements in 1969 consisted of assets purchased during 1967 which were scrapped. An analysis of the equipment account reveals the following:

Year	Beginning Balance	Additions	Retirements	Ending Balance
1967	—	$550,000	—	$550,000
1968	$550,000	10,000	—	560,000
1969	560,000	150,000	$60,000	650,000

(d) The bonds were issued in 1967 and the marketable securities were purchased fairly evenly over 1969. Other operating expenses and interest are assumed to be incurred evenly throughout the year.

(e) Assume that Gross National Product Implicit Price Deflators (1958 = 100) were as follows:

Annual Averages		Index	Conversion Factors (1969 4th Qtr. = 1.000)
1966		113.9	1.128
1967		116.8	1.100
1968		121.8	1.055
1969		126.7	1.014
Quarterly Averages			
1968	4th	123.5	1.040
1969	1st	124.9	1.029
1969	2nd	126.1	1.019
1969	3rd	127.3	1.009
1969	4th	128.5	1.000

Required:

(1) Prepare a schedule to convert the equipment account balance at December 31, 1969, from historical cost to general price-level adjusted dollars.

(2) Prepare a schedule to analyze in historical dollars the equipment—accumulated depreciation account for the year 1969.

(3) Prepare a schedule to analyze in general price-level dollars the equipment—accumulated depreciation account for the year 1969.

(4) Prepare a schedule to compute Skadden, Inc.'s general price-level gain or loss on its net holdings of monetary assets for 1969 (ignore income tax implications). The schedule should give consideration to appropriate items on or related to the balance sheet and the income statement.

(From the CPA exam.)

8-33. ***CONSTANT DOLLAR EARNINGS PER SHARE*** To obtain a more realistic appraisal of his investment, Martin Arnett has asked you to adjust certain financial data of the Glo-Bright Company for price-level changes. On January

1, 1969, he invested $50,000 in the Glo-Bright Company in return for 1,000 shares of common stock. Immediately after his investment the trial balance appeared as follows:

	Debit	Credit
Cash and receivables	$ 65,200	
Merchandise inventory	4,000	
Building	50,000	
Accumulated depreciation—building		8,000
Equipment	36,000	
Accumulated depreciation—equip.		7,200
Land	10,000	
Current liabilities		50,000
Capital stock, $50 stated value		100,000
	$165,200	$165,200

Balances in certain selected accounts as of December 31 of each of the next three years were as follows:

	1969	1970	1971
Sales	$39,650	$30,000	$42,350
Inventory	4,500	5,600	5,347
Purchases	14,475	16,350	18,150
Operating expenses (excluding deprec.)	10,050	9,050	9,075

Assume the 1969 price-level as the base year and that all changes in the price-level take place at the beginning of each year. Further assume that the 1970 price-level is 10% above the 1969 price-level and that the 1971 price-level is 10% above the 1970 level.

The building was constructed in 1965 at a cost of $50,000 with an estimated life of twenty-five years. The price-level at that time was 80% of the 1969 price-level.

The equipment was purchased in 1967 at a cost of $36,000 with an estimated life of ten years. The price-level at that time was 90% of the 1969 price-level.

The LIFO method of inventory valuation is used. The original inventory was acquired in the same year the building was constructed and was maintained at a constant $4,000 until 1969. In 1969 a gradual buildup of the inventory was begun in anticipation of an increase in the volume of business.

Mr. Arnett considers the return on his investment as the dividend he actually receives. In 1971 Glo-Bright paid cash dividends in the amount of $8,000.

Required:

(a) Compute the 1971 earnings per share of common stock in terms of 1969 dollars.

(b) Compute the percentage return on investment for 1969 and 1971 in terms of 1969 dollars.

(From the CPA exam.)

8-34. ***PRICE-LEVEL ADJUSTMENT OF FINANCIAL STATEMENTS*** Consider the following financial information for the Baxter Corporation:

(a) Sales and purchases were uniform throughout the year.

(b) FIFO inventory costing is used.

(c) The physical assets cost $260,000 and had an estimated life of twenty years.

(d) Dividends were paid on December 31 of each year.

COMPARATIVE INCOME STATEMENTS

	1972		1973	
Sales		$1,200,000		$1,550,000
Cost of goods sold:				
Beginning inventory	180,000		240,000	
Purchases	860,000		1,020,000	
Goods available for sale	1,040,000		1,260,000	
Less: ending inventory	240,000	800,000	190,000	1,070,000
Gross profit		400,000		480,000
Expenses:				
Selling	290,000		310,000	
Administrative	37,000		41,000	
Depreciation	13,000	340,000	13,000	364,000
Net operating income		60,000		116,000
Income tax (40%)		24,000		46,400
Net income after taxes		$36,000		$69,600

COMPARATIVE STATEMENTS OF RETAINED EARNINGS

	1972	1973
Retained earnings, January 1	$141,350	$134,850
Add: Net income after taxes	36,000	69,000
	177,350	204,450
Less: Dividends paid	42,500	48,000
Retained earnings, December 31	$134,850	$156,450

COMPARATIVE BALANCE SHEETS

	1971	1972	1973
ASSETS:			
Cash	$ 16,400	$ 13,000	$ 32,500
Receivables	98,270	111,890	154,720
Investments	50,000	40,000	60,000
Inventory	180,000	240,000	190,000
Physical assets (net)	195,000	182,000	169,000
Total assets	$539,670	$586,890	$606,220
LIABILITIES:			
Current	48,320	72,040	69,770
Long-term	70,000	100,000	100,000
STOCKHOLDERS' EQUITY:			
Capital stock (28,000 shares at $10/share)	280,000	280,000	280,000
Retained earnings	141,350	134,850	156,450
Total equities	$539,670	$586,890	$606,220

Assume the following index values:

At start of business: 100

1969 – 1st Quarter: 108

1971 – 4th Quarter: 115 1971 – average: 114

1972 – 4th Quarter: 122 1972 – average: 120

1973 – 4th Quarter: 130 1973 – average: 126

Required:

(1) Compute the purchasing power gain or loss for 1972 and 1973, using 1973 prices.
(2) Adjust all comparative statements in terms of 1973 prices.
(3) Compute the average unadjusted and adjusted return on stockholders' investment for 1972 and 1973 (use 1973 prices for adjusting).
(4) Compute the unadjusted and adjusted book value per share for 1972 and 1973 (use 1973 prices for adjustment). What is the net gain or loss on stockholders' investment?

UNIT III

ACCOUNTING INFORMATION FOR RESOURCE MANAGEMENT

A *resource* is any supply that will meet a need. In accounting terminology, *resource* is often restrictively defined as an asset,[1] that is, any physical object (tangible) or right (intangible) having money value. From an information system's viewpoint, we seek a broader definition: any supply upon which the firm may draw to meet its objectives.

In this unit, we are concerned with resources that are commonly accounted for in the management of business enterprises: financial, equity, operating, credit, and personnel. In terms of the balance sheet equation, A = E, equities (creditors' and owners') provide resources, while assets are the form in which resources are held or deployed.

These resource functions are like sub-systems because they are contained within and interact with the accounting information system. They are systems in that each type of resource has its own cycle and conforms to the basic model of input, transformation, output, feedback, and control. They are interrelated sub-systems in that they interface to provide data needed for economic decisions. For example, if management requires inventory, it could draw upon (alter the form of) an existing resource, as when inventory is purchased for cash:

[1]Eric L. Kohler, *A Dictionary for Accountants*, 3rd ed. (Englewood Cliffs, N.J.: Prentice-Hall, Inc., 1963), p. 428.

Debit: Inventory
Credit: Cash

or it could utilize credit for this purpose:

Debit: Inventory
Credit: Accounts payable

Management decisions are needed to determine the form in which resources are held. For example, if a business enterprise is formed with an owner's equity of $100,000, this sum is distributed among several asset accounts in order to have an operating business. A portion will be retained in cash, some in inventory, some in the form of fixed assets, and so forth. The ratio (or portfolio) in which resources are held can have vital importance to the efficiency and profitability of the enterprise.

Under this viewpoint, the balance sheet is a financial statement which shows the form in which resources are held (with an economic valuation), and the source from which they were obtained. Of course it is impossible, for practical purposes, to attempt to match specific sources with specific uses. Sources may be viewed as inputs to a melting pot, and uses as products from the pool:

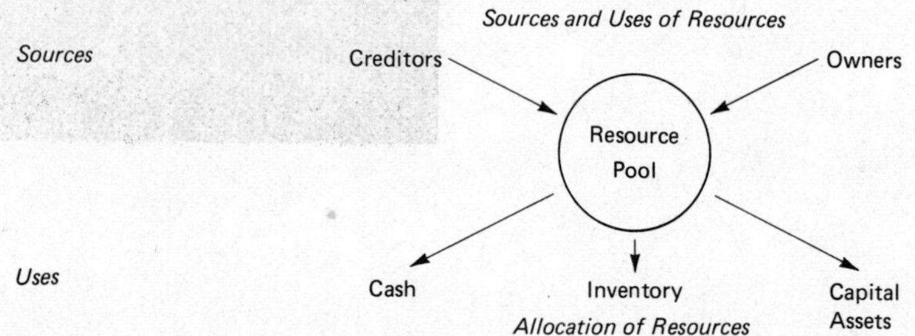

This viewpoint is admittedly different from the legalistic one in which resources are defined as assets, liabilities as claims against assets, and owners' equity as a residual interest in assets.[2] While we cannot deny that a legal obligation attaches to liabilities, this legalistic viewpoint places the emphasis on a relationship of secondary importance. The purpose of acquiring business resources is not to turn about and pay them out immediately to creditors and owners, but rather to consume them in the production of income, in which case more than the original inputs by creditors (the repayment includes interest) and owners (including dividends and retained earnings) is returned to them. If it were not for this expectation, there would be no creditors or stockholders. This view of creditors and owners as originators or investors in resources is not only more useful from a system's planning and operating viewpoint, but it also accords more closely with the going-concern assumption.

Financial resources include cash and cash equivalent assets. These resources contribute current operating capital and provide liquidity. *Capital equity* refers to the contributed and earned capital of stockholders, realized or potential. These accounts measure the extent of the investment of owners in the enterprise as a going concern

[2]Robert T. Sprouse and Maurice Moonitz, *A Tentative Set of Broad Accounting Principles for Business Enterprises,* Accounting Research Study No. 3 (New York: American Institute of Certified Public Accountants, 1962).

and the owners' residual interest in the assets in the event of dissolution, liquidation, or sale. *Credit* relates to receivables and payables transactions in which there is a delayed exchange of money, as well as creditor funding of current operations or capital (long-term) needs. Long-term credit is most often treated as part of the "capitalization" of the firm and we will adhere to that convention in this text. In this unit we also discuss accounting information as it relates to the management of *inventory* and *long-lived assets.*

CHAPTER

9

THE MANAGEMENT OF INVESTED CAPITAL

9.1 THE NATURE OF INVESTED CAPITAL

Economists define capital as (1) one of the factors of production, that is, goods produced by man and used for his consumption or in further production; or (2) wealth employed with a productive intent (more specifically, where an investment is made with the expectation of receiving a money income that exceeds the value of the investment).

Our use of the word *capital* conforms to the second definition. Accordingly, capital is wealth invested or held in an organization to assure its continuity for the benefit of investors. By *wealth* we refer to cash or other assets; by *invested* we mean a direct contribution of wealth, as well as capital that results when profits are "held" or retained by a firm: and by *continuity* we mean that wealth provided as capital is for the permanent or long-term endowment of the firm. Capital may come from *owners* or from *long-term creditors,* as we shall see later.

Basically, capital is viewed as a means for financing the operating assets of an organization. *Operating assets* are all assets other than intangible assets.

Capital is exercised through the employment of operating assets in the production and sale of goods and services. The ratio in which capital is distributed among the operating asset accounts (the asset portfolio question) is of great significance to the successful conduct of an enterprise. For example, the ratio of capital held in the form of cash, accounts receivable, merchandise inventory, or fixed assets has an important influence on earnings and on liquidity (the ability to meet obligations as they become due).

EXHIBIT 9-1 CAPITAL RESOURCE CYCLE

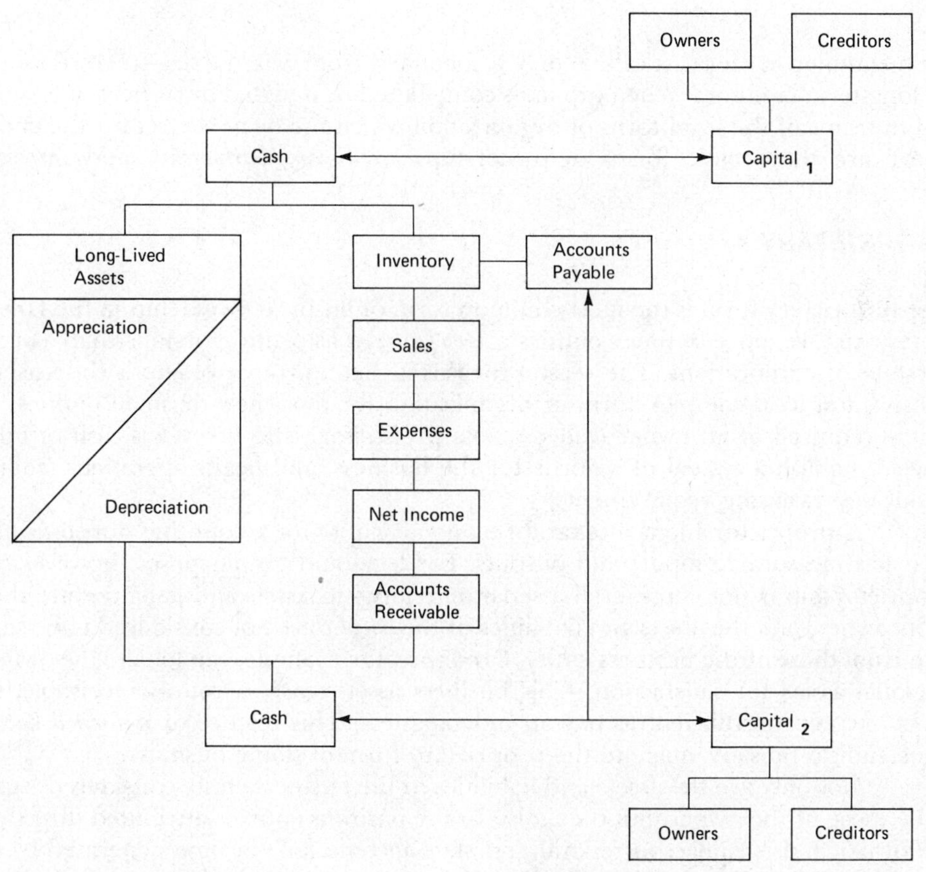

9.2 THE CAPITAL INVESTMENT

Capital is invested with expectation of a money return. This relationship is referred to as *return on investment.* Essentially return on investment (ROI) is computed by this formula:

$$R_i = \frac{I}{C}$$

where

R_i = return on investment
I = net income
C = capital invested

Capital investment in operating assets until its recovery through operations constitutes the capital resource cycle. This cycle is detailed in Exhibit 9-1. Exhibit 9-1 illustrates an important characteristic of the capital cycle; that is, that *real* return on investment includes *appreciation* in long-lived assets in addition to net income. This viewpoint accords with the Hicksian theory of *economic income* discussed in chapter 5.

9.3 TYPES OF CAPITAL INVESTMENT

We mentioned earlier that capital may be obtained from two sources—(1) owners and (2) long-term creditors. When capital is contributed or invested by owners, it is classified in terms of the legal form of organization which the owners elect for the entity. There are three basic forms of ownership: *proprietary, partnership,* and *corporate.*

PROPRIETARY

The proprietary form is the most common form of business ownership in the United States;[1] that is, more business entities are organized as proprietorships than as partnerships or corporations. The reason for this is that a proprietorship is the least expensive and least complex form of organization for most new or small entities. All that is required of an owner (called a sole proprietor) is to invest his cash or other assets, establish a system of records for the business, and begin operations (subject to business licensing requirements).

A proprietorship is a separate economic entity for accounting purposes; that is, it has measurable inputs and outputs. For legal and tax purposes, however, the proprietorship is not considered a separate entity—its assets and liabilities are those of its owner; and the assets and liabilities of the owner are not considered to be separate from those of the business entity. Creditors, for example, can look to the owner's personal assets for satisfaction if his business assets (cash, accounts receivable, fixtures, etc.) are insufficient to pay an indebtedness. This feature of *unlimited liability* is a significant disadvantage to the proprietary form of doing business.

Not only are the assets and liabilities of the business entity considered legally to be those of the owner, but the *income* of the business entity is attributed directly to the owner and is subject to federal and state income tax. Income generated by the entity is taxed to the owner regardless of whether he withdraws the income from the business or retains it as additional capital.

PARTNERSHIP

Often firms are formed by two or more individuals, and one form of multiple ownership is the partnership. Here, as with the proprietorship, the entity concept has not

[1]The U.S. Department of Commerce reports the following statistics on proprietorships, partnerships, and corporations registered in the United States in a recent year:

Form of Entity	Number	Gross Sales (in millions)
Proprietorship	9,142,000	$176,205
Partnerships	949,000	77,047
Corporations	1,074,000	772,915

changed; the partnership has its measurable inputs and outputs, and is otherwise considered a separate economic entity for accounting purposes. But again for legal and tax purposes, no entity is recognized. Creditors of a partnership may sue the partners *jointly* (as a group of partners) or *severally* (each partner individually). A partnership also has the negative feature of *unlimited liability.*[2] The personal assets of the partners may be attached in satisfaction of a creditor's claim where the assets of the partnership have been exhausted.

The legal life of a partnership terminates upon the admission or retirement of any partner. For example, if one partner dies, a partnership ceases. Although business operations may continue, even under an existing name, it does so under the form of a new partnership. The estate of the deceased partner joins the surviving partner(s) as a co-owner of the entity. The partnership interest may be willed to the deceased's heir(s), purchased by remaining partner(s), or sold to a new partner, according to the terms of the *partnership agreement.*

The laws of most states require that certain businesses be of the partnership form.[3] Generally these are professional groups—doctors, lawyers, and accountants. The largest accounting firms in the United States, for example, have two to three hundred partners. The death or disability of a partner in such large organizations does not impede the orderly flow of business, and in these cases the limited life concept has little practical significance.

As with the sole proprietorship, a partnership is not taxed as an entity; its income is taxed to the partners individually in terms of the ratio in which they share income. Again, this income to the partners is taxed whether or not they withdraw it.

CORPORATION

The corporate form of business derives its authority by state charter. Of the three types of ownership it alone is considered an entity separate from its owners for legal and tax purposes[4] as well as for accounting purposes. As such, the corporate form affords to its owners the benefits of limited liability. Unlike a proprietorship or partnership, shareholders (owners) of a corporation cannot be sued by creditors except in certain cases.[5] Unlike the other forms of business organization, a corporation's life is not affected by the death or disability of any of its owners.

As evidence of ownership, sole proprietors have all assets recorded in their names; partners have a written agreement which provides that title to assets be in the

[2]In a limited partnership, partners who are not active in managing the entity may have limited liability. But in a limited partnership there must always be at least one *general partner* whose personal liability is not limited.

[3] California Senate Bill 53, effective November 13, 1968, provides for the incorporation of dentists, physicians, and attorneys. Other states have adopted or are considering similar measures.

[4]The business as an entity in accounting, at law, and for tax purposes is summarized as follows:

	Accounting	Law	Tax
Proprietorship	Yes	No	No
Partnerships	Yes	Either	No
Corporations	Yes	Yes	Yes

[5]For example, when stockholders pay less than the "par" value of stock a *discount liability* results. In the event of liquidation, creditors may recover from stockholders personally a settlement equal to the discount liability.

names of partners individually or in the name of the partnership. Owners in a corporation have certificates called *shares of stock* as evidence of their ownership. Stock may be of two types: *preferred* and *common.*

9.4 TYPES OF CAPITAL STOCK

As the term suggests, preferred stock has certain priorities over common stock. Preferred stockholders are generally entitled to receive dividends, should any be declared, before dividends are distributed to holders of common stock. Preferred stockholders also have priority over common stockholders in the event of the liquidation of a corporation.

CUMULATIVE OR NONCUMULATIVE PREFERRED STOCK

Preferred stock may possess one or several distinctive features. It may be *cumulative* or *noncumulative.* If dividends are not declared in one or more years and payment of dividends is then resumed, holders of cumulative preferred stock are entitled to receive dividends for the year(s) in which no dividends were paid before there is any dividend distribution to common stockholders. Noncumulative preferred stock does not carry the provision for retroactive dividends.

PARTICIPATING OR NONPARTICIPATING PREFERRED STOCK

Preferred stock may be *participating* or *nonparticipating.* Preferred stock generally specifies a stated return or dividend on the certificate. For example, an issue of preferred stock may be titled: "5% cumulative participating preferred stock, $100 par value." This caption means that the holder of one share is entitled to a $5 dividend if one is declared (that is, 5% of the $100 par value of the stock). The *participating* feature means that after receiving the stated dividend, the stockholder has the right to participate to some degree with common stockholders in the distribution of dividends that remains after having satisfied the claims of the preferred stockholders. If the stock is *nonparticipating* the stockholders are limited to the return specified on the certificate.

NONVOTING AND CONVERTIBLE PREFERRED STOCK

Preferred stockholders are generally not entitled to vote in corporate matters; that is, their stock is *nonvoting.* In a sense preferred stockholders are similar to long-term creditors, who also have no voice in the management of a corporation and whose return on investment is limited to a specified interest rate. But preferred stockholders differ from long-term creditors in that the latter have claims on the firm that must be paid, while the corporation has no obligation to repay the capital invested by preferred stockholders. A corporation, however, usually reserves the right to recall (call or redeem) preferred stock on agreed terms, or give the holder the option to "convert" his preferred for common stock. Preferred stock containing this option is referred to as *convertible preferred stock.*

COMMON STOCK

By contrast, holders of *common* stock are not limited to a fixed dividend based upon a percentage of the face value of their stock. Also, voting rights generally attach to common and not to preferred stock. The right to vote is usually based on one vote per share of common stock. Common stockholders vote to elect the board of directors and on other matters requiring stockholder approval under state law.

Common stockholders usually have the right (called a "pre-emptive right") to purchase additional shares of stock, each time the corporation offers a new issue, on a pro rata basis with the present number of shares they own. The purpose of the pre-emptive right is to make it difficult for aggressive stockholders to gain control of a corporation by issuing new stock which they alone can purchase.

PAR, NO-PAR, STATED VALUE

When a corporation is formed, its officers file, with the state in which they intend to do business, two basic documents: (1) Articles of Incorporation and (2) By-Laws. The Articles describe the business activities in which the corporation intends to engage, provides information on its principal offices, and sets forth its authorized capital: the types, quantity, and value of preferred and common stock to be issued over the long term. The By-Laws detail the manner in which the corporation intends to conduct its affairs—voting rights of stockholders, types of boards and committees, duties and terms of officers, and so forth.

The clause on authorized capital appears as follows: "the corporation has an authorized capital of 1,000,000 shares of common stock of $10 par value." By *par value* we mean the nominal or face value of each share of stock. Stock that is sold is referred to as *issued* or *outstanding,* and it is customary for a corporation to issue only a part of its authorized capital at a time. It requires a vote of the stockholders, an amendment to the Articles, and approval by the state and, as to public issues, the Securities and Exchange Commission (SEC) to increase authorized capital.

Prior to its repeal in 1966, the federal stock transfer tax levied on the basis of the par value of registered stock caused many companies to set low par values ($10 or less, as opposed to $100) in the early 1900s. Common shares of some mining companies, for example, have par values in the pennies. Since par value and issue price to the public are often different, the par value only confused the prospective investor, particularly where the par value, such as $100, was actually printed on the stock certificate. Printing par value on a stock certificate led many investors to believe that the certificate had an intrinsic value, say $100, when the corporation may have issued it for say $70, and it was trading subsequently on the market at $60. There were other difficulties associated with par value stock:

1. *Discount Liability:* The par value constituted a "legal capital." If the company issued stock at less than par value, say $70, the purchaser was liable contingently for the

discount of $30 to creditors in the event the corporation was unable to meet its debt.

2. *Inflated Exchange Values:* Where the corporation received property in exchange for stock, such as fixed assets, the value of the assets was inflated in order to match the par value of the stock.

In 1912, New York State enacted legislation permitting corporations to issue *no-par* stock. Other states followed the example of New York. *No-par* stock was designed to eliminate the aforementioned problems associated with par value. There would be: (1) no money figure printed on the certificate, (2) no discount liability, (3) less incentive to over-value assets received in exchange for stock, and (4) no distinction between *legal* and *contributed* capital. The perceived problem with *no-par* stock was that it would no longer be necessary to distinguish between capital stock and paid-in premium or discount.

With the issue of par value stock above or below par, the premium or discount is recorded in a separate account. For example, if 100,000 shares of par value $10 are issued for $12, the notation in the balance sheet would be:

Contributed Capital	
Issued and outstanding 100,000 shares @ $10 par value	$1,000,000
Paid-in capital in excess of par value of common stock	200,000

If the shares are issued at $8 instead of par value $10, the notation would be:

Contributed Capital	
Issued and outstanding 100,000 shares @ $10 par value	$1,000,000
Discount on issue of capital stock	(200,000)

Because a premium or discount on the issue of stock may be an important indicator of public acceptance and confidence in a stock offering, most states require that no-par stock be given a *stated value.* Some states require that the entire amount received as stated value stock be credited to the capital stock account, in which case the distinction between capital stock and paid-in premium (or discount) is lost. Other states permit the board of directors to place a stated value on the stock. This value then applies to all shares issued. In this case premium or discount is recognized.

9.5 CAPITAL STOCK ACCOUNTS

The owners' equity (OE) section of the balance sheet recognizes two types of owners' capital: *contributed capital* and *earned capital.*

Contributed capital arises from the exchange of cash or other assets for capital stock. *Earned* capital arises from income generated by the firm net of dividends paid to the stockholders. Earned capital is most often referred to as *retained earnings.* Retained earnings at any given date represents net income earned since the inception of the firm, less cumulative cash and stock dividends issued.

After capital stock is issued originally—excluding subsequent issues—increases or decreases result from the following events:

1. Exercise of stock options, rights, and warrants.
2. Declaration of stock splits, including reverse splits.
3. Declaration of stock dividends.
4. Acquisition and retirement of treasury stock.

EXERCISE OF STOCK OPTIONS, RIGHTS, AND WARRANTS

A corporation may grant an individual the right to acquire shares of the corporation at some future date. When this right is evidenced by a certificate, such a right (and the applicable certificate) is called either a *right* or a *warrant,* depending on the length of the period in which the grantee (recipient of the right) has to exercise it (purchase the stock). These rights or warrants are themselves securities and are bought and sold in a manner similar to regular stock securities.

A *stock option* also involves the right to purchase a specified number of a corporation's shares at a stated price; however, options are not transferable like warrants and rights, but must be exercised by the person named. Options are often granted to officers of a corporation to purchase stock at a price lower than the prevailing or anticipated future price. In addition to the incentive of a lower price, there are also favorable income tax treatments for stock options which qualify under the applicable internal revenue service regulations. Options are said to be *exercised* when the holder purchases stock at the option price.

The difference between the market price and the price at the date of exercise (which is usually higher) can be thought of as additional compensation to the recipient.

STOCK SPLITS

As the market price of shares increases, a point is reached where the price exceeds the optimum trading range (say \$10–\$50 per share), in part because shares are generally traded in lots of 100. In order to bring the market value of the stock back within the optimum trading range and to distribute the stock more widely by having additional shares outstanding, a corporation—with the approval of its shareholders—may elect to *split the stock.* For example, in a 2:1 split, each shareholder receives two shares for each share he owns at the time of the split.

The stock split process is reversed when a corporation wishes to tighten the distribution of its stock or increase its market price. In a *reverse stock split* the number of shares is decreased, and the par or stated value is increased. But the total amount of a corporation's contributed capital has not changed in the process; it is simply divided among more (or fewer) shares.

STOCK DIVIDENDS

Instead of paying dividends in the form of cash, a corporation may elect to employ the funds internally. To give the shareholders some tangible reward the corporation issues a dividend in the form of stock instead of cash. In a *stock dividend,* shares are distributed instead of cash in proportion to the number of shares held by each stockholder on the date on which the stock dividend is declared. Stock dividends may range from 1% to 25% of the number of shares outstanding. When the stock dividend issue is 25% or above, there is a strong presumption of a stock split and the transaction should be treated as such.

It is important to distinguish between a stock dividend and a stock split. Neither increases or decreases owners' equity. However, in the case of a stock dividend, an amount equal to the total dividend is transferred from retained earnings to contributed capital. This transfer is based on an assumption that the shareholders would purchase additional shares if they received a cash dividend instead of a stock dividend.

TREASURY STOCK

When a corporation reacquires its own stock (through purchase or gift) we refer to this stock as *treasury stock.* The principal reasons for acquiring treasury stock are:

1. To reduce the contributed capital of the firm.
2. To use as collateral in acquiring other companies.
3. To use in support of stock options.
4. For resale, to avoid the time and cost of registering new issues.

Treasury stock is purchased either privately (from individual stockholders) or on the open market. Once acquired, it may be retired, held for other uses, or resold. If the stock is retired the transaction is treated as a *reverse* issue, and the appropriate division is made between the par value and any premium or discount.

There are two methods for accounting for treasury stock: the *par value method* and the *cost method.* The cost method is used most often in accounting for *common* treasury stock, while the par value method tends to be used more frequently for *preferred* treasury stock.

The difference between these methods is illustrated as follows.

A corporation has 100,000 shares outstanding with a par value of $10. They were issued for $12 each. And 10,000 shares of treasury stock are acquired for $15 per share. The owners' equity (OE) accounts following the transaction would appear as follows:

Cost Method

100,000 shares of common stock issued and outstanding	$1,000,000
Paid-in capital in excess of par value of common stock	200,000
	$1,200,000
Less: 10,000 shares of treasury stock	150,000
Contributed capital	$1,050,000
Retained earnings[6]	1,000,000
Owners' equity	$2,050,000

[6] Under the laws of certain states, a restriction may be placed on retained earnings equal to the cost of treasury stock. In this case retained earnings would be broken down into two parts:

Retained earnings restricted to treasury stock	$ 150,000
Unrestricted retained earnings	850,000
	$1,000,000

Par Value Method

100,000 shares of common stock issued and outstanding	$1,000,000	
Less: 10,000 shares of treasury stock	100,000	$ 900,000
Paid-in capital in excess of par value of common stock	200,000	
Less: 10,000 shares of treasury stock	20,000	180,000
Retained earnings	1,000,000	
Less: 10,000 shares of treasury stock	30,000	970,000
Owners' equity		$2,050,000

9.6 CAPITAL STOCK TRANSACTIONS ILLUSTRATED

An example of the impact of these transactions on the owners' equity (OE) accounts follows. The example is cumulative.

1. A corporation has an authorized capital of 1,000,000 shares of common stock @ $10 par = $10,000,000.
2. The corporation issues 100,000 shares @ $8 each. Directors receive 10,000 of these shares at no cost. The OE accounts reflect this transaction as follows:

100,000 shares issued & outstanding	$1,000,000
Discount on issue of capital stock	(280,000)
Contributed capital	720,000

Note that cash received was 90,000 shares @ $8 = $720,000. Immediately upon issue the value of a share of stock is

$$\frac{\$720{,}000}{100{,}000} = \$7.20$$

This feature is known as "dilution upon the issue of stock." The extent to which stock is diluted upon issue must be indicated in a company's prospectus.

3. The corporation issues a further 200,000 shares at $15 each. Directors receive 30,000 of these shares at no cost. The cumulative effect on OE accounts is:

300,000 shares issued & outstanding	$3,000,000
Paid-in capital in excess of par value of common stock	270,000
Contributed capital	$3,270,000

Cash proceeds of the second issue were 170,000 shares @ $15 = $2,550,000. This is added to the cash proceeds of $720,000 from the first issue to equal the current contributed capital of $3,270,000.

4. The corporation exercises a 2:1 stock split when the market value of the stock is $20 a share:

Authorized capital is restated to read: 2,000,000 shares of common stock @ $5 = $10,000,000. (Note that the total dollar volume of authorized capital is unaffected.)

OE accounts are affected as follows:

600,000 shares issued and outstanding	$3,000,000
Paid-in capital in excess of par value of common stock	270,000
Contributed capital	$3,270,000

5. The corporation now has *retained earnings* of $2,000,000. It declares a 10% *stock dividend* when the market value is $15:

OE accounts before stock dividend:

600,000 shares issued and outstanding	$3,000,000
Paid-in capital in excess of par value of common stock	270,000
Contributed capital	3,270,000
Retained earnings	2,000,000
Owners' equity	$5,270,000

OE accounts after stock dividend:

660,000 shares issued and outstanding	$3,300,000
Paid-in capital in excess of par value of common stock	870,000
Contributed capital	4,170,000
Retained earnings	1,100,000
Owners' equity	$5,270,000

The 10% is based on the number of shares already outstanding, i.e., .10(600,000). A stock dividend is treated as an *issue* of stock. The issue is for $15 a share × 60,000 shares = $900,000. The journal entry to record this event is:

Debit: Retained earnings	$900,000	
Credit: Shares issued & outstanding		$300,000
Paid-in capital in excess of par value of common stock		600,000

As no cash is involved in a stock option, the transaction consists of a transfer from retained earnings to the contributed capital accounts of an amount equal to the full value of the dividend.

6. The corporation acquires 20,000 shares of its own stock, i.e., *treasury stock* to cover a stock option plan. The market value on the date of acquisition is $20 a share. Following the transaction, the OE accounts are:

660,000 shares issued and outstanding	$3,300,000
Paid-in capital in excess of par value of common stock	870,000
	4,170,000
Less: 20,000 shares held in treasury	400,000
Contributed capital	$3,770,000
Retained earnings	1,100,000
Owners' equity	$4,870,000

(The *cost method* is used in this example.)

7a. The options are exercised when the market value per share is $25.

660,000 shares issued and outstanding	$3,300,000
Paid-in capital in excess of par value of common stock	870,000
Contributed capital	4,170,000
Retained earnings	1,100,000
Owners' equity	$5,270,000

The journal entry to record this transaction is:

Debit: Cash	$400,000	
Credit: Treasury stock		$400,000

In effect the persons holding the options have simply paid the firm the $20 per share needed to exercise the option. The $25 figure has no effect on the accounting system, although it is obvious the beneficiaries gain $5 per share by exercising the option.

7b. Return to instruction 6. The options are not exercised and the period expires. The firm elects to "retire" the treasury stock when the market value is $18. This transaction is in effect a *reverse issue.* Following this event the OE accounts are:

640,000 shares issued & outstanding	$3,200,000
Paid-in capital in excess of par value of common stock	570,000
Contributed capital	3,770,000
Retained earnings	1,100,000
Owners' equity	$4,870,000

7c. Return to instruction 6. The options are not exercised and the firm elects to sell the treasury stock. Net proceeds to the firm equal $22 per share. The journal entry to record this transaction is:

Debit: Cash	$440,000	
Credit: Treasury stock		$400,000
Gain on sale of treasury stock		40,000

OE accounts after this transaction are:

660,000 shares issued and outstanding	$3,300,000
Paid-in capital in excess of par value of common stock	870,000
Contributed capital	4,170,000
Retained earnings	1,140,000
Owners' equity	$5,310,000

The net effect of the gain on sale of treasury stock is to increase retained earnings. This gain would appear as an extraordinary item in the income statement and enter retained earnings as part of the normal income measurement process.

9.7 TYPES OF LONG-TERM DEBT

Capital derives not only from owners, but also from long-term creditors. By *long-term* we mean that the obligation matures after one year or one operating cycle of the firm, whichever period is longer.

Capital supplied by creditors, unlike that of owners, is borrowed and must be repaid. In addition to repaying the amount borrowed, the firm generally pays interest for the use of the borrowed funds. Long-term debt usually takes the form of bonds, long-term notes payable, or mortgages.

Long-term debt instruments are contracts which acknowledge the nature of the debt and detail the terms of interest and repayment of capital (principal). Bonds, however, are usually issued in standard units having a face value of $1,000 each, while notes are written for any sum.

Bonds are of two basic types: *secured* and *unsecured.* Secured bonds contain a claim on some type of *collateral,* usually property owned by the corporation, such as the rolling stock of railroads, or corporate real estate. This collateral right (called a *mortgage*) entitles the creditor to take the mortgaged property in satisfaction of the indebtedness. Unsecured bonds are called *debentures,* and their repayment rests upon the general credit of a corporation.

Bonds may contain a feature which eliminates the need for repayment; that is, a *conversion* feature. Convertible bonds may be exchanged for the corporation's capital stock, at the option of the bondholder, at specified dates and prices.

9.8 PROCESSING CAPITAL TRANSACTIONS

INPUT

The principal inputs of the capital equity cycle and related transaction documents are outlined in Exhibit 9-2. These documents provide evidence that accounting events involving capital have occurred and signal the accounting system to admit and process this information. For example, the receipt of owners' capital in the form of cash or other assets is recognized by issuing a stock *certificate;* whereas the receipt of creditors'

EXHIBIT 9-2 MAJOR CAPITAL INPUTS AND DOCUMENTS

EVENT	TRANSACTION DOCUMENTS	
	Owners' Capital	**Creditors' Capital**
A. Capital resources are received in the form of cash or other assets.	*Certificate* (issued in exchange for resources acquired—see stock register) a. Common shares b. Preferred shares	*Note* (issued in exchange for resources received) a. Notes payable b. Mortgages payable c. Bonds payable
B. Capital resources are relocated.	*Certificate* (issued for stock dividend or stock split)	*Note* (new note to replace existing note upon refunding) *Certificate* (issued when long-term debt is converted to capital stock)
C. Capital resources are decreased.	*Check* (treasury stock is acquired or cash dividends are paid)	*Check* (payment on debt is made)

capital in the form of cash or other assets is recognized by issuing a *note* (unsecured or secured by a mortgage, trust deed, or bond).

Similarly, the relocation of owner's capital is evidenced by the exchange of certificates, as in the case of stock splits and stock dividends. If existing creditors' capital is reformed, a new note is issued to retire the old one. Where creditors' capital is exchanged for owners' capital, as in the case of exercising a convertible bond, a certificate replaces the note. The opposite is true where owners' capital is converted into creditors' capital.

A check is the principal evidence for a decrease in capital. It is used to acquire treasury stock, pay dividends, and retire creditors' capital.

TRANSFORMATION$_1$

Establishing duality (or the cause-and-effect relationship) of capital transactions is the function of T_1. Typical T_1 capital entries for owners' events are shown in Exhibit 9-3 and for creditors' events in Exhibit 9-4.

There is a need to elaborate the T_1 process where: (1) there are numerous transactions involving only a few accounts; (2) there is a need for interim output from the accounting system; or (3) there are legal requirements that call for the maintenance of certain records.

The first need is met by using special journals (such as the *cash receipts* and *cash payments* journals referred to in chapter 4) to record the many detailed transactions involving (in this case) cash and the other accounts used most frequently in receiving and paying cash. Instead of posting each transaction to the ledger (the T_2 process), only totals from the special journals are posted.

Direct output (reports) from the accounting system may be required at T_1, as for example a daily report showing cash receipts, hours worked, sales, or the number of items in inventory. This output is for internal management purposes, but the data is retained in the system for further processing through T_2 and inculcation into other management reports and the financial statements.

Then there are legal requirements, which call for the maintenance of special T_1 records involving certain types of transactions. Accounting for capital is a case in point. Corporations that list their stock on securities exchanges are required by law to maintain a record of stock transactions and to employ the services of an *independent registrar.* The registrar's function is to protect stockholders against the fraudulent issue of stock certificates. Hence a certificate only becomes valid after it has been countersigned by the registrar. Before signing the certificate the registrar must be satisfied that the certificate is issued in accord with the articles and by-laws of a corporation, and has proper approval of its board of directors. He can approve new certificates up to the maximum number of shares authorized, or upon the surrender of old certificates, as in the case of certificates traded or treasury stock acquired.

Certificates are published by banknote companies in a format similar to checks—each certificate has a stub. On the stub is entered the information on the certificate (number, name of person to whom issued, and number of shares issued), and such additional information as the number of shares surrendered or issued previously.

The task of maintaining records on the details of current capital ownership is often delegated by a corporation to an authorized *transfer agent* (often a bank) who

EXHIBIT 9-3 THE DUALITY OF SOME TYPICAL OWNERS' CAPITAL EVENTS

Event	Transaction Document	(4) Date	Notation	(1) Doc. Code	(2) Trans. Code	(3) Acct. Code	Duality Instruction: Accounts	Amount: Debit	Amount: Credit
A. Capital resources are received from owners.	Certificate		a. Stock certificate(s) (common or preferred) issued in exchange for cash received.		10 10	11110 31120	Cash Capital Stock (common)	10,000	 10,000
	Certificate		b. Stock certificate(s) (common or preferred) issued in exchange for real property acquired.		10 10	12110 31120	Land Capital Stock (common)	90,000	 90,000
B. Capital resources from owners are relocated.	Certificate		c. Stock certificate(s) issued to existing shareholders as a distribution of earnings (stock dividend).		12 10	31210 31120	Retained Earnings Capital Stock	5,000	 5,000
	Certificate		d. Certificate(s) issued depending on ratio of stock split and number of shares held.			31120 31120	Capital Stock (original no. of shares and amount) Capital Stock (new shares and new par value)	-0-	 -0-
C. Capital resources are decreased.	Check		e. Outstanding shares are purchased (treasury stock) from shareholders and held for cancellation or future use.		10 12	31170 11110	Treasury Stock Cash	5,000	 5,000
	Adjustment		f. Cash dividends are declared.		12 10	31210 21530	Retained Earnings Dividends Payable	1,000	 1,000

EXHIBIT 9-4 THE DUALITY OF SOME TYPICAL CREDITORS' CAPITAL EVENTS

				Duality Instruction					
								Amount	
Event	Transaction Document	Date	Notation	Doc. Code	Trans. Code	Acct. Code	Accounts	Debit	Credit
A. Capital resources are received from creditors.	Note		g. Bond(s) secured by a long-term note payable is issued in exchange for cash received.		10	11110	Cash	10,000	
					10	21650	Long-term Liabilities (Bonds Payable)		10,000
	Note		h. Mortgage or trust deed secured by a long-term note payable is issued in exchange for land acquired.		10	12110	Land	20,000	
					10	21630	Long-term Liabilities (Mortgage Payable)		20,000
B. Capital resources are relocated.	Certificate(s)		i. Stock certificate(s) is issued in exchange for bonds converted to capital stock.		12	21650	Long-term Liabilities (Bonds)	5,000	
					10	31120	Capital Stock		5,000
C. Capital resources are decreased.	Check		j. Check is issued in repayment of bonds.		12	21650	Long-term Liabilities (Bonds)	2,000	
					12	11110	Cash		2,000
	Check		k. Check is issued for monthly installment (principal and interest) of mortgage payable.		10	80020	Interest Expense	100	
					12	21630	Long-term Liabilities (Mortgage Payable)	300	
					12	11110	Cash		400
							Total	$37,400	$37,400

(1) *Doc. Code: document code* or identification number that provides a trail to the original evidence.

(2) *Trans. code: a transaction code* is an arithmetic instruction that is needed for aggregation at T_2 – 10 = add, 12 = subtract. The $10,000 in event (a) is to be added to the cash account.

(3) *Acct. code:* an *account code* or number identifies the account to which an event is assigned.

(4) We have omitted dates in this example, but each event is dated.

maintains a record of outstanding ownership for dividend and voting purposes and effects transfers of certificates. The same independent party may serve as registrar and transfer agent.

TRANSFORMATION$_2$

The T_2 process (or posting) of the capital events shown in Exhibits 9-3 and 9-4 is illustrated in Exhibit 9-5. The T_2 process is also elaborated where: (1) there are numerous transactions involving certain accounts; (2) accounts change their characteristics frequently; or (3) there is a need for the maintenance of ledger records for legal or management purposes.

EXHIBIT 9-5 POSTING CAPITAL RESOURCE EVENTS TO T-ACCOUNTS

11110 Cash

	Debit		Credit
(a)	$10,000	(e)	$ 5,000
(g)	10,000	(j)	2,000
		(k)	400

31120 Capital Stock (Common)

	Debit		Credit
		(a)	$10,000
		(b)	90,000
		(c)	5,000
		(i)	5,000

12110 Land

	Debit		Credit
(b)	$90,000		
(h)	20,000		

31210 Retained Earnings

	Debit		Credit
(c)	$5,000		
(f)	1,000		

21530 Dividends Payable

	Debit		Credit
		(f)	$ 1,000

31170 Treasury Stock

	Debit		Credit
(e)	$5,000		

21650 Bonds Payable

	Debit		Credit
(i)	$ 5,000	(g)	$10,000
(j)	2,000		

80020 Interest Expense

	Debit		Credit
(k)	$ 100		

21630 Mortgage Payable

	Debit		Credit
(k)	$ 300	(h)	$20,000

Subsidiary ledgers meet the first two needs. For example, a firm with a large number of accounts receivable, the character of which changes rapidly as customers close and open accounts, will maintain a sub-ledger system for this purpose. Where subsidiary ledgers are used, only totals are posted to the general ledger for aggregation and summary. One purpose of a subsidiary ledger is to keep excess detail out of the general ledger; another purpose is to aid in work management, so that one unit of the organization can maintain accounts receivable records, another accounts payable records, and so forth.

The third need is for more information, such as personnel information on wages, leaves, pension plans, health insurance, or bonuses. Such a need exists in accounting for capital. A *stockholder's ledger* in the case of owners' capital, or bond and mortgage records in the case of creditors' capital, serve to keep track of transactions involving individual stockholders and creditors.

OUTPUT

The accounting information system generates various reports on the status of capital accounts. Most of these reports are internal and aid in the process of management planning and control. Reporting on the state of capital is also an integral part of the financial statements. Here, the *status* of capital accounts as of a particular date are disclosed in the balance sheet. *Changes* in owners' capital are shown in another statement known as: (1) statement of changes in capital (for proprietorships and partnerships), or (2) statement of retained earnings (for corporations).

Reporting characteristics in the financial statements for the respective types of organization are illustrated below.

Proprietorship

Assume that Mr. John Stone begins a business on January 1, 19*x*1, by investing capital in the form of cash and long-lived assets. A balance sheet at this point shows the *status* of proprietory capital as follows:

JOHN STONE DBA[7]
STONE DRUG STORE
BALANCE SHEET
JANUARY 1, 19x1

ASSETS		**EQUITIES**	
Current:		Capital	
Cash	$ 5,000	J. Stone	$15,000
Long-lived assets	10,000		
Total assets	$15,000	Total equities	$15,000

During 19*x*1, the business had a net income of $10,000. During the year Mr. Stone withdrew $5,000 from the business for his personal use:

JOHN STONE DBA
STONE DRUG STORE
STATEMENT OF CHANGES IN CAPITAL
FOR THE YEAR ENDED, DECEMBER 31, 19x1

Capital, January 1, 19x1	$15,000
Add: Net income for the year ended, December 31, 19x1	10,000
Total capital available	$25,000
Less: Capital withdrawn by owner for the year ended, December 31, 19x1	$ 5,000
Capital, December 31, 19x1	$20,000

[7] The designation *dba* ("doing business as") is used when a proprietorship or partnership adopts a fictitious name for its business.

The *status* of Mr. Stone's capital at the end of 19*x*1 appears in the owners' equity section of the balance sheet of that date:

EQUITIES

Capital:	
J. Stone	$20,000

Of the $10,000 in net income, Mr. Stone withdrew $5,000 for his personal use; the other $5,000 was "left in the business" and is added to his capital investment.

Partnership

On January 1, 19*x*2, Mr. Stone decides to take on a co-owner, and thus converts the proprietorship into a partnership. The incoming partner purchases a 50% interest in the capital and net income of the business for $15,000.

During 19*x*2 the business earns a net income of $20,000. *Changes* in capital for the year 19*x*2 would be shown as follows:

STONE AND ABLE DBA
STONE-ABLE DRUG COMPANY
STATEMENT OF CHANGES IN CAPITAL
FOR THE YEAR ENDED, DECEMBER 31, 19x2

	Stone	Able	Total
Capital, January 1, 19*x*2	$20,000	$ —	$20,000
Add: Additional investment	—	15,000	15,000
Net income for year ended December 31, 19*x*2 (divided equally)	10,000	10,000	20,000
Total available	$30,000	$25,000	$55,000
Less: Withdrawals (to equalize capital accounts)	15,000	10,000	25,000
Capital, December 31, 19*x*2	$15,000	$15,000	$30,000

Corporation

On January 1, 19*x*3, the partners decided to incorporate the business. They are attracted by the business having a life which is unaffected by a change in ownership, by the limited liability afforded to stockholders, and by the ease with which ownership can be transferred through stock certificates.

They decide to issue no-par common shares, with a stated value of $10 each. If Stone and Able each receive 500 shares for their $15,000 in capital, the owners' equity section of the balance sheet following the issue of capital stock to Stone and Able would show:

EQUITIES

OWNERS' EQUITY

Issued and outstanding		
1,000 shares—common stock @ $10 stated value	$10,000	
Paid-in capital in excess of stated value of common stock	20,000	$30,000

Assume that the corporation earns net income of $40,000 during 19*x*3 and pays $10,000 in dividends. *Changes* in capital for 19*x*3 would be disclosed as follows:

STONE-ABLE DRUG COMPANY, INC.
STATEMENT OF RETAINED EARNINGS
FOR THE YEAR ENDED, DECEMBER 31, 19x3

Retained earnings, January 1, 19*x*3	$ –
Add: Net income for the year ended, December 31, 19*x*3	40,000
Total available	40,000
Less: Dividends paid	10,000
Retained earnings, December 31, 19*x*3	$30,000

The owners' equity section of the December 31, 19*x*3, balance sheet would show the year-end *status* of owners' capital as follows:

OWNERS' EQUITY

Contributed capital:			
Issued and outstanding			
1,000 shares—common stock @ $10 stated value	$10,000		
Paid-in capital in excess of stated value of common stock	20,000	$30,000	
Retained earnings		30,000	$60,000

The financial statements do not disclose *changes* in creditors' capital, but the *status* of the long-term credit accounts (the balances owing) is disclosed in the balance sheet as follows:

LONG-TERM DEBT:

10-year, 5% first mortgage bonds outstanding, due January 1, 1975	$250,000	
Less: Unamortized bond discounts	5,000	
	245,000	
Serial 5% debentures, due June 3, 1972 to June 30, 1982, inclusive	100,000	
Purchase money obligations payable 1972 to 1978	50,000	$395,000

If the debt is to be paid through a sinking fund or is to be retired through refinancing, this type of information should be disclosed in the footnotes to the financial statements.

9.9 SYSTEMS CONTROLS FOR CAPITAL TRANSACTIONS

Stewardship and management controls are present in accounting for capital.

STEWARDSHIP CONTROLS

Stewardship controls are designed to ensure that:

1. Proper authorization exists for all capital transactions, such as:
   a. Issuance of certificates or notes.
   b. Payment of dividends or outstanding debt.
2. Separation of duties exists between the handling of funds and the maintenance of capital records.
3. Recording of capital transactions is in accordance with legal requirements and generally accepted accounting principles.

The use of a *registrar* and stock *transfer agent* in accounting for owners' capital provides for the stewardship controls that are necessary.

Because creditors' capital is usually accounted for internally, various records and procedures are established to maintain a proper stewardship of borrowed capital.

MANAGEMENT CONTROLS

The purpose of *management controls* is to optimize the employment of capital, and accordingly takes into account such considerations as:

1. Having the right amount of capital, so that the organization is neither over- nor under-capitalized.
2. Maintaining an optimum ratio between capital contributed by owners versus creditors.
3. Optimizing the rates and terms of borrowed capital.
4. Optimizing return on investment to owners.

Feedback, as we shall see presently, provides information as to whether or not these objectives are being met.

Optimum Capitalization

What is the right amount of capitalization? Essentially, capital is of a long-term nature; so it follows that *at least* the long-lived assets of a firm should be underwritten by capital. Most organizations are conservative and in addition also underwrite a portion of the current assets with capital equity.

While there is no generally applicable formula for determining the right amount of capital, the essentials of the problem can be structured as follows. Consider the balance sheet of a firm to consist of five parts—(1) current assets, (2) long-lived assets, (3) current liabilities, (4) long-term liabilities, and (5) owners' equity—as shown in Exhibit 9-6.

EXHIBIT 9-6 OPTIMIZING CAPITALIZATION

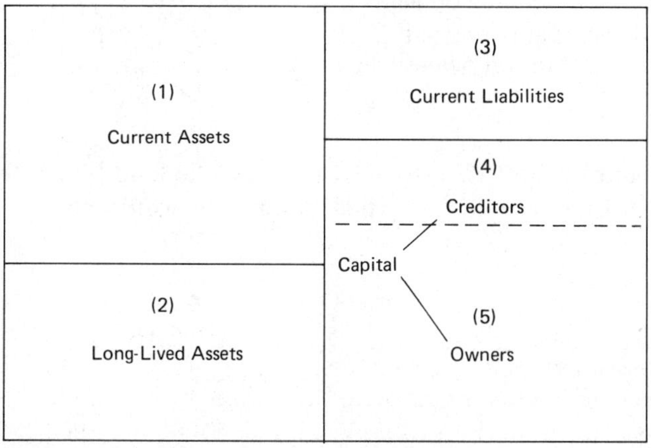

(1)
Current Assets

(2)
Long-Lived Assets

(3)
Current Liabilities

(4)
Creditors

Capital

(5)
Owners

Note in Exhibit 9-6 that capital covers all of the long-lived assets *plus* some of the current assets. Note also that owners contribute more capital than creditors. Say that a firm (A) has a long-lived/current asset ratio of 8:2, while the same ratio for another firm (B) is 2:8. Firm A requires considerably greater capitalization (80%+) than firm B (20% +). The extent to which capitalization exceeds the amount of long-lived assets (the "+" in the above) is based on such factors as risk, the firm's credit reputation, industry practices, undisclosed or understated asset values, or the state of the money market.

The owners in Exhibit 9-6 are shown as contributing more capital than creditors, which is illustrative of the fact that owners are responsible (through their elected officers) for operating the business, while creditors have no such responsibility. Therefore, owners should have sufficient capital invested in the business to repay the creditors fully if operations are not successful. This means that creditors are seldom willing to invest more than owners; so that equity/debt ratios of 7:3 or 6:4 are more common than a ratio of 1:1.

Financial Leverage

The maximum ratio of owners' versus creditors' capital, (say 6:4), is an overall constraint. Within this limit, management must decide on the extent to which it will borrow in terms of both incremental and total debt, and when it should borrow. These considerations are formalized through a procedure known as *financial leverage analysis*.

The basic notion of financial leverage can be grasped quite readily. If 8% can be earned on capital invested, and the interest rate on creditors' capital is 6%, then the 2% difference is additional income to the owners—this is *positive* leverage. On the other hand, if only 6% is earned on capital invested, and the cost of creditors' capital is 8%, then the 2% difference is an additional expense to the owners—this is *negative* leverage. The objective in the management of capital is to maximize positive financial leverage.

Consider this example of financial leverage: X invests $100 of his own funds in a business venture, with the following results:

Net income on sales	$ 10
Amount invested	$100
Return on owner's investment	10%

Encouraged by the 10% return, X induces Y to lend him $900 at 7% interest. If the same net income on sales is earned, the results would be:

	X	Y	X+Y
Net income on sales	$ 10	$ 90	$ 100
Less: Interest expense	–	63	63
Net income after interest expense	$ 10	$ 27	$ 37
Capital invested	$100	900	$1,000
Less: Capital contributed by creditors	–	(900)	(900)
Owner's investment	$100	–	$ 100
Return on owner's investment			37%

There is a 3% difference in what X can earn and the interest he pays Y. This 3% times the amount borrowed from Y (.03 × $900), which is $27, is added to the $10 earned on his $100 investment, to give him a total return of $37 (or 37% of $100). He has not invested any additional funds of his own, but he has used Y's capital to increase the return on his own investment.

A more complicated example follows. A company requires capital of $1,000,000. It may issue 100,000 shares at $10 per share (A), or it may borrow $200,000 of the $1,000,000 and issue stock for the balance (B), or it may borrow $400,000 and issue stock for the balance (C). The interest rate on the borrowed money is 7%. These options may be set forth as follows:

	(A) No Borrowing	(B) 20% Borrowing	(C) 40% Borrowing
Amount of owners' equity	$1,000,000	$800,000	$600,000
Number of shares	100,000	80,000	60,000
Creditors' equity	-0-	200,000	400,000
Interest expense	-0-	14,000	28,000

Earnings per share (EPS)—which is an expression of return on investment to owners—can be computed for various levels of *earnings before interest and taxes* (EBIT) where the interest is as shown above and a tax rate of 50% is assumed:

EBIT	Income After Interest (A)	(B)	(C)	Income After Tax (A)	(B)	(C)	EPS (A)	(B)	(C)
$ 28,000	$ 28,000	$ 14,000	$ –	$14,000	$ 7,000	$ –	$.14	$.09	$ .00
32,000	32,000	18,000	4,000	16,000	9,000	2,000	.16	.11	.03
56,000	56,000	42,000	28,000	28,000	21,000	14,000	.28	.26	.23
70,000	70,000	56,000	42,000	35,000	28,000	21,000	.35	.35	.35
140,000	140,000	126,000	112,000	70,000	63,000	56,000	.70	.79	.93
158,000	158,000	144,000	130,000	79,000	72,000	65,000	.79	.90	1.08

The leverage principle can be emphasized by a graphic illustration, as in Exhibit 9-7.

EXHIBIT 9-7 FINANCIAL LEVERAGE ILLUSTRATED

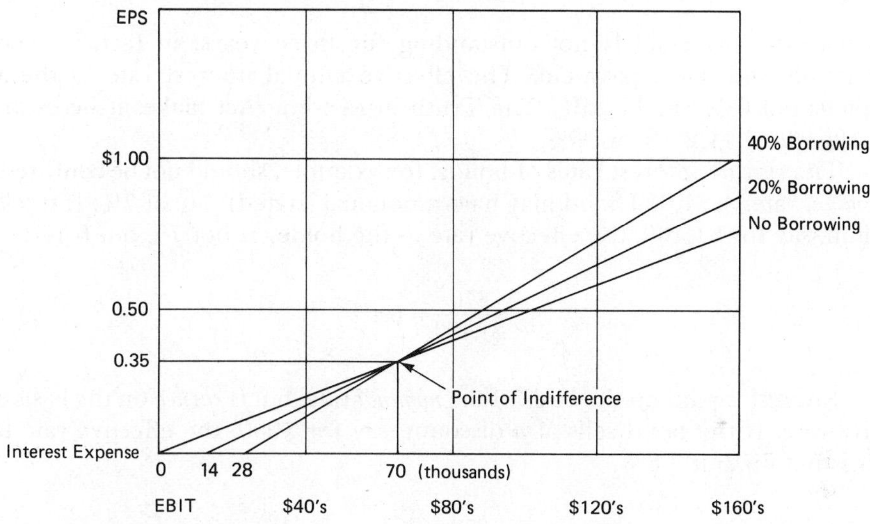

Note that the lines all pass through a common point. This is where EBIT equals the interest rate times the total capital required (.07 × $1,000,000 = $70,000). At this point the return on owners' investment is the same under any leverage option—$.35 per share. In leverage terms, the source of funds at this point is said to be *indifferent.*

Essential variables in the management control of creditors' capital are debt interest rates and terms. We show in chapter 10 how a cash discount expression such as 2/10, n/30 equates with a 36% effective annual interest rate. The Truth in Lending Act now makes it a matter of federal law for lenders to state the cost of credit in terms of an effective annual interest rate. This law should remove much of the confusion concerning interest rates.

Prior to the law, for example, a person seeking a $2,000 automobile loan would be offered (say) a 6% loan requiring payments of $65.56 per month for thirty-six months. The payment was computed as follows:

1st year: .06 × $2,000 = 120_i$
2nd year: .06 × $2,000 = 120_i$
3rd year: .06 × $2,000 = 120_i$

Total 3 years:

$$.18 \times \$2{,}000 = \$360_i + \$2{,}000_p = \$2{,}360_{i+p}$$

where

$$i = \text{interest}$$
$$p = \text{principal}$$

therefore:

$$\frac{2{,}360}{36 \text{ months}} = \$65.56 \text{ per month}$$

Of course, the principal is not outstanding for three years; in fact, it decreases progressively with each payment. The effective annual interest rate in the above example is not 6%, but 11.25%! The Truth in Lending Act makes it necessary for lenders to quote 11.25%, not 6%.

The *effective* interest rates of bonds, for example, should not be confused with the *nominal* rate. A $1,000 bond may have a nominal (stated) rate of 7%. If it sells at a premium, say for $1,100, the effective rate to the holder is not 7% but 6.4%:

$$\frac{\$70}{\$1{,}100} = 6.4\%$$

Interest is paid on the basis of the *nominal* rate, but is *earned* on the basis of the effective rate. If the bond sells at a discount, say for $900, the effective rate to the holder is not 7% but 7.8%.

$$\frac{\$70}{\$900} = 7.8\%$$

Debt terms are also important. For example, a loan may or may not call for periodic payments on principal—the alternative is an interest-only loan with principal all due at a certain date. A loan may secure real or personal property, or it may be given on the basis of the "general credit" of the borrower. A loan may or may not provide for an *acceleration* clause, which means that the entire unpaid balance of principal and interest is immediately payable upon the occurrence of a specified event, such as default on a payment. A loan may or may not provide for an *escalator clause,* which means that the interest rate can change on the basis of economic circumstances. A loan may be restricted to certain uses or it may be unrestricted. These matters are discussed further in chapter 17.

Optimizing Return on Investment

We began this chapter by asserting that owners invest capital in the expectation of making a profit on their investment. A dividend is only one form of return to stockholders; the other is appreciation in the market value of the shares they hold.

Dividends paid by the best-managed corporations (blue-chip), when considered alone, provide an insufficient return on investment; they average about 4 to 5% a year over the long run. If dividend income is the only expectation of the investor, he is advised to avoid the risks of the securities markets and earn 5 to 6% on his investment in a federally insured savings account. Ignoring the motivations of the speculator, increases in market value of shares over the long run is the added incentive to most investors.

Accordingly, return on stockholders' investment calls for a measurement that is broader than that of dividends earned. In fact, the appreciation in market value is a more important consideration than dividends in that it is non-taxable until realized (the shares are sold), and then it is taxed as a capital gain if the shares are held for more than six months. Capital gains tax is 50% of the regular tax rate of the individual to a maximum level of 25% in most cases.

Return on a stockholder's investment should therefore be computed on the basis of dividends received + appreciation in the market value of the shares during the year, or on an average basis over the course of several or many years (see chapter 17).

9.10 SYSTEMS FEEDBACKS FOR CAPITAL TRANSACTIONS

Feedback on capital resource management conforms to the general principles of feedback discussed in chapter 3. Accordingly, feedback furnishes users with (1) exception, (2) control, (3) comparative, and (4) interpretive reports.

As we have discussed previously, any material departure from plan is an *exception,* requiring special attention. Usually the difference between planned and actual results generates exceptions. In the area of capital resources such exceptions can result from the following circumstances:

1. A level of long-term borrowing has been budgeted based upon a planned level of investment in fixed assets (property, plant, and equipment). If the level of expenditures for fixed assets rises, resulting in a lower level of cash than was budgeted originally, an exception report is issued and the firm increases its planned level of long-term borrowing.
2. Suppose that due to market conditions, long-term funds are not available (e.g., a sluggish bond market). This may force the firm to seek funds from owners by selling additional shares of stock, thereby deviating from plans concerning earnings per share, rates of return, and other management control parameters.

Feedback on stewardship and management controls of capital resources can take several forms. Examples of feedback on *stewardship* controls include:

1. Reports detailing (or summarizing) the number of shares issued, the distribution of ownership, number of shares canceled, and other data concerning the exchange of certificates. Similar reports apply to long-term liabilities (e.g., notes and bonds payable).
2. Audit reports (either internal or external) detailing an examination of the stock certificate book and the stockholders' ledger, and examination of the cash system as it relates to the payment of dividends in the case of owners' equity and the payment of principal and interest in the case of creditors' equity.

Feedback on *management* controls include reports on the extent to which capital resources are employed to optimize return on equity and types of equity used to achieve the return. Feedback pinpointing rates of returns may be either *comparative* or *interpretive.*

Since the objective of investing capital resources is to earn a return, appropriate types of feedback on the management of capital resources are various measures of return. These measures are computations made from data contained in the financial statements. Return on investment analysis is discussed in chapter 7.

9.11 SUMMARY

Capital provides the means by which firms are formed and their assets acquired. Capital is supplied by owners and creditors, and in either case, a return on investment is expected. In the case of creditors, the return is expressed as, and limited to, an interest rate. In the case of owners the return is in the form of dividends plus appreciation in the value of shares held.

The principal stewardship controls involve proper authority and record-keeping. These functions are often carried out by independent specialists known as *registrars* and *transfer* agents.

The principal management controls have to do with how capital is raised and at what cost. Financial leverage analysis is a tool for determining an optimum ratio between owners' and creditors' capital.

Feedback on the management of capital provides information on the functioning of related controls and compares, analyzes, and interprets capital resource data in the light of present financial markets, past performance, competition, and management's plans and expectations.

CHAPTER 9 REFERENCES AND ADDITIONAL READINGS

Accounting Principles Board Opinion No. 10, Omnibus Opinion—1966, New York: American Institute of Certified Public Accountants, December 1966.

Accounting Principles Board Opinion No. 12, Omnibus Opinion—1967. New York: American Institute of Certified Public Accountants, December 1969.

Accounting Principles Board Opinion No. 14, Accounting for Convertible Debt and Debt Issued with Stock Purchase Warrants. New York: American Institute of Certified Public Accountants, March 1969.

Accounting Principles Board Opinion No. 15, Earnings per Share. New York: American Institute of Certified Public Accountants, May 1969.

Asher, Leslie I. "Accounting for Stock Ownership. *Management Accountant,* September 1968, pp. 17–22.

Asner, Theodore M. "Convertible Debentures—Tax and Financial Accounting Treatment Today." *The Tax Adviser,* January 1970, pp. 9–16.

Beaver, William H. "Reporting Rules for Marketable Equity Securities." *The Journal of Accountancy,* October 1971, pp. 57–61.

Bird, Francis A., and Jones, Phillip A. "A Decision-Tree Approach to Earnings Per Share." *The Accounting Review,* October 1970, pp. 779–83.

Block, Frank E. "The Place of Book Value in Common Stock Evaluation." *Financial Analysts Journal,* March–April 1964, pp. 29–33.

"Certifying Accountants' Review of Preliminary Proxy Material" (news report). *The Journal of Accountancy,* August 1970, p. 69.

Ellis, Charles D. "New Framework for Analyzing Capital Structure." *The Financial Executive,* April 1969, pp. 75–86.

Elliot, David C. "A New Index of Equity Values." *Financial Analysts Journal,* July 1969, pp. 341–43.

"Exchanges Drop Par Value Rule: Term's Use Depends on State Law" (news report). *The Journal of Accountancy,* August 1964, p. 17.

Hayes, Samuel L., and Reiling, Henry B. "Sophisticated Financing Tool: The Warrant." *Harvard Business Review,* January–February 1969, pp. 137–50.

Herrick, Anson. "Balance Sheet Presentation of Treasury Shares." *The Journal of Accountancy,* April 1963, pp. 74–75.

Imdieke, Leroy F., and Weygandt, Jerry J. "Accounting for that Imputed Discount Factor." *The Journal of Accountancy,* June 1970, pp. 54–58.

Paton, W. A. "Postscript on 'Treasury' Shares." *The Accounting Review,* April 1969, pp. 276–83.

Pfahl, John K.; Crary, David T.; and Howard, R. Hayden. "The Limits of Leverage." *The Financial Executive,* May 1970, pp. 48–56.

Pitt, James F. "Accounting for Reacquired Corporate Shares." *The Footnote,* December 1968, pp. 4–5.

Stephens, Matthew J. "Inseparability and the Valuation of Convertible Bonds." *The Journal of Accountancy,* August 1971, pp. 54–62.

Thompson, Howard E. "Capital Structure Coverage Ratios and the Rate of Return in Public Utilities." *Financial Analysts Journal,* January–February 1972, pp. 69–73.

Traum, Sydney S. "Accounting and Tax Aspects of Issuing Convertible Debenture Bonds." *New York Certified Public Accountant,* December 1967, pp. 931–34.

Waterman, Mervin H. "Capital Sources for Multinational Companies." *The Financial Executive,* May 1968, pp. 25–42.

West, Richard R. "An Alternative Approach to Predicting Corporate Bond Ratings." *Journal of Accounting Research,* Summer 1970, pp. 118–25.

Whitehurst, Frederick D. "The Predictability of Investor Cash Return from Historical Income Trends of Common Stocks." *The Accounting Review,* July 1970, pp. 553–64.

"Why Costs Should Be Assigned to Conversion Value—A Critique of APB Opinion No. 14." *CPA,* October 1970, pp. 826–29.

Young, Allan. "Financial, Operating and Security Market Parameters of Repurchasing." *Financial Analysts Journal,* July–August 1969, pp. 123–28.

CHAPTER 9 QUESTIONS, PROBLEMS, AND CASES

9- 1. What are two economic definitions of *capital?*

9- 2. Distinquish between *economic income* and *accounting income.* If the economic income is greater than the accounting income, what does the difference represent?

9- 3. "The ratio in which capital is distributed among the operating asset accounts is of great significance to the successful conduct of an enterprise." Why?

9- 4. From an economist's viewpoint revenue attaches during production; while from an accountant's viewpoint revenue is earned at the point of sale. Explain each viewpoint. What are some potential problems if the economists' viewpoint were adopted by accountants? What input rule serves as a basis for the accountant's recognition of revenue?

9- 5. What factors probably account for the popularity of the proprietary form of ownership?

9- 6. What factors will terminate a partnership's legal life?

9- 7. "A partnership is not taxed as an entity." How is its income taxed?

9- 8. Distinquish between a *stock split* and a *stock dividend.*

9- 9. What is *treasury stock?*

9-10. Distinquish between:
(a) Cumulative and noncumulative preferred stock
(b) Participating and nonparticipating preferred stock
(c) Nonvoting preferred stock and long-term creditors
(d) Convertible preferred stock and convertible bonds
(e) Secured an unsecured bonds

9-11. What is *positive leverage?* What is *negative leverage?*

9-12. Discuss two reasons for a stock split.

9-13. How does a stock dividend differ from a cash dividend?

9-14. What is a *discount liability?* How can it be avoided?

9-15. When a corporation is formed, what two documents must be filed with the state in which they intend to do business? What information does each document contain?

9-16. What are four difficulties associated with the use of par value stock that can be eliminated through the use of no-par stock?

9-17. Considering the difficulties resulting from the use of par values, why are *stated values* given to no-par stock?

9-18. Why is it desirable to maintain a distinction between capital stock and paid-in premium or discount?

9-19. Explain why stock options can be thought of as representing additional compensation to the recipient.

9-20. In what way does a stock right differ from a stock option? Define each.

9-21. Define or explain the use of the following terms or phrases:
(a) Wealth
(b) Liquidity
(c) Earning power
(d) Appreciation (realized and unrealized)
(e) Revenue
(f) Costs
(g) Expenses
(h) Unlimited liability
(i) Convertible preferred stock
(j) Pre-emptive right
(k) Authorized capital
(l) Inflated exchange value
(m) Contributed capital
(n) Earned capital
(o) Optimum trading range
(p) Collateral
(q) Transaction document
(r) Stockholder's ledger
(s) Acceleration clause
(t) Escalator clause

9-22. Why do corporations sometimes split their stock? What effect does a stock split have on the corporation's contributed capital? Why?

9-23. "It is important to distinquish between a stock dividend and a stock split." Why? What is the criterion used to make the distinction?

9-24. What are four principle reasons for acquiring treasury stock?

9-25. Since common stockholders have "a pre-emptive right," how do you suppose stock option plans work? Under this right, when options are granted to officers of a corporation, must they also be granted to all shareholders? Is treasury stock of importance in this issue?

9-26. How is an optimum capital position determined?

9-27. Indicate whether or not the following types of business entity are considered separate from their owners for accounting, legal, and tax purposes:

	Accounting		Legal		Tax	
	Yes	No	Yes	No	Yes	No
Proprietorships.........						
Partnerships.............						
Corporations............						

9-28. "If treasury stock is acquired for more than the original issue price, the excess reduces the amount of retained earnings." "If treasury stock is acquired for less than the original issue price, the difference between the two amounts is added to additional paid-in capital." Why is there a difference in the accounting treatment?

9-29. What is the function of:
(a) an independent registrar
(b) a transfer agent

9-30. Give two purposes of a subsidiary ledger.

9-31. What output report shows the status of capital? What output reports show the changes in capital of a single proprietor, partnership, and corporation?

9-32. Distinquish between *stewardship* controls and *management* controls. What are each type of controls designed to achieve? Give two examples of feedback on stewardship controls and two examples of feedback on management controls.

9-33. "At least the long-lived assets of a firm should be underwritten by capital." What are five factors that can account for the extent to which capitalization exceeds the amount of long-lived assets?

9-34. Distinquish between the *effective* interest rate of bonds and the *nominal* rate.

9-35. "A dividend is only one form of return to stockholders." What is another? Is this other form more important than dividends? Why?

9-36. A material departure from plan is an *exception*. In the area of capital, what circumstances can produce such exceptions?

9-37. How is book value measured? What does it represent? What are four deficiencies of book value measurement?

9-38. ***OPERATING ASSETS***

(a) Determine the total operating assets from the following balance sheet account balances:

Cash	$ 8,200
Notes receivable...................................	14,300
Accounts receivable	56,870
Marketable securities............................	20,000
Inventory	78,200
Prepaid insurance	1,200
Land	28,000
Buildings (net)	43,000
Equipment & machinery (net)	194,000
Goodwill...	6,000
Patents...	4,500
Copyrights..	2,800
Short-term notes payable......................	30,000
Accounts payable.................................	94,340
Accrued salaries payable.......................	31,230

Long-term notes payable	90,000
Federal income taxes payable	18,100
Common stock (17,000 shares issued and outstanding; $10 par value)	170,000
Retained earnings	23,400

(b) If the net income is $40,200, what is the return on investment? What is the earnings per share?

9-39. ***STOCK SPLIT VERSUS STOCK DIVIDEND*** Suppose the Landell Corporation has 25,000 shares of common stock outstanding. The par value of a share is $12 and the present market value is $32.
(a) If a 1.5:1 split is approved, prepare a journal entry to record the split.
(b) If a 25% stock dividend is distributed, prepare a journal entry to record the dividend.

9-40. ***EARNINGS PER SHARE*** Progresso Corporation has not reported earnings per share data in its annual reports to stockholders in the past. The president requested that you furnish information about the reporting of earnings per share data in the current year's annual report in accordance with generally accepted accounting principles.

Required:

(a) Define the term *earnings per share* as it applies to a corporation with a capitalization structure composed of only one class of common stock and explain how earnings per share should be computed and how the information should be disclosed in the corporation's financial statements.
(b) Discuss the treatment, if any, which should be given to each of the following items in computing earnings per share of common stock for financial statement reporting:
   (1) The declaration of current dividends on cumulative preferred stock.
   (2) The acquisition of some of the corporation's outstanding common stock during the current fiscal year. The stock was classified as treasury stock.
   (3) A two-for-one stock split of common stock during the current fiscal year.
   (4) A provision created out of retained earnings for a contingent liability from a possible law suit.
   (5) Outstanding preferred stock issued at a premium with a par value liquidation right.
   (6) The exercise at a price below market value but above book value of a common stock option issued during the current fiscal year to officers of the corporation.
   (7) The replacement of a machine immediately prior to the close of the current fiscal year at a cost 20% above the original cost of the replaced machine. The new machine will perform the same function as the old machine, which was sold for its book value.

(Adapted from the CPA exam.)

9-41. ***PRICE-EARNINGS RATIO*** If the market value per share is $21, and the net income is $630,000, what is the number of shares outstanding if the price-earnings ratio is 25:1?

9-42. ***T_1 JOURNAL ENTRIES—OWNERS' EVENTS*** Give the T_1 journal entries for each of the following owners' events:
(a) 7,000 shares of $5 par value stock were sold for $18 a share.
(b) A stock dividend of 4,000 shares was declared and paid. The par value is $5 and the market price at date of declaration is $23.

(c) A 3:1 stock split is approved.
(d) A building was acquired in exchange for $10,000 shares of $5 par stock. The market value per share is $15 at the time of exchange.
(e) $17,000 in cash dividends were declared.
(f) 2,000 shares of $5 par common stock was purchased for $27,000 from shareholders and will be held as treasury stock. The stock originally sold for $11 a share.
(g) A stockholder exercised his option to buy 800 shares of $5 par stock for $12 a share.
(h) 10,000 shares of no-par common stock was sold for $30 a share. The stated value is $16 per share.

9-43. ***T_1 JOURNAL ENTRIES—CREDITORS' EVENTS*** Give the T_1 journal entries for each of the following creditors' events:
(a) $100,000 in bonds are converted to 9,000 shares of $10 par value common stock.
(b) Land is acquired by assuming a mortgage debt of $70,000.
(c) $50,000 is borrowed from a local bank and is secured by a 6% note payable in three years.
(d) A year's interest is paid on a $5,000, 6% note.
(e) $5,000 long-term note is repaid.

9-44. ***FINANCIAL LEVERAGE—RETURN ON OWNERS' INVESTMENT*** The Paxton Corporation has a total owners' equity of $134,500 on December 31, 19*x*1. The net income from sales in 19*x*1 is $10,760. If the Paxton Corporation earns the same net income on sales, and each dollar of equity produces the same contribution to sales, what is the return on owners' equity if $80,000 is borrowed at 9% interest? Is positive or negative leverage produced from the borrowing?

9-45. ***FINANCIAL LEVERAGE*** Suppose the Clark Corporation requires additional capital of $500,000. Four plans are available:

Plan A: Issue 25,000 shares at $20 per share.
Plan B: Issue 15,000 shares at $20 per share and borrow $200,000 at 7% interest.
Plan C: Issue 10,000 shares at $20 per share and borrow $300,000 at 6% interest.
Plan D: Borrow $500,000 at 5.5% interest.

The Clark Corporation's present capital structure shows:

6% bonds: $300,000
Common stock (400,000 shares of $10 par stock, issued and outstanding): $4,000,000
Paid-in capital in excess of par: $240,000

Required:

Answer each of the following questions assuming a tax rate of 40%:
(a) If the company expects a net income before interest and taxes of $42,000, which plan should be undertaken if:
(1) earnings per share is to be maximized?
(2) income is to be maximized?

(b) If the company expects a net income before interest and taxes of $650,-000, which plan should be undertaken if:
 (1) earnings per share is to be maximized?
 (2) income is to be maximized?
(c) At what EBIT (earnings before interest and taxes) is the source of funds indifferent? In other words, where the EPS is the same under all leverage options.

9-46. ***EFFECTIVE INTEREST RATE*** Suppose a $200,000 bond has a nominal interest rate of 4%. What is the effective interest rate if:
(a) the bond sells for $160,000
(b) the bond sells for $250,000

9-47. ***PARTICIPATING PREFERRED STOCK*** The Everett Corporation has issued and outstanding 2,000 shares of common stock and 1,000 shares of 4% preferred stock, each with a par value of $100. Retained earnings are $50,000, and the directors declare a $25,000 cash dividend. Record the dividend declaration (for both common and preferred) assuming that:
(a) The preferred stock is cumulative and nonparticipating and there are no dividends in arrears.
(b) The preferred stock is cumulative and participates up to $3 per share above the regular 4% rate. (Participating means that the *remaining cash* after the 4% preferred dividend is subtracted is split among the common and preferred shares, but only up to $3 for the preferred.)
(c) The preferred stock is cumulative and fully participating, and there was no dividend declaration during the previous year. (In this instance, the preferred gets a portion of the remaining cash equally with the common, and with no upper limit.)

9-48. ***DETERMINING NET INCOME*** Finincial data of the Higgins Company include the following:

	December 31	
	1972	1971
Preferred stock, par $100	$ 75,000	$100,000
Common stock, par $10	150,000	100,000
Additional paid-in capital	40,000	30,000
Retained earnings	53,000	20,000

During early 1972, the company distributed a 50% stock dividend to the common stockholders. Later in the year, it retired 250 preferred shares at 120, of which $8 a share was charged to paid-in capital. Cash dividends paid during the year amounted to $12,000. Goodwill in the amount of $15,000 was written off to retained earnings. What was the net income for 1972?

9-49. ***OWNERS' EQUITY—BOOK VALUE*** The Nhung Mining Company issued 100,000 shares of $15 par common stock at par. Some time later the Nhung Company is in need of working capital. The stockholders agree to donate 10% of their holdings to the company. The shares are then reissued at $12 a share.

Required:

(a) Make the necessary journal entries to record the donation and reissue by the Nhung Company.
(b) Determine the following:
 (1) Total capital before the donation.
 (2) Book value per share before the donation.

(3) Total book value of 1,000 shares held by a particular stockholder before the donation (there is no preferred).
(4) Total paid-in capital after the donated stock is sold.
(5) Total capital after the donated stock is sold.
(6) Book value per share after the donated stock is sold.
(7) Total book value of the shares held by the stockholder in (3) after the donated stock is sold.

CHAPTER

10

THE MANAGEMENT OF CASH RESOURCES

10.1 THE NATURE OF CASH RESOURCES

The purpose of cash resources is to provide management with a liquidity buffer. *Liquidity* is a measure of financial soundness: it refers to a firm's ability to pay its obligations when they become due; and it denotes cash or other resources that can readily be converted into cash. Liquidity is measured in terms of a one-year (fiscal) period for organizations which have an operating cycle of one year or less; or as the natural operating cycle where it exceeds one year.

If it were not for the importance of liquidity there would be no incentive to hold resources in the form of cash or cash equivalents, as these assets have little or no earning power in most business enterprises. We discussed this point in chapter 7.

10.2 THE CASH RESOURCE CYCLE

The term *cycle* refers to the inception, transformation, and completion of a process. In *financial* terminology it refers to the amount of time it takes for data in one state to go through sequential steps and return to the original state. We should distinguish this from the use of the word in production management, where it means a series of operating sequences having similar end-products or services, where the elapsed time from the beginning to the end of the process is the cycle. In this chapter we use the financial meaning of the term.

The *cash cycle* of a merchandising enterprise which operates on a *cash* basis is shown in Exhibit 10-1. A cash cycle where credit transactions are recognized through the *accrual* method of accounting includes additional steps (Exhibit 10-2).

EXHIBIT 10-1 CASH CYCLE: CASH BASIS

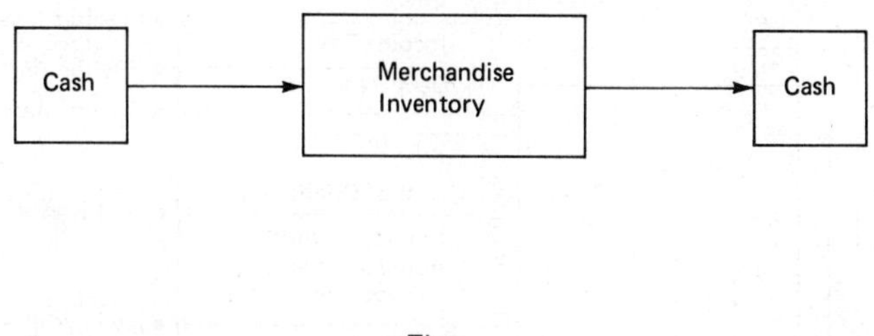

EXHIBIT 10-2 CASH CYCLE: ACCRUAL BASIS

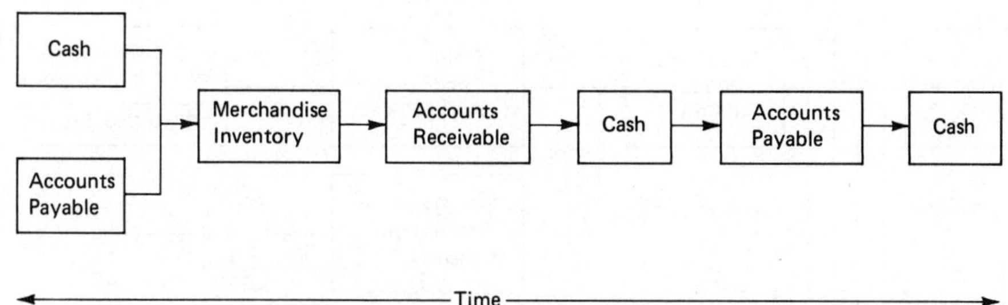

There are, of course, a number of other cash cycles; for example, cash is used to purchase fixed assets which are used in the production of income, from which cash expenses are deducted to arrive at a net operating cash balance. Or, cash may be placed into investments which in time are reconverted into cash. When we integrate these cash flows, the cycle becomes quite complex, as shown in Exhibit 10-3.

10.3 DEFINITION OF CASH

Cash includes money, negotiable money orders and checks, and balances in bank accounts net of adjustments for deposits in transit and checks outstanding. It does not include postage stamps, IOUs, post-dated checks or similar items that are frequently mingled with cash on hand. Following the systems approach outlined in Unit I, we are concerned here with inputs, transformation, outputs, feedback, and control of cash data within the accounting information system. The cash system plans and controls cash flow. It provides the basis for forecasting long-range and short-range cash needs; it monitors money receipts into the organization; it oversees the allocation of

EXHIBIT 10-3 INTEGRATED CASH CYCLE

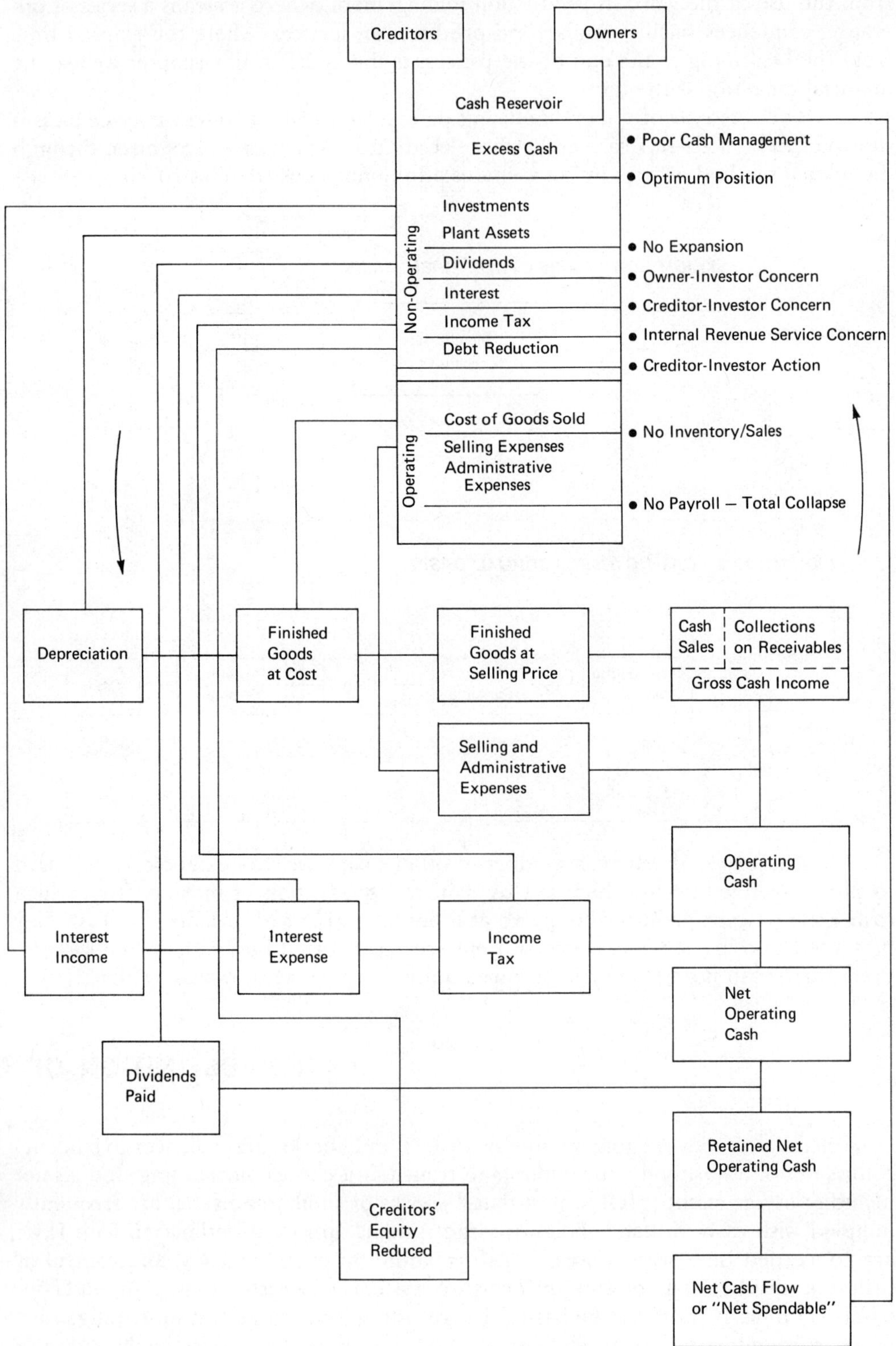

money between the several cash depositories; it optimizes cash position; and it provides authority for cash disbursements.

10.4 CASH SOURCES AND USES

There are several ways in which cash enters or exits the firm, as noted in chapters 6 and 7.

SOURCES:

1. Conversion of other assets into cash.
2. Increase in liabilities—cash loans, or credits which have the effect of postponing cash payments.
3. Increase in owners' equity through additional contributed cash, or through the net retention of cash from operations—cash from sales minus cash operating expenses, taxes, and dividends.

USES:

1. Investment in other assets.
2. Decrease in liabilities—payment of loans or the settlement of liability accounts.
3. Decrease in owners' equity through the repurchase of contributed capital (treasury stock), or through the net loss of cash from operations—excess of cash expenses, taxes, and dividends over cash from sales.

10.5 CASH FORECASTS AND BUDGETS

A "long-range" cash *forecast* covers the length of a cycle from investment of cash to its recovery from such items as plant and equipment, market development, and research. The period most commonly used for this purpose is from three to five years,[1] as this is viewed as being the maximum length of time for which sales trends, technology, and the products of market development and research can be projected with sufficient certainty to yield a reliable cash forecast. In cases where long-term cash flow is certain, as with ground rents, mortgage loans, or long-term leases, it may be projected accurately for periods up to ninety-nine years or more.

"Short-range" cash *budgets* cover the length of a cycle from investment of cash to its recovery in such items as inventory, receivables, and deferred charges. The period covered is generally the cash cycle referred to previously. As forecasts are extensions of budgets, but with less precision and detail (forecasts are generally stated in terms of years and in general categories of accounts, while budgets are for quarters or months, and are in more detail), we will concentrate here primarily on cash budgeting.

A format for a cash budget is contained in Exhibit 10-4, accompanied by explanatory notes. Its purpose is (1) to project *operating* cash position for a specified period, and (2) to enable management to plan for *non-operating* sources and uses given a knowledge of the operating cash deficiency or surplus. For example, in Exhibit 10-4

[1] *Cash Flow Analysis for Managerial Control,* Research Report No. 38 (New York: National Association of Accountants, 1961).

EXHIBIT 10-4

CASH BUDGET
FOR THE FISCAL YEAR, 19–

Details	[1] First Quarter	Second Quarter	Third Quarter	Fourth Quarter	Total
[2] **OPERATING SOURCES**					
Cash sales	$ 100,000	$ 100,000	$ 200,000	$ 500,000	$ 700,000
Collections on accounts receivable	900,000	800,000	1,200,000	1,700,000	4,600,000
Total operating sources	1,000,000	900,000	1,400,000	2,200,000	5,500,000
USES					
Cash purchases	80,000	80,000	150,000	200,000	510,000
[3] Payments on accounts payable	920,000	520,000	650,000	800,000	2,890,000
Cash operating expenses	400,000	400,000	500,000	600,000	1,900,000
Total operating uses	1,400,000	1,000,000	1,300,000	1,600,000	5,300,000
[4] NET OPERATING CASH	$ ⟨400,000⟩	$ ⟨100,000⟩ [8]	$ 100,000	$ 600,000	$ 200,000
NON-OPERATING SOURCES					
Interest income	$ 10,000	$ 10,000	$ 10,000	$ 8,000	$ 38,000
Sale of investments	–	–	100,000	–	100,000
Sale of fixed assets	50,000	–	–	–	50,000
Contributed capital	–	100,000	–	–	100,000
Loans, bonds, or other forms of long-term creditors' equity	340,000	–	–	–	340,000
Total non-operating sources	400,000	110,000	110,000	8,000	628,000
USES					
[5] Interest expense	–	5,000	5,000	5,000	15,000
Investments	–	–	–	100,000	100,000
Purchase of fixed assets	–	–	–	300,000	300,000
Repayment of creditors' equity	–	–	–	340,000	340,000
Dividends	–	–	–	50,000	50,000
Repurchase of owners' equity	–	–	–	–	–
Total non-operating uses	–	5,000	5,000	795,000	805,000
NET NON-OPERATING CASH	$ 400,000	$ 105,000	$ 105,000	$ ⟨787,000⟩	$ ⟨177,000⟩
NET CASH	–	5,000	205,000	⟨187,000⟩	23,000
[6] CASH BALANCE–BEGINNING	100,000	100,000	105,000	310,000	100,000 [7]
[6] CASH BALANCE–ENDING	$ 100,000	$ 105,000	$ 310,000	$ 123,000	$ 123,000 [7]

Notes to Exhibit 10-4:

1. Time intervals could be in months or even in weeks or days in the case of a monthly budget. In quarterly budgeting more information for immediate operating decisions can be obtained by breaking the next quarter into months. When one month remains in the existing quarter, the following quarter is broken down into three months.
2. It is important to recognize and separate the operating and non-operating cash budgets. The operating cash budget is less responsive to management decisions in the short run, and arriving at a net operating cash position enables management to make decisions if there is a projected cash shortage or surplus. The non-operating cash budget is much more responsive to management decisions; for example, the purchase of fixed assets can be postponed until there is sufficient operating cash available for the purpose. In Exhibit 10-4, it becomes clear that the optimum time for acquiring fixed assets is in the fourth quarter.
3. Payments on accounts payable do not necessarily relate to sales because of the normal time-lag involved. In Exhibit 10-4, first quarter payments on account, for example, relate to merchandise acquired in the fourth quarter.
4. As indicated in note 2 above, it is useful to calculate a "net operating cash" balance, as this figure is important in arriving at correct decisions relating to non-operating cash sources and uses. Projected for a year in advance, this balance gives management some time to plan to meet cash deficiencies or invest cash surpluses.
5. When loans are anticipated or approved, it is necessary to calculate the interest expense involved and to include this provision in the cash budget. If payments of principal are required in addition to interest, this should be provided for under "repayment of creditors' equity." In Exhibit 10-6, we have an interest only loan, taken out at the end of the first quarter, and paid in full at the end of the fourth quarter.
6. Some cash budgets have the beginning cash balance as the first item, in which case it is added to the operating sources. This tends to confuse the operating sources of a particular period with the cash balance from the last period. It is preferable to have the cash balances, beginning and ending, as balancing items in the position shown in Exhibit 10-4.
7. Beginning of the year cash balance and end of the year cash balance, respectively.
8. ⟨ ⟩ denotes negative balance.

an operating cash deficit of $400,000 is budgeted for the first quarter. A further deficit of $100,000 is indicated for the second quarter. In the third and fourth quarters respectively, surpluses of $100,000 and $600,000 are projected. Having this information in advance gives management guidance in cash planning. In the first quarter it elects to raise the needed cash by using its interest income, by selling fixed assets, and by securing a loan for $430,000. When clients apply for loans or lines of credit, bank loan officers use the cash budget as a principal device for determining the amount and terms of a loan. In our example, a short-term loan is indicated because of the firm's ability to repay it in the fourth quarter.

10.6 PROCESSING CASH TRANSACTIONS

INPUT

The principal cash events and their related documents are summarized in Exhibit 10-5.

EXHIBIT 10-5 MAJOR CASH EVENTS

EVENT	TRANSACTION DOCUMENT
A. Cash is received.	1. *Receipt* (the firm receives cash) 2. *Draft* (cash is deposited to the firm's credit in a bank)
B. Cash is relocated.	3. *Deposit* (relocation of cash to a bank account) 4. *Transfer* (relocation of cash from one station to another; relocation of cash from one bank account to another)
C. Cash is disbursed.	5. *Adjustment* (reduction from cash account for bank service charges and other fees and penalties) 6. *Petty cash* (for small cash disbursements) 7. *Check/money order* (an order to a bank to make a cash payment to the payee)

These documents initiate the processing of cash data. A *cash receipt* indicates that the firm has (or should have) received cash; a *check* indicates that a payment has been made; an *adjustment* (journal) document informs the system to record bank charges in an effort to reconcile a cash account with its related bank statement, and so forth.

TRANSFORMATION$_1$

The *duality* of cash input data is accomplished at T_1, as illustrated by the examples in Exhibit 10-6.

Cash Receipts and Payments Records

Because of numerous, repetitive events involving cash *receipts* (such as payments by customers of cash sales) and *payments* (such as payroll, rent, or accounts payable), it is useful to use specialized records (journals) for these items at the T_1 stage. The *cash receipts journal* is a specialized record for *all* cash receipts (see Exhibit 10-7). The *cash payments journal* is a specialized record for *all* cash disbursements (Exhibit 10-8).

Petty Cash and Imprest Fund Records

A *petty cash* or *imprest fund* record is used to record the many small cash or check payments that most organizations find it necessary to make for such items as postage stamps, taxicab fares, collect postage items, freight charges, and so forth. A petty cash or imprest fund permits immediate cash or check payment within a per-event limit (of say $5 to $10) without meeting the approval requirement for major cash or check disbursements. Where checks are used, a special petty cash checking account is maintained for that purpose.

The format for a *petty cash* or *imprest fund journal* is similar to that of the cash payments journal. There are minor differences between a petty cash fund versus an imprest fund:

Petty Cash:

1. In a petty cash fund, reimbursement is a fixed amount, say $100 per month, or whenever the fund balance is "low."
2. There is a periodic, usually month-end, transfer of expense items.

Imprest Fund:

1. In an imprest fund, reimbursement is an amount necessary to restore the fund to an approved maximum level, say $500, based on actual disbursements.
2. Expense items are transferred at the time reimbursement is requested.

In Exhibit 3-1 we indicated that there are certain outputs from the T_1 process:

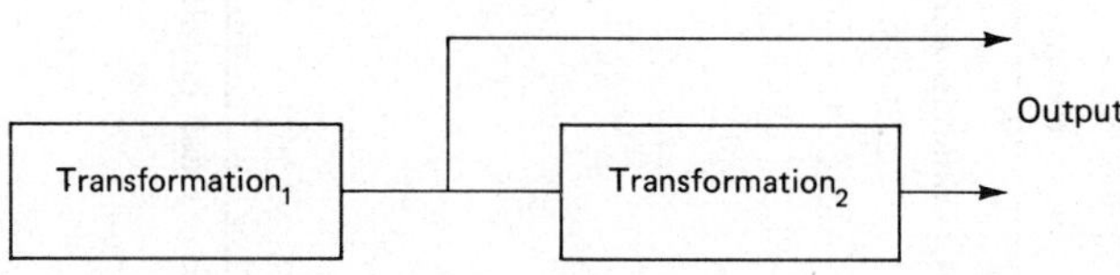

These specialized cash records are examples of this type of intermediate output. In some organizations, daily cash receipts and disbursement records are necessary for the proper management of financial resources.

EXHIBIT 10-6 THE DUALITY OF SOME TYPICAL CASH EVENTS

				(1)	(2)	(3)	Duality Instruction		
Event	Transaction Document	Date	Notation	Doc. Code	Trans. Code	Acct. Code	Accounts	Amount Debit	Amount Credit
								$	$
A. Cash is received.	Receipt		a. Capital provided in cash by owners.	1000	10	11100	Cash	10,000	
					10	31120	Capital		10,000
			b. Cash provided by long-term creditors in the form of debentures.	1001	10	11100	Cash	5,000	
					10	21650	Debentures Payable		5,000
			c. Customer makes a cash payment.	1002	10	11100	Cash	300	
					12	11210	Accounts Receivable		300
			d. A long-lived asset is sold for cash.	1003	10	11100	Cash	2,000	
					12	12110	Long-lived Assets		2,000
			e. A sale is made for cash.	1004	10	11100	Cash	3,000	
					10	41110	Sales		3,000
B. Cash is relocated.	Deposit		f. Cash is deposited in bank A.	2000	10	11110	Bank A	19,500	
					12	11100	Cash		19,500
			g. Cash is transferred from bank A to bank B.	2001	10	11110	Bank B	10,000	
					12	11110	Bank A		10,000
C. Cash is disbursed.	Adjustment		h. Bank A service charges are recorded.	3000	10	80090	Expenses	10	
					12	11110	Bank A		10

EXHIBIT 10-6 (CONTINUED)

		(4)		(1)	(2)	(3)	Duality Instruction		
Event	**Transaction Document**	**Date**	**Notation**	**Doc. Code**	**Trans. Code**	**Acct. Code**	**Accounts**	**Amount Debit**	**Amount Credit**
								$	$
	Petty Cash		i. Postage stamps are purchased.		10	70070	Expenses	100	
				3001	12	11100	Cash		100
	Check		j. Merchandise is purchased with a check from bank A.		10	11610	Merchandise Inventory	1,800	
				3002	12	11110	Bank A		1,000
			k. A payment is made to long-term creditors from bank A.		12	21650	Long-term Liabilities	1,000	
				3003	12	11110	Bank A		1,000
			l. An owner withdraws capital from the business; payment is from bank B.		12	31120	Capital	2,000	
				3004	12	11110	Bank B		2,000
			m. Payment is made to a vendor from bank B.		12	21110	Accounts Payable	500	
				3005	12	11110	Bank B		500
			n. A long-lived asset is purchased with a check drawn on bank B.		10	12110	Long-lived Assets	5,000	
				3006	12	11110	Bank B		5,000
			o. Wages, rent and other expenses are paid by checks drawn on bank B.		10	80090	Expenses	800	
				3007	12	11110	Bank B		800
							Total	$61,010	$61,010

(1) *Doc. Code: document code* or identification number that provides a trail to the original evidence.
(2) *Trans. code:* a *transaction code* is an arithmetic instruction that is needed for aggregation at T_2 (10 = add, 12 = subtract). The $10,000 in event (a) is to be added to the cash account.
(3) *Acct. code:* an *account code* or number identifies the account to which an event is assigned.
(4) We have omitted dates in this example, but each event is dated.

EXHIBIT 10-7 CASH RECEIPTS JOURNAL

			DEBITS							CREDITS			
Date	Notation	Doc. Code	Cash	Cash Discounts Taken	Other Accounts		Ref.	Other Accounts Title		Ref.	Other Accounts	Accounts Receivable	Sales
			$	$	$						$	$	$
	Capital provided by owners.	1000	10,000					Capital	√	31120	10,000		
	Proceeds from debentures.	1001	5,000					Debentures payable	√	21650	5,000		
	Customer makes a payment.	1002	300	20								320	
	Cash sale.	1004	3,000										3,000
	Payment is received in part cash and notes rec.	1005	1,000		2,000	√	114–10					3,000	
	Total		$19,300	$20	$2,000						$15,000	$3,320	$3,000
			√ Acct. Code 11100	√ Acct. Code 41170								√ Acct. Code 11210	√ Acct. Code 41100
(1)	(2)	(3)	(4)	(5)	(6)	(7)	(8)	(9)	(10)	(11)	(12)	(13)	(14)

(1) To record date of transaction.

(2) Explanation of accounting transaction.

(3) Document code or number.

(4) Itemized and total cash receipts transactions for the period. Only the total is posted to the cash account in the ledger; (13) and (14) are similar.

(5) Itemized and total cash discounts taken by customer. Journal is kept on a gross discount method. Under the *net discount* method there would be a credit account in the cash receipts journal called "cash discounts not taken."

(6) Other accounts to be debited. Each individual entry is posted to the ledger. The total is not posted; (12) is similar.

(7) √ indicates that an item has been posted; (10) is similar.

(8) Number of account in the ledger; (11) is similar.

(9) Title of "other accounts" to be debited or credited.

EXHIBIT 10-8 CASH PAYMENTS JOURNAL

			DEBITS						CREDITS				
Date	Notation	Doc. Code	Purchases	Accounts Payable	Other Accounts	Acct. Code		Other Accounts Title		Acct. Code	Other Accounts	Cash Discounts Taken	Cash
			$	$	$						$	$	$
	Purchase merchandise.	3002	1,800										1,800
	Officer obtains loan from company	3004			$ 2,000	11240	√	Accounts Receivable Officers					2,000
	Payment is made to vendor.	3005		$500								50	450
	Land is purchased.	3010			20,000	12110	√	Land Notes payable	√	21610	18,000		2,000
	Total		$1,800	$500	$22,000						$18,000	$50	$6,250
			√ Acct. Code 41810	√ Acct. Code 21110								√ Acct. Code 41340	√ Acct. Code 11100
(1)	(2)	(3)	(4)	(5)	(6)	(7)	(8)	(9)	(10)	(11)	(12)	(13)	(14)

(1) To record date of transaction.

(2) To explain transaction.

(3) Document code or number.

(4), (5), (13), and (14) Only totals are posted to the general ledger.

(6), (12) Only individual transactions are posted to the respective ledger accounts. Totals are not posted.

(7), (11) "Other accounts" numbers.

(9) "Other accounts" titles.

(8), (10) √ indicates posting to ledger.

TRANSFORMATION$_2$

The T_2 process (posting) consists of recording the T_1 events in the ledger accounts in accordance with the duality instruction. Using the T-account ledger format, the events in Exhibit 10-6 are posted in Exhibit 10-9.

EXHIBIT 10-9 POSTING CASH EVENTS TO T-ACCOUNTS

BALANCE SHEET T-ACCOUNTS (1)

(2) → 11100 Cash

(a)	$10,000	(f)	$19,500
(b)	5,000	(i)	100
(c)	300		
(d)	2,000		
(e)	3,000		
	20,300		$19,600
Bal.	$ 700		

11110 Bank A

(f)	$19,500	(g)	$10,000
		(h)	10
		(j)	1,800
		(k)	1,000
	19,500		$12,810
Bal.	$ 6,690		

11110 Bank B

(g)	$10,000	(l)	$ 2,000
		(m)	500
		(n)	5,000
		(o)	800
	10,000		$ 8,300
Bal.	$ 1,700		

11210 Accounts Receivable

(3) →	$ 1,200	(c)	$ 300
Bal.	$ 900		

(4) 11610 Merchandise Inventory (5)

(4) →	$ 3,000	(5)	$ 2,800
(j)	1,800		
	4,800		$ 2,800
Bal.	$ 2,000		

12110 Long-lived Assets

(n)	$ 5,000	(d)	$ 2,000
Bal.	$ 3,000		

21110 Accounts Payable (4)

(m)	$ 500	(4)	$ 3,000
		Bal.	$ 2,500

21650 Debentures Payable

(k)	$ 1,000	(b)	$ 5,000
		Bal.	$ 4,000

31120 Capital

(l)	$ 2,000	(a)	$10,000
		Bal.	$ 8,000

INCOME T-ACCOUNTS

41110 Sales (3)

		(3)	$ 1,200
		(e)	3,000
		Bal.	$ 4,200

80090 Expenses

(h)	$ 10		
(i)	100		
(o)	800		
Bal.	$ 910		

41310 Cost of Sales

(5) →	$ 2,800		

Notes:

1. A T-account is a simplified representation of a ledger account that is used to illustrate money flow under the debit-credit convention. Following is the typical format and content of a real ledger account:

Date	Document Code	Detail	Trans. Code	Batch/ Journal Code	Amount		
					Debit	Credit	Balance
–	1000	Capital	10		$10,000	–	$10,000
–	1001	Long-term liability	10		5,000	–	15,000
–	1002	Accounts receivable	10		300	–	15,300
–	1003	Long-lived assets	10		2,000	–	17,300
–	1004	Sales	10		3,000	–	20,300
–	2000	Bank A	12		–	$19,500	800
–	2001	Expenses	12		–	100	700

   The "batch/journal code" references the T_1 documentation of the entry. This code may be a journal page number, or in data processing systems, a "batch" number. In batch processing a certain number of accounting events (say 10) have their debit-credit amounts totaled and balanced on a batch summary voucher. This procedure enables the computer to identify specific batches that are out of balance.

2. In this example, we distinguish between "cash" and "bank" transactions. In other texts, and at other places in this text, cash is often used generically to refer to all forms of cash and checking transactions.
3. This entry does not involve cash at this point. A sale has been made "on account." The T_1 notation for the event is:

   Increase (Debit) Accounts receivable $1,200
   Increase (Credit) Sales $1,200

4. This is similar to the foregoing event; here merchandise inventory has been purchased "on account" with the following notation:

   Increase (Debit) Merchandise inventory $3,000
   Increase (Credit) Accounts payable $3,000

   Suppliers of inventories are called *vendors.*

5. There are two transactions for each sales event—recording the event at the *selling* price, and recording the event at the *cost* price. This entry records the cost of sales for the period:

   Increase (Debit) Cost of sales $2,800
   Decrease (Credit) Merchandise inventory.............. $2,800

Another way of looking at the transformation$_2$ process is to arrange the accounts in matrix form, one axis representing *debit* and the other *credit* entries. Matrix formulation of the foregoing events, as shown in Exhibit 10-10, enables us to record, aggregate, and summarize our cash events in one step.

EXHIBIT 10-10 EXAMPLE OF TRANSFORMATION$_2$ BY MATRIX

DEBITS (columns) / CREDITS (rows)

	Cash/ Banks	Accounts Receivable	Merchandise Inventory	Long-lived Assets	Accounts Payable	Long-term Liabilities	Capital	Sales	Cost of Sales	Expenses	Total	Balances
Cash/Banks	(f) 19,500 (g) 10,000		(j) 1,800	(n) 5,000	(m) 500	(k) 1,000	(l) 2,000			(h) 10 (i) 100 (o) 800	$40,710	–
Accounts Receivable	(c) 300										$ 300	–
Merchandise Inventory									(5) 2,800		$ 2,800	–
Long-lived Assets	(d) 2,000										$ 2,000	–
Accounts Payable			(4) 3,000								$ 3,000	$ 2,500
Long-term Liabilities	(b) 5,000										$ 5,000	$ 4,000
Capital	(a) 10,000										$10,000	$ 8,000
Sales	(c) 3,000	(3) 1,200									$ 4,200	$ 4,200
Cost of Sales											–	–
Expenses											–	–
Totals	$49,800	$1,200	$4,800	$5,000	$500	$1,000	$2,000	–	$2,800	$910	$68,010	–
Balances	$ 9,090	$ 900	$2,000	$3,000	–	–	–	–	$2,800	$910	–	$18,700

Notes:

1. The *columns* are debit entries; the *rows* are credit entries.
2. The balances are obtained by comparing the debit and credit totals of the same account. For example, the debit total for cash is $49,800, and the credit balance for cash is $40,710. Debit balance is therefore $49,800 – $40,710 or $9,090. Note that these cash balances include the bank accounts.

OUTPUT

Cash system data is combined with other sub-system data in producing the formal financial statements: the income statement, balance sheet, and statement of retained earnings (for corporations), or statement of changes in capital (for proprietors and partners).

Cash system output is not limited to the financial statements. The major share of the output, in fact, is for internal management purposes. Daily, weekly, and/or monthly cash reports are required in many organizations, as is data for cash budgeting and forecasting, as we have mentioned previously.

10.7 SYSTEMS CONTROLS FOR CASH TRANSACTIONS

There are stewardship and management controls in the cash system.

STEWARDSHIP CONTROLS

Stewardship controls are designed to accomplish two things:

1. The proper receipt of all cash to the organization.
2. The proper disbursement of all cash by the organization.

Cash is more susceptible to theft than any other asset, and a large percentage of business transactions involve the receipt or disbursement of cash. For these reasons, strict stewardship controls are needed to prevent malfeasance with regard to cash. Two forms of embezzlement should be noted:

1. Lapping: The theft of cash received from one customer, but credited to the customer's account at a later date by using cash received from another customer.
2. Kiting:
   a. Cashing an unrecorded check on one bank, and covering it with a check drawn on another bank.
   b. Opening a bank account with a fraudulent check (usually originating in a different city or state to lengthen clearing time), and then drawing most of the amount out before the bank discovers the error.

These and other forms of embezzlement can be guarded against by maintaining a system of internal control over the handling of cash. Some general principles for controlling *cash receipts* are:

1. The immediate separation of cash from its documentation (Exhibit 10-11).
2. The function of cash handling must be quite distinct from maintaining the accounting records. Neither party should have access to, or supervise, the record-keeping of the other.
3. If possible, there should be a daily deposit of *all* cash receipts to the bank. Deposit slips should contain sufficient detailed information to identify the individual items of the deposit. If petty cash is needed, it should be drawn by check from the bank, and not withheld from a deposit.

EXHIBIT 10-11 SEPARATION OF CASH FROM ITS DOCUMENTATION

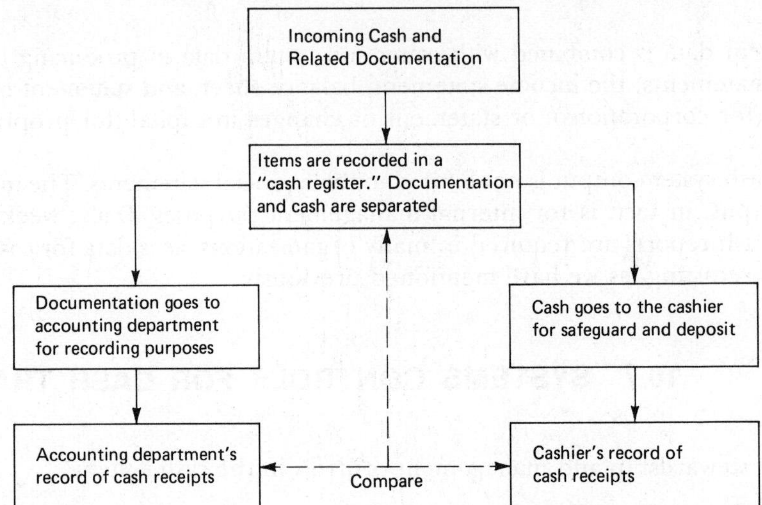

4. The party responsible for cash receipts should not also be responsible for cash disbursements.

Similarly, there are some general principles for controlling *cash disbursements:*

1. All disbursements should be made by check. Issuing a check should require the approval of more than one person. Payment by check provides a permanent record of disbursements, and a canceled check is proof that payment was made.
2. Checks should be pre-numbered. Spoiled checks should be marked "void" and maintained in numerical sequence. Only authorized check blanks should be used; the use of "counter checks" and other means for withdrawing cash, except by authorized checks, should be prevented.
3. If possible, checks should be signed by one person and countersigned by another.
4. Supporting invoices and other documentation should be perforated or marked "paid" in order to prevent double payment for the same item.
5. A system for approving payments should underlie the issuance of checks. The person who approves the payment should not be the person who issues the check.

Approving payments and issuing checks in some organizations is accomplished in accordance with *the voucher system.* The voucher system is a formal set of procedures for approving and issuing checks as illustrated in Exhibit 10-12.

EXHIBIT 10-12 THE VOUCHER SYSTEM

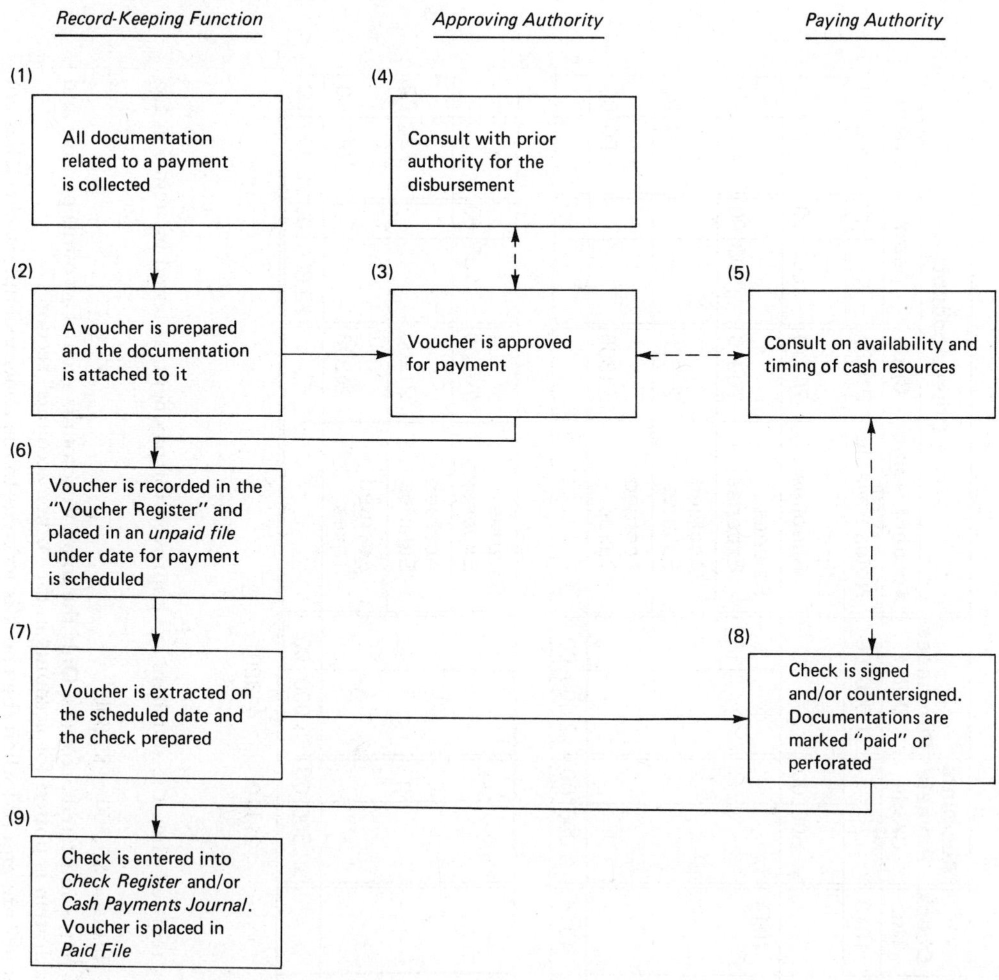

Notes:

1. In the case of a purchase, for example, the purchase requisition, the receiving report, the invoice, and the statement (if any) relating to the same event are all collated.
2. The documents are compared, the differences explained, and the voucher is prepared.

3-5. In authorizing the payment, the approving officer consults with prior authority for the disbursement, such as a committee action or the budget. He also consults with the paying officer as to availability and timing of cash resources.

6. An example of a voucher register is given in Exhibit 10-13.

7-8. The check is prepared on the scheduled date for payment and is forwarded to the paying authority together with the voucher and documentation. The paying officer has been consulted in step 4 regarding the scheduling of payment, and compares the timing. The check is signed.

9. The check is recorded in a check register (Exhibit 10-14).

EXHIBIT 10-13 A VOUCHER REGISTER

Date	Voucher Number	Payee	Date Paid	Check No.	Accounts Payable Credit	Purchases Debit	Other Accounts			
							Account Name	Code	Debit	Credit
1.1	400	City Bank	1.5	1013		1,000 00	Notes Payable	21620		1,000 00
1.5	401	Office Supply Company			500 00		Office Supplies	70010	500 00	
1.12	402	Payroll	1.15	1014			Salaries Expense	70020	900 00	
							Accrued Salaries	21200		720 00
							Accrued Taxes	21300		180 00
1.20	403	Ramon, Inc.	1.30	1015	2,000 00	2,000 00				
1.25	404	Payroll					Salaries Expense	70020	900 00	
							Accrued Salaries	21200		720 00
							Accrued Taxes	21300		180 00
					$2,500 00	$3,000 00			$2,300 00	$2,800 00
					21110 √	41820 √			√	√

Notes:

1. The entries are made in the voucher register when the vouchers are approved for payment, as noted by item 6 in Exhibit 10-12.
2. Debit entries equal credit entries, in this case $5,300 = $5,300.
3. Accounts are posted (√) periodically to the indicated accounts. Only the totals in accounts such as accounts payable and purchases above are posted, while each item is posted for accounts in the "other accounts" section.
4. The date of payment and check number are entered when the check is written. In the above example, a check has not yet been issued to Office Supply Company or for the 1.25 payroll.

EXHIBIT 10-14 A CHECK REGISTER

Date	Check Number	Payee	Voucher Number	Accounts Payable Debit	Cash Credit	Other Accounts: Account Name	Other Accounts: Code	Other Accounts: Debit	Other Accounts: Credit
1.5	1013	City Bank	400		1,000 00	Notes Payable	21620	1,000 00	
1.12	1014	Payroll Officer	402		720 00	Accrued Salaries	21200	720 00	
1.20	1015	Ramon, Inc.	403	2,000 00	1,960 00	Purchase Discounts Taken	41340		40 00
				$2,000 00	$3,680 00			$1,720 00	$40 00
				21110 √	11100 √			√	√

Notes:

1. When all payments are by check, this register serves the purpose of the cash payments journal discussed earlier.
2. A customary procedure for payroll is to issue one check for the entire payroll to a payroll officer who deposits it in a special payroll account and then issues individual checks to employees. Accrued taxes are remitted to the Internal Revenue Service on a customary quarterly basis.

As we note from the foregoing receipt and disbursement procedures, stewardship controls place a repeated emphasis on the principle of the *separation of duties.* Underlying this principle is the observed fact that the odds against dishonesty are improved significantly where an act requires the collusion of two or more persons.

MANAGEMENT CONTROLS

Management controls have a principal purpose—to *optimize* cash position. As mentioned earlier, excess cash may denote poor management, because these resources can usually produce a higher return if they are converted to some other asset form. Contrary to popular thinking, a large cash balance is not a reliable indicator of an organization's good state of health; it may indicate just the opposite. Too little cash is also hazardous and may require unscheduled borrowing of funds on adverse terms; or the untimely disposition of a firm's assets.

How do we optimize cash position? Some impressive results have attended the application of management controls in administering cash. In the following study, one company was able to sustain an increased sales volume with significantly smaller cash resources through the progressive application of management controls over a five-year period (Exhibit 10-15).

EXHIBIT 10-15 AN ILLUSTRATION OF CASH OPTIMIZATION

Year	Cash	Sales	% Cash Sales
1	$9,954,000	$67,080,000	14.8%
2	5,879,000	71,703,000	8.2
3	5,063,000	65,593,000	7.7
4	1,761,000	70,721,000	2.5
5	1,689,000	70,852,000	2.4

SOURCE: *Cash Flow Analysis for Managerial Control,* Research Report No. 38, p. 7.

Cash forecasts and budgets are the principal techniques for the management control of cash. Cash budgets may be prepared on a daily, weekly, quarterly, and/or annual basis. They serve as controls for the following reasons:

1. They emphasize the timing of future cash events.
2. They indicate periods when cash surpluses or shortages are likely to occur, thus enabling management to:
   a. Convert temporary surplus cash into investments.
   b. Arrange in advance for financing for periods where shortages are indicated.
3. They facilitate the scheduling of loan repayments.
4. By distinguishing postponable from non-postponable disbursements, they provide management with a basis for deciding priorities and for relating postponable needs to periods where optimum financing is possible.
5. They provide guidelines for controlling disbursements, in that expenditures for a particular account cannot exceed budget without special approval.

However, cash budgets do not necessarily indicate optimum cash position. One technique for doing this, where the cash inflow and outflow is fairly uniform, is:

1. To compute average daily cash disbursements by means of this formula:

$$D_a = \frac{D_t}{N_p}$$

where

$$D_a = \text{average daily disbursements}$$
$$D_t = \text{total disbursements for a period}$$
$$N_p = \text{number of days in the period}$$

2. Multiply this amount (D_a) by the desired number of days to arrive at the appropriate cash balance:

$$C_b = N_4 \times D_a$$

where

$$C_b = \text{cash balance}$$
$$N_r = \text{number of days covered by the cash reserve}$$

Example:

a. We wish to maintain a cash balance equal to 15 days of average daily disbursements.
b. Total disbursements for year are scheduled to be $900,000.
c. We will base our computations on the standard *financial year* of 360 days.

Accordingly:

$$D_a = \frac{\$900{,}000}{360}$$
$$D_a = \$2{,}500$$
$$C_b = 15 \times \$2{,}500$$
$$C_b = \$37{,}500$$

The fifteen days are determined by cash inflow. The assumption is that there will be an inflow of $37,500 in cash every fifteen days as illustrated graphically in Exhibit 10-16. A discussion of more elaborate models for determining cash position, where the cash inflow/outflow is uneven, is appended to this chapter.

There are two other management controls of cash that require our attention; namely, *cash discounts* and *float*.

Cash Discounts

Cash discounts are inducements to pay accounts within a specified period of time. Cash discount terms are usually quoted on vendor's invoices. For example, the cash discount expression 2/10, n/30 means that a 2% discount can be subtracted from the face amount of the invoice if payment is made within ten days of *the invoice date*. The

EXHIBIT 10-16 CASH POSITION MODEL

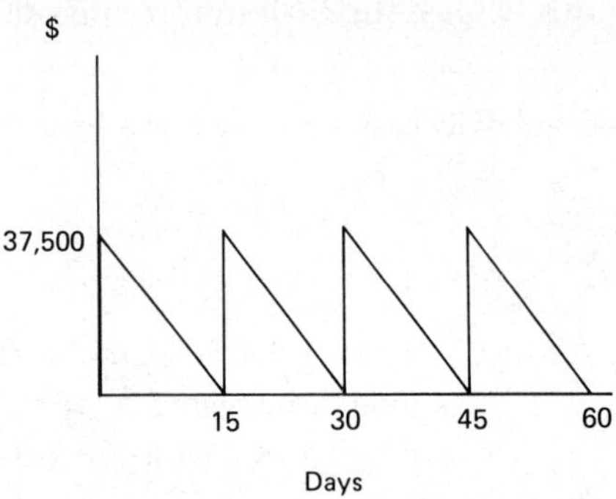

full amount is due within thirty days of the invoice date, and no discount is allowed if payment is made after the tenth day.

Cash discounts may be *received* where the firm purchases items, or *given* where the firm sells items. The accounting records may be kept on the assumption (1) that all discounts are taken (net price method), or (2) that all discounts are not taken (gross price method). An example of these methods follows:

> On June 25, 19–, X Company sells Y Company merchandise priced at $2,000 on terms 2/10, n/30. The invoice bears the same date.

1. Entries in X Company's records under the *net price method* would be:

	CASH		ACCOUNTS RECEIVABLE		SALES		CASH DISCOUNTS NOT TAKEN	
Date/Transaction	**Debit**	**Credit**	**Debit**	**Credit**	**Debit**	**Credit**	**Debit**	**Credit**
(a) June 25...........			$1,960			$1,960		
(b) July 5—if discount is taken...	$1,960			$1,960				
(c) July 25—if discount is not taken..............	$2,000			$1,960				$40

The entries in X Company's income statement if (b) or (c) occurs would be:

(b)	Sales	$1,960
(c)	Sales	$1,960
	Add: Cash discounts not taken by client(s)	$ 40
		$2,000

2. Entries in X Company's records under the *gross price method* would be:

Date/Transaction	CASH Debit	CASH Credit	ACCOUNTS RECEIVABLE Debit	ACCOUNTS RECEIVABLE Credit	SALES Debit	SALES Credit	CASH DISCOUNTS TAKEN Debit	CASH DISCOUNTS TAKEN Credit
(a) June 25...........			$2,000			$2,000		
(b) July 5—if discount is taken...	$1,960			$2,000			$40	
(c) July 25—if discount is not taken..............	$2,000			$2,000				

The entries in X Company's income statement if (b) or (c) occurs would be:

(b)	Sales...	$2,000
	Less: Cash discounts taken by client(s)	$ 40
		$1,960
(c)	Sales...	$2,000

3. Entries in Y Company's records under the *net price method* would be:

Date/Transaction	CASH Debit	CASH Credit	ACCOUNTS PAYABLE Debit	ACCOUNTS PAYABLE Credit	PURCHASES Debit	PURCHASES Credit	CASH DISCOUNTS NOT TAKEN Debit	CASH DISCOUNTS NOT TAKEN Credit
(a) June 25...........				$1,960	$1,960			
(b) July 5—if the discount is taken..............	$1,960		$1,960					
(c) July 25—if the discount is not taken..............		$2,000	$1,960				$40	

The entries in Y Company's income statement if (b) or (c) occurs would be:

(b)	Purchases (cost of sales).....................	$1,960
(c)	Purchases (cost of sales).....................	$1,960
	Add: Cash discounts not taken............	40
		$2,000

4. Entries in Y Company's records under the *gross price method* would be:

	CASH		ACCOUNTS PAYABLE		PURCHASES		CASH DISCOUNTS TAKEN	
Date/Transaction	**Debit**	**Credit**	**Debit**	**Credit**	**Debit**	**Credit**	**Debit**	**Credit**
(a) June 25...........				$2,000	$2,000			
(b) July 5–if the discount is taken..............		$1,960	$2,000					$40
(c) July 25–if the discount is not taken..............		$2,000	$2,000					

The entries in Y Company's income statement if (b) or (c) occurs would be:

(b)	Purchases (cost of sales)....................	$2,000
	Less: Cash discounts taken	40
		$1,960
(c)	Purchases (cost of sales)....................	$2,000

It is important to know which method the other party is using when it comes to reconciling their joint account; if they are using different cash discounting methods, the money amounts will not be the same. The choice of method should agree with management's policy regarding cash discounts. If the policy is to take discounts, then the net price method should be used in order to highlight exceptions to policy—that is, discounts not taken.

There is an implied interest rate in the discount formula. The 2% discount in the expression 2/10, n/30 is equivalent to a 36% annual interest rate. The formula for computing this is:

$$I_r = D_r \left(\frac{F_y}{O_p}\right)$$

where

I_r = Effective annual interest rate
D_r = Discount rate
F_y = Financial year consisting of 360 days
O_p = Option period

The firm will either pay on the 10th or on the 30th (there is no advantage to paying prior to the 10th, or between the 11th and 30th), and so the *option period* is twenty days. The cost of not taking the discount is 2% for twenty days. There are eighteen twenty-day periods in a year, hence 18 × 2% = 36% effective annual interest rate.

Example: Purchases subject to cash discounts on terms 3/10, n/30 totaled $1,200,000 during the twelve months of 1966. No cash discounts were taken. If the firm could borrow the necessary cash from a bank (at 6% interest) on the 10th of each month and repay the loan on the 30th of each month, what effect would this have on net income for the period?

Interest charged by the bank can be computed by this formula:

$$I_a = \frac{P_d}{F_y} \times I_r \times A$$

where

I_a = Interest amount
P_d = Period for which funds are borrowed (in days)
I_r = Annual interest rate
A = Amount borrowed

Hence:

$$I_a = \frac{20}{360} \times .06 \times \$1{,}164{,}000$$
$$I_a = \underline{\underline{\$3{,}880}}$$

Total amount borrowed would be $1,164,000 ($1,200,000 × .97) for a period of twenty days. In our example, the bank would charge $3,880. Cost of losing the cash discount can be computed:

$$.03 \times \$1{,}200{,}000 = \underline{\underline{\$36{,}000}}$$

Income would be improved by $32,120 ($36,000 − $3,880) if cash could be borrowed from the bank in order to take advantage of the cash discount. What rate would the bank have to charge on the $1,164,000 needed in order to equal the $36,000 of cash discounts lost?

$$I_r = \frac{I_a}{A\left(\frac{P_d}{F_y}\right)}$$

$$I_r = \frac{36{,}000}{1{,}164{,}000\left(\frac{20}{360}\right)} = .56 \text{ or } 56\%$$

Under what conditions should a firm offer cash discounts? The problem hinges on the inventory turnover cycle and profit margin, as these earlier receipts of cash can be used to acquire additional inventory. Take the specific question, "When should a firm offer the standard cash discount of 2/10, n/30?" If the average profit margin is 10%, we solve for the break-even inventory turnover cycle (holding period) as follows:

$$I_r = .02\left(\frac{360}{20}\right) = .36 \text{ or } 36\%$$

which is the effective annual rate of interest in the discount expression. The break-even turnover cycle in days (T_d) is computed by:

$$.36 = .10\left(\frac{360}{T_d}\right) = T_d = \frac{360}{.36/.10} = 100 \text{ days}$$

If the average profit margin on inventory is 10%, the firm will obtain positive leverage on a cash discount of 2/10, n/30 if the inventory cycle is less than 100 days. Obviously, more leverage is obtained as the inventory cycle is reduced.

Float

Float is cash in transit or suspense. For example, for the period between the time a check is written and the time it "clears" the payor's account, that amount of cash is float. Here are some other illustrations of float:

1. *Traveler's Cheques:* American Express Company trades its traveler's cheques for cash. The person takes a three-month vacation, during which time he periodically cashes the traveler's cheques. Meanwhile American Express Company has invested the cash it received. With a continuing stream of clients, it always has a substantial amount of float invested, earnings from which constitute the company's major source of income.
2. *Disneyland Coupons:* Visitors to Disneyland exchange money for coupons at the gate. They may not use all of the coupons in one day, and keep the rest for a return visit days, weeks, or months (or never) in the future. Disneyland, of course, has been paid for the unused coupons and so has at its disposal—float.
3. *"Trade Dollars":* A group of merchants wish to encourage business among themselves as a group. The promoters issue trade association dollars in exchange for real money. For as long as the "trade dollars" remain in circulation within the group, the promoters can benefit from the investment of the float.

These are examples of how float can be created. While most business firms do not create float, they can utilize it. For example, analysis of check-clearing processes can permit a judicious paring of cash reserves.

Bank reconciliations can be useful in developing statistical float data in addition to their usefulness in achieving agreement between the cash and bank accounts. Float works two ways in a checking account; when deposits are made, a float period of from two to three days is usually required before the checks clear the payors' accounts. This is *negative float,* for until the deposits are cleared the firm may not issue checks or effect withdrawals. On the other hand, checks issued by the firm are float until they have cleared the firm's bank account—this is *positive float.* The difference is *net negative* or *net positive* float. If the minimum float period is two days (based on mailing and clearing time), we can readily compute *minimum float.*

Float management should be developed in conjunction with statistical analysis. For example, a firm can collect data on the average transit periods of checks it issues (Exhibit 10–17).

EXHIBIT 10-17 RECORDING THE TRANSIT PERIODS OF CHECKS

Checks	Payee	1–2 days	3–4 days	5–6 days	7–8 days →
No. 80	A				$1,000
81	B			$2,000	
82	C			1,000	
83	D		$3,000		
84	E		1,000		
85	F	$ 1,000			
86	G	4,000			
87	H	5,000			
↓		$10,000	$4,000	$3,000	$1,000

With sufficient data and experience, we can calculating *probable* float on the basis of statistical probabilities as to typical in-transit periods.

10.8 SYSTEMS FEEDBACK FOR CASH TRANSACTIONS

Feedback on the cash system conforms to the general principles of feedback discussed in chapter 3. Accordingly, feedback furnishes users with (1) exception, (2) control, (3) comparative, and (4) interpretive reports.

EXHIBIT 10-18

CASH RECEIPTS AND DISBURSEMENTS REPORT FOR THE MONTH OF JANUARY, 19–

Items	Actual January	Budget January	Over Budget	%	Under Budget	%
Receipts						
Cash sales	$112,155	$110,000	$2,155	2.0%	–	–
Disbursements						
Purchases	65,165	60,000	5,165	8.6%	–	–
Payroll	32,000	34,000	–	–	$2,000	1.7%
Advertising	5,440	4,000	1,440	27.8%	–	–
Office expenses	8,113	9,000	–	–	887	9.8%
	110,718	107,000	6,605	6.2%	2,887	2.7%
Difference	$ 1,437	$ 3,000	$4,450	–	$2,887	–
Difference in expected and actual net cash Receipts	–	$ 3,000	–	–	$1,563	52.1%

Any material departure from plan is an *exception,* and all exceptions should receive special attention. Where a cash disbursement exceeds the authority of a person, approval should be obtained from higher levels in the organization. A widely used exception report is to show differences between actual and budgeted cash receipts and disbursements (Exhibit 10-18).

A second function of feedback is to report on cash stewardship controls; namely, that they are appropriate for the purposes to which they are applied, and that they are actually in effect. Feedback on cash management controls should indicate the extent to which budgetary control is in effect, and whether cash position is being optimized to the extent possible.

There are numerous forms of *comparative* feedback. For example, cash balances can be compared with those of previous periods, or with those of other firms. The relationship of cash to sales, to other asset accounts, or to current debt are useful comparisons. Reconciling accounts is another important form of comparative feedback. (*Reconciliation* is the determination of items necessary to bring the balances of two or more accounts into agreement.) The most prevalent reconciliation is between the bank account as recorded in a firm's books and the monthly bank statement. The items that generally give rise to adjustments between these balances are:

EXHIBIT 10-19 BANK RECONCILIATION ADJUSTMENTS

	ADJUSTMENT REQUIRED	
Item	**To the Book Balance**	**To the Bank Balance**
1. Deposits made but not yet recorded by the bank	none	increase
2. Checks outstanding: that is, checks issued by the firm which have not yet cleared the bank account	none	decrease
3. Checks returned for "nsf" (not sufficient funds) or other reasons	decrease	none
4. Bank service and other charges	decrease	none
5. Errors	increase or decrease	increase or decrease

In most cases, neither balance is correct, so the object of reconciliation is not only to have the balances agree, but also to arrive at the correct balance (Exhibit 10-20).

EXHIBIT 10-20 RECONCILIATION OF BANK AND BOOK BALANCES TO A CORRECT BALANCE

Bank Statement Adjustments

Balance as per bank statement, January 31, 19–		$3,000.00
Add: Deposit of January 28, 19–, not yet recorded		1,000.00
		$4,000.00
Less: Checks outstanding		
No. 101–Mr. X	$100.00	
No. 105–Mr. Y	400.00	
No. 111–Z Company	600.00	1,100.00
Correct balance		$2,900.00

Book Adjustment

Balance as per books, January 31, 19–		$3,105.00
Less: Bank service charge	$ 5.00	
Customer's check returned nsf	200.00	205.00
Correct balance		$2,900.00

The bank statement adjustments are timing differences and require no further effort. The items should appear on the February bank statement. The book adjustments do require a change in the records, which is accomplished by the following entries:

1. Increase (Debit) Office expense	$ 5.00	
Decrease (Credit) Cash		$ 5.00
<u>Notation:</u> Record bank service charges for the month of January, 19–.		
2. Increase (Debit) Accounts receivable	$200.00	
Decrease (Credit) Cash		$200.00
<u>Notation:</u> To reinstate an accounts receivable by reason of a nsf check.		

The purpose of *interpretive* feedback is to provide additional information for purposes of evaluating plans and results. For example, our exception report on cash receipts and disbursements (Exhibit 10–18) points to large variance with respect to advertising; and it is the purpose of interpretive feedback to explain why this and the other variances occurred. Interpretive feedback is a function that gives meaning to the statistical data in accounting reports.

10.9 MARKETABLE SECURITIES

Temporary cash surpluses, which will be required sometime within the operating cycle, should be invested in blue-chip, low-risk securities, which can readily be converted into cash when the need arises. The amount invested will usually differ from the current market quotation of the securities, and because these securities are a reserve source of cash, increases or decreases in market prices should be noted.

Accounting convention, where market is lower than cost, employs one of the following two forms of disclosure in the balance sheet:

1. Marketable Securities—at lower of cost or market 48,000
2. Marketable Securities—at cost (market value, $48,000)................50,000

Where market is higher than cost, the disclosure is usually made in a footnote to the financial statements.[2]

10.10 SUMMARY

The cash resource system is the most pervasive of the resource sub-systems in most organizations. The purpose of the system is to maintain a satisfactory state of liquidity in order for the firm to meet its cash obligations in an efficient and timely manner. But because cash has little or no earning power, it is unwise to maintain excess cash reserves. A management objective of the cash system therefore is to optimize cash position.

Because of the importance and vulnerability of cash resources, effective stewardship and management controls must be installed and maintained. Part of the function of feedback is to report on the functioning of controls; but in addition, feedback provides exception, comparative, and interpretive reports to users with a view toward improving the cash resource system.

[2]As noted in the Unit II Introduction, "marketable securities" was under consideration by the Accounting Principles Board as of the date of writing. Considerable pressure has been exerted on the Accounting Principles Board to relax the lower of cost or market rule in valuing marketable securities in favor of using only current market prices. See William H. Beaver, "Reporting Rules for Marketable Equity Securities," *The Journal of Accountancy*, October 1971, pp. 57–61.

CHAPTER 10 APPENDIX

*CASH MANAGEMENT MODELS**

Inventory-type models have been constructed to aid the financial manager in determining his firm's optimum cash balances. Four such models—those developed by Baumel, Miller and Orr, Beranek, and White and Norman—are presented in this appendix.

*The material in this appendix was prepared with the assistance of Richard A. Samuelson, assistant professor of accounting, Stanford University. It appears in this form in J. Fred Weston and Eugene F. Brigham, *Managerial Finance*, 4th ed., pp. 561–569.

THE BAUMOL MODEL[1]

The classic article on cash management by William J. Baumol applies the EOQ model to the cash management problem. Although Baumol's article emphasized the macroeconomic implications for monetary theory, he recognized the implications for business finance and set the stage for further work in this area. In essence, Baumol recognized the fundamental similarities of inventories and cash from a financial viewpoint. In the case of inventories, there are ordering and stock-out costs that make it expensive to keep inventories at a zero level by placing orders for immediate requirements only. But

[1]William J. Baumol, "The Transactions Demand for Cash: An Inventory Theoretic Approach," *Quarterly Journal of Economics*, LXVI (November 1952), 545–556.

there are also costs involved with *holding* inventories, and an optimal policy balances off the opposing costs of ordering and holding inventory.

With cash and securities the situation is very similar. There are order costs in the form of clerical work and brokerage fees when making transfers between the cash account and an investment portfolio. On the other side of the coin, there are holding costs consisting of interest foregone when large cash balances are held to avoid the costs of making transfers. Further, there are also costs associated with running out of cash, just as there are in the case of inventories. As with inventories, there is an optimal cash balance that minimizes these costs.

In its most operational form, the Baumol model assumes that a firm's cash balances behave, over time, in a saw-tooth manner, as shown in Exhibit A10-1.

EXHIBIT A10-1

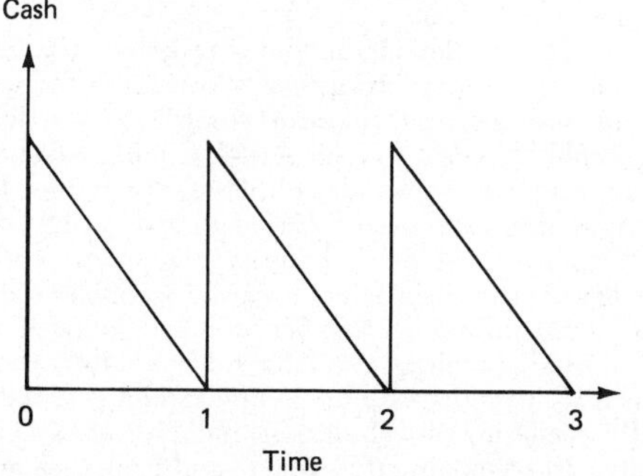

Receipts come in at periodic intervals, such as time 0, 1, 2, 3, and so forth; expenditures occur continuously throughout the periods. Since the model assumes certainty, the firm can adopt an optimal policy that calls for investing I dollars in a short-term investment portfolio at the beginning of each period, then withdrawing C dollars from the portfolio and placing it in the cash account at regular intervals during the period. The model must, of course, take into account both the costs of investment transactions and the costs of holding cash balances.

The decision variables facing the financial manager for a single period can be illustrated in Exhibit A10-2. At the beginning of the period, he has an amount of cash equal to T. A portion of the initial cash, $R = T - I$, is retained in the form of cash, and the balance, I, is invested in a portfolio of short-term liquid assets that earns a rate of return, i. The retained cash, R, is sufficient to meet expenditures during the period from t_0 to t_1. At time t_1, an additional C dollars will be transferred from the investment portfolio to the cash account to cover expenditures for the period from t_1 to t_2; C dollars will again be withdrawn at times t_2 and t_3. At t_4, receipts of T dollars again flow into the cash account, and the same process is repeated during the following period.

If the disbursements are assumed to be continuous, then $R = T - I$ dollars withheld from the initial cash receipt will serve to meet payments during $(T - I)/T$, a fraction of the period between receipts. Further,

EXHIBIT A10-2

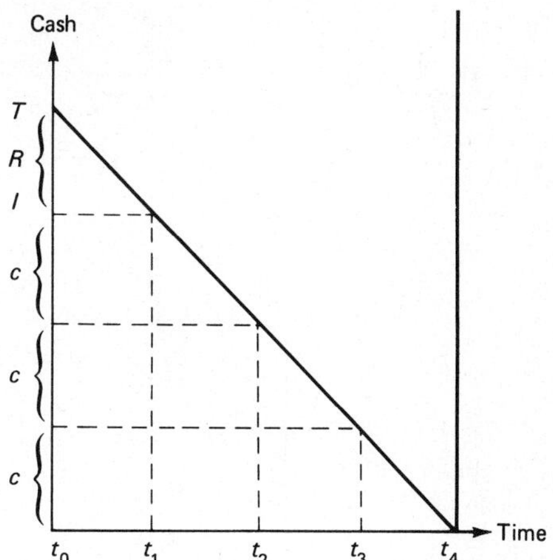

since the average cash holding for that time will be $(T - I)/2$, the interest cost (opportunity cost) of withholding that money will be

$$\left(\frac{T-I}{2}\right)i\left(\frac{T-I}{T}\right)$$

where i is the interest rate on invested funds. A brokerage fee is required to invest the I dollars invested, and this fee is equal to $b_d + K_d I$, where b_d and k_d are fixed and variable costs, respectively, of making deposits (investments).

The cost of obtaining cash for the remainder of the period is found, similarly, to be

$$\left(\frac{C}{2}\right)i\left(\frac{I}{T}\right) + \left(b_w + k_w C\right)\frac{I}{C}$$

The first term is the interest (opportunity) cost of holding the average amount $C/2$ of cash over the subperiod, and the second term is the brokerage cost of making withdrawals from the investment account.

Combining these component costs, the total cost function is given by:

$$Z = \left(\frac{T-I}{2}\right)i\left(\frac{T-I}{T}\right) + b_d + k_d I + \left(\frac{C}{2}\right)i\left(\frac{I}{T}\right) + (b_w + k_w C)\frac{I}{C} \quad \text{(A10-1)}$$

The optimal value for C is found by differentiating this function A10-1 with respect to C and setting the derivative equal to zero. This gives

$$C = \sqrt{\frac{2b_w T}{i}} \quad \text{(A10-2)}$$

R, the optimum cash balance to withold from the initial receipt, is found by differentiating equation A10-1 with respect to I, obtaining

$$R = T - I = C + T\left(\frac{k_w + k_d}{i}\right) \quad \text{(A10-3)}$$

EXHIBIT A10-3

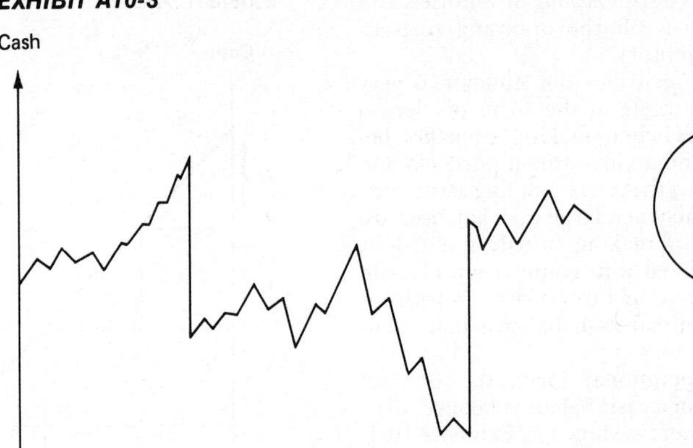

The financial manager, in order to minimize costs, will then withhold R dollars from the initial receipts to cover expenditures for the beginning of the period and will withdraw C dollars from his investment portfolio I/C times per period.

While the Baumol model captures the essential elements of the problem, its restrictive assumptions about the behavior of cash inflows and outflows are probably more applicable to an individual's situation than to a business firm's. For the firm, inflows are likely to be less lumpy, and outflows are likely to be less smooth. Instead, the behavior of cash balances might resemble the pattern of Exhibit A10-3. Daily changes in the cash balance may be up or down, following an irregular and somewhat unpredictable pattern. When the balance drifts upward for some length of time, a point is reached at which the financial officer orders a transfer of cash to the investment portfolio, and the cash balance is returned to some lower level. When disbursements exceed receipts for some period of time, investments are sold and a transfer is made to the cash account to restore the cash balance to a higher level. If this particular behavior is typical, then the certainty assumptions of the Baumol model are too restrictive to make it operational.

THE MILLER-ORR MODEL[2]

Recently Merton Miller and Daniel Orr expanded the Baumol model by incorporating a stochastic generating process for periodic changes in cash balances so that the cash pattern resembles that shown in Exhibit A10-3. In contrast to the completely deterministic assumptions of the Baumol model, Miller and Orr assume that net cash flows behave as if they were generated by a "stationary random walk." This means that changes in the cash balance over a given period are random, in both size and direction, and form a normal distribution as the number of periods observed increases. The model allows for a priori knowledge, however, that changes at a certain time have a greater probability of being either positive or negative.

The Miller-Orr model is designed to determine the time and size of transfers between an investment account and the cash account according to a decision process illustrated in Exhibit A10-4. Changes in cash balances are allowed to wander until they reach some level h at time t_1; they are then reduced to level z, the "return point," by investing $h - z$ dollars in the investment portfolio. Again the cash balance wanders aimlessly until it reaches the minimum balance point, r, at t_2, at which time enough earning assets are sold to return the cash balance to its return point, z. The model is based on a cost function similar to Baumol's and it includes elements for the cost of making transfers to and from cash and for the opportunity cost of holding cash. The upper limit, h, which cash balances should not be allowed to surpass, and the return point, z, to which the balance is returned after every transfer either to or from the cash account, are computed so as to minimize the cost function. The lower limit is assumed to be given, and it could be the minimum balance required by the banks in which the cash is deposited.

The cost function for the Miller-Orr model can be stated as $E(c) = bE(N)/T + iE(M)$, where $E(N)$ = the expected number of transfers between cash and the investment portfolio during the planning period; b = the cost per transfer; T is the number of days in the planning period; $E(M)$ = the expected average daily balance; and i = the daily rate of interest earned on the investments. The objective is to minimize $E(c)$ by choice of the variables h and z, the upper control limit and the return point, respectively.

The solution as derived by Miller and Orr becomes

$$z^* = \left(\frac{3b\sigma^2}{4i}\right)^{1/3}$$
$$h^* = 3z^* \qquad \text{(A10-4)}$$

for the special case where p (the probability that cash balances will increase) equals .5, and q (the probability that cash balances will decrease) equals .5. The variance of the daily changes in the cash balance is represented by

[2] Merton H. Miller and Daniel Orr, "A Model of the Demand for Money by Firms," *Quarterly Journal of Economics*, LXXX (August 1966), 413–435.

EXHIBIT A10-4

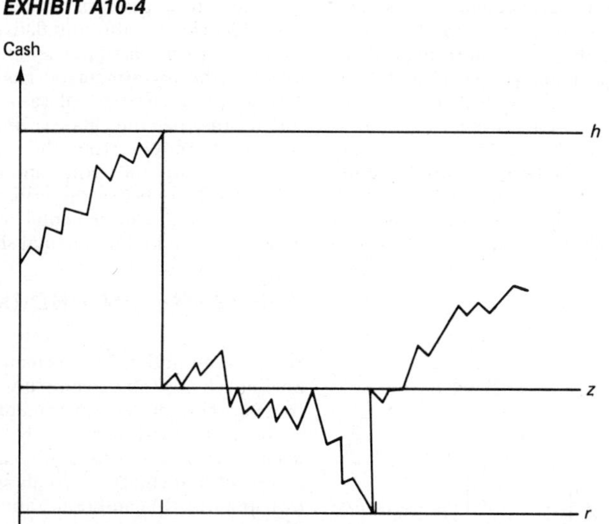

σ^2. As would be expected, a higher transfer cost, b, or variance, σ^2, would imply a greater spread between the upper and lower control limits. In the special case where $p = q = \frac{1}{2}$, the upper control limit will always be 3 times greater than the return point.

Miller and Orr tested their model by applying it to nine months of data on the daily cash balances and purchases and sales of short-term securities of a large industrial company. When the decisions of the model were compared to those actually made by the treasurer of the company, the model was found to produce an average daily cash balance which was about 40 percent *lower* ($160,000 for the model and $275,000 for the treasurer). Looking at it from another side, the model would have been able to match the $275,000 average daily balance with only 80 transactions as compared to the treasurer's 112 actual transactions.

As with most inventory control models, its performance depends not only on how well the conditional predictions (in this case the expected number of transfers and the expected average cash balance) conform to actuality, but also on how well the parameters are estimated. In this model, b, the transfer cost, is sometimes difficult to estimate. In the study made by Miller and Orr, the order costs included such components as "(a) making two or more long-distance phone calls plus fifteen minutes to a half-hour of the assistant treasurer's time, (b) typing up and carefully checking an authorization letter with four copies, (c) carrying the original of the letter to be signed by the treasurer and (d) carrying the copies to the controller's office where special accounts are opened, the entries are posted and further checks of the arithmetic are made."[3] These clerical procedures were thought to be in the magnitude of $20 to $50 per order. In the application of their model, however, Miller and Orr did not rely on their estimate for order costs; instead they tested the model using a series of "assumed" order costs until the model used the same number of transactions as did the treasurer. They could then determine the order cost implied by the treasurer's own action. The results were then used to evaluate the treasurer's performance in managing the cash balances, and, as such, provided valuable information to the treasurer.

The treasurer found, for example, that his action in purchasing securities was often inconsistent. Too often he made small-lot purchases well below the minimum of $h-z$ computed by the model, while at other times he allowed cash balances to drift to as much as double the upper control limit before making a purchase. If it did no more than give the treasurer some perspective about his buying and selling activities, the model was used successfully.

THE BERANEK MODEL[4]

William Beranek has devoted a chapter in his text, *Analysis for Financial Decisions,* to the problem of determining the optimal allocation of available funds between the cash balance and marketable securities. His approach differs from Baumol's in that he includes a probability distribution for expected cash flows and a cost function for the loss of cash discounts and deterioration of credit rating when the firm is caught short of cash. The decision variable in Beranek's model is the allocation of funds between cash and investments at the beginning of

[3] Merton H. Miller and Daniel Orr, *An Application of Control Limit Models to the Management of Corporate Cash Balances,* Proceedings of the Conference on Financial Research and Its Implications for Management, Alexander A. Robichek, ed. (New York: Wiley, 1967).

[4] William Beranek, *Analysis for Financial Decisions* (Homewood, Ill. Irwin, 1963), pp. 345–387.

the period. Withdrawals from investment are assumed possible only at the end of each planning period.

According to Beranek, it is more helpful for the analysis of cash management problems to regard cash *disbursements* as being directly controllable by management and relatively lumpy and to regard *receipts* as being uncontrollable and continuous. In the certainty case this pattern of cash balance behavior would be the reverse of the saw-tooth pattern assumed by Baumol, and it would look similar to the pattern illustrated in Exhibit A10-5. To rationalize this approach one can argue that institutional customs and arrangements might cause cash outflows to be concentrated at periodic intervals. Wages and salaries are ordinarily paid weekly or monthly, credit terms for merchandise purchases may allow payment on the tenth and final days of the month, and other significant outflows such as tax and dividend payments will be concentrated at regular intervals. Insofar as cash outflows are controllable and recur in a cyclical manner, the financial manager can predict his needs for cash over a planning period and can invest a portion of the funds that are not expected to be needed during the period.

EXHIBIT A10-5

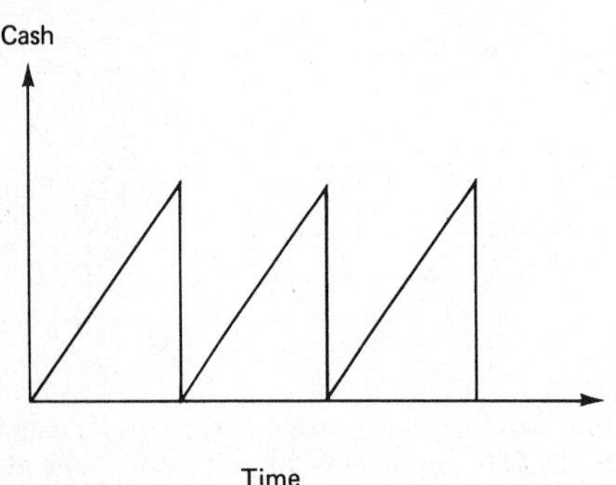

In Beranek's model, the financial manager is regarded as having total resources of k dollars available at the beginning of a planning period. He expects his net cash drain (receipts less disbursements) at the end of the period to be y dollars (either positive or negative), with a probability distribution $g(y)$. His objective of maximizing returns by investment in securities is constrained by transactions costs and the risk of being short of cash when funds are needed for expenditures. "Short costs" are regarded by Beranek as consisting of cash discounts foregone and the deterioration of the firm's credit rating when it is unable to meet payments in time. It might be more realistic, however, to think of "short costs" as the cost of borrowing on a line of credit, since the company would undoubtedly prefer short-term borrowing to foregoing cash discounts or allowing its credit rating to deteriorate.

Given the probability distribution of net cash flows, the costs of running short of cash, and the opportunity cost of holding cash balances, Beranek develops a cost function and differentiates it to find the optimal initial cash balance, or the amount of cash that should be on hand at the start of the period. His solution calls for setting the cash balance at a level where, if this critical level is set, the cumulative probability of running short of cash is equal to the ratio d/a, where d = net return on the investment portfolio and a = incremental cost of being short \$1 of cash. Stated in other words, this means that the financial manager should continue shifting resources from the opening cash balance to securities until the expectation that the ending cash balance will be below the critical minimum is equal to the ratio of the incremental net return per dollar of investment to the incremental short cost per dollar.

THE WHITE AND NORMAN MODEL[5]

D. J. White and J. M. Norman developed a model for an English insurance company very similar in spirit to the Beranek model. Investment decisions are assumed to be considered periodically, and cash inflows from premiums and outflows for claims and expenses are assumed to fluctuate randomly according to some known distribution. In addition, another cash outflow for "call-offs" by the stockbrokers is assumed to have an independent distribution function. A penalty rate on overdrafts (borrowings), analagous to Beranek's short-cost function, is also included in the model, while transactions costs are ignored (or implicitly considered in the net rate of return on investments). The opening cash balance that maximizes expected wealth at the end of the period is the relevant decision variable. The optimal solution is a function of Beranek's d, the incremental return per dollar of investment, and the interest rate on overdrafts.

A COMPARISON OF THE MODELS

The models described in this appendix differ in various details but more essentially in the emphasis given to certain costs effecting their solutions. The Baumol and Miller-Orr models give critical emphasis to the costs arising from transfers between the cash account and the investment portfolio. They ignore the alternative of borrowing and concentrate on the liquidation of investments to meet the needs for cash outflows. The Beranek and White-Norman models, however, give critical emphasis to the costs arising from the shortage of cash (the cost of borrowing, from one viewpoint), while transactions costs are only indirectly considered. The latter models ignore the alternative of liquidating investments to meet cash needs. A model that directly incorporates both the possibility of borrowing and the possibility of holding a portfolio of liquid assets would be desirable, since it is not clear that liquidation of investments would always be preferable to borrowing, or vice versa.

Of all the models, the Miller-Orr version appears to be the easiest to implement, if for no other reason than that its decision rules are so simple. Decision models are more likely to be used when their application is easily understood by management. In addition, the Miller-Orr decision model's planning period covers a longer period of time, so it would not have to be revised as often as the Beranek and Norman-White models. In

[5]D. J. White and J. M. Norman, "Control of Cash Reserves," *Operational Research Quarterly*, 16, No. 3 (September 1965).

the Beranek and Norman-White versions, information must be fed into the model and a decision derived each time a transfer between cash and securities is being considered. While this must be counted as a disadvantage of these models, it could result in better decisions by making the models more responsive to conditions existing at the time decisions are made.

The Miller-Orr model has an element of flexibility, however, that should not be overlooked. Expectations that cash balances are more likely to either increase or decrease over a given period can be incorporated into the calculation of the optimal values for the decision variables. Thus, if a business is subject to seasonal trends, the optimal control limits can be adjusted for each season by using different values for p and q, the probabilities that cash will increase and decrease, respectively.

The Miller-Orr model is built on the assumption that cash balances behave as if they were generated by a random walk. To the extent that this assumption is erroneous, the model would be of little use to management. If the timing of cash outflows (and perhaps even cash inflows) can be controlled significantly by management, then a model of the Beranek or Norman-White type may be more suitable. In this case, management should not have too much difficulty in forming the subjective probability distributions that are needed for these models. In reality, it would probably be true that cash flows are partly random and partly controllable, so that the applicability of any of the models could only be determined by testing them with actual data.

It should be remembered that decision models of the type discussed in this paper are not intended to be applied blindly. There are, of course, difficulties in estimating parameters and probabilities, as has been pointed out. But even more important, there is often information available to the financial manager that is not directly incorporated into the model. Thus, a model, acting ignorantly and unaware of other relevant information, might provide completely erroneous advice. On the other hand, despite their restrictive assumptions and errors, decision models often perform very well if they capture the essential elements in a decision problem. They should not, however, be used as the final answer to any particular decision; rather, cash management models should be used as a guide to intelligent decision-making, tempered with the manager's own good judgment.

CHAPTER 10 REFERENCES AND ADDITIONAL READINGS

Axford, Clinton B. "Cash Management vs. Compensating Balances." *Banking,* August 1970, pp. 43–44.

Baumol, William J. "The Transactions Demand for Cash: An Inventory Theoretic Approach." *Quarterly Journal of Economics* LXVI (November 1952).

Beranek, William. *Analysis for Financial Decision.* Homewood, Ill.: Richard D. Irwin, Inc., 1963, pp. 345–81.

Bowers, Richard L. "Managing the Company's Cash." *Management Accounting,* September 1971, pp. 22–26.

Carmichael, D. R. "Fraud in EDP Systems." *Internal Auditor,* May–June 1969, pp. 28–38.

Cash Flow Analysis for Managerial Control. Research Report No. 38. New York: National Association of Accountants, 1961.

Colt, Donald G. "Management Information Systems for Cash Management and Accounts Receivable Application." *Management Accounting,* June 1969, pp. 65–68.

Daniel, Art. "Shoplifting and Merchandise Fraud." *Retail Control,* January 1971, pp. 2–10.

Davidson, H. J.; Neter, J.; and Petran, A. S. "Estimating the Liability for Unredeemed Stamps." *Journal of Accounting Research,* Autumn 1967, pp. 186–207.

Drebin, Allan R. "Cash-Flowitis: Malady or Syndrome." *Journal of Accountancy,* Spring 1964, pp. 25–34.

Emery, John M. "Managing Cash for Profit." *The Financial Executive,* April 1968, pp. 17–25.

Eppen, Gary D., and Fama, Eugene F. "Solutions for Cash-Balance and Simple Dynamic-Portfolio Problems." *Journal of Business* 41, no. 1 (January 1968): 94–112.

Hewitt, LeRoy A. "An Inventory Technique Applied to Cash Management." *Management Services,* July-August 1970, pp. 37–43.

Jaedicke, Robert K. and Sprouse, Robert T. *Accounting Flows: Income, Funds, and Cash.* Englewood Cliffs, N.J.: Prentice-Hall, Inc., 1965.

King, Alfred M. *Increasing the Productivity of Company Cash.* Englewood Cliffs, N.J.: Prentice-Hall, Inc., 1969.

Lerner, Eugene M. "Simulating a Cash Budget." *California Management Review,* Winter 1968, pp. 79–86.

Lutz, Friedrich, and Lutz, Vera. *The Theory of Investment of the Firm.* Princeton, N.J.: Princeton University Press, 1951, pp. 205–211.

Mann, Everett J. "Cash Flow Earnings—New Concept in Security Analysis." *The Accounting Review,* July 1958, pp. 423–26.

Miller, Merton H., and Orr, Daniel. *An Application of Control Limit Models to the Management of Corporate*

Cash Balances. Proceedings of the Conference on Financial Research and Its Implications for Management, Stanford University, edited by Alexander A. Robichek. New York: John Wiley & Sons, Inc., 1967.

Miller, Merton H., and Orr, Daniel. "A Model of the Demand for Money by Firms." *Quarterly Journal of Economics,* August 1966, pp. 413–35.

Newhouse, Bertha S. "Short-Term Cash Forecasting." *The New York Certified Public Accountant,* August 1969, pp. 597–605.

Orgler, Yair E. *Cash Management Methods and Models.* Belmont, Calif.: Wadsworth Publishing Company, 1970.

Reed, Ward L. "Cash – The Hidden Asset." *The Financial Executive,* November 1970, pp. 54–60.

Stacey, Frederick C. "D. H. Holmes' Loss Prevention Effort." *Retail Control,* April–May 1971, pp. 2–14.

Tobin, J. "The Interest Elasticity of Transactions Demand for Cash." *Review of Economics and Statistics* XXXVIII (August 1956): 241–47.

Van Fenstermaker, Joseph. *Cash Management.* Kent, Ohio: Kent State University Press, 1967.

White, D. J., and Norman, J. M. "Control of Cash Reserves." *Operational Research Quarterly* 16, no. 3 (September 1965).

Wilkins, Edwin N. "Forecasting Cash Flow: Some Problems and Some Applications." *Management Accounting,* October 1967, pp. 26–30.

CHAPTER 10 QUESTIONS, PROBLEMS, AND CASES

10- 1. "The purpose of cash resources is to provide management with a liquidity buffer." Explain the meaning of this statement.

10- 2. Illustrate a graphical relationship between liquidity and earning power. Identify the position of major asset categories along the horizontal axis of the graph.

10- 3. Give two definitions of *liquidity.*

10- 4. Identify as many assumptions as you can that are implicit in the cash position model in Exhibit 10-16.

10- 5. Explain the term *effective annual interest rate.*

10- 6. "The term *cycle* refers to the inception, transformation, and completion of a process." What does a cycle refer to in financial terminology? In production management?

10- 7. Distinguish between a cash cycle operated on a *cash* basis and one operated on an *accrual* basis.

10- 8. Identify three of the principal cash cycles.

10- 9. Define or explain the use of the following terms or phrases:
(a) Negative float
(b) Positive float
(c) Cash discount
(d) Option period
(e) Comparative feedback
(f) Interpretive feedback

10-10. Name five functions of a cash system.

10-11. List five pertinent questions that are answered by a statement of sources and uses of cash.

10-12. What is the purpose of the following statements or records?
(a) A cash forecast (budget)
(b) Statement of sources and uses of cash (cash flow statement)
(c) Cash receipts journal
(d) Cash payments journal (check register)

(e) A voucher register
(f) A bank reconciliation statement

10-13. Distinguish and give examples of *stewardship* and *management* controls of cash.

10-14. Distinguish between the cash cycle of a long-range cash *forecast* and the cash cycle of a short-range cash *budget.*

10-15. What is the purpose of dividing the cash budget into *operating* and *non-operating* categories?

10-16. What are the differences, if any, between an imprest fund and a petty cash fund?

10-17. Define and distinguish *lapping* and *kiting.*

10-18. Identify and explain control procedures relating to cash receipts, cash relocation, and cash disbursements.

10-19. What are the considerations in attempting to optimize cash position?

10-20. Differentiate the use and abuse of float.

10-21. Distinguish a *voucher system* from the use of the word "voucher."

10-22. Describe the duties and obligations of the record-keeping function, the approving authority, and the paying authority in a voucher system.

10-23. "Contrary to popular thinking, a large cash balance is not a reliable indicator of an organization's good state of health; it may indicate just the opposite." Why isn't the cash balance a reliable indicator, and how can a large cash balance indicate an organization's poor state of health?

10-24. Give five reasons why cash budgets provide management control of cash.

10-25. Identify and explain four forms of comparative feedback.

10-26. Identify five items that generally give rise to adjustments between the bank account balance as recorded in the firm's books and the monthly bank statement.

10-27. Book adjustments from a bank reconciliation require a change in the records. Do bank statement adjustments require a similar change in the records? Why?

10-28. According to accounting convention, if the market price of marketable securities is lower than cost, the market price is disclosed in the balance sheet. Why isn't similar treatment accorded to a market price higher than cost?

10-29. Identify the following as *cash* or *non-cash* items:
(a) A check made payable to the company.
(b) Postage stamps.
(c) Traveler's cheques.
(d) Note payable to the company one year from now.
(e) Disneyland coupons.
(f) Ten boxes of unissued trading stamps (i.e., Blue Chip or S & H Green trading stamps).
(g) Note payable to company upon presentation to bank.
(h) Approved voucher.
(i) Cashier's check payable to Thurmond Goodrich, a company vice-president.

10-30. Identify the following as either a *source* or *use* of cash:
(a) Equipment with a book value of $20,000 is sold for $17,000.
(b) 2,000 shares of common stock were purchased as treasury stock.
(c) Bonds payable increased by $100,000.
(d) Net income is $58,000.
(e) Accrued taxes of $8,700 are paid.
(f) Depreciation on operating assets is $14,000.
(g) Cash dividends of $6,000 are paid to stockholders.
(h) 10,000 shares of $5 par value common stock were issued for $16 a share.

10-31. ***OPTIMUM CASH POSITION*** For both parts (a) and (b) assume the cash inflow and outflow is fairly uniform and the financial period is 360 days.

(a) If the firm maintains a cash balance equal to seven days of average daily disbursements, what is the optimal cash balance if total disbursements for the period are estimated to be $1,954,800?

(b) If the firm maintains a cash balance equal to fourteen days of average daily disbursements and the optimal cash balance is $6,300, what is the estimated total cash disbursements for the period?

10-32. ***AN ANALYSIS OF CASH*** The president of a small factory has come to you for advice. His bookkeeper tells him each year that the business has been just about breaking even. He said that the inventories, receivables, and payables have not varied much since the corporation was organized ten years ago but the cash has been constantly increasing. He thinks that the business has been making money and that there is an error. The president stated there has been no sale of assets, refinancing of indebtedness, or change in corporate structure such as sale of stock.

Required:

(a) Present briefly the explanation that you would give the president for the continued increase in cash.

(b) Give examples of transactions that would illustrate your explanation.

(c) What financial statements would you prepare for the president?

(From the CPA exam.)

10-33. ***TRANSFORMATION$_2$ BY MATRIX*** From the following events, determine the balances of all accounts using a matrix form:

(a) Owners invest $20,000 in cash.

(b) Customer pays $2,400 on his bill.

(c) A cash sale of $1,200 is made. The cost of merchandise was $800.

(d) The firm borrows $15,000 on a long-term note.

(e) Equipment is bought for $8,000 in cash and a $21,000 note.

(f) Bank service charge is $18.

(g) $10,500 of merchandise is bought on account.

(h) A payment of $2,500 is made on accounts payable.

(i) $4,720 in wages are paid in cash.

(j) A credit sale of $16,400 is made. The cost of merchandise sold was $9,000.

10-34. ***EFFECTIVE ANNUAL INTEREST RATE*** Assume the financial year consists of 360 days.

(a) What is the *effective annual interest rate* of not taking the following cash discounts:

(1) 3/10, n/30
(2) 2/15, n/45
(3) 1/10, n/40
(4) 2/10, n/60
(5) 3/20, n/60

(b) What is the *cash discount expression* when:

(1) The option period is twenty days, from the 10th, with effective annual interest of 24%?

(2) The discount rate is 15% up to the 20th and the effective annual interest rate is 48%?

(c) Cash discounts of 3/5, n/50 were not taken on $86,598 of purchases during 19x1.

(1) If the firm can borrow the necessary cash from the bank at 7% interest, how would income have been affected?

(2) What rate would the bank have to charge on the net amount ($86,598 − discount) to equal the cash discounts lost?

10-35. ***NET PRICE METHOD—GROSS PRICE METHOD*** Consider the following information:

On July 1, 19x1, the Seller Company sells 2500 lb. of merchandise #1 for $1 per pound to the Buyer Company on credit terms 3/20, n/40. The merchandise is shipped f.o.b. destination for $75.

On July 20, 19x1, the Seller Company sells 700 lb. of merchandise #2 for $2 per pound to the Buyer Company on credit terms 2/10, n/30. The merchandise is shipped f.o.b. shipping point for $20.

Required:

(a) Assume the Buyer Company records the July 1 purchase using the net price method. What amount is credited to accounts payable assuming the Seller Company pays the freight charges?

(b) Assume the Seller Company records the July 20 sale using the gross price method. What amount is credited to the sales account if the Seller Company pays the freight charges?

(c) Assuming the Buyer Company uses the net method to record purchases, what amount is recorded to purchases returns and allowances if 200 lb. of merchandise #1 is returned on July 3?

(d) Assume no purchases returns and allowances and the Seller Company does not pay any freight charges except those charges as specifically designated by the shipping arrangement. What amount is debited to accounts payable by the Buyer Company if the net method is used to record all purchases, and the full amount owed for both purchases (July 1 and July 20) is made on July 24?

(e) What amount of cash is paid by the Buyer Company in part (d)?

10-36. ***NET PRICE METHOD—GROSS PRICE METHOD*** Record the following transactions in *general journal form* assuming the Bailey Company uses the gross price method for recording sales and the Harned Company uses the net price method for recording purchases (record on books of both):

(a) January 8—The Bailey Company sold $35,000 of merchandise (sales invoice #101) to Harned Company on credit terms 2/10, n/30, f.o.b. destination. The Bailey Company paid the freight company $700 to ship the merchandise.

(b) January 10—The Harned Company returned $3,400 of defective merchandise (from sales invoice #101) to the Bailey Company upon receiving a credit memorandum from the Bailey Company.

(c) January 14—The Bailey Company sold $23,450 of merchandise (sales invoice #254) to the Harned Company on credit terms 4/10, n/30, f.o.b. shipping point. The Harned Company paid the freight company $683 to ship the merchandise.

(d) January 20—The Harned Company paid cash to the Bailey Company for the amount owed from invoice #101 and #254.

10-37. ***PAYMENTS AND RECEIPTS—SOURCES AND USES OF CASH*** The following financial data was furnished to you by the Relgne Corporation:

RELGNE CORPORATION
COMPARATIVE TRIAL BALANCES
AT BEGINNING & END OF FISCAL YEAR ENDED OCTOBER 31, 1969

	October 31 1969	Increase	Decrease	November 1 1968
Cash	$ 226,000	$176,000		$ 50,000
Accounts receivable	148,000	48,000		100,000
Inventories	291,000		$ 9,000	300,000
Unexpired insurance	2,500	500		2,000
Long-term investments at cost	10,000		30,000	40,000
Sinking fund	90,000	10,000		80,000
Land and building	195,000			195,000
Equipment	215,000	125,000		90,000
Discount on bonds payable	8,500		500	9,000
Treasury stock at cost	5,000		5,000	10,000
Cost of goods sold	539,000			
Selling and general expenses	287,000			
Income tax	32,000			
Loss on sale of equipment	1,000			
Capital gains tax	3,000			
Total debits	$2,053,000			$876,000
Allowance for doubtful accounts	$ 8,000	$ 3,000		$ 5,000
Accumulated depreciation—building	26,250	3,750		22,500
Accumulated depreciation—equipment	39,750	12,250		27,500
Accounts payable	55,000		5,000	60,000
Notes payable—current	70,000	50,000		20,000
Accrued expenses payable	18,000	3,000		15,000
Taxes payable	35,000	25,000		10,000
Unearned revenue	1,000		8,000	9,000
Note payable—long term	40,000		20,000	60,000
Bonds payable—long term	250,000			250,000
Common stock	300,000	100,000		200,000
Appropriation for sinking fund	90,000	10,000		80,000
Unappropriated retained earnings	94,000		18,000	112,000
Paid-in capital in excess of par	116,000	110,000		5,000
Sales	898,000			
Gain on sale of investments	12,000			
Total credits	$2,053,000			$876,000

The following information was also available:

(a) All purchases and sales were on account.
(b) The sinking fund will be used to retire the long-term bonds.
(c) Equipment with an original cost of $15,000 was sold for $7,000.
(d) Selling and general expenses includes the following expenses:

Expired insurance	$ 2,000
Building depreciation	3,750
Equipment depreciation	19,250
Bad debts expense	4,000
Interest expense	18,000

(e) A six-month note payable for $50,000 was issued towards the purchase of new equipment.
(f) The long-term note payable requires the payment of $20,000 per year plus interest until paid.
(g) Treasury stock was sold for $1,000 more than its cost.
(h) All dividends were paid by cash.

Required:

(1) Prepare schedules computing:
  a. Collections of accounts receivable.
  b. Payments of accounts payable.

(2) Prepare a statement of sources and uses of cash for the Relgne Corporation. Supporting computations should be given.

(From the CPA exam.)

10-38. ***STATEMENT OF SOURCES AND USES OF CASH*** Consider the comparative balance sheet data for 19*x*1 and 19*x*2:

Debit Balances	**19x1**	**19x2**
Cash	$ 12,340	$ 17,480
Marketable securities	50,000	60,000
Notes receivable—current	120,000	80,000
Accounts receivable	184,500	215,400
Merchandise inventory	101,700	146,350
Prepaid insurance	8,400	4,200
Land	80,000	80,000
Buildings	140,000	140,000
Machinery & equipment	218,000	250,000
Treasury stock	—	20,000

Credit Balances	**19x1**	**19x2**
Accumulated deprec.—buildings	$ 56,000	$ 63,000
Accumulated deprec.—mach. & equip.	120,000	56,000
Notes payable—current	40,000	60,000
Accounts payable	87,320	94,770
Long-term notes payable	200,000	50,000
Deferred taxes payable	15,000	19,000
Preferred stock, $10 par value	40,000	40,000
Common stock, $5 par value	200,000	275,000
Paid-in capital	120,000	315,000
Retained earnings	36,620	40,660

Other data:

(a) Operating income for 19*x*2 was $26,040.
(b) The company purchased 1,000 shares of its own preferred stock for $20 per share.
(c) Sold machinery for $24,000. The machinery had an original cost of $100,000 and an accumulated depreciation of $80,000.
(d) Purchased new machinery for $132,000.
(e) Paid cash dividends of $30,000.
(f) 15,000 shares of common stock were sold for $18 per share.

Required:

(1) Prepare a statement of changes in financial position.
(2) Prepare a cash flow statement.

10-39. ***CASH FORECAST*** The Standard Mercantile Corporation is a wholesaler and ends its fiscal year on December 31. You have been requested in early January 1972 to assist in the preparation of a cash forecast. The following information is available regarding the company's operations:

(a) Management believes the 1971 sales pattern is a reasonable estimate of 1972 sales. Sales in 1971 were as follows:

January	$ 360,000
February	420,000
March	600,000
April	540,000
May	480,000
June	400,000
July	350,000
August	550,000
September	500,000
October	400,000
November	600,000
December	800,000
	$6,000,000

(b) The accounts receivable at December 31 total $380,000. Sales collections are generally made as follows:

During month of sale	60%
In first subsequent month	30%
In second subsequent month	9%
Uncollectible	1%

(c) The purchase cost of goods averages 60% of selling price. The cost of inventory on hand at December 31 is $840,000, of which $30,000 is obsolete. Arrangements have been made to sell the obsolete inventory in January at half of the normal selling price on a C.O.D. basis.

The company wishes to maintain the inventory as of the first of each month at a level of three months' sales as determined by the sales forecast for the next three months. All purchases are paid for on the tenth of the following month. Accounts payable for purchases at December 31 total $370,000.

(d) Recurring fixed expenses amount to $120,000 per month including depreciation of $20,000. For accounting purposes the company apportions the recurring fixed expenses to the various months in the same proportion as that month's estimated sales bears to the estimated total annual sales. Variable expenses amount to 10% of sales. Payments for expenses are made as follows:

	During Month Incurred	Following Month
Fixed expenses	55%	45%
Variable expenses	70%	30%

(e) Annual property taxes amount to $50,000 and are paid in equal installments on December 31 and March 31. The property taxes are in addition to the expenses in item (d).

(f) It is anticipated that cash dividends of $20,000 will be paid each quarter on the fifteenth day of the third month of the quarter.

(g) During the winter unusual advertising costs will be incurred which will require cash payments of $10,000 in February and $15,000 in March. The advertising costs are in addition to the expenses in item (d).

(h) Equipment replacements are made at the rate of $3,000 per month. The equipment has an average estimated life of six years.

(i) The company's income tax for 1971 is $230,000. A Declaration of Estimated Income Tax was filed for 1971. The declaration estimated the company's total 1971 tax as $210,000 and payments were made as prescribed by income tax regulations. The balance of the tax due will be paid in equal installments.

For 1972, the company will file a declaration estimating the total tax as $220,000.

(j) At December 31, 1971, the company had a bank loan with an unpaid balance of $280,000. The loan requires a principal payment of $20,000 on the last day of each month plus interest at 1/2% per month on the unpaid balance at the first of the month. The entire balance is due on March 31, 1972.

(k) The cash balance at December 31, 1971, is $100,000.

Required:

Prepare a cash forecast statement by months for the first three months of 1972 for the Standard Mercantile Corporation. The statement should show the amount of cash on hand (or deficiency of cash) at the end of each month.

(Adapted from the CPA exam.)

10-40. ***CASH RECEIPTS AND DISBURSEMENTS—RECONCILIATION*** Consider the following data for the Bailey Teapot Company:

	October	November
Balance per bank statement	$8,489.00	$ 2,204.31
Balance per books	7,997.00	1,622.02
Total receipts per bank statement		34,178.43
Total receipts per books		34,512.03
Total disbursements per bank statement		41,003.12
Total disbursements per books		40,887.01
Bank service charge	4.80	5.60
Checks marked nsf	110.00	54.30
Deposits in transit	330.40	500.00
Outstanding checks at month end:		
Oct. #123 $287.00		
#129 424.00		
#141 10.00		
#163 56.40		
#164 111.02		
#170 48.78	937.20	
Nov. #129 $424.00		
#164 111.02		
#181 78.00		
#184 121.63		
#193 21.54		756.19
Error on bank statement in entering deposit of November 4:		
Correct amount $873.12		
Entered as 837.12		36.00
Deposit of Dailey Sodacracker Co. credited by bank to Bailey Co.		412.00
Check #180 written Nov. 7 erroneously recorded on the check register as $93.00. The correct amount is $83.00.		10.00

Required:

Assume service charges and nsf checks are recorded on the books in the following month, and bank statements are received on the fifth of each month.

(a) What is the *correct* total for:
   (1) Cash receipts in November?
   (2) Cash disbursements in November?

(b) Prepare a reconciliation of the November book balance and the bank balance to a *correct* balance.

(c) Reconciling from the bank statement balance to the book balance, show how you would treat each item. Indicate whether it is an addition or subtraction from the bank balance by an "X."

	Oct.		Receipts		Disb.		Nov.	
	Add	Sub	Add	Sub	Add	Sub	Add	Sub
Bank service charge—Oct.								
Bank service charge—Nov.								
Nsf checks—Oct.								
Nsf checks—Nov.								
Deposits in transit—Oct.								
Deposits in transit—Nov.								
Outstanding checks—Oct.								
Outstanding checks—Nov.								
Error by bank in entering deposit of Nov. 4								
Deposit of Dailey Sodacracker Co. credited to Bailey								
Erroneous recording of check #180								

10-41. ***BANK RECONCILIATION*** The following information is obtained from an analysis of the cash receipts and disbursements of the Tuck Company as of December 31, 1971:

(a) The bookkeeper's bank reconciliation at November 30, 1971.

Balance per bank statement		$19,400
Add deposit in transit		1,100
Total		20,500
Less outstanding checks		
#2540	$140	
1501	750	
1503	480	
1504	800	
1505	30	2,300
Balance per books		$18,200

(b) A summary of the bank statement for December 1971.

Balance brought forward	$ 19,400
Deposits	148,700
	168,100
Charges	132,500
Balance, December 31, 1971	$ 35,600

(c) A summary of the cash book for December 1971, before adjustments.

Balance brought forward	$ 18,200
Receipts	149,690
	167,890
Disbursements	124,885
Balance, December 31, 1971	$ 43,005

(d) Included with the cancelled checks returned with the December bank statement were the following:

Number	**Date of Check**	**Amount of Check**	
#1501	November 28, 1971	$75	This check was in payment of an invoice for $750 and was recorded in the cash book as $750.
#1503	November 28, 1971	$580	This check was in payment of an invoice for $580 and was recorded in the cash book as $580.
#1528	December 12, 1971	$800	This check replaced #1504 that was returned by the payee because it was mutilated. Check #1504 was not cancelled on the books.
–	December 19, 1971	$200	This was a counter check drawn at the bank by the president of the company as a cash advance for travel expense. The president overlooked informing the bookkeeper about the check.
–	December 20, 1971	$300	The drawer of this check was the Tuck Company.
#1535	December 20, 1971	$350	This check had been labeled nsf and returned to the payee because the bank had erroneously believed that the check was drawn by the Tuck Company. Subsequently the payee was advised to redeposit the check.
#1575	January 5, 1972	$10,000	This check was given to the payee on December 30, 1971, as a postdated check with the understanding that it would not be deposited until January 5. The check was not recorded on the books in December.

(e) The Tuck Company discounted its own sixty-day note for $9,000 with the bank on December 1, 1971. The discount rate was 6%. The bookkeeper recorded the proceeds as a cash receipt at the face value of the note.

(f) The bookkeeper records customers' dishonored checks as a reduction of cash receipts. When the dishonored checks are redeposited they are recorded as a regular cash receipt. Two nsf checks for $180 and $220 were returned by the bank during December. The $180 check was redeposited but the $220 check was still on hand at December 31. Cancellations of Tuck Company checks are recorded by a reduction of cash disbursements.

(g) December bank charges were $20. In addition a $10 service charge was made in December for the collection of a foreign draft in November. These charges were not recorded on the books.

(h) Check #2540 listed in the November outstanding checks was drawn in 1968. Since the payee cannot be located, the president of Tuck Company agreed to the suggestion that the check be written back into the accounts by a journal entry.

(i) Outstanding checks at December 31, 1971, totaled $4,000, excluding checks #2540 and #1504.

(j) A deposit of $2,400 was not recorded on the December bank statement.

The bookkeeper had recorded this deposit on the books on December 31, 1971, and then mailed the deposit to the bank.

Required:

(1) What is the *correct* total for:
   a. Cash receipts in December?
   b. Cash disbursements in December?

(2) Prepare a reconciliation of the cash receipts and cash disbursements recorded on the bank statement and on the company's books for the month of December 1971. The reconciliation should agree with the cash figure that will appear in the company's financial statements.

(Adapted from the CPA exam.)

CHAPTER

11

CREDIT MANAGEMENT

11.1 NATURE OF CREDIT

Credit is the ability to transact business currently in consideration of the promise of a future money exchange. It is characterized by such slogans as "buy now—pay later." Virtually every type of business transaction can be handled on a credit basis. Here are some activities which serve to illustrate the broad range of credit:

1. Goods or services are purchased now—payment is made at a later date.
2. A loan is obtained and is repayed in installments.
3. A credit card is used to purchase goods or services, with payment made upon receiving a statement from the credit card company.
4. Professional people, such as doctors and lawyers, provide services and agree to "send the bill."
5. Banks provide a line of credit, such as a "ready-reserve account" to honor overdraft checks within a certain limit.

Credit is so pervasive in certain advanced societies that it has been said that "about ninety-nine percent of all commercial transactions in the United States and Canada are on credit terms."[1]

Credit, in most business and personal situations, works in two directions: credit is given—credit is received. For example, a business purchases merchandise from a vendor "on account," and then sells the merchandise to a customer "on account."

11.2 PURPOSE OF CREDIT

OBTAINING CREDIT

A primary purpose for using credit in a business is to normalize cash flow. Without credit (usually in the form of accounts payable), a firm would have to pay for its purchases of goods and services as received—"cash on delivery" (C.O.D.). Credit allows a firm to predict and control the outflow of cash and thereby optimize cash position. As indicated earlier, cash has no earning power. Any balance not required for planned operating and non-operating uses should be converted to income-producing purposes (such as conversion into securities, merchandise inventory, or plant and equipment). Exhibit 11-1 shows how the use of credit can stabilize cash flow, and thereby reduce the average cash balance.

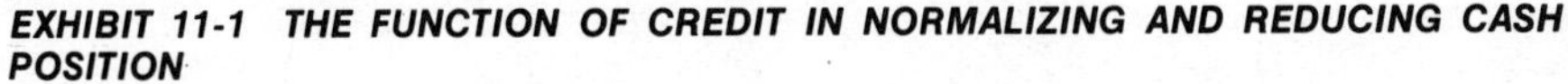

EXHIBIT 11-1 THE FUNCTION OF CREDIT IN NORMALIZING AND REDUCING CASH POSITION

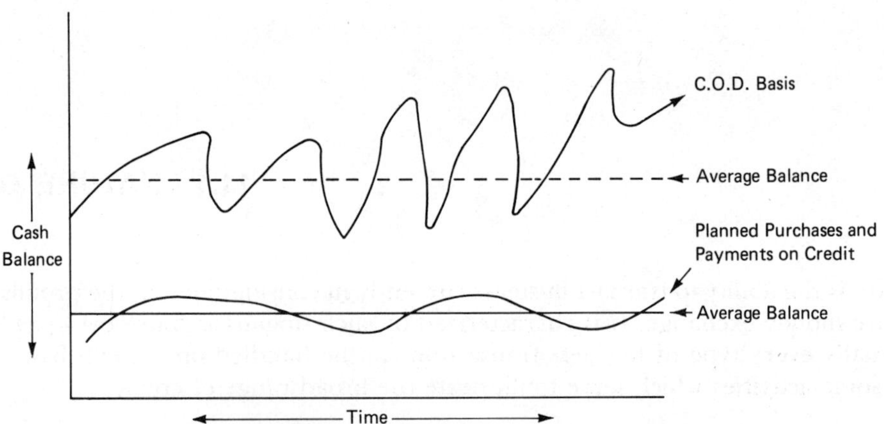

Sales usually fluctuate on the basis of monthly or seasonal demand. The burgeoning of sales at Christmas is a well-known example. This means that inventory must be accumulated (either bought or produced) and other costs incurred in anticipation of peak sale periods. In the absence of credit, cash would have to be paid prior to receiving revenue from sales. Although a firm's sales may be profitable (sales exceed costs and expenses), the difference in the *timing* of cash outlays and inflows

[1] *How to Build Profits by Controlling Costs* (New York: Dun & Bradstreet, Inc., 1959), p. 43.

EXHIBIT 11-2 NORMALIZING CASH FLOW THROUGH THE USE OF CREDIT

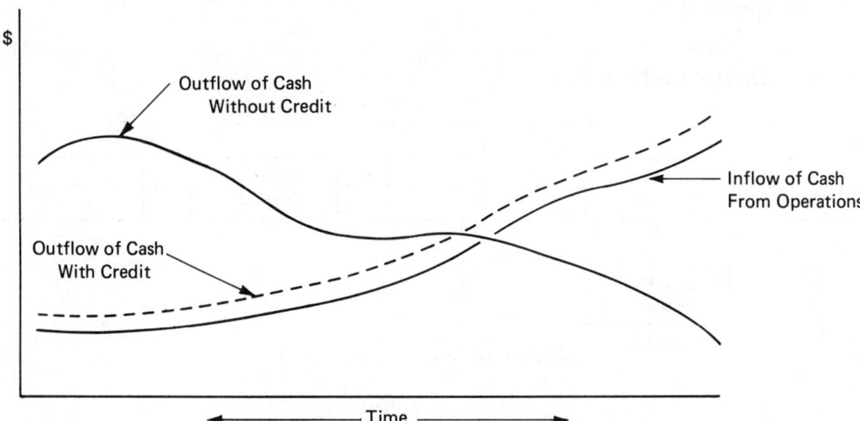

can pose serious liquidity problems. As shown in Exhibit 11-2, credit smooths out the disparity between cash outlays and inflows caused by timing differences between peak purchases and peak sales.

EXTENDING CREDIT

Most firms prefer to sell on a cash basis because of the lack of collection problems, bad-debt losses, and because there is no time lag between sale and receipt of payment. Customers, however, prefer delayed payments for several reasons:

1. *Convenience:* It is inconvenient and risky to carry sums of cash. It is also inconvenient to write checks at every stop. Ordering by telephone or by mail is also inconvenient when payment is C.O.D.
2. *More purchasing power:* Customers can purchase more goods and services when payments are in installments. Most persons, for example, do not have enough ready cash to pay the full price of an automobile. However, they do purchase automobiles based on payments that are scaled to their budgets.

Depending on prevailing practices in an industry, most new firms find that they must extend credit in order to compete. Later a firm usually expands its credit in order to increase sales volume.

11.3 THE CREDIT CYCLE

RECEIVABLES

As with other resources, there is a credit cycle. Credit given and credit received each have their own cycle. The cycle for credit given (which is usually in the form of accounts receivable) is shown in Exhibit 11-3. As illustrated, receivables are created through the sale of goods and services where the buyer is allowed to pay later on specified terms. Such receivables are called *trade receivables,* since they arise from the trading activities of a firm.

EXHIBIT 11-3 CREDIT GIVEN CYCLE

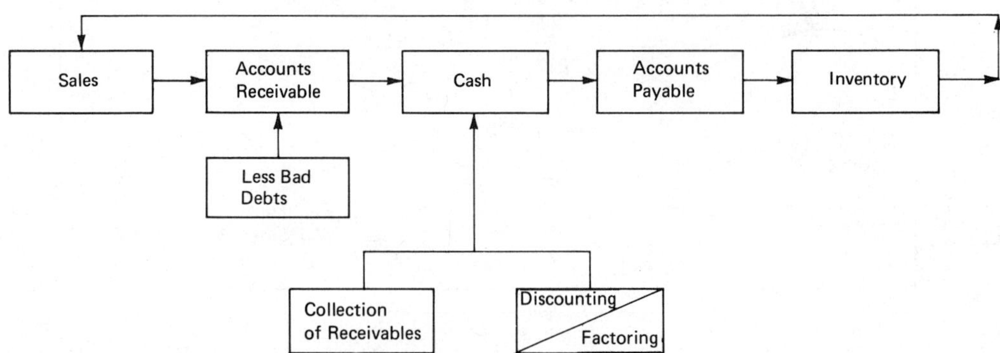

Receivables are ultimately either converted into cash or become uncollectible ("bad debts"). The conversion to cash is accomplished: (1) through collection of accounts receivable, (2) by using receivables as collateral for a loan, or (3) by selling the receivables outright.

Cash inflow from receivables is available to pay vendors, establish credit, make additional purchases of inventory. From this point inventory is sold, and payment is received on account to restart the cycle.

PAYABLES

Credit received is called *payables.* While the majority of payables arise from goods and services purchased on credit (called *trade accounts payable*), there are other types of payables for which no bills are received to fix the obligation. At any given date, a firm has outstanding obligations on such items as payroll, interest on notes, and taxes. This class of payables is called *accruals* and will be discussed later.

Like receivables, payables have a cycle, as shown in Exhibit 11-4. Goods and services are obtained on a credit basis and converted into inventory for sale or are used for other operating purposes. Inventory is sold in exchange for credit given, which is later converted into cash. The payables are settled with collections on receivables. The combination of cash and credit is used to obtain additional goods and services to restart the cycle.

11.4 TYPES OF CREDIT

Credit received and given may exist in several forms. The usual form of credit received is a purchase *on account.* This arrangement is in the nature of an unsecured debt on the part of the purchaser which is evidenced by an invoice and is usually payable within thirty to sixty days, before applying interest or carrying charges, depending on industry practice. To obtain open account credit from a seller, the debtor (borrower) usually completes an application, which is reviewed by a credit agency within the firm and/or by an independent agency such as the Retail Credit Merchants Association or Dun & Bradstreet. Upon determining that the applicant is a sound risk, a specified credit arrangement is granted.

EXHIBIT 11-4 CREDIT RECEIVED CYCLE

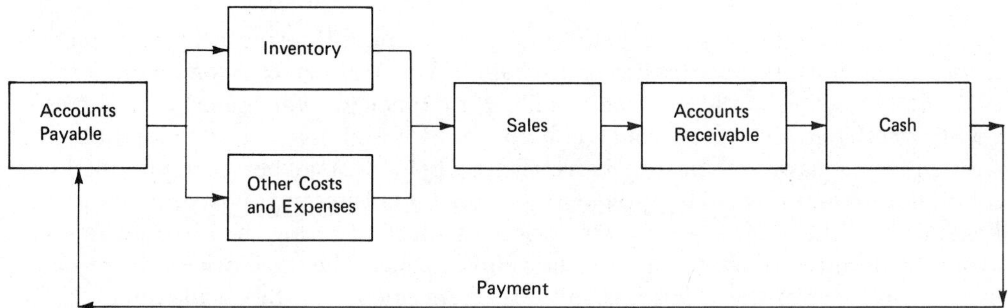

When the amount of a purchase is substantial and/or the payment period is more than thirty to sixty days, the purchaser may be asked to sign a *note* as evidence of the transaction. While open or trade accounts discussed above are informal understandings, signed notes constitute a formal contract or promise to pay a certain amount on a certain date. The debtor acknowledges in writing the amount of the debt, interest (if any), and the terms of payment. The creditor (extender of credit) may endorse the signed note in favor of a bank and receive the amount of the note less a discount. This process of discounting notes is discussed in more detail below.

Notes may be payable in one lump sum or in installments. One type of installment note is called a *conditional sales contract,* which entitles the purchaser to the use of the property purchased, but where title does not pass until the full amount has been paid.

Another form of credit which is common in certain industries (usually in retail trades) is *consignment.* Goods are furnished by a manufacturer or wholesaler (the *consignor*) to a retailer (the *consignee*), on an understanding that payment is due only when goods are sold. This permits a retailer to finance inventory through credit and return the goods to the consignor if he cannot sell them. The consignor does not report a sale when the goods are consigned to the retailer, but when the consignee sells them.

Still another form of credit is the *line of credit.* This is an arrangement between an extender of credit and the recipient that the latter may borrow (or purchase) up to a certain amount without further authorization. Business firms usually have lines of credit with banks which permit them to borrow cash up to an agreed limit. They may borrow and repay in whatever amounts and time intervals they wish, as long as they do not exceed the maximum amount as stipulated by the line of credit. In the case of money lines of credit, the interest rate is usually specified so that subsequent fluctuations in rate do not affect the arrangement. Banks usually charge a fee (or "points"), say 1% to 1½% of the maximum amount, to set up the line of credit. This fee is paid regardless of whether or to what extent the line of credit is used.

Lines of credit have been formalized for the consuming public in the form of *credit cards* and other revolving charge plans. A customer is rated by a firm and/or a credit agency as to risk and is assigned a *credit limit.* Purchases may be made up to this limit and payment is made on the basis of, say, 10% of the balance owed at each billing date. Again, purchases may be made to the extent that the balance owing is less than the credit limit. The whole or any part of the balance in excess of the minimum payment can be paid at any time without penalty.

CREDIT TERMS AND ALLOWANCES

Credit terms include the amount and timing of payment. The most common of credit terms, *cash discounts,* was discussed in chapter 10. Another class of credit terms is *trade discounts.* This is the practice of billing a retailer (or wholesaler) at a suggested retail price from which a percentage discount is allowed to arrive at a merchant's net cost. Different classes of consumers (retailers, wholesalers, jobbers) are provided with different discount rates to be applied to the billed retail amount. This provides pricing flexibility for the seller; he may vary prices by simply altering the discount rate and avoid the necessity of changing price lists and catalogs. The retail price is *not* recorded by the purchaser or the seller; it is only a reference point for the calculation of the net or actual price.

It should be noted that the Robinson-Patman Act of 1936 and other federal laws prohibit discrimination in pricing in interstate commerce and allow discounts only on the basis of the quantity ordered or similar factors.

FACTORING AND DISCOUNTING

As we discussed earlier, the extender of credit prefers to deal in cash but extends credit in order to compete and grow. There are various methods available by which a firm may extend credit and secure immediate cash.

One method is through the *sale of accounts receivable.* Certain business organizations known as *factors* will purchase accounts receivable for cash and assume the risk of collection. The sale of receivables (called *factoring*) involves several costs to the seller. The factor (purchaser) charges both interest on the amount borrowed and a percentage of collections on the receivables. In addition, the factor retains at all times a fixed percentage (from 5 to 10%) of the balance of uncollected receivables (a factor or dealer's reserve). This is done to protect the factor against sales returns, allowances, and bad accounts. In some cases the factor assumes the risk of collection, in other cases he reserves the right to charge bad accounts back to the seller by means of the factor's reserve.

A firm may also convert accounts receivable to cash by pledging or assigning them to a lender as collateral for a loan. Generally, repayment of the loan is made from collections on the receivables, with the lender having recourse to the assigned receivables in the event of the borrower's failure to pay. The assigned receivables would not be available to any other creditors for satisfaction of their debts and cannot be used as collateral for other loans.

DISCOUNTING NOTES RECEIVABLE

Notes receivable can also be sold, pledged as security for a loan, or assigned. They are generally discounted in the process of sale, as mentioned earlier.

When a note is discounted, the borrower (assignor) has a *contingent liability* for the amount of the note if the note is with *recourse.* No contingent liability is present if the note is *without recourse.* In the case of notes with recourse, the actual liability does not exist until the maker fails to pay; and since it is a contingent liability, a footnote to the balance sheet is sufficient disclosure.

Because notes have a specific term, their value at any time prior to maturity is less than the maturity value. The difference in value is a function of time to maturity and an interest rate.

For example, X Company receives a $1,000 (face value) note from Mr. Y payable in sixty days *without* interest. The bank discount rate is 6%. If, after thirty days, X Company wishes to discount the note with the bank, it will receive in cash proceeds the following amount:

$$\$1{,}000 - \left(\frac{6}{100} \times \frac{30 \text{ days}}{360 \text{ days}} \times \frac{\$1{,}000}{1}\right) = \$995$$

If X Company discounts the note on the forty-fifth day, the proceeds would be as follows (note that the proceeds increase as we approach the maturity date):

$$\$1{,}000 - \left(\frac{6}{100} \times \frac{15}{360} \times \frac{1{,}000}{1}\right) = \$997.50 \text{ Proceeds}$$

In computing the term of a note, some banks count both the first and last days, although the customary practice is to omit either the first or last day; usually the latter.

Now assume that the note is interest-bearing at an annual interest rate of 9%. If X Company holds the note for the full term (sixty days), its proceeds would be:

$$\$1{,}000 + \left(\frac{9}{100} \times \frac{60}{360} \times \frac{1{,}000}{1}\right) = \$1{,}015.00 \text{ Proceeds}$$

If X Company discounts the note alternatively on the thirtieth or forty-fifth day, based on a bank discount rate of 6 %, its proceeds would be:

$$\text{30th:}\quad \$1{,}015.00 - \left(\frac{6}{100} \times \frac{30}{360} \times \frac{1{,}015.00}{.\,1}\right) = \$1{,}009.92 \text{ Proceeds}$$

$$\text{45th:}\quad \$1{,}015.00 - \left(\frac{6}{100} \times \frac{15}{360} \times \frac{1{,}015.00}{1}\right) = \$1{,}012.46 \text{ Proceeds}$$

On an interest-bearing note we observe that the discount is based on *maturity value* and not on *face value.*

11.5 PROVIDING FOR DOUBTFUL ACCOUNTS

Extending credit involves the risk that some people will not pay. In order to provide for this contingency an *allowance for doubtful accounts* is established to cover uncollectibles that arise in the future out of present sales.

An allowance for doubtful accounts offsets accounts receivable in the balance sheet presentation as follows:

1. Accounts receivable	$100,000	
Less: Allowance for doubtful accounts	5,000	$95,000

or

2. Accounts receivable (net of allowance for doubtful accounts)	$95,000

The allowance account is increased by charges to *bad debt expense,* which is an income statement account listed under *general and administrative expense.* The entry to increase the allowance account is:

Increase (Debit) Bad debt expense	$	
Increase (Credit) Allowance for doubtful accounts		$

When a bad debt materializes, after efforts to collect have been exhausted, the loss is charged to the allowance account:

Decrease (Debit) Allowance for doubtful accounts	$	
Decrease (Credit) Accounts receivable		$

This entry eliminates the related receivables and decreases the allowance account. Efforts to collect may continue, and if they are successful they give rise to the following entries:

1. *Restore the receivable* (this entry reverses the former one)

Increase (Debit) Accounts receivable............	$	
Increase (Credit) Allowance for doubtful accounts		$

2. *Record the payment*

Increase (Debit) Cash	$	
Decrease (Credit) Accounts receivable		$

By restoring the receivable, the above procedure recognizes that an account has been restored and settled.

There are two basic methods for providing an allowance for doubtful accounts.

Sales Method: Bad debts may be viewed as incomplete sales and therefore bear

EXHIBIT 11-5

PERCENTAGE OF SALES

Procedure: A stated percentage of credit or total sales is set aside as an allowance for uncollectibles. The percentage figure is adjusted in the light of subsequent experience; thus, if the allowance account tends to decrease rapidly, a higher percentage rate of sales is applied, and *vice versa.*

Advantages: This method is computationally easy, and it provides the closest matching of the estimated bad debts with sales.

Disadvantages: This method does not require a close analysis of accounts receivable as an integral procedure.

RECEIVABLES

1. Percentage of Receivables

Procedure: A stated percentage representing expected uncollectibles is applied to receivables outstanding.

Advantages: The method is computationally easy once the initial percentage rate is obtained.

Disadvantage: As with the percentage of sales method, this method does not require an ongoing analysis or aging of receivables as an integral procedure.

2. Aging of Receivables

Procedure: The receivables are classified in terms of age and experience loss rates are applied to the respective age groups, e.g.,

	Balance	Loss Rate	Allowance
0–30 Days	$100,000	1%	$1,000
31–60 Days	10,000	3	300
61–90 Days	2,000	10	200
91–120 Days	1,000	30	300
Over 120 Days	2,000	80	1,600
	$115,000		$3,400

Each time the aging process is undertaken, the previous allowance is eliminated and the new allowance is substituted in its place.

Advantages: This method requires the periodic analysis of all accounts receivables.

Disadvantages: The method is computionally difficult (although much less so through computer applications), and it may fail to assign bad debt losses to their related sales periods.

a relationship to sales activity. Under this theory, a firm sets aside a small percentage of sales, say one-half of one percent—based on industry averages or a firm's experience—as an allowance to cover bad debts that arise from those sales. The percentage is usually based on credit sales only, but some firms base it on total sales.

Receivables Method: Or, bad debts may be viewed as arising from an error in credit judgment, so that the "allowance" should be based on accounts receivable outstanding rather than on sales. This is done by adjusting the allowance account to equal a percentage of the accounts receivable balance, or by setting the allowance account equal to the probability of collection based on "aging" the accounts receivable.

These methods are summarized and compared in Exhibit 11-5. Exhibit 11-6 gives some basic data on sales, receivables, and bad debts over a four-year period.

EXHIBIT 11-6

	19x4	19x3	19x2	19x1
1. Credit sales	$3,200,000	$2,600,000	$2,100,000	$2,400,000
2. Accounts receivable outstanding (end of year)	800,000	900,000	700,000	600,000
3. Aged: 0–30 days	400,000	500,000	400,000	350,000
31–60 days	200,000	220,000	210,000	150,000
61–90 days	150,000	140,000	70,000	40,000
Over 90 days	50,000	40,000	20,000	60,000
4. Actual bad debts	$ 35,000	$ 29,000	$ 25,000	$ 6,000

Applying percentage rates based on industry or a firm's own experience, allowances are calculated as in Exhibit 11-7.

EXHIBIT 11-7

Based On	**19x4**	**19x3**	**19x2**	**19x1**
1. 1% of credit sales	$32,000	$26,000	$21,000	$24,000
2. 4% of average* balance in receivables	34,000	32,000	26,000	24,000
3. Aging receivables:				
1%—0—30 days	4,000	5,000	4,000	3,500
3%—31—60 days	6,000	6,600	6,300	4,500
10%—61—90 days	15,000	14,000	7,000	4,000
20%—Over 90 days	10,000	8,000	4,000	12,000
Total aging	$35,000	$33,600	$21,300	$24,000

$$\text{*Average receivables} = \frac{\text{Beginning Balance} + \text{Ending Balance in Receivables}}{2}$$

The allowance for doubtful accounts record for the four-year period based on percentage of sales would be:

EXHIBIT 11-8 ALLOWANCE FOR DOUBTFUL ACCOUNTS BASED ON PERCENTAGE OF SALES

	19x4	19x3	19x2	19x1
Beginning balance	$11,000	$14,000	$18,000	-0-
Amount added during the year	32,000	26,000	21,000	24,000
Amount available during the year	43,000	40,000	39,000	24,000
Less: Bad debts	(35,000)	(29,000)	(25,000)	(6,000)
Ending balance	$ 8,000	$11,000	$14,000	$18,000
Ending balance as a percentage of sales	.25%	.42%	.66⅔%	.75%

Increments are made to the allowance account during each year in proportion to sales. In both absolute terms and as a percentage of sales, the decreasing balance of the allowance account shows the rate of 1% is too low. The rate is adjusted—in this case to provide for a higher allowance—when a trend is apparent. In the typical case it may take several years before a trend becomes apparent.

The allowance account record for the four-year period based on receivables (aging) would be:

EXHIBIT 11-9 ALLOWANCE FOR DOUBTFUL ACCOUNTS BASED ON AGING OF RECEIVABLES

	19x4	19x3	19x2	19x1
Beginning balance and amount available during the year	$33,600	$21,300	$24,000	$ -0-
Less: Bad debts	(35,000)	(29,000)	(25,000)	(6,000)
Balance net of bad debts	(1,400)	(7,700)	(1,000)	(6,000)
Adjustment to the allowance account [±]	36,400	41,300	22,300	30,000
Ending balance required (based on analysis of accounts receivable)	$35,000	$33,600	$21,300	$24,000

Under aging, no increment is made to the allowance account during the year. Receivables are aged and analyzed at the end of the year, and the existing balance in the allowance account is adjusted by an amount necessary to bring the balance of the account into agreement with the analysis of probable bad debts.

Notice that net income for the four years would be different by virtue of this option:

EXHIBIT 11-10 IMPACT ON NET INCOME OF THE SALES VERSUS RECEIVABLES METHODS OF PROVIDING FOR DOUBTFUL ACCOUNTS

	Charge to Income		Income: Net Difference	Income: Cumulative Difference
	Sales	**Receivables (Aging)**	**(S > R)**	**(S > R)**
19x1	$ 24,000	$ 30,000	$ 6,000	$6,000
19x2	21,000	22,300	1,300	7,300
19x3	26,000	41,300	15,300	22,600
19x4	32,000	36,400	4,400	27,000
TOTAL	$103,000	$130,000	$27,000	

This example is illustrative of the manner in which choices from among many acceptable accounting methods can be used to influence net income.

11.6 PROCESSING CREDIT TRANSACTIONS

INPUT

The principal credit system events and transaction documents are shown in Exhibit 11-11.

TRANSFORMATION$_1$

Establishing duality or the cause-and-effect relationship of credit events is the function of T_1. Typical T_1 entries for credit events are shown in Exhibits 11-12 and 11-13.

Related T_1 Records and Journals

Because of numerous, repetitive events involving credit transactions, it is useful to use specialized records (journals) for these items at the T_1 stage. The *sales journal* (Exhibit 11-14) is a specialized record for *all sales.*

EXHIBIT 11-11 MAJOR CREDIT INPUTS

EVENT	TRANSACTION DOCUMENT	
	Credit Received (Payables)	**Credit Given (Receivables)**
A. Credit is received/given.	1. *Invoice*—Purchase of goods. 2. *Adjustment*—Expense accruals (i.e., accrued payroll).	1. *Sales Invoice*—Sale of goods. 2. *Check*—Loan to employee.
B. Credit is relocated.	3. *Adjustment*—Return of goods purchased. 4. *Note*—30-day open account converted to note payable.	3. *Adjustment*—Set up allowance for doubtful accounts.
C. Credit is discharged.	5. *Check*—Payment of credit received. 6. *Adjustment*—Payment of credit received by a non-cash asset such as inventory or other asset.	4. *Check*—Factoring receivables or discounting notes. 5. *Check*—Bad debt recoveries.

EXHIBIT 11-12 THE DUALITY OF SOME TYPICAL CREDIT EVENTS (CREDIT GIVEN)

Event	Transaction Document	Date	Notation	Codes			Accounts	Amount	
				Doc.	Trans.	Acct.		Debit	Credit
A. Credit is given.	Invoice		a. Sale is made on open account.		10 10	11210 41110	Accounts Receivable Sales	$3,500*	 $3,500
	Note		b. 90-day note is received for sale of merchandise.		10 10	11410 41110	Notes Receivable Sales	1,000*	 1,000
B. Credit is relocated.	Adjustment		c. Set up allowance for doubtful accounts.		10 10	60090 11300	Bad Debts Expense Allowance for Doubtful Accounts	1,500	 1,500
	Adjustment		d. Uncollectible account is written off.		12 12	11300 11210	Allowance for Doubtful Accounts Accounts Receivable	125	 125
	Adjustment		e. Certain accounts receivable are assigned as collateral on a loan.		10 12	11260 11210	Assigned Accounts Receivable Accounts Receivable	1,200	 1,200*
C. Credit is discharged.	Check		f. Payment is received on account.		10 12	11110 11210	Cash Accounts Receivable	150	 150*
	Check		g. Note received from customer is discounted (non-interest-bearing).†		10 10 12	11110 80030 11410	Cash Financing Expense Notes Receivable	970 30	 1,000*

*These transactions are also recorded in a customer's file, where separate records, known as *accounts and notes receivable—subsidiary ledger*, are maintained for each customer.

†If the note is interest-bearing, it would be recorded as follows:	Check		g. Note received from customer is discounted (interest-bearing note).		10 10 12 12	11110 80030 41210 11410	Cash Financing Expenses Interest Income Notes Receivable	986 38	 25 1,000

EXHIBIT 11-13 THE DUALITY OF SOME TYPICAL CREDIT EVENTS (CREDIT RECEIVED)

Event	Transaction Document	Date	Notation	Codes			Accounts	Amount	
				Doc.	Trans.	Acct.		Debit	Credit
A. Credit is received.	Invoice		h. Purchase of goods on 30-day open account.		10 10	41810 21110	Purchases Accounts Payable	\$6,000*	 \$6,000
	Adjustment		i. Expenses owed at a given date are recorded (payroll between payment dates).		10 10	41820 21200	Labor Accrued Payroll	950	 950
B. Credit is relocated.	Adjustment		j. Goods purchased on open account are returned.		12 12	21110 41840	Accounts Payable Purchase Returns	675*	 675
	Adjustment		k. 30-day open account converted to a note payable.		12 10	21110 21610	Accounts Payable Notes Payable	1,250*	 1,250*
C. Credit is discharged.	Check		l. Paid balance owed to supplier and deducted discount of 2%.		12 12 10	21110 11110 41170	Accounts Payable Cash Discounts on Purchases	200*	 196 4

*These transactions are also recorded in a vendor's file known as *accounts and notes payable—subsidiary ledger,* where separate records are maintained for each vendor.

EXHIBIT 11-14 SALES JOURNAL

Cash Dr.	Accounts Receivable Dr.	Date		Description	Sales Cr.	Sales Taxes Payable Cr.
	2,100 00	Jan.	1	Sale on account	2,000 00	100 00
550 00				Cash sales for the day	500 00	50 00
	2,415 00		31	Sale on account	2,300 00	115 00
860 00			31	Cash sales for the day	800 00	60 00
1,410 00	4,515 00				5,600 00	325 00
(11100) √	(11210) √				(41100) √	(21430) √

We mentioned earlier that cash sales are often recorded in the cash receipts journal. However, when a sales journal is used, *all* sales are recorded in the sales journal.

Similarly, when a *purchases journal* is used, *all* purchases are recorded in the purchases journal (Exhibit 11-15), including cash purchases.

EXHIBIT 11-15 PURCHASES JOURNAL

Purchases Dr.	Date	Purchase Order No.	Description	Accounts Payable Cr.	Cash Cr.
	1970				
1,595.20	Jan. 10	70	UCLA Corporation	1,595.20	
227.30	15	71	Downtown Store		227.30
5,270.00	22	72	J. T. Robinson	5,270.00	
1,777.00	25	73	Grimm Co.	1,777.00	
220.00	30	74	Hatfield Co.		220.00
9,089.50				8,642.20	447.30
(41810) √				(21110) √	(11100) √

TRANSFORMATION$_2$

Using the T-accounts, the events Exhibits 11-12 and 11-13 are posted at T_2 as shown in Exhibit 11-16.

EXHIBIT 11-16 POSTING CREDIT EVENTS TO T-ACCOUNTS

11110 Cash

	Debit		Credit
(f)	$ 150	(l)	$ 196
(g)	970		

41110 Sales

	Debit		Credit
		(a)	$3,500
		(b)	1,000

EXHIBIT 11-16 (CONTINUED)

11210 Accounts Receivable

(a)	$3,500	(d)	$ 125
		(e)	1,200
		(f)	150

41810 Purchases

(h)	$6,000		

11260 Assigned Accounts Receivable

(e)	$1,200		

41840 Purchase Returns

		(j)	$ 675

11300 Allowance for Doubtful Accounts

(d)	$ 125	(c)	$1,500

41340 Discounts on Purchases

		(l)	$ 4

11410 Notes Receivable

(b)	$1,000	(g)	$1,000

80030 Financing Expense

(g)	$ 30		

21110 Accounts Payable

(j)	$ 675	(h)	$6,000
(k)	1,250		
(l)	200		

41820 Labor

(i)	$ 950		

21200 Accrued Payroll

		(i)	$ 950

60090 Bad Debts Expense

(c)	$1,500		

21610 Notes Payable

		(k)	$1,250

In addition to posting credit sales events to the ledger (or as a concurrent EDP process known as an *accounts receivable updating run*), each sale is recorded again on a record for each customer. This record, called an *accounts receivable subsidiary ledger* (Exhibit 11-17), may be in the form of index cards, ledger sheets, machine-readable cards, or magnetic tape. Each customer's record contains a history of sales, payments, and the current balance owing.

EXHIBIT 11-17 ACCOUNTS RECEIVABLE SUBSIDIARY LEDGER (RECORD)

NAME: UCLA STORE
ADDRESS:

Date 19x1		Explanation	Trans. Code	Debit		Credit		Balance	
Jan.	1	Balance						200	00
	5	Purchases		300	00			500	00
	10	Payment				200	00	300	00

Credit purchases are likewise posted individually to an *accounts payable subsidiary ledger* (Exhibit 11-18), in addition to being posted to the general ledger accounts. In this subsidiary ledger a separate account is maintained for each vendor showing purchases, payments, and current balance.

EXHIBIT 11-18 ACCOUNTS PAYABLE SUBSIDIARY LEDGER (RECORD)

NAME: CLEVELAND SALES COMPANY
ADDRESS: 5000 HELROSE AVE., LOS ANGELES, CALIF.

Date 19x1		Explanation	Trans. Code	Debit		Credit		Balance	
Jan.	1	Balance						240	00
	5	Purchase				400	00	640	00
	12	Payment		240	00			400	00

OUTPUT

The accounting information system generates statements reporting the status of credit given and credit received. The general ledger accounts for accounts receivable and accounts payable report the aggregate balances at any given date. These balances are an integral part of the financial statements.

For internal reporting, however, management needs more detailed information than aggregate balances provide. The information system, therefore, produces detailed lists of individual accounts receivable and accounts payable balances which support the aggregate general ledger balances.

The primary credit resource system outputs are: aged trial balance of accounts receivable, and aged trial balance of accounts payable.

Accounts Receivable

An aged trial balance of accounts receivable lists a customer's name, number (if any), the individual invoices not yet paid, the total balance owing, and the past due status of account. This list is tabulated from the individual accounts receivable subsidiary ledger discussed earlier and agrees in total with the general ledger account.

Accounts Payable

The primary output relating to credit received is a list of accounts payable showing the vendor's name, number (if any), date, amount and number of invoices not yet paid. This list is compiled from the subsidiary accounts payable ledger and agrees in total with the general ledger account. This list also shows the dating (due date) of the invoices outstanding and potential discounts available.

Other internal credit reports are discussed under the section on *feedback* (p. 448).

11.7 SYSTEMS CONTROLS FOR CREDIT TRANSACTIONS

There are *stewardship* and *management* controls in the credit resource system.

STEWARDSHIP CONTROLS

Credit Given

Stewardship controls are designed in general to safeguard assets. With respect to credit sales, proper stewardship controls insure against large credit losses which could stem from the following deficiencies:

1. Credit sales made without prior approval from the credit department.
2. Shipments made without bills being rendered to the customer.
3. Price and quantity errors on invoices.
4. Sales invoices that are not accounted for by number or that are omitted from the journals.
5. Collections that are not properly accounted for.
6. Returns that are not properly authorized and recorded.

Such deficiencies are usually cured by segregating duties – requiring different departments (or individuals) to have responsibility for such functions as:

a. Sales order preparation.
b. Credit approval.
c. Issuance of inventory from stock.
d. Shipment to customer.
e. Billing or invoice preparation.
f. Invoice audit.
g. Accounts receivable subsidiary posting.
h. General ledger controlling accounts.

Credit Received

The objectives of the stewardship controls relating to credit received are to avoid overpayment to suppliers and to record properly all credit received.

Stewardship controls in this area are also implemented, in part, by segregating duties into functional areas:

1. *Purchasing Entity:* Purchases are ordered by the purchasing department through the use of serially-numbered *purchase orders.*
2. *Receiving Entity:* The receiving department issues *receiving reports* for all goods received and is independent of purchasing.
3. *Accounts Payable Entity:* Compares receiving reports and purchase orders with

invoices received. Invoices are tested for proper price and quantity and approved for payment.

4. *Disbursing Entity:* Checks are prepared upon submission of verified supporting documents.
5. *Recording Entity:* Subsidiary records and general ledger recording are separated, and their details are matched with balances of the controlling accounts.

MANAGEMENT CONTROLS

Credit Given

Management controls in the area of the extension of credit have the following purposes: to minimize credit losses, and to optimize the level of receivables.

Minimizing credit losses: This is generally the function of the credit department, whose responsibilities are the following:

1. *Establishment and implementation of credit policies:* Involves determination of acceptable risk classes and the nature of adjustments allowed.
2. *Credit investigation and approval:* The securing and evaluation of information concerning customers' financial worth and authorization of current purchases. This function also includes the setting of credit limits discussed earlier under line of credit.
3. *Discount policies and other adjustments:* The evaluation of discounts taken by customers and the resolution of other problems, such as returns.
4. *Collection:* The collection and follow-up of delinquent accounts.
5. *Write-off of bad debts:* This action is usually initiated by the credit department.

Optimizing the level of receivables: The key to minimizing credit losses rests with the proper evaluation and monitoring of a customer's credit status.

The basis for the evaluation of credit risk has often been termed the *C's of credit:*[2]

1. *Character:* Refers to the probability that the customer will honor his obligations. The existence of a criminal record, for example, would be a negative indication. His past credit record is a good gauge of character.
2. *Capacity:* The determination of the customer's ability to repay credit granted. The nature and extent of earnings is the best indicator of capacity.
3. *Capital:* Refers to a customer's financial position at the time of evaluation, i.e., his assets and liabilities.
4. *Collateral:* Refers to the property which a customer may offer as security for the credit granted.
5. *Conditions:* Refers to external economic factors (i.e., industry layoff) which may affect the future ability of the customer to repay his obligation.

The information necessary for this evaluation can generally be obtained from the following sources:

[2]These five C's of credit reduce to "character" and "capacity," as noted in Appendix A to this chapter.

a. Credit associations which exchange credit information under the guidance of the National Association of Credit Management.
b. Credit-reporting agencies such as Dun & Bradstreet, National Credit Office, Lyon Furniture Mercantile Agency, and others.

Credit Insurance

As with other business hazards, abnormal credit losses can be offset by insurance coverage. Credit insurance, while helping to minimize credit losses, has the following limitations:

1. *Primary loss:* Insurance will not cover losses below the average bad debt loss ratio for the industry.
2. *Coinsurance:* A certain portion of the loss must be borne by the insured.
3. *Maximum coverage:* Losses from any one customer are subject to a maximum recovery usually related to the account's credit rating (admissible losses).
4. *Cost:* Cost may range between 1/20 and 1/5 of one percent of covered sales and is an additional cost to be weighed. In general, however, firms with a large amount of sales to a small number of customers should include credit insurance in any sound program of credit management.

Credit Received

Management controls in the area of credit received have as their objective proper purchasing policies, including securing both the lowest possible prices and the best credit terms.

1. *Prices:* Securing the best possible prices for purchased goods is the function of the purchasing department. Generally this goal requires that a specified number of competitive bids be obtained from vendors, prior to the establishment of any purchasing relationship. In addition some firms have a policy of changing the assignments of purchasing agents periodically to avoid any real or potential conflicts of interest resulting from a relationship between a purchasing agent and a vendor.
2. *Terms:* The negotiation of credit terms involves such considerations as scheduling of payments to suit the firm's budget, and trade and cash discounts.

11.8 SYSTEMS FEEDBACK FOR CREDIT TRANSACTIONS

Feedback on the credit resource system furnishes users with (1) exception, (2) control, (3) comparative, and (4) interpretive reports.

EXCEPTIONS

Exception reports outline any material departure from plan; all exceptions require special attention. When credit given to a customer exceeds his credit limit, an exception report is issued. For example, a credit limit is printed on certain credit cards. When a customer wishes to charge an amount over, say, $50, a merchant contacts a computer facility to determine if the customer will exceed his credit limit with the new purchase. If the answer is negative, the merchant makes the charge sale; if positive, the sale must be for cash or is disallowed.

With credit received, exception reports can be generated when vendors' invoices are paid after the discount period has elapsed. The exception report would show cash discounts lost.

CONTROLS

Feedback on stewardship and management controls can take several forms. Feedback on *stewardship controls* over credit resources include:

1. Aged trial balance of accounts receivables and payables matched to the general ledger control accounts.
2. Internal and external audits tracing sales invoices and purchase orders from initiation to destruction. Invoices are tested for price and quantity, for supporting documents such as shipping and receiving reports, and for proper authorization, such as credit approval in the case of sales orders and approval to disburse in the case of purchase orders or invoices.

Feedback on *management controls* reports the extent to which:

Credit given is *optimized* and *credit losses* are *minimized.*
Credit received is obtained on best prices and terms.

Credit Granted

Management control reports relating to credit losses would contain:

1. An analysis of bad accounts written off.
   a. Detail of bad accounts charged off and reasons for the write-off, such as bankruptcy or "skipped town."
   b. Detail of recoveries of bad debts showing reasons for recovery, such as court judgment.
2. An analysis of collection costs incurred either internally by the credit department, or externally by independent collection agencies, showing the effectiveness of various types of collection effort.

Credit Received

Management control reports on credit received would provide information on:

1. The volume of purchases made for a period—classified in terms of the volume of business conducted with each vendor.
2. Discounts taken and discount lost on purchase invoices.

COMPARISONS

There are several types of *comparative* feedback. One type is to confirm receivable and payable balances with other firms. Since the accounts receivable of one firm constitute accounts payable of other firms, correspondence with debtors or creditors will confirm balances.

Comparative feedback also results from comparison of current activity with that of prior periods. For example, the ratio of credit sales to total sales for the current period can be compared to prior periods. Current collections can be compared to prior collections. And the current level of payables can be compared to payables in prior periods.

Another type of comparative feedback is the computation of ratios. A test of the credit department's efficiency is the average collection period or the average daily sales represented in receivables. This is computed as follows:

$$\frac{\left(\begin{array}{c}\text{Net Trade}\\ \text{Accounts Receivable}\end{array}\right) + (\text{Trade Notes Receivable})}{\text{Net Sales}} \times \begin{array}{c}\text{Days}\\ \text{in}\\ \text{Period}\end{array} = \text{Average Collection Period}$$

INTERPRETATIONS

Interpretive feedback employs data developed under other types of feedback and gives meaning to the data. For example, an increase in the days sales in receivables over a prior period must be analyzed for possible causes:

1. Has collection efficiency (effectiveness) decreased?
2. Have economic conditions changed in a manner that affects paying practices?
3. Has there been a change in credit policies?

11.9 SUMMARY

The credit resource system provides for a delay in paying for goods and services. In most situations credit is given—and credit is received (used). *Open credit* is unsecured (it has no collateral) and is based on reputation and an agreement to pay. *Secured credit* has collateral in the form of other tangible property that is surrendered in payment of the debt in the face of default. Credit is recognized in most businesses by creating and maintaining records, systems, and reports on *accounts receivable* (credit given) and *accounts payable* (credit received).

In view of the probable default of some accounts, it is good business practice to maintain an *allowance account* to cover bad debts. This practice has a theoretical propriety in that it "matches" defaults with the time period in which the sale was made (the conditions for the default created).

The purposes of controls over credit generally seek to minimize credit losses and maximize credit benefits (interest rates, discounts).

Feedback supplies meaningful (interpretive) information on the functioning of controls, on exceptions, and on internal and external comparative facts and figures.

CHAPTER 11 APPENDIX A

THE CREDIT MODEL

This presentation has a dual purpose: (1) to propose a method for developing credit models, and (2) to show how a systemic approach can resolve problems of this type. The model presented here, as the word "systemic" suggests, is a product-mix of three disciplines—marketing, statistics, and accounting—with traces of measurement, information, and decision theories. This appendix illustrates why an interdisciplinary effort is needed to tackle complex problems.

11A.1 THE MARKETING MODEL[1]

The function of the marketing model is to differentiate credit risks in quantitative terms. Immediately we face the problem of measuring subjective matters such as "character" and "capacity."[2] We turn to measurement theory for an answer. We find that complex principles such as character and capacity cannot be measured directly. Instead, surrogates or representative measures are used for this purpose.[3] Most complex principles call for several surrogates, and each one should be capable of objective measurement.

Our search for surrogates is guided by information and decision theories. Our inquiry is inductive.[4] By studying information flows which have led to good (or bad) credit decisions in a sufficient number of cases, we begin to generalize as to an optimum decision structure.

Assume, for example, that the following surrogates are cited for character and capacity:

EXHIBIT 11A-1 ILLUSTRATIVE SURROGATES FOR CHARACTER AND CAPACITY

	Character*	Capacity
	Occupation	Earnings
	Specific credit record†	Dependents
	General credit record	Debt load
Stability	Age	Savings
Stability	Personal references	Equity (wealth)
Stability	Length of residence	
Stability	Length of employment	
Stability	Marital status	

*Race, creed, etc., although they may bear on credit character, must be omitted for legal reasons.

†A *specific* credit record is distinguished from a *general* credit record in that most persons have their own debt-paying priorities. Some will pay a mortgage or utility bill before a department store account. Others may reverse this order. It is important then to look to the person's credit performance in those areas most closely related to the creditor's line of business.

[1] This discussion is based on a marketing model for individuals, but a similar process would be used for firms.

[2] "Character" (the *intent* to pay promptly) and "capacity" (the *ability* to pay promptly) should be viewed somewhat independently, as one quality does not presume the other. Some persons with great capacity are poor credit risks because they lack the *will* to pay, while other persons of best intentions are poor credit risks because they lack the *means* to pay.

Data assembled by the National Credit Bureaus Inc. (see Appendix B of this chapter) suggest a strong relationship between occupation and character. Data analysis of this type leads to the selection of better surrogates.

[3] For a more extensive treatment of principals and surrogates see Yuji Ijiri, *The Foundations of Accounting Measurement* (Englewood Cliffs, N.J.: Prentice-Hall, Inc., 1967), pp. 3–31, and S. I. Hayakawa, *Language in Thought and Action,* 2nd ed. (New York: Harcourt, Brace & World, Inc., 1964).

[4] *Inductive* inquiry begins with systematic observations in the real world. Patterns of consistency in these observations lead to the development of theories. *Deductive* inquiry, on the other hand, begins with theories which may or may not be supportable. These theories are then tested in the real world to determine their validity.

Next, these surrogates must be ranked in order of their importance, as they are unlikely to be of equal value. For example, *earnings* may be a much more significant surrogate for capacity than is *savings*. Again, these weights are derived inductively.

EXHIBIT 11A-2 WEIGHTED SURROGATES

Character	%	Capacity	%
Occupation	40	Earnings	50
Specific credit record	20	Dependents	15
General credit record	10	Debt load	15
Age	10	Savings	10
Personal references	5	Equity (wealth)	10
Length of residence	5		
Length of employment	5		
Marital status	5		
	100%		100%

Weighting makes it apparent that we need not exhaust the universe of surrogates. Once we have accounted for a high percentage of our measure, additional data adds little to the decision structure. For example, we can reduce the number of character surrogates to four without losing much statistical significance (Exhibit 11A-3). The same could be done for capacity.

EXHIBIT 11A-3 SIGNIFICANT CHARACTER SURROGATES

Original Weights %		Revised Weights %
40	Occupation	50
20	Specific credit record	25
10	General credit record	12½
10	Age	12½
20	Others	–
100%		100%

We shall see presently that some firms need more credit information than others. The ability to expand or contract the number of surrogates enables us to have a more or less *sensitive* model as the situation requires.

The marketing model is used to accept or reject a credit risk and to minimize accepted risks. The latter objective is met in part by assigning persons to *credit risk groups* in which the credit limit per person decreases in relation to increased risk.

Credit risk groups can be identified by a factor which expresses the ratio of incremental costs to sales. Hence the designation "10% credit risk group" means that the cost of extending credit equals 10% of the sales to that group.

The credit risk factor is a composite of three types of cost, or:

$$F = \Sigma(r, n, e)$$

where

F = credit risk factor
r = cost of capital
n = normal credit costs
e = extraordinary credit costs

Let us examine the nature of these costs in more detail.

1. *Cost of Capital:* This is the cost of carrying receivables. The firm's internal rate of return or some opportunity cost of capital can be used as an index. The cost of capital increases in re-

lation to added risk in that capital is outstanding for longer periods in the event of tardy payments. Thus, while the cost of capital index is itself a constant, the total cost of capital will vary among credit risk groups in relation to collection periods.

2. *Normal Credit Costs:* These are the normal costs of supporting a credit function, such as credit department costs. These costs will increase slightly in relation to risk, e.g., several reminders are required with lower credit groups.
3. *Extraordinary Credit Costs:* This category includes legal, collection agency, and other expenses of settling overdue accounts, as well as uncollectible amounts ("bad debts"). Extraordinary credit costs rise sharply in relation to increased risk.

As stated, the credit risk factor is a complex index comprising three subordinate factors, as illustrated in Exhibit 11A-4.

EXHIBIT 11A-4 COMPOSITION OF THE CREDIT RISK FACTOR

Cost of Capital %	+	Normal Credit Costs %	+	Extraordinary Credit Costs %	=	Credit Risk Factor %
5		2		3		10
6		3		6		15
7		4		9		20
8		5		12		25
.		.		.		.
.		.		.		.
.		.		.		.

The credit risk factor can be depicted graphically as a cost function which increases as a percentage of credit sales in relation to increased risk (Exhibit 11A-5).

EXHIBIT 11A-5 THE MARKETING MODEL

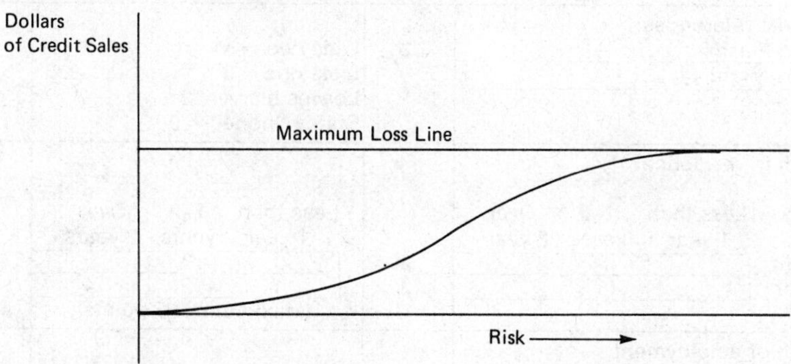

Numbers obtained from credit application forms can now be used to classify risks into credit groups. Let us examine this process. Our surrogates in Exhibit 11A-2 are the bases for developing the application form and scoring procedure shown in Exhibit 11A-6.[5] The maximum score in our example is 200 points. Assume that the application is for a major department store credit card. Our applicant—a hypothetical college professor—scores 159.

The scoring process utilizes decision theory. In most cases *decision rules* (referred to as "scoring procedures" in our example) are explicit. But as illustrated by items 2 and 3, subjective judgment is desirable to some extent. While it is possible to specify decision rules for items 2 and 3, it is important from a behavioral point of view to leave room for the exercise of judgment to prevent making the process entirely mechanical and hence void of human interest.

[5] Appendix C of this chapter illustrates a proposed scoring form for business, as opposed to personal, credit.

EXHIBIT 11A-6 APPLICATION FORM & SCORING PROCEDURE

Application Form	Scoring Procedure		Score	
	Verify*	Compute Score	Sub-total	Total
1. State your occupation: college professor	1	Multiply the percentage in Appendix B by 40 in each case. The college professor rates .87 × 40 =		35
2. List the department store credit cards you have at present: Sears	1	0 for none 5 to 10 for one depending on record 10 to 20 for two or more depending on record (Maximum of 20 points.)		10
3. Do you have the following accounts? With whom?†		*Checking account* 0 to 10 based on average balance & number of overdrafts	10	
Checking ☒ Wells Fargo	1			
Savings ☒ Home S & L	1	*Savings account* 5 to 20 based on average balance & withdrawal record	5	
Loan ☐	1	*Loan Account* −10 to 0 based on amount, duration, and purpose (such as refinancing)	0	
		(Maximum of 20 points.)		15
4. Age:				
Over 65 ☐	3	4		
61–65 ☐		8		
36–60 ☒		10		10
25–35 ☐		6		
Under 25 ☐		2		
5. Personal references: John Flash, Rudy Might	2	Lists two = 5 Lists one = 3 Leaves blank = 2 States "none" = 0		5
6. Length in residence: Less than 1 year / 1–2 years / Over 2 years		Less than 1 year / 1–2 years / Over 2 years		
Present: — / — / ×	2	1 / 3 / 5	5	
Former: — / — / ×	3	1 / 2 / 4	4	
		(Maximum of 5 points.)		5
7. Length of employment: Less than 1 year / 1–5 years / Over 5 years		Less than 1 year / 1–5 years / Over 5 years		
Present: — / — / ×	1	1 / 3 / 5	5	
Former: — / — / ×	2	0 / 2 / 4	4	
		(Maximum of 5 points.)		5

EXHIBIT 11A-6 (CONTINUED)

8. Marital status: Married [X] Single or widowed [ ] Divorced or separated [ ]	3	[5] [3] [1]		5
9. Gross earnings per annum of head of household: $17,000	1	Over $20,000 [50] $15,000 to $20,000 [40] $10,000 to $14,999 [30] $ 7,200 to $ 9,999 [20] Under $7,200 [10]		40
10. Number of dependents, excluding self 1 [ ] 2 [ ] 3 [X] 4 [ ] 5 [ ] Over 5	3	[15] [12] [9] [6] [3] [0]		9
11. Debt load: House payment/rent is $300 per month Total monthly installment debt is $300	2 3	Total debt load as a percentage of gross income Under 25% = 15 26 to 50% = 10 51 to 75% = 0 Over 75% = −10 Minus 10 points if house payments (rent) exceed 25% of earnings	o.k.	10
12. Equity Do you (own) ~~rent~~ your home?	3	own = 10, rent = 0		10
		Total....................................		159

*Verification index: 1 = verification is standard procedure.
2 = verify only in cases where total score is at the upper or lower credit risk group limits.
3 = do not verify except in most unusual cases.

†Note that we are using bank and savings and loan references for general credit record purposes. Item 3 on the application form combines the character general credit record factor, having a maximum of ten points, with the capacity savings factor, also with a maximum of ten points, making a twenty-point total for item 3. This demonstrates that it is possible to combine a character and capacity factor through the use of one source of information.

By means of our marketing model we recognize the need for credit risk groups and are able to quantify the attributes of credit risk in terms of numerical scores. However, to close the link between scores and credit risk groups we need a statistical model.

11A.2 THE STATISTICAL MODEL

The statistical model furnishes us with knowledge (or assumptions) as to the attributes of a population. We need this information to extend our credit model. Actually we should refer to statistical *models*—as many are available.[6] Only three of these are pertinent to our credit model: the *uniform*,[7] *Gaussian*, and

[6]Statistical distribution models can be classified into three groups: (1) *distributions of a discrete variable:* uniform, binomial, multinomial, hypergeometric, Poisson, and geometric; (2) *distributions of a continuous variable:* uniform, normal, beta, gamma, exponential, log-normal, and Weibull; and (3) *distributions which express relationships among other distributions:* Chi-square, F, and t distributions.

[7]The uniform distribution derives from an analysis of population attributes. Its properties are not known mathematically. Where population attributes are not known, the *Gaussian* model should be used.

Poisson distributions. The uniform model should be used with large populations whose attributes are known. The Gaussian model should be used with large populations whose attributes are not known but where they are presumed to conform to a normal distribution. The Poisson model should be used to screen relatively small groups of low credit risk.

We proceed in terms of large populations whose attributes are known. Because we are seeking to classify our population into groups, the *uniform* distribution expressed as a histogram is appropriate. We assume that the population consists of eleven credit risk groups, identified A through K (Exhibit 11A-7).

EXHIBIT 11A-7 A HISTOGRAM OF A UNIFORM DISTRIBUTION OF CREDIT RISKS

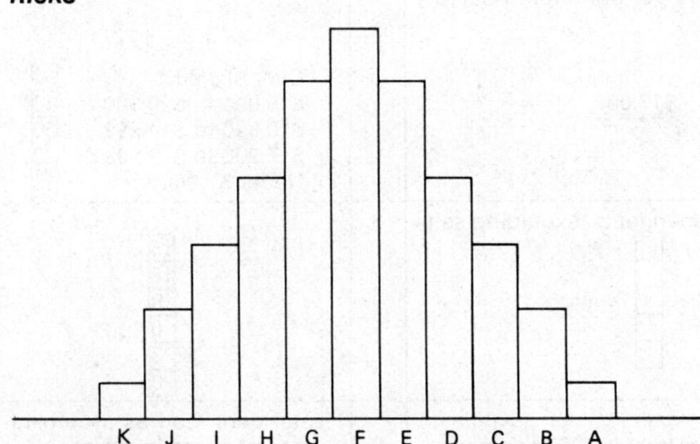

"A" customers can be defined as *cash* customers, in which event there are no credit costs. "K" customers are deemed to have credit risk factors of 100%. The other credit risk groups, B through J, range between these values as shown in Exhibit 11A-8.

EXHIBIT 11A-8 PROPERTIES OF OUR ASSUMED CREDIT RISK GROUPS

Score	Credit Risk Factor	Credit Risk Group	Potential Number of Persons	Average Sales Per Person* (Limit)	Total Potential Sales
None	0%	A	1,000	$100	$ 100,000
180–200	10	B	2,000	900	1,800,000
160–179	20	C	3,000	800	2,400,000
140–159	30	D	4,000	700	2,800,000
120–139	40	E	5,000	600	3,000,000
100–119	50	F	6,000	500	3,000,000
80– 99	60	G	5,000	400	2,000,000
60– 79	70	H	4,000	300	1,200,000
40– 59	80	I	3,000	200	600,000
20– 39	90	J	2,000	100	200,000
0– 19	100	K	1,000	0	0

*(1) In practical terms the limit may be different from average sales, but we are assuming these expressions to be equal in our example.
(2) A point to be stressed is that credit risk factors assume a distribution of risk, e.g., if all of the sales in group B are to a very few persons, the 10% factor would no longer be applicable. Geographical dispersion and enforcing credit limits are two ways in which to assure a distribution of risk.
(3) The limit of $100 in the case of group A is a purchasing power rather than a credit limit.

Exhibit 11A-8 prescribes the information which is needed to complete the statistical model. We need to know how many potential customers are in each credit risk group, as well as their purchasing or credit power. From this data we derive total potential sales. The score column relates application data to credit risk groups. In our example we assign scores to the full range of credit risk. In practice, of course, it is not necessary to differentiate risks below a *cut-off* point. For example, if we declined all risks under group E, we would not need to relate scores to credit risk groups below that level (Exhibit 11A-9).

EXHIBIT 11A-9 CUT-OFF OF CREDIT RISKS

	Score	Credit Risk Factor	Credit Risk Group
	None	0%	A
	180–200	10	B
Accept	160–179	20	C
	140–159	30	D
	120–139	40	E
Reject	Below 120		

Our college professor, with a score of 159, falls into group D. But as he is at the upper limit of D, some secondary verification, as mentioned in the footnote to Exhibit 11A-6, and/or a review of the subjective analysis in items 2 and 3 of the application can be employed to see if he should be placed in group C. This action is only of consequence to the professor in the event that he wishes to have his credit limit raised from $700 to $800. However, a change in category is more important to the firm, as it affects the accept-reject decision as well as sales forecasts and credit controls.

The statistical model enables us to segment a population into credit risk groups. It also furnishes us with sales forecast data and allows us to disperse risk through the medium of the credit limit. While our systemic credit model is greatly refined through the application of statistics, it is still incomplete. The remaining question relates to *cut-off.* But this is an important question, for it deals with (1) which risks to accept or reject, and (2) the extent to which we need credit information. For these answers we turn to an accounting model.

The statistical model can also be represented graphically, as in Exhibit 11A-10. It shows that on a

EXHIBIT 11A-10 THE STATISTICAL MODEL

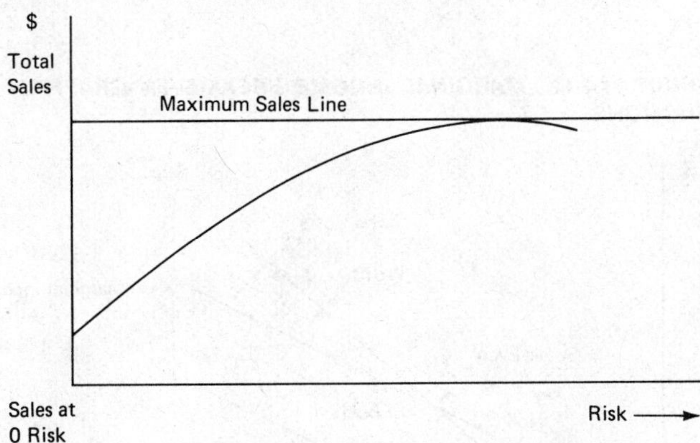

cumulative basis the more risk a company is willing to accept the higher its cumulative sales potential will be. The sales slope will peak out partly because, as Exhibit 11A-8 shows, the higher risk groups have progressively less purchasing power, and partly because there is a limit where the granting of credit ceases to be a sales inducement.

11A.3 THE ACCOUNTING MODEL

The *cost-volume-profit* (CVP) model discussed in chapter 18 is applicable to this problem. Underlying the CVP model is the observed fact that some costs, such as rents and salaries, relate to time periods and are *fixed* in terms of volume. That is, fixed costs do not vary in relation to changes in activity level. For example, rents and property taxes do not vary as a function of sales. Other costs do vary in relation to volume, such as production costs, the cost of acquiring goods and services, or sales commissions. These *variable* costs are responsive to changes in activity level. For example, a sales commission of 5% is paid out of every sales dollar, hence this cost item will always be 5% of sales, whereas a fixed salary will not change in relation to sales volume. We will not dwell on this concept of cost behavior, as it is discussed more fully in later chapters.

The CVP model is readily depicted by conventional break-even graphs (Exhibit 11A-11).

EXHIBIT 11A-11 BREAK-EVEN GRAPHS ILLUSTRATE COST-VOLUME-PROFIT RELATIONSHIPS

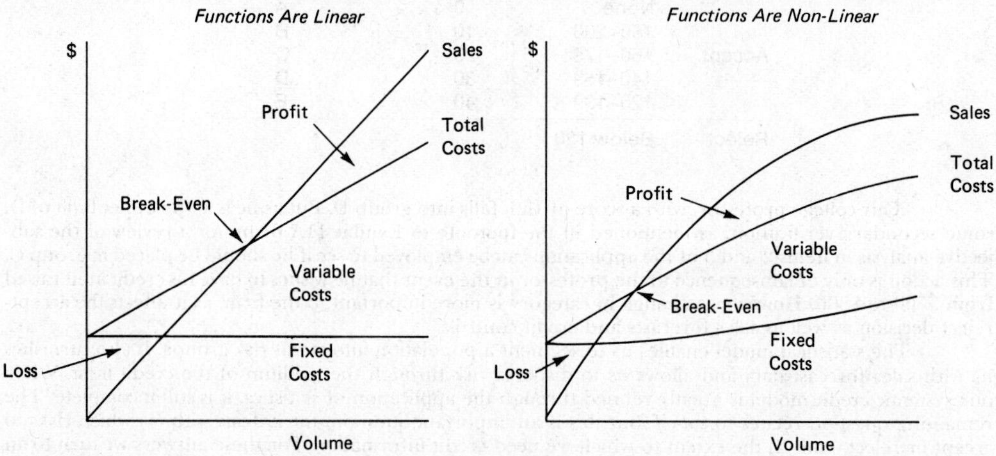

We will limit our discussion to linear CVP functions, in which case fixed costs do not vary *at all* in relation to volume, and variable costs change in *direct proportion* to changes in volume. By reversing the position of fixed and variable costs we have what is called a *marginal income* break-even graph (Exhibit 11A-12).

EXHIBIT 11A-12 MARGINAL INCOME BREAK-EVEN GRAPH OF LINEAR FUNCTIONS

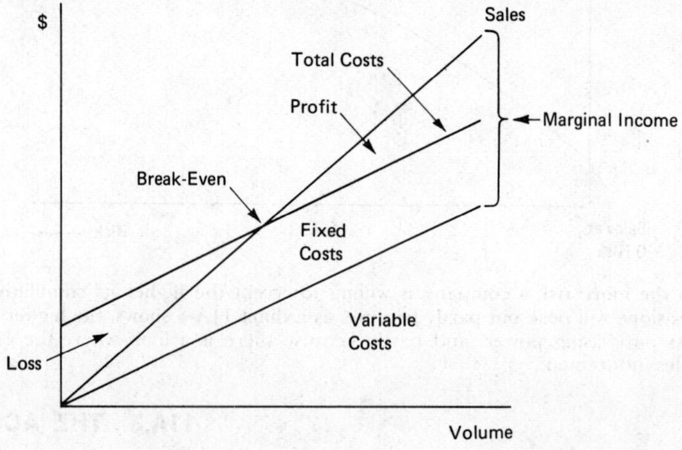

This graph is of interest to us in that it readily shows that marginal income + variable costs = sales, and that marginal income = fixed costs + profit (or − loss). This leads to the *marginal income statement*, which has this structure:

EXHIBIT 11A-13 MARGINAL INCOME STATEMENT

Sales
− Variable Costs
= Marginal Income
− Fixed Costs
= Profit

The distinction between *marginal income* and *profit* is crucial. In a linear CVP model, both variable costs and marginal income are fixed percentages of sales regardless of volume, given a fixed relationship between two factors: (1) selling price and (2) variable cost rate. A change in these factors leads to the following consequences where volume is held constant:

EXHIBIT 11A-14 EFFECT OF CHANGES IN SELLING PRICE OR VARIABLE COST RATE

		CHANGE IN SELLING PRICE		CHANGE IN VARIABLE COST RATE	
	Basic	Increase (10%)	Decrease (10%)	Increase (10%)	Decrease (10%)
Sales	$10,000	$11,000	$9,000	$10,000	$10,000
Variable costs	6,000	6,000	6,000	6,600	5,400
Marginal income	4,000	5,000	3,000	3,400	4,600
Fixed costs	3,000	3,000	3,000	3,000	3,000
Profit	$ 1,000	2,000	0	400	1,600

This feature of the CVP model means that once fixed costs are covered, changes in marginal income have a direct impact on profit (Exhibit 11A-15):

EXHIBIT 11A-15 INCREASES IN MARGINAL INCOME, AFTER RECOVERY OF FIXED COSTS, RESULTS IN DIRECT INCREASES TO PROFIT (Volume Increases 20%)

	Old Volume		Increase		New Volume	
	$	%	$	%	$	%
Sales	10,000	100	2,000	100	12,000	100
Variable costs	6,000	60	1,200	60	7,200	60
Marginal income	4,000	40	800	40	4,800	40
Fixed costs	3,000	30	–		3,000	25
Profit	1,000	10	800	40	1,800	15

Because marginal income is a constant ratio of sales (while profit is not), and because of the difficulties in attempting to apportion fixed costs, it is useful to analyze projects in terms of their "contribution to margin" rather than their contribution to profit. Conditions being equal, the project with a higher marginal income ratio would be selected.

Let us return to the credit model. Credit risk factors are variable costs. These variable costs must be added to the basic variable costs, as previously defined, to reach total variable costs. The basic CVP behavior of the firm can be viewed best in terms of a cash structure in which there are no variable credit costs. Suppose that the basic cash structure is:

		%
Sales	$10,000	100
Variable costs	6,000	60
Marginal income	4,000	40
Fixed costs	3,000	30
Profit	$ 1,000	10

The basic variable costs in our example are 60% of sales. Using the credit risk factors in Exhibit 11A-8, the total variable costs for each credit risk group would be as follows (Exhibit 11A-16).

EXHIBIT 11A-16 TOTAL VARIABLE COSTS OF CREDIT RISK GROUPS

Group	Basic Variable Rate	Credit Risk Factor	Total Variable Rate
A	60%	0%	60%
B	60	10	70
C	60	20	80
D	60	30	90
E	60	40	100
F	60	50	110
G	60	60	120
H	60	70	130
I	60	80	140
J	60	90	150
K	60	100	160

The cut-off problem is now clarified. If we decide on a minimum contribution to margin of 10%, credit would only be extended to groups A through D. Given our basic structure, suppose that potential sales to each credit group is $10,000. *Pro forma* income statements would appear as follows (Exhibit 11A-17).

EXHIBIT 11A-17 **PRO FORMA** ***INCOME STATEMENTS ON A MARGINAL BASIS***

	Group A	Group B	Group C	Group D	Total
Sales	$10,000	$10,000	$10,000	$10,000	$40,000
Variable costs	6,000(60%)	7,000(70%)	8,000(80%)	9,000(90%)	30,000
Marginal income	4,000	3,000	2,000	1,000	10,000
Fixed costs	–	–	–	–	3,000
Profit	–	–	–	–	$ 7,000

PRO FORMA ***INCOME STATEMENTS ON A CUMULATIVE BASIS***

Sales	$10,000	$20,000	$30,000	$40,000
Variable costs	6,000	13,000	21,000	30,000
Marginal income	4,000	7,000	9,000	10,000
Fixed costs	–	–	–	3,000
Profit				$ 7,000

It is clear that the contribution to margin decreases with lower credit groups. The determinant of cut-off is not the greatest contribution to margin ratio (as this would restrict us to cash customers only), but rather to some minimum rate, such as 10%. Given the fact that group A recovers the fixed costs of $3,000, the marginal income of each of the other groups contributes directly to increases in profit. Extending credit to group E would be a break-even proposition, while the inclusion of groups F through K would result in increasing reductions to profit.

The CVP model provides the key to cut-off, as mentioned before. We can dramatize this point by using two extreme "basic" structures (Exhibit 11A-18).

EXHIBIT 11A-18 DIFFERENT CVP STRUCTURES

	Structure X (High Variable Costs) $	%	Structure Y (High Fixed Costs) $	%
Sales	10,000	100	10,000	100
Variable costs	8,000	80	1,000	10
Marginal income	2,000	20	9,000	90
Fixed costs	1,000	10	8,000	80
Profit	1,000	10	1,000	10

While the basic profit ratio is the same, X and Y are radically different organizations insofar as credit management is concerned. Given a minimum 10% contribution to margin in both cases, note the difference in cut-off.

EXHIBIT 11A-19 DIFFERENCE IN CUT-OFF BASED ON CVP STRUCTURES

Credit Groups	Total Variable Cost Ratios: Structure X	Structure Y
A	80	10
B	90	20
	——— cut-off	
C	100	30
D	110	40
E	120	50
F	130	60
G	140	70
H	150	80
I	160	90
		——— cut-off
J	170	100
K	180	110

The nature of the credit problem can be viewed as a continuum with respect to CVP structures (Exhibit 11A-20).

EXHIBIT 11A-20 THE CVP-CREDIT CONTINUUM

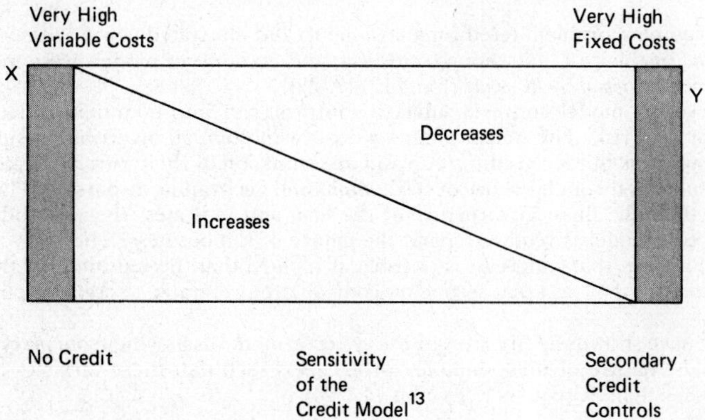

[13] We mentioned earlier that a model could be made more or less sensitive by changing the number of surrogates, i.e., by requiring more or less information.

No credit problem exists at the extreme of X. In industries such as retail food, margins are so low that the credit function is essentially ruled out. Below the extreme, very sensitive models are needed, as we are screening for a rather small number of low credit risks from a very large population. National, general-purpose credit card companies tend toward high-X. As we move down the continuum, less sensitive credit models are required. At the extreme of Y we need no credit screening mechanism. Our CVP structure is such that we assume the distribution of credit risks inherent in the population as a whole.[8] Instead of screening, we rely on secondary controls such as terminating service if payments are not made on time. Most utilities follow this approach.

In general terms, capital intensive industries tend toward Y, while personal service and retail organizations tend toward X. Given the enormous investment in plant and equipment, for example, what does it cost a utility or telephone company to service one additional customer? Magazine publication is another example which tends toward extreme Y. If the circulation of *TV Guide* is 8,500,000 (1970 figure), what is the risk of extending credit to the television viewing population as a whole, given that mailing of the *Guide* can cease after one or two issues in the event of nonpayment? Financing automobiles, building homes, and repairing automobiles are examples which tend toward high-X. The variable costs of providing these services is a high percentage of sales. Firms engaged in these activities require sensitive credit models.

The accounting model completes the loop. It provides the elements which are needed to complete our systemic credit model, i.e., (1) where to make the cut-off, and (2) how sensitive a credit model is required.

The basic CVP model in accounting, with credit costs added, appears in Exhibit 11A-21.

EXHIBIT 11A-21 THE ACCOUNTING MODEL WITH CREDIT COSTS ADDED

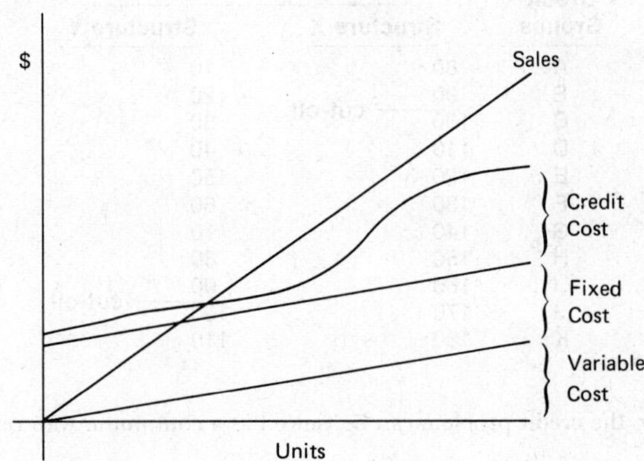

11A.4 SUMMARY

We have taken a complex problem (credit management), and illustrated why a systems approach is necessary to its solution. In this case marketing, statistical, and accounting models were integrated to achieve what we have called a *systemic credit model* (Exhibit 11A-22).

The marketing model converts subjective information into quantitative data which is used to identify classes of credit risk. The statistical model deals with population attributes and yields estimates as to the number of persons in each credit group and an estimation of their purchasing power. Statistics also leads us to distribute risk through the use of credit limits and geographic dispersion. The accounting model (CVP) scrutinizes the basic financial structure of the firm and indicates where cut-off should occur, and how sensitive a credit model is required given the nature of the business. The CVP-credit continuum in Exhibit 11A-20 illustrates that no credit is possible at high-X, that the sensitivity of the credit model decreases as we move toward Y, and that secondary controls are preferable to credit applications and screening at high-Y.

While we have shown the progress of the systemic model as moving from marketing to accounting (Exhibit 11A-23), the nature of these complex problems is such that these variables must be considered simultaneously rather than in sequence (Exhibit 11A-24).

[8]The distribution of credit risks in the total population of the United States, within the definition of legal age, is probably Gaussian in nature. This means that there are just as few very poor risks as there are very good risks.

This exercise points to the need for close cooperation between various specialists in solving complex problems. In addition, the systemic credit model which is developed in this appendix should have practical value to those who face the problem of designing or managing credit functions.

EXHIBIT 11A-22 THE SYSTEMIC CREDIT MODEL

COMPOSITE OF THE MARKETING, STATISTICAL, AND ACCOUNTING MODELS

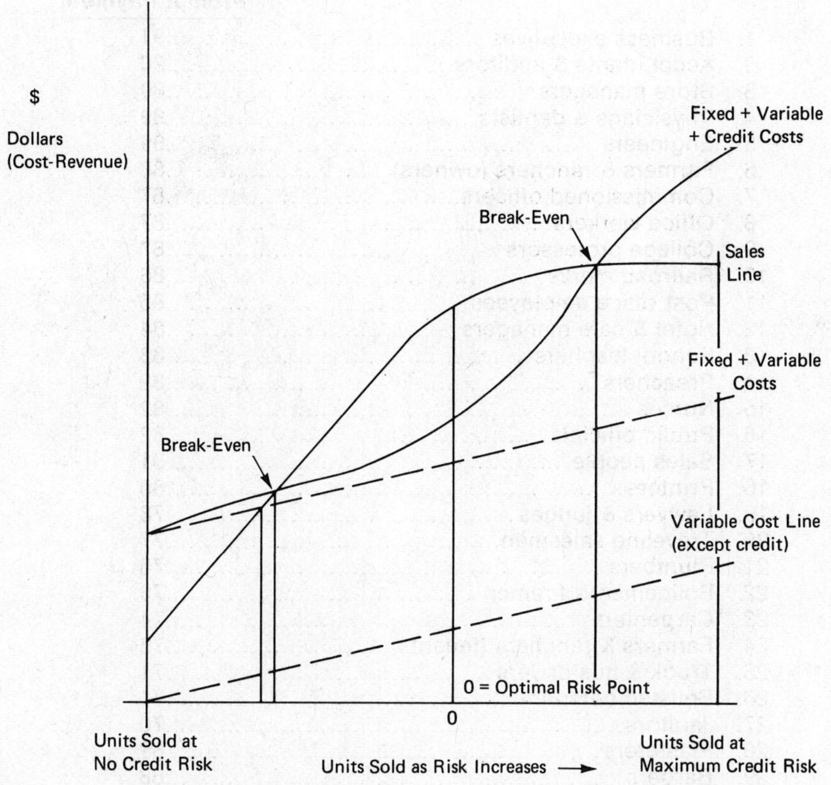

EXHIBIT 11A-23

Marketing ⟶ Statistics ⟶ Accounting ⟶ Systemic Credit Model

EXHIBIT 11A-24

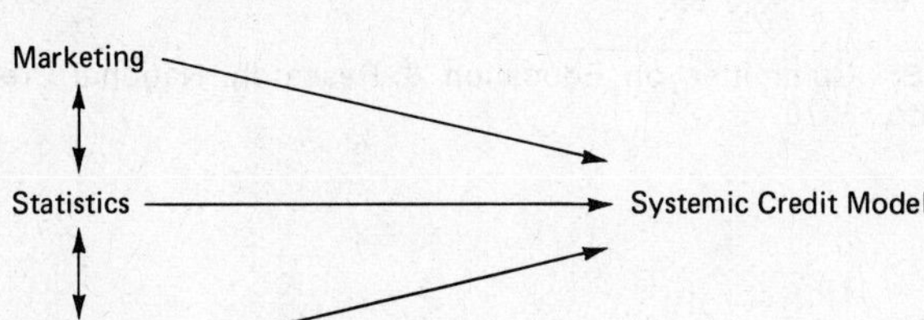

CHAPTER 11 APPENDIX B

NATIONAL STATISTICS ON PAYING HABITS OF VARIOUS OCCUPATIONS

		% of Prompt Payment
1.	Business executives	91
2.	Accountants & auditors	90
3.	Store managers	89
4.	Physicians & dentists	89
5.	Engineers	89
6.	Farmers & ranchers (owners)	88
7.	Commissioned officers	87
8.	Office workers	87
9.	College professors	87
10.	Railroad clerks	86
11.	Post office employees	85
12.	Hotel & cafe managers	84
13.	School teachers	83
14.	Preachers	82
15.	Nurses	82
16.	Public officials	82
17.	Sales people	81
18.	Printers	80
19.	Lawyers & judges	78
20.	Traveling salesmen	77
21.	Plumbers	76
22.	Policemen & firemen	76
23.	Carpenters	74
24.	Farmers & ranchers (tenants)	73
25.	Truck & bus drivers	71
26.	Enlisted personnel	71
27.	Janitors	70
28.	Plasterers	69
29.	Barbers	68
30.	Bartenders	63
31.	Musicians	63
32.	Painters	61
33.	Laborers	60
34.	Cooks	60
35.	Waitresses	59
36.	Laundry workers	58
37.	Housekeepers	58
38.	Models	58
39.	Actors	54
40.	Singers	53
41.	Loggers	52

SOURCE: Committee on Education & Research, National Credit Bureaus, Inc., 1970.

CHAPTER 11 APPENDIX C

PROPOSED CREDIT SCORING GUIDE FOR COMMERCIAL LOANS

Age of Business	Under 1 year 1	1–3 years 7	4–7 years 19	8–12 years 36	13–21 years 49	Over 21 years 67
Years of Present Management	Under 1 year 1	1–3 years 6	4–7 years 17	8–12 years 32	13–21 years 45	Over 21 years 50
Successive Years of Increased Profit	Loss −10	2–3 years 5	4–5 years 12	6–8 years 30	9–12 years 47	Over 12 years 62
Number of Days Inventory	Over 210 1	150–209 4	90–149 10	60–89 22	30–59 53	Under 30 72
Number of Days Receivables	Over 210 1	150–209 4	90–149 11	60–89 28	30–59 57	Under 30 70
Debt to Net Worth	Over 10:1 1	9:1 to 5:1 4	4:1 to 2:1 20	1:1 35	1:2 52	1:3 or better 70
Trade Reports	Suits & judgments 1	All slow 2	Mixed slow & satisfactory 5	All satisfactory 20	Pays promptly & takes all discounts 40	—
Industry Groups*	I 1	II 5	III 10	IV 15	V 19	VI 24
Audit	Own audit 1	Qualified audit 20	Unqualified audit by unknown CPA firm 40	Unqualified audit by known CPA firm 60	—	—

* Banks could set up industrial groupings to reflect their preferences in the granting of credit. If, for example, a bank has had very poor experience with a particular industry, the industry could be categorized as "Group 1" and given a correspondingly low score. Conversely, industries with good past records would be categorized by a group receiving a high score.

SOURCE: W. T. Maloan, "What Bankers are Now Looking for In Financial Statements," *The Practical Accountant,* January–February 1970, pp. 40–46. Used with permission.

CHAPTER 11 REFERENCES AND ADDITIONAL READINGS

Ackoff, Russell L. *A Concept of Corporate Planning.* New York: John Wiley & Sons, Inc., 1970.

Amstutz, A. E. *Computer Simulation of Competitive Marketing Response.* Cambridge, Mass.: MIT Press, 1967.

Bartels, Robert. *Credit Management.* New York: The Ronald Press Company, 1967.

Beckman, Theodore N., and Foster, Ronald S. *Credits and Collections: Management and Theory.* New York: McGraw-Hill Book Company, 1955.

Bowen, Richard L. "Application of Margin Rates to Credit Analysis." *Management Accounting,* November 1966, pp. 26–31.

Britt, S. H., and Boyd, H. W. Jr., *Marketing Management and Administrative Action.* New York: McGraw-Hill Book Company, 1963.

Brown, Victor. "Managing the Cost of Credit." *Retail Control,* September 1971, pp. 2–21.

Chamberlain, Neil W. *The Firm: Micro-Economic Planning and Action.* New York: McGraw-Hill Book Company, 1962.

Churchman, C. West. *The Systems Approach.* New York: Dell Publishing Co., Inc., 1968.

Clark, W. A., and Sexton, D. E. Jr. *Marketing and Management Science: A Synergism.* Homewood, Ill.: Richard D. Irwin, Inc., 1970.

Cohen, Kalman J., and Hammer, Frederick S. *Analytical Methods in Banking.* Homewood, Ill.: Richard D. Irwin, Inc., 1966.

Cremer, Richard. "Bank Credit Cards and Their Impact on Retailers." *Retail Control,* June 1970, pp. 25–33.

Donelly, J. H. Jr., and Ivancevich, J. M. *Analysis for Marketing Decision.* Homewood, Ill.: Richard D. Irwin, Inc., 1970.

Freund, John E., and Williams, Frank J. *Modern Business Statistics.* Englewood Cliffs, N. J.: Prentice-Hall, Inc., 1958.

Gold, Michael H. "Domestic and Export Credit Insurance." *New York Certified Public Accountant,* September 1971, pp. 661–65.

Horngren, Charles T. *Cost Accounting: A Managerial Approach.* 2nd ed. Englewood Cliffs, N.J.: Prentice-Hall, Inc., 1967.

Horrigan, James O. "The Determination of Long-Term Credit Standing with Financial Ratios." *Empirical Research in Accounting: Selected Studies 1966,* Supplement to the *Journal of Accounting Research* 4, pp. 44–70.

Ijiri, Yuji. *The Foundations of Accounting Measurement.* Englewood Cliffs, N. J.: Prentice-Hall, Inc., 1967.

Kaplan, Robert M. "Credit Risks and Opportunities." *Harvard Business Review,* March–April 1967, pp. 83–88.

Kotler, P. *Marketing Management.* Englewood Cliffs, N. J.: Prentice-Hall, Inc., 1967.

Marrah, George L. "Managing Receivables." *The Financial Executive,* July 1970, pp. 40–44.

Mateer, William H. *The Checkless Society: Its Cost Implications for the Firm.* East Lansing, Mich.: MSU Business Studies, Michigan State University Press, 1969.

Miller, D. W., and Starr, M. K. *Executive Decisions and Operations Research.* Englewood Cliffs, N. J.: Prentice-Hall, Inc., 1960.

Montgomery, D. B., and Urban, G. L., eds. *Applications of Management Science in Marketing.* Englewood Cliffs, N. J., Prentice-Hall, Inc., 1970.

Naitove, Irwin. *Modern Factoring.* New York: American Management Association, 1969.

Smith, D. W. "Efficient Credit Management with Timesharing." *The Financial Executive,* March 1971, pp. 29–30.

Smith, S. V.; Brien, R. H.; and Stafford, J. E. *Readings in Marketing Information Systems.* New York: Houghton Mifflin Company, 1968.

CHAPTER 11 QUESTIONS, PROBLEMS, AND CASES

11- 1. "A primary purpose for using credit in a business is to normalize cash flow." Explain the meaning of this statement.

11- 2. Distinguish between the *maturity value* and *face value* of a note. Which value is used in discounting a note?

11- 3. What is the purpose of an allowance for bad debts account?

11- 4. Why do most sellers prefer to sell for cash while most buyers prefer delayed payments? Give at least two reasons for the preference of each party.

11- 5. Distinguish between a *cash discount* and a *trade discount.* Why is the trade discount calculated on retail price? What is the usual basis for granting trade discounts? What noted federal law prohibits discrimination in pricing?

11- 6. What is the function of a *sales journal?* A *purchases journal?*

11- 7. What is the purpose of having credit risk groups? How are such groups distinguished from one another? How are persons placed into a group?

11- 8. Distinguish between *fixed costs* and *variable costs.*

11- 9. Given a basic marginal income statement for firms X and Y below, which one has the greater credit management problem? Explain.

Basic Marginal Income Statement	**X**	**Y**
Sales	$10,000	$10,000
Variable costs	8,000	2,000
Marginal income	2,000	8,000
Fixed costs	1,000	7,000
Profit	$ 1,000	$ 1,000

11-10. Describe three means for conversion of receivables into cash.

11-11. "While the majority of payables arise from goods and services purchased on credit, there are other types of payables for which no bills are received." Identify this class of payables. Give four examples of these payables.

11-12. Distinguish between the *cash basis* of accounting and the *accrual basis* of accounting. Does the cash basis mean that a firm does not use or give credit?

11-13. What *output rule* promotes the use of accrual basis accounting? Explain the rule.

11-14. "The usual form of credit received is a purchase on account." What is the:
(a) Nature of the arrangement
(b) Evidence of debt
(c) Usual payment period
(d) Process for obtaining credit

11-15. Explain how *consignment* is a form of credit. In the credit arrangement, who is the *consignee* and who is the *consignor?* How is a sale recorded under this arrangement?

11-16. (a) Name the parts of the credit given cycle:

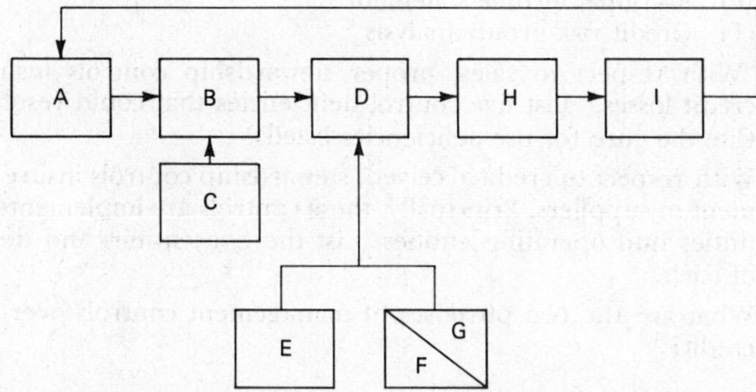

(b) Name the parts of the credit received cycle:

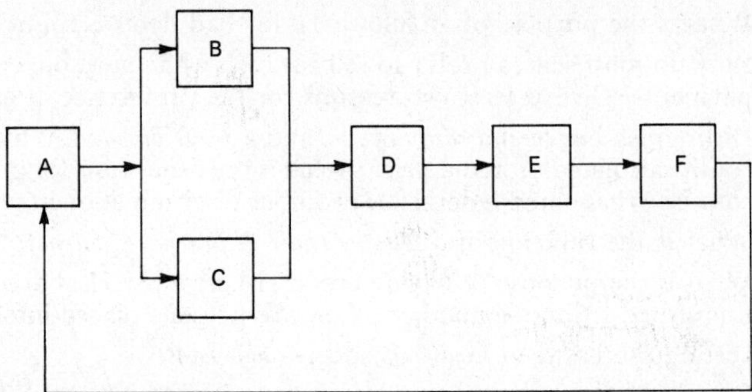

11-17. Define or explain the use of the following terms or phrases:
- (a) Trade receivables
- (b) Trade accounts payable
- (c) An accrual
- (d) A deferral
- (e) Credit agency
- (f) Conditional sales contract
- (g) Line of credit
- (h) "Points"
- (i) Factoring
- (j) Assignment
- (k) Open credit
- (l) Secured credit
- (m) Contribution to margin

11-18. What are the costs to the seller for factoring accounts receivable?

11-19. What are the two basic methods for providing an allowance for doubtful accounts? Explain the rationale behind each method and the procedure for calculating the allowance. What are the advantages and disadvantages of each?

11-20. In addition to posting credit sales and purchase events to the ledger, they are also posted again on a record for each customer or each vendor respectively. What are these individual records called and what form may these records assume? Why are two postings required—one to the general ledger account and one to the individual record? Isn't this posting redundant, and doesn't it cause the trial balance to be out of balance?

11-21. What is the purpose of the following statements or records:
- (a) Aged trial balance of accounts receivable
- (b) Aged trial balance of accounts payable
- (c) Accounts receivable subsidiary ledger
- (d) Cash customer marginal income statement (MIS)
- (e) Marginal income statement
- (f) Credit risk group analysis

11-22. "With respect to sales, proper stewardship controls insure against large credit losses." List five control deficiencies that could result in credit losses. Cite the cure for the deficiencies listed.

11-23. With respect to credit received, stewardship controls insure against overpayment to suppliers. Principally, these controls are implemented by segregating duties into operating entities. List the five entities and describe the duties of each.

11-24. What are the two purposes of management controls over the extension of credit?

11-25. List five functions of a firm's credit department.

11-26. Identify and explain four limitations of credit insurance.

11-27. In order to meet the 2/10, n/30 discount terms of its supplier, the Zeebee Corporation submits a non-interest-bearing note as payment. The note is for the net price. Should the supplier allow a cash discount to the Zeebee Corporation? If the note were interest-bearing, should the discount be allowed?

11-28. Just as the allowance for doubtful accounts serves to offset the accounts receivable balance, should *anticipated* cash discounts also serve as an offset? Suppose you anticipate that cash discounts will be allowed on 80% of the accounts receivable balance. Is your answer still the same?

11-29. Give at least two examples of each credit resource system feedback report:
(a) Exception reports
(b) Control reports
(c) Comparative reports
(d) Interpretive reports

11-30. What is the content of management control reports relating to credit granted?

11-31. Identify and explain the three costs of extending credit. What is the principal cost of not extending credit?

11-32. Describe the correlation to credit risk of the following characteristics:
(a) Credit and delinquency costs
(b) The amount that persons will buy
(c) The number of persons per group
(d) Total expected sales
(e) Credit limit of a group

11-33. "The point of maximum profit is where the credit risk group factor is equal to the marginal income rate of the basic firm." Explain.

11-34. ***DISCOUNTING NOTES RECEIVABLE*** Suppose a $900, forty-five-day note is discounted at the bank for 8%. The note was acquired on March 1 and discounted on March 28. If the proceeds from the bank are $902, what annual interest rate is the note bearing?

11-35. ***DISCOUNTING NOTES RECEIVABLE***
(a) Suppose an $800, forty-day, 9% note is acquired from a customer on December 1, 19*x*1.
 (1) If the note is discounted at the bank on December 16, at a discount rate of 6%, how much cash is received from the bank?
 (2) If the discounted note in (1) is dishonored by the maker, how much must be paid to the bank?
(b) Suppose a $2,200, ninty-day, 6% note is acquired from a customer on October 1. If the note is discounted on November 20 at 9%, what are the proceeds from the note?

11-36. ***ALLOWANCE FOR DOUBTFUL ACCOUNTS*** At the end of the current year the accounts receivable account has a debit balance of $100,000 and net sales for the year total $1,200,000. Determine the amount of bad debts expense under each of the following assumptions:
(a) The allowance account before adjustment has a credit balance of $300,
 (1) and the bad debts expense is estimated at 1% of net sales?
 (2) and an analysis of the accounts in the customers' ledger indicates bad accounts of $11,400?
 (3) and bad debts expense is estimated at 7% of the accounts receivable balance?
(b) The allowance account before adjustment has a debit balance of $1,400,
 (1) and bad debts expense is estimated at 3/4 of 1 % of net sales?

(2) and an analysis of the accounts in the customers' ledger indicates bad accounts of $9,100?
(3) and bad debts expense is estimated at 5% of the accounts receivable balance?

11-37. ***ALLOWANCE FOR DOUBTFUL ACCOUNTS*** Consider the following aging schedule for the ending balance of accounts receivable:

ACCOUNTS RECEIVABLE BY AGE GROUPS

	Amount	Percent Considered Uncollectible
Not yet due	$16,000	1%
0–4 months	9,000	3%
4–6 months	4,350	10%
6–10 months	1,450	50%
Total acc. rec.	$33,600	

Other data:

(a) Credit sales for the period are $450,000.
(b) The allowance for doubtful accounts has a debit balance of $1,200.

Required:

(1) Indicate the amount of adjustment to the allowance for doubtful accounts using the aging method for estimating uncollectibles.
(2) Indicate the amount of adjustment to the allowance for doubtful accounts if such adjustment is based on an uncollectible accounts expense estimated as 1% of credit sales.

11-38. ***JOURNAL ENTRIES—FACTORING AND DISCOUNTING*** Journalize the following events for the Naver Corporation and identify the transaction document for each event:

April 4: A 90-day, 5% note for $1,400 was received from a customer.
April 5: Purchased $1,600 of merchandise on an open account with credit terms of 3/10, n/30.
April 7: Factored $20,000 of accounts receivable. Proceeds from the factor were $18,200.
April 10: Returned $150 of defective merchandise bought on April 5.
April 13: A 40-day, 7% note for $600 was received from a customer.
April 15: Paid the balance owed from the April 5 purchase.
April 22: Borrowed $30,000 from the bank and pledged $35,000 of accounts receivable as collateral.
May 19: Discounted the note received April 4 at 4%.
May 22: A 60-day, 4% note for $2,200 was received from a customer.
May 23: Received the proceeds from the note dated April 13.
May 31: Discounted the May 22 note at a 6% discount rate.

11-39. ***PARTICIPATING IN A CREDIT CARD PLAN*** The Macias Company operates a full-line department store which is dominant in its market area, is easily accessible to public and private transportation, has adequate parking facilities, and is near a large permanent military base. The president of the company seeks your advice on a recently received proposal.

A local bank in which Macias Company has an account recently affiliated with a popular national credit-card plan and has extended an invitation to Macias Company to participate in the plan. Under the plan, affiliated banks mail credit-card applications to persons in the community who have good credit ratings, regardless of whether they are bank customers. If the recipient wishes to receive a credit card, he completes, signs, and returns the application and installment credit agreement. Holders of cards thus activated may charge merchandise or services at any participating establishment throughout the nation.

The bank guarantees payment to all participating merchants on all presented invoices which have been properly completed, signed, and validated with the impression of credit cards that have not expired or been reported stolen, or otherwise canceled. Local merchants, including your client, may turn in all card-validated sales tickets or invoices to their affiliated local bank at any time and receive immediate credits to their checking accounts of 96.5% of the face value of the invoices. If card users pay the bank in full within thirty days for amounts billed, the bank levies no added charges against them. If they elect to make their payments under a deferred payment plan, the bank adds a service charge which amounts to an effective interest rate of 18% per annum on unpaid balances. Only the local affiliated banks and the franchiser of the credit-card plan share in these revenues.

The 18% service charge approximates what the Macias Company has been billing customers who pay their accounts over an extended period on a schedule similar to that offered under the credit card plans. Participation in the plan does not prevent the Macias Company from continuing to carry on its credit business as in the past.

Required:

(a) What are the positive and negative financial- and accounting-related factors that the Macias Company should consider in deciding whether to participate in the described credit card plan? Explain.

(b) If the Macias Company does participate in the plan, which income statement and balance sheet accounts may change materially as the plan becomes fully operative?

(Adapted from the CPA exam.)

11-40. ***CREDIT RISK ANALYSIS*** You have generated the following credit management information:

Basic Financial Structure: (Group A)		**Credit Groups**		
			Credit Risk Factor	**Sales**
Sales	$10,000	A	0%	$10,000
Variable costs	6,000	B	5%	20,000
Fixed costs	4,000	C	10%	30,000
		D	20%	40,000
		E	30%	30,000
		F	50%	20,000
		G	70%	10,000

Required:

(a) Which is the last group to be included on a break-even contribution to margin basis?

(b) Which is the last group to be included on a cut-off of a minimum 10% contribution to margin?

(c) What would total *net income* be if our clientele consists of A through E in the sales amounts indicated?

(d) What is the contribution to margin of group A?
(e) What is the contribution to margin of group B?
(f) What is the average contribution to margin of A + B?

11-41. ***ALLOWANCE FOR DOUBTFUL ACCOUNTS*** Consider the three-year data for the Hanafee Company:

		19x3	19x2	19x1
(a) Credit sales		$6,910,000	$7,130,000	$6,820,000
(b) Accounts receivable (end of year balance)		1,060,000	1,200,000	970,000
(c) Aged:				
% considered uncollectible				
1%	0–30 days	550,000	600,000	500,000
2%	31–60 days	300,000	370,000	230,000
6%	61–100 days	160,000	170,000	140,000
15%	over 100 days	50,000	60,000	100,000
(d) Actual bad debts		45,200	62,000	37,400

Required:

(1) Using the sales method, prepare a schedule computing each year's ending balance for the allowance account, assuming 3/4 of 1% of credit sales are uncollectible.

(2) Using the receivables method, prepare a schedule:
   a. Computing each year's adjustment to the allowance account assuming 5% of accounts receivable outstanding will be uncollectible.
   b. Computing each year's adjustment to the allowance account based on an aging of the accounts receivable balance.

(3) Prepare a schedule calculating the net difference in income and cumulative difference in income (for each year) between the sales method and the aging method.

11-42. ***CREDIT RISK ANALYSIS*** Part (a): Suppose the following information is available:

CREDIT RISK GROUP ANALYSIS

		Cost Factor Expressed as a % of Sales			
Group	Necessary Attribute Score	Credit Cost	Delinquency	Total	Total Expected Sales per Annum
A	None	0%	0%	0%	$ 50,000
B	180+	6%	10%	16%	180,000
C	160–179	8%	10%	18%	270,000
D	140–159	8%	16%	24%	300,000
E	120–139	9%	23%	32%	350,000
F	119 or less	9%	35%	44%	190,000

Other data:

(1) Expected fixed costs are $15,000.
(2) Basic variable cost ratio (for cash sales) is .60.

Required: Part (a)

a. On the basis of the above information, which credit risk groups should be extended credit?

b. If a group must contribute a minimum of 10% to profit, which credit risk groups should be extended credit? If the contribution must be 20%, which groups are extended credit?

Part (b): Suppose Mr. Reynolds has applied for credit and gives you the following information:

Marital status	married
Age	31
Residence	renting a house
Time at residence	1.5 years
Time at previous residence	1 year
Occupation	Draftsman
Length of employment	2 years
Annual income	$11,200
No. of dependents (excluding self)	2
Debt load	house rental payment $200/mo. installment debt $370/mo.
Credit cards	Sears (good record) Master Charge (good record) Center Dept. Store (good record) "Zoom" Oil Company (good record)
Credit reference	City Natl. Bank Checking: average balance $200, good record City Savings & Loan Savings: $800 balance Loan: $5,000 car loan, good record
Personal references	Michael Hariff

Required: Part (b)

c. Using the score sheet in Exhibit 11A-6 of Appendix A, assign Mr. Reynolds to a credit group from Part (a).

d. If a group must contribute a minimum of 5% to profit, should Mr. Reynolds be granted credit?

CHAPTER

12

INVENTORY MANAGEMENT

12.1 THE NATURE OF INVENTORY

Inventory consists of physical things that: (1) are held for sale in the ordinary course of business; (2) enter into the production of salable goods; or (3) are expensed or capitalized in the ordinary course of business.

These definitions have a common element; i.e., inventory is a *stock* or *reservoir* of physical things.

The intent may be to sell these things to others, in which case the term *merchandise inventory* applies; or the things may be held for use in running an organization (such as maintenance supplies), in which case the cost of the supplies is charged to the income statement ("expensed" or "charged to income") as the supplies are used. Other supplies and materials (e.g., construction items) may become part of a long-lived asset (e.g., building). Inventory of this type is added to the cost of the long-lived asset ("capitalized") as it is requisitioned for use.

To explore the nature of inventory more closely, let us follow the flow of goods and services through the various sectors of a modern, industrial economy (Exhibit 12-1). Looking first at business enterprises, we observe that physical things

EXHIBIT 12-1 MAJOR SECTORS OF A MODERN ECONOMY

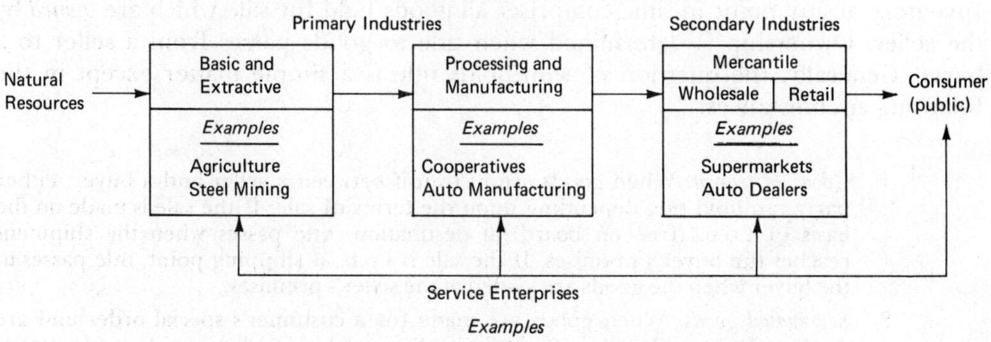

(unprocessed products and raw materials) flow from basic to manufacturing industries. Supplies of these things (unprocessed products and raw materials) that are ready for sale comprise the inventory of basic enterprises.

Unprocessed products and raw materials enter as *inventory* into the accounts of processing and manufacturing businesses. Further effort is now required to convert this inventory into salable goods for the consumer market. Accordingly, a manufacturing firm has three inventory accounts, as shown in Exhibit 12-2.

EXHIBIT 12-2 THE THREE INVENTORIES OF MANUFACTURING FIRMS

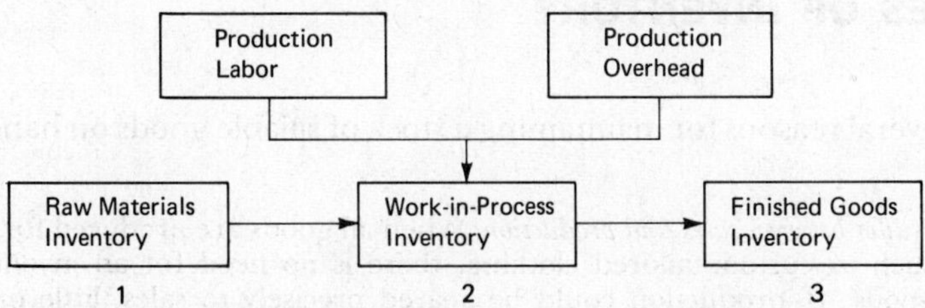

Production labor and other expenses ("overhead") are required to convert the raw material(s) into finished goods. Units that are completely finished are classified as *finished goods inventory,* while units that have started through the conversion process but are not yet finished are classified as *work-in-process inventory.*

Finished goods are sold to wholesalers or directly to retailers. These *mercantile* enterprises have only one inventory account—*merchandise inventory.*

All types of business enterprise carry supplies and materials that are not intended for resale. These items should be distinguished from merchandise inventory, and a caption such as "supplies" is often used for this purpose.

Service organizations do not specialize in the sale of physical things; hence, they have little or no merchandise inventory. Where they do have inventory, it is accounted for on the same basis as with mercantile enterprises. Materials and supplies in such cases are handled in the manner discussed above.

12.2 COMPOSITION AND OWNERSHIP OF INVENTORY

Inventory at any point in time comprises all goods held for sale which are *owned* by the seller. Ownership is determined when title to goods passes from a seller to a buyer. Generally, the question of who holds title is a simple matter except in the following circumstances:

1. *Goods in transit:* When goods are in transit between a seller and a buyer, either party can hold title depending upon the terms of sale. If the sale is made on the basis of f.o.b. (free on board) at destination, title passes when the shipment reaches the buyer's premises. If the sale is f.o.b. at shipping point, title passes to the buyer when the goods are loaded at the seller's premises.
2. *Segregated goods:* When goods are made for a customer's special order and are separated (set aside) from the seller's other salable inventory, title to the goods passes to the buyer at the time of separation even though they are being held ("set aside" or laid-away) at the seller's premises.
3. *Consignments:* Consignment sales are where a buyer (consignee) has possession of goods, but title does not pass until such goods are sold to a customer. Consigned goods are included in the inventory of the shipper (consignor) until they are sold by the consignee in part or in whole.
4. *Conditional and installment sales:* When goods are sold on a *conditional* or *installment sales contract,* title to the goods remains with the seller until the buyer has paid the contract price. However, since these contracts are normally paid in the ordinary course of business, the seller generally considers such goods as sold and excludes them from inventory. The buyer includes such goods in inventory even though the seller holds legal title.

12.3 PURPOSES OF INVENTORY

There are several reasons for maintaining a stock of salable goods on hand (inventory).

1. *Buffer between sales and production:* When all goods are produced for special orders, such as custom-tailored clothing, there is no need for an inventory of salable goods. If production could be geared precisely to sales, little or no inventory would be needed. But since sales fluctuate, production must also fluctuate in order to avoid the accumulation of inventory. If these fluctuations between sales and purchases can be synchronized, inventory could be reduced. However, there is generally a time-lag in information relating to fluctuations in sales or production. An important objective of management is to analyze sales and production trends and determine their significance one to the other at any early date:
   a. A buildup in sales requires a buildup in production, or there will be loss of sales until the production rate can match current demand.
   b. A slowdown in sales signals a slowdown in production, otherwise goods will be produced for which there is no ready market.

   Major fluctuations or trends must be recognized to avoid these problems. Where fluctuations are seasonal or of a minor nature, it is more economical to produce goods evenly throughout the year and use inventories as the *buffer* between production and sales. Uneven production requires spotty hiring, overtime, layoffs, and irregular purchasing practices, all leading to an increase in production costs.
2. *Buffer between production and supply of raw materials:* A sufficient supply of raw materials must be maintained in order to permit production to continue between

orders and the delivery of raw material. When sources of supply are unreliable, such as ore mined in a foreign country, the inventory of raw material (buffer) must be greater in order to insure a consistent level of production.

3. *As a hedge against higher prices:* In periods of rising prices, one purpose of holding inventory is to acquire raw materials or finished goods at relatively lower prices: (1) to gain a competitive advantage when prices increase (by selling at lower prices), or (2) to increase gross profit by matching a lower cost price against a higher sales price, as shown in Exhibit 12-3.

EXHIBIT 12-3 INVENTORY HOLDING GAIN

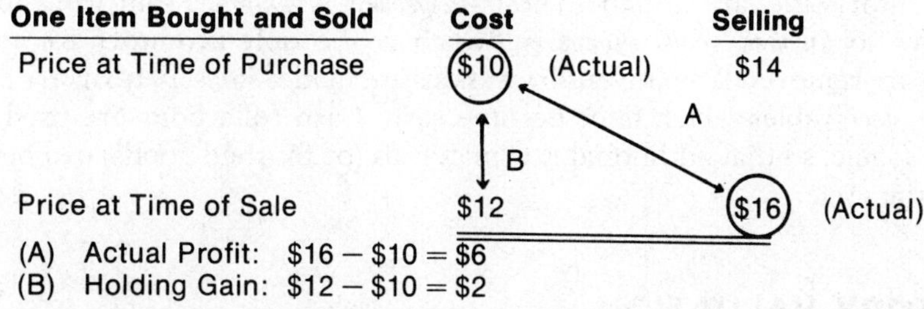

Of the $6 profit, $2 results from *holding* the inventory while the other $4 is the "normal" margin between cost and selling price.

In periods of falling prices, *holding losses* would materialize.

4. *Advertising:* Even though some industries do not sell merchandise from stock, a certain amount of inventory must be maintained for display or sampling purposes. For example, a sales office (or showroom) solicits orders to be shipped from a factory or warehouse but carries no merchandise inventory other than that

EXHIBIT 12-4 THE INVENTORY RESOURCE CYCLE

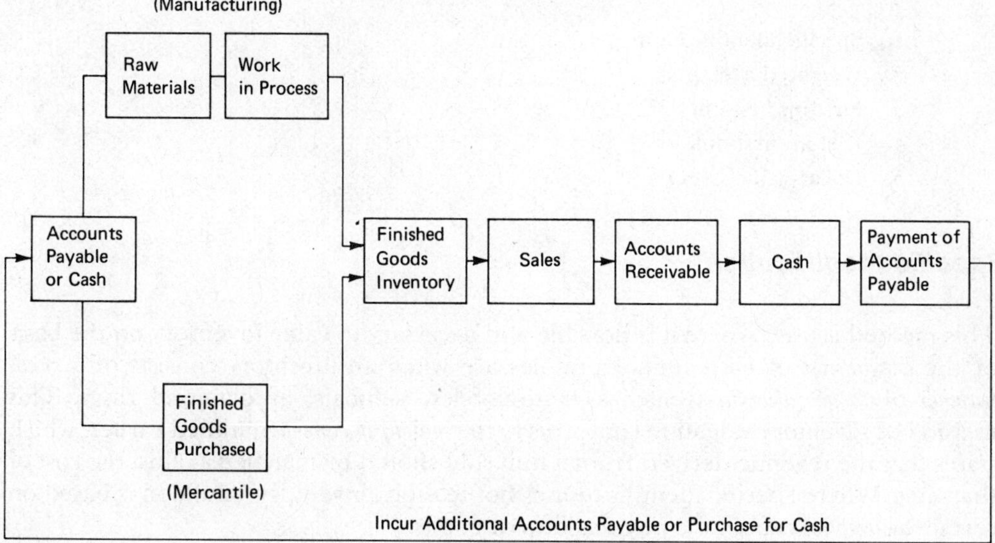

required for display or sampling. Obviously, a greater variety of products calls for a higher inventory for these showroom purposes.

12.4 THE INVENTORY RESOURCE CYCLE

As in the case of other resources, inventory passes through sequential steps called the *inventory resource cycle* (Exhibit 12-4).

Raw materials are purchased for credit or cash and placed into *raw materials inventory*. As materials are requisitioned for use, they are subtracted from raw materials inventory and are added to *work-in-process inventory*. From work-in-process, goods move to *finished goods inventory* (which is the only inventory for mercantile firms) and are removed from inventory as sales are made. Sales, in turn, are evidenced by cash or receivables which later become cash. Cash collections are used to repay accounts payable, so that additional raw materials (or finished goods) can be acquired to restart the cycle.

12.5 INVENTORY VALUATION

Having discussed earlier the composition of physical inventory, we now consider how a value is placed on the units in inventory and consequently on the units sold.

Inventory valuation (or "inventory pricing") methods can be classified into three basic classes: (1) those based on cost, (2) those based on market value, and (3) those based on the lower of cost or market.

COST-BASED METHODS

Five inventory valuation methods that are based on cost are:

1. Specific identification
2. Weighted average
3. First-in, first-out
4. Last-in, first-out
5. Dollar-value LIFO

Specific Identification

This method is used where it is possible and necessary to value inventory on the basis of the *actual cost* of each unit. Examples are when an inventory consists of a *small number* of *large-value items* such as automobiles, sailboats, or diamond rings. This method of inventory valuation conforms to the *matching concept* outlined earlier, which states that the revenue derived from a unit sold should be matched against the cost of that unit. Where specific identification is not feasible, inventory valuation is based on certain *assumptions* about the physical flow of goods.

Weighted Average

The weighted average method of valuing inventories assumes that goods are commingled, therefore inventory is valued according to the *average price* paid during a period. Each price paid is multiplied by the number of units purchased at that price; for example:

Date	Batch	No. of Units	Unit Price	Total
January 1	A	100	$10	$1,000
15	B	200	11	2,200
26	C	300	12	3,600
TOTAL		600		$6,800

Weighted average price is $6,800/600 = $11.33 per unit. This value is used to determine the cost of goods sold, and to value the inventory on hand.

If a continuous or *perpetual* record of inventory purchases and sales (or receipts and issuances) is maintained, the result will be a *moving average* with the unit cost changing each time a new purchase is made. For instance, if 200 units were sold or issued on January 17 and 200 units on January 29, the unit averages would be as follows:

Date	Batch	No. of Units	Unit Prices of Purchases or Issuances	Cost of Purchases or Issuances	Cumulative Inventory Quantity	Cost of Inventory	Unit Average Price
Jan. 1 Purchase	A	100	$10	$1,000	100	$1,000	$10
Jan. 15 Purchase	B	200	11	2,200	300	3,200	10.67
Jan. 17 Issuance		(200)	10.67	2,133	100	1,067	10.67
Jan. 26 Purchase	C	300	12	3,600	400	4,667	11.67
Jan. 29 Issuance		(200)	11.67	2,334	200	2,333	11.67

The ending inventory of 200 units would be valued at $11.67 per unit.

First-In, First-Out (FIFO)

A logical assumption about inventory flow for most businesses is that goods are sold in the order in which they are purchased. If 400 of the units in the preceding example are sold, first-in, first-out (FIFO) would assign value to cost of goods sold and to ending inventory as follows:

Cost of goods sold................$4,400
A: 100 @ $10 = $1,000
B: 200 @ 11 = 2,200
C: 100 @ 12 = 1,200
400 $4,400

Ending inventory $2,400
C: 200 @ $12 = $2,400

If a perpetual record of inventory purchases and issuances are maintained under a FIFO procedure, the same valuation of ending inventory will result:

	Batch A @ $10	Batch B @ $11	Batch C @ $12
Purchases:			
Jan. 1	100		
Jan. 15		200	
Issuances:			
Jan. 17	(100)	(100)	
Purchases:			
Jan. 26			300
Issuances:			
Jan. 29		(100)	(100)
	0	0	200

Ending inventory valuation.................$2,400
C: 200 @ $12 = $2,400

Last-In, First-Out (LIFO)

Another assumption about the physical flow of goods through a business is that last items purchased are sold first. While this assumption does not reflect the *actual* physical flow of goods in most businesses, this method of inventory valuation is adopted widely because of its effect on income.

If, in the foregoing instance, 400 units are sold, with the remaining 200 in ending inventory, prices would be assigned as follows:

Cost of goods sold..................$4,700
C: 300 @ $12 = $3,600
B: 100 @ 11 = 1,100
400 $4,700

Ending inventory $2,100
A: 100 @ $10 = $1,000
B: 100 @ 11 = 1,100
200 $2,100

LIFO charges cost of goods sold with the latest prices, while the earlier prices are assigned to the ending inventory.

If a perpetual record of inventory purchases and issuances are maintained under LIFO, a different ending inventory valuation may result due to the timing of issuances:

	Batch A @ $10	Batch B @ $11	Batch C @ $12
Purchases:			
Jan. 1	100		
Jan. 15		200	
Issuances:			
Jan. 17		(200)	
Purchases:			
Jan. 26			300
Issuances:			
Jan. 29			(200)
	100	0	100

Ending inventory valuation..................$2,200

A:	100 @ $10 =	$1,000
C:	100 @ 12 =	1,200
	200	$2,200

Dollar-Value LIFO

This method eliminates the need under conventional LIFO for specific identification of batches and batch prices. The ending inventory in units is simply priced at *current cost* and then adjusted to LIFO using a price index. Changes in inventory are determined at base-year prices. An increase indicates a *new batch* has been added, while a decline indicates a depletion from the *latest* batch (or batches). The batches comprising ending inventory are then restated using the price index for the year each batch was originally established. For example, suppose the following ending inventories and price levels are available:

Date	Inventory at Year-End Prices	Price Level Index
December 31, 1967	$400	100%
December 31, 1968	480	120%
December 31, 1969	330	110%
December 31, 1970	315	90%
December 31, 1971	525	105%
December 31, 1972	450	125%

Dividing by the appropriate price index, we can convert each year's ending inventory to base-year prices, and thus, determine the *real* increases and declines in inventory levels:

Date	Inventory at Year-End Prices	Price Level Index	Inventory at Base-Year Prices	Change in Inventory at Base-Year Prices
1967	$400	100%	$400	
1968	480	120%	400	0
1969	330	110%	300	(100)
1970	315	90%	350	50
1971	525	105%	500	150
1972	450	125%	360	(140)

Increases are treated as new batches, while declines are treated as reductions in the latest batch (or batches). In other words, a LIFO procedure is followed:

	1967	1970	1971
Beginning inventory	$400		
Decline in 1969	(100)		
Increase in 1970		$50	
Increase in 1971			$150
Decline in 1972			(140)
Ending inventory for 1972	$300	$50	$ 10

The batches comprising ending inventory are stated at base-year prices. They must be converted back to the prices prevailing when the batch was first established. This can be done using price indexes:

1967:	$300 × 100% =	$300.00
1970:	50 × 90% =	45.00
1971:	10 × 105% =	10.50
		$355.50

The 1972 ending inventory originally stated at a *current cost* of $450 is now converted to a LIFO cost of $355.50.

COMPARISON OF FIFO, WEIGHTED AVERAGE, AND LIFO

Assuming no beginning inventory, a sales revenue of $6,000, and *no* perpetual inventory records, comparative gross profit statements on the basis of FIFO, weighted average, and LIFO would be as follows:

EXHIBIT 12-5 COMPARATIVE GROSS PROFIT STATEMENTS

	FIFO		Weighted Average		LIFO	
Sales		$6,000		$6,000		$6,000
Beginning inventory	$ -0-		$ -0-		$ -0-	
Purchases	6,800		6,800		6,800	
Available	6,800		6,800		6,800	
Less: Ending inventory	2,400		2,266		2,100	
Cost of goods sold		4,400		4,534		4,700
Gross profit		$1,600		$1,466		$1,300

Note that *sales* and *purchases* are not affected by the inventory valuation method used. Note also that it is necessary to keep track of inventory batches under LIFO and FIFO, because unit prices of various batches are never averaged. A new batch is required each time the cost price changes on purchasing a particular item. Further comparisons between these inventory valuation methods are contained in Exhibit 12-6.

EXHIBIT 12-6 COMPARISON OF COST-BASED INVENTORY VALUATION METHODS

	FIFO	**Weighted Average**	**LIFO**
1. Inventory value:			
a. In periods of rising prices.	Highest Value	Between FIFO and LIFO	Lowest Value
b. In periods of falling prices.	Lowest Value		Highest Value
2. Balance sheet valuation as indication of current value.	Good	Fair	Poor
3. Income statement effect:			
a. In periods of rising prices.	Highest earnings	Lower than FIFO, higher than LIFO	Lowest earnings
b. In periods of falling prices.	Lowest earnings	Higher than FIFO, lower than LIFO	Highest earnings
4. Represents actual flow of goods.	Usually	Often	Rarely
5. Acceptable for income tax purposes.	Yes	Yes	Yes—but then LIFO must also be used in financial reporting.

In Exhibit 12-7 we follow FIFO, LIFO, and weighted average inventory valuation through one year of rising prices (19x1) and one year of falling prices (19x2).

EXHIBIT 12-7 COST-BASED INVENTORY VALUATION METHODS AND CHANGING PRICE-LEVELS

19x1

Purchases	**Batch**	**No. of Units**	**Unit Price**	**Total Price**
Jan. —Beginning inventory	A	1,000	$ 5	$ 5,000
Mar. 31—Purchases	B	1,500	6	9,000
June 15—Purchases	C	1,200	6	7,200
Sept. 19—Purchases	D	1,200	7	8,400
Dec. 1—Purchases	E	1,000	7	7,000
		5,900		$36,600

Sales				
Jan. —March 30—Sales	A	800	$ 8	6,400
Mar. 31—June 14—Sales	B	1,200	9	10,800
June 15—Sept. 18—Sales	C	1,000	9	9,000
Sept. 19—Nov. 30—Sales	D	1,200	10	12,000
Dec. 1—Dec. 31—Sales	E	1,000	10	10,000
		5,200		$48,200

EXHIBIT 12-7 (CONTINUED)

19x2

Purchases	Batch	No. of Units	Unit Price	Total Price
Jan. 1–Beginning inventory	F	700		
Mar. 31–Purchases	G	1,800	$ 7	$12,600
June 15–Purchases	H	1,500	6	9,000
Sept. 19–Purchases	I	1,200	5	6,000
Dec. 1–Purchases	J	1,000	5	5,000
		6,200		
Sales				
Jan. 1-March 30–Sales	F	600	$10	6,000
Mar. 31-June 14–Sales	G	1,500	10	15,000
June 15-Sept. 18–Sales	H	1,200	9	10,800
Sept. 19-Nov. 30–Sales	I	1,000	8	8,000
Dec. 1-Dec. 31–Sales	J	900	8	7,200
		5,200		$47,000

19x1 Gross Profit Statement

	FIFO		Weighted Average		LIFO	
Sales		$48,200		$48,200		$48,200
Beginning inventory	$ 5,000		$ 5,000		$ 5,000	
Add: Purchases	31,600		31,600		31,600	
	36,600		36,600		36,600	
Ending inventory	4,900	31,700	4,340	32,260	3,500*	33,100
Gross profit		$16,500		$15,940		$15,100

19x2 Gross Profit Statement

	FIFO		Weighted Average		LIFO	
Sales		$47,000		$47,000		$47,000
Beginning inventory	$ 4,900		$ 4,340		$ 3,500*	
Add: Purchases	32,600		32,600		32,600	
	37,500		36,940		36,100	
Ending inventory	5,000	32,500	5,960	30,980	5,600*	30,500
Gross profit		$14,500		$16,020		$16,500

*If a perpetual inventory is maintained, LIFO will produce an ending inventory valuation of $4,000 in 19*x*1 (A:200, B:300, C:200) and $5,900 in 19*x*2 (A:100, G:300, H:300, I:100, J:100).

As noted above, LIFO shows the lowest profit in a period of rising prices (19*x*1) and the highest profit in a period of falling prices (19*x*2). FIFO, on the other hand, shows the highest profit in a period of rising prices (19*x*1) and the lowest profit in a period of falling prices (19*x*2).

LIFO, then, is an anti-cyclical device: it curbs reported net income in an inflationary period and has the opposite effect in a period of recession or depression.

Firms that adopt LIFO during a period of rising prices to minimize taxable net income may not switch to FIFO during a period of falling prices; under the Internal Revenue Code, Regulation 1472–5:

An election made to adopt and use the LIFO inventory method is irrevocable, and the method once adopted shall be used in all subsequent taxable years, unless the use of another method is required by the Commissioner, or authorized by him pursuant to a written application therefore filed as provided in paragraph (e) of Reg.1.446–1.

Firms using LIFO for tax reporting purposes must also use LIFO in connection with published financial statements (Regulation 1.472–2[e]).

MARKET-BASED VALUATION METHODS

The cost of taking (that is, making an actual count of units on hand) and valuing inventories at frequent intervals is prohibitive where numerous small-value items are involved; e.g., in supermarkets. While generally accepted auditing standards—together with legal precedent and SEC regulations—require that a *physical inventory* (actual count) be taken at least once a year, specifically in the case of corporations, other methods for estimating the quantity and value of units of inventory on hand are needed for purposes of interim (monthly or quarterly) financial reports, as well as for internal management purposes. These methods are the *gross profit* method and the *retail* method.

Gross Profit Method

The value of inventory can be estimated by assuming an average gross profit percentage earned on sales (sales less cost of goods sold = gross profit). The average gross profit percentage used may be based on prior years' experience or on current markup. The value of ending inventory is deduced as follows:

Sales		$50,000
Gross profit (at an average percentage of 40%)		20,000
Costs of goods sold		30,000
Beginning inventory	$10,000	
Purchases	25,000	
Goods available for sale		35,000
Ending inventory		$ 5,000

Retail Method

The retail method provides a means of estimating the cost of an ending inventory stated at retail prices. The cost and retail price of goods available for sale in a given period are used to calculate a *cost-price ratio.* This ratio is then used subsequently to convert the retail price of ending inventory to an approximate cost.

The retail method eliminates the necessity for retail businesses to maintain or refer to cost records in order to calculate the cost of inventory items marked only with retail prices. The method, however, uses an *average* cost-price ratio, and consequently, its applicability to a year-end composite retail inventory is based upon two assumptions:

1. The retail method applied on a storewide basis assumes that ending inventory consists of the types and proportions of goods available during the year.
2. The markup percentage remains constant during the year.

The calculation of the cost-price ratio is the real crux of the retail method. Once formulated, it is simply applied to the ending inventory at retail to obtain a conversion to cost. For example, suppose the Hariff Company has a cost-price ratio of 70%, and the following schedule of last year's activity *at retail:*

Beginning inventory		$ 47,000
Add: Purchases (net)	$194,500	
Additional markups	12,000	
Markdown cancellations	7,000	213,500
		260,500
Less: Sales (net)	188,500	
Markup cancellations	3,000	
Markdowns	16,000	207,500
Ending inventory		$ 53,000
Ending inventory at cost = 70% × $53,000 = $37,100		

An understanding of the terminology used by retail businesses like the Hariff Company is essential, not only for the computation of ending inventory at retail, but also for the proper determination of a cost-price ratio. Ordinarily, the terms shown in the preceding schedule have the following meaning:

1. *Additional markup* is an increase in the original selling price.
2. *Markup cancellation* is a subsequent cancellation of an additional markup, but *not in excess* of such additional markup.
3. *Markdown* is a decrease in the original selling price.
4. *Markdown cancellation* is a subsequent cancellation of a markdown, but *not in excess* of such markdown.

There are *four* methods of calculating the cost-price ratio, and the application of each to the ending inventory at retail produces four different approximations of ending inventory: Lower of Cost or Market, Replacement Cost, LIFO, and FIFO.

METHOD 1: Lower of Cost or Market (the Conventional Method). Only additional markups are considered in the computation of the retail price of goods available for sale:

	Cost	Retail
Beginning inventory	$ 28,200	$ 47,000
Add: Purchases (net)	127,110	194,500
Additional markups		12,000
Less: Markup cancellations		(3,000)
Goods available for sale	$155,310	$250,500
Cost-price ratio = $155,310/$250,500 = 62%		

METHOD 2: Replacement Cost. Additional markups and markdowns are not considered in the computation of the retail price of goods available for sale:

	Cost	Retail
Beginning inventory	$ 28,200	$ 47,000
Add: Purchases (net)	127,110	194,500
Goods available for sale	$155,310	$241,500

Cost-price ratio = $155,310/$241,500 = 64%

METHOD 3: LIFO. The selling price of *goods purchased* is computed by considering additional markups and markdowns. The cost-price ratio is computed as the ratio between the cost and retail price of *goods purchased.* The ratio, then, is applicable only to any new incremental *inventory layer* added this period. The layers comprising any ending inventory are converted to cost using the cost-price ratio computed in the year in which the layer was added.

	Cost	Retail
Purchases (net)	$127,110	$194,500
Add: Additional markups		12,000
Markdown cancellations		7,000
Less: Markup cancellations		(3,000)
Markdowns		(16,000)
Goods purchased this period	$127,110	$194,500

Cost-price ratio = $127,110/$194,500 = 65%

METHOD 4: FIFO. The cost-price ratio is computed in the same manner as Method 3. Unlike Method 3, however, the ratio is applied to the entire ending inventory at retail to convert to cost.

Applying the cost-price ratios obtained from each method, the possible ending inventory costs of the Hariff Company are:

	Method: 1	2	4
Ending inventory at retail	$53,000	$53,000	$53,000
Cost-price ratio	62%	64%	65%
Ending inventory at cost	$32,860	$33,920	$34,450

Ending inventory at cost under Method 3:[1]

Beginning inventory	$28,200
New layer ($53,000 − $47,000): $6,000 × 65% =	3,900
Ending inventory at cost	$32,100

[1]Under Method 3 (LIFO), if the ending inventory is smaller than the beginning inventory, no new layer has been added but instead an old layer has been reduced. To find the ending inventory cost under this situation, assume ending inventory at retail is $42,000. The *cost* of ending inventory, then, should represent a fraction of the beginning inventory cost:

$$28{,}200 \times \frac{\$42{,}000}{\$47{,}000} = \$25{,}200$$

LOWER OF COST OR MARKET

When goods on hand no longer have the value evidenced by their original cost due to obsolescence or other factors, the loss in value should be reflected in the accounting period in which the loss becomes apparent. In these circumstances a departure from the cost rule is required by accounting convention.

An appropriate measure of value is the market price or current replacement cost of an item in inventory. When the market price or replacement cost of an item is lower than its original cost, indicating a decrease in anticipated sales revenue, the market price or replacement cost is used in valuing the inventory instead of original cost, subject to the following rules (Exhibit 12-8):

EXHIBIT 12-8 LOWER OF COST OR MARKET RULES

	COST	MARKET				
Case	**Original Cost**	**Replacement Cost**	**Floor (Estimated Sales Price Less Selling Expenses and Normal Profit)**	**Ceiling (Estimated Sales Price Less Selling Expenses)**	**Relevant Market Cost (Limited by Floor and Ceiling Values)**	**Lower of Cost of Market**
A	$.65	$ .70	$.55	$.80	$.70	$.65
B	.65	.60	.55	.80	.60	.60
C	.65	.50	.55	.80	.55	.55
D	.50	.45	.55	.80	.55	.50
E	.75	.85	.55	.80	.80	.75
F	.90	1.00	.55	.80	.80	.80

A: Market is not limited by floor or ceiling; cost is less than market.
B: Market is not limited by floor or ceiling; market is less than cost.
C: Market is limited to floor; market is less than cost.
D: Market is limited to floor; cost is less than market.
E: Market is limited to ceiling; cost is less than market.
F: Market is limited to ceiling; market is less than cost.

SOURCE: Simons & Karrenbrock, *Intermediate Accounting,* 4th ed. (Cincinnati: South-Western Publishing Company, 1964), p. 64. Copyright 1964 by South-Western Publishing Company. Used with permission.

You will notice in Exhibit 12-8 that the lower of cost or market rule is only applied within a range (between the floor and ceiling). There is only one cost price in each instance, but three possible market prices. We can illustrate the application of the lower of cost or market rule for each case A through F as follows:

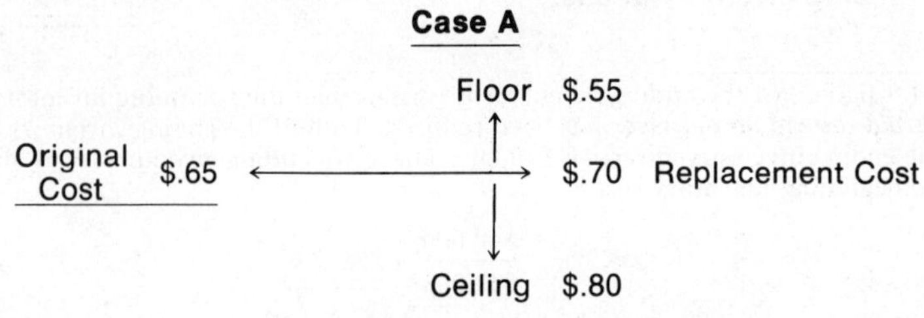

As the replacement cost of A falls within the range of floor to ceiling, it is the relevant market cost. The original cost of $.65 is selected because it is lower than the $.70 replacement cost.

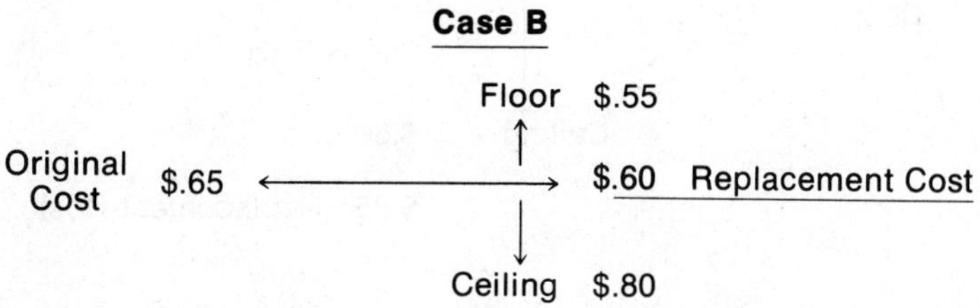

Again, replacement cost is within the floor-to-ceiling range. It is selected because it is lower than original cost.

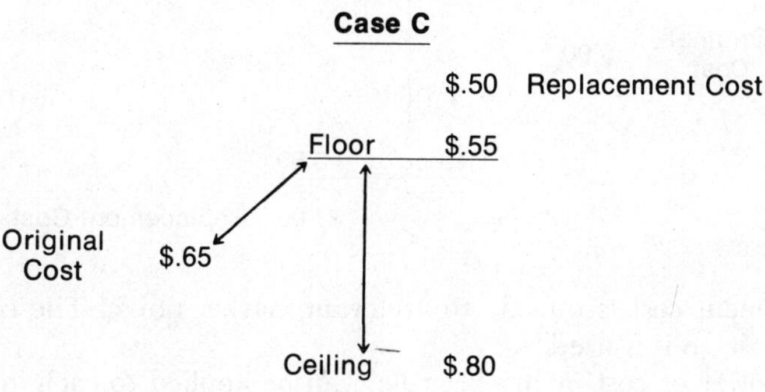

Replacement cost is below the floor in case C, hence the comparison is between original cost and floor. Floor is lower than original cost, so it is used.

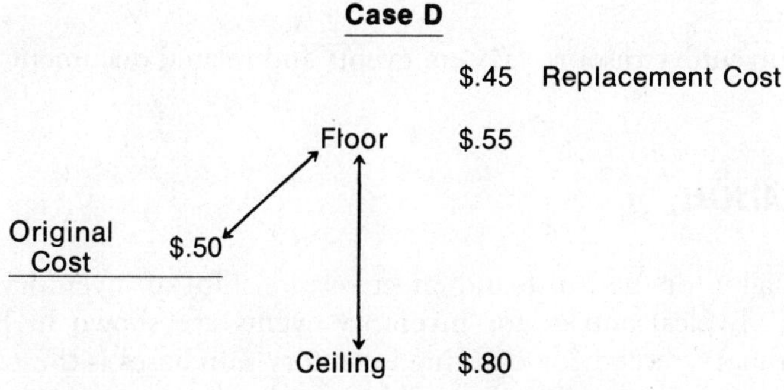

Replacement cost is below the floor, so the floor is compared with original cost. The latter is the lower figure, so it is used.

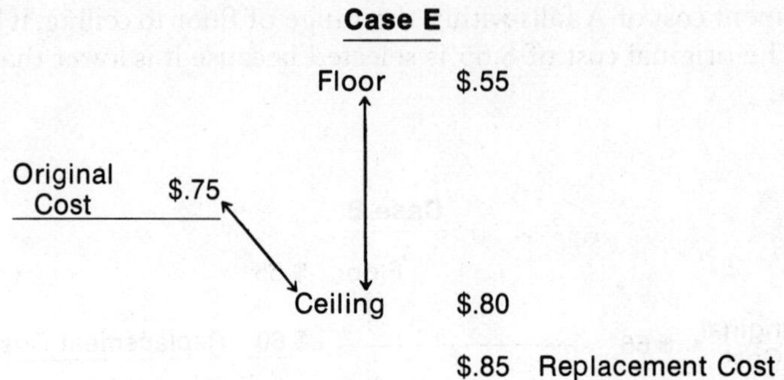

In Case E, replacement cost is outside the floor-to-ceiling range, so the comparison is between original cost and ceiling. Original cost is used because it is the lower figure.

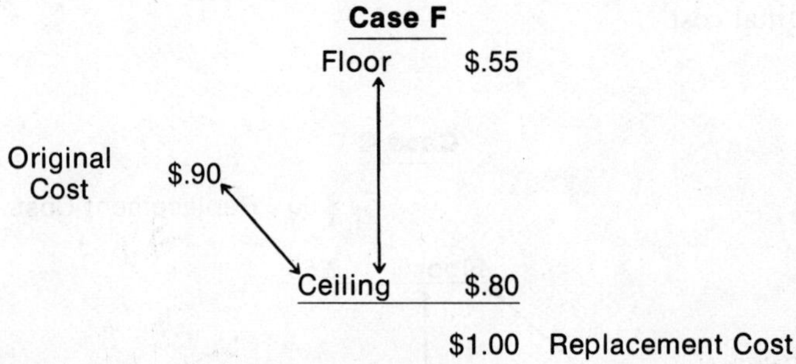

Again, replacement cost is outside the relevant market range. The ceiling is lower than original cost, so it is used.

The "lower of cost or market rule" can be applied to each item (or class of items) individually or to inventory as a whole.

12.6 PROCESSING INVENTORY TRANSACTIONS

INPUTS

The principal inventory resource system events and related documents are shown in Exhibit 12-9.

TRANSFORMATION$_1$

Establishing duality (or the cause-and-effect relationship) of inventory events is the function of T_1. Typical entries for inventory events are shown in Exhibit 12-10.

The primary record for entering inventory purchases is the *purchase journal* (or voucher register) discussed earlier. This journal records goods and services that are purchased on a *credit basis.* Most purchases in manufacturing and mercantile firms are for inventory items such as raw materials (manufacturing) or finished goods (mercantile).

EXHIBIT 12-9 MAJOR INVENTORY INPUTS AND DOCUMENTS

EVENT	TRANSACTION DOCUMENT	LIFO	Weighted Average	FIFO
A. Inventory is received.	1. *Invoice*—purchase of goods on credit.	at invoice cost	same	same
	2. *Check*—purchase of goods on C.O.D. basis.	same	same	same
B. Inventory is relocated.	3. *Requisition*—Raw materials are issued from stores to work-in-process.	at cost of latest purchase	at average cost to point of issue	in order of receipt
	4. *Adjustment*—Production labor and production overhead are added to raw materials in process.	at allocated cost	same	same
C. Inventory is sold or used.	5. *Invoice*—sale of goods.	at cost of latest complete unit	at weighted average cost	in order of production
	6. *Adjustment*—adjust book inventory to lower amount disclosed by physical count.			

EXHIBIT 12-10 THE DUALITY OF SOME TYPICAL INVENTORY EVENTS

Event	Transaction Document	Date	Notation	Codes			Accounts	Amount	
				Doc.	Trans.	Acct.		Debit	Credit
A. Inventory is received.	Invoice		a. Purchase of raw materials.		10	11610	Raw materials inventory	2,000	
					10	21110	Accounts payable		2,000
B. Inventory is relocated.	Requisition		b. Raw materials are issued from inventory to work-in-process.		10	11630	Work-in-process inv.	500	
					12	11610	Raw materials inv.		500
	Adjustment		c. Production labor and overhead are added to raw materials in process.		10	11630	Work-in-process inv.	1,700	
					12	41520	Direct labor		750
					12	50000	Manufacturing overhead		950
	Adjustment		d. Units in process are completed and transferred to finished goods inventory.		10	11650	Finished goods inventory	5,000	
					12	11630	Work-in-process inventory		5,000
C. Inventory is sold or used.	Invoice		e. Finished goods are sold on open account and the perpetual inventory is reduced.		10	11210	Accounts receivable	250	
					10	41110	Sales		250
					10	41300	Cost of goods sold	150	
					12	11650	Finished goods inventory		150
	Adjustment		f. Perpetual inventory records are decreased to conform to actual physical count.		10	41300	Cost of goods sold	2,000	
					12	11650	Finished goods inventory		2,000

The primary record for tracing the *movement* of inventories within a firm, such as the issue of raw materials from stock to work-in-process, is the *general journal.* This journal records events that are not entered into other journals. An increase in the cost of goods sold and the reduction in inventory accompanying a sale is recorded as an adjustment or *journal entry* in the general journal.

TRANSFORMATION$_2$

The T_2 process consists of recording the T_1 events in the ledger accounts in accordance with the rules of duality. Using the T-account format, the events in Exhibit 12-10 are posted as shown in Exhibit 12-11.

EXHIBIT 12-11 POSTING INVENTORY EVENTS TO T-ACCOUNTS

11210 Accounts Receivable

(e)	$ 250		

11610 Inventory—Raw Materials

Bal.*	$30,000	(b)	$ 500
(a)	2,000		

11650 Inventory—Finished Goods

Bal.	$50,000	(e)	$ 150
(d)	5,000	(f)	2,000

11630 Work in Process

Bal.	$ 8,000	(d)	$5,000
(b)	500		
(c)	1,700		

21110 Accounts Payable

		Bal.	$10,000
		(a)	2,000

41110 Sales

		Bal.	$75,000
		(e)	250

41300 Cost of Goods Sold

Bal.	$40,000		
(e)	150		
(f)	2,000		

41520 Direct Labor

Bal.	$15,000	(c)	$ 750

50000 Manufacturing Overhead

Bal.	$25,000	(c)	$ 950

* Balance prior to present entries.

In addition to posting inventory events to the ledger accounts, another posting is necessary for those companies that maintain a *perpetual inventory system.* This system (discussed later) requires that individual inventory events be posted to *subsidiary* inventory records in which detailed records of receipts and issues of each (major) inventory item or class of items are maintained.

OUTPUT

The accounting information system generates output consisting of data and reports concerning the status of inventory. These outputs are intended for two broad user groups: external and internal.

External Reporting

External users of financial statements are provided with information showing the status of inventories at the beginning and end of the period covered by the report. In addition to showing the value of inventory, the basis for valuing inventory must also be disclosed; for example, whether the firm is using average cost; first-in, first-out; last-in, first-out; or other inventory pricing methods.

Proper disclosure calls for such additional information as:

1. *Pledged inventories:* Disclosure should be made of inventory that is pledged to secure debt.
2. *Changes in pricing methods:* Changes in the method of valuing inventories (FIFO to LIFO, for example) should be disclosed as well as the effect of the change on the reported net income of the period.
3. *Break-down of inventory:* Manufacturing firms should disclose the composition of inventory such as the value of raw materials, work-in-process, and finished goods.

An example of disclosure of inventory in financial statements is the following:

INVENTORY (Valued at the lower of cost or market, with cost determined by the first-in, first-out method)

Finished goods	$125,000
Work-in-process	250,000
Raw materials	95,000
Factory supplies and repair parts	20,000
TOTAL INVENTORY	$490,000

Internal Reporting

For internal management purposes this general information is insufficient for planning and control. A basic report for internal use is the *stock status report.* This report provides a detailed analysis of the status of inventory, including the current status, the status last year, and the current rate of activity. Feedback from the inventory resource system is used to prepare other internal reports, as discussed later in this chapter.

12.7 SYSTEMS CONTROLS FOR INVENTORY TRANSACTIONS

Inventory, in most businesses, is a major asset. Therefore, controls over this resource are particularly crucial. As with other resources, controls in this area are of two types: stewardship and management.

STEWARDSHIP CONTROLS

Stewardship controls are designed in general to safeguard assets, that is, to prevent theft and fraud. In addition, stewardship controls insure the proper recording of inventory transactions.

Stewardship controls can be subdivided into (1) *custody* or *physical controls* and (2) *systems* or *records control.*

1. *Custody controls:* The essence of custody control or the physical control of assets lies in the segregation of duties. Allocation of responsibility for different stages in the flow of resources is the key to safeguarding assets. With respect to inventories, the following functions should be separated.
   a. *Receiving:* Goods received should be inspected for quantity and quality and forwarded to stores or warehouse.
   b. *Stores:* Goods received by stores should be vouched for independently of feedback on the receiving department. Additional control is provided by stores in that goods are only issued upon properly authorized requisitions, and the accounting department is notified directly by stores of quantities issued.
   c. *Work-in-process:* Unfinished goods are controlled by individuals in charge of production, usually foremen or superintendents. These individuals are responsible for the prompt reporting of defective units and scrap.
   d. *Shipping:* The shipping department provides control by requiring properly authorized shipping instructions.
2. *Systems control:* While a segregation of duties usually insures proper physical control, accounting for the physical movement of goods is the function of *systems control.* There are two basic controls of a systems nature: (a) the cost accounting system, and (b) the perpetual inventory system. Cost accounting systems will be discussed in later chapters of this text.

A firm may record sales and not reflect the issue of goods from inventory until a physical count is taken at the end of an accounting period. The amount of goods on hand is subtracted from goods available for sale during the period and the result is "cost of goods sold." This approach is referred to as a *periodic inventory* system.

Under a *perpetual inventory* system, the receipt and issue of each item of inventory is recorded on subsidiary records called *stock ledger cards.* These records are posted as part of the T_2 process in the same manner as other subsidiary ledger records (accounts receivable and accounts payable). Receipt of goods, recorded in the purchase journal, is posted to individual stock ledger cards. Decreases are usually recorded by posting *adjustments* (journal vouchers or entries), which are generated by the movements of inventory from one department to another (for example, raw materials from stores to work-in-process).

The balances on each of the stock ledgers should agree with the actual goods on hand. However, due to inevitable recording errors (or omissions such as scrap and defective units), it is rare that a physical count will agree with the *book* balances of the perpetual system.

MANAGEMENT CONTROLS

While stewardship controls safeguard inventories, management controls have as their objective the maintenance of optimum levels of inventory. The maintenance of optimum levels involves two basic issues: (1) determining the optimum quantity to be ordered or manufactured, and (2) determining the optimum time for placing the order. Inadequate attention to these two inventory decisions may result in carrying either excess or insufficient inventory, to which a cost is attached:

COSTS OF CARRYING EXCESS INVENTORIES:[2]

Property taxes.
Storage and handling.
Insurance.
Opportunity interest cost on capital tied up in excess inventory.
Risk of spoilage, theft, or obsolescence.
Administrative costs, e.g., paper work, physical inventory costs.

COSTS OF CARRYING INSUFFICIENT INVENTORIES:

Lost sales.
Additional administrative costs of rush orders.
Increased labor costs due to overtime work on rush orders, layoffs due to reduction in sales volume, and so forth.
Loss of goodwill.

Management also considers costs affected by the quantity ordered at one time. Certain costs increase with an increase in the size of an order, while other costs decrease with an increase in the quantity ordered.

COSTS THAT INCREASE WITH INCREASES IN THE QUANTITY ORDERED:

Cost of capital associated with incremental quantities.
Incremental storage and handling costs.
Increased insurance.
Additional risks of spoilage, theft, or obsolescence.

COSTS THAT DECREASE WITH INCREASES IN THE QUANTITY ORDERED:

Transportation charges per unit.
Trade and cash discounts.
Reduction in administrative costs (less paper work).

[2] As noted in chapter 7, the annual costs of carrying inventory have been estimated to equal 20% to 30% of the initial cost of acquiring the inventory. Excess inventory carried for a period of from three to five years would therefore have been paid for twice.

The optimum quantity is often referred to as the *economic order quantity* (EOQ). A convenient method for determining EOQ is the *average unit cost method* illustrated in Exhibit 12-12.

EXHIBIT 12-12 CALCULATING ECONOMIC ORDER QUANTITY

Order Size	Invoice Cost (Per Unit)		Costs that Decrease with Increased Quantity (Per Unit)		Costs that Increase with Increased Quantity (Per Unit)		Total Unit Cost
100	$10.00	+	$.50	+	$ .50	=	$11.00
200	9.50		.40		.60		10.50
500	9.00		.30		1.10		10.40
800	8.50		.20		1.80		10.50
1,000	8.00		.10		2.60		10.70

Economic Lot Size Based on an Annual Demand of 1,000 Units

Order Lot Size	Total Average Cost (Per Unit)	Total Costs for Maximum Order
100	$11.00	$11,000.00
200	10.50	10,500.00
500	10.40	10,400.00
800	10.50	10,500.00
1,000	10.70	10,700.00

This data can be plotted on a graph as shown below:

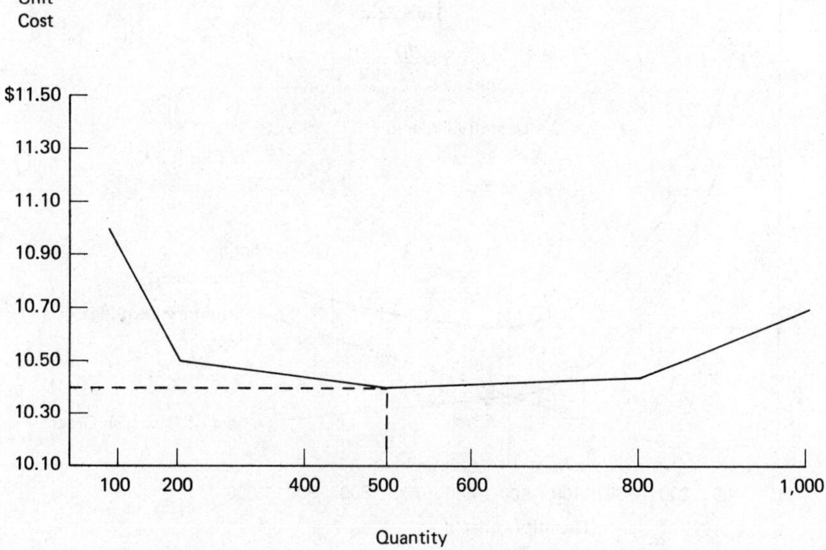

In general, if the annual demand for an item is a quantity, D (1000 items in the previous example), and the quantity ordered is Q (500 in the example), the firm will have to place $\frac{D}{Q}$ orders per year. If the cost (administrative, clerical, etc.) of placing an order is C, then $\frac{CD}{Q}$ is the annual cost of ordering a sufficient quantity of the item.

The simplest case, which we are considering, leads to an average inventory of $\frac{Q}{2}$. By letting the annual cost of carrying one unit in inventory be i (say, \$.10), the inventory carrying cost is $\frac{iQ}{2}$.

It follows that the costs which increase or decrease with the order size can be expressed by the formula:

$$T = \frac{CD}{Q} + \frac{iQ}{2} \qquad (1)$$

where

T = total cost (in dollars)
D = annual demand (in units)
i = cost of carrying one item in inventory for one year (in dollars)
Q = size of order (in units)
C = cost of placing an order

These relationships are illustrated in Exhibit 12-13.

EXHIBIT 12-13 INVENTORY COST RELATIONSHIPS

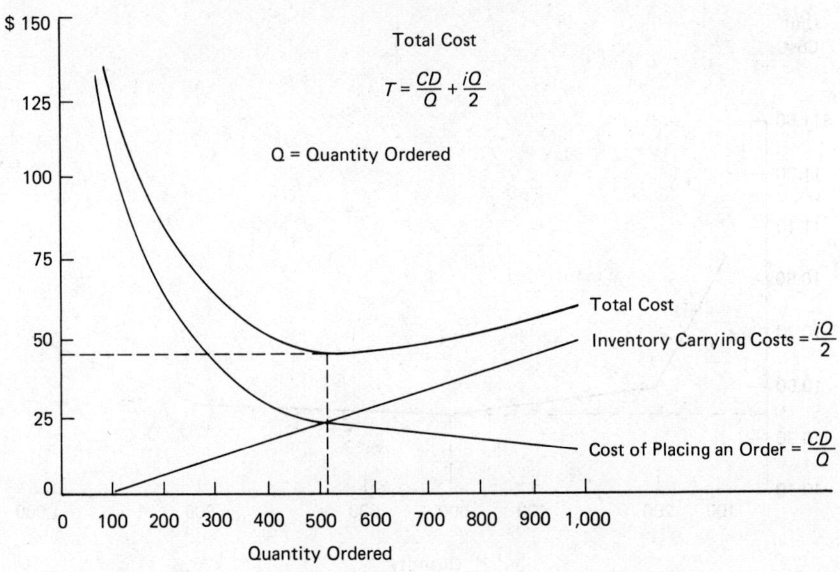

The objective of inventory management is to minimize T. Mathematically this can be done by differentiating T with respect to Q in equation (1) and setting the result equal to zero:

$$\frac{dT}{dQ} = \frac{CD}{Q^2} + \frac{i}{2} = 0 \tag{2}$$

And solving this equation for Q:

$$Q = \sqrt{\frac{2CD}{i}} \tag{3}$$

This last equation is known as the economic order quantity (EOQ) formula. For any demand D, ordering cost C, and carrying cost i, it provides the optimal order quantity Q.

To illustrate the use of the basic EOQ formula suppose:

Demand = 1,000 units for the year
Cost of placing and order = \$12.50
Cost of carrying one item in inventory for one year = \$.10

The economic order quantity would be:

$$\begin{aligned} Q &= \sqrt{\frac{2 \times 12.5 \times 1{,}000}{.10}} \\ &= \sqrt{\frac{25{,}000}{.10}} \\ &= \sqrt{250{,}000} \\ &= \underline{\underline{500 \text{ units}}} \end{aligned}$$

In setting up the previous model for inventory management, a number of assumptions were made:

1. Demand is known for certain in advance and is constant throughout the year.
2. Inventory stock is reduced to zero balance before it is replenished—there is no *safety stock.*
3. Replenishment is instantaneous—there is no *lead time.*
4. Inventory is used at a constant rate in each cycle.
5. Cost C is determined independently of the quantity Q ordered.
6. Cost i is determined independently of the quantity Q ordered.

Exhibit 12-14 shows the inventory behavior assumed in this basic model. Because of the certainty surrounding the basic EOQ model, it is known as a *deterministic model.*

The basic EOQ model can only be used as a starting point for inventory control. Most real-world situations are more complex and less certain than this model depicts.

EXHIBIT 12-14 BASIC EOQ INVENTORY BEHAVIOR

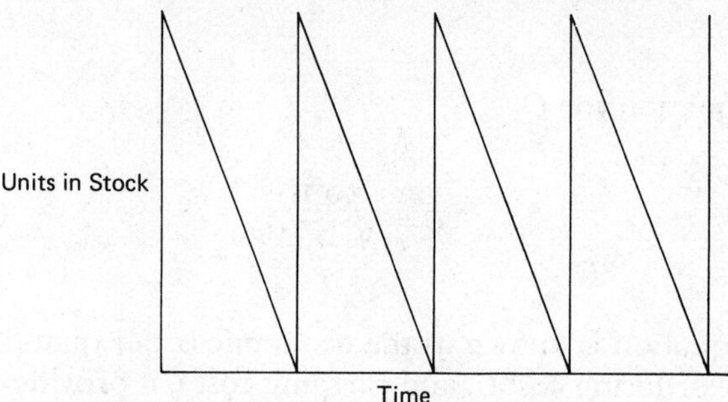

Let us extend the model slightly. Assume that the demand is not known with certainty, i.e., it is not deterministic; however, the demand *D* for last year is known and the factors that may cause a change in last year's *D* can be expressed as probabilities, as in Exhibit 12-15.

EXHIBIT 12-15 POISSON PROBABILITY DISTRIBUTION OF DEMAND (MEAN m = 10)

Demand *X*	Probability of Demand *X*	Probability of Demand For *X* or more
0	.0000	1.0000
1	.0004	1.0000
2	.0023	.9996
3	.0076	.9973
4	.0189	.9897
5	.0378	.9708
6	.0631	.9330
7	.0901	.8699
8	.1126	.7798
9	.1251	.6672
10	.1251	.5421
11	.1137	.4170
12	.0948	.3033
13	.0729	.2085
14	.0521	.1356
15	.0347	.0835
16	.0217	.0488
17	.0128	.0271
18	.0071	.0143
19	.0037	.0072
20	.0019	.0035
21	.0009	.0016
22	.0004	.0007
23	.0002	.0003
24	.0001	.0001
25	.0000	.0000

Consider that demand has a *Poisson* distribution with mean *m*. The probability *p* of having a demand of *X* units is given by the formula:

$$p(X) = \frac{m^X}{X!}\,e^{-m} \qquad X = 0, 1, 2, \ldots \tag{4}$$

The symbol $X!$ means "x factorial," which is $1 \cdot 2 \cdot 3 \cdot \ldots \cdot X$. For instance, $3! = 1 \cdot 2 \cdot 3 = 6$. Values of X can only be non-negative numbers, as the arithmetic progression $X = 0, 1, 2, \ldots$ suggests. The symbol e represents a number that frequently arises in natural phenomena and is approximately equal to 2.71828.[3]

We have now adjusted basic EOQ for probabilistic demand. Let us relax some other assumptions.

For example, after an order is placed a period of time elapses before the items are delivered. During this period, known as the *lead time,* inventory is still being consumed. Therefore an order must be placed early enough so that replenishment is made before the firm "runs out" of stock.

A *probabilistic model* must incorporate various levels of demand, the concept of lead time, provision for safety stock, and other factors. It solves for the optimum size order Q as well as reorder point r. Like all attempts to formalize complex behavior, the probabilistic model is also based on assumptions. But its assumptions are more realistic:

1. A range of probable demands is known.
2. The cost b of not being able to respond to an order immediately (that is, of having to back order) does not depend on time.
3. The lead time t is constant.
4. There are no quantity discounts.
5. Cost C is independent of both Q and r.
6. Cost i is independent of both Q and r.

Inventory now behaves as shown in Exhibit 12-16.

EXHIBIT 12-16 PROBABILISTIC INVENTORY BEHAVIOR

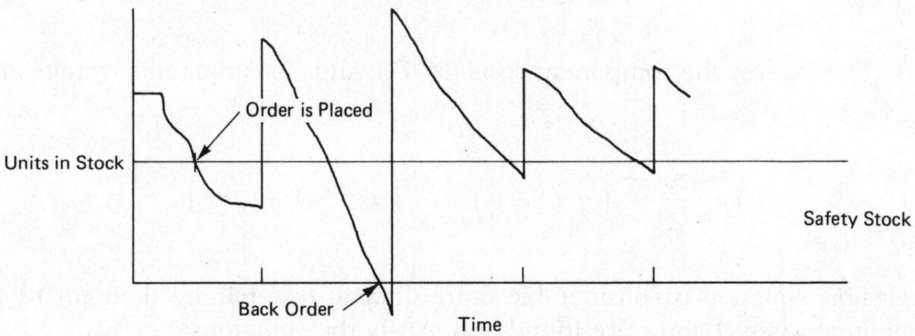

The average annual cost of placing orders is again

$$\frac{CD}{Q} \tag{5}$$

[3]The symbol e, in fact, forms the base for natural logarithms, $(1 + 1/h)^h \cong 2.71828$.

The quantity of stock expected to be in inventory when an order arrives is called *safety stock.* It is theoretically equal to the reorder point quantity (r) less the quantity demanded during the lead time (X). With a Poisson demand distribution, safety stock is:

$$S = \sum_{X=0}^{\infty} (r - X)\, p(X) = r \sum_{0}^{\infty} \frac{m^X}{X!} e^{-m} - \sum_{0}^{\infty} X \frac{m^X}{X!} e^{-m} = r - m \tag{6}$$

The average inventory level throughout a year is $\frac{Q}{2} + S = \frac{Q}{2} + r - m$; so the average annual inventory carrying cost is

$$i\left(\frac{Q}{2} + r - m\right) \tag{7}$$

The average number of back orders per year is the expected number of back orders per inventory cycle times the average number of cycles per year (D/Q). There are back orders only when the demand X during the lead time is greater than the reorder point r. The expected number of back orders per cycle is:

$$\sum_{X=r}^{\infty} (X - r)p(X) = mP(r-1) - rP(r) \tag{8}$$

where m is the mean of the Poisson distribution (as before) and $P(r)$ is the probability of demand for a quantity r or more.

Given the cost b of a single back order, the average annual cost of back orders is:

$$\frac{bD}{Q}\,[mP(r-1) - rP(r)] \tag{9}$$

The sum of the component costs (5), (7), and (9) is the total average annual cost:

$$T = \frac{CD}{Q} + i\left(\frac{Q}{2} + r - m\right) + \frac{bD}{Q}[mP(r-1) - rP(r)] \tag{10}$$

This equation is considerably more difficult to minimize than equation (1). T is minimal when Q and r are found that satisfy the equations:

$$Q = \sqrt{\frac{2D\{C + b[mP(r-1) - rP(r)]\}}{i}} \tag{11}$$

$$P(r) = \frac{Qi}{bD} \tag{12}$$

Fortunately, electronic computers enable iterative numerical methods to be used for finding Q and r. A computer-controlled inventory system involving a number of items is now possible, as depicted in Exhibit 12-17.

EXHIBIT 12-17

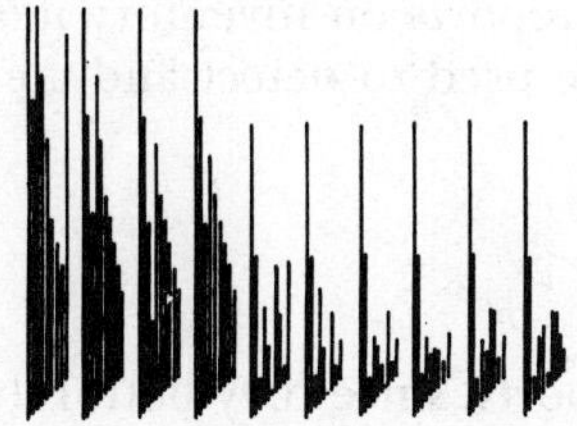

Variable		Range		Min Z	Max Z
X	2	200,000	650,000	400,000	200,000
Y	3	200,000	650,000	450,000	200,000
Z	74			196,700	458,780

Enter Display Option and Display Variables

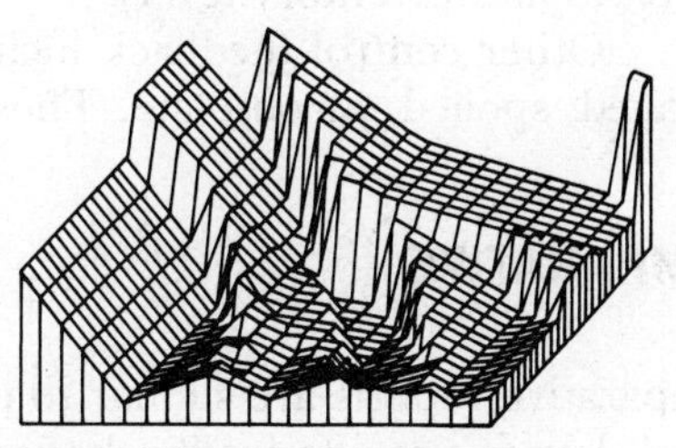

Variable		Range		Min Z	Max Z
X	3	200,000	660,000	480,000	280,000
Y	2	660,000	200,000	400,000	200,000
Z	24			189,500	475,400

Enter Display Option and Display Variables

SOURCE: Curtis H. Jones, "At Last: Real Computer Power for Decision Makers," *Harvard Business Review,* September–October 1970, pp. 75–89. Used with permission of the publisher and the author.

12.8 SYSTEMS FEEDBACK FOR INVENTORY TRANSACTIONS

Feedback on the inventory resource system furnishes users with (1) exception, (2) control, and (3) comparative reports.

EXCEPTION

Exception reports outline significant departures from plan which elicit special attention. When economic order quantities and reorder points have been determined for items in inventory, reorder details are entered into the information system. In an automated information system, this information is an integral part of the inventory system; while in a manual system, the reorder points and EOQs are recorded on perpetual inventory cards or are noted on cards placed in the various storage bins. When the level of goods on hand is reduced to the reorder point, a *buyer signal report* or *record of out of stock conditions* calls the attention of the purchasing department to the need to reorder. When inventory levels approach the reorder point, some systems provide for the automatic generation of a *purchase order,* which is forwarded to the vendor unless a "stop-order" intervenes.

CONTROL

Control reports with comparative prior period data are useful in determining whether current levels of inventory are over or under the levels necessary for effective operations. One type of report which is useful for control purposes is an *order analysis.* This report shows the current status and expected future requirements for each item in the inventory. It provides a complete analysis of items on hand and on order, as well as comparisons with stock levels for comparable prior periods. In addition the report shows projected stock positions for the next six months and provides control over purchases and inventory levels.

Other control feedback includes period reports on inventory items that are damaged, spoiled, or obsolete. These reports are used to detect and control waste.

COMPARATIVE

Comparative reports are similar to exception reports, since they both rely upon two sets of data to provide feedback. Feedback on the effectiveness of purchasing can be obtained by comparing actual prices with budget prices. These budget variances are designed into standard cost systems, which are discussed later.

Another comparative report shows returns of materials to suppliers for various inventory items. This may indicate either the purchase of inferior goods or the use of uneconomic lot sizes.

Another type of comparative feedback is provided by the computation of selected ratios, as discussed in chapter 7.

12.9 SUMMARY

Inventory represents a major resource for most industrial and mercantile firms. Inventory is comprised essentially of work-in-process or finished goods intended for sale in the ordinary course of business. The purpose of maintaining inventory is to provide a buffer between sales and production, to be used for advertising and display purposes, or as a hedge against future price increases.

Where inventory consists of a small number of large-value items, the cost of an item is *specifically* matched with its selling price. Where there is a large number of small-value items, inventory is generally maintained at retail value to avoid the maintenance of cost and selling price records. Cost of goods sold is computed by the use of an average markdown from selling price. Intermediate quantity-value inventories are priced on an "assumed cost basis" such as FIFO, weighted average, or LIFO. As these pricing methods yield different gross profit figures in relation to price changes, their use requires an understanding of the price-level issue.

Stewardship controls in inventory management involve (1) the application of consistent pricing methods, (2) maintaining inventory values at lower of cost or market in all instances other than LIFO, (3) adequate control and separation of duties with respect to the handling and custody of inventory, (4) a physical count of inventory balances at least once a year as witnessed by the firm's certified public accountants, and (5) the elimination of nonsalable items from inventory value.

Management controls have to do with the central issue of optimizing inventory balance and the quantity ordered. It seeks to avoid the problems of (1) holding too much or too little inventory, and (2) ordering in quantities that are too large or too small.

Feedback, as in other systems, involves exception, control, comparative, and interpretive reports.

CHAPTER 12 REFERENCES AND ADDITIONAL READINGS

INVENTORY VALUATION

Ageloff, Roy; Corcoran, A. Wayne; and Simpson, Richard H. "Dollar-Value LIFO Retail Inventory Pricing." *Management Services,* September–October 1969, pp. 46–51.

Bierman, Harold. "Inventory Valuation: The Use of Market Prices." *The Accounting Review,* October 1967, pp. 731–37.

Blair, Arthur H. "Switch to LIFO?" *The Journal of Accountancy,* December 1969, pp. 72–73.

Blakely, Edward J., and Thompson, Howard E. "Technological Change and Its Effect on Dollar-Value LIFO." *Management Accounting,* August 1969, pp. 33–38.

Brown, Robert O. "Inventory at Net Realizable Values?" *Management Accounting,* January 1968, pp. 43–44.

Cadenhead, Gary M. "Net Realizable Value Redefined." *Journal of Accounting Research,* Spring 1970, pp. 138–40.

Chasteen, Lanny G. "An Empirical Study of Differences in Economic Circumstances as a Justification for Alternative Inventory Pricing Methods." *The Accounting Review,* July 1971, pp. 504–8.

Fremgren, James M. "LIFO Inventory: What It Does and How to Use It for Greatest Tax Benefits." *Taxation for Accountants,* May–June 1970, pp. 120–26.

Gambling, Trevor E. "LIFO vs. FIFO Under Conditions of 'Certainty.'" *The Accounting Review,* April 1968, pp. 387–89.

Hirsch, A. Jay. "Dollar-Value and Retail LIFO: A Diagrammatic Approach." *The Accounting Review,* October 1969, pp. 840–42.

Most, Kenneth S. "The Value of Inventories." *Journal of Accounting Research,* Spring 1967, pp. 39–50.

Restall, Lawrence J., and Czajkowski, Peter. "Computation of LIFO Index: A Statistical Sampling Approach." *Management Accounting,* September 1969, pp. 43–48.

Staubus, George J. "Testing Inventory Accounting." *The Accounting Review,* July 1968, pp. 413–24.

Strohl, Raymond A. "Disclosing Inventory Holding Gains and Losses in Financial Statements." *National Public Accountant,* July 1969, pp. 22–28.

Wright, F. K. "Dual Variables in Inventory Measurement." *The Accounting Review,* January 1970, pp. 129–33.

INVENTORY CONTROL

Brown, Robert G. "Information, Decision Rules and Policy for Inventory Management." *Production and Inventory Management,* Third Quarter 1969, pp. 1–16.

Brown, Robert G. *Decision Rules for Inventory Management.* New York: Holt, Rinehart & Winston, Inc., 1967.

Buchan, Joseph, and Koenigsberg, Ernest. *Scientific Inventory Management.* Englewood Cliffs, N.J.: Prentice-Hall, Inc., 1963.

Bunch, Robert G. "The Effect of Payment Terms on Economic Order Quantity Determination." *Management Accounting,* January 1967, pp. 53–62.

Fabrycky, W. J., and Banks, Jerry. *Procurement and Inventory Systems: Theory and Analysis.* New York: Reinhold Publishing Corporation, 1967.

Hanssman, Fred. *Operations Research in Production and Inventory Control.* New York: John Wiley & Sons, Inc., 1962.

Hoffmann, Thomas R. "EOQ's for Aggregate Inventory Management." *Production and Inventory Management,* Third Quarter 1969, pp. 71–77.

Hottman, Raymond A. *Inventories: A Guide to Their Control, Costing and Effect Upon Income and Taxes.* New York: The Ronald Press Company, 1962.

Kahn, Robert. "A Checklist of Inventory Shortage Causes." *Retail Control,* March 1968, pp. 51–55.

Kaimann, Richard A. "EOQ vs. Dynamic Programming—Which One to Use for Inventory Ordering?" *Production and Inventory Management,* Fourth Quarter 1969, pp. 66–74.

Magee, John F. "Guides to Inventory Policy, No. 1: Functions and Lot Size." *Harvard Business Review,* January–February 1956, pp. 49–60.

———. "Guides to Inventory Policy, No. 2: Problems of Uncertainty." *Harvard Business Review,* March–April 1956, pp. 103–116.

Manes, R. P.; Samuels, J. M.; and Smyth, D. J. "Inventories and Sales: A Cross Section Study." *Empirical Research In Accounting: Selected Studies, 1967,* supplement to the *Journal of Accounting Research,* pp. 139–63.

Parsons, James A. "Input/Output Analysis." *Systems and Procedures Journal,* November–December 1968, pp. 26–27.

Perna, George D. "Inventory Systems Simulation—A Case Study." *Management Accounting,* July 1968, pp. 50–54.

Powell, George E. "Design Your Own EOQ Nomograph." *Production and Inventory Management,* October 1967, pp. 49–55.

Quinn, John P. "Creating an Effective System of Retail Inventory Control." *Retail Control,* January 1972, pp. 20–30.

Rinehard, Jack R. "Economic Purchase Quantity Calculations." *Management Accounting,* September 1970, pp. 18–20.

Simone, Albert J. "Theoretical Refinement and Practical Implementation of a Traditional Inventory Model." *Production and Inventory Management,* July 1967, pp. 15–31.

Vallario, Anthony A. "An Inventory Control System with Profitable By-Products." *Management Services,* January–February 1967, pp. 31–36.

Welch, W. Evert. "How to Prepare Practical EOQ Tables." *Production and Inventory Management,* Fourth Quarter 1969, pp. 1–6.

CHAPTER 12 QUESTIONS, PROBLEMS, AND CASES

12- 1. Merchandise firms have one inventory, while manufacturing firms have three inventories. Explain.

12- 2. Name three reasons for carrying inventory.

12- 3. Discuss the question of who holds title to inventory in each of the following circumstances:
   (a) Goods in transit
   (b) Segregated goods
   (c) Consignments
   (d) Conditional and installment sales

12- 4. What are the three basic classes of inventory pricing methods?

12- 5. What is a *holding gain?*

12- 6. Compare the cost-based inventory pricing methods—FIFO, weighted average, and LIFO—for each of the following characteristics:
   (a) *Inventory value*
      (1) in periods of rising prices
      (2) in periods of falling prices
   (b) *Balance sheet valuation as an indication of current value*
   (c) *Income statement effect*
      (1) in periods of rising prices
      (2) in periods of falling prices
   (d) *Represents actual flow of goods*
   (e) *Acceptable for income tax purposes*

12- 7. LIFO is an anti-cyclical device. Explain.

12- 8. "The cost of taking and pricing inventories at frequent intervals is prohibitive where numerous small-value items are involved." How is this problem solved in reference to interim financial statements and internal management reports?

12- 9. Define or explain the use of the following terms or phrases:
(a) Lower of cost or market
(b) Original cost
(c) Replacement cost
(d) Floor
(e) Ceiling
(f) Relevant market cost

12-10. Identify the components or sequential steps of the inventory resource cycle:

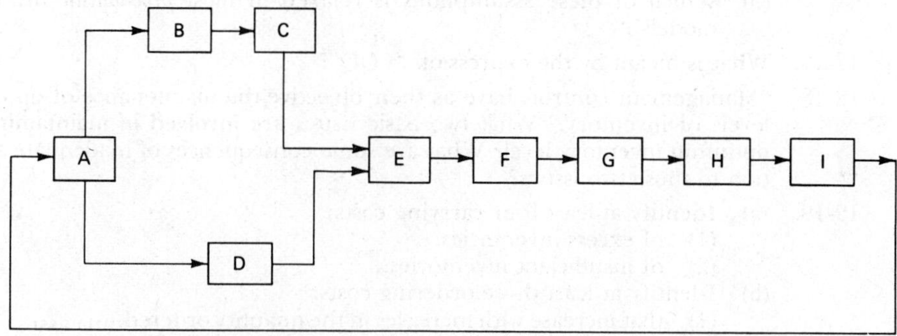

12-11. Define or explain the use of the following terms or phrases:
(a) f.o.b. destination
(b) f.o.b. shipping point
(c) Inventory holding gain
(d) Pledged inventory
(e) Stock status report
(f) Stock ledger card
(g) Economic lot size
(h) Lead time
(i) Safety stock
(j) Buyer signal report
(k) Order analysis

12-12. For external reporting, what information should be disclosed in addition to merely showing the value of total inventory?

12-13. What are inventory stewardship controls designed to accomplish? What are the two categories of stewardship controls? Distinguish between the two categories by identifying the functions of each and by giving some specific control examples under each category.

12-14. Distinguish between a *periodic inventory system* and a *perpetual inventory system.*

12-15. Inventory pricing is independent of the actual flow of goods. Explain.

12-16. (a) Indicate six assumptions which are implied by the following *deterministic* inventory model:

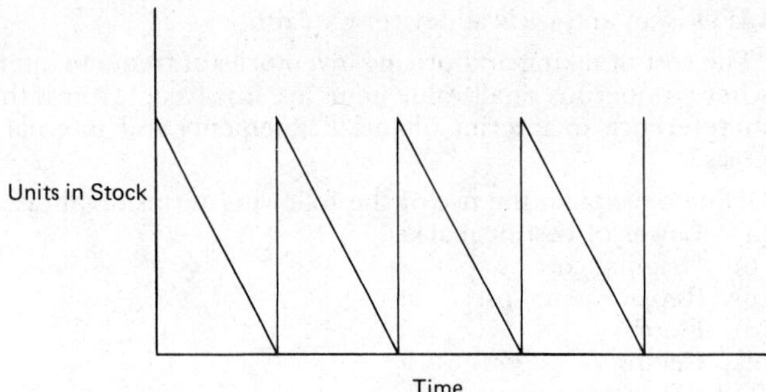

(b) Which of these assumptions is relaxed in most *probabilistic* inventory models?

12-17. What is meant by the expression "EOQ"?

12-18. "Management controls have as their objective the maintenance of optimum levels of inventory." What two basic issues are involved in maintaining an optimum inventory level? What are some consequences of inadequate attention to those two issues?

12-19. (a) Identify at least four carrying costs:
(1) of excess inventories.
(2) of insufficient inventories.
(b) Identify at least three ordering costs:
(1) that increase with increases in the quantity ordered.
(2) that decrease with increases in the quantity ordered.

12-20. Distinguish between *segregated* and *consigned* inventory.

12-21. Distinguish between the basic features of a *deterministic* and a *probabilistic* inventory model.

12-22. (a) Express the average annual inventory carrying cost as a formula assuming a probabilistic inventory model.
(b) Express the average annual cost of back orders as a formula assuming a probabilistic inventory model.

12-23. Define each of the following variables used in the probabilistic inventory model: X; m; D; $p(X)$; $X!$; C; Q; r.

12-24. Discuss the functions of an inventory system comparative report.

12-25. When reorder details are entered into a manual inventory system, explain how feedback exception reports are used.

12-26. ***INVENTORY PRICING*** A company valued the twelve items of product X in its December 31, 19*x*1 inventory at a total of $70 on the basis of the following:

Jan. 1	Balance	10 items at $5
April 25	Purchased	15 items at $6
Nov. 3	Purchased	5 items at $7

The market value (replacement cost) of one unit of product X was $7 on Dec. 31. What inventory pricing method was used by the company for this product?

12-27. ***ECONOMIC ORDER QUANTITY RELATIONSHIPS—PROBABILISTIC MODEL*** Suppose the following data is available:
(a) Demand data in Exhibit 12-15.
(b) Cost of a single back order is $18.

(c) Cost of placing an order is $10.
(d) Reorder point quantity is 14.
(e) Annual carrying costs of one unit is $.08.
(f) Annual demand is 450.

Required:

(1) Compute the economic order quantity.
(2) Compute the average annual costs of back orders.
(3) Compute the average annual inventory carrying cost.

12-28. ***INVENTORY RATIO ANALYSIS***

(a) If the projected sales for November are 261,300 units and the number of days supply in inventory is six days, what is the balance of inventory on November 1?
(b) If the number of days' supply in inventory is sixteen days and the balance of inventory on July 1 is 47,840 units, what are the projected sales in units for July?
(c) Suppose the beginning inventory is $40,000 and the ending inventory is $26,800. What is the inventory turnover if the cost of sales for the year is $684,700?
(d) Suppose the inventory turnover is sixteen times a year with sales of 1,120,000 units. What is the ending inventory in units if the beginning inventory is 83,000 units?

12-29. ***ECONOMIC ORDER QUANTITY RELATIONSHIPS—DETERMINISTIC MODEL***

(a) If the carrying cost is $.24 and the cost of placing an order is $20, what is the annual demand if the economic order quantity is 320 units?
(b) If the carrying cost is $.24 and the cost of placing an order is $10, what is the economic order quantity if the annual demand is 12,000 units?
(c) If the lead time is four days and the average demand per day is three units, what is the reorder point quantity if a safety stock of eight units is required?

12-30. ***LOWER OF COST OR MARKET*** The Paris Company manufactures and sells four products, the inventories of which are priced at cost or market, whichever is lower. A normal profit margin rate of 30% is usually maintained on each of the four products.

The following information was compiled as of December 31, 19*x*1:

Product	Original Cost	Cost to Replace	Estimated Cost to Dispose	"Normal" Selling Price*	Expected Selling Price
A	$35.00	$42.00	$15.00	$70.00	$ 80.00
B	47.50	45.00	20.50	95.00	95.00
C	17.50	15.00	5.00	35.00	30.00
D	45.00	46.00	26.00	90.00	100.00

*"Normal" selling price = original cost ÷ (100% − the normal 50% gross margin rate).

Required:

(a) Why are expected selling prices important in the application of the lower of cost or market rule?
(b) Prepare a schedule containing unit values (including "floor" and "ceiling") for determining the lower of cost or market on an individual product basis. The last column of the schedule should contain for each

product the unit value for the purpose of inventory valuation resulting from the application of the lower of cost or market rule.

(c) What effects, if any, do the expected selling prices have on the valuation of products A, B, C, and D by the lower of cost or market rule?

(From the CPA exam.)

12-31. ***GROSS PROFIT METHOD*** Treat each of the following as a separate case:

(a) Assume the beginning inventory is $30,000, the purchases of the period $87,500, and the net sales $102,000. The gross profit rate is assumed to have approximated 40% of net sales for the past several years. Estimate the ending inventory using the gross profit method.

(b) The Triplex Company reported sales of $400,000 during 19*x*1, while the merchandise available for sale during the period was $320,000 at cost. Assuming a gross profit rate of 37%, what is the estimated ending inventory for 19*x*1?

12-32. ***ECONOMIC ORDER QUANTITY*** You have been engaged to install an accounting system for the Kaufman Corporation. Among the inventory control features Kaufman desires as a part of the system are indicators of "how much" to order "when." The following information is furnished for one item, called a "komtronic," which is carried in inventory:

(a) Komtronics are sold by the gross (twelve dozen) at a list price of $800 per gross f.o.b. shipper. Kaufman receives a 40% trade discount off list price on purchases in gross lots.

(b) Freight cost is $20 per gross from the shipping point to Kaufman's plant.

(c) Kaufman uses about 5,000 komtronics during a 259-day production year and must purchase a total of thirty-six gross per year to allow for normal breakage. Minimum and maximum usages are twelve and twenty-eight komtronics per day, respectively.

(d) Normal delivery time to receive an order is twenty working days from the date a purchase request is initiated. A rush order in full gross lots can be received by air freight in five working days at an extra cost of $52 per gross. A stockout (complete exhaustion of the inventory) of komtronics would stop production, and Kaufman would purchase komtronics locally at list price rather than shut down.

(e) The cost of placing an order is $10; the cost of receiving an order is $20.

(f) Space storage cost is $12 per year per gross stored.

(g) Insurance and taxes are approximately 12% of the net delivered cost of average inventory and Kaufman expects a return of at least 8% on its average investment (ignore return on order and carrying cost for simplicity).

Required:

(1) Prepare a schedule computing the total annual cost of komtronics based on uniform order lot sizes of one, two, three, four, five, and six gross of komtronics. (The schedule should show the total annual cost according to each lot size.) Indicate the economic order quantity (economic lot size to order).

(2) Prepare a schedule computing the minimum stock reorder point for komtronics. This is the point below which reordering is necessary to guard against a stockout. Factors to be considered include average lead-period usage and safety stock requirements.

(3) Prepare a schedule computing the cost of a stockout of komtronics. Factors to be considered include the excess costs for local purchases and for rush orders.

(From the CPA exam.)

12-33. ***INVENTORY PRICING—PERIODIC VERSUS PERPETUAL*** Suppose the Hanafee Teapot Company handles its merchandise on a simple buy and sell basis. During 19*x*1 the inventory activity was as follows:

Jan. 1	Beginning inventory: 18,000 lb. @ $2.00 per unit
Jan. 20	Sale: 15,000 lb. @ $5.00 per unit
April 15	Purchase: 30,000 lb. @ $2.05 per unit
May 27	Sale: 25,000 lb. @ $5.10 per unit
July 16	Purchase: 20,000 lb. @ $2.10 per unit
Oct. 1	Sale: 15,000 lb. @ $5.15 per unit
Nov. 14	Purchase: 10,000 lb. @ $2.10 per unit
Dec. 2	Sale: 18,000 lb. @ $5.20 per unit

During 19*x*2, the company's activities with regard to the same product were as follows:

Jan. 15	Purchase: 30,000 lb. @ $2.10 per unit
April 15	Sale: 25,000 lb. @ $5.20 per unit
Sept. 16	Purchase: 20,000 lb. @ $2.25 per unit
Oct. 20	Sale: 28,000 lb. @ $5.25 per unit
Dec. 1	Purchase: 15,000 lb. @ $2.30 per unit
Dec. 13	Sale: 14,000 lb. @ $5.30 per unit

Required: What is

(a) the 19*x*1 gross profit figure if FIFO had been applied on a periodic inventory basis?
(b) the 19*x*1 gross profit figure if LIFO had been applied on a periodic inventory basis?
(c) the 19*x*1 cost of goods sold figure if LIFO had been applied on a perpetual inventory basis?
(d) the 19*x*1 cost of goods sold figure if the weighted average cost procedure had been used on a periodic basis?
(e) the 19*x*2 cost of goods sold figure under LIFO applied on a periodic basis?
(f) the 19*x*2 gross profit figure under FIFO applied on a periodic basis?
(g) For the year 19*x*2 how much higher would gross profit be on the LIFO periodic basis than on the weighted average periodic basis?

12-34. ***GROSS PROFIT METHOD OF INVENTORY VALUATION*** The Make Flight Company lost a significant portion of its inventory to thieves late in 19*x*2. The company determined that the inventory immediately after the theft amounted to $9,300. The following information was taken from the records of the company.

	19x2 to date of theft	**19x1**
Purchases	120,400	149,752
Purchase returns and allowances	6,100	8,000
Sales	183,200	216,180
Sales returns and allowances	2,200	4,780
Wages and salaries	27,400	33,500
Rent	3,200	3,200
Insurance	1,200	1,300
Advertising	1,840	4,400
Interest expense	4,130	2,120
Depreciation	1,400	1,700
Furniture & fixtures (net)	8,310	8,400
Misc. exp.	8,600	10,100
Beginning inventory	52,000	54,000
Machinery & equipment	18,400	19,160

Required:

From the above information, estimate the cost of the inventory stolen.

12-35. ***INVENTORY PRICING*** Assuming that the beginning inventory for 1965 = 0, compute the gross profit under FIFO and weighted average given the following data:

	1965	1966	1967
Gross profit under LIFO is	$20,000	$30,000	$15,000
Value of ending inventory under:			
LIFO is	40,000	50,000	60,000
Weighted average is	35,000	55,000	62,000
FIFO is	28,000	60,000	65,000

Required: Gross profit under:

(a) Weighted average for: (1) 1965
(2) 1966
(3) 1967

(b) FIFO for: (1) 1965
(2) 1966
(3) 1967

(c) Movement of prices was up, down, or stable in: (1) 1965
(2) 1966
(3) 1967

12-36. ***INVENTORY PRICING*** Consider the following inventory data of the Bailey Company during 19*x*1:

	No. of Units	Cost per Unit
Beginning inventory	10	$ 8.00
First purchase (Feb. 1)	7	9.00
Second purchase (Mar. 1)	5	9.00
Third purchase (April 1)	8	11.00
Fourth purchase (July 1)	4	10.00
Fifth purchase (Sept. 15)	10	12.00
Sixth purchase (Nov. 1)	6	12.50
Available for sale	50	
Units sold	34	
Units in ending inventory	16	

Required:

(a) What is the ending inventory valuation using: (1) weighted average cost per unit; (2) FIFO?

(b) What method causes the lowest net income for 19*x*1 – FIFO, LIFO, or weighted average?

(c) What is the cost of goods sold for 19*x*1 if LIFO is used to value ending inventory?

(d) If the replacement cost per unit of inventory is $10, the estimated selling price is $18, the estimated selling expense is $4, and the normal profit is $3, what is the value of the ending inventory if the lower of cost or market rule is applied and:

(1) LIFO is used?

(2) FIFO is used?

12-37. ***INVENTORY PRICING*** The ABC Corporation had the following merchandise transactions in 1972:

	Units	Unit Cost
Beginning inventory	600	$5
February 4 purchase	400	6
July 12 purchase	500	7
August 10 purchase	300	8
November 21 purchase	600	4

Sales	
January 15 sale	500
July 15 sale	600
September 15 sale	500

Required:

Calculate the ending inventory for December 31, 1972, under the following assumptions:

(a) LIFO method:
  (1) Periodic
  (2) Perpetual
(b) FIFO method:
  (1) Periodic
  (2) Perpetual

12-38. ***GROSS PROFIT METHOD OF ESTIMATING INVENTORIES*** On August 31, 1971, Lifters Corporation, a dealer in automotive parts, took a physical inventory. The management was surprised to discover that the inventory amounted to $10,400. Investigation revealed the night watchman, hired in February, 1971, cooperated with thieves to systematically loot the warehouse. The corporation books showed the following balances on August 31:

Sales	$66,000
Returned sales and allowances	3,400
Inventory, December 31, 1970	28,000
Purchases	36,000
Returned purchases and allowances	2,100

For the past four years Lifters Corporation has averaged a gross profit of 30% of net sales.

Required:

Compute the amount of the theft claim to be submitted to the insurance company. Present your computations in statement form.

12-39. ***LOWER OF COST OR MARKET RULE*** Indicate the unit inventory price in the following cases according to the interpretation of the lower of cost or market rule.

	Cases				
	1	2	3	4	5
Cost	$2.00	$2.00	$2.00	$2.00	$2.00
Ceiling	1.30	2.05	1.80	2.40	1.90
Floor	1.10	1.85	1.60	2.20	1.70
Market	1.20	2.10	1.85	2.15	1.60

12-40. ***ECONOMIC ORDER QUANTITY—DETERMINISTIC MODEL*** The Shelby Toy Company's best selling specialty item is a scale model diesel roadgrader. The toy uses special 1-inch rubber wheels bought from an outside supplier in sets of four tires. Total annual needs are 8,000 sets of tires at a rate of thirty-two sets of tires per working day. Also, the company has a policy of maintaining *safety stock of ten sets of tires.*

The following information is also available:

(a) The tire manufacturer offers the following discount rates:

Quantity of Sets	Discount
In order of 100 or less	none
101–699	.0010 per set
700–1499	.0015 per set
1500–4999	.0020 per set
5000–10,000	.0025 per set

(b) If the number of purchase orders is ten per year then the total annual carrying cost will be $20.50 and *total annual expenses* will be $76.00.

Required: Compute the following:

(1) Annual cost of carrying one set in stock one year.
(2) Cost of placing an order.
(3) The economic order quantity if order sizes of 200, 300, 500, 700, 1000, 3000, and 5000 are investigated (assume the carrying per set and the cost per purchase order is the same at any order size).
(4) The total expense incurred at the economic order size found in part (3).

12-41. ***INVENTORY PRICING—LOWER OF COST OR MARKET*** The Loton Company sells only three products: A, B, and C. The selling and purchasing activity for each of these products during 19*x*1 is as follows:

Product A	No. of Units	Cost per Unit
Beginning inventory	1,200	$7.00
First purchase	7,800	7.10
Second purchase	6,500	7.40
Third purchase	4,000	7.40
Fourth purchase	11,000	7.50
Fifth purchase	8,000	7.50
Available for sale	38,500	
Units sold	37,000	
Units in ending inventory	1,500	

Product B		
Beginning inventory	10,000	$2.30
First purchase	24,500	2.10
Second purchase	30,000	2.00
Third purchase	9,000	2.50
Fourth purchase	14,000	2.50
Available for sale	87,500	
Units sold	80,000	
Units in ending inventory	7,500	

Product C	No. of Units	Cost per Unit
Beginning inventory	2,300	$5.00
First purchase	1,500	5.20
Second purchase	3,400	5.20
Third purchase	3,000	5.20
Fourth purchase	2,500	5.10
Fifth purchase	2,400	5.10
Sixth purchase	1,500	5.05
Seventh purchase	1,000	5.05
Available for sale	17,600	
Units sold	15,000	
Units in ending inventory	2,600	

At the end of 19*x*1, the following additional information is available:

	A	B	C
Selling price per unit	$10.50	$4.50	$8.50
Replacement cost per unit	7.20	2.30	5.10
Est. selling exp. per unit	3.00	.50	2.00
Normal profit per unit	.50	.80	1.50

Required:

(a) Applying the lower of cost or market rule to each product individually, what is the total ending inventory valuation using:
  (1) FIFO
  (2) LIFO
  (3) Weighted average

(b) Applying the lower of cost or market rule to the inventory as a whole, what is the total ending inventory valuation using:
  (1) FIFO
  (2) LIFO
  (3) Weighted average

12-42. ***RETAIL METHOD*** Consider the following data:

	19x1	19x2
Beginning inventory at *retail*	$ 650	–
Beginning inventory at *cost*	500	–
Purchases at *retail*	8,120	9,540
Purchases at *cost*	6,900	7,190
Additional markups	400	–
Markdowns	350	750
Markdown cancellations	120	230
Gross sales	7,735	10,025
Sales returns and allowances	180	305

Required:

For each of the following, calculate the ending inventory cost for 19*x*1 and 19*x*2 using the retail method. (Round off the cost-price ratio to the nearest whole number.)

(a) Conventional method (lower of cost or market)
(b) Replacement cost
(c) LIFO
(d) FIFO

12-43. ***DOLLAR-VALUE LIFO*** The Rodney Corporation computes ending inventory using current costs. Suppose the company adopts the dollar-value LIFO method of costing inventory in 1973. Using a base year of 1966, the company computed price-level indexes for each year from 1966 to 1973. This information, together with the original ending inventory costs, is as follows:

End of:	Inventory at Year-End Prices	Price Level Index
1966	$126,000	100%
1967	143,000	110%
1968	155,250	115%
1969	165,000	125%
1970	174,000	120%
1971	149,600	110%
1972	136,500	105%
1973	147,400	110%

Required:

Compute the ending inventory cost for 1973 using the dollar-value LIFO method.

CHAPTER

13

THE MANAGEMENT OF LONG-LIVED ASSETS: PLANT AND EQUIPMENT

13.1 THE NATURE OF LONG-LIVED ASSETS

Long-lived assets comprise physical things that: (1) are of a fairly permanent nature; (2) will be used by or benefit the enterprise in future periods; and (3) are not acquired for the purpose of resale.

By "fairly permanent nature" we mean that these assets are held for more than one accounting period. In most cases they are held for many years.

By "benefitting" the enterprise, we mean that long-lived assets must be of value to the ongoing or probable future operations of a firm. Hence an irreparable, broken-down piece of equipment may have a continuing *physical life,* but it has no further *economic life* and therefore cannot be classified as a long-lived asset.

The major distinction between *long-lived assets* and *merchandise inventory* lies in the fact that the latter is acquired or produced with the intent to sell it in the ordinary course of business, while the former are purchased for the long-term use of the enterprise and not held for resale.

A classification of long-lived assets into their major types is shown in Exhibit 13-1.

EXHIBIT 13-1 A CLASSIFICATION OF LONG-LIVED ASSETS

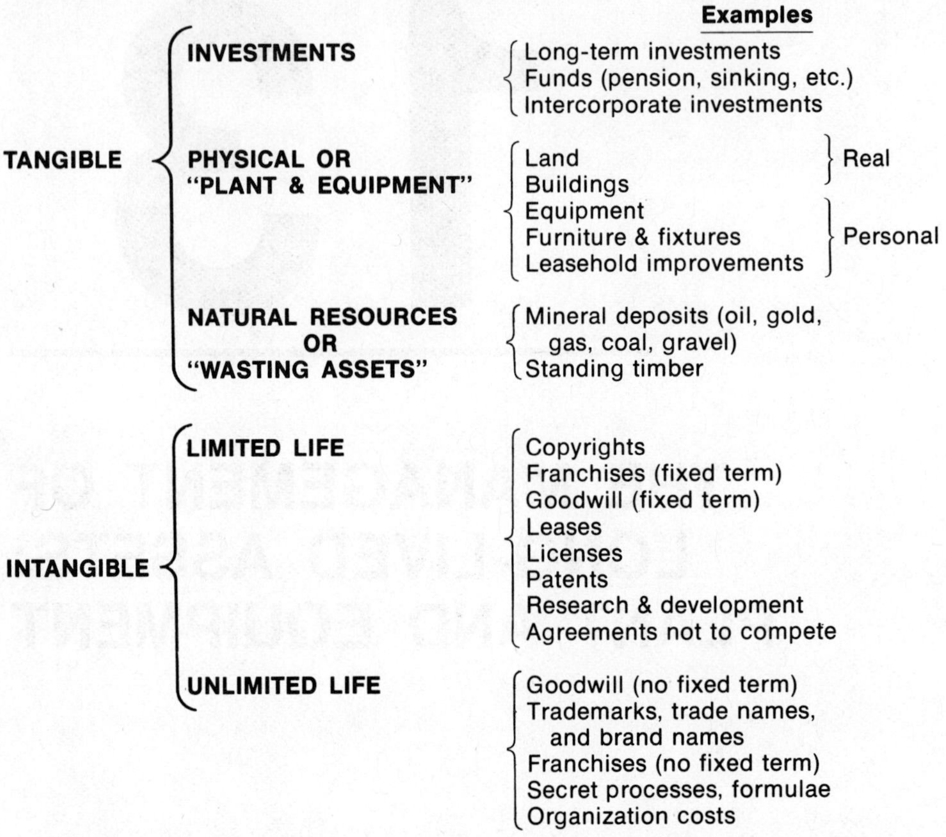

The terminology used to refer to increases and decreases in the value of long-lived assets is:

	Increases in Value	Decreases in Value
Physical assets	Appreciation	Depreciation
Natural resources	Accretion	Depletion
Intangible assets	Appreciation	Amortization

13.2 TANGIBLE LONG-LIVED ASSETS

As Exhibit 13-1 suggests, long-lived assets are of two major types: *tangible* and *intangible.* Tangible long-lived assets are in turn divided into three major groups.

1. *Investments:* We have previously stated that the reason for purchasing marketable securities is to earn a temporary return on excess cash. When such assets are not held for temporary purposes (liquidity), but for long-term growth, they are classified as investments.

Investments include portfolios of stocks and bonds held by a firm, long-term funds such as *pension plan funds,* and funds accumulated for the repayment of bonds, i.e., *sinking funds.*

In addition, a company may advance cash to or hold stock in affiliated companies such as subsidiaries; these items are also classified as investments.

2. *Plant and Equipment:* This group contains *real* and *personal property* items. *Real property* (or *real estate*) includes land and anything attached to land, such as buildings, fences, sidewalks, and other land improvements. (These items are known as *Sec. 1231* assets in the tax code.)

   Only those real property items employed in a firm's operations are classified as plant and equipment. When a firm holds undeveloped land either for a future building site or as an investment, that land cost is shown under investments rather than plant and equipment, because it is not employed in ongoing operations.

   Personal property refers to all other property items not included in real property. Typically the following items are included in personal property: machinery and equipment, furniture and fixtures, orchards, dairy and breeding animals. In short, personal property includes all of the nonreal property items owned by a firm and used in the production of revenues. (These items are known as *Sec. 1245* assets in the tax code.)
3. *Natural Resources or "Wasting Assets":* Natural resources which are subject to exhaustion through extraction are called *wasting assets.* Examples of wasting assets are mineral deposits (coal, sulphur, iron, copper, other types of ore), oil and gas deposits, and standing timber.

13.3 INTANGIBLE LONG-LIVED ASSETS

While tangible long-lived assets have certain physical characteristics, *intangibles* generally lack physical substance. Examples of intangible long-lived assets include items such as copyrights, trademarks, franchises, leaseholds, and goodwill. Although the long-lived assets classified as investments are considered legally to be intangibles, accountants restrict the term to those *special rights* or advantages which benefit future operations.

Intangible long-lived assets are in turn divided into two groups: intangibles with a limited life, and intangibles with unlimited life.

LIMITED LIFE

Certain intangibles have limited lives arising from government regulation or private agreement. The following are examples:

1. *Patents:* A patent is a grant by the federal government giving the holder the exclusive right to control the manufacture, sale, and other use of a particular discovery or invention for a period of *seventeen years.* A patent is not renewable, but the discovery or invention can be protected by new applications for patentable improvements in the original patented item.
2. *Copyrights:* A copyright is also a grant by the federal government which entitles the holder to control his literary, musical, or artistic works for a period of twenty-eight years, renewable for another twenty-eight years. Copyrights, like patents, can either be developed or purchased.

3. *Research and Development Costs:* Most large (and some small) companies support ongoing research and development programs to discover new products and/or improve existing ones. The costs of such programs represent either (a) an ongoing expense of current operations or (b) an asset which will benefit more than one operating period. It is often difficult to determine whether a given research program will have future benefits. If the result of such programs is patentable, then the accumulated program costs should be shown as *patent cost.* If research and development programs do not produce patentable results, then carrying forward accumulated costs depends on whether or not there will be future discernible benefits. If a company expects to have increased future sales as a result of research and development efforts, then the accumulated research costs should be carried forward and matched against future sales. The practice in most businesses is to treat research and development as a period cost, i.e., charged to income as the expenses are incurred.
4. *Leaseholds and Leasehold Improvements:* A lease (document) gives one party (lessee) the right (called a *leasehold*) to the use of real property for a specified time at an agreed amount of rent. The owner of the property (lessor) takes physical possession of the leased property at the expiration of the lease.

   Leases are written for a specified time period. Some parties may wish to write leases with an unlimited period; however, leases of land are limited to a period of ninty-nine years and leases to land improvements are limited to fifty-five years by California state law—which is typical of the laws of most other states in this regard.

   While the lease grants certain rights to the lessee, leases are generally not recorded on the books of either the lessee or the lessor (except for companies which are predominately engaged in leasing activities), because the lease is an executory contract, that is, a contract that requires subsequent performance by both parties. Often a lessee will make improvements to a property as required to suit his particular needs. The cost of such improvements benefit the lessee's operations over the period of the lease or the life of the improvements, whichever is shorter. For example, if leasehold improvements have an economic life of ten years but the lease is for five years, then the leasehold improvements are amortized over five years, since at the expiration of the lease the improvements become the property of the lessor.
5. *Other Limited-Life Intangibles:* Other intangibles such as franchises, licenses, or "agreements not to compete" generally have limited lives. Licenses and franchises, for example, are rights to do something for a specified period. A franchise grants a business an exclusive right to sell a particular product within a given area. Franchises are rarely granted for an indefinite period; therefore, the costs associated with obtaining one are amortized over its stated life.

UNLIMITED LIFE[1]

Certain intangibles have no natural fixed or limited life, of which the following are typical:

1. *Trademarks and Brand Names:* In markets with homogeneous products and similar prices, the competitive advantage rests with firms whose trademarks or brand names generate greater consumer appeal. Well-recognized trademarks and brand names such as "Coca Cola," "Polaroid," "Band-Aid," are of inestimable worth. No attempt is made to place a value on these intangibles in terms of their market appeal. Clearly, however, the costs of developing such trademarks and brand names benefit future operating periods, but since there is no time limit on trade-

[1] *APB Opinion No. 17,* issued in August 1970, requires that intangible assets which cannot otherwise be assigned a reasonable life be amortized over a maximum period of forty years.

marks or brand names as being the property of the registrant (the firm that registers the name with the United States Patent Office), the costs of obtaining trademarks and brand names are carried forward from year to year intact, until there is evidence of a loss in market appeal, at which time the cost of the trademark or brand name is amortized in full.

Certain trademarks and brand names increase in value (market appeal) over time, but such increases are not recognized for reporting purposes by present accounting convention.

However, it is considered an acceptable accounting practice not to capitalize the development costs of trademarks and brand names, but to expense them to income as they are incurred. The reasoning behind this treatment is that the future value (market appeal) of a trademark or brand name is not known at the time of registration, and that its value (market appeal) is as much a function of advertising (the costs of which are expensed immediately) as the name itself.

2. *Organization Costs:* These are costs that are incurred in forming a business entity. They include legal and accounting fees, state incorporation fees, stock certificate costs, and promotional and underwriting costs. Such costs benefit operations over the life of the firm. Unless the articles of incorporation and the resultant state charter specify a limited life, it is assumed that a corporation will continue in perpetuity. As such the related incorporation costs benefit an unspecified number of operating periods.

   Although such costs have an indefinite service life, most companies amortize (charge to expense) these costs over a period of five years or more following incorporation. This is now the required treatment for tax purposes (citation 1954, IRC). Prior to 1954 such costs were deductible only in the last year of a company's life.

3. *Other Specific Intangibles:* Other intangibles with unlimited lives include franchises, secret processes, and formulae. The treatment of these intangibles is similar to the ones mentioned above. The costs of development are carried forward to successive operating periods for as long as the value represented by cost is considered to be relevant. When a decline in value is recognized, a write-off can be authorized. Declines in value occur when a franchise is canceled by the granting authority, or where competitive secret processes and formulae are developed by others.

4. *Goodwill:* Conceptually "goodwill" sums up the intangible attributes (in addition to those discussed above) of a business which make it successful, such as a favorable location (prestigious neighbors, availability of parking, traffic density); good reputation; charm and ability of its management and staff; long-standing relationships with vendors, creditors, and customers. It is, of course, difficult to place a proper money value on these qualities—for this reason, internally-generated goodwill is not recognized by present accounting rules for financial recording and reporting purposes.

   Goodwill only enters the accounting system when it is *purchased* in connection with the acquisition of a business. Consider the purchase of a very small business—say a hamburger stand. It is listed for sale under "business opportunities" in the local newspaper for $1,000. Upon inquiring as to its assets (the items of value) we discover that:

   The seller will take his cash and inventory with him.

   The stand itself and the equipment is all leased, requiring monthly payments.

   What then are we paying for? Goodwill. Our balance sheet immediately after the acquisition reads:

BALANCE SHEET

ASSETS		EQUITY	
Goodwill...........	$1,000	Capital...........	$1,000

We would assess our investment inaccurately if we failed to record goodwill as an asset, and our cash outlay as equity. If we made $200 profit in the first year, return on investment is 20%; but failing to show our investment of $1,000 would make any attempt to measure return on investment meaningless.

Of course, *purchased goodwill* is recognized in the acquisition of large businesses as well, being the amount that is paid over and above the fair market value of all recorded assets. Another definition of *goodwill* is that it represents the *present value* of the discounted future earnings of the firm in excess of the value of tangible assets.

13.4 THE VALUATION OF LONG-LIVED ASSETS

The value of long-lived assets (as with other assets), for accounting purposes, are the costs attached to their development or acquisition. The bases for value of major categories of long-lived assets are shown in Exhibit 13-2.

EXHIBIT 13-2 THE BASES FOR VALUING LONG-LIVED ASSETS

		BASES FOR VALUE	
Asset	**Description**	**Where the Asset is Developed**	**Where the Asset is Purchased**
Investment	Commitment of funds for more than one operating period held in the form of stocks, bonds, or cash.	——	At cost, unless a "permanent" decline in value below cost is recognized, in which case investments are carried at a market value which is below cost.
Physical (Plant and Equipment)	Land, buildings, machinery, equipment, furniture employed in operations.	At cost of development including raw materials, labor, and overhead. (Less depreciation.)	At purchase price including freight, insurance, and installation. (Less depreciation.)
Natural Resources	Mineral deposits and standing timber	At cost of development including drilling costs, shaft costs, clearing costs. (Less depletion.)	At purchase price including drilling costs and other readying costs. (Less depletion.)
Intangibles	Property rights and special advantages benefiting future operating periods.	At cost of development including design salaries, legal and accounting costs in connection with applications to patent or register, litigation costs of successfully defending an infringement suit. (Less amortization when a loss in value is recognized.)	At purchase price including registration and litigation costs of successfully defending an infringement suit. (Less amortization when a loss in value is recognized.)

As shown in Exhibit 13-2, the original cost of an asset usually includes items in addition to the purchase price, e.g.:

1. *Land:* The cost of land includes brokers' commissions; and legal, title search, insurance, recording, and escrow fees. Unpaid taxes or interest owing by the previous owner may also be considered part of the original cost. In addition, certain costs incurred following the purchase of land are added to land value as they are incurred: clearing, grading, subdividing, landscaping, and other improvements such as fencing, lighting, sewers, sidewalks, and water mains.
2. *Building:* The cost of a building includes design and architectural fees, expenses in obtaining bids, permits, licenses and inspection fees. Where an existing building is purchased, the cost of remodelling, partitioning, etc., is added to the purchase price.
3. *Land and Building:*
   a. Where land and building are purchased together, the purchase price must be allocated between them. This is because depreciation is allowed on a building that is used for business purposes, while no depreciation of land is permissible. An acceptable method for allocating cost between land and building is by using the property tax assessment ratio. In most states property is assessed (its *assessed value*) at some fraction of *fair market value.* Most property tax assessments separate land, improvements (buildings), and personal property. For example, assume that the assessed value of land and improvements on the basis of 25% of fair market value is:

	Assessed Value	Ratio of L/I
Land	$ 20,000	.20
Improvements	80,000	.80
Total Assessed value	$100,000	

   Accordingly, if the property is purchased for $500,000, the new owner can allocate cost to land and building as follows:

	Purchase Price	Ratio
Land	$100,000	.20
Building	400,000	.80
Total	$500,000	

   Only the $400,000 assigned to the building can be depreciated.

   b. Where the land that is purchased contains an obsolete building that the new owner proposes to demolish in order to make the land suitable for other uses, the cost of removing the old building *is added to the cost of the land.*
   c. Where the land contains an old building, but where the new owner continues to use it and subsequently decides to demolish it and erect a new building, the cost of removing the old building *is added to the cost of constructing the new building.*
4. *Machinery, Equipment, Furniture, and Fixtures:* Recorded cost of items in this category include the purchase price, related taxes, freight charges, insurance while in transit, installation charges, and other costs of preparing the item for use.

Items within this group include manufacturing machinery, tools, patterns and dies, desks, chairs, display fixtures, and automobiles and trucks.

As with the removal of an old building, the cost of removing old machinery is added to the cost of the new machinery that replaces it.

5. *Natural Resources:* If natural resources are developed, only the development costs are capitalized. For example, costs of exploring for oil, drilling, etc., form the asset value of an oil natural resource (the cost of unsuccessful drillings may be added to the cost of a successful one). Similarly, the cost and nurture of seeds and seedlings form the asset value of standing timber.

   However, where natural resources are purchased—an oil interest or a forest—the purchase price is used as the asset value. Each of these methods is consistent with the cost-basis rule of accounting. Readers of financial statements should not expect that natural resources values as stated on the balance sheet represent the market value of these resources. They must obtain this type of information—oil reserves, value of standing timber—through other means.

6. *Intangibles:* Intangibles are also recorded at cost, which is composed of different items depending upon whether the asset is purchased or developed. If the asset is purchased, value is based on acquisition cost including registration, patent and legal fees, and expenses of defending successfully an infringement suit.

   If intangibles are developed internally (with the exception of goodwill), the recorded value includes accumulated development or design costs; filing, registration, and patent costs; legal and accounting fees, and expenses of defending successfully an infringement suit. When a company loses an infringement suit (relating to a patent, copyright, or trademark), the expense of litigation is written off as well as the recorded cost of the related intangible asset.

13.5 CAPITAL AND REVENUE EXPENDITURES

In an accrual accounting system, the purchase of a long-lived asset is referred to as a *capital expenditure;* that is, the cost is carried on the balance sheet rather than charged against income at the time of purchase. If the asset is depreciable, this cost is allocated over future income periods in the form of *depreciation* (for physical assets), *depletion* (for natural resources), or *amortization* (for intangible assets).

For example, a truck is purchased for $5,000 and is depreciated on a straight-line basis over its useful life of five years. The journal entries involved, and their effect on the income statement and balance sheet for each of the five years, would be as shown in Exhibit 13-3.

EXHIBIT 13-3 ALLOCATION OF THE COST OF A CAPITAL ASSET OVER ITS USEFUL LIFE

ENTRY			**Effect on Income Statement and Balance Sheet**
Y_0—Time of Purchase (for Cash)			**Y_0—Time of Purchase**
Increase (Debit)			1. Income Statement—no effect on income.
Equipment........................	$5,000		
Decrease (Credit)			2. Balance Sheet—would show this item under *long-lived assets:*
Cash...........................		$5,000	Equipment............................$5,000

EXHIBIT 13-3 (CONTINUED)

ENTRY	Effect on Income Statement and Balance Sheet
Y_1—End of First Year	**Y_1—End of First Year**
Increase (Debit) Depreciation expense ....$1,000 Increase (Credit) Accumulated depreciation on equipment $1,000	1. Income Statement—depreciation expense reduces income by $1,000. 2. Balance Sheet—would show these items under *long-lived assets:* Equipment ....$5,000 Less: Accumulated depreciation .... (1,000) $4,000 (the $4,000 is referred to as "book value.")
Y_2—End of Second Year	**Y_2—End of Second Year**
Same as Y_1	1. Income Statement—depreciation expense reduces income by $1,000. 2. Balance Sheet—would show these items under *long-lived assets:* Equipment ....$5,000 Less: Accumulated depreciation .... (2,000) $3,000 (The $3,000 is referred to as "book value.")
Y_3—End of Third Year	**Y_3—End of Third Year**
Same as Y_1	1. Income Statement—same as Y_2. 2. Balance Sheet—would show: Equipment ....$5,000 Less: Accumulated depreciation .... (3,000) $2,000
Y_4—End of Fourth Year	**Y_4—End of Fourth Year**
Same as Y_1	1. Income Statement—same as Y_2. 2. Balance Sheet—would show: Equipment ....$5,000 Less: Accumulated depreciation .... (4,000) $1,000
Y_5—End of Fifth Year	**Y_5—End of Fifth Year**
Same as Y_1	1. Income Statement—same as Y_2. 2. Balance Sheet—would show: Equipment ....$5,000 Less: Accumulated depreciation .... (5,000) —0—

Notes:

1. The original cost of the asset ($5,000) is carried intact for as long as the asset is owned and used by the business.
2. Depreciation is a method for expensing the cost of the asset to income over its anticipated useful life.
3. "Depreciation expense" is the income statement account that bears the depreciation to be charged against income in a particular year.
4. The corresponding duality account is "accumulated depreciation" in which successive depreciation amounts are aggregated and offset against the original cost of the asset. Accumulated depreciation is a *contra-account* in that it appears on the

asset side of the balance sheet while it is in the nature of an equity account (it has a natural credit balance).

5. No further depreciation is taken after the point where accumulated depreciation = original cost.
6. "Book value" may bear no relationship to "economic value." For example, at the end of the first year the economic value of the truck could be $3,000 or less; however, as the asset was not purchased for resale at the end of the first year, economic value is not the relevant yardstick, but rather the value of the truck on a five-year investment basis.
7. If the truck is sold for an amount greater than book value (say for $2,500 cash at the end of the third year), a gain on sale results, giving rise to this entry:

Increase (Debit) Cash	$2,500	
Decrease (Debit) Accumulated depreciation	3,000	
Decrease (Credit) Equipment		$5,000
Increase (Credit) Gain on sale of equipment		500
	$5,500	$5,500

The "gain on sale" is added to net income in the period of sale as an extraordinary gain.

8. If the truck is sold for less than book value (say for $1,500 cash at the end of the third year)—a loss on sale results, giving rise to this entry:

Increase (Debit) Cash	$1,500	
Decrease (Debit) Accumulated depreciation	3,000	
Increase (Debit) Loss on sale of equipment	500	
Decrease (Credit) Equipment		$5,000
	$5,000	$5,000

The "loss on sale" is subtracted from net income in the period of sale as an extraordinary loss.

Under the cash basis of accounting, the cost of a long-lived asset is charged to income at the time of purchase, per this entry:

Increase (Debit) Equipment purchase	$5,000	
Decrease (Credit) Cash		$5,000

Of course, under the cash system, significant fluctuations will occur in income as the result of purchasing fixed assets at periodic intervals. As most profit-seeking businesses operate on the accrual system of accounting, let us inquire as to when an expenditure is capitalized versus expensed.

There are four basic rules that underlie the capitalization of an expenditure:

1. The asset must be acquired for use in operations or be held as an investment and not for resale.
2. The asset item (or group of related items) is of a material (significant) amount.
3. Similar items (or group of related items) should be treated in the same manner—the rule of consistency.

4. The asset must benefit (be used or held for investment) more than one accounting period.

For example: (1) The purchase of inventory is not a capital expenditure in that it is acquired for the purpose of resale. (2) The cost of the asset (as an item or as a group of items) must be of a material amount. Some firms set an arbitrary level for materiality calling, say, for the capitalization of all long-lived assets over an amount of $100 or some other figure. (3) A single chair may not be of material amount, but twenty chairs purchased at one time would be; hence, chairs purchased in any quantity would be capitalized. (4) The overriding rule is that the asset benefit more than one accounting period.

Charges other than for ongoing maintenance of long-lived physical assets may be incurred. These charges are usually substantial and fall into two categories:

1. *Additions* include enlargement and extension of existing facilities and improvements in machinery which result in better performance. An example of an extension is the addition of a new wing to an existing building. A machine addition might be a new motor with more horsepower that increases its output.

   These additions are added to the cost of the original asset. When the addition has an estimated useful life different from the main property, the cost of the addition is allocated to expense over the life of the addition or the main asset, whichever is shorter.
2. *Betterments* are expenditures which rehabilitate certain assets or increase their service lives beyond the original estimate of useful life. These expenditures are not added to the original asset cost but are subtracted from accumulated depreciation.

13.6 THE PURPOSE OF LONG-LIVED ASSETS

There are several purposes for acquiring long-lived assets.

1. *Investments*[2] are long-term commitments of resources (a) externally or (b) internally.
   a. *External investments* are made for several reasons. A primary reason for the acquisition of another company's common stock is to achieve control of that firm. There are advantages to acquiring control of another company. Such an association could achieve better sources of material supply, or a better sales outlet. Currently a dominant reason for acquisitions is to diversify into unrelated fields ("conglomerate"). A company may wish to enter a field in which it has no operating experience. One method of entering a new field is to hire management talent knowledgeable in the new area and begin a new division. A more common method, however, is to acquire the stock of a firm already operating in the desired field.

      Investments may also include bonds issued by another firm. Such long-term investments are often held by insurance companies, banks, trust companies, and educational and charitable institutions. These securities are held primarily for their fixed return (interest) and for the relative stability of bond prices as compared with common stock prices.
   b. *Internal investments* include *funds* set apart for certain purposes. Examples are

[2]For a more complete treatment of investments see chapter 17, "Investment Analysis and Control."

sinking funds which are used to retire long-term debt. The purpose of such funds is to ensure that assets will not be used for operations but rather for the designated purpose. Lenders often require that such funds be set up. Other required funds include pension funds which provide for the retirement of employees.

2. *Plant and equipment* are needed for business operations. Management generally has two options with respect to plant and equipment—such items can be purchased or leased. The advantages of leasing are listed below:
   a. No heavy commitment of capital is required. Generally only the first and last month's rent is required.
   b. The lease "debt" is not recorded on the books of the lessee.
   c. The risk of obsolescence is shifted to the lessor.

   The advantages of purchasing equipment include the following:
   a. Purchasing may be cheaper than leasing, since the lessor must build into a lease both recapture of the original cost, interest, and a profit margin.

EXHIBIT 13-4 THE LONG-LIVED ASSET RESOURCE CYCLE

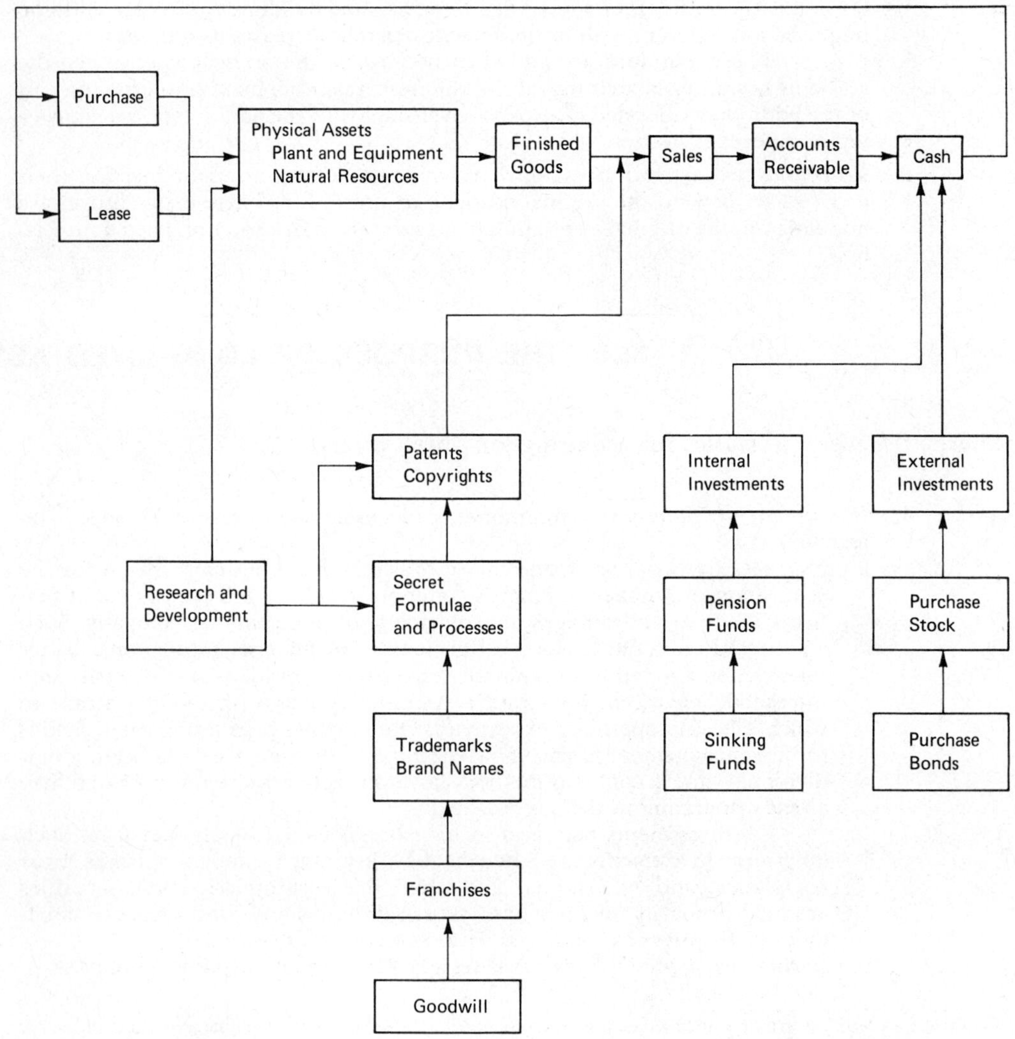

b. Previously, leasing gained popularity because of its favorable tax treatment. Only depreciation is deductible in a purchase, while the full amount of the lease payment can be deducted for tax purposes. However, current income tax provisions (accelerated depreciation) in many cases develop larger depreciation deductions in early years than rental payments.
c. Purchase of equipment on a deferred payment plan permits the buildup of equity, while rental payments are charged to expense and do not build up equity.

3. *Intangibles* are purchased and/or developed for several reasons. Patents, copyrights, franchises, and trademarks are intangibles in the form of government-granted monopolies. The purchase or development of such intangibles improves the competitive posture of a firm.

13.7 THE LONG-LIVED ASSET RESOURCE CYCLE

Like other resources, long-lived assets also pass through sequential steps which we shall refer to as the *long-lived asset resource cycle* (shown in Exhibit 13-4).

Physical assets are either purchased or leased, and with the addition of research and development, finished goods are produced for sale. Research and development may also result in patents, copyrights, trademarks, or secret formulae and processes that serve to increase sales. Sales are converted into accounts receivable and then into cash. Cash may then be used for the following capital purposes:

1. Purchase additional physical assets.
2. Finance more research and development.
3. Make investments—externally and internally.

With the purchase of additional physical assets, the cycle restarts.

13.8 DEPRECIATION OF LONG-LIVED ASSETS

DETERMINING DEPRECIABLE COST

The basis for valuing long-lived assets is:

Original Cost + Additions − Accumulated Depreciation (less betterments) = Book Value.

We have observed that a number of items may enter into "original cost," such as:

1. ORIGINAL COST OF LAND INCLUDES:

Purchase price of the land
Broker's commission
Title fees

Surveying fees
Delinquent real estate taxes if assumed by the buyer
Removal of obsolete building
Land improvements (sidewalks, utilities, paved surfaces, shrubbery)

2. ORIGINAL COST OF BUILDINGS MAY INCLUDE:

Actual construction costs
Fees to engineers and architects
Structural attachments (wiring, electrical fixtures, piping, elevators)
Insurance premiums during construction
(Note that interest on construction loans is charged to operations in the case of all businesses except utility companies.)

3. ORIGINAL COST OF MACHINERY AND EQUIPMENT:

Purchase price
Transportation of new equipment
Removal of old equipment to make room for new equipment

After acquiring long-lived assets there may be certain continuing expenditures in relation to maintaining or improving the asset. These expenditures are *capital* expenditures where they contribute to further life or increased capacity, or *revenue* expenditures where they maintain or restore the asset to its intended state.

As stated, assets are generally carried at their original cost. Under certain conditions, however (e.g., the sale of a business), it may be necessary to state assets in terms of their current market value. When various assets are acquired together, a reassignment of values is necessary, e.g., the following assets with a book value of $50,000 are purchased for $100,000:

	Book Value	Basis of Revaluation	Adjusted Value
Land	$10,000	(10,000/50,000 × 100,000)	$ 20,000
Building	30,000	(30,000/50,000 × 100,000)	60,000
Equipment	10,000	(10,000/50,000 × 100,000)	20,000
	$50,000		$100,000

The *realization* of increases or decreases in the value of fixed assets gives rise to capital gains or losses, while the *recognition* of increases or decreases in the value of fixed assets (without realization) gives rise to appraised capital if an increase occurs, or a reduction in retained earnings if a decrease occurs.

DEPRECIATION METHODS

Fixed assets decrease in value as the result of *physical* and *functional* factors. Physical factors are: (1) exhaustion, wear and tear; (2) deterioration; and (3) damage or destruction. Functional factors are: (1) inappropriateness or inadequacy; and (2) obsolescence. The *basic purpose of depreciation* in accounting is to *allocate* the cost of an asset to specific accounting periods over its useful life, hence, it is a method of *cost allocation* and not of *valuation.*

One of several methods of depreciation may be used for financial or tax purposes, and each method is also supported by a theory. The major methods of depreciation are:

1. *Straight-Line* (S-L)
2. *Units-of-Production* (U-P)
3. *Accelerated*
   a. Double-Declining Balance (D-D)
   b. 150% Declining Balance (150%)
   c. Sum-of-Years'-Digits (S-Y-D)
4. *Interest-Based*
   a. Internal Rate of Return (I-R)
   b. Annuity (A-M)
   c. Sinking Fund (S-F)

The selection of a depreciation method over other methods has an important bearing in determining:

1. Net income.
2. Income tax.
3. Whether or not a capital investment is profitable.
4. The relative profitability of operating assets through its influence on the operating ratios, analysis of working capital, return on investment, and other analytical measures.

The common denominator of all depreciation methods are three essential measurements:

1. *Depreciable Cost:* the amount to be depreciated in terms of original or assigned cost. (Original Cost − Salvage Value, if any, = Depreciable Cost.)
2. *Salvage Value:* the minimum economic worth of the asset at the end of its intended useful life.
3. *Useful Life:* the period of time benefiting from the employment of the asset.

Particular problems attend the estimation of useful life. For example, the standard of maintenance may well affect asset life, or the quality variances in similar products may result in different lives. Estimated useful life may be determined on the basis of past operating experience, by statistical methods (actuarial, turnover), or by mathematical methods, e.g., the point-rating method. For income tax purposes, of course, guidelines are available from the Internal Revenue Service for determining useful life.[3] Taxpayers using depreciation lives shorter than those of the Internal Revenue Service should be prepared to substantiate their reason for varying from the guidelines.

The means for computing depreciation under each of these several methods and its underlying theory are contained in Exhibit 13-5.

---

[3]Internal Revenue Service, *Revenue Procedure 62–21,* July 1962.

EXHIBIT 13-5 MAJOR DEPRECIATION METHODS: COMPUTATION AND THEORY

Method	**Computation**	**Description—Theory**
1. Straight-Line (S-L)	a. $\frac{100}{\text{No. of Years}}\% = $ S-L rate b. S-L Rate × Depreciable Cost = Annual Depreciation	Depreciable assets contribute equally to the generation of income in each of their useful lives.
2. Units-of-Production (U-P)	a. $\frac{\text{Depreciable Cost}}{\text{Miles, Hours, or Other Activity Scale}} = $ Rate Per Unit b. Rate × No. of Units used = Annual Depreciation	A direct measurement of the use to which an asset is put, such as mileage or operating hours, is the most accurate basis for computing depreciation, i.e., depreciation is a function of use, not of time or obsolescence.
3. Accelerated: a. Double-Declining Balance (D-D)	a. 2 × S-L Rate = D-D Rate b. D-D Rate × Declining Balance of Book Value = Annual Depreciation	1. That assets are more productive in early years than in later ones—hence, depreciation should be greater in early years.
b. 150% Declining Balance (150%)	a. 1.5 × S-L Rate = 150% Rate b. 150% Rate × Declining Balance of Book Value = Annual Depreciation	2. That maintenance increases as assets grow older, giving rise to a straight-line relationship when depreciation + maintenance are combined:
c. Sum-of-Years'-Digits (S-Y-D)	a. Add number of years, e.g., 1 + 2 + 3 + 4 + 5 = 15 total digits, or use the formula $D = \frac{n(n+1)}{2}$ where D = total digits n = no. of years therefore, $D = \frac{5(5+1)}{2} = 15$ b. $\frac{\text{Depreciable Cost}}{\text{Total Digits}} = $ Value of One Digit c. No. of Digits per year in Reverse Order × Value of One Digit = Annual Depreciation 1st Year Depreciation = 5 × Value of One Digit; 2nd Year Depreciation = 4 × Value of One Digit; etc.	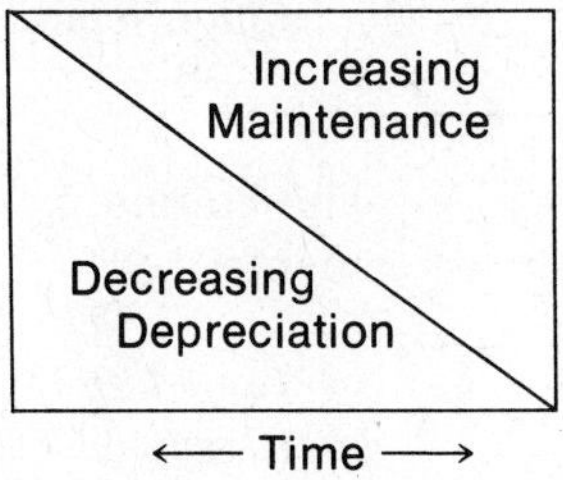 Increasing Maintenance Decreasing Depreciation ← Time →

EXHIBIT 13-5 (CONTINUED)

Method	Computation	Description—Theory
4. Interest-Based*		
a. Internal Rate (Declining Balance)	a. Compute the yield (internal rate of return) by means of the formula $\text{Rate} = 1 - \sqrt[\text{No. of Years}]{\dfrac{\text{Salvage Value}}{\text{Original Cost}}}$ b. Internal Rate × Declining Balance of Book Value = Annual Depreciation.	There is an implicit interest relationship in a depreciation problem; namely, to find an interest rate that discounts original cost to salvage value over the period of useful life.
b. Annuity Method	a. Compute the present value of $1 received at the end of each successive year of useful life at a given interest rate (obtain a present value factor). b. Salvage Value, if any, × Present Value Factor = Present Value of Salvage Value. c. Original Cost − Present Value of Salvage Value = Depreciable Cost. d. $\dfrac{\text{Depreciable Cost}}{\text{Present Value Annuity Factor}} =$ Constant Annual Depreciation Charge, which includes interest	The investment in a long-lived asset requires an investment of capital that becomes unavailable for other purposes, such as purchasing inventory. The declining book value of the asset should be charged with cost-of-capital (an interest rate). Because the depreciation amount covers the cost of the item plus an interest charge, the total amount is greater than the depreciable cost of the asset.
c. Sinking Fund (S-F)	a. Compute the future value of a $1 annuity in arrears for each successive year at a given interest rate (obtain a future value factor). b. $\dfrac{\text{Depreciable Cost}}{\text{Future Value Annuity Factor}} =$ Constant Annual Depreciation Charge, net of interest c. Compute simple Interest Per Annum (at the same interest rate) + Annual Depreciation Charge = Constant Annual Depreciation Charge + Interest.	If depreciation were set aside in an interest-bearing investment (sinking fund), less depreciation would be required inasmuch as the growing balance of accumulated depreciation would be earning, which could be used to offset the amount of depreciation necessary to recover the depreciable cost of the asset.

*Prior to studying the interest-based methods, the student should cover the material in Appendices B and C relating to logarithms, interest, annuities, and present and future values.

Depreciation formulae for the principal methods of depreciation—straight-line, double-declining, and sum-of-years'-digits—are given in Exhibit 13-6.

EXHIBIT 13-6 FORMULAE FOR PRINCIPAL DEPRECIATION CALCULATIONS

Depreciation Method	Computing Depreciation Charge for Any Year	Computing Amount of Accumulated Depreciation for Any Year	Computing Book Value for Any Year
Straight-Line	$D_t = \frac{A(1-s)}{N}$	$C_t = A(1-s)\frac{t}{N}$	$A_t = A\left[1 - \frac{t}{N}(1-s)\right] + s$
Double-Declining	$D_t = \gamma A(1-\gamma)^{t-1}$	$C_t = A[1-(1-\gamma)^t]$	$A_t = A(1-\gamma)^t$
Sum-of-Years'-Digits	$D_t = \frac{A(1-s) \times 2(N-t+1)}{N(N+1)}$	$C_t = A(1-s)t\left[\frac{2N-t+1}{N(N+1)}\right]$	$A_t = A\left[1 - \frac{(1-s)t \times (2N-t+1)}{N(N+1)}\right]$

Where

A = book value at initial point in time, or original asset cost in straight-line and sum-of-years'-digits

N = remaining life in years, except N is useful life in straight-line and sum-of-years'-digits

$s = \frac{\text{Salvage Value}}{\text{Initial Book Value, or original asset cost in straight-line and sum-of-years'-digits}}$

γ = depreciation rate

$D(t)$ = depreciation allowed for the tth year

$C(t)$ = accumulated depreciation for all years up to and including the tth year

$A(t)$ = book value at the end of the tth year

t = time in years measured from the initial point in time

s = salvage value

EXAMPLES OF DEPRECIATION METHODS

The foregoing depreciation methods are illustrated by means of the following example:

A truck is acquired for $10,000 and has an estimated useful life of five years or 100,000 miles; salvage value at the end of five years is estimated to be $1,000. During the five-year period the following mileage data is recorded:

Y_1	20,000 miles
Y_2	30,000 miles
Y_3	30,000 miles
Y_4	10,000 miles
Y_5	10,000 miles
Total	100,000 miles

Straight-Line Method

Under this method the cost of $10,000 minus the salvage value of $1,000 = $9,000 depreciable cost divided by the estimated useful life of five years to arrive at the annual depreciation charge of $1,800. Entries for the period in the asset accounts are:

EXHIBIT 13-7 STRAIGHT-LINE DEPRECIATION SCHEDULE

	ASSET ACCOUNT			–	ACCUMULATED DEPRECIATION ACCOUNT			=	BOOK VALUE
Period	**Debit**	**Credit**	**Balance**		**Debit**	**Credit**	**Balance**		
Y_0	$10,000	–	$10,000		–	–	–		$10,000
Y_1	–	–	10,000		–	$1,800	$1,800		8,200
Y_2	–	–	10,000		–	1,800	3,600		6,400
Y_3	–	–	10,000		–	1,800	5,400		4,600
Y_4	–	–	10,000		–	1,800	7,200		2,800
Y_5	–	–	10,000		–	1,800	9,000		1,000

Units-of-Production Method

Under this method the expected useful life of 100,000 is divided into the cost of $10,000 minus the salvage value of $1,000 = $9,000 to arrive at a mileage rate of 9¢ a mile. This rate is multiplied by the number of miles recorded for the period, e.g., for Y_1, 20,000 miles × .09 = $1,800. The asset accounts for the periods involved would show the following balances:

EXHIBIT 13-8 UNITS-OF-PRODUCTION DEPRECIATION SCHEDULE

	ASSET ACCOUNT			–	ACCUMULATED DEPRECIATION ACCOUNT			=	BOOK VALUE
Period	**Debit**	**Credit**	**Balance**		**Debit**	**Credit**	**Balance**		
Y_0	$10,000	–	$10,000		–	–	–		$10,000
Y_1	–	–	10,000		–	$1,800	$1,800		8,200
Y_2		–	10,000		–	2,700	4,500		5,500
Y_3	–	–	10,000		–	2,700	7,200		2,800
Y_4	–	–	10,000		–	900	8,100		1,900
Y_5	–	–	10,000		–	900	9,000		1,000

The units-of-production method can also be used in conjunction with operating hours or any similar activity scale.

Declining Balance–Internal Rate

Under this method it is necessary to find a uniform discount rate that will reduce the cost of $10,000 to the salvage value of $1,000 in five years. The formula for arriving at this rate is:

$$\text{Uniform Discount Rate} = 1 - \sqrt[\text{Period}]{\frac{\text{Salvage Value}}{\text{Original Cost}}}$$

or, in terms of our example:

$$\begin{aligned}
\text{Rate} &= 1 - \sqrt[5]{\frac{1{,}000}{10{,}000}} \\
&= 1 - \sqrt[5]{.10000} \\
&= 1 - \frac{1}{5}\,(\text{Log } .10) \\
&= 1 - \text{Antilog}\left(\frac{49.00000 - 50}{5}\right) \\
&= 1 - \text{Antilog } (9.80000 - 10) \\
&= 1 - .63 \\
&= 37\%
\end{aligned}$$

This uniform rate applied to the book value at the end of each period results in the following depreciation schedule.

EXHIBIT 13-9 INTERNAL RATE DECLINING BALANCE DEPRECIATION SCHEDULE

	ASSET ACCOUNT			−	ACCUMULATED DEPRECIATION ACCOUNT			=	BOOK VALUE
Period	**Debit**	**Credit**	**Balance**		**Debit**	**Credit**	**Balance**		
Y_0	$10,000	–	$10,000		–	$ –	$ –		$10,000
Y_1	–	–	10,000		–	3,700	3,700		6,300
Y_2	–	–	10,000		–	2,331	6,031		3,969
Y_3	–	–	10,000		–	1,468	7,499		2,501
Y_4	–	–	10,000		–	925	8,424		1,576
Y_5	–	–	10,000		–	576	9,007		1,000

*In practice no further depreciation is taken after the book value has been reduced to the amount of salvage value ($1,000).

Double-Declining Balance

Under this method the uniform percentage rate is computed at twice the straight-line rate, i.e., a five-year straight-line rate is 20%, hence the double-declining rate is 40%. Under this method we have the following asset balances:

EXHIBIT 13-10 DOUBLE-DECLINING DEPRECIATION SCHEDULE

	ASSET ACCOUNT			− ACCUMULATED DEPRECIATION ACCOUNT			= BOOK VALUE
Period	Debit	Credit	Balance	Debit	Credit	Balance	
Y_0	$10,000	—	$10,000	—	—	—	$10,000
Y_1	—	—	10,000	—	$4,000	$4,000	6,000
Y_2	—	—	10,000	—	2,400	6,400	3,600
Y_3	—	—	10,000	—	1,440	7,840	2,160
Y_4	—	—	10,000	—	864	8,704	1,296
Y_5	—	—	10,000	—	296	9,000	1,000

Sum-of-Years'-Digits

Under this method the cost of $10,000 minus the salvage value of $1,000 = $9,000 is divided by the sum of years (1 + 2 + 3 + 4 + 5 = 15) = $600 per digit. This figure is multiplied by 5 to compute the first year's depreciation of $3,000; by 4 to arrive at the second year's depreciation of $2,400; and so forth.

EXHIBIT 13-11 SUM-OF-YEARS'-DIGITS DEPRECIATION SCHEDULE

	ASSET ACCOUNT			− ACCUMULATED DEPRECIATION ACCOUNT			= BOOK VALUE
Period	Debit	Credit	Balance	Debit	Credit	Balance	
Y_0	$10,000	—	$10,000	—	$ —	$ —	$10,000
Y_1	—	—	10,000	—	3,000	3,000	7,000
Y_2	—	—	10,000	—	2,400	5,400	4,600
Y_3	—	—	10,000	—	1,800	7,200	2,800
Y_4	—	—	10,000	—	1,200	8,400	1,600
Y_5	—	—	10,000	—	600	9,000	1,000

Sinking Fund Method

Under this method it is assumed that the annual depreciation is placed in a hypothetical sinking fund at a given interest rate, and that the cost of the interest portion of depreciation is separated from the regular depreciation. The method involves the following procedures:

1. Find the future value of $1.00 annuity in arrears for five years at a 5% interest rate:[4]

$$\text{Future Value} = \text{Annuity}\left[\frac{(1 + \text{Interest Rate})^{\text{No. of Periods}} - 1}{\text{Interest Rate}}\right]$$

$$= 1\left[\frac{(1 + .05)^5 - 1}{.05}\right]$$

$$= 1\left(\frac{1.2763 - 1}{.05}\right)$$

$$= 5.526$$

[4]Or obtain future value factor from Table B-3 in Appendix B, at intersection of 5% and five years.

2. Divide cost of $10,000 minus salvage value of $1,000 = $9,000 by 5.526 = $1,628.77 to get uniform depreciation net of interest.

EXHIBIT 13-12 SINKING FUND DEPRECIATION SCHEDULE

	Asset Account Balance	Depreciation	5% Interest	Accumulated Depreciation	Book Value
Y_0	$10,000.00				$10,000.00
Y_1	10,000.00	$1,628.77	$ —	$1,628.77	8,371.23
Y_2	10,000.00	1,628.77	81.44	3,338.98	6,661.02
Y_3	10,000.00	1,628.77	166.95	5,134.70	4,865.30
Y_4	10,000.00	1,628.77	256.74	7,020.21	2,979.79
Y_5	10,000.00	1,628.77	351.02	9,000.00	1,000.00

Annuity Method

The annuity method is similar to the sinking fund method in that the interest factor is taken into account in computing depreciation. In this case, however, the interest rate is applied to the diminishing book value. The assumption is that the book value represents an investment. The method involves the following steps:

1. Compute the present value of $1 for five years at 5% interest.[5]

$$\text{Present Value} = 1\left[\frac{1}{(1+.05)}\right]^5 = .7835$$

2. Compute the present value of the salvage value, i.e., $1,000 × .7835 = $78.53.
3. Take cost of $10,000 minus $783.53 to get depreciable amount = $9,216.47.
4. Divide $9,216.50 by the present value of an annuity of $1 for five years at 5% ($4.3295) = $2,128.77 to get the annual depreciation charge.

The asset account balances now take the following form.

EXHIBIT 13-13 ANNUITY METHOD DEPRECIATION SCHEDULE

	Asset Account Balance	Depreciation Charge		Interest Based on Book Value		Accumulated Depreciation Added	Accumulated Depreciation Balance	Book Value
Y_0	$10,000.00							$10,000.00
Y_1	10,000.00	$2,128.77	−	$500.00	=	$1,628.77	$1,628.77	8,371.23
Y_2	10,000.00	2,128.77		418.56		1,710.21	3,338.98	6,661.02
Y_3	10,000.00	2,128.77		333.05		1,795.72	5,134.70	4,865.28
Y_4	10,000.00	2,128.77		243.26		1,885.51	7,020.21	2,979.79
Y_5	10,000.00	2,128.77		148.98		1,979.79	9,000.00	1,000.00

[5]Or obtain present value factor for .7835 from Table B-2, Appendix B, at intersection of 5% and five years.

Comparison of Methods

A comparison of annual depreciation expense resulting from the various depreciation methods is given below:

EXHIBIT 13-14 COMPARATIVE DEPRECIATION FLOWS

					S-F			A-M		
	S-L	**U-P**	**D-D**	**S-Y-D**	**Depr.**	**Int.**	**Total**	**Depr.**	**Int.**	**Total**
Y_1	$1,800	$1,800	$4,000	$3,000	$1,629 +	$ 0 =	$1,629	$2,129 –	$500 =	$1,629
Y_2	1,800	2,700	2,400	2,400	1,629 +	81 =	1,710	2,129 –	419 =	1,710
Y_3	1,800	2,700	1,440	1,800	1,629 +	167 =	1,796	2,129 –	333 =	1,796
Y_4	1,800	900	864	1,200	1,629 +	256 =	1,885	2,129 –	244 =	1,885
Y_5	1,800	900	296	600	1,629 +	351 =	1,980	2,129 –	149 =	1,980
	$9,000	$9,000	$9,000	$9,000			$9,000			$9,000

It should be noted that the choice of depreciation method:

> *Does not* lengthen or shorten the useful life of an asset.
> *Does not* increase or decrease the total amount of depreciation. However, it *does* alter the time-flow of depreciation, i.e., accelerated methods allow greater depreciation in early years and lower depreciation in later years as compared with straight-line depreciation.

It should also be noted that a business—under present income tax regulations—can use one method of depreciation for tax purposes (say D-D) in order to lower taxable income, while using another method (say S-L) for reporting to stockholders, thus showing a comparatively higher net income. The difference in tax paid on the basis of taxable versus reported net income gives rise to tax allocation as discussed below.

13.9 DEPRECIATION AND TAX ALLOCATION

From our previous example, the use of double-declining depreciation for tax purposes and straight-line for financial reporting purposes results in the following variations in net income and income tax expense over the five-year period, assuming a tax rate of 50%.

EXHIBIT 13-15 THE EFFECTS OF DEPRECIATION ALTERNATIVES ON INCOME AND INCOME TAXATION

	Y_1	Y_2	Y_3	Y_4	Y_5	**Total**
S-L Depreciation	$1,800	$1,800	$1,800	$1,800	$1,800	$9,000
D-D Depreciation	4,000	2,400	1,440	864	296	9,000
Income (F > T)	2,200	600	(360)	(936)	(1,504)	-0-
Tax (50%)	1,100	300	(180)	(468)	(752)	-0-
EAT	$1,100	$ 300	($ 180)	($ 468)	($ 752)	-0-

If the tax savings in early years are funded at an appropriate rate of interest, the after-tax benefits of using D-D for tax and S-L for financial purposes would be as follows, assuming an interest rate of 5%:

EXHIBIT 13-16 THE BENEFITS OF TAX ALLOCATION

	Tax Allocation Fund			Cumulative		EBT			Cum.
Period	**Debits**	**Credits**	**Balance**	**EAT**	**Total**	**(5%)**	**Tax**	**EAT**	**EAT**
Y_1	–	$1,100	$1,100	–	$1,100.00	$55.00	$27.50	$27.50	$27.50
Y_2	–	300	1,400	$27.50	1,427.50	71.38	35.69	35.69	63.19
Y_3	($180)	–	1,220	63.19	1,283.19	64.16	32.08	32.08	95.27
Y_4	(468)	–	752	95.27	847.27	42.36	21.18	21.18	116.45
Y_5	(752)	–	–	116.45	116.45*	5.82	2.91	2.91	119.36

*The $116.45 represents accumulated interest earned (after tax) and is not repayable.

So the benefit in postponing the tax difference is the use to which the tax savings can be placed until they are required to meet the tax obligation. Of course, in an asset with a much longer life, the turnaround point is about mid-life, which can mean a period of twenty years or more before repayment *starts,* and up to forty years or more before the tax allocation cycle is completed. Repayment of the tax differential can be delayed indefinitely if the firm's depreciable assets are growing.[6]

Under present income tax regulations, it is also permissible for a taxpayer to switch from an accelerated method to straight-line at the optimum point.

However, where an accelerated method of depreciation is applied to an asset, and the asset is disposed of, any gain on the sale is *ordinary income* (as opposed to being a capital gain) to the extent of the excess of accelerated depreciation over straight-line.[7] This is known as "depreciation recapture."

Under provisions of the 1969 Tax Reform Act there is a 100% recapture of post-1969 accelerated depreciation. As stated before, this means that the difference in the amount of depreciation taken under an accelerated form of depreciation and that taken under a straight-line depreciation is treated as ordinary income upon sale of the property.

13.10 TIMING DIFFERENCES BETWEEN ACCOUNTING AND DEPRECIATION PERIODS

Assets may not always be acquired at the beginning of an accounting period, giving rise to a difference between the accounting year and depreciation year:

[6] See John W. Buckley, *Income Tax Allocation: An Inquiry into Problems of Methodology and Estimation* (New York: Financial Executives Research Foundation, 1972).

[7] Internal Revenue Code, Sec. 1250.

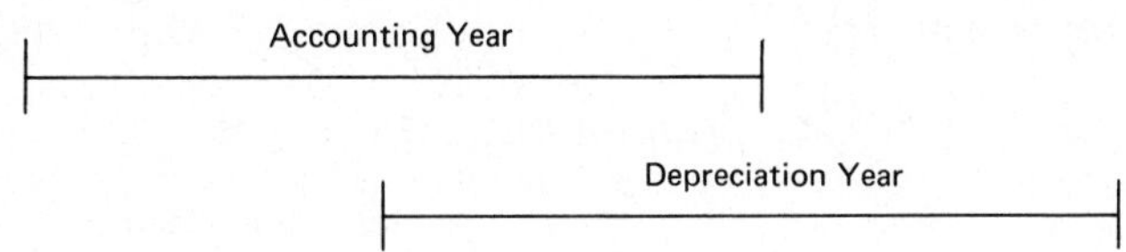

Firms will often take depreciation from the nearest half- or quarter-year. The assignment of depreciation to the proper period under (1) straight-line, (2) sum-of-years'-digits, and (3) double-declining is illustrated as follows:

A firm's accounting period is the calendar year. An asset costing $10,000, with a $1,000 salvage value (depreciable cost of $9,000) and a useful life of five years, is purchased on April 20, 19*x*1, with depreciation to take effect from April 1, 19*x*1.

EXHIBIT 13-17 ALLOCATION BETWEEN DEPRECIATION AND ACCOUNTING YEAR

A. STRAIGHT-LINE

		Accounting Year Depreciation Change is Based on		
	Depreciation Year	75% from Present Depreciation Year	25% from Previous Depreciation Year	Total
19*x*1	$1,800	$1,350 →	-0-	$1,350
19*x*2	1,800	1,350 →	$450	1,800
19*x*3	1,800	1,350 →	450	1,800
19*x*4	1,800	1,350 →	450	1,800
19*x*5	1,800	1,350 →	450	1,800
19*x*6	-0-	-0-	450	450
TOTAL	$9,000 ←	Depreciable Cost	→ TOTAL	$9,000

B. SUM-OF-YEARS'-DIGITS

		Accounting Year Depreciation Charge is Based on		
	Depreciation Year	75% from Present Depreciation Year	25% from Previous Depreciation Year	Total
19*x*1	$3,000	$2,250 →	$-0-	$2,250
19*x*2	2,400	1,800 →	750	2,550
19*x*3	1,800	1,350 →	600	1,950
19*x*4	1,200	900 →	450	1,350
19*x*5	600	450 →	300	750
19*x*6	-0-	-0-	150	150
TOTAL	$9,000 ←	Depreciable Cost	→ TOTAL	$9,000

EXHIBIT 13-17 (CONTINUED)

C. DOUBLE-DECLINING

		Accounting Year Depreciation Charge is Based on		
	Depreciation Year	**75% from Present Depreciation Year**	**25% from Previous Depreciation Year**	**Total**
19x1	$4,000	$3,000	$ -0-	$3,000
19x2	2,400	1,800	1,000	2,800
19x3	1,440	1,080	600	1,680
19x4	864	648	360	1,008
19x5	296	222	216	438
19x6	-0-	-0-	74	74
TOTAL	$9,000 ←	Depreciable Cost	→ TOTAL	$9,000

If depreciation took effect on June 1, 19*x*1, the accounting year would be charged with 50% of the present depreciation year and 50% from the previous depreciation year. If depreciation began in October 1, 19*x*1, the ratio would be 25% from the present depreciation year and 75% from the previous depreciation year.

13.11 GROUP AND COMPOSITE DEPRECIATION

Where a firm chooses not to keep depreciation records on individual assets, it may use *group* or *composite* depreciation methods.

GROUP DEPRECIATION

Group depreciation is used with (1) similar-type assets, (2) that have the same life, and (3) where the same depreciation method is used for all items in the group.

Illustration: A business purchases containers for $100,000. There is no salvage value. The probable lives of the containers have been computed as follows:

% of Containers	Probable Useful Lives
10%	3 years
20	4 years
40	5 years
20	6 years
10	7 years

The average life of the group is five years. Using straight-line depreciation, the balances of the group asset accounts over the seven-year period are as follows:

EXHIBIT 13-18 GROUP DEPRECIATION SCHEDULE—STRAIGHT-LINE

	ASSET ACCOUNT			ACCUM. DEPRECIATION ACCT.			BOOK
	Debit	Credit	Balance	Debit	Credit	Balance	VALUE
Y_0	$100,000	$ -0-	$100,000	$ -0-	$ -0-	$ -0-	$100,000
				(20%)			
Y_1	-0-	-0-	100,000	—	20,000	20,000	80,000
Y_2	-0-	-0-	100,000	-0-	20,000	40,000	60,000
Y_3	-0-	10,000	90,000	10,000	20,000	50,000	40,000
Y_4	-0-	20,000	70,000	20,000	18,000	48,000	22,000
Y_5	-0-	40,000	30,000	40,000	14,000	22,000	8,000
Y_6	-0-	20,000	10,000	20,000	6,000	8,000	2,000
Y_7	-0-	10,000	-0-	10,000	2,000	-0-	-0-

If the probability of the distribution of useful life is not symmetrical, as in the above example, average life can be computed by means of the weighted average procedure:

% of Items		Probable Useful Lives (Years)		Weighted Average
30%	×	4	=	120
30	×	5	=	150
10	×	6	=	60
10	×	7	=	70
10	×	8	=	80
10	×	9	=	90
100%				570

Average life of group = 570/100 = 5.7 years.

Additions to the Group Account

If, in the above example, $20,000 worth of containers with the same probability distribution as to average life are added at the end of the fifth year, the adjustment to the account for year 5 and beyond is:

EXHIBIT 13-19 GROUP DEPRECIATION: ADDITIONS

	ASSET ACCOUNT			ACCUMULATED DEPRECIATION ACCOUNT			BOOK VALUE
	Debit	**Credit**	**Balance**	**Debit**	**Credit**	**Balance**	
Y_5	$20,000	$40,000	$50,000	$40,000	$14,000	$22,000	$28,000
Y_6	-0-	20,000	30,000	20,000	10,000	12,000	18,000
Y_7	-0-	10,000	20,000	10,000	6,000	8,000	12,000
Y_8	-0-	2,000	18,000	2,000	4,000	10,000	8,000
Y_9	-0-	4,000	14,000	4,000	3,600	9,600	4,400
Y_{10}	-0-	8,000	6,000	8,000	2,800	4,400	1,600
Y_{11}	-0-	4,000	2,000	4,000	1,200	1,600	400
Y_{12}	-0-	2,000	-0-	2,000	400	-0-	-0-

Gain or Loss on Sale of Group Assets

No gain or loss on the sale of individual items in a group depreciation account is recognized until the last period. If, in our original example, Y_5 retirements of $40,000 are sold for $10,000 (a $10,000 gain), it decreases the charge to accumulated depreciation in that year and reflects itself as a $10,000 credit balance in book value in Y_7, as follows:

EXHIBIT 13-20 GROUP DEPRECIATION: GAIN ON SALE

	ASSET ACCOUNT			ACCUMULATED DEPRECIATION ACCOUNT			BOOK VALUE
	Debit	**Credit**	**Balance**	**Debit**	**Credit**	**Balance**	
.							
.							
.							
Y_5		$40,000	$30,000	$30,000	$14,000*	$32,000	$(2,000)
Y_6	-0-	20,000	10,000	20,000	6,000*	18,000	(8,000)
Y_7	-0-	10,000	-0-	10,000	2,000*	10,000	(10,000)

*The same depreciation schedule is maintained.

The receipt of the $10,000 in Y_5 gave rise to the entry:

Y_5

Increase (Debit) Cash	$10,000	
Decrease (Debit) Accumulated depreciation	30,000	
Decrease (Credit) Asset account		$40,000

The disposition of the gain in Y_7 is accomplished by the following entry:

Y_7

Decrease (Debit) Accumulated depreciation	$10,000	
Increase (Credit) Gain on sale of group assets		$10,000

A loss or a retirement that is greater than anticipated is handled in the reverse manner: e.g., \$50,000 is retired in Y_5 instead of \$40,000, with \$10,000 retired in each of the remaining years, and the loss of \$2,000 resulting from an earlier-than-expected retirement (or loss) is carried into Y_7 as shown.

EXHIBIT 13-21 GROUP DEPRECIATION: LOSS ON RETIREMENT

	ASSET ACCOUNT			ACCUMULATED DEPRECIATION ACCOUNT			BOOK VALUE
	Debit	**Credit**	**Balance**	**Debit**	**Credit**	**Balance**	
.							
.							
.							
Y_5	-0-	\$50,000	\$20,000	\$50,000	\$14,000	\$12,000	\$8,000
Y_6	-0-	10,000	10,000	10,000	4,000	6,000	4,000
Y_7	-0-	10,000	-0-	10,000	2,000	(2,000)	2,000

The entry in Y_7 to dispose of the loss is:

Increase (Debit) Loss on retirement of group assets	\$2,000	
Increase (Credit) Accumulated depreciation		\$2,000

Group Depreciation: Sum-of-Years'-Digits Method and Other Accelerated Methods

The previous examples have used straight-line depreciation, but group assets can be depreciated under any of the acceptable methods. The sum-of-years'-digits group depreciation method applied to the same problem is illustrated as follows:

1. Average group life is five years.
2. Number of digits is $= 5\left(\frac{5+1}{2}\right) = 15$
3. First-year depreciation is $\frac{5}{15} \times \$100{,}000 = \$33{,}333$.
4. Convert to a percentage rate, i.e., a 33⅓% rate.
5. Apply the rate to declining book value as follows:

EXHIBIT 13-22 GROUP DEPRECIATION: SUM-OF-YEARS'-DIGITS

	ASSET ACCOUNT			ACCUMULATED DEPRECIATION			BOOK
	Debit	**Credit**	**Balance**	**Debit**	**Credit**	**Balance**	**VALUE**
Y_0	$100,000	$	$100,000	$ -0-	$ -0-	$	$100,000
						(33⅓%)	
Y_1	-0-	-0-	100,000	-0-	33,333	33,333	66,667
Y_2	-0-	-0-	100,000	-0-	22,222	55,555	44,445
Y_3	-0-	10,000	90,000	10,000	14,815	60,370	29,630
Y_4	-0-	20,000	70,000	20,000	9,877	50,247	19,753
Y_5	-0-	40,000	30,000	40,000	6,584	16,831	13,169
Y_6	-0-	20,000	10,000	20,000	4,389	1,220	8,780
Y_7	-0-	10,000	-0-	10,000	8,780	-0-	-0-

Double-declining depreciation would be similar to the above, except that the rate would be 40% instead of 33⅓%.

COMPOSITE DEPRECIATION

Composite depreciation, on the other hand, is used with (1) dissimilar assets, (2) that have unequal lives, and (3) where the same or different methods of depreciation are used for the items in the composite account.

Illustration: A business purchases A-type assets for $10,000 with a salvage value of $1,000 and a useful life of three years; B-type assets for $15,000 with a salvage value of $3,000 and a useful life of four years; and C-type assets for $25,000 with a salvage value of $5,000 and a useful life of ten years.

EXHIBIT 13-23 COMPOSITE DEPRECIATION: SAME METHOD (STRAIGHT-LINE)

Asset	Cost	Salvage Value	Depreciable Cost	Estimated Life	First-Year Depreciation
A	$10,000	$1,000	$ 9,000	3 years	$3,000
B	15,000	3,000	12,000	4 years	3,000
C	25,000	5,000	20,000	10 years	2,000
	$50,000	$9,000	$41,000		$8,000

Composite depreciation rate is: $8,000 ÷ $50,000 = .16 or 16%.
The composite useful life is: $41,000 ÷ $8,000 = 5.125 years, which will hold true for any combination of methods.

EXHIBIT 13–24 COMPOSITE DEPRECIATION: SAME METHOD (DOUBLE-DECLINING)

			Double-Declining		Straight-Line	
Asset	Cost	Estimated Life	Rate	Amount 1st Year	Rate	Amount
A	$10,000	3 years	66⅔%	$ 6,700	33⅓%	$3,350
B	15,000	4 years	50	7,500	25	3,750
C	25,000	10 years	20	5,000	10	2,500
	$50,000			$19,200		$9,600

Composite depreciation rate is: $19,200 ÷ $50,000 = 38.4%.

EXHIBIT 13-25 COMPOSITE DEPRECIATION: DIFFERENT DEPRECIATION METHODS

						1st Year Depreciation	
Asset	Cost	Estimated Life	Method	Salvage Value	Depreciable Cost	Comp.	S-L
A	$10,000	3 years	S-L	$1,000	$ 9,000	$ 3,000	$3,000
B	15,000	4 years	D-D	3,000	12,000	7,500	3,000
C	25,000	10 years	S-Y-D	5,000	20,000	3,636	2,000
	$50,000			$9,000	$41,000	$14,136	$8,000

Composite depreciation rate is: $14,136 ÷ 50,000 = 28.3%.

An example of the use of composite depreciation is an apartment owner who can either depreciate the building, the elevator, and the furniture and fixtures separately or combine them into a single composite account.

As with group depreciation, additions and withdrawals, and gains and losses are absorbed within the account until the end of the composite period.

It should be noted with respect to both group and composite depreciation that (1) average life is determined by straight-line; (2) while the straight-line rate is computed on the basis of the declining balance in the asset account, all declining balance depreciation is computed on the basis of declining book value; (3) when straight-line is mixed with other methods in a composite account, a declining balance method results; and (4) sum-of-years'-digits converts into a declining balance method by dividing original book value into the first year's depreciation as calculated by the digit method.

13.12 DEPLETION

Natural resources may be depleted either on the basis of (1) cost, or (2) a statutory depletion allowance. Under the cost method, depletion is charged to income in the ratio of consumed resources to original cost. For example, if an oil well is estimated to contain 1,000,000 barrels of oil, and the costs of developing the oil well amount to $100,000, then depletion under the cost method can be charged at the rate of $\frac{\$100{,}000}{1{,}000{,}000} = \$.10$ per barrel of oil that is *sold.*

Statutory depletion is based on a percentage of sales as enacted by Congress. Some statutory rates for various resources are: oil, 22%; uranium 22%; coal, 10%; clay, 7½%. With an oil interest, for example, depletion can be charged against sales (net of transportation) at the rate of 22% for as long as sales are made without respect to the cost of developing or purchasing the oil interest. These alternatives are illustrated as follows:

Illustration: An oil company has a cost-basis of $105,000. Oil reserves are estimated at 1,500,000 barrels. During the current year it extracted 60,000 barrels, but only sold 50,000 barrels @ $3 per barrel (net of transportation costs). Operating expenses were $60,000.

Depletion Under the Cost Method

$$\frac{\$105{,}000 \text{ (total cost)}}{1{,}500{,}000 \text{ (total reserves)}} = 7¢ \text{ per barrel} \times 50{,}000 \text{ barrels sold.}$$

Total cost depletion.......... $ 3,500

Depletion Under Percentage of Sales Method

Gross income from oil sales	$150,000
Depletion 22% of $150,000 =	
Total percentage depletion	$ 33,000

Under existing tax laws, the company has the option of taking depletion by either method as long as the method does not result in a depletion deduction that exceeds 50% of taxable income.

Sales	$150,000
Operating expenses	60,000
Taxable income	90,000
50% of taxable income	45,000

As the percentage depletion method does not exceed 50% of taxable income, the entire depletion of $33,000 is permitted. Any excess above 50% of taxable income would be disallowed.

Because depletion (as with depreciation) does not involve a cash expenditure, it has the effect of sheltering earnings against income tax, thus producing a more substantial after-tax cash flow. Income and cash flow statements under cost and statutory depletion in the above example are provided in Exhibit 13-26.

On an income statement basis the statutory percentage method shows a lower net income, but note the significant difference in the amount of income tax paid and cash inflow after tax. Of course, oil companies can report on the statutory percentage method for tax purposes and use the cost method for financial reporting purposes. The effective tax rate in the financial statements in the above example is 32%, as computed below.

Income before taxes and depletion	$90,000	
Depletion (cost method)	3,500	
Taxable income	86,500	
Tax (statutory percentage method)	28,500	(32%)
Income reported for financial purposes	$58,000	

EXHIBIT 13-26 INCOME AND CASH FLOW STATEMENTS

a. Cost Method Depletion

Sales	$150,000	Sales	$150,000
Operating expenses	60,000	Operating expenses	60,000
Income before depletion and taxes	90,000	Cash flow before tax	90,000
Depletion (7¢ × 50,000 barrels)	3,500		
Taxable income	86,500		
Tax (50%)	43,250	Tax	43,250
Income after tax	$ 43,250	Cash flow after tax	$ 46,750

or, Income after tax	$43,250
Add-back depletion	3,500
= Cash flow after tax	$46,750

b. Statutory Percentage Method Depletion

Sales	$150,000	Sales	$150,000
Operating expenses	60,000	Operating expenses	60,000
Income before depletion and taxes	90,000	Cash flow before tax	90,000
Depletion (22% × $150,000)	33,000		
Taxable income	57,000		
Tax (50%)	28,500	Tax	28,500
Income after tax	$ 28,500	Cash flow after tax	$ 61,500

or, Income after tax	$28,500
Add-back depletion	33,000
= Cash flow after tax	$61,500

13.13 PROCESSING LONG-LIVED ASSET TRANSACTIONS

INPUT

The principle inputs of the long-lived asset resource system and related documents are outlined in Exhibit 13-27.

These documents provide evidence that accounting events involving long-lived assets have occurred, and signals the accounting system to admit and process this information. For example, the purchase of plant and equipment is usually evidenced by a check. The purchase of stock is evidenced by stock certificates.

The value of long-lived assets may increase or decrease. When the change is upward, the principal document signalling an increase in value is a check. Increases are only added to long-lived assets when additional costs are incurred; upward changes in the market value of long-lived assets are not recognized in the accounting system. When the value of a long-lived asset declines below original cost, the downward adjustment is recorded.

When long-lived assets are sold or are considered to be worthless, they are removed from the accounts by an *adjustment* entry.

EXHIBIT 13-27 LONG-LIVED ASSET INPUTS AND RELATED DOCUMENTS

	TRANSACTION DOCUMENT	
EVENT	**Tangibles**	**Intangibles**
A. Long-lived assets are purchased/developed.	*Check*—plant and equipment items are purchased. *Certificates*—another company's stock is purchased as a long-term investment.	*Letters Patent*—patent is granted by U.S. Patent Office. *Adjustment*—excess of cost over book value of stock acquired (goodwill) is recorded.
B. Long-lived assets change in value.	*Check*—funds are contributed to pension and sinking funds. *Check*—capital improvement is made to existing plant and equipment. *Adjustment*—permanent decline below cost of investment is recorded.	*Check*—costs of successfully litigating patent infringement are added to patent cost.
C. Long-lived assets are sold or used.	*Adjustment*—periodic depreciation and depletion is recorded. *Adjustment*—plant and equipment items are sold. *Adjustment*—mining properties are abandoned and written off.	*Adjustment*—periodic amortization is recorded. *Adjustment*—worthless intangibles are written off (worthless patent).

TRANSFORMATION$_1$

Establishing duality (or the cause-and-effect relationship) of long-lived asset transactions is the function of T_1. Typical T_1 long-lived asset events are shown for tangible assets in Exhibit 13-28 and for intangibles in Exhibit 13-29.

The primary T_1 records for recording long-lived asset transactions are the invoice record (or voucher register), the disbursements journal, and the general journal (adjustments). The purchase of a long-lived asset is handled through the purchases journal, or, when paid for in cash, through the cash disbursements journal. The cash receipts journal is rarely involved in accounting for long-lived asset events unless a long-lived asset is sold for cash.

TRANSFORMATION$_2$

The T_2 process or posting of the long-lived asset events in Exhibits 13-28 and 13-29 is shown in Exhibit 13-30.

EXHIBIT 13-28 THE DUALITY OF SOME TYPICAL LONG-LIVED ASSET EVENTS (TANGIBLE)

Event	Transaction Document	Date	Notation	Doc. Code	Trans. Code	Acct. Code	Accounts	Amount Debit	Amount Credit
A. Long-lived assets are purchased/developed.	Invoice		a. Machinery is purchased on account.		10	12410	Machinery	$ 1,500	
					10	21110	Accounts Payable		$ 1,500
	Work Orders & Material Requisitions		b. Warehouse is constructed using internal labor and materials (self-construction).		10	12210	Warehouse	150,000	
					10	21230	Accrued Payroll		80,000
					10	21110	Acounts Payable		40,000
					10	50000	Overhead Applied		30,000
	Certificate		c. Purchase of 1,000 shares of Y Company common stock @ $60.00.		10	11540	Investment in Y Co. stock	60,000	
					12	11110	Cash		60,000
	Grant Deed		d. Mining properties are acquired in exchange for common stock issued.		10	11550	Mining Properties	25,000	
					10	31120	Capital Stock		25,000
B. Long lived assets change in value.	Invoice		e. Capital improvement is made in existing equipment.		10	12460	Equipment	1,000	
					10	21110	Accounts Payable		1,000
	Adjustment		f. Share of net loss of Y Company is recorded and reduces the cost.		10	80040	Extraordinary Loss	5,000	
					12	11530	Investment in Y Company		5,000
C. Long-lived assets are sold or used.	Adjustment		g. Periodic depreciation is recorded.		10	50040	Depreciation and Depletion	10,000	
					10	12310	Accumulated Depreciation		10,000
	Receipt		h. Plant is sold for cash.		10	11110	Cash	50,000	
					12	12310	Accum.Depreciation	60,000	
							Plant		100,000
					10	41240	Gain on Sale		10,000

EXHIBIT 13-29 THE DUALITY OF SOME TYPICAL LONG-LIVED ASSET EVENTS (INTANGIBLE)

Event	Transaction Document	Date	Notation	Doc. Code	Trans. Code	Acct. Code	Accounts	Amount Debit	Amount Credit
A. Long-lived assets are purchased/developed.	Letters		i. Patent is purchased for cash.		10 12	13010 11110	Patent Costs Cash	$10,000	 $10,000
	Work order or invoice		j. Leasehold improvements are made.		10 12	12610 11110	Leasehold Improvements Cash	5,000	 5,000
	Check		k. Organization costs are paid.		10 12	12020 11110	Organization Costs Cash	1,000	 1,000
B. Long-lived assets change in value.	Adjustment		l. Patent is granted and development cost is reclassified at patent cost.		10 12	13010 50090	Patent Cost Research and Development Expense	60,000	 60,000
	Check		m. Costs of successful patent litigation added to patent cost.		10 12	13010 11110	Patent Cost Cash	10,000	 10,000
C. Long-lived assets are sold or used.	Adjustment		n. Periodic amortization is recorded.		10 10 10	50040 13110 13110	Amortization Accumulated Amortization –Patent Costs –Copyrights	2,000	 2,000
	Adjustment		o. Canceled franchise is written off.		10 12	41250 13140	Extraordinary Loss Unamortized Franchise Cost	3,000	 3,000

EXHIBIT 13-30 POSTING LONG-LIVED ASSET EVENTS TO T-ACCOUNTS

11110 Cash

	Debit		Credit
fwd*	$200,000	(c)	$60,000
(h)	50,000	(i)	10,000
		(j)	5,000
		(k)	1,000
		(m)	10,000

11530 Investment in "Y" Company

	Debit		Credit
(c)	$ 60,000	(f)	$ 5,000

12210, 12410 Plant and Equipment

(See plant ledger for detail)

	Debit		Credit
fwd*	$300,000	(h)	$100,000
(a)	1,500		
(b)	150,000		
(e)	1,000		

12310, 12510 Accumulated Depreciation

	Debit		Credit
		fwd*	$100,000
(h)	$ 60,000	(g)	10,000

11550 Mining Properties

	Debit		Credit
(d)	$ 25,000		

13010 Patent Costs

	Debit		Credit
(i)	$ 10,000		
(l)	60,000		
(m)	10,000		

12610 Leasehold Improvements

	Debit		Credit
(j)	$ 5,000		

13020 Organization Costs

	Debit		Credit
(k)	$ 1,000		

13040 Franchise Costs

	Debit		Credit
fwd*	$ 3,000	(o)	$ 3,000

13110 Accumulated Amortization

	Debit		Credit
		(n)	$ 2,000

21110 Accounts Payable

	Debit		Credit
		(a)	$ 1,500
		(b)	40,000
		(e)	1,000

21230 Accrued Payroll

	Debit		Credit
		(b)	$80,000

50000 Overhead Applied

	Debit		Credit
		(b)	$30,000

41250 Other Gains and Losses

	Debit		Credit
(f)	$ 5,000	(h)	$10,000
(o)	3,000		

50040 Depreciation, Depletion, & Amortization

	Debit		Credit
(g)	$ 10,000		
(n)	2,000		

50090 Research and Development Expense

	Debit		Credit
fwd*	$300,000	(l)	$60,000

31120 Capital Stock

	Debit		Credit
		(d)	$25,000

*Note: "fwd" indicates a balance forward from prior transactions.

As we mentioned earlier, the T_2 process may be elaborated under certain conditions. One of the conditions cited is the need to maintain ledger records for legal or management purposes. The Internal Revenue Service, for example, requires detailed records in support of depreciation and amortization charges.

For management control purposes, maintaining detailed records on individual, group, or composite long-lived assets is essential. The aggregate balances in the general ledger accounts do not provide sufficient information for control purposes; therefore, subsidiary accounts are maintained for individual (or for large groups of) long-lived assets.

The individual records are posted as part of the T_2 process and are called *property records* or, collectively, a *plant ledger* (Exhibit 13-31). The balances of the individual property records should agree with the general ledger accounts.

EXHIBIT 13-31 EXAMPLES OF PROPERTY RECORDS

Description ________ **Control Account** ________

Department ________ **Location** ________

Purchased from ________ **Manufacturer's No.** ________

Estimated life ________ **Depreciation Rate** ________ **Salvage Value** ________

Insurance ________ **Weight** ________ **Horsepower** ________

			Cost			Depreciation Allow			
Date	**Notation**	**Ref.**	**Dr.**	**Cr.**	**Bal.**	**Dr.**	**Cr.**	**Bal.**	**Net Book Value**

These records may be maintained on ledger cards, tabulating cards, or magnetic tape.

OUTPUT

The accounting information system generates various reports on the status of and changes in long-lived assets. Most of these reports are internal and aid in the process of management planning and control. Reporting on the state of long-lived assets is also an integral part of the financial statements. Here, the *status* of long-lived assets as of a particular date are disclosed in the balance sheet.

The balance sheet reports the cost of long-lived asset resources currently employed, less *accumulated depreciation, depletion,* and/or *amortization.* A representative listing of these items in a typical balance sheet format is shown in Exhibit 13-32.

A major internal output for long-lived assets is a report detailing the nature of the investment by type of equipment or cost center. Other reports which are useful for internal purposes include the following:

1. Reports on equipment utilization, including productive and nonproductive machine hours (machine downtime).
2. Reports showing repair and maintenance costs by various asset classifications.
3. Reports detailing asset acquisitions and retirements.

EXHIBIT 13-32 REPORTING OF LONG-LIVED ASSETS IN THE BALANCE SHEET

CURRENT ASSETS

(detail)

INVESTMENTS

Investment in Y Company, not consolidated, at cost, less decrease of $5,000 for share of loss of Y for year ended	$300,000
Sinking fund for retirement of bonds payable	150,000
Land held for future building site	200,000
Total investments	$650,000

PLANT AND EQUIPMENT—AT COST

	Cost	Accumulated Depreciation	Net
Machinery & equipment	$ 500,000	$250,000	$250,000
Buildings	800,000	500,000	300,000
Land	150,000	—	150,000
Total	$1,450,000	$750,000	$700,000

MINING PROPERTIES—AT COST	$350,000	
Less accumulated depletion	100,000	$250,000

INTANGIBLES

	Cost	Accumulated Amortization	Net
Patents, at cost of purchase and development	$ 250,000	$ 75,000	$175,000
Leasehold improvements	60,000	30,000	30,000
Goodwill, at cost, based upon value of shares given in exchange	300,000	150,000	150,000
Licenses, franchises, and other minor items	30,000	20,000	10,000
Total	$ 640,000	$275,000	$365,000

13.14 SYSTEMS CONTROLS FOR LONG-LIVED ASSET TRANSACTIONS

Stewardship and management controls are present in the management of long-lived assets.

STEWARDSHIP CONTROLS

Stewardship controls have as their objective the safeguarding of assets (custody) and the proper recording of transactions (systems or records control). Although plant and equipment and other long-lived assets may constitute a significant proportion of a firm's assets, the *safeguarding* aspect of stewardship controls are not as vital in this area as in *cash* or *credit* management. Most long-lived assets are not susceptible to fraud or theft, and thus the physical custody objective is met by the following procedures:

1. Maintenance of a subsidiary plant ledger coupled with periodic physical inventories to check the existence, location, and condition of all property.
2. A system of authorization prior to the acquisition and disposition of major items. Serially numbered and properly approved capital work orders are used to control the acquisition of physical assets. Serially numbered retirement work orders control dispositions.

While physical stewardship controls are important in the area of long-lived assets, the recording objective is more vital. Since depreciation, amortization, and depletion are often substantial amounts, their effect on income is large. Therefore, proper recording of transactions, including acquisitions, retirements, and changes in status, is essential to reporting income and the state of affairs correctly. Control over proper computing and recording of long-lived asset events is aided by the following procedures:

1. Transfers of property items should require prior approval, so that depreciation may be charged to the cost center that benefits from the use of the asset.
2. A definitive policy should be in effect to distinguish between capital and revenue expenditures.
3. Acquisition and disposition work orders should be controlled, so that additions and retirements are accounted for properly.

MANAGEMENT CONTROLS

While stewardship controls safeguard and provide for computing and recording long-lived asset events, management controls have as their objective:

1. The optimum selection of long-lived assets.
2. The effective utilization of long-lived assets.
3. The timely retirement and replacement of long-lived assets.
4. The selection of optimum depreciation policy in the light of tax and financial reporting considerations.

Selection of Long-Lived Assets

Management is concerned that long-lived assets are purchased at the right time, from the best source (or in the best possible location), for the best price or most favorable terms, and that the purchase is in accordance with a plan such as the cash budget or capital budget. If a firm is not sure of a new location, it may lease, or lease with an option to purchase until the opportunities become clear. Selection of assets in terms of financing (the amount of down payment versus full price, for example) or depreciation (whether or not it qualifies for new-owner double-declining depreciation) criteria constitute important management decisions.[8]

Utilization of Long-Lived Assets

Having acquired a long-lived asset, continuing management effort is required to maintain effective utilization of the asset. Controls include authorizing only trained personnel to operate sensitive equipment. In the case of buildings, policies are developed to maintain adequate occupancy. Break-down time, excessive maintenance, and similar disutilities in the use of long-lived assets are avoided wherever possible by purchasing items that have a manufacturer's guarantee, mounting programs of preventive maintenance, and by ensuring that the equipment is operated correctly. Excessive idle time or vacancy rate in buildings may lead to the disposal of excess plant and equipment.

Retirement and Replacement

With the exception of investments, which are held for the purpose of long-term growth, the retention of other long-lived assets—particularly plant and equipment—are solely for purposes of productivity. Accordingly, their retirement and replacement (or remodeling) is a matter that requires frequent review as to the need for modification or replacement. Manufacturing companies need to ensure that their asset retirement and replacement plans match the needs of competitive production. As depreciation itself (not being in the form of cash) does not provide for the replacement of assets, retained earnings or other funds ought to be earmarked for this purpose. In a period of rising prices, of course, the cost of replacing an equivalent asset increases, which means that replacement planning should take this factor into account in determining policies with respect to retained earnings or other capital sources that will be used to meet these asset replacement needs.

Depreciation Policy

We have already noted the significant effect that choices among methods of depreciation have on taxable and financial income. Also, the selection of a useful life from within a range of acceptable estimates may have just as significant an effect on taxable and financial income as does the choice among the various methods of depreciation. These matters enter into the formulation of depreciation policy, which serves as a control in selecting methods of depreciation and estimating the probable lives of assets.

From an income-tax perspective, another management control requirement is to see that the depreciation program meets the IRS's "reserve ratio test."[9] This reserve ratio test is used to determine the reasonableness of the accumulated deprecia-

[8] See chapter 17 on investment analysis.

[9] IRS, *Revenue Procedure 62–21*, July 1962.

tion account (or "reserve") and hence the depreciation rate itself. To show how the reserve ratio test works, consider the following example:

Illustration: The asset group has a class life of ten years. Straight-line depreciation is used:

Asset account balance, 10 years ago	$50,000
Accumulated depreciation account balance	36,850
Asset account balance, current	67,000

The Rate of Growth is

$$\text{Asset Ratio} = \frac{67{,}000}{50{,}000} = 1.34$$

{This measures the rate of growth of the asset account.

The Reserve Ratio is

$$\text{Reserve Ratio} = \frac{36{,}850}{67{,}000} = 55\%$$

{This formula expresses a ratio of the current balance in the accumulated depreciation account to the current asset account balance.

The growth rate is determined by the *Rate of Growth Conversion Table.* Locate the value 1.34 in the column for the ten-year class life, and read the rate of growth from the left-hand column. The growth rate is 3.

EXHIBIT 13-33

Rates of Growth	Class Life (Years)						
%	8	9	10	11	12	13	14
−1	.92	.91	.90	.90	.89	.88	.87
0	1.00	1.00	1.00	1.00	1.00	1.00	1.00
+1	1.08	1.09	1.10	1.12	1.13	1.14	1.15
2	1.17	1.20	1.22	1.24	1.27	1.29	1.32
3	1.27	1.30	1.34	1.38	1.43	1.47	1.51
4	1.37	1.42	1.48	1.54	1.60	1.66	1.73

The adequacy of the depreciation rate is then tested by reference to the *Reserve Ratio Table* (Exhibit 13-34).

EXHIBIT 13-34*

Test Life (Years)	Rate of Growth				
	−1	0	1	2	3
9	51 46–59	50 45–58	49 44–57	48 44–56	48 43–55
10	51 46–59	50 45–58	49 44–57	48 44–56	48 43–55

*If an accelerated depreciation method is used, a different Reserve Ratio Table is required. Refer to IRS, *Revenue Procedure 62–21,* July 1962.

As the reserve ratio is within the limits of the test (43–55%), the taxpayer's depreciation policy is considered adequate. If the reserve ratio exceeds the upper limit based on appropriate class life and rate of growth, the depreciation rate must be lowered and/or the excess depreciation may be disallowed, based on all of the facts and circumstances. On the other hand, the firm can increase its rate of depreciation if the reserve ratio falls below the lower limit.

13.15 SYSTEMS FEEDBACK FOR LONG-LIVED ASSET TRANSACTIONS

Feedback on the long-lived asset resource system furnishes users with (1) exception, (2) control, (3) comparative, and (4) interpretive reports, of which the former two are discussed below, while the latter conform to our previous comments with regard to comparative and interpretive reports.

EXCEPTION

Exception reports outline any material departure from plan. One type of exception report compares expenditures on long-lived assets with amounts previously *appropriated* and shown in a *capital budget.* When a disbursement in a given category exceeds the appropriated amount, an exception is recorded and investigated.

CONTROL

Feedback on stewardship and management controls can take several forms. Feedback on stewardship controls over long-lived assets include:

1. Trial balance of individual property records (plant ledger) agrees with aggregate general ledger amounts.
2. Internal audits tracing property items from authorization to disposition. Property records are tested for accuracy, including physical verification of the existence and condition of a property item.

Feedback on management controls include reports on the extent to which long-lived assets are (1) property selected, (2) effectively utilized, and (3) disposed (or replaced) in a timely fashion.

13.16 SUMMARY

In this chapter we have discussed the various types of long-lived assets: (1) tangible—investments, physical assets, and natural resources; and (2) intangible—limited and unlimited life. We have observed that the essential basis for valuing long-lived assets is original cost, which in most instances includes items in addition to the purchase price. We have noted that some long-lived assets (those classified as *capital assets* under the Internal Revenue Code) qualify for depreciation. There are several acceptable methods of depreciation, and the choice of method has a significant bearing on taxable income and financial reporting. (We noted that different methods could be used for tax versus financial reporting, thus giving rise to the need for tax allocation.) Assets are depreciable over estimated useful lives, the best source of which are the depreciation guidelines contained in *Revenue Procedure 62–21*. We noted that assets can be depreciated individually, or in *group* or *composite* accounts.

Major controls have to do with proper purchasing, custody, utilization, and replacement and retirement. Feedback, in common with other sub-systems, reports exceptions, reports on the effectiveness of controls, and provides decision makers with comparative and interpretive data so as to improve the long-lived asset management process.

CHAPTER 13 REFERENCES AND ADDITIONAL READINGS

Archibald, T. Ross. "The Return to Straight-Line Depreciation: An Analysis of a Change in Accounting Method." *Empirical Research in Accounting: Selected Studies, 1967*, Supplement to the *Journal of Accounting Research*, pp. 164–80.

Bierman, Harold Jr. "Accelerated Depreciation and Rate Regulation." *The Accounting Review*. January 1969, pp. 65–78.

Brief, Richard P. "Depreciation Theory and Capital Gains." *Journal of Accounting Research*, Spring 1968, pp. 149–52.

Brief, Richard P. "A Late Nineteenth Century Contribution to the Theory of Depreciation." *Journal of Accounting Research*, Spring 1967, pp. 27–38.

Brigham, Eugene F. "The Effects of Alternative Depreciation Policies on Reported Profits." *The Accounting Review*, January 1968, pp. 46–61.

Brown, Murray. "Depreciation and Corporate Profits." *Survey of Current Business*, October 1963, pp. 5–12.

Buckley, John W. *Income Tax Allocation: An Inquiry into Problems of Methodology and Estimation*. New York: Financial Executives Research Foundation, 1972.

Davey, Patrick J., and Walsh, Francis J. *Depreciation Accounting Practices*. The Conference Board, 1969.

Depreciation Policy and the Reserve Ratio Test—A Symposium. New York: National Association of Manufacturers, 1965.

Feinschreiber, Robert. "Accelerated Depreciation: A Proposed New Method." *Journal of Accounting Research*, Spring 1969, pp. 17–21.

Forney, Ross. "An Application of Composite Depreciation." *NAA Bulletin*, June 1965, pp. 42–43.

Hayes, Douglas A. "Depreciation Policies and Earning Power." In *Financial Analysis and Investment Management*, edited by Eugene M. Lerner. Homewood, Ill.: Richard D. Irwin, Inc., 1963.

Heath, John Jr. "Property Valuation Problems and the Accountant." *Journal of Accountancy*, January 1964, pp. 54–58.

Hogan, William T. *Depreciation Policies and Resultant Problems*. New York: Fordham University Press, 1967.

Ijiri, Yuji, and Kaplan, Robert S. "Probabilistic Depreciation and Its Implication for Group Depreciation." *The Accounting Review*, October 1969, pp. 743–56.

Livingstone, John L. "Accelerated Depreciation, Cyclical Asset Expenditures and Deferred Taxes." *Journal of Accounting Research*, Spring 1967, pp. 77–94.

Lucas, Harold. "The Calculus of Costs—V—Replacement Theory: Some Operational Research Aspects." *Accountancy* (England), December 1969, pp. 896–900.

______. "The Calculus of Costs—VI—Replacement Theory: Some Operational Research Aspects." *Accountancy* (England), January 1970, pp. 29–33.

Myers, John H. "Depreciation Manipulation for Fun and Profits." *Financial Analysts Journal,* November–December 1967, pp. 117–23.

Paton, William A. *Depreciation: Concept and Measurement.* Ann Arbor, Mich.: Bureau of Business Research, The University of Michigan, 1964.

Porter, Stanley P. *"Full Cost" Accounting: The Problem it Poses for the Extractive Industries.* New York: Arthur Young & Company, 1972.

Pye, Malcolm L. "Footnote on Declining-Balance Depreciation." *The Accounting Review,* April 1965, pp. 451–52.

Pyle, Robert L. "Depreciation—Accounting Concept or Political Tool." *Management Accounting,* February 1967, pp. 49–51.

Schwab, Bernhard, and Nicol, Robert E. G. "From Double-Declining-Balance to Sum-of-the-Years'-Digits: An Optimum Switching Rule." *The Accounting Review,* April 1969, pp. 292–96.

Sorter, George H.; Becker, Selwyn; Archibald, T. R.; and Beaver, W. H. "Corporate Personality as Reflected in Accounting Decisions." *Journal of Accounting Research,* Autumn 1964, pp. 183–96.

Staubus, George J. "Asset Lives: Three Comments." *Accountancy* (England), October 1967, pp. 658–60.

Surrey, Stanley S. "A Computer Study of Tax Depreciation Policy." *The Journal of Accountancy,* August 1968, pp. 57–63.

Wesman, Harvey B. "Market Evidence of Depreciation in Single-Family Homes." *The Appraisal Journal,* July 1969, pp. 341–43.

Wright, F. K. "Depreciation and Obsolescence in Current Value Accounting." *Journal of Accounting Research,* Autumn 1965, pp. 167–81.

———. "Toward a General Theory of Depreciation." *Journal of Accounting Research,* Spring 1964, pp. 80–90.

———. "An Evaluation of Ladelle's Theory of Depreciation." *Journal of Accounting Research,* Autumn 1967, pp. 173–79.

Young, T. N., and Pierson, C. G. "Depreciation—Future Services Basis." *The Accounting Review,* April 1967, pp. 338–41.

CHAPTER 13 QUESTIONS, PROBLEMS, AND CASES

13- 1. What are the attributes or nature of the physical things that comprise long-lived assets?

13- 2. Distinguish between the physical life and the economic life of equipment.

13- 3. Distinguish between a *capital* and a *revenue* expenditure.

13- 4. Can investments be included under the category of intangibles? Is there some distinction between the two or are investments simply a special class of intangibles? Explain.

13- 5. Define or explain the implication of the following terms and phrases:
(a) Wasting assets
(b) Executory contract
(c) Property tax-assessment ratio
(d) Book value
(e) Salvage value
(g) Useful life
(h) Plant ledger
(i) Capital budget

13- 6. What are the major group classifications of tangible long-lived assets and the major group classifications of intangible long-lived assets? What are the characteristics of each group? What are the costs involved with each valuation?

13- 7. What is the criteria for classifying real property either as an investment or as plant and equipment?

13- 8. Distinguish between *real* and *personal* property.

13- 9. What is *goodwill?* When is it recognized in the accounts?

13-10. Define and discuss the following limited-life intangibles:
(a) Copyrights
(b) Leasehold
(c) Research and development costs
(d) Patents
(e) Franchise (limited life)

13-11. Classify the following asset examples as:
(a) Investments
(b) Plant and equipment
 (1) Real
 (2) Personal
(c) Natural resources
(d) Limited-life intangible
(e) Unlimited-life intangible

Asset Examples:
(1) Copyrights
(2) State incorporation fees
(3) The "Last Ditch" zinc mine
(4) Employees' pension fund
(5) 10 desks used by the secretaries
(6) 50-year lease on the factory building
(7) 10-year franchise
(8) 5 acres of land rented for commercial use
(9) 1000 acres of forest land bought for extracting lumber
(10) Land on which the factory was built

13-12. Identify the terms that refer to increases or decreases in value of the following types of long-lived assets:

	Increases in Value	Decreases in Value
Physical (plant) assets	________	________
Natural resources	________	________
Intangible assets	________	________

13-13. Define and discuss the following unlimited-life intangibles:
(a) Trademarks and brand names
(b) Organization costs
(c) Goodwill

13-14. Why do you suppose increases in the value of trademarks and brand names are not recognized for reporting purposes? Why is it considered an acceptable accounting practice not to capitalize the development costs of such intangibles?

13-15. "Internally-generated goodwill is not recognized by present accounting rules for financial recording and reporting purposes." Why?

13-16. Identify the principle types of long-lived assets and explain their purpose in the organization.

13-17. What are five costs of land acquisition that are included in the recorded cost? What are three costs incurred following the purchase of land that are added to the recorded cost of land?

13-18. Beyond the basic cost of a building, what are three costs that may be added to the recorded cost?

13-19. It is said that the use of statutory depletion as compared with cost depletion has, in most cases, produced a lower taxable income but a higher after-tax cash flow. Explain.

13-20. Describe the situation when the cost of removing an old building is added to the cost of the land, and the situation when it is added to the cost of constructing a new building.

13-21. What are the four basic rules that underlie the capitalization of an expenditure? Which of the following expenditures should be capitalized:
(a) A $7 hand tool (two-year useful life)
(b) $10,000 in merchandise for resale
(c) $10 in postage stamps
(d) $600 in supplies
(e) A $5,000 machine (four-year useful life)
(f) A $5,000 machine (one-year useful life)
(g) 100 $8 hand tools used in production activities (two-year useful life)

13-22. "Intangibles are recorded at cost, which is composed of different items depending upon whether the asset is purchased or developed." List at least three items comprising the cost of a purchased intangible and three items comprising the cost of intangibles developed internally.

13-23. Define *depreciation* and *accumulated depreciation.* What are the purposes of each?

13-24. Distinguish between *betterments* and *additions* by citing specific examples and discussing the accounting treatment for each.

13-25. List and explain at least four purposes for acquiring external investments.

13-26. Compare the advantages of leasing equipment with the advantages of purchasing.

13-27. What are the physical and functional factors that can account for a decrease in the value of fixed assets?

13-28. Discuss the problems of estimating the useful life of an asset.

13-29. What is meant by *depreciation recapture?*

13-30. Identify the following sequential steps of the long-lived asset resource cycle:

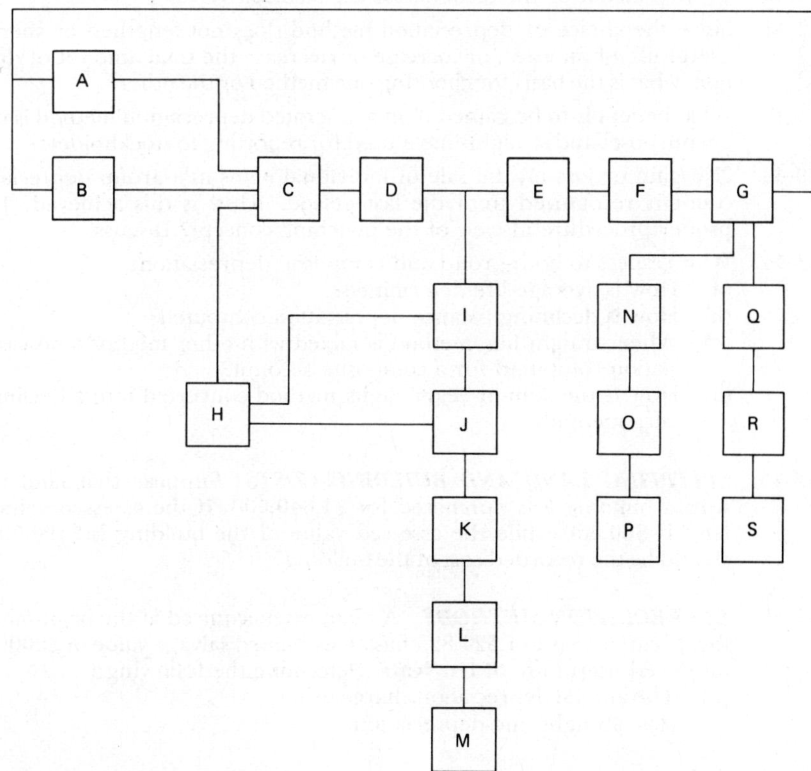

13-31. For each of the following depreciation methods: (1) describe the theory for its use, and (2) indicate the method of computing annual depreciation:
(a) Straight-line
(b) Units-of-production
(c) Double-declining balance
(d) 150% declining balance
(e) Sum-of-years'-digits
(f) Internal rate
(g) Annuity method
(h) Sinking fund method

13-32. What is the *reserve ratio test?* Demonstrate how it works.

13-33. "Readers of financial statements should not expect that natural resources values as stated on the balance sheet represent the market value of these resources." Why?

13-34. Distinguish between *group* and *composite* depreciation by citing the characteristics of assets suitable for each method.

13-35. Describe the stewardship controls by which the physical custody objective for long-lived assets is met.

13-36. "A major internal output for long-lived assets is a report detailing the nature of the investment by type of equipment or cost center." Identify three other reports that are useful for internal purposes.

13-37. "While physical stewardship controls are important in the area of long-lived assets, the recording objective is more vital." Why is it more vital? Identify three controls that aid in the control of computation and recording.

13-38. Identify and discuss the four objectives of management controls over long-lived assets.

13-39. Identify and discuss two possible forms of feedback on stewardship controls over long-lived assets.

13-40. What is meant by the term *income-tax allocation?*

13-41. Since the choice of depreciation method does not lengthen or shorten the useful life of an asset, or increase or decrease the total amount of depreciation, what is the basis for choosing one method or the other?

13-42. What benefit is to be gained if an accelerated depreciation method is used for tax purposes and straight-line is used for reporting to stockholders?

13-43. "No gain or loss on the sale of individual items in a group depreciation account is recognized until the last period." How is this achieved? Is this a proper procedure in view of the matching concept? Discuss.

13-44. With respect to both group and composite depreciation:
(a) How is average life determined?
(b) How is declining balance depreciation computed?
(c) When straight-line method is mixed with other methods, how is depreciation computed for a composite account?
(d) How is the sum-of-years'-digits method converted into a declining balance method?

13-45. ***SPLITTING LAND AND BUILDING COSTS*** Suppose that land together with a building was purchased for $1,040,000. If the assessed value of the land is $60,000 while the assessed value of the building is $190,000, what should be the recorded cost of the building?

13-46. ***DEPRECIATION METHODS*** A plant asset acquired at the beginning of the fiscal year at a cost of $24,825 has an estimated salvage value of $2000 and an estimated useful life of ten years. Determine the following:
(a) The annual depreciation charge using:
(1) Straight-line depreciation.

(2) Annuity method assuming 6% interest.
(3) Sinking fund method assuming 6% interest.

(b) The amount of depreciation for the *second year* computed by the 150% declining balance method.
(c) The amount of depreciation for the *second year* computed by the sum-of-years'-digits method.

13-47. ***LONG-LIVED ASSET TRANSACTIONS***

(a) If a milling machine with a five-year life is bought for $10,000 on April 1, 1966, what would be the credit balance in the accumulated depreciation account on December 31, 1967, assuming straight-line depreciation is used and the machine has an estimated residual value of $300 at the end of five years?
(b) What would be the accumulated depreciation balance assuming double-declining balance depreciation is used in (a)?
(c) If equipment with a five-year life is bought on July 1, 1964, for $45,000 and sold on October 1, 1967, for $12,000, what is the gain or loss on the sale assuming the equipment had a salvage value of $4,000 at the end of five years and straight-line depreciation method is used?
(d) What is the gain or loss in (c) if the equipment is sold for $20,000?
(e) What is the depreciation expense reported in 1967 in (c)?
(f) If an old machine with an original cost of $7,000 and an accumulated depreciation of $6,200 is exchanged for a new machine costing $5,000, what is the gain or loss to be recognized in the exchange assuming a trade-in allowance on the new machine of $1,450?
(g) How much cash must be paid on the exchange in (f)?
(h) Assume in (f) that the accumulated depreciation of the old machine is $6,800 and the trade-in allowance was $150. What is the recorded cost of the new machine if no gain or loss is to be recognized?

13-48. ***DEPRECIATION CALCULATIONS—PRINCIPAL METHODS*** Consider the following data:

Purchased a Xerox machine on March 1, 1966, for $5,640.
Useful life is estimated at six years.
Estimated disposal value at the end of the six years is $1,200.

Required:

(a) What is the depreciation expense for the second year (1967) using straight-line depreciation?
(b) What is the balance of the accumulated depreciation account on January 1, 1970, using straight-line depreciation?
(c) What is the balance of the accumulated depreciation account on January 1, 1968, using double-declining balance depreciation method?
(d) What is the depreciation expense reported in the first year using sum-of-the-years'-digits method?
(e) Which depreciation method reports the highest net income in 1966?
(f) Assume that at the beginning of the fifth year (1970) the machine was substantially modified, thus increasing its useful life by another two years beyond its original estimated life. If the extraordinary repair cost $900, what will be the depreciation expense reported for the fifth year assuming straight-line depreciation was originally used (and is continued), and the disposal value at the end of the extra two years is the same as the original?

13-49. ***CALCULATING BOOK VALUE AND GAIN OR LOSS*** On April 1, 1968, the Williamson Company buys a tape-controlled drill press. The details of the purchase and other pertinent data are as follows:

Cost:	$128,000
Life:	5 years
Salvage value:	$4,000
Deprec. method:	Double-declining balance

On October 1, 1972, the Williamson Company trades in the tape-controlled drill press on a newer and improved version. The details of the new purchase are as follows:

Cost:	$152,000
Life:	8 years
Salvage value:	$2,000
Deprec. method:	Sum-of-the-years'-digits
Trade-in for old machine:	*$12,000*

Required:

(a) Book value of first machine on Dec. 31, 1971.
(b) Gain or loss on trade-in.
(c) Depreciation expense for *1973* assuming *no gain or loss* is recognized on the exchange.
(d) Book value of second machine on Dec. 31, 1973, assuming *gain or loss is recognized* on the exchange.
(e) Assuming the *first machine* uses straight-line depreciation instead of double-declining balance, will the depreciation expense for 1973 be higher or lower than reported in (c)?

13-50. ***COMPREHENSIVE PROBLEM—DEPRECIATION METHODS*** An item of new equipment acquired at a cost of $36,000 at the beginning of a fiscal year has an estimated life of four years and an estimated salvage value of $3,000.

Required:

(a) Determine for each of the four years the book value of the equipment at the end of the year by each of the following methods:

Depreciation Method	1	2	3	4
Straight-Line				
150% Declining Balance				
Double-Declining Balance				
Sum-of-Years'-Digits				
Internal Rate Declining Bal.				
Sinking Fund (at 6%)				
Annuity Method (at 6%)				

(b) On July 1 of the fourth year the equipment was traded in for similiar equipment priced at $40,000. The trade-in allowance on the old equipment was $6,800 and a note was given for the balance. For the first three depreciation methods above, journalize the entry to record the transaction and the accrued depreciation to date assuming:
(1) Any gain or loss on the transaction is recognized.
(2) Any gain or loss on the transaction is not recognized, but absorbed into the recorded cost of the new equipment.

13-51. ***JOURNAL ENTRIES*** Journalize the following events:

Jan. 1, 19*x*1 Machine A is purchased for $34,000. The machine has a six-year life and an estimated salvage value of '$4,000. Sum-of-years'-digits depreciation will be used.

Jan. 12, 19x1 A bill of $600 for installing machine A was received.

Oct. 1, 19x1 Machine B is purchased for $21,000. The machine has a five-year life and an estimated salvage of $2,000. Double-declining balance depreciation will be used. Old equipment with a book value of $4,000 and accumulated depreciation of $16,000 was removed and sold for $2,500. The cost of removal was $800.

Dec. 31, 19x1 Depreciation expense for 19x1 is recorded.

July 1, 19x2 The operating capacity of machine A is increased by 30% through the addition of a loading apparatus with a useful life of ten years. The addition of the loader cost $7,500. Sum-of-years'-digits depreciation will be used.

Dec. 31, 19x2 Depreciation expense for 19x2 is recorded.

April 1, 19x3 Machine B breaks down. The repair bill amounts to $5,000. The majority of the cost was for a new motor. The estimated life of the motor is five years.

July 1, 19x3 Machine B is not operating up to standards and the management decides to replace it. The machine is sold for $15,000 and machine C is purchased for $28,000. The new machine has a useful life of four years and an estimated salvage value of $6,000; 150% declining balance depreciation will be used.

Dec. 31, 19x3 Depreciation expense for 19x3 is recorded.

13-52. ***DEPRECIATION AND TAX ALLOCATION***

(a) Suppose the Northridge Company acquired a new machine for $80,000. The machine has an estimated life of four years and an estimated salvage value of $2,000. Assuming the Northridge Company uses sum-of-years'-digits for tax purposes and straight-line for financial reporting purposes, what are the after-tax benefits if the tax rate is 40% and an interest rate of 6% is applicable? Set up a schedule showing tax differences and interest computations.

(b) Assuming the Northridge Company uses the internal rate declining balance, what are the after-tax benefits? Set up a new schedule.

(c) Suppose the machine as depreciated in (a) is sold at the end of three years for $12,000 in cash. What part of the gain is *ordinary income* under the recapture rule of the internal revenue code?

13-53. ***DEPRECIATION CALCULATIONS*** The Wade Corporation purchased a machine on Oct. 1, 19x1, at a cost of $850. In addition, the corporation paid $40 to have the machine delivered and $160 to have it installed. The estimated useful life of the machine is three years with a residual value of $150 at the end of that time.

Required:

What are the annual depreciation charges for the three-year period under each of the following methods:

		Depreciation Expense		
Depreciation Method	**19x1 Oct. 1–Dec. 31**	**19x2 Jan. 1–Dec. 31**	**19x3 Jan. 1–Dec. 31**	**19x4 Jan. 1–Sep. 30**
Straight-Line				
Sum-of-Years'-Digits				
Sinking Fund Method (at 5%)				
Internal Rate Declining Bal.				

13-54. ***GROUP DEPRECIATION—STRAIGHT-LINE***
Part (a): The Bailey Company buys twenty typewriters for $230 each. There is no salvage value. The probable lives of the typewriters have been computed as follows:

% of Typewriters	Probable Useful Lives
30	3 years
40	4 years
30	5 years

The Bailey Company does not wish to keep depreciation records on individual assets, so it elects the *group method* using *straight-line* depreciation.

During the next five years the Bailey Company experiences the following *actual disposals:*

No. of Typewriters	Disposed at End of	Proceeds from Disposal
3	2 years	$400
6	3 years	500
8	4 years	400
3	5 years	0

Required: Part (a)

(a) Compute the balance of accumulated depreciation at end of year 4.
(b) Compute the gain or loss to be recognized at the end of the group life.

Part (b): Three years from the date of original purchase, the Bailey Company buys ten more typewriters for $250 each. These machines are added to the group and are expected to have the same probable lives as the first machines. The actual disposals on the first machines are the same as indicated earlier, and the actual disposals on the new machines are as follows:

No. of Typewriters	Disposed at End of	Proceeds from Disposal
3	2 years	$300
5	3 years	100
2	4 years	0

Required: Part (b)

(a) Compute the balance of accumulated depreciation at end of year 4 (the fourth year from the *start* of the group).
(b) Compute the *gain or loss* to be recognized at the end of the group life.

13-55. ***GOODWILL—PURCHASED*** The Royer Company is planning to acquire the Olliff Corporation and must determine the amount to be paid for the net assets and goodwill. The following is data of the Olliff Corporation:

Assets at appraised value (before goodwill)	$130,000
Liabilities	45,000
Capital	$ 85,000

Net earnings:

1966	$10,000
1967	11,500
1968	15,000
1969	12,500
1970	13,500
	$62,500

Required:

Calculate the amount to be paid for goodwill under each of the following assumptions:

(a) Average earnings are capitalized at 12% in arriving at the business worth.
(b) A return of 8% is considered normal on net assets at appraised value; excess earnings are to be capitalized at 15%.
(c) A return of 10% is considered normal on net assets at appraised value; goodwill is valued at the present value of five years' excess earnings (the present value of $1 received for five years in the future is $3.79).

13-56. ***AVERAGE GROUP LIFE*** Using the weighted average procedure, compute the average group life for asset types A and B.

ASSETS A

% of Items	Probable Useful Life
15%	2
20%	3
25%	4
25%	5
10%	6
5%	7

ASSETS B

% of Items	Probable Useful Life
5%	1
8%	2
24%	3
30%	4
22%	5
8%	6
3%	7

13-57. ***RESERVE RATIO TEST*** Suppose the following information is available for firms A and B:

	Class Life	Asset Acct. Balance One Class Life Ago	Accum. Deprec.	Current Asset Balance
Firm A	15 yrs.	784,000	540,000	1,345,000
Firm B	9 yrs.	63,500	34,290	76,200

Required:

By referring to Exhibits 13-33 and 13-34, determine whether the depreciation policy of each firm is proper according to IRS guidelines.

13-58. ***GROUP DEPRECIATION*** The Block Corporation acquired twenty similar machines at the beginning of 1960 for $30,000. The machines had an average life of five years and no salvage value. The group depreciation method was used. Machines were retired as follows:

2 machines at the end of 1962

5 machines at the end of 1963

6 machines at the end of 1964
5 machines at the end of 1965
2 machines at the end of 1966

Complete the following schedule using straight-line depreciation:

	ASSET ACCOUNT			ACCUM. DEPRECIATION			BOOK VALUE
	Debit	Credit	Balance	Debit	Credit	Balance	
1/01/1960							
12/31/1960							
12/31/1961							
12/31/1962							
12/31/1963							
12/31/1964							
12/31/1965							
12/31/1966							

13-59. ***GROUP DEPRECIATION*** Each year a company has been investing an increasingly greater amount in machinery. Since there are a large number of small items with relatively similar useful lives, the company has been applying straight-line depreciation of a uniform rate to the machinery as a group. The ratio of this group's total accumulated depreciation to the total cost of the machinery has been steadily increasing and now stands at .75 to 1.00. What is the most likely explanation of this increasing ratio?

(Adapted from the CPA exam.)

13-60. ***DEPLETION*** The Nautral Resources Company has invested $312,000 in developing the Up-River Coal Preserve. Coal reserves are estimated at 600,000 tons. In 19*x*1, 30,000 tons were contracted and sold at $40 a ton.

Required:

(a) Compute the depletion under the cost method.
(b) Compute the depletion under the percentage of sales method if the statutory depletion is 10% and operating expenses are:
   (1) $1,000,000
   (2) $800,000
(c) If operating expenses are $950,000, compute the cash flow after tax for both the cost method and the statutory percentage method.
(d) What is the *effective tax rate* from (c) if the cost method is used for financial reporting and the statutory percentage method is used for tax purposes?

13-61. ***DEVELOPMENT COSTS–AMORTIZATION*** The Fendo Company has incurred significant costs in the development of EDP programs (i.e., software) for major segments of the sales and production scheduling systems.

The EDP program development costs will benefit future periods to the extent that the systems change slowly and the program instructions are compatible with new equipment acquired at three- to six-year intervals. Their service value of the EDP programs is affected almost entirely by changes in the technology of systems and EDP equipment and does not decline with the number of times the program is used. Since many system changes are minor, program instructions frequently can be modified with only minor losses in program efficiency. The frequency of such changes tends to increase with the passage of time.

Required:

(a) Discuss the propriety of classifying the unamortized EDP program development costs as:
   (1) Prepaid expense.
   (2) An intangible fixed asset with limited life.
   (3) A tangible fixed asset.

(b) Numerous methods are available for amortizing assets that benefit future periods. Each method (like a model) presumes that certain conditions exist and, hence, that method is most appropriate under those conditions. Discuss the propriety of amortizing the EDP program development costs with:
   (1) The straight-line method.
   (2) An increasing-charge method (e.g., the annuity method).
   (3) A decreasing-charge method (e.g., the sum-of-the-years'-digits method).
   (4) A variable-charge method (e.g., the units-of-production method).

(Adapted from the CPA exam.)

13-62. ***GROUP DEPRECIATION—DOUBLE DECLINING BALANCE***

Part (a): The Highrise Company buys 100 budget-priced secretarial desks for $140 each. There is no salvage value. The probable lives of the secretarial desks have been computed as follows:

% of Desks	Probable Useful Life
10%	1 year
30%	2 years
40%	3 years
15%	4 years
5%	5 years

In order to minimize record keeping, the Highrise Company elects the group method of depreciation using double-declining balance computation.

During the next four years the Highrise Company experiences the following actual disposals:

No. of Desks	Disposed at End of	Proceeds from Disposal
12	1 yr.	$ 500
35	2 yrs.	$1,100
48	3 yrs.	$ 600
5	4 yrs.	$ 10

Required:

(a) Prepare a schedule showing the *activity* in the asset account, the accumulated depreciation account, and the book value each year.

(b) Give the journal entry at the end of the group life showing the disposition of any gain or loss.

Part (b): Two years from the date of original purchase, the Highrise Company buys twenty more desks for $160 each. The desks are added to the group, and are expected to have the same average life as the original desks. The actual disposals on the first desks are the same as indicated earlier, and the actual disposals on the new desks are as follows:

No. of Desks	Disposed at End of	Proceeds from Disposal
6	2 yrs.	$400
8	3 yrs.	$250
3	4 yrs.	$ 50
3	5 yrs.	0

Required:

(a) Prepare a schedule showing the *activity* in the asset account, the accumulated depreciation account, and the book value each year.
(b) Give the journal entry at the end of the group life showing the disposition of any gain or loss.

13-63. ***INTANGIBLES*** The amortization and write-down or write-off of intangible assets involve basic accounting principles of balance sheet presentation and income determination.

Required:

(a) Give the two broad classifications or types of intangible assets and indicate the factors you would consider in classifying them.
(b) State the generally accepted accounting procedures for the amortization and write-down or write-off of the two classifications of intangible assets.
(c) It has been argued on the grounds of conservatism that all intangible assets should be written off immediately after acquisition. Give the accounting arguments against this treatment.

(From the CPA exam.)

13-64. ***COMPOSITE DEPRECIATION*** Mr. Rent, an apartment owner, chooses to depreciate his investment holdings by combining them into a single composite account. The costs, estimated useful lives, and depreciation methods are as follows:

Asset	Cost	Estimated Life	Depreciation Method	Salvage Value
Building	$600,000	40.0 yrs.	S-L	$50,000
Elevator	20,000	10.0 yrs.	S-Y-D	5,000
Furniture & Fixtures	90,000	4.0 yrs.	D-D	3,000

Required:

Compute the following:

(a) Composite depreciation rate.
(b) Composite depreciation life (without salvage).
(c) Compute the depreciation for each of the first five years assuming the furniture and fixtures are disposed at the end of the fourth year for $4,500 in cash.

UNIT IV

ACCOUNTING INFORMATION FOR OPERATIONS MANAGEMENT

In Unit III we discussed the management of several resources which are crucial to most enterprises: capital, cash, credit, inventory, and long-lived assets (primarily plant and equipment). While the management of resources as discrete entities is important, of even greater significance is the ability to coalesce resources towards purposive ends.

The objective is not merely to hold resources, but to utilize them effectively in order that enterprises may realize their goals. The goal of business enterprises is to maximize return on investment within societal parameters. Nonbusiness enterprises seek the common goal of maximizing the effectiveness of their social services, whether they are cultural, educational, civic, medical, religious, or charitable.

So we move from the study of static resources to their dynamics, for it is in the conjunction and employment of resources that organizations reach their objectives.

The employment of resources in organizations is called *operations management.* In this unit we are concerned primarily with the role of accounting in operations management. As stated in chapters 4 and 5, one of the functions of accounting is to aid, and report on, the management of resources. The income statement, for example, attempts to show how effectively resources have been managed during a specific time period. For this reason the income statement is often referred to as an *operating statement.* This title is quite appropriate to non-profit organizations in which the measurement of "income" is not a key objective. The purpose of the income statement is to report on operations management to persons external to the firm. But the accounting information system plays an even larger role in facilitating operations management within the firm.

In chapter 14, on production operations, we discuss ways in which the accounting systems aids in the production function. We not only discuss the traditional link between accounting and production, but also suggest how accounting data is needed for several operations research techniques relative to production. The purpose is to show that accounting can and must be allied with other disciplines in order to grapple with operational problems of increasing complexity.

In chapter 15, on marketing operations, we consider the relationship of accounting to the marketing function. Again we discuss the traditional link between accounting and marketing, and then go on to show how accounting joins with other analytical tools in planning and controlling complex marketing operations.

In chapter 16, on personnel and administration, we study the role of accounting in aiding the function of administration and the management of our most vital resource: people.

The growing complexity of modern organizations is making operations management more scientific. In turn, operations managers are insisting on more timely and relevant data from the accounting system. The purpose of this unit is to give the student in accounting insight and sensitivity for some of the demands which contemporary operations management is likely to make upon the accounting function.

CHAPTER 14

ACCOUNTING INFORMATION FOR PRODUCTION MANAGEMENT

14.1 THE NATURE OF PRODUCTION MANAGEMENT

The production function is an input-output system. The inputs are resources to the system which include materials, machines, men, and capital. These inputs are transformed through a set of operations into outputs. The outputs of the system are finished products, serviced customers, or completed missions. The transformation processes are not confined to a manufacturing environment. They can also be found in supermarkets, hospitals, and, to some extent, branches of governments. Exhibit 14-1 illustrates a basic production system. Operations in the system differ by the type of business a firm does. In a manufacturing firm, these operations are purchasing of raw materials and supplies; recruiting work force; storing raw material, work-in-process, and finished goods; various machining works, inspection, packaging, and shipment. For a mercantile firm, the operations are purchasing, storing, and sales of products. In a service organization, the production operations are receiving clients and performing services. Operations may occur in series. For example, when finished products are shipped from the factory to a warehouse, they leave the factory sub-system to enter a warehouse sub-system. In this way, the two sub-systems are part of

EXHIBIT 14-1 A GENERAL PRODUCTION SYSTEM

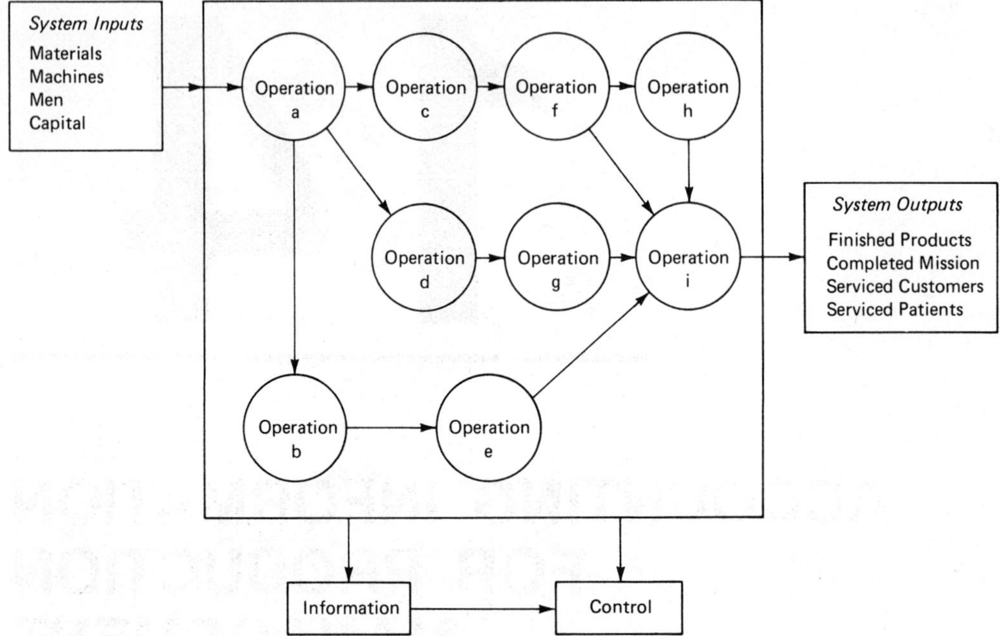

one production system. Operations also may occur in parallel, such as when a number of factories produce similar products to supply several market areas.

The management of these transformation processes is called *production management.* It deals with decision making related to a production system so that the resulting goods or services can be produced to its specification, on time, at a minimum cost.

The principle objectives of production management are to:

1. Satisfy customers concerning delivery dates and quality.
2. Produce and distribute the products at the lowest possible cost.
3. Invest capital efficiently to generate the highest possible return.

These objectives are often mutually inconsistent. For example, the sales department may clamor for quick deliveries and rush orders; the production people want long runs and uninterrupted schedules. It is the responsibility of operations management to coordinate all concerned functions to achieve overall efficiency.

In coordinating the concerned departments, decisions must be made by management. A decision is simply a selection from two or more courses of action. Generally speaking, a decision made at the present time is based upon historical data or experience and establishes a course of action that will result in some future outcome. The outcome can often be represented by a relative value. The sophistication of decision making for a given area depends upon the level of knowledge within the area and the complexity of the decisions to be made. Sometimes we find that criteria and values are clear and straightforward, data are readily obtainable, future values are quite predictable, and risks are fairly clear. In this case, decision making is almost automatic.

In other instances, criteria and values are vague, relevant data are hard to collect, risk and future performance are difficult to predict. The decision will be made by balancing off conflicting values. In all cases, decision making is the attempt to choose those courses of action which have the greatest net value.

In chapter 2, we discussed the general decision making process. We shall briefly review the analytic approach to decision making as a systematic study and quantitative evaluation of the past and future. Intuition is oriented in the present but it incorporates knowledge of the past and estimates of what may happen in the future. It is a reasonable assumption that the analytical approach is more reliable. The process of analytical decision making is shown in Exhibit 14-2.

EXHIBIT 14-2 FLOW OF DECISION MAKING PROCESS

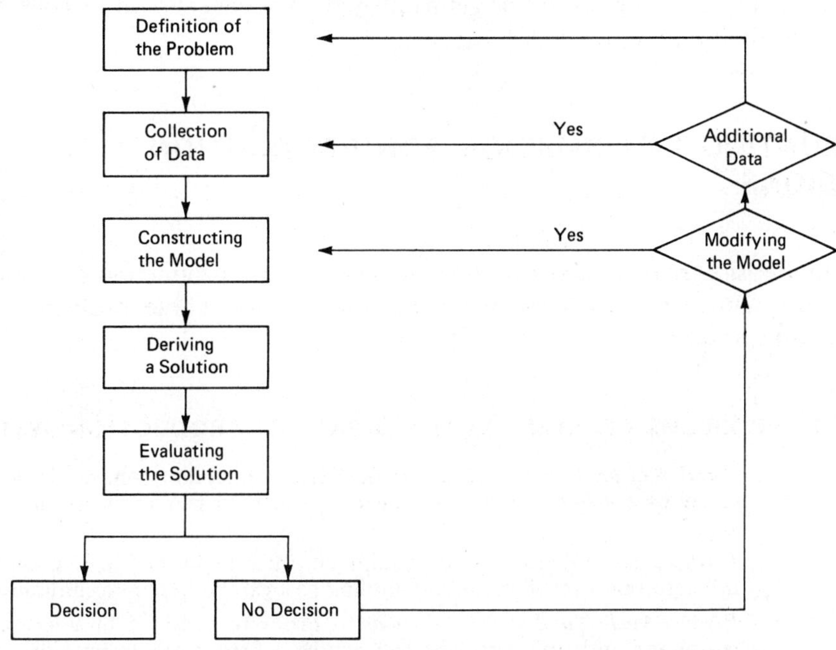

To define a problem, the decision maker should have an exact statement of objectives and alternative ways of pursuing them. Once a problem is defined, quality data from the environment must be collected. There are often factors in a decision situation that cannot be translated into dollars and cents with any pretense of accuracy. The decision maker must recognize that these intangible factors influence a decision just as persuasively as tangible ones.

A model is a representation of the real world. We begin to formulate our model when we develop objectives and alternatives. The model shows the relationship between cause and effect, between objectives and constraints. It is manipulated to show the end product we can expect from following a given course of action. There are physical models, such as a scale-model car; schematic models, like organization charts; and mathematical models. We have discussed some mathematical models in the previous chapters. These include cash flow, inventory, and depreciation models. We will introduce here models that are useful in operations management.

Model builders are confronted with conflicting objectives: to make the model as easy to solve as possible and to make it as accurate as possible. They must also keep in mind the mathematical complexity of the solution, because the decision maker must understand the solution and be capable of using it. Solutions are derived from the model and must be evaluated. The merit of a model is determined by how well it represents the real world. The ultimate test of predicted behavior comes when the predictions are exposed to reality. The veracity of a model can be checked initially by applying it to historical data. If the objective is to predict sales, the data from two years ago can be used as input to predict last year's sales. An agreement between the forecast and actual sales figures indicates that the model can be used for current predictions, provided the decision environment essentially is unchanged.

When the solution from the model is tested, the final authority is the decision maker. He must evaluate the accuracy and reliability of the data and the model. If he is not satisfied, the model should be reformulated, new data should be collected, or the problem should be redefined.

14.2 ACCOUNTING INFORMATION FOR PRODUCTION DECISIONS

As in any decision making process, the management of a production function must identify the nature of problems in production systems. These problems can be divided into two categories:

1. PROBLEMS RELATED TO THE DESIGN OF PRODUCTION SYSTEMS:

a. *Location of production facility.* Location of a production facility should be decided by considering the cost factors related to proximity to markets and supplies.
b. *Facility layout.* Operations and equipment must be located in relation to each other so that overall material-handling cost can be kept at a minimum.
c. *Product mixing and design selection.* In order to satisfy a broader range of customers and utilize facilities efficiently, a firm needs to provide a variety of products or services. Selection of products and their design must be planned carefully in line with productive capability and total profitability.

2. PROBLEMS RELATED TO THE OPERATION AND CONTROL OF PRODUCTION SYSTEM:

a. *Inventory and production control.* Decisions must be made concerning the allocation of production capacity with respect to demand and inventory policy. Feasible schedules must be worked out and performance must be controlled.
b. *Maintenance of facility.* To avoid costly break-downs, maintenance effort must be carried out at a proper level.
c. *Quality control.* Permissible levels of risk for shipping bad products to customers must be established by considering the balance between inspection cost and cost of the loss of sales.
d. *Cost control.* Labor, material, and overhead costs must be controlled.

The relative importance of these problems depends upon the nature of individual firms. However, every production operation has these problems in some degree. When a production manager has identified his problem, pertinent information must be collected for evaluation of alternative courses of action. The most important information is product costs.

Product Costs are all the costs incurred in the creation of a unit of output. They are generally divided into three components of cost: labor, materials, and overhead.

Labor and materials are called *prime costs.* These are costs directly traceable to a unit of output. Labor is called direct labor when the time spent on each unit of production is recorded. Indirect labor is a component of overhead and refers to supervision, janitorial, clerical, and other labor costs that are not traced to units of production.

Direct materials are those materials and supplies which can be clearly identified with physical unity of output. Indirect materials such as paint, grease, and oil are not traceable to any particular unit of production.

Overhead includes all non-traceable manufacturing expenses, indirect materials, and indirect labor associated with production operations. Examples include depreciation of manufacturing facilities and equipment, supervision, utilities, and other expenses that are not directly identified with a unit of output.

The kinds of *cost systems* commonly used are:

1. Job order cost system: determines the cost of each order that is completed.
2. Process cost system: primarily used in continuous manufacturing and involves the determination of average costs per work center.

Under either system, a company may use an actual or a standard cost approach. Under the *actual* method, total costs of a production order are determined by adding up the actual material, labor, and overhead costs incurred during the manufacture of the product. Under the *standard cost* approach, synthetic costs are predetermined and serve as a basis of comparison against actual costs. These matters are discussed further in chapters 18–20.

14.3 ACCOUNTING RULES AND PROCEDURES

Production is subject to certain accounting rules and procedures. Other functional areas closely related to production are research and development and purchasing activities. These areas are subject to the accounting rules and procedures outlined below.

Product research and development expenses: Research and development activities have as their objective the development of new products, improvement of existing products, and improvement in production methods and processes.

Research and development costs can be accounted for in two ways: either expensed or capitalized.

1. *Expensing research and development costs:* Arguments for charging research and development costs to expense when incurred include the following:

a. Where research and development programs are continuous, ongoing programs, such costs should be charged to expense because they are recurring annual costs similar to advertising and administrative expenses.
b. The useful life or beneficial life of research and development costs is usually difficult to estimate. Indeed, it is often impossible to predict whether or not any useful benefits will arise from research and development investments.

2. *Capitalizing research and development costs:* There are also arguments in favor of capitalizing research and development costs.
a. Research and development activities may result in improvements which will benefit future periods, and if such costs are expensed, future revenues will not be matched against their proper costs.
b. When research and development programs are undertaken for other firms or for the government, such costs are capitalized. In some cases, such costs represent reimbursable costs similar to accounts receivable.

14.4 PURCHASING

The accounting rules and procedures concerning purchasing activities deal with the following points:

ITEMS INCLUDED IN PRODUCT COST

The cost of manufacturing a product includes three distinct elements: (a) materials costs, (b) labor costs, and (c) overhead or burden. When different products are processed together, problems as to cost allocation arise. Often product costs are assigned to products on an arbitrary basis because there is no way of determining actual costs, or because it is too difficult to do so (chapter 18).

When finished goods are acquired rather than manufactured, their cost consists of the invoiced price less applicable discounts; in other words, the net purchase price including freight charges.

ITEMS EXCLUDED FROM PRODUCT COST

We have included in the product cost both *direct* and *indirect* product costs; the former are directly associated with units of output, while the latter are not directly associated with separate units of output but *are* incurred in the manufacturing (or purchasing) process. Items excluded from product cost include *selling* expenses and *general and administrative* expenses. These expenses are generally associated with ongoing functional activities not related to the creation of physical output.

COST OF GOODS SOLD

In an income statement, an amount designated as "cost of goods sold" is subtracted from sales to yield gross profit or gross margin. The former amount constitutes the total of all product costs which are considered to apply to goods sold in a given period. All other product costs applicable to goods not yet sold are carried forward in the balance sheet as merchandise inventory. Cost of goods sold contains only product costs and not selling and general and administrative expenses.

ADJUSTMENTS AND OFFSETS TO COST OF GOODS SOLD

There are certain adjustments and offsets to cost of goods sold. These include *discounts* and *returns and allowances* which arise out of purchasing activities.

1. *Discounts:* Purchases of raw materials, finished goods, and supplies often provide for discounts to be taken upon payment. For example, cash discounts are offered by vendors for prompt payment. Any discounts which reduce amounts payable for purchases are deducted from gross purchases on the income statement. Firms enter purchases in their records at gross or net prices. We discussed accounting for cash discounts under the net and gross price methods in chapter 10.
2. *Returns and allowances.* Occasionally goods purchased must be returned to a vendor for various reasons, such as:
   a. Goods are damaged, do not meet specifications or otherwise are unacceptable.
   b. Shipments contain goods not ordered.
   c. Purchaser is overstocked and cannot carry goods at the time.

   The amount of returns in a given period is subtracted from gross purchases.

For similar reasons, a vendor often makes allowances to a purchaser in lieu of receiving returned goods. Such allowances also reduce gross purchases.

14.5 PROCESSING PRODUCTION TRANSACTIONS

Processing production and related transactions involves inputs, transformations, and outputs.

INPUTS

The principal production transactions and related documents are shown in Exhibit 14-3. This exhibit shows the acquisition of raw materials (manufacturing) and finished goods (mercantile), the relocation of goods within a firm, and ultimate sale.

EXHIBIT 14-3 PRODUCTION EVENTS AND RELATED DOCUMENTS

EVENT	TRANSACTION DOCUMENT
A. Raw materials (manufacturing) or finished goods (mercantile) are purchased.	1. *Purchase order* or *invoice.* 2. *Adjustment.* Discounts are taken on purchases as allowable.
B. Goods are relocated.	3. *Requisition.* Raw materials are released. 4. *Credit memo.* Unacceptable goods are returned for credit.
C. Goods are sold.	5. *Invoice* or *shipping order.* Goods are sold and removed from inventory.

EXHIBIT 14-4 THE DUALITY OF SOME TYPICAL PRODUCTION AND RELATED EVENTS

Event	Transaction Document	Date	Notation	Codes			Accounts	Amount	
				Doc.	Trans.	Acct.		Debit	Credit
A. Goods are purchased.	Invoice		a. Raw materials are purchased on account by a manufacturing firm.			11610 21110	Raw Materials Accounts Payable	5,000	5,000
	Invoice		b. Finished goods are purchased by a mercantile firm.			11650 21110	Finished Goods Accounts Payable	3,000	3,000
	Check		c. Paid for purchases after deducting allowable discount.			21110 11110 41170	Accounts Payable Cash Discounts on Purchases	1,000	970 30
B. Goods are relocated.	Adjustment		d. Raw materials are released from stores to work-in-process.			11630 11610	Work in Process Raw Materials	4,000	4,000
	Credit Memo		e. Unacceptable goods are returned.			21110 11610	Accounts Payable Raw Materials	500	500
C. Goods are sold.	Invoice		f. Finished goods are sold and removed from inventory.			41310 11650	Cost of Goods Sold Finished Goods	250	250

TRANSFORMATIONS

Production data undergo two transformations in the accounting system.

Transformation$_1$: Establishing duality or the cause-and-effect relationship of sales events is the function of T_1. Typical T_1 entries for production events are shown in Exhibit 14-4.

Transformation$_2$: Using the T-accounts, the events in Exhibit 14-4 are posted at T_2 as shown in Exhibit 14-5.

EXHIBIT 14-5 POSTING PRODUCTION AND RELATED EVENTS TO T-ACCOUNTS

11110 Cash

fwd	$10,000	(c)	$970

21110 Accounts Payable

(c)	$1,000	(a)	$5,000
(e)	500	(b)	3,000

11610 Raw Materials

(a)	$5,000	(d)	$4,000
		(e)	500

41310 Cost of Goods Sold

(f)	$250		

11650 Finished Goods

(b)	$3,000	(f)	$250

41170 Discounts on Purchases

		(c)	$30

11630 Work in Process

(d)	$4,000		

OUTPUTS

The accounting information system generates statements reporting production and related activities. These reports are of two types:

1. *Financial reports* show purchasing and production activity during a specified period as an integral part of an income statement. Most published annual reports show one amount designated as cost of goods sold (or simply *cost of sales*). However, few published statements show the detail leading to total cost of goods sold and therefore they are not informative about production and purchasing activities.
2. *Management reports* provide detailed break-downs of production costs. Production operations are analyzed in terms of material usage, labor utilization, and overhead application. The structure of output for management depends upon requirements for information. Since the primary purpose of producing output for management is to assist in control of operations, some of the forms of output are discussed in the next section.

14.6 ANALYTICAL TOOLS FOR PRODUCTION MANAGEMENT

Research in war operations by the armed forces during World War II produced new mathematical and computational techniques for solving complex problems. These techniques were adapted and extended by industries after the war. The development of high-speed computers, combined with these techniques, made possible the solution of many large-scale, complex problems in production operations. The function of Operations Research is to apply the scientific method to problems involving the control of organized systems, so as to provide solutions which best serve the purposes of the organization as a whole. An operations research (O.R.) team aids the management in formulating problems, constructing models, deriving solutions, evaluating solutions, and implementing the solutions. Some O.R. techniques are extensively used in solving production problems. These include:

1. Linear Programming
2. Queuing Theory
3. Simulation
4. Quality Control
5. Transfer Pricing

14.7 LINEAR PROGRAMMING

Linear programming (LP) is a mathematical technique for determining the optimum allocation of resources and obtaining a particular objective when there are alternative uses of the resources. Resources may be capital, materials, manpower, machines, or other facilities. Objectives in resource allocation problems are either minimization of cost or maximization of profit.

Since its development two decades ago, LP has been applied successfully in many types of production problems. Some examples are:

1. *Mixing problems:* A product is composed of several ingredients yielding the desired characteristics of the product with varying cost. The objective is to obtain the least costly mix of ingredients which meets the characteristic requirements of the product. Gasoline blending at refineries and cattle feed mixing on farms are examples of this type of problem.
2. *Capacity allocation problems:* The objective is to allocate limited capacity to products so that the profit is maximized.
3. *Assignment problems:* A number of jobs must be handled by various men and/or machines. The objective is to determine the least costly assignment.[1]
4. *Transportation problems:* This type of problem deals with the selection of a minimum cost shipment schedule from various plants with given capacities and costs to various distribution centers with given demands and transportation costs.[2]
5. *Purchasing problems:* For example, a manufacturer wants to know which parts to make and which to buy to maximize profit within plant capacity restrictions.

EXAMPLE OF LINEAR PROGRAMMING

To illustrate the basic concepts of linear programming, let us examine the following simplified example.

[1] For further discussion, refer to chapter 16, section 16.2.

[2] See chapter 15, section 15.4.

A small machine shop makes two products, P1 and P2; they must be processed by three machines, M1, M2, and M3. The times required to make a unit of each product are given in Exhibit 14-6. A unit of P1 yields a profit of $9, and P2 yields $10.

Assuming that any combination of P1 and P2 can be sold, how much of P1 and P2 should be manufactured each month in order to maximize total profit?

EXHIBIT 14-6 TIME REQUIREMENTS (IN MINUTES)

	Machine 1	Machine 2	Machine 3
Product 1	11	7	6
Product 2	9	12	16
Monthly Time Available	9,900	8,400	9,600

The objective in this example is to maximize profit; let us call x_1 the number of units of product P1, and x_2 the number of units of P2. Then, z is the function to be maximized, where:

$$z = 9x_1 + 10x_2 \quad (1)$$

Because there is no meaning for negative x_1 and x_2, we must have

$$x_1 \geqslant 0,\ x_2 \geqslant 0 \quad (2)$$

Since the total time required on the machines must not exceed their available capacities, we have the following constraints:

$$11x_1 + 9x_2 \leqslant 9{,}900 \text{ for Machine M1} \quad (3)$$
$$7x_1 + 12x_2 \leqslant 8{,}400 \text{ for Machine M2} \quad (4)$$
$$6x_1 + 16x_2 \leqslant 9{,}600 \text{ for Machine M3} \quad (5)$$

Let us explore what the constraints mean in geometrical terms. In Exhibit 14-7, we draw the following straight lines:

$$L_1 = 11x_1 + 9x_2 = 9{,}900 \quad (6)$$
$$L_2 = 7x_1 + 12x_2 = 8{,}400 \quad (7)$$
$$L_3 = 6x_1 + 16x_2 = 9{,}600 \quad (8)$$

By constraint (2), our solution must lie in the first quadrant formed by the x_1 and x_2 axes. Constraints (3), (4), and (5) restrict our solution to the unshaded portion. Let us consider, for example, the solution $x_1 = 450$, $x_2 = 100$ (point S_1), which gives us:

$$z = 9 \times 450 + 10 \times 100 = 5{,}050 \text{ (dollars)}$$

EXHIBIT 14-7 GRAPHIC SOLUTION OF SAMPLE PROBLEM

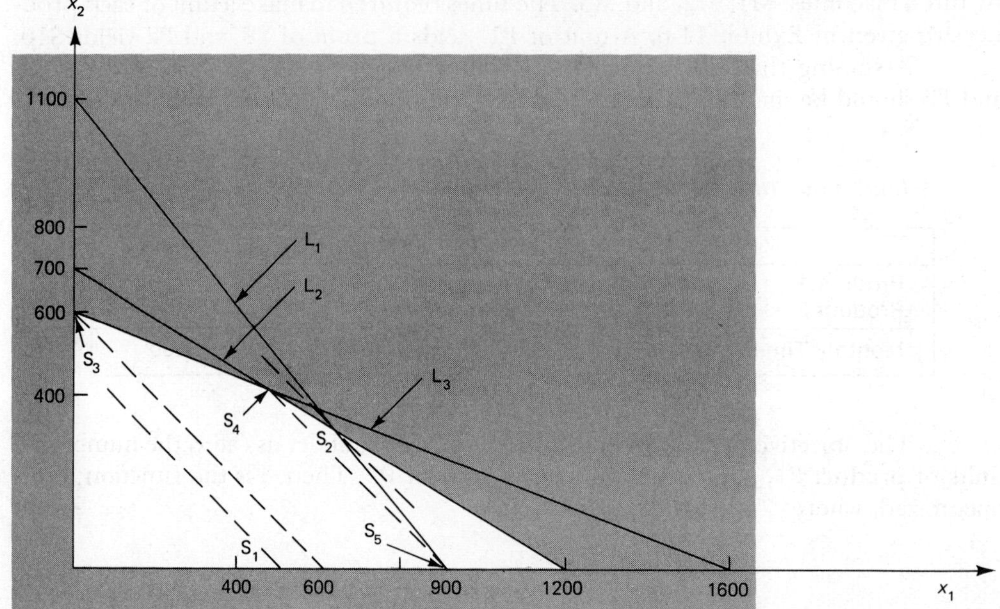

It is obvious that this is not maximum, since if we move in the direction of the arrow we increase the value of z while continuing to meet the requirements of the constraints.

Let us use a dotted line to represent the function (1) for a particular value of z. Since the coefficients 9 and 10 are invariant, this line will remain parallel to itself when the value of z is changed.

When we shift the line corresponding to z, we note that at point S_2, where the L_1 and L_2 intersect, we have the highest value for z; thus:

$$\text{Max. } z = 9 \times 626 + 10 \times 334 = 8{,}974 \text{ (dollars)}$$

It should be observed that the maximum must always correspond to one of the corners of the feasible region, that is, S_2, S_3, S_4, or S_5. This provides us with a graphical method for solving problems with two variables. By analogy the *Simplex Method* for computing more complex problems was developed.

The solution $x_1 = 626$, $x_2 = 334$ (rounded to the nearest integers) corresponds to the full use of machines M1 and M2, but machine M3 has idle time of

$$9{,}600 - (6 \times 626 + 16 \times 334) = 500 \text{ (minutes)}$$

From Exhibit 14-7, we observe that the three machines would be fully used only if the three lines representing the constraints intersect at a single point.

A solution with just as many variables permitted to be nonzero as there are constraints, with all other variables being forced to be zero, is called a *basic solution.* The variables that are permitted to be nonzero are called *basic variables;* together they form a *basis.* If basic variables also satisfy the constraints and are non-negative, they represent a point in the feasible region, and we have a *basic feasible solution.*

As in our example, the constraints are often in inequality form. To convert them into equations, auxiliary variables are introduced. Such a variable is called a *slack variable.* Sometimes we introduce another type of auxiliary variable to form an initial basis. Once the value of such a variable becomes zero, it is driven out of the basis. This type of variable is called an *artificial variable.*

Other terms used in a normal formulation of an LP problem are illustrated in Exhibit 14-8.

EXHIBIT 14-8 THE TERMINOLOGY USED IN DESCRIBING THE NORMAL FORMULATION OF A LINEAR PROGRAMMING PROBLEM (MATRIX FORMULATION)

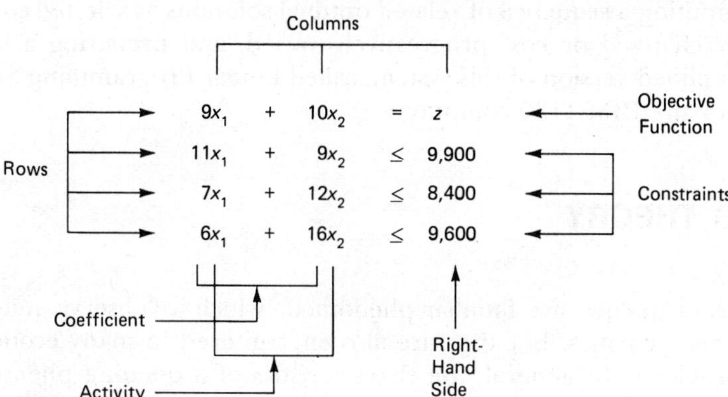

CHARACTERISTICS OF LINEAR PROGRAMMING

LP is a powerful tool but it is not a cure-all. The following limitations should be kept in mind when applying linear programming:

1. A problem must have a definite, identified, numerical goal. The goal, or objective function, has to be stated as the sum of a series of terms, each consisting of the product of the activity level and a constant multiplier which is the cost or profit per unit of that activity. The goal can only be to maximize the total profit or minimize total cost, whichever is appropriate. Problems like "increase efficiency" or "improve customer service" cannot be solved by LP.
2. There must be separate and identifiable activities, and the level of each activity must be measurable in numerical terms. In our example, the activities are the amount of each product to be manufactured.
3. The activities must be interrelated. For instance, the two products in our example must share the same type of machines in different levels. If they require entirely different machines, we cannot formulate it as a linear programming problem.
4. All activities must appear in linear combinations only, both in the objective function and in the constraints. It is not permissible for two or more variables to be multiplied together, squared, or assume any other nonlinear forms.
5. All constraints must be identified and stated in numerical terms. Statements like "the bottleneck is the polishing machine" cannot be considered as a constraint. We must know just how many hours per day or month are available. Failure to state all the constraints will lead to misleading results.

Some of these limitations can be overcome. For example, in many problems, we can use linear approximation for nonlinear activities without loss of validity. However, these limitations must be kept in mind in selecting linear programming methods to solve problems.

Computer programs have been developed to solve large LP problems. These programs are easy to use and can solve problems with several thousands of rows and virtually unlimited numbers of columns. For example, the Mathematical Programming System/360 (MPS/360) developed for the IBM System 360 computers can solve problems with 300 constraints in a matter of hours. Use of MPS/360 involves building the mathematical model, finding an optimal solution, determining the ranges of the objective function elements and right-hand side elements for which the solution is optimal, computing a sequence of related optimal solutions as selected constraints are progressively changed or cost progressively varied, and preparing a management report. A simplified version of this system, called Linear Programming System (LPS), is available for the IBM 1130 computers.

14.8 QUEUING THEORY

Waiting lines, or queues, are familiar phenomena which we observe quite frequently in our personal activities, but they are also encountered in many economic, social, and other problems. In general, the characteristics of a queuing phenomenon are:

1. Units arrive, at regular or irregular intervals of time, at a place called the service center.
2. One or more service channels or service stations are assembled at the service center.
3. Units wait in the service center, according to a certain priority rule, to be serviced and then leave the service center.

Exhibit 14-9 shows some examples of queuing phenomena.

EXHIBIT 14-9 EXAMPLES OF QUEUING PHENOMENA

ARRIVALS	NATURE OF SERVICE	SERVICE STATIONS
Customers	Check out groceries	Check-out counters
Ships	Unloading	Docks
Planes	Landing	Runways
Telephone calls	Conversation	Telephone circuits
Defective machines	Repairs	Mechanics
Patients	Treatment	Beds in hospital

Whenever waiting lines form in an economic system there is reason to question the situation. A line-up means congestion. The cost of congestion may be directly observable, as ships waiting for unloading, or the costs may be more subtle, as when a potential customer leaves a barber shop that has a waiting line. But there is also a cost associated with relieving congestion. Providing more services, more docks, or more barbers eliminates congestion at the risk of creating excess service capacity. A queuing problem consists of either *scheduling arrivals* or *providing facilities*, or both, to minimize the sum of the costs of waiting customers and idle facilities.

STRUCTURE OF QUEUING SYSTEM

Let us define the following notations:

m = number of units in the total situation; it may be finite or infinite.
n = number of units in the system, including those waiting in line or being served.
v = number of units waiting in line.
j = number of units being served.
p = number of idled service stations.
s = number of service stations.

With these notations, we illustrate a general queuing problem in Exhibit 14-10.

EXHIBIT 14-10 STRUCTURE OF A GENERAL QUEUING SYSTEM

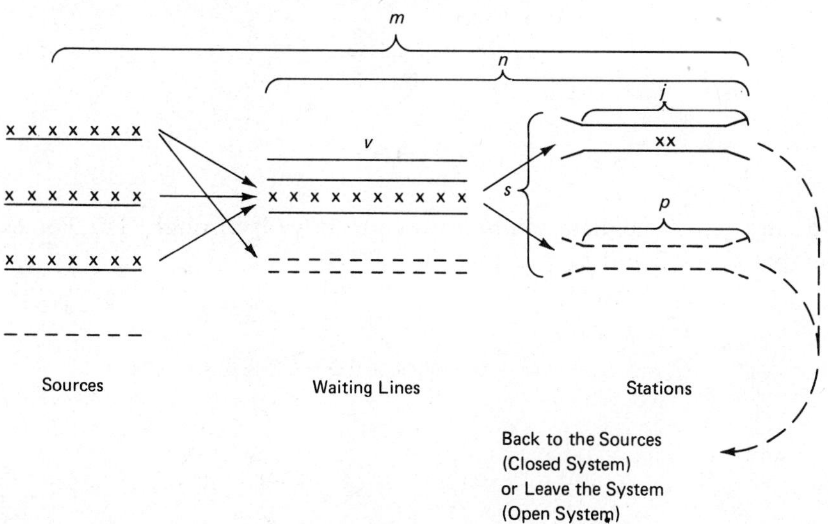

The basic concept in the analysis of a queuing process is that of a *state* of the system. A state is a description of the system that provides a sufficient basis for predicting future behavior probabilistically. The essential point about such predictions is that they do not require information about how the state came about, only what it is. This concept might be more clear by examining an example.

Assume a maintenance man checks on machines each month and that past experience shows that if a machine broke down last month, the chance of the same machine breaking down this month is p_1, and if there was no break-down last month, then the chance is p_0. Let us define the first month as month 0, the second month as month 1, and so on. Then in any month after the first one, each machine must be in one of two states:

State 0 = no break-down last month
State 1 = one break-down last month

If we know a machine's present state and p_0, p_1, we can predict its future behavior.

Let U_n be the probability of a break-down in month n for a machine which had no break-down in the first month, and W_n be the corresponding probability for a machine which had a break-down in the first month. We can construct the following equation for a machine which was in State 0 in month 1:

$$U_{n+1} = p_1 U_n + p_0(1 - U_n) \qquad n > 0 \tag{9}$$

for a machine which was in State 1 in month 1, the equation is

$$W_{n+1} = p_1 W_n + p_0(1 - W_n) \qquad n > 0 \tag{10}$$

Notice that

$$U_1 = p_0 \tag{11}$$

and

$$W_1 = p_1 \tag{12}$$

Given p_0 and p_1, we tabulate solutions to equations (9) through (12). For example, suppose that $p_0 = 0.2$ and $p_1 = 0.4$, we obtain

$$U_1 = p_0 = 0.2$$
$$U_2 = p_1 U_1 + p_0(1 - U_n) = 0.4 \times 0.2 + 0.2 \times 0.8 = 0.24$$

and

$$W_1 = p_1 = 0.4$$
$$W_2 = p_1 W_1 + p_0(1 - W_1) = 0.4 \times 0.4 + 0.2 \times 0.6 = 0.28$$

Exhibit 14-11 shows the results for $n = 1, 2, \ldots, 6$.

EXHIBIT 14-11 STATE PROBABILITIES

n	1	2	3	4	5	6
U_n	0.2	0.24	0.248	0.2496	0.2499	0.2500
W_n	0.4	0.28	0.256	0.2561	0.2503	0.2500

Examination of Exhibit 14-11 suggests that both U_n and W_n settle down to the same value as n becomes larger. When we reach this state, $U_n = W_n$, we call it the *steady-state* probability. One interpretation of a steady-state probability is that in the long run, independent of the state in the initial month, there will be a break-down 25% of the time.

Steady-state probabilities are of considerable interest because they are useful in predicting long-run profits and costs. Unless we know that the queuing process will terminate before it reaches a steady state, knowledge of the steady-state probabilities is usually sufficient to solve the queuing problem. To arrive at these steady-state probabilities, it often involves the solution of partial differential equations.

For most practical problems, it is assumed that the arrival pattern follows a Poisson distribution and service times follow an exponential distribution. The following formulae are applicable to this type of problem:

$$\text{Length of queue} = \frac{A^2}{S(S-A)} \tag{13}$$

$$\text{Average waiting time in queue} = \frac{A}{S(S-A)} \tag{14}$$

$$\text{Average waiting time in queue and service} = \frac{1}{S-A} \tag{15}$$

where A is the arrival rate and S is the service rate.

We shall demonstrate the application of these equations with a simplified example.

EXAMPLE OF A QUEUING PROBLEM[3]

Logging trucks arriving at a lumber mill follow a Poisson distribution with an average of three trucks each hour. After the trucks arrive, they unload the logs in a pond at an exponential rate averaging four per hour. The lumber mill is considering the replacement of the present log dump with a new unloading facility which is expected to provide an exponential service rate of S = six trucks per hour. The initial cost would be \$200,000 with no salvage value at the end of its ten-year life. The cost of an idle truck is \$20 per hour. With cost of capital valued at 10% and no salvage expected from the present facility, should the investment be made? From (13) we have:

$$\frac{3^2}{4(4-3)} = \frac{9}{4} = 2.25 \text{ trucks waiting in line}$$

From (14), the average time a truck waiting in queue is

$$\frac{3}{4(4-3)} = \frac{3}{4} = 0.75 \text{ hour}$$

[3]The example is from James L. Riggs, *Economic Decision Models for Engineers and Managers* (New York: McGraw-Hill Book Company, 1968), pp. 322–23. Used with permission.

From (15), the logging trucks on the average spent

$$\frac{1}{4-3} = 1 \text{ hour}$$

at the unloading dock.

Based on a forty-hour week with fifty working weeks per year, the annual waiting time cost for the present facility is:

Arrival rate × Waiting at unloading dock × cost of idle truck × hours per year
$= 3 \times 1 \times 20 \times (40 \times 50) = \$120{,}000$

The same cost for the new facility will be

$$3 \times \frac{1}{6-3} = 20 \times 2000 = \$40{,}000$$

Hence, the annual savings for the new unloader are:

$$\$120{,}000 - \$40{,}000 = \$80{,}000$$

14.9 SIMULATION

Many real-life management problems are difficult if not impossible to solve analytically. A variety of queuing-type problems are in this category. When decisions involve the number of servers at a service facility, efficiency of the servers, or the number of service facilities, we have to select the appropriate probability distribution for the pattern of arrivals and for the service times before we can choose a proper queuing model. To obtain these probability distributions, sufficient statistical data must be collected. Even if this could be accomplished, we still have to make some generalization of the problem in order to solve it analytically.

The technique of simulation involves the construction of a model which is largely mathematical in nature. The simulation model describes the operation of a system in terms of individual events or components of the system. The system is divided into elements whose behavior can be predicted, at least by probability distributions, for each of the various possible states of the system and its inputs. Thus, simulation provides a means of dividing the model-building job into smaller component parts, and then combining these parts in their logical order to study their interaction on each other. After constructing the model, it is then activated by generating input data to simulate the actual operation of the system and record its aggregate behavior. By repeating this for different alternative design configurations and comparing their performances, we can identify the most promising configuration.

One problem in production operation which has been frequently simulated is the *job shop.* A primary characteristic of a job shop is the great diversity of jobs to be performed. A job shop produces primarily to customer orders. Each job requires a different set and sequence of operations. Only very limited analytical procedures are available for helping to solve this problem.

The main considerations in designing and operating a job shop are the cost of having idle machine and labor capacity, the cost of work-in-process inventory, and the need to meet the specified completion dates. Unfortunately, these considerations tend to conflict with each other. For example, one can have a low cost of idle machine and labor capacity by providing only a minimum amount of machinery and manpower. But this would result in considerable delay, and thus increase work-in-process inventories and slippage in delivery.

Simulating a job shop can be helpful in many ways. First, it can identify potential bottlenecks of a given operating design which can be resolved before actual operation. Second, it provides a means for testing suggested changes regarding machine and labor capacity. Third, it can be used to forecast workloads in various work areas of the job shop and thereby develop more realistic schedules and estimated completion dates. Finally, various job dispatch rules can be simulated to compare their effect on the performance of the system and thereby determine which one meets management's objectives most closely.

A thorough understanding of the real operation of the system is needed in order to construct a simulation model. The designer begins by reducing the real system to a logical flow diagram. Ultimately, the system is decomposed into a set of elements for which operating rules are given. These operating rules predict the events that will be generated by the corresponding elements. At this stage, random numbers are generated according to probability distributions. After specifying these elements, rules, and logical linkages, the model should be tested thoroughly piece by piece. If any information is available regarding the aggregate behavior of some form of the real system, it is worthwhile to verify that this behavior is predicted reasonably well by the corresponding simulated system.

Due to the complexities of most real systems formulated by simulation models, computers must be used. Since the purpose of simulation studies is to compare alternatives, computer programs for simulation must be flexible enough to accommodate readily the alternatives that are being considered. Most of the instructions in a simulation program are logical operations, whereas the relatively little actual arithmetic work required is usually of a very simple nature. These considerations motivated the development of general simulation programming languages in the early 1960s. These languages are designed to expedite the kind of programming unique to simulation. They also provide some type of internal timing and control mechanism to assist in the kind of bookkeeping that is required when executing a simulation run.

For all of these reasons, a simulation program almost always should be written in one of these simulation languages rather than a general programming language. Some of the best known general simulation languages are SIMSCRIPT, GPSS, and DYNAMO.

14.10 PRODUCTION AND QUALITY CONTROL

Generally speaking, the control of production operations involves control over the *amount produced, quality control,* and *cost control.* The amount to produce in a given period depends upon the most economical combination of capacities in relation to demand. Analytical techniques such as linear programming, queuing theory, simulation, and inventory theory are useful in planning the amount of production. Once the amount of production is planned and scheduled, and information system should be established to feed back current information on the status of production for control purposes.

Cost control is concerned with the day-to-day operating decisions which affect production cost. Costs are a result and function of activities involved. If activities are controlled properly, then resulting costs are controlled.

The control of quality is based on the design of processes and the selection of equipment. The basic quality capabilities must be designed into the production system. Given these basic capabilities, desired quality levels are controlled by selecting adequately trained personnel, maintaining suitable plant and equipment, and controlling raw materials and quality characteristics of finished products.

The techniques of quality control are centered in inspection methods and statistical control methods. Statistical control methods fall into two categories; (1) acceptance sampling and (2) process control. *Acceptance sampling* involves the determination of the probability that the entire lot of materials or products meets quality standards on the basis of a few samples. *Process control* involves a continuous or periodic sampling of the output of a process to check if quality standards are within limits.

In order to be sure of the quality of each item in a lot, it is necessary to inspect every item. If the product has been processed under quality-control conditions, a good idea of the average quality of the products in a lot can be formed by merely inspecting a sample taken at random from the lot. Hence, the purpose of sampling is to reduce the cost of inspection without sacrificing too much of the quality of the product. In any sampling operation, there are always some errors or risks involved. The risk that a bad lot will be accepted is called the *consumer's risk.* Similarly, a good lot may be rejected from time to time, this type of risk is called the *producer's risk.*

Military Standard Inspection plans are available which can be used in quality control. These plans are based on binomial and Poisson distributions. When using these plans it is necessary to decide the acceptable quality level. This is a nominal value expressed in terms of percent defective.

Another way to specify a particular sampling plan is to indicate the random size, n, and the number of defectives in the sample, c, permitted before the entire lot is rejected. The operating characteristic (OC) curve for a particular combination of n and c shows how well the plan discriminates between good and bad lots. Exhibit 14-12 shows an OC curve for a sampling plan with $n = 50$ and $c = 1$. This curve shows the probability of acceptance of a lot for various values of percent defectives in the lot. For example, if the actual lot quality were 2%, samples of $n = 50$ would accept the lot as satisfactory about 73% of the time and reject it about 27% of the time.

There are two reasons why a production process may result in variations from normal performance. One is due to a combination of minor causes, none of which can account for any significant part of the outcome. This is called *random* or *chance cause.* The other is due to specific traceable causes and is called *assignable cause.* When a process is in a state of statistical control, defective items are due to chance variation only. With the control chart, when variations due to one or more assignable causes occur, they will appear on the chart, thus prompting proper attention.

Control charts are based on the theory that the occurrence of defective items follows a certain probability distribution. Usually a binomial, a Poisson, or a normal distribution is used. The mean of the selected distribution indicates the average

EXHIBIT 14-12 OC CURVE FOR SAMPLING PLAN (n = 50 AND c = 1)

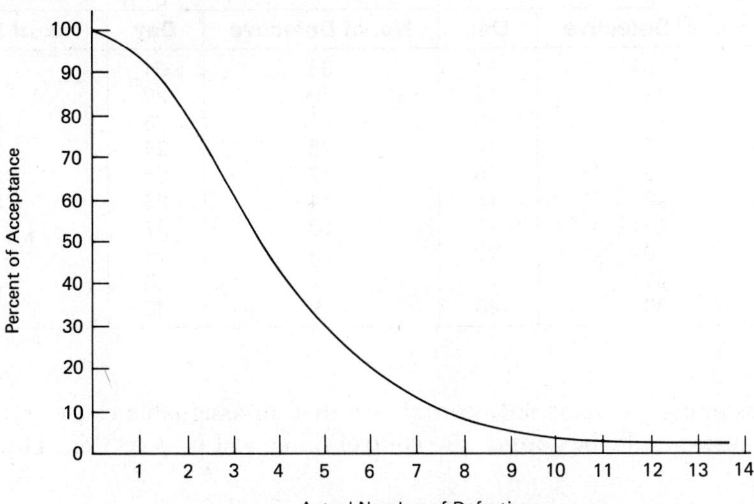

process. The control limits are set at the process average plus and minus a given number of standard deviations, depending on the tightness of the control. When the control limits are exceeded, the process is *out of control* but most likely has an assignable cause.

Exhibit 14-14 shows a control chart for the proportion of defectives (p-charts) based on the binomial distribution. The mean of a binomial distribution is:

$$\bar{p} = \frac{x}{n} = \frac{\text{total number of defectives}}{\text{total number observed}} \tag{16}$$

and the standard deviation is:

$$S_p = \sqrt{\frac{\bar{p}(1-\bar{p})}{n_d}} \tag{17}$$

where n_d is the number of observations made in one day.

Exhibit 14-13 shows the results of the production and inspection of 100 items a day for thirty days. Based on these data, we obtain:

$$\bar{p} = \frac{549}{30 \times 100} = 0.183$$

and

$$S_p = \sqrt{\frac{0.183 \times (1-0.183)}{100}} = 0.039$$

EXHIBIT 14-13 RESULTS OF INSPECTION OF 100 ITEMS DAILY FOR 30 DAYS

Day	No. of Defective	Day	No. of Defective	Day	No. of Defective
1	6	11	33	21	12
2	11	12	39	22	4
3	20	13	25	23	23
4	22	14	18	24	27
5	9	15	17	25	31
6	40	16	14	26	33
7	12	17	13	27	16
8	10	18	5	28	14
9	31	19	7	29	11
10	30	20	9	30	7

Assuming we want 99% confidence that an assignable cause (rather than a random cause) would be found, the control limits will be $p \pm 3\ S_p$. Thus we have:

$$\text{Mean} = \bar{p} = 0.183$$
$$\text{Upper Control Limit (UCL)} = \bar{p} + 3\ S_p = 0.3$$
$$\text{Lower Control Limit (LCL)} = \bar{p} - 3\ S_p = 0.066$$

These data are plotted in Exhibit 14-14.

EXHIBIT 14-14 CONTROL CHART FOR PROPORTION OF DEFECTIVES

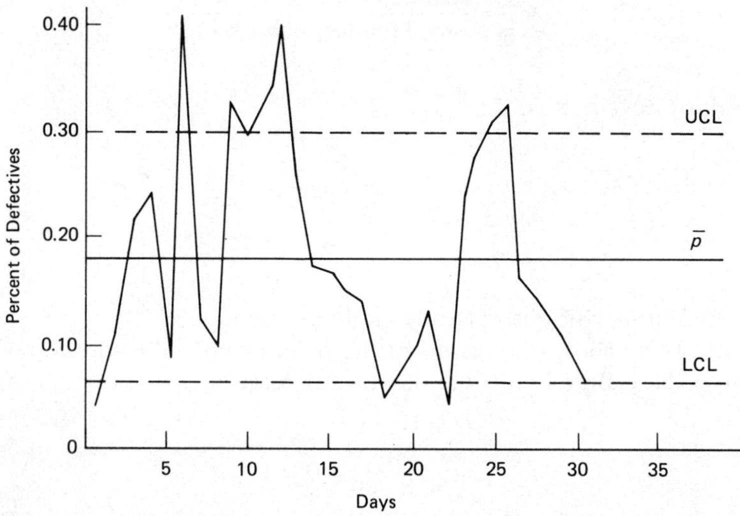

14.11 TRANSFER PRICING

In a divisionalized company, whenever transactions among divisions make up more than a negligible proportion of the total transactions, the division's relative profitability can be affected by the policy used for pricing inter-divisional business. Since transfer prices are an essential part of profit measurement, they should help management evaluate the performance of the divisions or profit centers viewed as separate entities. They must also motivate them to act in a manner which is conducive to the success of the company as a whole.

There are three commonly used methods in determining transfer prices among divisions: (1) market price, (2) marginal cost, and (3) shadow price.

MARKET PRICE

The theoretical grounds for the *market price* method is that in a competitive market for transferred products, a division can satisfy its needs for intermediate products by buying them outside at the going price. It would be in the company's interest to do so to prevent another division from incurring incremental costs of a greater amount in supplying the intermediate product. If the transfer price for the intermediate product is set at its market price, the transferor division can supply as much as it wishes, leaving the transferee division to acquire any additional supplies it may need by outside purchase. Similarly, the transferor division may be able to supply more of the intermediate product at the market price than the consuming division can use. This postulates a highly theoretical condition that the total profit of the company would not be affected if the supplier division did no business with the other divisions, but sold all of the output on the market, leaving the consuming divisions to buy all their requirements outside. However, in real life, such behavior would not be likely to leave the company's profit unchanged. The supplier division would incur selling expenses in making outside sales which would not occur on interdivisional transfers. On the other hand, it would probably cost the consuming divisions no more to buy from another company than to buy from another division of their own company. In recognition of this fact, many companies modify the market price method by deducting from the market price a margin estimated to cover either the whole, or a part, of the selling and collection expenses. Thus the transferee division saves on internal transfers as compared with outside sales.

The drawback of the market price method is the difficulty of determining intermediate prices. Several factors, such as the sensitivity of market demand to quantities and the discount for particular types of traders, create this situation. All these factors are due to the rare existence of perfectly competitive markets. In a perfectly competitive market there would be one price for one product, and that price would not be sensitive to the quantities bought or sold by the divisions of a single company. For basic raw materials, such as steel, wood pulp, lumber, and the like, with the modest degrees of imperfection, market price can be an appropriate basis for transfer pricing.

MARGINAL COST

If a good competitive market for the intermediate product is lacking, or if for any other reason there is not a well-defined market for it independently of the quantity bought or sold by the divisions of the company themselves, then another basis of transfer pricing has to be found. The transfer price conducive to maximizing the corporation's profits is the *marginal* or *incremental cost* of the transfer division for that output at which this marginal cost equals the transfereė division's net marginal revenue from using the transferred products.

The method of marginal or incremental cost works the same way as in the make-or-buy decisions within a division. The company will compare the cost of buying from outside with the incremental cost of producing by another division. The assumptions of the marginal cost method are:

1. The cost of the intermediate products transferred among divisions is a continuous function of the volume of the output of the transferor division.
2. The transferor division always has the capacity to meet all demands made on it up to the point where the incremental cost of further output equals the incremental value of the output to the company.

If production facilities are inadequate, or other resources constitute a bottleneck which restricts the output of the intermediate below what is needed to satisfy the consuming division, the marginal cost method will not result in a satisfactory allocation of the intermediate product.

SHADOW PRICES

The existence of capacity constraints in the divisions making intermediate products complicates the transfer pricing problem. The development of linear programming and other mathematical programming techniques contributes two remarkable things in solving this problem. One is the optimal allocation of resources, as we discussed earlier. The other is to provide a set of values to be attached to the scarce resources limiting output. These values are called *shadow prices.* The shadow prices indicate the amount by which total profits would be increased if the producing division could increase its productive capacity by a unit. Most of the existing computer programs for solving mathematical programming problems will yield these shadow prices under the subject of post-optimization analysis.

The shadow prices could not be used directly as transfer prices. To turn shadow prices into transfer prices, we would have to add on the variable cost of the materials.

14.12 SYSTEMS CONTROLS FOR PRODUCTION OPERATIONS

Production operations are subject to stewardship and management controls.

STEWARDSHIP CONTROLS

Stewardship controls are designed to safeguard assets and insure proper recording of transactions. With regard to production operation, the following areas are important control points:

Bids, Quotations, Contracts

It is the function of a purchasing department to obtain bids and quotations and to let contracts. A goal of stewardship controls is to prevent improper purchasing resulting in "kickbacks" to purchasing officials. Fair purchasing requires obtaining independent bids and impartially selecting the lowest bid. In order to ensure that feedback exists, contracts should be negotiated and let by someone not involved with obtaining and comparing bids.

Acquisition and Requisition

Acquisition of goods and supplies purchased should be made by a separate receiving department which prepares a *receiving report.* The receiving report is then compared with the original purchase order for quality and completeness.

After acquisition by a receiving department, goods must be moved immediately to *stores,* where they are safeguarded until required by production operations. Materials are issued only upon receipt of an authorized *requisition.* Such requisitions are generally prepared in triplicate: one copy goes to the storekeeper, another copy is retained by the department making the request, and another copy moves to the accounting department for keeping track of goods within the firm.

Scrap

Most manufacturing operations generate scrap, which consists of small pieces of material which are unusable in operations. Managing scrap is a control problem relating to production efficiency. Disposing of scrap is a stewardship control problem. Scrap is generally salable and therefore its disposition must be approved by responsible authorities.

MANAGEMENT CONTROLS

Management controls have as their objective the reduction of production costs and the achievement of optimum purchasing activities. Management controls include the following:

Standards and Budgets[4]

The essence of any management control system is the setting of standards and comparison of actual amounts against budgets. In production operations the setting of standards for materials and labor involves analysis of all phases of production. Such

[4]For further discussion, refer to chapter 23.

analysis often brings benefits in itself. Insights are gained in the process of setting standards because of the close review of operations. Standards are set for the price and quantity of materials and the price and quality of labor. Such standards are used by management as "yardsticks" against which actual results are compared; any significant differences between actual and standard amounts (called variances) are investigated.

Standards are incorporated into budgets, which are operating plans expressed in dollars. Forecasting the future is vital to all businesses and to most individuals. Such forecasting, when put into quantitative terms, is a *budget.* Actual operations are compared to budgeted amounts and any significant deviations are investigated for cause. Sometimes deviations may be caused by unrealistic budgeting practices; usually, however, deviations from budget reflect poor implementation of managerial policies. This, then, is the way in which budgets aid in managerial control.

Variances

We have already discussed above that the differences between actual and standard costs are called *variances.* When management is aware of such variances and can analyze them, they are an invaluable aid in management control of production operations.

Standards are usually set for each one of the three components of manufacturing or product cost:

1. *Materials.* Standards are set for *material usage* and for *material price.* If excessive materials are consumed in production operations, the accounting information system generates material usage variances which point up such usage. Similarly, if prices paid for materials acquired exceed predetermined standards, material price variances will result. The output of such variances signals the need for investigation.
2. *Labor.* Standards are also set for labor utilization and labor rates. Should either utilization or rates deviate from standard, variances will result. Such variances could be either *favorable* or *unfavorable.* If favorable, the variance is in the company's favor; that is, rates or prices utilization achieved are lower than standard. Unfavorable variances constitute increases over standard. Both favorable and unfavorable variances should be investigated, because continued favorable variances could suggest that standards have been set too low.
3. *Overhead.* As we discussed before, overhead consists of all manufacturing costs not included under direct materials and labor. Standards should also be set for such costs based upon what costs should be under standard production. Overhead variances can be computed in a number of ways. Under certain methods, two overhead variances would be generated; under other methods three and four variances are generated to analyze different aspects of overhead costs.

Applied Overhead

Since overhead costs usually do not accumulate in direct proportion to production, estimated amounts of overhead are charged to production on some rational basis.

This process is called *applying overhead.* When actual overhead costs for a period are accumulated and compared with the amounts applied to production, there is usually either more or less applied than was actually incurred. When more overhead is applied than incurred, the *over-applied* amount could suggest greater production than anticipated, overestimation of overhead costs, or a combination of those factors. Similarly, *under-applied* amounts suggest the reverse: less production than anticipated, underestimation of overhead costs.

Best Source

The objective of purchasing activities is to secure materials at the best possible *prices* and on the best possible *terms.* Included in this objective is that the best source of supply should be obtained. A source of supply (vendor) is rated according to the following factors:

1. Ability to supply the quantities required: in other words, is the supplier able to deliver a large order, or must he gear up capacity?
2. Ability to deliver in accordance with time schedules.
3. Quality requirements: are shipments of a consistent acceptable quality?
4. Prices: are prices and terms competitive?

The selection of suppliers should be made on the basis of these factors. Periodically, the selection of suppliers should be reviewed to determine whether any bias is evident in the selection process.

14.13 SYSTEMS FEEDBACK FOR PRODUCTION OPERATIONS

Feedback on production operations include the following types of reports which are generated by the accounting information system: (1) control reports, (2) exception reports, (3) comparative reports, and (4) interpretive reports.

CONTROL REPORTS

Feedback on stewardship and management controls exist in several forms. Feedback on stewardship controls of production operations include:

1. Cost of goods manufactured and sold sections of income statements.
2. Detailed schedules containing analyses of material purchases, direct labor categories, and manufacturing overhead break-downs.
3. Reports of auditors examining manufacturing cost records, purchasing records, and other production purchasing data.

Feedback on management controls include reports detailing the following items:

1. Material usage and scrap produced.
2. Labor utilization in terms of production hours, idle time, overtime, and other statistics.
3. Statistics concerning the number of units produced, average quality factors, and number of rejects.

EXCEPTION REPORTS

Exception reports outline any material departure from plan. Material, labor, and overhead *variances* constitute exceptions. Such variances point up the differences between actual conditions and planned or standard amounts. Significant variances require investigation; insignificant variances do not fall within the meaning of *exception reporting* and usually do not require investigation.

COMPARATIVE REPORTS

Comparative reports show current results against (1) results of prior periods and (2) planned levels. For example, a weekly material cost report would show current costs of materials consumed, prior period material costs, and comparison with standard costs. Such reports aid in evaluating a firm's current operating position.

INTERPRETIVE REPORTS

Interpretive reports contain explanations of differences shown in the reports listed above. For example, a weekly labor report which shows actual and standard hours would be an interpretive report if the variances shown were analyzed in terms of causes such as training time, waiting due to lack of material, and machine break-down.

14.14 SUMMARY

The production function is an input-output system. The management of production operations deals with decision making related to efficient use of resources to transform inputs into outputs.

Cost information is essential to production management. It assists management in identifying problems. It provides foundations for analyzing problems and selecting alternative courses of action. Costs related to production operations are subject to accounting rules and procedures.

The development of Operations Research techniques, since the end of World

War II, greatly improved the analytical tools for the analysis of production problems. Basic concepts of linear programming, queuing theory, simulation, and statistical quality control were presented in this chapter. It is aimed to equip the reader with some fundamental knowledge about these subjects rather than to give a complete treatment of their theories.

Transfer pricing is important to divisionalized control. Three methods for setting up transfer prices between producing and consuming divisions were discussed. These are market price, marginal cost, and shadow prices.

Stewardship and management controls are vital to production operations. Control, exception, comparative, and interpretive reports generated by the accounting information system provide feedback on production operations.

CHAPTER 14 REFERENCES AND ADDITIONAL READINGS

GENERAL

Abramovitz, Irving. *Production Management.* New York: The Ronald Press Company, 1967.

Bock, Robert H., and Holstein, William K. *Production Planning and Control.* Columbus, Ohio: Charles E. Merrill Publishing Co., 1963.

Buffa, Elwood S. *Modern Production Management.* New York: John Wiley & Sons, Inc., 1969.

Buffa, Elwood S. *Models for Production and Operations Management.* New York: John Wiley & Sons, Inc., 1963.

Corcoran, A. Wayne. *Mathematical Applications in Accounting.* New York: Harcourt, Brace & World, Inc., 1968.

Daverio, Paul V., and Goslin, Lewis N. "Innovation in Production Technology." *Business Horizons,* June 1968, pp. 47–54.

Enrick, Norbert L. "Sales Production Coordination through Mathematical Programming." *Management Services,* September–October 1964, pp. 21–29.

Hillier, F. S., and Lieberman, G. J. *Introduction to Operations Research.* San Francisco: Holden-Day, Inc., 1968.

Holstein, William K. "Production Planning and Control Integrated." *Harvard Business Review,* May–June 1968, pp. 121–40.

Link, Philip A. "The Role of Production Control in Cost Control." *Industrial Management,* July 1969, pp. 3–10.

Moore, Roger L. "Manufacturing Management: Planning for Production Control." *The Journal of Accountancy,* August 1969, pp. 82–84.

Niebel, Benjamin W., and Baldwin, Edward N. *Designing for Production.* Homewood, Ill.: Richard D. Irwin, Inc., 1963.

Plossl, G. W., and Wight O. W. *Production and Inventory Control.* Englewood Cliffs, N. J.: Prentice-Hall, Inc., 1967.

Riggs, J. L. *Economic Decision Models for Engineers and Managers.* New York: McGraw-Hill Book Company, 1968.

Schrier, Elliot. "Production Planning in a Multiplant System." *California Management Review,* Summer 1969, pp. 69–78.

Solomons, David. *Divisional Reporting: Measurement and Control.* Homewood, Ill.: Richard D. Irwin, Inc., 1965.

Staley, John D., and Delloff, Irving A. *Improving Individual Productivity.* New York: American Management Association, Inc., 1963.

Techniques for Forecasting Product Demand. Management Services Technical Study No. 7. New York: American Institute of Certified Public Accountants, 1968.

Theil, Henri; Boot, John C. G.; and Kloek, Teun. *Operations Research and Quantitative Economics.* New York: McGraw-Hill Book Company, 1965.

Walter, John R. "Computer-Based Production Control." *Canadian Chartered Accountant,* August 1966, pp. 108–111.

LINEAR PROGRAMMING

Adams, Tom H. "Use of Linear Programming in the Selection of Optimal Shipping Points." *Transportation Journal,* Spring 1969, pp. 11–20.

Demski, Joel S. "An Accounting System Structured on a Linear Programming Model." *The Accounting Review,* October 1967, pp. 701–712.

Dorfman, Robert; Samuelson, Paul A.; and Solow, Robert M. *Linear Programming and Economic Analysis.* New York: McGraw-Hill Book Company, 1958.

Feltham, Gerald A. "Some Quantitative Approaches to Planning for Multi-product Production Systems." *The Accounting Review,* January 1970, pp. 11–26.

Raun, Donald L. "Product-Mix Analysis by Linear Programming." *Management Accounting,* January 1966, pp. 3–13.

Szandtner, T. A. B. "The Transportation Problem—A Special Case of Linear Programming." *Canadian Chartered Accountant,* February 1970, pp. 127–30.

Thompson, Gerald E. *Linear Programming.* New York: The Macmillan Company, 1971.

Tummins, Marvin. "A Simple Method of Linear Programming." *Management Services,* January–February 1966, pp. 44–50.

QUEUING THEORY

Coffman, E. G. "Studying Multiprogramming Systems." *Datamation,* June 1967, pp. 47, 49–51.

MacLachlan, Duncan. "Operations Research and Servicing Problems." *Canadian Chartered Accountant,* April 1963, pp. 266–70.

Shuchman, Abe, ed. *Scientific Decision Making in Business: Readings in Operations Research for Nonmathematicians.* New York: Holt, Rinehart & Winston, Inc., 1963.

SIMULATION

Cremeans, John E. "The Trend in Simulation." *Computers and Automation,* January 1968, pp. 44–48.

Kay, Ira M. "An Executive's Primer on Simulation." *Data Processing Magazine,* October 1966, pp. 52–57.

Marland, Robert E. "A Simulation Model for Determining Scrap Decision Rules in the Metal Processing Industry." *Production and Inventory Control,* First Quarter 1970, pp. 29–35.

Story, Richard M. "The Use of Simulation to Solve a Queueing Problem." *Management Services,* January–February 1968, pp. 58–61.

Tyran, Michael R. "A Computerized Decision Simulator Model." *Management Accounting,* March 1971, pp. 19–26.

Zivan, Seymour M. "The Zerox Model for Long-Range Planning." *Business Economics,* Spring 1967, pp. 52–55.

QUALITY CONTROL

Adams, Charles F. "Quality Control and the Challenge of Change." *Industrial Management,* May 1969, pp. 6–8.

McElwee, Leonard F. "Sustaining Error-Free Performance." *Management Accounting,* December 1967, pp. 42–50.

Nigra, Alphonse L. "Quality Control of Data Through Statistical Control." *Management Services,* May–June 1970.

Perry C. R. "Zero Defects as a Motivational Tool." *Systems and Procedures Journal,* March–April 1967.

TRANSFER PRICING

Bierman, Harold Jr., and Dyckman, Thomas R. "Transfer Pricing." In *Managerial Cost Accounting*, Bierman and Dyckman. New York: The Macmillan Company, 1971, pp. 219–42.

Hass, J. E. "Transfer Pricing in a Decentralized Firm." *Management Science*, February 1968, pp. 310–11.

Hirschleifer, J. "On the Economics of Transfer Pricing." *Journal of Business*, July 1956, pp. 172–84.

Ronen, J., and Copeland, R. "Transfer Pricing for Divisional Autonomy." *Journal of Accounting Research*, Spring 1970, pp. 99–112.

CHAPTER 14 QUESTIONS, PROBLEMS, AND CASES

14- 1. Describe the purposes of production management.

14- 2. Describe the production operations of the transformation process found in a:
(a) Manufacturing firm
(b) Mercantile firm
(c) Service organization

14- 3. Identify the two broad categories of problems in a production system and give specific examples under each. How is the identification of these problems important to the production function?

14- 4. Explain how the following account balances are handled in the income statement:
(a) Purchases discounts lost
(b) Freight charges on purchases
(c) Indirect production labor
(d) Research and development costs
(e) Salesmen's commissions
(f) Sales discounts
(g) Purchases returns and allowances
(h) Purchases discounts

14- 5. "The role of accounting in production management is limited to generating the information needed to prepare the cost of goods sold section in the income statement." Discuss.

14- 6. Define or explain the use of the following linear programming terms or phrases:
(a) Slack variable
(b) Artificial variable
(c) Basic solution
(d) Basic variables
(e) Basic feasible solution
(f) Objective function

14- 7. Identify and describe five limitations to the application of linear programming.

14- 8. Distinguish among *physical, schematic,* and *mathematical* models. Give examples of each in accounting.

14- 9. Cite five types of production problems to which linear programming has been successfully applied.

14-10. Describe the analytic approach to decision making. How does it differ from simple intuition? Identify the parts of the analytic decision making process:

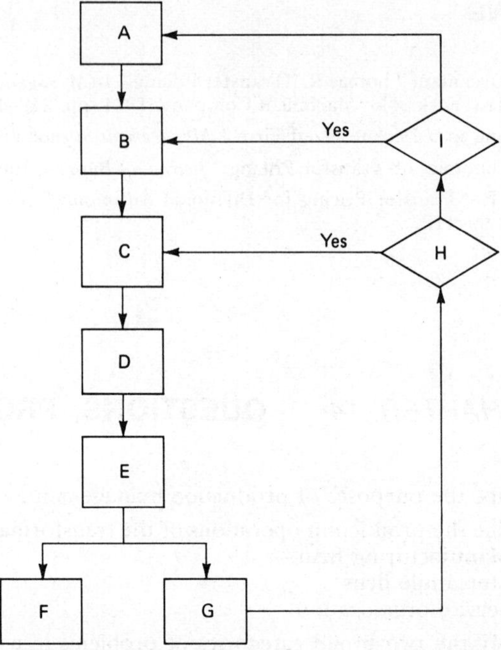

14-11. Cite the three principle objectives in production management. "These objectives are often mutually inconsistent." Explain these inconsistencies by giving specific examples.

14-12. What accounting treatment is given to the following production events:
(a) Discounts, trade, and cash
(b) Returns
(c) Raw materials enter work-in-process

14-13. Give the rudimentary distinction between:
(a) Job order cost system and process cost system
(b) Actual cost approach and standard cost approach

14-14. (a) Describe the type of problem that is the objective of each of the following operations research techniques:
(1) Linear programming
(2) Queuing theory
(3) Simulation
(4) Quality control
(5) Transfer pricing

(b) Describe how each one of these techniques can be used to solve an accounting-related problem in areas other than production.

14-15. Identify the parts of the normal formulation of a linear programming problem:

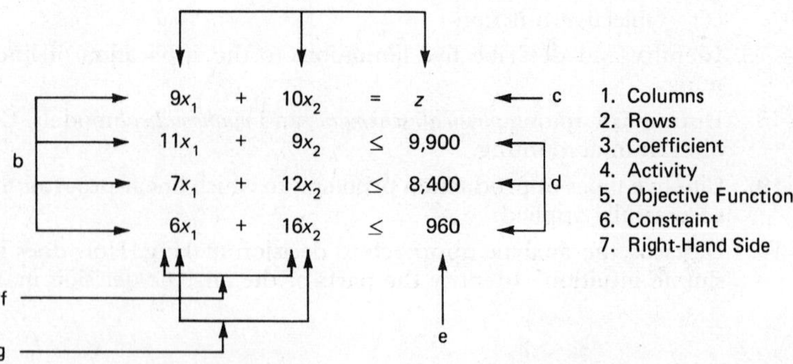

14-16. Define or explain the use of the following terms or phrases:
(a) Prime costs
(b) Acceptance sampling
(c) Process control
(d) Military standard inspection plans
(e) Random or chance cause
(f) Assignable cause
(g) Upper control limit
(h) Lower control limit
(i) Shadow prices
(j) Receiving report
(k) Material requisition
(l) Scrap

14-17. What are three general characteristics of a queuing phenomenon? Give several specific examples of the phenomena.

14-18. In a queuing process, what is the significance of "the state of the system"?

14-19. "Steady-state probabilities are of considerable interest because they are useful in predicting long-run profits and costs." What is a steady-state probability and how is it used for prediction?

14-20. Explain the process of constructing a simulation model.

14-21. One frequently simulated production operation is the *job shop*. Explain at least four operational benefits to be derived from this simulation model.

14-22. With a quality control procedure based upon statistical sampling, there are some risks involved. Distinguish between the *consumer's risk* and the *producer's risk*.

14-23. Explain the theory and construction of a *control chart*.

14-24. What are the two principle assumptions underlying the marginal cost method for determining transfer prices between divisions?

14-25. Discuss four factors used in rating a source of materials supply.

14-26. Cite arguments in favor of *expensing* and *capitalizing* research and development costs.

14-27. ***TRANSFER PRICING*** The Denes Company has two internal divisions, A and B. The revenues and expenses of both are combined to determine the net income of the company. In the past, division B has always purchased division A's output. Division A sells its output of component parts for $2 apiece. This year, however, the market price for a comparable component part dropped to $1.80. Will the company benefit or lose if division B purchases its needed 6,000 component parts from an outside supplier, providing division A can produce a different component part with only a 5¢ increase in variable costs (no change in fixed costs) and can sell at least 6,500 to an outside buyer at $1.90? Currently, division A's variable cost per unit is $1.80 and total fixed costs are $4,000.

Required:

Give the *dollar amount* of benefit or loss to the Denes Company if B purchases from an outside supplier.

14-28. ***QUEUING THEORY*** MacKenzie Park has recently experienced costly production slowdowns due to maintenance problems in its assembly department. There are four machines in the department and one repairman to service them. Experience indicates that the repairman can service ten machines in one eight-hour day if necessary and that three machines generally require his services during any one day.

Management is considering the employment of a second repairman for the department and has asked for your advice. It has been decided that the company will hire the second repairman if it is found that the average time a machine lies idle waiting to be serviced exceeds one hour.

Should a second repairman be hired? Will one additional repairman be enough to reduce the idle waiting time to less than one hour? Show the computations supporting your conclusions.

(Adapted from the CPA exam.)

14-29. ***JOURNALIZING*** Give the journal entry for each of the following events and determine the ending balance of each account affected (assume zero beginning balances).

(a) \$7,000 in raw materials are purchased on account with terms of 3/10, n/30, f.o.b. shipping point. The company pays the freight of \$300. The purchase is recorded using the net method.
(b) \$2,400 in raw material is purchased for cash. The freight of \$75 is paid by the seller.
(c) The purchase in (a) is paid for within the discount period.
(d) \$4,200 in raw materials are requisitioned into production.
(e) \$800 of the raw materials purchased in (b) are defective. The seller notifies the company that an allowance of \$650 will be credited against the debt.
(f) \$1,600 in raw materials are requisitioned into production.
(g) \$8,000 in direct labor was expended on production this period.
(h) 18,000 units of production are finished. The cost of this production is \$8,100.
(i) 14,000 units with a cost of \$6,300 are sold for \$9,800.

14-30. ***QUEUING THEORY—STEADY-STATE PROBABILITY*** The Syverson Company uses an automatic conveyor system for transporting raw materials into the production area. Since the conveyor is constantly in operation, it breaks down frequently and with an average lost production time of three hours. In order to evaluate the cost of production and compile suitable budget figures, the company wishes to formulate the steady-state probability of the conveyor system break-down during any given week. From past experience the company has estimated that if the conveyor broke down in one week, it has a 50% chance of breaking down the next week. If there is no break-down in one week, however, the chance of break-down the next week is 80%.

Required:

Compute the steady-state probability that the Syverson Company's conveyor system will break down in any given month (compute answer to four significant digits).

14-31. ***LINEAR PROGRAMMING*** Beekley, Inc. manufactures widgets, gadgets, and trinkets and has asked for advice in determining the best production mix for its three products. Demand for the company's products is excellent, and management finds that it is unable to meet potential sales with existing plant capacity.

Each product goes through three operations: milling, grinding, and painting. The effective weekly departmental capacities in minutes are: milling —10,000; grinding—14,000; and painting—10,000.

The following data is available on the three products:

	Selling Price Per Unit	Variable Cost Per Unit	Per Unit Production Time (in Minutes) Milling	Grinding	Painting
Widgets	$5.52	$4.45	4	8	4
Gadgets	5.00	3.90	10	4	2
Trinkets	4.50	3.30	4	8	2

Required:

(a) Determine the following in equation form:
  (1) The objective function.
  (2) The capacity constraints.
  (3) The non-negativity requirements.

(b) Describe the linear programming problem in normal form (matrix form), including any slack variables.

(Adapted from the CPA exam.)

14-32. ***LINEAR PROGRAMMING*** Suppose the Tanner Corporation produces two products—a high-quality tennis racket (Model Q) and a budget tennis racket (Model B). The company has only twelve production workers, each working an eight-hour day for 250 days in a year. There are three stringing machines that are operated full-time by three of the production workers. A special nylon string used on both models is in short supply and only 12,000 yards are available per year.

Model Q (the high-quality tennis racket) yields a profit of $18 per racket, while Model B (the budget tennis racket) yields a profit of $3 per racket. Some time and material specifications of each model are as follows:

	Model Q	Model B
Labor hours to complete one frame	20	4
Time to string one frame	3	2
Yards of string per racket	10	8

Required:

(a) If the Tanner Corporation wishes to maximize profit it can set up a linear programming model. For such model, determine:
  (1) The objective function.
  (2) The constraints.

(b) Set up the objective function and constraints in normal format (matrix formulation).

(c) Determine the approximate quantities of Model Q and Model B that should be produced to maximize profit. Present a graphical solution.

14-33. ***LINEAR PROGRAMMING*** The cost accountant of the Stangren Corporation, your client, wants your opinion of a technique suggested to him by a young accounting graduate he employed as a cost analyst. The following information was furnished you for the corporation's two products, trinkets and gadgets:

(a)

EXHIBIT A
DAILY CAPACITIES IN UNITS

	Cutting Department	Finishing Department	Sales Price Per Unit	Variable Cost Per Unit
Trinkets	400	240	$50	$30
or				
Gadgets	200	320	$70	$40

(b) The daily capacities of each department represent the maximum production for *either* trinkets *or* gadgets. However, any combination of trinkets and gadgets can be produced as long as the maximum capacity of the department is not exceeded. For example, two trinkets can be produced in the Cutting Department for each gadget not produced and three trinkets can be produced in the Finishing Department for every four gadgets not produced.
(c) Material shortages prohibit the production of more than 180 gadgets per day.
(d) Exhibit B is a graphic expression of simultaneous linear equations developed from the production information above.

EXHIBIT B
GRAPH OF PRODUCTION RELATIONSHIPS

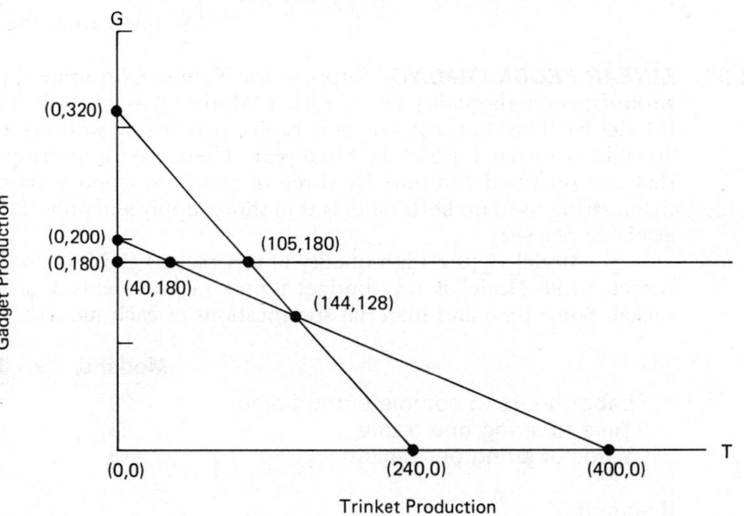

Required:

(1) For what kinds of decisions are contribution margin data (revenue in excess of variable cost) useful?
(2) Comparing the information in Exhibit A with the graph in Exhibit B, identify and list the graphic location (coordinates) of the:
   a. Cutting Department's capacity.
   b. Production limitation for gadgets because of the materials shortage.
   c. Area of feasible (possible) production combinations.
(3) a. Compute the contribution margin per unit for trinkets and gadgets.
   b. Compute the total contribution margin of each of the points of intersections of lines bounding the feasible (possible) production area.
   c. Identify the best production alternative.

(From the CPA exam.)

14-34. ***QUEUING THEORY*** Customers arrive at the Save-More Market following a Poisson Distribution at an average rate of eighty customers per hour. After shopping the customer can go through any of the open check-out stands. Normally, five check-out stands are open and can handle an average of twenty customers per hour at each stand (check-out times follow an exponential distribution). If customers have to wait at the check-out stands too long, some will begin shopping at other markets. The Save-More Market manager estimates that for every two hours of time spent by customers in the check-out lines and for service, the store will lose $50 worth of monthly shopping.

Required:

(a) Compute the length of a check-out queue.
(b) Compute the average waiting time in a queue.
(c) Compute the average waiting time in the queue and for service.
(d) Based on a 365-day operation for ten hours a day, what is the annual waiting time cost for the Save-More Market?
(e) Compute parts (a) through (d) if each check-out stand handles an average of only eighteen customers per hour.

14-35. ***LINEAR PROGRAMMING*** A company markets two products, Alpha and Gamma. The marginal contributions per gallon are $5 for Alpha and $4 for Gamma. Both products consist of two ingredients, D and K. Alpha contains 80% D and 20% K, while the proportions of the same ingredients in Gamma are 40% and 60% respectively. The current inventory is 16,000 gallons of D and 6,000 gallons of K. The only company producing D and K is on strike and will neither deliver nor produce them in the foreseeable future. The company wishes to know the numbers of gallons of Alpha and Gamma that it should produce with its present stock of raw materials in order to maximize its total revenue.

Required:

(a) Express the following in equation form:
    (1) The objective function.
    (2) The constraint imposed by the quantity of D.
    (3) The constraint imposed by the quantity of K.
    (4) The non-negativity requirement.
(b) With a graphical analysis, determine the production of Alpha and Gamma which will maximize total revenue of the company.
(c) Assuming that the marginal contributions per gallon are $7 for Alpha and $9 for Gamma, what quantities of Alpha and Gamma should be produced to maximize total revenue?

(Adapted from the CPA exam.)

14-36. ***QUALITY CONTROL CHART*** The Marflex Corporation produces glass jars for sale to jam and jelly manufacturers. At the end of the production process a quality control inspector visually inspects a sample of glass jars for quality impairment. Approximately 300 jars per day are inspected at various staggered times throughout the day. If the number of defectives exceed the acceptable control limit for two succeeding days, production is stopped and the production machinery is overhauled. After each overhaul, new quality control limits are established based upon the inspection results for the first twenty days of new operations. Following the last overhaul, the first twenty days inspection results were:

Day	No. of Defective	Day	No. of Defective
1	24	11	40
2	16	12	27
3	12	13	12
4	38	14	18
5	26	15	51
6	10	16	102
7	70	17	23
8	58	18	15
9	13	19	61
10	42	20	46

Required:

(a) Compute the *upper* and *lower* quality control limits for the period following the last overhaul, based on control limits set at ±2 standard deviations.

(b) For each of the following inspection samples indicate whether the production quality is acceptable:

(1) 104
(2) 16
(3) 180
(4) 34
(5) 56

CHAPTER

15

ACCOUNTING INFORMATION FOR MARKETING MANAGEMENT

15.1 THE NATURE OF MARKETING MANAGEMENT

The Committee on Definitions of the American Marketing Association defines *marketing* as: "The performance of business activities that direct the flow of goods and services from producer to consumer or user."[1] The foundation for marketing operations is the satisfaction of these consumer wants. The creation and satisfaction of these wants provides the rationale for a firm's existence, and the degree to which they are satisfied provides information as to the efficiency of the firm.

Frequently the study of marketing management is viewed along quite narrow lines. For example, the management of sales operations must be blended with consideration of other subjects such as product planning, pricing, advertising, personal selling, and distribution. The management of sales operations alone should not be referred to as marketing management. Providing accounting information for marketing decisions within this broad context is the subject of this chapter.

[1] R. S. Alexander et al., *Marketing Definitions: A Glossary of Marketing Terms* (New York: American Marketing Association, 1960), p. 15; reprinted in "Report of The Definitions Committee," *Journal of Marketing* 13 (October 1948): 202.

EXHIBIT 15-1 THE MARKETING CYCLE

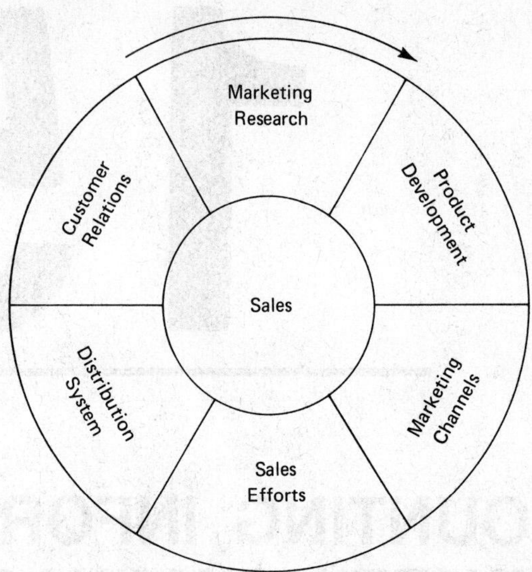

Marketing operations proceed through successive stages which will be called the *marketing cycle.* As illustrated in Exhibit 15-1, the cycle begins with marketing research, with the mission of analyzing market demands. Product development involves the manufacture or purchase of goods in demand or goods for which demand will be created. Marketing channels are analyzed and an optimum network of intermediaries is established. The network of marketing intermediates is connected with the distribution system which allows a firm to supply goods and meet demand. Sales effort is required to create and maintain demand. In order to maintain demand a program of good customer relations must be established. All of these activities contribute to making *sales,* which is the prime objective of marketing operations.

Before we discuss the scope of marketing management and some of the tools used in making decisions regarding various marketing activities, let us distinguish *revenue* from *sales. Revenue* is defined as those accounting events which give rise to an increase in retained earnings. *Sales* is a form of revenue that arises from the sale of a firm's goods or services in the ordinary course of business. Exhibit 15-2 contains examples to clarify the difference between these terms.

EXHIBIT 15-2 EXAMPLES OF REVENUE AND SALES

Transaction	Revenue	Sales
1. Sales of goods or services in the ordinary course of business:		
(a) on credit.	X	X
(b) for cash.	X	X
2. Gain on sale of long-lived assets.	X	
3. Settlement of a liability for less than its face value.	X	
4. Non-operating income.	X	

15.2 TIMING REVENUE: RECOGNITION VERSUS REALIZATION

Revenue is recognized when a transaction is admitted to the accounting system. There are several criteria for recognizing revenue. If a credit sale is made, for example, the revenue (sale) could be recorded (recognized) at the point of sale *or* only when payment is received (realized). In this example, the recognition of revenue precedes realization.

Revenue timing, in part, is determined by accounting convention. Firms that use the *cash basis* of accounting recognize revenue at the point of realization; while those that use the *accrual basis* of accounting recognize revenue at the point where there is a legal right to receive payment, e.g., where title is deemed to have passed from seller to buyer. Under the accrual method of accounting the *sales basis* of recognizing revenue is the customary accounting role. However, there are certain exceptions to the sales basis of recognizing revenue.

1. *Post sale:* In some cases, revenue may be recognized after a sale. This is common in the case of *installment* or contract sales. Such sales are made subject to a series of periodic payments (installments), with the seller retaining legal title to the goods. Due to the long period of collections, revenue is recognized as payments are received.[2]

   Installment sales is an important aspect of economic growth–it allows sales to be greatly expanded without the requirement of immediate realization. The buyer promises to pay for goods or services in installments over an extended period of time. In the case of real or personal property, the seller generally attempts to reduce the risk of noncollection by retaining legal title to the goods until full payment is eventually received.

   The problem, from an accounting viewpoint, centers on the question of profit recognition. Two methods are widely used: either (a) recognize profit at the time of sale or (b) defer recognition over the life of the contract. The first method treats an installment sale as a regular credit sale, while the second–the installment method of accounting–treats each cash installment (including down payment) as a partial return of cost and a partial realization of gross profit. For example, if goods costing $900 are sold for $1,200, the deferred gross profit is $300. The cost–gross profit ratio of 75:25 is used to divide all subsequent cash collections into a recovery of cost and a *realization* of deferred gross profit. If a $160 installment payment is received, $120 (75% of $160) is regarded as recovery of cost, and $40 (25% of $160) is regarded as a realization of gross profit. By the time the last installment payment is received, deferred gross profit will have been reduced to zero.

   For a *nondealer sale,* the deferred gross profit account balance is established *immediately* as the difference between selling price and *all* costs and expenses from the sale. For example, suppose the Perkins Company sells land for $25,000. Commissions and other expenses are $2,000, and the original cost of the land is $18,000:

			% of Selling Price
Selling price		$25,000	100%
Less: Original cost	$18,000		
Commissions & other	2,000	20,000	80%
Gross profit		$ 5,000	20%

[2]The installment method of recognizing revenue is permitted for federal income tax purposes.

At the end of the year, an amount equal to 20% of the year's cash collections on installments is transferred from the deferred gross profit account into the realized gross profit account.

For a *dealer sale,* the deferred gross profit account is established at the *end of the year* as the difference between total installment sales and the cost of installment sales:

Total installment sales	$240,000	100%
Less: Cost of installment sales	168,000	70%
Gross profit	$ 72,000	30%

The average gross profit percentage is computed from this relationship and used to determine the amount transferred to the realized gross profit account. A new percentage is computed each year and is applied selectively to cash collections from sales originating in that year. For instance, suppose the last four years had gross profit rates of 20%, 22%, 18%, and 25% respectively. For collections received in 19*x*4, the amount of gross profit realized is:

	Cash Collections in 19x4	Gross Profit Rate	Realized Gross Profit
19*x*1 installment sales	$120,000	20%	$ 24,000
19*x*2 installment sales	190,000	22%	41,800
19*x*3 installment sales	175,000	18%	31,500
19*x*4 installment sales	230,000	25%	57,500
Total cash collections in 19x4	$715,000		
Total gross profit realized			$154,800

2. *Prior to sale:* In some cases, revenue is recognized prior to a sale when realization is assured and the amount can be determined. Revenue in this case is recognized during production and/or at the end of production, but before actual sale. Two primary examples are (a) long-term contracts such as construction, and (b) in extractive industries such as mining gold.[3] With long-term contracts, it is an acceptable accounting practice to recognize revenue on the basis of *percentage of completion* of the contract. These percentages of completion are based on production schedules and may differ from periodic payments under the contract. Two methods are in current use: the percentage of completion may be based on (a) an engineering estimate of the proportion of work completed, or (b) the relationship between costs incurred and estimated total completion costs.[4]

As an example of the second method, suppose the High-Rise Corporation is constructing an office building complex for a contract price of $20 million. Applicable data for the first two years are:

	19x1	19x2
Construction costs	$ 4,200,000	$4,600,000
Estimated costs to complete	13,300,000	9,000,000
Collections from contract billings	4,700,000	5,050,000

[3] In extractive industries it is also an acceptable practice to recognize sale of gold or other specie (1) where a firm contract of sale exists, and (2) where production is assured.

[4] There is some theoretical difficulty justifying this treatment since many construction projects require substantial initial outlays for material even before there has been any distinguishable progress toward completion.

The *revenue* and *gross profit* earned by the High-Rise Corporation in 19*x*1 and 19*x*2 are calculated as follows:

19x1

1. **Percentage of Completion**

Actual costs (cumulative)	$ 4,200,000
Estimated costs to complete the contract	13,300,000
Total estimated costs	$17,500,000

% of Completion = Actual Cost/Total Estimated Costs
% of Completion = $4,200,000/$17,500,000
% of Completion = 24%

2. **Revenue and Gross Profit**

Revenue = % of Completion × Contract Price
Revenue = 24% × $20,000,000
Revenue = $4,800,000

Gross Profit = Earned Revenue − Actual Costs
Gross Profit = $4,800,000 − $4,200,000
Gross Profit = $600,000

19x2

1. **Percentage of Completion**

Actual costs (cumulative)	$ 8,800,000
Estimated costs to complete the contract	9,000,000
Total estimated costs	$17,800,000

% of Completion = Actual Cost/Total Estimated Costs
% of Completion = $8,800,000/$17,800,000
% of Completion = 49%

2. **Revenue and Gross Profit**

Revenue = (% of Completion × Contract Price) −
Revenue Recognized in Prior Periods
Revenue = (49% × $20,000,000) − $4,800,000
Revenue = $9,800,000 − $4,800,000
Revenue = $5,000,000

Gross Profit = Earned Revenue − Actual Costs
Gross Profit = $5,000,000 − $4,600,000
Gross Profit = $400,000

There is uncollected revenue of $100,000 (total earned revenue less total collections) in 19*x*1 and $50,000 in 19*x*2. For financial statement purposes, these amounts are shown as receivables in their respective years.[5] If the contract billings exceed the total accumulated construction cost, the excess is shown as a liability. The propriety of this dual treatment lies in the effort to recognize the earned

[5]Normally, accountants will distinguish between the "billed" and "unbilled" portion of the receivable with the unbilled portion representing the unreimbursed construction costs.

revenue still to be received, while at the same time recognizing the liability for a return of gross profit if the contract is not satisfactorily completed.

Service companies sell services, not products. The basis for recognizing revenue for service companies is the point at which a service is rendered. Generally a billing is made when the service is complete, but billing may be made at various stages of completion. Sometimes a billing may be made prior to the rendering of a service (i.e., retainers); such billings are not taken into earned revenue until the service is performed.

The timing of revenue recognition may differ in tax reporting versus financial accounting reporting. Timing differences arising from the use of different depreciation methods were discussed in chapter 13. Here we note that timing differences can also arise in the area of revenue recognition. For example, it is acceptable for financial reporting purposes under accrual accounting to recognize the face value of a long-term installment contract as revenue at the time of sale provided there is a significant down payment (around 10%); while for tax reporting purposes revenue can be recognized as principal payments are made per each installment, provided the down payment does not exceed 29%. A summary of major timing differences is contained in Exhibit 15-3.

In Exhibit 15-4 we summarize the conventional bases for recognizing revenue for various types of sales.

15.3 THE SCOPE OF MARKETING MANAGEMENT

As with any management process, marketing management consists of determining objectives, developing plans to achieve the objectives, organizing a system to put the plans into action, implementing the plans, and controlling the operation.

DETERMINING MARKETING OBJECTIVES

The basic objective of a firm is to acquire a part of the market by offering some product or service. Since only rarely can a product or service be all things to all people, market segmentation is very important to most firms. By *market segmentation* we mean the strategy of dividing a market into smaller sections so that it can be conquered by the firm. Market segmentation is based on the concept that the market for a product is not homogeneous as to its needs and wants. Different marketing strategies must be employed in selling to the various parts. A firm must set up a continuous policy of looking for differences in the total market, geographically or otherwise. Often these differences are quite marginal, and their exploitation may require imaginative thinking on merchandising and promotion.

It is generally true that total sales can be increased with a more diversified product line sold through more diversified channels. However, we must consider whether the product line can be expanded profitably.

Objectives may be either acquisitive or retentive. For example, a firm may want to obtain a dominant share of its market or it may want to retain the dominant share it already has. Profitability is commonly used as the most important considera-

EXHIBIT 15-3 SOME MAJOR TIMING DIFFERENCES RESULTING FROM THE USE OF DIFFERENT METHODS FOR TAX AND FINANCIAL REPORTING

Item	Method (T = Tax, F = Financial)	Option	Function	Category	Nature of Difference
Advance Royalties	F—Royalty payments made in advance of production to secure oil property are booked as a receivable and recovered as a reduction of production royalties.	R		B	Credit
	T—Royalty is expensed as paid.	R	•		
Amortization of Leasehold Improvements	F—Improvements are amortized over the lease period by an accelerated method.	O		A	Credit
	T—Where asset life is longer than lease life, deduction is limited to a pro rata amount.	R			
Contested State Taxes	F—All contingent tax assessments relating to a given year are expensed.	R	•	C	Debit
	T—Tax may not be deducted until the assessment meets allowance requirements.	R	•		
Debenture Repurchase	F—When debentures are repurchased at a discount, the difference between face amount and that paid is booked as miscellaneous income.	R	•	B	Credit
	T—The amount of discount reduces depreciation expense for debenture-related assets spread over asset life.	O			
Deferred Compensation (Profit Sharing, Additional Compensation, Vacation, etc.)	F—Expenses are accrued for applicable fiscal period.	R		A (Alt. C)	Debit
	T—Compensation is deducted when paid.	R			
Depreciation	F—Accelerated method and/or short asset life is used to calculate depreciation expense.	O		A	Debit
	T—Straight-line and/or long asset life is used to calculate depreciation deduction. OR	O			

EXHIBIT 15-3 ***(CONTINUED)***

Item	Method (T = Tax, F = Financial)	Option	Function	Category	Nature of Difference
	F—Straight-line and/or long asset life is used to calculate depreciation expense.	O		A	Credit
	T—Accelerated method and/or short asset life is used to calculate deduction.	O			
Earnings of Foreign Subsidiaries	F—Income is recognized by parent in year earned.	R	•	C	Credit
	T—Taxable income occurs when payment is remitted by subsidiary to parent company.	R	•		
Estimated Expenses of Settling Pending Lawsuits	F—Estimated expenses are recorded when reasonably ascertainable.	R	•	C	Debit
	T—Tax deduction is taken when payment is made.	R	•		
Estimated Losses on Disposal of Facilities	F—Estimated losses are recorded when anticipated and determinable.	R	•	C	Debit
	T—Tax deduction is taken when loss is incurred.	R	•		
Estimated Inventory Losses (and Purchase Commitments)	F—Estimated losses are recorded when reasonably anticipated.	R	•	C	Debit
	T—Losses are deducted when incurred.	R	•		
Fees, Dues, and Service Contracts	F—Income is deferred to later periods when earned.	R		B	Debit
	T—Income is taxed when received.	R	•		
Exploration Costs of Unoperated Units	F—Geophysical and geological costs incurred prior to leasing oil property are expensed in the year incurred.	O	•	B	Debit
	T—Costs which were expensed when incurred are reinstated for a unit subsequently leased. If no oil is found, the expense is again taken; otherwise, costs are capitalized and amortized over production.	R	• ( )		

Item	Method (T = Tax, F = Financial)	Option	Function	Category	Nature of Difference
Gains on Sales of Property Leased Back	F—Gains are deferred and amortized over the lease period.	O	⊔⊔⊔⊔⊔	B	Debit
	T—Gains are taxed at date of sale.	R	•		
Guarantees and Warranties	F—Estimated costs of contracts are recorded at date of sale.	R	•	B	Debit
	T—Costs are deducted when incurred.	R	⊔⊔⊔⊔⊔		
Installment Sales	F—Profits are recorded at date of sale.	R	•		
	T—Income is reported as installments are collected.	O	⊔⊔⊔⊔⊔	B	Credit
Interest and Taxes During Construction	F—Construction costs are capitalized.	R	⊔⊔⊔⊔⊔	B	Credit
	T—Costs are deducted as incurred.	R	•		
Interest on Federal Income Tax Deficiencies	F—Interest expense on expected tax deficiencies (tax paid less tax due if all doubtful items were taxed) is accrued.	O	•	C	Debit
	T—Interest is deducted when paid.	R	•		
Leasing Activities	F—Revenue is recorded in lessor's accounts based on the financing method.	R	⊔⊔⊔⊔⊔	A	Credit
	T—Revenue taxed is rent received.	R	⊔⊔⊔⊔⊔		
Marketing Program Expenses	F—Costs of closing out old model lines (where model year does not coincide with fiscal year) is spread over year's production and includes costs accrued for units sold in current year but incurred in following year.	R	•	C	Varies
	T—Closing costs are deducted when incurred.	R	•		
Long-Term Contracts	F—Revenues are recorded on percentage of completion basis.	O	⊔⊔⊔⊔⊔	B	Credit
	T—Revenues are taxed on a completed contract basis.	O	•		
Organization Costs	F—Costs are expensed as incurred.	O	•		
	T—Costs are amortized over five years or more.	R	⊔⊔⊔⊔⊔	B	Debit
Pension Costs	F—Expenses are recorded when accrued.	R	•		
	T—Deduction is allowed when contribution is made to the pension fund.	R	•	C	Debit

***EXHIBIT 15-3* (CONTINUED)**

Item	Method (T = Tax, F = Financial)	Option	Function	Category	Nature of Difference
Pre-Operating Expenses	F—Expenses are amortized.	O	|_|_|_|_|	B	Credit
	T—Expenses are deducted when incurred.	R	•		
Proceeds on Sales of Oil or Ore Payments	F—Proceeds are recorded as revenue when production occurs.	R	|_|_|_|_|	B	Debit
	T—Proceeds are taxed at date of sale.	R	•		
Profits on Inter-Company Transactions	F—Profits on assets remaining within the consolidated group are eliminated in the financial statements.	R	|_|_|_|_|	B	Debit
	T—Profits are taxed when reported in separate returns.	R	•		
Promotional Accruals (Coupons, Premiums, etc.)	F—A reserve for contests, etc., in process is accrued.	O	•	C	Debit
	T—Expenses are deducted when incurred.	R	•		
Property Taxes	F—Taxes are accrued over fiscal year of taxing authority.	R	•	C	Credit
	T—Taxes are deducted at lien date.	O	•		
Provision for Gas Revenue Refund	F—Where unapproved rate increase is in effect, lower rate is recorded as income, the increase being deferred.	R	•	B	Debit
	T—Revenue is taxed at the higher rate.	R	|_|_|_|_|		
Provision for Major Repairs	F—Provisions are accrued on a systematic basis.	O	|_|_|_|_|	B	Debit
	T—Expenses are deducted when paid.	R	•		
Rents and Royalties	F—Revenue is deferred to periods when earned.	R	|_|_|_|_|	B	Debit
	T—Revenue is taxed when collected.		•		
Research and Development	F—Costs are deferred and amortized.	O	|_|_|_|_|	B	Credit
	T—Costs are deducted when incurred.	R	•		

Item	Method (T = Tax, F = Financial)	Option	Function	Category	Nature of Difference
Reserve for Doubtful Accounts and Cash Discounts	F—Revenues are reduced by amount expected to be "bad" and for cash discounts on outstanding receivables.	O	•	C	Debit
	T—Bad debt expense exceeds allowable and discounts are written off as taken.	R	•		
Self-Insurance Expense	F—Based on consistent computations, expense is accrued for insurance.	R	⊔⊔⊔⊔	B	Debit
	T—Deduction is allowed when loss occurs.	R	•		
Trademarks and Patents	F—Costs are expensed in year incurred.	O	•	B	Debit
	T—Costs are amortized over asset life.	R	⊔⊔⊔⊔		
Unamortized Discount Issue Cost	F—Costs are deferred and amortized.	R	⊔⊔⊔⊔	B	Credit
	T—Costs are deducted when bonds are refunded.	R	•		
Unoperated Acreage Amortization	F—Bonus paid to obtain oil rights is amortized over the expected life of relevant oil rights.	O	⊔⊔⊔⊔	B	Debit
	T—Bonus is deducted when oil rights are surrendered.	R	•		

Notes:

1. Under the *method* column, "F" indicates the method of accounting used for financial reporting, while "T" indicates the method of accounting, for the same item, used for tax reporting.
2. In some cases, indicated by an "O" in the *option* column, tax regulations or accounting principles (as the case may be) allow for a choice or option as to the method used; in other cases the particular treatment is required, as noted by an "R" in this column.
3. These timing differences fall into three categories, which can be described in general terms as follows:

   Category A: The time-flow of revenue (or expense) is for more than one accounting period for both tax and financial reporting. However, one time-flow is more accelerated than the other.

   Category B: Revenue (or expense) is reported as a lump sum (indicated by a dot) for one purpose, while a time-flow is used for the other purpose.

   Category C: Revenue (or expense) is reported as a lump sum for both financial and tax purposes, but at different points in time.
4. The difference is defined in terms of the impact on financial reporting. A "debit" difference means that financial income is lower than tax income, and *vice versa*.

EXHIBIT 15-4 TIMING OF REVENUE RECOGNITION BY TYPES OF SALES

TYPES OF SALES	TIME WHEN REVENUE IS RECOGNIZED
1. Cash sales	Receipt of cash.
2. Cash on delivery (C.O.D.) sales	a. When shipment is made, or b. When payment is made, or c. Set up a C.O.D. sales account to record shipment and transfer to regular sales account upon receipt of payment.
3. Credit (charge) sales	When sales are made.
4. Conditional sales	a. When sales are made, or b. On an installment basis.
5. Consignment sales	When recipient (consignee) makes a sale.
6. Installment sales	a. When sales are made, or b. When payments are received.
7. Intra-company sales	Do not constitute sales, merely shown as transfers.
8. Inter-company sales	Recorded as sales by selling company and estimated when the accounts of the affiliated companies are consolidated.
9. Long-term contracts	a. Completed contract method: revenue and costs are deferred until the contract is complete, or b. Percentage of completion method: revenue is recognized in stages as the contract moves toward completion.
10. Short sales	When delivery is made.
11. Undelivered sales	a. When billed, or b. When delivery is made.
12. Export sales	Same as credit sales, adjust exchange fluctuation through foreign exchange account if necessary.
13. Approval sales	When billing is made.
14. Will-call sales	a. Record deposit as a liability, record sales when balance is paid, or b. Record as sales when a deposit is made.
15. Backlog	This is the total of unfilled orders at any point in time. It does not represent complete transactions.

tion in determining a firm's marketing objectives. But profit is often ill defined. By changing the firm's accounting system, profit can be destroyed or created. Therefore profit is not a matter of fact, it is merely a matter of accounting and financial policy. Profitability can be operationally defined and transformed into objectives by constructing a functional relationship in terms of measurable elements. For example, if we define profitability as:

$$\text{Profitability} = \frac{\text{Income per year} - \text{Losses per year}}{\text{Investment}}$$

we must break "income" and "losses" into factors that produce them. Only in this way can we understand the objective and control the implementation of the objective.

DEVELOPING MARKETING PLANS

Once a firm has specified its marketing objectives, it must develop a plan by which it hopes to accomplish them. Planning is a decision making process. It is concerned both with avoiding future incorrect actions and with reducing the frequency of failure to exploit opportunities.

The network of decisions which constitute a marketing plan must deal with opportunities and obstacles in the market, with values and objectives, with the marketing organization and the resources available to it. It must also deal with the time and place at which specified activities are to occur.

To develop a marketing plan, the planner must first analyze the market position from a functional view of the firm. A firm's market position is defined in terms of customers, suppliers, and competition. In general, the firm has to function in such a way as to give satisfactory service to both customers and suppliers. Otherwise, it may be bypassed because of pressures building up on one side of the market or the other. Competition can invade the firm's market position by taking advantage of these pressures. For many a firm the best way to meet competition is to apply itself everlastingly to improving its services to customers and suppliers.

Second, the planner must generate strategies to enhance and enlarge the firm's position. There are usually sharply contrasting alternatives to be considered, such as producing a high-quality product for an exclusive market as compared to a stripped-down product at a cheaper price. Analytical techniques are available for predicting the outcome of alternatives.

Third, the planner must design a marketing program to give effect to the chosen strategy. Program design begins by laying out a sequence of activities to take place over a stated period of time. At the programming stage the planner must distinguish between the analytical and administrative views of the plan. The *analytical view* utilizes an operating model to evaluate the likelihood of achieving the expected outputs. The *administrative view* translates the plan into detailed working instructions. The analytical view gives confidence that the plan will work and the administrative view is the instrument for actually putting it to work.

The final step of planning is the implementation of the strategy and program. The implementation of a plan means presenting it to the organization which will carry it out. It also means training the people who will execute the plan.

IMPLEMENTING MARKETING PLANS

No matter how completely objectives are defined, or how carefully marketing strategies are planned, nothing happens if they are merely left on paper. The firm must put the plans into action.

The marketing research function determines the projects on which it can work most profitably and then carries out the actual data collection and analysis. Advertising programs must be determined. Actual advertisements will then be developed in conjunction with an advertising agency. Proper media are selected to put these advertising programs in front of the consumers.

Salesmen must be recruited, trained, supervised, and paid. Plans for these activities are developed in the planning stage. Such plans will take into account salesforce needs in view of the objectives. If more salesmen are needed to accomplish the sales objective, the plan will call for this increase. The recruiting, selecting, and training programs must be carried out to send salesmen into the field.

Distribution channels must be established. Physical distribution of the product must be accomplished. Products must be made available when customers' orders arrive.

ORGANIZING THE MARKETING FUNCTION

Behavioral scientists interested in human organizations have developed many different philosophies regarding business firms. It is clear that an organization which is market-oriented should have substantially different characteristics than one which is production-oriented.

Since the marketing function usually serves as the firm's line of communication with the market, it is essential that the firm's overall organization should permit the flow of relevant information between its marketing department and other departments.

Whether the marketing function is centralized or decentralized, whether it is geographically oriented or product-oriented, a marketing department should perform market operations and market services. *Market operations* include field sales, sales training and administration, distribution, product services, and customers. *Market services* consist of advertising, sales promotion, sales forecasting, public relations, marketing research, and office administration.

Organizational changes within the marketing department must occur if the marketing concept is changed. The impact of marketing generally makes itself felt in attitudinal changes that affect the ways in which individuals cooperate with each other. These attitudinal changes ultimately find their way into new procedures which prescribe relationships among departments.

CONTROLLING THE MARKETING OPERATION

By control we mean following up to determine whether the actual operations are proceeding according to plan. Management must be kept informed on both long-range market trends and short-run changes in the strategies employed by competitors.

Control in marketing is extremely difficult because so much of what is done in marketing can be viewed only as a combination of activities. Many companies use market-share as a tool for measuring their operation. The reason is the belief that such measurements separate changes in sales resulting from forces outside the firm from those for which the management of the firm can be held responsible. The outside forces are general recession or prosperity, shortage of goods, changes in government purchases, or shifts in foreign demand. However, market-share does not indicate how a defective situation might be corrected or how management might capitalize on a success.

The mounting cost of marketing and the use of high speed computers have encouraged an increased flow of information about profitability. Factors contributing to profit (or loss), such as product lines, salesmen, advertising, pricing, distribution, and others, can be monitored and analyzed faster than ever before. This enables the management to take corrective action quickly.

Later in the chapter we shall discuss the control aspect of marketing operation, both from the analytical and the administrative viewpoints.

15.4 ANALYTICAL ASPECTS OF MARKETING MANAGEMENT

The increasing complexity of marketing decision problems make it impossible for marketing executives to make reasonable judgments based solely on their intuition or experiences. The virtually unlimited strategic possibilities in formulating marketing decisions, compounded by the uncertainty of competitors' movements, make it very difficult to determine the outcome of any strategy. This situation encourages the marketing manager to take a more analytical approach to marketing decisions. This type of approach to marketing problems generally considers only a few factors at a time rather than the entire problem. Therefore, it is a valuable addition to the experience, judgment, and intuition of the decision maker.

We shall discuss some of the analytical approaches to major marketing activities.

MARKETING RESEARCH

Marketing research is the beginning of any marketing effort. It involves studying consumer preferences and practices. Marketing research can be divided into three stages of research: (1) preliminary or exploratory research, (2) analytical or descriptive research, and (3) market testing.

Preliminary or Exploratory Research

This is the gathering of basic data about a marketing problem. The approach is generally unstructured but includes a review of literature about the industry being examined. There are many sources for published background information on any industry. There are firms specializing in conducting market surveys and selling the raw data or sorted information to interested parties.

Additional first-hand information to be used as background for the solution of a marketing problem can be obtained from interviews with executives in the industry, with bankers, and with accountants who regularly deal with that industry.

The objective at this point is to secure basic overall data and isolate fundamental relationships.

Analytical or Descriptive Research

This phase of marketing research attempts to crystallize a specific problem. This is done in terms of a product profile which interrelates who buys a product, when, where, how, and why. Factors such as geographical dispersions, family size, income levels, and others are analyzed.

Sampling techniques have been applied to the movement of certain classes of products through retail channels. There are many market survey firms which collect data on retailers' sales and inventories by time periods, type of store, product class, individual brand, and geographic area. They either sell the raw data to an interested firm or perform some kind of basic analysis for their clients. The approach they use is to select randomly a certain number of samples through direct interviews or consumer panels, either relying on continuous or one-time survey, to predict the movement of certain products or the shift in market share distribution.

Another analytical method frequently used in market research is statistical forecasting (chapter 22). The sales forecast is one of the most important pieces of corporate information because so many decisions depend on it. Budgets are set, manufacturing plans are laid, raw materials are bought, people are hired, advertising contracts are signed, all on the basis of expected sales.

For example, let us assume a company has fifteen years of annual sales figures for product X and wants to come up with a five-year sales projection. The market research department examines the historical data and decides to do a straight-line projection by setting:

Forecast = sales at year 0 + trend × multiple of forecast interval or

$$y = a + bX$$

The reader may observe the familiarity of this equation. It is a simple linear regression problem. Using the least square method applied to the data in Exhibit 15-5, we find that:

$$a = 4.5 \text{ and } b = 10.4$$

Exhibit 15-5 shows the data and the results. Exhibit 15-6 illustrates the trend of past sales data and the projection.

From Exhibit 15-6, we notice that the actual sales figures do not match the linear projection very well. The difference between actual and projected figures is called the forecast error. Forecast error[6] is caused by an improper forecast model and/or other factors. There are other techniques, such as time series, exponential smoothing, or input-output analysis, for forecasting sales (chapter 22). If the proper technique is used, sales can be projected reasonably with mathematical models consisting of pertinent factors.

Market Testing

While analytical research may uncover cause-and-effect relationships, it is not designed primarily to determine such relationships. The isolation of cause-and-effect relationships is the function of market testing.

[6]The forecast error expressed as a percentage of the actual outcomes is computed by the formula:

$$\frac{\text{Forecast} - \text{Actual}}{\text{Actual}}$$

EXHIBIT 15-5 SALES OF PRODUCT X (IN THOUSANDS OF DOLLARS)

YEAR	ACTUAL SALES	STRAIGHT-LINE PROJECTION	ERROR
1956	10	5	5
1957	30	15	15
1958	25	25	0
1959	30	36	−6
1960	50	46	4
1961	40	57	−17
1962	60	67	−7
1963	70	78	−8
1964	70	88	−18
1965	110	99	11
1966	120	109	11
1967	120	119	1
1968	140	130	10
1969	150	140	10
1970	140	151	−11
1971		161	
1972		172	
1973		182	
1974		193	
1975		203	

EXHIBIT 15-6 STRAIGHT-LINE SALES PROJECTION (IN THOUSANDS OF DOLLARS)

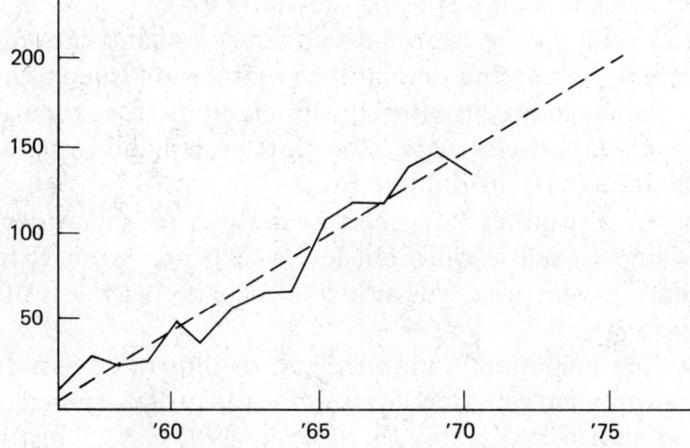

PRICING

One of the most important and complex marketing decision problems is the determination of the "best" price for a product or service. The determination of price is, in classical economic theory, the result of supply and demand relations. But many factors which influence the demand for a product cannot be accounted for in such broad terms.

It is important for us to recognize the distinction between price and cost. *Costing* a product utilizes data that is primarily internal to a firm, e.g., the cost of materials, labor, overhead; *pricing* a product involves a host of factors external to a firm,

EXHIBIT 15-7 DEMAND CURVE

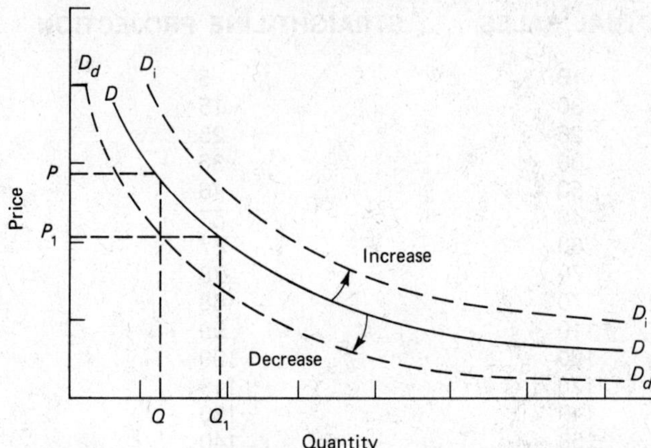

such as competition, demand, consumer preferences, and legal environment. The costing variables are much more stable and predictable than the pricing variables.

The *demand* for a product can be defined as the various quantities of it that consumers will take off the market given a number of factors. The most important ones are: the price of the product, the income levels of prospective purchasers, the purchasers' preferences, the range of products available for consumption. Exhibit 15-7 shows a demand curve. From this curve, a decrease in price from P to P_1 increases quantity purchase from Q to Q_1. This increase should not be viewed as a change in demand since it is on a specific demand curve.

A change in some of the factors which affect demand can shift the entire demand curve to the left (decreasing demand) or to the right (increasing demand). For example, higher incomes may cause the consumers to increase their rate of purchase at each alternative price and *vice versa.* The shift in demand in both directions is illustrated by the dotted curves in Exhibit 15-7.

The *supply* of a product is defined as the various quantities of the product that sellers are willing to sell at different levels of price. From Exhibit 15-8, it can be seen readily that a lower price will induce a seller to place less of the product on the market and *vice versa.*

A shift in the total amount supplied can be illustrated as a downward or upward shift in the supply curve. A downward shift in supply indicates an increase in the total supply (as shown in Exhibit 15–8) from SS to S_iS_i. This means that more goods will be supplied at the same prices.

The demand and supply curves for a particular product can be shown in a single diagram to illustrate the variables which influence the market price. The demand curve depicts what the consumers are willing to buy while the supply curve indicates what the sellers are willing to supply. The supply and demand curves are presented jointly in Exhibit 15-9.

At a price-level of P_1 the buyers are demanding Q_5 quantity of the product, but the seller is willing to place Q_1 quantity on the market. The difference between the quantity demanded and the quantity supplied forms a surplus of the product if the price, P_1, is set by the seller. If each seller perceived the surplus as accumulated, he would assume that he could sell a greater quantity of the product if he lowers the

EXHIBIT 15-8 SUPPLY CURVE

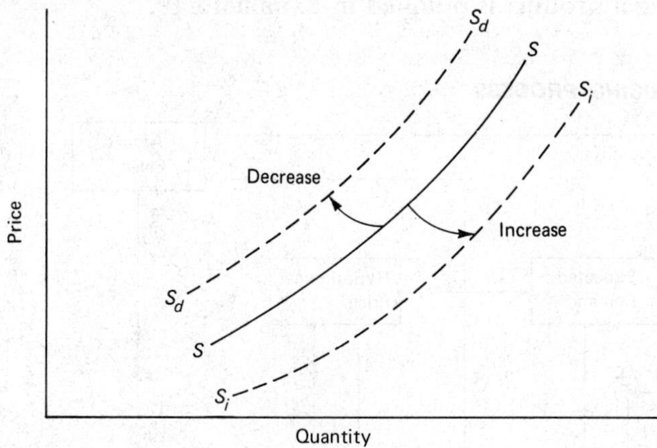

EXHIBIT 15-9 SUPPLY AND DEMAND CURVES

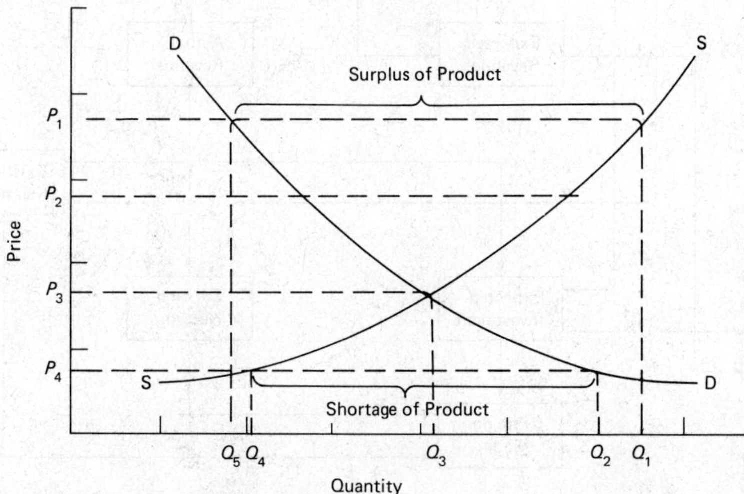

price. Eventually, when the price is reduced to P_3, the buyer will buy all the product that the seller is willing to place on the market at that particular price-level.

On the other hand, if the seller initially set a price of P_4 for the product, the buyer would be willing to purchase Q_2 quantity of the product. However, the seller would only place Q_4 quantity of the product on the market at that price. This difference in willingness to produce more and the intense demand for the product would theoretically force the buyers to bid against each other to purchase the product. The bidding would stop at the P_3 price-level. This price is called the *equilibrium price.*

Determining consumer behavior rests upon economists' concepts of *price elasticity* and *demand schedules,* and upon psychological and sociological factors.

There are quite significant analytical models developed in recent years for pricing products. These models use break-even analysis, decision trees, risk analysis, sensitivity analysis, and simulation techniques to relate selected factors with a mathematical model to predict the impact of price on profit. Inputs to these models and the process of pricing a product is outlined in Exhibit 15-10.

EXHIBIT 15-10 PRICING PROCESS

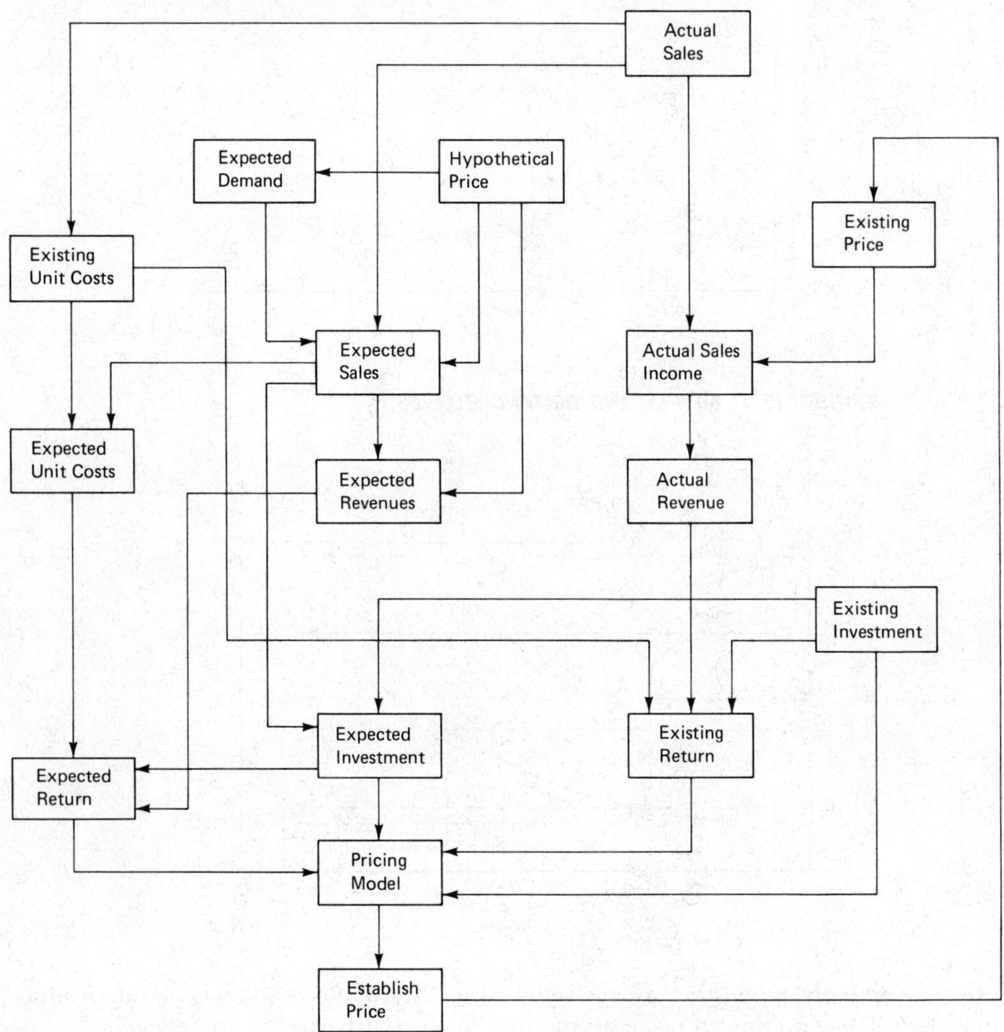

ADVERTISING

Advertising is mass, paid communication, the purpose of which is to influence buyer attitudes and induce action beneficial to the advertiser. The development of effective advertising is a major function of marketing operations. This entails determining the size of the advertising budget, media selection, and the timing of advertising.

Planning of advertising budget is subject to the same principles of marginal analysis that apply to production problems. Because the relevant considerations for deciding how much to advertise are not measurable, intuitive guesses have to take their place. Under these circumstances, rival methods, though not strictly relevant, have been used. Most companies use the "fixed percentage of sales" methods to determine their advertising budget. This is irrational for two reasons. First, this approach means that increased sales causes increased advertising, not that increased advertising causes increased sales. Second, advertising is a stimulus and purchasing is a response. Other companies use the "all-you-can-afford" approach which reflects a blind faith in advertising. Still others use the "investment" or "in response to competitive effort" approaches. All these methods hide rather than highlight the economic issues in the advertising problem. Recent development in analytical techniques, such as industrial dynamics, statistical decision theory, and mathematical programming makes it possible to yield a more ideal approximation.

The media selection problem is to allocate a limited advertising fund among competing channels of communication. In order to express the media selection objective in quantitative terms, several criteria can be used. These are total exposures, frequency, and coverage. These criteria are relatively easy to measure but are removed from profit and sales results. Again, analytical techniques, especially linear programming, have provided a systematic framework for solving this problem.

PERSONAL SELLING

Personal selling allows the salesman to get immediate reaction from the prospective buyer and then adjust his presentation to follow the mood and attitude of the buyer to accomplish a sale. Personal salesmanship can involve each of the major phases of selling: persuasion, information, and motivation.

How many salesmen does a firm need? Which salesman should be assigned to what area? These are two important questions management must answer. To the first problem a simple criterion is to stop adding new salesmen when the cost of adding a new salesman equals the profit on the sales volume he is expected to bring in. This can be expressed by the following formula:

$$S \times P = C$$

where

S = sales volume that an additional salesman is expected to produce
P = the expected profit margin on this sales volume
C = the total cost of maintaining this salesman in the field

Information about the operating profit margin on each dollar of added volume and the total cost of maintaining each additional salesman in the field are readily available from accounting records. However, the sales volume which one additional man might be expected to produce is difficult to determine.

Assignment of salesmen to cultivate new accounts in a particular geographical area has an impact upon future sales revenue. Developments in operations research techniques have aided in sales-force allocation decisions. These allocation techniques will be taken up in the next chapter.

DISTRIBUTION

Another major task in marketing management is the physical movement of goods from plant to customers. A product must be made available when the buyer desires it and where he can obtain it conveniently. Distribution includes selection of marketing channels, logistics of dispersing goods, and management of inventories.

Market Channels

A market channel is the combination of institutions through which a seller markets his products. The simplest channel is one where goods are moved directly from factory to customer. Most industrial products use this direct selling approach. However, for most consumer products numerous middlemen may comprise this channel.

In selecting channels of distribution, management must decide on the general type of channel to be used. If middlemen are going to be used, the type of outlet and intensity of distribution must also be decided. To solve this problem, break-even

EXHIBIT 15-11 INFORMATION FLOW IN LOGISTIC DECISION

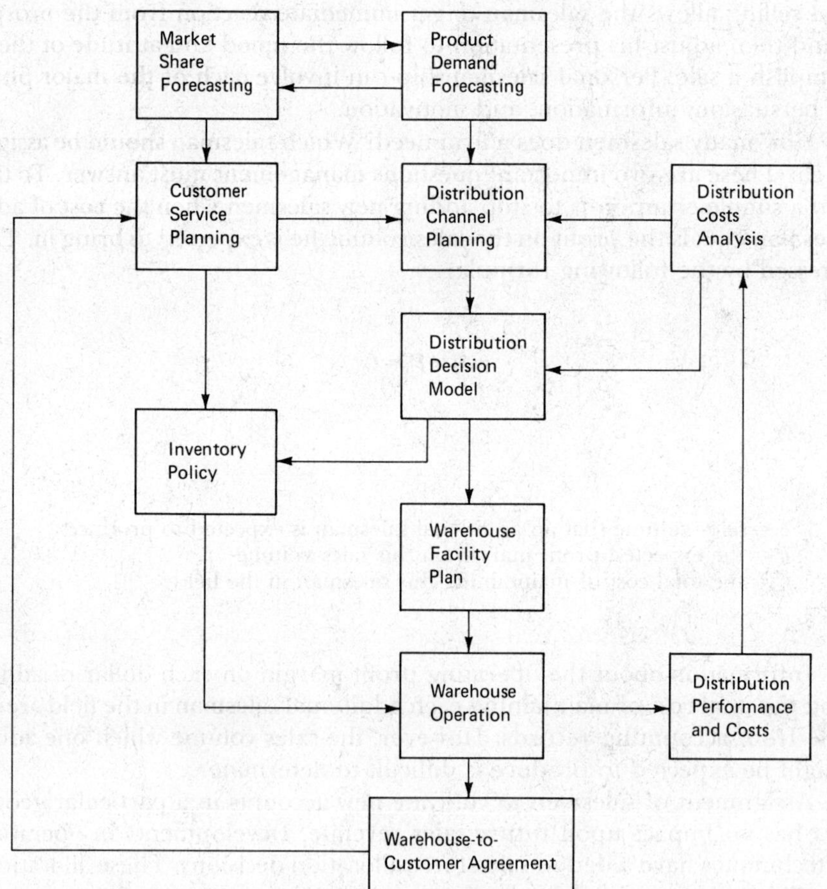

analysis and statistical decision theory are frequently used. However, most corporate accounting systems fail to meet the information needs for making this type of decision. They readily provide the total costs for order processing, freight, or warehousing; but when management wants to know how these costs would be affected by a realignment of distribution channels, the accounting system has not had the answers.

Logistics of Distribution

Exhibit 15-11 illustrates the dimensions of a basic logistic information flow. The logistics of distribution involves the design of a distribution system for getting goods to the customer at a minimum cost to the firm. The ideal distribution system is one which minimizes product (including material) handling, information handling, and transportation costs.

Operations research techniques have demonstrated their great potential in solving logistics problems. For example, the transportation problem, which involves the selection of the cheapest routes to ship goods from supply sources to demand destinations, can be solved by a special application of linear programming called the *transportation method.* This method provides a means for identifying optimal transportation routes; that is, transportation routes resulting in minimum shipping cost. The method provides the best decision for transporting a given quantity of a *single commodity* to its destination. Formulation of the decision requires that we know:

1. The amount and location of supplies.
2. The quantities requested at each destination.
3. The cost of transporting.

For example, the Haring Company has a logistics problem involving three warehouses and four marketing areas. Suppose the following actual and estimated data is available:

ACTUAL QUANTITIES AVAILABLE:

Warehouse 1 (W1) has 45 units
Warehouse 2 (W2) has 60 units
Warehouse 3 (W3) has 75 units

ESTIMATED MARKET DEMAND:

Market Area 1 (M1) needs 30 units
Market Area 2 (M2) needs 50 units
Market Area 3 (M3) needs 55 units
Market Area 4 (M4) needs 45 units

ESTIMATED TRANSPORTATION COST PER UNIT (as a function of the distance from warehouse to market area):

Warehouse	Market Area			
	M1	M2	M3	M4
W1	10	12	26	20
W2	24	8	12	18
W3	14	17	9	6

First, the logistics problem should be set up in the form of a *transportation matrix:*[7]

Origin	Destination				
	M1	M2	M3	M4	
W1	10	12	26	20	45
W2	24	8	12	18	60
W3	14	17	9	6	75
	30	50	55	45	180 / 180

The columns represent the market destinations and the rows represent the commodity origins. The cells linking origins and destinations contain the per unit transportation cost in the upper left-hand corner, thus leaving room in each cell for the subsequent allocation of commodity supplies. Total available quantities of each origin are contained in the far right column, and total quantities required by each destination are shown in the bottom row. These supply-and-demand quantities are called *rim requirements.*

Using this transportation matrix, we can develop an *initial feasible solution* that will satisfy the rim requirements. That is, the quantity allocated to a given cell may not exceed the supply available nor exceed the quantity requested. In other words, the sum of occupied cells on *each* column and row may not exceed the rim requirement for that column or row. In addition to rim requirements, there are two others that must be met:

1. The number of occupied cells (cells containing allocated commodities) must equal one less than the sum of the number of origins and destinations:

$$C_o = O + D - 1$$

where

[7] In this example, the total commodity supply equals demand. In an unequal situation, *dummy* origins or destinations must be included in the transportation matrix. Shipping costs to or from a dummy destination or origin is zero. The excess supply or demand is entered as a rim requirement for the dummy destination or origin, respectively.

C_o = number of occupied cells
O = number of origins
D = number of destinations

2. The occupied cells must be in independent positions. This requirement is met if it is *impossible* to make a round trip (without reversing) from each allocation back to itself by making only horizontal and vertical movements between occupied cells.

The objective of the transportation method is to formulate the *least-cost* solution of a logistics problem. An initial feasible solution is obtained in *three steps:*

STEP 1: Allocate commodity units to $O+D-1$ cells starting in the cell with the least transportation cost and allocating to successively higher cost cells taking care in each instance not to exceed the rim requirements. If two or more cells have the same per unit transportation cost, make a selection by examining the consequences on later allocations.

In our example, we can follow this sequential process:

a. Cell W3,M4 is the starting point. According to our rim requirements, 45 units should be allocated to the cell, leaving 30 units in W3.
b. Cell W2,M2 has the next lowest cost of $8 per unit. Again, adhering to rim requirements, 50 units should be allocated, leaving 10 units in W2.
c. Cell W3,M3 is next. Rim requirements indicate that M3 can use 55 units; but only 30 units are left in W3 (45 units were allocated in part a). Allocate 30 units to W3,M3.
d. Cell W1,M1 is next. Allocate 30 units. W1 is now left with 15 units.
e. Cell W1,M2 and W2,M3 have the same unit cost of $12. M2's demand, however, is already satisfied; hence, cell W2,M3 is next. M3 still needs 25 units; but W2 has only 10 units remaining. Allocate 10 units to cell W2,M3.
f. W1 is the only warehouse with a remaining supply and M3 is the only market area still in need. The remaining 15 units should be allocated to W1,M3.

The completed transportation matrix is:

Origin	**Destination** M1	M2	M3	M4	
W1	10 / 30	12 /	26 / 15	20 /	45
W2	24 /	8 / 50	12 / 10	18 /	60
W3	14 /	17 /	9 / 30	6 / 45	75
	30	50	55	45	180 / 180

STEP 2: This step checks for adherence to feasibility requirements:

a. Are rim requirements met? *Yes.*

The totals of rows and columns do not exceed the supply and demand indicated by the rim requirements.

b. Are the occupied cells in independent positions? *Yes.*

It is impossible to make a round trip from each occupied cell back to itself.

c. Does $C_o = O + D - 1$? *Yes.*

Proof: $6 = 3 + 4 - 1$

STEP 3: Compute the total shipping cost.

a. For each occupied cell, determine the total shipping cost: (e.g., W1,M1 = 10 × 30 = $300)

	Destination			
Origin	M1	M2	M3	M4
W1	300		390	
W2		400	120	
W3			270	270

b. Add the total for each market area (destination):

M1:	=	$ 300
M2:	=	400
M3: 390 + 120 + 270	=	780
M4:	=	270
		$1,750

c. The total from b can be corroborated by adding the total for each warehouse (origin):

W1:	300 + 390 =	$ 690
W2:	400 + 120 =	520
W3:	270 + 270 =	540
		$1,750

The initial feasible solution is to supply each marketing area as follows:[8]

M1: Total demand is estimated at 30 units.

Solution: Ship 30 units from W1.

[8] An improved initial feasible solution (of lesser cost) can be obtained using Vogel's approximation. This method is more highly structured and is based upon a minimization of penalty costs.

M2: Total demand is estimated at 50 units.
Solution: Ship 50 units from W2.

M3: Total demand is estimated at 55 units.
Solution: Ship 15 units from W1.
Ship 10 units from W2.
Ship 30 units from W3.

M4: Total demand is estimated at 45 units.
Solution: Ship 45 units from W3.

This solution was obtained by an informal inspection method. Enactment of this solution will result in a transportation cost of $1,750. This solution, however, is not necessarily the *optimal* or least-cost solution. It is merely an initial *feasible* solution and must be tested for optimality.

Starting with the initial solution, a refinement is possible when a unit transfer from an occupied cell to an unoccupied cell results in a positive opportunity cost. The iterative procedure involved in the actual refinement is very detailed and often results in only a small cost reduction.[9] Consequently, for practical purposes we can use our initial feasible solution as a good *approximation* of the optimal solution.

15.5 ANALYSIS OF MARKETING BEHAVIOR

Failure rate of new products varies between 75% and 95%, depending on the samples and definitions used.[10] This high mortality rate indicates the challenging tasks of marketing management. A firm must first be able to identify the public's expected demand. It must then develop the "right" product at the right time to satisfy this demand. The marketing management also has to understand the continuous changes in marketing conditions. For example, the consumer attitude change toward a certain product may indicate improper pricing or that the product has reached its declining stage. To generate the right information at the right time for marketing decisions, a marketing information system is necessary. By *marketing information system* we mean a structured operation which utilizes people, machines, and procedures to collect, scan, and analyze pertinent information to be used as the basis for making marketing decisions.

The simulation procedure is very useful in the analysis of marketing behavior. Simulation involves constructing and employing an abstract model which replicates some aspect of the operations. If a marketing manager is attempting to describe and evaluate some characteristic of a given operation, he can use a properly constructed simulation model by changing its inputs to see the resultant outputs. Through such experimentation a large number of input combinations and their impact upon output can be carefully scrutinized. The ability to perform the experimental procedure allows

[9] In the example just illustrated, this iterative procedure is not difficult. An improved solution of $1600 can be obtained by shifting fifteen units from cell W1,M3 to cell W1,M2, and correspondingly, shifting fifteen units from cell W2,M2 to cell W2,M3. This produces a net positive opportunity cost of $10 per unit, hence 15 × $10 results in a total cost reduction of $150.

[10] J. T. O'Meara, Jr., "Selecting Profitable Products," *Harvard Business Review,* January–February 1961, p. 83.

the decision maker to test his theories and plans of marketing action on an abstract model instead of on the firm's ongoing marketing system.

Depending on the complexity of the problem, simulation can be a manual, machine, or man-machine process. Once a simulation process has been validated to the satisfaction of the user of the model, the model can act as a kind of synthetic test to screen alternative strategies.

With the development in high-speed computers and quantitative techniques, the complex marketing behavior will soon be better understood by marketing managers. This is particularly true in the areas of advertising and promotion, sales training, competitive gaming, and marketing planning.

15.6 ACCOUNTING RULES AND PROCEDURES

Accounting for the revenues and costs of marketing operations is subject to certain rules and procedures.

MARKETING RESEARCH EXPENSES

Market research expenses comprise the costs of performing the three stages of research discussed earlier. Such costs include the salaries of research personnel and related payroll benefits, travel costs, telephone, costs of periodicals and other research materials, and clerical and other office costs incidental to completing research projects. Often firms employ outside marketing consultants on a fee basis to perform market research; such costs are properly classified as *outside marketing services,* or some such descriptive title. Usually, a firm's regular salesmen perform marketing research tasks as part of their normal duties. They may market test products either on their regular sales calls or as a separate mission. Salesmen also participate in product development discussion and other phases of market research. For purposes of analysis, it may be useful to allocate salesmen's salaries and other costs to market research cost on a fair basis. One fair basis is salesmen's time, which may be reported on a time sheet filled in weekly as a part of the payroll procedure.

SALES

Sales are the monetary expression of the aggregate value of goods and services transferred by an enterprise to its customers during a specified time period. Because of the predominance of accrual accounting, sales comprise all legally completed transactions, lacking only the final collection of proceeds. Usually a sale involves delivery of goods with a concurrent passage of title. Some significant exceptions to this general concept exist in the case of conditional sales and long-term contracts. Deposits received do not represent sales transactions unless a sale is made at the time a deposit is received. Sales include only transactions that take place in connection with the principal operations of a business. Sales of machinery and equipment by a business not primarily engaged in the sale of such assets is not considered a *sale.*

Any gains or other revenue not primarily connected with the principal income-producing activities of a business are excluded from sales. Thus interest income earned by a manufacturing firm is excluded from sales, and is recorded as *nonoperating income.*

Certain items are offset against sales. These items are considered as adjustments to sales, rather than as reductions or expenses against sales.

Returns

When goods are returned for cash or credit, such returns represent a cancellation of the original sales transactions and could properly reduce sales directly. However, for analytical purposes, sales returns are classified separately and offset against sales as follows:

Sales	$100,000
Less sales returns	8,000
Net sales	$ 92,000

Allowances

Allowances are reductions in sales price after sales are made, usually prior to collection of the proceeds. Allowances are made to customers for two basic reasons:

1. Allowances on certain products to allow for shortages in shipments, breakages, spoilage, inferior quality, and other errors.
2. General price allowances to avoid a loss in volume and to retain customers.

Some authorities feel that the first type should be offset against sales, while the latter allowances should reduce sales directly. However, generally both types of allowances are offset against sales as follows:

Sales	$100,000
Less sales allowances	5,000
Net sales	$ 95,000

Discounts

Discounts are generally reductions in invoiced prices or price lists.

1. *Cash discounts.* Cash discounts represent reductions in invoiced prices which the seller allows for prompt payment. An older accounting treatment of discounts was to consider them as financial expenses, such as interest. Current treatment would consider cash discounts a *sales adjustment.*

2. *Trade discounts.* Such discounts are used to determine the price charged to a particular class of consumer with reference to one price list. For example, a standard price list would show a piece of merchandise at $100 list price. A wholesaler might be entitled to subtract a 40% discount, while a retailer might be entitled to subtract a 30% discount. Trade discounts are used merely to compute the *actual purchase* price and thus sales are entered at the *net purchase* price; trade discounts are rarely shown.
3. *Employee discounts.* Generally employees are permitted a discount on purchases made from their employer. These discounts can be shown as *employee benefits,* or more commonly they are considered *sales adjustments.*
4. *Bad debts.* When the proceeds of a sale are not collectible, there has really been a cancellation of an original sale. Common sense, then, would dictate that bad debts can be *offset against sales.* However, this is rarely done in practice. Current practice treats bad debts either as (1) a financial expense or (2) a selling or administrative expense.

   The first treatment is justified by the theory that initial claims (accounts receivable) arise from financial consideration; therefore, the subsequent loss should be charged against financial expense. The second treatment allocates bad debts to the department which has responsibility either for credit extension or follow-up collections. If such responsibility lies with the selling or marketing group, then selling expenses are charged. If collection is an administrative function, then it is charged with bad debts.
5. *Non-cash contributions.* When goods or services are donated, there is an accounting problem. Some businesses ignore non-cash donations for accounting purposes. Other firms would like to show the cash equivalents of donations by a charge to contributions and a reduction of inventories if goods were donated, or a reduction of salaries and other expenses if services were donated. Federal income tax regulations permit a deduction for the *fair market value of goods* (not services) contributed to approved charitable institutions.
6. *Warranties.* Warranties are extended to purchasers of certain products to cover the repair or replacement of defective parts within a specified period and in compliance with certain conditions such as regular service (automobiles) and lack of abuse. The manufacturer generally reimburses the service center (or distributer) for costs incurred in servicing claims under warranties. The manufacturer generally provides for such costs either by a deduction from sales or by a charge to operating expenses.
7. *Freight on sales.* When freight is billed separately (as a separate item) to the customer, the freight cost will be reimbursed and may be treated as a reduction of sales. When the seller assumes the freight cost (f.o.b. destination) and such cost is not added specifically to a customer's bill, the freight cost should appear as an expense of distribution (selling expenses).

ADVERTISING EXPENSES

Accounting for advertising expenditures generally involves a charge to advertising expense, properly broken down as to type of media such as television, commercials, newspaper ads, and others. However, an accounting problem does arise with costs of *major advertising and promotional campaigns.* In most cases, the benefits of such costs will be realized in subsequent accounting periods and such costs should be deferred (or capitalized) in order to be *matched* with the revenues produced. It is difficult to select the proper or fair period over which such costs should be amortized (charged off to expense). Therefore, in most cases such costs are charged to the current period even though there is clearly a benefit to future periods.

DISTRIBUTION EXPENSES

Most traditional accounting texts discuss marketing costs under the caption of distribution costs. In our discussion, distribution expenses will consist of only those costs incurred in storing and delivering goods.

OTHER REVENUE

Increases in net assets which do not result from sales are considered as *other revenue items.* Such items are reported on an income statement after *net earnings from operations.* Other revenue items include the following:

1. *Gains:* Gains on sales of assets which are not held for sale in the ordinary course of business are reported as other revenue. Such items include gains on the sale of fixed assets, investment securities, or assets other than inventories.
2. *Accretion and appreciation:* Increases in the values of assets are generally not recognized in the accounts until they are *realized;* that is, until such assets are sold or exchanged in an arm's-length transaction. Some assets do increase in value (*appreciate*) over time. Land, for example, may increase due to conditions of supply and demand. In addition to increases in values of specific assets, some assets increase in quantity. This occurs with natural resources such as timber and with livestock. While there is generally no question that increases in value have occurred, current practice avoids recognition before sale.
3. *Non-operating revenue:* A business may receive revenue from sources other than normal operating revenues. Such items are shown below net operating income, since they are not connected with the major revenue-producing activities of a firm. Included among such items are the following:
   a. *Interest income* received by non-financial business (other than banks, insurance companies, finance companies) is non-operating revenue.
   b. *Dividends* received by businesses other than securities dealers and other financial institutions are non-operating revenue.
   c. Similar treatments for *rents* and *royalties.*
4. *Forgiveness of debt* (*reduction in liability*): When debt previously recognized in the accounts is cancelled, some authorities would recognize the amount forgiven as revenue. An example would be the retirement of bonds payable at less than book value; such gain on retirement would be shown as *other revenue.* When debt arose originally out of an expense item, treatment as revenue in the period the debt is forgiven would not be technically correct. This is really a restatement of a prior year's profit. Some authorities feel that revenue is not realized from cancellation of debt; they feel that such gains are *gifts of capital* and should be treated as *additional paid-in* or *donated capital.*
5. *Contributions or donations to capital:* Conscience payments and reductions in liabilities outlined above are revenue items and pass through the income statement. Contributions or donations to capital do not pass through the income statements. While both classes of items result in increases in net assets, revenues result from *operations* (even non-operating revenues) and increases in paid-in capital result from *investment.*

15.7 PROCESSING SALES TRANSACTIONS

Processing sales transactions involves inputs, transformations, and outputs.

EXHIBIT 15-12 SALES EVENTS AND RELATED DOCUMENTS

EVENT	TRANSACTION DOCUMENT
A. Sales are made.	1. *Sales ticket* or *sales invoice.* Goods are sold for cash or credit. 2. *Installment* or *conditional sales contract.* Goods are sold on a deferred payment plan. 3. *Adjustment.* Periodic revenue from long-term contracts is recorded.
B. Sales are adjusted.	4. *Adjustment.* Merchandise previously sold is returned for cash refund or credit. 5. *Adjustment.* Allowances are granted to customers for shortages, defects, breakage, or other errors.

EXHIBIT 15-13 THE DUALITY OF SOME TYPICAL SALES TRANSACTIONS

Event	Transaction Document	Date	Notation	Codes			Accounts	Amount	
				Doc.	Trans.	Acct.		Debit	Credit
A. Sales are made.	Invoice		a. Sale is made on open account.		10 10	11210 41110	Accounts Receivable Sales	3,500	3,500
	Invoice		b. Sale is made for cash.		10 10	11110 41110	Cash Sales	250	250
	Note		c. Sale is made on a deferred payment basis.		10 10	11410 41110	Installment Notes Receivable Sales	2,000	2,000
B. Sales are adjusted.	Adjustment		d. Goods previously sold are returned for credit.		10 12	41310 11210	Sales Returns Accounts Receivable	100	100
			e. Allowance is granted to a customer for breakage, shortage, or some other reason.		10 12	41140 11210	Sales Allowances Accounts Receivable	300	300

INPUTS

The principal sales transactions and related documents are shown in Exhibit 15-12. This figure shows that sales are made in various ways and that sales are adjusted because of returns and allowances. Sales expenses are treated in a manner similar to administrative expenses, which are discussed in chapter 16.

TRANSFORMATIONS

Sales data undergoes two transformations in the accounting system:

Transformation$_1$: Establishing duality or the cause-and-effect relationship of sales events is the function of T_1. Typical T_1 entries for sales events are shown in Exhibit 15-13.

Transformation$_2$: Using the T-accounts, the events in Exhibit 15-13 are posted at T_2 as shown in Exhibit 15-14.

OUTPUTS

The accounting information system generates statements reporting sales and selling expenses. These reports are of two types:

1. *Financial reports* show sales made and selling expenses incurred during a specified period as an integral part of the income statement. In annual reports to stockholders, some companies break down sales by major products or product lines, by divisions, or other material segments. Other firms, particularly diversified companies, have been criticized for not disclosing sales by major classifications.

   Selling expenses are rarely detailed in published reports; in some reports selling expenses are not shown at all but are aggregated with administrative expenses and reported as one item.
2. *Management reports* provide detailed break-downs of sales by products, by customers, by divisions, and by other meaningful segments. Selling expenses are broken down into classifications such as sales, salaries, travel, media advertising, and other meaningful accounts. Such detailed information is used for planning and control of marketing operations.

EXHIBIT 15-14 POSTING SALES EVENTS TO T-ACCOUNTS

11110 Cash			
(b)	$250		

11210 Accounts Receivable			
(a)	$3,500	(d)	$100
		(e)	300

11410 Installment Notes Receivable			
(c)	$2,000		

41110 Sales			
		(a)	$3,500
		(b)	250
		(c)	2,000

41310 Sales Returns			
(d)	$100		

41140 Sales Allowances			
(e)	$300		

15.8 SYSTEMS CONTROLS FOR MARKETING OPERATIONS

There are *stewardship* and *management controls* applicable to marketing operations.

STEWARDSHIP CONTROLS

Stewardship controls are designed to safeguard assets and insure proper recording of transactions. With respect to marketing operations, stewardship controls include the following objectives:

Control of Cash and Credit Transactions

We have previously discussed stewardship control of cash. Credit transactions make up the bulk of sales transactions in most circumstances (other than retail sales). The dominant control is *segregation* of the following *duties:*

1. *Sales order department,* which is responsible for establishing control over all orders received, screening and editing orders, obtaining credit approvals, preparing shipping and back orders.
2. *Credit department* is responsible for approving credit transactions based upon an evaluation of a customer's financial status.
3. *Shipping department* must see that nothing leaves the premises without proper authorization in the form of shipping orders or other release forms.
4. *Billing department* is responsible for the preparation of customer invoices. This is usually done upon receipt of a copy of a shipping order. It is the responsibility of this department to see that all shipments are billed.

Authority for and Control of Discounts and Price Changes

These controls are essential in safeguarding sales transactions. Fraud and errors can occur when discounts are mishandled. Company policy should be established with respect to discount conditions; certain discounts are allowed to various classes of customers with specified payment dates. Discounts taken are normally recorded upon collection and should be tested by an internal audit department on a periodic basis.

Price changes must be properly authorized and applied by the billing department. To check on the accuracy of invoices rendered by a billing department, some companies maintain a separate department to *audit invoices* for their propriety. Pricing is checked against authorized price lists, and extensions and totals are tested for accuracy.

Cut-Off

Cut-off in recording sales transactions allocates sales to the period in which they are made. Shipments made prior and after the close of an accounting period are traced to the sales journal to see if they have been recorded in the proper period. Entries in the sales journal are also traced to shipping documents to see that goods entered as sales were shipped in the proper period.

Matching

Matching requires that revenues and applicable costs be allocated to the same accounting period in order to determine fairly periodic income. The cost of a major advertising campaign should not be charged to expense when incurred, but rather deferred to be matched against future sales generated by the campaign. Often such matching is arbitrary because the stream of benefits resulting from a marketing expenditure is not susceptible of close estimation. Therefore, costs are generally charged off over an arbitrary period.

MANAGEMENT CONTROLS

Management controls have as their objectives the optimizing of sales versus marketing costs. Some specific management control areas include the following:

Marketing Research Cost-Effectiveness

Analyses of the effectiveness of monies expended on marketing research requires estimates of future benefits from each product or project, matched against their respective costs. While market testing a product through distributing free samples may be an effective way of evaluating consumer preferences, it may also be the most expensive method of testing. Other methods of testing include questionnaires (for example, these are less expensive than personal interviewing and can reach a wide test group but may be less effective because of failure to reply) and opinion surveys.

Advertising Cost-Effectiveness

Advertising cost-effectiveness compares the costs and benefits of various types of advertising. Management controls aim at an optimum relationship of costs and benefits. Evaluation of advertising costs is made in terms of measures such as number of units of advertising space or time used in various media versus the type and number of persons reached.

Distribution Cost Analysis

Distribution cost analysis evaluates the costs of various methods of delivering goods to customers against benefits such as speed, convenience, and storage factors.

Product Line Analysis

Product line analysis evaluates the strengths and weaknesses of component members of a product line. Additions to and deletions from a product line are evaluated in terms of product profitability and the necessity of offering a complete line.

Budget and "Quota" Controls

Budget and "quota" controls are generally the only workable controls available to cover expenditures. When expenses cannot be related directly to physical units of output, such expenses are controlled through budgets and quotas. Salesmen, for example, may be allowed to spend up to a certain amount for a given sales trip. When this quota is exceeded, the excess expenses may be disallowed or examined critically. Other expenses, such as market research expenses, may be budgeted with expenditures, not to exceed such amount without executive review and approval. One difficulty with budgets and quotas is that individuals tend to spend up to such amounts even if it is unnecessary, in order to obtain at least an equal amount in the next budget.

New Products

New products must be developed continuously and introduced in order to maintain and improve competitive position. Product development requires a great deal of data generally not contained within the formal accounting information system. Information on the size of the total market, the market's growth pattern, the locations of the market, the competitive position, and product life-cycle must be sought outside the accounting information system. In addition to analyzing the demand criteria surrounding a proposed product, cost factors must also be analyzed. Production costs are not the only factors to be included in an analysis; promotional costs, such as first-year advertising, can be extremely large.

15.9 SYSTEMS FEEDBACK FOR MARKETING OPERATIONS

Feedback on marketing operations furnishes users with (1) exception, (2) control, (3) comparative, and (4) interpretive data.

EXCEPTION

Exception reports outline any material departure from plans. To evaluate and control salesmen's performance, for example, a sales analysis by salesman is common. This report shows which salesmen are under quota or budgeted sales by over or under a certain amount, say 5%. This report would be the basis for beginning a review of the performance of the salesmen listed. Factors such as the number of calls per day, the average amount sold per order, and others would be considered in evaluating performance.

CONTROL

Control reports show the extent to which stewardship and management controls are in effect. Stewardship controls are evidenced by a detailed income statement supported by reports of internal and independent auditors. The auditors' reports state that sales revenues and selling expenses have been verified, that all transactions have been recorded, and that income is fairly stated.

Management control reports state the extent to which sales revenues and selling expenses have been optimized. Such control reports are in the form of special analyses showing costs expended and benefits received. Salesmen's salaries can be compared with orders turned in; or pieces of an advertising mail-out can be compared with mail orders received.

COMPARATIVE

Comparative feedback can result from a comparison of current activity with that of prior periods or with the performance of competitors. The most common report is a comparative statement of sales. This shows current sales compared with those of prior years and compared with sales budget. Similar comparisons can also be made of selling expenses.

Another type of comparative feedback is the computation of ratios and per unit costs, such as the following:

1. Selling cost as a percent of net sales
2. Cost per dollar of gross profit
3. Cost per sales transaction
4. Cost per order received
5. Cost per shipment
6. Cost per mile traveled
7. Number of advertising pieces mailed

INTERPRETATIVE

Interpretative feedback employs data developed under other types of feedback and gives meaning to the data. Exception reports may show that certain salesmen are significantly *above* quota. This condition must be analyzed for causes. Perhaps management has undervalued the territory, and the quota should be raised. Perhaps these salesmen are pushing high-volume but low-profit items. All possibilities raised by an exception report should be investigated.

15.10 SUMMARY

Marketing is the overall activity of creating and maintaining demand for a firm's goods and services. The major functions of marketing operations are marketing research, product development, marketing channels, sales efforts, distribution systems, and customer relations.

The term *revenue* is different from *sales* in that the former refers to all accounting events which increase retained earnings, while the latter refers to revenue arising only from disposition of the firm's goods versus services in the ordinary course of business. Depending upon the form of sales, timing of revenue recognition is different.

Marketing management, as any other management process, consists of determining objectives, developing plans, organizing the marketing system, implementing plans, and controlling marketing operation.

The development of high-speed computers and analytical techniques made it more important for accounting systems to provide the pertinent cost information in the appropriate fashion to aid management in making marketing decisions. The discussion of the analytical aspect of some marketing activities intends to give the reader some insight as to what kind of accounting information the marketing management needs.

Accounting rules and procedures regarding marketing operation as well as the processing of sales transactions are described.

Stewardship and management controls are essential to marketing operation. The feedback on marketing operation provides management with important information for decision making.

CHAPTER 15 REFERENCES AND ADDITIONAL READINGS

GENERAL, MARKETING

Ackoff, R. L. *A Concept of Corporate Planning.* New York: John Wiley & Sons, Inc., 1970.

Amstutz, A. E. *Computer Simulation of Competitive Marketing Response.* Cambridge, Mass.: MIT Press, 1967.

Britt, S. H., and Boyd, H. W. Jr. *Marketing Management and Administrative Action.* New York: McGraw-Hill Book Company, 1963.

Clark, W. A., and Sexton, D. E. Jr. *Marketing and Management Science: A Synergism.* Homewood, Ill.: Richard D. Irwin, Inc., 1970.

Donnelly, J. H. Jr., and Ivancevich, J. M. *Analysis for Marketing Decision.* Homewood, Ill.: Richard D. Irwin, Inc., 1970.

Ferguson, R. O., and Sargent, L. F. *Linear Programming: Fundamentals and Applications.* New York: McGraw-Hill Book Company, 1958.

Kotler, P. *Marketing Management.* Englewood Cliffs, N.J.: Prentice-Hall, Inc., 1967.

Looba, N. P. *Linear Programming: An Introductory Analysis.* New York: McGraw-Hill Book Company, 1964.

Miller, D. W., and Starr, M. K. *Executive Decisions and Operations Research.* Englewood Cliffs, N.J.: Prentice-Hall, Inc., 1960.

Montgomery, D. B., and Urban, G. L., eds. *Applications of Management Science in Marketing.* Englewood Cliffs, N.J.: Prentice-Hall, Inc., 1970.

Riggs, J. L. *Economic Decision Models for Engineers and Managers.* New York: McGraw-Hill Book Company, 1968.

Sasieni, M.; Yaspan, A.; and Friedman, L. *Operations Research: Methods and Problems.* New York: John Wiley & Sons, Inc., 1960.

Shuchman, A., ed. *Scientific Decision-Making in Business.* New York: Holt, Rinehart & Winston, Inc., 1963.

Simon, L. S., and Freimer, M. *Analytical Marketing.* New York: Harcourt, Brace & World, Inc., 1970.

Smith, S. V.; Brien, R. H.; and Stafford, J. E. *Readings in Marketing Information Systems.* New York: Houghton Mifflin, 1968.

INCOME RECOGNITION

American Accounting Association 1964 Concepts and Standards Research Committee—The Realization Concept. "The Realization Concept." *The Accounting Review,* April 1965, pp. 312–22.

Arnett, Harold E. "Recognition as a Function of Measurement in the Realization Concept." *The Accounting Review,* October 1963, pp. 733–41.

Blackman, William W. Jr. "Accounting Principles for Long-Term Construction Contracts." *New York Certified Public Accountants,* November 1960, pp. 759–67.

Comiskey, Eugene E., and Mlynarczyk, F. A. "Recognition of Income by Finance Companies." *The Accounting Review,* April 1968, pp. 248–56.

Hendriksen, Eldon S. "Revenues and Expenses, Gains and Losses." In *Accounting Theory,* E. S. Hendriksen. Homewood, Ill.: Richard D. Irwin, Inc., 1970, pp. 159–99.

Landry, M. "The Income Recognition Problem for a Finance Company." *Canadian Chartered Accountant,* February 1970, pp. 111–16.

Thomas, Arthur L. *Revenue Recognition.* Ann Arbor, Mich.: Bureau of Business Research, University of Michigan, 1966.

Windal, Floyd. *The Accounting Concept of Realization.* East Lansing, Mich.: Bureau of Business and Economic Research, Michigan State University, 1961.

GENERAL, ACCOUNTING AND MARKETING

Barry, John. "The Accountant's Role in Marketing." *Management Services,* January–February 1967, pp. 43–50.

Fox, Harold W. "Accounting Concepts for Marketing Operations." *The National Public Accountant,* December 1968, pp. 12–14.

Goodman, Sam R. "Management Accounting and the Marketing Concept." *Budgeting,* January–February 1968, pp. 20–22.

Kennedy, C. "The Responsibility of the Accountant in Marketing Management." *Cost and Management* (Canada), November 1967, pp. 19–22.

Martin, B. P. "Marketing Looks at the Accountant." *The Australian Accountant,* April 1970, pp. 134–38.

Weigand, Robert E. "The Accountant and Marketing Channels." *The Accounting Review,* July 1963, pp. 584–90.

ADVERTISING

Dietrich, A. O., "Checking the Advertising, Sales and Cost Relationships." *Industrial Marketing,* June 1964, pp. 107–8.

Kelly, William T. "Advertising Control: A Computer Application." *Management Services,* September–October 1967, pp. 41–48.

Lambeth, George. "Developing the Statistics for Cost Comparisons." *Industrial Marketing,* June 1964, p. 109.

Morrill, John E. "Industrial Advertising Pays Off." *Harvard Business Review,* March–April 1970, pp. 4–14.

Schwerin, Horace S. "Can Advertising Expenditures be 'Quality Controlled.'" *The Financial Executive,* March 1966, pp. 28–35.

Whitney, John W. "Better Results from Retail Advertising." *Harvard Business Review,* May–June 1970, pp. 111–20.

DISTRIBUTION STRATEGY

Bursk, Edward C., and Chapman, John F., eds. *New Decision Making Tools for Management: Mathematical Programming as an Aid in the Solving of Business Problems.* Cambridge, Mass.: Harvard University Press, 1963, pp. 224–46.

Gwinner, Robert F. "Coordinating Strategy and Tactics in Sales Administration." *MSU Business Topics,* Summer 1970, pp. 56–62.

Hennessy, J. H. "Considerations in Remodeling a Physical Distribution System." *The Financial Executive,* April 1969, pp. 64–73.

Morse, Leon. "The Changing Anatomy of Industrial Sales Distribution." *Dun's Review and Modern Industry,* January 1963, pp. 37–38.

Pirasteh, Ross. "Prevent Blunders in Supply and Distribution." *Harvard Business Review,* March–April 1969, pp. 113–27.

CHAPTER 15 QUESTIONS, PROBLEMS, AND CASES

15- 1. For each type of sale, explain the conventional bases for recognizing revenue:
(a) Cash sales
(b) Cash on delivery (C.O.D.) sales
(c) Credit (charge) sales
(d) Conditional sales
(e) Consignment sales
(f) Installment sales
(g) Long-term contracts
(h) Short sales
(i) Undelivered sales
(j) Export sales
(k) Approval sales
(l) Will-call sales

15- 2. Explain the concept of *market segmentation.*

15- 3. "Objectives may be either acquisitive or retentive." Explain the meaning of this statement.

15- 4. "Once a firm has specified its marketing objectives, it must develop a plan by which it hopes to accomplish them." What are the four steps or phases in developing a marketing plan?

15- 5. "Whether the marketing function is centralized or decentralized, whether it is geographically oriented or product-oriented, a marketing department should perform market operations and market services." Distinguish between *market operations* and *market services* by citing examples of each.

15- 6. Why is market-share often used as a tool for measuring the success of marketing operations? What are the limitations of its use?

15- 7. Describe the *analytical approach* to formulating a marketing decision.

15- 8. Explain how sampling techniques and statistical forecasting can be used in marketing research.

15- 9. Most corporate accounting systems fail to meet the information needs for selecting channels of distribution. Describe how they fail to meet such needs and suggest possible remedies.

15-10. Give two reasons for the irrationality of using a *fixed percentage of sales* for determining an advertising budget. Identify some alternative approaches for determining the advertising budget.

15-11. Distinguish between revenue *recognition* and *realization.*

15-12. What is the conventional accounting treatment for these items:
(a) Returns & allowances
(b) Cash discounts
(c) Trade discounts
(d) Employee discounts
(e) Bad debts
(f) Contributions (cash & non-cash)
(g) Warranties
(h) Freight on sales
(i) Advertising expenses
(j) Appreciation in value
(k) Forgiveness of debt

15-13. Identify the relationships of supply and demand functions:

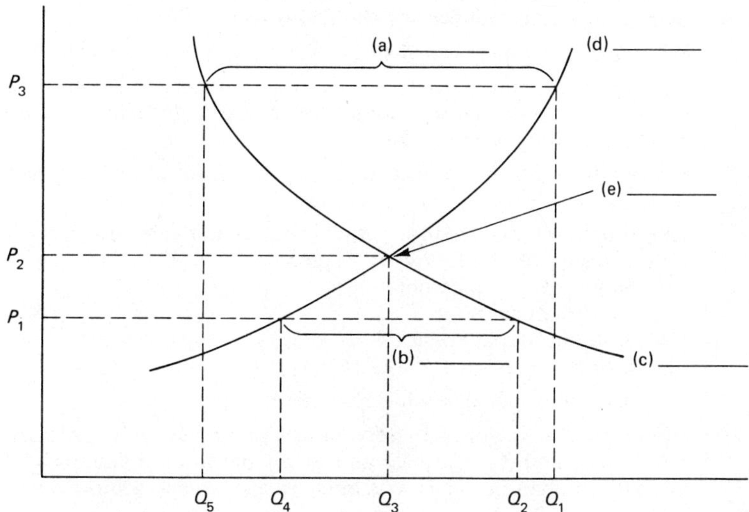

1. Demand function
2. Supply function
3. Equilibrium price
4. Surplus of product
5. Shortage of product

15-14. Identify and explain the three stages of marketing research.

15-15. Define or explain the use of the following terms or phrases:
(a) Product profile
(b) Forecast error
(c) Demand
(d) Supply
(e) Equilibrium price
(f) Advertising
(g) The media selection problem

15-16. Distinguish between a change in demand caused by a decrease or increase in price, and a change or shift in demand caused by a change in the income level of the customer or a change in buying preference. Illustrate this distinction graphically.

15-17. To answer the question of how many salesmen a firm needs, "a simple criterion is to stop adding new salesmen when the cost of adding a new salesman equals the profit on the sales volume he is expected to bring in." Is this an adequate and reasonable criterion? Explain the reasoning behind your response.

15-18. What are the principle activities included in the distribution operation?

15-19. Discuss the application and usefulness of linear programming for marketing distribution problems, and simulation models for an analysis of marketing behavior.

15-20. Discuss the propriety of capitalizing marketing research expenses and then amortizing such costs to the periods benefited.

15-21. What are two basic reasons for granting sales allowances to customers?

15-22. Since the benefits of a major advertising or promotional campaign will accrue to future accounting periods, should the costs of such advertising and promotion be capitalized and then amortized in subsequent periods? Discuss the propriety and feasibility of this accounting treatment.

15-23. Appreciation of assets is not recognized in the accounts until realized. Explain the possible rationale behind this treatment.

15-24. What are four objectives of stewardship controls over marketing operations?

15-25. "Authority for and control of discounts and price changes are essential in safeguarding sales transactions." What are some possible consequences if authority and/or control is lacking?

15-26. Discuss the necessary interaction between marketing and production management.

15-27. The dominant stewardship control over credit sales transactions is segregation of duties by the following departments:
(a) Sales order department
(b) Credit department
(c) Shipping department
(d) Billing department

Describe the duties of each department.

15-28. Identify six management control areas in the marketing information system. Since management controls aim at an optimum relationship of costs and benefits, explain how each control area attempts to achieve such an aim.

15-29. Identify the parts of a basic logistic information flow.

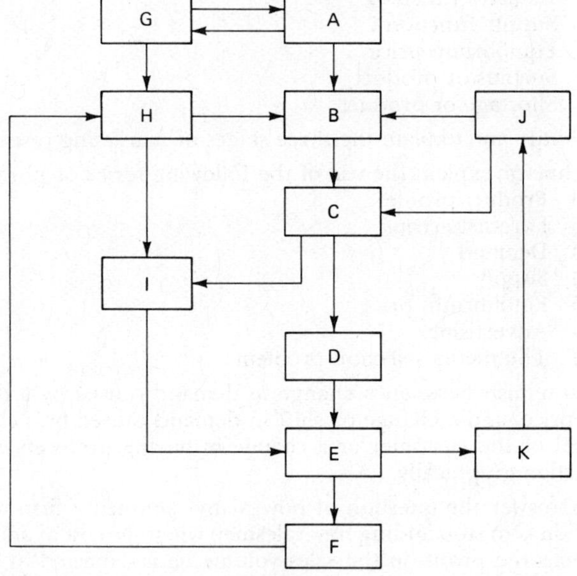

15-30. In a marketing information system, what is the typical content of the following feedback reports:
(a) Exception reports
(b) Control reports
(c) Comparative reports
(d) Interpretive reports

15-31. ***REVENUE RECOGNITION*** Bonanza Trading Stamps, Inc., was formed early this year to sell trading stamps throughout the Southwest to retailers who distribute the stamps gratuitously to their customers. Books for accumulating the stamps and catalogs illustrating the merchandise for which the stamps may be exchanged are give free to retailers for distribution to stamp recipients. Centers with inventories of merchandise premiums have been established for redemption of the stamps. Retailers may not return unused stamps to Bonanza.

The following schedule expresses Bonanza's expectations as to percentages of a normal month's activity which will be attained. For this purpose, a "normal month's activity" is defined as the level of operations expected when expansion of activity ceases or tapers off to a stable rate. The company expects that this level will be attained in the third year and the sales of stamps will average $2,000,000 per month throughout the third year.

Month	Actual Stamp Sales Percent	Merchandise Premium Purchases Percent	Stamp Redemptions Percent
6th	30%	40%	10%
12th	60	60	45
18th	80	80	70
24th	90	90	80
30th	100	100	95

Bonanza plans to adopt an annual closing date at the end of each twelve months of operations.

Required:

(a) Discuss the factors to be considered in determining when revenue should be recognized in measuring the income of a business enterprise.
(b) Discuss the accounting alternatives that should be considered by Bonanza Trading Stamps, Inc., for the recognition of its revenues and related expenses.
(c) For each accounting alternative discussed in (b) above, give balance sheet accounts that should be used and indicate how each should be classified.

(From the CPA exam.)

15-32. ***MAJOR ADVERTISING—PROMOTIONAL DISPLAY*** Kwik-Bild Corporation sells and erects shell houses. These are frame structures that are completely finished on the outside but are unfinished on the inside except for flooring, partition studding, and ceiling joists. Shell houses are sold chiefly to customers who are handy with tools and who have time to do the interior wiring, plumbing, wall completion and finishing, and other work necessary to make the shell houses livable dwellings.

Kwik-Bild buys shell houses from a manufacturer in unassembled packages consisting of all lumber, roofing, doors, windows, and similar materials necessary to complete a shell house. Upon commencing operations in a new area, Kwik-Bild buys or leases land as a site for its local warehouse, field office, and display houses. Sample display houses are erected at a total cost of from $3,000 to $7,000 including the cost of the unassembled packages. The chief element of cost of the display houses is the unassembled packages, since erection is a short-low-cost operation. Old sample models are torn down or altered into new models every three to seven years. Sample display houses have little salvage value because dismantling and moving costs amount to nearly as much as the cost of an unassembled package.

Required:

(a) A choice must be made between:
  (1) Expensing the costs of sample display houses in the period in which the expenditure is made, and

(2) Spreading the costs over more than one period.
Discuss the advantages of each method.

(b) Would it be preferable to amortize the cost of display houses on the basis of
(1) The passage of time or
(2) The number of shell houses sold?
Explain.

(From the CPA exam.)

15-33. ***INSTALLMENT SALES*** The Whitewall Appliance Company, your client, has followed the policy of selling its merchandise at retail for cash only. During the past year it expanded its line of appliances to include higher-priced items and provided an eighteen-month installment payment plan for its customers.

Under Whitewall's installment payment plan the customer's contract includes a financing charge of 10% of the sales price of the merchandise. Whitewall has decided to retain the installment contracts receivable and not discount them with a finance company. Whitewall intends to obtain the necessary additional working capital by short-term bank loans.

You learn that Whitewall has decided to report the unearned portion of the 10% finance charges as a current liability in the balance sheet with full disclosure in a footnote, an acceptable treatment. You know that the unearned portion of the finance charges might be reported by alternative accounting procedures.

Required:

(a) What arguments do you expect from Whitewall to support its decision to report the unearned portion of the 10% finance charges as a current liability?
(b) What reasons would you offer Whitewall for reporting the unearned portion of the finance charges as deferred income in a section of the balance sheet between liabilities and stockholders' equity?
(c) The unearned portion of the finance charges may be reported as a deduction from the total contracts receivable on the asset side of the balance sheet. What reasons would you offer for this procedure?
(d) Discuss the validity of the arguments for the three methods. Which method do you recommend?
(e) Whitewall has not given any consideration to the accounting method to be used for recognizing revenue on the installment sales. Give the methods of recognizing revenue (you may write in terms of gross profit) from installment sales and discuss the acceptability of each method.

(From the CPA exam.)

15-34. ***INSTALLMENT SALES*** The Fairdeal Appliance Company sells all merchandise by installment contracts. Legal title to an appliance is not relinquished until the customer completes his installment payments. A summary of selling activity for the last four years is:

	19x1	19x2	19x3	19x4
Sales (installments)	$875,000	$934,000	$918,000	$963,000
Beginning inventory	26,000	28,500	27,000	29,000
Ending inventory	28,500	27,000	29,000	26,400
Purchases	676,250	699,000	727,220	787,060
Cash collections:				
19x1 sales	322,500	294,000	222,500	32,000
19x2 sales		330,800	280,000	268,700
19x3 sales			384,300	321,000
19x4 sales				394,600

Required:

(a) Compute the gross profit percentage for each year.
(b) Compute the amount of gross profit realized in each year.
(c) Compute the balance of deferred gross profit for each year.

15-35. ***INSTALLMENT SALES*** The Good Deal Appliance Company began business on January 1, 1972. All sales of new merchandise are made on installment contracts. The company recognizes income from the sale of new merchandise under the installment method and employs the periodic inventory system. The following information was extracted from the company's accounts at December 31 for the years indicated:

	1973	1972
Installment contracts receivable:		
1972 contracts	$ 17,300	$ 42,000
1973 contracts	56,000	
Cash sales of trade-ins	20,500	
Installment sales	310,000	221,000
Purchases—new merchandise	176,700	170,180
Inventory, new merchandise—Jan. 1	42,000	
Operating expenses	65,803	53,718
Loss from defaulted contracts	10,400	

A further review of company records disclosed the following additional information:

(a) The inventory of new and repossessed merchandise on hand at December 31, 1973, was $36,432 and $4,100 respectively.
(b) When a customer defaults on a contract the company records the repossessed merchandise at its approximate wholesale market value in a separate account. Differences between the unpaid balance on the contract and the wholesale market value are charged to the loss from defaulted contracts account. Repossessed merchandise is sold on the installment contract basis.
(c) The wholesale value of repossessed goods is determined as follows:
    (1) Goods repossessed during year of sale are valued at 40% of original sales price.
    (2) Goods repossessed subsequent to the year of sale are valued at 20% of original sales price.
(d) There were no defaulted contracts during 1972. An analysis of contracts defaulted and charged off during 1973 follows:

	Original Sales Price	Unpaid Contract Balance
1972 contracts	$19,500	$10,500
1973 contracts	11,000	8,200

(e) On January 1, 1973, the company began granting allowances on merchandise traded in as part payment on new sales. During 1973 the company granted trade-in allowances of $22,600. The wholesale value of traded-in merchandise was $15,800. All merchandise traded in during the year was sold for cash.
(f) The company uses the installment method of reporting income on goods sold on the installment basis for both book and tax purposes. Assume the income tax rate is 48%.

Required:

(1) Prepare a schedule of unrealized gross profit at December 31, 1973 and 1972, from contract sales. Include a supporting schedule calculating the gross profit percentage for contract sales for both years.

(2) Compute the adjustment (if any) that you would recommend be made to the loss from defaulted contracts account.

(3) Prepare a statement of income for The Good Deal Appliance Company for the year ended December 31, 1973. Supporting schedules computing the realized gross profit from (a) 1972 sales and (b) sales of traded-in merchandise should be in good form.

(Adapted from the CPA exam.)

15-36. ***PERCENTAGE OF COMPLETION*** The High-Way Company constructs modern freeways. It is presently working on an $8 million highway for the state of Montana. The three-year-old project is expected to take another two years. Data for the three years is as follows:

	19x1	19x2	19x3
Construction costs	$2,700,000	$1,400,000	$1,500,000
Estimated costs to complete	4,900,000	3,550,000	2,000,000
Contract billings	2,500,000	1,200,000	1,600,000
Collections from contract billings	1,800,000	1,500,000	1,900,000

Required:

Assuming the High-Way Company uses the percentage of completion method based on estimated cost, determine the gross profit recognized in each of the three years and the applicable receivable and liability balances for each year.

15-37. ***PERCENTAGE OF COMPLETION*** The Metro Construction Company commenced doing business in January 19*x*1. Construction activities for the year 19*x*1 are summarized as follows:

Project	Total Contract Price	Contract Expenditures to Dec. 31, 19x1	Estimated Costs to Complete Contracts	Cash Collections to Dec. 31, 19x1	Billings to Dec. 31, 19x1
A	$ 310,000	$187,500	$ 12,500	$155,000	$155,000
B	415,000	195,000	255,000	210,000	249,000
C	350,000	320,000	—	300,000	350,000
D	300,000	16,500	183,500	—	4,000
	$1,375,000	$719,000	$451,000	$665,000	$758,000

The company is your client. The president has asked you to compute the amounts of revenue for the year ended December 31, 19*x*1, that would be reported under the completed contract method and the percentage of completion method of accounting for long-term contracts.

The following information is available:

(a) All contracts are with different customers.

(b) Any work remaining to be done on the contracts is expected to be completed in 19*x*2.

(c) The company's accounts have been maintained on the completed contract method.

Required:

(1) Prepare a schedule computing the amount of revenue by project for the year ended December 31, 19*x*1, that would be reported under
 a. The completed contract method.
 b. The percentage of completion method.

(2) Prepare a schedule under the completed contract method computing the

amounts that would appear in the company's balance sheet at December 31, 19x1, for (a) costs in excess of billings and (b) billings in excess of costs.

(3) Prepare a schedule under the percentage of completion method that would appear in the company's balance sheet at December 31, 19x1, for (a) costs and estimated earnings in excess of billings and (b) billings in excess of costs and estimated earnings.

(4) The company adopted the percentage of completion method for financial reporting purposes and the completed contract method for income tax purposes. Assume that income before provision for taxes for the year ended December 31, 19x1, under the percentage of completion method is $80,000 and the taxable income is $20,000. The income tax rate is 50%. Prepare the journal entry that you would recommend to record the income tax liability at December 31, 19x1.

(Adapted from the CPA exam.)

15-38. ***PERCENTAGE OF COMPLETION*** Weinstein Contractors, Inc., undertakes long-term, large-scale construction projects and began operations on October 15, 19x1, with contract No. 1, its only job during 19x1. A trial balance of the company's general ledger at December 31, 19x2, follows:

WEINSTEIN CONTRACTORS, INC.
TRIAL BALANCE
DECEMBER 31, 19x2

Cash	$ 68,090	
Accounts receivable	136,480	
Costs of contracts in progress	421,320	
Plant and equipment	35,500	
Accumulated depreciation		$ 8,000
Accounts payable		70,820
Deferred income taxes		1,908
Billings on contracts in progress		459,400
Capital stock		139,000
Retained earnings		2,862
Selling and administrative expenses	20,600	
	$681,990	$681,990

The following information is available:

(a) At December 31, 19x2, there were three jobs in progress, the contract prices of which had been computed as follows:

	Contract 1	Contract 2	Contract 3
Labor and material costs	$169,000	$34,500	$265,700
Indirect costs	30,000	5,500	48,000
Total costs	$199,000	$40,000	$313,700
Add: Profit in contract	40,000	3,000	30,300
Total contract price	$239,000	$43,000	$344,000

During the year, billings are credited to billings on contracts in progress; at year-end this account is charged for the amount of revenue to be recognized.

(b) All job costs are charged to cost of contracts in progress. Cost estimates are carefully derived by engineers and architects and are considered reliable. Data on costs to December 31, 19x2, follow:

Contract	Original Estimate	Incurred to Date: Total	Labor & Materials	Indirect
1	$199,000	$115,420	$ 92,620	$22,800
2	40,000	32,000	26,950	5,050
3	313,700	313,700	265,700	48,000
Totals	$552,700	$461,120	$385,270	$75,850

(c) At December 31, 19*x*1, accumulated costs on contract 1 were $39,800; no costs had accumulated on contracts 2 and 3.

Required:

(1) Prepare a schedule computing the percentage of completion of contracts in progress at December 31, 19*x*2.
(2) Prepare a schedule computing the amounts of revenue, related costs, and net income to be recognized in 19*x*2 from contracts in progress at December 31, 19*x*2.

(Adapted from the CPA exam.)

15-39. ***TRANSPORTATION METHOD*** The Sherfy Company assembles small digital computers at three plant locations. Its customers are located in five marketing areas: Detroit, New York, Denver, Seattle, and Los Angeles. The transportation cost for one computer from plant to market is as follows:

	Detroit	New York	Denver	Seattle	Los Angeles
Plant 1	$20	$14	$30	$35	$38
Plant 2	18	25	15	24	16
Plant 3	22	34	19	10	12

For 19*x*1 the *production* of each plant and the *demand* of each marketing area is expected to be:

Plant 1: 350 units
Plant 2: 200 units } *Supply*
Plant 3: 300 units

Detroit: 160 units
New York: 255 units
Denver: 85 units } *Demand*
Seattle: 110 units
Los Angeles: 240 units

Required:

Using the transportation method, determine the best logistics scheme for transporting the assembled computers to market areas.

15-40. ***TRANSPORTATION METHOD*** Delaney, Inc., manufactures dictating machines in its three factories and ships them to warehouses in three cities. Shipping costs were uniform throughout the fiscal year ending June 30, 19*x*1. A schedule of shipping costs follows:

COST OF SHIPPING ONE FINISHED UNIT
DURING FISCAL YEAR ENDED JUNE 30, 19x1

To Warehouses in	From Factories in: Red City	Bluefield	Green Valley
Blacktown	$3	$8	$5
Orange	5	4	2
Indigo	4	7	3

Sales of the Delaney machine have been excellent and the company has had to operate its three plants at full capacity to fill orders. During the year the following shipments were made:

UNITS SHIPPED TO WAREHOUSES DURING FISCAL YEAR ENDED JUNE 30, 19x1

To Warehouses in	From Factories in Red City	Bluefield	Green Valley	Total
Blacktown	5,000	7,000		12,000
Orange		3,000	13,000	16,000
Indigo		7,000	2,000	9,000
Total shipments	5,000	17,000	15,000	37,000

Management is aware that the above allocation of production probably did not result in the lowest possible total cost of freight and is concerned about the impact of this on the valuation of the June 30, 19*x*1, finished goods inventory. The company wishes to value inventories at the cost of manufacturing plus the freight charges applicable under an allocation of production scheme which would result in the lowest total cost of freight.

At June 30, 19*x*1, Delaney had the following finished goods inventories:

In Blacktown warehouse	3,000 units	(all from Red City)
In Orange warehouse	1,000 units	(all from Green Valley)
In Indigo warehouse	2,000 units	(all from Bluefield)
Total finished goods	6,000 units	

The cost of manufacturing a dictating machine is $78 at Red City and $80 at both Bluefield and Green Valley.

Required:

(a) Prepare a schedule computing the actual cost of finished goods inventory in warehouses, including freight, at June 30, 19*x*1. The company uses the first-in, first-out method.

(b) Prepare a schedule showing the manner in which production during fiscal 19*x*1 should have been shipped to warehouses to minimize total freight costs.

(c) Prepare a schedule computing the cost of finished inventory at June 30, 19*x*1, including the cost of freight which would have been applicable if the company had followed the lowest-cost allocation in (b). Assume for any warehouse receiving shipments from more than one factory that the units on hand pertain to the production of the factory from which the freight cost is minimal.

(d) Assume that the 1,000 units in the Orange warehouse were shipped there from the Blacktown warehouse at a shipping cost of $7 per unit and that the units had originally been shipped to Blacktown from the factory in Bluefield. At what amount should these 1,000 units be valued in inventory? Why?

(Adapted from the CPA exam.)

CHAPTER

16

ACCOUNTING INFORMATION FOR PERSONNEL AND ADMINISTRATIVE OPERATIONS

16.1 THE NATURE OF PERSONNEL AND ADMINISTRATIVE OPERATIONS

While marketing and production operations are essential to the survival of an enterprise, personnel and administrative operations provide the necessary services for reaching its goals. In this chapter we will discuss accounting information for personnel and administrative operations.

ADMINISTRATION

Administration is an activity whose goal is the effective coordination of functional areas within an organization in order to reach its objectives. These objectives may be expressed in profit or nonprofit terms. *Administration* and *management* are terms often used interchangeably. Both terms refer to the overall planning and control required by an organization. Executives concerned with the administration of a firm are not directly responsible for specific functional areas. The responsibilities for those areas rest with executives who are specialized in the various functions.

Administrative expenses are all expired costs not included in product or manufacturing costs. In other words, all costs not included in costs of goods sold are considered administrative expenses. Such expenses are classified into the following categories:

1. *Selling expenses* were discussed previously. These are the expenses incurred in the process of moving finished products to consumers. These include costs of creating and maintaining demand for a firm's products, as well as the distribution costs incurred in delivering goods.
2. *General and administrative expenses* (G & A) include all expenses incurred in running a firm, except those expenses classified as costs of goods sold or as selling expenses. Examples of general and administrative expenses include officers' salaries, legal and accounting fees, business licenses, office supplies, postage, telephone, and other general expenses.
3. *Financial expenses* are costs incurred in connection with or for the use of money. An example is interest expense arising from a firm's indebtedness.

PERSONNEL ADMINISTRATION

Personnel administration is an activity concerned with the management of a firm's most valuable resource—personnel. The basic objective of personnel administration is the maintenance of sound relationships between a firm and its employees.

The costs in personnel administration are called *payroll expenses,* which include:

1. *Salary* expense refers to compensation paid to supervisors, clerical and other white-collar workers, and managers. Such compensation is usually higher than *wages* (discussed below) and is generally computed on the basis of a month or a year. Most salaried workers are exempt from overtime regulations.
2. *Wages* are compensation paid to hourly-rated or other nonsupervisory and nonclerical employees. Wage earners are generally found in manufacturing operations and are subject to the provisions of the Fair Labor Standards Act concerning overtime pay. Wage rates can be computed on an hourly basis or on a piece-work basis.
3. *Fringe benefits* include supplementary forms of compensations which employees receive in addition to stated wages or salaries. Such fringe benefits include employer contributions to insurance premiums, retirement plans, taxes paid by the employer for old-age pensions (F.I.C.A.), and unemployment insurance. Other fringe benefits include employer-provided services such as cafeterias, employee publications, health facilities, and moving expenses.

THE ADMINISTRATIVE SUB-SYSTEM

As we defined it in the beginning of this chapter, administration is fundamentally a process of planning, organizing, staffing, directing, and controlling activities which will lead to an effective fulfillment of organizational objectives. The nature of the administrative operations in an organization can be viewed as a sub-system of the total organizational system (Exhibit 16-1).

EXHIBIT 16-1 ADMINISTRATIVE SUB-SYSTEM

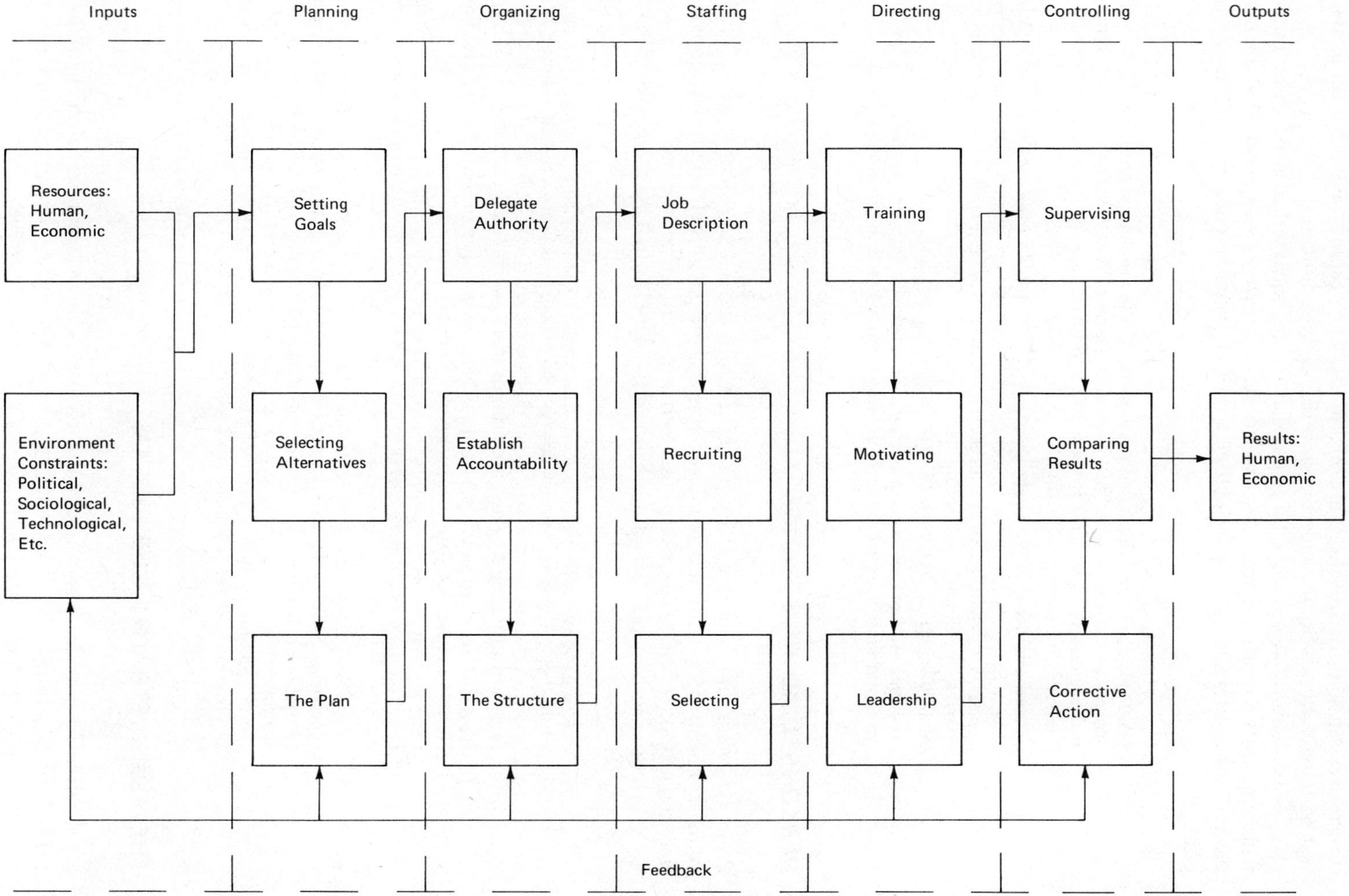

Inputs

As illustrated in Exhibit 16-1, *inputs* to this sub-system are human and other economic resources. These resources are taken from an environment which the management cannot completely control, either in quality or amount. There are political, sociological, technological, and various other forms of constraints in the environment which can affect the management of an organization.

Planning

The first function of administration is planning. *Planning* is basic to all management operations and consists of setting goals and selecting courses of action from competing alternatives. Issues such as deciding which business to be in and how much business to strive for are primary planning problems. Secondary planning issues include specific ways of arriving at fundamental goals. The distinction between *strategic* and *operational* planning should be understood:[1]

1. *Strategic Planning* involves major decisions such as long-range planning, adding or deleting a product line, entering or exiting a marketing area, and major expansion or reduction in size.
2. *Operational Planning* refers to relatively unusual and continuing operations, as well as to short-term forecasts. Minor changes in products, market areas, etc., can be accommodated under operational planning.

Organizing

The second function of administration is organizing. *Organizing* is concerned with grouping activities in a manner that will facilitate the accomplishment of goals. When these goals require the efforts of multiple personnel, we are concerned with the task of establishing some type of relationship among them, and between the group and the common goal.

Central to any scheme of organization is the delegation of authority. Authority must always go hand in hand with responsibility, which is the obligation to get something done. The source for delegating responsibility is one's superior in the organization. When a superior delegates responsibility to a subordinate, he creates a relationship based on obligation between himself and the subordinate. Delegating does not relieve the superior of the original responsibility; it only allows for someone else to do the work.

Exhibit 16-2 indicates that the objective determines the work to be performed. The total work consists of a number of activities. These activities are works that can be identified and separated from other works. Individual jobs are created by selecting and grouping activities into individual assignments. The basic principle governing this process is functional similarity. This principle is also applied to the creation of sections, departments, and divisions.

Authority is the right to perform and command. If one has been delegated a

[1]See Robert N. Anthony, *Planning and Control Systems—A Framework for Analysis* (Cambridge, Mass.: Harvard University Press, 1965).

EXHIBIT 16-2 CREATION OF JOBS

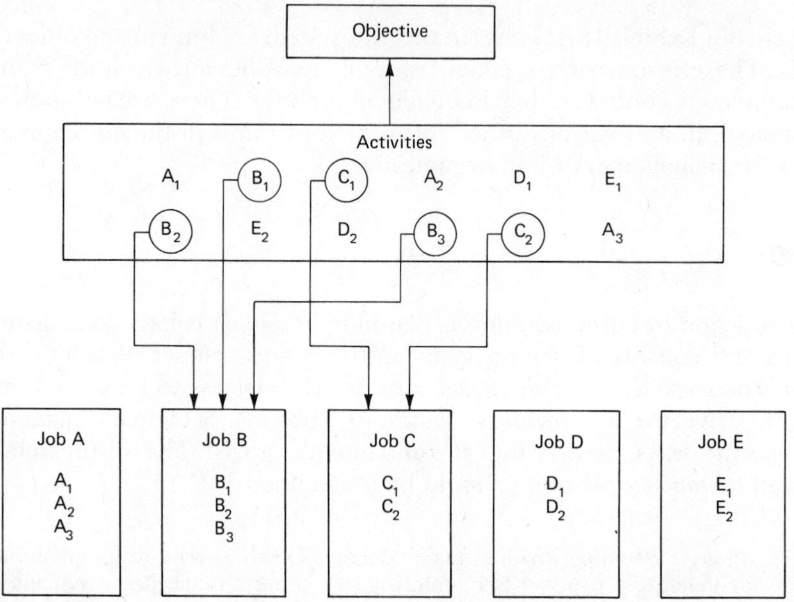

sufficient amount of authority to enable fulfillment of his responsibility, he is reasonably accountable to his superior for results.

The increasing complexity of decision making in top level management in large corporations has led to reorganization of the presidential office. The concept of a plural president has been reported in such organizations as General Motors, General Electric, Scott Paper, and others.

With increasing size of organization, the tendency is in the direction of greater decentralization of authority and responsibility as well as for more precise descriptions of these relationships.

Staffing

Staffing is the focus of personnel operations. It starts with the preparation of job descriptions. Once a job is defined, recruiting begins. Recruiting is searching for suitable candidates and encouraging them to apply for a position. The process of selection consists of interviewing and testing. Certain preferences previously used to exclude applicants are now forbidden under various federal and state fair employment practices acts, such as discrimination on the basis of sex, race, creed, or national origin. Major activities of personnel operations will be discussed later in this chapter.

Directing

Plans have been made, and an organization has been created and staffed. The next logical function of management is to stimulate the employee to undertake the work required. This function is referred to as *directing*.

Training is the process of increasing the skill and knowledge of employees to improve existing performance or to prepare for a new assignment. It plays an important role in directing the efforts of subordinates toward the rationally determined objectives of the organization. The organization hopes to benefit from training with increased productivity, reduced supervision, increased stability, and heightened morale. The employee can gain from training through increased compensation from better productivity, greater freedom and security, and better job satisfaction.

The motivation to act cannot be observed. It can only be inferred by observing and analyzing actual behavior. In order to motivate his subordinates in a positive manner, the manager must have available a series of rewards. He must also insure that desired behavior and the rewards are effectively related. Proper communication must be established to make sure that the employee understands what is expected from him and how he will be rewarded.

Leadership is another major element of direction and is concerned with the relationships among the leader, the followers, and the situation. Leadership at top management requires conceptual skills in establishing the basic goals and image of the organization. Lower management requires more technical skill.

Controlling

The last function of administration is controlling. *Control* is the process that ensures that activities conform with established rules and standards. It requires the monitoring of operative performance and the effectiveness of resource utilization. This is often accomplished through supervision. Since a supervisor is the direct link between management and its employees, the supervisory position is a very sensitive one. Too much supervision is often detrimental to good employee relations and too little encourages loose conduct.

To close the control loop, critical information with respect to established standards must be provided. This feedback operation involves direct overseeing by immediate supervisors, periodic collection of data from significant activities, and systematic comparison with standards. When an intolerable event occurs, corrective action must be taken. Standard control devices include the Gantt Chart and PERT for quantity and time, statistical control charts for quality, and budgets for control of costs.

Outputs

The *outputs* of the administrative system are performance results in both human and economic terms. It is by these outputs that society judges the success of the organization. Organizations exist by permission of society and will fail if the results produced are inappropriate or too costly.

16.2 MAJOR ACTIVITIES IN PERSONNEL OPERATIONS

The objective of personnel management is to maximize the utilization of human resources of the organization. The major activities in personnel management are manpower development, manpower planning, compensation, and organization planning. These activities should be treated in an integrated and systematic manner.

MANPOWER DEVELOPMENT

Manpower development involves job definition and clarification, training, periodic appraisal, and various other developmental activities. Instead of discussing these activities individually, we shall outline some of the problems which exist today in the manpower development area.

We have mentioned the importance of *training* to an organization. Firms have used movies, programmed learning, classroom teaching, sensitivity training, and other approaches to supplement on-the-job training. However, the effectiveness of such tools cannot be evaluated with available theories. Many training activities may not be worth the time, the resources, and the effort. But without the means to evaluate them, one cannot identify the most satisfactory supplementary techniques for manpower development.

Success of individual performance has been measured in terms of salary, job level, and various performance ratings. These criteria, however, cannot be used to predicate successful performance in initial selection, but are useful in periodic appraisals of individuals for promotion and further development.

Psychological tests attempt to identify potential talent, to predict turnover among employees, and to predict employee performance under business pressures. Validations of tests must be replicated as conditions for their use change. Personnel managers need to screen useful tests to meet the specific needs of their organizations and to develop new tools when unusual needs exist.

Perhaps *motivation* is the most complex matter of all the areas of human behavior. It is generally true that proper rewards will motivate people. But for most people material rewards are ineffective beyond the subsistence level as discussed in chapter 2.

MANPOWER PLANNING

Manpower planning refers to the rather complex task of forecasting and planning for the right numbers and kinds of people at the right places and times to perform activities which will benefit both the organization and its employees. It is the process of determining manpower requirements and the means for meeting those requirements in order to carry out the plans of the organization. This process is illustrated in Exhibit 16-3.

At the beginning of the manpower planning process, the organizational objectives and plans must be formulated. The fundamental *objective of manpower planning* is to provide the organization with the personnel to perform the activities that will achieve organizational goals. Therefore, it must be integrated with total organizational planning.

Once the organizational objectives are defined, the gross manpower requirements should be forecasted. *Manpower forecast* involves a complete definition of types, numbers, location, and timing of manpower skills needed throughout the organization for the planning period. The techniques used in manpower forecasting are ex-

EXHIBIT 16-3 MANPOWER PLANNING PROCESS

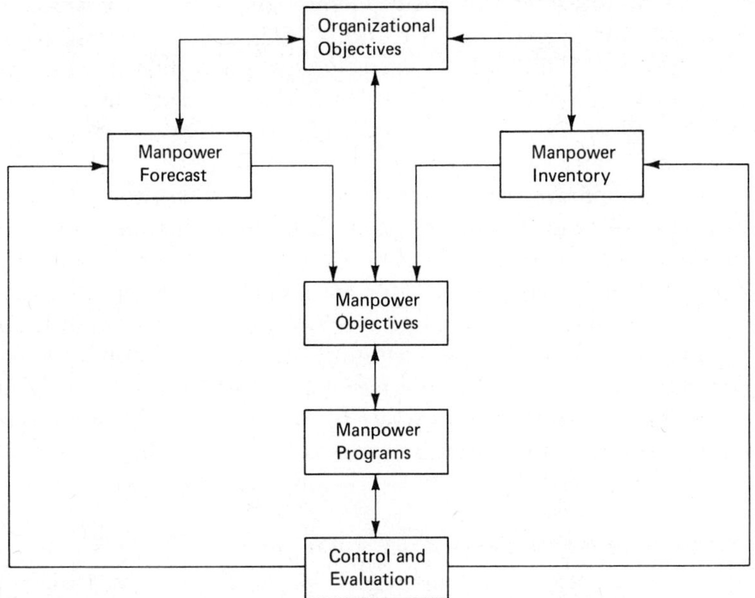

pert estimate, historical comparison, task analysis, and mathematical modeling, depending on the special requirements of an organization.

It is becoming an increasingly common practice in large organizations to develop a data bank of employee skills which can be matched against any perceived needs. For example, if a new product is developed, the skills needed can be identified and compared against the *manpower inventory* in an effort to find the most qualified persons for a particular job, and to assist in relocating employees who may have completed assignments on other projects. With particular regard to available manpower supply within an organization, computers have come of age. The U.S. armed forces have clearly demonstrated the possibilities of developing complete personnel data systems. The automated Air Force Personnel Data System, for example, yields demographic, training, career progress, and quality analyses of 135,000 officers—analyses used in officer assignment, retirement, promotion, and separation, and, to a limited degree, in personnel analysis. A similar personnel data system serves airmen. The navy has a battery of classification tests coupled with a computerized assignment system, called COMPASS, which matches qualified enlisted men with jobs and school assignments. The system also permits research on such things as retention, performance, and optimal petty officer ratios. A simulation model, COSIMO, lets one look at all interactions between selected decision variables to determine the effects that a given decision has upon cost and effectiveness over time within a given system.[2]

Many companies have set up computer-based manpower inventory systems designed along the same principles as the military systems. For example, North American Rockwell has a "skill index" which lists the following information about each employee: present assignment, past experience, appropriate next assignment, education, foreign language skills, years of management experience, publications, patents,

[2] J. W. Walker, "Forecasting Manpower Needs," *Harvard Business Review,* March–April 1969, pp. 152–64.

and military status.[3] IBM has a comprehensive personnel data system (PDS) that has been proved to be an effective tool in supporting corporate objectives as well as fulfilling the more traditional personnel functions. This system contains up to 400 data elements on each of the 150,000 IBM employees in the United States. The PDS file is updated according to payroll frequency at each location. With the accurate, current-data base, IBM is able to evaluate its pension plan, conduct its manpower and long-range salary planning, and other analyses.[4]

The *assignment of manpower* to various operating tasks should be made under a plan that contributes to a minimization of total cost or to a maximization of total profit. Such an assignment scheme can be devised using a special application of linear programming called the *assignment method.* Men (or machines) can be assigned to various jobs in a manner that minimizes performance cost. Jobs can vary in duration and can range from miniscule assembly and machining operations to operations combined into tasks. Assignments are made on the basis of an individual worker's hourly wage rate (or a machine's rate) and on an estimate of the time he will take to complete each job. There are, however, two prerequisites to an application of the assignment method:

1. Each worker may be assigned to only one job.
2. The number of workers must equal the number of jobs. If there is an extra worker, we must add a *dummy* job to those available. By assuming a zero cost for any worker to complete this job, we can express an *indifference* as to which worker is assigned. Subsequently, the analysis will result in the least desirable worker being assigned to the dummy job. If there is an extra job, a similar procedure is followed.

Suppose the Hendrick Company has *four* jobs to complete (J1, J2, J3, J4) and *four* workers (W1, W2, W3, W4) capable of completing any one of them. The hourly wage for workers 1 through 4 is $2.00, $2.50, $1.75, and $2.40, respectively; and the proficiency of each is as follows:

Performance Time in Hours

	W1	W2	W3	W4
J1	11.0	7.2	5.7	7.1
J2	5.0	3.6	8.6	6.7
J3	9.0	6.0	5.7	5.4
J4	4.0	3.6	10.3	5.4

The solution to this assignment problem follows five steps:

STEP 1: Set up a *job-worker matrix* showing the cost for each worker to complete each job. Multiplying the performance time by the appropriate hourly wage yields the cost matrix:[5]

---

[3] Ibid.

[4] W. R. Liebtag, "How An EDP Personnel Data System Works For Corporate Growth," *Personnel,* July–August 1970, pp. 15–21.

[5] If the problem had involved *profits* instead of *costs,* a cost matrix could have been constructed by determining the *relative cost* of each cell. These costs are obtained by subtracting the value of each cell from the largest value in any cell.

	W1	W2	W3	W4
J1	$22	$18	$10	$17
J2	10	9	15	16
J3	18	15	10	13
J4	8	9	18	13

STEP 2: Treating each *row* separately, subtract the least-cost cell from every cell on that row. This subtraction will produce at least one zero on each row, with the remaining cell figures representing the *opportunity cost* of non-optimal assignments.

	W1	W2	W3	W4
J1	12	8	0	7
J2	1	0	6	7
J3	8	5	0	3
J4	0	1	10	5

STEP 3: Check for a solution by drawing the *minimum number* of vertical and/or horizontal lines so that *all zeroes* in the matrix are covered. If the number of lines equals the number of rows (or columns, since the matrix is square) a solution has been obtained. The location of the zero opportunity costs discloses the solution. First, assign facilities for which there is no choice. After the assignment, check for any newly created no-choice assignments. Make additional assignments and then check again for newly created no-choice assignments. Continue the procedure until all assignments are made. If the *last remaining* assignments invoice a choice, then factors such as employee seniority and personality must be the deciding influences.

	W1	W2	W3	W4
J1	12	8	0	7
J2	1	0	6	7
J3	8	5	0	3
J4	0	1	10	5

The *minimum number of lines* necessary to cover all zeroes is three; therefore, a solution is not yet obtained.

STEP 4: Treating each *column* separately, subtract the least-cost cell from every cell in that column. This subtraction will produce at least one zero in each column, with the remaining cell figures representing the opportunity cost of not assigning an individual worker to his "best" task.

	W1	W2	W3	W4
J1	12	8	0	4
J2	1	0	6	4
J3	8	5	0	0
J4	0	1	10	2

STEP 5: Repeat step 3 by again checking for a solution.
If a solution is not obtained:

1. *Subtract* the *smallest* uncovered number in the matrix from all uncovered numbers.
2. *Add* the *smallest* uncovered number in the matrix to all numbers appearing at line intersections.
3. Repeat step 3 by again checking for a solution.

	W1	W2	W3	W4
J1	12	8	0	4
J2	1	0	6	4
J3	8	5	0	0
J4	0	1	10	2

The least number of lines that can be drawn is four. The choice of horizontal lines is purely arbitrary. Any combination of horizontal and/or vertical lines are acceptable so long as they represent the minimum number of lines. In this instance, regardless of the combinations, four lines must still be drawn. *A solution has been obtained.* We can now make the assignments according to the procedure specified in step 3 and calculate the cost of this optimal solution by using assignment costs obtained from the original cost matrix in step 1:

Assign W1 to J4 at a cost of	$ 8
Assign W2 to J2 at a cost of	9
Assign W3 to J1 at a cost of	10
Assign W4 to J3 at a cost of	13
	$40

Manpower programs entail all of the traditional personnel functions, which include employment, supporting, and information, as shown in Exhibit 16-4. These programs must be designed specifically for different types of skills, and usually the programs will be highly dissimilar. For example, training programs for managerial skills will be different from those for production workers.

For the manpower planning process to operate effectively, there must be feedback and control. There must be continuous *evaluation* to assure that programs are being achieved and that they are proper for providing personnel to meet organizational objectives.

COMPENSATION

Compensation is intended to maintain or enhance employee performance. It is clear that monetary rewards can motivate employees to a certain degree, but financial rewards alone do not satisfy many of the human needs. For example, a high salary does not guarantee relaxation to an overworked executive. A high wage does not insure that the individual's desire for self-fulfillment is satisfied. Thus, management should

EXHIBIT 16-4 PERSONNEL FUNCTIONS

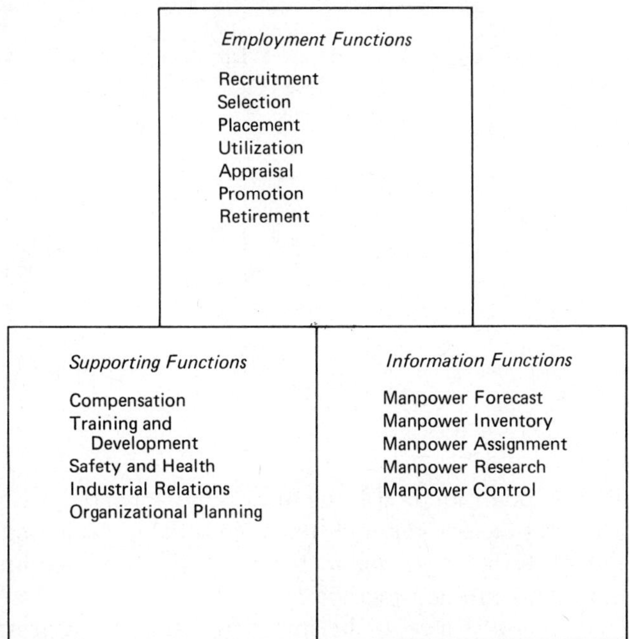

be concerned about various non-monetary rewards, including recognition, appreciation, participation, authority, challenging work, promotion, pleasant working conditions, and latitude for initiative. Unfortunately, research on the effectiveness of both monetary and non-monetary compensation programs is almost entirely lacking.

We have defined the terms *wages* and *salaries* earlier in this chapter. In recent years, a few companies, including IBM and Texas Instruments, have placed production and maintenance workers on salaried status. Although most such changes have been initiated by management, unions are beginning to demand salaried status for workers. For example, the United Auto Workers, the United Rubber Workers, and the Steelworkers have made such demands during negotiations in recent years.

The major problems involved in shifting large groups of employees from wage to salaried status relate to the consequent changes in fringe benefits. The shift is frequently accompanied by increasing supplemental benefits such as sick leave, major medical insurance, severance pay, group life insurance, and time off for personal business. Another problem may be the reaction of those employees presently on salaried payroll. If part of their income has been higher status and more liberal privileges and fringe benefits than those of hourly-paid employees, they may react by agitating for reestablishment of some kind of differential or for higher salaries.

In general, wage and salary payments within the organization are determined by a sequence of events. As illustrated in Exhibit 16-5, it starts with job analysis. *Job analysis* is the systematic investigation of a job in order to reduce its essential characteristics to a written job description. There are three techniques commonly used in job analysis; namely, observation, interview, and questionnaire. Many organizations use a combination of these techniques in obtaining information about the job.

Job evaluation is the process of determining the relative worth of the various jobs within the organization, so that differential wages or salaries may be paid to jobs

EXHIBIT 16-5 WAGE AND SALARY DETERMINATION PROCESS

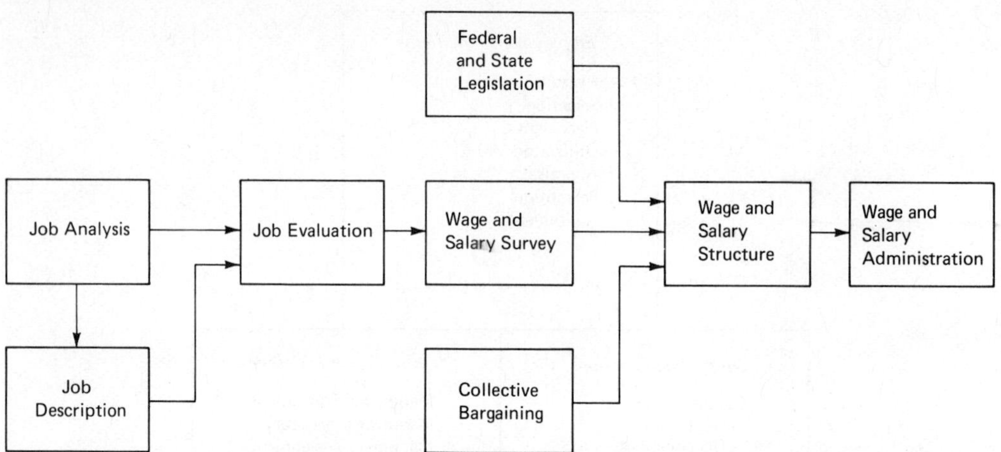

of different worth. The point method is the most popular method used in job evaluation. It examines several factors common to the jobs being evaluated and rates each job along a scale of each factor. Other methods are the factor-comparison method, classification method, and ranking method.

Wage and salary surveys involve the survey and analysis of prevailing wage and salary levels in the community or industry. These surveys may be made by mail, telephone, or interview. Survey results are also published periodically by various trade and professional associations such as the National Industrial Conference Board, American Management Association, and United States Bureau of Labor Statistics.

Wage and salary structure are made on the bases of job evaluation, prevailing practices, organizational problems, federal and state legislation, collective bargaining, and pressures of the labor market. In addition to basic wages and salaries, there are a wide variety of fringe benefits and incentive payments. Because of the continued pressure from organized labor, the increased leisure time available to all workers, the higher level of affluence, new medical advances, and further social legislation by the government, employees will regard benefits as rights in the future even more so than at present.

Wage and salary administration deals with general adjustment, translating merit-rating into dollars, and maintaining some control over wage and salary expenditures.

Executive compensation refers to fringe benefits provided to a firm's executives. Such benefits are necessary to recruit, retain, and motivate top executives. Examples of executive fringe benefits include deferred compensation, stock options, insurance, bonuses, profit-sharing plans, and so forth. Since an executive is generally in a high income tax bracket, the selection of executive compensation plans is very sensitive to tax laws. The Tax Reform Act of 1969 made qualified stock options a less popular means for extra compensation. A study by McKinsey and Company,[6] sampling 165 large companies in a wide mix of industries, shows that while 65% of the companies with option plans were giving qualified stock options in January 1970, that figure dropped to 58% by the year's end. But more significantly, when companies get around to making the changes they say they are working on, the percentage of qualified option plans could fall to as low as 38%. On the other hand, the use of tandem

[6] "Top Men Demand New Kinds of Pay," *Business Week*, January 23, 1971, p. 65.

option plans, a combination of both qualified and non-qualified options, more than doubled during 1970. Similarly, the use of phantom stock, which is essentially a fancier way of giving a deferred bonus, grew by more than 100% in 1970.

The stock option had its heyday in the 1950s and early 1960s, when the top personal tax rate was as high as 91%. But when a highly paid executive sold stock he picked up through options, he paid no more than a 25% tax on the gain. Beginning in 1972, earned income such as salary was taxed at no more than 50%, while the capital gains rate on such items as option gains moved up to 35%. And the executive also may have to pay an additional 10% minimum tax on a portion of extremely large preference income items, which include one-half of long-term capital gains as well as any paper gain on the difference between an option's exercise price and the stock's market value.

Because the complexities of various compensation items are interrelated in terms of tax effects, some companies are setting up tax sheltered investments, such as apartment complexes and other real estate ventures, in which top management participates. However, an executive compensation plan must focus on performance and motivation rather than devise gimmicky plans that maximize tax advantages.

ORGANIZATIONAL PLANNING

Organizational planning has traditionally been concerned with the description and design of formal organizational relationships through organization charts. The bases for this planning have been established both by directions from line managers concerning how the company should be organized and by principles of organization inherited from decades of management thought and practice.

Organizing has been described as the process of establishing relationships among personnel. The primary formal relationships involved are responsibility, authority, and accountability. In theory, an organization structure should be designed in such a way that each person's efforts will add to, but do not duplicate or offset, the efforts of others in his unit. The efforts of each unit then merge effectively with those of other units to maximize accomplishment of departmental and organizational goals. The major types of structures are *line, line and staff,* and *functional.*

In line organizations, all personnel perform basic functions, or are located in a chain of command above these functions. The line and staff form introduces the complexities of specialists in an advisory capacity.

The primary consideration in developing an organization structure is that the selected pattern will contribute to the attainment of the organization's goals. Ideally, the structure in effect at any given time will be the one that makes a maximal contribution. Unfortunately, no one can predict the future exactly—hence, no one knows what the ideal is. Several guidelines can be used in planning a better organization structure. For example:

1. Reduce conflict through clear managerial role prescriptions.
2. Design organizational structures and establish role prescriptions in accord with existing abilities, skills, and personality characteristics.
3. Understand the nature of the business, and design a structure that can respond to external constraints and pressures.

Organizational planning should be carried out by staff specialists and managers. Staff specialists serve to complement a manager's knowledge of a situation with broader norms for organization.

HUMAN RESOURCE VALUATION

People are the essential ingredient in all organizations, whether they are business, educational, governmental, or religious, and the way in which people are recruited and utilized by the organization largely determines whether the organization will survive to achieve its objectives. The effective management of people means that manpower planning must be a part of overall organizational strategy. In recent years, there are more and more large corporations purchasing small, technically oriented companies—not for their equipment, but for their skilled engineers and scientists. Business organizations are spending ever-increasing sums of money to retrain their managers. Financial analysts are giving more attention to the quality of their managers than to any other factor in the valuation of a company's securities.

The ability to increase profits is limited not only by investment dollars, but also by the availability of experienced salesmen, skilled engineers, and capable top level managers. Decisions based solely on the monetary aspects, ignoring the personnel factors, are likely to be non-optimal ones. For example, the executive vice president of a large distribution organization is evaluating the performance of two divisional sales managers. Both divisions are set up as investment centers, with Division A showing a 20% return on investment and Division B an 11% return. However, when the two divisions were established in the preceding year, all of the company's experienced salesmen were assigned to Division A. The Division B manager has had to hire and train new salesmen. In this case, the conventional return-on-investment approach would show that Division A is superior to B. However, the executive vice president would or should rate Division B better than A.[7]

Although many executives already recognize the significance of limited availability of certain key skills, the existing accounting systems treat people as an expense item. The only reference to people on the profit-and-loss statement or balance sheet is under the heading of wages and salaries. In principle, the problem of measuring the value of people should be approached in the same way as that of measuring the value of other resources, by applying the so-called economic theory of value. In these terms, the value of human resources can be conceived of and measured as the present worth of their expected future services. Since the concept of value is an abstraction which is difficult, if not impossible, to measure, resources are typically measured in terms of surrogates. There are several possible surrogate measures of the value of people to organizations, including acquisition cost, replacement cost, current cost, compensation, and performance indices.

1. *Acquisition cost:* The reason for using this historical cost is that the price actually paid for an asset by a purchaser reflects his assessment of its value to him at the time of acquisition.
2. *Replacement cost:* Replacement cost refers to the sacrifice that would have to be in-

[7] J. S. Hekimian and C. H. Jones, "Put People On Your Balance Sheet," *Harvard Business Review,* January–February 1967, pp. 105–113.

curred by a given organization in order to replace an existing resource with another one capable of providing an equivalent set of services.

3. *Current cost:* Current cost refers to the current price that exists for a resource in the market in which it is bought and sold.
4. *Compensation:* Compensation is the price paid for the use of units of human services, not the price or market value of the whole human asset.
5. *Performance indices:* Since performance indices constitute an index of an individual's effectiveness in achieving his responsibilities, they are intended to measure the contribution an individual makes to the goals of an organization by rendering services in his present position.

16.3 ACCOUNTING RULES AND PROCEDURES

Accounting for personnel and administrative operations follows certain rules and procedures.

COSTS AND EXPENSES

The distinction between *costs* and *expenses* should be clarified at this point. Costs are the amounts paid for the acquisition of goods and services. When the benefits to be derived from the goods and services acquired have not yet been realized, such future benefits are called *unexpired costs* or *prepaid expenses.* The term *expense* refers to an expired cost. For example, when a month's rent has been paid at the beginning of a month, such a cost is considered unexpired. When the month is over, the unexpired cost is considered an expense.

Some costs are never considered expenses, because theoretically they never expire. The costs of acquiring or producing merchandise for sale does not expire, but rather is transferred into sales.

The costs of personnel and administrative operations are generally considered expenses when incurred. Salaries of officers, for example, represent payment for services rendered for a past period, rather than a cost to be applied to future periods.

REVENUE AND CAPITAL EXPENDITURES

When expenditures are classified as assets, such costs are called *capital* expenditures; the term that describes the addition to assets is called *capitalizing* a transaction. The alternative to capitalizing is *expensing* a transaction. Costs are capitalized because they benefit future operations: that is, the goods or services acquired will not be exhausted in one fiscal period. Technically, the office chair will probably last more than one fiscal period; however, for expediency, amounts smaller than a specified amount are written off to expense. The costs of office chairs acquired, for example, are considered capital costs and are included in the asset *office furniture.* However, it may be the policy of a firm not to capitalize costs below a specified amount but rather to consider such costs as expenses or, as they are often called, *revenue expenditures.* In our previous example, if a firm buys one chair for $45, that cost may be treated as an expense because it does not meet the $50 capital expenditure limit.

The twin rules of *materiality* and *consistency* govern in *capital* versus *revenue* expenditure decisions. We have said that if an item is less than a certain amount, it will be expensed rather than capitalized—this is *materiality*. Consistency dictates that all items of a similar nature be expensed. For example, if one chair is purchased and expensed because of immateriality, the purchase of 100 chairs should be treated in like manner even though the total dollar sum may be material.

16.4 ACCOUNTING FOR PERSONNEL ADMINISTRATION

Accounting for human resources covers the following items:

1. *Trust funds* are sums of money which are held by a company, either for its employees or for the government. A company collects money from employees and holds the funds in a *fiduciary* capacity. Such funds include *mandatory* deductions under various federal and state regulations such as state disability acts, Federal Insurance Contribution Act, and federal and state income taxes to be withheld. Optional deductions include savings deposits, purchases of savings bonds, health and accident insurance premiums, life insurance premiums, pension plan contributions, charitable contributions, and others. Such deductions, including contributions of an employer's share, are liabilities on a company's records. The compound entry to record such funds is made when a payroll is disbursed, as follows:

Debit (Increase):	Wages and/or salaries expense (for total gross wages and salaries before deductions)
Credit (Increase):	Payroll taxes payable (mandatory payroll deductions)
Credit (Increase):	Other deductions (optional)
Credit (Decrease):	Cash (net payroll paid out)

2. *Deferred Salary* is a type of executive compensation. It represents salaries and/or bonuses which are to be paid at a later date although earned presently. At the time earned, such deferred compensation is recorded as a current expense and a liability. This liability remains on the records until paid. A typical entry for deferred compensation is as follows:

Debit (Increase):	Executive salaries
Credit (Increase):	Deferred executive compensation payable

3. *Insurance* for executives may be of two types, depending upon the beneficiary (the person to whom benefits are to be paid). If a company pays the premiums for insurance on its executives, the amount of such premiums are an expense deduction for federal income tax purposes only if the company is not the beneficiary. If the company is the beneficiary, the premiums may be considered an expense of operations for financial statement purposes, but not for income tax purposes. If the beneficiary is someone named by the insured executive (other than the com-

pany), the premiums paid (or a portion thereof) represent additional compensation to the executive.

4. *Other fringe benefits* available to executives include company-owned automobiles, expense accounts, company-owned apartments and homes, loans at low interest rates, purchase of company products at cost, and company-paid education.

16.5 PROCESSING PERSONNEL AND ADMINISTRATIVE TRANSACTIONS

Processing personnel and administrative transactions involves inputs, transformation, and outputs.

INPUTS

The principal personnel and administrative events and related documents are shown in Exhibits 16-6 and 16-7. There are two basic events in these areas: (1) the rendering of service to a firm and (2) payment for such services.

EXHIBIT 16-6 PERSONNEL EVENTS AND RELATED DOCUMENTS

EVENT	TRANSACTION DOCUMENT
A. Personnel render service to a firm.	1. *Time cards* in the case of hourly workers. 2. *Employment authorization* in the case of salaried employees.
B. Payroll is paid.	3. *Check* or *receipt for cash received.* Documents are issued when payroll is disbursed. 4. *Adjustment.* Deferred compensation and fringe benefits are allocated to eligible employees.

EXHIBIT 16-7 ADMINISTRATIVE EVENTS AND RELATED DOCUMENTS

EVENT	TRANSACTION DOCUMENT
A. Administrative expense.	1. *Invoice.* Services are rendered by parties outside a firm. 2. *Time cards* and *employment authorization.* Services are rendered by administrative personnel. 3. *Adjustment.* To record administrative depreciation and amortization.
B. Administrative expenses are paid.	4. *Check.* Payment is made for expenses incurred.

EXHIBIT 16-8 *THE DUALITY OF SOME TYPICAL PERSONNEL EVENTS*

Event	Transaction Document	Date	Notation	Codes: Doc.	Codes: Trans.	Codes: Acct.	Accounts	Amount: Debit	Amount: Credit
PERSONNEL									
A. Personnel render services to a firm.	Time cards		a. Production workers earn wages.		10 10	41820 21230	Manufacturing Labor Accrued Payroll	12,000	 12,000
	Payroll authorization		b. Administrative personnel earn salaries.		10 10	70020 21230	Admin. Salaries Accrued Payroll	5,000	 5,000
B. Accrued Payroll is paid.	Check		c. Accrued payroll is paid weekly and proper deductions are taken.		12 10 12	21230 21300 11110	Accrued Payroll Accrued Payroll Taxes Cash in Bank	17,000	 2,000 15,000
			d. Company liability for contribution to employee pension plan based on 15% of total compensation is recorded.		10 10	50020 21700	Employee Benefits Pension Plan (Special Reserve)	2,550	 2,550
ADMINISTRATIVE									
A. Administrative expenses are incurred.	Invoice		e. Invoice is received for legal services.		10 10	70000 21130	Legal Services Accounts Payable	1,000	 1,000
	Adjustment		f. Administrative depreciation and amortization.		10 10	70040 12320	Depreciation and Amortization Accumulated Depreciation	 1,500	 1,500

TRANSFORMATIONS

Personnel and administrative data undergo two transformations in the accounting system.

Transformation$_1$: Establishing duality or the cause-and-effect relationship of personnel and administrative events is the function of T_1. Typical T_1 entries for such events are shown in Exhibit 16-8.

Transformation$_2$: Using T-accounts, the events in Exhibit 16-8 are posted at T_2 as shown in Exhibit 16-9.

EXHIBIT 16-9 POSTING PERSONNEL AND ADMINISTRATIVE EVENTS TO T-ACCOUNTS

11110 Cash in Bank

fwd	$30,000	(c)	$15,000
		(g)	1,000

12320 Accumulated Depreciation

		(f)	$1,500

21700 Pension Plan

		(d)	$2,550

70040 Depreciation and Amortization

(f)	$1,500		

21230 Accrued Payroll

(c)	$17,000	(a)	$12,000
		(b)	5,000

21130 Accounts Payable

		(e)	$1,000

21300 Accrued Payroll Taxes

		(c)	$2,000

41820 Manufacturing Labor

(a)	$12,000		

70020 Administrative Salaries

(b)	$5,000		

50020 Employee Benefits

(d)	$2,550		

70000 Legal Services

(e)	$1,000		

OUTPUTS

The accounting information system generates statements reporting personnel and administrative activities. These reports are of two types:

1. *Financial reports* show personnel and administrative expenses during a specified period as an integral part of the income statement. Some published financial statements show personnel costs (*wages, salaries,* and related benefits) as a separate item; other statements allocate manufacturing wages to *cost of goods sold,* salesmen's salaries to *selling expenses,* and administrative salaries to *general and administrative expenses.*
2. *Management reports* provide detailed information for analysis and action by management. Such information includes detailed break-downs of personnel and administrative expenses. In addition, management reports include non-financial information concerning personnel and administrative operations. Such informa-

tion includes personnel statistics such as turnover rates, absenteeism, productivity rates, and others.

16.6 SYSTEMS CONTROLS FOR PERSONNEL AND ADMINISTRATIVE OPERATIONS

Personnel and administrative operations are subject to stewardship and management controls.

STEWARDSHIP CONTROLS

Stewardship controls are designed to safeguard assets and insure proper recording of transactions.

Administrative

With regard to administrative expenses, stewardship controls coincide with controls over *purchasing activities* (chapter 14) and *disbursement activities* (chapter 10).

Control of purchasing insures that administrative expenses have been authorized and that invoices have been approved for payment. Controls of disbursements insure that payments are made only for properly authorized purposes. Other controls common to both areas are the proper recording of transactions. One such control is a *detailed Chart of Accounts* with a manual explaining to which account items are to be charged.

Personnel

Stewardship controls in personnel operations have the following objectives.

1. *Compliance with federal and state laws.* In the area of personnel operations, stewardship controls are also required to insure compliance with federal and state laws such as the following:
   a. *Fair Labor Standards Act* requires employers engaged in interstate commerce to pay workers a minimum wage of $1.60 per hour effective February 1, 1968.
   b. *Social Security Act* requires deductions from employees and a matching contribution from employers for the payment by the federal government of pensions to retired persons.
   c. *State Unemployment.* Most states require contributions by employers to provide a fund to make subsistence payments to unemployed employees. Quarterly employers' returns are usually required.
   d. *Internal Revenue Service.* Regulations issued by the Internal Revenue Service are concerned mainly with reporting income of employees and payment of withholding taxes deducted from employees.
2. *Authority of personnel actions.* A system of authorizations constitute an important stewardship control of personnel operations, which require that actions involving compensation be properly authorized.

a. *Pay raises and related charges of status* must be authorized by proper officials. Generally the *personnel department* hires, terminates, and makes changes of status. The *payroll department,* which is responsible for making up payroll, computes a pay raise only upon authorization from personnel.
b. *Fringe benefits* are generally of two types: those for which all employees are eligible and those which only pertain to selected employees (executives). Examples of the former include health and accident insurance coverage, parking privileges, purchase of goods at discounts, and others. Such benefits are generally authorized at the time of employment by the personnel department. The other class of benefits are generally reserved for those with executive status and can either be authorized by personnel or by special authorization of a highly placed executive.
c. *Executive compensation* is generally authorized at the highest level by a board of directors or by approval of stockholders. If a specified scale of executive compensation is in force, a personnel department may put an authorization into effect after being informed of an employee's advancement in executive ranks. If executive compensation is discretionary, such an authorization usually comes from the highest level in a company, such as president or vice president.

3. *Custodianship of trust funds.* Personnel operations generate several types of trust funds. These are funds which a company holds for the benefit of its employees. Such funds are of two types: mandatory funds and voluntary funds.

Mandatory funds are those funds which an employer is required by law to maintain, such as withholding taxes and related payroll deductions.

Voluntary funds are established at the discretion of management or under the provisions of union agreements. Such funds are benefit plans for employees and these in turn may be of two types: qualified and nonqualified plans.

a. *Qualified plans* are benefit plans such as pension or profit-sharing plans which meet the requirements of the Internal Revenue Code and are approved by the Internal Revenue Service. Generally such funds are administered by an independent trustee such as a bank or insurance company and, therefore, stewardship controls pose few problems.
b. *Non-qualified plans* are discretionary employee benefit plans which do not meet the requirements of the Internal Revenue Service and such plans are generally administered by the company itself. Stewardship controls are concerned with protection of money in the fund, payments to employees, and accounting for income of the fund.

4. *Payroll controls* are concerned with the payment of proper amounts to proper employees. Such controls insure that correct amounts are paid to employees, that proper payroll deductions are taken, that terminated employees are dropped from the payroll, and that unclaimed wages are guarded. The essential element of control with respect to payroll is segregation of duties. The timekeeping department, for example, is separate from the department which computes wages and issues payroll checks.

MANAGEMENT CONTROLS

Management controls have as their objective the achievement of an optimum cost-effectiveness condition with respect to administrative and personnel costs.

Administrative Costs

Management controls over administrative costs consist of the following.

1. *Budgetary control* is a measure used to control all areas of expenditure, including administrative costs. Administrative costs are much harder to control than most other costs because there is generally no direct relationship between such costs and measures of output. Thus, while factory labor costs can be related to units of production, administrative costs cannot. Many administrative costs are difficult to predict and others cannot be standardized.

   The use of budgets, however, can aid in exercising control over such costs. A prerequisite to achieving budgetary control is assigning responsibility for administrative costs to appropriate employees. After responsibility has been assigned, each responsible employee submits a budget request in which he states his requirements for a coming period. Such requests are examined, modified, and then incorporated into an overall administrative budget. This budget becomes the standard against which expenditures are matched. Amounts exceeding budget require explanations from the responsible employee. The difficulty in this process is determining whether the initial budget is reasonable, since many administrative costs are not capable of being measured against workable standards.
2. *Allocation of G & A.* Some general and administrative (G & A) expenses are allocable to other activities. In controlling G & A expenses, management should determine if any of these expenses can be related directly to other activities.

Personnel Costs

Management controls over personnel costs include the following.

1. *Cost data and output analysis.* The foundation of management control of personnel costs is data on all personnel costs. When such costs are related to output, the resulting relationships can be used as standards to evaluate subsequent costs. In order to relate output with costs, the various phases of obtaining output are often analyzed. Time and motion studies can be used to break down an individual operation into basic elements. For example, an operation in which a factory worker bolts one piece to another may be analyzed in terms of its components: turning, reaching for a bolt, fitting two pieces together, and so forth. Each motion and its related time is then studied to determine if modifications could make it more efficient. For example, turning away from the production line is an inefficient motion. Perhaps supplies could be elevated over the production line to avoid the necessity of a wasted motion.

   Even administrative and clerical costs[8] can be evaluated in terms of output analysis as in the following example:

Function	Unit of Output Measurement
Filing	Number of pieces filed
Typing	Number of lines typed
Mail Handling	Number of pieces handled
Keypunching	Number of cards punched

2. *Quality control.* Management control of personnel operations is concerned not only with control of costs, but with control of costs *consistent* with *quality* of output.

[8]Determining output measures for administrative and clerical operations has presented a continuing problem to those who are concerned with improving organizational efficiency. A concerted effort to remedy this problem in federal government has been initiated recently. *Measuring and Enhancing Productivity in the Federal Sector,* issued in June 1972, summarizes the activities of a joint project involving the U.S. Civil Service Commission, General Accounting Office, Office of Management and Budget, and seventeen participating agencies (U.S. Government Printing Office, 1972, 723–825/73 1–3).

Management must continually monitor output to assure itself that quality standards are being maintained. This is true not only of the output of production personnel (physical products), but also of the output of marketing and administrative personnel.

Quality control of production personnel consists of testing by supervisors or quality control engineers for deviations from acceptable minimum standards. A product may be too long, too short, too heavy, too light, function too fast or too slowly, and so forth. The appearance of a defect signals the need for production to halt until the condition causing such a defect is found and corrected.

Quality control in other areas, such as marketing and administrative operations, consists of periodically evaluating units of output. We have previously mentioned types of measurement units available for evaluating administrative operations. Marketing personnel can also be evaluated in terms of solicitation costs per customer, collection costs per customer, and so forth.

3. *Personnel inventory skills.* It has often been said that the most valuable asset of most companies is their management or personnel. More specifically, the talents or skills of a company's personnel are most essential. Many companies, therefore, maintain a record of the specific skills or talents of its personnel. Such a listing is called a *personnel skills inventory.* Among the items included in the typical inventory are:
   a. Level of education, including degrees held and fields of concentration.
   b. Language capabilities.
   c. Previous work experience in terms of acquaintance with foreign countries.
   d. Special skills.

   If management needs, for example, a Ph.D. in chemistry who can speak Arabic for a travel assignment to an oil field in the Middle East, it need only search its skill inventory to see if any present employee has all or most of those skills. The ability to fill an opening by a transfer from within is always cheaper than recruiting an outsider, and, as mentioned earlier, this route is available in terms of labor union relations if not by basic employee relations.

16.7 SYSTEMS FEEDBACK FOR PERSONNEL AND ADMINISTRATIVE OPERATIONS

Feedback on personnel and adminstrative operations furnishes users with (1) control, (2) exception, (3) comparative, and (4) interpretive reports.

CONTROL

Feedback on stewardship and management controls of personnel and administrative operations can take several forms. Examples of feedback on stewardship controls include:

1. Reports detailing costs of personnel and administrative operations.
2. Reports of internal and external auditors covering their examination of these areas with respect to the following points:
   a. Assurance that all disbursements allegedly for personnel and administrative operations *were* in fact made for those areas.
   b. Assurance that personnel and administrative costs have been properly accounted for.

Feedback on management controls includes those reports discussed under the following points.

EXCEPTION

Exception reports list any material departure from plans. Such exception reports are the basis for investigation of the area reporting the exception. Manpower plans may call for a certain number of employees. An exception report may be issued showing the current level of employees significantly higher than planned levels. Such a condition requires investigation. Responsible executives are called upon to explain the reasons for exceptions. Possible negative causes for such conditions include poor control of hiring, poor control over productivity of present employees, and failure to change plans in accordance with changing conditions.

COMPARATIVE

Comparative reports show one set of data against another. In the case of personnel and administrative operations, comparative reports might show current costs against similar costs for a prior period, such as a year ago or a previous month. Comparisons of current costs against planned costs are related to *exception* reports discussed above. Such comparisons are *internal; external* comparisons can also be made and reported upon. External data showing general industry experience can be included in comparison reports.

INTERPRETIVE

Interpretive reports employ the data developed under other types of feedback and give meaning to that data. For example, if a *comparison report* shows that employee turnover has increased in a current period over that of a prior period, an interpretive report would seek to answer questions such as the following:

1. Do the company's pay scales need revision in response to changes in the industry?
2. Are working conditions below industry standards?
3. Are recruitment practices failing to keep pace with work requirements?

16.8 SUMMARY

Personnel and administrative operations are the service ends of an organization. The purpose of this chapter, like those on production and marketing (chapters 14 and 15), is to outline the essential activities in the subject matter and to explain the related accounting rules and procedures. By outlining the essential activities, we hope that the reader can understand the needs for accounting information in solving operating problems and to improve current practices, if they are inadequate.

Administration and management are terms frequently used interchangeably. Either can be viewed as the process of planning, organizing, staffing, directing, and controlling.

Personnel operations involve the management of the most valuable resources of an organization—human resources. The major activities are manpower development, manpower planning, compensation, and organization planning.

In recent years, active research efforts in human resource accounting have been both interesting and encouraging. Even though there is still no accurate method for measuring the value of human resources, the modeling effort for human resource valuation has shown significant contributions.

Accounting rules and procedures regarding general and administrative (G & A) costs, including the distinctions between costs and expenses, revenue and capital expenditures, and accruals and deferrals, are important in accounting. Within the accounting rules and procedures, processing of personnel and administrative transactions undergo two transformations.

Controls of personnel and administrative operations involve stewardship and management controls. These include control, exception, comparative, and interpretive reports to feed back the efforts and results.

CHAPTER 16 REFERENCES AND ADDITIONAL READINGS

GENERAL REFERENCES

Boyd, B. B. *Management-Minded Supervisor.* New York: McGraw-Hill Book Company, 1968.

Coleman, B. P. "An Integrated System For Manpower Planning." *Business Horizons,* October 1970.

Ferguson, R. O., and Sargent, L. F. *Linear Programming: Fundamentals and Applications.* New York: McGraw-Hill Book Company, 1958.

Flippo, E. B. *Management: A Behavioral Approach.* 2nd ed. Boston: Allyn & Bacon, Inc., 1970.

French, W. *The Personnel Management Process: Human Resources Administration.* 2nd ed. Boston: Houghton Mifflin, 1970.

Herzberg, F.; Mansner, B.; and Snyderman, B. *The Motivation to Work.* 2nd ed. New York: John Wiley & Sons, Inc., 1959.

Looba, N. P. *Linear Programming: An Introductory Analysis.* New York: McGraw-Hill Book Company, 1964.

Maslow, A. H. *Motivation and Personality.* New York: Harper & Row, 1954.

Miner, J. B. *Personnel and Industrial Relations: A Managerial Approach.* New York: The Macmillan Company, 1969.

Riggs, J. L. *Economic Decision Models for Engineers and Managers.* New York: McGraw-Hill Book Company, 1968.

Sasieni, M.; Yaspan, A.; and Friedman, L. *Operations Research: Methods and Problems.* New York: John Wiley & Sons, Inc., 1960.

Shuchman, A. *Scientific Decision-Making in Business.* New York: Holt, Rinehart & Winston, Inc., 1963.

Walker, J. W. "Trends in Manpower Management Research." *Business Horizons,* August 1968.

Weber, M. *The Theory of Social and Economic Organization.* New York: Oxford University Press, 1967.

ADMINISTRATIVE AND GENERAL EXPENSES

Smollen, William J. "Budgeting General and Administrative Expenses." *Managerial Planning,* November–December 1969, pp. 24–28.

Trentin, H. George, and Jones, Reginald L. *Budgeting General and Administrative Expenses.* Management Bulletin No. 74. New York: American Management Association, 1966.

PERSONNEL RELATIONS AND EXECUTIVE COMPENSATION

Accounting Principles Board Opinion No. 8. Accounting for the Cost of Pension Plans. New York: American Institute of Certified Public Accountants, 1966.

Bueschel, Richard T. *EDP and Personnel.* Management Bulletin No. 86. Jersey City, N.J.: American Management Association, 1966.

"Business Management's Fourth Annual Executive Compensation Report." *Business Management,* January 1969, pp. 22–29.

Cook, Fred. "The Changing Goals of Compensation." *Business Management,* February 1970, pp. 23–24.

"Cost of Management Study—1967." *Business Management,* January 1967, pp. 32–43.

Crystal, Graef S. "The Ten Commandments of Executive Compensation." *The Financial Executive,* August 1970, pp. 52–64.

"Executive Income Index: President's Pay by Sales and Industry." *Business Management,* February 1970, pp. 17–22.

"Executive Salaries Continue Upward." *The Financial Executive,* December 1969, p. 12.

Fischer, Harry C. *The Uses of Accounting in Collective Bargaining.* Los Angeles, Calif.: Institute of Industrial Relations, University of California, Los Angeles, 1969.

Gordon, T. J., and LeBleu, R. E. "Employee Benefits, 1970–1985." *Harvard Business Review,* January–February 1970, pp. 93–107.

Hettenhouse, George W. "Cost/Benefit Analysis of Executive Compensation." *Harvard Business Review,* July–August 1970, pp. 114–24.

Hicks, Ernest L. *Accounting for the Cost of Pension Plans.* Accounting Research Study No. 8. New York: American Institute of Certified Public Accountants, 1965.

"How Individual Executives Feel About Their Pay Level, Pay Progress, Company's Pay Policy." *Business Management,* January 1967, pp. 58–74.

Lewellen, William G. *Executive Compensation in Large Industrial Corporations.* New York: National Bureau of Economic Research, 1968.

Perhman, John C. "Phantom Stock: Better than Options?" *Dun's Review,* September 1970, pp. 32–35, 89.

Wolf, Gordon, and Leo, Mario. "A Systems Approach to Total Compensation." *Business Management,* February 1970, pp. 44–48.

Wood, Ernest O.; Cerny, John F.; and Rafuse, H. Avery. *Tax Aspects of Deferred Compensation.* New York: Arthur Young & Company, 1965.

HUMAN RESOURCES ACCOUNTING

Brummet, R. Lee. "Accounting for Human Resources." *The Journal of Accountancy,* December 1970, pp. 62–66.

Brummet, R. Lee; Flamholtz, Eric G.; and Payle, William C. "Human Resource Measurement—A Challenge for Accountants." *The Accounting Review,* April 1968, pp. 217–24.

Flamholtz, Eric, "A Model for Human Resource Valuation: A Stochastic Process with Service Rewards." *The Accounting Review,* April 1971, pp. 253–67.

Flamholtz, Eric G. "Should Your Organization Attempt to Value Its Human Resources?" *California Management Review,* Winter 1971, pp. 40–45.

Golbert, Michael H. "The Asset Value of the Human Organization." *Management Accounting,* July 1970, pp. 25–28.

Likert, Rensis, and Pyle, William C. "Human Resources Accounting." *Financial Analysts Journal,* January–February 1971, pp. 75–87.

"People are Capital Investments at R. G. Barry Corp." *Management Accounting,* November 1971, pp. 53–55.

Schwartz, Baruch, and Schwartz, Aba. "On the Use of the Economic Concept of Human Capital in Financial Statements." *The Accounting Review,* January 1971, pp. 103–112.

Winpisinger, William. "Human Resources." *Managerial Planning,* September–October 1971, pp. 24–28.

CHAPTER 16 QUESTIONS, PROBLEMS, AND CASES

16- 1. Distinguish between *strategic* and *operational* planning.

16- 2. Identify the categories of administrative expense and explain the nature of the specific expenses found in each category.

16- 3. Define or explain the use of the following terms and phrases:
(a) Administrative expenses
(b) Personnel administration
(c) "Functional similarity"
(d) Authority
(e) Responsibility
(f) "Plural president"

16- 4. Define the following costs of personnel administration:
(a) Salary
(b) Wages
(c) Fringe benefits

16- 5. What is *human resource accounting?*

16- 6. Dintinguish between *cost* and *expense.*

16- 7. Describe the program you would develop to measure the cost-effectiveness of clerical operations.

16- 8. "Administration is fundamentally a process of planning, organizing, staffing, directing, and controlling activities which will lead to an effective fulfillment of organizational objectives." Explain the content of each administrative activity. What are the inputs and constraints which affect administrative activities?

16- 9. "Authority must be commensurate with responsibility." Explain what is meant by this statement.

16-10. What is meant by a *personnel skills inventory?*

16-11. "With increasing size of organization, the tendency is in the direction of greater decentralization of authority and responsibility as well as more precise descriptions of these relationships." Cite some possible reasons that support this tendency.

16-12. Delineate and explain the activities involved in the staffing process.

16-13. Define and explain the role of the following tasks as they relate to the *directing* activity of administration:
(a) Training
(b) Motivation
(c) Leadership

16-14. Explain the major activities in personnel operations:
(a) Manpower development
(b) Manpower planning
(c) Compensation
(d) Organization planning

16-15. "Manpower planning refers to the rather complex task of forecasting and planning for the right numbers and kinds of people at the right places and times to perform activities which will benefit both the organization and its employees." In the following diagram identify the parts of the manpower planning process. Describe the function of each part.

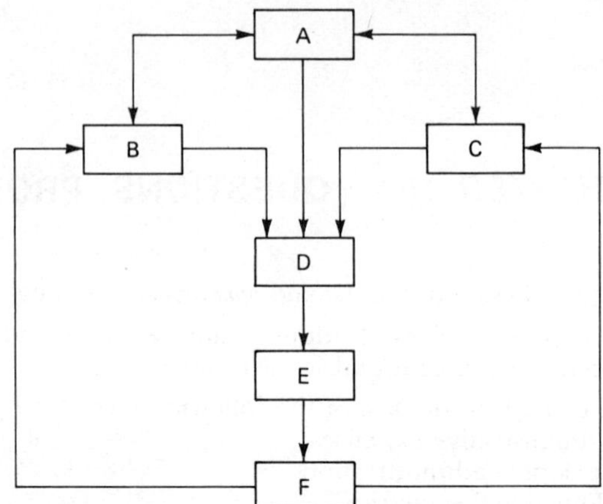

16-16. Manpower programs entail all of the traditional personnel functions—employment, supporting, and information. Identify the activities of each function.

16-17. "Critics of computerized personnel information retrieval systems have held that the costs far outweigh the benefits." Discuss.

16-18. "For the manpower planning process to operate effectively, there must be feedback and control. There must be continuous evaluation to assure that programs are being achieved and that they are proper for providing personnel to meet organizational objectives." What are some control features and feedback reports that might be found, or could be instituted, on the manpower planning process?

16-19. "It is clear that monetary rewards can motivate employees to a certain degree, but financial rewards alone do not satisfy many of the human needs." What various non-monetary rewards should management be concerned with?

16-20. Define and explain the role of the following tasks as they relate to the compensation of employees:
(a) Job analysis
(b) Job evaluation
(c) Wage and salary surveys
(d) Wage and salary structure
(e) Wage and salary administration

16-21. "The major problems involved in shifting large groups of employees from wage to salaried status relate to the consequent changes in fringe benefits." What are the fringe benefits that frequently accompany this shift?

16-22. Identify the parts of the wage and salary determination process:

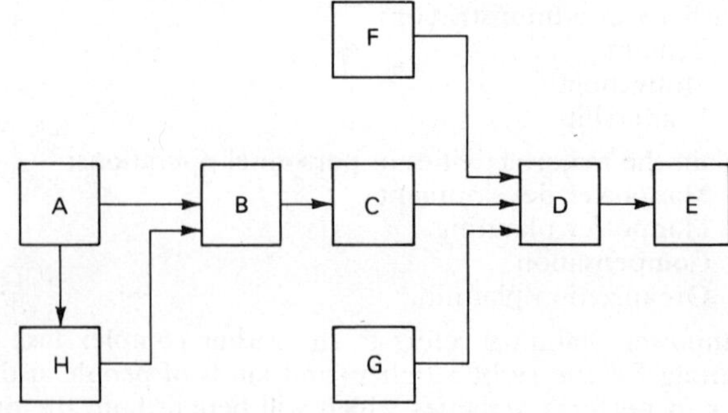

16-23. What are three guidelines for planning a better organization structure?

16-24. "Managers are typically handicapped by the lack of relevant, timely, and reliable information about their human resources. They do not have the essential information as well as the basic quantitative decision and evaluation-oriented tools needed to facilitate human resource management." How should the problem of measuring the value of people be approached?

16-25. What are five possible surrogate measures of the value of people to organizations?

16-26. Distinguish between *revenue* and *capital* expenditures. Explain how the rules of materiality and consistency apply in this distinction.

16-27. If the end of a payroll period does not correspond with the end of the accounting period, what accounting difficulties are presented by this situation? How are they solved?

16-28. "A company collects money from employees and holds the funds in a *fiduciary* capacity." Explain what is meant by a fiduciary capacity. Cite some specific mandatory and optional deductions that a company might withhold from the gross pay of employees. How are such deductions recorded on the company's records?

16-29. If a company pays the premiums for insurance on its executives, how can such premiums be treated for federal income tax purposes?

16-30. What are the related documents of the following *personnel events:*
(a) Personnel render service to a firm
(b) Payroll is paid

16-31. What are the related documents of the following *administrative events:*
(a) Administrative expense
(b) Administrative expenses are paid

16-32. In the area of personnel operations, what federal and state laws are stewardship controls most likely to be concerned with?

16-33. What are the objectives of stewardship controls in personnel operations?

16-34. There are two types of voluntary funds created by management for the benefit of employees—qualified plans and non-qualified plans. Distinguish between the two plans.

16-35. ***ASSIGNMENT METHOD*** The Rosemeed Corporation produces powerboats. There are four assembly operations involved in the production of eighteen-foot hulls. A crew of four workers produce all the eighteen-foot hulls. The average performance time (in hours) of each worker for each assembly operation is as follows:

	Assembly Operations			
	1	**2**	**3**	**4**
J. Hyatt	5.2	6.1	6.8	5.6
V. Mundat	4.8	7.0	6.2	5.2
B. Nevell	5.6	6.8	7.0	5.0
C. Powers	5.0	6.4	6.5	6.1

Required:

If the hourly wage of Hyatt, Mundat, Nevell, and Powers is $3.50, $3.00, $3.70, and $4.00, respectively, determine the worker-operation assignments that will minimize the production cost of boat hulls.

16-36. ***ASSIGNMENT METHOD*** Employee vacations are taken during six "slow" periods throughout the year. In order to maintain high employee morale, the personnel manager has asked each of the six employees to rank their vacation preferences from 1 to 5, with 1 being most desirable and 5 the least desirable. The results are as follows:

Vacation Period	Employee 1	2	3	4	5	6
1/1–1/15	2	5	1	4	1	1
4/15–4/31	6	4	5	6	5	3
7/1–7/15	1	3	2	5	6	4
8/1–8/15	4	2	4	1	3	5
8/15–8/31	5	1	3	2	4	6
12/15–12/31	3	6	6	3	2	2

Required:

Assign each employee to a vacation time so that overall morale is maximized.

UNIT V

ACCOUNTING INFORMATION FOR CONTROL

We have discussed resource management in both static and dynamic terms. Our treatment to this point has had a distinct bias in favor of the external and functional uses of accounting information systems.

We turn now to the role of accounting for internal management purposes. The information needs discussed in Units V and VI do not stem from external requirements primarily, but rather from the need to plan and control internal operations. Unit V deals with accounting information for control, while Unit VI deals with accounting information for planning. As Unit VI has its own introduction, we will focus here on the use of accounting information in controlling organization activities.

We stated in chapter 1 that the purpose of control is to assure that activities conform to plans. In terms of our GPS Complex in chapter 1, controls arise in response to goals. Their purpose is to constrain processes and systems, so that the activities of the enterprise are geared to the fulfillment of goals.

In our concept of the tri-process (Exhibit 1-12) and the tri-system (Exhibit 1-16) structures in chapter 1, we note that control is imposed on activity as follows:

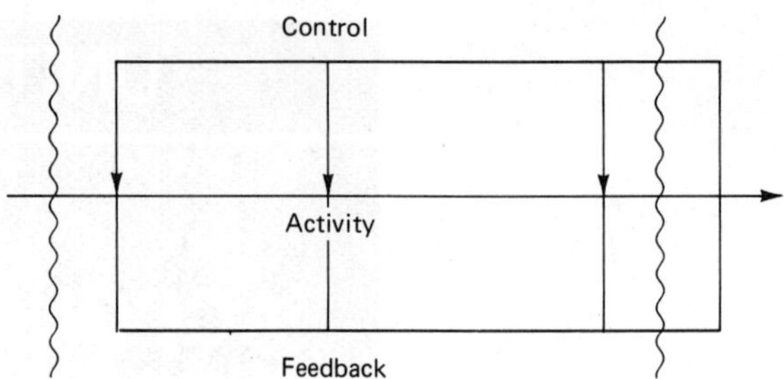

This operating definition of control should be distinguished from the use of the term as it relates the total *control climate* in an organization. In this latter sense control refers to the sum of management efforts relative to all activities of an enterprise. In this context, *planning* looks to future operations while *control* is the management of current activities in accordance with plans. The study of control in its broad meaning comprises at least the entire curricula of a modern business education, with a focus in management. We are necessarily constrained to more modest objectives in this text, and especially in Unit V.

The objective of Unit V is to introduce students to some specific, operating control models in which accounting information is integral.

In chapter 17 we discuss controls relative to investment decisions. We identify the ingredients of investment decisions and illustrate how investment models are used for three types of decisions: (a) investments in bonds, (b) investments in stocks, and (c) investment in real estate. The principles of investment control discussed in connection with these decisions can be extended to other applications. The appendix to chapter 17 contains some additional investment resource data.

In chapters 18, 19, and 20 we cover subject matter that is referred to as *cost accounting.* Cost accounting has been termed the analytic arm of accounting. It is in this area that accounting has made most progress toward its designation as a *science.* It is in cost accounting, rather than financial accounting, that we can come to grips readily with such concepts as cost-effectiveness or input-output. Cost accounting was born and nurtured in manufacturing firms, so students should expect to see most illustrations drawn from manufacturing problems. However, cost accounting is rapidly finding applications in mercantile firms and in service organizations such as governments, schools, and hospitals. In fact what is known as "programmed budgeting" or "program, planning, and budgeting systems" (PPBS) is largely cost accounting in the setting of not-for-profit organizations. Because of the growing importance of service organizations, students of cost accounting should consciously think of ways in which the models they encounter in manufacturing can be transferred or adapted to service enterprises.

Chapter 18 lays a foundation for cost accounting. Basic terms and concepts are defined. The cost accounting classification of data is discussed in depth leading to "cost behavioral" models.

Chapter 19 extends the treatment of cost accounting to the discussion of three types of cost systems: (1) job, (2) process, and (3) departmental. The problem of allocating overhead in these situations is accentuated.

In chapter 20 we turn our attention to standard costing, in which the cost of products (or services) is computed in advance of production and sale. These standards are used as a basis for determining and analyzing variances between expected and actual performance.

Cost accounting models and techniques, like computers or operations research techniques, have a particular appeal to students (and managers) with analytic propensity. We must mention that cost accounting models can be abused in a manner analogous to the use of computers or operations research models. There are some tendencies that should be avoided in this context: (1) the use of more elaborate and costly models than are needed to control the activity in question, (2) the displacement of archaic models with more exotic ones for "intellectual" rather than pragmatic reasons, (3) the idolization of models as the ends rather than the means by which broader organizational objectives are reached.

Controls, like other economic activities, must be responsive to the general principle of cost-effectiveness. For this reason controls should be examined periodically to determine whether or not they are needed, whether costs are proportionate to their benefits, and whether or not they are being used as intended.

CHAPTER

17

INVESTMENT ANALYSIS AND CONTROL

17.1 THE NATURE OF INVESTMENT DECISIONS

An *investment* is an economic outlay where there is the expectation of a money return above the amount invested. The accounting system relates to investment decisions in a number of ways. It provides data when an investment is planned, making it possible for management to assess the cost-benefit of various alternatives and to select the best opportunity. Accounting data aids in the continuing management of an investment and in its final disposition.

The discussion of accounting for investments, while being of primary importance to business management, is also quite pertinent to the investments that we make as individuals.

17.2 INVESTMENT VERSUS SPECULATION

When does an investment become speculation? The question turns upon the degree of risk involved. This makes it difficult to find a specific demarcation. What is speculation to one investor may be within the range of normalcy for another.[1] Certainly the size of an investment relative to one's total resources is important in this regard. Most of us would be willing to gamble and lose a few dollars without pain. But size of total resources relative to an investment is not the only criterion. Some investors with large resources are very conservative in making even small investments, and *vice versa.* Psychological as well as financial factors are part of an investor's makeup.

While it may be difficult to mark the threshold of investment versus speculation, there are some unquestioned examples of each. Buying a government bond or placing funds in a savings account that is guaranteed by FDIC (Federal Deposit Insurance Corporation) certainly qualify as investments by any definition. Other conservative investments include the stock of "blue-chip" corporations as well as prime real estate.

On the other hand, it is clear that a round at the blackjack table is speculative, as is horse racing and other forms of gambling. Investments in new "glamor" enterprises tend to be viewed as speculative, as are investments in research projects from which marketable products may or may not emerge.

Within these borders the issue is determined on an individual basis, depending on what is known as an investor's *utility function* or *risk aversion index.* This index is theoretical at present, but efforts to formalize it are being made. The index is a composite of the factors which make one person willing to risk more than another. If the index can be formalized it will be a useful tool in predicting investor behavior.

17.3 TYPES OF INVESTMENTS

There are many types of investments opportunities available to business firms and to us as individuals. In this chapter we will discuss the basic principles of investment and give some pertinent examples. We will not attempt to discuss the various types of investments in depth.

Three general classes of investments can be recognized: *proprietary, equity,* and *possessory.*

1. **PROPRIETARY** (where the investor is or tends to be the sole owner):
   a. *Real estate* is sole property when title is held "in severalty," which means *sole ownership.*
   b. *Proprietary business investment* where the investor is the sole owner of the business he establishes.
   c. *Research and development* tends to be the sole property of the person funding the investment, but this is not always the case. Sometimes more than one party will fund a research project under agreement to share in the proceeds.
   d. *Capital assets other than real estate,* e.g., equipment and transportation vehicles. In the case of automobile ownership most state vehicle registration codes require that the vehicle be owned by only one person at a time.
   e. *Insurance policies.* Generally the investor is the owner of the policy unless he specifically executes an assignment in favor of another person. The owner of a policy should not be confused with the beneficiary. A policy generally requires the designation of only one beneficiary, which can be the owner's estate.

[1]This concept is often referred to as an individual "preference" or "utility" function. See Herman Chernoff and Lincoln E. Moses, *Elementary Decision Theory* (New York: John Wiley & Sons, Inc., 1959), pp. 79–118, and D. Davidson et al., *Decision Making: An Experimental Approach* (Stanford, Calif.: Stanford University Press, 1957).

2. **EQUITY** (where the investment represents an undivided interest in a larger entity):
   a. *Real estate* where title is held under "joint tenancy" or "tenancy in common," which represent two forms in which real estate can be held by more than one person. Between joint tenancy and tenancy in common the difference is right of survivorship or the lack of such right, respectively. Two other forms of co-ownership of real estate include "tenancy by the entirety" and "community property," the latter being limited to husband-and-wife situations.
   b. *Cooperatives and condominia in real estate.* A stock cooperative in real estate is where the investor owns stock representing his interest in a particular real estate project. He does not have title to any real estate. In order to transfer his interest he must sell his stock. A cooperative apartment project, for example, may give the investor a *possessory* right to use a specific apartment, but he does not own it.

      In a condiminium, on the other hand, the investor does own title to his specific real estate. In addition he generally has an undivided interest in the common areas. His interest is transferred by conveying title.
   c. *Cooperatives other than real estate.* An example is a farmers' cooperative. A group of farmers invest collectively in a business that processes and distributes their produce. Interest is held in the form of stock and is transferrable as such.
   d. *Stocks and bonds.* Investments in the stocks and bonds of public corporations or the bonds of governments represents a fractional equity interest on the part of the investor. He does not own any specific assets of the company he is investing in.
   e. *Joint ventures.* Here two or more investors contribute resources to a common endeavor, upon completion of which they dissolve the business and share the proceeds.
   f. *Partnership.* Doing business as a partner represents an equity investment. A particular partner has a fractional interest in the partnership as a whole but not in any of its specific assets.

3. **POSSESSORY** (where the investment does not represent ownership but rather the right to use something):
   a. *Leaseholds.* A tenant does not own the property that he lives in or uses, but he has the right of possession and "quiet enjoyment" for as long as the lease is in force.
   b. *Chattels.* Chattels (personal property) are often acquired by installment purchases, such as automobiles, refrigerators, office equipment, or many similar assets. Until payment is complete, the person holding the financing contract, which is called a *security agreement* under the Uniform Commercial Code, is the owner of the chattel. But the person making the payments has a possessory interest.
   c. *Real estate under "land contract."* Under a land contract (also known as a "contract of sales") the purchaser only receives title when certain conditions are met—usually, this involves a certain number of payments. Until that point he has possessory interest in the real estate.
   d. *Life estate.* Life estates are usually created by will, where the survivor is given the earnings from an investment for life, but does not have the right to invade the *corpus* of the estate. Such a right is possessory.
   e. *Franchise.* In this case the investor has the exclusive right to engage in a particular business in a stated area. Examples of franchise investments include automobile agencies, insurance representatives, food retail outlets, and restaurants.

The accountant is often called upon to assist persons or businesses in making investment decisions. The investment techniques presented in this chapter will be of value in analyzing most types of investment decisions.[2] Investments are also influenced to a great extent by prevailing tax law. Our discussion of the role of tax law on investments will of necessity be quite cursory.

---

[2]"Capital budgeting decisions" is the subject of chapter 24.

17.4 REASONS FOR INVESTING

Investments are made for a variety of reasons, and these reasons to a large extent determine the type of investment that is made. Reasons range from "making a quick buck" to minimizing taxes. Availability of funds, financial risk, interest rates, investment experience and philosophy, and many other factors contribute to the complex psychology of investments. Any investment model which can encompass all of these variables would be of little practical value.

The general purpose of investments is to obtain an overall return on investment, as stated earlier. However, here are some more specific reasons for investing.

IMMEDIATE VERSUS DELAYED INCOME

Some investors require immediate returns which may include interest, principal, or both. This requirement can be met through the purchase of treasury bonds or real estate under lease, so that rent payments are forthcoming.

Other investors do not require immediate returns. For example, parents may wish to provide for their children's education through purchasing an insurance policy many years in advance of the need. Investors who do not have immediate cash needs have opportunities which range from raw land that may have future subdivision potential to life insurance policies which provide retirement income.

OBTAIN A STREAM OF FUTURE CASH BENEFITS

Many investments are made for the purpose of obtaining a stream of future cash benefits. The stream of benefits may be in the form of an *annuity* (equal periodic payments) or of *unequal periodic payments.*

An *annuity* refers to an equal sum of money that is *paid* or *received* at equal time intervals. The interval may be in days, months, years, or any other stated period. Monthly rent or home mortgage payments are examples of *annuities payable.* Monthly salary is an example of an *annuity receivable.*

Exhibit 17-1 depicts an annuity receivable, and Exhibit 17-2 represents an *annuity payable.*

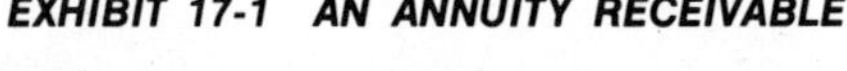
EXHIBIT 17-1 AN ANNUITY RECEIVABLE

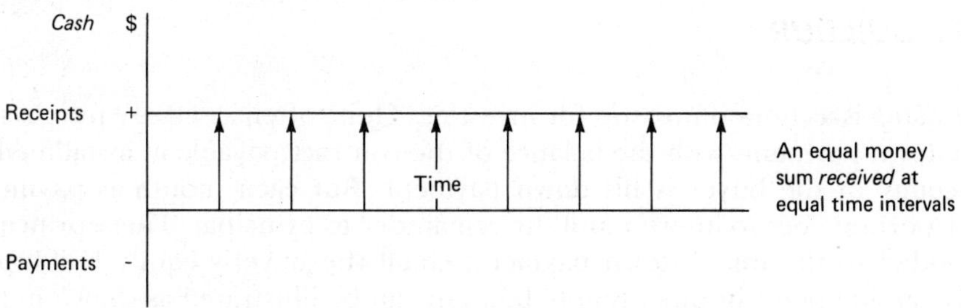

EXHIBIT 17-2 AN ANNUITY PAYABLE

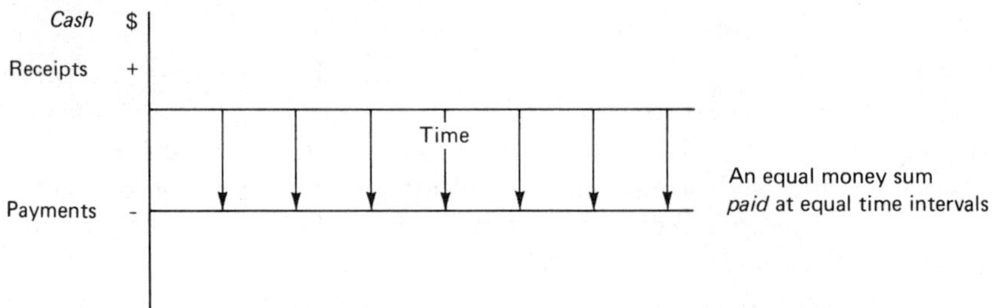

A stream of future cash benefits may not consist of equal money amounts and/or of regular periodic intervals, although the former is more typical. Such uneven cash streams are called *unequal periodic payments.* Again, the cash benefits may be payable or receivable. An illustration of unequal periodic payments receivable is shown in Exhibit 17-3.

EXHIBIT 17-3 UNEQUAL PERIODIC PAYMENTS RECEIVABLE

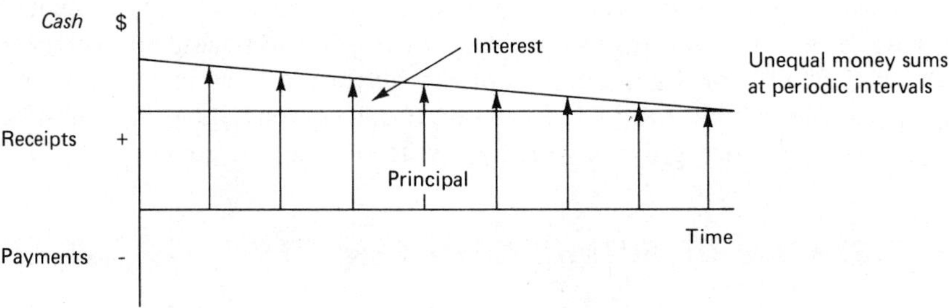

A good example of an unequal periodic payment contract is a real estate loan which calls for equal principal payments per period plus interest on the unpaid balance. Suppose we have a loan for $10,000 paid in annual installments of $1,000 principal plus 7% interest. The first year the payment will be $1,700, which is $1,000 principal + .07 ($10,000) interest. The second year the payment will be $1,630, which is $1,000 principal + .07 ($9,000) interest, and so forth.

A stream of future cash benefits is equal to something of value now. The *present value* of a stream of future cash benefits is obtained by discounting the future cash sums by means of a specific interest rate. Similarly, it is possible to compute the *future value* of a stream of money amounts. Students who are not familiar with computing present and future values are referred to Appendix B.

EQUITY BUILDUP

Equity buildup is a common reason for investing. Quite often assets are purchased with a small down payment, with the balance of the contract payable in installments. The initial equity of the buyer is his down payment. But each month as payments are made, a portion goes to interest and the remainder to principal. These principal portions, added to the initial down payment, equal the buyer's equity buildup in the property at any point in time. Equity buildup can be illustrated as shown in Exhibits 17-4 and 17-5.

EXHIBIT 17-4 EQUITY INCREASE WITH EQUAL PAYMENTS

EXHIBIT 17-5 EQUITY BUILDUP AS A PERCENT OF PURCHASE PRICE

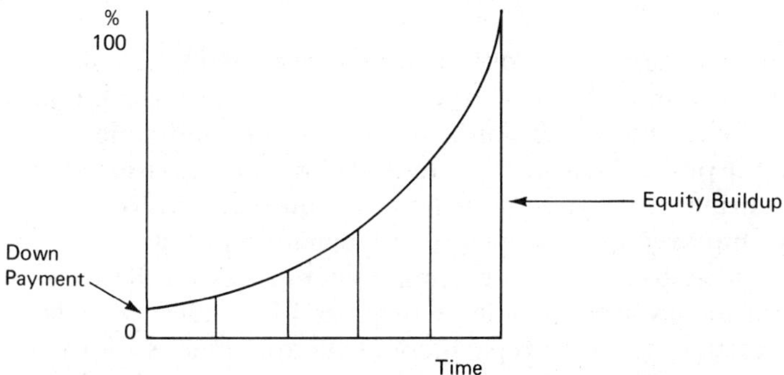

Equity in a property is the difference between its net market value at any point in time and the indebtedness against the property. If a property is appreciating in value, equity will exceed equity buildup. If a property is losing value, real equity will be less than equity buildup.

APPRECIATION

An asset *appreciates* when it increases in value above its purchase price. Investment in common stocks and in real estate are often made in the expectation of appreciation. Appreciation in the value of common stocks, as we shall see presently, is of equal or greater importance to investors than is dividends. In real estate, great fortunes have been made by purchasing land in the path of development and subdividing and selling it at the opportune time.

MAINTAIN OR IMPROVE MARKET POSITION

Investments in research and development projects are designed to maintain or improve a firm's market position. Having a successful product now does not guarantee a future market. On the one hand successful products are emulated by competitors even within the framework of patent law, and on the other hand consumer patterns change, making it unlikely that a successful product in the past will continue to be such in the future. This type of investment is not optional—it is essential.

Investment in future markets requires a money outlay for human talent, facilities, and equipment in present periods, and successful outcomes are not always assured. In this connection it is important to separate *pure* research from *applied* research. The former has a long payoff, a higher risk of failures, and intermediate progress is difficult to measure. However, it is through pure research that many important breakthroughs have occurred. Applied research has a shorter horizon and primarily involves improvements to existing products plus the development of promising ideas which have emerged through pure research.

Because of the difficulty in measuring the results of research and development, this area of investment has yielded most reluctantly of all to formal models.

ESTABLISH A RESERVE FOR FUTURE COMMITMENTS OR CONTINGENCIES

Some investments are made to cover future commitments or contingencies. *Pension plans* are a good example. Most plans consist of a fund to which both employer and employee contribute. These pension funds should not and generally cannot be used for operating purposes. Instead the funds are invested to insure that payments will be made to retiring employees according to contract. Pension funds are often administered by employee groups, including labor union trusts.

Sinking funds to retire corporate indebtedness is another form of investment. Suppose a firm incurs a bond indebtedness of $1,000,000 payable in ten years. A conservative practice to ensure repayment at the due date is for the firm to set aside an amount each year, which, when added to the interest the fund will earn, will total $1,000,000 in ten years. If the fund earns 8% interest per annum, the amount to be set aside each year would be $69,029.[3]

17.5 THE INVESTMENT CYCLE

The investment cycle is portrayed in Exhibit 17-6. An investor, most often with the assistance of financing, secures the needed capital to make an investment. The flow of earnings are reduced by expenses pertinent to the investment, as well as by income taxes. In addition to earnings, the investment should return the capital outlay. If the investment is made in a depreciable asset, the value of the asset can be reduced annually through depreciation. This depreciation is a deductible operating expense, hence it reduces the amount of earnings otherwise subject to the income tax. Depreciation in this context is referred to as a *tax shield* or *shelter*. The amount of income protected by depreciation is exempt from income taxation until the asset is disposed of, at which time the amount of depreciation is taxable on a capital gains basis. The capital gains tax rate is 50% of a taxpayer's regular rate up to a maximum of 25%. We will discuss the concept of a tax shield in further detail later.

An investment cannot be assessed fully until the point of disinvestment—when the investment is liquidated. In making investments it is necessary, therefore, to base calculations on the anticipated life-cycle of the investment.

Net cash flow after tax is applied first to the repayment of the financed debt, the balance accruing to the benefit of the investor. Most financing agreements stipu-

[3]This type of sinking fund problem is solved through the use of *future value tables* as illustrated in Appendix B.

late that the financier becomes the owner of the investment in the event that debt payments are not made on time.

EXHIBIT 17-6 THE INVESTMENT CYCLE

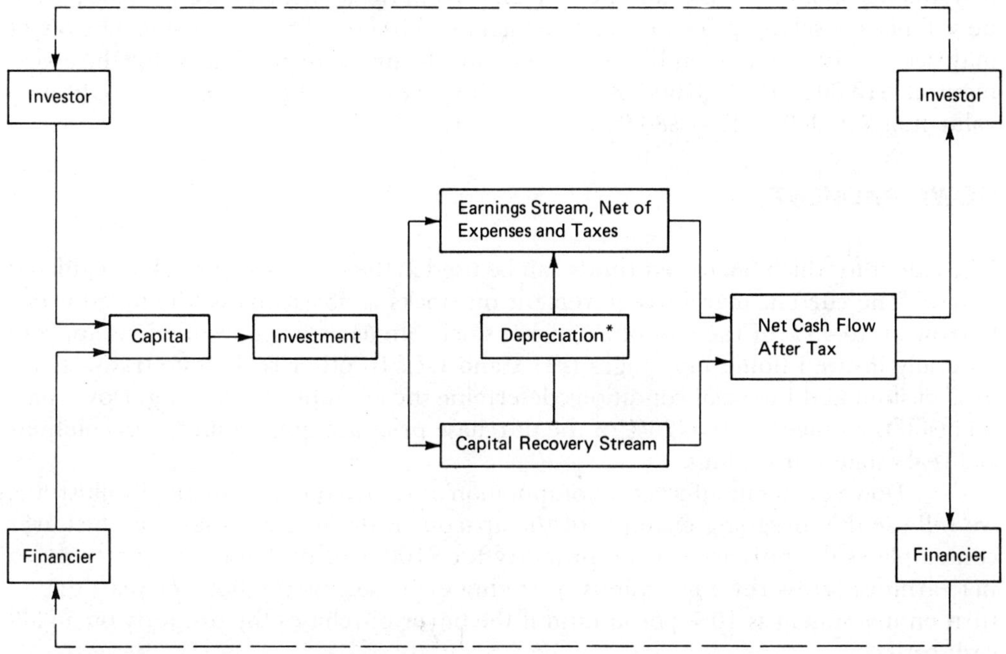

*Depreciation of capital assets shelters earnings otherwise subject to income tax, but these earnings are taxed later as capital gains at the point of disinvestment.

17.6 THE INVESTMENT DECISION

These are the common ingredients of investment decisions:

1. Cost of the investment
2. Down payment
3. Financing, including term and rate
4. Earnings and cash flow
5. Depreciation
6. Tax strategy

Let us take a brief look at these factors in turn.

COST OF THE INVESTMENT

In an investment decision the cost or price of the investment is a derived value. It is determined by the expectations of the buyer and by the willingness of a seller to trade at that price. The price that one is willing to pay for stocks or bonds is based on the expected performance of a company. The price of real estate is based on the expected profits the investment will yield.

For example, if the present owner of an apartment building computes his investments on an 8% basis, and net earnings from the apartment are $10,000 a year, he will place a selling price on the apartment of $10,000/.08 = $125,000. The buyer may desire a 10% return on his investment, in which case he will only value the apartment at $10,000/.10 = $100,000. An investor seeking a 12½% return would only value it at $10,000/.125 = $80,000, and so forth.

DOWN PAYMENT

The extent to which borrowed funds can be used in the purchase of stock is regulated by law. The current margin requirement on stocks is 55%; that is, the investor can borrow up to 45% of the cost of acquiring stock. Similar margin regulations apply to federally insured home mortgages (FHA and GI). In other real estate transactions, local custom and financial conditions determine the amount of financing. Down payments in the range of 10 to 20% of the purchase price are quite common in commercial real estate transactions.

Down payment affects the computation of return on investment. To illustrate, we will use the foregoing example of the apartment house. Let us say that the buyer contemplates the purchase of the property for $100,000. In that the property shows net earnings (gross revenues minus operating expenses) of $10,000 per year, the return on investment is 10% per annum if the buyer purchases the property on an all-cash basis.

Suppose that the transaction instead is structured as follows:

Selling price	$100,000
Down payment	10,000
Note secured by a 1st Trust Deed on the following terms. Payment to be made in equal monthly installments of $753 ($9,036 per annum) including principal and interest at 8% for a 20-year period.[4]	$ 90,000

The buyer has paid 10% down and financed $90,000 on the above terms. The $10,000 in net earnings must first cover mortgage payments before the buyer has any return on his investment:

Net earnings	$10,000
Annual mortgage payments	9,036
Net spendable	$ 964

Percent return on the buyer's investment is $\frac{\$\ 964}{\$10{,}000} = 9.64\%$.

[4] Loan amortization is computed by using the table in Exhibit 17-7, i.e., 8% at twenty years = .1004($90,000) = $9,036 per annum/12 = $753 per month.

EXHIBIT 17-7 TABLE OF CONSTANT ANNUAL PERCENT NEEDED TO AMORTIZE A PRINCIPAL AMOUNT CALCULATED ON A MONTHLY BASIS.

Multiply appropriate "constant" below times loan amount to determine annual payment, then divide by twelve to determine amount of monthly payments.

Rate / Years	7	7 1/8	7 1/4	7 3/8	7 1/2	7 5/8	7 3/4	7 7/8
5	23.77	23.84	23.91	23.98	24.05	24.12	24.19	24.26
6	20.46	20.54	20.61	20.68	20.75	20.83	20.90	20.97
7	18.12	18.19	18.26	18.34	18.41	18.49	18.56	18.63
8	16.37	16.44	16.52	16.59	16.67	16.74	16.82	16.89
9	15.01	15.09	15.16	15.24	15.32	15.40	15.47	15.55
10	13.94	14.02	14.09	14.17	14.25	14.33	14.41	14.49
11	13.07	13.14	13.22	13.30	13.38	13.46	13.54	13.62
12	12.35	12.43	12.51	12.59	12.67	12.75	12.83	12.91
13	11.74	11.82	11.91	11.99	12.07	12.15	12.24	12.32
14	11.23	11.31	11.40	11.48	11.56	11.65	11.73	11.82
15	10.79	10.87	10.96	11.04	11.13	11.21	11.30	11.39
16	10.41	10.50	10.58	10.67	10.75	10.84	10.93	11.02
17	10.08	10.17	10.25	10.34	10.43	10.52	10.61	10.69
18	9.79	9.88	9.97	10.06	10.14	10.23	10.32	10.41
19	9.54	9.62	9.71	9.80	9.89	9.98	10.08	10.17
20	9.31	9.40	9.49	9.58	9.67	9.76	9.86	9.95
21	9.11	9.20	9.29	9.38	9.47	9.57	9.66	9.76
22	8.93	9.02	9.11	9.21	9.30	9.39	9.49	9.58
23	8.76	8.86	8.95	9.05	9.14	9.24	9.33	9.43
24	8.62	8.71	8.81	8.90	9.00	9.10	9.19	9.29
25	8.49	8.58	8.68	8.78	8.87	8.97	9.07	9.17
26	8.37	8.46	8.56	8.66	8.76	8.86	8.96	9.06
27	8.26	8.36	8.46	8.55	8.65	8.75	8.85	8.96
28	8.16	8.26	8.36	8.46	8.56	8.66	8.76	8.86
29	8.07	8.17	8.27	8.37	8.47	8.58	8.68	8.78
30	7.99	8.09	8.19	8.29	8.40	8.50	8.60	8.71
31	7.91	8.02	8.12	8.22	8.32	8.43	8.53	8.64
32	7.85	7.95	8.05	8.16	8.26	8.36	8.47	8.58
33	7.78	7.89	7.99	8.09	8.20	8.31	8.41	8.52
34	7.72	7.83	7.93	8.04	8.15	8.25	8.36	8.47
35	7.67	7.78	7.88	7.99	8.10	8.20	8.31	8.42
36	7.62	7.73	7.84	7.94	8.05	8.16	8.27	8.38
37	7.58	7.68	7.79	7.90	8.01	8.12	8.23	8.34
38	7.54	7.64	7.75	7.86	7.97	8.08	8.19	8.30
39	7.50	7.61	7.72	7.82	7.93	8.04	8.16	8.27
40	7.46	7.57	7.68	7.79	7.90	8.01	8.12	8.24
41	7.43	7.54	7.65	7.76	7.87	7.98	8.10	8.21
42	7.40	7.51	7.62	7.73	7.84	7.96	8.07	8.18
43	7.37	7.48	7.59	7.71	7.82	7.93	8.05	8.16
44	7.35	7.46	7.57	7.68	7.80	7.91	8.02	8.14
45	7.32	7.43	7.55	7.66	7.77	7.89	8.00	8.12
46	7.30	7.41	7.53	7.64	7.75	7.87	7.98	8.10
47	7.28	7.39	7.51	7.62	7.74	7.85	7.97	8.08
48	7.26	7.37	7.49	7.60	7.72	7.83	7.95	8.07
49	7.24	7.36	7.47	7.59	7.70	7.82	7.94	8.05
50	7.23	7.34	7.46	7.57	7.69	7.80	7.92	8.04

EXHIBIT 17-7 (CONTINUED)

Rate / Years	8	8 1/8	8 1/4	8 3/8	8 1/2	8 5/8	8 3/4	8 7/8
5	24.34	24.41	24.48	24.55	24.62	24.70	24.77	24.84
6	21.04	21.12	21.19	21.27	21.34	21.41	21.49	21.56
7	18.71	18.78	18.86	18.93	19.01	19.08	19.16	19.24
8	16.97	17.05	17.12	17.20	17.28	17.35	17.43	17.51
9	15.63	15.71	15.78	15.86	15.94	16.02	16.10	16.18
10	14.56	14.64	14.72	14.80	14.88	14.96	15.04	15.13
11	13.70	13.78	13.87	13.95	14.03	14.11	14.19	14.28
12	12.99	13.08	13.16	13.24	13.33	13.41	13.49	13.58
13	12.40	12.49	12.57	12.65	12.74	12.82	12.91	13.00
14	11.90	11.99	12.07	12.16	12.24	12.33	12.42	12.50
15	11.47	11.56	11.65	11.73	11.82	11.91	12.00	12.09
16	11.10	11.19	11.28	11.37	11.46	11.55	11.64	11.73
17	10.78	10.87	10.96	11.05	11.14	11.24	11.33	11.42
18	10.50	10.60	10.69	10.78	10.87	10.96	11.06	11.15
19	10.26	10.35	10.44	10.54	10.63	10.72	10.82	10.91
20	10.04	10.14	10.23	10.32	10.42	10.51	10.61	10.71
21	9.85	9.94	10.04	10.14	10.23	10.33	10.43	10.52
22	9.68	9.78	9.87	9.97	10.07	10.16	10.26	10.36
23	9.53	9.62	9.72	9.82	9.92	10.02	10.12	10.22
24	9.39	9.49	9.59	9.69	9.79	9.89	9.99	10.09
25	9.27	9.37	9.47	9.57	9.67	9.77	9.87	9.97
26	9.16	9.26	9.36	9.46	9.56	9.66	9.77	9.87
27	9.06	9.16	9.26	9.36	9.47	9.57	9.67	9.78
28	8.97	9.07	9.17	9.28	9.38	9.48	9.59	9.69
29	8.88	8.99	9.09	9.20	9.30	9.41	9.51	9.62
30	8.81	8.91	9.02	9.13	9.23	9.34	9.45	9.55
31	8.74	8.85	8.95	9.06	9.17	9.28	9.38	9.49
32	8.68	8.79	8.90	9.00	9.11	9.22	9.33	9.44
33	8.63	8.73	8.84	8.95	9.06	9.17	9.28	9.39
34	8.57	8.68	8.79	8.90	9.01	9.12	9.23	9.34
35	8.53	8.64	8.75	8.86	8.97	9.08	9.19	9.30
36	8.49	8.60	8.71	8.82	8.93	9.04	9.15	9.26
37	8.45	8.56	8.67	8.78	8.89	9.00	9.12	9.23
38	8.41	8.52	8.63	8.75	8.86	8.97	9.09	9.20
39	8.38	8.49	8.60	8.72	8.83	8.94	9.06	9.17
40	8.35	8.46	8.57	8.69	8.80	8.92	9.03	9.15
41	8.32	8.43	8.55	8.66	8.78	8.89	9.01	9.12
42	8.30	8.41	8.52	8.64	8.75	8.87	8.99	9.10
43	8.27	8.39	8.50	8.62	8.73	8.85	8.97	9.08
44	8.25	8.37	8.48	8.60	8.71	8.83	8.95	9.07
45	8.23	8.35	8.46	8.58	8.70	8.81	8.93	9.05
46	8.21	8.33	8.45	8.56	8.68	8.80	8.92	9.03
47	8.20	8.31	8.43	8.55	8.67	8.78	8.90	9.02
48	8.18	8.30	8.42	8.54	8.65	8.77	8.89	9.01
49	8.17	8.29	8.40	8.52	8.64	8.76	8.88	9.00
50	8.16	8.27	8.39	8.51	8.63	8.75	8.87	8.99

How to find what percentage of a loan will be paid off at any time prior to maturity:

1. Find the Constant Annual Percent (above) for the original loan.
2. Now find the Constant Annual Percent that would fully pay off (amortize) the same loan, only for the shorter period. (The shorter period being the term for which you want the balance.)
3. Subtract the interest rate from both constants.
4. Now divide the larger number into the smaller.
5. The resulting percentage is the percent of the original loan which is paid off in the shorter period.

EXHIBIT 17-7 ***(CONTINUED)***

Rate / Years	9	9 1/8	9 1/4	9 3/8	9 1/2	9 5/8	9 3/4	9 7/8	10
5	24.92	24.99	25.06	25.13	25.21	25.28	25.35	25.43	25.50
6	21.64	21.71	21.78	21.86	21.93	22.01	22.09	22.16	22.24
7	19.31	19.39	19.46	19.54	19.62	19.69	19.77	19.85	19.93
8	17.59	17.66	17.74	17.82	17.90	17.98	18.06	18.13	18.21
9	16.26	16.34	16.42	16.50	16.58	16.66	16.74	16.82	16.90
10	15.21	15.29	15.37	15.45	15.53	15.61	15.70	15.78	15.86
11	14.36	14.44	14.52	14.61	14.69	14.78	14.86	14.94	15.03
12	13.66	13.75	13.83	13.92	14.00	14.09	14.17	14.26	14.35
13	13.08	13.17	13.25	13.34	13.43	13.52	13.60	13.69	13.78
14	12.59	12.68	12.77	12.86	12.95	13.03	13.12	13.21	13.30
15	12.18	12.27	12.36	12.45	12.54	12.63	12.72	12.81	12.90
16	11.82	11.91	12.00	12.09	12.18	12.28	12.37	12.46	12.56
17	11.51	11.60	11.70	11.79	11.88	11.98	12.07	12.16	12.26
18	11.24	11.34	11.43	11.53	11.62	11.72	11.81	11.91	12.00
19	11.01	11.10	11.20	11.29	11.39	11.49	11.58	11.68	11.78
20	10.80	10.90	11.00	11.09	11.19	11.29	11.39	11.49	11.59
21	10.62	10.72	10.82	10.92	11.01	11.11	11.21	11.31	11.41
22	10.46	10.56	10.66	10.76	10.86	10.96	11.06	11.16	11.26
23	10.32	10.42	10.52	10.62	10.72	10.82	10.93	11.03	11.13
24	10.19	10.29	10.39	10.50	10.60	10.70	10.81	10.91	11.01
25	10.08	10.18	10.28	10.39	10.49	10.59	10.70	10.80	10.91
26	9.97	10.08	10.18	10.29	10.39	10.50	10.60	10.71	10.82
27	9.88	9.99	10.09	10.20	10.31	10.41	10.52	10.63	10.73
28	9.80	9.91	10.01	10.12	10.23	10.34	10.44	10.55	10.66
29	9.73	9.83	9.94	10.05	10.16	10.27	10.38	10.48	10.59
30	9.66	9.77	9.88	9.99	10.10	10.20	10.31	10.43	10.54
31	9.60	9.71	9.82	9.93	10.04	10.15	10.26	10.37	10.48
32	9.55	9.66	9.77	9.88	9.99	10.10	10.21	10.32	10.44
33	9.50	9.61	9.72	9.83	9.94	10.05	10.17	10.28	10.39
34	9.45	9.56	9.68	9.79	9.90	10.01	10.13	10.24	10.36
35	9.41	9.53	9.64	9.75	9.86	9.98	10.09	10.21	10.32
36	9.38	9.49	9.60	9.72	9.83	9.95	10.06	10.17	10.29
37	9.34	9.46	9.57	9.69	9.80	9.92	10.03	10.15	10.26
38	9.31	9.43	9.54	9.66	9.77	9.89	10.00	10.12	10.24
39	9.29	9.40	9.52	9.63	9.75	9.86	9.98	10.10	10.22
40	9.26	9.38	9.49	9.61	9.73	9.84	9.96	10.08	10.19
41	9.24	9.35	9.47	9.59	9.71	9.82	9.94	10.06	10.18
42	9.22	9.33	9.45	9.57	9.69	9.80	9.92	10.04	10.16
43	9.20	9.32	9.43	9.55	9.67	9.79	9.91	10.03	10.15
44	9.18	9.30	9.42	9.54	9.66	9.77	9.89	10.01	10.13
45	9.17	9.29	9.40	9.52	9.64	9.76	9.88	10.00	10.12
46	9.15	9.27	9.39	9.51	9.63	9.75	9.87	9.99	10.11
47	9.14	9.26	9.38	9.50	9.62	9.74	9.86	9.98	10.10
48	9.13	9.25	9.37	9.49	9.61	9.73	9.85	9.97	10.09
49	9.12	9.24	9.36	9.48	9.60	9.72	9.84	9.96	10.08
50	9.11	9.23	9.35	9.47	9.59	9.71	9.83	9.95	10.07

Example: What percent of a twenty-five year loan at 5% interest will be paid off in twenty years?

	Constant		**Interest**		
5% 25 yrs:	7.02	minus	5.00	= 2.02	= .691, say 69%
5% 20 yrs:	7.92	minus	5.00	= 2.92	

69% of the loan is paid off in twenty years.

SOURCE: The William Wilson Company, Division of R. A. Roman, 918 East Green Street, Pasadena, California. Used by permission of the publisher.

FINANCING AND INTEREST RATES

The financier is rewarded by charging *interest* on the money sums he advances. The money sum that is loaned or borrowed is called *principal.* Of course, in addition to earning interest on the amount loaned, the financier is concerned with getting his principal back. *Amortization* of a loan means that principal and interest are repaid in regular installments. In Exhibit 17-7 we note that the *constant* rate necessary to amortize a 7% loan over thirteen years is 11.74% of the total amount of the loan. The difference between the 7% interest rate and the 11.74% "constant" represents the return of capital. If the amount of the loan is $100,000, an *amortization schedule* showing annual totals, but based on monthly payments of $979.17, is computed as follows (Exhibit 17-8):

EXHIBIT 17-8 AMORTIZATION SCHEDULE

Terms: $100,000 at 7% payable monthly over thirteen years.

	Interest	Principal	Total Payment	Accumulated Principal	Balance Outstanding
Y_0	–	–	–	–	$100,000.00
Y_1	$ 6,844.60	$ 4,905.40	$ 11,750.00	$ 4,905.40	95,094.60
Y_2	6,489.99	5,260.01	11,750.00	10,165.41	89,834.59
Y_3	6,109.74	5,640.26	11,750.00	15,805.67	84,194.33
Y_4	5,702.01	6,047.99	11,750.00	21,853.66	78,146.34
Y_5	5,264.80	6,485.20	11,750.00	28,338.86	71,661.14
Y_6	4,795.98	6,954.02	11,750.00	35,292.88	64,707.12
Y_7	4,293.28	7,456.72	11,750.00	42,749.60	57,250.40
Y_8	3,754.23	7,995.77	11,750.00	50,745.37	49,254.63
Y_9	3,176.21	8,573.79	11,750.00	59,319.16	40,680.84
Y_{10}	2,556.41	9,193.59	11,750.00	68,512.75	31,487.25
Y_{11}	1,891.81	9,858.19	11,750.00	78,370.94	21,629.06
Y_{12}	1,179.16	10,570.84	11,750.00	88,941.78	11,058.22
Y_{13}	414.99	11,058.22	11,473.21	100,000.00	–0–
Total	$52,473.21	$100,000.00	$152,473.21	–	–0–

An amortization schedule for the first year on a monthly basis would be as shown in Exhibit 17-9:

You will notice that interest is computed first and deducted from the total payment to obtain the principal reduction portion of the payment. This means that a high proportion of early payments is attributable to interest, with the principal portion increasing steadily through the life of the contract.

EXHIBIT 17-9 AMORTIZATION SCHEDULE FIRST YEAR

Terms: $100,000 at 7% payable monthly over thirteen years.
Monthly interest rate is .07/12 = .00583.

	Interest	Principal	Total Payment	Accumulated Principal	Balance Outstanding
M_0	—	—	—	—	$100,000.00
M_1	$ 583.33	$ 395.84	$ 979.17	$ 395.84	99,604.16
M_2	581.02	398.15	979.17	793.99	99,206.01
M_3	578.70	400.47	979.17	1,194.46	98,805.54
M_4	576.36	402.81	979.17	1,597.27	98,402.73
M_5	574.02	405.15	979.17	2,002.42	97,997.58
M_6	571.65	407.52	979.17	2,409.94	97,590.06
M_7	569.27	409.90	979.17	2,819.84	97,180.16
M_8	566.89	412.28	979.17	3,232.12	96,767.88
M_9	564.48	414.69	979.17	3,646.81	96,353.19
M_{10}	562.06	417.11	979.17	4,063.92	95,936.08
M_{11}	559.63	419.54	979.17	4,483.46	95,516.54
M_{12}	557.19	421.94	979.13*	4,905.40	95,094.60
Total	$6,844.60	$4,905.40	$11,750.00	—	—

*Rounded.

Some loans are *interest-only*, with full principal due and payable at a certain specified date. Other loans may call for a *balloon payment.* For example, the foregoing loan could be amortized on the basis set forth in Exhibit 17-8 "with the balance outstanding at the end of the tenth year all due and payable." This means that at the end of the tenth year the outstanding balance of $31,487.25 is due.

Simple Interest

Interest based on a principal sum which remains unchanged during the period for which the interest is to be calculated is known as *simple interest.* The simple interest formula is:

$$S = P \times R \times n = PRn$$

where

S = simple interest
P = principal
R = interest rate
n = number of periods

The simple interest on $1,000 loaned at an annual interest rate of 6% for one year is:

$$S = (\$1{,}000)\ (.06)\ (1) = \$60$$

Interest on the same loan for three months would be:[5]

$$S = (\$1{,}000)\ (.06)\ (.25) = \$15$$

Interest on the same loan for eighteen months would be:

$$S = (\$1{,}000)\ (.06)\ (1.5) = \$90$$

Generally speaking, simple interest is charged for amounts borrowed for a year or less and *compound* interest for longer periods, but there are many exceptions to this rule.

Compound Interest

Compound interest is computed at the end of stated periods and becomes part of the principal upon which the interest for the following period is determined.

The compound interest formula is:

$$F = P\ (1 + R)^n$$

where

F = compounded amount or future value of principal plus accumulated interest
P = principal
R = interest rate
n = number of periods

How much will $1,000 grow in two years at 8% interest?

$$\begin{aligned} F &= \$1{,}000\ (1 + .08)^2 \\ &= \$1{,}000\ (1.08)^2 \\ &= \$1{,}000\ (1.1664) \\ &= \underline{\underline{\$1{,}166.40}} \end{aligned}$$

Compound interest problems can also be solved through the use of *future value tables* as illustrated in Appendix B. In addition, they can be solved through the

[5] *Ordinary* interest assumes a financial year of 360 days divided into twelve months of 30 days each, hence fractions of years can be used as in the above example.

Exact interest is based on the actual calendar year of 365 days and requires the computation of the actual number of days in a loan period.

use of *logarithms.* (Common logarithm tables and instructions for their use are contained in Appendix C.)

Here is an example of a compound interest problem solved by means of logarithms: To what amount will a deposit of \$1,000 grow in twenty years if it is invested at 6% interest?

$$F = \$1{,}000\ (1 + .06)^{20}$$

Solving for $(1.06)^{20}$ by means of logarithms

$$\begin{aligned} \log 1.06 &= 0.025306 \\ 20 \log 1.06 &= 0.50612 \\ \text{antilog of } 0.50612 &= 3.20714 \end{aligned}$$

therefore

$$\begin{aligned} F &= \$1{,}000\ (3.20714) \\ &= \underline{\underline{\$3{,}207.14}} \end{aligned}$$

Compound interest alone could be accumulated according to the following polynomial equation:

$$P(R^n + R^{n-1} + R^{n-2} + \cdots + R^1) = P\left(\sum_{k=1}^{n} R^k\right)$$

where all exponents must equal or be greater than one and where P, R, and n are defined as above.

Compounding the Interest Rate

You will frequently hear the expression "compounded quarterly" or "compounded daily," as in the statement "at 6% interest compounded quarterly." In this case the 6% figure is referred to as the *nominal* annual interest rate. The *effective* annual interest rate is computed by this formula:

$$R_e = \left(1 + \frac{R}{f}\right)^f - 1$$

where

R_e = effective annual interest rate
R = nominal annual interest rate
f = number of compounding periods, e.g., quarterly = 4; monthly = 12; daily = 360; quarterly for 4 years = 16; etc.

The effective annual rates of our 6% nominal rate for various compounding periods would be:

Semiannual:

$$\begin{aligned} R_e &= \left(1 + \frac{.06}{2}\right)^2 - 1 \\ &= (1 + .03)^2 - 1 \\ &= (1.0609) - 1 \\ &= \underline{\underline{.0609 \text{ or } 6.09\%}} \end{aligned}$$

Quarterly:[6]

$$\begin{aligned} R_e &= \left(1 + \frac{.06}{4}\right)^4 - 1 \\ &= (1.015)^4 - 1 \\ &= (1.0613636) - 1 \\ &= \underline{\underline{.0613636 \text{ or } 6.14\%}} \end{aligned}$$

Monthly:

$$\begin{aligned} R_e &= \left(1 + \frac{.06}{12}\right)^{12} - 1 \\ &= (1.005)^{12} - 1 \\ &= (1.0616778) - 1 \\ &= \underline{\underline{.0616778 \text{ or } 6.17\%}} \end{aligned}$$

Daily:

$$\begin{aligned} R_e &= \left(1 + \frac{.06}{360}\right)^{360} - 1 \\ &= (1.000166)^{360} - 1 \\ &= (1.0618314) - 1 \\ &= \underline{\underline{.0618314 \text{ or } 6.18\%}} \end{aligned}$$

Notice that the compound interest formula *divides* the nominal rate by the number of conversion periods while at the same time multiplying the number of years by the same conversion factor to obtain the applicable periods (the exponent). The present and future value tables in Appendix B can be handled in this way for compounding purposes. That is, the applicable number of compounding periods is

[6]Logarithms can be used to obtain approximate solutions to this type of problem, and the "monthly" and "daily" problems.

the number of conversion periods per year (f) multiplied by the number of years (n). In effect, a problem is solved by the following formula:[7]

$$F = P\left(1 + \frac{R}{f}\right)^{fn}$$

where

F = compounded amount or future value of principle plus accumulated interest

How much will $1,000 invested in a fund that earns 6% interest compounded quarterly grow in four years?

$$\begin{aligned} F &= \$1{,}000\left(1 + \frac{.06}{4}\right)^{4(4)} \\ &= \$1{,}000\ (1.015)^{16} \\ &= \$1{,}000\ (1.269) \\ &= \underline{\underline{\$1{,}269}} \end{aligned}$$

The same sum compounded annually would amount to $1,262.50.

EARNINGS AND CASH FLOW

Earnings and cash flow can be quite different in investments that include financing and depreciation. The earnings figure is important because it provides the basis for income tax computation. The cash flow figure is perhaps more important because it reflects the amount of cash that an investor receives from his project.

A typical statement of earnings and cash flow for a real estate investment is illustrated in Exhibit 17-10 (p. 715).

From Exhibit 17-10 you will notice that through the net operating income figure there is no difference between earnings and cash flow. The difference thereafter results from two items:

1. Only the *interest expense* portion of the loan payment can be deducted from earnings. The *entire loan payment* is deducted for cash flow purposes.
2. Depreciation is deductible from earnings, but as it *does not represent a cash outlay* it is not deductible from cash flow.

In our example we have a net loss before income tax of $24,835. For a taxpayer in a 50% bracket this means a tax *credit* of $12,418. This credit will shelter other earnings of the taxpayer, saving in effect $12,418 in cash outflow. This cash savings

---

[7] Since $F = P(1 + R)^n$ and $R_e = \left(1 + \frac{R}{f}\right)^f - 1$, we can substitute the equation for R_e (effective interest) in place of R in our compound interest formula, thereby obtaining a new compound interest formula.

resulting from the tax credit is added to the net cash flow before tax of $3,620, yielding $16,038 in *after tax* cash flow.

In this example a *net loss on earnings* corresponds with a favorable *cash flow after tax.* This relationship is typical in the early years of a real estate investment because of high interest expense and accelerated depreciation. Each successive year we would have *more* earnings and *less* cash flow as these shelters decrease in effectiveness. The twenty-fifth year of our motel example would yield the following data:

	Earnings	**Cash Flow**
NET OPERATING INCOME	$ 37,620	$ 37,620
LESS:		
Financing ($400,000, 7%, 25 yrs)		
Interest expense (25th year)	1,428	1,428
Principal payment (25th year)	–	32,572
Total	1,428	34,000
Depreciation (S-Y-D, 25th year)	1,385	–
Total financing & depreciation	2,813	34,000
NET BEFORE INCOME TAX	34,807	3,620
INCOME TAX (50%)	(17,404)	(17,404)
NET AFTER TAX	$ 17,403	$(13,784)

In the twenty-fifth year, much decreased interest expense and depreciation shields result in higher taxable earnings and, therefore, income tax. Cash flow to meet the income tax obligation is only $3,620, so the owner has to obtain $13,784 from other sources.

This explains why many real estate investments are not held for the full mortgage term. The general practice is to sell the investment between the eighth and twelfth years and purchase a new property in order to maximize earning shelters. Of course it is possible to extract additional cash out of a real estate investment by refinancing the loan. The additional funds raised through refinancing are tax free at that point.

Stocks and bonds do not have the depreciation feature, nor is financing prominent in these types of investments.

DEPRECIATION

Depreciation methods were discussed in depth in chapter 13. Here we are concerned with the role of depreciation in investment decisions. We have shown how depreciation shelters earnings. In straight-line depreciation there would be a uniform shelter throughout the life of the investment, although interest expense—the other shelter—would decrease progressively.

A comparison of the percentage of cost recovered by the four most common methods of depreciation is shown in Exhibit 17-11. Income tax law restricts the use of accelerated depreciation in certain instances. Prior to 1969 double-declining depreciation was limited to certain assets of which the investor was the *first owner.* The 1969 Tax Reform Act further restricts the double-declining method to newly constructed residential rental housing:

EXHIBIT 17-10 EARNINGS VERSUS CASH FLOW IN REAL ESTATE

A 100-Unit Motel* (First Year)	Earnings	Cash Flow
Income		
Room rentals & miscellaneous	$100,000	$100,000
Operating Expenses		
Salaries and wages	$ 24,290	$ 24,290
Manager's compensation	4,560	4,560
Laundry	2,820	2,820
Linen, china, glassware	1,440	1,440
Advertising, printing	3,810	3,810
Payroll taxes & insurance	1,760	1,760
Heat, light & power	5,800	5,800
Repairs & maintenance	3,550	3,550
Cleaning and other supplies	2,060	2,060
Telecommunications	1,640	1,640
Other misc. operating expenses	4,580	4,580
Property taxes	3,730	3,730
Insurance	2,340	2,340
	$ 62,380	$ 62,380
NET OPERATING INCOME	37,620	37,620
LESS:		
Financing ($400,000, 7%, 25 yrs)		
Interest expense (1st year)	27,840	27,840
Principal payment (1st year)	–	6,160
Total	27,840	34,000
Depreciation (S-Y-D, 25 years)	34,615	–
Total financing & depreciation	62,455	34,000
NET BEFORE INCOME TAX	(24,835)	3,620
INCOME TAX (50%)	12,418	12,418
NET AFTER TAX	$ (12,417)	$ 16,038

Net cash flow after tax as a % return on owner's down payment of $100,000 $\frac{16,038}{100,000} = 16.04\%$

*This is a typical statement for a 100-unit motel. Full price = $500,000. Depreciable assets $450,000, using S-Y-D on a composite life of twenty-five years. (Mortgage payments are quarterly at $8,500; the annual payments are 4 ($8,500) = $34,000.)

1. All other newly constructed real estate acquired after July 24, 1969, is limited to 150% declining balance.
2. Used real estate acquired after July 24, 1969, is limited to straight-line depreciation, with the exception of used residential rental housing which will be limited to 125% declining balance provided the remaining life is at least twenty years.
3. Non-residential real estate which is sold at a gain after December 31, 1969, is subject to full recapture of the excess of accelerated over straight-line depreciation for periods after December 31, 1969, but is limited to the amount of the gain.

   Residential rental property receives different recapture treatment as to accelerated depreciation claimed after December 31, 1969: post-1969 depreciation in excess of straight-line is 100% recapture if the property is held for 100 months or less, and for each month the property is held beyond 100 months, the recapture percentage decreases by 1% per month.

EXHIBIT 17-11 COMPARISON OF VARIOUS DEPRECIATION METHODS (TWENTY-FIVE-YEAR ASSET)

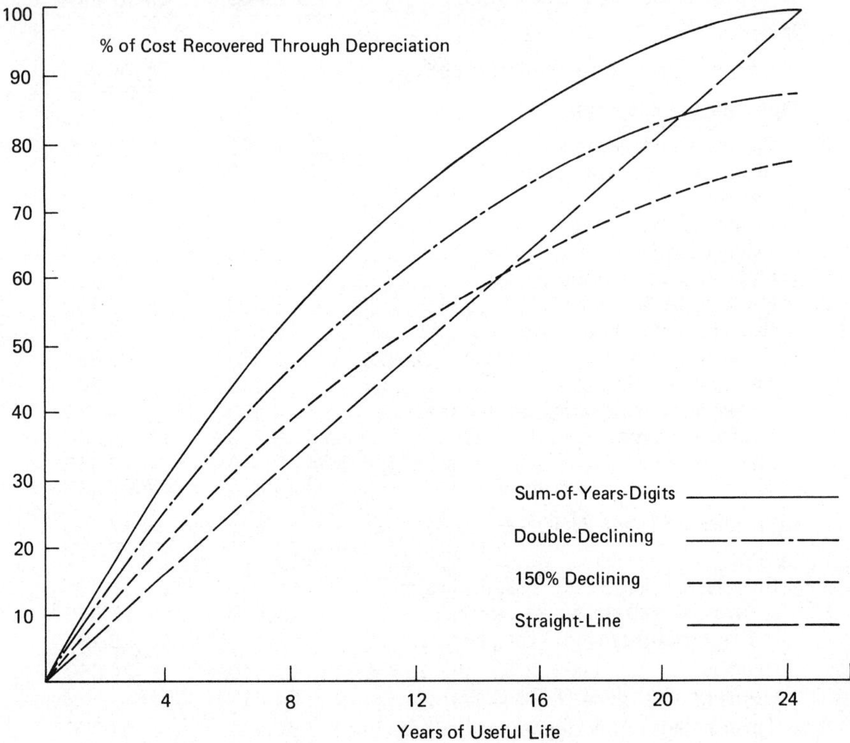

The 1969 Tax Reform Act effectively reduced the influence of accelerated depreciation in real estate investments, with the exception of residential rental property.

Another key variable in determining the amount of depreciation is the allowable useful life of the asset. The Internal Revenue Service has set forth *guidelines* for *new* assets (the current guidelines for useful lives are contained in Exhibit 17-12), but these do not apply to the second owner or subsequent owners of an asset. For example, a first owner may own an apartment building for its full useful life, depreciating it over the guideline period of forty years. If he sells it at this point the new owner acquires a depreciable asset.[8] He must depreciate it over some useful life, but forty years would not be reasonable. In these second and subsequent owner situations the following factors are used in practice for determining useful life—they are listed in the order of importance, e.g., if no. 1 is present, it overrides no. 2, and so forth:

1. A master lease to a single-purpose tenant.
2. The useful life allowed by the Internal Revenue Service or tax courts in a comparable situation.
3. A master lease to a multi-purpose tenant.
4. The financing term, specifically where new financing is obtained upon change of ownership.
5. The longest lease where there are several tenants.

[8]Where land and building are purchased together, and convention is to use the tax assessment ratio for apportioning value between land (which is non-depreciable) and building.

EXHIBIT 17-12 GUIDELINES OF USEFUL LIVES

GROUP ONE: GUIDELINES FOR DEPRECIABLE ASSETS USED BY BUSINESS IN GENERAL

1. Office Furniture, Fixtures, Machines, and Equipment ....10 years
2. Transportation Equipment
   (*a*) *Aircraft (air frames and engines, except aircraft of air transport companies)* .... 6 years
   (*b*) *Automobiles, including taxis* .... 3 years
   (*c*) *Buses* .... 9 years
   (*d*) *General-purpose trucks:*
   Light (actual unloaded weight less than 13,000 pounds) .... 4 years
   Heavy (actual unloaded weight 13,000 pounds or more) .... 6 years
   (*e*) *Railroad cars* .... 15 years
   (*f*) *Tractor units (over-the-road)* .... 4 years
   (*g*) *Trailers and trailer-mounted containers* .... 6 years
   (*h*) *Vessels, barges, tugs and similar water transportation equipment* .... 18 years
3. Land Improvements .... 20 years
4. Buildings (including structural components and integral service equipment)

Apartments .... 40 years	Loft Buildings .... 50 years
Banks .... 50 years	Machine Shops .... 45 years
Dwellings .... 45 years	Office Buildings .... 45 years
Factories .... 45 years	Stores .... 50 years
Garages .... 45 years	Theaters .... 40 years
Grain Elevators .... 60 years	Warehouses .... 60 years
Hotels .... 40 years	Other buildings .... facts and circumstances

5. Subsidiary Assets (jigs, dies, returnable containers, pallets, glassware, etc.).—Taxpayer may use method of accounting other than depreciation method based on useful life. If depreciation on useful life method is used, life is to be based on facts and circumstances.

GROUP TWO: GUIDELINES FOR NONMANUFACTURING ACTIVITIES, EXCLUDING TRANSPORTATION, COMMUNICATIONS, AND PUBLIC UTILITIES

1. Agriculture
   (*a*) *Machinery and Equipment* .... 10 years
   (*b*) *Animals*
   Cattle, breeding or dairy .... 7 years
   Horses, breeding or work .... 10 years
   Hogs, breeding .... 3 years
   Sheep and goats, breeding .... 5 years
   Other animals .... facts and circumstances
   (*c*) *Trees and Vines* .... facts and circumstances
   (*d*) *Farm Buildings* .... 25 years
2. Contract Construction
   (*a*) *General Contract Construction* .... 5 years
   (*b*) *Marine Contract Construction* .... 12 years
3. Fishing .... facts and circumstances
4. Logging and Sawmilling
   (*a*) *Logging* .... 6 years
   (*b*) *Sawmills* .... 10 years
   (*c*) *Portable Sawmills* .... 6 years
5. Mining .... 10 years
6. Recreation and Amusement .... 10 years
7. Services .... 10 years
8. Wholesale and Retail Trade .... 10 years

EXHIBIT 17-12 (CONTINUED)

GROUP THREE: GUIDELINES FOR MANUFACTURING

1. Aerospace Industry .... 8 years
2. Apparel and Fabricated Textile Products .... 9 years
3. Cement Manufacture .... 20 years
4. Chemicals and Allied Products .... 11 years
5. Electrical Equipment
   (a) *Electrical Equipment* .... 12 years
   (b) *Electronic Equipment* .... 8 years
6. Fabricated Metal Products .... 12 years
7. Food and Kindred Products Except Grain and Grain Mill Products, Sugar and Sugar Products, and Vegetable Oil Products .... 12 years
8. Glass and Glass Products .... 14 years
9. Grain and Grain Mill Products .... 17 years
10. Knitwear and Knit Products .... 9 years
11. Leather and Leather Products .... 11 years
12. Lumber, Wood Products, and Furniture .... 10 years
13. Machinery Except Electrical Machinery, Metalworking Machinery, and Transportation Equipment .... 12 years
14. Metalworking Machinery .... 12 years
15. Motor Vehicles and Parts .... 12 years
16. Paper and Allied Products
   (a) *Pulp and Paper* .... 16 years
   (b) *Paper Finishing and Converting* .... 12 years
17. Petroleum and Natural Gas
   (a) *Drilling, Geophysical and Field Services* .... 6 years
   (b) *Exploration, Drilling and Production* .... 14 years
   (c) *Petroleum Refining* .... 16 years
   (d) *Marketing* .... 16 years
18. Plastics Products .... 11 years
19. Primary Metals
   (a) *Ferrous Metals* .... 18 years
   (b) *Nonferrous Metals* .... 14 years
20. Printing and Publishing .... 11 years
21. Professional, Scientific, and Controlling Instruments; Photographic and Optical Equipment; Watches and Clocks .... 12 years
22. Railroad Transportation Equipment .... 12 years
23. Rubber Products .... 14 years
24. Ship and Boat Building .... 12 years
25. Stone and Clay Products Except Cement .... 15 years
26. Sugar and Sugar Products .... 18 years
27. Textile Mill Products Except Knitwear
   (a) *Textile Mill Products, Excluding Finishing and Dyeing* .... 14 years
   (b) *Finishing and Dyeing* .... 12 years
28. Tobacco and Tobacco Products .... 15 years
29. Vegetable Oil Products .... 18 years
30. Other Manufacturing .... 12 years

GROUP FOUR: GUIDELINES FOR TRANSPORTATION, COMMUNICATIONS, AND PUBLIC UTILITIES

1. Air Transport .... 6 years
2. Central Steam Production and Distribution .... 28 years
3. Electric Utilities
   (a) *Hydraulic production plant* .... 50 years
   (b) *Nuclear production plant* .... 20 years

EXHIBIT 17-12 (CONTINUED)

(*c*) *Steam production plant* .... 28 years
(*d*) *Transmission and distribution facilities* .... 30 years

4. Gas Utilities
   (*a*) *Distribution facilities* .... 35 years
   (*b*) *Manufactured gas production plant* .... 30 years
   (*c*) *Natural gas production plant* .... 14 years
   (*d*) *Trunk pipelines and related storage facilities* .... 22 years
5. Motor Transport—Freight .... 8 years
6. Motor Transport—Passengers .... 8 years
7. Pipeline Transportation .... 22 years
8. Radio and Television Broadcasting .... 6 years
9. Railroads
   (*a*) *Machinery and equipment* .... 14 years
   (*b*) *Structures and similar improvements* .... 30 years
   (*c*) *Grading and other right-of-way improvements* .... facts and circumstances
   (*d*) *Wharves and docks* .... 20 years
   (*e*) *Power plant and equipment*
   Electric generating equipment
   Hydraulic .... 50 years
   Nuclear .... 20 years
   Steam .... 28 years
   Steam, compressed air, and other power plant and equipment .... 28 years
10. Telephone and Telegraph Communications ..... FCC rates or facts and circumstances
11. Water Transportation .... 20 years
12. Water Utilities .... 50 years
13. Electrified Railroads, Including Electrified Street Railways... facts and circumstances

SOURCE: Adapted from Internal Revenue Service, *Revenue Procedure 62–21,* July 1962. Based on Reg. § 1.167(a)–8. Prior to July 1962 the Treasury Department used *Bulletin F* as the guide to depreciation lives.

Even if the first owner sells the apartment after ten years, there is no compulsion for the new owner to use a thirty-year useful life if the above considerations point to a shorter life. It has been a reality in real estate investments for second and subsequent owners to reduce useful lives substantially, thus increasing their depreciation tax shields.

The alternatives of depreciating assets separately or in a composite account should be tested in each instance. For example, with straight-line depreciation separate accounts will yield higher depreciation in early years, as shown below.

	Cost	Guideline Years	Straight-Line Depreciation: Separate	Straight-Line Depreciation: Composite
Building	$400,000	40	$10,000	$10,000
Furniture & fixtures	100,000	10	10,000	10,000
Total	$500,000		$20,000	$20,000
Depreciation:				
1st year			$20,000	$20,000 (.04 × $500,000)
2nd year			20,000	19,200 (.04 × $480,000)
3rd year			20,000	18,432 (.04 × $460,800)
4th year			20,000	17,695 (.04 × $442,368)
(etc.)				

However, the use of 150% declining balance will produce the opposite outcome:

	150% Declining Balance	
Depreciation:	**Separate**	**Composite**
1st year	$30,000	$30,000 (.06 × $500,000)
2nd year	27,188	28,200 (.06 × $470,000)
3rd year	24,734	26,508 (.06 × $441,800)
4th year	22,587	24,918 (.06 × $415,292)
(etc.)		

Generally, depreciation methods applied against cost (i.e., straight-line and sum-of-years'-digits) will produce higher depreciation in early years if separate accounts are used. On the other hand, declining balance depreciation methods will produce higher depreciation in early years if composite accounts are used.

The depreciation tax shield effect can be extended by switching from accelerated depreciation to straight-line at the optimum time. Exhibit 17-11 indicates the switch-over point from 150% to straight-line at fifteen years, and from double-declining to straight-line at twenty years. After these years straight-line depreciation would be higher. There is no switch-over from S-Y-D to straight-line, as can be seen in Exhibit 17-11.

TAX STRATEGY

Tax strategy plays an important role in investments. Changes in tax law can alter the form of investments. For example, the 1969 Tax Reform Act encourages investment in low-rental residential property to meet the critical shortage in low-rental housing in the United States in that period.

Of course, tax exempt investors such as employee pension funds need not concern themselves with tax strategy. But the number of tax exempt investors is decreasing continually. The 1969 Tax Reform Act calls for tax on the investments of foundations and the business property of churches and other tax-exempt organizations.

There are three tax provisions which play a major role in investment decisions.

1. *Long-term capital gains:* The gain on sale of capital assets that are held for six months or more is 50% of the taxpayer's regular tax rate with a limit of 25%. Real estate and stocks qualify. Capital losses are only deductible against short-term (less than six months) or long-term capital gains, except that individuals may deduct capital losses at the rate of $1,000 per year on joint returns ($500 per year on separate returns) from ordinary taxable income.
2. *Depreciation tax shield:* A depreciable property shelters earnings as stated before. Straight-line depreciation taken during the life of an asset is taxable at the point of sale on a capital gains basis. The difference between accelerated and straight-line depreciation, under the provisions of the 1969 Tax Reform Act, is taxable as ordinary income at the point of sale.
3. *Net operating loss:* A net operating loss, such as the $24,835 figure in our example in Exhibit 17-10 can be used to shelter income from other sources, i.e., it is

transferrable. If there is no other income to shelter, it can be carried back three years to recover taxes paid during that prior period; and if it is not yet exhausted, it can be carried forward five years to shelter future earnings. Unlike capital losses, net operating losses can be deducted from ordinary income as stated above.

These income tax considerations will be illustrated in the examples which follow. Because tax laws change and tax courts are continually interpreting tax law, investors are advised to seek the assistance of tax attorneys or certified public accountants who specialize in taxes before making commitments.

17.7 EXAMPLES OF INVESTMENTS

Three types of investments will be used to illustrate the application of the foregoing material: (1) bonds, (2) stocks, and (3) real estate.

BONDS

Bonds have four basic financial characteristics: (1) face value, (2) nominal or coupon rate, (3) market value, and (4) effective interest or yield.

The *face value* is the official value of the bond, and generally this value is printed on the bond. The *coupon* rate is the official interest which is paid periodically on the bond. But a bond may sell for more (at a premium) or for less (at a discount) than its face value. This is referred to as the *market* value of a bond. Obviously if the bond is sold at a discount, the *yield* of the bond will be higher than the coupon rate.

Example: If a \$1,000 bond with a coupon rate of 5% sells for \$800, the yield to the holder will be 6.25% instead of 5% per annum, i.e., $\$1{,}000 \times .05 = 50/800 = .0625$.

If the bond is sold at a premium, the yield of the bond will be lower than the coupon rate.

Example: If a \$1,000 bond with a coupon rate of 5% sells for \$1,200, the yield to the holder will be 4.17% instead of 5% per annum, i.e., $\$1{,}000 \times .05 = 50/1{,}200 = .0417$.

There is one other consideration, however. If the buyer holds the bond to maturity in the first instance he will receive an additional \$200, which would increase his yield above 6.25% per annum. In the second example he would lose \$200 at maturity, which would decrease his yield below 4.16%. Even if he does not hold his bond to maturity, it is unlikely that he will sell it for exactly the amount that was paid for it. Therefore the gain or loss on sale must be part of the *yield* figure.

The table in Exhibit 17-13 allows for computation of bond yields provided they are held for maturity.

EXHIBIT 17-13 BOND VALUES AND YIELDS

YEARS AND MONTHS

Yield	19–5	19–6	19–7	19–8	19–9	19–10	19–11	20–0
.00	197.08	197.50	197.92	198.33	198.75	199.17	199.58	200.00
.25	189.97	190.35	190.72	191.10	191.48	191.85	192.23	192.61
.35	187.21	187.58	187.94	188.30	188.66	189.02	189.38	189.74
.40	185.85	186.21	186.56	186.92	187.27	187.62	187.98	188.33
.45	184.50	184.85	185.20	185.55	185.89	186.24	186.59	186.93
.50	183.17	183.51	183.85	184.19	184.53	184.87	185.21	185.54
.55	181.84	182.18	182.51	182.84	183.17	183.51	183.84	184.17
.60	180.53	180.86	181.18	181.51	181.83	182.16	182.48	182.81
.65	179.23	179.55	179.87	180.18	180.50	180.82	181.14	181.46
.70	177.94	178.25	178.56	178.87	179.19	179.50	179.81	180.12
.75	176.66	176.97	177.27	177.58	177.88	178.19	178.49	178.80
.80	175.39	175.69	175.99	176.29	176.59	176.88	177.18	177.48
.85	174.14	174.43	174.72	175.01	175.30	175.60	175.89	176.18
.90	172.89	173.18	173.46	173.75	174.03	174.32	174.60	174.89
.95	171.66	171.94	172.22	172.49	172.77	173.05	173.33	173.61
1.00	170.43	170.71	170.98	171.25	171.52	171.80	172.07	172.34
1.05	169.22	169.49	169.75	170.02	170.29	170.55	170.82	171.09
1.10	168.02	168.28	168.54	168.80	169.06	169.32	169.58	169.84
1.15	166.82	167.08	167.34	167.59	167.85	168.10	168.36	168.61
1.20	165.64	165.89	166.14	166.39	166.64	166.89	167.14	167.39
1.25	164.47	164.72	164.96	165.20	165.45	165.69	165.93	166.18
1.30	163.31	163.55	163.79	164.02	164.26	164.50	164.74	164.98
1.35	162.16	162.39	162.63	162.86	163.09	163.32	163.55	163.79
1.40	161.02	161.25	161.47	161.70	161.93	162.15	162.38	162.61
1.45	159.89	160.11	160.33	160.55	160.77	161.00	161.22	161.44
1.50	158.77	158.98	159.20	159.42	159.63	159.85	160.07	160.28
1.55	157.65	157.87	158.08	158.29	158.50	158.71	158.92	159.13
1.60	156.55	156.76	156.97	157.17	157.38	157.58	157.79	158.00
1.65	155.46	155.66	155.86	156.06	156.27	156.47	156.67	156.87
1.70	154.38	154.58	154.77	154.97	155.16	155.36	155.56	155.75
1.75	153.30	153.50	153.69	153.88	154.07	154.26	154.45	154.64
1.80	152.24	152.43	152.61	152.80	152.99	153.17	153.36	153.55
1.85	151.18	151.37	151.55	151.73	151.91	152.09	152.28	152.46
1.90	150.14	150.32	150.49	150.67	150.85	151.02	151.20	151.38
1.95	149.10	149.28	149.45	149.62	149.79	149.96	150.14	150.31
2.00	148.07	148.24	148.41	148.58	148.75	148.91	149.08	149.25
2.05	147.05	147.22	147.38	147.55	147.71	147.87	148.04	148.20
2.10	146.04	146.21	146.36	146.52	146.68	146.84	147.00	147.16
2.15	145.04	145.20	145.35	145.51	145.66	145.82	145.97	146.13
2.20	144.05	144.20	144.35	144.50	144.65	144.80	144.96	145.11
2.25	143.07	143.21	143.36	143.51	143.65	143.80	143.95	144.09
2.30	142.09	142.23	142.38	142.52	142.66	142.80	142.95	143.09
2.35	141.12	141.26	141.40	141.54	141.68	141.81	141.95	142.09
2.40	140.16	140.30	140.43	140.57	140.70	140.84	140.97	141.11
2.45	139.21	139.34	139.47	139.60	139.73	139.86	140.00	140.13
2.50	138.27	138.40	138.52	138.65	138.78	138.90	139.03	139.16
2.55	137.33	137.46	137.58	137.70	137.83	137.95	138.07	138.20
2.60	136.41	136.53	136.65	136.76	136.88	137.00	137.12	137.24
2.65	135.49	135.61	135.72	135.83	135.95	136.07	136.18	136.30
2.70	134.58	134.69	134.80	134.91	135.02	135.14	135.25	135.36

EXHIBIT 17-13 (CONTINUED)

YEARS AND MONTHS

Yield	19–5	19–6	19–7	19–8	19–9	19–10	19–11	20–0
2.75	133.67	133.78	133.89	134.00	134.11	134.22	134.33	134.44
2.80	132.78	132.89	132.99	133.09	133.20	133.30	133.41	133.52
2.85	131.89	131.99	132.09	132.19	132.30	132.40	132.50	132.60
2.90	131.01	131.11	131.21	131.30	131.40	131.50	131.60	131.70
2.95	130.14	130.23	130.33	130.42	130.52	130.61	130.71	130.80
3.00	129.27	129.36	129.45	129.55	129.64	129.73	129.82	129.92
3.05	128.41	128.50	128.59	128.68	128.77	128.85	128.94	129.04
3.10	127.56	127.65	127.73	127.82	127.90	127.99	128.07	128.16
3.15	126.72	126.80	126.88	126.96	127.05	127.13	127.21	127.30
3.20	125.88	125.96	126.04	126.12	126.20	126.28	126.36	126.44
3.25	125.05	125.13	125.20	125.28	125.36	125.43	125.51	125.59
3.30	124.23	124.30	124.38	124.45	124.52	124.59	124.67	124.75
3.35	123.41	123.49	123.55	123.62	123.69	123.76	123.84	123.91
3.40	122.60	122.67	122.74	122.81	122.87	122.94	123.01	123.08
3.45	121.80	121.87	121.93	122.00	122.06	122.13	122.19	122.26
3.50	121.00	121.07	121.13	121.19	121.25	121.32	121.38	121.45
3.55	120.22	120.28	120.34	120.40	120.45	120.51	120.58	120.64
3.60	119.43	119.50	119.55	119.61	119.66	119.72	119.78	119.84
3.65	118.66	118.72	118.77	118.82	118.88	118.93	118.99	119.04
3.70	117.89	117.95	117.99	118.05	118.10	118.15	118.20	118.26
3.75	117.13	117.18	117.23	117.28	117.32	117.37	117.43	117.48
3.80	116.37	116.42	116.47	116.51	116.56	116.61	116.65	116.70
3.85	115.62	115.67	115.71	115.75	115.80	115.84	115.89	115.94
3.90	114.88	114.92	114.96	115.00	115.05	115.09	115.13	115.18
3.95	114.14	114.18	114.22	114.26	114.30	114.34	114.38	114.42
4.00	113.41	113.45	113.49	113.52	113.56	113.60	113.64	113.78
4.05	112.68	112.72	112.76	112.79	112.82	112.86	112.90	112.94
4.10	111.97	112.00	112.03	112.06	112.10	112.13	112.17	112.20
4.15	111.25	111.29	111.32	111.34	111.38	111.41	111.44	111.47
4.20	110.55	110.58	110.60	110.63	110.66	110.69	110.72	110.75
4.25	109.84	109.88	109.90	109.92	109.95	109.98	110.01	110.04
4.30	109.15	109.18	109.20	109.22	109.25	109.27	109.30	109.33
4.35	108.46	108.49	108.51	108.53	108.55	108.57	108.60	108.62
4.40	107.78	107.80	107.82	107.84	107.86	107.88	107.90	107.93
4.45	107.10	107.12	107.14	107.15	107.17	107.19	107.21	107.23
4.50	106.42	106.45	106.46	106.47	106.49	106.51	106.53	106.55
4.55	105.76	105.78	105.79	105.80	105.82	105.83	105.85	105.87
4.60	105.10	105.11	105.12	105.13	105.15	105.16	105.18	105.19
4.65	104.44	104.46	104.46	104.47	104.48	104.50	104.51	104.57
4.70	103.79	103.80	103.81	103.82	103.83	103.84	103.85	103.86
4.75	103.14	103.16	103.16	103.17	103.17	103.18	103.19	103.20
4.80	102.50	102.51	102.52	102.52	102.53	102.53	102.54	102.55
4.85	101.87	101.88	101.88	101.88	101.88	101.89	101.90	101.91
4.90	101.24	101.25	101.25	101.25	101.25	101.25	101.26	101.27
4.95	100.61	100.62	100.62	100.62	100.62	100.62	100.62	100.63
5.00	100.00	100.00	100.00	99.99	99.99	99.99	100.00	100.00
5.05	99.38	99.38	99.38	99.37	99.37	99.37	99.37	99.38
5.10	98.77	98.77	98.77	98.76	98.76	98.75	98.75	98.76

EXHIBIT 17-13 (CONTINUED)

YEARS AND MONTHS

Yield	19–5	19–6	19–7	19–8	19–9	19–10	19–11	20–0
5.15	98.17	98.17	98.16	98.15	98.15	98.14	98.14	98.14
5.20	97.57	97.57	97.56	97.55	97.54	97.54	97.53	97.53
5.25	96.97	96.97	96.96	96.95	96.94	96.93	96.93	96.93
5.30	96.39	96.38	96.37	96.36	96.35	96.34	96.33	96.33
5.40	95.22	95.21	95.20	95.18	95.17	95.16	95.15	95.14
5.50	94.07	94.06	94.05	94.03	94.01	94.00	93.99	93.98
5.60	92.95	92.94	92.91	92.89	92.88	92.86	92.85	92.84
5.70	91.84	91.82	91.80	91.78	91.76	91.74	91.72	91.71
5.75	91.29	91.27	91.25	91.23	91.21	91.19	91.17	91.15
6.00	88.62	88.60	88.56	88.54	88.51	88.49	88.46	88.44
6.50	83.58	83.55	83.51	83.47	83.44	83.40	83.37	83.34
7.00	78.93	78.90	78.85	78.80	78.76	78.72	78.68	78.64

A formula and example for approximating the value and yield of a bond (bonds are generally valued on a yield basis) follow:

	Discount	**Premium**
1.	$\bar{I}=I+\frac{d}{n}$	$\bar{I}=I-\frac{p}{n}$

2. $\bar{C}=\frac{C+M}{2}$

3. $Y=\frac{\bar{I}}{\bar{C}}$

where

$\bar{I}$ = average income
$\bar{C}$ = average cost
Y = yield (approximate)
I = coupon interest (average total)
M = maturity or face value
d = discount
p = premium
n = number of years to maturity
C = cost of bond

Example: A twenty-year, 5% bond with a face value of $1,000 is purchased for $97. What is the approximate yield to maturity?[9]

1. $\bar{I}=\$50+\frac{\$30}{20}=\$51.50$

[9] Bonds generally have a standard face value of $1,000 each.

2. $\overline{C} = \dfrac{\$970 + \$1{,}000}{2} = \$985$

3. $Y = \dfrac{\$51.50}{\$985} = 5.23\%$ per annum (approximate)

A more precise *yield* can be obtained from Exhibit 17-13, which is based on present values. Interpolating for values between 5.20 and 5.25 produces the figure 5.244%.

The coupon interest per annum is taxable as ordinary income. If the bond is held for six months or more, there is a long-term capital gain in the amount of the discount and *vice versa* for premium.

STOCKS

In a sense the four characteristics of a bond are present in stocks. A share of stock has a *book* or *face* value (par or stated). *Nominal* interest is paid in the form of dividends. The *market value* is what the stock is selling for at any point in time. *Yield* is computed on the basis of dividends received plus any gain or loss on the sale of stock.

Example: An investor purchases 100 shares of common stock in X company in 19*x*1 for $25 a share. He receives dividends at the end of each of five years as shown below:

	Dividends Per Share	Total
Y_1	$1.25	$125
Y_2	.90	90
Y_3	1.10	110
Y_4	1.40	140
Y_5	1.00	100

At the end of five years he sells his shares for $40 each. The *exact yield* on his investment can be computed by means of a trial and error procedure, using Table B-2, Appendix B. What we have is a stream of unequal payments that need to be discounted to the current outlay of $2,500.[10]

	Dividend Income		Sale of Stock		Total	Capital Gain
Y_1	$125	⟶				
Y_2	90	⟶				
Y_3	110	⟶				
Y_4	140	⟶				
Y_5	100	+	$4,000	=	$4,100	$1,500
Total	$565	+	$4,000	=	$4,565	$1,500

The exact yield is 13.66%.

The formulae for estimating the yield on bonds can also be used for stock,

[10] Refer to the discussion of time-adjusted rate of return in chapter 24.

where $\bar{I}$ equals average dividends and $\bar{C}$ is average investment, which is calculated by adding the purchase price to the selling price and dividing by two.

$$1.\quad \bar{I} = \$113 + \frac{\$1{,}500}{5} = \$413$$

$$2.\quad \bar{C} = \frac{\$2{,}500 + \$4{,}000}{2} = \$3{,}250$$

$$3.\quad Y = \frac{\$413}{\$3{,}250} = 12.7\%$$

The dividend income is taxed as ordinary income. If the stock is held for six months or more, we have a long-term capital gain if it is sold for an amount in excess of cost. Any loss on sale, regardless of the length of ownership, is a capital loss.

REAL ESTATE

The following data is provided for our real estate example:

Purchase price	$120,000
Value assigned to land	15,000
Value assigned to building	105,000
Depreciation method	S-L
Useful life	21 years
Down payment	20,000
Amount financed	100,000
Net operating income per annum	11,000
Tax rate	50%
Property increases in value at the rate of 5% a year.	

The amortization schedule for the amount financed is contained in Exhibit 17-14.

EXHIBIT 17-14 AMORTIZATION SCHEDULE

Terms: $100,000, amortized in equal monthly payments of $728.33 ($8,740 per annum) including principal and interest at 6½% until paid in full.

	Annual Totals		
	Interest	**Principal**	**Balance**
Y_0	$ –	$ –	$100,000
Y_1	6,432	2,308	97,692
Y_2	6,277	2,463	95,229
Y_3	6,112	2,628	92,601
Y_4	5,937	2,804	89,797
Y_5	5,749	2,992	86,805
Y_6	5,548	3,192	83,613

EXHIBIT 17-14 (CONTINUED)

	Annual Totals		
	Interest	**Principal**	**Balance**
Y_7	5,335	3,406	80,208
Y_8	5,107	3,634	76,574
Y_9	4,863	3,877	72,697
Y_{10}	4,603	4,137	68,560
Y_{11}	4,326	4,414	64,146
Y_{12}	4,031	4,710	59,436
Y_{13}	3,715	5,025	54,411
Y_{14}	3,379	5,361	49,050
Y_{15}	3,020	5,721	43,329
Y_{16}	2,637	6,104	37,226
Y_{17}	2,228	6,512	30,713
Y_{18}	1,792	6,949	23,765
Y_{19}	1,326	7,414	16,351
Y_{20}	830	7,910	8,440
Y_{21}	300	8,440	—

Integrated earnings and cash flow data are developed in Exhibit 17-15.

Assume a sale at the end of year 10:

Selling price[11] ($120,000 × 1.6289)	$195,468
Less: Balance outstanding on loan	68,560
Cash flow before tax	$126,908

Computation of Capital Gain:

Method 1	Original price of property	$120,000	
	Less: Cumulative deprec.	50,000	
	Tax basis	$ 70,000	
	Selling price of property	$195,468	
	Less: Tax basis	70,000	
	Capital gain	$125,468	
Method 2	Appreciation in value	$ 75,468	
	Cumulative depreciation	50,000	
	Capital gain	$125,468	
	Capital gain tax (.25 × $125,468)		$31,367
	CASH FLOW ON SALE AFTER TAX		$95,541

The yield on the investment is 23.39% per annum, which is computed from Table B-2, Appendix B, as follows:

[11] Property value increases by 5% per annum, hence the future value factor for ten years (1.6289) is used. See Table B-2, Appendix B.

Computation of Yield (After Tax)

	Net Spendable	Cash Flow After Tax	Total	PV @ 24%	PV @ 22%
Y_1	$ 2,476	–	$ 2,476 × .806 =	$ 1,996 × .820 =	$ 2,030
Y_2	2,398	–	2,398 × .650 =	1,559 × .672 =	1,611
Y_3	2,316	–	2,316 × .524 =	1,214 × .551 =	1,276
Y_4	2,228	–	2,228 × .423 =	942 × .451 =	1,005
Y_5	2,134	–	2,134 × .341 =	728 × .370 =	790
Y_6	2,034	–	2,034 × .275 =	559 × .303 =	616
Y_7	1,927	–	1,927 × .222 =	428 × .249 =	480
Y_8	1,813	–	1,813 × .179 =	325 × .204 =	370
Y_9	1,691	–	1,691 × .144 =	244 × .167 =	282
Y_{10}	1,561	$95,677	97,238 × .116 =	11,280 × .137 =	13,322
	$20,578	$95,677	$116,225	$19,275	$21,782

Note: interpolate between 24% and 22% for yield. (Interpolation is discussed in chapter 24.)

Investment analysis data relative to this example is summarized in Exhibit 17-16.

Exhibit 17-16 should be interpreted in this way: if the property is sold in the ninth year, yield per annum is 24.32%; if the property is sold in the eleventh year, yield per annum is 22.55%; and so forth. As noted, the highest yield is in the first year, but there are practical as well as financial constraints such as brokerage fees and depreciation recapture which make it wise to hold the investment for a number of years.

The importance of the tax rate should be emphasized in real estate investments. In this example we have used a 50% rate. Note how cash flow after tax (or "net spendable") as shown in Exhibit 17-15 for the first year would differ under alternative tax rates of 70% and 20%:

Tax Rate	Taxable Income	Tax	Earnings After Tax	Add-Back Deprecia-tion	Less: Principal Payments	Net Spendable (Cash Flow After Tax)	% Return
70%	($432)	$302	($130)	$5,000	($2,308)	$2,562	12.81
50%	(432)	216	(216)	5,000	(2,308)	2,476	12.38
20%	(432)	86	(346)	5,000	(2,308)	2,346	11.73

The advantage in favor of a high tax bracket increases in relation to the size of the taxable loss—a high taxable loss will result in a much greater return to persons in high as opposed to low tax brackets. To illustrate this point, assume that the taxable loss in the above example is $4,320 rather than $432:

Tax Rate	Taxable Income	Tax	Earnings After Tax	Add-Back Depreciation	Less: Principal Payments	Net Spendable	% Return
70%	($4,320)	$3,020	($1,300)	$5,000	($2,308)	$1,392	6.96
50%	(4,320)	2,160	(2,160)	5,000	(2,308)	532	2.66
20%	(4,320)	860	(3,460)	5,000	(2,308)	(768)	(3.84)

EXHIBIT 17-15 INTEGRATED STATEMENT OF EARNINGS AND CASH FLOW

	EARNINGS						CASH FLOW			
	Net Operating Income	Less: Interest Payments	Less: Depreciation (S-L)	Taxable Income	Tax (50%)	Earnings After Tax	Add-Back Depreciation	Less: Principal Payments	Net Spendable* (Cash Flow After Tax)	% Return†
Y_1	$11,000	($6,432)	($5,000)	($ 432)	$ 216	($ 216)	$5,000	($ 2,308)	$ 2,476	12.38%
Y_2		(6,277)		(277)	139	(139)		(2,463)	2,398	11.99
Y_3		(6,112)		(112)	56	(56)		(2,628)	2,316	11.58
Y_4		(5,937)		63	(32)	32		(2,804)	2,228	11.14
Y_5		(5,749)		251	(126)	126		(2,992)	2,134	10.67
Y_6		(5,548)		452	(226)	226		(3,192)	2,034	10.17
Y_7		(5,335)		665	(333)	333		(3,406)	1,927	9.63
Y_8		(5,107)		893	(447)	447		(3,634)	1,813	9.06
Y_9		(4,863)		1,137	(568)	568		(3,877)	1,691	8.46
Y_{10}		(4,603)		1,397	(698)	698		(4,137)	1,561	7.81
Y_{11}		(4,326)		1,674	(837)	837		(4,414)	1,423	7.11
Y_{12}		(4,031)		1,969	(985)	985		(4,710)	1,275	6.38
Y_{13}		(3,715)		2,285	(1,142)	1,142		(5,025)	1,117	5.59
Y_{14}		(3,379)		2,621	(1,311)	1,311		(5,361)	949	4.75
Y_{15}		(3,020)		2,980	(1,490)	1,490		(5,721)	770	3.85
Y_{16}		(2,637)		3,363	(1,682)	1,682		(6,104)	578	2.89
Y_{17}		(2,228)		3,772	(1,886)	1,886		(6,512)	374	1.87
Y_{18}		(1,792)		4,208	(2,104)	2,104		(6,949)	156	0.78
Y_{19}		(1,326)		4,674	(2,337)	2,337		(7,414)	(77)	(0.39)
Y_{20}		(830)		5,170	(2,585)	2,585		(7,910)	(325)	(1.63)
Y_{21}	11,000	(301)	(5,000)	5,700	(2,850)	2,850	5,000	(8,439)	(589)	(2.95)
	$231,000	$(83,548)	$(105,000)	$42,452	$(21,226)	$21,226	$105,000	$(100,000)	$26,226	

*The term *net spendable* is often used for "net cash flow after tax."

†Percent return per annum on the down payment of $20,000. These percentages do not represent "yield."

EXHIBIT 17-16 INVESTMENT DATA ON REAL ESTATE EXAMPLE

	(1) Cumulative Deprecia-tion	(2) Cumulative Apprecia-tion	(3) Capital Gain	(4) C.G.After Tax (75%)	(5) Tax Basis Less Loan Balance	(6) Cash Flow on Sale	(7) Cumulative Net Spendable	(8) Total Cash Flow After Tax	(9) Yield
Y_1	$ 5,000	$ 6,000	$ 11,000	$ 8,250	$17,308	$ 25,558	$ 2,476	$ 28,034	40.08%
Y_2	10,000	12,300	22,300	16,725	14,771	31,496	4,874	36,370	36.48%
Y_3	15,000	18,915	33,915	25,436	12,399	37,835	7,190	45,025	33.66%
Y_4	20,000	25,861	45,861	34,396	10,203	44,598	9,418	54,016	31.39%
Y_5	25,000	33,154	58,154	43,615	8,195	51,810	11,552	63,362	29.51%
Y_6	30,000	40,811	70,811	53,109	6,387	59,495	13,586	73,081	27.92%
Y_7	35,000	48,852	83,852	62,889	4,792	67,681	15,513	83,194	26.56%
Y_8	40,000	57,295	97,295	72,971	3,426	76,397	17,326	93,723	25.37%
Y_9	45,000	66,159	111,159	83,370	2,303	85,673	19,017	104,690	24.32%
Y_{10}	50,000	75,468	125,468	94,101	1,440	95,541	20,578	116,119	23.39%
Y_{11}	55,000	85,241	140,241	105,181	854	106,035	22,001	128,036	22.55%
Y_{12}	60,000	95,503	155,503	116,627	564	117,191	23,276	140,467	21.80%
Y_{13}	65,000	106,278	171,278	128,458	589	129,047	24,393	153,440	21.11%
Y_{14}	70,000	117,592	187,592	140,694	950	141,644	25,342	166,986	20.48%
Y_{15}	75,000	129,471	204,471	153,354	1,671	155,024	26,112	181,136	19.90%
Y_{16}	80,000	141,945	221,945	166,459	2,774	169,233	26,690	195,923	19.37%
Y_{17}	85,000	155,042	240,042	180,032	4,287	184,318	27,064	211,382	18.87%
Y_{18}	90,000	168,794	258,794	194,096	6,235	200,331	27,219	227,550	18.41%
Y_{19}	95,000	183,234	278,234	208,676	8,649	217,325	27,142	244,467	17.98%
Y_{20}	100,000	198,396	298,396	223,797	11,560	235,357	26,817	262,173	17.57%
Y_{21}	105,000	214,316	319,316	239,487	15,000	254,487	26,226	280,713	17.19%

While the investment still yields a positive return to the person in the 70% tax bracket, the return is negative for investors who are in the 50% and 20% tax brackets.

17.8 SUMMARY

We defined *investment* as an economic outlay in the expectation of a money return above the amount invested. The amount invested is *principal.* The amount in excess of principal is *interest.* In making investment decisions there should be assurance that principal will be returned. Losing a few percentages in interest is less catastrophic than losing 100% of principal.

Investors' behavior patterns which can be normalized in terms of a theoretical *risk aversion index* combine a host of economic and psychological considerations.

Reasons for investing may differ depending on the investor's needs. These needs may determine whether the investment is short-term or long-term, whether there is an immediate or delayed cash flow, or whether equity buildup is desired. Appreciation in value is a common goal of investing, and such appreciation must be added to current earnings in order to compute the true yield of the investment. This requires that we look at the whole life-cycle of an investment.

We discussed important ingredients common to most investment decisions: (1) cost of the investment, (2) down payment, (3) financing, (4) earnings and cash flow, (5) depreciation, and (6) tax strategy.

We looked at examples of computing yields on investments in bonds, stocks, and real estate.

CHAPTER 17 APPENDIX

INVESTMENT ANALYSIS INFORMATION AND STATISTICS

The purpose of this Appendix is to provide students with some sources of investment information. In addition some standard statistics relative to investments in real estate, bonds, and stocks is included for educational purposes.

SOURCES OF INVESTMENT INFORMATION AND STATISTICS

1. GENERAL REAL ESTATE AND URBAN ECONOMICS

Apartment Houses, Institute of Real Estate Management, 155 East Superior Street, Chicago, Illinois, 60611. Publishes periodic data on apartment houses.

The Appraisal Journal (Quarterly), American Institute of Real Estate Appraisers, National Association of Real Estate Boards, 155 East Superior Street, Chicago, Illinois, 60611.

Buildings (Monthly), STAMATS Publishing Company, 427 Sixth Avenue, Cedar Rapids, Iowa, 52406.

Economic Geography (Quarterly), Commonwealth Press, 44 Portland Street, Worcester, Massachusetts.

Hotels & Motels, Laventhol, Krekstein, Horwath & Horwath, 1845 Walnut Street, Philadelphia, Pennsylvania, 19103. This certified public accounting firm publishes an annual statistical volume on the lodging industry.

Journal of American Institute of Planners (Bimonthly), American Institute of Planners, Port City Press, Baltimore, Maryland, 21208.

Journal of Property Management (Bimonthly), American Institute of Real Estate Appraisers, National Association of Real Estate Boards, 155 East Superior Street, Chicago, Illinois, 60611.

Journal of Regional Science (April, August, December), Regional Science Research Institute, Department of Regional Science, Wharton School, University of Pennsylvania.

Land Economics (Quarterly), University of Wisconsin Press, Madison, Wisconsin.

Mobile Home Park Management (Bimonthly), J. Brown Hardison, Publisher, 6229 Northwest Highway, Chicago, Illinois, 60631.

Office Buildings, rental income and operating costs for office buildings are analyzed annually by The Accounting and Exchange Committee, Building Owners and Managers Association, 134 South LaSalle Street, Chicago, Illinois, 60603.

Residential Research Reports (Periodically), Residential Research Committee of Southern California, 13437 Ventura Blvd., Sherman Oaks, California, 91403.

Skyscraper Management (Quarterly), Building Owners and Management Association International, 134 South LaSalle, Chicago, 60603.

2. GENERAL INDUSTRY AND FINANCE

Dun's Review and Modern Industry (Monthly), Dun & Bradstreet Publications Corporation, P.O. Box 3088, Grand Central Station, New York, N.Y., 10017.

Investment Dealer's Digest (Weekly), Investment Dealers Digest Incorporated, 150 Broadway, New York, N.Y., 10038.

Moody's Bond Survey (Weekly), Moody's Investors Service, Inc., 99 Church Street, New York, N.Y., 10007.

Standard Bond Reports Standard & Poors Corporation, 449 Boston Post Road, Orange, Connecticut, 06477.

Standard N.Y.S.E. Stock Reports (Daily), Standard & Poors Corporation.

Standard Corporation Records (Daily), Standard & Poors Corporation.

3. SELECTED ORGANIZATIONS

American Aviation (Biweekly), American Aviation Publications, Inc., 1156 15th Street N. W., Washington, D.C., 20005.

Aerospace Facts & Figures (Annual), Aero Publishers, Inc., 329 Aviation Road, Fallbrook, California, 92028.

Wards Automotive Yearbook (Annual), Powers and Company, Inc., 550 West Fort Street, Detroit, Michigan, 48226.

Broadcasting (Weekly), Broadcasting Publications, Inc., 1735 De Sales Street, N. W., Washington, D.C., 20036.

Construction Review (Monthly), U.S. Department of Commerce, Superintendent of Documents, U.S. Government Printing Office, Washington, D.C., 20402.

Chain Store Age (Monthly), Lebhar-Friedman Publications, Inc., 500 North Dearborn Street, Chicago, Illinois, 60610.

Foreign Operations: Barclays Overseas Review (Monthly) Barclays Bank, D.C.O., 54 Lombard Street, London, E.C. 3.

Federal Reserve Bulletin (Monthly), Division of Administrative Services, Board of Governors of the Federal Reserve System, Washington, D.C., 20551.

Quarterly Financial Report for Manufacturing Corporations, Federal Trade Commission, Securities and Exchange Commission, Superintendent of Documents, U.S. Government Printing Office, Washington, D.C., 20402.

SELECTED INVESTMENT STATISTICS

See Exhibits 17A-1–17A-9.

EXHIBIT 17A-1 MOTEL OPERATING STATISTICS—1968–69 (ALL FIGURES ARE MEDIANS.)

	ANNUAL AMOUNTS PER ROOM				**RATIOS TO ROOM SALES**			
	No Operated Restaurant		**Restaurant Operated**		**No Operated Restaurant**		**Restaurant Operated**	
	1969	**1968**	**1969**	**1968**	**1969**	**1968**	**1969**	**1968**
Income								
Guest room rentals	$3,610	$3,477	$3,759	$3,610	100.0%	100.0%	100.0%	100.0%
Public room rentals	24	21	46	37	.7	.6	1.2	.9
Restaurant								
Operating income			353	443			8.2	10.5
Lease income	236	270			6.7	7.8		
Other income (net)	28	26	48	34	.8	.7	1.3	.9
Total	3,855	3,681	4,234	4,197	106.4	106.3	112.0	112.6
Operating Expenses								
Payroll (excluding restaurant)	895	848	1,112	1,058	26.0	25.2	29.0	28.1
Payroll taxes and employee benefits	81	73	100	82	2.2	2.1	2.9	2.6
Total	978	919	1,212	1,143	28.2	27.4	31.8	30.9
Housekeeping	319	295	337	330	8.9	8.7	9.1	8.9
Administrative	336	217	302	269	8.1	6.8	8.3	7.8
Advertising	170	132	187	177	4.1	3.3	5.0	5.4
Heat, light and power	182	169	218	213	4.6	4.6	5.7	6.0
Repairs and maintenance	169	160	199	188	4.5	4.1	5.2	5.3
Total	2,128	1,926	2,517	2,327	59.8	58.0	65.8	66.3
House income (before taxes, interest, depreciation, etc.)	$1,681	$1,705	$1,833	$1,828	48.5%	50.3%	49.6%	50.5%
Percentage of occupancy	75.70%	71.69%	72.15%	70.84%				
Average rate per occupied room	$13.49	$12.47	$14.32	$13.56				
Ratios to total sales, including restaurant rental income and other income								
Payroll (including restaurant)	23.1%	23.1%	29.4%	28.1%				
Payroll taxes and employee benefits	1.8	1.8	3.0	2.7				
Total	25.1%	24.8%	32.0%	30.5%				
Administrative expenses	7.0%	5.8%	4.4%	4.3%				
Advertising	3.9	2.8	2.8	2.8				
Heat, light and power	4.0	4.1	3.1	3.3				
Repairs and maintenance	3.9	3.8	3.0	2.9				
House income	43.0	44.5	25.7	26.9				

SOURCE: Laventhol, Krekstein, Horwath & Horwath, *Lodging Industry* (1970 edition), p. 15. Used with permission.

EXHIBIT 17A-2 HOTEL OPERATING STATISTICS—1968–69

	MEDIAN AMOUNTS PER AVAILABLE ROOM						RATIOS OF MEDIAN AMOUNTS TO ROOM SALES					
	Under 300 Rooms		300–600 Rooms		Over 600 Rooms		Under 300 Rooms		300–600 Rooms		Over 600 Rooms	
	1969	1968	1969	1968	1969	1968	1969	1968	1969	1968	1969	1968
Rooms												
Sales	$2,221	$1,777	$3,668	$3,211	$4,195	$3,855	100.0%	100.0%	100.0%	100.0%	100.0%	100.0%
Departmental expenses												
Payroll and related expenses	647	550	792	751	766	737	29.1	31.0	21.6	23.4	18.3	19.1
Other	230	188	275	281	349	329	10.4	10.6	7.5	8.8	8.3	8.5
Total	829	738	1,087	1,046	1,119	1,050	37.3	41.5	29.6	32.6	26.7	27.2
Departmental income	1,333	1,068	2,541	2,158	3,105	2,788	60.0	60.1	69.3	67.2	74.0	72.3
Food and beverages												
Sales												
Food	1,504	1,773	2,068	1,988	2,436	2,241	78.1	77.0	71.7	72.3	73.8	70.4
Beverages	489	568	873	760	961	917	25.4	24.7	30.2	27.7	29.1	28.8
Total	1,926	2,302	2,886	2,748	3,302	3,182	100.0	100.0	100.0	100.0	100.0	100.0
Cost of sales												
Food	610	715	741	712	728	668	40.6	40.3	35.8	35.8	29.9	29.8
Beverages	154	187	266	234	254	241	31.5	32.9	30.5	30.8	26.4	26.3
Total	760	877	966	888	971	914	39.5	38.1	33.5	32.3	29.4	28.7
Gross profit	1,166	1,347	1,926	1,816	2,301	2,210	60.5	58.5	66.7	66.1	69.7	69.5
Other income	18	14	52	47	41	42	.9	.6	1.8	1.7	1.2	1.3
Gross profit and other income	1,166	1,354	2,015	1,816	2,376	2,230	60.5	58.8	69.8	66.1	72.0	70.1
Departmental expenses												
Payroll and related expenses	809	1,074	1,398	1,288	1,334	1,282	42.0	46.7	48.4	46.9	40.4	40.3
Other	153	174	262	254	244	237	7.9	7.6	9.1	9.2	7.4	7.4
Total	966	1,215	1,721	1,524	1,595	1,526	50.2	52.8	59.6	55.5	48.3	48.0
Departmental income	202	170	470	374	653	724	10.5	7.4	16.3	13.6	19.8	22.8
Ratio of departmental income to room sales							9.1	9.6	12.8	11.6	15.6	18.8
Net income (loss) from minor operated departments and other income	(17)	(19)	42	62	121	106	(.8)	(1.1)	1.1	1.9	2.9	2.7
Gross income	1,518*	1,219*	3,053*	2,594*	3,879*	3,618*	68.3	68.6	83.2	80.8	92.5	93.9
Undistributed operating expenses												
Administrative and general												
Payroll and related expenses	237	240	298	292	305	282	10.7	13.5	8.1	9.1	7.3	7.3
Other	243	232	297	290	377	321	10.9	13.1	8.1	9.0	9.0	8.3
Total	457	437	530	587	641	549	20.6	24.6	14.4	18.3	15.3	14.2
Advertising and promotion	102	103	198	231	274	265	4.6	5.8	5.4	7.2	6.5	6.9
Heat, light and power	346	323	316	310	289	271	15.6	18.2	8.6	9.7	6.9	7.0
Repairs and maintenance	205	213	333	329	441	380	9.2	12.0	9.1	10.2	10.5	9.9
Total undistributed expenses	1,119*	925*	1,657*	1,216*	1,609*	1,650*	50.3	52.1	45.1	37.9	38.4	42.8
House income	399	294	1,396	1,378	2,270	1,968	18.0	16.5	38.1	42.9	54.1	51.1
Store rentals	54	71	64	62	84	67	2.4	4.0	1.7	1.9	2.0	1.7
Gross operating income	$ 458	$ 318	$1,396	$1,398	$2,390	$2,102	20.6%	17.9%	38.1%	43.5%	57.0%	54.5%

*For clarity in presentation, all totals marked with an asterisk are not medians but computed figures.

SOURCE: Laventhol, Krekstein, Horwath & Horwath, *Lodging Industry*, pp. 28–29. Used with permission.

EXHIBIT 17A-3 MOBILE HOME STATISTICS

MOBILE HOME PARK CONSTRUCTION COSTS

100 Spaces: Eight to Ten Spaces Per Acre

	Ranges
Space Costs: \$1,500 to \$1,900 per space. Includes utilities, engineering, paving, grading, pro-rated costs of streets, fencing and off-site improvements. Does not include land and buildings.	\$150,000–\$190,000
Buildings: Recreation hall with office and kitchen, utility building including laundry room and storage room.	30,000– 70,000
Pool: 900-1,000 sq. ft.	4,000– 8,000
Shuffleboard Courts: (2) \$400 to \$700 each.	800– 1,400
Equipment: 8 to 10 washers with 3 or 4 dryers, car or truck for park use, garden and office equipment.	10,000– 15,000
Professional Services:	
General contractor (8% to 10% of construction costs.)	15,000– 27,000
Architect or designer (5% to 7% of construction costs.)	9,000– 19,000
TOTAL	\$219,000–\$330,000

MOBILE HOME PARK INCOME AND EXPENSES

	Income:	**Range**
(1)	Rents	84.0%–89.0%
(2)	Washing & vending machines	1.0 – 2.5
(3)	Utilities	11.0 –16.0
	Total income	100.0%
	Expenses:	
	Salaries & wages	7.0–11.0
(3)	Utilities	11.5–15.0
	Maintenance & repairs	2.0– 4.0
(4)	Pool cleaning	0.5– 1.0
(5)	Supplies	0.7– 2.0
(6)	Advertising & promotion	0.2– 1.0
	Office expenses	0.1– 0.5
(7)	Telephone	0.4– 1.0
(8)	Association dues & permits	0.2– 1.0
	Legal & accounting	0.3– 0.7
(9)	Insurance	0.5– 1.6
(10)	Land & property taxes	6.0–12.0
(11)	Depreciation	10.0–20.0
(12)	Interest on loan payments	6.0–11.0
	Total expenses	45.0–58.0
	Net operating profit	42.0–55.0
	Income tax	
(12)	Loan payments	

Note: Data not additive vertically. Low figures in one category may be compensated by high figures in another, bringing total expenses to the ranges indicated.

SOURCE: "Mobile Home Parks," *Small Business Reporter* 7, no. 10 (San Francisco: Bank of America, 1970). Used with permission.

EXHIBIT 17A-4 SHOPPING CENTER STATISTICS

(a)
REGIONAL SHOPPING CENTERS BY AGE GROUP
OPERATING RESULTS IN RELATION TO TOTAL CAPITAL COST

	Dollars per sq. ft. of GLA		Percent of total capital cost	
	Median	**Middle Range**	**Median**	**Middle Range**
1–3 Years				
Total Capital Cost	$23.48	$16.91–$25.03	100.0%	– –
Operating Receipts	2.36	2.02– 3.21	11.9	9.0%–14.5%
Operating Expenses	.70	.52– .95	3.3	2.5 – 3.9
Operating Balance	1.61	1.37– 2.20	8.1	6.8 –10.3
4–6 Years				
Total Capital Cost	$16.63	$16.02–$22.00	100.0%	– –
Operating Receipts	2.22	1.67– 2.81	12.8	10.1%–15.2%
Operating Expenses	.71	.60– .86	4.0	2.9 – 4.7
Operating Balance	1.42	1.22– 1.86	8.2	7.4 –10.5
7–9 Years				
Total Capital Cost	$17.66	$13.58–$21.96	100.0%	– –
Operating Receipts	2.01	1.92– 2.60	13.3	10.2%–14.7%
Operating Expenses	.64	.57– .76	3.7	3.1 – 4.4
Operating Balance	1.38	1.19– 1.87	9.6	7.3 –10.5
10 Years and Over				
Total Capital Cost	$17.83	$13.59–$24.79	100.0%	– –
Operating Receipts	2.24	1.88– 2.85	13.0	11.6%–15.6%
Operating Expenses	.80	.56– .99	4.6	4.1 – 5.4
Operating Balance	1.38	1.24– 2.01	8.5	6.6 –11.6

(b)
COMMUNITY SHOPPING CENTERS
OPERATING RESULTS IN RELATION TO TOTAL CAPITAL COST

	Dollars per sq. ft. of GLA		Percent of total capital cost	
	Median	**Middle Range**	**Median**	**Middle Range**
Total Capital Cost	$12.80	$11.00–$14.63	100.0%	– –
Operating Receipts	1.85	1.58– 2.18	14.1	12.6%–17.3%
Operating Expenses	.59	.46– .83	4.5	3.4 – 5.6
Operating Balance	1.26	1.08– 1.48	9.5	8.3 –12.0

SOURCE: ULI—the Urban Land Institute, The Dollars and Cents of Shopping Centers, 1972 (Washington, D.C.: Urban Land Institute, 1967). Used with permission.

EXHIBIT 17A-5 FINANCING NEW CORPORATE STOCK ISSUES (IN BILLIONS OF DOLLARS)

	1964	1965	1966	1967	1968	1969	1970	1971 (est.)	1972 (proj.)
USES									
Gross new issues									
Manufacturing and mining	.7	1.3	1.9	2.5	2.8	3.8	3.5	3.9	2.9
Transportation	.1	.1	.8	.3	.2	.3	.2	.7	.4
Electric, gas and water	.6	.6	.6	.7	.9	1.4	2.9	4.1	4.5
Communication	1.8	.6	.6	.5	.2	.3	.1	1.6	1.9
Finance and real estate	.4	.4	.2	.2	.6	1.7	1.5	2.0	1.8
Commercial and other	.1	.2	.2	.5	1.3	1.9	.9	1.7	1.2
Total	3.7	3.2	4.2	4.7	6.1	9.3	9.2	14.0	12.7
Less: Retirements									
Exchanges for debt	.2	.2	.7	.2	2.4	2.1	.2	.2	.2
Other*	2.1	3.0	2.3	2.2	4.6	2.9	2.2	1.0	1.5
Total	2.3	3.2	3.0	2.4	7.0	5.0	2.4	1.2	1.7
Net new issues	1.4	–	1.2	2.3	–.9	4.3	6.8	12.8	11.0
Funds raised by:									
Financial intermediaries									
Financial corporations	–	–	–	–	.1	.9	.9	1.7	1.5
Commercial banks	–	–.1	–	–	–.1	–	–	–	–
Total	–	–.1	–	–	–	.9	.9	1.7	1.5
Nonfinancial corporations	1.4	–	1.2	2.3	–.9	3.4	5.9	11.1	9.5
SOURCES									
Savings institutions—contractual-type									
Life insurance companies	.4	.7	.3	1.0	1.4	1.7	2.0	3.7	3.3
Private noninsured pension funds	2.2	3.1	3.5	4.6	4.8	5.4	4.7	8.9	6.7
State and local government retirement funds	.3	.4	.5	.7	1.3	1.7	2.1	3.0	2.6
Fire and casualty insurance companies	.3	–.1	.2	.9	.6	.7	1.1	2.0	1.6
Total	3.2	4.1	4.5	7.2	8.0	9.5	9.9	17.6	14.2
Mutual savings banks	.1	.2	–	.2	.3	.2	.3	.3	.3
Mutual funds	.7	1.2	1.0	1.5	1.5	2.5	1.1	.7	1.5
Total savings institutions	4.0	5.5	5.5	8.9	9.8	12.2	11.3	18.6	16.0
Foreign investors	–.3	–.4	–.3	.8	2.3	1.5	.6	.4	2.5
Residual: Individuals and others	–2.2	–5.1	–4.0	–7.4	–13.0	–9.4	–5.2	–6.2	–7.5
Total	1.4	–	1.2	2.3	–.9	4.3	6.8	12.8	11.0
MEMORANDUM									
Net new issues	1.4	–	1.2	2.3	–.9	4.3	6.8	12.8	11.0
Conversions (Table 10)	.2	.4	.5	1.1	1.0	1.2	.8	1.9	2.0
Net of conversions	1.2	–.4	.7	1.2	–1.9	3.1	6.0	10.9	9.0

*Called for payment, repurchases and retirements in connection with liquidations, reorganizations and mergers.

SOURCE: Securities and Exchange Commission. These statistics are compiled and published annually in *Bankers Trust Investment Outlook* (New York: Bankers Trust Company, P.O. Box 318, Church Street Station, 10015). The above is from Table 11 of the 1972 edition of the *Outlook*. Used with permission.

EXHIBIT 17A-6 FINANCING NEW CORPORATE BOND ISSUES (IN BILLIONS OF DOLLARS)

	1964	1965	1966	1967	1968	1969	1970	1971 (est.)	1972 (proj.)
USES									
Gross new issues									
Manufacturing and mining	3.1	4.7	6.4	9.7	7.0	6.4	9.1	9.4	7.5
Transportation	.9	1.0	1.7	2.0	1.7	1.8	2.2	1.9	2.0
Electric, gas and water	2.1	2.1	3.3	4.2	4.3	5.2	7.8	7.4	7.5
Communication	.6	.7	1.7	1.8	1.7	1.9	5.1	4.2	3.5
Financial and real estate	3.3	3.4	1.6	2.2	2.0	2.6	3.7	6.0	5.2
Commercial and other	.6	.9	.9	1.5	2.6	1.6	1.6	2.6	1.5
Total	10.7	12.7	15.6	21.3	19.4	19.5	29.5	31.5	27.2
Less: Retirements									
Conversions	.2	.4	.5	1.1	1.0	1.2	.8	1.9	2.0
Other	3.9	4.2	4.0	4.2	4.4	4.6	5.9	6.2	6.5
Total	4.1	4.6	4.5	5.3	5.4	5.8	6.7	8.1	8.5
Net new issues	6.6	8.1	11.1	16.0	14.0	13.8	22.8	23.4	18.7
Funds raised by:									
Financial intermediaries									
Financial corporations	2.1	1.9	.8	1.0	.8	1.6	2.6	2.8	1.7
Commercial banks*	.5	.8	.1	.3	.3	.1	–	1.5	1.5
Total	2.6	2.7	.9	1.3	1.1	1.7	2.6	4.3	3.2
Nonfinancial corporations	4.0	5.4	10.2	14.7	12.9	12.1	20.2	19.1	15.5
SOURCES									
Savings institutions—contractual-type									
Life insurance companies	1.9	2.4	2.2	3.7	3.7	1.6	1.2	4.2	3.6
Private noninsured pension funds	1.9	1.7	2.1	1.1	.6	.6	2.0	–1.2	.5
State and local government retirement funds	1.9	2.1	2.5	3.4	2.5	3.0	3.9	4.6	5.8
Fire and casualty insurance companies	.3	.8	.7	.6	1.2	.8	1.5	1.1	.7
Total	6.0	7.0	7.4	8.8	8.0	6.0	8.6	8.7	10.6
Mutual savings banks	–.2	–.1	.2	1.9	1.1	–	1.1	3.3	1.8
Mutual funds	.4	.4	.4	–	.4	.2	.7	.1	.2
Total savings institutions	6.2	7.4	8.1	10.7	9.5	6.2	10.5	12.1	12.6
Commercial banks	.1	–.1	.1	–	–	–	.2	1.0	–
State and local general funds	.4	.3	.7	1.1	.9	.5	.5	.5	–
Foreign investors	.2	–.2	.2	–.3	–.3	–.2	–.2	–.3	–
Residual: Individuals and others	–.3	.7	2.0	4.5	3.8	7.2	11.9	10.1	6.1
Total	6.6	8.1	11.1	16.0	14.0	13.8	22.8	23.4	18.7
MEMORANDUM									
Convertible bonds									
Gross new issues offered for cash	.4	1.3	1.9	4.5	3.3	4.0	2.7	3.6	3.8
Conversions (Table 11)	.2	.4	.5	1.1	1.0	1.2	.8	1.9	2.0
Net increase in outstandings†	.2	.9	1.4	3.4	2.3	2.8	1.9	1.7	1.8

* Includes affiliates.

† Excludes convertible bonds issued in exchange for stocks.

SOURCE: Securities and Exchange Commission. These statistics are compiled and published annually in *Bankers Trust Investment Outlook* (New York: Bankers Trust Company, P.O. Box 318, Church Street Station, 10015). The above is from Table 10 of the 1972 edition of the *Outlook.* Used with permission.

EXHIBIT 17A-7 FINANCING MORTGAGES (IN BILLIONS OF DOLLARS)

	1964	1965	1966	1967	1968	1969	1970	1971 (est.)	1972 (proj.)
USES									
Residential mortgages									
Home	15.4	15.4	10.4	12.5	15.3	15.6	13.4	27.5	26.5
Multifamily	4.6	3.6	3.1	3.6	3.4	4.9	5.8	9.8	9.5
Total	20.0	19.0	13.5	16.1	18.7	20.5	19.2	37.3	36.0
Commercial mortgages	3.8	4.5	5.6	4.7	6.6	5.4	5.5	8.7	9.0
Farm mortgages	2.1	2.3	2.1	2.2	2.0	2.0	1.7	2.3	2.1
Total	25.8	25.7	21.3	22.9	27.4	27.8	26.4	48.3	47.1
SOURCES									
Savings institutions—contractual-type									
Life insurance companies	4.6	4.9	4.6	2.9	2.5	2.1	2.3	1.2	1.9
Private noninsured pension funds	.6	.6	.5	.2	–	.2	.1	–.6	–
State and local government retirement funds	.5	.7	.8	.5	.4	.3	.9	.4	.5
Total	5.7	6.2	5.9	3.6	2.8	2.5	3.3	1.0	2.4
Saving institutions—deposit-type									
Savings and loan associations	10.4	9.0	3.8	7.5	9.4	9.6	10.4	25.3	21.8
Mutual savings banks	4.3	4.1	2.7	3.1	2.8	2.5	2.0	4.5	4.0
Credit unions	.1	.1	.1	.1	.2	.2	.2	.5	.4
Total	14.8	13.2	6.6	10.7	12.4	12.3	12.7	30.3	26.2
Total savings institutions	20.4	19.3	12.5	14.3	15.2	14.8	16.0	31.3	28.6
Commercial banks	4.5	5.6	4.6	4.6	6.7	5.2	2.5	9.0	7.5
Financial corporations	.4	.5	–.6	.4	.7	1.4	1.8	1.5	1.5
Government									
U.S. Government	–.1	–.1	.8	.9	1.1	.7	.3	–.1	.2
Non-Budget agencies	.3	1.1	2.6	1.8	2.2	4.4	5.4	3.7	6.1
State and local general funds	.2	.2	.1	.1	.3	.1	.5	2.5	2.5
Total	.4	1.2	3.5	2.8	3.6	5.2	6.2	6.1	8.8
Residual: Individuals and others	.1	–.9	1.4	.9	1.2	1.2	–.1	.4	.7
Total	25.8	25.7	21.3	22.9	27.4	27.8	26.4	48.3	47.1
MEMORANDA									
Private housing starts									
Number (in thousands of units)	1,529	1,473	1,165	1,292	1,508	1,467	1,434	2,048	2,050
Construction outlays	20.0	20.1	16.6	18.7	22.6	22.8	22.1	32.9	35.1
Private residential construction put in place									
New housing units	21.8	21.7	19.4	19.0	24.0	25.9	24.2	34.3	34.0
Other	6.2	6.2	6.4	6.6	6.5	7.3	7.6	8.0	8.5
Total	28.0	27.9	25.7	25.6	30.6	33.2	31.7	42.3	42.5

SOURCES: Federal Reserve, Federal Home Loan Bank Board, and Bureau of the Census, U.S. Department of Commerce. These statistics are compiled and published annually in *Bankers Trust Investment Outlook* (New York: Bankers Trust Company, P.O. Box 318, Church Street Station, 10015). The above is from Table 7 of the 1972 edition of the *Outlook.* Used with permission.

EXHIBIT 17A-8 FINANCING HOME MORTGAGES (IN BILLIONS OF DOLLARS)

	1964	1965	1966	1967	1968	1969	1970	1971 (est.)	1972 (proj.)
USES*									
Government-backed mortgages									
FHA-insured	3.3	3.7	2.8	2.6	3.2	3.9	5.4	7.0	6.5
VA-guaranteed	–	.2	.2	1.2	1.3	1.8	1.7	4.2	4.0
Total	3.3	3.9	3.0	3.8	4.5	5.7	7.1	11.2	10.5
Conventional mortgages	12.0	11.5	7.5	8.6	10.8	10.1	6.1	16.3	16.0
Total	15.4	15.4	10.4	12.5	15.3	15.6	13.4	27.5	26.5
SOURCES†									
Savings institutions—contractual-type									
Life insurance companies	1.2	1.1	.6	–.5	–.7	–1.1	–1.4	–1.8	–1.7
Private noninsured pension funds	.2	.2	.2	.1	–	–	.1	–.2	–
Total	1.4	1.3	.8	–.4	–.7	–1.1	–1.3	–2.0	–1.7
Savings institutions—deposit-type									
Savings and loan associations	8.2	7.1	2.9	6.0	7.2	7.8	7.5	18.5	16.0
Mutual savings banks	2.7	2.7	1.6	1.8	1.4	1.4	1.2	3.5	2.8
Credit unions	.1	.1	.1	.1	.2	.2	.2	.5	.4
Total	11.0	9.8	4.6	7.9	8.9	9.5	8.9	22.5	19.2
Total savings institutions	12.4	11.1	5.4	7.5	8.1	8.4	7.6	20.5	17.5
Commercial banks	2.3	3.1	2.4	2.4	3.5	3.0	.9	4.8	3.8
Financial corporations	.4	.5	–.6	.4	.6	.3	.1	–.5	.2
Government									
U.S. Government	–.1	–.1	.6	.7	.8	.1	–.1	–.2	–
Non-Budget agencies	–.1	.5	1.9	1.1	1.6	3.8	4.6	2.2	4.5
State and local general funds	–	–	–	–	.1	–	.1	.3	.3
Total	–.2	.4	2.5	1.9	2.6	3.9	4.6	2.3	4.8
Residual: Individuals and others	.5	.3	.7	.3	.5	–	.2	.4	.2
Total	15.4	15.4	10.4	12.5	15.3	15.6	13.4	27.5	26.5
MEMORANDA									
Private 1-family housing starts									
Number (in thousands of units)	970	964	778	844	900	811	813	1,148	1,170
Average cost per unit (in thousands of dollars)	15.4	16.2	16.8	17.3	18.5	19.2	18.3	19.6	20.8
Construction outlays	15.0	15.6	13.0	14.6	16.7	15.6	14.9	22.5	24.3
Manufacturers' shipments of mobile homes (in thousands of units)	191	216	217	240	318	413	401	490	550

*Comprises 1- to 4-family mortgages.

† Ownership of GNMA-guaranteed pass-through mortgage pools has been allocated among the private institutional investors.

SOURCES: Federal Reserve, Federal Home Loan Bank Board, Bureau of the Census, U.S. Department of Commerce, Mobile Homes Manufacturers Association, and Government National Mortgage Association. These statistics are compiled and published annually in ***Bankers Trust Investment Outlook*** (New York: Bankers Trust Company, P.O. Box 318, Church Street Station, 10015). The above is from Table 8 of the 1972 edition of the *Outlook.*

EXHIBIT 17A-9 BOND YIELDS AND INTEREST RATES: 1929 TO 1964*

Year	U.S. Government Security Yields: 3-month Treasury Bills[1]	U.S. Government Security Yields: 3–5 Year Issues[2]	U.S. Government Security Yields: Taxable Bonds[3]	High-Grade Municipal Bonds (Standard & Poor's)	Corporate Bonds (Moody's): Aaa	Corporate Bonds (Moody's): Baa	Prime Commercial Paper, 4–6 Months	FHA New Home Mortgage Yields[4]
1929				4.27	4.73	5.90	5.85	([5])
1930				4.07	4.55	5.90	3.59	([5])
1931	1.402			4.01	4.58	7.62	2.64	([5])
1932	.879			4.65	5.01	9.30	2.73	([5])
1933	.515	2.66		4.71	4.49	7.76	1.73	([5])
1934	.256	2.12		4.03	4.00	6.32	1.02	([5])
1935	.137	1.29		3.40	3.60	5.75	.75	([5])
1936	.143	1.11		3.07	3.24	4.77	.75	([5])
1937	.447	1.40		3.10	3.26	5.03	.94	([5])
1938	.053	.83		2.91	3.19	5.80	.81	([5])
1939	.023	.59		2.76	3.01	4.96	.59	([5])
1940	.014	.50		2.50	2.84	4.75	.56	([5])
1941	.103	.76		2.10	2.77	4.33	.53	([5])
1942	.326	1.13	2.46	2.36	2.83	4.28	.66	([5])
1943	.373	1.34	2.47	2.06	2.73	3.91	.69	([5])
1944	.375	1.33	2.48	1.86	2.72	3.61	.73	([5])
1945	.375	1.18	2.37	1.67	2.62	3.29	.75	([5])
1946	.375	1.16	2.19	1.64	2.53	3.05	.81	([5])
1947	.594	1.32	2.25	2.01	2.61	3.24	1.03	([5])
1948	1.040	1.62	2.44	2.40	2.82	3.47	1.44	([5])
1949	1.102	1.43	2.31	2.21	2.66	3.42	1.49	4.34
1950	1.218	1.50	2.32	1.98	2.62	3.24	1.45	4.15
1951	1.552	1.93	2.57	2.00	2.86	3.41	2.16	4.23
1952	1.766	2.13	2.68	2.19	2.96	3.52	2.33	4.30
1953	1.931	2.56	2.94	2.72	3.20	3.74	2.52	4.65
1954	.953	1.82	2.55	2.37	2.90	3.51	1.58	4.60
1955	1.753	2.50	2.84	2.53	3.06	3.53	2.18	4.65
1956	2.658	3.12	3.08	2.93	3.36	3.88	3.31	4.80
1957	3.267	3.62	3.47	3.60	3.89	4.71	3.81	5.44
1958	1.839	2.90	3.43	3.56	3.79	4.73	2.46	5.49
1959	3.405	4.33	4.08	3.95	4.38	5.05	3.97	5.77
1960	2.928	3.99	4.02	3.73	4.41	5.19	3.85	6.16
1961	2.378	3.60	3.90	3.46	4.35	5.08	2.97	5.78
1962	2.778	3.57	3.95	3.18	4.33	5.02	3.26	5.60
1963	3.157	3.72	4.00	3.23	4.26	4.86	3.55	5.46
1964	3.549	4.06	4.15	3.22	4.40	4.83	3.97	5.45

*Percent per annum.

[1] Rate on new issues within period.

[2] Selected note and bond issues. Prior to 1941 these were tax-exempt issues.

[3] Series includes: April 1953 to date, bonds due or callable 10 years and after; April 1952–March 1953, bonds due or callable after 12 years; October 1941–March 1952, bonds due or callable after 15 years.

[4] Based on the maximum permissible interest rate (5¼% since May 1961), and 25-year mortgages paid in 12 years, until 1962. From 1962, 30-year mortgage paid in 15 years.

[5] Not available.

Data Sources: Treasury Department, Board of Governors of the Federal Reserve System, Federal Housing Administration, Standard & Poor's Corporation, and Moody's Investors Service.

SOURCE: Edwin B. Cox, ed., *Basic Tables in Business and Economics* (New York: McGraw-Hill Book Company, 1967), p. 347, Table 12–14. Used with permission.

EXHIBIT 17A-10 COMMON STOCK PRICE INDEXES, YIELD AND EARNINGS

	PRICE INDEX[1]						Dividend Yield[2] (percent)	Price Earnings Ratios[3]
		Industrials						
Period	Total	Total	Capital Goods	Consumers' Goods	Public Utilities	Railroads		
				1941–43 = 10				
1929	26.02	21.35	21.48	22.49	59.33	46.15	3.47	13.32
1930	21.03	16.42	16.24	15.67	53.24	39.62	4.51	15.81
1931	13.66	10.51	8.81	11.41	37.18	23.72	6.15	13.31
1932	6.93	5.37	3.99	6.19	20.65	8.75	7.43	16.80
1933	8.96	7.61	6.33	8.27	19.72	12.75	4.21	22.95
1934	9.84	9.00	7.62	9.85	15.79	14.05	3.72	19.39
1935	10.60	10.13	8.91	11.18	15.15	11.78	3.82	14.18
1936	15.47	14.69	13.96	14.90	22.47	17.71	3.44	15.44
1937	15.41	14.97	15.34	13.81	19.07	16.86	4.86	12.38
1938	11.49	11.39	11.26	10.77	14.17	9.15	5.18	18.38
1939	12.06	11.77	11.91	11.88	16.34	9.82	4.05	13.80
1940	11.02	10.69	11.07	11.34	15.05	9.41	5.59	10.24
1941	9.82	9.72	10.21	9.80	10.93	9.39	6.82	8.26
1942	8.67	8.78	8.93	8.56	7.74	8.81	7.24	8.80
1943	11.50	11.49	10.87	11.65	11.34	11.81	4.93	12.84
1944	12.47	12.34	11.23	13.43	12.81	13.47	4.86	13.66
1945	15.16	14.72	13.66	16.46	16.84	18.21	4.17	16.33
1946	17.08	16.48	15.86	19.22	20.76	19.09	3.85	17.69
1947	15.17	14.85	14.27	16.38	18.01	14.02	4.93	9.36
1948	15.53	15.34	14.67	15.75	16.77	15.27	5.54	6.90
1949	15.23	15.00	14.14	15.76	17.87	12.83	6.59	6.64
1950	18.40	18.33	18.07	18.97	19.96	15.53	6.57	6.63
1951	22.34	22.68	22.54	20.99	20.59	19.91	6.13	9.27
1952	24.50	24.78	23.04	21.40	22.86	22.49	5.80	10.47
1953	24.73	24.84	23.46	21.91	24.03	22.60	5.80	9.69
1954	29.69	30.25	29.93	24.85	27.57	23.96	4.95	11.25
1955	40.49	42.40	42.55	32.28	31.37	32.94	4.08	11.50
1956	46.62	49.80	48.79	34.55	32.25	33.65	4.09	14.05
1957	44.38	47.63	47.01	32.48	32.19	28.11	4.35	12.89
1958	46.24	49.36	47.93	36.33	37.22	27.05	3.97	16.64
1959	57.38	61.45	63.93	47.35	44.15	35.09	3.23	17.05
1960	55.85	59.43	59.75	47.21	46.86	30.31	3.47	17.09
1961	66.27	69.99	67.33	57.01	60.20	32.83	2.97	21.06
1962	62.38	65.54	58.15	54.96	59.16	30.56	3.37	16.68
1963	69.87	73.39	63.30	62.28	64.99	37.58	3.17	17.62
1964	81.37	86.19	76.32	73.83	69.91	45.46	3.01	....

[1] Includes 500 common stock, 425 are industrials; 50 are public utilities; and 25 are railroads.

[2] Aggregate cash dividends (based on latest known annual rate) divided by the aggregate monthly market value of the stocks in the group. Annual yields are averages of monthly data. Weekly data are Wednesday figures.

[3] Ratio of price index for last day in quarter to quarterly earnings (seasonally adjusted annual rate). Annual ratios are averages of quarterly data.

Data Source: Standard and Poor's Corporation.

SOURCE: Edwin B. Cox, ed., *Basic Tables in Business and Economics* (New York: McGraw-Hill Book Company, 1967), p. 347, Table 12–13. Used with permission.

EXHIBIT 17A-11 RATES OF PROFIT AFTER TAXES ON STOCKHOLDERS' EQUITY IN MANUFACTURING CORPORATIONS: 1947 TO 1964[1]

Industry Group	1947	1950	1955	1958	1959	1960	1961	1962	1963	1964
Total	15.6	15.4	12.6	8.6	10.4	9.2	8.8	9.8	10.2	11.6
Durable goods	14.5	16.8	13.8	8.0	10.4	8.6	8.1	9.6	10.1	11.8
Transportation equipment	11.0	21.5	20.2	8.8	12.9	11.7	10.6	15.0	15.2	15.8
Electrical machinery, equipment, and supplies	19.0	20.8	12.3	10.2	12.4	9.5	8.9	10.0	10.0	11 2
Other machinery	15.8	14.0	10.3	6.8	9.7	7.6	7.8	9.1	9.6	12.5
Other fabricated metal products	17.7	15.9	10.0	7.2	8.0	5.6	5.9	7.9	8.3	10.1
Primary metal industries	12.2	14.5	14.1	6.8	8.0	7.2	6.4	6.2	7.2	9.2
Stone, clay, and glass products	14.0	17.6	15.6	10.1	12.7	9.9	8.8	8.8	8.6	9.6
Furniture and fixtures	18.1	15.1	9.2	6.2	8.8	6.5	4.9	7.9	8.2	10.1
Lumber and wood products, exc. furniture	22.9	17.4	11.1	5.7	9.3	3.6	4.0	5.6	8.2	10.0
Instruments and related products	14.4	16.7	12.5	10.6	13.0	11.6	10.5	12.0	12.0	14.3
Misc. manufacturing, and ordnance	14.0	12.2	8.6	8.0	9.2	9.2	9.8	9.3	8.8	9.5
Nondurable goods	16.6	14.0	11.4	9.2	10.4	9.8	9.6	9.9	10.4	11.5
Food and kindred products	17.6	12.3	8.9	8.7	9.3	8.7	8.9	8.8	9.0	10.0
Tobacco manufactures	10.1	11.5	11.4	13.5	13.4	13.4	13.6	13.1	13.4	13.4
Textile mill products	19.5	12.6	5.7	3.5	7.6	5.8	5.0	6.2	6.0	8.5
Apparel and other finished products	18.9	10.1	6.2	4.9	8.6	7.7	7.0	9.3	7.7	11.7
Paper and allied products	22.1	16.1	11.5	8.0	9.5	8.5	7.8	8.1	8.1	9.3
Printing and publishing, exc. newspapers	17.2	11.5	10.2	9.0	11.4	10.6	8.5	10.2	9.1	12.6
Chemicals and allied products	16.0	17.8	14.7	11.4	13.6	12.2	11.8	12.4	12.9	14.4
Petroleum refining and related industries	14.8	13.8	13.2	9.9	9.8	10.1	10.3	10.0	11.2	11.4
Rubber and misc. plastics products	12.4	16.7	13.2	9.1	11.0	9.1	9.3	9.6	9.2	10.6
Leather and leather products	14.1	10.9	8.5	5.6	8.4	6.3	4.4	6.9	6.9	10.5

[1] Percent. Includes Alaska and Hawaii. Data are averages of quarterly figures at annual rates. Based on sample; see source for discussion of methodology. Excludes newspapers.

SOURCE: Federal Trade Commission and Securities and Exchange Commission; *Quarterly Financial Report for Manufacturing Corporations.*

EXHIBIT 17A-12 TOTAL ACQUISITION OF FUNDS 1970–1971 AND DEMAND FOR FUNDS, 1972 (NET OF REPAYMENTS)

	Actual		Projected	Change From Prior Year		
Long-Term Funds	**1970**	**1971**	**1972**	**1969–1970**	**1970–1971**	**1971–1972**
	(billions of dollars)					
Corporate and Foreign Bonds	$ 21.1	$ 20.3	$ 16	$ 7.8	$–0.8	$–4.3
Corporate Stock	6.8	13.4	14	2.0	6.6	0.6
State and Local Government Securities	11.8	20.2	17	3.7	8.4	–3.2
Mortgages	25.8	47.0	53	–2.1	21.2	6.0
Total Long-Term Funds	$ 65.5	$100.9	$100	$11.4	$35.4	$–0.9
Short and Intermediate Term Funds						
Bank Loans	$ 2.7	$ 13.0	$ 15	$–13.0	$10.3	$ 2.0
Open Market Paper and Other	12.2	6.5	10	– 2.9	–5.7	3.5
Consumer Credit	4.3	10.4	12	– 5.0	6.1	1.6
U.S. Government (public debt securities)	12.9	26.0	28	14.2	13.1	2.0
Federal Agency Debt	8.8	3.2	10	0.7	–5.6	6.8
Total Short and Intermediate Term Funds	$ 40.9	$ 59.1	$ 75	$– 6.0	$18.2	$15.9
Total Demand For Funds	$106.4	$160.0	$175	$ 5.4	$53.6	$15.0

SOURCE: Raymond Jallow, "Demand for Funds in U.S. Financial Markets—A Record Level in 1972," Research and Planning Division (Los Angeles: United California Bank, June 1972), p. 6. Used by permission of the author.

CHAPTER 17 REFERENCES AND ADDITIONAL READINGS

Barlow, Robin et al., *Economic Behavior of the Affluent.* Washington, D.C.: The Brookings Institution, November 1966.

Cagan, Phillip. *Changes in the Cyclical Behavior of Interest Rates.* New York: National Bureau of Economic Research, Occasional Paper 100, 1966.

Conard, Joseph W. *The Behavior of Interest Rates: A Progress Report.* New York: National Bureau of Economic Research, General Series 81, 1966.

Determinants of Investment Behavior. New York: National Bureau of Economic Research, Universities National Bureau Conference, Series 18, 1967.

Freund, William C. *Investment Fundamentals.* New York: The American Bankers Association, 1966.

Hart, William L. *Mathematics of Investment.* 4th ed. Boston: D.C. Heath & Company, 1958.

Herzog, John P., and Earley, James S. *Home Mortgage Delinquency and Foreclosure.* New York: National Bureau of Economic Research, General Series 91, 1970.

Holland, Daniel M. *Dividends Under the Income Tax.* New York: National Bureau of Economic Research, Fiscal Studies 7, 1962.

Landsberg, Hans H. et al., *Resources in America's Future: Patterns of Requirements and Availabilities, 1960–2000.* Baltimore, Md.: The Johns Hopkins Press, 1963.

Salomon Brothers & Hutzler, *An Analytical Record of Yields and Yield Spreads.* New York: Salomon Brothers & Hutzler, 1969.

CHAPTER 17 QUESTIONS, PROBLEMS, AND CASES

17- 1. The Internal Revenue Service has published guidelines applicable to "new" depreciable assets. What rules govern the assignment of useful life to second and subsequent owners?

17- 2. Define or explain the use of the following terms and phrases:
(a) Risk aversion index
(b) Security agreement
(c) Annuity
(d) Present value
(e) "Equity buildup"
(f) Appreciation
(g) Tax shield
(h) Principal
(i) Amortization
(j) "Balloon payment"
(k) IRS depreciation guidelines

17- 3. There are three general classes of investments—proprietary, equity, and possessory. For each class, describe the status of the investment in terms of its distinguishing features, and identify and discuss at least five examples under each classification.

17- 4. Distinguish between a real estate investment held under *joint tenancy* or *tenancy in common.*

17- 5. What is a real estate stock cooperative? Compare the possessory right of a cooperative with that of a condiminium.

17- 6. Distinguish between *investment* and *speculation.* Give examples of each.

17- 7. "The general purpose of investments is to obtain an overall return on investment." Identify and explain at least five more specific reasons.

17- 8. What are some relevant factors contributing to the psychology of investments?

17- 9. Explain the concept of *equity buildup* by a diagram showing equity increase from equal payments. Under what circumstance can equity exceed equity buildup? Define *equity.*

17-10. "Appreciation in the value of common stock is of equal or greater importance to investors than is dividends." Why?

17-11. "An investment cannot be assessed fully until the point of disinvestment—when the investment is liquidated." Discuss.

17-12. Distinguish between the characteristics of *pure* and *applied* research.

17-13. Identify the parts or steps of the investment cycle:

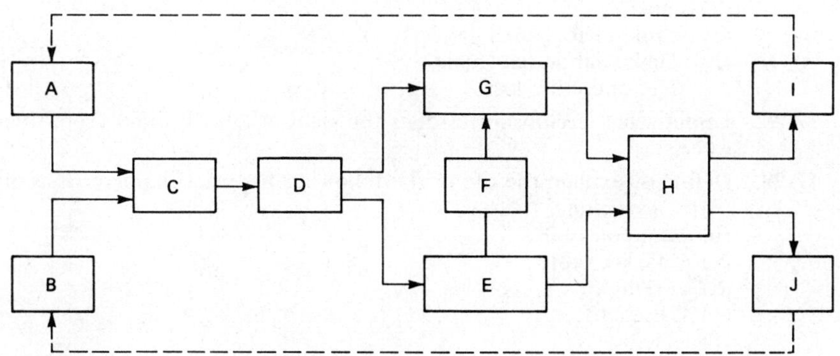

17-14. What are the six common ingredients of an investment decision?

17-15. Illustrate how a *tax shelter* works. Cite examples.

17-16. Distinguish between *equity buildup* and *appreciation.*

17-17. "The extent to which borrowed funds can be used in the purchase of stock is regulated by laws." Is such regulation necessary, and what are the supporting arguments for your viewpoint?

17-18. What do the factors in Exhibit 17-7 represent? How are they used and for what applications?

17-19. What does the *return of capital* represent? How is the percentage rate computed?

17-20. Cite some reasons for making investments. Do these reasons make different types of investments more desirable? Discuss.

17-21. Distinguish between the *nominal annual interest rate* and the *effective annual interest rate.* Which is higher and why?

17-22. "In an investment decision the cost (or price) of the investment is a derived value." Discuss.

17-23. How does the *yield* of a bond differ from the *coupon rate?*

17-24. What are the factors that account for a difference between the earnings flow and cash flow from a financed real estate investment? Which flow is probably higher in the earlier years of the investment and which is probably higher in the later years? What accounts for this condition? What generalization can you make concerning the ideal length of time for holding a financed real estate investment?

17-25. "The 1969 Tax Reform Act effectively reduced the influence of accelerated depreciation in real estate investments with the exception of residential rental property." What are the specific restrictions for each of the following assets under the 1969 Tax Reform Act:
(a) The depreciation restriction on newly constructed real estate acquired after July 24, 1969.
(b) The depreciation restriction on used real estate acquired after July 24, 1969.
(c) The recapture treatment for non-residential real estate which is sold at a gain after December 31, 1969.
(d) The recapture treatment for residential rental property depreciated after December 31, 1969.
(e) The depreciation restriction on used residential rental housing.

17-26. "The depreciation tax shield effect can be extended by switching from accelerated depreciation to straight-line at the optimum time." What is the optimum time? There is always an optimum time for switch-over to straight-line from a declining balance depreciation, but never such a time for switching from sum-of-the-years'-digits depreciation. Explain this situation.

17-27. Discuss the nature of the following tax provisions and their role in investment decisions:
(a) Long-term capital gain
(b) Depreciation tax shield
(c) Net operating loss

17-28. Under what circumstances does the yield of a bond differ from the coupon rate?

17-29. Define or explain the use of the following financial characteristics of bonds:
(a) Face value
(b) Coupon rate
(c) Market value
(d) Premium
(e) Discount
(f) Yield

17-30. ***SINKING FUND*** By referring to Table B-3 (future value of a $1 annuity), determine:

(a) The amount required to be set aside each year if:

(1) The fund balance should total $20,000 in eight years, with an applicable interest of 6% per annum.

(2) The fund balance should total $4,000,000 in twenty years, with an applicable interest of 8% per annum.

(b) The interest that must be earned if the amount set aside is $3,975 per year for ten years, and the fund balance required at the end of ten years is $50,000.

17-31. ***COST OF INVESTMENT***

(a) What selling price should an *owner* place on an investment if it returns $42,000 a year in net earnings and the owner computes his investments on a 6% basis.

(b) From part (a), would a *buyer* be willing to accept the offer if he desires an 8% return on his investment? What price should he be willing to accept? What arguments can he use to persuade the seller to adjust his price?

(c) Suppose the owner sets a selling price of $500,000 and requires a down payment of 20% with the balance financed by a thirty-year installment note at 7½% interest. Using Exhibit 17-7, compute the percentage return on the buyer's investment. If the buyer desires an 8% return on his investment, should he accept the seller's terms?

17-32. ***AMORTIZATION OF A LOAN***

(a) Suppose Robert Plascoe was granted a loan of $20,000 with principle and interest to be repaid in equal monthly installments of $253.50 for ten years. Compute the annual interest rate of Mr. Plascoe's loan (use Exhibit 17-7 in your calculations).

(b) If a 9½%, thirty-year note is repaid in equal monthly installments of $808, what is the amount of the loan?

17-33. ***COMPOUND INTEREST—LOAN REPAYMENT*** Suppose Mr. Collins borrows $40,000 at an interest rate of 7½% with the stipulation that he repay the loan (interest and principle) in five equal annual installments of $6,000, and the balance at the end of six years. What balance will be payable at the end of six years? (Use the tables in Appendix B.)

17-34. ***COMPUTING INTEREST*** Determine the following:

(a) Simple interest on $38,000 loaned at an annual interest rate of 9%.

(b) Simple interest per year on $38,000 loaned at a quarterly interest rate of 9%.

(c) The value of an $8,000 investment at the end of five years if interest is earned at 8% annually. (Use the tables in Appendix B.)

(d) Same as (c) only at 8% compounded daily. (Again use logarithms to obtain a solution.)

(e) The effective annual interest rate when the nominal rate is:

(1) 8% compounded monthly

(2) 7% compounded semiannually

(Use logarithms to obtain a solution.)

17-35. ***BOND YIELD*** Compute the following:

(a) The approximate yield to maturity of a ten-year, 6%, $1,000 bond purchased for 103.

(b) The coupon interest rate of a fifteen-year, $1,000 bond purchased for 94 and yielding 6.19%.

(c) The number of years to maturity of a 7%, $1,000 bond purchased for 109 and yielding 6.22%.

17-36. ***REAL ESTATE INVESTMENT–COMPUTATION OF YIELD*** Coleman and Associates bought a twelve-story office building and have provided the following information:

(a) Purchase price–$3,600,000.
(b) 5% of purchase price assigned to land value.
(c) Depreciation method is sum-of-years'-digits.
(d) Useful life is forty-five years.
(e) Down payment is 20% of purchase price.
(f) 80% of purchase price is financed with a 7% note secured by a first trust deed.
(g) Net operating income per annum is expected to be $300,000.
(h) Tax rate is 40%.
(i) The property is expected to increase in value by 4% a year.

After eight years, Coleman and Associates sell the office building.

Required:

(1) Prepare an amortization schedule for the first eight years based upon equal annual payments including principle and interest.
(2) Prepare an integrated statement of earnings and cash flow for the first eight years of the building's life.
(3) Prepare a computation of any capital gain or loss assuming property is sold at the end of eight years.
(4) Compute the cash flow after tax resulting from the sale at end of year 8. Assume a capital gains tax of 25%.
(5) Compute the approximate *yield* on the building investment through a trial-and-error procedure using Table B-2 in Appendix B.

17-37. ***COMPOSITE DEPRECIATION*** Mr. Lentman acquired an office building for $730,000. An itemization of the cost, useful lives, and salvage value is as follows:

	Cost	Salvage	Estimated Useful Life in Years
Building	$560,000	2,000	30
Elevators	50,000	10,000	20
Fixtures	25,000	5,000	10
Metal furniture	60,000	12,000	10
Fabric & wood furniture	35,000	1,000	8
	$730,000		

Required:

(a) Using the composite depreciation method, determine the useful life of the group.
(b) With straight-line depreciation, determine the total amount of depreciation for the first five years of the investment's life using:
    (1) Separate accounts
    (2) A common composite account
(c) If 150% declining balance depreciation is used, determine the total amount of depreciation for the first five years of the investment's life using:
    (1) Separate accounts
    (2) A common composite account
(d) If Mr. Lentman has a choice of depreciation methods, and can depreciate the assets separately or as a composite group, what combination is most advantageous:

(1) If he expects to sell his investment in five years?
(2) If he expects to keep the building indefinitely?

17-38. ***STOCK YIELD*** The Joseph Thompson Investment Company purchased 15,000 shares of Able Company in 1968 for $35 a share, and 18,000 of Baker Company in 1950 for $24 a share. The per share dividends received since 1968 are as follows:

	Dividends Per Share	
	Able Co.	**Baker Co.**
1968	$2.45	
1969	2.20	
1970	1.80	$ .90
1971	1.40	1.30
1972	1.60	1.70
1973	2.00	2.10

At the end of 1973, the Joseph Thompson Investment Company liquidates its investment in Able Co. for $38 a share and its investment in Baker Company for $40 a share.

Required: Determine the following:

(a) The approximate *yield* for:
  (1) Able Company
  (2) Baker Company
(b) What apparent factor or factors account for the difference in yield? What type of stock investment—speculative or established company stock—is likely to produce a higher yield during favorable economic conditions? To stabilize its overall yield at the highest possible level, what type of stock investments are desirable?

17-39. ***STOCK YIELD*** Using the approximate method, identify the yield of the following investment:

Investment in stock in $Y_0 = \$2,000$
Dividends received, end of

$Y_1 = \$\ 80$
$Y_2 = 110$
$Y_3 = 60$
$Y_4 = 70$

Sale of investment, end of $Y_4 = \$2,800$
Ignore taxes

Required: Compute the approximate yield.

17-40. ***EARNING AND CASH FLOW IN REAL ESTATE*** Land Consultants Inc., a real estate investment firm, has just acquired an office building for $2,400,000 (the portion attributable to land is $400,000). The building has a thirty-year serviceable life and is expected to have net operating income of $260,000 per year. Land Consultant's Inc. paid 20% of the purchase price as a down payment and incurred an indebtedness for the remainder with a thirty-year, 7½% note.

Required:

Answer the following using Exhibit 17-7:

(a) Compute the percent return on Land Consultant's investment.

(b) Assuming an income tax rate of 40%, and sum-of-the-years'-digits depreciation on the building, what is the after tax cash flow in the first year?

17-41. ***AMORTIZATION OF A LOAN***

(a) Calculate the loan balance outstanding after eight *monthly* payments (payments include principle and interest) on a 9%, twenty-five-year loan of $32,000.

(b) Calculate the loan balance for part (a) after eight years. Suggestion: use the procedure described in footnote to Exhibit 17-7.

(c) Calculate the total amount of interest that will be paid on the $32,000 loan.

CHAPTER

18

COST ACCOUNTING CONCEPTS AND RELATIONSHIPS

18.1 THE NATURE AND PURPOSE OF COST ACCOUNTING

Cost accounting is the analytic arm of accounting.[1] It has two principal objectives: (1) to provide managers with the information they need to plan and control the operations of an organization; and (2) to provide the data that is needed to "cost" the goods and services produced by a firm.

Much of the traditional literature discusses cost accounting in the manufacturing context and contributes to its image as being "production accounting." Actually the principles of cost accounting are applicable to all of the activity areas of a

[1]Eric L. Kohler, *A Dictionary for Accountants* (Englewood Cliffs, N.J.: Prentice-Hall, Inc., 1970), pp. 128–29 provides a more comprehensive definition of "cost accounting" as being:

> That branch of accounting dealing with the classification, recording, allocation, summarization and reporting of current and prospective costs. Included in the field of cost accounting are the design and operation of cost systems and procedures; the determination of costs by departments, functions, responsibilities, activities, products, territories, periods, and other units, of forecasted future cost and standard or desired cost; the comparison of costs of different periods, of actual with estimated or standard costs, and of alternative costs; the presentation and interpretation of cost data as an aid to management in controlling current and future operations.

Used with permission.

firm (e.g., marketing and administration) as well as to all types of organizations, including governmental and not-for-profit entities.

Let us consider the two principal objectives of cost accounting in further detail.

PROVIDE FINANCIAL DATA FOR MANAGEMENT PLANNING AND CONTROL

The formal financial statements of a firm do not meet the information needs of managers. First, the statements are only published annually, at which time the data is history. Managers need information on a current and continuing basis and cannot wait for monthly or annual summaries. The formal financial statements do not provide a basis for control because they deal with organizations as a whole. For control purposes differential data is needed to evaluate one element within a firm versus another, such as the performance of persons, products, departments, or divisions. This type of information is quite detailed and is generally highly confidential even within an organization.

The formal financial statements do not provide a basis for planning future operations. History is only one ingredient of forecasting, and reliance on extrapolation as the principal tool of planning is diminishing rapidly.

Of course, the scope of financial accounting is broader than the formal financial statements. It includes the sub-functions of payroll, accounts receivable, accounts payable, treasury, and many others. While these sub-functions are necessary and important to the management of all types of organizations, they do not serve the analytic purpose performed by cost accounting. In fact, the cost accounting function relates to the financial accounting functions as part of the feedback-control loops (Exhibit 18-1).

EXHIBIT 18-1 FINANCIAL AND COST ACCOUNTING IN SYSTEMS RELATIONSHIP

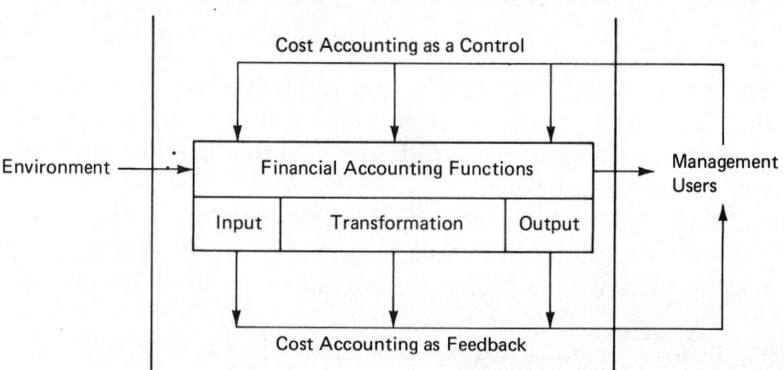

Let us look at a very simple example of how cost accounting can put meaning into accounting data. Our example deals with the way in which accounting data is classified. Financial accounting uses a *primary classification* of accounts. This means that accounting events are placed into accounts that can be thought of as being "generic" or "natural." For example, all salaries go into a salaries expense account;

all rents go into a rent expense account, and so forth. Exhibit 18-2 shows an income statement of a company on a primary account basis.

EXHIBIT 18-2 PRIMARY ACCOUNT CLASSIFICATION

Sales		$100,000
Cost of sales		50,000
Gross profit		50,000
Selling expenses	$20,000	
Administrative exp.	20,000	40,000
Net income		$ 10,000

Assume that the company has four product lines. Exhibit 18-2 gives us a view of the organization as a whole, but it tells us nothing about the performance of the four product lines. To give us product line information we need a different account classification. For example, each of the product lines produces sales, has a cost of sales, and incurs selling and administrative expenses. To give us this information we need a *functional account classification.* Each product line, as it were, becomes a business entity. Let us look at the same data in terms of a functional classification

EXHIBIT 18-3 FUNCTIONAL ACCOUNT CLASSIFICATION

	Product A	Product B	Product C	Product D	Total
Sales	$40,000	$20,000	$10,000	$30,000	$100,000
Cost of sales	(25,000)	(9,000)	(6,000)	(10,000)	(50,000)
Gross profit	15,000	11,000	4,000	20,000	50,000
Selling expenses	(10,000)	(3,000)	(1,500)	(5,500)	(20,000)
Administrative expenses	(8,000)	(4,000)	(2,000)	(6,000)	(20,000)
Net income	$ (3,000)	$ 4,000	$ 500	$ 8,500	$ 10,000
Ratio of net income to sales	(7.5%)	20%	5%	28.3%	10%

(Exhibit 18-3). These figures speak for themselves. Needless to say, the management of our company would benefit more from the information in Exhibit 18-3 than that in 18-2. We are now able to evaluate the four product lines and make decisions that will improve the overall performance of the firm.

The above example still deals with historical data, however. Part of the function of cost accounting is to put more meaning into historical data. But a more important function is to prevent serious losses from occurring. This is done by monitoring activities on a constant basis and analyzing and reporting variances from planned operations. A third function is to provide cost data for planning decisions. These functions will be discussed in further detail in this chapter and in the two that follow.

PROVIDE DATA FOR COSTING GOODS AND SERVICES

Costing a product should be distinguished at once from pricing a product. Information for *costing* purposes is generated within a firm while *pricing* decisions hinge primarily on external factors (Exhibit 18-4).

EXHIBIT 18-4 DERIVATION OF COSTING VERSUS PRICING

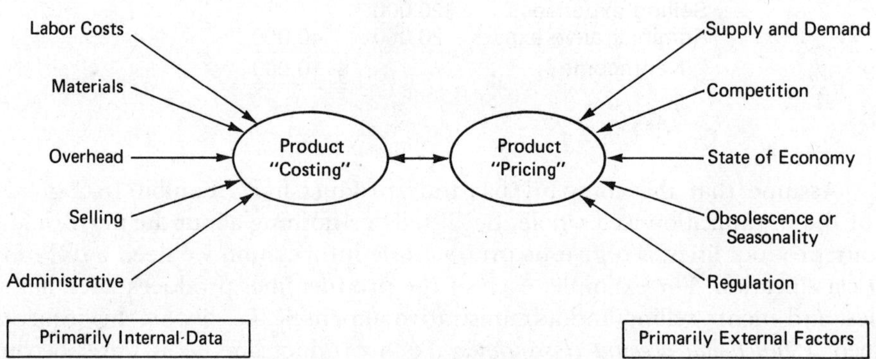

In the long run, of course, the price of a product must exceed its cost if operations are to be profitable. In the short run, however, prices sometimes fall below cost for competitive or other reasons, e.g., inventory sales or the gasoline wars with which we are familiar. In the inventory sale, fashions may have changed, so the reduction in price can be viewed as a salvage operation. In fact in these industries a certain salvage factor is built into the price, so that those persons buying early in the season subsidize those who buy later. In the gasoline war the objective of price-reduction is more sinister, i.e., to reduce the number of stations at a particular locale by straining the resources of the weakest competitor.

Product pricing in some industries is regulated by law. Telephone rates are set by the Federal Communications Commission (FCC); railroad freight and passenger rates are set by the Interstate Commerce Commission (ICC); brokerage fees on stock transactions are regulated by the Securities and Exchange Commission (SEC); and airline rates are approved by the Civil Aeronautics Board (CAB), just to mention a few of the regulatory practices in the United States.

But even in those industries where direct regulation is not present, antitrust and other federal laws play an important role in pricing. We have often thought that a very large automobile manufacturer could, through economies of scale, price its products much lower than a small automobile manufacturer. But if the smaller manufacturer is driven out of business by the big one, what is likely to happen? It is even odds that the antitrust laws will force the big manufacturer to break up into a number of individual companies in order to "keep the market competitive." Paradoxically, "the market is kept competitive" by the big manufacturer charging the same prices as are necessary to keep the little manufacturer in business.

This is to say that all of our indulgence in "costing" may have little bearing on the prices that pertain—which is not to say that costing is unimportant, but rather that the cost accountant should realize that his efforts to influence price may not always be successful.

EXHIBIT 18-5 COST CATEGORIES

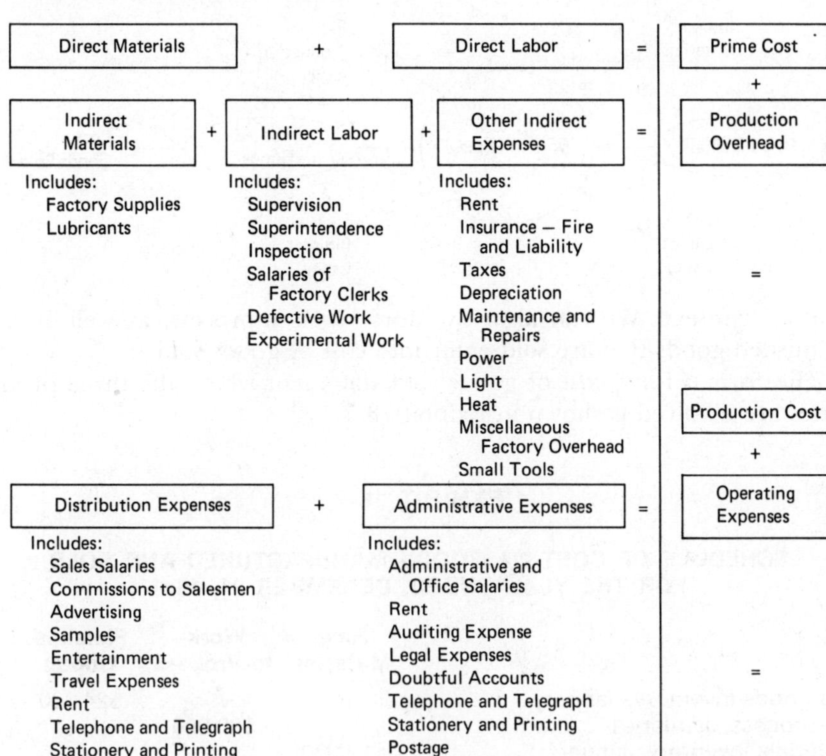

SOURCE: Adapted from Matz, Curry and Frank, *Cost Accounting,* 4th ed. (Cincinnati: South-Western Publishing Company, 1967), p. 29. Used with permission.

Various types of cost enter into the final cost of a product. By convention these costs have been classified into the categories in Exhibit 18-5.

In manufacturing accounts, there are three inventories instead of one:

1. Raw materials
2. Work-in-process
3. Finished goods

The production costs defined in Exhibit 18-5 flow through these inventories as depicted in Exhibit 18-6. As noted in the exhibit, transformation takes place at the work-in-process stage. It is here that the various resources are merged into a product. However, it is not necessary to inventory all of these resources. Labor, indirect materials, and factory overhead do not lend themselves to being inventoried.[2] Raw materials, on the other hand, represent physical things that can be controlled in

[2]Although labor "skill inventories" are being developed in certain industries, as discussed briefly in chapter 16.

EXHIBIT 18-6 FLOW OF COSTS THROUGH PRODUCTION INVENTORIES

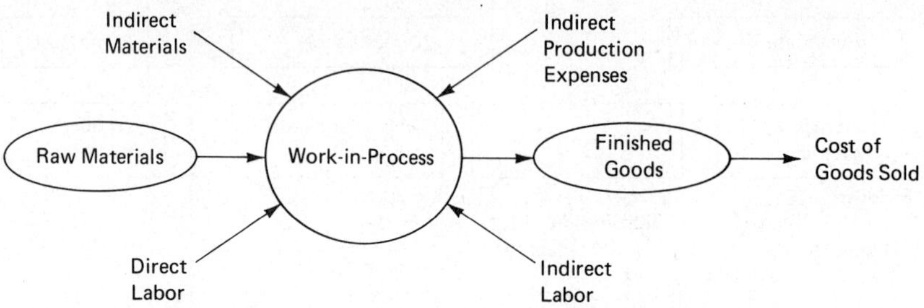

an inventory context. We can also inventory work-in-process, as well as finished goods Finished goods that are sold enter into cost of goods sold.

The format for a cost of goods sold statement where the three production inventories are involved is shown in Exhibit 18-7.

EXHIBIT 18-7

SCHEDULE OF COST OF GOODS MANUFACTURED AND SOLD FOR THE YEAR ENDED, DECEMBER 31, 19x1

	Raw Material	Work-In-Process	Finished Goods	
Finished goods inventory, January 1			$24,000	
Work-in-process, January 1		$30,000		
Raw materials inventory, January 1	$12,000			
Purchases during the year	15,000			
Raw materials available	27,000			
Raw materials inventory, December 31	15,000			
Raw materials requisitioned & used during 19x1		12,000		
Direct labor		13,800		
Production overhead		5,520		
Total work-in-process during 19x1		$61,320		
Work-in-process, December 31		14,800		
Work finished during the year			46,520	
Total finished goods			$70,920	
Finished goods inventory, December 31			35,800	
Cost of goods manufactured and sold				$35,120

This is contrasted with the inventory accounts of mercantile firms which have only one inventory, i.e., finished goods:

Inventory, January 1	50,000	
Inventory purchased during year	110,000	
Total inventory available	160,000	
Inventory, December 31	70,000	
Cost of goods sold		$90,000

Because of the detail required for a manufacturing cost of goods sold statement, it is most generally presented as a *schedule* to the income statement:

Sales	$60,000
Cost of goods manufactured and sold (Schedule A)	35,120
Gross profit	$24,880

18.2 COST ACCOUNTING TERMS AND CONCEPTS

The importance of control in the management of enterprises is reflected by the extensive vocabulary of terms and concepts in cost accounting. The more frequently used terms are defined and categorized below.

EXHIBIT 18-8 COST ACCOUNTING TERMS AND DEFINITIONS

1. **TIME-ORIENTED COSTS:** these are costs that bear a specific relationship to periods of time.
   a. *Historical cost:* The actual exchange price that was paid, i.e., cost to the present owner at the time of acquisition.
   b. *Sunk cost:* A past cost that is irrelevant to a current economic decision.
   c. *Estimated cost:* A future cost that can be reasonably ascertained at present.
   d. *Standard cost:* A predetermination of what costs should be under projected conditions. Often referred to as "engineered costs."
   e. *Period cost:* An expenditure that relates to a time rather than to an activity index.
2. **TRACEABILITY-ORIENTED COSTS:** these costs are distinguished by our ability to trace them to activity areas.
   a. *Direct cost:* A cost that is internal to a given cost center.
   b. *Indirect cost:* A cost that benefits more than one cost center.
   c. *Product cost:* A cost that can be traced to a given product center.
   d. *Prime cost:* Direct materials and direct labor attributable to a given product center.
   e. *Joint cost:* The common cost of facilities or services employed in the output of two or more simultaneous products of major commercial significance.
   f. *By-product cost:* The cost associated with marketing a secondary product. A by-product does not carry part of the basic production costs as does a joint product.
3. **CONTROL-ORIENTED COSTS:** these terms are distinguished by our ability to control costs.
   a. *Controllable cost:* A direct cost for which one person has complete responsibility.
   b. *Noncontrollable cost:* A cost for which one person does not have complete responsibility.
   c. *Opportunity cost:* The cost of an alternative, often restricted in definition to the next best alternative.
   d. *Differential or marginal cost:* The cost of adding one additional unit of effort. More broadly defined as the difference between costs at two activity levels.
   e. *Imputed cost:* The subjective and arbitrary determination of cost in the absence of factual data.
   f. *Postponable cost:* A cost that can be delayed without serious injury to the enterprise.
   g. *Out-of-pocket cost:* That portion of total cost which is represented by the physical outlay of cash.
4. **BEHAVIORALLY-ORIENTED COSTS:** these costs are recognized by the degree of responsiveness to activity indexes.
   a. *Fixed cost:* A cost which has no recognized activity index or fails to respond to one.
   b. *Variable cost:* A cost that changes in direct proportion to an activity index.
   c. *Semi-variable cost:* A cost that changes with respect to an activity index, but not in direct proportion.

These cost categories are not mutually exclusive, but they do place the terms into a meaningful classification and help to explain why we have so many cost terms.

18.3 TIME-ORIENTED COSTS

Some costs have a strong relationship to time rather than to activity indices. For example, a salary is paid somewhat irrespective of what a person produces in one time period versus another; the same amount of rent is paid each month whether or not a facility is used. There are many examples of time-oriented costs, of which the list below is illustrative:

EXHIBIT 18-9 TIME-ORIENTED OR PERIOD COSTS

Salary
Rent
Property tax
Property insurance premiums
Depreciation, other than the units-of-production method

The accounting convention is that *period* costs (or revenues) should be assigned to the time periods to which they belong. If we pay first and last month's rent, for example, that portion belonging to the last month is considered prepaid rent until we reach the time period to which it belongs, at which time it becomes rent expense. This convention is adhered to even though we recognize that some present period costs may give rise to future revenues.

These time-oriented costs are generally *fixed* in nature.

HISTORICAL COST

Historical cost is the sum that was actually paid for an item. As mentioned in chapter 3, financial accounting records are maintained on an historical cost basis. The alternatives to historical cost are:

Replacement cost: What it would cost at the present time to replace an asset.

Earning power cost: Cost based on the earnings of an asset discounted to its present value, as illustrated in chapters 5 and 17.

Current market value: What we could sell an asset for at the present time in the open market.

While historical cost underlies financial accounting as it is practiced at present, in cost accounting we have more freedom to experiment with other cost bases, as our data is consumed only within the firm. For management purposes, historical cost may not be the best guide to value, and so these other valuation techniques are necessary. In fact, it is sometimes useful to reflect values in a number of different ways.

SUNK COST

A *sunk cost* is an historical cost, but in addition it is a cost which does not have relevance to a current economic decision. For example, in selling a house, what was paid for it originally may be of some interest to the seller, but it surely has no bearing on what the property is worth. The house could have been purchased originally in excess of its value. The fact that the first buyer made a mistake does not mean that his error can be passed on to the second buyer. Or the property could have been purchased for much less than its market value, in which case the first buyer is unlikely to share his profits with the second buyer. The concept of sunk costs is critical to capital budgeting decisions, as we point out in chapter 24.

ESTIMATED AND STANDARD COSTS

Most modern business activity is based on what products *should cost* rather than on what they *do cost.* It is generally necessary to price a product before actual costs are known. To the extent that pricing relies on cost data, we have to use estimated rather than actual costs for this purpose. For example, the cost of making a particular model automobile is based on this computation:

$$\frac{\text{Total costs of production}}{\text{Number of automobiles produced}} = \text{Cost per automobile}$$

The above data is not available until the end of the business year, but it is necessary that we cost the automobile at the beginning of the year. We use estimated (standard) costs for this purpose. Likewise, a school budget is based on the estimated cost of educating a certain number of students a year. The rates that a hospital charges are based on estimates of patient load and intensity of care needed. Insurance premiums are based on an estimate of the number of claims. In fact, all major organizations operate on the basis of estimated costs.

The difference between estimated and standard costs turns upon the degree of precision used. *Standard costs* are carefully structured costs, using engineering estimates which break operations down into minute tasks, e.g., how long it should take to produce a certain part on a machine lathe, or the average time needed to install the steering assembly onto an automobile chassis on an assembly line.

Estimated costs are accompanied by less precision, as one might expect in a school or hospital budget.

18.4 TRACEABILITY-ORIENTED COSTS

COST CENTERS

Our definitions in this category refer to cost or product centers. A *cost center* is a unit of the organization to which costs are assigned and within which they are aggregated. Cost centers are like systems—we have one within another. At the highest level the

EXHIBIT 18-10 COST CENTERS

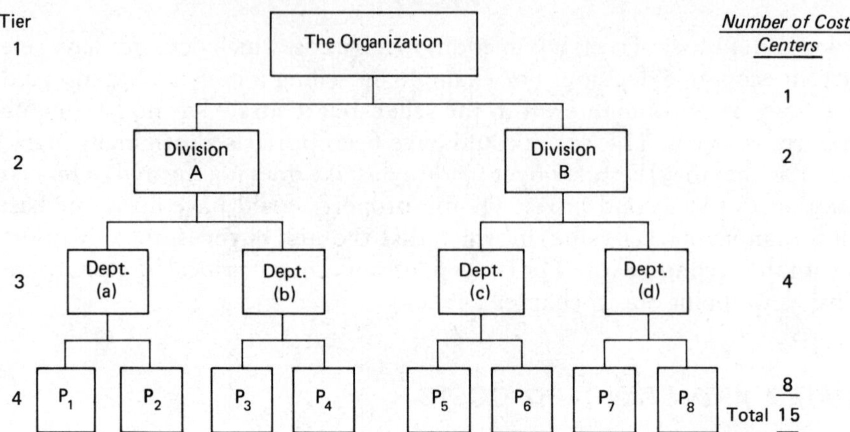

whole organization is a cost center. If it has two divisions, they are each cost centers, and there are many cost centers at lower levels, right down to specific jobs or products (Exhibit 18-10). With the designation of fifteen cost centers, we can cost (1) the organization as a whole, (2) each of its divisions, (3) each of its departments, and (4) each of its product lines.

DIRECT AND INDIRECT COSTS

Direct costs are traceable 100% to *one* cost center. It is obvious that at tier 1 in Exhibit 18-10 *all* costs are *direct.* At other tiers, only those costs that are traceable to a center can be called direct.

Indirect costs are those costs that are shared by one or more cost centers. For example, at the division level, the salary of the president of the organization cannot be traced entirely to division A or B. Headquarters expenses such as this are considered indirect and are allocated to division A and B on some arbitrary basis:

	Division A	**Division B**
Direct costs	$100,000	$120,000
Administrative overhead	30,000	40,000
Total costs	$130,000	$160,000

If total headquarter costs are $70,000, this sum would be allocated to the two divisions upon some agreed basis.

PRODUCT AND PRIME COSTS

Prime costs are direct material and labor costs that can be traced to a particular product or job. Production overhead comprises those other costs of production that cannot be traced to a particular product, hence overhead is indirect. Some typical production overhead expenses are detailed in Exhibit 18-5.

JOINT PRODUCT COSTS

Joint costs are allocated by convention to products in the ratio of dollar volume of sales. Once again, each product may have its direct costs, so we are referring only to the common costs of production when we speak of joint costs. Suppose there are five products, where the joint costs total $100,000. This sum, as stated above, is apportioned among the five products in the ratio of their sales volume (Exhibit 18-11).

EXHIBIT 18-11 ALLOCATION OF JOINT COSTS

	Sales Volume	Ratio	Direct Costs	Joint Costs
Product A	$ 300,000	.30		$ 30,000
Product B	150,000	.15		15,000
Product C	100,000	.10		10,000
Product D	250,000	.25		25,000
Product E	200,000	.20		20,000
Total	$1,000,000	1.00	↓	$100,000

BY-PRODUCT COST

In costing a by-product, all of the fixed costs of production are allocable to the major products. A by-product is charged only with the cost of preparing it for market, and with the selling and administrative expenses directly attributable to its sales. For example, sawdust is a by-product of lumber. The expenses necessary to make sawdust a viable commercial product are assigned to that operation, but it is not charged with the basic costs of milling lumber.

Some by-products in time become major products (gasoline was once a by-product of kerosene) and *vice versa,* but no general rule has been developed to determine when a by-product should bear its share of general overhead.

18.5 CONTROL-ORIENTED COSTS

CONTROLLABLE VERSUS NON-CONTROLLABLE

A *controllable cost* is a direct cost for which one person has complete responsibility. A *responsibility accounting system* is where this type of control climate is in effect.

A *non-controllable cost* is a cost for which one person does not have complete responsibility. It may be direct or indirect. There may be costs within a cost center over which no one person in the cost center has complete responsibility, such as rental of space which is negotiated on a central basis.

A responsibility accounting system calls for the separation of costs for which one person is responsible from those over which he has little or no control. Obviously, evaluation of executive performance is influenced most by the ability to manage controllable costs.

OTHER CONTROL-ORIENTED COSTS

Generally speaking several alternatives are considered in arriving at a choice. The alternatives that were discarded were in effect other ways in which to achieve the same objective. The choice may have been made by the narrowest of margins. It is often useful to look back and inquire what might have happened had some other alternative been selected instead. *Opportunity costing* performs this function. It not only deals with past alternatives, but also with current and future ones.

Differential costs (marginal) are the costs that change between two activity points. This concept is allied to variable costs which we discuss in the next section.

Imputed costs are costs assigned to an object through subjective analysis. For example, a piece of equipment may have been donated to a firm, but in order to value its contribution to the organization it is helpful to impute a value. Imputed costs underlie much of the simulation currently applied to business operations, where arbitrary values are assigned and function as variables which can be tested under different assumed operating conditions.

Postponable costs (or *discretionary costs*) are those costs that can be delayed without injury to operations. It separates things that it "would be nice to have" from things that are "really needed." For example, the purchase of a new typewriter can be postponed for a while without injury to performance. Non-operating and capital expenditures contain more postponable items than operating expenses.

Out-of-pocket refers to the specific cash outlay involved in a transaction. If you make a $300 down payment on a $3,000 automobile, the $300 is out-of-pocket. This concept is used in capital budgeting and investment analysis for purposes of measuring return on investment.

18.6 BEHAVIORALLY-ORIENTED COSTS

When we speak of the *behavior* of costs we refer to their degree of responsiveness to an activity scale. Take depreciation of a truck as a case in point. If we use the straight-line method, the same amount of depreciation will be charged each period without regard to the number of miles we drive the truck. If we use the units-of-production method, however, the depreciation charge is a direct function of mileage. In the former case we have a non-responsive cost, while in the latter case we have a fully responsive cost.

Fixed Costs: do not respond at all to a change in an activity index.

Variable Costs: change in direct proportion to a change in an activity index.

Semi-Variable Costs: change in relation to an activity index, but not in direct proportion.

We can represent these three types of behavioral costs in graphic form as in Exhibit 18-12.

There is no single profile of a semi-variable cost. The graph in Exhibit 18-12 represents a decreasing cost function, e.g., electricity consumption where there is a

EXHIBIT 18-12 GRAPHS OF COST BEHAVIOR

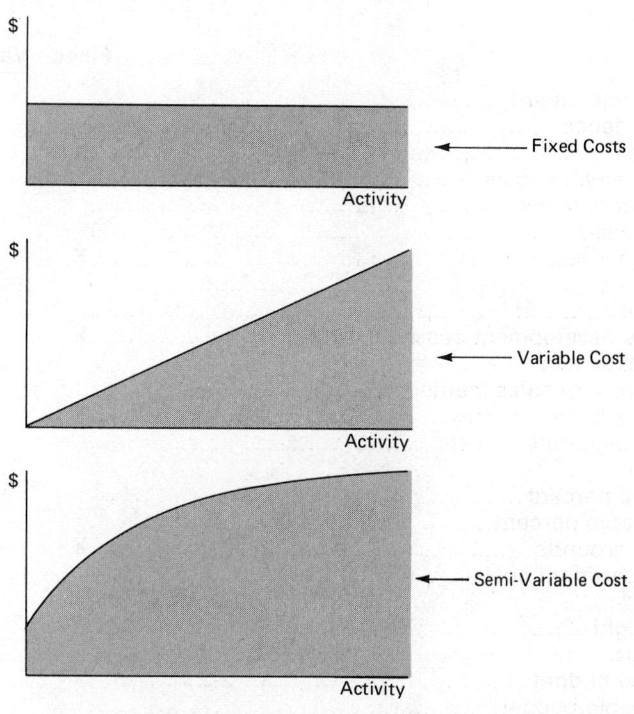

decreasing rate as we increase use. You will also observe that semi-variable costs intersect the *Y* axis, which means that they contain some degree of fixedness.

IDENTIFYING FIXED, VARIABLE, AND SEMI-VARIABLE COSTS

Exhibit 18-13 shows a list of accounts classified as being either fixed, variable, or semi-variable. It should help you to identify and classify costs on a behavioral basis.

EXHIBIT 18-13 CLASSIFYING FIXED, VARIABLE, AND SEMI-VARIABLE COSTS

	Fixed	Variable	Semi-Variable
1. Straight-line depreciation	X		
2. Units-of-production depreciation		X	
3. Accelerated depreciation methods			X
4. Comissions to salesmen:			
(a) straight commission		X	
(b) salary plus, or changing commission rate			X
5. Executive salaries	X		
6. Repairs to building	X		
7. Fire insurance on facilities	X		
8. Group health insurance			X
9. Power for machinery:			
(a) constant rate		X	
(b) sliding rate			X

EXHIBIT 18-13 (CONTINUED)

	Fixed	Variable	Semi-Variable
10. Repairs to equipment			X
11. Superintendence			X
12. Property tax	X		
13. Inventory carrying costs			X
14. Social security taxes			X
15. Direct materials		X	
16. Legal retainer fees	X		
17. Indirect labor			X
18. Direct labor		X	
19. Research & development costs	X		
20. Bad debt expense:			
(a) percent of sales method		X	
(b) aging of receivables			X
21. Personnel department costs			X
22. Royalties:			
(a) fixed percent		X	
(b) variable percent			X
23. Upkeep of grounds	X		
24. Payroll department costs			X
25. Rent	X		
26. Heat and light			X
27. Advertising:			
(a) fixed budget	X		
(b) variable budget			X
28. Bonuses and incentives			X

Now use your skill to match the graphs in Exhibit 18-14 with the appropriate descriptions. The answers are given at the bottom of p. 767.

EXHIBIT 18-14 IDENTIFYING COST BEHAVIOR GRAPHS

The vertical axes of the graphs represent *total* dollars of expense and the horizontal axes represent production. In each case the zero point is at the intersection of the two axes. The graphs may be used more than once.

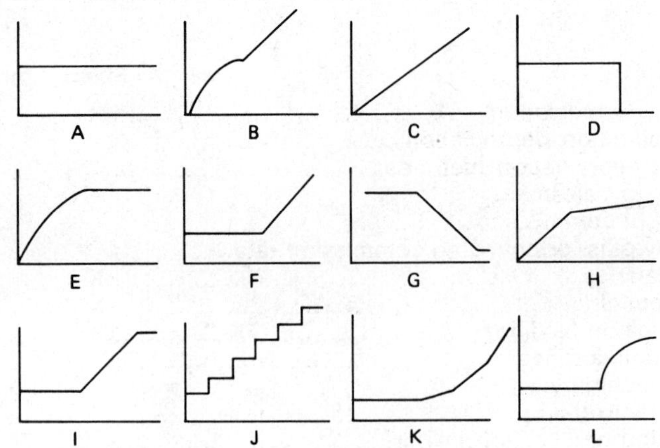

EXHIBIT 18-14 (CONTINUED)

1. Depreciation of equipment, where the amount of depreciation charged is computed by the machine hours method.
2. Electricity bill—a flat fixed charge, plus a variable cost after a certain number of kilowatt hours are used.
3. City water bill, which is computed as follows:

First 1,000,000 gallons or less	$1,000 flat fee
Next 10,000 gallons	.003 per gallon used
Next 10,000 gallons	.006 per gallon used
Next 10,000 gallons	.009 per gallon used
etc.	

4. Cost of lubricant for machines, where cost per unit decreases with each pound of lubricant used (for example, if one pound is used, the cost is $10.00; if two pounds are used, the cost is $19.98; if three pounds are used, the cost is $29.94; with a minimum cost per pound of $9.25).
5. Depreciation of equipment, where the amount is computed by the straight-line method. When the depreciation rate was established it was anticipated that the obsolescence factor would be greater than the wear and tear factor.
6. Rent on a factory building donated by the city, where the agreement calls for a fixed fee payment unless 200,000 man-hours are worked, in which case no rent need be paid.
7. Salaries of repairmen, where one repairman is needed for every 1,000 hours of machine hours or less (i.e., 0 to 1,000 hours requires one repairman, 1,001 to 2,000 hours requires two repairmen, etc.).
8. Federal unemployment compensation taxes for the year, where labor force is constant in number throughout year (average annual salary is $6,000 per worker).
9. Cost of raw material used.
10. Rent on a factory building donated by county, where agreement calls for rent of $100,000 less $1 for each direct labor hour worked in excess of 200,000 hours, but minimum rental payment of $20,000 must be paid.

SOURCE: Uniform Certified Public Accountant Examination, May 1959, Copyright 1959, American Institute of Certified Public Accountants, Inc. Used by permission.

ACTIVITY INDICES

We have made repeated reference to activity indices. You may have recognized by now that there are many activity indices. Activity indices for the variable and semi-variable accounts identified in Exhibit 18-13 are listed in Exhibit 18-15.

Although there are many activity indices, each organization has a *macro-activity index.* This macro-index relates to the principal *production function* of an organization. Every organization has a production function—it is descriptive of the real purpose of an organization. It is only by comparing resources consumed against the macro-index that we are able to make efficiency judgments on organizations.[3] Exhibit 18-16 gives some illustrative macro-indices.

If we look at the total fixed, variable, and semi-variable costs of an organization, the macro-index becomes the scale of the *X* axis. Dollars is uniformly the scale of the *Y* axis (Exhibit 18-17).

[3]This illustrates the process-system relationship discussed in chapter 1.

EXHIBIT 18-15 ACTIVITY INDICES

Account*	Activity Index
2. Units-of-production depreciation:	
(a) on a truck	mileage
(b) on a production machine	operating hours
4. Commissions to salesmen	sales volume
8. Group health insurance	number of employees
9. Power for machinery	kilowatts used
10. Repairs to equipment	operating hours
11. Superintendence	number of employees
13. Inventory carrying costs	quantity/cost
14. Social security taxes	employee earnings
15. Direct materials	number of units
17. Indirect labor	direct labor hours
18. Direct labor	number of units
20. Bad debt expense:	
(a) percent of sales methods	sales volume
(b) aging of receivables	formulae
21. Personnel department costs	number of employees
22. Royalties	sales volume
24. Payroll department costs	number of employees
26. Heat and light	units of energy used
27. Advertising (variable budget)	no uniform index
28. Bonuses and incentives	number of units or sales volume

*The numbers in Exhibit 18-13 are used to facilitate reference.

EXHIBIT 18-16 MACRO-INDEX OF VARIOUS ORGANIZATIONS

Type of Organization	Macro-Index
1. Manufacturing firms	number of units produced
2. Commercial firms	number of units sold
3. Elementary schools	pupil-hours
4. High schools	student-hours
5. Universities and colleges	full-time equivalent student ("student FTE")
6. Hospitals	patient days
7. Utilities	number of units sold
8. Libraries	number of volumes loaned
9. Railroads	revenue miles
10. Airlines (passenger service)	passenger revenue miles

EXHIBIT 18-17 MACRO-INDEX OF INDUSTRIAL ORGANIZATIONS

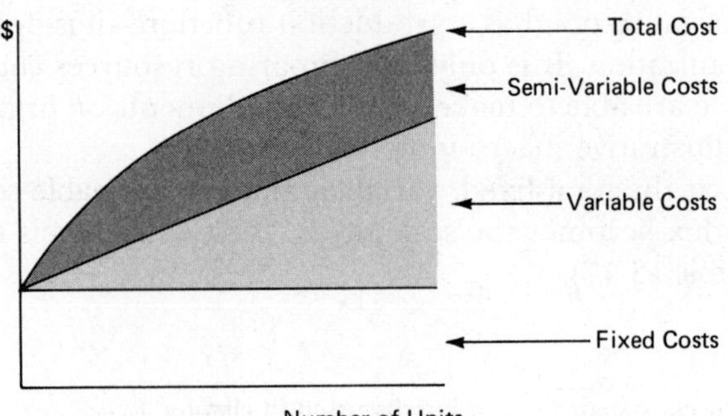

While each organization has a macro-activity index, it also has numerous minor ones. We make the bold assumption in cost accounting that the minor ones are *surrogates*[4] of the macro-index, as depicted in Exhibit 18-18.

EXHIBIT 18-18 MICRO-INDICES AS SURROGATES OF MACRO-INDEX

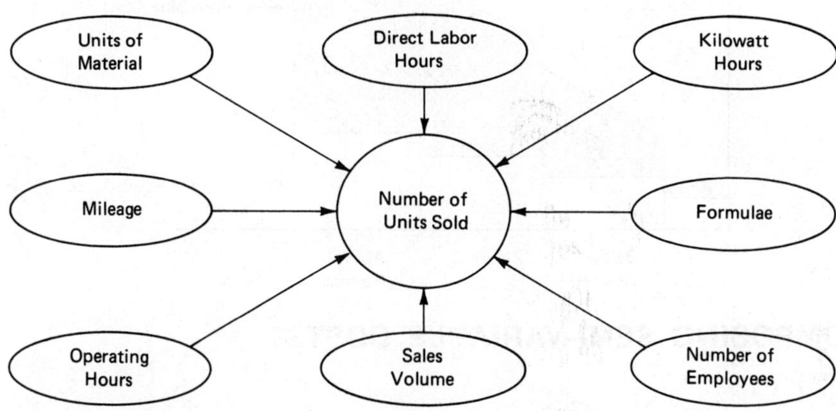

TWO ASSUMPTIONS OF BEHAVIORAL COSTS

Our ability to separate costs in terms of behavior rests upon two important assumptions:

1. A time period of one year.
2. A normal macro-activity range.

Fixed costs are assumed to be fixed for one year. Executive salaries, property tax, and other fixed costs change from year to year, but they are relatively stable during each year. This assumption is important, because in the long run all costs are *variable;* while in the very short run all costs are *fixed.*

Then there is the assumption of a normal macro-activity range. Obviously fixed costs will not remain constant if we drop to zero activity. If we exceed the *normal capacity* of organization, additional fixed costs need to be incurred to handle the overload.

In fact, we can recognize a series of ranges, as illustrated in Exhibit 18-19. These ranges are important in developing a *flexible budget,* which we discuss in chapters 20 and 23.

[4]Recognizing surrogates for the measurement of complex principles was discussed in chapter 1.

ANSWERS TO EXHIBIT 18-14

1.	C	6.	D
2.	F	7.	J
3.	K	8.	H
4.	B	9.	C
5.	A	10.	G

Fixed = A
Variable = C
Semi-variable = B,D,E,F,G,H,I,J,K,L.

EXHIBIT 18-19 RANGES IN MACRO-ACTIVITY

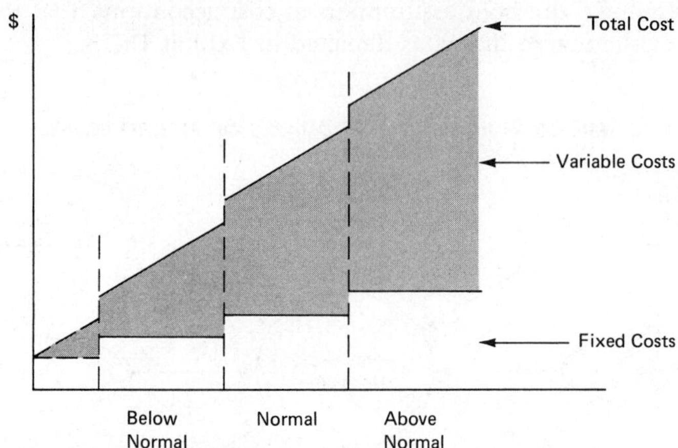

18.7 DECOMPOSING SEMI-VARIABLE COSTS

Fixed and variable costs are linear by definition, while the profiles of semi-variable costs differ markedly. Because it is useful to work with linear relationships, we are concerned here with the problem of resolving semi-variable costs into fixed and variable costs. We start with three types of behavioral cost and end with two (Exhibit 18-20).

EXHIBIT 18-20 RESOLVING SEMI-VARIABLE COSTS

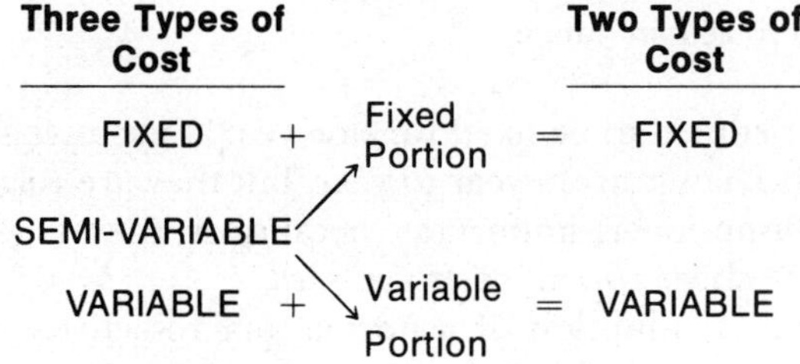

Each semi-variable cost consists of a fixed and a variable element. We will discuss three methods for separating the fixed and variable parts of a semi-variable cost:

1. High and low point
2. Scattergraph
3. Least squares

Let us use cost data from the fringe-benefit account (Exhibit 18-21) for our example. You will notice that it is necessary to have both activity and cost data. How do we recognize this account as being semi-variable? If it were fixed, the dollar amounts would be the same regardless of changes in volume. If it were variable, the dollar amounts would vary in direct proportion to changes in volume. Neither of these conditions exists—so the account is semi-variable.

EXHIBIT 18-21 A SEMI-VARIABLE ACCOUNT

Month	Direct Labor Hours	Fringe-Benefit Costs
1	700	$ 750
2	800	840
3	900	930
4	1,000	1,015
5	1,100	1,090
6	1,200	1,170
7	1,350	1,205
8	1,250	1,200
9	1,150	1,130
10	950	970
11	850	900
12	750	800
Total	12,000	$12,000

HIGH AND LOW POINT

These are the steps in applying the high and low point method:

1. Select the *highest activity* point with its corresponding dollar amount, which incidentally need not be the highest dollar figure.
2. Select the *lowest activity* point with its corresponding dollar amount, which in turn need not be the lowest dollar figure.
3. Find the difference in activity and in dollars.
4. Divide the difference in activity into the difference in dollars to get the variable rate.
5. Multiply high and low activity points by the variable rate and subtract the product from the respective dollar amounts in 1 and 2 above.
6. The remainder in each instance is *fixed* cost. It should be the same amount for the high and low levels of activity.

We apply these steps to the foregoing problem:

	Hours	Cost
1. High activity	1,350	$1,205
2. Low activity	700	750
3. Difference	650	$ 455

4. Find variable rate $\frac{\$455}{650} = \$.70$ per direct labor hour

	High Activity	Low Activity	
Cost data	$1,205	$ 750	
5. Variable cost:			
High (.70 × 1,350)	⟨945⟩		
Low (.70 × 700)		⟨490⟩	
6. Fixed cost	$ 260	$ 260	per month

The variable cost rate can also be obtained by using this formula:

$$V_r = \frac{(H_c - L_c)}{(H_a - L_a)}$$

where

V_r = variable rate
H_c = cost corresponding with high point
L_c = cost corresponding with low point
H_a = high activity
L_a = low activity

Accordingly

$$V_r = \frac{(\$1{,}205 - \$750)}{(1{,}350 - 700)} = \frac{\$455}{650} = \$.70 \text{ per direct labor hour}$$

Then use steps 5 and 6 as above.

A graph of the high and low points method would show fixed costs as intersecting the *Y* axis at $260, as in Exhibit 18-22.

EXHIBIT 18-22 GRAPH OF HIGH AND LOW POINTS METHOD

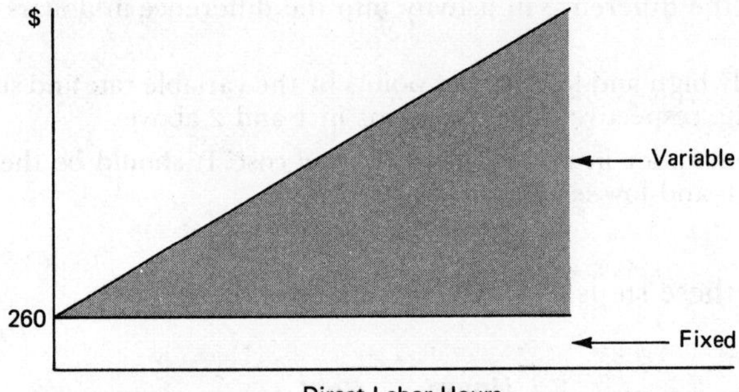

The advantage of the high and low points method lies in its simplicity in calculations. Its disadvantage is that it draws a regression line on the basis of only two data points and assumes that the other points lie on a straight line between the high and low points.

SCATTERGRAPH

The scattergraph method employs a graphic solution. It requires that we plot the coordinates of each set of activity-cost data. The specific steps of the scattergraph method are enumerated as follows:

1. Draw a graph to scale, with the axes extending beyond the highest activity and cost points.
2. Plot the coordinates of each set of data, which may be marked M_1, M_2, . . . for each period for purposes of identification.
3. Visually draw a regression line that appears to represent the thrust of the data.
4. The fixed cost level is determined where the regression line intersects the *Y* axis.
5. The variable cost rate is determined conventionally as follows:
   a. Take the dollar amount at the high activity point.
   b. Subtract fixed costs as obtained in 4 above.
   c. The remainder is variable cost at the high activity point.
   d. Divide variable cost by the high activity figure to get the variable cost rate.

The scattergraph method is applied to our fringe-benefit account as depicted in Exhibit 18-23.

EXHIBIT 18-23 THE SCATTERGRAPH

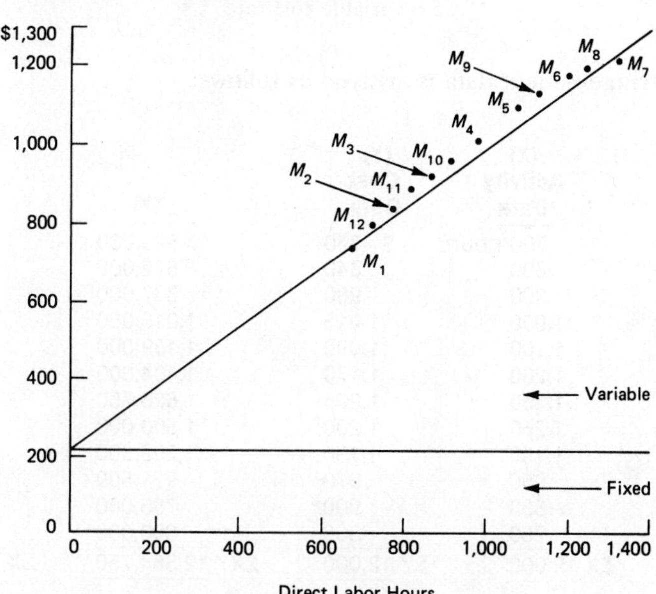

Compute the variable cost rate (as in point 5 above):

a. Cost corresponding with high activity level $1,205
b. Fixed cost per graph 230
c. Variable cost .... $ 975

d. Variable cost rate $= \frac{\$975}{1{,}350}$ hours $=$ \$.72 per direct labor hour

In drawing the regression line, it is *not* necessary to have an equal number of points above and below the line. The objective, as stated before, is to draw a line that represents the thrust of the coordinates.

The scattergraph does take into account all of the data. Its disadvantage lies in one's ability to draw an accurate line of regression.

LINEAR REGRESSION METHOD (LEAST SQUARES)

The method of least squares computes the weight or value of each coordinate in arriving at the line of regression. The formula for this type of solution involves a pair of simultaneous linear equations:

$$\Sigma XY = a\Sigma X + b\Sigma X^2 \quad (1)$$
$$\Sigma Y = na \quad + b\Sigma X \quad (2)$$

where

X = activity data
Y = cost data
n = number of periods
a = fixed cost
b = variable cost rate

Our fringe-benefit data is arrayed as follows:

(*n*) Months	**(*X*) Activity Data**	**(*Y*) Cost Data**	**(*XY*)**	**(X^2)**
1	700 hours	$ 750	525,000	490,000
2	800	840	672,000	640,000
3	900	930	837,000	810,000
4	1,000	1,015	1,015,000	1,000,000
5	1,100	1,090	1,199,000	1,210,000
6	1,200	1,170	1,404,000	1,440,000
7	1,350	1,205	1,626,750	1,822,500
8	1,250	1,200	1,500,000	1,562,500
9	1,150	1,130	1,299,500	1,322,500
10	950	970	921,500	902,500
11	850	900	765,000	722,500
12	750	800	600,000	562,500
	ΣX 12,000	ΣY 12,000	ΣXY 12,364,750	ΣX^2 12,485,000

Substitute the above values in equations (1) and (2)

$$12{,}364{,}750 = 12{,}000a + 12{,}485{,}000b \quad (1)$$
$$12{,}000 = \quad 12a + \quad 12{,}000b \quad (2)$$

To eliminate (a): Repeat (1)

$$12{,}364{,}750 = 12{,}000a + 12{,}485{,}000b \quad (3)$$

Multiply (2) by −1,000

$$\underline{-12{,}000{,}000 = -12{,}000a - 12{,}000{,}000b} \quad (4)$$

Adding

$$364{,}750 = 485{,}000b \tag{5}$$

$$b = \frac{364{,}750}{485{,}000} \tag{6}$$

$$b = .752 \text{ or } 75.2\% \text{ variable } \underline{\text{cost rate}} \tag{7}$$

To solve for (a): Substitute .752 for (b) in equation (2)

$$12{,}000 = 12a + 12{,}000\ (.752) \tag{8}$$

$$12{,}000 = 12a + 9{,}024 \tag{9}$$

$$12a = 12{,}000 - 9{,}024 \tag{10}$$

$$a = \frac{2{,}976}{12} \tag{11}$$

$$= \underline{\$248 \text{ fixed cost}} \tag{12}$$

Linear regression by means of least squares gives us a more accurate solution to the problem. Its disadvantage is the amount of manual computation involved, which presents no problem if calculators or computers are used.

In separating the fixed and variable portions of semi-variable costs, we can compute each account independently by means of its own activity index *or* we can group all semi-variable accounts together and regress the total cost data on the basis of the best or most frequent index. In this latter instance the macro-activity index is usually the best one to use.

18.8 BREAK-EVEN ANALYSIS

Having separated semi-variable costs, we can construct a linear break-even graph including a revenue function, as in Exhibit 18-24.

EXHIBIT 18-24 BREAK-EVEN CHART

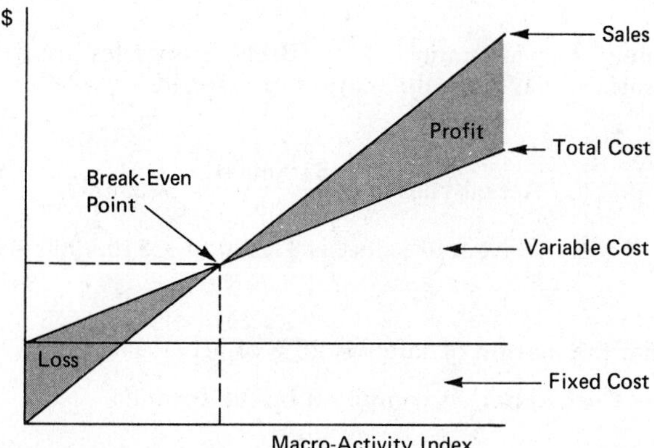

EXHIBIT 18-25 MARGINAL BREAK-EVEN CHART

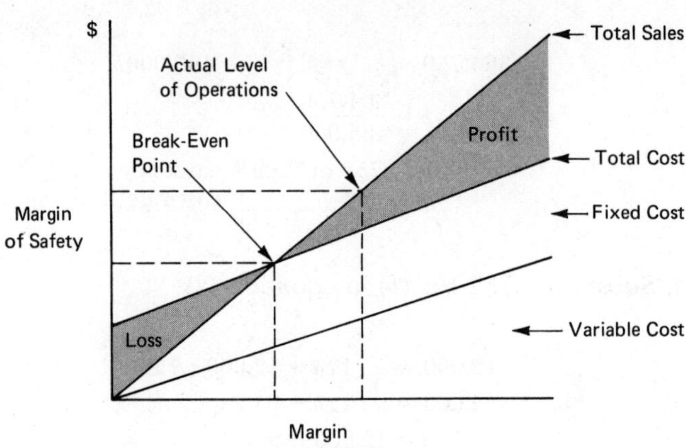

Our break-even chart can be converted into a *marginal* break-even chart (Exhibit 18-25) by reversing the positions of fixed and variable costs. A marginal break-even chart conforms with the marginal income statement which we discussed in chapter 5 and the appendix to chapter 11.

This marginal break-even chart contains some relationships which are important to the discussion of cost-volume-profit analysis which follows:

1. **Margin of Safety:** the difference between actual operations (above the level of break-even) and the break-even point.
2. **Margin of Safety Ratio:** is computed by the formula

$$M_s = \frac{(S_a - S_b)}{S_a}$$

where

M_s = Margin of safety ratio (MS ratio)
S_a = Actual sales
S_b = Sales at the break-even point

Example: The MS ratio is 20%. Break-even sales are \$100,000. (a) What are actual sales? (b) What is the margin of safety?

a. Actual sales are $\frac{\$100{,}000}{.80} = \$125{,}000$

b. Margin of safety is \$125,000 − \$100,000 = \$25,000

Note that the margin of safety is 20% of actual sales.

3. **Variable Cost Ratio:** is computed by the formula

$$V_r = \frac{V}{S}$$

where

V_r = Variable cost ratio (VC ratio)
V = Variable costs
S = Sales

4. **Marginal Income Ratio:** is computed by the formula

$$M_r = \frac{(S - V)}{S} = \frac{M}{S}$$

where

M_r = Marginal income ratio (MI ratio)
S = Sales
V = Variable cost
M = Marginal income

You will recall that the format for a marginal income statement (chapter 5) is:

Sales	$10,000
Less: Variable costs	6,000
Marginal income	4,000
Less: Fixed costs	3,000
Profit	$ 1,000

In this example the VC ratio is .60 (or 60%) and the MI ratio is .40 (or 40%). You will notice that:[5]

Fixed Costs	Fixed Costs
+ Profit	− Loss
= Marginal Income	= Marginal Income

At the break-even point marginal income = fixed costs, as there is no profit or loss.

18.9 COST-VOLUME-PROFIT ANALYSIS

With these relationships in mind we attend to cost-volume-profit changes. There are five variables in cost-volume-profit analysis:

[5]The VC and MI ratios are always complementary.

1. *Volume:* the number of units sold
2. *Selling price* per unit
3. *Variable cost rate* or cost per unit
4. *Fixed costs*
5. *Profit*

We can change any four variables simultaneously and solve for the fifth. Four examples are given below.

EXAMPLES OF FORMULA APPROACH

EXAMPLE 1: From the present marginal income statement (N_1) compute a projected one (N_2) based on the changes indicated.

	(Given) Present (N_1)	Changes	(Required) Projected (N_2)
Sales	$10,000	+ 10% in unit selling price	$17,400 (100.0%)
Variable costs	6,000	+ 20% in unit variable cost	11,400 (65.5%)
Marginal income	4,000		6,000 (34.5%)
Fixed costs	3,000	+ $1,000 in fixed cost	4,000 (23.0%)
Profit	$ 1,000	+ $1,000 in profit required	$ 2,000 (11.5%)

A four-stage formula can be used for solving this type of problem.

$$MR_2 = \frac{(U_r \times S_1) - (U_r \times V_1)}{(U_r \times S_1)} \tag{1}$$

$$M_2 = (F_1 \pm A) + (P_1 \pm A) \tag{2}$$

$$S_2 = \frac{M_2}{MR_2} \tag{3}$$

$$V_2 = S_2 - M_2 \tag{4}$$

where

MR = Marginal income ratio
U_r = Unit multiplier
S = Sales
V = Variable cost
M = Marginal income
A = Adjustment amount
P = Profit
N = Period
$_{1,2}$ = Period 1 or period 2

Accordingly:

$$MR_2 = \frac{(1.10 \times \$10{,}000) - (1.20 \times \$6{,}000)}{(1.10 \times \$10{,}000)} = \frac{\$11{,}000 - \$7{,}200}{\$11{,}000} = \frac{\$3{,}800}{\$11{,}000} = \underline{.345} \quad (1)$$

$$M_2 = (\$3{,}000 + \$1{,}000) + (\$1{,}000 + \$1{,}000) = 4{,}000 + 2{,}000 = \underline{\$6{,}000} \quad (2)$$

$$S_2 = \frac{\$6{,}000}{.345} = \underline{\$17{,}400} \quad (3)$$

$$V_2 = \$17{,}400 - \$6{,}000 = \underline{\$11{,}400} \quad (4)$$

Change in the number of units sold between N_1 and N_2 is:

$$N_2 \text{ volume} = \frac{S_2}{U} = \frac{17{,}400}{1.10} = \underline{15{,}818} \text{ unit equivalents}$$

$$N_1 \text{ volume} = \frac{S_1}{U} = \frac{10{,}000}{1.00} = \underline{10{,}000} \text{ unit equivalents}$$

$$\text{Increase } N_2 > N_1 = \underline{5{,}818} \text{ unit equivalents or } 58\%$$

As we do not know how many units we have in N_1, we speak in terms of "unit equivalents." We know that in order to meet the required changes we need a 58% increase in the number of units sold.

EXAMPLE 2: Let us use the same N_1 statement and change data as in Example 1 except for the profit requirement, which we will state in terms of a percentage rather than dollar change:

	N_1	Change
Profit	\$1,000	25% of sales at N_2

Our foregoing formula is modified:

$$MR_2 = \frac{(U_r \times S_1) - (U_r \times V_1)}{(U_r \times S_1)} \quad (1)$$

$$F_r = MR_2 - P_r \quad (2)$$

$$F_2 = (F_1 \pm A) \quad (3)$$

$$S_2 = \frac{F_2}{F_r} \quad (4)$$

$$M_2 = MR_2 \times S_2 \quad (5)$$

$$V_2 = S_2 - M_2 \quad (6)$$

where new symbols are

F_r = Fixed cost rate at N_2
P_r = Profit expressed as a percentage of sales at N_2

Accordingly:

$$MR_2 = (1) \text{ is the same as before} = \underline{.345} \quad (1)$$

$$F_r = .345 - .25 = \underline{.095} \quad (2)$$

$$F_2 = (\$1{,}000 + \$3{,}000) = \underline{\$4{,}000} \quad (3)$$

$$S_2 = \frac{\$4{,}000}{.095} = \underline{\$42{,}100} \quad (4)$$

$$M_2 = .345 \times \$42{,}100 = \underline{\$14{,}500} \quad (5)$$

$$V_2 = \$42{,}100 - \$14{,}500 = \underline{\$27{,}600} \quad (6)$$

The N_2 statement under Example 2 is:

Sales	$42,100	(100.0%)
Variable costs	27,600	(65.5%)
Marginal income	14,500	(34.5%)
Fixed costs	4,000	(9.5%)
Profit	$10,500	(25.0%)

The answers are approximate, i.e., with slide-rule accuracy. With problems of this sort high accuracy is not required, and in fact can be misleading in that it suggests a precision to the data that does not exist in fact.

In Example 2 a 283% increase in the number of units sold would be required to accommodate the changes, including a profit that is 25% of sales. As the marginal income ratio is only 34.5% and the profit change calls for 25%, only 9.5% is available for fixed costs. It is this relationship of 9.5% to $4,000 in fixed costs that provides the key to solving problems of the Example 2 type.

EXAMPLE 3: In this example we move backward from N_2 to N_1.

	(Required) N_1		**Changes from N_1 that resulted in N_2**	**(Given) N_2**	
Sales	$5,850		− 10% unit selling price	$10,000	
Variable costs	2,350	(40.0%)	+ 10% unit variable cost	5,000	(50.0%)
Marginal income	3,500	(60.0%)		5,000	(50.0%)
Fixed costs	2,000		+ $2,000 in fixed costs	4,000	
Profit	$1,500		− $500 in profit	$ 1,000	

The formula in Example 1 is converted into this form:

$$MR_1 = \frac{\left(\frac{S_2}{U_r}\right) - \left(\frac{V_2}{U_r}\right)}{\left(\frac{S_2}{U_r}\right)} \quad (1)$$

$$M_1 = (F_2 \mp A) + (P_2 \mp A) \quad (2)$$

$$S_1 = \frac{M_1}{MR_1} \quad (3)$$

$$V_1 = S_1 - M_1 \quad (4)$$

The symbols are consistent. Accordingly:

$$MR_1 = \frac{\left(\frac{10,000}{.90}\right) - \left(\frac{5,000}{1.10}\right)}{\left(\frac{10,000}{.90}\right)} = \frac{11,111 - 4,545}{11,111} = \frac{6,566}{11,111} = \underline{.60} \quad (1)$$

$$M_1 = (\$4,000 - \$2,000) + (\$1,000 + \$500) = \underline{\$3,500} \quad (2)$$

$$S_1 = \frac{\$3,500}{.60} = \underline{\$5,850} \quad (3)$$

$$V_1 = \$5,850 - \$3,500 = \underline{\$2,350} \quad (4)$$

The change in units sold is computed as before.

EXAMPLE 4: Working backwards again, with the same data as above except for profit, which was 15% of sales in N_1.

MR_1 is the same as Example 3 (1)

$$F_r = MR_1 - P_r \quad (2)$$

$$F_1 = F_2 \mp A \quad (3)$$

$$S_1 = \frac{F_1}{F_r} \quad (4)$$

$$M_1 = MR_1 \times S_1 \quad (5)$$

$$V_1 = S_1 - M_1 \quad (6)$$

where

F_r = Fixed cost rate at N_1

P_r = Profit expressed as a percentage of sales at N_1

So,

$MR_1 = \underline{.60}$ as before (1)

$$F_r = .60 - .15 = \underline{.45} \quad (2)$$

$$F_1 = \$4,000 - \$2,000 = \underline{\$2,000} \quad (3)$$

$$S_1 = \frac{\$2,000}{.45} = \underline{\$4,450} \quad (4)$$

$$M_1 = .60 \times \$4,450 = \underline{\$2,670} \quad (5)$$

$$V_1 = \$4,450 - \$2,670 = \underline{\$1,780} \quad (6)$$

The N_1 statement on this basis is:

Sales	$4,450	(100.0%)
Variable costs	1,780	(40.0%)
Marginal income	$2,670	(60.0%)
Fixed costs	2,000	(45.0%)
Profit	$ 670	(15.0%)

Cost-volume-profit problems of this sort may be solved by plotting changes on graph paper drawn to scale, as shown for Example 4 in Exhibit 18-26.

EXHIBIT 18-26 PLOTTING COST-VOLUME-PROFIT CHANGES BY GRAPH

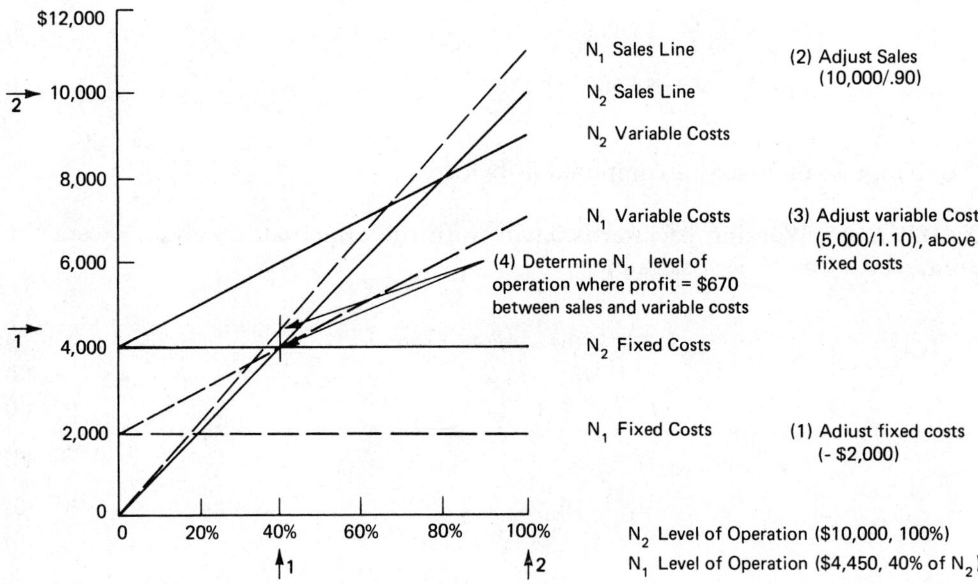

NON-FORMULA APPROACH

A non-formula approach to solving this type of problem is presented below:

1. We are given an existing statement and proposed changes.

		Changes
Sales	$1,000	− 10% in unit selling price
Variable costs	500	+ 10% in unit variable costs
Marginal income	500	
Fixed costs	400	+ $100 in fixed costs
Profit	$ 100	$200 in profit is required

A marginal income statement based on these changes is required.

2. Our basic relationships (variable expense and marginal income ratios) have changed. Step 1 in our analysis is to hold volume constant and compute the new relationships:

	Original	(Ratio)	(Changes)	New Statement Holding Volume Constant	(Ratio)
Sales	$1,000		(−10%)	$ 900	
Variable costs	500	(50%)	(+10%)	550	(60%)
Marginal income	500	(50%)		350	(40%)
Fixed costs	400		+$100	500	
Profit (loss)	$ 100			$(150)	

As we have not met our profit requirement of $200, a change in volume (number of units sold) is needed.

3. To obtain the solution to this problem, let us start with known facts:

Profit required is	$200
Fixed costs are	500
Marginal income is	$700

We also know that marginal income is 40% of sales, hence, the revised sales figure is $700/.40 = $1,750. The revised marginal income statement is:

PRO FORMA
MARGINAL INCOME STATEMENT

Sales	$1,750
Variable costs	1,050 (60%)
Marginal income	700 (40%)
Fixed costs	500
Profit	$ 200

Note that the volume necessary to achieve $200 net income in the face of the proposed changes is a 94% increase in the number of units sold, 1,750/.90 − 1,000/1.00 = 944 or 94% of 1,000. (N_2 volume is 194% of N_1 volume.)

4. A variation of the problem is to state the profit requirement as a percentage of sales instead of a fixed amount. Returning to Step 1, let us modify the changes:

		Changes
Sales	$1,000	− 10% in unit selling price
Variable costs	500	+ 10% in unit variable costs
Marginal income	500	
Fixed costs	400	+ $100 in fixed costs
Profit	$ 100	Profit equal to 25% of new sales is required

5. We proceed through Step 2 above, and note that our ratios have changed:

   VC ratio from 50% to 60%
   MI ratio from 50% to 40%

6. Marginal income covers fixed expenses and net income (or loss), hence, 40% of sales is available for fixed expenses *and* net income. As we require net income = 25% sales, only 15% of sales is available for fixed expenses, hence:

$$\left(\frac{\$500}{.15}\right) = \text{New Sales of } \$3{,}333$$

7. Our *pro forma* marginal income statement in response to the changes in 4 is:

		% of Sales
Sales	$3,333	
Variable costs	1,998	(60%)
Marginal income	1,335	(40%)
Fixed costs	500	(15%)
Profit	$ 835	(25%)

MARGINAL INCOME ANALYSIS AND CONTRIBUTION TO PROFIT

Another important use of marginal income analysis is to determine "contribution to profit." This approach enables us to evaluate projects or departments on the basis of their contribution to profit, by which we really mean "contribution to marginal income" (fixed expenses and profit). Because variable expenses generally can be traced directly to their respective projects or departments, the *marginal income* figure is a more valid measure of operating efficiency than is *net income.* To arrive at project or departmental net income, it is necessary to allocate fixed expenses to the various projects or departments on some appropriate basis. For example, rent paid—which is a fixed expense—can be apportioned among departments in the ratio of the space they occupy.

To illustrate the contribution to profit idea, consider the example of a lumber company that has the following marginal income statement.

LUMBER COMPANY
MARGINAL INCOME STATEMENT

Sales	$100,000	
Variable costs	30,000	
Marginal income	70,000	
Fixed costs	60,000	
Profit	$ 10,000	(10%)

Suppose that sawdust, which was previously a waste product, can now be marketed. Sales of sawdust are expected to be $10,000 a year, and the variable costs of operating the sawdust department are expected to amount to $5,000 a year.

If we are asked to cost the sawdust department by itself, it might be considered rational to allocate 10% of the fixed costs of $60,000 to this new operation, in that sawdust sales are 10% of lumber sales. The resulting statement would show sawdust to be unprofitable.

SAWDUST DEPARTMENT
MARGINAL INCOME STATEMENT

Sales	$10,000
Variable costs	5,000
Marginal income	5,000
Fixed costs	6,000
Profit	$ (1,000)

This is a misleading picture, because the $6,000 was allocated from lumber and does not represent additional costs of doing business. Looking at both departments under the new assumption is necessary in order to evaluate the impact of sawdust operations on the firm as a whole:

LUMBER-SAWDUST COMPANY
MARGINAL INCOME STATEMENT

	Lumber	Sawdust	Total
Sales	$100,000	$10,000	$110,000
Variable costs	30,000	5,000	35,000
Marginal income	70,000	5,000	75,000
Fixed costs	54,000	6,000	60,000
Profit	$ 16,000	$ (1,000)	$ 15,000 (14%)

We now have a clearer picture of operations as a whole. Sawdust has increased the net income ratio from 10% to 14%. There is no question the firm is better off financially under the new arrangement. But we have not yet solved the measurement problem at the departmental level. Would a department head of sawdust be content or be motivated by showing his operations at a net loss? Of course not. So we could manipulate fixed costs until we reached a ratio which was agreeable to both depart-

LUMBER-SAWDUST COMPANY
MARGINAL INCOME STATEMENT

	Lumber	Sawdust	Total
Sales	$100,000	$10,000	$110,000
Variable costs	30,000	5,000	35,000
Marginal income	70,000	5,000	75,000
	(70%)	(50%)	
Fixed costs			60,000
Profit			$ 15,000

Contribution to profit (Fixed expenses & profit) $\frac{\$70,000}{75,000} = 93\%$ $\frac{\$5,000}{75,000}$ (7%)

ment heads. Or, preferably, we could recognize the arbitrary nature of allocating fixed costs[6] and the dubious value of comparing departmental performance on the basis of profit, and instead compare performance on the basis of marginal income as a percentage or ratio of profit.

Another application of marginal cost analysis is presented in the appendix to chapter 11 where it is used to determine cut-off in credit risks.

18.10 SUMMARY

The function of cost accounting is to provide management with the data it needs for the planning and control of operations. We distinguished between *costing* and *pricing*, recognizing that factors other than cost enter into pricing decisions.

We discussed cost accounting concepts in the context of four categories: (1) time-oriented, (2) traceability-oriented, (3) control-oriented, and (4) behaviorally-oriented. These categories are not exclusive. For example, rent expense is a *period* cost in (1); it might be *direct* or *indirect* in (2), depending upon whether or not it relates to one *cost center* or more than one; it would be a *controllable* cost in (3) if one person had complete responsibility for determining rent; and it is a *fixed* cost in (4).

The behavioral category consists of fixed, semi-variable, and variables accounts. Fixed costs are not responsive to changes in an activity index, semi-variable costs do change but not in direct proportion, while variable costs change in direct proportion. Every firm has a macro-activity index, with many minor ones which operate as surrogates of the major one.

To reduce behavioral costs to linear relationships, we separate the fixed and variable elements of semi-variable costs. Three methods for doing this were discussed: (1) high and low points, (2) scattergraph, and (3) method of least squares.

We are now able to construct the conventional break-even chart and convert it into a marginal break-even chart. The key items in a marginal break-even chart are: (1) margin of safety, (2) margin of safety ratio, (3) variable cost ratio, and (4) marginal income ratio.

This leads us into cost-volume-profit analysis, where we can alter four of five variables simultaneously to measure the effect of changes on *pro forma* operations. The variables are (1) number of units sold, (2) unit selling price, (3) unit variable cost, (4) fixed costs, and (5) profit.

We discussed four examples using a multi-step formula approach and illustrated a graphic solution to Example 4 in Exhibit 18-26.

[6] The allocation of fixed costs or overhead is important in determining the "full cost" of various cost centers, as discussed in chapter 19.

CHAPTER 18 REFERENCES AND ADDITIONAL READINGS

GENERAL

Benston, George J. *Contemporary Cost Accounting and Control.* Belmont, Calif.: Dickenson Publishing Company, 1970.

Bierman, Harold Jr., and Dyckman, Thomas R. *Managerial Cost Accounting.* New York: The Macmillan Company, 1971.

Cooper, W. W. *Historical and Alternative Costs: A Study in Some Relations between the Economic Theory of the Firm and Accounting Control of Operations.* Pittsburgh: Carnegie Institute of Technology, 1950.

Dean, Joel. "Cost Structure of Entreprises and Break-Even Charts." *American Economic Review Supplement* 38, no. 2 (May 1948); 153–64.

Dearden, John. *Cost and Budget Analysis.* Englewood Cliffs, N.J.: Prentice-Hall, Inc., 1962.

Horngren, Charles T. *Cost Accounting: A Managerial Emphasis.* Englewood Cliffs, N.J.: Prentice-Hall, Inc., 1962.

Ijiri, Yuji. *Management Goals and Accounting for Control.* Chicago: Rand McNally & Co., 1965.

Luoma, Gary A. *Accounting Information in Managerial Decision-Making for Small and Medium Manufacturers.* Research Monograph 2. New York: National Association of Accountants, 1967.

Matz, Adolph; Curry, Othel J.; and Frank, George W. *Cost Accounting.* 4th ed. Cincinnati: South-Western Publishing Company, 1967.

Terrill, William A., and Patrick, Albert W. *Cost Accounting for Management.* New York: Holt, Rinehart & Winston, Inc., 1965.

BREAK-EVEN AND COST-VOLUME-PROFIT ANALYSIS

Arnstein, William E., and Mack, Edgar A. "A New Approach to the Break-Even Chart." *Management Services,* March–April 1964, pp. 60–62.

Bell, Albert L. "Break-Even Charts Versus Marginal Graphs." *Management Accounting,* February 1969, pp. 32–35, 48.

Brault, Rejean. "Utility of the Classical Break-Even Chart: A Critique." *Cost and Management* (Canada), March–April 1969, pp. 24–27.

Charnes, A.; Cooper, W. W.; and Ijiri, Y. "Break-Even Budgeting and Programming to Goals." *Journal of Accounting Research,* Spring 1963, pp. 16–43.

Chumachenko, Nikolai G. "Once Again: The Volume-Mix-Price/Cost Budget Variance Analysis." *The Accounting Review,* October 1968, pp. 753–62.

Dow, Alice S., and Johnson, Orace. "The Break-Even Point Concept: Its Development and Expanding Applications." *Management Accounting,* February 1969, pp. 29–31, 48.

Ferrara, William L. "Break-Even for Individual Products, Plants, and Sales Territories." *Management Services,* July–August 1964, pp. 38–47.

Givens, Horace R. "An Application of Curvilinear Break-Even Analysis." *The Accounting Review,* January 1964, pp. 141–43.

Goggans, Travis P. "Break-Even Analysis with Curvi-linear Functions." *The Accounting Review,* October 1965, pp. 867–71.

Jaedicke, Robert K., and Robichek, Alexander A. "Cost-Volume-Profit Analysis Under Conditions of Uncertainty." *The Accounting Review,* October 1964, pp. 917–26.

Jenkins, David O. "Cost-Volume-Profit Analysis." *Management Services,* March–April 1970, pp. 55–57.

Manes, Rene. "A New Dimension to Break-Even Analysis." *Journal of Accounting Research,* Spring 1966, pp. 87–100.

Mitchell, G. B. "Break-Even Analysis and Capital Budgeting." *Journal of Accounting Research,* Autumn 1969, pp. 332–38.

Moore, Carl L. "An Extension of Break-Even Analysis." *Management Accounting,* May 1969, pp. 55–58.

Morrison, Thomas A., and Kaczka, Eugene. "A New Application of Calculus and Risk Analysis to Cost-Volume-Profit Changes." *The Accounting Review,* April 1969, pp. 330–43.

Raun, Donald L. "Volume-Cost Analysis—The Multiple Regression Analysis Approach." *Management Accounting,* December 1966, pp. 53–55.

Vernon, Thomas H. "Airlines and the Elusive B-E Point." *The Financial Analysts Journal,* May–June 1969, pp. 51–57.

Weiser, Herbert J. "Break-Even Analysis: A Re-Evaluation." *Management Accounting,* February 1969, pp. 36–41.

FIXED AND VARIABLE COSTS

Gynther, R. S. "Improving Separation of Fixed and Variable Expenses." *NAA Bulletin,* June 1963, pp. 29–38.

Jensen, Robert E. "A Multiple Regression Model for Cost Control—Assumptions and Limitations." *The Accounting Review,* April 1967, pp. 265–73.

Pierce, Richard F. "The Importance of the Distinction Between Fixed and Variable Costs." *NAA Bulletin,* May 1964, pp. 19–26.

Tingey, Sherman. "Difficulties in Identifying Fixed and Variable Costs." *Budgeting,* March–April 1968, pp. 25–28.

RESPONSIBILITY ACCOUNTING SYSTEMS

Beyer, Robert. *Profitability Accounting for Planning and Control.* New York: The Ronald Press Company, 1963.

Cooke, Robert B. "Responsibility Reporting of Return on Investment." *Management Accounting,* July 1967, pp. 24–29.

Ferrara, William L. "Responsibility Accounting—A Basic Control Concept." *NAA Bulletin,* September 1964, pp. 11–19.

O'Connell, Neil F., "Responsibility Accounting and Reports," *The Journal of Accountancy,* September 1968, pp. 81–84.

Pintado, Jose Manuel. "Responsibility Accounting." *Management Services,* March–April 1965, pp. 34–40.

CHAPTER 18 QUESTIONS, PROBLEMS, AND CASES

18- 1. "*Fixed* and *variable* costs are linear by definition, while the profiles of *semi-variable* costs differ markedly." Discuss.

18- 2. What are the two principle objectives of *cost accounting?*

18- 3. "The formal financial statements of a firm do not meet the information needs of managers." Specifically, what are the shortcomings of formal statements?

18- 4. How does the cost accounting function relate to the financial accounting functions? Show your answer as a diagram depicting financial and cost accounting in a systems relationship.

18- 5. Distinguish between a *primary* and a *functional* classification of accounts. Which classification yields more useful information from a managerial viewpoint? Why?

18- 6. Describe how each of the following cost accounting functions are achieved:
(a) Putting meaning into historical data.
(b) Prevention of serious losses.
(c) Providing cost data for planning decisions.

18- 7. "The principles of cost accounting are applicable to all of the activities of a firm, e.g., marketing and administration, as well as to all types of organizations, including governmental and not-for-profit entities." Discuss.

18- 8. For each of the following pricing situations, indicate the regulatory agency involved:
(a) Railroad freight and passenger rates
(b) Airline rates
(c) Telephone rates
(d) Brokerage fees

18- 9. To avoid antitrust suits, the market is kept competitive by the big manufacturer charging the same prices as are necessary to keep the little manufacturer in business. Explain the paradox of this situation.

18-10. Give at least five examples of specific expenses found in the following cost categories:
(a) Administrative expenses
(b) Indirect labor
(c) Production overhead (excluding indirect labor)
(d) Distribution expenses

18-11. Identify the lettered parts of a diagram depicting the flow of costs through production inventories:

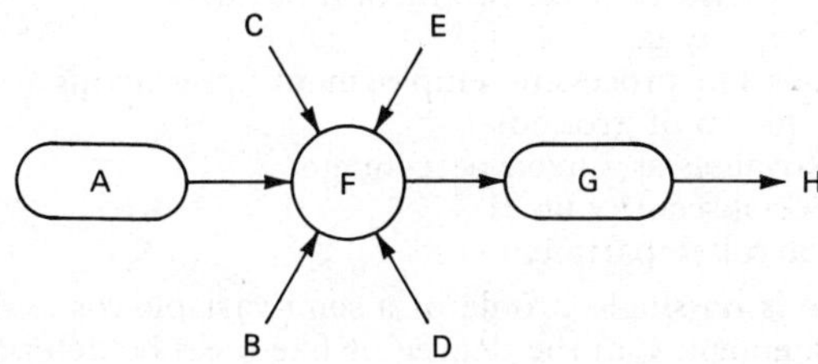

18-12. Define or explain the use of the following terms and phrases:
(a) "Salvage factor" (when reduction in price is anticipated)
(b) Standard cost
(c) "Prime" production costs
(d) Joint product
(e) By-product
(f) "Controllable" cost
(g) "Non-controllable" cost
(h) Differential cost
(i) Imputed cost
(j) Out-of-pocket cost
(k) Postponable costs
(l) Production function
(m) Normal capacity

18-13. What two assumptions underlie the classification of behavioral costs?

18-14. Explain the characteristics of costs found in each of the following categories, and identify and define the most frequently used sub-classifications under each:
(a) Time-oriented costs
(b) Traceability-oriented costs
(c) Control-oriented costs
(d) Behaviorally-oriented costs

18-15. "While historical cost underlies financial accounting as it is practiced at present, in cost accounting we have more freedom to experiment with other cost bases, as our data is consumed only within the firm." Identify and explain some alternative cost bases and point out instances in which such cost bases are an improvement over historical cost for management purposes.

18-16. Explain the meaning and relevancy of *sunk costs* for making decisions in the present or future.

18-17. "Most modern business activity is based on what products should cost rather than on what they do cost." Explain the meaning of this statement and cite a few examples.

18-18. In terms of the degree of precision for preparation, distinguish between *standard* costs and *estimated* costs.

18-19. Give one example of a situation for each graph in Exhibit 18-14. (Note: Do not use the same examples given in the illustrative text problem.)

18-20. Classify the following items as either fixed, variable, or semi-variable and where applicable identify a possible activity index for each:
(a) Sum-of-the-years'-digits depreciation
(b) Building repairs
(c) Electricity consumption—constant rate
(d) Rent
(e) Legal retainer fees
(f) Superintendence
(g) Fire insurance on production facilities
(h) Property tax
(i) Costs of processing employment applications
(j) Upkeep of grounds
(k) Royalties at a fixed percentage
(l) Social security taxes
(m) Payroll department costs

18-21. "There is no single profile of a semi-variable cost." Explain the meaning of this statement. Can the degree of fixedness be determined from a graphical profile? How?

18-22. Explain why *costing* a product is different from *pricing* a product. Show the distinction with a diagram.

18-23. Distinguish between *direct* and *indirect* costs by explaining their traceability to various levels or tiers of cost centers.

18-24. Distinguish between *joint product* costs and *by-product* costs. What is the conventional means of accounting for each type of cost? What is included in the inventoriable cost of a by-product? Suggest a rule determining when a particular product is a by-product and when it is a joint product.

18-25. What is a *responsibility accounting system?* What is the principle characteristic of the system? What benefits can be derived by instituting such a system in a production environment?

18-26. Explain the concept of *opportunity* cost and how such a concept can be usefully applied to the control of operations and to the planning of future operations and/or asset acquisitions.

18-27. Define and graphically illustrate the degree of responsiveness of the following costs to an activity index.
(a) Fixed cost
(b) Variable cost
(c) Semi-variable cost

18-28. Define a *cost center.* In what respect is a cost center analogous to a system?

18-29. Distinguish between *marginal income* and *profit.*

18-30. Identify a possible macro-index of activity for each of the following types of organizations:

(a) Commercial firms
(b) High schools
(c) Airlines
(d) Libraries
(e) Hospitals

18-31. "It is only by comparing resources consumed against the macro-index that we are able to make efficiency judgments on organizations." What are the efficiency judgments that should concern us? How is this comparison against the macro-index illustrative of the process-system relationship first discussed in chapter 1?

18-32. "While each organization has a macro-activity index, it also has numerous minor ones. We make the bold assumption in cost accounting that the minor ones are *surrogates* of the macro-index." What are the possible advantages and disadvantages arising from such an assumption? What is the practical necessity of making such assumption?

18-33. "Our ability to separate costs in terms of behavior rests upon two important assumptions:
(a) A time period of one year.
(b) A normal macro-activity range."

Explain what is meant by each assumption and the importance of such assumptions in determining our ability to separate costs by behavior. If operations fall outside of our normal macro-activity range, what are the consequences on cost behavior?

18-34. Given the cost data of a particular account, what conditions would you look for in determining the account's cost behavior?

18-35. Describe the six steps in applying the high and low point method for separating the fixed and variable portions of a semi-variable cost.

18-36. Define and distinguish:
(a) Fixed costs
(b) Variable costs
(c) Semi-variable costs

Give three examples of each.

18-37. What are the five variables in cost-volume-profit analysis? What is the purpose of cost-volume-profit analysis?

18-38. Describe the five steps in applying the scattergraph method for separating the fixed and variable portions of a semi-variable cost.

18-39. Identify the lettered parts of the marginal break-even chart.

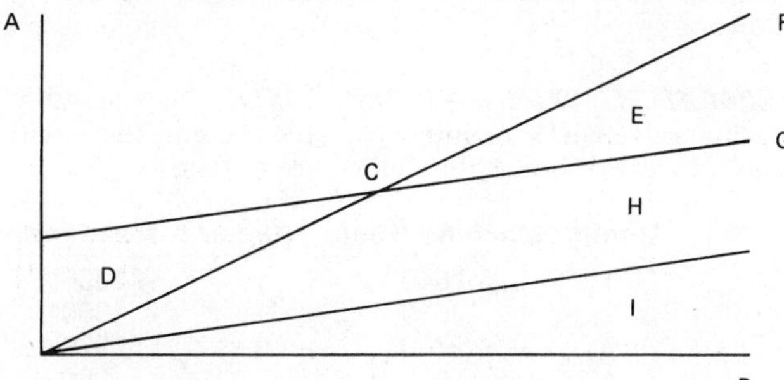

18-40. Define and explain the use of the following relationships for marginal break-even analysis:
(a) Margin of safety
(b) Margin of safety ratio
(c) Variable cost ratio
(d) Marginal income ratio

18-41. What is meant by an *activity index?* Distinguish between a *macro-* and *micro-* activity index.

18-42. ***SCHEDULE OF COST OF GOODS MANUFACTURED AND SOLD*** From the following account balances prepare a schedule of cost of goods manufactured and sold for 19*x*2:

	Dec. 31 19x1	Dec. 31 19x2
Raw materials inv.	17,420	16,960
Raw materials used	88,310	96,740
Work-in-process	34,750	26,220
Finished goods	74,700	91,400
Production overhead	51,910	58,130
Direct labor	124,600	144,700

18-43. ***BEHAVIORALLY-ORIENTED COSTS*** The Shullman Production Corporation used the number of units produced as a *macro-index* of activity. The corporation produces only one product, a high-quality, compact electric wall heater. Some selected operating data for the last two years is as follows:

	19x1	19x2
Production in units	12,400	13,800
Salesmen's salary	$ 58,000	$ 59,260
Misc. selling expenses	40,460	42,770
Advertising	17,488	17,656
Packing costs	29,264	32,568
Direct materials	322,400	358,800
Direct labor	173,600	193,200
Indirect labor	61,000	64,500
Depreciation	14,700	14,700
Indirect materials	13,732	14,684
Heat and light	5,608	5,846
Equipment repairs	5,292	5,404

The management of Shullman Production Corporation wants to know what the balances of each of the selected accounts would have been if the company had produced 14,500 units in 19*x*2. Assuming that only the past two year's data is relevant, compute the balance for each selected account.

18-44. ***SEPARATING SEMI-VARIABLE COSTS*** The monthly postings to the machinery repair & maintenance account, and the monthly production activity expressed in machine hours, are as follows:

Month	Machine Hours	Repair & Maintenance Cost
1	2640	$366
2	2510	350
3	2700	370
4	1820	280
5	1900	268
6	2140	330
7	1800	284
8	1620	240
9	1780	320
10	2110	350
11	2300	337
12	2600	414

Required:

(a) Determine the variable cost rate per machine hour and the fixed monthly cost of repair and maintenance of machinery using each of the following methods:
  (1) High and low point
  (2) Scattergraph
  (3) Linear regression (least-squares procedure)

(b) Explain the advantages and disadvantages of each method and indicate which method you prefer in this circumstance. Explain the rationale for your preference.

18-45. ***BREAK-EVEN ANALYSIS*** If the break-even point is 2,000 units at a selling price of $24 per unit and 3,400 units at a selling price of $18 per unit, what is the *break-even point in dollars* at a selling price of $22 per unit (in all instances, assume a zero desired profit)?

18-46. ***COST-VOLUME-PROFIT ANALYSIS*** The Gleason Manufacturing Co. produces two products, A and B. The unit costs and unit selling prices are shown below. The fixed cost per unit is based on a normal activity of 20,000 units of A and 30,000 units of B per year.

	A	B
Selling price per unit	1.10	1.20
Direct material cost per unit	.40	.60
Direct labor cost per unit	.30	.20
Variable manufacturing overhead	.14	.06
Fixed manufacturing overhead	.10	.12
Variable selling & administrative	.08	.10
Fixed selling & administrative	.06	.04

Assume the Gleason Co. is currently producing 22,000 units of A and 25,000 units of B and expects to continue this activity level for an indefinite period. In addition, the company sells all that it produces during any one period. Is there an advantage to dropping production of product B and adding product C if 45,000 units of C could be produced without disturbing the present output of product A and without any increase in the capacity of the plant? Product C could be sold at a unit price of $1.00 and produced at a *prime unit cost* (labor & materials) which is 10% lower than the prime unit cost of product B. However, all other variable costs for C will increase by 20% per unit over what is now incurred by product B per unit. Express your answer as an *increase* or *decrease* in net income, and *indicate the dollar amount.*

18-47. ***BREAK-EVEN ANALYSIS*** Carey Company sold 100,000 units of its product at $20 per unit. Variable costs are $14 per unit (manufacturing costs of $11 and selling costs of $3). Fixed costs are incurred uniformly throughout the year and amount to $792,000 (manufacturing costs of $500,000 and selling costs of $292,000). There are no beginning or ending inventories.

Required: Compute the following:

(a) The break-even point for this product.
(b) The number of units that must be sold to earn a net income of $60,000 for the year before income taxes.
(c) If the income tax rate is 40%, the number of units that must be sold to earn an after-tax income of $90,000.
(d) If labor costs are 50 % of variable costs and 20 % of fixed costs, what is the increase in the number of units required to break even if there is a 10 % increase in wages and salaries?

(Adapted from the CPA exam.)

18-48. ***COST OF GOODS MANUFACTURED***

	Case 1	Case 2	Case 3	Case 4
Sales	325,000	J	88,300	CC
Direct labor	105,000	10,000	T	DD
Variable production overhead	28,000	K	7,100	10,750
Work-in-process 1/1/71	2,000	2,500	1,300	EE
Fixed selling & admin. expenses	25,000	L	12,150	14,000
Raw materials used	A	M	8,500	17,500
Fixed production overhead	B	2,500	3,100	4,750
Raw materials purchased	C	17,900	8,850	FF
Variable selling & admin. expenses	D	16,300	U	9,500
Raw materials inventory 1/1/71	2,000	1,100	V	4,500
Total production overhead	E	8,000	W	GG
Finished goods inventory 12/31/71	11,000	N	3,400	6,500
Raw materials inventory 12/31/71	3,000	O	2,100	3,000
Work-in-process 12/31/71	17,000	1,500	2,500	13,250
Goods completed during year	195,000	35,000	Y	72,750
Prime costs	140,000	Q	30,500	46,500
Operating expenses	G	29,500	35,200	II
Cost of goods manufactured & sold	H	42,500	Z	JJ
Gross profit	I	45,250	AA	KK
Finished goods inventory 1/1/71	16,000	17,000	2,800	7,800
Net income	65,000	R	BB	33,500

Required:

Find values for each letter, considering each case independently.

18-49. ***BREAK-EVEN ANALYSIS—COST-VOLUME-PROFIT RELATIONSHIPS*** Consider the following four *independent situations:*

(a) If fixed costs are \$800 and the break-even point in dollars is \$2,600 (desired income is zero), what volume of *sales in dollars* must be achieved to earn a profit of \$100?

(b) When the Hanafee Company has sales of \$9,600, there is a net profit of \$1,000; when sales are \$13,200, profit is \$2,200. What is the Hanafee Company's break-even point in dollars?

(c) Suppose teapots have a unit contribution margin (UCM) of \$1.25 and a break-even point of 176,000 units (with zero net income). If the desired net income is \$78,000, what number of units must be sold?

(d) Suppose the variable cost ratio (VCR) is .70 and the income is \$57,000 when sales are \$378,000. What is the break-even point in dollars (with a desired net income of zero)?

18-50. ***MARGINAL INCOME—BREAK-EVEN ANALYSIS*** Ruidoso Ski Lodge operates a ski shop, restaurant, and lodge during the 120-day ski season from November 15 to March 15. The proprietor is considering changing his operations and keeping the lodge open all year.

Results of the operations for the year ended March 15, 1969, were as follows:

	Ski Shop		Restaurant		Lodge	
	Amount	Percent	Amount	Percent	Amount	Percent
Revenue	$27,000	100%	$40,000	100%	$108,000	100%
Costs:						
Costs of goods sold	14,850	55	24,000	60		
Supplies	1,350	5	4,000	10	7,560	7
Utilities	270	1	1,200	3	2,160	2
Salaries	1,620	6	12,000	30	32,400	30
Insurance	810	3	800	2	9,720	9
Property taxes on building	540	2	1,600	4	6,480	6
Depreciation	1,080	4	2,000	5	28,080	26
Total costs	20,520	76	45,600	114	86,400	80
Net income or (loss)	$ 6,480	24%	$ (5,600)	(14)%	$ 21,600	20%

(a) The lodge has 100 rooms and the rate from November 15 to March 15 is $10 per day for one or two persons. The occupancy rate from November 15 to March 15 is 90%.

(b) Ski shop and restaurant sales vary in direct proportion to room occupancy.

(c) For the ski shop and restaurant, cost of goods sold, supplies, and utilities vary in direct proportion to sales. For the lodge, supplies and utilities vary in direct proportion to room occupancy.

(d) The ski shop, restaurant, and lodge are located in the same building. Depreciation on the building is charged to the lodge. The ski shop and restaurant are charged with depreciation only on equipment. The full cost of the restaurant equipment became fully depreciated on March 15, 1969, but the equipment has a remaining useful life of three years. The equipment can be sold for $1,200 but will be worthless in three years. All depreciation is computed by the straight-line method.

(e) Insurance premiums are for annual coverage for public liability and fire insurance on the building and equipment. All building insurance is charged to the lodge.

(f) Salaries are the minimum necessary to keep each facility open and are for the ski season only, except for the lodge security guard, who is paid $5,400 per year.

Two alternatives are being considered for the future operation of Ruidoso Ski Lodge:

(1) The proprietor believes that during the ski season the restaurant should be closed because "it does not have enough revenue to cover its out-of-pocket costs." It is estimated that lodge occupancy would drop to 80% of capacity if the restaurant were closed during the ski season. The space utilized by the restaurant would be used as a lounge for lodge guests.

(2) The proprietor is considering keeping the lodge open from March 15 to November 15. The ski shop would be converted into a gift shop if the lodge should be operated during this period with conversion costs of $1,000 in March and $1,000 in November each year. It is estimated that revenues from the gift shop would be the same per room occupied as revenues from the ski shop, that variable costs would be in the same ratio to revenues and that all other costs would be the same for the gift shop as for the ski shop. The occupancy rate of the lodge at a room rate of $7 per day is estimated at 50 percent during the period from March 15 to November 15 whether or not the restaurant is operated.

Required:

(Ignore income taxes and use thirty days per month for computational purposes.)

a. Prepare a projected income statement for the ski shop and lodge from November 15, 1969, to March 15, 1970, assuming the restaurant is closed during this period and all facilities are closed during the remainder of the year.
b. Assume that all facilities will continue to be operated during the four-month period of November 15 to March 15 of each year.
   1. Assume that the lodge is operated during the eight months from March 15 to November 15. Prepare an analysis which indicates the projected marginal income or loss of operating the gift shop and lodge during this eight-month period.
   2. Compute the minimum room rate which should be charged to allow the lodge to break even during the eight months from March 15 to November 15, assuming the gift shop and restaurant are not operated during this period.

(From the CPA exam.)

18-51. ***COST-VOLUME-PROFIT RELATIONSHIPS—FORWARD ANALYSIS*** The Tolkien Company had the following marginal income statement for 19*x*1:

Sales	$270,000
Variable costs	180,000
Marginal income	90,000
Fixed costs	75,000
Profit	$ 15,000

The company has acquired your help in determining the financial consequences of the following changes:
(a) 15% increase in unit selling price
(b) 5% decrease in unit variable cost
(c) $12,000 increase in fixed cost
(d) $20,000 increase in profit

Required:

(1) Compute the following:
   a. The 19*x*2 sales in dollars.
   b. The required percentage increase in the number of units sold in 19*x*2.
(2) Suppose the new profit requirement is expressed as 18% of the new sales revenue. Compute the following:
   a. The 19*x*2 sales in dollars.
   b. The 19*x*2 variable cost.
   c. The required percentage increase in the number of units sold in 19*x*2.

18-52. ***COST-VOLUME-PROFIT ANALYSIS***
(a) Reconstruct the *old* marginal income statement, given those changes which resulted in the new one:

Old	Changes based on old statement	New
Sales	+10% in unit selling price	$11,000
Variable costs	−10% in unit variable cost	5,400
Marginal income		5,600
Fixed costs	−$1,000	4,000
Profit	Old profit was 20% of old sales	$ 1,600

(b) If old volume (no. of units sold) = 100%, what does new volume equal?
(c) What is the margin of safety ratio based on *new* sales?
(d) What is the margin of safety ratio based on *old* sales?

18-53. ***BREAK-EVEN ANALYSIS*** Metal Industries, Inc., operates its production department only when orders are received for one or both of its two products, two sizes of metal discs. The manufacturing process begins with the cutting of doughnut-shaped rings from rectangular strips of sheet metal; these rings are then pressed into discs. The sheets of metal, each four feet long and weighing thirty-two ounces, are purchased at $1.36 per running foot. The department has been operating at a loss for the past year as shown below.

Sales for the year	$172,000
Expenses	177,200
Net loss for the department	$ 5,200

The following information is available:
(a) Ten thousand four-foot pieces of metal yielded 40,000 large discs, each weighing four ounces and selling for $2.90, and 40,000 small discs, each weighing 2.4 ounces and selling for $1.40.
(b) The corporation has been producing at less than "normal capacity" and has had no spoilage in the cutting step of the process. The skeletons remaining after the rings have been cut are sold for scrap at $.80 per pound.
(c) The variable conversion cost of each large disc is 80% of the disc's direct material cost and variable conversion cost of each small disc is 75% of the disc's direct material cost. Variable conversion costs are the sum of direct labor and variable overhead.
(d) Fixed costs were $86,000.

Required:
(1) For each of the parts manufactured, prepare a schedule computing:
a. Unit material cost after deducting the value of salvage.
b. Unit variable conversion cost.
c. Unit contribution margin.
d. Total contribution margin for all units sold.
(2) Assuming you computed the material cost for large discs at $.85 each and for small discs at $.51 each, compute the number of units the corporation must sell to break even based on a normal production capacity of 50,000 units. Assume no spoiled units and a product mix of one large disc to each small disc.

(From the CPA exam.)

18-54. ***COST-VOLUME-PROFIT RELATIONSHIPS—BACKWARD ANALYSIS*** The Nulty Company had the following marginal income statement for 19*x*2:

Sales	$92,000
Variable costs	63,000
Marginal income	29,000
Fixed costs	20,000
Profit	$ 9,000

Last year, after acquiring your expert advice, the company instituted the following changes in the financial operation of 19*x*1:
(a) There was a 7% increase in unit selling price.
(b) There was a 10% increase in unit variable cost.
(c) Fixed cost was reduced by $8,000.
(d) Profit increased by $2,000.

Required:

(1) Compute the following:
  a. The 19x1 sales in dollars.
  b. The 19x1 variable cost.
  c. The 19x1 profit.
  d. The percentage increase or decrease in the number of units sold in 19x2.

(2) If the profit for 19x1 was 6% of sales for 19x1, compute the following:
  a. The 19x1 sales in dollars.
  b. The 19x1 variable cost.
  c. The percentage increase or decrease in the number of units sold in 19x2.

18-55. ***MARGINAL BREAK-EVEN ANALYSIS*** The Martin Company produces only one product. Operating data for this product is as follows:

(a) Selling price per unit $24.00

(b) Variable manufacturing costs per unit:

Direct materials	8.00
Direct labor	4.50
Variable overhead	2.70
	$15.20

(c) Fixed overhead $154,600
(d) Variable selling and administrative cost per unit $2.40
(e) Fixed selling and administrative $89,800
(f) Estimate sales for 19x1 are 47,800 units

Required: Compute the following:

(1) Break-even point in sales dollars.
(2) Margin of safety.
(3) Margin of safety ratio.
(4) Variable cost ratio.
(5) Marginal income ratio.

18-56. ***JOINT PRODUCT COSTS*** A, B, and C are joint products. Their cost for November, up to the point of separation, was $486. The following additional data is also available:

	A	B	C
Sales for November (in units)	18	32	12
Inventory of finished units on November 1	10	6	2
Selling price per unit	$10	$12	$ 6

There are no beginning or ending work-in-process inventories. FIFO is used for transferring out of finished goods inventory.

Required:

(a) If the November 30 inventory of A is six units, B is four units, and C is five units, what is the value of these ending inventories using the relative sales value technique?
(b) Assuming the same information as in part (a) and that the beginning inventory (November 1) of A is valued at $72, B at $21, and C at $14, what is the gross margin of each product line?
(c) If C is a by-product, what is the ending inventory valuation of C assuming the same information as in part (a)?

(d) What would be your answer for part (a) if there are further processing costs incurred beyond the split-off point for total production:
A: $50 B: $95 C: $40

18-57. ***COST-VOLUME-PROFIT ANALYSIS*** The president of Beth Corporation, which manufactures tape decks and sells them to producers of sound reproduction systems, anticipates a 10% wage increase on January 1 of next year to the manufacturing employees (variable labor). He expects no other changes in costs. Overhead will not change as a result of the wage increase. The president has asked you to assist him in developing the information he needs to formulate a reasonable product strategy for next year.

You are satisfied by regression analysis that volume is the primary factor affecting costs and have separated the semi-variable costs into their fixed and variable segments by means of the least-squares criterion. You also observe that the beginning and ending inventories are never materially different.

Below are the current year data assembled for your analysis:

Current selling price per unit	$ 80.00
Variable cost per unit:	
Material	$ 30.00
Labor	12.00
Overhead	6.00
Total	$ 48.00
Annual volume of sales	5,000 units
Fixed costs	$51,000

Required:

Provide the following information for the president, using cost-volume-profit analysis:

(a) What increase in the selling price is necessary to cover the 10% wage increase and still maintain the current profit-volume-cost ratio?

(b) How many tape decks must be sold to maintain the current net income if the sales price remains at $80.00 and the 10% wage increase goes into effect?

(c) The president believes that an additional $190,000 of machinery (to be depreciated at 10% annually) will increase present capacity (5,300 units) by 30%. If all tape decks produced can be sold at the present price and the wage increase goes into effect, how would the estimated net income before capacity is increased compare with the estimated net income after capacity is increased? Prepare computations of estimated net income before and after the expansion.

(From the CPA exam.)

18-58. ***SCHEDULE OF COST OF GOODS MANUFACTURED—COST BEHAVIOR ANALYSIS*** Using the following information, prepare a schedule of cost of goods manufactured:

Direct material used: $1,720
Manufacturing overhead:
Fixed: $400
Variable: $520
Selling & administrative expenses:
Fixed: $200
Variable: $380
Direct materials purchased: $1,840

Sales: $4,680
Direct material inventory *beginning* is 60% of direct material inventory *ending*
Work-in-process inventory:
Beginning: $100
Ending: $100
Break-even point in dollars: $3,120
There is no beginning or ending finished goods inventory.

Hint: Use the break-even point in dollars to calculate direct labor.

18-59. ***SEPARATING SEMI-VARIABLE COSTS*** The Carlson Manufacturing Company uses units of production as a *macro-index* of activity. Over the past five years the total semi-variable production cost and the total production is as follows:

Year	Production in Units	Semi-Variable Cost
1	48,000	$ 93,200
2	52,000	89,000
3	56,000	114,000
4	66,000	135,000
5	80,000	136,400

Required:

(a) If the production next year is planned at 86,000 units, what is the expected total for semi-variable production costs using:
(1) Linear regression by least squares.
(2) High and low point method.

(b) If there is any variation between the expected semi-variable costs and the actual, what are the plausible reasons?

(c) Suppose the machine hours for the five years are as follows:

Year	Machine Hours
1	38,400
2	40,300
3	48,800
4	55,100
5	60,000

Using machine hours as an activity base, what is the expected total semi-variable product costs next year if 86,000 units are planned and the method for separating the semi-variable cost is:
(1) Linear regression by least squares.
(2) High and low point method.

(d) Which activity index—units-of-production or machine hours—produces the best separation of fixed and variable costs?

18-60. ***COST-VOLUME-PROFIT RELATIONSHIPS*** The Playrite Golf Supply Company has a branch store that sells only special order golf shoes. The following financial data is available for the branch store:

	Per Pair
Selling price	$16.00
Variable costs:	
Direct labor (@ $2.00/hr)	$ 4.00
Raw material	5.00
Salesman's commission	1.60
	$10.60
Fixed expenses:	
Rent on store	$ 4,000
Manager's salary	7,500
Advertising (local)	1,500
Other fixed costs	2,000
Salesman's salaries	13,000
	$28,000

Required:

Consider each question independently. Present all calculations to the nearest pair of shoes or nearest dollar.

(a) What is the break-even point in sales dollars and in number of shoes?

(b) If the company policy is that each store must submit 10% of gross sales to the central office for nation-wide advertising, what would be the break-even point?

(c) The store manager feels he can sell 3,000 more pairs by lowering the price by $2.50 and raising the salesman's commissions by $.35 per pair. Would the increase in volume compensate for the lowering of the price?

(d) Another alternative is to reduce the salesman's salaries to $9,500 and increase their commission to 15% of sales. How would these changes affect the store's break-even point (in pairs of shoes and dollar sales)?

(e) If the company requires the store to have a net income before taxes of $27,000, what sales volume would be necessary to generate such an income? In your calculations, consider the information in part (b) to be applicable.

CHAPTER

19

COST ACCOUNTING SYSTEMS

19.1. TYPES OF COST ACCOUNTING SYSTEMS

In this chapter we discuss three major types of cost accounting systems: (1) departmental, (2) job, and (3) process. Specifically, we are concerned with the problems of cost measurement and allocation incident to departmental, job, and process cost accounting.

The concept of a cost center and of direct and indirect costs are central to our discussion of these systems. We have said that a *cost center* is a unit of an organization in which we aggregate costs for purposes of control. The whole organization is certainly a cost center; but in most instances we want controls at lower levels, so we organize divisions, departments, product lines, jobs, and other activity centers into specific cost centers.

We have said that *direct* costs are incurred entirely within a cost center, while *indirect* costs are shared among cost centers. Indirect costs are generally referred to as *overhead* or *burden.*

19.2 ACCOUNTING FOR OVERHEAD

Overhead costs are incurred for the benefit of more than one cost center. Generally, overhead extends to all cost centers. Some examples of overhead are:

1. *Rent:* where more than one cost center shares a common facility.
2. *Maintenance:* janitorial, building, grounds, and equipment maintenance which benefit several cost centers.
3. *Cafeteria:* services the needs of various cost centers.
4. *Advertising:* some advertising may be direct, i.e., it relates to a single product. Other advertising may be general, designed to maintain or improve the image of the firm as a whole.
5. *General administration:* head office expenses which benefit all operations of an organization. This type of overhead is often referred to as "G & A," i.e., general and administration.

We observe that some overhead activities, such as maintenance, cafeteria, and G & A, form cost centers in their own right. Other overhead activities, such as rent or supervision, are not organized as cost centers. The cost centers which serve as overhead to other departments or units are referred to as *service cost centers.* Their sole purpose is to service *production cost centers.*

Again, the term *production* is used here in its broadest meaning. As stated before, every organization has a production function, which may be organized into many cost centers. This distinction between *production* and *service* centers is critical in departmental cost accounting, as we shall see presently.

ALLOCATING OVERHEAD

In order to arrive at the full cost of running a production cost center, overhead that benefits many cost centers must be allocated to each of them in an equitable manner. By *full cost* we mean the cost that the production cost center would incur internally if overhead services were not available. For example, if space were not provided for all centers, each center would have to rent its own facilities. If janitorial services were not provided centrally, each center would have to contract for its own services, and so forth. The purpose in allocating overhead is to spread the burden of common services over a number of benefitting production centers. Presumably the cost of pooling services should be less than having each cost center negotiate for its own needs.

ALLOCATION BASES

One way of allocating overhead to production cost centers is to use a different basis for each type of overhead (Exhibit 19-1).

These bases for allocating overhead are the ones which appear to be most typical in practice; however, there are suitable alternatives for each item. In fact, there is no general rule as to which basis should be used in a particular case. Each organization wrestles constantly with these bases in an effort to achieve equity.

EXHIBIT 19-1 BASES FOR ALLOCATING OVERHEAD

I. UNSTRUCTURED (Overhead activities that are not organized into cost centers.)

Type of Overhead	Illustrative Basis of Allocation to Production Cost Centers
1. Rent	Square footage.
2. Depreciation – buildings	Square footage.
3. Heating & cooling	Square footage.
4. Lighting	Kilowatt-hours or number of fixtures.
5. Telecommunications	Number of employees, or number of outlets.
6. Supervision	Number of employees.
7. Depreciation – equipment	Operating hours.
8. Indirect materials and supplies	Number of units or centers.
9. Property tax	Square footage.
10. Inspection	Number of units completed.

II. STRUCTURED (Overhead activities that are organized into cost centers.)

Type of Overhead	Illustrative Basis of Allocation to Production Cost Centers
1. General and administration	Number of employees or prime cost.
2. Cafeteria	Number of employees.
3. Payroll	Number of employees.
4. Personnel	Number of employees.
5. Insurance & retirement	
a. Fire insurance	Square footage.
b. Health insurance	Number of employees.
c. Workmen's compensation	Number of employees.
d. Retirement	Number of employees.
6. Transportation	Number of employees.
7. Maintenance	Square footage.
8. Recreation	Number of employees.
9. Purchasing	Units of direct material.
10. Advertising (general)	Number of employees, prime cost, or sales volume.
11. Legal	Number of employees.
12. Computer services	Number of employees.
13. Research & development	Prime cost.
14. Storage	Material quantity.
15. Labor relations	Number of union employees.

Rather than use a separate basis for each type of overhead, some organizations prefer to use one basis for all overhead. An example illustrative of this approach follows.

Example: Our company manufactures mobile homes. It makes four basic models, and to ease computation we assume that only one mobile home in each category is manufactured in a typical one-month period. We are provided with the information below. Our objective is to allocate the $30,000 of overhead among the four products by using a single basis.

OPERATING DATA	Model A	Model B	Model C	Model D	Total
Prime costs:					
Direct materials	$3,000	$ 5,000	$ 8,000	$ 4,000	$20,000
Direct labor costs	5,000	8,000	10,000	7,000	30,000
Total prime costs	8,000	13,000	18,000	11,000	50,000
Overhead	–	–	–	–	30,000
Total cost	$ –	$ –	$ –	$ –	$80,000
Direct labor hours	2,000	4,000	4,000	2,000	12,000
Average labor rate	2.50	2.00	2.50	3.50	

At this point we do not have a *full* cost for any model, so we are unable to measure the extent to which each model is profitable. We need to allocate the $30,000 in overhead to the four models. Notice that total costs remain unchanged by allocation. The total cost of the four models will remain $80,000 after allocation.

The $30,000 of overhead is comprised of the following items:

Overhead Accounts

Supplies & indirect materials	$2,000	Rent	$ 3,000
Advertising (general)	3,000	Utilities	2,000
Maintenance	2,000	Property tax	1,000
Executive salaries	4,000	Insurance:	
Secretarial	2,000	Plant	2,000
General office expenses	2,000	Workmen's comp.	1,000
Supervision	2,000	Depreciation on equipment	2,000
		Total overhead	$30,000

What we are seeking is *one basis* for allocating total overhead. Here are six suggested methods:

1. Direct material cost
2. Direct labor cost
3. Prime costs
4. Direct labor hours
5. Selling price
6. Contribution to margin

The selling price of each model is determined by competition:

	Model A	Model B	Model C	Model D	Total
Selling price	$15,000	$24,000	$31,000	$20,000	$90,000
Total costs	–	–	–	–	(80,000)
Profit	–	–	–	–	$10,000
% of sales					11.1%

Direct Material Cost

We have $30,000 in overhead and $20,000 in direct material cost, so the overhead allocation rate per dollar of direct materials is $30,000/$20,000 = $1.50. Under this method, overhead assigned to A is $1.50 × $3,000 = $4,500; B is $1.50 × $5,000 = $7,500; C is $1.50 × $8,000 = $12,000; and D is $1.50 × $4,000 = $6,000.

	Model A	Model B	Model C	Model D	Total
Selling price	$15,000	$24,000	$31,000	$20,000	$90,000
Prime costs	8,000	13,000	18,000	11,000	50,000
Overhead	4,500	7,500	12,000	6,000	30,000
Total cost	(12,500)	(20,500)	(30,000)	(17,000)	(80,000)
Profit	$ 2,500	$ 3,500	$ 1,000	$ 3,000	$10,000
% of sales	16.7%	14.6%	3%	15.0%	11.1%

Under this method of allocating overhead, Model C appears to be least profitable.

Direct Labor Costs

Direct labor costs = $30,000 versus $30,000 in overhead, so the allocation rate is $30,000/$30,000 = $1.00. Overhead is therefore the same as direct labor cost for each model.

	Model A	Model B	Model C	Model D	Total
Selling price	$15,000	$24,000	$31,000	$20,000	$90,000
Prime costs	8,000	13,000	18,000	11,000	50,000
Overhead	5,000	8,000	10,000	7,000	30,000
Total cost	(13,000)	(21,000)	(28,000)	(18,000)	(80,000)
Profit	$ 2,000	$ 3,000	$ 3,000	$ 2,000	$10,000
% of sales	13.3%	12.5%	9.7%	10.0%	11.1%

Prime Costs

Prime costs total $50,000 versus $30,000 in overhead, so the allocation rate is $30,000/$50,000 = .60. The overhead assigned to A is .60 × $8,000 = $4,800; B is .60 × $13,000 = $7,800; C is .60 × $18,000 = $10,800; and D is .60 × $11,000 = $6,600.

	Model A	Model B	Model C	Model D	Total
Selling price	$15,000	$24,000	$31,000	$20,000	$90,000
Prime costs	8,000	13,000	18,000	11,000	50,000
Overhead	4,800	7,800	10,800	6,600	30,000
Total costs	(12,800)	(20,800)	(28,800)	(17,600)	(80,000)
Profit	$ 2,200	$ 3,200	$ 2,200	$ 2,400	$10,000
% of sales	14.7%	13.3%	7.1%	12.0%	11.1%

Direct Labor Hours

Direct labor hours total 12,000. The overhead allocation rate is $30,000/12,000 = $2.50 per hour. Overhead allocated to A is 2,000 hrs. × $2.50 = $5,000; B is 4,000 hrs. × $2.50 = $10,000; C is 4,000 hrs. × $2.50 = $10,000; and D is 2,000 hrs. × $2.50 = $5,000.

	Model A	Model B	Model C	Model D	Total
Selling price	$15,000	$24,000	$31,000	$20,000	$90,000
Prime costs	8,000	13,000	18,000	11,000	50,000
Overhead	5,000	10,000	10,000	5,000	30,000
Total costs	(13,000)	(23,000)	(28,000)	(16,000)	(80,000)
Profit	$ 2,000	$ 1,000	$ 3,000	$ 4,000	$10,000
% of sales	13.3%	4.2%	9.7%	20.0%	11.1%

Selling Price

Total selling price is $90,000 versus $30,000 in overhead. The allocation rate is $30,000/$90,000 = 33.3%. Overhead allocated to A is $15,000/3 = $5,000; B is $24,000/3 = $8,000; C is $31,000/3 = $10,300; and D is $20,000/3 = $6,700.

	Model A	Model B	Model C	Model D	Total
Selling price	$15,000	$24,000	$31,000	$20,000	$90,000
Prime costs	8,000	13,000	18,000	11,000	50,000
Overhead	5,000	8,000	10,300	6,700	30,000
Total costs	(13,000)	(21,000)	(28,300)	(17,700)	(80,000)
Profit	$ 2,000	$ 3,000	$ 2,700	$ 2,300	$10,000
% of sales	13.3%	12.5%	8.7%	11.5%	11.1%

Contribution to Margin

The contribution to "margin" (overhead and profit) of each model is its selling price minus prime costs, i.e., A, $7,000; B, $11,000; C, $13,000; and D, $9,000. This totals $40,000, which is equal to overhead + profit. The overhead allocation rate is $30,000/$40,000 = .75. Overhead assigned to A is .75 × $7,000 = $5,250; B is .75 × $11,000 = $8,250; C is .75 × $13,000 = $9,750; and D is .75 × $9,000 = $6,750.

	Model A	Model B	Model C	Model D	Total
Selling price	$15,000	$24,000	$31,000	$20,000	$90,000
Prime costs	8,000	13,000	18,000	11,000	50,000
Overhead	5,250	8,250	9,750	6,750	30,000
Total costs	(13,250)	(21,250)	(27,750)	(17,750)	(80,000)
Profit	$ 1,750	$ 2,750	$ 3,250	$ 2,250	$10,000
% of sales	11.7%	11.5%	10.5%	11.25%	11.1%

COMPARISON OF METHODS

We can summarize the six methods on the basis of their profit margins:

	Model A	Model B	Model C	Model D	Total
1. Direct materials cost	16.7%	14.6%	.3%	15.0%	11.1%
2. Direct labor cost	13.3	12.5	9.7	10.0	11.1
3. Prime costs	14.7	13.3	7.1	12.0	11.1
4. Direct labor hours	13.3	4.2	9.7	20.0	11.1
5. Selling price	13.3	12.5	8.7	11.5	11.1
6. Contribution to margin	11.7	11.5	10.5	11.25	11.1
Range	5.0%	10.4%	10.2%	10.0%	0

The selection of a basis for allocating overhead has an important bearing on how we evaluate the four models. Our opinion of Model C, for example, would differ markedly between methods 1 and 6.

Which method is correct? There is no precise answer to this question. On the one hand, it can be said that no method is correct since the choice of any method is arbitrary. On the other hand, just *any* method does not appear to be satisfactory, because some appear to be better than others. This suggests that some selection process is possible. Obviously the managers of the production cost centers would want to play an active role in deciding on the basis to be used.

One "theoretical" approach would be to analyze the composition of overhead items and choose the basis that is common to most items.

The authors' preference is the contribution to margin method, as this assigns overhead to production cost centers based on their ability to bear it. The disadvantage is that this method penalizes those centers which make the greatest contribution to margin by allocating to them relatively higher amounts of overhead. For this reason managerial performance should be based on contribution to margin statistics rather than on final profit.

A portion of the $30,000 of overhead is *fixed.* If we eliminate one model, fixed overhead will have to be borne by three models instead of four. This is an important consideration in deciding whether or not to discontinue a cost center.

19.3 APPLYING OVERHEAD

The overhead allocation rate is determined for an advance period of time, usually for the ensuing year. Using our preceding example, overhead for the next month was estimated at $30,000. If we use *direct labor hours* as the basis for allocating overhead, the *applied overhead rate* is $30,000/12,000 = $2.50 per hour. This means that for every direct hour that is charged to a job, $2.50 is included in the rate to cover overhead.

The *effective* labor rates for the four models are:

	Model A	Model B	Model C	Model D	Average
Direct labor rates	$2.50	$2.00	$2.50	$3.50	$2.50
+ Applied overhead rate	2.50	2.50	2.50	2.50	2.50
= Effective labor rate	$5.00	$4.50	$5.00	$6.00	$5.00

The rate that is charged to a customer is the *effective rate;* the employee is paid the *direct labor rate;* and the *applied overhead rate* is retained by the organization to cover its expected overhead.

Apart from changes in rate, the number of actual hours can vary from the 12,000 expected hours, and/or we can incur more or less overhead than expected. Observe what happens to overhead from a variance in hours.

1. Excess Labor Hours, No Change in Overhead

Suppose it takes 14,000 hours to complete the models.

a. Direct labor cost will be 14,000 × \$2.50 = \$35,000

b. Applied overhead will be 14,000 × 2.50 = 35,000

If the four products are sold for \$90,000 and there is no change in direct materials cost, the income statement for the period would be:

				Alternative Method
Sales		$90,000		$90,000
Cost of goods sold:				
Direct materials	$20,000			
Direct labor	35,000			
Applied overhead	35,000	90,000	90,000	
*Less adjustment for overapplied overhead			5,000	85,000
Gross profit on basis of applied overhead		0		
*Add: Overapplied overhead		5,000		
Gross profit		$ 5,000		$ 5,000

*The adjustment may be made to cost of goods sold or to gross profit.

2. Less Labor Hours, No Change in Overhead

Suppose it takes 10,000 hours to complete the models:

a. Direct labor cost will be 10,000 × \$2.50 = \$25,000

b. Applied overhead will be 10,000 × 2.50 = 25,000

The resulting income statement would be:

Sales		$90,000
Cost of goods sold:		
Direct materials	$20,000	
Direct labor	25,000	
Applied overhead	25,000	70,000
Gross profit on the basis of applied overhead		20,000
Less: Underapplied overhead		(5,000)
Gross profit		$15,000

We see that where actual is greater than applied, we have *under-applied* overhead. Where applied is greater than actual, we have *over-applied* overhead. As noted above, the adjustment is made in the income statement either to cost of goods sold *or* to gross profit.

When direct labor hours is used as the basis for applying overhead, an efficiency in labor hours will result in underapplying overhead, other conditions remaining stable. An excess in labor hours will produce a "profit" in overhead. As the responsibility for overhead and labor reside at two different places in most organizations, this cause-and-effect relationship needs to be understood and monitored if counter-productive behavior is to be minimized.

19.4 DEPARTMENTAL COST SYSTEMS

Earlier we distinguished between *productive* and *service* cost centers. In commercial organizations the production cost centers are often referred to as *profit* centers in that their activities are revenue-producing.

The production centers in an educational institution would be those departments where learning and research takes place. Supporting those educational functions are a variety of service centers such as (1) administration, (2) maintenance, (3) food service, (4) traffic and police, (5) student residence, and (6) athletics. It must be remembered that these service centers are not indispensable. It is always possible to contract for outside services. It is the production functions in organizations that are indispensable if an entity is to survive.

In addition to servicing production cost centers, service centers also minister to each other.

In order to estimate the *full* cost of each center, proration of costs from service centers to production centers and from service centers to each other is necessary.

EXAMPLE: TWO SERVICE DEPARTMENTS

Consider a school with four departments: education department 1 (A); education department 2 (B); a cafeteria (X), and a transportation department (Y).

	Producing Centers		Service Centers		
	A	B	X	Y	Total
Direct costs	$12,000	$15,000	$10,000	$8,000	$45,000
Unstructured overhead[1]	3,000	4,000	2,000	1,000	10,000
Total center costs	$15,000	$19,000	$12,000	$9,000	$55,000

The distribution of effort by the two service departments is represented as follows:

[1] "*Unstructured overhead*" is defined in Exhibit 19-1. This type of overhead is assigned to departments first, based on the overhead allocation discussed previously.

Basis	A	B	X	Y
Number of employees	40%	50%	(100%)	10%
Number of persons	35%	45%	20%	(100%)

40% of the persons who use the cafeteria are employees of department A, 50% from department B, and 10% from department Y. The cost of feeding department X employees is absorbed by the other three departments, because no "X's" would eat if the cafeteria service were contracted from without.[2] Also, 35% of the persons transported are from department A, 45% from department B, and 20% from department X.

This type of problem is solved through a set of simultaneous equations:

$$X = \$12{,}000 + .20Y \qquad (1)$$
$$Y = \$\ 9{,}000 + .10X \qquad (2)$$

1. Ordering the symbols we have:

$$X - .20Y = \$12{,}000 \qquad (3)$$
$$-.10X + Y = 9{,}000 \qquad (4)$$

2. Eliminate X by retaining (3) and multiplying (4) by 10 times:

$$X - .20Y = \$\ 12{,}000 \qquad (5)$$
$$-X + 10.00Y = 90{,}000 \qquad (6)$$
$$9.80Y = \$102{,}000 \qquad (7)$$
$$Y = \frac{\$102{,}000}{9.80} \qquad (8)$$
$$Y = \underline{\underline{\$10{,}400}} \qquad (9)$$

3. Solve for X by substituting \$10,400 for Y in equation (3):

$$X - .20(\$10{,}400) = \$12{,}000 \qquad (10)$$
$$X - \$2{,}080 = \$12{,}000 \qquad (11)$$
$$X = \underline{\underline{\$14{,}080}} \qquad (12)$$

4. Distribute service centers to producing centers to obtain *full* cost of producing centers. The *full* cost of service centers was computed above, i.e., $Y = \$10{,}400$; $X = \$14{,}080$:

[2]There is no allocation by a service department to itself, the reason being that if that department were eliminated there would be no need for the department to service its own needs.

	Producing Centers		Service Centers		
	A	B	X	Y	Total
Total center costs	$15,000	$19,000	$12,000	$ 9,000	$55,000
Distribute Y	3,640	4,680	2,080	(10,400)	–
Distribute X	5,640	7,040	(14,080)	1,400	–
Full cost of producing centers	$24,280	$30,720	–	–	$55,000
Full cost of service centers			$14,080	$10,400	

Production centers A and B now bear the total cost of $55,000. The full costs of service centers X and Y appear below the line—they are not part of the $55,000. They are memoranda items only.

If the trustees of the school contemplate contracts for food service and/or transportation, the relevant costs are:

The point of indifference[3] is:	
1. For department X	$14,080
2. For department Y	10,400
3. For departments Y and X	$24,480

Notice that the *unstructured overhead* is included in the full cost of the service centers. If these costs are not recovered through contracting for services, they would be reallocated to the remaining departments, thereby increasing their costs.

Interpreting the Data

What do the figures $14,080 and $10,400 mean? Consider a decision as to an outside contract for X. The $14,080 is the break-even point (if the outside bid is less than $14,080, the contract offer should be accepted; if it exceeds $14,080, we should continue to operate X) where the following assumptions are present:

1. There will be no residual costs of X, i.e., the contract will alleviate all costs associated with operating department X, and
2. Department Y can reduce its costs by extent of prior service to X, which amounts to $2,080 in this example.

Of course, other assumptions are possible. To compute the break-even point of decisions of this type, the following framework is of value:

1. The present out-of-pocket costs of operating all service departments (in this case, two departments with a total of $21,000) should not be exceeded.

[3]The *point of indifference* is analogous to break-even. In the above example, any bid that is lower than the point of indifference should be accepted; any bid that is higher should be rejected.

2. Prepare a tableau in which X, Y, and B-E are variables which in sum must not exceed the present out-of-pocket amount ($21,000). Given values for X and Y, B-E can be ascertained readily, where various assumptions exist.

A DECISION REGARDING X

Total	Y	X	B-E		Assumptions
$21,000 =	$9,000 +	$ 0 +	$12,000	a.	X has no residual costs. Y cannot reduce costs at all by reason of eliminating X.
$21,000 =	$9,000 +	$1,000 +	$11,000	b.	X has $1,000 in residual costs. Y cannot reduce costs at all.
$21,000 =	$6,920 +	$1,000 +	$13,080	c.	X has $1,000 in residual costs. Y can reduce costs to the extent of prior service to X ($9,000 − $2,080 = $6,920).
$21,000 =	$6,920 +	$ 0 +	$14,080	d.	X has no residual costs. Y can reduce costs to the extent of prior service to X.

It follows that a replacement decision involving one service department requires an analysis of all service departments. An elimination decision involving a producing department requires an analysis of all producing *and* service departments.

EXAMPLE: THREE SERVICE DEPARTMENTS

In this more comprehensive example, four methods for allocating costs are illustrated. Methods 1 and 2 do not result in full costing of service centers, hence we do not advocate their use. These methods are of historical significance, but students may still encounter these methods in practice.

You will notice that as problems of this type become more complex, solution by simultaneous equations is increasingly tedious. It is for this reason that Method 3 has value. Under this method we use iterative arithmetic to allocate costs. Three successive "cycles" is usually adequate. On the fourth or last cycle we use the step-down method to close out the service centers. Method 3 lends itself to computer programming. By iteration we can handle organizations with numerous departments. Matrix algebra also provides a solution to cost-allocation problems of this type, but this method is not illustrated.

The four methods we do illustrate are:

1. Method 1 – Direct Allocation
2. Method 2 – Step-down Allocation
3. Method 3 – Iterative Allocation
4. Method 4 – Simultaneous Equations Allocation

Example: A corporation has three *producing* departments: grinding, forming, and finishing; and three *service* departments: building services, office services, and employee services. The following data is provided.

Department	Direct Department Expense	Labor Hours	Square Feet	No. of Employees
A. Grinding	$10,000	3,000	700	60
B. Forming	8,000	2,500	600	40
C. Finishing	7,000	2,050	400	30
D. Office services	5,000	2,500	300	30
E. Building services	6,000	4,000	200	20
F. Employee services	9,000	4,000	200	40
Total	$45,000	18,050	2,400	220

Bases for allocating *service* department expenses to *producing* departments are:

Service Department	Basis of Allocation
D. Office services	Labor Hours
E. Building services	Square Feet
F. Employee services	No. of Employees

Allocation under the four methods mentioned follows:

Method 1—Direct Allocation

Rule: No service department expenses are allocated to other service departments—allocation is made only to producing departments. The order of "closing" service departments is unimportant where this method is used:

	Producing			Service			
	A	B	C	D	E	F	Total
Direct costs	$10,000	$ 8,000	$ 7,000	$5,000	$6,000	$9,000	$45,000
Allocate F	4,160	2,760	2,080	–	–	(9,000)	–
Allocate E	2,460	2,120	1,420	–	(6,000)	–	–
Allocate D	1,990	1,650	1,360	(5,000)	–	–	–
Producing centers	$18,610	$14,530	$11,860	–	–	–	$45,000
Service centers				$5,000	$6,000	$9,000	$20,000

Computations: As there is no reciprocal allocation among service centers, only production center data is used in the allocation process:

1. *Department F* costs are allocated on the basis of number of employees in A, B, and C. The total number of employees in these departments is 130. Accordingly

$$\frac{60}{130}(\$9{,}000) \text{ is assigned to A; } \frac{40}{130}(\$9{,}000) \text{ to B; and } \frac{30}{130}(\$9{,}000) \text{ to C}$$

2. *Department E.* Using square footage as the basis,

$\frac{7}{17}$ (\$6,000) is assigned to A; $\frac{6}{17}$ (\$6,000) to B; and $\frac{4}{17}$ (\$6,000) to C

3. *Department D.* Using labor hours as the basis,

$\frac{300}{755}$(\$5,000) is assigned to A; $\frac{250}{755}$(\$5,000) to B; and $\frac{205}{755}$(\$5,000) to C

Method 2—Step-Down Allocation

Rule: There is a partial distribution of service departments expenses to other service departments under this method. The general practice is to distribute the service department with the highest total costs first. "Highest" total cost is based on a comparison of direct costs. The order in which departments are closed is important in this method:

	Producing			Service			
	A	B	C	D	E	F	Total
Direct costs	$10,000	$ 8,000	$ 7,000	$5,000	$6,000	$9,000	$45,000
Allocate F	3,000	2,000	1,500	1,500	1,000	(9,000)	—
Allocate E	2,450	2,100	1,400	1,050	(7,000)	—	—
Allocate D	3,000	2,500	2,050	(7,550)	—	—	—
Producing centers	$18,450	$14,600	$11,950	—	—	—	$45,000
Service centers				$7,550	$7,000	$9,000	$23,550

Computations: Service centers are closed in the order of greatest costs.

1. *Department F* is allocated to A, B, C, D, and E.

$$A = \frac{60}{180}(\$9{,}000);\ B = \frac{40}{180}(\$9{,}000);\ C = \frac{30}{180}(\$9{,}000);\ D = \frac{30}{180}(\$9{,}000);\ \text{and}$$

$$E = \frac{20}{180}(\$9{,}000)$$

As we are closing F, it is excluded from allocation.

2. *Department E* is allocated to A, B, C, and D.

$$A = \frac{7}{20}(\$7{,}000);\ B = \frac{6}{20}(\$7{,}000);\ C = \frac{4}{20}(\$7{,}000);\ D = \frac{3}{20}(\$7{,}000)$$

3. *Department F* is allocated to A, B, and C.

$$A = \frac{300}{755}(\$7{,}550);\ B = \frac{250}{755}(\$7{,}550);\ C = \frac{205}{755}(\$7{,}550)$$

Distribution Matrix—Methods 3 and 4

Before illustrating allocation under methods 3 and 4, it is necessary to prepare a distribution matrix which indicates the extent to which the service departments serve each other as well as the producing departments; in this case:

Service Distribution Matrix

	Producing			Service		
Service Dept.	**A**	**B**	**C**	**D**	**E**	**F**
D	19%	16%	13%	(100%)	26%	26%
E	32	27	18	14	(100)	9
F	33	22	17	17	11	(100)

Computations: There is reciprocal allocation among all service departments.

1. *Department D* service is distributed as follows:

$$A = \frac{300}{1{,}555} = 19\%;\ B = \frac{250}{1{,}555} = 16\%;\ C = \frac{205}{1{,}555} = 13\%;$$

$$E = \frac{400}{1{,}555} = 26\%;\ \text{and } F = \frac{400}{1{,}555} = 26\%$$

2. *Department E* is allocated as follows:

$$A = \frac{7}{22} = 32\%;\ B = \frac{6}{22} = 27\%;\ C = \frac{4}{22} = 18\%;$$

$$D = \frac{3}{22} = 14\%;\ \text{and } F = \frac{2}{22} = 9\%$$

3. *Department F* is allocated as follows:

$$A = \frac{6}{18} = 33\%;\ B = \frac{4}{18} = 22\%;\ C = \frac{3}{18} = 17\%;$$

$$D = \frac{3}{18} = 17\%;\ \text{and } E = \frac{2}{18} = 11\%$$

Method 3—Iterative Allocation

Rule: Each service department allocates to other service departments as well as to producing departments on the basis of the diminishing balances. Theoretically there is no limit to the number of "cycles" that can be used, but for practical purposes 3 to 4 "cycles" is adequate. The significance of the order in which service departments are closed is relatively unimportant.

		Producing			Service			
Cycle	**Detail**	**A**	**B**	**C**	**D**	**E**	**F**	**Total**
	Direct	$10,000	$ 8,000	$ 7,000	$5,000	$6,000	$ 9,000	$45,000
1	Allocate F	3,000	2,000	1,500	1,500	1,000	(9,000)	–
	Allocate E	2,240	1,890	1,260	980	(7,000)	630	–
	Allocate D	1,420	1,200	970	(7,480)	1,945	1,945	–
2	Allocate F	857	566	438	438	276	(2,575)	–
	Allocate E	710	600	400	311	(2,221)	200	–
	Allocate D	142	120	97	(749)	195	195	–
3*	Allocate F	130	88	66	66	45	(395)	–
	Allocate E	84	72	48	36	(240)	–	–
	Allocate D	40	34	28	(102)	–	–	–
Producing centers		$18,623	$14,570	$11,807	–	–	–	$45,000
Service centers (add items in parentheses)					$8,331	$9,461	$11,970	$29,762

*Use step-down method on the last iteration.

Method 4—Simultaneous Equations Allocation

Rule: The allocation of costs among service departments and to producing departments is determined by simultaneous equations. Three techniques are available: (1) elimination by addition or subtraction; (2) the canonical method; and (3) a multidimensional coordinate graph system. Elimination by addition or subtraction is illustrated:

Computations: Basic equations are developed from the matrix on p. 814:

$$
\begin{aligned}
D - .14E - .17F &= 5{,}000 && (1)\\
-.26D + E - .11F &= 6{,}000 && (2)\\
-.26D - .09E + F &= 9{,}000 && (3)
\end{aligned}
$$

1. Eliminate F between (1) and (2):

$$
\begin{aligned}
-11 \times (1) \quad & -11.00D + 1.54E + 1.87F = -55{,}000 && (4)\\
17 \times (2) \quad & -4.42D + 17.00E - 1.87F = 102{,}000 && (5)\\
& -15.42D + 18.54E = 47{,}000 && (6)
\end{aligned}
$$

2. Eliminate F between (2) and (3):

$$
\begin{aligned}
100 \times (2) \quad & -26.00D + 100.00E - 11.00F = 600{,}000 && (7)\\
11 \times (3) \quad & -2.86D - .99E + 11.00F = 99{,}000 && (8)\\
& -28.86D + 99.01E = 699{,}000 && (9)
\end{aligned}
$$

3. Solving for D
   Eliminate E between (6) and (9):

$$
\begin{aligned}
-99.01 \times (6) \quad & 1{,}526.73D - 1{,}835.65E = -4{,}653{,}470 && (10)\\
18.54 \times (9) \quad & -535.06D + 1{,}835.65E = 12{,}959{,}460 && (11)\\
& 991.67D = 8{,}305{,}990 && (12)\\
& D = \$8{,}376 && (13)
\end{aligned}
$$

4. Solving for E
Substitute $8,376 for D in (10):

$$1{,}526.73(8{,}376) - 1{,}835.65E = -4{,}653{,}470 \quad (14)$$
$$1{,}835.65E = 17{,}441{,}360 \quad (15)$$
$$E = \$9{,}502 \quad (16)$$

5. Solving for F
Substitute $8,376 for D and $9,502 for E in (3):

$$-.26\ (8{,}376) - .09\ (9{,}502) + F = 9{,}000 \quad (17)$$
$$F = \$12{,}033 \quad (18)$$

6. Summarizing:

$$D = \$\ 8{,}376$$
$$E = 9{,}502$$
$$F = 12{,}033$$

7. Check:

$$8{,}376 - .14(9{,}502) - .17(12{,}033) = 5{,}000$$
$$8{,}376 - 1{,}330 - 2{,}046 = 5{,}000$$
$$5{,}000 = 5{,}000$$
$$-.26(8{,}376) + 9{,}502 - .11(12{,}033) = 6{,}000$$
$$-2.178 + 9{,}502 - 1{,}324 = 6{,}000$$
$$6{,}000 = 6{,}000$$
$$-.26(8{,}376) - .09(9{,}502) + 12{,}033 = 9{,}000$$
$$-2{,}178 - 855 + 12{,}033 = 9{,}000$$
$$9{,}000 = 9{,}000$$

8. Distribute:

	Producing			Service			
	A	B	C	D	E	F	Total
Direct costs	$10,000	$ 8,000	$ 7,000	$5,000	$6,000	$ 9,000	$45,000
Allocate F	3,971	2,647	2,046	2,046	1,324	(12,033)	–
Allocate E	3,041	2,565	1,710	1,330	(9,502)	855	–
Allocate D	1,591	1,340	1,089	(8,376)	2,178	2,178	–
Producing centers	18,603	14,552	11,845	–	–	–	$45,000
				$8,376	$9,502	$12,033	$29,911

You will notice that the iterative allocation method approximates the correct solution after three "cycles." Each additional cycle would bring the Method 3 solution into closer agreement with Method 4.

Methods 1 and 2 do not give us the information needed to *full cost* the service centers.

19.5 JOB VERSUS PROCESS COST SYSTEMS

In *job* costing each job or unit of production is a cost center. In *process* costing all identical units of production *together* constitute a cost center.

Only overhead is allocated to the units of production in job costing, while all of the elements of production costs are allocated to units of production in process accounting (Exhibit 19-2).

EXHIBIT 19-2 ALLOCATION OF COSTS TO UNITS OF PRODUCTION

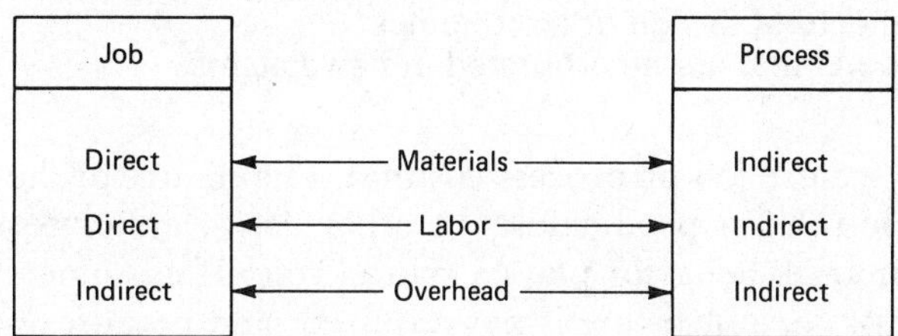

In job costing we are able to trace direct materials and direct labor to each job. Only overhead is allocated.

Example: In automobile service repair, mechanics' time is charged directly to each repair job, as are spare parts. Overhead is traditionally added to the direct labor rate. Labor and materials are *direct*—overhead is *indirect* or allocated.

In process costing it is not possible to trace direct materials or direct labor to any particular unit of production. Product lines are treated as cost centers rather than units within product lines. Production costs are assigned on an average basis. Overhead is allocated by some acceptable method, most often on the basis of number of units produced:

$$\frac{\text{Material} + \text{Labor} + \text{Overhead}}{\text{Number of Units Produced}} = \text{Cost Per Unit}$$

Example: In a bakery, it is not possible to trace the precise labor or materials in every loaf of bread. Labor, materials, and overhead are averaged over all of the loaves of bread.

Some cost systems are hybrid—they combine job and process costing in either order. Exhibit 19-3 lists some examples of typical cost systems:

EXHIBIT 19-3 EXAMPLES OF COST SYSTEMS

JOB

Highway construction	Prototypes
Major buildings	Medical and legal care
Custom printing	Automobile repair
Custom home construction	Advertising

EXHIBIT 19-3 (continued)

PROCESS

Petroleum production	Student education
Agricultural production	Lumber production
Automobile production	Gross printing
Tract homes	

HYBRID PROCESS-JOB (Job superimposed on a process)

Options added to basic automobile production.
Customizing basic airframe construction.

HYBRID JOB-PROCESS (Process superimposed on a job)

Architectural design of tract homes.
Cartoons that are incorporated in newspapers.

When do we use job or process costing? The nature of the activity is one determinant; e.g., petroleum production. In other cases, either cost system could be employed. Here market behavior plays a critical role. If customers are not willing to pay a differential price, job costing is not required; and because a job system is more costly, a good alternative is process costing. For example, customers would probably not be willing to pay more for one identical "basic" automobile than another, simply because more labor was charged to the job. However, they are willing to pay for automobile options, which makes *basic price + options* an ideal cost system for automobile manufacturers.

19.6 JOB COSTING SYSTEMS

The processing of accounting data through a job costing system is illustrated below:

A corporation has raw materials inventory of $12,000 on January 1, 19*x*6, and the following jobs finished and in process.

JOBS-IN-PROCESS
JANUARY 1, 19x6

Job No.	Direct Materials	Direct Labor	Applied Overhead	Total
C	$2,000	$ 3,000	$1,200	$ 6,200
D	3,000	4,000	1,600	8,600
E	4,000	8,000	3,200	15,200
	$9,000	$15,000	$6,000	$30,000

JOBS FINISHED
JANUARY 1, 19x6

Job No.	Direct Materials	Direct Labor	Applied Overhead	Total
A	$5,000	$6,000	$2,400	$13,400
B	4,000	5,000	2,000	11,000
	$9,000	$11,000	$4,400	$24,400

During the month of January, 19x6, the following transactions took place:

1. Jobs A and B were delivered to their customers.
2. Job D was finished and delivered to its customer.
3. Jobs C, E, and F were finished but were not delivered to customers.
4. Jobs G and H were still in process at the end of the month.
5. Materials costing $15,000 were purchased during January and added to raw materials inventory.
6. Job order costs were incurred by or distributed to the various jobs worked on during the month as follows:

Job No.	Direct Materials	Direct Labor	Applied Overhead	Total
C	$ 2,000	$ 1,000	$ 400	$ 3,400
D	1,000	800	320	2,120
E	—	1,000	400	1,400
F	4,000	4,000	1,600	9,600
G	3,000	3,000	1,200	7,200
H	2,000	4,000	1,600	7,600
	$12,000	$13,800	$5,520	$31,320

This information flows through the *Job Cost Records:*

JOB COST RECORDS

Job No. A		Materials	Labor	Overhead	Total	Status*		
						I	F	D
	Balance, Jan. 1	$5,000	$6,000	$2,400	$13,400			
	Added during January	—	—	—	—			
	Total, Jan. 31	$5,000	$6,000	$2,400	$13,400	x	x	x

Job No. B		Materials	Labor	Overhead	Total	Status		
						I	F	D
	Balance, Jan. 1	$4,000	$5,000	$2,000	$11,000			
	Added during January	—	—	—	—			
	Total, Jan. 31	$4,000	$5,000	$2,000	$11,000	x	x	x

Job No. C		Materials	Labor	Overhead	Total	Status		
						I	F	D
	Balance, Jan. 1	$2,000	$3,000	$1,200	$ 6,200			
	Added during January	2,000	1,000	400	3,400			
	Balance, Jan. 31	$4,000	$4,000	$1,600	$ 9,600	x	x	

*Status: I—In Process (EOM); F—Finished but not delivered (EOM); D—Finished and delivered (EOM); EOM—End of Month.

JOB COST RECORDS (CONTINUED)

Job No. D

	Materials	Labor	Overhead	Total	Status I	Status F	Status D
Balance, Jan. 1	$3,000	$4,000	$1,600	$ 8,600			
Added during January	1,000	800	320	2,120			
Balance, Jan. 31	$4,000	$4,800	$1,920	$10,720	x	x	x

Job No. E

	Materials	Labor	Overhead	Total	Status I	Status F	Status D
Balance, Jan. 1	$4,000	$8,000	$3,200	$15,200			
Added during January	—	1,000	400	1,400			
Balance, Jan. 31	$4,000	$9,000	$3,600	$16,600	x	x	

Job No. F

	Materials	Labor	Overhead	Total	Status I	Status F	Status D
Balance, Jan. 1	—	—	—	—			
Added during January	$4,000	$4,000	$1,600	$ 9,600			
Balance, Jan. 31	$4,000	$4,000	$1,600	$ 9,600	x	x	

Job No. G

	Materials	Labor	Overhead	Total	Status I	Status F	Status D
Balance, Jan. 1	—	—	—	—			
Added during January	$3,000	$3,000	$1,200	$ 7,200			
Balance, Jan. 31	$3,000	$3,000	$1,200	$ 7,200	x		

Job No. H

	Materials	Labor	Overhead	Total	Status I	Status F	Status D
Balance, Jan. 1	—	—	—	—			
Added during January	$2,000	$4,000	$1,600	$ 7,600			
Balance, Jan. 31	$2,000	$4,000	$1,600	$ 7,600	x		

The cost of jobs manufactured and sold report for the month of January would be as follows (assume actual overhead for January is $6,120):

COST OF JOBS MANUFACTURED AND SOLD REPORT
JANUARY 31 19x6

	Finished goods inventory, January 1			$24,400	
	Jobs-in-process, January 1		$30,000		
	Raw materials inventory, January 1	$12,000			
	Purchases during January	15,000			
	Raw materials available	27,000			
	Raw materials inventory, January 31	15,000			
	Raw materials used during January		12,000		
	Direct labor		13,800		
	Applied overhead		5,520		
	Total jobs-in-process for January		$61,320		
S1	Jobs-in-process, January 31		14,800		
	Jobs finished during January			46,520	
	Total finished jobs			$70,920	
S2	Finished goods inventory, January 31			35,800	
S3	Cost of jobs manufactured and sold				$35,120
S4	Add: Adjustment for under-applied overhead				690
	Cost of goods sold				$35,810

S1—SCHEDULE OF JOBS-IN-PROCESS
JANUARY 31, 19x6

Job No.	Direct Materials	Direct Labor	Applied Overhead	Total
G	$3,000	$3,000	$1,200	$ 7,200
H	2,000	4,000	1,600	7,600
Total	$5,000	$7,000	$2,800	$14,800

S2—SCHEDULE OF FINISHED JOBS
JANUARY 31, 19x6

Job No.	Direct Materials	Direct Labor	Applied Overhead	Total
C	$ 4,000	$ 4,000	$1,600	$ 9,600
E	4,000	9,000	3,600	16,600
F	4,000	4,000	1,600	9,600
Total	$12,000	$17,000	$6,800	$35,800

S3—SCHEDULE OF JOBS SOLD
JANUARY 31, 19x6

Job No.	Direct Materials	Direct Labor	Applied Overhead	Total
A	$ 5,000	$ 6,000	$2,400	$13,400
B	4,000	5,000	2,000	11,000
D	4,000	4,800	1,920	10,720
Total	$13,000	$15,800	$6,320	$35,120

S4–SCHEDULE OF APPLIED AND ACTUAL OVERHEAD

Overhead was applied on the basis of 40¢ per $1 of direct labor cost (40% × $13,800)	$5,520
Actual overhead for January was	6,210
Under-applied overhead was	$ 690

The overhead rate for January was too low to cover actual overhead; a rate of 45¢ per $1 of direct labor cost would have been adequate (45% × $13,800 = $6,210).

19.7 PROCESS COSTING SYSTEMS

Process costing would present very few problems if all units that were started in a period were also finished in that same period. We would sum materials, labor, and overhead costs and divide it by the number of units completed to arrive at the finished cost per unit. But this condition is not typical. Generally there are units at many different stages of completion at any particular point in time. For control purposes, we need to assess work-in-process at frequent intervals, not only at year-end.

Valuing work-in-process is the most difficult part of process costing. Often the process does not stop in fact, but we are asked as cost accountants to assume that operations do stop at a specific moment, during which time we are to value the work-in-process.

In chapter 1 we discussed the problem of measuring processes. We mentioned that the key to measuring a process is to adopt a scale (Exhibit 19-4). While there may be units at an infinite number of points in the process, the scale makes it possible for us to assume that all units are at one or another of the recognized stages of completion. In Exhibit 19-4, the directional arrow between the stages indicates that once an item has started at stage 0, it is *immediately* assumed to be at stage 1. All work-in-process between stages 1 and 2 is assumed to be at stage 2, and so forth.

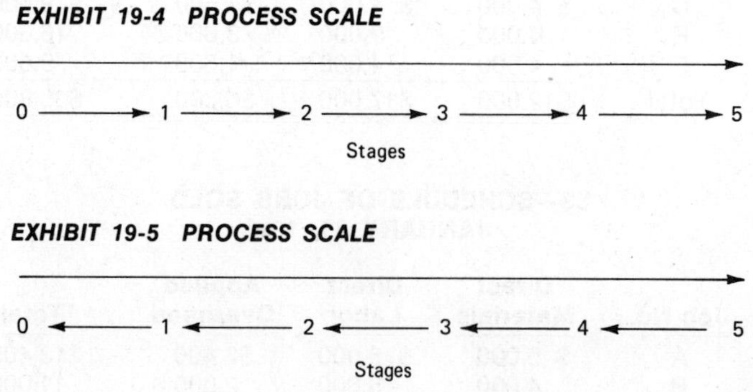

If the arrows are in the opposite direction, as in Exhibit 19-5, we assume that all units between 0 and 1 are at 0.

Both of these assumptions present us with problems: (1) The Exhibit 19-4 forward flow means that once an item has left stage 4 it is finished. But such items are not finished and additional costs must be incurred to finish them. (2) The Exhibit 19-5 reverse flow means that all the costs incurred on items between 0 and stage 1 are assigned to items at other stages, because theoretically we have no units between 0 and 1.

To overcome this problem we generally use forward flow until the next to last stage, as illustrated in Exhibit 19-6.[4]

When units have left stage 3 they are assumed to be at stage 4, and all units between stages 4 and 5 are assumed to be at stage 4. Only units that are 100% complete are at stage 5. The scale that is used in process costing is most commonly *percentage of completion* as shown in Exhibit 19-6.

EXHIBIT 19-6 PROCESS SCALE AND PERCENTAGE COMPLETION

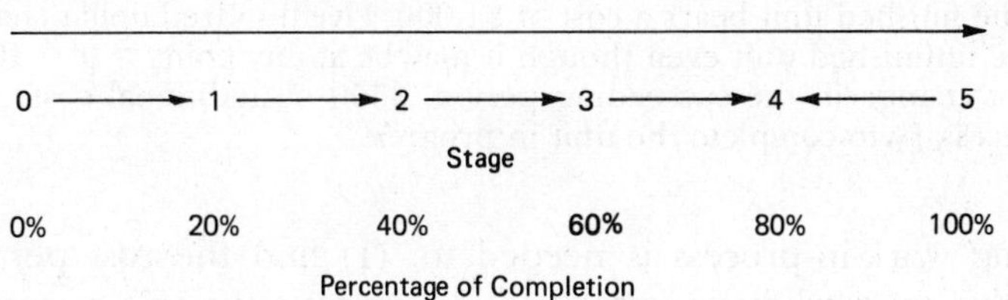

EQUIVALENT UNITS

The standard for measuring work-in-process is *equivalent units*, or more precisely, *equivalent finished units*. Let us illustrate this concept with a very simple example.

1. We have a process with only two stages of completion, 50% and 100%

   0 → 50% ← 100%

2. One item is finished (at stage 100%), the other item is in process and is assumed to be at stage 50%. (It could be anywhere between 0% and 100%)
3. Instead of one unit finished and one unit half finished, for cost accounting purpurposes we say that we have two units that are each 75% complete:

$$\begin{array}{lcl} 1 \text{ unit} & @\ 100\,\% = & 100 \\ \underline{1} \text{ unit} & @\ \ 50\ \ \ = & \underline{\ 50} \\ 2 \text{ units} & & \underline{150 = 75\,\% \text{ each}} \end{array}$$

4. We know the costs for the period from our accounting records: i.e., materials requisitioned, labor charges, and overhead.

[4]It would be conceptually equivalent to use reverse flow at all stages except 0 ↔ 1, where items in process would be assigned to 1, i.e., 0 → 1.

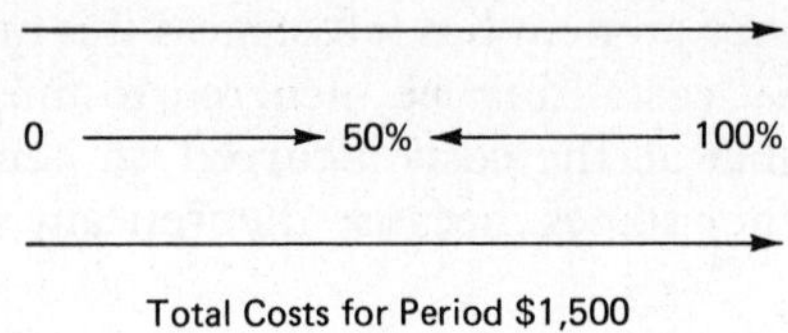

5. Two units that are 75% complete equate with 1.5 *equivalent full units,* and we divide this into the costs for the period to obtain the *cost per finished unit:*

$$\frac{\$1{,}500}{1.5} = \$1{,}000$$

6. The finished unit bears a cost of $1,000. Five hundred dollars has been spent on the unfinished unit even though it may be at any point $> 0 < 100\%$. If costs do not change in the succeeding period, $500 in additional costs is *assumed* to be necessary to complete the unit in progress.

Costing work-in-process is needed to: (1) find the cost per finished unit; (2) place a value on work-in-process; and (3) compute the cost of completing work-in-process.

Rather than measure work-in-process on the basis of total cost flow, we recognize three distinct cost flows: materials, labor, and overhead. This distinction is necessary where these cost flows are different, as shown in Exhibit 19-7.

EXHIBIT 19-7 PROCESS COST FLOWS

Heavy Materials Light

Light Labor Heavy

Uniform Overhead Uniform

Time →

Typically, there is a heavy input of materials early in the process. Labor generally intensifies toward the end of the process. Overhead flow depends on the basis of allocation used. In Exhibit 19-7 a units-of-production basis is assumed, as is an even distribution of units throughout the process. If a labor cost basis is used, overhead flow will be the same as the labor cost flow.

Computing *equivalent units* on the basis of distinct cost flows is illustrated below:

Example: Compute (1) cost per finished unit, and identify the materials, labor, and overhead components of finished costs; (2) compute the total value of work-in-process, and identify the materials, labor, and overhead components of work-in-process; and (3) compute total costs necessary to complete work-in-process in the succeeding period, and identify the materials, labor, and overhead components of costs needed to complete the work-in-process.

Costs for the period from the accounting records are:

Materials	$ 78,000
Labor	104,000
Overhead	30,000
	$212,000

One hundred units were started in process, twenty units were finished.

ADDITIONAL PROCESS DATA

0 ⟶ A ⟶ B ⟶ C ⟶ D ⟵ E

	0	A	B	C	D	E	
Number of units at each stage	0	20	20	20	20	20 =	100 total
Engineered cost flows expressed in cumulative percentages:							
Materials	0	50%	70%	80%	90%	100%	
Labor	0	20%	30%	40%	70%	100%	
Overhead	0	20%	40%	60%	80%	100%	

COMPUTATION OF EQUIVALENT UNITS

	Materials			Labor			Overhead		
	Units	**Cum. %**	**Weighted Average**	**Units**	**Cum. %**	**Weighted Average**	**Units**	**Cum. %**	**Weighted Average**
A	20 ×	.50 =	10	20 ×	.20 =	4	20 ×	.20 =	4
B	20 ×	.70 =	14	20 ×	.30 =	6	20 ×	.40 =	8
C	20 ×	.80 =	16	20 ×	.40 =	8	20 ×	.60 =	12
D	20 ×	.90 =	18	20 ×	.70 =	14	20 ×	.80 =	16
E	20 ×	1.00 =	20	20 ×	1.00 =	20	20 ×	1.00 =	20
	100		78	100		52	100		60
% completion	$\frac{78}{100}$ = .78 or 78%			$\frac{52}{100}$ = .52 or 52%			$\frac{60}{100}$ = .60 or 60%		
Equivalent Units (EU)*	.78 × 100 = 78			.52 × 100 = 52			.60 × 100 = 60		

*Percentage completion is multiplied by the *total* number of units to obtain *equivalent* units. In this case we have a total of 100 units, so .78 × 100 = equivalent units (material). If percentage completion is 80% and we have a total of 20,000 units, equivalents units = 16,000.

Answers to our problem are:

1. *Finished Goods:* 20 units

			Cost Per Finished Unit		Units Finished		Total
Material:	$\frac{\$78,000}{78}$	=	$1,000	×	20	=	$20,000

		Cost Per Finished Unit		Units Finished		Total
Labor:	$\frac{\$104{,}000}{52} =$	2,000	×	20	=	40,000
Overhead:	$\frac{\$30{,}000}{60} =$	500	×	20	=	10,000
Total		$3,500	×	20	=	$70,000

2. *Work-In-Process:* 80 units

	Total Costs	−	Finished Goods	=	Work-In-Process
Materials	$ 78,000	−	$20,000	=	$58,000
Labor	104,000	−	40,000	=	64,000
Overhead	30,000	−	10,000	=	20,000
Total	$212,000	−	$70,000	=	$142,000

Note: Percentage completion may be expressed as a function of total units or it may be restricted in reference to work-in-process. A comparison of percentage completion in these two contexts, using the above data, follows:

	Percentage Completion Based on Total Units					Percentage Completion Based on Work-in-Process								
	Percent		Number of Total Units		Total EU	Percent		Units in W-I-P		EU in W-I-P		EU in Finished Goods		Total EU
Materials	.78	×	100	=	78	.725	×	80	=	58	+	20	=	78
Labor	.52	×	100	=	52	.40	×	80	=	32	+	20	=	52
Overhead	.60	×	100	=	60	.50	×	80	=	40	+	20	=	60

Percentage completion based on work-in-process is most commonly used in cost accounting problems. It derives in fact from the computation based on total units, e.g., of the 78 total EU in materials, 20 are known to be finished. This leaves 58 in process. As the number of units in process is 80, the percentage completion factor is

$$\frac{58}{80} = .725 \text{ or } 72.5\%$$

An alternative method for computing percentage completion on the basis of work-in-process can be illustrated by repeating the procedure on p. 825 but removing finished units (100%) from the calculation. Percentage completion on work-in-process for materials would be:

	Units	Cum. %		Weighted Average
A	20 ×	.50	=	10
B	20 ×	.70	=	14
C	20 ×	.80	=	16
D	20 ×	.90	=	18
	80			58/80 = .725 or 72.5%

3. *Required to Complete Work-In-Process:* Complete the 80 units at the same rates of production.

	Equivalent Units to Complete	×	Cost per Finished Unit	=	Total Cost
Materials	...100 − 78 = 22	×	$1,000	=	$ 22,000
Labor	.........100 − 52 = 48	×	2,000	=	96,000
Overhead	...100 − 60 = 40	×	500	=	20,000
Total	....		$3,500	=	$138,000

4. *Proof:*

100 units fully completed should cost a total of....................	$350,000*
Costs incurred in the current period were............................	212,000
Costs needed to complete work-in-process	$138,000

*100 units × $3,500 each.

Notice that we have (1) *equivalent finished units* and (2) *equivalent units* (EU) to be finished. Expressed as percentages, these two EU's are complementary. If we have 52% EU completion for labor in period_1, then 48% EU of labor remains to be completed in period_2.

This formula can be used for computing equivalent units of production:

$$\text{EU} = F - \%_1 (W/P_1) + \%_2 (W/P_2)$$

where

EU = equivalent units
F = units finished or transferred to next department
$\%_1$ = percentage completion of beginning work-in-process
W/P_1 = number of units in beginning work-in-process
$\%_2$ = percentage completion of ending work-in-process
W/P_2 = number of units in ending work-in-process

PROCESS COSTING THROUGH DEPARTMENTS

Many processes are departmentalized, i.e., the units travel through various departments before they are completed. Automobile manufacturing departments would be assembly, finishing and painting, and testing. In a bakery, departments would be mixing, baking, and wrapping.

Each department is a cost center. Finished goods for one department are raw input to the next department.

In some processes, losses such as shrinkage, breakage, or evaporation are normal. In these cases the number of units that exit a department will be less than those that enter. In order to recover costs, the units that remain must bear the full costs. Therefore, units lost are subtracted from total units to arrive at equivalent units. Also, the department in which the losses occur must make the adjustment.

Assume that we have only one type of cost and two departments. All units except those which are lost are finished:

Dept.	Units Started	Units Lost	Units Finished	Total Cost
A	11,000	1,000	10,000	$20,000
B	10,000	2,000	8,000	40,000
				$60,000

Department A transfers 10,000 units to B at $2 each for a total of $20,000. Because 2,000 additional units are lost in B, department B makes this adjustment to units received from A:

	Units	Unit Cost	Total Cost
Units received	10,000	$2.00	$20,000
Units lost	(2,000) +	.50	–*
Adjusted for units lost in department B	8,000	2.50	20,000†
Dept. B costs	8,000	5.00	40,000
Finished goods	8,000	$7.50	$60,000

*The 2,000 units lost in department B add $.50 to each unit that remains.

†8,000 remaining units need to carry the full cost from department A.

The standard process cost report is called a *cost of production schedule*. It consists of seven parts:

1. Quantity schedule.
2. Cost from preceding department.
3. Beginning work-in-process.
4. Current production costs.
5. Transfer costs to next department or to finished goods inventory.
6. Ending work-in-process.
7. Percentage completion, beginning and ending work-in-process.

Following is an example of departmental process costing. The information that is given for period$_1$ is shown in Exhibit 19-8. A completed cost of production schedule is contained in Exhibit 19-9.

EXHIBIT 19-8 COST OF PRODUCTION SCHEDULE FOR PERIOD 1 (WITH DATA THAT IS GIVEN)

	Department A		**Department B**		**Department C**	
1. Quantity schedule	**Units**	**Units**	**Units**	**Units**	**Units**	**Units**
Beginning inventory		0		0		0
Units started		11,000				
Units/previous dept				8,000		6,000
Units lost	1,000		1,000		1,000	
Units transferred to next dept	8,000		6,000		4,000	
Units in process	2,000		1,000		1,000	
Total	11,000	11,000	8,000	8,000	6,000	6,000

2. Input from preceding department	**Equiv. Units**	**Unit Cost**	**Total Cost**	**Equiv. Units**	**Unit Cost**	**Total Cost**	**Equiv. Units**	**Unit Cost**	**Total Cost**
Cost/previous dept	–	–	–		$	$		$	$
Adj. for units lost	–	–	–						
Adj. cost/prev. dept	–	–	–						
3. Beginning work-in-process									
4. Current production costs	none	none	none	none	none	none	none	none	none
Materials			$49,500			34,000			20,000
Labor			25,800			44,800			27,000
Overhead			16,800			39,000			18,000
	–		92,100	–		117,800	–		65,000
	–		$92,100	–		$201,800	–		$245,000
5. Transferred cost									
Transferred to next department or to finished goods									
6. Ending work-in-process									
From prev. dept	–	–	–						
Present department									
Materials									
Labor									
Overhead									
Total W-I-P									
Total	–	–	$92,100	–	–	$201,800	–	–	$245,000

EXHIBIT 19-8 (CONTINUED)

7. Percentage completion (based on work-in-process)	Department A	Department B	Department C
a. Beginning work-in process	none	none	none
b. Ending work-in-process Materials........	50%	80%	100%
Labor.............	30%	40%	50%
Overhead........	20%	50%	50%

		Department A Equivalent Units		Department B Equivalent Units		Department C Equivalent Units
Computation of Equivalent Units:	%	In-Proc. Trans. Total	%	In-Proc. Trans. Total	%	In-Proc. Trans. Total
Materials...............	50%	1,000 + 8,000 = 9,000	80%	800 + 6,000 = 6,800	100%	1,000 + 4,000 = 5,000
Labor....................	30	600 + 8,000 = 8,600	40	400 + 6,000 = 6,400	50	500 + 4,000 = 4,500
Overhead..............	20	400 + 8,000 = 8,400	50	500 + 6,000 = 6,500	50	500 + 4,000 = 4,500

The example is continued through period$_2$. Again, Exhibit 19-10 gives the information that is available from the accounting records, while Exhibit 19-11 shows a completed schedule for period$_2$.

In this example, as with most problems in process costing, percentage completion data for each element of cost is furnished.

EXHIBIT 19-9 COST OF PRODUCTION SCHEDULE FOR PERIOD 1 (COMPLETED)

	Department A		Department B		Department C	
1. Quantity schedule	**Units**	**Units**	**Units**	**Units**	**Units**	**Units**
Beginning inventory		0		0		0
Units started		11,000				
Units/previous dept.				8,000		6,000
Units lost	1,000		1,000		1,000	
Units transferred to next dept.............	8,000		6,000		4,000	
Units in process	2,000		1,000		1,000	
Total	11,000	11,000	8,000	8,000	6,000	6,000

EXHIBIT 19-9 (CONTINUED)

	Department A			Department B			Department C		
2. Input from preceding department	**Equiv. Units**	**Unit Cost**	**Total Cost**	**Equiv. Units**	**Unit Cost**	**Total Cost**	**Equiv. Units**	**Unit Cost**	**Total Cost**
Cost/previous dept.	–	–	–	8,000	$10.50	$ 84,000	6,000	$30.00	$180,000
Adj. for units lost	–	–	–	–1,000	+1.50		–1,000	+6.00	
Adj. cost/ prev. dept.	–	–	–	7,000	12.00	84,000	5,000	36.00	180,000
3. Beginning work-in-process	–	–	–	–	–	–	–	–	–
4. Current production costs									
Materials	9,000	$ 5.50	$49,500	6,800	5.00	34,000	5,000	4.00	20,000
Labor	8,600	3.00	25,800	6,400	7.00	44,800	4,500	6.00	27,000
Overhead	8,400	2.00	16,800	6,500	6.00	39,000	4,500	4.00	18,000
Sub-total	–	10.50	92,100	–	18.00	117,800	–	14.00	65,000
Total costs	–	$10.50	$92,100	–	$30.00	$201,800	–	$50.00	$245,000
5. Transferred Cost									
Transferred to next department or to finished goods	8,000	$10.50	$84,000	6,000	$30.00	$180,000	4,000	$50.00	$200,000
6. Ending work-in-process									
From prev. dept.	–	–	–	1,000	12.00	12,000	1,000	36.00	36,000
Present department									
Materials	1,000	5.50	5,500	800	5.00	4,000	1,000	4.00	4,000
Labor	600	3.00	1,800	400	7.00	2,800	500	6.00	3,000
Overhead	400	2.00	800	500	6.00	3,000	500	4.00	2,000
Total W-I-P	–		8,100			21,800			145,000
Total costs	–	–	$92,100	–	–	$201,800	–	–	$245,000

7. Schedule of Completion and Equivalent Units

	%	Department A Equivalent Units In-Proc. Trans. Total	%	Department B Equivalent Units In-Proc. Trans. Total	%	Department C Equivalent Units In-Proc. Trans. Total
Materials	50%	1,000 + 8,000 = 9,000	80%	800 + 6,000 = 6,800	100%	1,000 + 4,000 = 5,000
Labor	30	600 + 8,000 = 8,600	40	400 + 6,000 = 6,400	50	500 + 4,000 = 4,500
Overhead	20	400 + 8,000 = 8,400	50	500 + 6,000 = 6,500	50	500 + 4,000 = 4,500

Notes on Exhibit 19-9

A. *Computing Equivalent Units:* Percentage figures are based on ending work-in-progress. EU for materials in Department A:

Percentage Completion		Total Units in Ending W-I-P		EU in Ending W-I-P		EU in Finished Goods		Total EU
.50	×	2,000	=	1,000	+	8,000	=	9,000

B. *Computing Unit Cost:* The total cost for the current period, e.g., $49,500 for materials in department A, is given. Unit cost is obtained by dividing the current cost by EU computed in (A) above:

$$\frac{\$49{,}500}{9{,}000} = \$5.50 \text{ unit cost}$$

C. *Adjusting for Units Lost:* The units lost in department A were taken into account in arriving at the EU in that department, e.g., 9,000 total EU for materials. If no units had been lost in department A, EU would have been 10,000 instead of 9,000. The 9,000 units are bearing the full current production costs of materials in department A.

Additional units are lost in department B. Input from department A needs to be adjusted accordingly in department B, as described on p. 828.

D. *Accounting for Total Costs:* Total costs are accumulated in Sections 2, 3, and 4 comprising:

2. Input from preceding department.....
3. Beginning work-in-process ....
4. Current production costs ....____
   Total costs....................................═══

This total cost is accounted for in Sections 5 and 6.

5. Units transferred to next department or finished goods..........
6. Ending work-in-process.................____
   ═══

These totals must always agree.

E. *Cost Aggregation:* The unit costs from the preceding department are added to the unit costs for the current period from within the department, to give total cumulative unit cost. In department C the cumulative unit cost from departments A and B (after adjustment for units lost) is $36.00. This is added to the $14.00 of unit costs for department C, to total cumulative unit costs of $50.00 for all three departments.

Similarly the totals of sections 2, 3, and 4, when added together, equate with cumulative total costs where there are preceding departments.

F. *Ending Work-In-Process: Units from Preceding Department:* In computing ending work-in-process it is important to include units from the preceding department. In department B, for example, we have a total of 7,000 units, of which 6,000 are transferred to department C. The 1,000 units in ending work-in-process in department B are those remaining from the 7,000 adjusted units from department A at the adjusted unit cost rate of $12.00.

G. *Ending Work-In-Process: EU and Unit Costs:* EU in ending work-in-process is the difference between EU under current production costs *less* units transferred:

	Department A				
	EU Under Current Production Costs	−	**EU Transferred**	=	**EU in Ending Work-In-Process**
Materials	9,000	−	8,000	=	1,000
Labor	8,600	−	8,000	=	600
Overhead	8,400	−	8,000	=	400

The unit cost in ending work-in-process is the same as the unit cost under current production costs.

EXHIBIT 19-10 COST OF PRODUCTION SCHEDULE FOR PERIOD 2 (WITH DATA THAT IS GIVEN)

	Department A		Department B		Department C	
1. Quantity schedule						
Beginning W-I-P		2,000		1,000		1,000
Units started		15,000				
Units from preceding dept.				14,000		12,000
Units lost	1,000		1,000		1,000	
Units trans./next dept.	14,000		12,000		10,000	
Ending W-I-P	2,000		2,000		2,000	
Total	17,000	17,000	15,000	15,000	13,000	13,000

	Dept. A Equiv. Units	Dept. A Unit Cost	Dept. A Total Cost	Dept. B Equiv. Units	Dept. B Unit Cost	Dept. B Total Cost	Dept. C Equiv. Units	Dept. C Unit Cost	Dept. C Total Cost
2. Input from preceding department									
Cost/prec. dept.	–	–	–						
Adj for units lost	–	–	–						
Adj. cost/prec. dept.	–	–	–						
3. Beginning W-I-P									
Preceding dept.	–	–	–						
Present: Materials									
Labor									
Overhead									
Sub-total	–	–		–	–		–	–	
4. Current production costs									
Materials			76,680			60,480			48,840
Labor			49,700			94,500			61,800
Overhead			29,820			71,250			42,800
Sub-total	–		$156,200	–		$226,230	–		$153,440
Total costs	–			–			–		

5. Transferred cost									
Transferred/next dept.: Finish beginning W-I-P									
Units started & finished in current period									
Total									
6. Ending W-I-P									
Preceding dept.	–	–	–						
Present: Materials									
Labor									
Overhead									
Total W-I-P									
Total costs	–	–		–	–		–	–	

	Department A			Department B			Department C		
	Mat.	**Labor**	**O.H.**	**Mat.**	**Labor**	**O.H.**	**Mat.**	**Labor**	**O.H.**
7. Percentage completion (based on work-in-process)									
Beginning W-I-P	50%	30%	20%	80%	40%	50%	100%	50%	50%
Ending W-I-P	60%	40%	30%	70%	50%	50%	100%	40%	60%

EXHIBIT 19-11 COST OF PRODUCTION SCHEDULE FOR PERIOD 2 (COMPLETED)

	Department A		Department B		Department C	
1. Quantity schedule						
Beginning W-I-P		2,000		1,000		1,000
Units started		15,000				
Units/prec. dept.				14,000		12,000
Units lost	1,000		1,000		1,000	
Units trans./next dept.	14,000		12,000		10,000	
Ending W-I-P	2,000		2,000		2,000	
	17,000	17,000	15,000	15,000	13,000	13,000

	Dept. A Equiv. Units	Dept. A Unit Cost	Dept. A Total Cost	Dept. B Equiv. Units	Dept. B Unit Cost	Dept. B Total Cost	Dept. C Equiv. Units	Dept. C Unit Cost	Dept. C Total Cost
2. Input from preceding department costs									
Cost/prec. dept.	–	–	–	14,000	$10.98	$153,760	12,000	$29.85	$358,210
Adj. for units lost	–	–	–	⟨1,000⟩	+ .85	–	⟨1,000⟩	+ 2.71	–
Adj. cost/prec. dept.	–	–	–	13,000	11.83*	153,760	11,000	32.56*	$358,210
3. Beginning W-I-P									
Preceding dept.	–	–	–	1,000	12.00	12,000	1,000	36.00	36,000
Present: Materials	1,000	$ 5.50	$ 5,500	800	5.00	4,000	1,000	4.00	4,000
Labor	600	3.00	1,800	400	7.00	2,800	500	6.00	3,000
Overhead	400	2.00	800	500	6.00	3,000	500	4.00	2,000
Sub-total	–	–	8,100	–	–	21,800	–	–	45,000
4. Current production costs									
Materials	14,200	5.40	76,680	12,600	4.80	60,480	11,000	4.44	48,840
Labor	14,200	3.50	49,700	12,600	7.50	94,500	10,300	6.00	61,800
Overhead	14,200	2.10	29,820	12,500	5.70	71,250	10,700	4.00	42,800
Sub-total	–	11.00	156,200	–	18.00	$226,230	–	14.44	$153,440
Total cumulative costs	–	$11.00	$164,300	–	$29.83	$401,790	–	$47.00	$556,650

(A) (B)

5. Transferred cost									
Transferred/next dept.: Finish beginning W-I-P	2,000	10.88	21,760	1,000	30.08*	30,080	1,000	50.00	50,000
Units started & fin.	12,000	11.00	132,000	11,000	29.83	328,130	9,000	47.00	423,000
Total	14,000	10.98	153,760	12,000	29.85	358,210	10,000	47.30	473,000
6. Ending W-I-P:									
Preceding dept.	–	–	–	2,000	11.83	23,660	2,000	32.56*	65,170
Present: Materials	1,200	5.40	6,480	1,400	4.80	6,720	2,000	4.44	8,880
Labor	800	3.50	2,800	1,000	7.50	7,500	800	6.00	4,800
Overhead	600	2.10	1,260	1,000	5.70	5,700	1,200	4.00	4,800
Total W-I-P	–	–	10,540	–	–	43,580	–	–	$ 83,650
Total	–	–	$164,300	–	–	$401,790	–	–	$556,650

(C) (D) (E)

	Department A			Department B			Department C		
	Mat.	**Labor**	**O.H.**	**Mat.**	**Labor**	**O.H.**	**Mat.**	**Labor**	**O.H.**
7. Percentage completion (based on work-in-process)									
Beginning W-I-P	50%	30%	20%	80%	40%	50%	100%	50%	50%
Ending W-I-P	60%	40%	30%	70%	50%	50%	100%	40%	60%

*Approximate

Notes on Exhibit 19-11

A. *Beginning Work-In-Process:* Beginning work-in-process is given. In this case, the ending work-in-process in Exhibit 19-9 is carried forward to Exhibit 19-11. This would be true of all continuation problems.

B. *Computing Equivalent Units:* Use the formula on p. 827. For materials in department A:

$$\begin{aligned} EU &= 14{,}000 - .50(2{,}000) + .60(2{,}000) \\ &= 14{,}000 - 1{,}000 + 1{,}200 \\ &= 14{,}200 \end{aligned}$$

C. *Computing Transferred Cost:*

Method 1: Compute ending work-in-process and subtract from total cost. For department A:

	Total cost	$164,300	
	Ending W-I-P	10,540	
	Transferred cost	153,760	comprising
Less:	12,000 in current period at $11.00 each	132,000	
	2,000 from beginning work-in-process	21,760	= $10.88 each

Method 2: Unit costs changed in period 2 over period 1. All of the 12,000 started and finished in period 2 have a uniform cost of $11.00. However, the 2,000 units that make up beginning work-in-process have mixed costs of period 1 and 2. The $10.88 average cost can be computed as follows:

		EU	Unit Cost	Total Cost		Weighted Average Unit Cost
Materials	Beginning W-I-P	1,000	$5.50	$ 5,500		
	To complete	1,000	5.40	5,400		
		2,000		$10,900	=	$ 5.45
Labor	Beginning W-I-P	600	3.00	1,800		
	To complete	1,400	3.50	4,900		
		2,000		$ 6,700	=	$ 3.35
Overhead	Beginning W-I-P	400	2.00	800		
	To complete	1,600	2.10	3,360		
		2,000		$ 4,160	=	$ 2.08
						$10.88

D. *Equivalent Units in Ending Work-In-Process:* Where beginning work-in-process is included in the problem, those units are added to units in current production in order compute total units available for the period. Remember the basic inventory computation:

Beginning inventory	
Purchases for the period....................	_______
= Total available	
− Units transferred or sold	_______
= Ending inventory..................................	_______

EU for ending work-in-process in department C is:

	EU in Beginning W-I-P		EU in Current Production		Total EU		Less EU Transferred		EU in Ending W-I-P
Preceding Department	1,000	+	11,000	=	12,000	−	10,000	=	2,000
Materials	1,000	+	11,000	=	12,000	−	10,000	=	2,000
Labor	500	+	10,300	=	10,800	−	10,000	=	800
Overhead	500	+	10,700	=	11,200	−	10,000	=	1,200

E. *Inventory Pricing Methods:* As illustrated in note (C), a change of unit costs between periods impacts on the transferred cost. In process costing the major inventory methods may be used. Under LIFO, period 1 costs would not be transferred but would be retained in ending work-in-process. The opposite is true of FIFO. What we have illustrated in the above example is the *weighted average method* of pricing inventory.

19.8 SUMMARY

We have discussed problems of cost measurement and allocation in three principal cost systems: departmental, job, and process. These systems are not mutually exclusive.

We distinguished between *production* and *service* centers, and we found that *full cost* data is needed in deciding whether or not to continue a center.

The problem of allocating overhead is common to all cost systems. Overhead should be allocated on a fair and realistic basis. One way to allocate overhead is to use a separate basis for each type of overhead. Obviously, this is a costly approach. A practical alternative is to use one method for allocating all overhead to jobs, units in process, or departments.

In departmental accounting, service centers minister to each other as well as to production centers. *Full costing* requires that we allocate service center costs to each other and to producing departments. Iterative and simultaneous equation methods were illustrated.

In job costing, materials and labor can be traced to each job, and only overhead is allocated.

A critical problem in process costing is to value work-in-process. The concept of *equivalent units* provides the solution to this problem. The flow of process costs through departments was illustrated. A *cost of production schedule* provides the information that is needed to control departmental process costs and to compute the cost of finished goods and ending work-in-process.

CHAPTER 19 REFERENCES AND ADDITIONAL READINGS

OVERHEAD AND COST ALLOCATION

Barton, Richard F. "An Experimental Study of the Impact of Competitive Pressures on Overhead Allocation Bids." *Journal of Accounting Research,* Spring 1969, pp. 116–22.

Carroll. *Overhead Cost Control.* New York: McGraw-Hill Book Company, 1964.

Chaump, Donald G. "Reducing Overhead Through the Task-Activity Cycle Ratio Matrix Analysis." *Management Accounting,* February 1967, pp. 23–32.

Corcoran, A. Wayne. *Mathematical Applications in Accounting.* New York: Harcourt, Brace & World, Inc., 1968, pp. 158–90.

Dick, William G. "A Suggested Flexible Overhead Distribution Plan." *Management Accounting,* September 1965, pp. 48–50.

Fails and Associates. *Overhead Application Rates.* Raleigh, N.C.: Fails and Associates, Inc., 1965.

Harper, W. M. "Apportionment of Overheads—the Problem of Reciprocal Service Departments." *Accountancy* (England), December 1966, pp. 879–81.

Joyce, James E. "The Overhead Mystique." *Management Accounting,* November 1968, pp. 43–46.

Kaplan, Robert S., and Thompson, Gerald L. "Overhead Allocation via Mathematical Programming Models." *The Accounting Review,* April 1971, pp. 352–64.

Livingstone, John Leslie. "Input-Output Analysis for Cost Accounting, Planning and Control." *The Accounting Review,* January 1969, pp. 48–64.

Livingstone, John Leslie. "Matrix Algebra and Cost Allocation." *The Accounting Review,* July 1968, pp. 503–8.

Mautz, Robert K., and Skousen, K. Fred. "Common Cost Allocation in Diversified Companies." *Financial Executive,* June 1968, pp. 15–25.

Van Tatenhove, James M. "Managing Indirect Costs in the Aerospace Industry." *Management Accounting,* September 1969, pp. 36–42, 48.

Willard, Bruce K. "Cost Distribution Using Infinitely Variable Averages." *Management Accounting,* October 1969, pp. 12–15.

JOB COSTING SYSTEMS

Horngren, Charles T. *Cost Accounting: A Managerial Emphasis.* Englewood Cliffs, N.J.: Prentice-Hall, Inc., 1967, pp. 68–95.

Matz, Adolph; Curry, Othel J.; and Frank, George W. *Cost Accounting.* 4th ed. Cincinnati: South-Western Publishing Company, 1967, pp. 378–80.

Terrill, William A., and Patrick, Albert W. *Cost Accounting for Management.* New York: Holt, Rinehart & Winston, Inc., 1965, pp. 173–95.

PROCESS COSTING SYSTEMS

Horngren, Charles T. *Cost Accounting: A Managerial Emphasis.* Englewood Cliffs, N.J.: Prentice-Hall, Inc., 1967, pp. 628–51.

Matz, Adolph; Curry, Othel J.; and Frank, George W. *Cost Accounting.* 4th ed. Cincinnati: South-Western Publishing Company, 1967, pp. 378–440.

Terrill, William A., and Patrick, Albert W. *Cost Accounting for Management.* New York: Holt, Rinehart & Winston, Inc., 1965, pp. 36–139.

CHAPTER 19 QUESTIONS, PROBLEMS, AND CASES

19- 1. Under what conditions should a job or process cost system be employed?

19- 2. "Overhead costs are incurred for the benefit of more than one cost center." If costs are incurred for one specific cost center, are they overhead costs? Why? In your discussion cite some typical examples of overhead costs.

19- 3. Distinguish between a *service cost center* and a *production cost center.* Why is this distinction between service and production centers critical in departmental cost accounting?

19- 4. Explain the purpose in allocating overhead to production centers as it relates to the notion or concept of "full cost."

19- 5. What methods are used currently for allocating service department costs to producing departments? Which method do you prefer and why? What is the reason for allocating service department costs to each other and to producing departments?

19- 6. What is the purpose and use of overhead application rates? If an under- or over-application results, how is the situation remedied? What are the consequences of making no end-of-period adjustment?

19- 7. Distinguish between the *effective rate,* the *applied overhead rate,* and the *direct labor rate.*

19- 8. Define or explain the use of the following terms and phrases:
(a) Cost center
(b) Direct cost
(c) Overhead
(d) "Full cost"
(e) "Contribution margin"
(f) Under-applied overhead
(g) Over-applied overhead
(h) Profit center
(i) Point of indifference

19- 9. In the allocation of structured overhead, why is it necessary to first determine the *full cost* of service departments? Can an equitable distribution be achieved without first determining the full cost?

19-10. If the full cost of a service department is not recovered through contracting for services, how are the remaining departments affected?

19-11. Define *overhead.* Give some examples of *unstructured* and *structured* overhead, and for each example suggest a possible basis for allocation to production cost centers.

19-12. Explain the concept of an *equivalent unit.*

19-13. Why are the direct allocation method and the step-down method less desirable than a solution by simultaneous equations? Can a "point of indifference" be established for service centers using direct allocation or step-down method? Why?

19-14. State the allocation rule for each method of allocating structured overhead:
(a) Direct
(b) Step-down
(c) Iterative
(d) Simultaneous equations

19-15. What is the distinction between *process* costing and *job order* costing in regard to the allocation of production costs?

19-16. Indicate whether the following production cost elements are direct or indirect in job versus process costing:

Cost Element	Job	Process
Materials...........		
Labor................		
Overhead		

19-17. Give examples of hybrid job-process systems:
(a) Job imposed on a process.
(b) Process imposed on a job.

19-18. "Valuing work-in-process is the most difficult part of process costing." What makes this valuation so difficult and why is it necessary that we attach a value to work-in-process?

19-19. Explain the assumptions inherent in a process scale based on percentage of completion. Draw a diagram of this process scale and a diagram of its conceptual equivalent.

19-20. Typically, in a process cost flow, what is the difference in behavior between material and labor consumption over time?

19-21. "There is one true method for allocating overhead to organizational units." Discuss.

19-22. How do we cope with the basic measurement problem underlying process costing, i.e., how do we measure processes?

19-23. Indicate the assumptions about a unit's stage of completion with each process scale:

Forward Flow:

0 ⟶ 1 ⟶ 2 ⟶ 3 ⟶ 4

Reverse Flow:

0 ⟵ 1 ⟵ 2 ⟵ 3 ⟵ 4

What are the problems inherent in these assumptions and what is a possible solution?

19-24. Why are units lost in one department treated as an adjustment to the cost of units received from the supplying department?

19-25. Identify the seven parts of a *cost of production schedule.*

19-26. "It must be remembered that service centers are not indispensable. It is always possible to contract for outside services. It is the production functions in organizations that are indispensable if an entity is to survive." Discuss.

19-27. Distinguish *applying overhead* from *allocating overhead.*

19-28. In the chapter illustrations of process costing, the weighted average method is used for pricing inventories. What potential computational and procedural difficulties could have arisen if the method chosen had been LIFO or FIFO? With LIFO or FIFO, it is necessary to segregate into production lots when computing the total cost of ending work-in-process inventory? What about when transferring goods from one department to another?

19-29. *ITERATIVE ALLOCATION OF STRUCTURED OVERHEAD* Suppose the following *service distribution matrix* is available:

Service Dept.	Producing			Service		
	A	B	C	D	E	F
F	30%	20%	20%	15%	15%	(100%)
E	25	35	10	10	(100)	20
D	10	20	40	(100)	5	25

Required:

Complete the iterative allocation schedule for four cycles using the stepdown method on the fourth cycle:

	Producing			Service		
	A	B	C	D	E	F
Direct costs	$50,000	$70,000	$15,000	$14,000	$12,000	$8,000
Allocate F						
Allocate E						
Allocate D						

19-30. ***ALLOCATING UNSTRUCTURED OVERHEAD*** The Elia Company makes five different size aluminum window casings. Financial data for 19*x*1 operations is as follows:

	Size				
	2′ × 2′	2′ × 4′	2′ × 6′	4′ × 6′	6′ × 6′
Sales	$187,000	$260,000	$162,000	$451,000	$145,000
Prime costs:					
Direct materials	63,000	91,000	60,000	172,000	60,000
Direct labor	36,000	52,000	41,000	118,000	37,000
Direct labor hours	15,000	20,600	16,400	45,700	14,300

The total overhead is $280,000

Required:

(a) Determine the allocation of the $280,000 in overhead to each size of window casing using:
(1) Direct material cost
(2) Direct labor cost
(3) Prime costs
(4) Direct labor hours
(5) Sales revenue
(6) Contribution to margin

(b) Which basis (or bases) for allocation appears to be the most equitable? Discuss the reasons for your choice.

19-31. ***APPLIED OVERHEAD*** The following information is available at the *end* of 1970 for the Wilson Teapot Company operations. (The company's only product is a low-cost stainless steel teapot.)

Selling price per unit: $2.20.
Actual factory overhead incurred was $53,000.
Under-applied overhead is $4,400.
Actual units produced in 1970 was 108,000.

Required:

Supply the missing *budget figures* for the Wilson Company's 1970 budget, assuming that overhead is applied on a per unit basis:

Sales in units	______
Sales in dollars	______
Total selling & administrative expenses	$35,500
Net income	$ 6,648
Direct labor cost per unit	______

Total direct labor cost	$40,552
Direct material cost per unit	$ 1.00
Total direct material cost	______
Factory overhead:	
Variable	______
Fixed	$30,000
Inventories	none

Remember that you are looking for budget figures at the beginning of the period by using end-of-period actual data.

19-32. ***ALLOCATION OF STRUCTURED OVERHEAD—TWO SERVICE DEPARTMENTS*** The Mulloney Corporation has three production departments—machining, assembly, and finishing—and two service departments—payroll and janitorial services. Some selected financial data for 19*x*1 is as follows:

	Machining	Assembly	Finishing	Payroll	Janitorial Services	Total
Direct materials	$ 48,600	$123,400	$ 8,000		$ 3,500	$ 183,500
Direct labor	112,000	240,000	97,000	$12,000	22,000	483,000
Total prime costs	$160,600	$363,400	$105,000	$12,000	$25,500	$ 666,500
Unstructured overhead						340,000
Total cost						$1,006,500

Assume that each service department does not require its own services and also the distribution of service department costs is on the basis of *number of employees* for the payroll department and *square feet of floor space* for janitorial services. The applicable information for allocating service department costs is:

	Machining	Assembly	Finishing	Payroll	Janitorial Services	Total
Floor space (in sq. ft.)	4,400	7,000	5,000	600	—	17,000
No. of employees	14	48	34	—	4	100

Required:

(a) Using total prime cost as a basis, determine the allocation of unstructured overhead to each department.

(b) Determine the full cost of each production department by using simultaneous equations allocation.

(c) Should the company contract for an outside payroll preparation (bank service) if the yearly charge is:
(1) $20,000
(2) $12,500
(3) $18,400

(d) Should the company contract for outside janitorial services if yearly charge is:
(1) $37,000
(2) $49,000
(3) $34,000

(e) What is the *point of indifference* if the company contracts for both services?

(f) Determine the full cost of each production department by allocating the costs of each service department using:
(1) Direct allocation
(2) Step-down allocation
(3) Iterative allocation

(g) For this company, which of the four allocation methods produces the most accurate determination of full costs for production departments? Explain your response.

19-33. ***ALLOCATION OF STRUCTURED OVERHEAD—MULTIPLE SERVICE DEPARTMENTS*** Meddock Corporation has three producing departments and three service departments. Financial data for the first month of 19*x*1 is as follows:

Department	Direct Department Expense	Labor Hours	Square Feet	No. of Employees
Prod-1	$ 8,000	2,500	2,000	60
Prod-2	6,000	1,200	800	30
Prod-3	12,000	3,000	3,200	75
Serv-1	1,000	500	400	12
Serv-2	3,000	1,120	800	30
Serv-3	500	80	200	3
Total:	$30,500	8,400	7,400	210

The unstructured overhead for the first month was $5,800. All unstructured overhead is allocated on the basis of labor hours. The bases used by the Meddock Corporation for allocating service department expenses to producing departments are:

Service Departments	Basis of Allocation
Serv-1	Labor hours
Serv-2	Square feet
Serv-3	No. of employees

Required:

(a) Determine the allocation of unstructured overhead to departments.
(b) Determine the full cost of each production department using:
 (1) Direct allocation
 (2) Step-down allocation
 (3) Iterative allocation
 (4) Simultaneous equations allocation

19-34. ***JOB COSTING*** The Coldspar Corporation produces heavy machinery by special order. On January 1, 19*x*1, the corporation had a raw materials inventory of $53,000 and the following jobs finished and in process:

JOBS-IN-PROCESS
JANUARY 1, 19x1

Job No.	Direct Materials	Direct Labor	Applied Overhead	Total
D	18,400	37,000	25,900	81,300
E	26,100	51,000	35,700	112,800
G	13,200	28,000	19,600	60,800
H	22,500	43,000	30,100	95,600
	80,200	159,000	111,300	350,500

JOBS FINISHED
JANUARY 1, 19x1

Job No.	Direct Materials	Direct Labor	Applied Overhead	Total
A	33,400	60,000	42,000	135,400
B	27,000	54,000	37,800	118,800
C	31,500	55,000	38,500	125,000
F	25,400	38,000	26,600	90,000
	117,300	207,000	144,900	469,200

During the first six months of 19*x*2 the following information is available:

(a) Jobs A, C, and F were delivered to customers.
(b) Jobs E and H were finished and delivered to customers.
(c) Job D was finished but still undelivered.
(d) Raw materials of $75,400 were purchased during the six months.
(e) Overhead was applied at $.70 per direct labor dollar.
(f) Actual overhead for the six months was $96,000.
(g) Job order costs for the six-month period are as follows:

Job No.	Direct Materials	Direct Labor
D	7,800	11,000
E	4,200	4,000
G	6,800	15,000
H	10,000	9,000
I	24,600	34,000
J	18,200	29,000
K	25,000	42,000

Required:

(1) Prepare a schedule of jobs-in-process on June 30, 19*x*2.
(2) Prepare a schedule of finished jobs on June 30, 19*x*2.
(3) Prepare a schedule of jobs sold during the first six months of 19*x*2.
(4) Compute the amount of under- or over-applied overhead for the six months ended June 30, 19*x*2.
(5) Prepare a schedule of cost of goods manufactured and sold.

19-35. ***EQUIVALENT UNITS—NON-DEPARTMENTALIZED*** Consider the following process data for the Kurtig Engineering Company:

	0 ⟶	A ⟶	B ⟶	C ⟵	D
Number of units at each stage......	0	480	560	200	1,320
Cumulative percentage cost flows:					
Material....................................	0	70%	80%	95%	100%
Labor..	0	10%	60%	80%	100%
Overhead	0	30%	60%	70%	100%

Required:

(a) Compute *equivalent finished units* with regard to:
  (1) Material
  (2) Labor
  (3) Overhead

(b) Compute *equivalent units to be finished* with regard to:
(1) Material
(2) Labor
(3) Overhead

19-36. ***PROCESS COSTING—NON-DEPARTMENTALIZED*** The Taste-Bud Food Processing Company produces a special chicken-potpie through a secret six-stage process. The current engineered *cumulative* cost flows (expressed as percentages) for each production stage are:

	0 →	A →	B →	C →	D →	E ←	F
Materials	0	20%	30%	80%	90%	90%	100%
Labor	0	40%	70%	85%	85%	95%	100%
Overhead	0	10%	20%	40%	60%	80%	100%

For 19*x*1, 2,000,000 units were started in process and 1,970,000 units were finished. The number of units remaining at each production stage are as follows:

	0 →	A →	B →	C →	D →	E ←	F
No. of units at each stage	0	2,000	6,000	5,000	8,000	9,000	

From the accounting records for 19*x*1, the following production costs were incurred:

Materials	$420,000
Labor	148,000
Overhead	510,000

Required:

(a) Compute *equivalent finished units* with regard to:
(1) Material
(2) Labor
(3) Overhead

(b) Compute *equivalent units to be finished* with regard to:
(1) Material
(2) Labor
(3) Overhead

(c) Compute the *cost per finished unit* and identify the materials, labor, and overhead cost components.

19-37. ***PROCESS COSTING THROUGH TWO DEPARTMENTS*** The Risenex Corporation has two production departments. Applicable data for 19*x*1 and 19*x*2 is:

	Department A		Department B	
	19x1	**19x2**	**19x1**	**19x2**
Quantity Data				
Beg. W-I-P inv.—units	0	220	0	70
Units started	1,200	1,100		
Units from previous dept.			900	1,000
Units lost	80	120	50	60
Units transferred	900	1,000	780	950
Units in process	220	200	70	60

	Department A		Department B	
	19x1	**19x2**	**19x1**	**19x2**
Current Production Costs:				
Materials	$5,928	$5,566	$6,744	$8,469
Labor	$2,580	$2,964	$2,828	$3,332
Overhead	$4,242	$4,429	$3,204	$3,812
Percentage Completion for Ending Work-in-Process				
Materials	40%	50%	90%	90%
Labor	60%	60%	40%	50%
Overhead	50%	70%	30%	40%

Required:

(a) Prepare a cost of production schedule for each year (using weighted average method of pricing inventory).

(b) Compute the cost of ending work-in-process inventory for 19*x*2 if the applicable inventory pricing method is:

(1) LIFO

(2) FIFO

19-38. ***PROCESS COSTING THROUGH THREE DEPARTMENTS*** The Astro-Labs Corporation has three production departments. Applicable data for 19*x*1 and 19*x*2 is:

	Department A		Department B		Department C	
	19x1	**19x2**	**19x1**	**19x2**	**19x1**	**19x2**
Quantity Data:						
Beg. W-I-P inv.—units	0	700	0	500	0	100
Units started	8,700	9,000				
Units from previous dept.			7,600	8,400	6,900	8,200
Units lost	400	500	200	100	0	100
Units transferred	7,600	8,400	6,900	8,200	6,800	7,900
Units in process	700	800	500	600	100	300
Current Production Costs:						
Materials	$63,040	$72,420	$29,200	$28,770	$ 6,900	$10,250
Labor	26,845	30,420	21,750	22,988	27,360	36,045
Overhead	23,650	27,430	25,200	27,060	27,480	30,438
Percentage Completion for Ending Work-in-Process:						
Materials	40%	50%	80%	70%	100%	100%
Labor	10%	15%	70%	60%	40%	50%
Overhead	40%	40%	60%	50%	70%	60%

Required:

Prepare a cost of production schedule for each year (using weighted average method of pricing inventory).

19-39. ***PROCESS COSTING*** The Thompson Processing Company had work-in-process at the beginning and end of 19*x*1 as follows:

	Percentage of Completion	
	Material	**Conversion Costs**
January 1, 19x1 – 3,500 units	50%	20%
December 31, 19x1 – 2,000 units	70%	30%

The company completed 50,000 units of finished goods during 19*x*1. Manufacturing costs incurred during 19*x*1 were:

Materials	$242,600
Conversion costs	$435,400

Inventory at January 1, 19*x*1, was carried at a cost of $12,200 (materials, $6,800; conversion costs, $5,400).

Required:

(a) Using the weighted average method, compute the equivalent production for 19*x*1 for materials and conversion.
(b) Using the weighted average method, what is the proper cost of ending goods-in-process inventory?

19-40. ***OVERHEAD ALLOCATION*** A and B are producing departments. X and Y are service departments representing cafeteria and transportation respectively. Prior to any cost allocation the direct costs of X = $9,090 and Y = $6,000. Service department costs are distributed in this manner:

X costs	Y costs
To Y = 10%	To X = 20%
To A = 30%	To A = 40%
To B = 60%	To B = 40%

Required:

(a) Compute:
  (1) The *total* cost to be allocated from X.
  (2) The *total* cost to be allocated from Y.
(b) Suppose, in continuation of the above problem, that we are considering an outside bid for cafeteria services:
  (1) If X costs are fully reducible, but Y costs are not reducible at all, what is the point of indifference?
  (2) Suppose $1,000 of X costs cannot be eliminated by virtue of the proposed contract services, and Y costs are not reducible – what is the point of indifference?
  (3) Assume the data in (2) except that Y costs are reducible in the amount of service previously rendered to X – what is the point of indifference?

19-41. ***PROCESS COSTING*** The Quality Paint Company uses a process-cost system. Materials are added at the beginning of a particular process and conversion costs are incurred uniformly. Work-in-process at the beginning and end is assumed 50% complete for materials and 30% complete for conversion. One gallon of material makes one gallon of product. In addition, the following data is available:

Beginning inventory	900 gallons
Materials added	9,900 gallons
Ending inventory	390 gallons
Conversion costs incurred	$16,000

Cost of materials added $18,600
Conversion costs, beginning inventory ....$ 800
Cost of materials, beginning inventory........$ 1,450

Required:

(a) Using the weighted average method, what are the equivalent units of production for:
(1) Materials
(2) Conversion
(b) Using the weighted average method, what is the cost per equivalent unit for:
(1) Materials
(2) Conversion
(c) Using the weighted average method, what is the value of the ending work-in-process inventory?

19-42. ***PROCESS COSTING*** Ballinger Paper Products manufactures a high quality paper box. The box department applies two separate operations—cutting and folding. The paper is first cut and trimmed to the dimensions of a box form by one machine group. One square foot of paper is equivalent to four box forms. The trimmings from this process have no scrap value. Box forms are then creased and folded (i.e., completed) by a second machine group. Any partially processed boxes in the department are cut box forms that are ready for creasing and folding. These partly processed boxes are considered 50% complete as to labor and overhead. The materials department maintains an inventory of paper in sufficient quantities to permit continuous processing, and transfers to the box department are made as needed. Immediately after folding, all good boxes are transferred to the finished goods department.

During June 1971, the materials department purchased 1,210,000 square feet of unprocessed paper for $244,000. Conversion costs for the month were $226,000. A quantity equal to 30,000 boxes was spoiled during paper cutting and 70,000 boxes were spoiled during folding. All spoilage has a zero salvage value, is considered normal and cannot be reprocessed. All spoilage loss is allocated between the completed units and partially processed boxes. Ballinger applies the weighted average cost method to all inventories. Inventory data for June are given below.

Inventory	Physical Unit	June 30, 1971 Units on Hand	June 1, 1971 Units on Hand	June 1, 1971 Cost
Materials Department:				
paper	square feet	200,000	390,000	$76,000
Box Department:				
boxes cut, not folded	number	300,000	800,000	55,000*
Finished Goods Department:				
completed boxes on hand	number	50,000	250,000	18,000

*Materials $35,000
Conversion costs......... 20,000
$55,000

Required: Prepare the following for the month of June 1971:

(a) A report of cost of paper used for the materials department.
(b) A schedule showing the physical flow of units (including beginning and ending inventories) in the materials department, in the box department, and in the finished goods department.
(c) A schedule showing the computation of equivalent units produced for materials and conversion costs in the box department.
(d) A schedule showing the computation of unit costs for the box department.
(e) A report of inventory valuation and cost of completed units for the box department.
(f) A schedule showing the computation of unit costs for the finished goods department.
(g) A report of inventory valuation and cost of units sold for the finished goods department.

(From the CPA exam.)

19-43. ***PROCESS COSTING***

/——→/——→/——→/——→/←——/

	A	B	C	D	E	
No. of units	200 +	200 +	200 +	200 +	200 =	1,000
Flow of:						
Materials	60%	70%	80%	90%	100%	
Labor	30%	40%	70%	70%	100%	
Overhead	20%	40%	60%	80%	100%	

(cumulative percentages)

Costs of current period (P_1)

Materials	$160,000
Labor	232,500
Overhead	60,000
Total	$452,500

Required:

(a) Compute the cost of finished goods for P_1.
(b) Compute the value of work-in-process for P_1.
(c) Compute the costs needed to complete the work-in-process at P_1 prices.

19-44. ***COST ALLOCATION***

	Producing		Service	
			Cafe	Transport
	A	B	X	Y
Direct costs	$40,000	$55,000	$20,000	$12,700
Distribution of X's services	40%	30%	(100%)	30%
Y's services	40%	40%	20%	(100%)

Required:

What is the point of indifference regarding a "make or buy" decision involving department X:

(a) If X's costs are fully reducible, but Y cannot reduce its costs at all?
(b) If $2,000 of X's costs are fixed, but Y cannot reduce its costs at all?
(c) If $2,000 of X's costs are fixed, and Y can reduce its costs to the extent of its prior service to X?
(d) If X's costs are fully reducible, and Y can reduce its costs to the extent of its prior service to X?

CHAPTER

20

STANDARD COSTS AND VARIANCE ANALYSIS

20.1 THE NATURE OF STANDARD COSTS

A *standard cost* is a predetermined cost. In defining this concept in chapter 18 we explained that much modern business activity is conducted on the basis of what costs *should be* rather than what costs *are.* The cost of educating a student is not known until the end of the academic year, but it is necessary to establish fees, rates, and appropriations at the beginning of the year. The cost of treating a patient is not known until the end of the fiscal year, but again hospitals need to estimate costs for rate-setting purposes. In fact the cost of any product is not known until all of this information is in hand.

$$\frac{\text{Total Costs for the Period}}{\text{Number of Units Produced}} = \text{Cost Per Unit}$$

Determining the standard cost of a product is more complex than simply carrying forward its cost from the preceding period. While historical costs certainly play a role in setting standards, many other factors must be taken into account as depicted in Exhibit 20-1.

Except for historical costs, all of these factors deal with future events. Future labor rates have to be estimated, and assumptions must be made regarding the availability of the required quantity and quality of manpower skills. Changes in plant layout may require modification of prior standards.

EXHIBIT 20-1 SOME FACTORS ENTERING INTO STANDARD COSTING

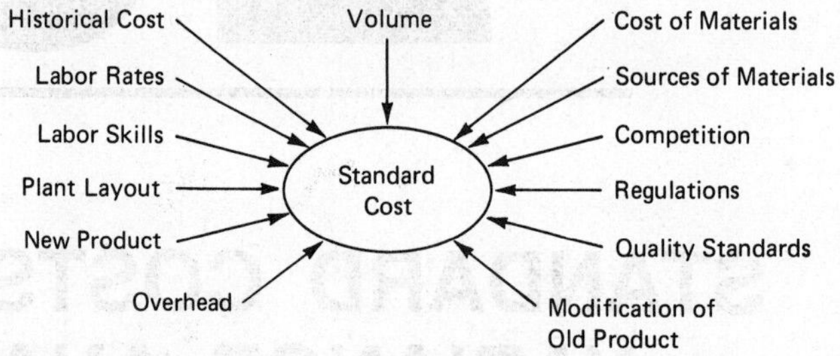

Historical Cost
Volume
Cost of Materials
Labor Rates
Sources of Materials
Labor Skills
Competition
Plant Layout
Standard Cost
Regulations
New Product
Quality Standards
Overhead
Modification of Old Product

New products or major changes to old products often call for an extensive re-engineering of standards. Overhead items such as rents, salaries, insurance, taxes, and others may be expected to change during the production period. Feedback on products sold may lead to changes in quality standards.

Regulations and laws may come into effect which require changes in standards. Expected behavior of competitors during the production period must be considered in developing standards. There may be anticipated changes in the cost of materials or in the sources from which we obtain them. These expectations are part of the standard costing decision.

The expected level of activity for the period is an important factor in developing standards. The activity or volume level influences labor personnel and rates, overhead, and costs and discounts relative to materials. This factor is so critical that standards are often developed for a series of activity levels. This procedure is referred to as *flexible budgeting*.

20.2 SETTING STANDARDS

Standards comprise the three major types of production cost: materials, labor, and overhead. Energy-activity data supports each of these cost elements (Exhibit 20-2). A formal statement of a materials standard (Exhibit 20-3) would include all of the activity-energy data shown in Exhibit 20-2.

The description and quality portion of the statement is considerably more detailed than represented. This part of the standard does not enter formally into the accounting system because it is non-quantitative in nature. Inspection and other control routines attend to this facet of the standard.

A labor cost standard is similar to the one for materials (Exhibit 20-4). Again,

EXHIBIT 20-2 COMPOSITION OF STANDARD COSTS

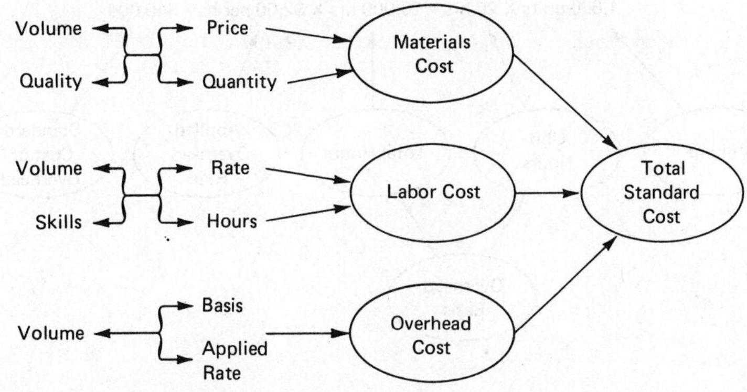

*The importance and interdependence of activity-energy data in making efficiency judgments is discussed in chapter 1.

EXHIBIT 20-3 A MATERIALS STANDARD

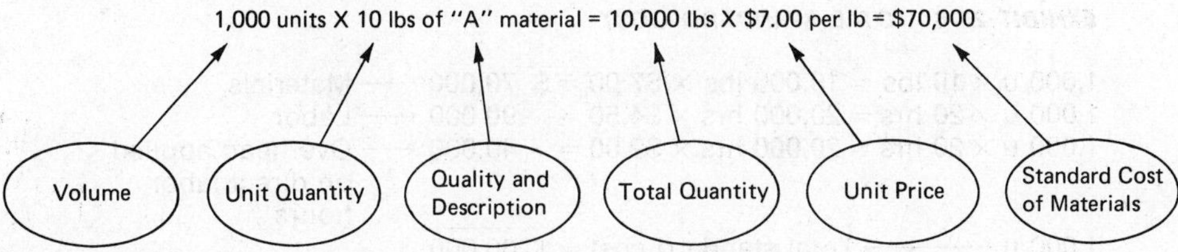

EXHIBIT 20-4 A LABOR COST STANDARD

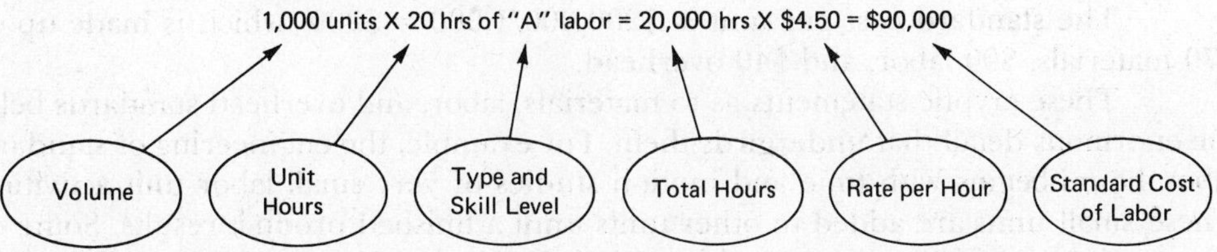

the type of labor (carpenter, electrician, accountant, engineer, etc.) and the skill level (Grade I, II, etc.), is defined in more detail than we show above. As with materials description and quality, this portion of the labor standard is not a formal part of the cost accounting system. Human resource management is most commonly the responsibility of personnel departments.

The standard cost of overhead derives from an estimate of overhead costs at a particular volume level. This amount is then applied to units of production on some acceptable basis.

Throughout this chapter we will assume that overhead is allocated on the basis of *direct labor hours.* Standard labor hours at a volume level of 1,000 units is 20,000 hours. If overhead at that volume is expected to be $40,000, the applied overhead rate is $2.00 per direct labor hour (Exhibit 20-5).

EXHIBIT 20-5 OVERHEAD STANDARD

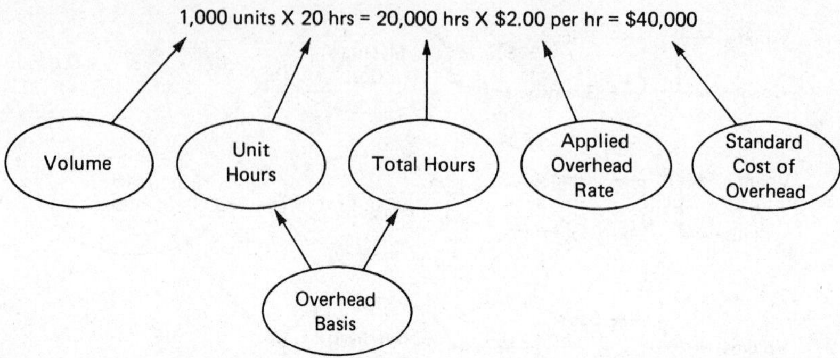

The "total standard cost" for the 1,000 units is the sum of the standards costs of materials, labor, and overhead:

EXHIBIT 20-6 TOTAL STANDARD COST

1,000 u × 10 lbs = 10,000 lbs × $7.00 =	$ 70,000 ←	Materials
1,000 u × 20 hrs = 20,000 hrs × $4.50 =	90,000 ←	Labor
1,000 u × 20 hrs = 20,000 hrs × $2.00 =	40,000 ←	Overhead applied on direct labor hours
1,000 u ⟶ Total standard cost =	$200,000	

The standard cost per unit is $200,000/1,000 = $200; which is made up of $70 materials, $90 labor, and $40 overhead.

These cryptic statements as to materials, labor, and overhead standards belie the enormous detail that undergirds them. For example, the engineering of standard labor hours begins with time and motion studies of very small labor unit activities. These small units are added to other units until a finished product results. Some of these units are common to several products. By developing standard costs for very small packages we are able to aggregate them in various combinations into many products.

Developing labor standards is illustrated in the Exhibits 20-7 through 20-11.[1]

A flow chart for setting labor time standards used by a major manufacturer is shown in Exhibit 20-12.

Similar processes are involved in setting labor rates, and material quantities and price. These concurrent processes meet in arriving at the total standard cost (Exhibit 20-13).

We conclude that setting standards is a complex process requiring the involvement and cooperation of every organizational unit.

[1]Exhibits 20-7 through 20-12 are from an address by J. O. Foreman, "Standardized Corporate-Wide Methodology for Pricing Parts," 1968. By permission of North American Rockwell Corp.

EXHIBIT 20-7 DETAILED TIME AND MOTION STUDY OF A MINOR LABOR ACTIVITY

FABRICATION OF CERAMIC PRINTED SUBSTRATE (C.P.S.)

Code	Item No.	Description of Operation	Per Occ.	Set-up	Run-time
		SECTION II			
E-12	6.	FIRING OF CIRCUITRY (TWO SIDED):			
		A. Run Time			
		1. Load and unload substrate from oven.			.0012
		Base Run Time			.0012
		Weighted Run Time	C.P.S.		.002
E-13	7.	TOUCH UP OF PLATED THROUGH HOLES AND PADS (TWO SIDED):			
		A. Run Time			
		1. Touch up plated through holes. Walk to oven or hot plate with or to obtain fiberglass plate of parts and return. Pick up fired C.P.S.' from tray receiver at end of oven, stack in hand, orienting each part to align circuit to each other, for a total of (102) parts.			.0283
		Base Run Time			.0283
		Weighted Run Time	C.P.S.		.038
E-14	8.	SCREENING OF RESISTORS (HAND) INK VALUE (TWO SIDED):			
		A. Set Up			
		1. Obtain screen, position in machine and tighten in place with (4) screws.		.019	
		2. Obtain jar of ink or maskant and mix with small spatula.		.028	
		3. Pick up jar of ink and apply to screen with putty knife.		.013	
		4. Run (7) substrates and check for alignment.		.017	
		5. Walk to oven or hot plate with, or to obtain fiberglass plate of parts and return.		.023	
		6. Obtain C.P.S., walk to hot plate 10′, position on plate, dry and return to screen area. Walk to comparator 15′ position C.P.S. on comparator, check and return to screen area. Adjust screen by loosening screws on one side and tightening on the opposite side.		.004	

EXHIBIT 20-8 OPERATION 7 IS INCORPORATED INTO A LARGER UNIT

FABRICATION OF CERAMIC PRINTED SUBSTRATE (C.P.S.)

Code	Item No.	Description of Operation	Per Occ.	Set-up	Run-time
		SECTION II			
Sec. II M-6	6.	FIRING OF CIRCUITRY:			
		Load and unload from oven.			.002
		Total	C.P.S.		.002
Sec. II M-7	7.	TOUCH UP OF PLATED THROUGH HOLES AND PADS:			
		A. Touch holes and pads place in oven and fire.			.038
		Total	C.P.S.		.038
Sec. II M-8	8.	SCREENING OF RESISTORS (1) INK VALUE:			
		A. Screen resistors (1) ink value–(2) sided.		.510	.004
		Total	C.P.S.	.510	.004
Sec. II M-9	9.	SCREENING OF RESISTORS (2) INK VALUE:			
		A. Screen resistors (2) ink values–(2 sided)		1.021	.007
		Total	C.P.S.	1.021	.007
Sec. II M-10	10.	SCREENING OF RESISTORS (3) INK VALUES.			
		A. Screen resistors (3) ink values–(2) sided.		1.533	.011
		Total	C.P.S.	1.533	.011
Sec. II M-11	11.	SCREENING OF RESISTORS (4) INK VALUES:			
		A. Screen resistors (4) ink values–(2) sided.		2.043	.015
		Total	C.P.S.	2.043	.015

EXHIBIT 20-9 OPERATION 7 IS NOW PART OF EVEN A LARGER UNIT OF LABOR ACTIVITY AS WE BUILD TOWARD COMPLETION OF A BASIC WORK UNIT

PAGE 1 of 2

DERIVATION FORM TITLE **TWO-SIDED FABRICATION OF CERAMIC PRINTED SUBSTRATES (CPS)**

DERIVATION FORM NO. ______ **DATE SEPTEMBER 1, 1966**

Deriv. Line Item	Corporate Ref.	Dated	Item	Operation	Set-up Unit Meas	Set-up Std Hrs	Run Unit Meas	Run Std Hrs	Remarks
1	S-200-E-02	9–1–66	1	Mount substrate to backing plate.	Rel.	.023	CPS	.011	
	S-200-E-02	9–1–66	2	Drill through holes.	Rel.	.089	CPS	.057	
	S-200-E-02	9–1–66	3	Clean after drilling			CPS	.005	
	S-200-E-02	9–1–66	4	Penetrant dye check after drill			CPS	.006	
	S-200-E-02	9–1–66	6	Firing of circuitry			CPS	.002	
	S-200-E-02	9–1–66	14	Machine dip solder	Rel.	.034	CPS	.006	
	S-200-E-02	9–1–66	15	Touch-up pad build-up & clean after dip solder			CPS	.006	Constant items occur once on each CPS.
	S-200-E-02	9–1–66	18	Attach terminal wires (handling)			CPS	.005	
	S-200-E-02	9–1–66	20	Coat terminal wires			CPS	.016	
	S-200-E-02	9–1–66	21	Trim terminal wires			CPS	.007	
	S-200-E-02	9–1–66	22	Sub. (Internal inspect)			CPS	.014	
	S-200-E-02	9–1–66	23	Flourescent dye check & clean			CPS	.004	
	S-200-E-02	9–1–66	24	Package (T-200-T-289)			CPS	.001	
5	S-200-E-02	9–1–66	5	Screening of circuitry	Rel.	.329	CPS/side	.008	
7	S-200-E-02	9–1–66	7	Touch-up of plated thru-holes & pad			CPS	.038	
8	S-200-E-02	9–1–66	8	Screening of resistors (1) ink value	Rel.	.510	CPS	.004	
9	S-200-E-02	9–1–66	9	Screening of resistors (2) ink values	Rel.	1.021	CPS	.007	
10	S-200-E-02	9–1–66	10	Screening of resistors (3) ink values	Rel.	1.533	CPS	.011	
11	S-200-E-02	9–1–66	11	Screening of resistors (4) ink values	Rel.	2.043	CPS	.015	
12	S-200-E-02	9–1–66	12	Firing of resistors	Rel.	.236	CPS	.004	

EXHIBIT 20-10 A BASIC LABOR UNIT IS COMPLETE—IT INCLUDES OPERATION 7

TIME STANDARD DERIVATION FORM

PAGE 1 OF 1

TITLE: "TWO SIDED"-FABRICATION OF CERAMIC PRINTED SUBSTRATE (CPS)

PART NO.	**CHG. LTR. DEPT.**	**ESTIMATOR**
PART NAME	**MODEL**	**DATE**

	Operation	**Unit of Measure**	**Oper**	**Set-up Occ**	**Set-up Hrs**	**Run Occ**	**Run Hrs**	**Sub-Total Set-up**	**Sub-Total Run**
1	Constant per C.P.S.	CPS		1	.146	1	.140	.146	.140
2									
3									
4									
5	Screening of circuitry	CPS/Side			.329		.008		
6									
7	Touch up of plated thru-holes & pad	CPS					.038		
8	Screening of resistors (1) ink value	CPS			.510		.004		
9	Screening of resistors (2) ink values	CPS			1.021		.007		
10	Screening of resistors (3) ink values	CPS			1.533		.011		
11	Screening of resistors (4) ink values	CPS			2.043		.015		
12	Firing of resistors	CPS					.002		
13	Screening & curing of solder maskant	CPS			.236		.004		
14									
15									
16	Resistor adjust	Res.			.030		.004		
17	Final resistance value check	Res.					.001		
18									
19	Attach terminal wires (solder)	Wire Pad					.002		
20									
21									
42									
43									
44								.146	.140
							SUB-TOTAL		
							FUNCTIONAL TEST		
							TOTAL STANDARD HOURS		

COMPLEXITY CODE

A B C D

SET-UP CODE

A B C D E F G H J K L

EXHIBIT 20-11 THE PERSONS PERFORMING OPERATION 7 MAINTAIN A RECORD OF ACTUAL TIME AND GIVE REASONS FOR ANY VARIANCES. THIS TYPE OF RECORD IS MAINTAINED CONTINUOUSLY. A STUDY OF THE REASONS FOR VARIANCES OVER A PERIOD OF TIME WILL INDICATE WHETHER OR NOT THE STANDARDS SHOULD BE CHANGED. A CONSTANT MONITORING OF STANDARDS LEADS TO IMPROVED WORK MEASUREMENT.

RECORD OF VARIANCES

SPEC ______ FABRICATION OF PAGE 1 OF 3

CERAMIC PRINTED SUBSTRATE (CPS) "TWO SIDED-THRU HOLE"

FILE NO. ______ DATE SEPTEMBER 1, 1966

Deriv. Line Item	Date	Application Instructions	Std. Time Set-up	Std. Time Run	Act. Time Set-up	Act. Time Run	Explanation of Variances
1.		MOUNT (WAX) SUBSTRATE TO BACKING PLATE					
		Set-Up					
		a. Apply per release					
		Run					
		a. Apply per each CPS					
2.		DRILL THRU HOLES					
		Set-Up					
		a. Apply per release					
		Run					
		a. Apply per each CPS Note: All holes are drilled simultaneously					
3.		CLEAN AFTER DRILLING					
		Run					
		a. Apply per each CPS					
4.		PENETRANT DYE CHECK & FIRE AFTER DRILLING					
		Run					
		a. Apply per each CPS					
5.		SCREENING OF CIRCUITRY					
		Set-Up					
		a. Apply per each side requiring circuitry					
		Run					
		a. Apply per each side requiring circuitry					
6.		FIRING OF CIRCUITRY					
		Run					
		a. Apply per CPS					
7.		TOUCH-UP OF PLATED THRU-HOLES & PADS	–	.038			
		Run					
		a. Apply per each CPS					
8,9,10,11		SCREENING OF RESISTORS					
		Set-Up					
		a. If resistors are required, do the following:					
		b. Check "RESISTOR DATA CHART" on the face of the drawing.					

EXHIBIT 20-12 FLOW CHART OF PROCEDURES IN DEVELOPING LABOR TIME STANDARDS

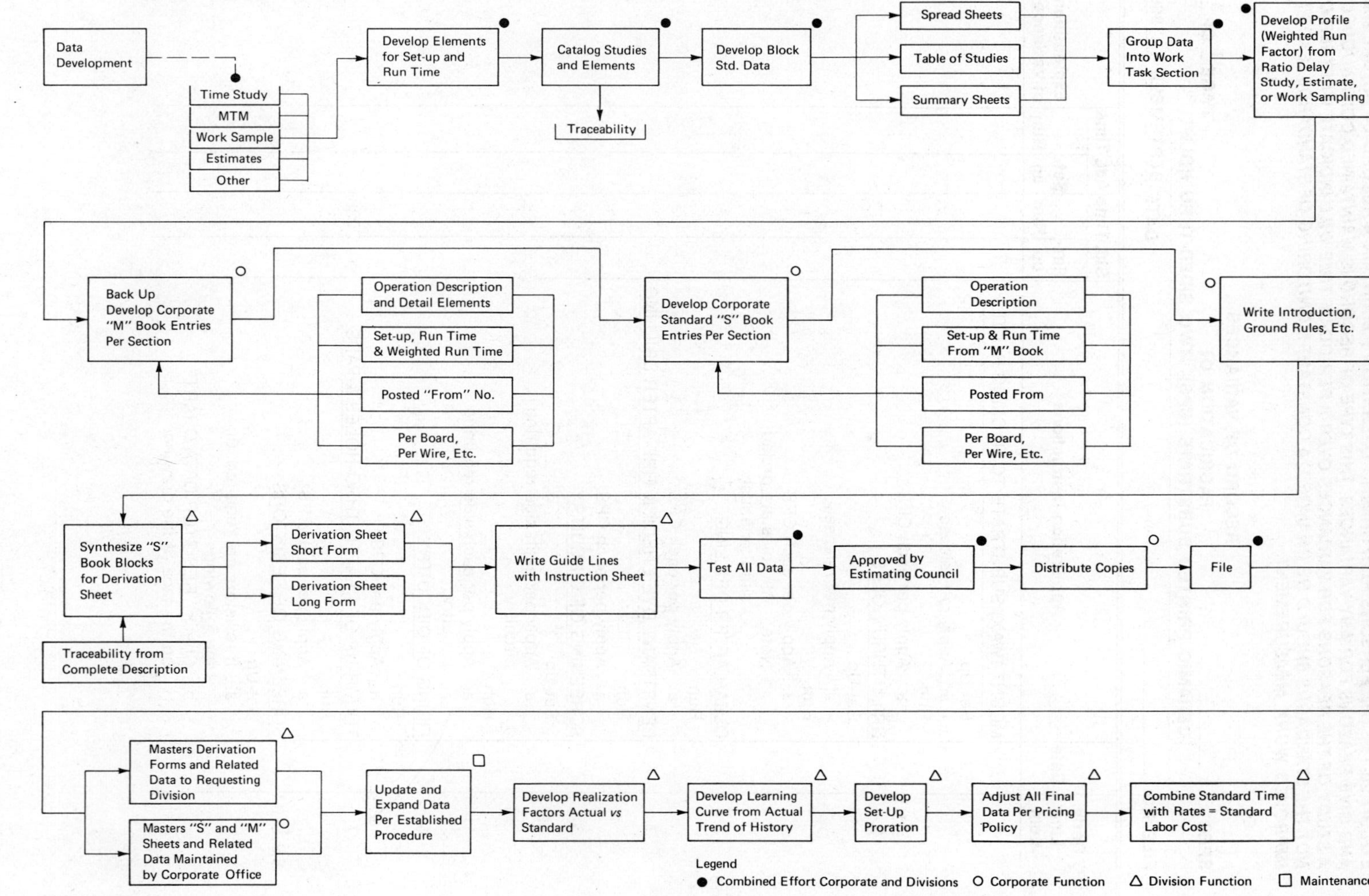

EXHIBIT 20-13 CONCURRENT PROCESSES FOR TOTAL STANDARD COST

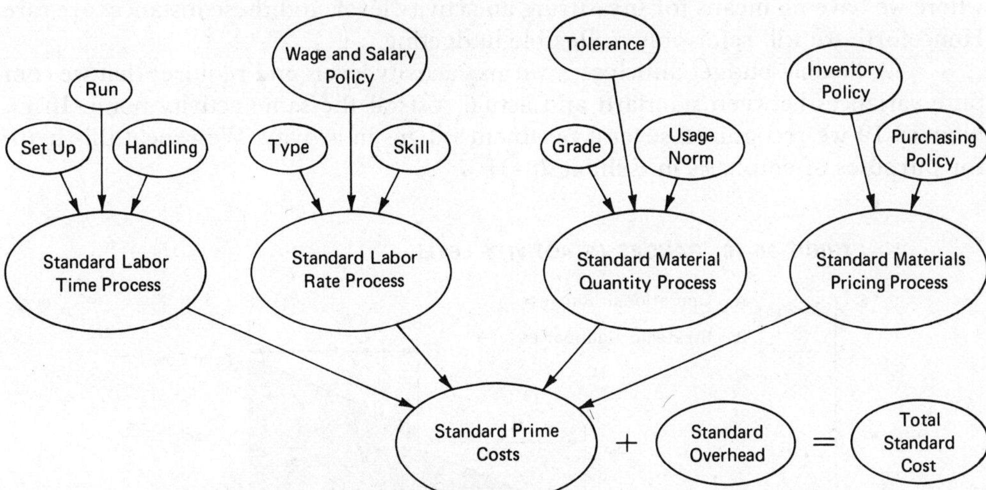

20.3 FIXED AND FLEXIBLE BUDGETS

A *fixed* budget assumes no variance in the level of activity. A *flexible* budget establishes a series of standard costs for various activity levels.

In our previous example (Exhibit 20-6) we anticipated the completion of 1,000 units at a total standard cost of $200,000. Suppose we complete only 900 units at a total cost of $200,000. Fixed budget variance analysis ignores the difference in activity level:

EXHIBIT 20-14 FIXED BUDGET ANALYSIS

Standard cost	$200,000
Actual cost	200,000
Variance	$ 0

Assuming that all costs are variable, flexible budget variance analysis would report the situation differently:

EXHIBIT 20-15 FLEXIBLE BUDGET ANALYSIS

Standard cost restated for 900 units	$180,000
Actual cost for 900 units	200,000
Unfavorable variance	$ (20,000)

The fixed budget format fails to report the fact (1) that less units were produced or (2) that it cost more to produce the units than was expected. For these reasons, fixed budget analysis is not recommended. It only has legitimacy in situations where we have no means for measuring an activity level, and these instances are rare. Henceforth we will refer only to flexible budgeting.

A flexible budget anticipates various activity levels and requires that we compute variances between standard and actual costs at the same activity point. In Exhibit 18-19 we recognized several pertinent ranges in activity. We repeat this figure for purposes of emphasis in Exhibit 20–16.

EXHIBIT 20-16 RANGES IN ACTIVITY LEVEL

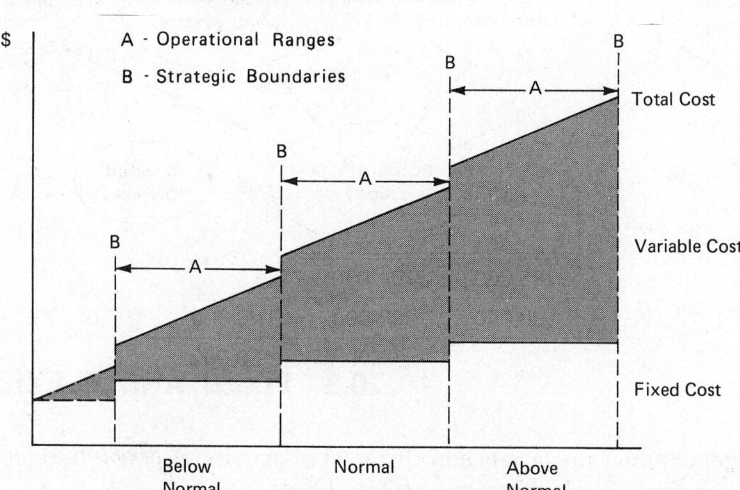

We have distinguished previously between *operational* and *strategic* events. The former term refers to a range of normalcy in which certain relationships will hold constant; e.g., the price of material. Therefore the notion of operationality applies only to the short-run predictable future, which in cost accounting we limit to a one-year period.

A strategic event is either a long-term event, or an event that occurs outside of the range of normalcy in the short run. All long-range planning is fraught with uncertainty which makes strategic decisions imperative. Major departures from normalcy in the short run also require strategic decision making. For example, if the activity level falls below a certain percentage it may be necessary to close down part of the plant, lay off employees, and take other major actions. A *full-range* flexible budget, such as the one contained in Exhibit 20-17, provides for the contingency of abnormal operations, either above or below normal. A *normal-range* flexible budget assumes no departures from normalcy, and hence it generally covers a smaller range of change in activity level.

In Exhibit 20-17 we have provided for three ranges of activity in our flexible budget: (1) normal: 90–110%; (2) below normal: 65–85%; and (3) above normal: 115–135%.

Within each range our relationships are constant. In the *normal range,* fixed costs are constant at $20,000 for any level of activity within the range. The price of material is $7.00 per lb for quantities between 9,000 and 11,000 lb. And the labor rate is constant at $4.50 per hour for total hours in the range of 18,000 to 22,000. The unit cost will vary within the range because fixed costs are stable.

EXHIBIT 20-17 A FLEXIBLE BUDGET

Standard Cost Elements	Below Normal Range				
	65%	**70%**	**75%**	**80%**	**85%**
Materials	$ 52,000	$ 56,000	$ 60,000	$ 64,000	$ 68,000
Labor	65,000	70,000	75,000	80,000	85,000
Prime Costs	$117,000	$126,000	$135,000	$144,000	$153,000
Overhead					
Fixed	15,000	15,000	15,000	15,000	15,000
Variable	14,300	15,400	16,500	17,600	18,700
Total Overhead	29,300	30,400	31,500	32,600	33,700
Total Standard Costs	$146,300	$156,400	$166,500	$176,600	$186,700
Standard Cost Per Unit	$225	$223	$222	$221	$220
Activity & Unit Cost Data:					
No. of Units	650	700	750	800	850
Direct Labor Hours	13,000	14,000	15,000	16,000	17,000
Unit Price – Materials	$8.00	$8.00	$8.00	$8.00	$8.00
Unit Rate – Labor	5.00	5.00	5.00	5.00	5.00
Variable Cost Rate	1.10	1.10	1.10	1.10	1.10

Standard Cost Elements	Normal Range Normal Capacity				
	90%	**95%**	**100%**	**105%**	**110%**
Materials	$ 63,000	$ 66,500	$ 70,000	$ 73,500	$ 77,000
Labor	81,000	85,500	90,000	94,500	99,000
Prime Costs	$144,000	$152,000	$160,000	$168,000	$176,000
Overhead					
Fixed	20,000	20,000	20,000	20,000	20,000
Variable	18,000	19,000	20,000	21,000	22,000
Total Overhead	38,000	39,000	40,000	41,000	42,000
Total Standard Costs	$182,000	$191,000	$200,000	$209,000	$218,000
Standard Cost Per Unit	$202	$201	$200	$199	$198

EXHIBIT 20-17 (CONTINUED)

	Normal Range				
	Normal Capacity				
	90%	**95%**	**100%**	**105%**	**110%**
Activity & Unit Cost Data:					
No. of Units	900	950	1,000	1,050	1,100
Direct Labor Hours	18,000	19,000	20,000	21,000	22,000
Unit Price – Materials	$7.00	$7.00	$7.00	$7.00	$7.00
Unit Rate – Labor	4.50	4.50	4.50	4.50	4.50
Variable Cost Rate	1.00	1.00	1.00	1.00	1.00

	Above Normal Range				
Standard Cost Elements					
	115%	**120%**	**125%**	**130%**	**135%**
Materials	$ 69,000	$ 72,000	$ 75,000	$ 78,000	$ 81,000
Labor	92,000	96,000	100,000	104,000	108,000
Prime Costs	$161,000	$168,000	$175,000	$182,000	$189,000
Overhead					
Fixed	30,000	30,000	30,000	30,000	30,000
Variable	20,700	21,600	22,500	23,400	24,300
Total Overhead	50,700	51,600	52,500	53,400	54,300
Total Standard Costs	$211,700	$219,600	$227,500	$235,400	$243,300
Standard Cost Per Unit	$184	$183	$182	$181	$180
Activity & Unit Cost Data:					
No. of Units	1,150	1,200	1,250	1,300	1,350
Direct Labor Hours	23,000	24,000	25,000	26,000	27,000
Unit Price – Materials	$6.00	$6.00	$6.00	$6.00	$6.00
Unit Rate – Labor	4.00	4.00	4.00	4.00	4.00
Variable Cost Rate	.90	.90	.90	.90	.90

The *normal capacity* of the firm is equated with 100%. The flexible budget pivots from this point. In Exhibit 20-17 we have illustrated variances from normal capacity in 5% intervals. We have also made assumptions as to the range of normalcy. These factors will change from one situation to another. Some firms may find it useful to develop their flexible budget in intervals other than 5%. Their range of normalcy may be smaller or greater than 90 to 110%. In fact, the range of normalcy is not determined by some specific percentage range, but rather by changes in the fundamental cost relationships: (1) an increase or decrease in the quantity or price of materials; (2) an increase or decrease in labor hours or rate per unit of activity; and (3) an increase or decrease in fixed or variable overhead.

In Exhibit 20-17 we have depicted a *below normal range* of 65 to 85%. If activity level drops below 90%, the normal range cost relationships are expected to change. New cost relationships will take effect and be constant within the lower range.

In the below normal range the cost of materials is expected to be constant at $8.00 per lb. The increase in the price paid for materials can be explained in part by the loss of quantity discounts. In this range, the labor rate is expected to be $5.00 per hour, which can be explained by the fact that lower paid workers are laid off, raising the average rate of those with seniority who remain. A reduction in fixed costs can be expected in this range, including reduced maintenance, rents, executive salaries, and other fixed expenses. The variable overhead rate is depicted as increasing, which may be explained by the fact that such items as labor fringe benefits cannot be reduced in proportion to the reduction in the labor force, resulting in an increase in overhead rate per remaining labor hours.

In the *above normal range* similar assumptions are made regarding cost behavior. Increased quantities of materials can be expected to lower the price per pound from $7.00 to $6.00. The labor force is expanded by hiring less experienced persons, reducing the average hourly rate from $4.50 to $4.00. New fixed costs can be anticipated in the form of increased maintenance, rents, executive salaries, and so forth. And the variable overhead rate can be expected to drop because a non-proportional increase in variable overhead can be spread over more labor hours.

A cardinal value of a flexible budget is its ability to plan for contingent actions in the event that normal expectancies do not materialize. Its value as a *planning* tool is augmented by its value as a *control* tool. The flexible budget can be detailed in terms of much shorter periods than a year; i.e., monthly, weekly, or even daily. Actual operations can be contrasted with planned operations on a continuous basis in order to monitor variances. These variances can be analyzed to determine whether or not they are "controllable." A *controllable* variance such as labor inefficiency can be corrected through personnel action or improved training and supervision. If detected early, many controllable variances can be rectified without serious consequence to planned operations. A *noncontrollable* variance, such as an increase in the price of material or an increase in negotiated labor rates, cannot be corrected. Such variances will affect operating results. And the consequence of noncontrollable variances to planned operations should be ascertained promptly.

In Exhibit 20-18 we illustrate how actual results can be plotted against planned operations. In this example standard cost and activity are assumed to be uniform throughout the year. If there are varying levels of cost or activity for different periods, the graph should be proportioned accordingly.

In our example, we produced less units at greater cost at AM_1 than was planned for SM_1. This was apparently a controllable variance, as the situation was corrected through about AM_5. At that point a noncontrollable trend set in, which carried through the remainder of the year. At AM_{12} we had only produced about 870 units, but at a total cost in excess of $200,000. As a matter of fact, the change of circumstances at AM_5 were of a strategic nature, causing actual operations to move outside of the normal range.

You will notice that the ranges narrow toward the point of origin. This makes it more difficult to predict whether early variances will be within a particular range. The ranges in Exhibit 20-17 are plotted in Exhibit 20-19 for purposes of emphasizing this point.

EXHIBIT 20-18 ACTUAL VERSUS STANDARD OPERATIONS: BASED ON NORMAL CAPACITY

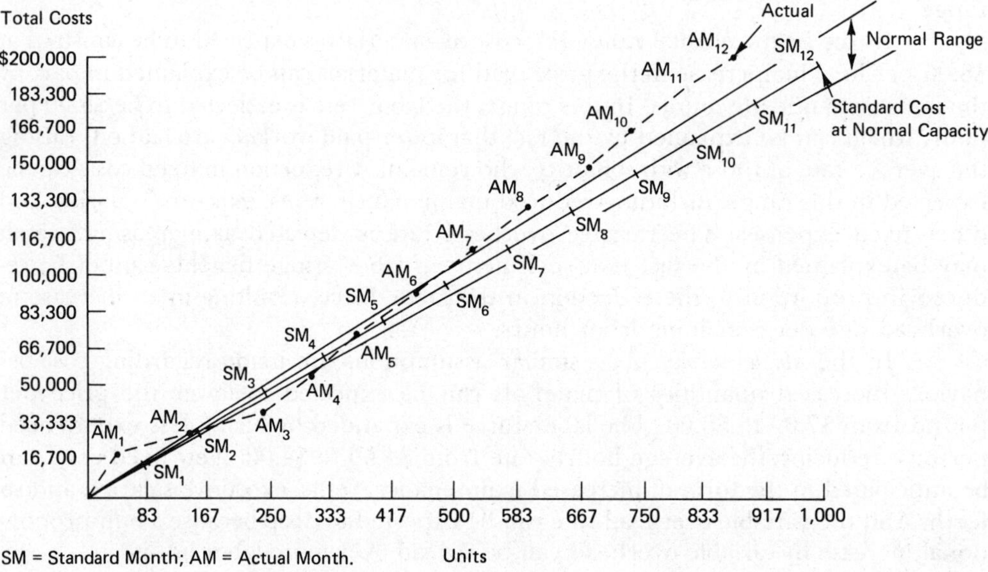

SM = Standard Month; AM = Actual Month.

EXHIBIT 20-19 RANGES NARROW TOWARD THE POINT OF ORIGIN

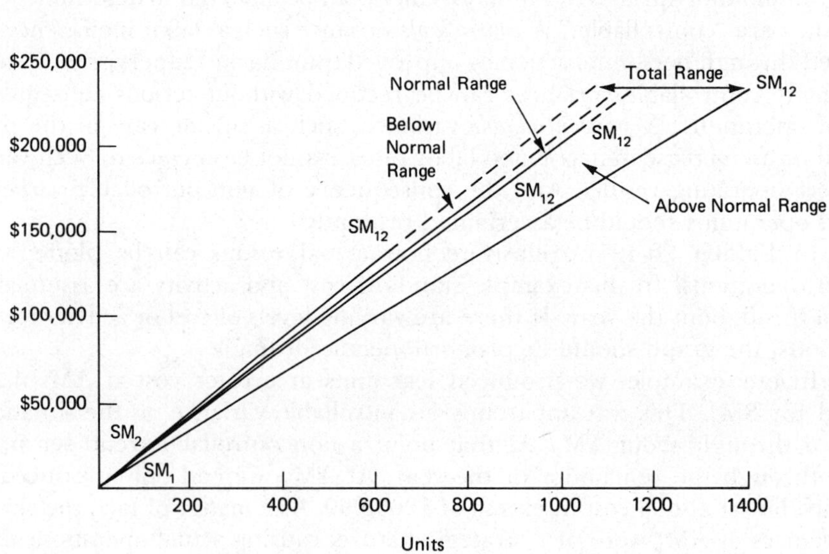

20.4 COMPUTING VARIANCES

FORMAL APPROACH

The difference between *standard* and *actual* is termed *variance,* as mentioned previously. We consider here the manner in which variances are computed. Let us use the materials element of our preceding example to illustrate the computation of variances.

Our materials standard is:

$$1{,}000 \text{ u} \times 10 \text{ lb} = 10{,}000 \text{ lb} \times \$7.00 = \$70{,}000$$

Let us begin by assuming no change in activity level, i.e., we planned and achieved a production *volume* of 1,000 units. The variables therefore relate to (1) what quantity of materials we used, and (2) the price paid for materials. We have three conditions—(1) more; (2) less; or (3) the same—when we contrast actual price and quantity with standard price and quantity. Therefore, $3 \times 3 = 9$ combinations, which are detailed as follows:

POSSIBLE PRICE-QUANTITY COMBINATIONS

1. $Pa = Ps$, $Qa = Qs$, i.e., same price, same quantity.
2. $Pa > Ps$, $Qa = Qs$, i.e., actual price more than standard, same quantity.
3. $Pa < Ps$, $Qa = Qs$, i.e., standard price more than actual, same quantity.
4. $Pa > Ps$, $Qa > Qs$, i.e., actual price more than standard, actual quantity more than standard.
5. $Pa > Ps$, $Qa < Qs$, i.e., actual price more than standard, actual quantity less than standard.
6. $Pa < Ps$, $Qa > Qs$, i.e., actual price less than standard, actual quantity more than standard.
7. $Pa < Ps$, $Qa < Qs$, i.e., actual price less than standard, actual quantity less than standard.
8. $Pa = Ps$, $Qa > Qs$, i.e., same price, actual quantity more than standard.
9. $Pa = Ps$, $Qa < Qs$, i.e., same price, actual quantity less than standard.

These combinations form the basis for computing variances as illustrated by means of the graphs in Exhibit 20-20.

Labor rate and efficiency variances behave in precisely the same manner as materials price and quantity variances. The only distinction is in terminology. With labor variances we use rate instead of price and efficiency instead of quantity.

If actual exceeds standard in any of these categories, we speak of an *unfavorable* variance. Conversely, if standard exceeds actual in any of these categories, we speak of a *favorable* variance.

We note from the nine possible combinations in Exhibit 20-20 that 4 and 7 have a "mixed" variance. This occurs when price *and* quantity exceed their standards and where price *and* quantity are below their standards.

EXHIBIT 20-20 COMPUTING VARIANCES BY GRAPH

1. $Pa = Ps, Qa = Qs$

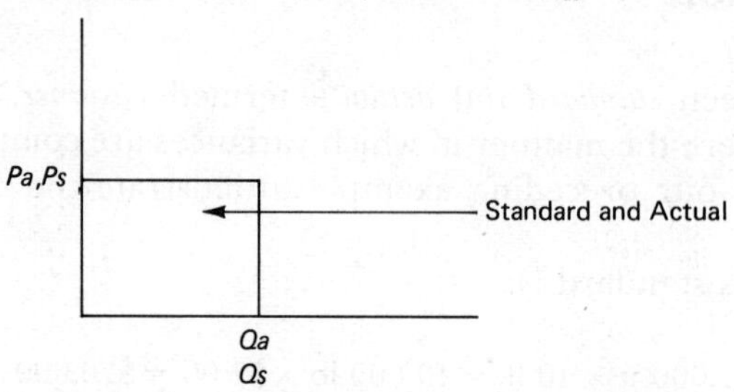

There is no variance in this situation.

2. $Pa > Ps, Qa = Qs$, or

3. $Pa < Ps, Qa = Qs$

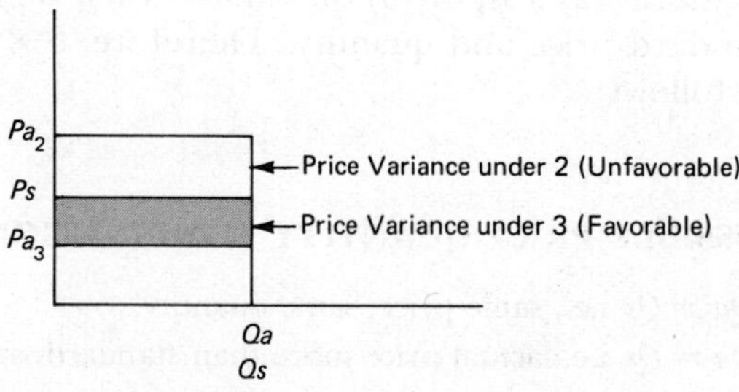

Formula for computing variances, where V_p = price variance; V_q = quantity variance. Negative result = unfavorable variance; Positive result = favorable variance.

$$V_p = Qs(Pa - Ps)$$
$$V_q = Ps(Qa - Qs)$$

In 2 and 3 there is no V_q variance, as $Qa - Qs = 0$

4. $Pa > Ps, Qa > Qs$, or

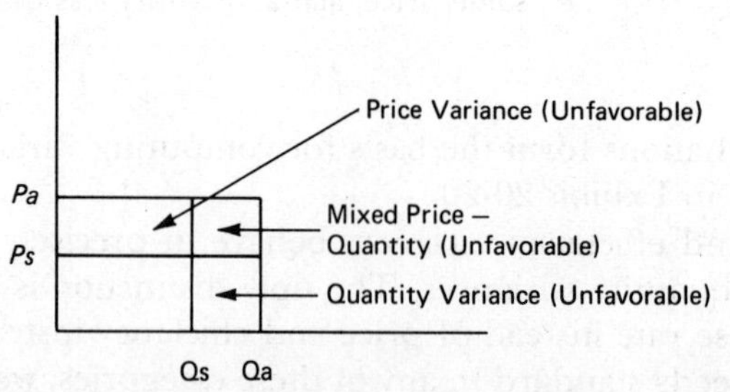

Formula: (V_{pq} = mixed price-quantity variance)

$$V_{pq} = (Pa - Ps)(Qa - Qs)$$
$$V_p = Qs(Pa - Ps)$$
$$V_q = Ps(Qa - Qs)$$

EXHIBIT 20-20 (CONTINUED)

5. *Pa > Ps, Qa < Qs*

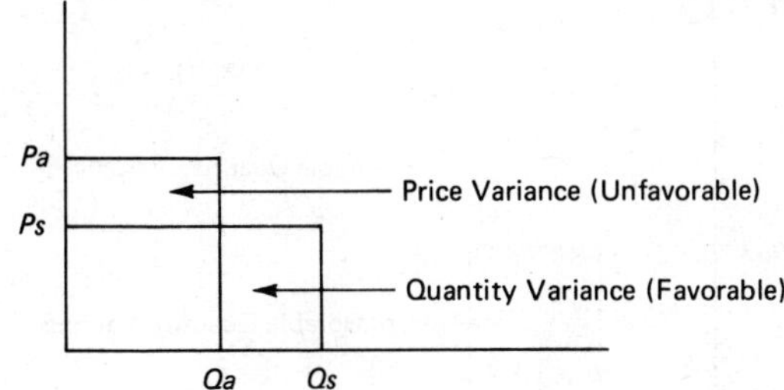

Formula:

$$V_p = Qa(Pa - Ps)$$
$$V_q = Ps(Qs - Qa)$$

6. *Pa < Ps, Qa > Qs*

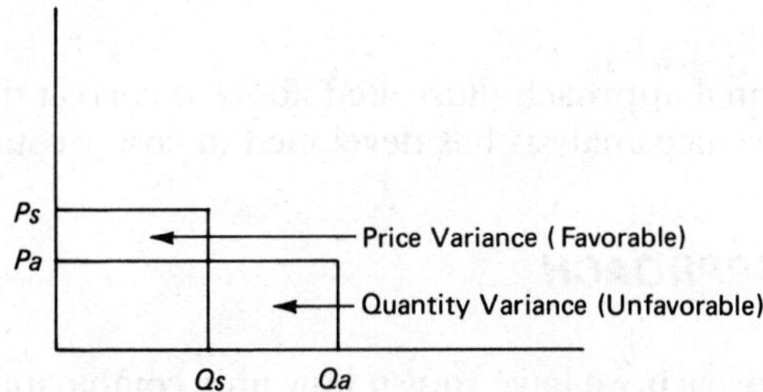

Formula:

$$V_p = Qs(Ps - Pa)$$
$$V_q = Pa(Qs - Qa)$$

7. *Pa < Ps, Qa < Qs*

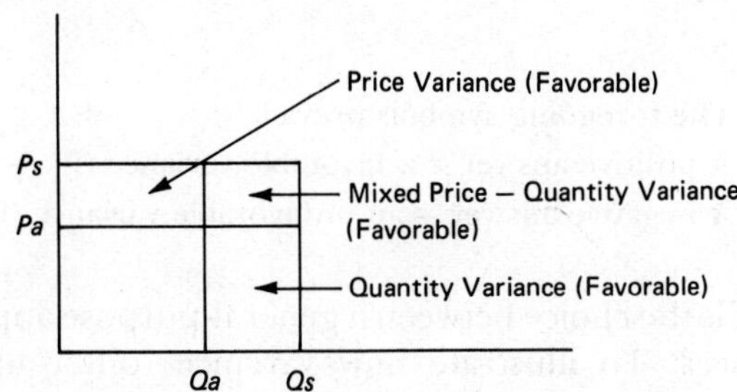

Formula:

$$V_{pq} = (Ps - Pa)(Qs - Qa)$$
$$V_p = Qa(Ps - Pa)$$
$$V_q = Pa(Qs - Qa)$$

EXHIBIT 20-20 (CONTINUED)

8. $Pa = Ps$, $Qa > Qs$, or
9. $Pa = Ps$, $Qa < Qs$

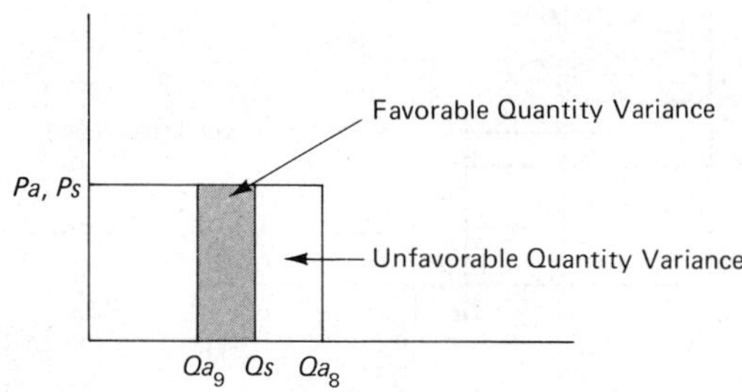

Formula:

$$V_p = Qs(Ps - Pa)$$
$$V_q = Ps(Qs - Qa)$$

In 8 and 9 there is no V_p variance, as $Ps - Pa = 0$

While the formal approach illustrated above is correct theoretically, a practical convention for variance analysis has developed in cost accounting.

CONVENTIONAL APPROACH

Under the formal approach we have shown how nine combinations of price-quantity variances can be solved by the means of a number of formulae. The practical convention in cost accounting analyzes price-quantity (and rate-efficiency) variances by means of these formulae:

$$V_p = Qa(Ps - Pa)$$
$$V_q = Ps(Qs - Qa)$$

where

The foregoing symbols prevail.
A positive answer = a favorable variance (F).
A negative answer = an unfavorable variance (U).

The trade-off is the choice between a general-purpose approach and precision in computing variances. To illustrate how variances differ under these two approaches, we assume the materials standard stated previously and allow for changes in price and quantity as follows:

Volume	Alternative Quantities			Alternate Prices		
1,000 units	9,000 *a*	10,000 *s*	11,000 *a*	\$6.00 *a*	\$7.00 *s*	\$8.00 *a*

A *net variance* is the difference between total standard and actual cost. Net variance is the same under either method. We compute net variance for the nine combinations as a first step:

1. $Pa = Ps,\ Qa = Qs$

Standard	1,000 u × 10 lb = 10,000 lb × $7.00 =	$70,000
Actual	1,000 u × 10 lb = 10,000 lb × 7.00 =	70,000
Net variance		-0-

2. $Pa > Ps,\ Qa = Qs$

Standard	1,000 u × 10 lb = 10,000 lb × $7.00 =	$70,000
Actual	1,000 u × 10 lb = 10,000 lb × 8.00 =	80,000
Net variance		$(10,000) (U)

3. $Pa < Ps,\ Qa = Qs$

Standard	1,000 u × 10 lb = 10,000 lb × $7.00 =	$70,000
Actual	1,000 u × 10 lb = 10,000 lb × 6.00 =	60,000
Net variance		$10,000 (F)

4. $Pa > Ps,\ Qa > Qs$

Standard	1,000 u × 10 lb = 10,000 lb × $7.00 =	$70,000
Actual	1,000 u × 11 lb = 11,000 lb × 8.00 =	88,000
Net variance		$(18,000) (U)

5. $Pa > Ps,\ Qa < Qs$

Standard	1,000 u × 10 lb = 10,000 lb × $7.00 =	$70,000
Actual	1,000 u × 9 lb = 9,000 lb × 8.00 =	72,000
Net variance		$ (2,000) (U)

6. $Pa < Ps,\ Qa > Qs$

Standard	1,000 u × 10 lb = 10,000 lb × $7.00 =	$70,000
Actual	1,000 u × 11 lb = 11,000 lb × 6.00 =	66,000
Net variance		$ 4,000 (F)

7. $Pa < Ps,\ Qa < Qs$

Standard	1,000 u × 10 lb = 10,000 lb × $7.00 =	$70,000
Actual	1,000 u × 9 lb = 9,000 lb × 6.00 =	54,000
		$16,000 (F)

8. $Pa = Ps,\ Qa > Qs$

Standard	1,000 u × 10 lb = 10,000 lb × $7.00 =	$70,000
Actual	1,000 u × 11 lb = 11,000 lb × 7.00 =	77,000
Net variance		$ (7,000) (U)

9. $Pa = Ps,\ Qa < Qs$

Standard	1,000 u × 10 lb = 10,000 lb × $7.00 =	$70,000
Actual	1,000 u × 9 lb = 9,000 lb × 7.00 =	63,000
Net variance		$ 7,000 (F)

The composition of "net variance" differs in certain instances by using the conventional approach rather than the formal one, as illustrated in Exhibit 20-21 for the foregoing example.

EXHIBIT 20-21 COMPARISON OF FORMAL VERSUS CONVENTIONAL METHODS FOR COMPUTING VARIANCES

		Formal			Conventional	
	Net Variance	**Price**	**Quantity**	**Mixed PQ**	**Price**	**Quantity**
1.	–	–	–	–	–	–
2.	$10,000 (U)	$10,000 (U)	–	–	$10,000 (U)	–
3.	10,000 (F)	10,000 (F)	–	–	10,000 (F)	–
* 4.	18,000 (U)	10,000 (U)	$7,000 (U)	$1,000 (U)	11,000 (U)	$7,000 (U)
5.	2,000 (U)	9,000 (U)	7,000 (F)	–	9,000 (U)	7,000 (F)
* 6.	4,000 (F)	10,000 (F)	6,000 (U)	–	11,000 (F)	7,000 (U)
* 7.	16,000 (F)	9,000 (F)	6,000 (F)	1,000 (F)	9,000 (F)	7,000 (F)
8.	7,000 (U)	–	7,000 (U)	–	–	7,000 (U)
9.	7,000 (F)	–	7,000 (F)	–	–	7,000 (F)

* Instances where the methods differ.

In most instances the conventional method yields the same sub-variances as the formal approach, supporting the case for a trade-off between some precision and the utility of a general purpose approach. Accordingly, we will use the conventional approach for computing variances throughout the remainder of this chapter.

COMPUTING MATERIAL VARIANCES

Let us proceed with the above example but change the volume of units produced, e.g.:

Standard: 1,000 u × 10 lb = 10,000 lb × $7.00 = $70,000
Actual: 900 u × 11 lb = 9,900 lb × 6.50 = 64,350

Under the concept of flexible budgeting, the difference between these total costs ($70,000 − $64,350 = $5,650) is meaningless because we are comparing the cost of producing 1,000 units in the first instance versus 900 units of actual output. The objective is to compare costs at the same level of activity. This is done by *restating* standard costs in terms of actual volume:

~~Original standard: 1,000 u × 10 lb = 10,000 lb × $7.00 = $70,000~~
(The original standard is irrelevant.)

Standard restated to actual volume:[2]	900 u × 10 lb = 9,000 lb × $7.00 =	$63,000
Actual costs:	900 u × 11 lb = 9,900 lb × $6.50 =	64,350
Net variance	=	$ 1,350 (U)

[2] As we are still within the normal range of our example, the cost relationships are constant. We will hereafter assume that we are always within the normal range.

Sub-variances:

Quantity: $V_q = Ps(Qs - Qa)$	900 lb × \$7.00 =	6,300 (U)
Price: $V_p = Qa(Ps - Pa)$	9,900 lb × .50 =	4,950 (F)
Net variance (Proof)		\$ 1,350 (U)

By restating the standard to actual volume, we allow for a valid comparison. We actually used more material than the standard called for, hence the 900 additional lb are charged with the standard cost of material of \$7.00. Because we used *more* material than standard, the variance is *unfavorable*. The price per pound was less than expected. We purchased 9,900 lb at a savings of 50¢ per lb, which yields our *favorable* price variance of \$4,950.

COMPUTING LABOR VARIANCES

We take the labor costs in Exhibit 20-6 as our standard, and compare it with actual labor costs (given):

~~Original standard:~~	~~1,000 u × 20 hrs = 20,000 hrs × \$4.50 = \$90,000~~		
(The original standard is not used in computing variances.)			
Standard restated to actual volume:[3]	900 u × 20 hrs = 18,000 hrs × 4.50 =	81,000	
Actual costs	900 u × 18 hrs = 17,100 hrs × 5.00 =	85,500	
Net Variance:		\$ 4,500	(U)
Sub-variances:			
Efficiency: $V_e = Rs(Hs - Ha)$	900 hrs × \$4.50 =	4,050	(F)
Rate: $V_r = Ha(Rs - Ra)$	17,100 hrs × .50 =	8,550	(U)
Net variance (Proof)	=	\$ 4,500	(U)

where

V_e = Efficiency variance
R = Rate, standard or actual respectively
H = Hours, standard or actual respectively

We used *less* hours than expected. These 900 *favorable* hours are multiplied by the standard rate to give us the efficiency variance of \$4,050. The change in rate was *unfavorable*. The difference in rate of 50¢ per hour is multiplied by the total actual hours of 17,100 to yield the rate variance of *\$8,550*.

By observing the direction in which quantity (hours) or price (rate) vary, you should have no difficulty in deciding whether variances are favorable or unfavorable.

COMPUTING OVERHEAD VARIANCES

While there is a generally accepted convention for computing materials and labor variances, many techniques have been proposed for computing overhead variances.

[3] Actual volume is the same for all elements of cost: materials, labor, and overhead.

This area of cost does not lend itself readily to analysis or to the assignment of responsibility for variances to specific persons in an organization.

We will illustrate a three-variance approach to analyzing overhead. We continue the foregoing example, adding actual overhead data to the standard overhead figures contained in Exhibit 20-6:

Standard		
	1000 u/20,000 hrs × \$1.00 F_{or} =	\$20,000 Fixed O.H.
	1000 u/20,000 hrs × \$1.00 V_{or} =	20,000 Variable O.H.
	1000 u/20,000 hrs × \$2.00 A_{or} =	40,000 Total O.H.

where

F_{or} = Fixed overhead rate. This rate can only be computed at normal capacity level:

$$\frac{\text{Normal Capacity Fixed O.H.}}{\text{Normal Capacity Hours}} = \frac{\$20{,}000}{20{,}000} = \$1.00$$

V_{or} = Variable overhead rate. This rate will be constant within a normal range.

$$\frac{\text{Normal Capacity Variable O.H.}}{\text{Normal Capacity Hours}} = \frac{\$20{,}000}{20{,}000} = \$1.00$$

A_{or} = Applied overhead rate. The sum of $F_{or} + V_{or}$.

$$\frac{\text{Normal Capacity Total O.H.}}{\text{Normal Capacity Hours}} = \frac{\$40{,}000}{20{,}000} = \$2.00$$

Actual overhead incurred during the period is given as:

Fixed	\$21,000
Variable	19,000
Total	\$40,000

We recall that overhead is allocated on the basis of direct labor hours:

Standard hours at 1,000 u	= 20,000
Standard hours at 900 u	= 18,000
Actual hours (given)	= 17,100

Overhead variances can now be computed as follows:

EXHIBIT 20-22 OVERHEAD VARIANCE ANALYSIS

	Basis	Fixed	Variable	Total
(1) ~~Original standard applied overhead~~	~~1000 u/20,000 hrs~~	~~\$20,000~~	~~\$20,000~~	~~\$20,000~~
(2) Restated on basis of *standard applied overhead*	900 u/18,000 hrs	18,000	18,000	36,000
(3) Flexible budget overhead at actual volume	900 u/18,000 hrs	20,000	18,000	38,000
(4) Actual applied overhead	900 u/17,100 hrs	17,100	17,100	34,200
(5) Actual overhead	900 u/17,100 hrs	21,000	19,000	40,000
(6) Net variances (2–5)		\$ 3,000 (U)	\$ 1,000 (U)	\$ 4,000 (U)

EXHIBIT 20-22 (CONTINUED)

	Fixed	Variable	Total
(7) **Sub-variances**			
(8) *Budget* overhead variances (2–3)	$2,000 (U)	$ 0	$2,000 (U)
(9) *Efficiency* overhead variances (3–4)	2,900 (F)	900 (F)	3,800 (F)
(10) *Controllable* overhead variances (4–5)	3,900 (U)	1,900 (U)	5,800 (U)
Net variances (Proof)	$3,000 (U)	$1,000 (U)	$4,000 (U)

Notes to Exhibit 20-22

1. Items 1 and 2 are the same if there is no change in volume. Original standard applied overhead is irrelevant where volume has changed.
2. *Standard Applied Overhead.* Overhead in this example is applied at the rate of $2.00 per hour. The actual volume of 900 units allows for 18,000 hours, hence:

$$18{,}000 \times \$1.00\ F_{or} = \$18{,}000 \text{ Fixed}$$
$$18{,}000 \times \$1.00\ V_{or} = \underline{18{,}000} \text{ Variable}$$
$$18{,}000 \times \$2.00\ A_{or} = \underline{\$36{,}000} \text{ Total}$$

3. *Flexible Budget at Actual Volume:* The flexible budget based on 900 units provides for overhead as follows (See Exhibit 20-16):

Fixed	$20,000
Variable	18,000
Total	$38,000

If volume variance is within the normal range, fixed costs will remain constant. The variable cost *rate* will also be constant in relation to the basis of allocation.

4. *Actual Applied Overhead.* Only 17,100 hours were used in the production of 900 units. Overhead *is* applied on actual hours.

$$17{,}100 \times \$1.00\ F_{or} = \$17{,}100 \text{ Fixed}$$
$$17{,}100 \times \$1.00\ V_{or} = \underline{17{,}100} \text{ Variable}$$
$$17{,}100 \times \$2.00\ A_{or} = \underline{\$34{,}200} \text{ Total}$$

5. *Actual Overhead:* These amounts are obtained from the accounting records of the period.
6. *Net Variances:* These are computed between steps 2 and 5.
7. *Sub-Variances:* Our approach generates three overhead variances: (1) budget, (2) efficiency, and (3) controllable.
8. *Budget Overhead Variance:* The difference between steps 2 and 3. We can also compute this variance by the formula:

$$V_{ob} = [B_s \times A_{or}] - [F + (B_s \times V_{or})]$$

where

V_{ob} = Budget overhead variance.
A_{or} = Applied overhead rate (see p. 876)
V_{or} = Variable overhead rate (see p. 876)
B_a = Actual basis (number of units or hours depending upon which is used as the basis for allocating overhead)
B_s = Standard basis at actual volume
F = Fixed costs
P_n = Percentage of normal capacity attained by actual production

To illustrate we solve for the *budget* variance for total overhead in our example:

$$\begin{aligned} V_o &= [18{,}000 \times \$2] - [\$20{,}000 + (18{,}000 \times \$1)] \\ &= [\$36{,}000] - [\$20{,}000 + (\$18{,}000)] \\ &= \$36{,}000 - \$38{,}000 \\ &= \underline{-\$2{,}000} \text{ or } \underline{\$2{,}000 \text{ (U)}} \end{aligned}$$

The "fixed" component of the *budget* variance is computed by a modification of the above formula:

$$V_{ob(f)} = [B_s \times A_{or}] - F$$

The "variable" component of the *budget* can be isolated by:

$$V_{ob(v)} = [B_s \times A_{or}] - [B_s \times V_{or}]$$

9. *Efficiency Overhead Variance:* The difference between steps 3 and 4; or we can use this formula:

$$V_{oe} = [F + (B_s \times V_{or})] - [B_a \times A_{or}]$$

where

V_{oe} = Efficiency overhead variance
B_a = Actual basis (number of units or hours or other basis that is used for allocating overhead—in this case, "actual hours")
F = Fixed costs per flexible budget
V_{or} = Variable overhead rate
A_{or} = Applied overhead rate
B_s = Standard basis at actual volume

Solving for total *efficiency* variance in Exhibit 20-22:

$$\begin{aligned} V_{ob} &= [\$20{,}000 + (18{,}000 \times \$1)] - [17{,}100 \times \$2] \\ &= \$38{,}000 - \$34{,}200 \\ &= \underline{\$3{,}800} \text{ (F)} \end{aligned}$$

The "fixed" component of the *efficiency* variance can be obtained by modifying the formula:

$$V_{oe(f)} = F - (B_a \times F_{or})$$

The formula for the "variable" component of the *efficiency* variance is:

$$V_{oe(v)} = (B_s \times V_{or}) - (B_a \times V_{or})$$

10. *Controllable Overhead Variance:* The difference between steps 4 and 5 in Exhibit 20-22; or we can use this formula:

$$V_{oc} = (B_a \times A_{or}) - A$$

where

V_{oc} = Controllable overhead variance
A = Actual overhead
(other symbols as before)

Solving for total *controllable* variance in our example:

$$\begin{aligned} V_{oc} &= (17{,}100 \times \$2) - \$40{,}000 \\ &= \$34{,}200 - \$40{,}000 \\ &= \underline{-\$5{,}800} \text{ or } \underline{\$5{,}800 \text{ (U)}} \end{aligned}$$

The "fixed" component of the *controllable* variance is computed by:

$$V_{oc(f)} = (B_a \times F_{or}) - A_f$$

where

A_f = Actual fixed costs

The "variable" component of the *controllable* variance is computed by:

$$V_{oc(v)} = (B_a \times V_{or}) - A_v$$

where

A_v = Actual variable costs

The construction of Exhibit 20-22 is such that if an amount is smaller than the one above it, we have a *favorable* variance. If an amount is higher than the one above it the variance is *unfavorable.* This is because we move progressively in Exhibit 20-22 from standard to actual overhead. For example:

Computing Net Variance of Fixed Costs:

Item (2) is lower than item (5) = \$18,000 − \$21,000 = \$3,000 (U)

Computing Efficiency Overhead Variance of Variable Costs:

Item (3) is greater than item (4) = \$20,000 − \$17,100 = \$2,900 (F)

The use of an overhead table such as the one depicted in Exhibit 20-22 permits us to compute overhead variances in the body of the table (Exhibit 20-23).

EXHIBIT 20-23 STRUCTURED METHOD FOR COMPUTING OVERHEAD

			Fixed	Variable	Total
(2)	Standard applied overhead....		\$18,000	\$18,000	\$36,000
		Budget	>\$2,000 (U)	>\$ 0	>\$2,000 (U)
(3)	Flexible budget overhead at actual volume		20,000	18,000	38,000
		Efficiency	> 2,900 (F)	> 900 (F)	> 3,800 (F)
(4)	Actual applied overhead		17,100	17,100	34,200
		Controllable	> 3,900 (U)	> 1,900 (U)	> 5,800 (U)
(5)	Actual overhead		21,000	19,000	40,000
(6)	Net variances (sum of sub-variances)		\$3,000 (U)	\$1,000 (U)	\$4,000 (U)

Where there is no break down of overhead into its fixed and variable components, our analysis is limited to *total* variances.

DATA SUMMARY AND SCHEDULE OF VARIANCES

Let us summarize the data that is needed for variance analysis from our preceding example and develop the *schedule of variances* (Exhibit 20-24), which is a typical format for reporting variances.

DATA SUMMARY

	"Original" Standard ("Normal Capacity")	"Revised" Standard At Actual Volume	Actual
Number of units....................................	1,000 units	900 units	900 units
Total materials cost..............................	\$70,000	\$63,000	\$64,350
Quantity (total)	10,000 lb	9,000 lb	9,900 lb
Price per lb	\$7.00	\$7.00	\$6.50
Total labor cost	\$90,000	\$81,000	\$85,500
Hours (total)......................................	20,000 hrs	18,000 hrs	17,100 hrs
Rate per hour	\$4.50	\$4.50	\$5.00
Overhead – total cost............................	\$40,000	\$36,000*	\$40,000
Fixed	\$20,000	\$18,000*	\$21,000
Variable	\$20,000	\$18,000*	\$19,000
Overhead rates	\$1.00 F_{or}		
	\$1.00 V_{or}	same	same
	\$2.00 A_{or}		

* Revised standard overhead is based on "applied overhead" per standard hours at actual volume.

EXHIBIT 20-24 SCHEDULE OF VARIANCES

Cost Element	Standard at Actual Volume	Actual Cost	Net (F) Variance (U)	Sub-Variances (F) (U)	
				Type	**Amount**
→ Materials	$63,000	$64,350	$1,350 (U)	Quantity	$6,300 (U)
				Price	$4,950 (F)
→ Labor	$81,000	$85,500	$4,500 (U)	Efficiency	$4,050 (F)
				Rate	$8,550 (U)
Fixed Overhead	$18,000	$21,000	$3,000 (U)	Budget	$2,000 (U)
				Efficiency	$2,900 (F)
				Controllable	$3,900 (U)
Variable Overhead	$18,000	$19,000	$1,000 (U)	Budget	$ 0
				Efficiency	$ 900 (F)
				Controllable	$1,900 (U)
→ Total Overhead	$36,000	$40,000	$4,000 (U)	Budget	$2,000 (U)
				Efficiency	$3,800 (F)
				Controllable	$5,800 (U)
→ Total Costs	$180,000	$189,850	$9,850 (U)	—	—

20.5 AN ILLUSTRATION IN COMPUTING VARIANCES

We will begin with a typical set of data provided in standard costing problems:

Standard Data:

Normal capacity: 2,000 units.
Materials: 10 lb per unit @ $4.00 per lb.
Labor: 20 hours per unit @ $2.50 per hour.
Overhead: Fixed, $20,000; Variable, $1.00 per direct labor hour.

Actual Data:

Units produced: 1,900.
Materials requisitioned and used: 18,000 lb.
Materials inventory data:

Beginning inventory		4,000 lb @ $4.00 per lb.
Purchases	(A)	10,000 lb @ 4.10 per lb.
	(B)	12,000 lb @ 4.20 per lb.

Materials inventory pricing method: FIFO.
Labor: A total cost of $98,400 based on 41,000 hours.
Overhead: Actual total overhead $57,000, comprising $19,500 fixed and $37,500 variable.

Required: Compute materials, labor, and overhead variances.

We illustrate a systematic solution to this problem.

STEP I: Prepare a data summary schedule for purposes of organizing the information and to ensure that we have all of the data that is needed to compute variances. This step can be dispensed with as you gain experience in solving standard costing problems:

DATA SUMMARY

	Standard at Normal Capacity	Standard at Actual Volume	Actual
Number of units	2,000	1,900	1,900
Total materials cost	$ 80,000	$76,000	$73,800
Quantity (total)	20,000	19,000	18,000
Price per lb	$4.00	$4.00	$4.10
Total labor cost	$100,000	$95,000	$98,400
Hours (total)	40,000	38,000	41,000
Rate per hour	$2.50	$2.50	$2.40
Overhead–total cost	$ 60,000	$57,000*	$57,000
Fixed	20,000	19,000*	19,500
Variable	40,000	38,000*	37,500
Overhead rates	$.50 F_{or}		
	1.00 V_{or}	same	same
	$1.50 A_{or}		

*Based on standard applied overhead.

Some routine calculations are necessary to complete the data summary.

STEP II: Compute variances:

(A) Materials

Standard at actual volume	1,900 u × 10 lb = 19,000 lb × $4.00 =	$76,000
Actual*	18,000 lb × 4.10 =	73,800
Net variance		$ 2,200 (F)
Quantity variance	1,000 lb × $4.00 =	$ 4,000 (F)
Price variance	18,000 lb × .10 =	$ 1,800 (U)

(B) Labor

Standard at actual volume	1,900 u × 20 hrs = 38,000 hrs × $2.50 =	$95,000
Actual	41,000 hrs × 2.40 =	98,400
Net variance		$ 3,400 (U)
Efficiency variance	3,000 hrs × $2.50 =	$ 7,500 (U)
Rate variance	41,000 hrs × .10 =	$ 4,100 (F)

*It is not necessary to compute the actual unit quantity. In this case it averaged about 9.5 lb per unit.

(C) Overhead	Fixed	Variable	Total
Standard applied overhead	$19,000	$38,000	$57,000
Budget variance	>$1,000 (U)	> 0	>$1,000 (U)
Flexible budget overhead at actual volume	20,000	38,000	58,000
Efficiency variance	>$ 500 (U)	>$3,000 (U)	>$3,500 (U)
Actual applied overhead	20,500	41,000	61,500
Controllable variance	>$1,000 (F)	>$3,500 (F)	>$4,500 (F)
Actual overhead	19,500	37,500	57,000
Net variances	$ 500 (U)	$ 500 (F)	0

STEP III: Complete the schedule of variances, using the above data:

EXHIBIT 20-25 SCHEDULE OF VARIANCES

Cost Element	Standard at Actual Volume	Actual Costs	Net (F) Variance (U)	Sub-Variances (F) (U) Type	Amount
→ Materials	$76,000	$73,800	$2,200 (F)	Quantity	$4,000 (F)
				Price	$1,800 (U)
→ Labor	$95,000	$98,400	$3,400 (U)	Efficiency	$7,500 (U)
				Rate	$4,100 (F)
Fixed Overhead	$19,000	$19,500	500 (U)	Budget	$1,000 (U)
				Efficiency	$ 500 (U)
				Controllable	$1,000 (F)
Variable Overhead	$38,000	$37,500	500 (F)	Budget	0
				Efficiency	$3,000 (U)
				Controllable	$3,500 (F)
→ Total Overhead	$57,000	$57,000	0	Budget	$1,000 (U)
				Efficiency	$3,500 (U)
				Controllable	$4,500 (F)
→ Total Costs	$228,000	$229,200	$1,200 (U)		
Unit Cost	$120.00*	$120.63*			

*Based on standard applied overhead.

20.6 ANALYSIS AND INTERPRETATION OF VARIANCES

There are several important reasons for computing variances:

1. To validate the standard.
2. To improve the future standard.
3. To determine whether or not variances were controllable.
4. To trace variances to the appropriate responsibility center.

VALIDATE THE STANDARD

Before computing variances, a reassessment of the standard is necessary if a valid comparison is to be made. Any basic inaccuracies in the assumptions or data underlying the standard should be brought to light. While the original standard is still used in computing variances, that portion of the variance(s) due to inaccuracies in the standard should be separated for purposes of determining controllability or responsibility. Validation of a past standard is an important step in preparing a future standard.

IMPROVE FUTURE STANDARD

In addition, new events may have occurred during the period that affect a future standard. In analyzing variances it is important to distinguish *repetitive* causes from *non-repetitive* ones. For example, an increase in the price of materials is usually repetitive as it will affect future purchases, while the malfunction of a machine may cause a temporary inefficiency in the use of material but will not affect future operations if the machine is repaired.

As we pointed out earlier in this chapter, analysis of variances is only one aspect in setting a standard. Predictions as to future events must also be taken into account. Variance analysis does not provide this exogenous information.

DETERMINE CONTROLLABILITY

A fundamental reason for computing variances is to assess managerial performance. Accordingly, it is important to separate noncontrollable variances from controllable ones. A *controllable* variance is one over which a designated person has complete responsibility. It is a variance which reflects on management ability: a *favorable* variance connotes effective management, while an *unfavorable* variance connotes ineffective management. Generally speaking, material quantity, labor efficiency, and the *controllable* variance in overhead are considered controllable. However, these variances need to be examined in detail before concluding the issue of controllability.

Important breakthroughs such as innovative use of materials or labor may lead to significant *favorable* variances in the period in which they occur. Future standards are revised accordingly, which means that credit for the breakthrough is pertinent to the current period only. Future innovation is necessary to create favorable variances in future periods.

DETERMINE RESPONSIBILITY

The responsibility for sub-variances generally resides in different places in an organization, e.g.:

Type of Variance	Responsibility Center
Materials quantity	Production or primary function
Materials price	Purchasing
Labor efficiency	Production or primary function
Labor rate	Personnel – (wage and salary administration)
Overhead budget	Production or primary function
Overhead efficiency	Production or primary function
Overhead controllable	Administration

The nature of material and labor variances can be comprehended readily: more or less quantity (hours) were used than was allowed by standard, and at a price (rate) lower or higher than standard. Overhead variances need more detailed explanation.

20.7 ANALYZING OVERHEAD VARIANCES

BUDGET OVERHEAD VARIANCE

This variance comprises only the *fixed* component of overhead. It measures the burden of fixed costs relative to a change in volume. If actual production is less than normal, this variance will always be unfavorable. If production exceeds normal capacity, this variance will always be favorable. Within a specific volume range, fixed costs do not vary – hence a lower volume will carry a relatively higher burden of fixed costs, while a higher volume will carry a relatively lower burden of fixed costs. Because this variance is a derivative of a volume change, it is generally *noncontrollable.* Changes in volume stem from production or marketing factors in most instances, although inefficient purchasing or use of labor may be causative, which means that this variance can be traced to some primary function.

EFFICIENCY OVERHEAD VARIANCE

This variance measures the extent to which a change in the basis for applying overhead results in *over-* or *under-*application. For example, in the illustrative problem beginning on p. 881 there was an efficient use of labor to the extent of 2,000 hours (40,000 − 38,000). As overhead in the example was *applied* at the rate of $1.50 per direct labor hour, this efficiency in the use of labor resulted in an under-application to the extent of $3,500 (U) (which is 2,000 hours × $1.50 per hour). This variance will always be unfavorable where we have labor efficiency and *vice versa.* The primary responsibility for this variance rests with that part of the organization which has authority for labor usage or whatever other basis is used to assign overhead.

CONTROLLABLE OVERHEAD VARIANCE

The responsibility for this variance rests with administration. Monitoring of direct labor hours (or whatever basis is used to assign overhead) is needed on a continuous basis to determine whether or not the applied overhead rate requires modification in order to recoup overhead expenses, *or* to determine what steps can be taken to reduce overhead in the event that volume drops and the applied rate cannot be altered for competitive reasons. Generally speaking, an efficient use of labor (assuming this basis of allocation) will automatically result in lower overhead due to a reduction in an indirect labor portion of overhead—overtime, fringe benefits, etc. The applied overhead rate can be adjusted to recover the non-labor-related overhead. For example, if $36,000 in overhead is expected to be recovered from 18,000 hours of labor at $2.00 an hour, a reduction in labor hours to 15,000 hours would call for an applied rate of $2.40 to recover the same amount in overhead. It is an administrative responsibility to monitor the interplay between labor efficiency and overhead and to take whatever steps are necessary to control the recovery of overhead.

The importance of computing sub-variances relates to our need to identify responsibility for variances. We caution that sub-variances should always be computed, even in those instances where the net variance is zero or negligible. Often a small net variance can result from two offsetting variances of material significance. For example, a favorable labor efficiency variance may completely offset an unfavorable rate variance. In Exhibit 20-25 we found that a zero net variance in overhead involved substantial sub-variances.

20.8 INVESTIGATING VARIANCES

Computing variances is only the first analytic step. Once significant variances are detected, the search for causes begins. Each of the cost elements can be investigated further, as illustrated in Exhibit 20-26.

Computerized search routines are available (such as QUICK-QUERY) so that data can be rearranged into various formats in order to zero in on the precise causative factor. For example, a materials quantity variance can be traced progressively to a division, a department, a work unit, and down to a specific employee or machine.

The investigation of variances should be responsive to the cost-benefit constraint. Variances should not be investigated in cases where we have a highly probable cause, or where the cost of searching for causes exceeds the benefits that will result. As to the former, if we are 99% certain that a particular factor caused the variance, the cost of obtaining the additional 1% assurance is probably out of all proportion

EXHIBIT 20-26 EXTENDED COST VARIANCE ANALYSIS

1. **Further Analysis of Material Quantity Variance**
   a. Analysis by cost center: department, area, worker.
   b. Analysis by type of material.
   c. Analysis by process-line.
   d. Analysis by job-line.
   e. Analysis by spoiled goods report.
2. **Further Analysis of Material Price Variance**
   a. Analysis by type of material.
   b. Analysis by ordering methods: economic lot size, lead time, etc.
   c. Analysis by supplier.
   d. Analysis of controllable vs. uncontrollable price variances.
3. **Further Analysis of Labor Efficiency Variance**
   a. Analysis by cost center: department, area, worker.
   b. Analysis by process-line.
   c. Analysis by product-line.
   d. Analysis by spoiled goods report.
4. **Further Analysis of Labor Rate Variance**
   a. Analysis by labor skill.
   b. Analysis by cost center: department, area, worker.
   c. Analysis of controllable vs. uncontrollable rate variances.
5. **Further Analysis of Overhead Variances**
   a. Analysis by bases of allocation.
   b. Analysis by cost center: department, area, worker.
   c. Analysis of direct (controllable) vs. indirect (noncontrollable) overhead.
   d. Analysis by process-line.
   e. Analysis by product-line.

to the benefits. As to the latter point, it is senseless to invest effort in searching for causes where (1) no future benefits will stem from the investigation, or (2) where the cause falls within an acceptable range of behavior.

Both favorable and unfavorable variances should be subject to investigation. We respond readily to the need to investigate unfavorable variances. Here are some examples of good reasons for investigating favorable ones:

1. *Materials Quantity:* A favorable materials quantity variance may mean that quality is being compromised. Lowering the quality of a product may have long-range market implications.
2. *Overhead Controllable Variance:* In an effort to reduce overhead, necessary maintenance may be deferred. For lack of adequate maintenance in the current period, future operations may be impaired.

The need for investigating variances on an efficient basis has led to the creation of a number of statistical models, which in most cases are aided by the power of the computer. The purpose of these models is to determine which variances to investigate based on two criteria: (1) whether a variance falls within an acceptable range of variation, and (2) whether the benefits of investigating exceeds the cost.

The structure of this type of model can be described most briefly as follows:

1. A distribution of cost behavior is established. The *normal, Poisson,* or other dispersion mode can be used depending on its perceived relevance to the data in question.
2. The standard deviation is computed.
3. The probability that the variance is acceptable or unacceptable is determined by relating the standard deviation to a table of distribution values.
4. Decision rules incorporating cost-benefit data are constructed to determine whether or not to investigate the unacceptable variances under point 3.

Students who are interested in the statistical analysis of standard cost variances are referred to the references at the end of this chapter.

20.9 PRODUCT-MIX VARIANCES

Certain manufacturing processes involve mixing proportions of various ingredients together, e.g., a bakery mixes flour, milk, yeast, etc., to yield loaves of bread. Product-mix variance analysis is used to identify cost differences due to (1) *mix:* the actual amount of various ingredients used as compared with the standard amount; (2) *price:* the actual amount paid for the various materials as compared with the standard price; and (3) *yield:* the actual amount of yield as compared with standard yield.

Illustration: A company with three materials in its product-mix has developed the following standard cost:

STANDARD DATA

Type of Materials	Std. Mix (Input)	Std. Cost Per lb	Total Input Cost	Std. Ave. Input Cost	Standard Shrinkage	Std. Yield (lb)	Std. Yield Cost Per lb
A	100 lb	$.90	$ 90.00	–	–	–	–
B	90 lb	.60	54.00	–	–	–	–
C	60 lb	.60	36.00	–	–	–	–
Total	250 lb	–	$180.00	$.72	10%	225 lb	$.80

ACTUAL DATA

Raw Materials Put Into Process	Cost Per lb	Total Cost	Actual Yield
A 200,000 lb	$.85	$170,000	–
B 150,000 lb	.64	96,000	–
C 100,000 lb	.74	74,000	–
450,000 lb		$340,000	410,000 lb

In this problem we are dealing with *material* variances only. Instead of two variances (*price* and *quantity*), we have three: *price, mix,* and *yield.* The *price* variance in product-mix problems is computed by the conventional materials price variance formula (p. 872):

$$V_p = Qa(Ps - Pa)$$

The *mix* variance is the same as the *quantity* variance. *Qs* and *Qa* are based on ratios of *input* quantities:

$$V_q = Ps(Qs - Qa)$$

The *yield* variance is computed by the formula:

$$V_y = U_s(A_y - S_y)$$

where

V_y = yield variance
U_s = standard price per completed unit
S_y = standard yield
A_y = actual yield
(A positive result indicates a *favorable* yield variance, a negative result indicates an *unfavorable* yield variance.)

COMPUTATION OF NET VARIANCES:

	Input Quantity (lb)	Shrinkage %	Shrinkage Amount (lb)	Output Quantity (lb)	Average Price per Output Unit (lb)	Total Cost
(1) Original standard..........	250	10	25	225	\$.80	\$180
(2) Standard for actual volume[4]...........	450,000	10	45,000	405,000	\$.80	\$324,000
(3) Standard cost based on actual yield	450,000	8.9 (approx.)	40,000	410,000	\$.80	\$328,000
(4) Actual..........................	450,000	8.9 (approx.)	40,000	410,000	\$.83 (approx.)	\$340,000
(5) Net variance................. (Items 3–4)						\$ 12,000 (U)

COMPUTATION OF SUB-VARIANCES:

(6) *Price variance:* $V_p = Qa(Ps - Pa)$

Ingredient	Qa	(Ps − Pa)	Total	
A	200,000 ×	\$.05 (F) =	\$10,000 (F)	
B	150,000 ×	.04 (U) =	6,000 (U)	\$10,000 (U) *Price*
C	100,000 ×	.14 (U) =	14,000 (U)	

[4] Alternative calculation of standard yield:

$$S_y = \left(\frac{450,000}{250}\right) \times 225 = 405,000$$

(7) *Mix variance:* $V_q = Ps(Qs - Qa)$

Ingredient	$(Qs - Qa)$[5] Ps	
A	20,000 (U) × .90 = $18,000 (U)	
B	12,000 (F) × .60 = 7,200 (F)	$ 6,000 (U) *Mix*
C	8,000 (F) × .60 = 4,800 (F)	

(8) *Yield variance:* $V_y = U_s(S_y - A_y)$
.80(410,000 − 405,000) $ 4,000 (F) *Yield*

(9) Net variance (proof) $12,000 (U)

Our previous discussion on the analysis and interpretation of variances is pertinent to product mix variances. In our example the $12,000 (U) net variance between what 410,000 output units should have cost ($328,000) and what they did cost ($340,000) is explained by the sub-variance analysis. The cost of materials was reduced for A, but the increases in B and C led to a net $10,000 (U) price variance. Attention should focus particularly on the price increase of C.

The mix was not in the standard proportion; we used 20,000 more pounds of A which was offset by 20,000 less pounds of B and C. Quantity variances should always net to zero as we are simply restating the standard mix in terms of the actual quantity in order to get these quantity differences. As ingredient A was the most costly one, the mix trade-off resulted in a net unfavorable variance of $6,000.

Given 450,000 lb of input, we should have obtained 405,000 lb of output per the standard. We actually yielded 410,000. So yield was favorable. The 5,000 lb of favorable yield are costed at the standard cost per finished product (.80 in this case) to give us the yield variance.

20.10 SUMMARY

Standard costing underlies most modern business activity. The cost of a product needs to be ascertained prior to production for price-setting and control purposes. The three major elements of cost—materials, labor, and overhead—enter into the setting of standards.

Actual data is compared with standard data on an ongoing basis and variances are computed and analyzed. The types of variances illustrated in this chapter are:

- Materials
  - Price
  - Quantity (or mix in product-mix problems)
  - Yield (in product-mix problems)
- Labor
  - Efficiency
  - Rate

[5] $Qs - Qa$ is computed as follows:

	Standard Mix	Actual Mix	Difference
A	180,000	200,000	20,000 (U)
B	162,000	150,000	12,000 (F)
C	108,000	100,000	8,000 (F)
Total	450,000	450,000	−0−

Overhead
  Budget
  Efficiency
  Controllable

Computing variances is only the first step in the analytic process. Variances need to be analyzed and interpreted in greater depth in order to: (1) validate past standards; (2) improve future standards; (3) determine whether variances are controllable or not; and (4) trace variances to the appropriate responsibility center.

The processing of standard and actual cost data can be accomplished in one of two ways:

1. *Standard as a Budget:* Under this method standard cost data is not entered formally into the accounting records, but actual data is periodically compared with standard data for purposes of determining variances:

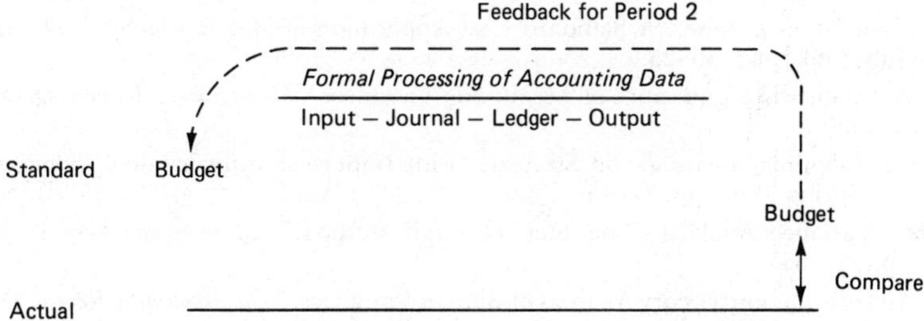

2. *Standard as Actual:* Under this method standard data as well as actual data is processed formally through the accounting system:

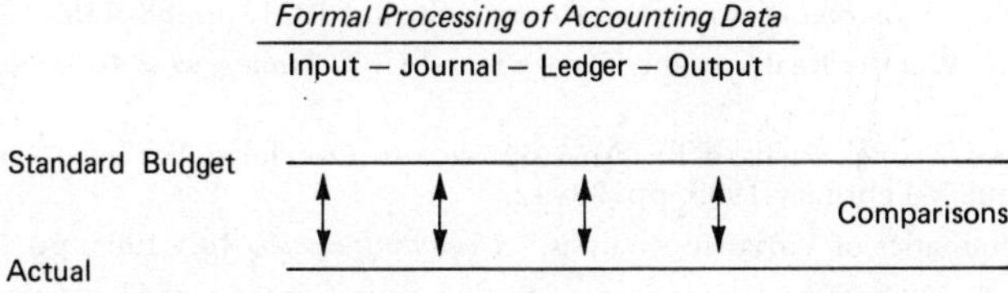

The former system is the less costly of the two, but the advantage of processing standard data through the records allows for more frequent or even continuous comparisons and is therefore a better control device.

The purpose of standard costing and variance analysis is to improve the costing of goods and services through the careful engineering of costs and the search for the causes of variances.

CHAPTER 20 REFERENCES AND ADDITIONAL READINGS

Bierman, H. Jr., and Dyckman, T. R. *Managerial Cost Accounting.* New York: The Macmillan Company, 1971.

Dopuch, N., and Birnberg, J. G. *Cost Accounting: Accounting Data for Management's Decisions.* New York: Harcourt, Brace & World, Inc., 1969.

Henrici, S. B. *Standard Costs for Manufacturing.* New York: McGraw-Hill Book Company, 1960.

Horngren, C. T. *Cost Accounting: A Managerial Emphasis,* Englewood Cliffs, N.J.: Prentice-Hall, Inc., 1967.

How Standard Costs are Being Used Currently. Research Report No. 11–15. New York: National Association of Accountants, 1948.

Stedry, A. C. *Budget Control and Cost Behavior.* Englewood Cliffs, N.J.: Prentice-Hall, Inc., 1960.

ANALYSIS OF VARIANCES

Bailey, A. R. "A Computerized Standard Cost and Variance Analysis Model for Improved Cost Control" (Ph.D. dissertation, UCLA, 1969).

Bierman, H. Jr.; Fouraker, L. E.; and Jaedicke, R. K. "A Use of Probability Statistics in Performance Evaluation." *The Accounting Review,* July 1961, pp. 409–417.

Demski, Joel S. "Optimizing the Search for Cost Deviation Sources." *Management Science,* April 1970, pp. 486–94.

Dopuch, N.; Birnberg, J. G.; and Demski, J. "An Extension of Standard Cost Variance Analysis." *Accounting Review,* July 1967, pp. 526–36.

Duvall, R. M. "Rules for Investigating Cost Variances." *Management Science,* June 1967, pp. 631–41.

Frank, Werner, and Manes, Rene. "A Standard Cost Application of Matrix Algebra." *The Accounting Review,* July 1967, pp. 516–25.

Juers, Donald A. "Statistical Significance of Accounting Variances." *Management Accounting,* October 1967, pp. 20–25.

Kaplan, Robert S. "Optimal Investigation Strategies with Imperfect Information." *Journal of Accounting Research,* Spring 1969, pp. 32–43.

Kirby, Fred M. "Variance Analysis—The 'Step-Through Method.'" *Management Services,* March–April 1970, pp. 51–54.

Lev, Baruch. "An Information Theory Analysis of Budget Variances." *The Accounting Review,* October 1969, pp. 704–10.

Luh, F. "Controlled Cost: An Operational Concept and Statistical Approach to Standard Costing." *The Accounting Review,* January 1968, pp. 123–32.

Ozan, T., and Dyckman, T. R. "A Normative Model for Investigation Decisions Involving Multi-Origin Cost Variances." *Journal of Accounting Research,* Spring 1971, pp. 88–115.

Partridge, R. William. "Will the Real Variance Please Stand Up?" *Management Accounting,* November 1966, pp. 3–9.

Peppet, Russell F., and Troxel, Richard B. "An Approach to Overhead Variance Analysis." *Management Services,* January-February 1969, pp. 38–42.

Weber, C. "The Mathematics of Variance Analysis." *Accounting Review,* July 1963, pp. 534–39.

Zannetos, Z. S. "Standard Costs as a First Step to Probabilistic Control: A Theoretical Justification, and Extension and Implications." *Accounting Review,* April 1964, pp. 296–304.

Zannetos, Z. S. "On the Mathematics of Variance Analysis." *Accounting Review,* July 1963, pp. 528–33.

CHAPTER 20 QUESTIONS, PROBLEMS, AND CASES

20- 1. Define *standard cost.* What is the purpose of standard costing?

20- 2. "Determining the standard cost of a product is more complex than simply carrying forward its cost from the preceding period." Why is it more complex and what additional factors should be considered in establishing standards?

20- 3. What is the activity-energy data for the following major cost elements:
(a) Material
(b) Labor
(c) Overhead

How is each data used in making efficiency judgments?

20- 4. The description and quality of materials and labor is not a formal part of the cost accounting system. Should this data be included? State your arguments.

20- 5. Distinguish between *operational* and *strategic* events and relate such distinction to activity ranges.

20- 6. What is the purpose of flexible budgeting? How does it differ from fixed budgeting? What are the limitations of a fixed budget variance analysis?

20- 7. Define or explain the use of the following terms and phrases:
(a) Activity-energy data
(b) Time and motion study
(c) Flexible budgeting
(d) Strategic boundaries
(e) Operational ranges
(f) Range of normalcy
(g) Normal capacity
(h) Net variance
(i) Yield variance
(j) Mix variance

20- 8. Distinguish between a *full-range flexible budget* and a *normal-range flexible budget.*

20- 9. "The range of normalcy is not determined by some specific percentage range, but rather by changes in the fundamental cost relationship." What are these changes?

20-10. Identify the concurrent processes for arriving at a total standard cost.

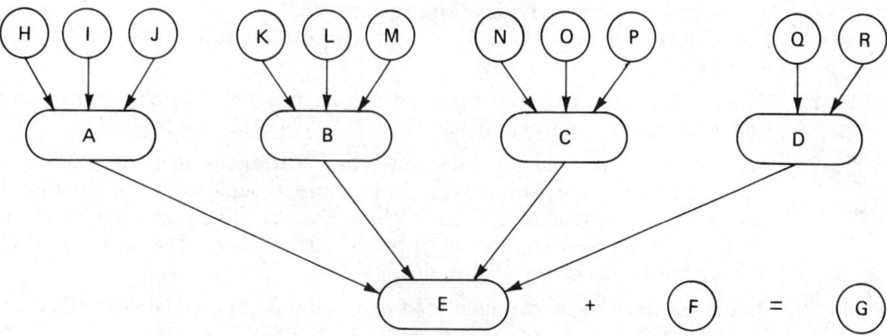

20-11. What are the possible explanations for an increase in variable costs per unit as activity declines from the above normal range, and the explanations for a decrease in variable costs per unit as activity increases from the below normal range?

20-12. "A cardinal value of the flexible budget is its ability to plan for contingent actions in the event that normal expectancies do not materialize." Explain the meaning of this statement.

20-13. Differentiate between *noncontrollable* and *controllable* variances by citing examples of each. How is it possible to distinguish between a variance that signals a change in underlying circumstances and one that merely reflects a correctable situation?

20-14. Under the *formal approach* to computing variances, and assuming attained activity (production volume) equals planned activity, list all possible rate-efficiency combinations for labor.

20-15. Under the formal approach to computing variances, explain how a mixed price-quantity variance for materials is produced. What is the control significance of this variance? When changing to the *conventional* approach, what happens to the mixed price-quantity variance?

20-16. Cite and discuss the reasons for using the conventional method of variance analysis over the formal method.

20-17. Identify two ways in which to develop an accounting system that handles both standard and historical cost data.

20-18. Why is it necessary to restate the standard or expected production to actual production before proceeding with the calculation of variances?

20-19. "While the original standard is still used in computing variances, that portion of the variance(s) due to inaccuracies in the standard should be separated for purposes of determining controllability or responsibility." Propose a method for identifying and separating such inaccuracies.

20-20. Give four reasons for computing and analyzing variances.

20-21. Identify as many different types of organizations (or industries) as you can in which standard costing is needed.

20-22. Indicate how you would extend your investigation of the following variances—whether favorable or unfavorable:

(a) Materials price
(b) Materials quantity
(c) Labor price
(d) Labor efficiency
(e) Budget overhead
(f) Efficiency overhead
(g) Controllable overhead
(h) Materials price in product-mix
(i) Materials quantity in product-mix
(j) Materials yield in product-mix

20-23. "The engineering of standard labor hours begins with time and motion studies of very small labor unit activities. These small units are added to other units until a finished product results. Some of these units are common to several products. By developing standard costs for very small packages we are able to aggregate them in various combinations into many products." Discuss.

20-24. What is the importance of distinguishing repetitive causes from non-repetitive ones in the analysis of variances?

20-25. "A fundamental reason for computing variances is to assess managerial performance. Accordingly, it is important to separate noncontrollable variances from controllable ones." What are the distinguishing characteristics of a controllable variance as opposed to a noncontrollable one? Why is it important to make the distinction?

20-26. Is it necessary to investigate zero or negligible net variances? Why?

20-27. Explain what is *measured* by the isolation of a:
(a) Budget overhead variance
(b) Efficiency overhead variance
(c) Controllable overhead variance

20-28. "If actual exceeds standard in computing variances, we speak of *unfavorable* variance. If standard exceeds actual, we speak of a *favorable* variance." Discuss. Does *unfavorable* refer to a "bad" or "noncontrollable" situation? Conversely, does *favorable* always refer to "good" or "controllable" differences?

20-29. Indicate the organizational group having responsibility for the following sub-variances:

Type of Variance	Responsibility Center
Materials quantity	
Materials price	
Labor efficiency	
Labor rate	
Overhead budget	
Overhead efficiency	
Overhead controllable	

20-30. "Variances should not be investigated in cases where we have a highly probable cause, or where the cost of searching for causes exceeds the benefits that will result." Discuss.

20-31. Identify the variances relevant to:
(a) Materials
(b) Labor
(c) Overhead

20-32. What are the three variances encountered in product-mix problems?

20-33. Should favorable variances be investigated? Cite some specific reasons to support your response.

20-34. What are two criteria used in statistical models for determining which variances to investigate? Describe the structure of these statistical models.

20-35. ***VARIANCE COMPUTATION—COMPREHENSIVE PROBLEM*** The Keldsen Company uses a standard cost system for its production activity. Standard cost data applicable to 19*x*1, and actual data for 19*x*1, are as follows:

Standard Data:
Normal capacity: 112,500 units
Materials: 30 lb per unit @ $1.50 per lb
Labor: 8 hours per unit @ $3.00 per hour
Overhead: Fixed, $900,000; Variable, $2.00 per direct labor hours

Actual Data:
Units produced: 120,000 units
Materials requisitioned and used: 3,750,000 lb
Materials inventory data:

Beginning inventory		80,000 lb @	$1.60
Purchases:	(A)	1,200,000 lb @	1.40
	(B)	1,440,000 lb @	1.50
	(C)	1,100,000 lb @	1.70

Labor: A total cost of $2,929,500 based on 945,000 hours.
Overhead: Actual total overhead $2,560,000, comprising $850,000 fixed and $1,710,000 variable.

Required:

Compute the material, labor, and overhead variances.

20-36. ***FORMAL VERSUS CONVENTIONAL APPROACH TO VARIANCE ANALYSIS*** Consider the following data:
(a) Actual and planned volume is 1600 units
(b) *Standard Costs Per Unit:*
Material: 14 lb @ $5 per lb
Labor: 2 hours @ $3 per hour
(c) *Actual Data:*

	Alternative Quantities in lb			Alternative Prices		
Material	19,000 *a*	22,400 *s*	26,000 *a*	$4 *a*	$5 *s*	$6 *a*

	Alternative Efficiency in hours			Alternative Rates		
Labor	3,000 *a*	3,200 *s*	3,300 *a*	$2.50 *a*	$3 *s*	$5 *a*

Required:

Prepare a schedule showing the computation of the nine combinations of price-quantity variances for material, and the nine combinations of efficiency-rate variances for labor. The schedule should show a computation of net variances and a comparison of formal versus conventional methods for variance computation.

20-37. ***THREE-VARIANCE METHOD FOR OVERHEAD*** The Rollins Manufacturing Company uses the three-variance method for analyzing overhead. The standard cost card for its only product is:

STANDARD COST CARD	
Materials:	$108
Labor: 4 hours @ $8.00 per hour	32
Overhead:	
Variable: $3.50 per labor hour	14
Fixed: $1.00 per labor hour (rate based on normal capacity)	4
Total standard cost per unit	$158

Other data is as follows:

Normal capacity:	40,000 units
Units produced:	38,000 units
Actual labor hours:	155,000 hours
Actual fixed overhead:	$162,000
Actual variable overhead:	$580,000

Required:

Prepare an overhead variance analysis table showing the computation of three variances of variable overhead and three for fixed overhead.

20-38. ***STANDARD COST VARIANCE ANALYSIS***

(a) Determine the *efficiency variance* in direct labor hours, given the following:

Variable overhead efficiency variance is $112 (F).

Actual hours worked were 238 hours.

Flexible budget at actual volume is $1.064.

(b) Determine the *normal capacity* of this plant (in labor hours), given the following:

Direct labor efficiency variance is $30 (F).

Standard labor rate of $2.50 per hour.

Actual direct labor hours incurred was 112 hours.

Production in standard labor hours was below normal capacity by 18 hours.

20-39. ***STANDARD COST VARIANCE ANALYSIS***

	Standard Data	Actual Data
No. of units		1,000
Materials quantity	10 lb per unit	10,450 lb, total
Materials price	$2.00 per unit	$19,855, total
Labor hours	8 hrs per unit	7,410 hrs, total
Labor rate	$4.00 per hour	$4.10 per hour
Overhead	$16,000	$15,000

Required:

Using flexible budgeting analysis, compute:
(a) The materials quantity variance.
(b) The materials price variance.
(c) The labor efficiency variance.
(d) The labor rate variance.
(e) The over- or under-application of overhead.

20-40. ***DIRECT COSTING VERSUS ABSORPTION COSTING*** Consider the following information:
Basic production data at *standard cost per unit:*

Direct material	$10
Direct labor	5
Variable overhead	4
Fixed overhead (based on normal capacity)	3

Sales price per unit	$40
Normal activity	18,000 units
Actual production for 1970	16,000 units
Beginning inventory	4,000 units
Sales in units	15,000 units

Actual costs were:

Material	$168,000
Labor	78,000
Variable factory overhead	65,600
Fixed factory overhead	54,000
Selling and administrative expense, assumed as being all fixed	150,000

All variances are charged to income as an adjustment to cost of goods sold.

Required:

(a) Compute the difference in net income between an income statement using the direct costing approach and an income statement using the traditional absorption costing approach.
(b) Compute the ending inventory valuation using the direct costing approach and using the absorption costing approach.

20-41. ***STANDARD COST VARIANCE ANALYSIS*** Consider the following information:

Actual total labor cost is	$ 3,944.85
Actual total material cost is	9,350.00
Actual total variable overhead cost is	9,381.00
Actual total fixed overhead is	12,010.00

Labor efficiency variance	$160.80 (U)
Labor rate variance	130.05 (U)
Material price variance	$784 (F)
Material quantity variance	538 (F)
Variable overhead budget variance	0 (U)
Variable overhead efficiency variance	489 (U)
Variable overhead controllable variance	161 (F)
Fixed overhead budget variance	162 (U)
Fixed overhead efficiency variance	522 (U)
Fixed overhead controllable variance	1,202 (F)

Additional information:

> The standard direct labor hours per unit is *3 hours.*
> Variable overhead varies in relation to direct labor hours.
> *Normal capacity is 705 direct labor hours.*
> Only one type of labor is used, and only one type of material is used.
> All material purchased during the period is used in production. There are no beginning or ending material inventories.

Required:

(a) Compute the actual production in units.
(b) On the basis of the above information, complete the following standard cost card for *one unit of output.*

STANDARD COST CARD	
	Total
Direct material	$____
Direct labor: 3 hours @ $____	$____
Variable overhead: $____ per direct labor hour	$____
Fixed overhead: $____ per direct labor hour	$____

20-42. ***STANDARD COST VARIANCE ANALYSIS—SCHEDULE OF VARIANCES*** The Ross Manufacturing Company has established standard costs for the processing department, in which one size desk lamp is produced. The standard costs are used in interpreting actual performance. The standard costs of producing one of these lamps are shown below:

STANDARD COST CARD	
Lamp, Style B12	
Direct material: 15 pounds @ 21¢	$ 3.15
Direct labor: 6 hours @ $2.00	12.00
Indirect costs:	
Variable overhead: $1.20 per direct labor hour	7.20
Fixed overhead: $.85 per direct labor hour	5.10
	$27.45

The fixed overhead rate of $.85 per direct labor hour is based on normal monthly activity of 120,000 direct labor hours of operation.

The costs of operations to produce 19,500 of these lamps during March are stated below (there were no initial inventories):

Materials purchased: 300,000 pounds @ 22¢	$ 66,000
Materials used: 296,000 pounds	
Direct labor: 120,000 hours (actual)	252,000
Indirect costs:	
Variable overhead	141,000
Fixed overhead	103,500

Required:

Compute the material, labor, and overhead variances.

20-43. ***STANDARD COST VARIANCE ANALYSIS*** The Wade Company uses a standard cost system. The standard cost card for its only product, a four-drawer dresser, is as follows:

Materials: Lumber—59 board feet @ 10¢	$ 5.00
Direct labor: 3 hours at $2.00	6.00
Indirect costs:	
Variable overhead—$1.00 per direct labor hour	3.00
Fixed overhead—$.50 per direct labor hour	1.50
	$15.50

During the month of January, 400 dressers were produced. A summary of operating activity showed the following variances:

Material price variance	$250 (U)
Material quantity variance	100 (U)
Direct labor rate variance	110 (F)
Direct labor efficiency variance	200 (F)
Fixed overhead:	
Budget variance	80 (U)
Controllable variance	70 (U)
Efficiency variance	130 (F)
Variable overhead:	
Efficiency variance	100 (F)
Budget variance	0
Controllable variance	140 (U)

Required: Compute the following:

(a) Materials used (board feet of lumber).
(b) Accrued payroll for January.
(c) Actual variable overhead incurred.
(d) Actual fixed overhead incurred.
(e) Normal activity (in direct labor hours).
(f) Actual direct labor hours used.
(g) Actual direct labor rate per hour.

20-44. ***OVERHEAD VARIANCES*** The Craft Manufacturing Company produced 750 units of product Y during July 1973. A portion of the standard cost card for the product shows (to produce *one* unit of Product Y):

Labor: 10 direct labor hours at $4.30 per hour	
Factory overhead:	
Variable (based on direct labor hours)	$30.00
Fixed (based on direct labor hours)	15.00
Total standard factory overhead per unit	$45.00

During the month the *total* factory overhead incurred was $33,975. The fixed overhead variances were as follows:

Fixed overhead *budget* variance:	$450 (U)
Fixed overhead *efficiency* variance:	225 (F)
Fixed overhead *controllable* variance:	375 (F)

Required: Compute the following:

(a) *Normal capacity* in labor hours.
(b) *Actual labor hours* for July.
(c) Variable overhead budget variance.
(d) Variable overhead efficiency variance.
(e) Variable overhead controllable variance.

20-45. ***STANDARD COST VARIANCE ANALYSIS*** Ross Shirts, Inc., manufactures short- and long-sleeved men's shirts for large stores. Ross produces a single quality shirt in lots to each customer's order and attaches the store's label to each. The standard costs for a dozen long-sleeved shirts are:

Direct materials	24 yards @ $ .55	$13.20
Direct labor..........................	3 hours @ $2.45	7.35
Manufacturing overhead.........	3 hours @ $2.00	6.00
Standard cost per dozen ...		$26.55

During October 19*x*1, Ross worked on three orders for long-sleeved shirts. Job cost records for the month disclose the following:

Lot	Units in Lot	Material Used	Hours Worked
30	1,000 dozen	24,100 yards	2,980
31	1,700 dozen	40,440 yards	5,130
32	1,200 dozen	28,825 yards	2,890

The following information is also available:

(a) Ross purchased 95,000 yards of material during the month at a cost of $53,200. The materials price variance is recorded when goods are purchased and all inventories are carried at standard cost.

(b) Direct labor incurred amounted to $27,500 during October. According to payroll records, production employees were paid $2.50 per hour.

(c) Overhead is applied on the basis of direct labor hours. Manufacturing overhead totaling $22,800 was incurred during October.

(d) A total of $288,000 was budgeted for overhead for the year 19*x*1, based on estimated production at the plant's normal capacity of 48,000 dozen shirts per year. Overhead is 40% fixed and 60% variable at this level of production.

(e) There was no work-in-process at October 1. During October lots 30 and 31 were completed, and all material was issued for lot 32, which was 80% completed as to labor.

Required:

(1) Prepare a schedule computing the standard cost for October 19*x*1 of lots 30, 31, and 32.

(2) Prepare a schedule computing the materials price variance for October 19*x*1, and indicate whether the variance is favorable or unfavorable.

(3) Prepare schedules for each lot produced during October 19*x*1, computing (and indicating whether the variances are favorable or unfavorable):
   a. Materials quantity variance in yards.
   b. Labor efficiency variance in hours.
   c. Labor rate variance in dollars.

(4) Prepare a schedule computing the total controllable, efficiency, and budget overhead variances for October 19*x*1, and indicate whether the variances are favorable or unfavorable.

(Adapted from the CPA exam.)

20-46. ***PRODUCT-MIX VARIANCES*** The following data is available for Ever-Last Paint Company:

	Standard Data		Actual Data	
Input:	300 lb A × $1.00 =	$ 300	3,200 lb A × $1.10 =	$ 3,520
	500 lb B × 2.00 =	1,000	5,100 lb B × 1.90 =	9,690
	200 lb C × 3.50 =	700	1,700 lb C × 3.40 =	5,780
	1,000 lb	$2,000	10,000 lb	$18,990
Yield	100 Units		900 Units	

Required: Compute:

(a) The *price* variance.
(b) The *mix* variance.
(c) The *yield* variance.
(d) The standard cost of the total units actually produced.

20-47. ***PRODUCT-MIX VARIANCES*** Consider the product-mix data for the Labate Bakery:

Standard mix	Standard yield	Actual mix	Actual yield
A 150 lb @ $1.10	100 units	A 3,600 lb @ $4,032	2,100 units
B 100 lb @ 2.05		B 2,400 lb @ 4,896	
C 250 lb @ 1.50		C 4,800 lb @ 7,680	

Required: Compute the *price, mix,* and *yield* variances.

20-48. ***PRODUCT-MIX VARIANCES FOR MATERIAL*** The Rushmore Bakery Products Company produces a world-famous Shepherd's Bread. The company uses four basic ingredients and has the following standards per loaf:

	Standard Data				
Material	Standard Mix		Standard Cost per Pound	Standard Shrinkage	Standard Yield
A	.10 lb	@	$1.25	—	—
B	.45 lb	@	.75	—	—
C	.65 lb	@	.50	—	—
D	.30 lb	@	.60	—	—
	1.50 lb			20%	1.20 lb

During 19*x*1, the Rushmore Bakery produced and sold 3,770,000 loaves of bread. The materials used in baking and the actual prices of materials are as follows:

Material	Material Put in Process	Cost per Pound	Actual Yield
A	350,000 lb	$1.25	
B	1,585,000 lb	.85	
C	2,750,000 lb	.45	
D	1,200,000 lb	.70	
	5,885,000 lb		4,472,600 lb

Required:

(a) Compute the net variance for materials.
(b) Compute the sub-variances for materials:
    (1) Price
    (2) Mix
    (3) Yield
(c) Compute the standard cost of 19*x*1 production.

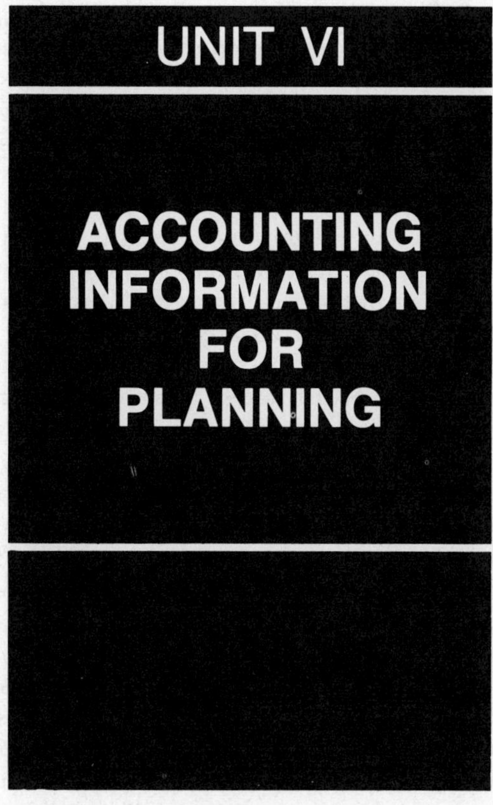

In chapter 4 we represented a total information system as comprising a cube with the following characteristics:

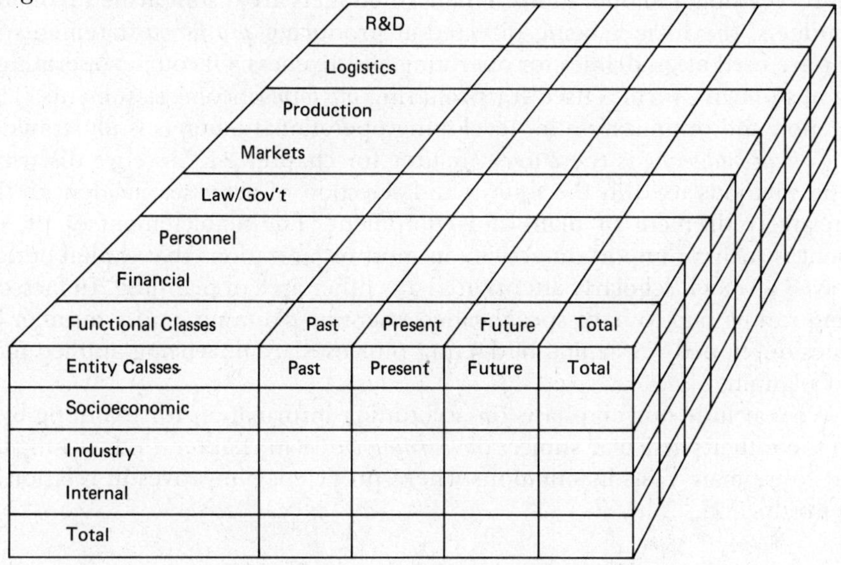

We depicted accounting as being a principal part of the financial "slice" of the MIS cube. Historically, accounting provided "past" information about the firm itself (internal data), so that its role in the cube was quite limited. It is now recognized that accounting must play a larger role in MIS by concerning itself with the present and the future in addition to reporting on the past. In fact, of the total quantity and quality of accounting information, those portions relative to the present and the future are growing in size and importance at a rapidly increasing pace.

The organization of this text has paralleled this development. Following our introduction of accounting as an information system, we focused on the role of accounting in financial reporting. We then turned our attention to the control aspects of accounting which are concerned with the conformance of ongoing activities in accordance with the objectives of the enterprise. We now turn our attention more specifically to the role of accounting in planning.

We begin by discussing *tax planning and administration* in chapter 21. We are concerned here not only with tax planning for firms (micro), but also tax planning for the United States as a whole (macro). The chapter also contains an historical perspective on tax planning and administration in the United States and refers on occasion to tax practices in other countries. So while the chapter is concerned with planning, the inclusion of this other material in the text is intended to stimulate student interest in this subject with a hope that more work will be done to improve the tax structure in the United States.

Chapter 22 deals with *forecasting.* Some general principles of budget forecasting are discussed, and then several forecasting techniques are treated in more detail: (1) *unstructured* techniques consisting of personal observation, group consensus, and user's expectation; and (2) *structured* techniques consisting of simple moving average, weighted moving average, exponential smoothing, and correlation analysis. While looking into the future is always accompanied by uncertainty, the forecasting techniques which are being developed and used today have brought a surprising degree of science to a practice that was formerly thought to be an art.

In chapter 23 we extend our discussion to *operational budgeting.* The purpose of operational budgeting is to control actual performance. It serves as an interphase between forecasting and operations. Financial budgets are distinguished from operational budgets, the former being directed at producing *pro forma* statements, while the latter are used as guidelines for operating effectiveness. Of course, operating budget data in summary form is used for preparing *pro forma* income statements. The use of simulation and optimization in developing operational budgets is illustrated.

Capital budgeting is the subject matter for chapter 24. Here we discuss principles and methods used in the timing and selection of activities incident to the acquisition and retirement of plant and equipment. The management of plant and equipment is such an important activity in most organizations that capital budgeting has received as much scholarly attention as any other area of planning. In fact, capital budgeting can be said to have spearheaded scientific planning, and a number of the techniques developed for capital budgeting purposes are now being applied to other forms of planning.

We conclude our emphasis on accounting information for planning by dealing with the rather particular subject of *learning curves* in chapter 25. Learning curves are used to estimate costs in situations where proficiency improves in relation to increased production.

In all of these subject areas our emphasis is on the role of accounting information in planning activities. The extension of accounting into future activities broadens the field considerably. As this incursion is only in its infancy, students of accounting will find this area to be one in which they can contribute more extensively than in the more traditional areas.

CHAPTER

21

TAX PLANNING AND ADMINISTRATION

21.1 THE FUNCTION OF TAXATION

Taxation appears to be a necessary economic institution. Archaeologists assure us that taxation is as old as the most primitive of our social institutions. Certainly taxation anteceded writing and money in most cultures. That taxation is of overriding contemporary importance speaks to its vitality. There are several reasons why taxation is necessary, including: (1) providing essential services such as schooling and medical care, (2) protecting the country, (3) administering the law, (4) regulating domestic and foreign commerce, (5) regulating the economy, and (6) distributing income and wealth.

As students and citizens we are concerned not only with the total tax burden, but also with the equity with which taxes are raised, the programs which tax revenues support, the effectiveness of those programs, and the efficiency of tax processes and government services. Let us consider these matters in turn. We will discuss taxation on a macro-scale, then briefly consider some tax planning issues for businesses and individuals.

21.2 THE TAX STRUCTURE IN THE UNITED STATES

TAXATION BY THE FEDERAL, STATE, AND LOCAL GOVERNMENT

There are several tax jurisdictions in the United States, classified for most purposes into two groups: (1) *federal government,* and (2) *state and local government,* consisting of states, counties, cities (municipalities and townships), school districts, and special districts (flood, water, utilities).

Federal government receipts and outlays for some recent years are depicted in Exhibits 21-1 and 21-2, while those of state and local government are contained in Exhibits 21-3 and 21-4.

EXHIBIT 21-1 FEDERAL BUDGET RECEIPTS AND OUTLAYS: 1954 TO 1971

For years ending June 30

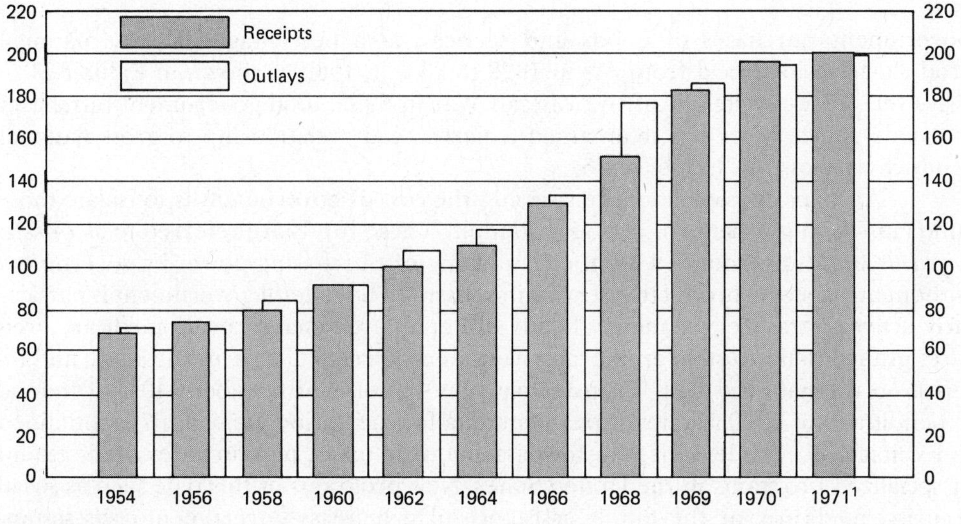

[1] Estimated.

SOURCE: Chart prepared by Dept. of Commerce, Bureau of the Census. Data from Executive Office of the President, Bureau of the Budget.

These data show substantial increases in government services, and while we may be concerned with the growth of the federal budget, state and local expenditures have risen even more rapidly in the past two decades. The question as to whether government is too costly or not is a pressing one for which ready answers are not available. Nor can we contemplate this issue in much depth within our cursory tax treatment. But one way in which to view this issue is to measure government costs against gross national product. This would indicate whether government costs are rising faster than the economy as a whole. Over the long run, the answer is definitely yes.

EXHIBIT 21-2 THE ANNUAL FEDERAL BUDGET: 1967–70

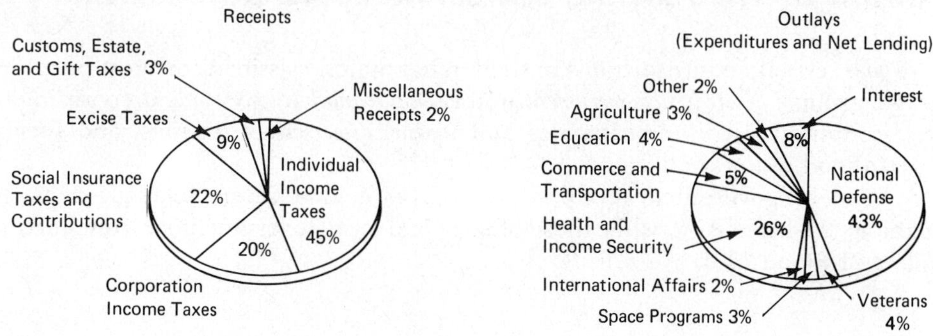

SOURCE: Chart prepared by Dept. of Commerce, Bureau of the Census. Data from Executive Office of the President, Bureau of the Budget.

Government purchases of goods and services, as a percentage of gross national product, have increased from 8% in 1929 to 23% in 1969 as shown in Exhibit 21-5. However, since the height of the Korean War in 1952, total government purchases of goods and services has maintained a fairly steady relationship to gross national product, as shown in Exhibit 21-6.

Another consideration in assessing the cost of government is to isolate those funds in which government acts as a conduit. These funds are referred to as *transfer payments* and can be defined as "the channeling of purchasing power by government without any specific productive service in return." The federal government is particularly active in transfer payments. Ready examples are social security, medicare, welfare, grants-in-aid to state and local government, foreign aid, farm subsidies, and interest on the national debt. Transfer payments accounted for about 40% of federal expenditures in 1970. Transfer payment data for the period 1954–1967 is contained in Exhibit 21-7. The level of transfer payments is in major part an index of the extent of socialized programs in the United States. New programs of this type such as social security, medicare, or the family assistance plan increase government costs significantly. If there is a presumption that these matters were taken care of formerly in the private sector, then these programs must be viewed as strategic shifts in the economy rather than as operational increases in government costs.

A BRIEF HISTORY OF FEDERAL INCOME TAX IN THE UNITED STATES

Taxation, as we now know it in the United States, is a fairly recent phenomenon. For example, there was no income tax prior to March 1, 1913. Because corporate and individual income taxes account for some 60% of total government revenue (Exhibits 21-8 and 21-30), we will take a brief excursion into the history of federal income tax in the United States as part of our discussion of the U.S. tax structure.

EXHIBIT 21-3 FEDERAL, STATE, AND LOCAL GOVERNMENT RECEIPTS, OUTLAYS, AND DEBT OUTSTANDING

In millions of dollars, except as indicated. Prior to 1960, excludes Alaska and Hawaii. Excludes intergovernmental revenue and expenditure. Local government amounts are estimates subject to sampling variation; see source. See also *Historical Statistics, Colonial Times to 1957,* series Y 384–681.

ITEM AND YEAR	All governments	FEDERAL		STATE AND LOCAL			PER CAPITA[1] (dollars)		
		Total	Percent of all govt.	Total	State	Local	Total	Federal	State and local
Revenue									
1942	28,352	16,062	56.7	12,290	6,012	6,278	181	110	71
1950	66,680	43,527	65.3	23,153	11,480	11,673	386	264	121
1955	106,404	71,915	67.6	34,489	16,678	17,811	564	395	169
1960	153,102	99,800	65.2	53,302	26,094	27,209	726	484	242
1965	202,585	125,837	62.1	76,748	38,506	38,242	876	551	325
1966	225,547	141,142	62.6	84,405	43,000	41,405	962	605	357
1967	252,563	161,351	63.9	91,211	46,793	44,419	1,045	661	383
1968	265,639	165,239	62.2	100,400	52,525	47,875	1,087	667	421
Expenditure									
1942	45,576	34,662	76.1	10,914	3,563	7,351	322	254	68
1950	70,334	42,429	60.3	27,905	10,864	17,041	400	250	150
1955	110,717	70,342	63.5	40,375	14,371	26,004	592	388	204
1960	151,288	90,289	59.7	60,999	22,152	38,847	714	426	288
1965	205,550	118,996	57.9	86,554	31,334	55,221	896	511	385
1966	224,813	129,907	57.8	94,906	34,195	60,711	967	544	423
1967	257,800	151,821	58.9	105,978	39,704	66,274	1,096	624	472
1968	282,645	166,411	58.9	116,234	44,304	71,930	1,182	670	512
Debt Outstanding[2]									
1942	91,759	72,422	78.9	19,337	3,257	16,080	680	537	143
1950	281,472	257,357	91.4	24,115	5,285	18,830	1,856	1,697	159
1955	318,641	274,374	86.1	44,267	11,198	33,069	1,928	1,660	268
1960	356,286	286,331	80.4	69,955	18,543	51,412	1,979	1,591	383
1965	416,786	317,274	76.1	99,512	27,034	72,478	2,150	1,637	513
1966	426,958	319,907	74.9	107,051	29,564	77,487	2,180	1,633	547
1967	439,880	326,221	74.2	113,659	32,472	81,185	2,223	1,649	574
1968	468,736	347,578	74.2	121,158	35,666	85,492	2,345	1,739	606

[1] Based on estimated population as of July 1, including Armed Forces abroad through 1955. Refers to general revenue and expenditure excluding intergovernmental amounts. [2] As of end of fiscal year.

SOURCE: Dept. of Commerce, Bureau of the Census; *Historical Statistics on Governmental Finances and Employment;* Census of Governments: 1967, Vol. 4, No. 5, *Compendium of Government Finances;* and annual report, *Governmental Finances.*

Early Development of the Federal Income Tax

While a federal income tax was proposed as early as 1815, the first income tax law was the Revenue Act of 1861 (which provided a personal exemption of $800 and the following rates: residents 3%, nonresident citizens 5%, interest on U.S. securities 1 1/2%), but no revenue was actually collected under this act.

The income taxes collected during the Civil War period (1863–1873) were based on the Revenue Acts of 1862 and 1864. The 1862 act reduced the personal ex-

EXHIBIT 21-4 SOURCES AND USES OF STATE AND LOCAL GOVERNMENT REVENUES

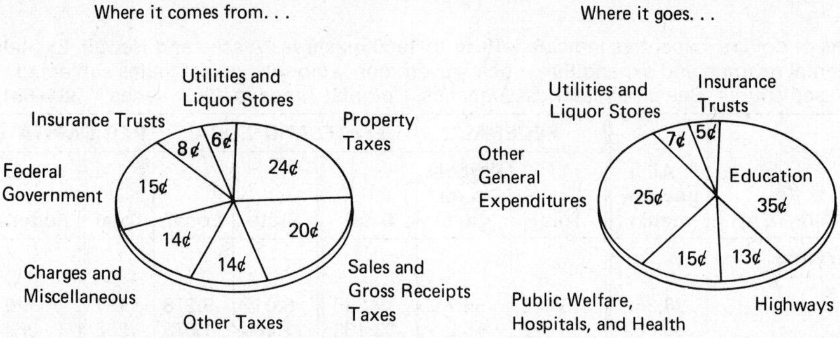

Where it comes from. . .

Utilities and Liquor Stores 6¢
Insurance Trusts 8¢
Property Taxes 24¢
Federal Government 15¢
Charges and Miscellaneous 14¢
Other Taxes 14¢
Sales and Gross Receipts Taxes 20¢

Where it goes. . .

Utilities and Liquor Stores 7¢
Insurance Trusts 5¢
Education 35¢
Other General Expenditures 25¢
Public Welfare, Hospitals, and Health 15¢
Highways 13¢

SOURCE: Dept. of Commerce, Bureau of the Census.

emption to $600 and the basic rate continued to be 3% except that a 5% rate was applied to those having an income in excess of $10,000. The 1864 act removed the discriminatory rate against nonresident citizens and provided for further income graduations as follows: $600 to $5,000 at 5%; $5,000 to $10,000 at 7 1/2%; and over $10,000 at 10%.

The history of the present law, however, properly begins with the Revenue Act of 1894 which was promptly challenged in the *Pollock* v. *The Farmers' Loan and Trust Company* case, and was declared invalid nine months after its passage. The issue was simple. The Constitution provides that "no capitation or other direct tax shall be laid unless in proportion to the census or enumeration hereinbefore directed to be taken." Obviously, an income tax cannot be apportioned in terms of this provision. (For example, tax collected in a state whose population entitled it to thirty representatives would have to be three times as great as the amount of tax collected in another state whose population entitled it to, say, ten representatives). The Supreme Court therefore held that "the tax . . . so far as it falls on the income of real estate, and of personal property, being a direct tax, within the meaning of the constitution, and therefore unconstitutional and void, because not apportioned according to representation, all these sections constituting one entire scheme of taxation, are necessarily invalid."

This ruling made a constitutional amendment necessary in order to impose a direct income tax. Meanwhile, however, an ingenious scheme was devised to impose a tax on corporations, and the Corporation Excise Tax of 1909 was successful in taxing corporate net income in excess of $5,000 at a rate of 1%.

The Sixteenth Constitutional Amendment

The Sixteenth Amendment was passed by Congress on July 12, 1909, and ratified by the required number of state legislatures early in 1913. This amendment provided that "the Congress shall have power to lay and collect taxes on incomes, from whatever source derived, without apportionment among the several States, and without regard to any census or enumeration." (The constitutionality of the 1913 act was upheld in *Brushaber* v. *Union Pacific Railroad Co.*) Ratification was obtained by February 25, 1913, and income was taxed beginning March 1, 1913.

EXHIBIT 21-5 GROSS NATIONAL PRODUCT—SUMMARY: 1929 TO 1969

In billions of dollars. Prior to 1960, excludes Alaska and Hawaii.

Item	1929	1930	1933	1935	1940	1945	1950
Gross national product	103.1	90.4	55.6	72.2	99.7	211.9	284.8
By type of expenditure:							
Personal consumption expenditures	77.2	69.9	45.8	55.7	70.8	119.7	191.0
Gross private domestic investment	16.2	10.3	1.4	6.4	13.1	10.6	54.1
Net exports of goods and services	1.1	1.0	.4	.1	1.7	−.6	1.8
Government purchases of goods and services	8.5	9.2	8.0	10.0	14.0	82.3	37.9
By major type of product:							
Goods output	56.1	46.9	27.0	39.9	56.0	128.9	162.4
Services	35.6	34.2	25.7	28.3	35.4	76.5	87.0
Structures	11.4	9.2	2.9	4.0	8.3	6.5	35.4
By sector:							
Business	95.1	82.4	48.9	64.1	89.1	172.3	256.3
Households and institutions	2.9	2.7	1.7	1.9	2.4	4.1	6.4
Rest of the world	.8	.7	.3	.4	.4	.4	1.2
General government	4.3	4.5	4.7	5.9	7.8	35.2	20.9
	1955	**1960**	**1965**	**1966**	**1967**	**1968**	**1969 (prel.)**
Gross national product	398.0	503.7	684.9	749.9	793.4	865.7	932.3
By type of expenditure:							
Personal consumption expenditures	254.4	325.2	432.8	466.3	492.3	536.6	576.0
Gross private domestic investment	67.4	74.8	108.1	121.4	116.0	126.3	139.6
Net exports of goods and services	2.0	4.0	6.9	5.3	5.2	2.5	2.1
Government purchases of goods and services	74.2	99.6	137.0	156.8	180.1	200.3	214.7
By major type of product:							
Goods output	216.4	259.6	347.2	383.3	398.4	431.1	459.9
Services	132.6	187.3	262.9	289.1	316.7	347.5	377.5
Structures	49.0	56.8	74.8	77.5	78.4	87.1	95.0
By sector:							
Business	352.9	440.7	594.4	648.9	681.0	740.6	795.4
Households and institutions	9.1	13.2	18.5	20.2	22.7	25.2	28.6
Rest of the world	1.8	2.4	4.2	4.1	4.5	4.7	4.2
General government	34.2	47.5	67.8	76.6	85.3	95.2	104.1

SOURCE: Dept. of Commerce, Office of Business Economics; *The National Income and Product Accounts of the United States, 1929–1965*, and *Survey of Current Business*, July 1969 and February 1970.

EXHIBIT 21-6 GROSS NATIONAL PRODUCT AND THE GOVERNMENT'S SHARE (IN CONSTANT 1958 DOLLARS)

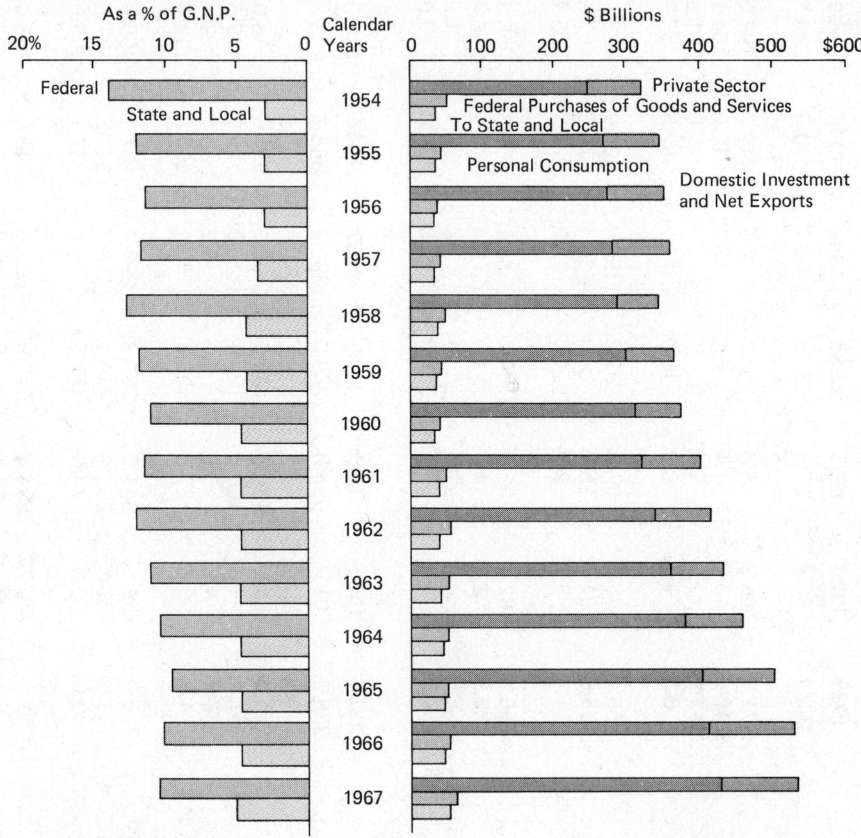

SOURCE: Data from the U.S. Department of Commerce, compiled by the National Industrial Conference Board, *The Federal Budget: Its Impact on the Economy* (New York: National Industrial Conference Board, 1969), p. 47. Used by permission of The Conference Board.

Sixty Years of Federal Income Tax: 1913–1972

Since the 1913 act, over forty revenue acts and other laws containing tax provisions have been enacted. Early in 1939, all of the provisions of the various acts still in force were incorporated in the *Internal Revenue Code.* The 1939 code also contained numerous sections of the Revised Statutes and other laws relating to internal revenue.

The *Internal Revenue Code of 1954* completely overhauled the federal tax laws, making radical changes in the form and arrangement of the 1939 code, and effecting extensive and fundamental changes in the substantive rules of taxation. Despite the complete rewriting of tax laws in 1954, numerous amendments and changes have been made since that time. For example, the Revenue Act of 1962 enacted provisions that prevented diversion of U.S. source income to foreign sources and taxed foreign investment income as it is earned; it also granted a 7% investment credit on the acquisition of certain business equipment.

EXHIBIT 21-7 FEDERAL TRANSFER PAYMENTS BY TYPE OF RECIPIENT

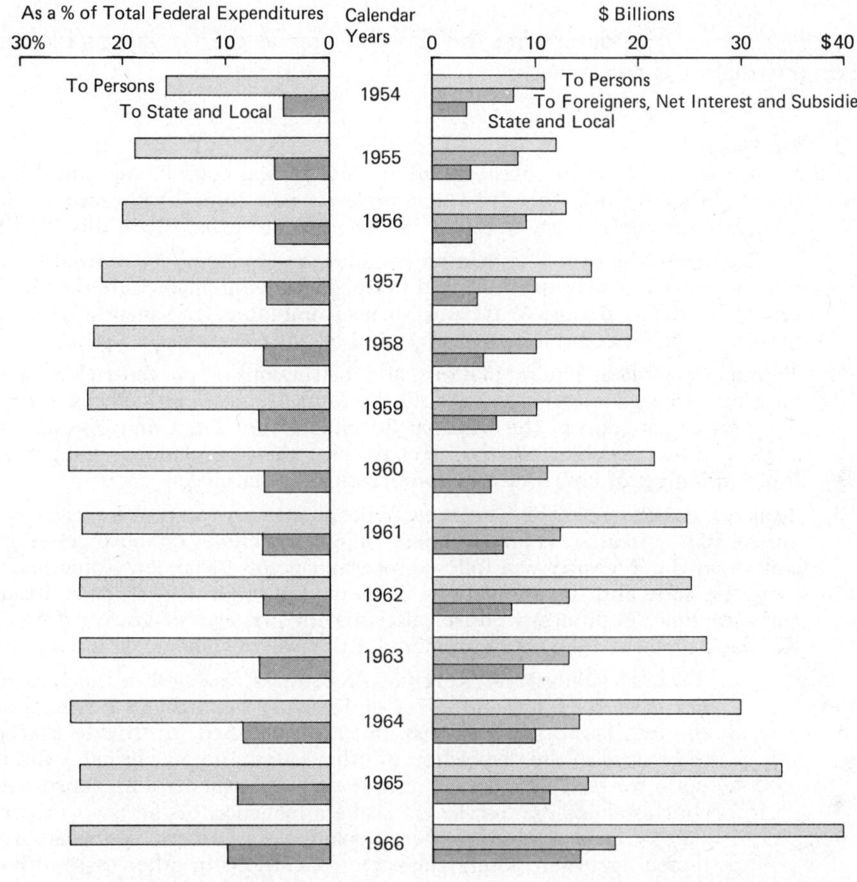

SOURCE: Data from the U.S. Department of Commerce, compiled by the National Industrial Conference Board, *The Federal Budget: Its Impact on the Economy* (New York: National Industrial Conference Board, 1969), p. 50. Used by permission of The Conference Board.

The Revenue Act of 1964 was designed to reduce the impact of taxes on the whole economy of the country. It provided the largest individual and corporate tax rate reduction since the passage of the 1913 act. Other important changes were made, including (1) income averaging provisions, (2) raising the minimum income subject to tax, (3) introducing a new concept of the standard deduction based on dependency exemptions, and (4) other provisions aimed at reducing tax avoidance and removing inequities among classes of taxpayers.

The Tax Reform Act of 1969 constituted a particularly vigorous amendment to the tax code. A number of loopholes were closed (e.g., "hobby losses") and some incentives were created, particularly in the areas of low-cost housing. For the first time private foundations were required to pay a tax equal to 4% of their net investment income, and tax-exempt organizations, including churches, became subject to income tax on their "business" activities. There were changes in exemptions, substantial changes in filing requirements, and lower tax rates for single persons and heads of household.

THE SOURCES OF "FEDERAL TAX LAW"

There are *four sources* that determine the "law" insofar as the taxpayer's federal tax liability on any matter is concerned:

1. *The Statute:*
   a. *General.* In 1939 the existing federal tax law was consolidated into "The Internal Revenue Code." In 1954, a completely new Internal Revenue Code was adopted, and the present statutory tax law is found primarily in this 1954 code.
   b. *Legislative Meaning.* The meaning behind the law cannot be minimized and is often obscured. A taxpayer may find useful background material in the published reports of the (1) House Ways and Means Committee, (2) Senate Finance Committee, (3) public committee hearings, and (4) the *Congressional Record.*
2. *Treasury Regulations:* The regulations, and instructions on tax return blanks which have the weight of regulations, are the Treasury Department's official interpretation and explanation of the Internal Revenue Code. The Commissioner is specifically authorized by statute to prepare and issue regulations. They have the force and effect of law, unless in conflict with the statute.
3. *Administrative Rulings:* The Treasury Department and Internal Revenue Service are constantly issuing "rulings." These rulings sometimes establish general principles that the Treasury will follow on certain points of tax law, sometimes construe the code and the regulations in their application to particular instances, and sometimes outline procedures affecting the taxpayer's rights or duties. The IRS has issued the following statement on the weight to be given to rulings:

   > Revenue rulings and Revenue Procedures reported in the Bulletin do not have the force and effect of Treasury Department Regulations (including Treasury Decisions), but are published to provide precedents to be used in the disposition of other cases, and may be cited and relied upon for that purpose. . . . Since each published ruling represents the conclusion of the Service as to the application of the law to the entire state of facts involved, Service personnel and others concerned are cautioned against reaching the same conclusions in other cases unless the facts and circumstances are substantially the same.
4. *Court Decisions:* Court decisions arise either from original jurisdiction or from appellate. IRS officials are not bound by these decisions until the whole round of appeals is accomplished. Generally, these decisions, like Revenue Rulings, tend to apply to a specific, identifiable entity of facts.

LEGISLATIVE HISTORY OF A REVENUE ACT

Tax legislation originates in the House of Representatives and more specifically with its Ways and Means Committee. During the formulative period of a bill, hearings are held and recommendations are made by the Treasury Department, the Joint Committee on Internal Revenue Taxation, other official bodies, and private individuals and organizations. The bill is reported to the House by the Ways and Means Committee and is subject to amendments from the floor.

After the House has passed a bill, it goes to the Senate Finance Committee, and similar hearings are held. Once again, further changes may be made when the bill comes before the Senate. If the final Senate version differs sufficiently from the House version, a joint committee of Senators and Representatives is formed to work out a compromise. Usually the resulting "conference committee bill" is passed promptly by both houses and submitted to the president for signature.

If the president signs the bill it becomes law. If he fails to sign it within ten days it still becomes law (unless Congress adjourns before the expiration of the ten-day period, in which event a "pocket veto" occurs). The president may veto the bill, in which case he sends it back to the House of Representatives with his stated objections. The bill must then be passed by two-thirds of the membership of each House meeting independently; and if this is accomplished, the bill becomes law. If the vote in either house falls short of the necessary two-thirds endorsement, the veto stands.

ADMINISTRATION OF THE FEDERAL INCOME TAX

The Office of the Commissioner of the Internal Revenue was created in 1862, and until 1952 the tax administrative organization under his direction was called the "Bureau of Internal Revenue," at which time (1952) the name was changed to the "Internal Revenue Service." The Internal Revenue Service functions as a division of the Treasury Department; it is organized internally into seven regions and fifty-eight districts, with the district office as the primary functioning unit of the system.

The greatest change in the mechanics of administering the tax occurred in 1962 with the installation of the nationwide National Computer Center near Martins-

EXHIBIT 21-8 RECEIPTS, EXPENDITURES, AND EMPLOYMENT OF THE INTERNAL REVENUE SERVICE: 1863–1963

Fiscal Year	Receipts (millions)	Expenses (millions)	% Cost of Collection	Number of Employees
1863	39.1	?		4,000
1873	113.5	6.6	5.814%	5,136
1883	144.6	5.1	3.527	4,341
1893	161.0	4.2	2.609	3,744
1903	230.7	4.8	2.081	3,960
1913	344.4	5.5	1.597	4,000
1923*	2,621.7	36.5	1.392	17,613
1933	1,619.8	30.0	1.853	11,524
1943	23,227.3	98.6	.424	36,338
1953	69,686.5	268.6	.386	53,463
1963	105,925.4†	490.0	.462	59,000

SOURCE: Lillian Doris, ed., *The American Way in Taxation: Internal Revenue 1863–1963* (Englewood Cliffs, N.J.: Prentice-Hall, Inc., 1963), p. 34 (adapted). Used with permission.

*Excludes costs and employees involved in prohibition and narcotics enforcement.

†Revenue derived as follows:

Corporations	$ 22,336,134,000
Ind.—not withheld	15,204,971,000
Ind.—withheld	51,838,632,000
Unemployment Ins.	948,464,000
Estate and gift	2,187,547,000
Excise taxes	13,409,737,000
Total	$105,925,395,000
Less refunds	6,535,249,000
Trans. to trust fds	948,464,000
Net tax receipts	$ 98,441,682,000

burg, West Virginia. Systematic conversion to EDP has been made necessary by the burgeoning increase in tax returns (96 million in 1962, to 111 million in 1970, to a projected 135 million in 1980) and by the increasing complexity of the tax law. Eventually a master file on each business and individual will be maintained at the National Computer Center, and IRS hopes that the new system will provide even lower collection costs, more rapid and accurate processing of returns, and a better check of delinquent taxpayers.

Some indication of the growth and efficiency of the tax administration system over the years is reflected in Exhibit 21-8.

THE CHANGING PHILOSOPHY IN INCOME TAX ADMINISTRATION

Over the years the philosophy in tax administration has changed from one of *enforcement* to *voluntary compliance* (with 97% of the tax now obtained through voluntary compliance and only 3% through enforcement). The essence of this new philosophy is contained in the following statement by the former Commissioner of Internal Revenue, Mortimer M. Caplin, in May 1964: "At the heart of administration is interpretation of the Code. It is the duty . . . of each person in the Service . . . to try and find the true meaning of the statutory provision and not to adopt a strained construction in the belief that he is 'protecting the revenue.'" (See Appendix C to this chapter.)

FEDERAL INCOME TAX PROCESSES

The regions, districts and data processing centers of the Internal Revenue Service are depicted in Exhibit 21-9. As stated previously, the basis of the income tax structure in the United States is "voluntary compliance," which means that taxpayers estimate and pay their tax liability. Enforcement is in effect for those who seek to evade their tax obligation and to assess the degree of voluntary compliance (compliance audits).

The income tax is based on a "pay-as-you-earn" philosophy. Most businesses estimate and pay their tax liability quarterly, while "withholding" from wages and salaries (Exhibit 21-10) is the principal vehicle for collecting federal income taxes from individuals. However, most individuals are still required to file a "return" prior to April 16 of each year. Their total tax liability is computed for the year ended December 31, and any difference between the tax computation and withholding is accounted for by means of a refund (withholding exceeds tax liability) or an additional tax payment.

These returns are routed through the district office to a regional computing center (Exhibit 21-9). At this point the audit process begins.

Most income is reported twice. Organizations report on payments made to individuals using: (1) Form W-2 for wages and salaries, and (2) Form 1099 for interest and other payments. The first audit step is to compare income as reported by the individual versus income reported by the organizations from which he has received payments. Additional audit steps include verifying arithmetic accuracy, selecting a number of returns for routine compliance audits, and testing for the reasonableness of deductions. These audit procedures are sketched in Exhibit 21-11.

EXHIBIT 21-9 *REGIONS, DISTRICTS, AND DATA PROCESSING CENTERS OF THE INTERNAL REVENUE SERVICE (7 REGIONS, 58 DISTRICTS)*

SOURCE: Reproduced by permission from the 1972 *Federal Tax Course,* p. 2706, published and copyright 1971, by Commerce Clearing House, Inc., Chicago, Ill. 60646.

EXHIBIT 21-10 ILLUSTRATIVE WITHHOLDING SCHEDULE

MONTHLY PAYROLL PERIOD

MARRIED PERSON

Wages less exemptions:		**Income tax to be withheld:**	
Not over $17		0	
Over–	**But not over–**		**of excess over–**
$17	$100	14%	$17
$100	$367	$11.62, plus 15%	$100
$367	$733	$51.67, plus 17%	$367
$733	$1,475	$113.89, plus 20%	$733
$1,475	$1,833	$262.29, plus 25%	$1,475
$1,833		$351.79, plus 30%	$1,833

SINGLE PERSON–
UNMARRIED HEAD OF HOUSEHOLD

Wages less exemptions:		**Income tax to be withheld:**	
Not over $17		0	
Over–	**But not over–**		**of excess over–**
$17	$58	14%	$17
$58	$100	$5.74, plus 15%	$58
$100	$367	$12.04, plus 17%	$100
$367	$733	$57.43, plus 20%	$367
$733	$917	$130.63, plus 25%	$733
$917		$176.63, plus 30%	$917

For wages paid after 12/31/69 (without surcharge).

For self-employed persons it is sometimes necessary for the IRS to use indirect methods such as observing a standard of living or measuring the activity in bank accounts to verify earnings. This procedure is exemplified by the following report in the *Wall Street Journal:*[1]

> **BANK DEPOSITS that a couple can't explain lead to tax troubles.**
> If a taxpayer's bank account opened the year with $1,412, chalked up $239,283 in deposits, and contained $7.49 at year-end, how much did the taxpayer earn that year? About $224,590 more than he declared on his tax return, the IRS answered. Wrong, the Tax Court ruled. Actually, the man and his wife were kiting checks, it said. At least $184,078 in deposits merely reflected one check written to cover another falling due.
>
> In this case, the IRS had questioned the couple's income and applied a method known as "bank deposits and cash expenditures" to make its own estimate. The taxpayer, a blind attorney, protested that in fact they were badly in debt and making payments to ten lenders. In a desperate effort to keep up, they "availed themselves" of the time lag between when a check is cashed and when it is presented for payment. They devised at least eight ways to cash a check somewhere and make a quick deposit before previous checks bounced.
>
> *The Tax Court drastically chopped the IRS estimate, but it still found $34,889 in deposits and cash outlays unexplained. It was forced to conclude the sum was unreported income, the court said.*

[1] *The Wall Street Journal,* November 25, 1970, p. 5.

EXHIBIT 21-11 THE IRS AUDIT PROCESS

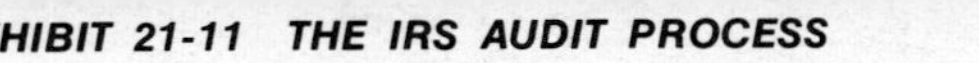

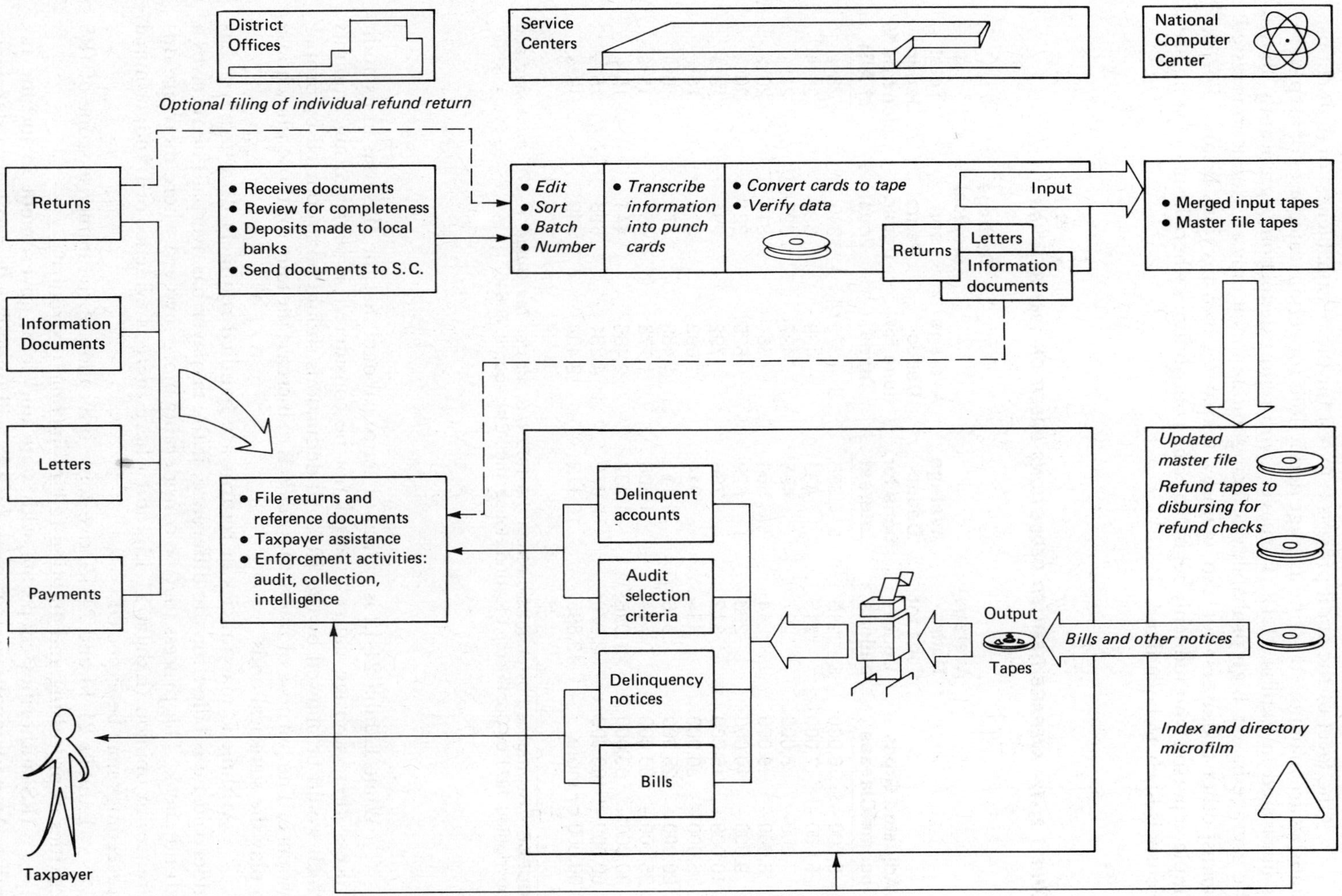

District Offices

Service Centers

National Computer Center

Optional filing of individual refund return

Returns

Information Documents

Letters

Payments

- Receives documents
- Review for completeness
- Deposits made to local banks
- Send documents to S.C.

- *Edit*
- *Sort*
- *Batch*
- *Number*

- *Transcribe information into punch cards*

- *Convert cards to tape*
- *Verify data*

Input

Returns

Letters

Information documents

- Merged input tapes
- Master file tapes

Updated master file

Refund tapes to disbursing for refund checks

Bills and other notices

Index and directory microfilm

Output

Tapes

Delinquent accounts

Audit selection criteria

Delinquency notices

Bills

- File returns and reference documents
- Taxpayer assistance
- Enforcement activities: audit, collection, intelligence

Taxpayer

SOURCE: John S. Bubula, "Tax Administration by Computer—How it Works, What is Coming?" *Journal of Taxation* 25, no. 4 (October 1966): 205–9. Used by permission of the publisher and the author.

One facet of the audit process is to test for the reasonableness of deductions. Statistics are maintained on the average deductions for certain categories of taxpayers, as illustrated in Exhibit 21-12. Taxpayers who report deductions significantly above the average have a high probability of being audited. Not only are deductions tested against other taxpayers, but also against a taxpayer's own previous history. For example, a person who suddenly begins to claim contributions where he made none previously is likely to be audited.

EXHIBIT 21-12 AVERAGE ITEMIZED DEDUCTIONS BASED ON 1968 RETURNS

Adjusted Gross Income Classes	Average Deductions for Contributions	Average Deductions for Interest	Average Deductions for Taxes	Average Medical and Dental Deductions	Total Deductions as % of AGI
$ 5,000–$ 6,000	$ 213	$ 368	$ 370	$340	23%
6,000– 7,000	215	439	439	326	22%
7,000– 8,000	232	495	497	327	21%
8,000– 9,000	244	564	564	314	20%
9,000– 10,000	268	629	625	321	20%
10,000– 15,000	312	736	792	294	18%
15,000– 20,000	434	914	1,093	316	16%
20,000– 25,000	586	1,111	1,453	372	16%
25,000– 30,000	714	1,308	1,778	451	15%
30,000– 50,000	1,096	1,732	2,486	444	15%
50,000– 100,000	2,276	2,975	4,231	628	15%
100,000 or more	13,895	10,112	12,404	949	19%

SOURCE: Reproduced by permission from the 1972 *U.S. Master Tax Guide*, p. 376, published and copyrighted 1971 by Commerce Clearing House, Inc., Chicago, Ill. 60646.

While Exhibit 21-12 is typical of statistical data that the IRS uses in its audit process, these average figures should not be considered as representing amounts which would be allowed by the IRS. All deductions should be supported by proper evidence. The purpose of *compliance audits* is to increase the ante for those who choose to play the statistical odds.

Arithmetic inaccuracies in returns are handled routinely. If a taxpayer has underpaid he is billed for the difference; if the taxpayer has overpaid he receives a refund check. The process may be considerably more involved where there are differences in opinion (Exhibit 21-13), and where there is evidence of fraud, criminal proceedings may be expected.

Exhibits 21-14 and 21-15 give some indication of the immense scope of IRS activities in processing and auditing federal income tax returns.

IRS authorities cooperate with state and local government in income tax audits. An additional tax assessment by IRS will undoubtedly result in a deficiency notice from state or local jurisdictions as IRS audit information is furnished to them.

EXHIBIT 21-13 INCOME TAX APPEAL PROCEDURE—INTERNAL REVENUE SERVICE

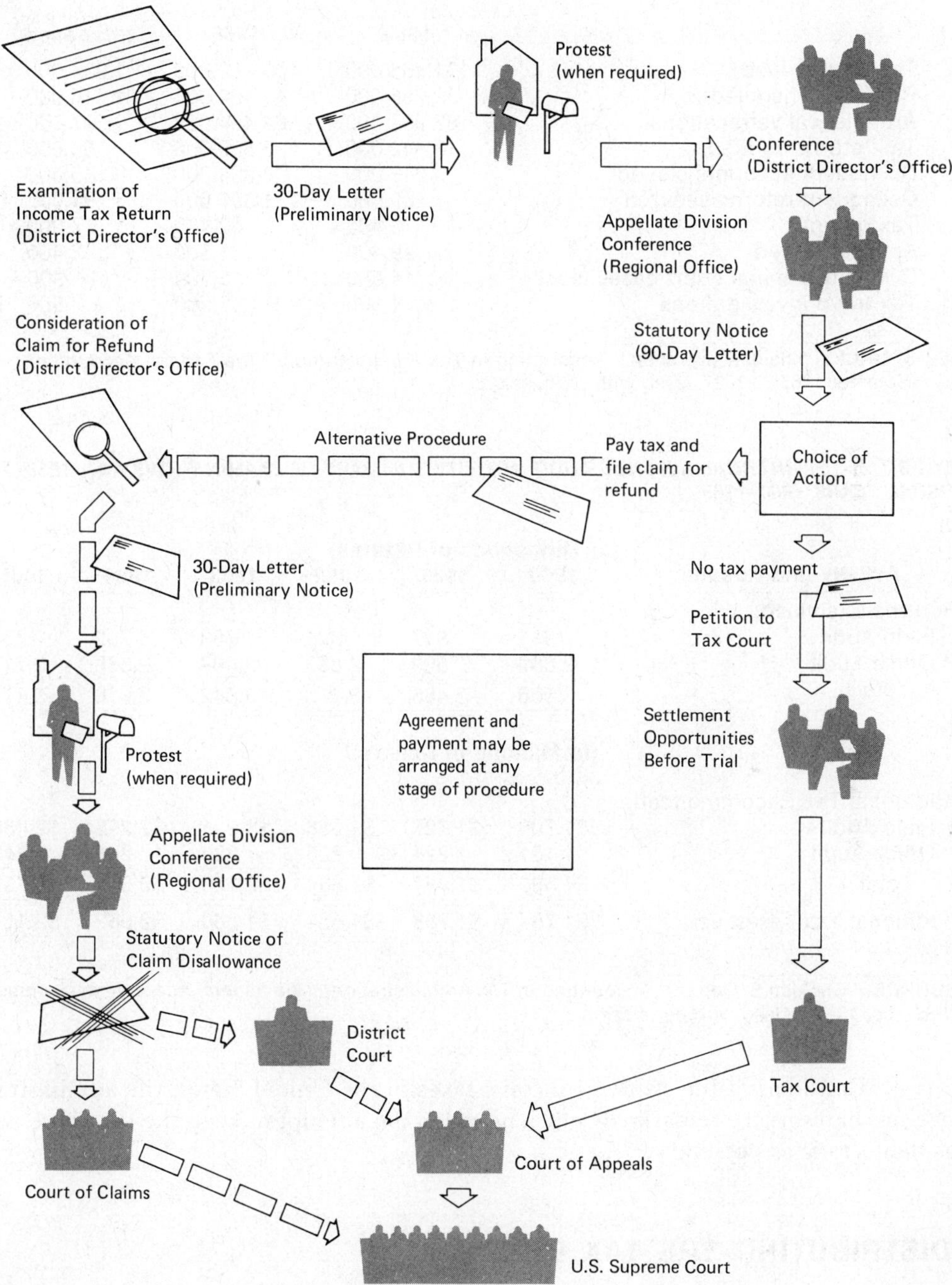

SOURCE: Reproduced by permission from the *1972 Federal Tax Course*, p. 2709, published and copyrighted 1971 by Commerce Clearing House, Inc., Chicago, Ill. 60646.

EXHIBIT 21-14 ACTIVITY IN FEDERAL INCOME TAX RETURNS, 1965–66 (NUMBER OF RETURNS)

	1965	1966	Increases
Tax returns filed	101,865,000	103,799,000	1,934,000
Refunds scheduled	39,258,000	41,104,000	1,846,000
Arithmetical verifications	62,957,000	64,484,000	1,527,000
Tax returns audited	3,442,000	3,530,000	88,000
Delinquent accounts closed	3,249,000	3,394,000	145,000
Delinquent returns secured	1,209,000	1,300,000	91,000
Tax rulings	75,400	82,400	7,000
Appeals settled	29,400	31,800	2,400
Civil and criminal court cases closed	14,800	15,700	900
Tax fraud investigations	14,300	15,200	900

SOURCE: Sheldon S. Cohen, "Accounting in Tax Administration," *The Federal Accountant* (Summer 1965): 10–27. Used with permission.

EXHIBIT 21-15 INTERNAL REVENUE AUDIT ACTIVITY SUMMARY OF EXAMINATIONS AND RESULTS FISCAL YEARS 1960–1965

Activity and Results	1960	1961	1962	1963	1964	1965
	(In Thousands of Returns)					
Returns Examined:						
Field Audit	911	917	804	753	752	755
Office Audit	2,089	2,569	2,668	3,088	2,858	2,716
Total	3,000	3,486	3,473	3,842	3,610	3,471
	(In Millions of Dollars)					
Additional Tax Recommended:						
Field Audit	$1,700	$1,727	$1,656	$1,924	$2,296	$2,486
Office Audit	181	224	228	236	254	243
Total	$1,880	$1,951	$1,884	$2,160	$2,550	$2,729
Additional Tax Assessed	$1,787	$1,788	$1,631	$1,860	$2,062	$2,151

SOURCE: Sheldon S. Cohen, "Accounting in Tax Administration," *The Federal Accountant* (Summer 1965), pp. 10–27. Used with permission.

Considering the scope of income taxes in the United States, the administrative mechanisms are remarkably efficient, given the attempt to keep the tax processes as democratic as possible.

21.3 DISTRIBUTING THE TAX BURDEN

Terms referring to the distribution of tax burden, such as *progressive* or *regressive,* are common to our everyday language. Their technical meaning is less well understood. Actually these tax equity concepts of progression and regression have two meanings:

1. *Technical:* In a technical sense a tax is said to be *progressive* if the tax rate increases for higher levels of wealth or income. The tax is *proportional* if the same tax rate

EXHIBIT 21-16 COMBINED FEDERAL INDIVIDUAL NORMAL TAX AND SURTAX RATES, BY TAXABLE INCOME BRACKET: 1939 TO 1970

In percent. For selected income years. Actual rates rounded to nearest whole percent. The normal tax rates were 4 percent for 1939 and 3 percent for 1944–53 before adjustment for reductions from tentative tax in 1946–50. The Internal Revenue Code of 1954 combined the normal tax and surtax rates into a single rate schedule.

Taxable Income[1]	1939	1944–45	1948–49[2]	1952–53	1954–63	1964	1965–67	1968[3]	1969[3]	1970[3]
0–$2,000	4	23	17	22	20	16–18	14–17	14–19	14–20	14–18
$2,001–$4,000	4	25	19	25	22	20	19	21	21	20
$4,001–$6,000	8	29	23	29	26	24	22	24	24	23
$6,001–$8,000	9	33	26	34	30	27	25	27	28	26
$8,001–$10,000	10	37	30	38	34	31	28	30	31	29
$10,001–$12,000	11	41	33	42	38	34	32	34	35	33
$12,001–$14,000	12	46	38	48	43	38	36	39	40	37
$14,001–$16,000	13	50	41	53	47	41	39	42	43	40
$16,001–$18,000	15	53	44	56	50	45	42	45	46	43
$18,001–$20,000	17	56	47	59	53	48	45	48	50	46
$20,001–$22,000	19	59	49	62	56	51	48	52	53	49
$22,001–$26,000	21	62	52	66	59	54	50	54	55	51
$26,001–$32,000	23	65	55	67	62	56	53	57	58	54
$32,001–$38,000	25	68	57	68	65	59	55	59	61	56
$38,001–$44,000	28	72	61	72	69	61	58	62	64	59
$44,001–$50,000	31	75	63	75	72	64	60	65	66	62
$50,001–$60,000	35–39	78	66	77	75	66	62	67	68	64
$60,001–$70,000	39–47	81	69	80	78	69	64	69	70	66
$70,001–$80,000	47–51	84	71	83	81	71	66	71	73	68
$80,001–$90,000	55	87	74	85	84	74	68	73	75	70
$90,001–$100,000	59	90	77	88	87	75	69	74	76	71
$100,001–$150,000	62	92	78–80	90	89	77	70	75	77	72
$150,001–$200,000	64	93	81	91	90	77	70	75	77	72
$200,001–$300,000	66–68	94	82	92	91	77	70	75	77	72
$300,001–$500,000	70–72	94	82	92	91	77	70	75	77	72
$500,001 or more	79	94	82	92	91	77	70	75	77	72

X Not applicable. [1] Income after exclusions, deductions, and exemptions. For 1948–70, joint returns double the tax on one-half of their taxable income. For 1954–70, the same treatment is provided for a surviving spouse. For 1952–70 heads of households compute their tax by use of a rate schedule which provides for about one-half the split income benefits allowed married couples filing joint returns.

[2] Includes effect of percentage reductions of tentative tax, which is tax computed from rate schedule before application of percentage reductions. [3] Includes effect of 7.5 percent, 10 percent, and $2\frac{1}{2}$ percent tax surcharge imposed for 1968, 1969, and 1970, respectively.

SOURCE: U.S. Congress. Staff of the Joint Committee on Internal Revenue Taxation. Adapted from tabular release, June 4, 1969.

EXHIBIT 21-17 MONEY INCOME—PERCENT DISTRIBUTION OF FAMILIES AND UNRELATED INDIVIDUALS, BY INCOME LEVEL AND RACE, IN CONSTANT (1968) DOLLARS: 1950 TO 1968

Prior to 1960, excludes Alaska and Hawaii

ITEM AND INCOME LEVEL	WHITE					NEGRO AND OTHER RACES				
	1950	1955	1960	1965	1968	1950	1955	1960	1965	1968
Families	**100.0**	**100.0**	**100.0**	**100.0**	**100.0**	**100.0**	**100.0**	**100.0**	**100.0**	**100.0**
Under $3,000	23.4	18.4	15.5	12.1	8.9	55.4	45.7	40.5	31.4	22.8
$3,000–$4,999	26.8	19.4	15.5	12.9	11.0	29.7	26.9	22.7	24.7	21.9
$5,000–$6,999	22.9	23.3	20.6	16.1	14.3	9.2	15.4	16.1	16.7	16.5
$7,000–$9,999	16.6	23.1	24.5	25.6	24.0	3.7	9.4	12.9	15.3	17.7
$10,000–$14,999	10.2	11.8	16.8	21.9	26.1	2.1	2.3	6.3	9.4	14.7
$15,000 and over		4.1	7.2	11.4	15.7		0.3	1.6	2.6	6.3
Median income	$4,985	$5,991	$6,857	$7,995	$8,936	$2,704	$3,320	$3,794	$4,419	$5,590
Ratio, Negro and other to white	(X)	(X)	(X)	(X)	(X)	0.54	0.55	0.55	0.55	0.63
Unrelated Individuals	**100.0**	**100.0**	**100.0**	**100.0**	**100.0**	**100.0**	**100.0**	**100.0**	**100.0**	**100.0**
Under $1,500	48.4	44.0	38.6	32.6	27.2	59.0	57.2	55.2	42.8	39.5
$1,500–$2,999	19.0	21.4	21.2	23.5	23.3	21.5	24.4	19.9	24.3	22.9
$3,000–$4,999	21.7	19.6	18.3	16.8	19.1	15.2	14.3	13.8	15.8	17.8
$5,000–$6,999	7.6	9.2	13.0	12.7	12.2	3.1	3.1	8.2	10.9	10.7
$7,000–$9,999	2.1	4.1	6.2	9.3	10.6	1.2	0.7	2.1	5.3	7.1
$10,000 and over	1.2	1.6	2.4	5.1	7.5	–	0.1	0.8	1.0	2.0
Median income	$1,613	$1,830	$2,187	$2,478	$2,952	$1,190	$1,264	$1,332	$1,847	$1,999
Ratio, Negro and other to white	(X)	(X)	(X)	(X)	(X)	0.74	0.69	0.61	0.75	0.68

– Represents zero. X Not applicable.

SOURCE: Dept. of Commerce, Bureau of the Census; *Current Population Reports,* Series P–60, and unpublished data.

applies to all levels of wealth or income, and the tax is *regressive* if the tax rate increases for lower levels of income or wealth.

a. *Example of a progressive tax:* In this technical sense the federal income tax is progressive. As shown in Exhibit 21-16, the tax rate increases for higher levels of income.

b. *Example of a proportional tax:* An example of a technical proportional tax is the property tax in most jurisdictions. While the value of property (wealth) may vary considerably, the same property tax rate (stated in mills per $1 of value) is generally fixed. Thus if the rate is ten mills, a property assessed at $10,000 would pay $1,000, while a property assessed at $20,000 would pay $2,000 in property taxes per annum. (As we have stated earlier, assessed value is usually a fraction of market value. In California, for example, assessment at 25% of market value is the rule.)

c. *Example of a regressive tax:* There are few ready examples of a technical regressive tax in the United States. An example would be a mass transportation tax to support local government. As most users of the transportation system would be from lower economic groups, they would be paying to support local government.

2. *Socioeconomic:* A more important framework for studying the distribution of the tax burden utilizes the concepts of "progression" and "regression" in a different context. Under this concept a *progressive* tax improves the relative socioeconomic status of the lower income-wealth groups. A *neutral* tax maintains the status quo, while a *regressive* tax improves the relative position of the higher income-wealth groups.

   This concept recognizes that the population is distributed over a range of income-wealth categories, as illustrated by the income distribution data in Exhibit 21-17.

   Under the socioeconomic concept of tax distribution, *shifts* in tax scales are as important as the scales themselves. For example, let us start with a given tax distributed as illustrated in Exhibit 21-18.

EXHIBIT 21-18

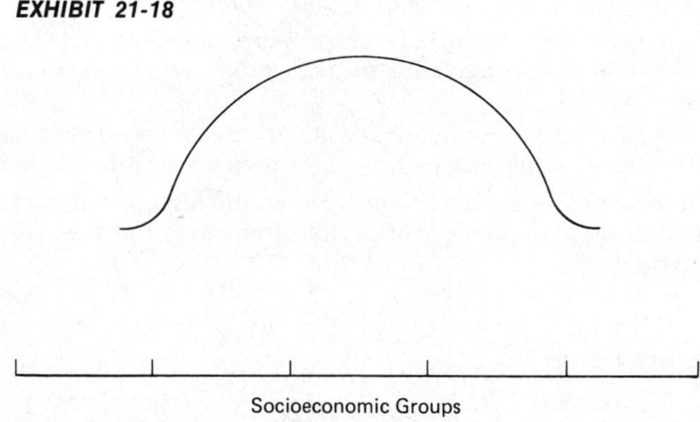

If the tax burden becomes skewed to the right, as in Exhibit 21-19, we refer to the shift as being *regressive.*

EXHIBIT 21-19

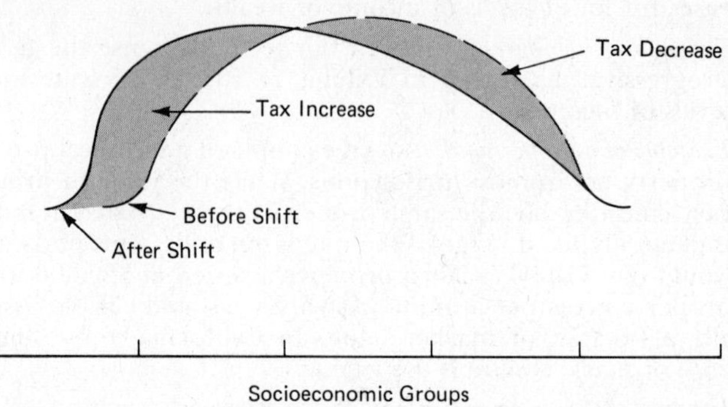

If the tax burden becomes skewed to the left, as in Exhibit 21-20, the shift is *progressive.*

EXHIBIT 21-20

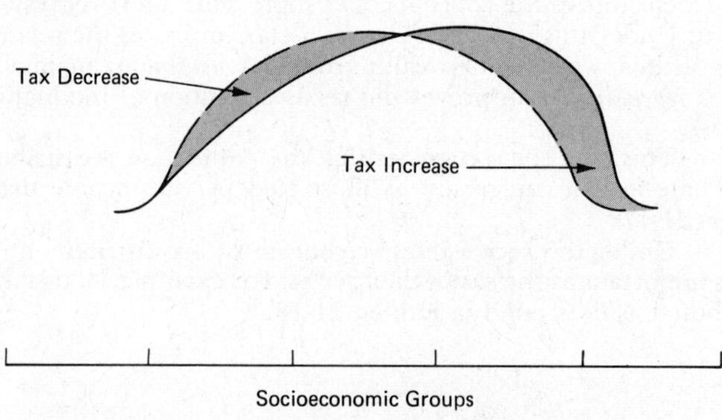

There are some ready examples of socioeconomic shifts:

a. *Progressive shift:* An increase in property tax offset by a decrease in the sales tax would be a progressive shift, as property owners are a higher socioeconomic group.

b. *Regressive shift:* An increase in the sales tax, as opposed to raising property or income tax, would place a heavier burden on the lower socioeconomic groups.

The trade-off does not have to be between the highest and lowest groups; in fact, the middle socioeconomic groups are often caught in the crunch, as illustrated in Exhibit 21-21.

EXHIBIT 21-21

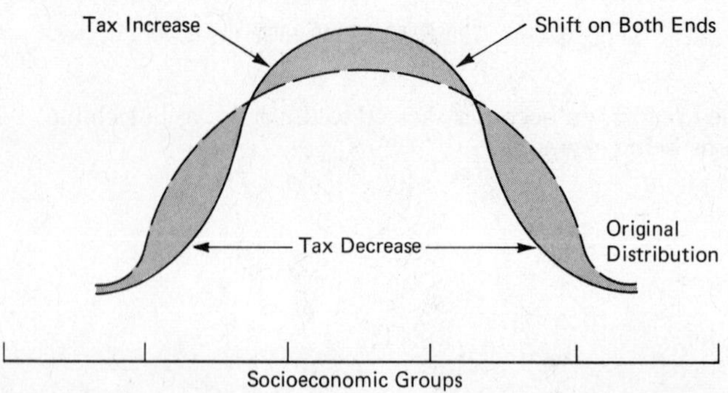

EXHIBIT 21-22 INDIVIDUAL INCOME TAX RETURNS, BY ADJUSTED GROSS INCOME CLASSES: 1960, 1967, AND 1968

Number of returns in thousands: money figures in millions of dollars. Includes Puerto Rico and Virgin Islands. Includes returns of resident aliens; based on a sample of returns as filed, unaudited.

ADJUSTED GROSS INCOME CLASS	NUMBER OF RETURNS			ADJUSTED GROSS INCOME			INCOME TAX AFTER CREDITS		
	1960	1967	1968 (prel.)	1960	1967	1968 (prel.)	1960	1967	1968[1] (prel.)
Total	60,593	71,283	73,363	316,558	506,642	556,278	39,464	62,920	76,579
Taxable returns	48,061	58,673	61,315	297,152	487,445	538,348	39,464	62,920	76,579
Under $1,000	1,353	623	651	1,123	586	611	39	5	5
$1,000–$1,999	4,170	5,002	5,098	6,222	7,454	7,560	490	374	380
$2,000–$2,999	5,034	4,351	4,450	12,677	10,901	11,092	1,096	793	861
$3,000–$3,999	5,794	4,904	4,852	20,307	17,170	16,993	1,886	1,384	1,474
$4,000–$4,999	6,401	4,969	4,874	28,812	22,380	21,915	2,764	1,914	2,015
$5,000–$9,999	19,998	23,425	22,975	138,455	172,615	170,386	15,362	16,600	17,933
$10,000–$14,999	3,637	10,363	11,963	42,752	124,171	144,292	6,159	14,627	18,300
$15,000–$49,999	1,549	4,709	6,069	35,278	101,676	129,013	7,283	16,844	22,428
$50,000–$99,999	101	260	300	6,648	17,162	19,842	2,273	5,055	6,182
$100,000–$499,999	23	64	78	3,808	10,356	12,685	1,607	4,014	5,176
$500,000–$999,999	1	2	3	486	1,383	1,808	226	605	815
$1,000,000 and over	(z)	1	1	584	1,590	2,150	281	707	1,011
Nontaxable returns	12,532	12,610	12,048	19,405	19,196	17,930	(x)	(x)	(x)

X Not applicable. Z Less than 500.
[1] Includes investment credit and tax surcharge.

SOURCE: Treasury Dept., Internal Revenue Service; *Statistics of Income, Individual Income Tax Returns.*

In Exhibit 21-22 you will notice that most of the federal income tax is raised from persons in the $5,000 to $15,000 brackets. In the series of tax rate changes in Exhibit 21-14, the highest group received a significant decrease (from 91% in 1963 to 70% in 1970), while the lowest group experienced a decrease from 20% to 14%. By contrast the $12,001–$14,000 group decreased only 3% from 1963 through 1969.

There are other ways of evaluating the tax distribution. For example, the steady increase in welfare costs (including such auxiliary programs as the food stamp program), cause us to question whether the economic resources of the United States are distributed equitably (Exhibit 21-23).

EXHIBIT 21-23

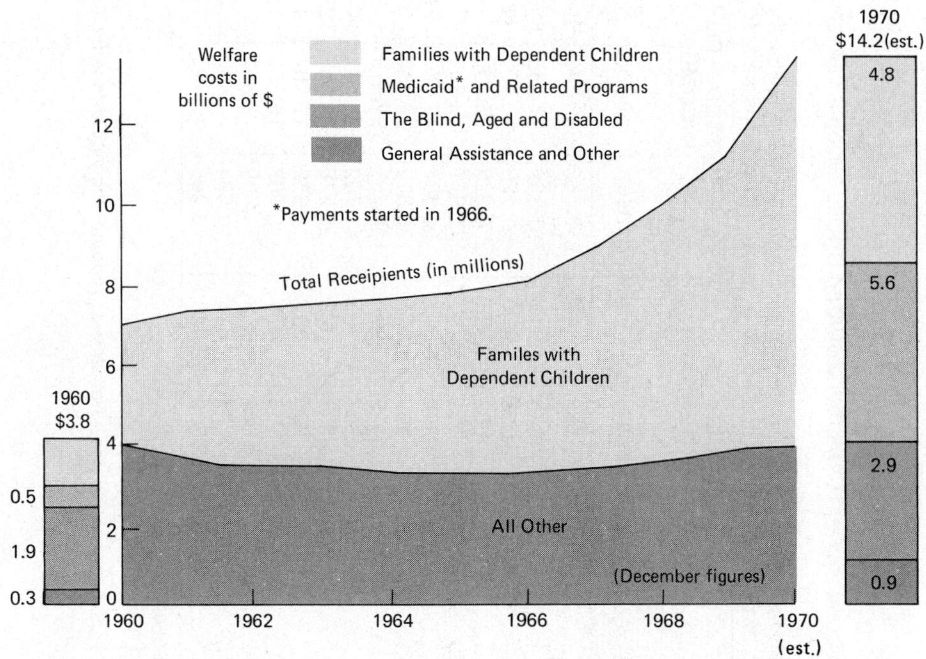

SOURCE: *TIME*, February 8, 1971. Reprinted by permission from *TIME*, The Weekly Newsmagazine; © Time Inc.

Tabulations which show that low-income persons in the United States pay comparatively lower taxes than their counterparts in most European countries (Exhibit 21-24) is of small consolation to low-income groups in this country.

The dilemma in distributing the tax burden is clearly one of avoiding social inequity on the one hand while preserving economic incentive on the other. There is no absolute truth in this matter. In fact, the problem of distributing the tax burden is analogous to the problem of allocating overhead to benefitting units in an organization (chapter 18). In each case many alternatives are available and the choices depend on sociopolitical strategy. For this reason it is likely that "tax lobbying" of one sort or another will remain a fundamental part of our economic fabric.

In part the question of equitable tax distribution hinges on the total economic

EXHIBIT 21-24 PERCENT OF GROSS INCOME PAID IN NATIONAL AND LOCAL TAXES IN UNITED STATES VERSUS SEVERAL EUROPEAN COUNTRIES (1961)

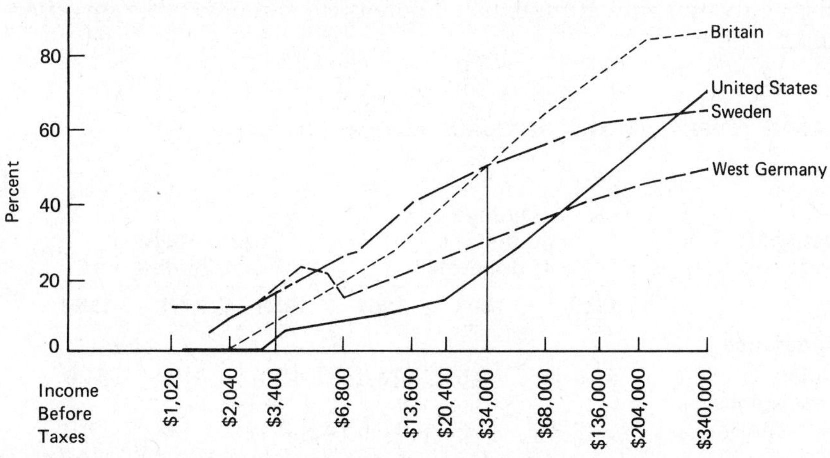

SOURCE: National Institute Economic Review, Britain. Appeared in *Business Week,* August 25, 1962, pp. 52–66, in an article entitled, "How Taxes Compare—A Close Look at the Tax Bite, Here and in Europe." Copyright 1962 by *Business Week.* Used with permission.

picture, especially the cost of living. If a particular socioeconomic group requires all of its income to sustain a subsistance standard of living, the imposition of any tax would cause a social injustice. Defining an adequate subsistance level is now receiving overdue attention.[2] Given sufficient goodwill on the part of all concerned, and with adequate expertise, we can make progress in improving tax distribution in the United States, while retaining the incentives which have undergirded the economy.

21.4 PROGRAMS SUPPORTED BY TAX REVENUES

Taxpayers should and do have an interest in the programs supported by tax revenues. Their ability to influence resource allocation via taxation is *indirect;* that is, they can elect representatives who support their social goals. A direct link between taxation and programs is absent. In short, it would call for taxpayers to indicate how they would like their tax contributions distributed over various existing or suggested programs. Great flexibility would be required in government administration to execute priorities in terms of the indicated preferences of taxpayers. It would be interesting to conduct such inquiries periodically to observe what program choices taxpayers would make *if* they were given the opportunity of direct tax-program representation. It may be that choices made on April 15—the tax filing date—would differ from those made in November elections. Certainly a tax-program plebiscite would have the advantage in that (1) taxpayers would have to make choices between programs in the light of scarce resources, and (2) programs could be separated from the charisma of political personalities.

But even within our existing system of indirect tax-program relationship,

[2] President Nixon's "Family Assistance Program" (FAP) was aimed at this problem.

shifts in program priorities are observed, even though the pace of change may at times appear to be inexorably slow. For example, the period 1959 to 1969 saw the beginning of a major shift from national defense to domestic programs, as indicated in Exhibit 21-25.

EXHIBIT 21-25 FEDERAL BUDGET RESOURCE ALLOCATION: 1959–69

Functional Categories	Outlays (in billions of dollars)			Percentage Distribution			Change: 1959 to 1969 (in billions of dollars)
	1959	1964	1969	1959	1964	1969	
National defense							
DOD, military	41.5	49.6	77.8	45.0	41.8	41.9	36.3
Military assistance program (MAP)	2.2	1.2	0.6	2.4	1.0	0.3	−1.6
Subtotal, military and MAP	43.7	50.8	78.4	47.4	42.8	42.2	34.7
(Support of Southeast Asia operations)	(−)	(−)	(28.8)	(−)	(−)	(15.5)	(28.8)
Other	2.9	2.8	2.6	3.2	2.4	1.4	−.3
Subtotal, national defense	46.6	53.6	81.0	50.6	45.2	43.6	34.4
Civilian Programs							
International affairs and finance	3.3	4.1	4.0	3.5	3.5	2.1	0.7
Space	.1	4.2	4.2	0.2	3.5	2.3	4.1
Agriculture and natural resources	6.6	7.2	9.0	7.1	6.0	4.9	2.4
Human resources programs	19.6	28.4	58.1	21.3	24.0	31.3	38.5
Veterans	5.4	5.7	7.7	5.9	4.8	4.2	2.3
Other civilian programs	5.6	8.5	11.0	6.1	7.2	5.9	5.4
Subtotal, civilian programs	40.6	58.1	94.1	44.1	49.0	50.7	53.4
Interest							
Undistributed intragovernmental transactions	−2.2	−2.9	−5.1	−2.4	−2.5	−2.8	−2.9
Total	92.1	118.6	185.6	100.0	100.0	100.0	93.5

Note: Detail will not necessarily add to totals because of rounding.

SOURCE: Testimony of Robert P. Mayo, Budget Director of the United States, before the Subcommittee on Economy in Government, Joint Economic Committee of the Congress, June 3, 1969.

In addition to program support, the tax structure can serve wittingly or unwittingly as a regulator of socioeconomic behavior. Notice the patterns of exemptions in Exhibit 21-26. There have been steady increments in the incentive to marry and bear children since the income tax was instituted in 1913.

EXHIBIT 21-26 MAJOR CHANGES IN PERSONAL EXEMPTIONS SINCE 1913

Year	Single Persons	Married Persons: Amount	Married Persons: As percent of single persons' exemption	Children: Amount	Children: As percent of single persons' exemption
1913	$3,000	$1,400	133%	$ 0	0%
1917	1,000	2,000	200	200	20
1921	1,000	2,500	250	400	40
1925	1,500	3,500	233	400	27
1932	1,000	2,500	250	400	40
1940	800	2,000	250	400	50
1941	750	1,500	200	400	53
1942	500	1,200	240	350	70
1944	500	1,000	200	500	100
1948	600	1,200	200	600	100
1970	625	1,250	200	625	100
1971	650	1,300	200	650	100
1972	700	1,400	200	700	100
1973	750	1,500	200	750	100

It is suggested that social goals such as decreasing birth rate can be achieved—partially at least—by creating tax disincentives rather than incentives.

The tax structure has also been used as an administrative vehicle for the social security and welfare programs in the United States. Payroll deductions and the annual reporting requirement apply to F.I.C.A. (Federal Insurance Contributions Act) in the same reporting format as federal income taxes. The growing number of social programs and the increasing rates of contributions are shown in Exhibit 21-27, reflecting use of the tax structure to implement social goals. Piggybacking new programs on existing administrative structures is generally more efficient than setting up separate reporting and processing systems for each new tax or tax-supported program.

21.5 TAX ADMINISTRATION

As illustrated in Exhibit 21-27, the Internal Revenue Service prides itself on the low cost of collecting taxes. The IRS can operate at that level only because the burden of recording-keeping is placed on the taxpayer rather than government. The total cost of accounting services relative to various tax requirements—both personal and business—is enormous and grows as tax law becomes increasing complex. Maintaining records and preparing the annual tax return is an onerous task for most individuals, who must turn increasingly to experts for assistance. The effort is compounded enormously for businesses, which must maintain detailed records on employees in addition to every other facet of their business. They must meet the reporting requirement of many taxing jurisdictions. Changes in the filing requirement for individuals are recorded in Exhibit 21-28. You will notice that the burden of record-keeping and filing was extended to more and more persons until—for the first time, effective 1970—a reverse trend was detected.

While the 1970 change in the filing requirement will not affect most taxpayers, it will remove the need for record-keeping and filing returns for persons in very low income groups, who can least afford to share in the cost of administering the tax structure.

One of the frustrations of the tax structure in the United States is the multiplicity of taxes and taxing jurisdictions. What started out as a fairly clearcut partition-

EXHIBIT 21-27 THE F.I.C.A. TAX RATE

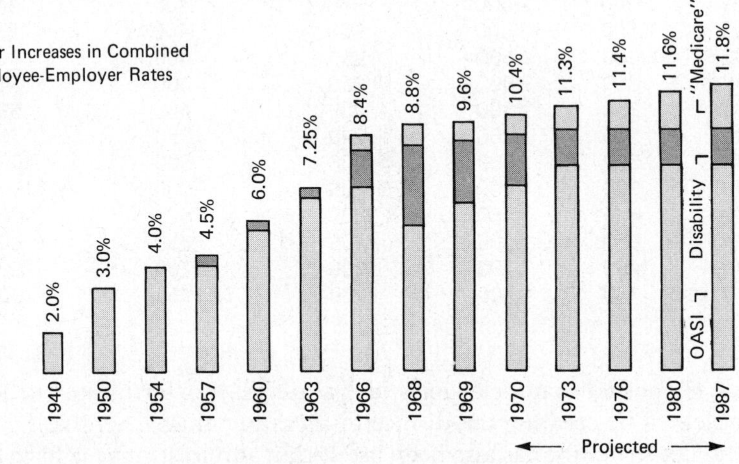

SOURCE: Data from the Social Security Administration, compiled by the National Industrial Conference Board, *The Federal Budget: Its Impact on the Economy* (New York: National Industrial Conference Board, 1969), p. 28. Used by permission of The Conference Board.

EXHIBIT 21-28 MAJOR CHANGES IN THE REQUIREMENTS FOR FILING INCOME TAX RETURNS SINCE 1913*

	Return required if net or gross income equalled or exceeded amount specified	
Period	**Single, or married and not living with spouse**	**Married couple, joint return**
1913–1916	Net, $3,000	Net, $3,000
1917–1920	Net, 1,000	Net, 2,000
1921–1923	Net, 1,000/Gross, $5,000	Net, 2,000/Gross, $5,000
1924	Net, 1,000/Gross, 5,000	Net, 2,500/Gross, 5,000
1925–1931	Net, 1,500/Gross, 5,000	Net, 3,500/Gross, 5,000
1932–1939	Net, 1,000/Gross, 5,000	Net, 2,500/Gross, 5,000
1940	Gross, $800	Gross, $2,000
1941	Gross, 750	Gross, 1,500
1942–1943	Gross, 500	Gross, 1,200
1944–1947	Gross, 500	Gross, 500 each spouse
1948–1953	Gross, 600	Gross, 600 each spouse
1954–1957	Gross, 600	Gross, 600 each spouse
1958–1969	Gross, 600	Gross, 600 either spouse
1970–*	Gross, 1,700 (under 65)	Gross, 2,300
	Gross, 2,300 (over 65)	Gross, 2,900 (either spouse over 65)
		Gross, 3,500 (both spouses over 65)

*The $600 income requirement is unchanged (1970–) for married persons filing separate returns and/or living apart, or if any other taxpayer is entitled to claim a dependency exemption for the spouse.

ing of sources (federal, income and excise; states, sales; counties and cities, property) has burgeoned into a potpourri in which every agency is extending its reach to virtually every source, as illustrated in Exhibit 21-29.

There is also a constant search for new tax sources, ranging from a "tippler's

EXHIBIT 21-29 TAX REVENUE, BY SOURCE AND LEVEL OF GOVERNMENT: 1942 TO 1968

In millions of dollars, except as indicated. Prior to 1960, excludes Alaska and Hawaii. Local government amounts are estimates subject to sampling variation; see source. See also *Historical Statistics, Colonial Times to 1957,* series Y 386–391, Y 448–458, Y 522–527, Y 581–592, and Y 654–659.

SOURCE AND YEAR	All government	Federal	STATE AND LOCAL Total	State	Local	PER CAPITA[1] (dollars) Total	Federal	State and local
Total:[2]								
1942	20,793	12,265	8,528	3,903	4,625	154	91	63
1950	51,100	35,186	15,914	7,930	7,984	337	232	105
1955	81,072	57,589	23,483	11,597	11,886	491	348	142
1960	113,120	77,003	36,117	18,036	18,081	628	428	201
1965	144,953	93,710	51,243	26,126	25,116	748	483	264
1966	160,742	104,095	56,647	29,380	27,267	821	531	290
1967	176,121	115,121	61,000	31,926	29,074	890	582	308
1968	185,126	117,554	67,572	36,400	31,171	926	588	338
Individual income:								
1942	3,481	3,205	276	249	27	26	24	2
1950	16,533	15,745	788	724	64	109	104	5
1955	29,984	28,747	1,237	1,094	143	181	174	7
1960	43,178	40,715	2,463	2,209	[3] 254	240	226	14
1965	52,882	48,792	4,090	3,657	[3] 433	273	252	21
1966	60,206	55,446	4,760	4,288	[3] 472	307	283	24
1967	67,352	61,526	5,826	4,909	[3] 916	340	311	29
1968	76,034	68,726	7,308	6,231	[3] 1,077	380	344	37
Corporation income:[3]								
1942	4,999	4,727	272	269	3	37	35	2
1950	11,081	10,488	593	586	7	73	69	4
1955	18,604	17,861	744	737	7	113	108	5
1960	22,674	21,494	1,180	1,180	(3)	126	119	7
1965	27,390	25,461	1,929	1,929	(3)	141	131	10
1966	32,111	30,073	2,038	2,038	(3)	164	154	10
1967	36,198	33,971	2,227	2,227	(3)	183	172	11
1968	31,183	28,665	2,518	2,518	(3)	156	143	13
Sales, gross receipts, and customs:								
1942	5,776	3,425	2,351	2,218	133	43	25	17
1950	12,997	7,843	5,154	4,670	484	86	52	34
1955	17,221	9,578	7,643	6,864	779	104	58	46
1960	24,452	12,603	11,849	10,510	1,339	136	70	66
1965	32,904	15,786	17,118	15,059	2,059	170	81	88
1966	33,726	14,641	19,085	17,044	2,041	172	75	97
1967	36,336	15,806	20,530	18,575	1,956	184	80	104
1968	39,186	16,275	22,911	20,979	1,932	196	81	115

EXHIBIT 21-29 (CONTINUED)

SOURCE AND YEAR	All govern-ment	Federal	STATE AND LOCAL Total	State	Local	PER CAPITA[1] (dollars) Total	Federal	State and local
Property:								
1942	4,537	(X)	4,537	264	4,273	34	(X)	34
1950	7,349	(X)	7,349	307	7,042	48	(X)	48
1955	10,735	(X)	10,735	412	10,323	65	(X)	65
1960	16,405	(X)	16,405	607	15,798	91	(X)	91
1965	22,583	(X)	22,583	766	21,817	117	(X)	117
1966	24,670	(X)	24,670	834	23,836	126	(X)	126
1967	26,047	(X)	26,047	862	25,186	132	(X)	132
1968	27,747	(X)	27,747	912	26,835	139	(X)	139
Other taxes, including licenses:								
1942	2,000	908	1,092	903	189	15	7	8
1950	3,140	1,110	2,030	1,643	387	21	7	13
1955	4,527	1,402	3,125	2,490	634	27	8	19
1960	6,411	2,191	4,220	3,530	692	36	12	23
1965	9,191	3,670	5,521	4,715	807	47	19	28
1966	10,029	3,935	6,094	5,177	917	52	20	32
1967	10,188	3,818	6,370	5,354	1,016	51	19	32
1968	10,976	3,889	7,087	5,760	1,327	55	19	35

X Not applicable.

[1]Based on estimated population as of July 1, including Armed Forces abroad through 1955.
[2]Federal amounts include excess profits tax, normal tax, surtax, and, for 1942, unjust enrichment tax.
[3]Corporation included with individual income tax collections.

SOURCE: Dept. of Commerce, Bureau of the Census; *Historical Statistics on Governmental Finances and Employment;* Census of Governments: 1967, Vol. 4, No. 5, *Compendium of Government Finances;* and annual report, *Governmental Finances.*

tax" on cocktails (Los Angeles),[3] to sewer taxes, inventory tax, and many others. The search for new sources is prompted by the desire to avoid confrontation with taxpayer groups which are defending established territory. For example, any effort to raise the property tax raises queries and often opposition from well-organized property taxpayer associations. In staking out specific territories the total range of taxes is not challenged, and when a new source is discovered it can be implemented, as there is no organized opposition. Whether the growing consumer movement in the United States will concern itself in time with the total tax burden and its distribution is a poignant question.

Several interesting attempts to simplify the taxation process are being observed in other countries. Australia, for example, has a centralized tax-collection system. Allocations are then made to the federal government and to the provinces and territories in accordance with formulae. In Europe, within the framework of The Organisation for Economic Co-operation and Development (OECD), there has been steady progress and adoption of a value-added tax (VAT) in preference to other forms of taxation including income, sales, and cascade. The structure and differences between VAT, sales, and cascade are illustrated in Exhibits 21-30 and 21-31. France

[3]The tippler's tax was declared unconstitutional after being in effect for several years.

EXHIBIT 21-30 SIMPLIFIED DIAGRAM SHOWING COLLECTION MECHANISM OF A VAT* (VALUE-ADDED TAX)

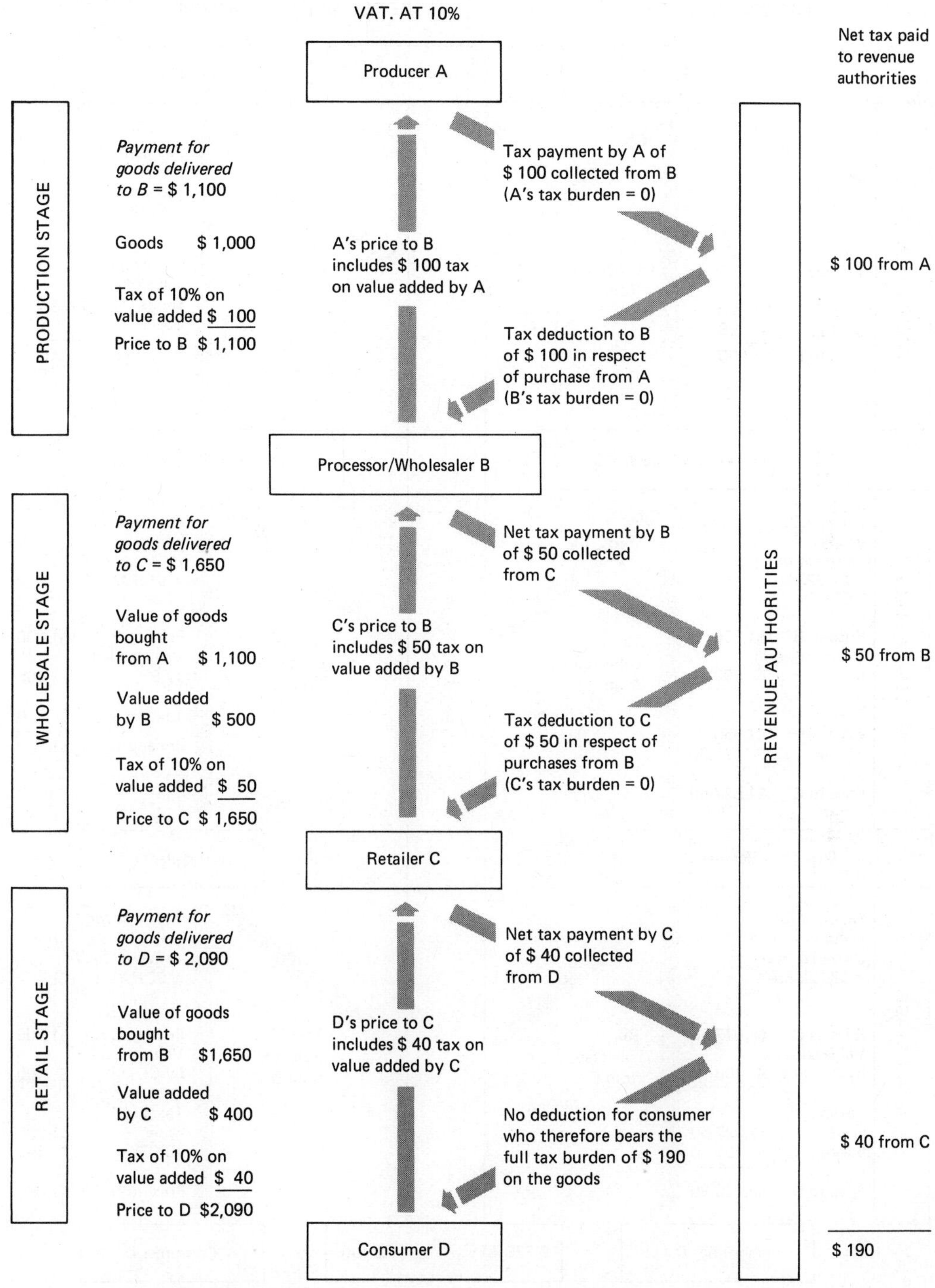

*It is assumed that (a) VAT is at 10% of the tax exclusive value, (b) the tax exclusive value of goods sold by A is $1,000, (c) the value added by B (processing, packing, labour, costs, and profits) is $500, (d) the value added by C (labour costs and profits) is $400. The possibility of backwards shifting or taxe occulte is not taken into account, nor the fact that in practice tax will usually have been paid on components supplied to A.

SOURCE: "Changing to a Value-Added Tax," *The OECD Observer* 44 (February 1970):14–15. Used with permission.

EXHIBIT 21-31 SIMPLIFIED DIAGRAM SHOWING COLLECTION MECHANISM OF A CASCADE TAX AND A RETAIL SALES TAX*

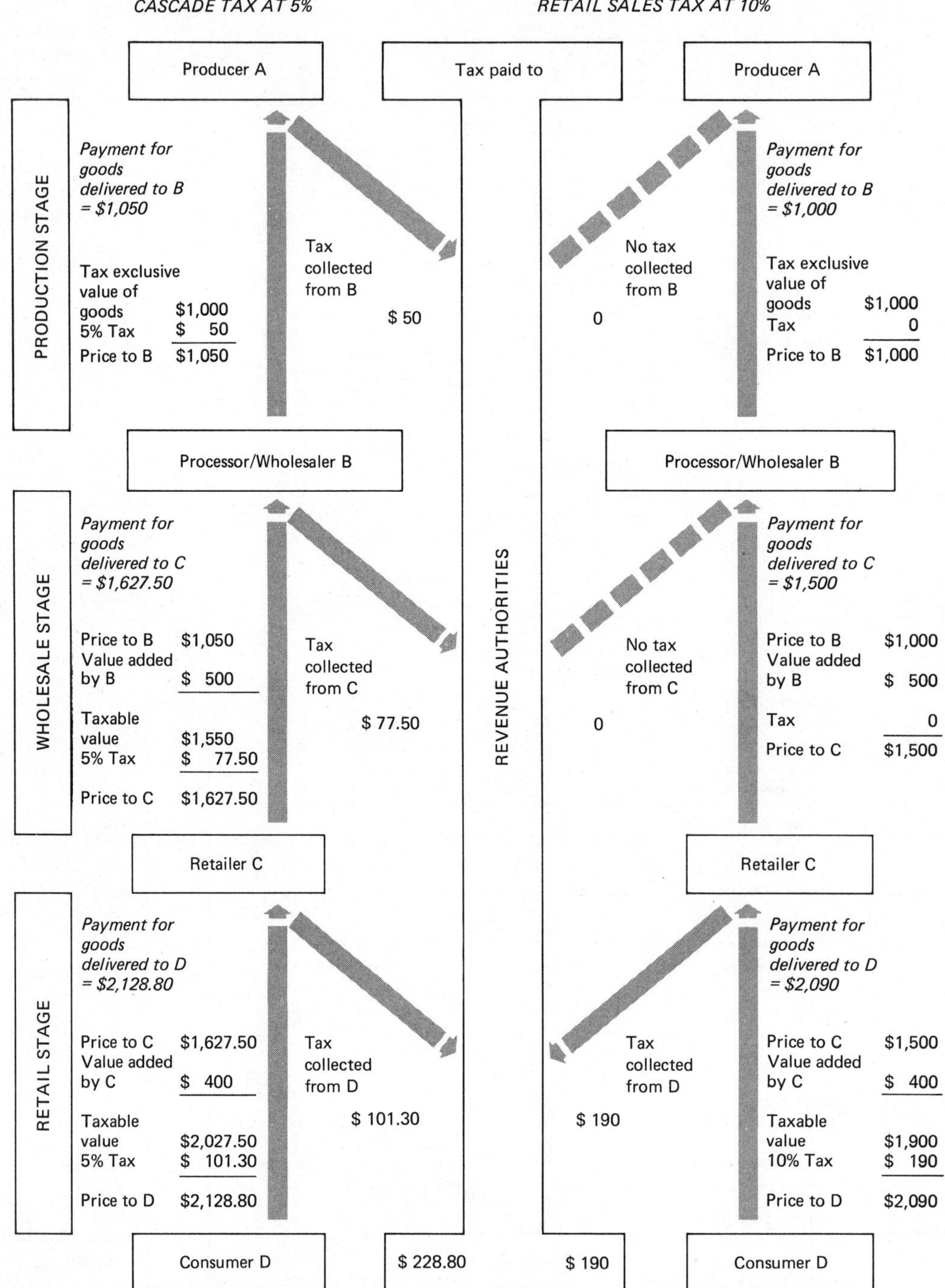

*Simplifications and assumptions as in Exhibit 21-30. In practice cascade systems are sometimes levied at lower rates at wholesale stage and sometimes not levied at all at retail stage, but as tax levied at preproduction stages is not taken into account in the chart, the relative yields are fairly realistic.

SOURCE: "Changing to a Value-Added tax," *The OECD Observer* 44 (February 1970): 15. Used with permission.

and Germany established a comprehensive VAT system as of January 1, 1968. Denmark introduced the measure on July 3, 1967; and the Netherlands and Sweden on January 1, 1969. Belgium and Italy were scheduled to institute VAT in 1971 and 1972 respectively.

This development is of particular interest to United States taxation in that Congressman Wilbur D. Mills, chairman of the House Ways and Means Committee, introduced H.R. 13713 in September 1969 calling for legislation which would allow the Secretary of the Treasury to refund ". . . such local, State, and Federal taxes as he determines are directly or indirectly borne by such exported article. . . . "

In theory the VAT tax has merits in that it would allow for few exceptions and exclusions, and hence simplify the enormous burden of tax administration by businesses. Additional arguments in favor of VAT include the points that the existing corporate income tax is a tax on efficiency (businesses showing losses are not taxed, and in fact are rewarded), and that expenses can be inflated in order to minimize taxes. The principal argument against VAT is that it may be regressive in nature. For example, taxation will be based on sales volume rather than profit, so that high-volume, low-profit products will bear an increased tax burden. As it is these products which are generally geared to low-income groups, the latter would pay more for their goods and services. It is perhaps for this last reason that the AFL-CIO submitted the following statement to the two political conventions in 1968:[4]

> All efforts to make inroads on the progessivity of the federal tax structure should be repulsed. These include proposals for a national sales, transactions, or value-added tax.

At the time of writing, this issue has come into clear focus and presages a widening dialogue on a more efficient administrative tax structure in the United States. Perhaps the growing debate on revenue-sharing, begun in 1971, will lead, if not to VAT, to a single administrative system as exemplified by Australia.

21.6 TAX PLANNING

We now turn to tax planning for businesses and individuals. The items discussed illustrate typical ways to avoid tax by planning transactions to fit the IRS requirements for beneficial treatment.

Avoidance is distinguished from *evasion.* One may avoid taxes by engaging in transactions favored by the Internal Revenue Code; whereas evasion operates outside the law. Direct methods of evasion consist of doctoring actual figures—"padding expenses" or not disclosing revenues. A more subtle form of evasion is where a non-favored transaction is made to appear like one deserving of tax benefits. For example, where a transaction occurs for the express reason of reaping benefits allowed under the Internal Revenue Code with no business purpose, the courts are empowered to look beyond bookkeeping to substance. Finding none, they may disallow the benefit. Most of our tax litigation centers in the grey area between avoidance and evasion.

Federal income tax is levied on corporations, individuals, estates, and trusts.

[4] B. Kenneth Sanden, "A Look at Value-Added Taxation," *The Price Waterhouse Review* XV, no. 3, (Autumn 1970): 30–37.

Income of a proprietorship is reported on the return of the proprietor. A partnership reports its income to the IRS but is not taxed. Each partner is taxed as an individual for his portion of partnership income.

While the tax rate for corporations is 22%, a surtax of 26% brings the actual maximum rate to 48%. As a fiscal device an additional surcharge, recently 10%, may be levied or removed as needed to curb inflation or help balance the budget.

Tax rates for individuals are shown in Exhibit 21-14. Rates for income retained by estates and trusts are the same as for individuals.

Various alternatives exist in reporting income, which result in widely differing income taxes.

SUB-CHAPTER S ELECTION

A business may be organized as a corporation with all the legal protection which accrues to that form of business and yet elect to be taxed as a partnership if certain qualifications are met:

1. There are ten or less shareholders who are:
   a. Individuals or decedent estates, and
   b. Not nonresident aliens.
2. It files the election at the appropriate time.
3. It is a domestic corporation which is not consolidated with some other business entity.
4. It has one class of stock.
5. At least 80% of income is derived from domestic sources.
6. Not more than 20% of income is derived from rents, interest, royalties, dividends, gains from sale of securities or annuities.

The advantage of this election is to remove one tax layer through which income must pass. To illustrate, assume two shareholders in the 20% bracket own a corporation which in its first year of operation earned taxable income of $25,000 and distributed $12,500 to each of its shareholders.

Taxes as a corporation would be:

Corporation $25,000 × 22%	$ 5,500
Individual A $12,500 × 20%	2,500
Individual B $12,500 × 20%	2,500
TOTAL TAXES AS CORPORATION	$10,500

Taxes under sub-chapter S would be:

Corporation 0	
Individual A $12,500 × 20%	$2,500
Individual B $12,500 × 20%	2,500
TOTAL TAXES UNDER SUB-CHAPTER S	$5,000

Conversely, a corporation's net operating loss would be divided among the shareholders and would be available to offset their earned income—an especially advantageous situation for those in the high brackets.

CAPITAL GAINS

Capital gains and losses result from the sale of capital assets. An individual's capital assets are his residence and investments, such as stock or vacant land. All corporate assets, except for (1) receivables, (2) inventory, and (3) non-depreciable assets such as land (that is, all section 1231 assets), are considered capital assets and benefit from capital gains treatment.

For tax purposes capital gains and losses are divided further into short term (held less than six months) and long term (held six months or more). Short-term gains and losses are taxed as ordinary income. Long-term capital gains and losses are netted against each other and taxed at half the taxpayer's rate to a maximum of 25%. In addition, short-term and long-term gains and losses must be netted together and the remainder taxed appropriately.

The need to plan purchases and sales to minimize taxes can be illustrated as follows. Suppose a taxpayer in the 50% bracket purchases stock for $100,000. The difference in tax between his two options is as follows, given a sale for $150,000:

	Gain	Rate	Tax
Short-term sale	$50,000	50%	$25,000
Long-term sale	$50,000	25%	12,500
Tax saving			$12,500

A variation of capital gains taxation is allowed under Section 1231 of the Internal Revenue Code. Where a company sells its operating property, either real or depreciable personal property, it may take any gain as a capital gain. Assuming no other capital transactions, the company may deduct a loss on sale from ordinary income. In effect, gains are treated as capital gains and losses deducted at ordinary income rates. This provision encourages enterprises to update their facilities and thus maintain a high level of productivity.

ALTERNATIVE ACCOUNTING METHODS

For several categories of assets, alternative accounting methods may be used to attain tax savings. Differences in methods relating to inventory, depreciation, depletion, and amortization are the main variables.

Inventory Valuation

As we have noted before, inventory (and cost of goods) may be priced by any of several methods; specific identification, FIFO, weighted average, or LIFO. Where tax and book methods are similar, a taxpayer may elect the method which results in the lowest tax. Once the method is elected, permission must be granted by the IRS before a change may be effected. In periods of rising prices, LIFO method creates lower income, hence lower tax.

Because inventory is being continually replaced by higher priced items, the chances of having to pay the taxes saved in years past are remote. Should prices begin a downswing, taxes would be greater than under LIFO—in a disadvantageous economic climate.

Accelerated Depreciation

All depreciation methods discussed so far are permissible for tax purposes. Depending on income flow, of course, taking the accelerated methods results in tax savings.

Use of 200% accelerated depreciation is restricted by the Revenue Code to depreciable personal property and new residential rental housing (whereas used apartments are limited to straight-line). All other real property may be depreciated at a maximum of 150%.

An additional 20% first year's depreciation (up to a maximum of $10,000 per taxpayer) is permitted but reduces an asset's depreciable basis. This benefit was combined with the better known investment tax credit as an incentive for purchasing new facilities.

Until 1970 the investment tax credit of 7% on qualified investments was allowed on all personal property except residential and hotel furnishings. The amount of credit depends on estimated asset life and whether the asset is new or used, the highest credit going to new assets with estimated lives in excess of seven years. In the case of disposal before expiration of the estimated life, a pro rata recapture of the investment tax credit is required.

Two provisions have been added which favor the purchase of operating capital. For assets purchased between January 1 and June 30, depreciation may begin January 1. For assets purchased between July 1 and December 31, depreciation may begin July 1. Thus, if an asset is sold on December 31, the seller may take depreciation for all twelve months and the buyer for six.

The second provision involves IRS guidelines for depreciable asset lives. These range from three years for taxis to sixty years for warehouses and grain elevators. Taxpayers are now allowed to shorten the original guideline lives by 20% for operating plant and equipment.

Because depreciation rarely reflects the change in value of real property, it has been beneficial to use the most accelerated depreciation method and realize capital gains upon the sale of the property. This effectively converts the difference between depreciation allowed under straight-line and that taken under accelerated methods from ordinary income to capital gains. To close this loophole the law requires property to be held for 100 months before one may reap this benefit. Depreciation recapture decreases by 1% for each month the property is held. Such property fell under Sections 1250 and 1245. Under the 1970 law, residential rental property is the only real estate which still receives this favored treatment. For all others the difference between accelerated depreciation and straight-line taken after December 31, 1969, is subject to recapture (up to the amount of any gain) and is taxed at ordinary income rates.

Depletion

We have discussed the difference between statutory depletion and amortization of development costs. The function of statutory depletion is to subsidize, through tax reduction, the exploration and development costs of natural resources. As long as property produces gross income, a percentage thereof (up to 50% of net income) can be deducted. The 1969 Tax Reform Act lowered oil and gas depletion allowances from 27 1/2% to 22%.

Sale of Stocks Versus Bonds

When a corporation requires money for expansion or debt reduction, several options are available: obtaining loans, issuing bonds, or selling stock.

Because the interest paid to bondholders is deductible from revenues for tax purposes while dividends are not, there is a tax advantage to floating bond issues. Assume the sale of 6% preferred stock versus 6% bonds for the purpose of raising $100,000 after issuing costs.

Stock sale:		
Net income	$25,000	
Tax	5,500	
Net income after tax	19,500	
Less: Preferred stock dividend	6,000	
INCREASE IN RETAINED EARNINGS		$13,500
Bond sale:		
Net operating income	$25,000	
Interest expense	6,000	
Net income	19,000	
Tax	4,180	
Net income after tax	14,820	
INCREASE IN RETAINED EARNINGS		14,820
Difference in methods		$ 1,320

STOCK OPTION PLANS

Qualified stock option plans permit an employee to purchase his company's (parent or subsidiary) stock below market price and be taxed at capital gains rates upon sale. Non-qualified stock options give no such tax benefit. In either case the employer corporation does not receive a tax deduction if the terms of the option are respected; but it does if the stock is sold prematurely (see requirements below).

In order to qualify for this tax favor, a stock option plan must:

1. Offer stock at a price not less than market value on the date of the option.
2. The plan must be approved by shareholders within twelve months before or after adoption.
3. The option cannot extend beyond ten years.

4. The number of shares available and number of employees entitled to options must be stated in the plan approved by the stockholders.
5. The plan must be open to persons holding no more than 5% of the company's stock.
6. The plan must include these requirements:
   a. Limit each option to a five-year period.
   b. Limit the option to an individual or his lawful estate.
   c. Ban exercise of new options while prior options are still outstanding.
7. The employee must hold stock for at least three years after exercising the option.

Qualified stock option plans differ from non-qualified plans in the amount of income taxed at capital gains rates.

	Market Value when Option Granted	Market Value when Option Exercised	Actual Proceeds on Sale
Qualified	$10,000	$12,000	$15,000
	↑	Capital gain—$5,000	↑
Non-qualified	10,000	12,000	15,000
	↑ Ordinary income $2,000 ↑	↑ Capital gain $3,000 ↑	

21.7 SUMMARY

Tax planning and administration on either a macro or micro basis is a significant area of study in its own right. It does, however, pervade and interact with accounting; accordingly, we believe that it is important to include an introduction to taxation as an integral part of the study of accounting.

In this chapter we have discussed both macro and micro tax planning and administration at a superficial level. We discussed the tax structure in the United States, distribution of the tax burden—progressive, regressive, and neutral taxation, program-tax relationships, and efficiency of the taxation processes in the United States. In this last connection we pointed to the centralized system used in Australia and the VAT in Europe.

We turned next to a very brief discussion of tax planning for individuals and businesses. Among the topics covered were (1) sub-chapter S election, (2) capital gains and losses, (3) inventory pricing, (4) accelerated depreciation, (5) depletion, (6) sale of stocks versus bonds, and (7) stock option plans.

With the complexity of taxation in modern economics, tax planning is a necessity. The material in chapter 21 is insufficient as a guide to comprehensive tax planning, but it does introduce salient concepts and will serve as a basis for further studies in taxation.

CHAPTER 21 APPENDIX A

THE BASIC TAX REPORTING FORMAT FOR FORM 1040

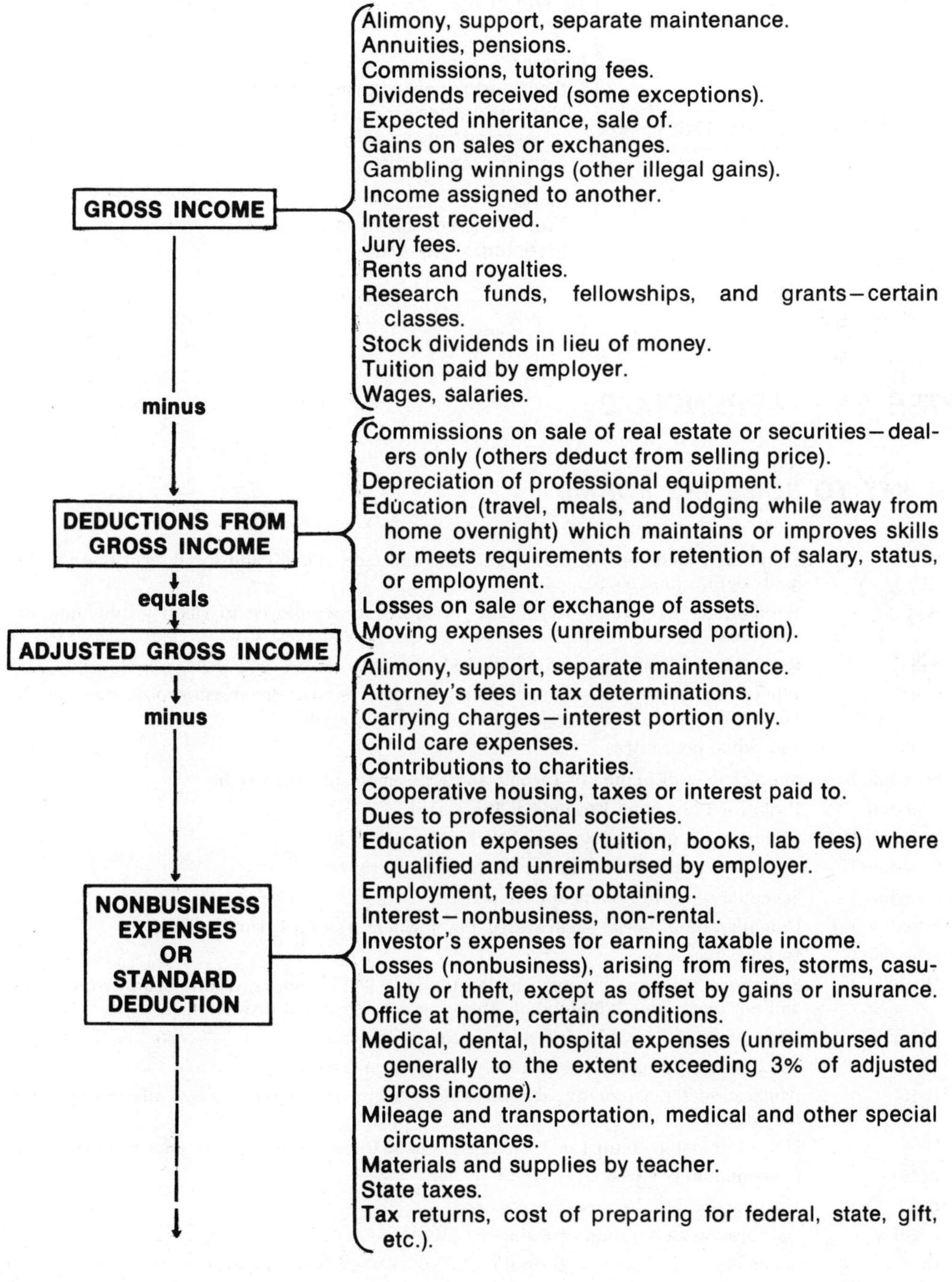
GROSS INCOME
Alimony, support, separate maintenance.
Annuities, pensions.
Commissions, tutoring fees.
Dividends received (some exceptions).
Expected inheritance, sale of.
Gains on sales or exchanges.
Gambling winnings (other illegal gains).
Income assigned to another.
Interest received.
Jury fees.
Rents and royalties.
Research funds, fellowships, and grants—certain classes.
Stock dividends in lieu of money.
Tuition paid by employer.
Wages, salaries.
minus
DEDUCTIONS FROM GROSS INCOME
Commissions on sale of real estate or securities—dealers only (others deduct from selling price).
Depreciation of professional equipment.
Education (travel, meals, and lodging while away from home overnight) which maintains or improves skills or meets requirements for retention of salary, status, or employment.
Losses on sale or exchange of assets.
Moving expenses (unreimbursed portion).
equals
ADJUSTED GROSS INCOME
minus
NONBUSINESS EXPENSES OR STANDARD DEDUCTION
Alimony, support, separate maintenance.
Attorney's fees in tax determinations.
Carrying charges—interest portion only.
Child care expenses.
Contributions to charities.
Cooperative housing, taxes or interest paid to.
Dues to professional societies.
Education expenses (tuition, books, lab fees) where qualified and unreimbursed by employer.
Employment, fees for obtaining.
Interest—nonbusiness, non-rental.
Investor's expenses for earning taxable income.
Losses (nonbusiness), arising from fires, storms, casualty or theft, except as offset by gains or insurance.
Office at home, certain conditions.
Medical, dental, hospital expenses (unreimbursed and generally to the extent exceeding 3% of adjusted gross income).
Mileage and transportation, medical and other special circumstances.
Materials and supplies by teacher.
State taxes.
Tax returns, cost of preparing for federal, state, gift, etc.).

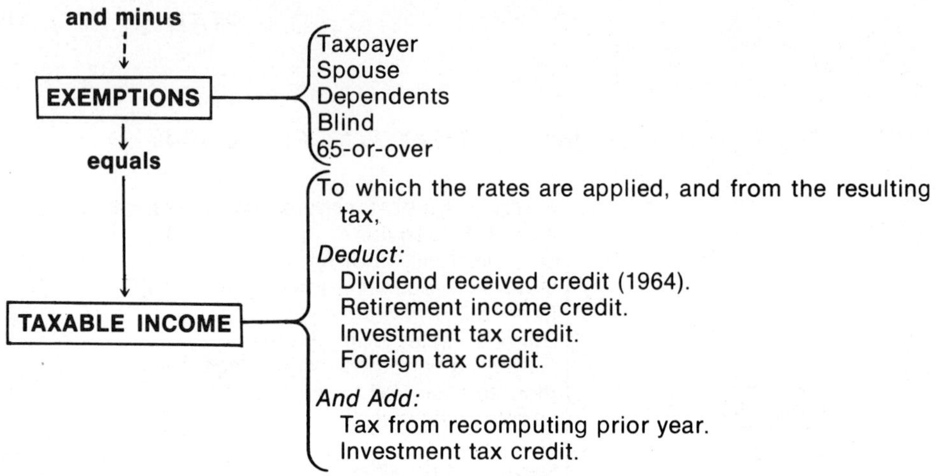

CHAPTER 21 APPENDIX B

A KEY TO SOME IRS FORMS

W-2	Employer's statement of total wages paid, and federal taxes and social security withheld, on or before January 31.
W-4	Withholding Exemption Certificate—furnished by employee to claim withholding exemptions.
843	Refund claim form for net loss carryback.
936	Where one spouse is absent and cannot sign joint return, the absent spouse may execute Form 936: "Authorization—Joint Return or Declaration."
1040	Individual tax return.
Schedule B:	Supplemental Schedule of Income and Retirement Income Credit.
Schedule C:	Profit (or Loss) from Business or Profession.
Schedule C-3:	Computation of Social Security Self-Employment Tax.
Schedule D:	Gains and Losses from Sales or Exchanges of Property.
Schedule F:	Schedule of Farm Income and Expense.
Schedule F-1:	Computation of Social Security Self-Employment Tax on Farm Earnings.
Schedule G:	Income Averaging
1040A	Short form for wages earners with less than $10,000 income consisting mainly from wages and not more than $200 total of other wages, interest and dividends.
1040ES	Declaration of Estimated Income Tax for Individuals.
1041	U.S. Fiduciary Income Tax Return (for estates and trusts).
1045	Application for a tentative carryback adjustment on prior-year taxes affected by a net operating loss carryback.
1065	U.S. Partnership Return of Income (also used for syndicates, pools, joint ventures, etc.).
1116	Computation of foreign tax credit.
1120	U.S. Corporation Income Tax Return.
1120ES	Corporation Declaration of Estimated Tax.
1310	Statement of Claimant to Refund on Behalf of Deceased Taxpayer.
2106	Schedule of Deductible Transportation, Travel, and Outside Salesman Expenses.

2119	Statement Concerning Sale or Exchange of Personal Residence (a more detailed form than 1040-Schedule D).
2120	Waiver to Claim of Dependent where multiple-support agreements are in effect.
2440	Statement to Support Exclusion of Sick Pay.
2441	Form claiming expenses in connection with housekeeping or maid-caring for dependent.
2688	Application for Extension of Time to File.
2948	Medical and Dental Expense Statement (May be filed with Form 1040).
3909	Moving Expense Adjustment (May be filed with Form 1040).
3468	Computation of Investment Credit.

CHAPTER 21 APPENDIX C

*STATEMENT ON SOME PRINCIPLES OF INTERNAL REVENUE TAX ADMINISTRATION**

The function of the Internal Revenue Service is to administer the Internal Revenue Code. Tax policy for raising revenue is determined by Congress.

With this in mind, it is the duty of the Service to carry out that policy by correctly applying the laws enacted by Congress; to determine the reasonable meaning of various Code provisions in light of the Congressional purpose in enacting them; and to perform this work in a fair and impartial manner, with neither a government nor a taxpayer point of view.

At the heart of administration is interpretation of the Code. It is the responsibility of each person in the Service, charged with the duty of interpreting the law, to try and find the true meaning of the statutory provision and not to adopt a strained construction in the belief that he is "protecting the revenue." The revenue is properly protected only when we ascertain and apply the true meaning of the statute.

The Service also has the responsibility of applying and administering the law in a reasonable, practical manner. Issues should only be raised by examining officers when they have merit, never arbitrarily or for trading purposes. At the same time, the examining officer should never hesitate to raise a meritorious issue. It is also important that care be exercised not to raise an issue or to ask a court to adopt a position inconsistent with an established Service position.

Administration should be both reasonable and vigorous. It should be conducted with as little delay as possible and with great courtesy and considerateness. It should never try to overreach, and should be reasonable within the bounds of law and sound administration. It should, however, be vigorous in requiring compliance with the law and it should be relentless in its attack on unreal tax devices and fraud.

CHAPTER 21 REFERENCES AND ADDITIONAL READINGS

TAX GUIDES

Commerce Clearing House, Inc., Chicago, Illinois, publishes annually:

U.S. Master Tax Guide

Federal Tax Course

Prentice-Hall, Inc., Englewood Cliffs, New Jersey, publishes annually:

Prentice-Hall Federal Tax Handbook

Federal Tax Course

*A statement issued by the Commissioner of Internal Revenue, Mortimer M. Caplin, on Friday, May 1, 1964, and published in the *Internal Revenue Bulletin,* no. 1964–22, June 1, 1964.

U.S. Treasury Department, Internal Revenue Services, publishes annually:
Your Federal Income Tax
Tax Guide for Small Business

GENERAL REFERENCES

Barnes, William S., director. *World Tax Series.* Harvard Law School, International Program in Taxation. Chicago: Commerce Clearing House, Inc., 1963.

Black, Duncan. *The Incidence of Income Taxes.* London: The Macmillan Company, 1939.

Dickerson, Leo D. *Federal Income Tax Fundamentals.* Belmont, Calif.: Wadsworth Publishing Company, 1961.

Doris, Lillian, ed. *The American Way in Taxation: Internal Revenue 1863–1963.* Englewood Cliffs, N.J.: Prentice-Hall, Inc., 1963.

Gaa, Charles. *Contemporary Thought on Federal Income Taxation.* Belmont, Calif.: Dickenson Publishing Company, 1968.

Holzman, Robert S. *Tax Basis for Managerial Decisions.* New York: Holt, Rinehart & Winston, Inc., 1965.

Jacoby, Neil. *Canada's Tax Structure and Economic Goals.* Toronto: York University Press, 1967.

Joint Committee on the Economic Report. *The Federal Revenue System: Facts and Problems.* 84th Cong. 1st sess. Washington, D.C.: U.S. Government Printing Office, 1956.

THE ACCOUNTANT AND TAX PRACTICE

Barnes, William T. "The CPA's Responsibilities in Tax Practice." *The Journal of Accountancy,* March 1968, pp. 27–33.

Blake, Mathew F. "Tax Practice: Responsibilities and Interrelationships." *The Journal of Accountancy,* March 1967, pp. 31–37.

Coffee, Melvin A. "Accountant's Role When a Client Faces Criminal Tax Fraud Investigation by Special Agent." *Taxation for Accountants,* July 1970, pp. 152–56.

Division of Federal Taxation of the American Institute of Certified Public Accountants. *Statements on Responsibilities in Tax Practice* (a series of statements). New York: American Institute of Certified Public Accountants.

Farber, Paul. *Working with the Revenue Code—1969.* New York: American Institute of Certified Public Accountants, 1969.

Finkston, Herbert. "The Work of the AICPA Tax Division." *The Tax Adviser,* February 1970, pp. 123–26.

Golub, Steven, and Larson, Robert E. "Accountant's Responsibility in the Preparation of Federal Income Tax Returns." *The New York Certified Public Accountant,* March 1967, pp. 218–22.

Kess, Sidney, and Kess, Lydia. "What It's Like to Work in the Tax Department of a Giant CPA Firm." *Taxation for Accountants,* November–December 1968, pp. 320–22.

Levy, M. H. "How to Apply for a Tax Ruling: The Step-by-Step Procedure." *The Practical Accountant,* August 1970, pp. 34–39.

Schreiber, Irving. *How to Handle Tax Audits, Requests for Rulings, Fraud Cases, and Other Procedures Before I.R.S.* New York: The Macmillan Company, 1967.

Tanner, Stephen D. "Corporation Estimated Income Tax Headaches." *The Journal of Accountancy,* February 1970, p. 80.

Wald, Leslie H. "Danger Signals of Fraud When Preparing Returns." *The Practical Accountant,* September–October 1969, pp. 10–13.

SELECTED TAX TOPICS

Battersby, Mark E. "Tax Return Filing by Computer." *Computer and Automation,* January 1971, pp. 19, 20.

Due, John F. "The Institutional Environment and the Tax Structure in Developing Economies." *The International Journal of Accounting Education and Research,* Fall 1968, pp. 17–27.

Elsberry, Donald G. "ADP: Its Significance to the Tax Practitioner." *The National Public Accountant,* January 1965, pp. 5, 19.

Gunder, Roger W. "What Management Expects from the Tax Department." *The Tax Executive,* October 1969, pp. 22–27.

Hertzog, R. P. "RIRA—The IRS' New Electronic Weapon in Litigating Tax Cases: How It Works." *Taxation for Accountants,* January–February 1967, pp. 362–63.

"IRS Officials Discuss Data Processing and Compliance Procedures" (news feature). *The Journal of Accountancy,* January 1966, pp. 19–24.

Kelly, Robert R. "Sales and Use Taxation in Interstate Commerce." *Management Accounting,* March 1967, pp. 29–35.

Miles, Jesse M. "Foreign Taxes and U.S. Tax Implications." *The Journal of Accountancy,* May 1966, pp. 46–52.

Moonitz, Marice. "Can Laws Coerce Accounting?" *Journal of Accounting Research,* Spring 1967, pp. 129, 130.

Morrison, Thomas A. "Taxation of International Investments." *The Accounting Review,* October 1966, pp. 704–713.

Smith, Paul W. *Tax Management in Action.* New York: American Management Association,.Inc., 1964.

Surrey, Stanley S. "The United States Income Tax System—The Need for a Full Accounting." *The Journal of Accountancy,* February 1968, pp. 57–61.

Taylor, Howard D. "Automatic Data Processing in the Internal Revenue Service." *The Journal of Accountancy,* March 1965, pp. 53–56.

CHAPTER 21 QUESTIONS, PROBLEMS, AND CASES

21- 1. How would you answer the question as to whether taxation in the United States is excessive or not?

21- 2. Define or explain the implication or use of the following terms and phrases:
- (a) Transfer payments
- (b) *Brushaber* v. *Union Pacific Railroad Co.*
- (c) Compliance audit
- (d) "Pay-as-you-earn philosophy"
- (e) Form 1099
- (f) Form W-2
- (g) Proportional tax rate
- (h) Neutral tax
- (i) Tax lobbying
- (j) VAT tax
- (k) Sub-chapter S election
- (l) Additional first year depreciation
- (m) 7% investment credit

21- 3. "The question as to whether government is too costly or not is a pressing one for which ready answers are not available." What are two methods for assessing the cost of government?

21- 4. Cite five examples of transfer payments. What proportion of federal expenditures is represented by transfer payments?

21- 5. Distinguish between "technical" and "socioeconomic" definitions of *progressive, proportional or neutral,* and *regressive* taxation.

21- 6. Explain the organizational structure of the Internal Revenue Service.

21- 7. "Over the years the philosophy in tax administration has changed from one of enforcement to voluntary compliance." Discuss the immergence of this new philosophy.

21- 8. Explain the audit process applied to individual income tax returns upon reaching a regional computing center. Approximately what percentage of total returns are audited? What percentage of total returns are investigated for tax fraud?

21- 9. How is the audit of self-employed persons accomplished?

21-10. "One facet of the audit process is to test for the reasonableness of deductions." How is this test accomplished?

21-11. Answer the following questions about the history of federal income tax in the United States:
   (a) What were the personal exemption provisions and tax rates of the Revenue Act of:
      (1) 1861
      (2) 1862
      (3) 1864
   (b) The Revenue Act of 1894 was challenged in the *Pollock* v. *The Farmers' Loan and Trust Company* case, and was declared invalid nine months after its passage. What was the issue that caused the act to be declared invalid?
   (c) What was the tax rate imposed by the Corporation Excise Tax Law of 1909?
   (d) What constitutional amendment gives Congress the power to lay and collect taxes on income? When was the amendment ratified by the required number of states? What court case upheld the constitutionality of this revenue act?
   (e) "The Revenue Act of 1964 was designed to reduce the impact of taxes on the whole economy of the country." What are five important changes resulting from this act?
   (f) In general terms, highlight the important changes in income tax law provided by the Tax Reform Act of 1969.

21-12. Identify and discuss the four sources that determine the income tax law insofar as the taxpayer's federal tax liability on any matter is concerned.

21-13. Trace the legislative history of a tax bill from its inception to eventual enactment into law.

21-14. Distinguish between *avoidance* and *evasion.*

21-15. Explain the income tax appeal procedure by diagraming or listing the steps involved from the IRS's original examination of the return to an eventual disposition by the United States Supreme Court.

21-16. "Considering the scope of income taxes in the United States, the administrative mechanisms are remarkably efficient, given the attempt to keep the tax processes as democratic as possible." Discuss the efficiency of tax administration and support your views with statistical data from tables and diagrams presented in this chapter.

21-17. "Under the socioeconomic concept of tax distribution, *shifts* in tax scales are as important as the scales themselves." Demonstrate the importance of shifts in the tax scale by diagrams showing the relative tax burden of socioeconomic groups. Give some examples of each socioeconomic shift. Which socioeconomic group accounts for most of the federal income tax revenue?

21-18. "The dilemma in distributing the tax burden is clearly one of avoiding social inequity on the one hand while preserving economic incentives on the other." Discuss this dilemma and those tax schemes which are specifically designed to best handle the problem of social equity and economic incentives. Discuss the role of *tax lobbying* and *subsistance level income* in the final distribution of tax burden.

21-19. Indicate the tax benefits of the following items:
   (a) Sub-chapter S election
   (b) Capital gains
   (c) Inventory pricing
   (d) Accelerated depreciation

(e) Depletion
(f) Stock options

21-20. "The taxpayers' ability to influence resource allocation via taxation is *indirect;* that is, they can elect representatives who support their social goals." What is the practicality of instituting a direct link between taxes and program choices? What are the possible advantages and disadvantages of a tax program plebiscite? Is our present indirect tax program relationship responsive to shifts in program priorities?

21-21. "In addition to program support, the tax structure can serve wittingly or unwittingly as a regulator of socioeconomic behavior." Discuss and cite some specific examples of regulation by taxation.

21-22. Discuss the propriety of using the existing tax structure as an administrative vehicle for social security and welfare programs.

21-23. Originally, what were the designated revenue sources for the:
(a) Federal government
(b) State government
(c) Counties and cities

21-24. "The search for new tax sources is prompted by the desire to avoid confrontation with taxpayer groups which are defending established territory. Whether the growing consumer movement in the United States will concern itself in time with the total tax burden and its distribution is a poignant question." Discuss your reaction to this possibility.

21-25. What effect does the 1970 change in filing requirements have upon the cost burden of administering the tax structure? Since the IRS has an audit procedure, why is it necessary for individuals and companies to maintain records and file returns? Should the IRS maintain detailed earnings records and simply bill each taxpayer? Would this procedure produce a more equitable distribution of the costs of administering the tax structure?

21-26. Briefly describe the nature and scope of sources and uses of tax revenue by federal, state, and local government in the United States.

21-27. What are the advantages and disadvantages of a VAT tax? Name some countries that have adopted a VAT system.

21-28. Under sub-chapter S election, what are the six qualifications that a corporation must meet in order to be taxed as a partnership? What is the advantage of a corporation electing to be taxed as a partnership?

21-29. Identify the items classified as capital assets of:
(a) An individual
(b) A corporation

21-30. Comment on the efficiency of the tax system in the United States.

21-31. Describe the tax treatment of long-term capital gains and losses compared with short-term capital gains and losses.

21-32. When a company sells its operating assets, what is the tax provision of Section 1231 (of the Internal Revenue Code) concerning the treatment of gains and losses? What business incentive is provided by this provision?

21-33. Discuss how alternative accounting methods may be used to attain tax savings in situations relating to:
(a) Inventory
(b) Depreciation
(c) Depletion
(d) Stock versus bond sale
(e) Stock option plans

21-34. What are the restrictions of the Internal Revenue Code on the use of 200% accelerated depreciation?

21-35. Distinguish between a VAT, sales, and cascade tax.

21-36. "Most taxing jurisdictions are reaching out to tap most available sources." Discuss.

21-37. "Two provisions have been added which strongly favor the purchase of operating capital." One provision involves depreciation calculation, the other involves the IRS guidelines for determining the depreciable life of operating assets. Explain these provisions.

21-38. The use of accelerated depreciation effectively converts the difference between depreciation allowed under straight-line and that taken under accelerated methods from ordinary income to capital gains. How was this loophole closed by the 1970 law?

21-39. How could we strengthen the link between taxation and social goals?

21-40. "The function of statutory depletion is to subsidize through tax reduction the exploration and development costs of natural resources." Discuss the propriety of this type of government subsidy in relation to social goals.

21-41. What are the seven provisions that a stock option plan must meet in order to qualify for favored tax treatment? How is the capital gain computed under a qualified plan versus a non-qualified plan?

21-42. If stock purchased under a qualified stock option plan is sold prematurely by the employee, the corporation will receive a tax deduction that it would otherwise not receive. Explain why the corporation would receive a tax deduction, and how such deduction would be calculated.

21-43. "The level of transfer payments is in major part an index of the extent of socialized programs in the United States. New social programs such as social security, medicare, or the family assistance plan increase government costs significantly. If there is a presumption that these matters were taken care of formerly in the private sector, then these programs must be viewed as strategic shifts in the economy rather than as operational increases in government costs." Discuss.

21-44. ***ESTABLISHING A SYSTEM OF TAXATION*** Hogland is an independent sovereign country. The only product produced by Hogland's citizens is pork. However, since all citizens of Hogland are vegetarians, all pork is exported to neighboring countries.

In Hogland there are 300 small hog ranches that account for all the raising and breeding of hogs. The fourteen slaughter houses of Hogland handle all the slaughtering, packing, and transporting needs of Hogland's ranchers. All pork products are exported in processed and packaged form. Annually, about 8 million hogs are processed in Hogland.

The government of Hogland is presently small and has only modest expenditures of about $100,000. Future planning, however, calls for more public assistance to retired ranch workers, resurfacing of ranchland access roads, new school buildings, etc. For the past twenty years the government of Hogland has been supported by donations from the fourteen slaughter houses.

In order to finance new expenditures, Hogland's government officials have decided to institute a system of taxation that would *equitably* distribute the burden to all citizens. Suggest what type of tax should be instituted, and how the tax system can be administered.

21-45. ***QUALIFIED STOCK OPTION PLAN*** The following information is available with respect to an option granted to William Doran by his employer pursuant to a qualified stock option plan:

Fair market value and the option price on the date of grant, October 30, 1968	$ 50

Fair market value on date of exercise, June 5, 1969	$ 60
Selling price on November 15, 1970	$ 75
Number of shares acquired by exercise	200
Number of shares sold November 15, 1970	100

Required:

Determine the effect of the November 15 sale on Mr. Doran's 1970 taxable income.

(Adapted from the CPA exam.)

CHAPTER

22

FORECASTING

22.1 THE FORECASTING PROCESS

Forecasting is the process of estimating future events. Recording the *accounting significance* of the *outcome* of such events is *budget planning.* The significance of planning and the dependency of organizations upon forecasting is obvious if we again view the organization diagram presented in the introduction to Unit I. Exhibit 22-1 shows the importance of planning to a goal-oriented entity.

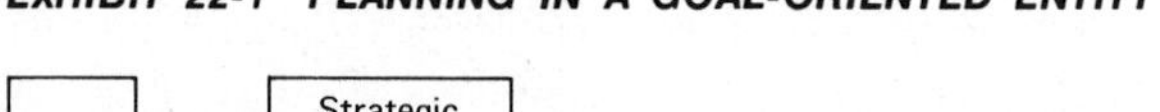
EXHIBIT 22-1 PLANNING IN A GOAL-ORIENTED ENTITY

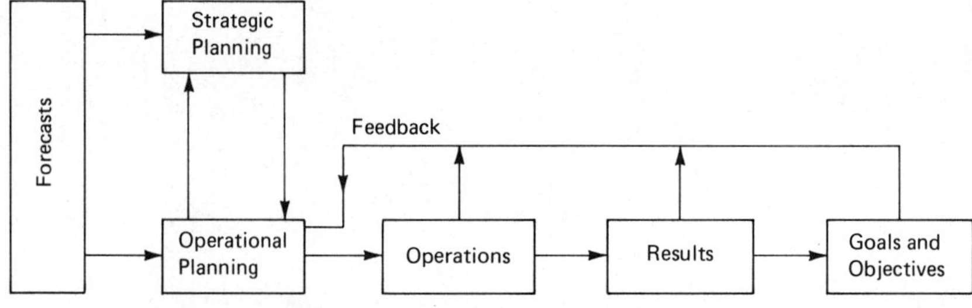

The decision maker in this organization searches for courses of action to attain company objectives. The *function of a budget* is to provide data relevant to the choice among alternatives; and the *function of forecasting* is to provide a precursory data base for generating budget values.

22.2 EFFECTIVENESS

A budget should represent the most effective means for reaching the company's financial objectives. The most effective budget is a budget of *alleged values*, that is, values which if employed in the decision process would lead to the correct decision.[1] For example, suppose that a decision maker uses a budget to guide his operating activities. In doing so, he uses a fixed set of decision rules which call for the alignment of activity to match the budgeted standard. With the decision rules represented by line *A* in Exhibit 22-2, a budgeted standard *b* would call for the action indicated by *y*.

EXHIBIT 22-2 RELATIONSHIP BETWEEN BUDGETED STANDARDS AND ACTIONS TAKEN

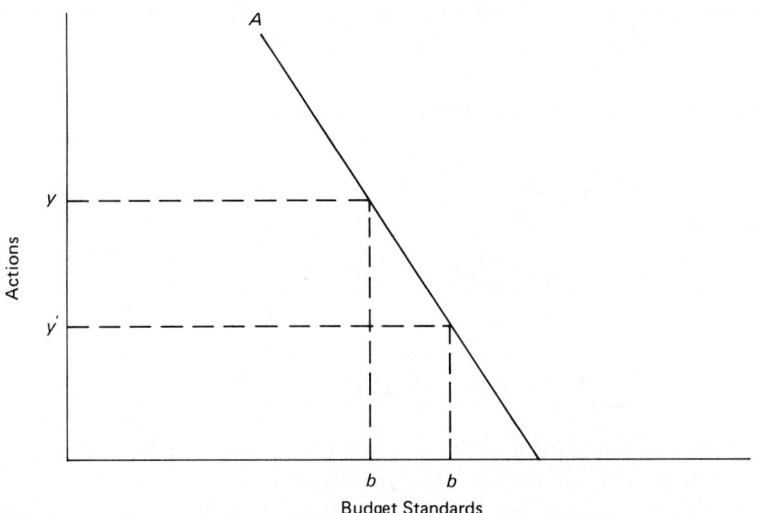

However, suppose further that the action called for by *y* does not yield an optimal operating activity, but the action called for by *y*′ does. The proper budgeted standard from the decision maker's viewpoint, then, is *b*′, not *b*. In other words, he alleges that the budgeted standard *b*′ will lead to the optimal operating activity, given his set of decision rules.

An ideal or optimal budget composed of alleged values is represented by a straight line in Exhibit 22-3, where alleged values are those budgeted standards which if used according to designated decision rules, will lead the decision maker to the proper result. The optimal budget represented by this straight line promotes the most *effective* action for reaching the organization's objectives. We are assured of such ac-

[1] The term "alleged value" is employed by Yuji Ijri in *The Foundations of Accounting Measurement* (Englewood Cliffs, N.J.: Prentice-Hall, Inc., 1967), p. 139.

tion, since the decision rules are highly structured and known in advance to be the alignment of action to the budgeted standard. In this instance, if we could always produce the alleged values we would be sure that the pursuance of goals would be accompanied by the optimal consumption of company resources.

EXHIBIT 22-3 STABLE BUDGETING—OPTIMAL EFFECTIVENESS

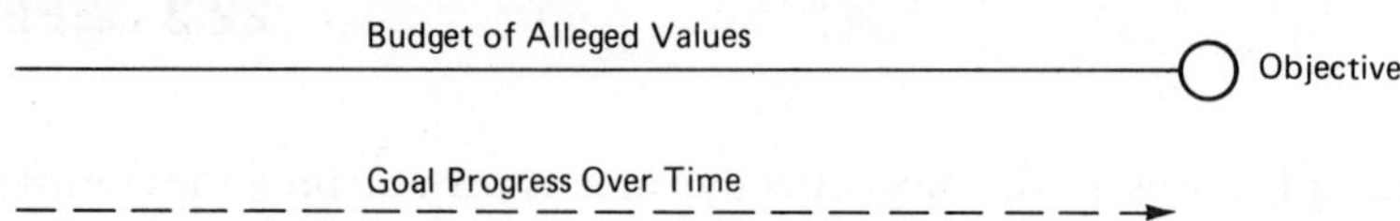

The use of standards other than those represented by the optimal budget line will result in inappropriate actions, since our decision rules allege optimality. Unfortunately, many of today's businesses, if not all, are simply unable to produce these alleged values. This inability results from the nature of an uncertain future, from the great difficulty in quantifying those qualitative factors that affect operational activity, and from the fact that decision makers may not have identical decision rules. Theoretically, *true values* or optimal budgeted standards are not attainable on a practical basis except by accident. Alleged values do exist for an optimal budget, but we simply are unable to say with certainty that we have successfully measured them. We are left with a situation as diagramed in Exhibit 22-4, in which budget values such as those represented by b in Exhibit 22-2 are plotted.

EXHIBIT 22-4 UNSTABLE BUDGETING—NON-OPTIMALITY

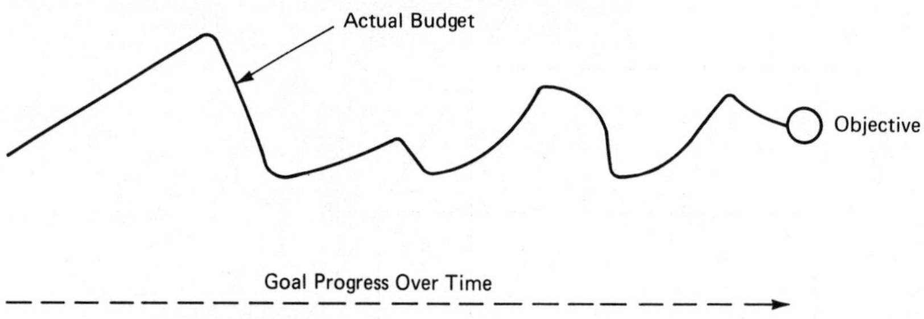

The situation represented by Exhibit 22-4 is due, in part at least, to a short-run focus resulting from ineffective forecasting and a fixation on short-run operating objectives. Since "going concern" is a fundamental concept, however, effectiveness cannot be optimal unless planning is oriented toward the long run. Unstable budgeting can be avoided, at least partially, if the development of budget standards are coordinated with long-run plans, even if this involves an apparent sub-optimization in the short run.

If we superimpose Exhibit 22-4 upon 22-3 we can readily observe the consequences of ineffective planning. Line ab in Exhibit 22-5 represents a *bias* caused by the use of inappropriate budgeted standards in the decision process.

The ab line of Exhibit 22-5 represents the same bias as indicated by the distance between the alleged value b' and the value b in Exhibit 22-2. As a practical matter, we can expect all budgets to contain built-in bias as exemplified by the non-alignment of the actual budget line with the budget of alleged values. It is important that we minimize this bias, since the use of an ineffective budget, no matter how closely we adhere to it, will not enable us to make the best use of company resources.

EXHIBIT 22-5 BIAS CAUSED BY UNSTABLE BUDGETING

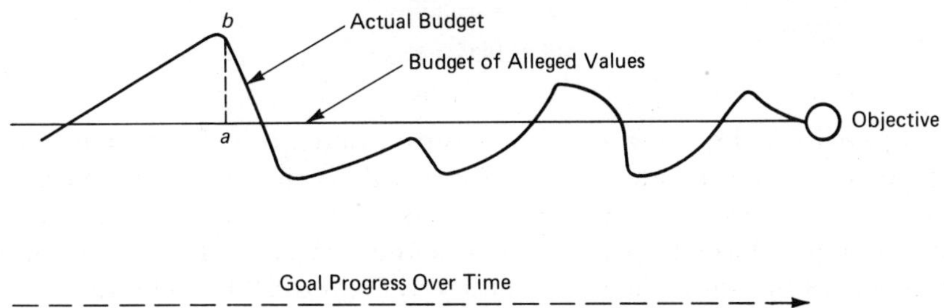

Bias can be reduced provided we carefully select our forecasting techniques; however, because of the uncertainty of future events (both exogenous and endogenous), we must accept the premise of a near-optimal budget as representing our best estimate of the future.

22.3 RELIABILITY

Budgets must be user-oriented. That is, they must provide the user with those values necessary to operate *effectively* within the context of his decision apparatus. For instance, let us take the example of an airplane pilot and his plane. Together they represent a system whose objective is to fly to different locations. The pilot is aware of a ten-degree calibration error in his navigational compass and automatically adjusts for the difference. In other words, he has developed decision rules for this compass. Even though the compass is producing erroneous values, it is producing those values necessary to cause the desired result. If a new and properly functioning compass were installed without the pilot's knowledge, he would fly in the wrong direction, for this compass does not produce the alleged values required by his decision rules. Consequently, even though the new compass is properly calibrated, and hence is more objective, it does not produce the alleged values which the old compass is capable of producing. It is not as reliable. The point is, a measurement does not have to be accurate or objective *per se* to produce the desired result—rather, it must be useful to the decision maker in enabling him to take the proper action. The reliability of a budgeted standard is determined by both its objectivity and the bias (indicated in Exhibit 22-5). Professor Ijiri[2] states this relationship mathematically as:

$$R = V + B$$

where

[2] Yuji Ijiri and R. K. Jaedicke, "Reliability and Objectivity of Accounting Measurements," *The Accounting Review* XLI, No. 3 (July 1966): 481. Variability is synonymous with "objectivity" in this equation. See Harold Bierman, Jr. and Thomas R. Dyckman, *Managerial Cost Accounting* (New York: The Macmillan Company, 1971), pp. 19–21. These authors define objectivity as:

$$O = \tfrac{1}{n}[\textstyle\sum_i (X_i - \overline{X})^2]$$

where X_i represents the individual observations and $\overline{X}$ represents the average of the observations. Bias is defined as $B = (\overline{X} - \mu)$, where μ is the value to be estimated. Reliability is $R = \tfrac{1}{n}[\sum_i (X_i - \overline{X})^2] + (\overline{X} - \mu)^2$.

R = reliability
V = variability
B = bias

Objectivity is the *consensus* of a measured value. It is reflected in Exhibit 22-6 as the dispersion about the mean in a symmetrical distribution. It is a measure of the variability of responses and indicates the consensus of observations. Exhibit 22-6a represents a highly objective measure because the variability about the mean is not as great relatively as the variability represented by Exhibit 22-6b. The forecasted value $\overline{X}$ in Exhibit 22-6b is more subjective than the $\overline{X}$ of Exhibit 22-6a because there is

EXHIBIT 22-6 OBJECTIVITY AS THE DISPERSION ABOUT THE MEAN

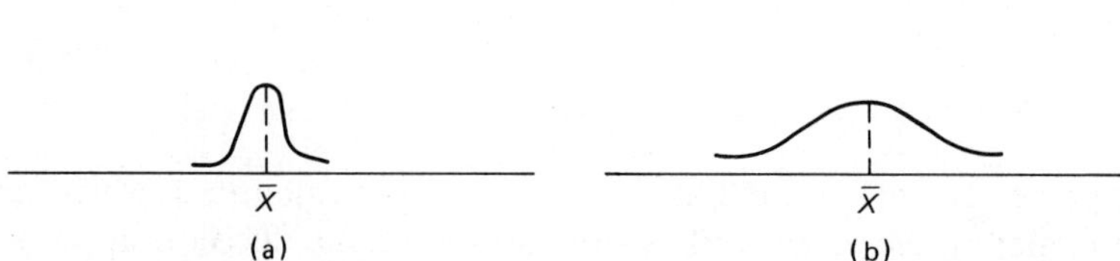

less agreement and hence more dispersion of responses. This does not mean the forecasted $\overline{X}$ is an inferior budget estimate, for as we have learned, there are two determinates of a reliable forecast: bias and objectivity. Therefore, if the subjective $\overline{X}$ (Exhibit 22-6b) produces less bias than the objective $\overline{X}$ (Exhibit 22-6a), it may be more reliable, and hence, more desirable as a budgeted standard. Exhibit 22-7 represents such a situation.[3]

EXHIBIT 22-7 COMPARATIVE RELIABILITY

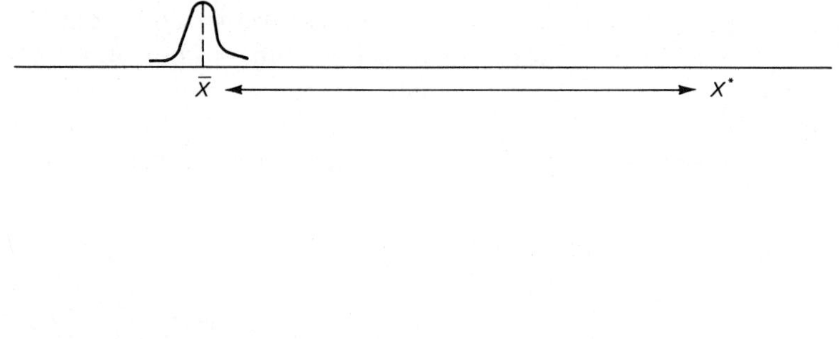

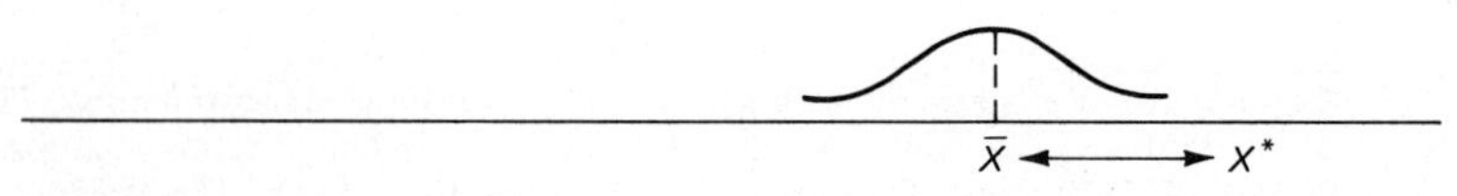

In Exhibit 22-7, X^* is the alleged value and the distance between $\overline{X}$ and X^* is the bias. Speaking relatively, then, the upper diagram of Exhibit 22-7 represents a

[3]Diagram from Ijiri and Jaedicke, "Accounting Measurements," p. 482. Used by permission of the publisher and the authors.

highly objective forecast but with a large bias, while the lower diagram represents a subjective forecast but with a small bias. Hence, due to the relationship $R = V + B$, the $\overline{X}$ of the lower diagram would be the preferred forecast. The point is, a forecast should not be rejected simply because it is more subjective than another. Forecasting techniques should be chosen for their ability to produce objective values and to produce values which closely approximate the user's alleged values.

Our objective in budget construction should be the measurement of budgeted standards which are reliable. This reliability is partly determined from bias caused by the user's decision rules and partly by the objectivity of the forecast. We know in a budgeting system that our decision rules are highly structured and dictate the alignment of action to budgeted standards. That is, we assume that a decision maker, knowing the outcome of an activity (forecasted value), will take the proper action to produce such outcome. This assumption of equivalency between alleged and forecasted values allows a budget to be used for planning as well as control.

We should take advantage of this knowledge and produce user-oriented forecasts by reducing bias and increasing objectivity. This will involve the careful selection of forecasting techniques, since objectivity by itself does not assure the reduction of bias.

22.4 FORECASTING METHODS[4]

The methods we discuss are of two general types—unstructured and structured (or non-algorithmic and algorithmic). In the unstructured category we are concerned with three methods:

1. Personal observation
2. Group consensus
3. User's expectation

In the structured category we are concerned with four methods:

1. Simple moving average
2. Weighted moving average
3. Exponential smoothing
4. Correlation analysis

All of these methods generate forecasts of *single-point values.* The value, in each instance, represents the most likely future outcome. As such, of course, there is a degree of uncertainty surrounding its occurrence. We are saying that it will most likely be this value, but possibly the outcome could be higher or lower. Consequently, we devise a means to formulate quantitatively the uncertainty of these single-point values, and with this added knowledge, refine our forecasts by computing *expected values.*

[4]It must be emphasized that no particular forecasting technique is best under all conditions. The nature of the data in large measure determines the method that should be used. This problem is discussed further in chapter 23.

The objective in using any of the above methods is to forecast single-point values (most likely values) necessary for the construction of a budget of alleged values. This involves an analysis of many factors: (1) the firm's past accounting data; (2) possibly economic indicators such as industry data, and national statistics such as gross national product; (3) competitor's activities; (4) supplier's activities; (5) government regulations—existing and proposed; (6) plant capacity—existing and as proposed in the capital budget; (7) market surveys; (8) advertising and promotional campaigns; and (9) corporate personalities. All these factors, while important, are difficult to weigh relative to one another. Also, many are non-quantifiable. Hence, while the more subjective forecasting methods are capable of handling a greater variety of factors, they are not systematic and consistent in associating the factors. Some influences may dominate simply because of personal whims and preferences of the forecaster. Objective methods, on the other hand, are algorithmic and deal with only quantifiable factors. It is probably a blending of the two methodologies that will produce the best estimates of the values needed to construct a budget of alleged values.[5]

PERSONAL OBSERVATION

This is a method whereby one person comes up with an estimate of a future value by using hunches, intuition, and other inarticulated background data to temper his evaluation of historical accounting data or other quantified economic data. The weight given to any specific data item is based purely on his judgment. Some people are very successful guessers and somehow are able to perceive future events clearly. There are some, on the other hand, whose estimating ability is very poor because they are unable to assimilate the relevant factors and mentally assign the proper weights. Those persons able to interpret available data correctly by employing their background knowledge successfully are referred to as "experts." We should attempt to assign the forecasting task to those with demonstrated predictive ability or those possessing the requisite background knowledge to qualify as experts.

While this method is very subjective, it is not always the least reliable. To illustrate, let us use a poignant example by Olaf Helmer involving expert judgment in medical diagnostics:[6]

> A patient, let us assume, exhibits a pattern of symptoms such that it is virtually certain that he has either ailment A or ailment B, with respective probabilities of 0.4 and 0.6, where these probabilities derive from the statistical record of past cases. Thus the entire body of explicit symptomatic evidence is (by hypothesis) such as to indicate a margin in favor of the prediction that the patient suffers from disease B rather than A, and thus may respond positively to a corresponding course of treatment. But it is quite possible that an examining physician, taking into consideration not only the explicit indicators that constitute the symptoms (temperature and blood pressure, for example) but also an entire host of otherwise inarticulated background knowledge with regard to this particular patient (such as the circumstances of the case) may arrive at a diagnosis of disease A rather than B. Thus the use of background information, in a way that is not systematized but depends entirely on the exercise of informal expert

[5]Since the weightings which attend objective methods are probably subjectively determined, this blending is already partially achieved.

[6]O. Helmer and N. Rescher, *On the Epistemology of the Inexact Sciences* (Santa Monica, Calif.: The RAND Corporation, R-353, February 1960), p. 23. Used by permission of the publisher and the authors.

judgment, may appropriately lead to predictive conclusions in the face of prima facie evidence that points in the opposite direction.

Even though this technique is very subjective, its use appears valid in isolated incidents, especially if forecasts are made by experts recognized for their past predictive success. The inconsistency of formulation inherent in this technique, however, most probably will produce unstable budgeting over the long run by reflecting an inordinate influence from personal bias.

GROUP CONSENSUS

It is generally agreed that personal observations by themselves result in very parochial estimates, whereas group forecasting, especially by those managers responsible for adhering to budget standards, can produce better forecasts and more attainable standards. The problems in producing a reliable group estimate, though, arise mainly from the committee framework where specious persuasion and status biases interfere with information flow and reasoning.

The deleterious effects of the committee structure on group consensus can be overcome by employing the *Delphi process.* This process replaces a direct face-to-face confrontation of committee members with a carefully designed series of questionnaires interspersed with information feedback. The feedback between rounds contains the median response, interquartile range, and arguments for values lying outside the interquartile range. Diagrammatically, the interquartial range is shown in Exhibit 22-8 as the middle 50% of the responses.

EXHIBIT 22-8 THE INTERQUARTILE RANGE OF A FREQUENCY DISTRIBUTION

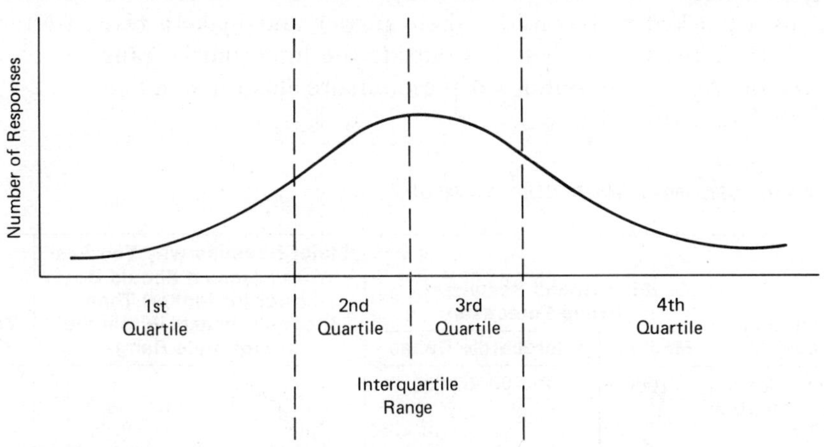

With information provided between each round, and with the same question being repeated, hopefully each respondent can: (1) give a more informed response in each round; (2) in the final round, together with the other respondents, produce a median value which closely approximates the alleged value; (3) cause a convergence of opinions by reducing the opinion spread evidenced by the interquartile range; and (4) cause the direction of convergence to be toward the alleged value. For instance, the round-one questionnaire illustrated in Exhibit 22-9 would be completed anonymously by each group member. This question calls for an estimate of 1971 sales by the Bentley Electronics Company of portable color TV sets.

EXHIBIT 22-9 FIRST-ROUND QUESTIONNAIRE

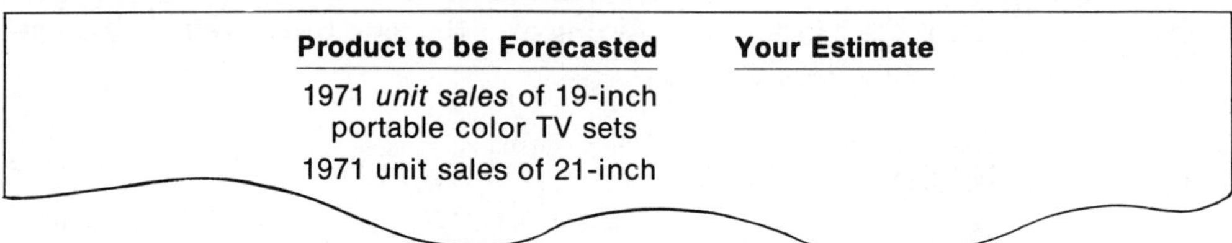

Product to be Forecasted	Your Estimate
1971 *unit sales* of 19-inch portable color TV sets	
1971 unit sales of 21-inch	

The opinion of each participant is tallied in the form of a frequency distribution and a consensus estimate chosen as representative of the group's collective opinion. This consensus, or measure of central tendency, is subject to error, and the subjective measure of that probable error is the dispersion or spread of possible outcomes on either side of the single figure. The precise measure of this uncertainty is really not our concern, but rather the width of the interquartile range as defined by its high and low value. This width gives us some measure of the divergence of opinion and hence a measure of the objectivity of the median response.[7] We know this median response, as an estimate of sales, can be made more reliable if we increase the objectivity of its measurement (since $R = V + B$) and reduce or maintain the present bias. The real concern is not whether the median is a good representative of group opinion, but whether it is a reliable estimate of the alleged value. With this in mind, the second-round questionnaire provides the participants with the group median of the first-round responses and the interquartile range. Using this feedback information, the participants are asked to reconsider their answer and make a revised estimate. In addition, if their revised estimate lies outside the interquartile range, they must indicate a reason. Again, the round-two questionnaire illustrated in Exhibit 22-10 would be completed anonymously.

EXHIBIT 22-10 SECOND-ROUND QUESTIONNAIRE

Product to be Forecasted	First-Round Results of Group Forecasts: Median	First-Round Results of Group Forecasts: Interquartile Range	Major Reasons Why You Feel Your Forecast Should Be Lower (or Higher) Than Those Forecasts Within the Interquartile Range	Your New Forecast
1971 *Unit Sales* of 19-inch Portable Color TV	35,000	23,500–57,000		――
1971 Unit Sales of 21-inch Portable Color TV				――

[7] The median response is chosen as representative of group opinion since it is the middle value of a response distribution. Half the group thinks the proper value is less than or equal to it and the other half thinks it is greater than or equal to it.

The reasons given by respondents for holding viewpoints which differ from 75% of the group (values lying in the first or fourth quartiles) are summarized, and together with the new median and interquartile range, they are returned to the participants in a third-round questionnaire as illustrated in Exhibit 22-11. This time the respondents are asked to offer counter-arguments if they find the reasons from the second-round unconvincing enough to bring their estimate into the interquartile range.

EXHIBIT 22-11 THIRD-ROUND QUESTIONNAIRE

Product to be Forecasted	Second-Round Results of Group Forecasts		Major Reasons Given by Those Whose Forecasts Are Lower (or Higher) Than Those Within the Interquartile Range	Your Opinion for Each Reason You Find Unacceptable in Making Your Own Forecast	Your New Forecast
	Median	Interquartile Range			
1971 *Unit Sales* of 19-inch Portable Color TV	36,500	28,000–47,500	Lower: Current reports showing high X-ray emission from color TV sets. . . . Higher: Expanded color broadcasts, improved picture tube. . . .		——

Critiques of round-three reasons, together with a new median and interquartile range, are returned to the respondents in a round-four questionnaire illustrated in Exhibit 22-12. The respondents now have one last opportunity to revise their estimates.

EXHIBIT 22-12 FOURTH-ROUND QUESTIONNAIRE

Product to be Forecasted	Third-Round Results of Group Forecasts		Major Reasons Given by Those Whose Forecasts Are Lower (or Higher) Than Those Within the Interquartile Range	Summary of Critiques of Reasons Given by Those Who Found the Major Reasons Unacceptable	Your Final Forecast
	Median	Interquartile Range			
1971 *Unit Sales* of 19-inch Portable Color TV	37,200	29,400–45,000	Lower: Current reports showing high X-ray emission from color TV sets. . . . Higher: Expanded color broadcasts, improved picture tube. . . .	Reports show X-ray emission well below standard. . . . Expanded for sports events only. . . .	——

Experimental use of this consensus technique has produced exceptionally good approximations of true values.[8] In these experiments the median usually converged toward the alleged value (thus reducing bias), and the interquartile range shrank dramatically. This situation is shown diagrammatically in Exhibit 22-13.

EXHIBIT 22-13 INCREASING OBJECTIVITY AND DECREASING BIAS CAUSED BY THE DELPHI PROCESS

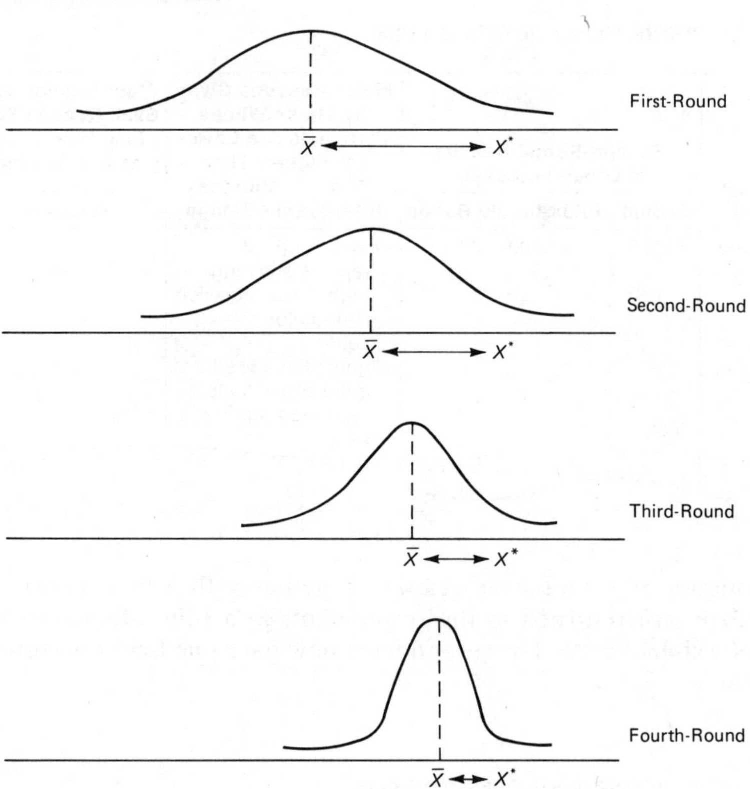

On particular questions, it can be demonstrated experimentally that some respondents are more "expert" than others. These experts by themselves often produce better approximations of the alleged value than the group median. Knowing this, a median value obtained by applying the Delphi technique can be improved upon by choosing respondents carefully. Recognized experts can be used and/or respondents can be instructed to identify their degree of expertise for each estimate. From these self-competence ratings, an elite sub-group can be selected. The median response of this sub-group promises an even better approximation than does the Delphi technique alone; therefore, estimates of alleged values should be predicated upon such refinement.

[8] Refer to B. Brown and O. Helmer, *Improving the Reliability of Estimates Obtained from a Consensus of Experts* (Santa Monica, Calif.: The RAND Corporation, P–2986, September 1964). The "true value" is equated with the alleged value.

USERS' EXPECTATION METHOD

Under this method, supplier companies solicit the intentions of their buyers. Companies serving industrial customers, or operating in a market dominated by a few large buyers, are particularly amenable to this method. It provides a low-cost means of obtaining useful forecast information and perhaps gains customer goodwill by accommodating production activity to the needs of buyers.

SIMPLE MOVING AVERAGE

This method is a smoothing process which uses the most recent *n* observations to compute an average. This average will be an estimate of the most likely future outcome. For example, given the monthly sales data in Exhibit 22-14, the forecast procedure, using an eight-month average, is:

$$\frac{\underset{\text{Nov.}}{26.0} + \underset{\text{Dec.}}{28.0} + \underset{\text{Jan.}}{32.0} + \underset{\text{Feb.}}{27.0} + \underset{\text{Mar.}}{28.5} + \underset{\text{Apr.}}{34.0} + \underset{\text{May}}{29.8} + \underset{\text{Jun.}}{30.3}}{8} = 29.45 \text{ or } \$29{,}450 \quad \text{(Forecast for July)}$$

EXHIBIT 22-14 MONTHLY SALES DATA

Month	Actual Sales ($)
November	26,000
December	28,000
January	32,000
February	27,000
March	28,500
April	34,000
May	29,800
June	30,300

Since the July forecast of $29,450 is an average, we can expect some forecast error to occur. In this instance, if actual July sales are $31,000, then a forecast error of $1,550 has occurred. This occurrence may be partly attributable to:

1. Random fluctuations.
2. The mean of the sales generating process was already higher than our estimate.
3. The mean of the process actually rose in July.

In order to obtain a quicker response to the most recent sales trends, it may be wise to limit our observations to the four most recent months:

$$\frac{\underset{\text{Mar.}}{28.5} + \underset{\text{Apr.}}{34.0} + \underset{\text{May}}{29.8} + \underset{\text{Jun.}}{30.3}}{4} = 30{,}650 \quad \text{(Forecast for July)}$$

We have reduced our forecast error to $350 by placing heavier emphasis on June sales. When eight months were employed, each month had an equal weight of 1/8—consequently, the earliest months through May received a weight of 7/8, compared with a June weight of 1/8. When we changed the average to include only the latest four months, March through May received a weight of 3/4 and June a weight of 1/4. The weight applied to the June observation increased by 100% from a 50% reduction in the number of observations. Hence, the number of months used in computing the average has a direct effect on the weight applied to current data.

Moving average acquires its name by the successive addition of new data and the corresponding deletion of old data. For instance, the next forecast for August will employ July's actual sales and delete November's sales:

Dec.	Jan.	Feb.	Mar.	Apr.	May	Jun.	Jul.	Forecast for August
28.0 +	32.0 +	27.0 +	28.5 +	34.0 +	29.8 +	30.3 +	31.0	

$$\frac{28.0 + 32.0 + 27.0 + 28.5 + 34.0 + 29.8 + 30.3 + 31.0}{8} = 30{,}075$$

The numerator, then, is moving and always including the latest eight months.[9] When the actual sales for August is available, it will be included in the September forecast and December will be deleted, and so on. In the four-month average, any forecast will always be made with the latest four months.

Better filtering of random fluctuations is possible by employing greater numbers of observations. Unfortunately, with increased observations we discount the immediate past more heavily. We conclude that three problems are inherent with the moving average method:

1. All observations are given equal weight, including those from a possibly remote past.
2. The smoothing effect causes a slower detection of changes in the underlying process.
3. A large number of observations must be carried from one forecast period to the next.

We can, however, be flexible in the number of observations employed, and hence may diminish the effects of such problems. Choosing the number of periods employed in the moving average is clearly an indication of the importance we attach to old and new data. We can employ a large number of observations if we feel the process is changing slowly and desire to filter out "noise," or employ a smaller number of observations if we wish to obtain a greater response in recent trends.

WEIGHTED MOVING AVERAGE

This technique is the same as simple moving average except that a selected weighting is assigned to the current data regardless of the number of observations comprising

[9]The numerator can consist of any two or more observations.

the average. For example, using the data of Exhibit 22-14 and an eight-month moving average, we apply a 50% weight to June's data:

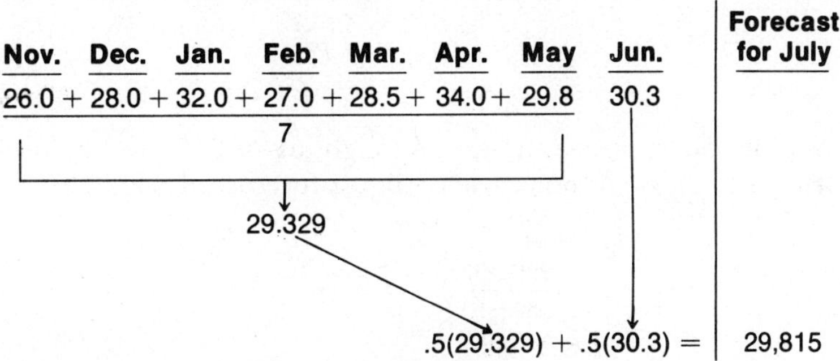

With this type of moving average, as with simple moving average, the same procedure is applied for each new forecast (deleting the oldest month and adding the new) while always maintaining a fixed number of observations. For example, using an actual sales figure of $31,000 for July, the August forecast is computed as:

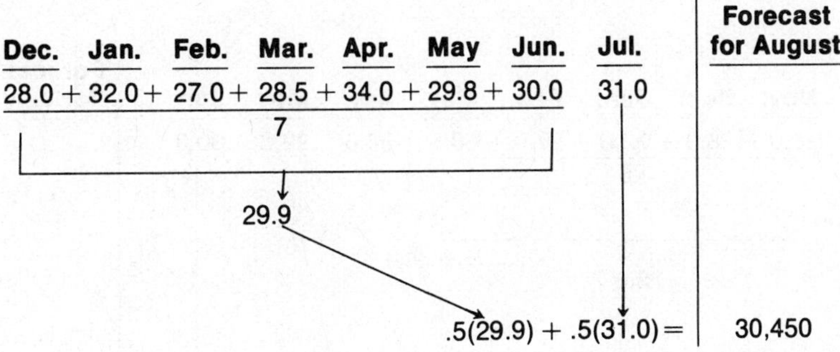

The percentage weighting of the current item can be changed to reflect a lesser influence in the forecast by simply applying a heavier weight to the earlier seven months. For example, the August forecast could be changed by giving a 25% weight to July's actual sales:

$$.75(29{,}900) + .25(31{,}000) = 30{,}175$$

The general formula for this *one-place weighted moving average* is:

Let

n = number of past observations comprising the moving average.
A = the average of the earliest $n - 1$ observations
x = a past observation
A_w = weighted average
P = percentage applied to the latest observation

$$A = \frac{\sum_{t=2}^{n} x_t}{n-1} \tag{1}$$

$$A_w = A(1 - P) + Px_1 \tag{2}$$

Giving our latest observation, x_1, a weighting of 25%, we can use the general two-step formula to arrive at our earlier August forecast of $30,175:

$$A = \frac{209{,}300}{8-1}$$
$$A = 29{,}900$$
$$A_w = 29{,}900(1 - .25) + .25(31{,}000)$$
$$A_w = 30{,}175$$

The formula as developed, and our example problems, have thus far been only one-place. That is, only one observation is assigned a selective weighting. Suppose we wished to assign a 25% weight to the last three observations:

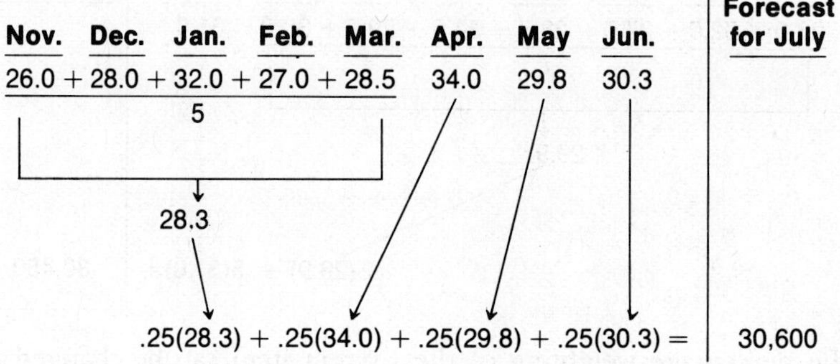

Further, suppose we wished to assign varying weights to the last four observations—40% to June, 20% to May, 10% to April, and 5% to March:

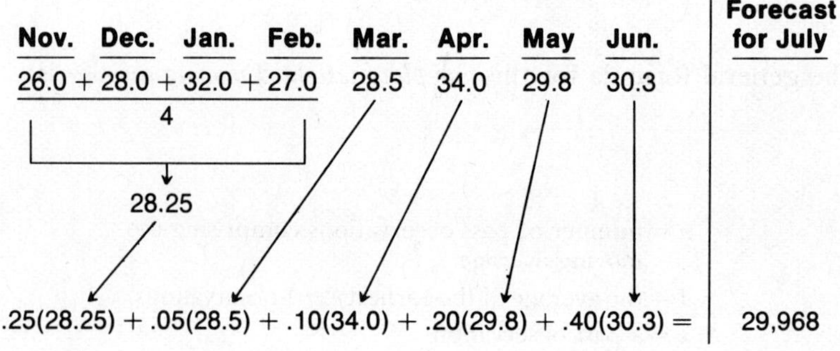

The general formula for this *multiple-place weighted moving average* is:

Using the same variables described earlier, except let

b = the number of observations to which weights will be applied
A = the average of the earliest $n - b$ observations

$$A = \frac{\sum_{t=b+1}^{n} x_t}{n - b} \tag{3}$$

$$A_w = A\left(1 - \sum_{a=1}^{b} P_a\right) + \sum_{a=1}^{b} P_a x_a \tag{4}$$

Using the various weights assigned to the latest four months in our last example, we use the general two-step formula to arrive at our earlier July forecast of \$29,968:

$$A = \frac{113{,}000}{8 - 4}$$
$$A = 28{,}250$$
$$A_w = 28{,}250(1 - .75) + 22{,}905$$
$$A_w = 29{,}968$$

With this selective weighting procedure we have overcome the main drawback of simple moving average—the ability to weight *only* the latest observation exclusively. One problem, however, still has not been overcome—the necessity to carry a number of observations forward from period to period.

EXPONENTIAL SMOOTHING

This technique is designed to overcome the potentially serious drawback of carrying large numbers of past observations. Only the old forecast and the new observations are required. But even with this modest requirement, *all* past observations are considered, not just n observations as with the moving average. In effect, past observations are weighted geometrically in inverse relation to their ages. The new observation is assigned a selected percentage weight while the old forecast is assigned the remainder from 100%.

Let

α = percentage weighting to current observation
F_n = new forecast
F_o = old forecast (forecast of previous period)
x_c = current observation

Then

$$F_n = \alpha x_c + (1 - \alpha)F_o \tag{5}$$

Assume a new forecast is the fifth in a sequence and current data is to be weighted 30%. The new forecast, then, is:

$$F_5 = .3x_4 + (1 - .3)F_4$$

By referring to Exhibit 22-15 we observe the effects of a 30% weight on current data.

EXHIBIT 22-15 EXPONENTIAL SMOOTHING EFFECTS RESULTING FROM A 30% WEIGHTING ON CURRENT DATA

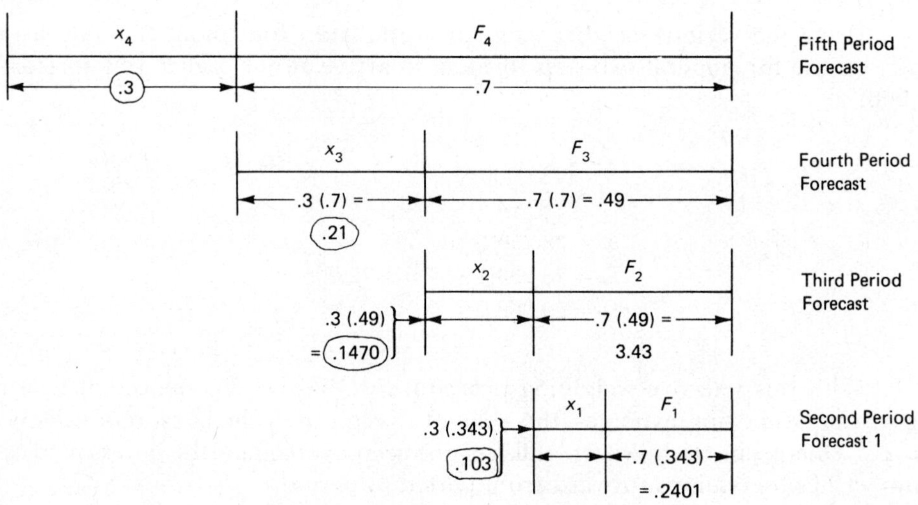

*The exponential smoothing process must begin with an initial forecast F_1.

Summarizing, the *effective weighting* applied to components of the fifth period forecast are:[10]

x_4	x_3	x_2	x_1	F_1	
.3	.21	.1470	.103	.2401	$= F_5$

Mathematically, we can simply expand our general formula to show the same relationship:

$$F_5 = \alpha x_4 + \alpha(x_3)(1 - \alpha) + \alpha(x_2)(1 - \alpha)^2$$
$$+ \alpha(x_1)(1 - \alpha)^3 + (1 - \alpha)^4 F_1$$

[10] If plotted, these effective weights to *past data* will form an exponential curve; hence, the name "exponential smoothing" is derived.

Intuitively, we note that *all* past observations are weighted according to:

	Weight
Current Observation	α
1 period old	$\alpha(1-\alpha)$
2 periods old	$\alpha(1-\alpha)^2$
3 periods old	$\alpha(1-\alpha)^3$
n periods old	$\alpha(1-\alpha)^n$

That is, as each observation becomes older it has a smaller and smaller influence in the new forecast. For a few selected current weights, Exhibit 22-16 lists the resulting weights which the formula effectively assigns to past data.

EXHIBIT 22-16 EFFECTIVE WEIGHTING FACTORS

Observations	**Weights**			
Current period	.3	.4	.6	.8
1 period old	.21	.24	.24	.16
2 periods old	.147	.144	.096	.032
3 periods old	.103	.074	.038	.006
4 periods old	.072	.045	.015	.001

Obviously, from Exhibit 22-16 we note that the smaller the weight for the current observation, the more significant the role past data will play in the new forecast. The selection of the initial weight is important for this reason, but also because a smaller and smaller weight has the equivalent effect of carrying larger and larger numbers of observations in the moving average method. Intuitively, we grasp the fact that a smaller initial weight will generate larger comparative weights all the way back to where the number of observations approaches zero. This is analogous to the selection of a larger number of observations in computing a moving average. An equivalency formula has been developed for this purpose:[11]

$$\alpha = \frac{2}{n+1} \tag{6}$$

With this formula we can determine the number of observations (n) necessary in a moving average to yield the exponential smoothing forecast using α as the weighting constant. Exhibit 22-17 shows the number of observations needed in a moving average to duplicate the results of exponential smoothing.

CORRELATION ANALYSIS

Frequently in business we observe a relationship between the movement of economic factors. Correlation analysis is an attempt to formulate a functional relationship be-

[11]Refer to C. McMillan and R. F. Gonzalez, *Systems Analysis: A Computer Approach to Decision Models* (Homewood, Ill.: Richard D. Irwin, Inc., 1965), p. 220.

tween some independent variable and the variable we wish to predict. Some of the more elementary forms of this method[12] have already been presented in chapter 18—the high and low point, scattergraph, and linear regression using least squares.

EXHIBIT 22-17 MOVING AVERAGE VERSUS EXPONENTIAL SMOOTHING

Smoothing Constant	Number of Observations Needed with Moving Average
.001	1999
.01	199
.05	39
.25	7
.30	5.7
.40	4
.60	2.3

Two types of correlations yield significant forecasting information—*time correlation* and *data correlation.* Time correlation is the formulation of a *trend* over time. We observe the movement of some economic data over time and *extrapolate* into the future. Time is our independent variable. For example, possibly a linear correlation could result between time and sales as shown in Exhibit 22-18. Graphically

EXHIBIT 22-18 SALES TREND LINE

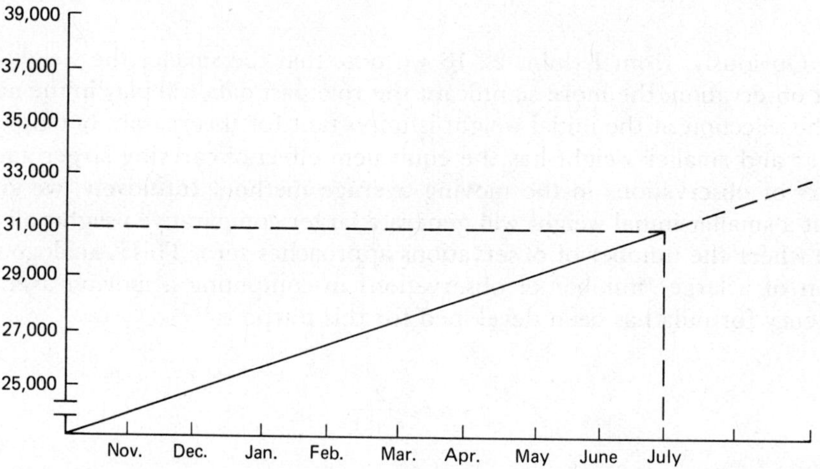

this correlation represents a trend line which we will extrapolate into the future and obtain a forecast for July. With *data correlation* the independent variable is another data item rather than time. In this instance, the correlation or functional relationship will be used to predict the dependent value from a given independent value as shown in Exhibit 22-19. Data correlation involves the derivation of a predicted value from an *interpolation* within our range of experience. This is in contrast to time correlation, which involves extrapolation out of our experience range. In both instances, however, we assume that the same underlying process for generating the dependent variable is intact.[13]

[12]Regression and correlation analysis are essentially the same technique.

[13]The *coefficient of correlation* (r) can be found by the formula $r = \frac{\Sigma(X-\overline{X})(Y-\overline{Y})}{\sqrt{\Sigma(X-\overline{X})^2 (Y-\overline{Y})^2}}$ and its significance by $z = 1/2[\log_e(1+r) - \log_e(1-r)]$, where z corresponds to values in a cumulative frequency table.

EXHIBIT 22-19 DATA CORRELATION*

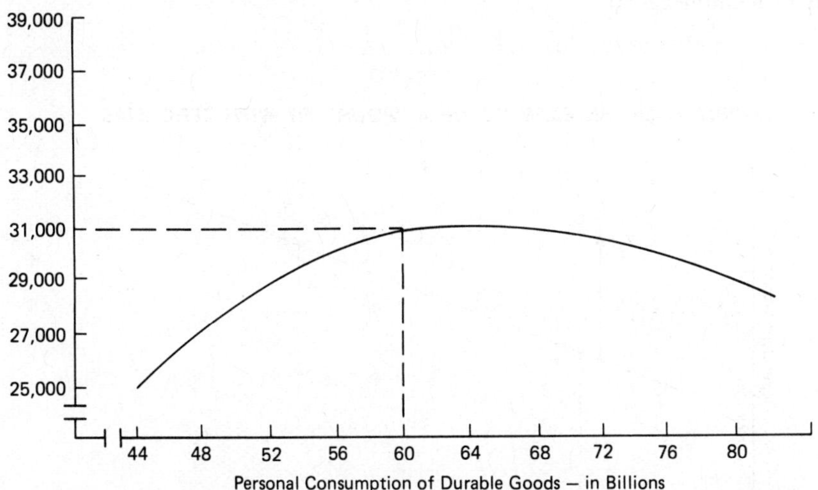

*With data correlation, the independent value (personal consumption of durable goods) can be an actual figure or predicted. If actual, then the prediction based on the correlation is a *lag prediction.* The movement of this independent variable leads the movement of the dependent variable. In this situation, all predictions from a certain correlation are predictions for a fixed lag period. For instance, if we wished to predict the sales three months from now based upon the current value of the independent variable, we must use a correlation with a lag of three months. The data points comprising the correlation are actual independent and dependent values three months apart.

With correlation by least squares, this relationship is expressed as an equation in which we solve for the dependent value given a value for the independent variable. Our objective in finding a functional equation is either to: (1) interpolate the value of the dependent variable corresponding to some value that lies between two independent historical values, or (2) extrapolate the value of the dependent variable corresponding to an independent value lying outside the range of our past experience. To meet these objectives we find the best fitting polynomial for a given set of observed data by reducing the bias between our historical values and the values obtained from the curve. We express this relationship in the form of an equation.

The total bias of a curve is the sum of the deviations at each *X*-data point between the historical *Y*-value and the *Y*-value obtained from the functional equation. This bias determines the objectiveness of the equation and the "goodness" of fit to the historical data. The most appealing situation is when the bias is as small as possible. Using Y^1 as the value obtained from the functional equation, the bias is expressed as:

$$B = \sum_{i=1}^{n} (Y_i - Y_i') \tag{7}$$

where

n = the number of data points

This expression of bias has some inherent flaws, however, when we fit a line to two points as in Exhibit 22-20.

EXHIBIT 22-20 AN EXAMPLE OF A "POOR" FIT WITH ZERO BIAS

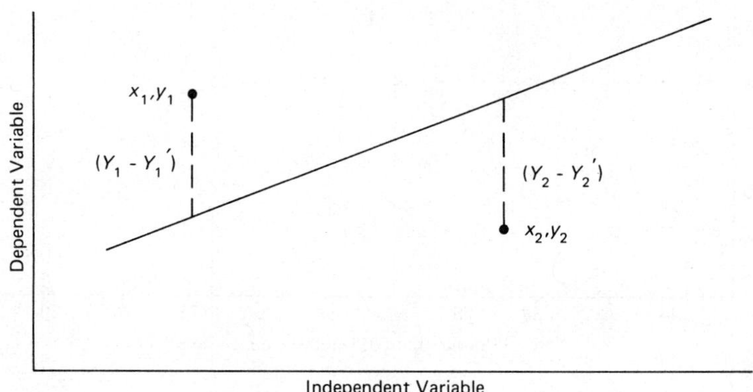

We find that minimizing the bias is not a satisfactory condition for producing the best fit unless we square the deviations or express them as absolute values before obtaining the sum. Since we must differentiate to find a minimum, and since the absolute-value function has no derivative at its minimum,[14] we are left, then, with the least-squares method, in which the bias is expressed as:

$$B = \sum_{i=1}^{n} (Y_i - Y_i')^2 \tag{8}$$

The correlation equation represented by minimizing the sum of the squared deviations inherently provides the best fitting curve to the historical values used in the analysis. Unless we obtain a perfect correlation, we expect some historical values to lie above the curve and others below. The sum of these deviations, however, will always equal zero, but more importantly, the sum of these same deviations squared will produce a bias lower than any other curve. For example, in Exhibit 22-21 the sum of both positive and negative deviations from either curve equals zero. The bias, however, of curve *a* is considerably less than that of curve *b*. Curve *a* has a bias of 10 $[(+1)^2 + (-1)^2 + (0)^2 + (-2)^2 + (0)^2 + (+2)^2]$ and curve *b* a bias of 68 $[(+6)^2 + (+2)^2 + (+1)^2 + (-3)^2 + (-3)^2 + (-3)^2]$. Curve *a*, then, is the correct choice, for it represents the best or most reliable fit and will assure a minimization of forecast errors, especially if such forecast requires an extrapolation of dependent values beyond our range of experience.[15]

[14]We can derive a minimum bias from an absolute-value function using the Chebyshev approximation.

[15]Example from R. A. Knapp, "Forecasting and Measuring with Correlation Analysis," *Financial Executive*, May 1963, p. 17. Copyright 1963 by *Financial Executive*. Used with permission.

EXHIBIT 22-21 COMPARISON OF CURVES WITH DIFFERING BIAS

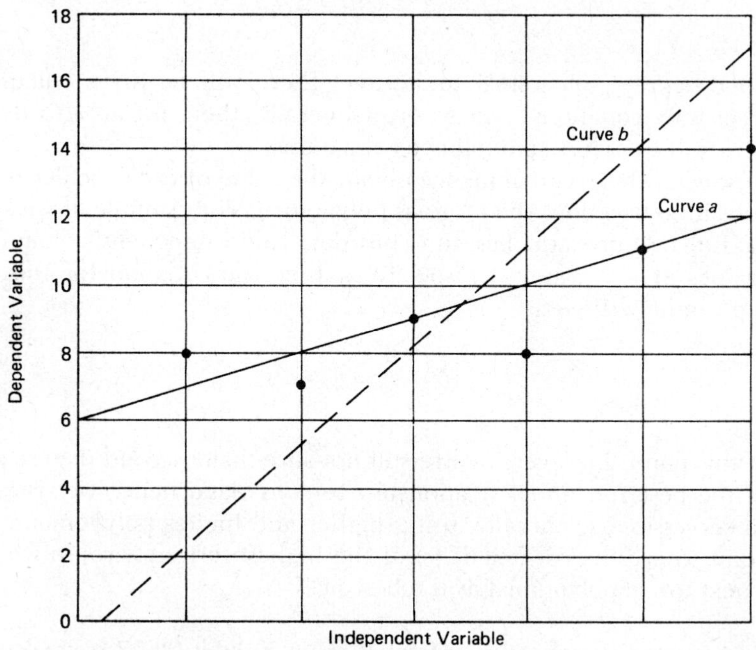

Reproduced from Knapp, "Forecasting and Measuring," p. 17. Copyright 1963 by *Financial Executive.* Used with permission.

From the least-squares equation we produce a system of simultaneous equations called "normal equations" by fitting a particular function to our data points. In our analysis, we will fit only polynomials:[16]

First Degree Polynomial:	$Y_i' = c_1 + c_2X_i$
Second Degree Polynomial:	$Y_i' = c_1 + c_2X_i + c_3X_i^2$
Third Degree Polynomial:	$Y_i' = c_1 + c_2X_i + c_3X_i^2 + c_4X_i^3$
m th Degree Polynomial:	$Y_i' = c_1 + c_2X_i + c_3X_i^2 + \cdots + c_{m+1}X_i^m$

For example, using a first-degree polynomial and substituting into our least squares equation we obtain:

$$B = \sum_{i=1}^{n} (Y_i - c_1 - c_2X_i)^2 \tag{9}$$

Since our goal is to minimize B (bias), we do so by first differentiating B with respect to c_1, and then with respect to c_2. By setting each result equal to zero and rearranging, we obtain a group of simultaneous equations referred to as *normal equations:*

[16] We could fit other functions, such as an exponential: $y = ax^b$. In doing so, however, we must use logarithms to avoid the generation of non-linear normal equations.

$$nc_1 + (\Sigma X_i)c_2 = \Sigma Y_i \qquad (10)$$
$$(\Sigma X_i)c_1 + (\Sigma X_i^2)c_2 = \Sigma(X_iY_i)$$

For a second-degree polynomial (quadratic) there will be three equations, for a third-degree, four equations, and so on. Generally, then, for an mth degree polynomial there will be $m + 1$ simultaneous equations.

By solving these equations we obtain the value of each coefficient (c), which we then substitute back into the original polynomial. For example, if we assume that a quadratic function gives the best fit to our data, and subsequently obtain 10, 4, and 2 as the values of c_1, c_2, and c_3 respectively, then the equation for this functional relationship can be written as:

$$10 + 4X + 2X^2 = Y$$

At this point, however, we are still not sure that a second-degree polynomial represents the best functional relationship for our data, hence we try other polynomials in succession. Eventually, using higher and higher polynomials, we should reach a point where the coefficient (c) of the highest term is zero; in which case we select the next lower polynomial as the best fit.[17]

Example: Suppose the monthly information in Exhibit 22-22 is chosen randomly from past financial records of the Astro Corporation.

EXHIBIT 22-22 SOME SELECTED MONTHLY DATA FOR THE ASTRO CORP. (IN THOUSANDS)

Production in Units	Production Payroll in Dollars
12.5	$176
13.0	165
10.0	82
11.5	125
10.0	75
13.5	190
15.0	240
11.0	90
11.5	115

A plot of this data appears in Exhibit 22-23.

[17] Due to roundoff errors, computer programs will produce nonzero off-diagonal terms. In general, however, they will be very small compared with the diagonal terms and, hence, may be treated as zero.

EXHIBIT 22-23 PLOT OF SELECTED MONTHLY DATA FOR THE ASTRO CORP.

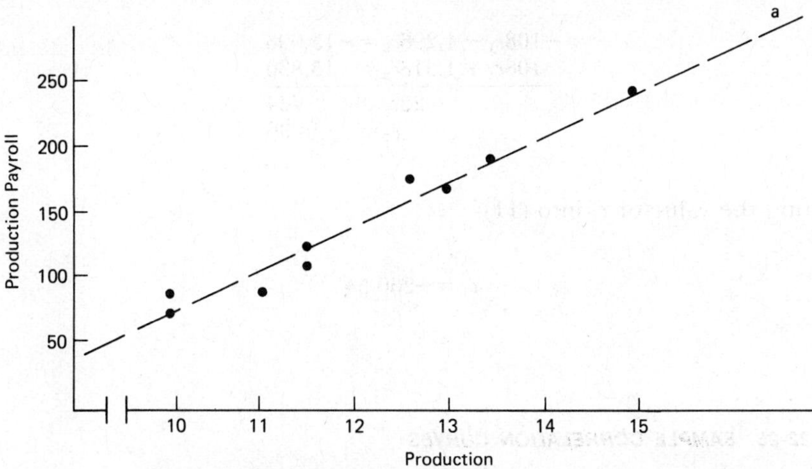

From the plot of our data, it appears that the straight line *a* best explains the relationship between production and production payroll. The equation for this line is found by the following procedure:

STEP 1: Find the best fitting first-degree polynomial (linear equation) by solving the normal equations for values of c_1 and c_2, and substituting c_1 and c_2 into the equation for a first-degree polynomial. To solve the normal equations, we must prepare the table in Exhibit 22-24.

EXHIBIT 22-24 TABLE OF REQUIRED VALUES—FIRST DEGREE POLYNOMIAL

X (Production in Units)	Y (Production Payroll)	XY	X^2
12.5	176	2,200	156.25
13.0	165	2,145	169.00
10.0	82	820	100.00
11.5	125	1,437.5	132.25
10.0	75	750	100.00
13.5	190	2,565	182.25
15.0	240	3,600	225.00
11.0	90	990	121.00
11.5	115	1,322.5	132.25
108.0	1,258	15,830.0	1,318.00

Substituting the values from Exhibit 22-24 into our normal equations and solving, we obtain:

$$9c_1 + 108c_2 = 1{,}258 \tag{11}$$
$$108c_1 + 1{,}318c_2 = 15{,}830 \tag{12}$$

Multiply equation (11) by −12 and add the result to equation (12):

$$\begin{aligned} -108c_1 - 1{,}296c_2 &= -15{,}096 \\ 108c_1 + 1{,}318c_2 &= 15{,}830 \\ \hline 22c_2 &= 734 \\ c_2 &= 33.36 \end{aligned}$$

substituting the value of c_2 into (11):

$$c_1 = -260.54$$

EXHIBIT 22-25 SAMPLE CORRELATION CURVES

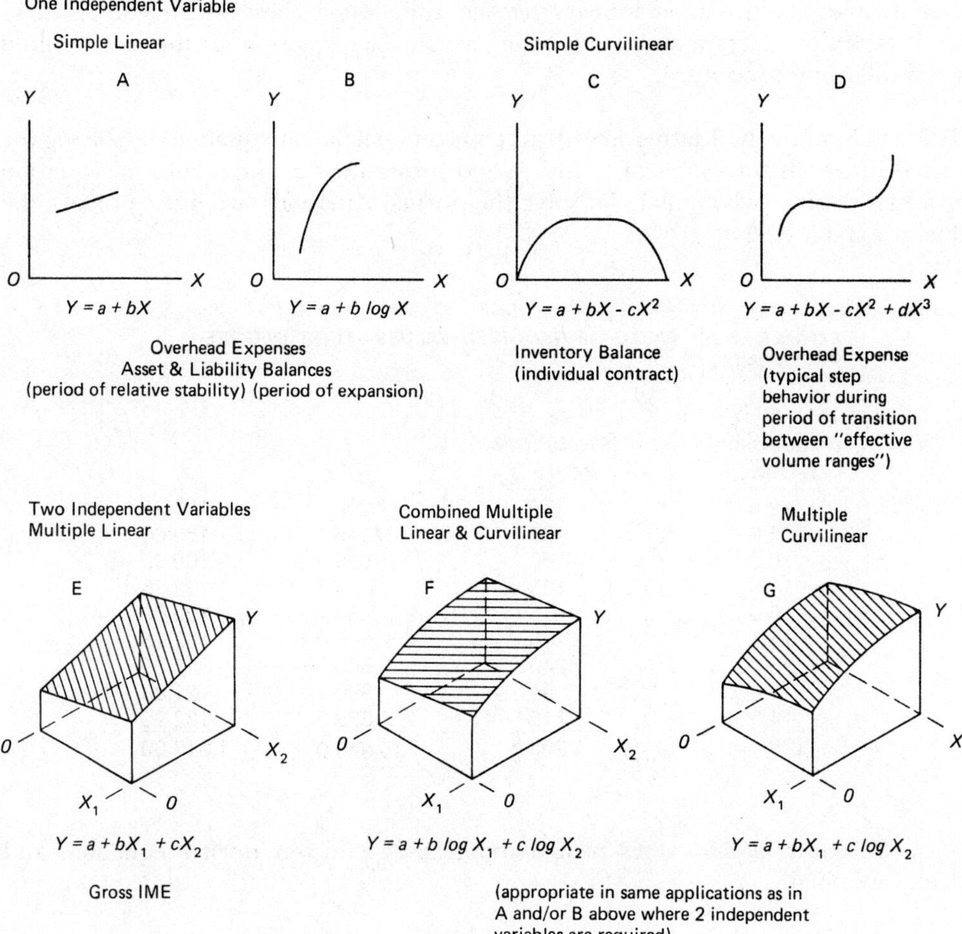

These values are substituted into the first-degree polynomial to obtain a functional relationship between production and production payroll:

$$Y = -260.54 + 33.36X$$

STEP 2: Find the best fitting second-degree polynomial by solving the following normal equations for values of c_1, c_2, and c_3:

$$nc_1 + (\Sigma X_i)c_2 + (\Sigma X_i^2)c_3 = \Sigma Y_i$$
$$(\Sigma X_i)c_1 + (\Sigma X_i^2)c_2 + (\Sigma X_i^3)c_3 = \Sigma(X_iY_i)$$
$$(\Sigma X_i^2)c_1 + (\Sigma X_i^3)c_2 + (\Sigma X_i^4)c_3 = \Sigma(X_i^2Y_i)$$

In this example, we would expect c_3 to equal zero, in which case we would choose the first-degree polynomial as our best fitting curve.

A similar procedure can be applied to any set of data points and a best fitting correlation equation will result. A sampling of the wide variety of such equations is shown in the top half of Exhibit 22-25. The lower half of this same exhibit shows a dependent variable as a function of two independent variables. Although we have not illustrated the procedure for multiple correlation, the substance of the least squares method is applicable.

Exhibit 22-26 shows one company's experience with correlation analysis. The results give an insight into the value of this method.

EXHIBIT 22-26 CORRELATION ANALYSIS COMPARED WITH OTHER METHODS

Forecasts with Correlation Analysis				**Experienced % Error Using Other Methods**		
Item Forecasted	**Source Period of Data Correlated**	**Year Forecasted**	**% Error**	**1961**	**Least**	**Previous 2 yrs. Average**
Customers receivables	Oct. 58–Oct. 60	1961	2.5	NA	23.2	41.9
Accounts payable	Jan. 58–Oct. 60	1961	9.0	NA	16.9	27.2
Gross IEM	Nov. 58–Oct. 60	1961	5.4	10.7	9.7	17.8
Gross IEM	Nov. 58–Aug. 61	1961	1.6	2.3	NA	NA

SOURCE: Knapp, "Forecasting and Measuring," p. 17. Copyright 1963 by *Financial Executive.* Used with permission.

22.5 ESTIMATING THE UNCERTAINTY OF SINGLE-POINT VALUES

The single-point estimates from our previous analyses represent our best estimate of the most likely future occurrence. That is, in reality our estimate is the *modal value* of a distribution of possible outcomes, even though the structured forecasting techniques rely on the *mean* to achieve this outcome. Forecasting the dispersion about the mode provides a means for examining the uncertainty associated with single-point estimates by evaluating subjectively the outcome of an estimating process.

For instance, if we employed the least squares technique to forecast sales for October, we would determine a functional relationship between sales and time and solve for Y when $X = 10$ (tenth month):

$$Y = 4 + 9X$$
$$Y = \$94{,}000$$

The least squares method gives us the best fitting equation for all of our historical values. We know, however, that for any one month, the actual value could vary from the value obtained by using the equation. The possible variation for a randomly chosen month, or from a projected month, is determined by the distribution of each past value around the value obtained from the equation. The variance for each actual value can be expressed as a percentage of the value obtained from the equation and tallied to form a frequency distribution. Pictorially, the dispersion appears in Exhibit 22-27. In obtaining our forecast for October we should evaluate the historical degree of variation so as to evaluate subjectively the possible variation of our estimate.

EXHIBIT 22-27 VARIATION AROUND THE MODAL VALUE

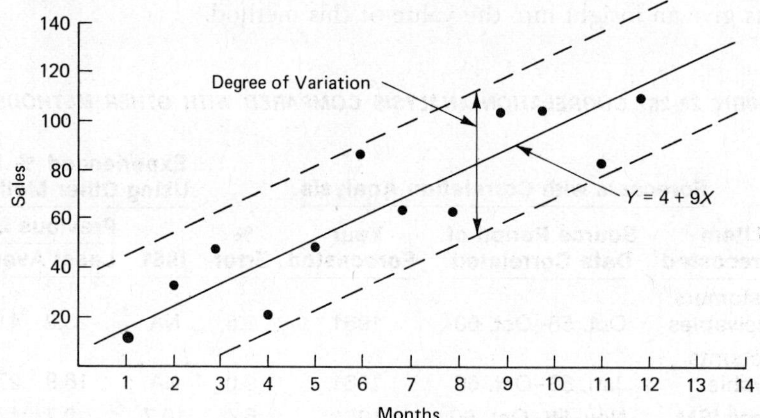

Ideally, we should estimate the frequency of occurrence by classes. That is, the total range of possible outcomes is broken down into discrete classes and the frequency of occurrence by class is estimated. For example, suppose sales range from 0 to 500,000 as an outside limit. We could divide the range into five classes:

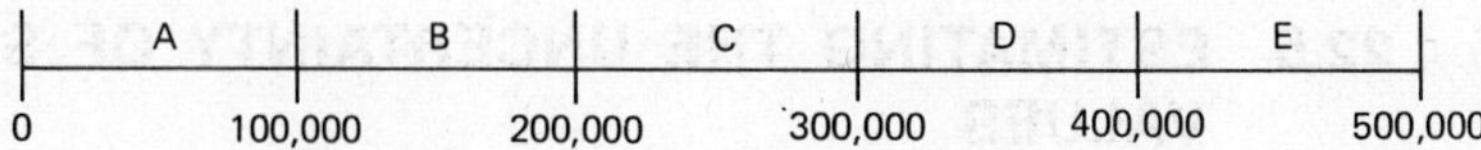

The frequency with which sales fall within each class is estimated subjectively. This estimate, in the form of a *histogram*, is presented in Exhibit 22-28. We expect sales to fall within class A 10% of the time, within B 25% of the time, within C 35% of the time, within D 20% of the time, and within E 10% of the time. The sum of the probabilities

EXHIBIT 22-28 FREQUENCY DISTRIBUTION OF SALES BY CLASSES

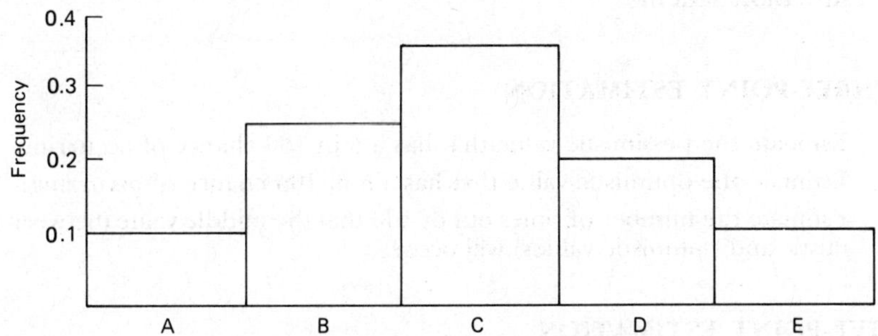

must equal one. If it is less, not all classes are represented; if more, an impossible situation of greater than a 100% frequency is present.

The form of the uncertainty dispersion in Exhibit 22-28 can be improved. We cannot evaluate the uncertainty of the mode unless we somehow express our frequency in discrete values. A possible solution involves *compressing* the classes into their middle values. This midpoint of the class then becomes representative of the class and assumes the probability of the entire class. Compression of classes is shown in Exhibit 22-29.

EXHIBIT 22-29 COMPRESSION OF CLASSES

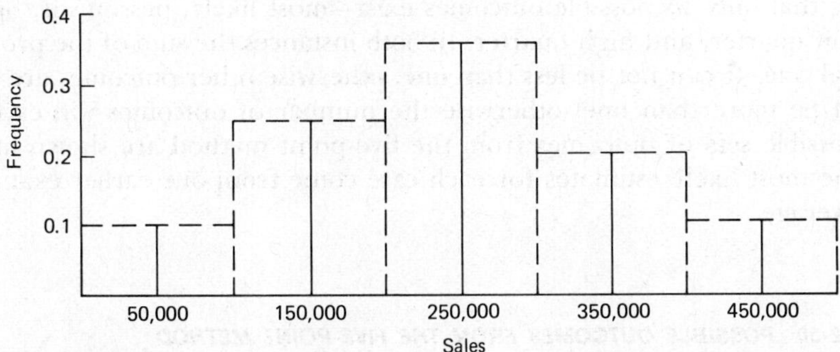

This procedure is fine for deriving subjective probabilities. However, we are attempting to evaluate the uncertainty of our most likely value (mode); therefore, it must be represented as one of the discrete points. Remember, these discrete values merely represent their class and take on the probability of that class, but by themselves have a very minute possibility of occurring. This is in sharp contrast to the mode, which by itself has a high probability of occurring. Since our objective is to measure the uncertainty of this occurrence, the mode must be represented in the discrete distribution as one of the possible outcomes. This being the case, we must amend our forecasting procedure to (1) estimate the probable occurrence of the mode, and (2) find a schema by which its inclusion will not cause the sum of the probabilities to exceed one.

The solution is to employ single-point estimates to measure the uncertainty of a single-point estimate. By a subjective evaluation procedure (possibly the Delphi technique) we forecast the number of times out of 100 we expect our single-point estimate to occur. The evaluative procedure may take the form of a three-point or five-point estimation scheme:

THREE-POINT ESTIMATION

1. Estimate the pessimistic value that has a 5 in 100 chance of occurring.
2. Estimate the optimistic value that has a 5 in 100 chance of occurring.
3. Estimate the number of times out of 100 that the middle value (between the pessimistic and optimistic values) will occur.

FIVE-POINT ESTIMATION

1. Estimate the pessimistic value that has a 5 in 100 chance of occurring.
2. Estimate the optimistic value that has a 5 in 100 chance of occurring.
3. Estimate the number of times out of 100 that the middle value (between the pessimistic and optimistic values) will occur.
4. Estimate the number of times out of 100 that the *low* quarter value will occur. The low quarter value is midway between the pessimistic value and the middle value.
5. Estimate the number of times out of 100 that the *high* quarter value will occur. The high quarter value is midway between the optimistic value and the middle value.

With three-point estimation we are saying that only *four* possible outcomes exist—most likely, pessimistic, optimistic, and middle. With five-point estimation we are saying that only *six* possible outcomes exist—most likely, pessimistic, optimistic, middle, low quarter, and high quarter. In both instances the sum of the probabilities must equal one. It can not be less than one, otherwise other outcomes are possible; nor can it be more than one, otherwise the number of outcomes will exceed 100.

Possible sets of outcomes from the five-point method are shown in Exhibit 22-30. The most likely estimates for each case come from our earlier example with moving average.

EXHIBIT 22-30 POSSIBLE OUTCOMES FROM THE FIVE-POINT METHOD

		CASE 1		CASE 2		CASE 3	
		Outcome	Prob.	Outcome	Prob.	Outcome	Prob.
	Most Likely	29,475	.35	30,700	.40	30,018	.40
Five-Point Method	Pessimistic	27,500	.05	27,400	.05	24,500	.05
	Lower Quarter	29,375	.30	29,050	.25	26,375	.05
	Middle	31,250	.15	30,700	.40	28,250	.15
	Upper Quarter	33,125	.10	32,350	.25	30,125	.30
	Optimistic	35,000	.05	34,000	.05	32,000	.05

In each case, the estimate of five points represents a possible dispersion of outcomes around the most likely estimate. Graphically, each case appears as in Exhibit 22-31.

EXHIBIT 22-31

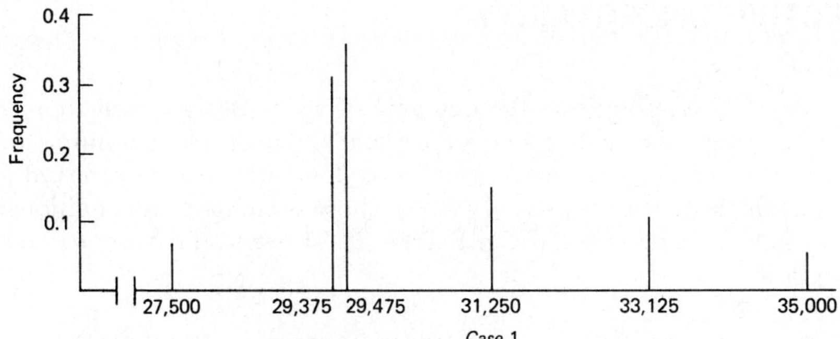

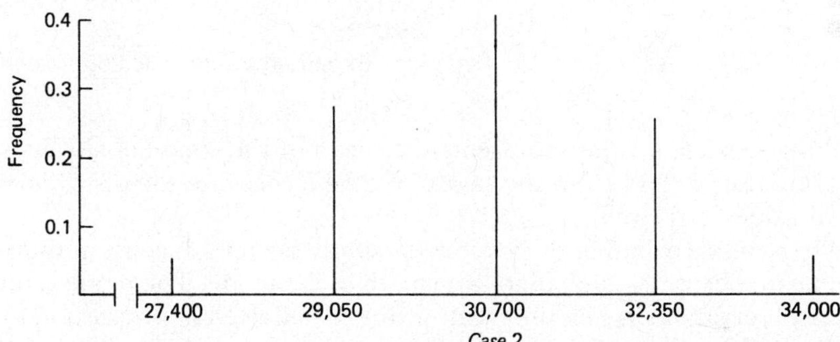

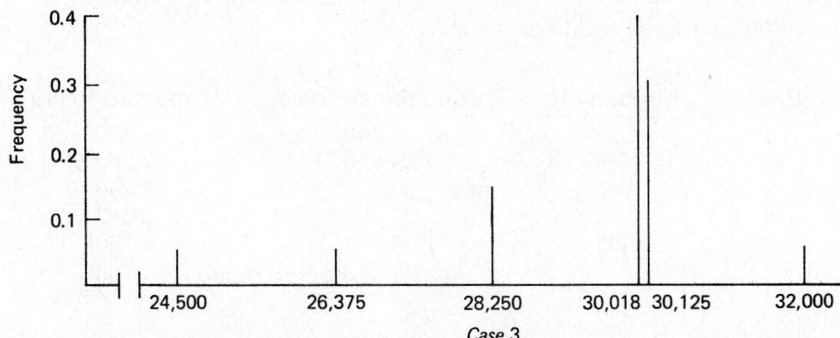

The distribution in Case 1 is *skewed to the right,* Case 3 is *skewed to the left,* and Case 2 is *symmetrical.* The skewness of the distribution reveals the location of the *mean* relative to the mode (most likely value). For a distribution skewed to the left, the mean is a smaller value than the mode; and *vice versa* when the skewness is to the right. In a symmetrical distribution the mode and mean are identical.

22.6 DETERMINING SINGLE-POINT ESTIMATES FROM SUBJECTIVE UNCERTAINTY

We now take the viewpoint that the outcome of a single-point estimation process is incomplete and must be carried one step further, that is, by computing an *expected value* as the *mean* of all possible outcomes. Possible outcomes are referred to as *conditional values* because they represent values whose occurrence is conditional upon a stated probability. Using Case 1 from Exhibit 22-31, we would compute an expected value as follows:

Event	Probability	Conditional Value	Expected Value
1	.05	27,500	1,375
2	.30	29,375	8,813
3	.35	29,475	10,316
4	.15	31,250	4,688
5	.10	33,125	3,313
6	.05	35,000	1,750
		Expected Value =	30,255

The resulting expected value represents the mean of the conditional values. In this example the mean differs from the mode of 29,475 because the distribution of the conditional values is skewed.

When the distribution of possible outcomes is skewed, many authorities consider the mean a better single-point estimate than the mode. The mode is unaffected by extreme observations, while the mean is directly affected in proportion to the frequency of extreme values. For this reason the mean is more representative of the entire distribution and is a better figure for comparative purposes.

If the distribution is not skewed, but is symmetrical as in Case 2 of Exhibit 22-31, then the mean is *identical* to the mode, in which case it becomes unnecessary to perform any further calculations for an expected value. If we did, however, we could verify the equality of the mode and mean:

Event	Probability	Conditional Value	Expected Value
1	.05	27,400	1,370
2	.25	29,050	7,262.5
3	.40	(mode) 30,700	12,280
4	.25	32,350	8,087.5
5	.05	34,000	1,700
		Expected Value =	30,700

The expected values in both cases represent the mean of a distribution of conditional values. By this representation we mean that given a long enough period of time we would expect the average of all the actual outcomes to equal this expected value. Hence, expected values are forecasts based on long-run experience and as such may sometimes yield inappropriate forecasts for short-run purposes.[17] On such oc-

[17] It may also be inappropriate to use such forecasts in an analysis involving non-linear functions. Refer to Harvey M. Wagner, *Principles of Operations Research* (Englewood Cliffs, N.J.: Prentice-Hall, Inc., 1969), chapter 16, sections 16.2 and 16.3.

casions it may be desirable to revert back to the mode as an expected value, remembering, of course, that in doing so we tend to overemphasize short-run experience and consequently run the risk of unstable budgeting.

22.7 SUMMARY

We discussed the concepts of effectiveness and reliability as they relate to the generation of budgeted standards. Effective standards are those which allow us to meet objectives through optimal consumption of resources. Reliable standards are those which are capable of producing the correct decision, given the framework of a particular decision apparatus.

Personal observation was cited as an obvious forecasting technique. Its relative subjectiveness does not negate its value in isolated incidents, but it could be seriously deficient in providing systematic forecasts. The solution was simply to pool the opinion of many observers. The method chosen was the Delphi technique. This approach avoids the entanglements of specious persuasion by maintaining the anonymity of responses. Using several rounds of questionnaires, with feedback between rounds, we expect a convergence of opinion toward the alleged value and the final emergence of a forecast closely approximating the "ideal" value. If the company has few buyers, a simpler and more direct forecasting route is solicitation of the expected demand of users.

Systematic techniques are referred to as *structured* forecasting methods. They are algorithmic in nature. Moving averages produce a forecasted value as the mean of a fixed number of historical values. Each new forecast is based on the latest historical values taken chronologically. By varying the number of values comprising the average, or by selective weighting, we can designate the influence of one or more historical values. Further, we can eliminate the main drawback of this method—carrying historical values from one forecast period to the next—by adopting exponential smoothing. By this technique, we arbitrarily assign a weight to the latest actual value and assign its reciprocal to last period's forecast. The result is the next period's forecast. The final structural technique—correlation analysis—also involves a reliance upon past data. The method establishes a functional relationship between a dependent variable and an independent variable. The equation of this relationship is used to generate a forecasted value.

Uncertainty of forecasts is measured subjectively as the dispersion around the most likely value. By considering this uncertainty when the distribution is skewed, we can produce a new estimate called an expected value. This value is the mean of all possible outcomes.

CHAPTER 22 REFERENCES AND ADDITIONAL READINGS

American Management Association. *Materials and Methods of Sales Forecasting.* Special Report No. 27. New York: American Management Association, Inc., 1957.

Anton, Hector H., and Firmin, Peter A. *Contemporary Issues in Cost Accounting.* Boston: Houghton Mifflin, 1966.

Argyris, Chris. *The Impact of Budgets on People.* New York: Controllerships Foundation, 1952.

Ayres, Robert U. *Technological Forecasting and Long-Range Planning.* New York: McGraw-Hill Book Company, 1969.

Becker, Selwyn, and Green, David Jr. "Budgeting and Employee Behavior." *Journal of Business,* October 1962, pp. 392–402.

Bierman, Harold Jr. "Probability, Statistical Decision Theory and Accounting." *The Accounting Review,* July 1962, pp. 400–405.

Broster, E. J. "Trend Forecasting—A Proposed New Technique." *The Accountant,* February 25, 1967, pp. 236–40.

Brown, Bernice, and Helmer, Olaf. *Improving the Reliability of Estimates Obtained from a Consensus of Experts.* Santa Monica, Calif.: RAND Corporation, 1964.

Brown, R. G. *Smoothing, Forecasting, and Prediction of Discrete Time Series.* Englewood Cliffs, N. J.: Prentice-Hall, Inc., 1963.

Campbell, Robert M., and Hitchin, David. "The Delphi Technique: Implementation in the Corporate Environment." *Management Services,* November–December 1968, pp. 37–42.

Daily, R. Austin. "Reporting Forecasted Information." *The Accounting Review,* October 1971, pp. 686–92.

DeSalvia, Donald N. "Exponential Smoothing: A Pragmatic Approach to Production Planning." *Production and Inventory Management,* First Quarter 1968, pp. 15–29.

Doofe, Henry C. "A Case Study in Financial Forecasting." *Cost and Management* (Canada), February 1966, pp. 51–66.

Dressel, R. L. "Input-Output Relationships as a Forecasting Tool." *NAA Bulletin,* June 1962, pp. 25–32.

Gershefski, George W., and Harvey, Allan. "Corporate Models—The State of the Art." *Management Science,* February 1970, pp. B303–B321.

Grenander, U., and Rosenblatt, M. *Statistical Analysis of Stationary Time Series.* New York: John Wiley & Sons, Inc., 1957.

Hamburg, Morris, and Atkins, Robert J. "Computer Model for New Product Demand." *Harvard Business Review,* March–April 1967, pp. 107–115.

Helmer, Olaf, and Rescher, Nicholas. *On the Epistemology of the Inexact Sciences.* Santa Monica, Calif.: RAND Corporation, 1960.

Hoag, R. V., and Craig, A. T. *Introduction to Mathematical Statistics.* New York: The Macmillan Company, 1965.

Horngren, Charles T. *Cost Accounting: A Managerial Emphasis.* Englewood Cliffs, N.J.: Prentice-Hall, Inc., 1967.

Ijiri, Yuji. *The Foundations of Accounting Measurement: A Mathematical, Economic, and Behavioral Inquiry.* Englewood Cliffs, N.J.: Prentice-Hall, Inc., 1967.

Ijiri, Y.; Kinard, J. C.; and Putney, F. B. "An Integrated Evaluation System for Budget Forecasting and Operating Performance with a Classified Budgeting Bibliography." *Journal of Accounting Research,* Spring 1968, pp. 1–28.

Ijiri, Y.; Levy, F. K.; and Lyon, R. C. "A Linear Programming Model for Budgeting and Financial Planning." *Journal of Accounting Research,* Autumn 1963, pp. 198–212.

Ijiri, Y., and Robicheck, Alexander. "Cost-Volume-Profit Analysis Under Conditions of Uncertainty." *The Accounting Review,* October 1964, pp. 917–26.

Isenson, Raymond S. "Technological Forecasting—A Management Tool." *Business Horizons,* Summer 1967, pp. 37–46.

Kahle, R. V. "Mathematical Techniques in Corporate Planning." *Business Economics,* Winter 1965–66, pp. 58–61.

Kimball, William L. "Planning with Mathematical Models." *Managerial Planning,* March–April 1969, pp. 14–17.

Knapp, Robert A. "Forecasting and Measuring with Correlation Analysis." *Financial Executive,* May 1963, pp. 13–19.

Knight, W. D., and Weinwurm, E. H. *Managerial Budgeting.* New York: The Macmillan Company, 1964.

Lazzaro, Victor. *Systems and Procedures: A Handbook for Business and Industry.* Englewood Cliffs, N.J.: Prentice-Hall, Inc., 1968.

Lenz, Ralph C., and Lanford, H. W. "The Substitution Phenomenon." *Business Horizons,* February 1972, pp. 63–68.

Leontief, Wassily W. "A Proposal for Better Business Forecasting." *Harvard Business Review,* November–December 1964, pp. 166–67.

Levine, Alan H. "Forecasting Techniques." *Management Accounting,* January 1967, pp. 31–36.

McCracken, Daniel D., and Dorn, William S. *Numerical Methods and Fortran Programming.* New York: John Wiley & Sons, Inc., 1964.

McMillan, Claude, and Gonzalez, Richard F. *Systems Analysis: A Computer Approach to Decision Models.* Homewood, Ill.: Richard D. Irwin, Inc., 1965.

Manthey, Philip S. "Profit Planning Using Forecast Schedules." *Management Accounting,* January 1967, pp. 13–30.

Neter, John, and Wasserman, William. *Fundamental Statistics for Business and Economics.* Boston: Allyn & Bacon, Inc., 1966.

O'Neal, Charles R. "New Approaches to Technological Forecasting—Morphological Analysis." *Business Horizons,* December 1970, pp. 48–58.

Osborne, Harlow. "Characteristics of Sales Forecasts Based on Gross National Product." *Financial Analysts Journal,* September–October 1970, pp. 39–46, 59, 60.

Panaro, J. Richard. "The Future of Computerized Sales Forecasting." *Management Accounting,* August 1967, pp. 46–48.

Riggs, James L. *Economic Decision Models for Engineers and Managers.* New York: McGraw-Hill Book Company, 1968.

Schussel, George. "Simulation and Sales Forecasting." *Datamation,* June 1967, pp. 40–45.

Sord, B. H., and Welsch, Glen A. *Business Budgeting.* New York: Controllership Foundation, Inc., 1958.

Vancil, Richard F. "The Accuracy of Long-Range Planning." *Harvard Business Review,* September–October 1970, pp. 98–101.

Vazsonyi, Andrew. "Statistical Techniques for Financial Planning and Forecasting." *Controller,* May 1957, pp. 216–22, 244–48.

Weston, J. Fred. "Forecasting Financial Requirements." *The Accounting Review,* July 1958, pp. 427–40.

CHAPTER 22 QUESTIONS, PROBLEMS, AND CASES

22- 1. Explain what is meant by *bias.* How does it relate to unstable budgeting? How is it caused?

22- 2. With a moving average forecasting method, forecast errors may be attributable to what causes?

22- 3. Distinguish between *forecasting* and budgeting. What is the function of each?

22- 4. What is the relationship between *effectiveness* and *reliability?*

22- 5. Define or explain the use of the following terms and phrases:
(a) Alleged value
(b) Effectiveness
(c) Reliability
(d) Objectivity
(e) Expected values
(f) Single-point values
(g) Delphi process
(h) Trend line
(i) Extrapolation
(j) Interpolation
(k) "Normal equations"
(l) Histogram
(m) Symmetrical
(n) Skewed distribution

22- 6. In the determination of an *alleged value* explain the interaction of decision rules, budget standards, and operating activity. Are the alleged values of every decision maker identical?

22- 7. In exponential smoothing, which best filters out the effects of random fluctuations, a large or small weighting constant? Why?

22- 8. "If we could always produce the alleged values we would be sure that the pursuance of goals would be accompanied by the optimal consumption of company resources." Discuss.

22- 9. When using a budget, a company hopes to attain a responsive reaction from the decision maker that will yield an optimal operating activity. Ideally the budget should be constructed of alleged values. Is this construction possible in view of the fact that each decision maker may not have identical decision rules? Discuss.

22-10. Explain the distinction between *stable* and *unstable* budgeting. Which type of budgeting situation is most prevalent? What is the importance of a long-run orientation in budgeting?

22-11. "The use of standards other than those represented by the optimal budget will result in inappropriate actions, since our decision rules allege optimal standards." Explain the meaning of this statement.

22-12. "As a practical matter, we can expect all budgets to contain built-in bias." Why? Is it important that we minimize such bias? Why? What are the means of reducing bias?

22-13. Budgets should provide the user with those values necessary to operate effectively within the context of his decision apparatus. What is meant by effective operation?

22-14. Is it necessary for an alleged value to be mathematically accurate? Is *accuracy* equated with *reliability?* Explain your responses.

22-15. "A measurement does not have to be accurate or objective *per se* to produce the desired result—rather, it must be useful to the decision maker." Discuss.

22-16. How is the concensus of a measured value used to determine the subjectivity or objectivity of that value? Is a subjectively determined value inferior to an objectively determined value as a budget estimate? Use diagrams in explaining your response.

22-17. Why is *class compression* necessary in evaluating the uncertainty of an estimated modal value?

22-18. With correlation analysis, why can't we find the best fitting curve by simply minimizing the bias? What is the solution?

22-19. Reliability is the overriding consideration in constructing budget standards. Discuss your reaction to this statement.

22-20. What are five factors that could be of possible use in forecasting single-point values?

22-21. Objective forecasting methods are algorithmic and associate only quantifiable information by pre-set weightings. How are the pre-set weightings determined? If the weights are determined subjectively, does this negate the objectivity of the forecasting method?

22-22. What are the impediments to producing reliable group estimates through a committee structure?

22-23. Why is the Delphi process concerned with the width of the interquartile range rather than with a precise measure of the uncertainty of the median value? What means is used by the Delphi process to shrink the interquartial range and what means is used to reduce the bias?

22-24. "The use of background information, in a way that is not systematized but depends entirely on the exercise of informal expert judgment, may appropriately lead to predictive conclusions in the face of prima facie evidence that points in the opposite direction." Explain the meaning of this statement. In forecasting, how is an *expert* distinguished from other forecasters? The exclusive use of personal judgment will probably result in unstable budgeting in the long-run. Why?

22-25. What kind of feedback is given between rounds of the Delphi consensus process? What are the objectives in providing such feedback information?

22-26. Using a long-run analysis, is the *most likely value* also the *expected value?*

22-27. Is an objectively determined value always reliable? Explain.

22-28. What three problems are inherent in simple moving average forecasting?

22-29. Why is simple moving average referred to as a smoothing process?

22-30. With the simple moving average method, "better and better filtering of random fluctuations is possible by employing greater numbers of observations." How is this filtering accomplished? Is it a desirable trait?

22-31. With the moving average method "we can employ a large number of observations if we feel the process is changing slowly and desire to filter out any noise, or employ a smaller number of observations if we wish to obtain a greater response to recent trends. Explain and demonstrate the truth of this statement.

22-32. The smaller the smoothing constant in exponential smoothing, the more significant part our past data will play in the new forecast. Explain.

22-33. What are the two types of correlation analysis? Differentiate between the two. What is the independent variable of each?

22-34. With data correlation analysis, explain what is meant by a *lag prediction.*

22-35. Identify and explain the two uses of an equation representing the functional relationship between an independent and dependent variable.

22-36. How is the total bias of a curve (or functional relationship) determined? What does this bias represent? How is the bias expressed with the least squares method?

22-37. Explain how the normal equations are obtained from the least squares criterion (bias equation)?

22-38. "Forecasting the dispersion about the mode provides a means of examining the uncertainty associated with single-point estimates by subjectively evaluating the outcome of an estimating process." Describe the subjective evaluation procedure for obtaining a measure of the uncertainty. How can the uncertainty of an estimate be computed from past data?

22-39. When our objective is to measure the uncertainty of the modal value, why must the mode be represented in the discrete distribution as one of the possible outcomes?

22-40. Describe the three-point and five-point estimation schemes.

22-41. Distinguish between an *expected value* and a *conditional value.*

22-42. "When the distribution of possible outcomes is skewed, many authorities consider the mean a better single-point estimate than the mode." Why?

22-43. What moving average drawback is overcome by using exponential smoothing?

22-44. ***EXPONENTIAL SMOOTHING***

(a) Compute a forecast for the next period assuming the actual data last period was $181,300, the forecast last period was $170,000, and the exponential smoothing constant is:
(1) .30
(2) .80
(3) .05

(b) Compute a forecast for the next period assuming the actual data last period was $94,350, the forecast last period was $115,400, and the exponential smoothing constant is:
(1) .40
(2) .90
(3) .10

(c) Determine the *weights* effectively assigned to data for the *past five periods* if the exponential smoothing constant is:
(1) .10

(2) .50
(3) .75

(d) Determine the number of observations necessary in a moving average to yield the exponential smoothing forecast when the smoothing constant is:
(1) .20
(2) .0005

22-45. ***DETERMINING BIAS*** The Rodney Company has two correlation curves *a* and *b*. The historical values taken from company financial records are indicated as black dots on the graph.

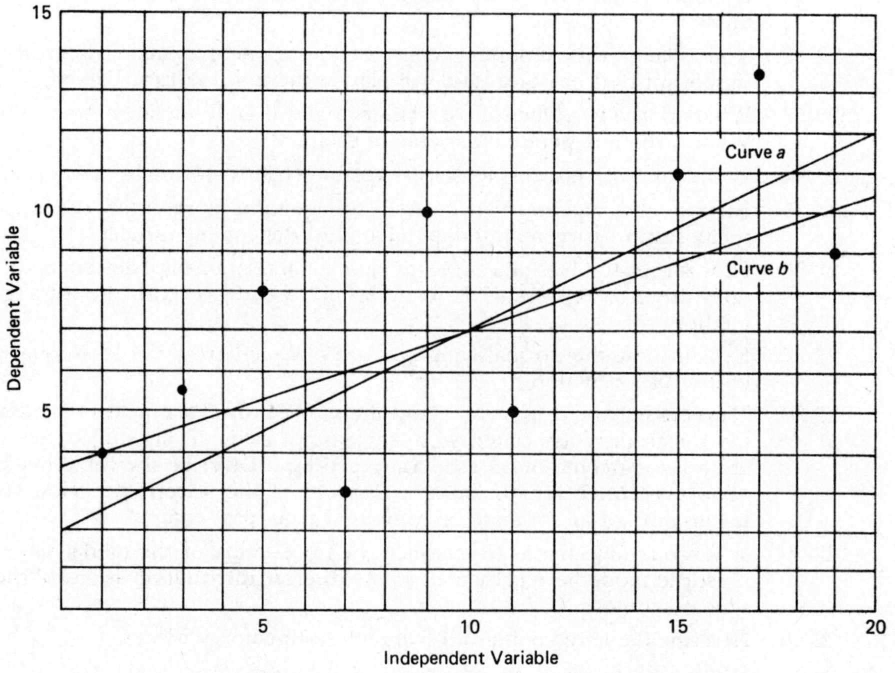

Required:

Using the least squares criterion, determine the *bias* of each curve. Which curve represents the best fit of Rodney Company historical data?

22-46. ***MOVING AVERAGE FORECASTING*** The following monthly sales data is taken from the financial records of the Hanafee Corporation:

	Month	Actual Sales
19x1	Jan.	$ 87,400
	Feb.	73,200
	Mar.	96,000
	Apr.	95,000
	May	98,500
	June	101,400
	July	110,300
	Aug.	104,000
	Sept.	96,000
	Oct.	94,700
	Nov.	98,000
	Dec.	102,000

	Month	Actual Sales
19x2	Jan.	101,400
	Feb.	90,200
	Mar.	96,400
	Apr.	97,000

(a) Using a six-month *simple moving average,* compute the *forecast* error for:
(1) February 19x2
(2) March 19x2
(3) April 19x2
(b) Using an eight-month *simple moving average,* compute the forecast for May 19x2.
(c) From an inspection of the historical sales data, how many months should the *simple moving average* contain in order to produce the best forecast for May 19x2?
(d) Using a fourteen-month *one-place weighted moving average,* compute the *forecast* for March 19x2 and April 19x2 by applying a 60% weight to the current data.
(e) Using a fourteen-month *multiple-place weighted moving average,* compute the forecast for March 19x2 and April 19x2 by applying the following weights:
(1) 50% to current data X_1
(2) 20% to X_2
(3) 10% to X_3
(f) What smoothing constant must be used in exponential smoothing to give an equivalent forecast to that obtained by simple moving average, using all the historical data provided in this problem?

22-47. ***CORRELATION ANALYSIS—DATA CORRELATION*** The financial records of Hillary Corporation show the following relationship between production and variable manufacturing overhead:

Production in Units	Variable Overhead
84,000	$250,000
83,000	299,000
96,000	270,000
78,000	250,000
56,000	196,000
88,000	220,000
72,000	245,000
91,000	255,000

Required:

(a) Find the best fitting first-degree polynomial using the method of least squares.
(b) When production is expected to be 94,000 units, what is the forecast of variable overhead using the equation developed in part (a)?
(c) Find the best fitting second-degree polynomial using the method of least squares. (Refer to chapter 18, p. 815, for an example using *elimination by addition or subtraction* for solving simultaneous equations.)
(d) What is the forecast for part (b) using the second-degree polynomial equation?

22-48. ***CORRELATION ANALYSIS—TIME CORRELATION*** The sales of the Holly Company for the last ten quarters are as follows:

	Quarter	Sales
19x1	1	$142,000
	2	164,000
	3	205,000
	4	220,000
19x2	1	238,000
	2	260,000
	3	290,000
	4	304,000
19x3	1	330,000
	2	360,000

Required:

(a) Find the best fitting first-degree polynomial using the method of least squares.

(b) Forecast the sales for the third and fourth quarters of 19*x*3 using the first-degree polynomial developed in part (a).

22-49. ***EXPECTED VALUES*** Using exponential smoothing, the Frazer Company forecasted 19*x*1 sales of $80,000 for product A, $440,000 for product B, and $135,000 for product C. The company wished, however, to refine these forecasts and obtain an expected value from an analysis of the uncertainty surrounding each forecast.

Using the Delphi process and a five-point estimation scheme, the sales staff of the Frazer Company made the following estimates of the uncertainty surrounding the sales forecasts of company products.

	Product A		Product B		Product C	
	Outcome	Prob.	Outcome	Prob.	Outcome	Prob.
Pessimistic	50,000	.05	190,000	.05	100,000	.05
Lower quarter	72,500	.20	287,500	.05	122,500	.25
Middle	95,000	.25	385,000	.10	145,000	.15
Upper quarter	117,500	.10	482,000	.15	167,500	.10
Optimistic	140,000	.05	580,000	.05	190,000	.05
Forecasted sales	80,000	.35	440,000	.60	135,000	.40

Required:

Compute the 19*x*1 *expected* sales for products A, B, and C.

22-50. ***EXPECTED VALUE ANALYSIS*** Food Products, Inc., posed the following problem to your firm and requested guidelines which can be applied in the future to obtain the largest net income.

A Food Products plant on the coast produces a food product and ships its production of 10,000 units per day by air in an airplane owned by Food Products. The area is sometimes fogbound and shipment can then be made only by rail. The plant does not operate unless shipments are made. Extra costs of preparation for rail shipment reduce the marginal contribution of this product from $.40 per unit to $.18 per unit and there is an additional fixed cost of $3,100 for modification of packaging facilities to convert to rail shipment (incurred only once per conversion).

The fog may last for several days, and Food Products normally starts shipping by rail only after rail shipments become necessary to meet commitments to customers.

A meteorological report reveals that during the past ten years the area has been fogbound 250 times for one day and that fog continued 100 times for a second consecutive day and 10 times for a fifth consecutive day. Occasions and length of fog were both random. Fog never continued more than five days and there were never two separate occurrences of fog in any six-day period.

Required:

(a) Prepare a schedule presenting the computation of the daily marginal contribution (ignore fixed conversion cost)
  (1) When there is no fog and shipment is made by air.
  (2) When there is fog and shipment is made by rail.

(b) Prepare a schedule presenting the computation of the probabilities of the possible combinations of foggy and clear weather on the days following a fogbound day. Your schedule should show the probability that, if fog first occurs on a particular day,
  (1) The next four days will be foggy.
  (2) The next three days will be foggy and day 5 will be clear.
  (3) The next two days will be foggy and days 4 and 5 will be clear.
  (4) The next day will be foggy and days 3, 4, and 5 will be clear.
  (5) The next four days will be clear.

(c) Assume you determine it is probable that it would be unprofitable to start shipping by rail on either the fourth or fifth consecutive foggy day. Prepare a schedule presenting the computation of the probable marginal income or loss that should be expected from rail shipments if rail shipments were started on the third consecutive foggy day and the probability that the next two days will be foggy is .25, the probability that the next day will be foggy and day 5 will be clear is .25, and the probability that the next two days will be clear is .50.

(d) In this engagement you should consider the reliability of the data upon which you base your conclusions. What questions should be considered regarding
  (1) Financial data reliability?
  (2) Meteorological data reliability?

(Adapted from the CPA exam.)

22-51. ***DELPHI PROCESS*** Fifteen participants in the Delphi forecasting method were asked to give their estimate of 1971 new-customer orders for products A, B, and C. In addition, each participant was asked to indicate his degree of competence for each forecast by estimating whether his response will fall in the first, second, third, or fourth quartile (of distributed responses) in relation to the actual new customer orders. For instance, if a respondent thought his estimate would fall within the first quartile of responses in relation to the actual value, he would rate his competence as 1. The responses from the first-round questionnaire are as follows:

Respondent	Self Competence Rating	Product A	Self Competence Rating	Product B	Self Competence Rating	Product C
1	1	102,000	4	60,000	1	545,000
2	3	170,000	3	40,000	2	500,000
3	3	108,000	2	45,000	2	600,000
4	3	164,000	1	80,000	3	800,000
5	3	86,000	2	42,000	3	460,000
6	3	120,000	3	38,000	2	480,000
7	2	95,000	3	25,000	2	390,000
8	1	110,000	1	90,000	1	550,000
9	2	85,000	2	100,000	1	450,000
10	1	115,000	2	35,000	3	400,000
11	3	130,000	3	30,000	3	600,000
12	1	110,000	1	45,000	2	500,000
13	2	100,000	2	70,000	3	620,000
14	3	150,000	3	35,000	1	430,000
15	3	150,000	2	95,000	2	570,000

Required:

(a) From the first-round results, determine the feedback information for the second round. What instructions should be given to the respondents on this second-round questionnaire?
(b) After the second-round responses are received and tallied, what instructions should be given to the respondents on the third-round ques-
(c) From the self-competence ratings select one elite sub-group for each product and determine a forecast of new customer orders for each product based upon a concensus of each elite sub-group. An elite sub-group should contain eight respondents who have indicated the highest competency.

CHAPTER

23

OPERATIONAL BUDGETING

23.1 THE BUDGET AS A CONTROL

The preparation of formal planning documents for controlling the operating phases of a business is referred to as operational budgeting. These documents consist of alleged values[1] which are used as reference points for determining operational *efficiency*. This control aspect of budgeting was discussed in Unit V. Variances were calculated as the difference between actual performance and expected or budgeted performance, and as such, they became measures of operating efficiency. The *purpose* of operational budgeting is to control actual performance, as illustrated in Exhibit 23-1.

Control is administered through *performance reports* which highlight variances from budget figures. Exhibit 23-2 contains a sample performance report for the assembly department of the Pratt Company. This document provides a means of instituting *responsibility accounting* in which those responsible for the incurrence of certain costs are given information concerning optimal expenditure levels and data as to their performance in meeting such levels. The responsible person may redirect or adjust his performance so as to adhere to budgeted plans.

[1] Refer to chapter 22 for a discussion of alleged values.

EXHIBIT 23-1 BUDGETARY CONTROL OF OPERATIONS

Actual Performance

Control

Operational Budgets

Requisite to control is a planning document containing our alleged values; that is, values which cause the decision maker to take an optimal action. With a budget used for both planning and control, these alleged values are forecasted values of *expected future outcomes.* A budget is effective if it is constructed of alleged values and reliable if it enables the company to reach its objectives.

23.2 FIXED AND FLEXIBLE BUDGETS

The performance report of Exhibit 23-2 shows variances calculated from a *fixed budget* —that is, from a budget constructed of values explicitly formulated for a given level of operating activity. If the budgeted level of activity had been attained, the budget variances would have been meaningful. As evidenced by actual production, the budget quota was not attained; consequently, some variances have been inappropriately calculated, for we expect some costs to vary directly with attained activity. These costs are *variable costs.*[2] From Unit V we recall that variable costs by definition are constant on a per unit basis, and hence can be expected to vary directly with activity levels, as indicated in Exhibit 23-3.

Other costs remain unchanged over a wide range of production activity. These costs are *fixed.* We can recognize the relationship of cost to production activity by constructing a *flexible budget*—that is, a budget specifically designed for the attained activity. For example, suppose we isolated variable and fixed costs of Pratt's assembly department and constructed a budget for an attained production of 5,500 units. The budget value for each variable cost is calculated by multiplying the actual production by the unit cost. On the other hand, the fixed costs, not being influenced by activity levels, remain unchanged. The new flexible budget is shown in Exhibit 23-4.

It appears from our example that a fixed budget gives quite erroneous re-

[2] We recognize that not all variable costs are *strictly variable;* some are *step-variable,* as shown:

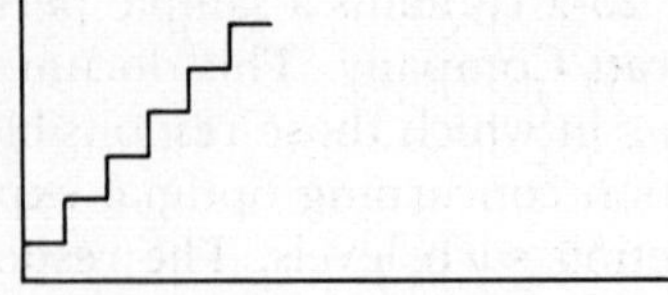

These costs represent the acquisition of *activity increments* rather than the acquisition of exact activity needs. Labor cost is a good example, where indivisible chunks of service potential are acquired.

EXHIBIT 23-2 PERFORMANCE REPORT FOR ASSEMBLY DEPARTMENT OF PRATT COMPANY

	Budget		Actual		Variance	
	This Month	**Year-to-date**	**This Month**	**Year-to-date**	**This Month**	**Year-to-date**
Units produced	6,000	24,000	5,500	22,500	(500)	(1,500)
Direct material	180,000	720,000	176,000	720,000	4,000	0
Direct labor	156,000	624,000	145,750	596,250	10,250	27,750
Overhead						
Indirect labor	16,200	64,800	15,400	58,500	800	6,300
Setup	200	800	180	760	20	40
Rework	5,100	20,400	4,620	19,800	480	600
Supplies	1,800	7,200	1,870	6,300	(70)	900
Maintenance	800	3,200	840	3,200	(40)	0
Depreciation	21,000	84,000	19,250	78,750	1,750	5,250
Property taxes	270	1,080	270	1,080	0	0
R & D	2,400	9,600	2,200	9,400	200	200
Employee training	4,200	16,800	3,700	15,200	500	1,600

EXHIBIT 23-3 VARIABLE COST BEHAVIOR

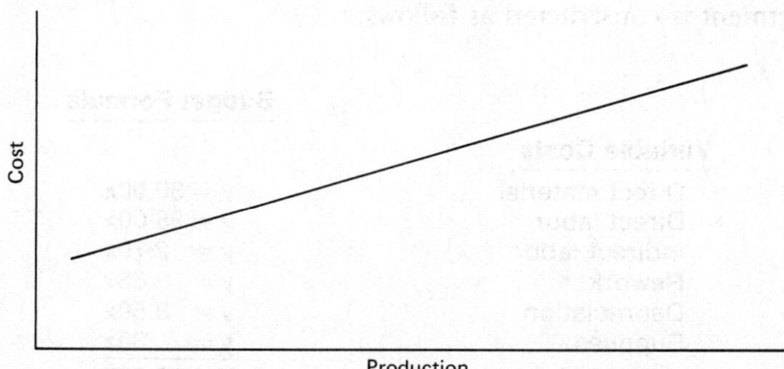

EXHIBIT 23-4 PERFORMANCE REPORT FOR AN ASSEMBLY OF 5,500 UNITS THIS MONTH, 22,500 TO DATE

	Budget		Actual		Variance	
	This Month	**Year-to-date**	**This Month**	**Year-to-date**	**This Month**	**Year-to-date**
Variable Costs						
Direct material	165,000	675,000	176,000	720,000	(11,000)	(45,000)
Direct labor	143,000	585,000	145,750	596,750	(2,750)	(11,250)
Indirect labor	14,850	60,750	15,400	58,500	(550)	(2,250)
Rework	4,675	19,125	4,620	19,800	55	(675)
Depreciation*	19,250	78,750	19,250	78,750	0	0
Supplies	1,650	6,750	1,870	6,300	(220)	450
Fixed Costs						
Set up	200	800	180	760	20	40
Maintenance	800	3,200	840	3,200	(40)	0
Property taxes	270	1,080	270	1,080	0	0
R & D	2,400	9,600	2,200	9,400	200	200
Employee training	4,200	16,800	3,700	15,200	500	1,600

* Based on units-of-production.

sults because the variability of some costs is ignored. The underproduction of assembled units is a very important variance by itself; however, we know that underproduction should not be the cause of *favorable* variances as suggested by the fixed budget. Thus, in order to get a true measure of the *efficiency* of production activities, we must base such measure upon *actual* production. In this way we measure the efficiency of actual activity, not desired activity.

There are three things to note from this new budget:

1. We have again formalized a budget for one activity level.
2. All variable costs are thought to relate directly to production as an activity indicator.
3. Fixed costs do not relate to activity of the assembly department; hence, they may not be *controllable* at this level of operations.

Instead of formalizing the flexible budget into budgets for each possible production level, a more advantageous expression is a *budget formula.* With this formula, performance reports may be prepared when actual production is known. In this way we avoid the possibility of preparing a useless budget. A budget formula for the assembly department is constructed as follows:

	Budget Formula
Variable Costs	
Direct material	$y = 30.00x$
Direct labor	$y = 26.00x$
Indirect labor	$y = 2.70x$
Rework	$y = .85x$
Depreciation	$y = 3.50x$
Supplies	$y = .30x$
Total variable per unit	$Y = 63.35X$
Fixed Costs	
Set up	$y = 200$
Maintenance	$y = 800$
Property taxes	$y = 270$
R & D	$y = 2{,}400$
Employee training	$y = 4{,}200$
Total fixed costs per month	$Y = 7{,}870$

Total Budget = \$7,870 per month + \$63.35 per unit

$$Y = 7{,}870 + 63.35X$$

This formula is valid as long as actual production activity falls within a *normal* or *relevant range.* The relevant range is described in Exhibit 23-5 as the activity interval in which production facilities are not altered. It is the range defined by present or planned plant capacity.

We observe that a change in the *scale of activity* abruptly alters fixed costs and causes variable cost per unit to assume a new value. The budget formula thus becomes invalid. A new formula is required, since the underlying process which generates production activity (and its associated costs) has changed.

Variable costs in our flexible budget vary in relation to activity. The applicable activity, however, is not necessarily production itself, but could be another related

EXHIBIT 23-5 RELEVANT OPERATING RANGE

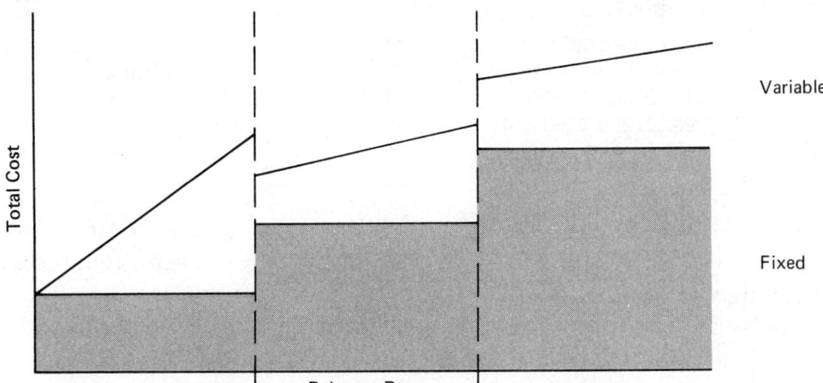

*These boundaries can be thought of as "strategic boundaries."

activity such as: direct labor hours, machine hours, killowatt hours consumed, elapsed time. The point is that our flexible budget and hence our budget formula is probably more complicated than first visualized. Each type of variable expense could have its own activity base. For example, the *x* of the individual budget formula for direct labor may be hours rather than units, for depreciation it may be machine hours, and so on:

Variable Costs	**Budget Formula**	**Activity Base**
Direct material	$y = 30.00x$	units produced
Direct labor	$y = 2.75x$	labor hours
Indirect labor	$y = .72x$	machine hours
Rework	$y = .09x$	labor hours
Depreciation	$y = .93x$	machine hours
Supplies	$y = .08x$	machine hours

Fixed costs should be budgeted but should not be shown in performance reports unless they are *controllable.* A controllable cost is *discretionary;* that is, its incurrence is directly controlled by, or at the discretion of, the person to whom it is reported. A *noncontrollable* cost is a cost whose incurrence is at the discretion of a higher-level cost center.[3] It is a *committed* cost. Only the discretionary fixed costs should appear in the flexible budget of a cost center.

It might be apparent, at this point, that we have still prepared a somewhat naive budget, because in each category of costs listed for the assembly department there could be many further classifications, each with its own budget formula. For instance, direct materials may contain a hundred different items of material, each used in different proportions, each with a different price, and each with a different activity base:

[3]Cost centers are discussed in chapter 18.

	Budget Formula	Activity Base
Variable Costs		
Direct material		
Type A lug bolt	$y = .03x$	no. of lug bolts
No. 3 flux solder	$y = .12x$	ounces
No. 012 copper wire	$y = .015x$	inches
(etc.)		

Labor could have the same problem. Recognizing this situation, we have some appreciation for the possible complexity of operating budgets, even though on a practical basis, budgeting tends to be more general and formulae are usually conceived only on a unit-of-production basis.[4] This is particularly true when a standard cost system is used. In this instance, production inputs—labor, materials, and overhead—are specified on a per unit base, not on number of inches, pounds, labor hours, or other indicators of consumption. Generally speaking, direct labor hours is used as an activity base, because it is common to all goods produced, and hence provides a reference base not available on a per unit basis when heterogenous goods are produced.

23.3 BUDGET VALUES—DOLLARS OR UNITS

Budgets are used to control the internal operations of a business, and thus should be expressed in terms most meaningful to persons in charge of operations. Often the most meaningful data to a foreman is budgeted *labor hours* or budgeted *quantities* of raw materials. These figures are more meaningful because they relate to usage. Unless a foreman is aware of all labor rates and material prices, he cannot gauge his adherence to budget standards.

In most cases, the appropriateness of dollar or quantity figures is self-evident. For instance, a budget for purchasing should contain dollar values, since prices of quantities purchased is the criteria for measuring the performance of this responsibility center. Likewise a production center is concerned with the quantity of raw materials consumed in attaining a given output, not necessarily the cost of usage.[5]

23.4 THE BUDGETING PROCESS

A budgeting process is illustrated in Exhibit 23-6. The input is the *sales forecast,* the transformation is the construction of *formal budgets,* and the output is *pro forma statements.*

Budgets represent an emulated transformation—that is, a duplication of the actual system expected to exist during the budgeting period as well as the "state" of

[4]Units-of-production is an appropriate macro-activity scale for manufacturing organizations. Refer to the discussion in chapter 18.

[5]Unless, of course, the *sales mix* (the proportion of production factors specified for a given output) is controllable, or the substitution of higher priced labor or raw materials is allowable.

EXHIBIT 23-6 THE BUDGETING PROCESS

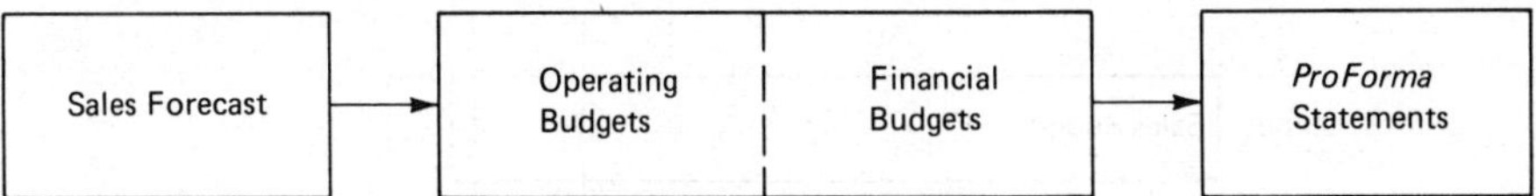

such transformation at discrete time intervals. For control, the state of the actual transformation is compared with the state of the budget.

At the operating level two types of budgets are distinguishable—operating and financial. By referring to Exhibit 23-7 we observe this budgeting dichotomy. *Operating budgets* are formal statements of the expected activity in all phases of a business directly relating to its principle cycles—buying, production, and selling. *Financial budgets,* on the other hand, are budgets of cash receipts and disbursements, and as such are concerned with the financing of business operations. These cash budgets, as discussed earlier, have a balance sheet orientation. That is, the output of cash budgeting is represented by the cash balance on the pro forma balance sheet. Quite naturally though, operating budgets, representing the operational phases of the business, culminate as *pro forma* income statements. It is the budgeting system output which ultimately reveals the focus of operational budgeting as opposed to financial or cash budgeting.

EXHIBIT 23-7 OPERATING AND FINANCIAL BUDGETS

Operating Budgets	Financial Budgets
Sales Budget	Cash Receipts
Production Budget Quotas	Cash Disbursements
Material Usage Budget	
Material Purchases Budget	
Direct Labor Usage Budget	
Overhead Budget	
Ending Inventory Budget	
Selling & Admin. Exp. Budget	

Sales forecasts represent input data which is transformed through operational budgets into *pro forma* financial statements. The *pro forma* statements exemplify the end result of the budgeting process, and as such represent the *financial objectives* of the company. These objectives should correspond *exactly* with our stated objectives if budget construction is optimal. The *pro forma* statements take the same form as our regular income statement, balance sheet, and funds statement, but they contain budget values rather than actual.

23.5 FUNCTIONAL AND PROGRAM BUDGETING

Functional budgeting, or budgeting for an organization's functional activities, is called *vertical budgeting;* while program budgeting, or budgeting for specifically established programs with *sub-goal orientation,* is *horizontal budgeting.* Profit oriented organizations, because of their functional activity structure, use vertical budgeting. Not-for-profit organizations use program or horizontal budgeting. Both, however,

EXHIBIT 23-8 FUNCTIONAL AND PROGRAM MASTER BUDGETS

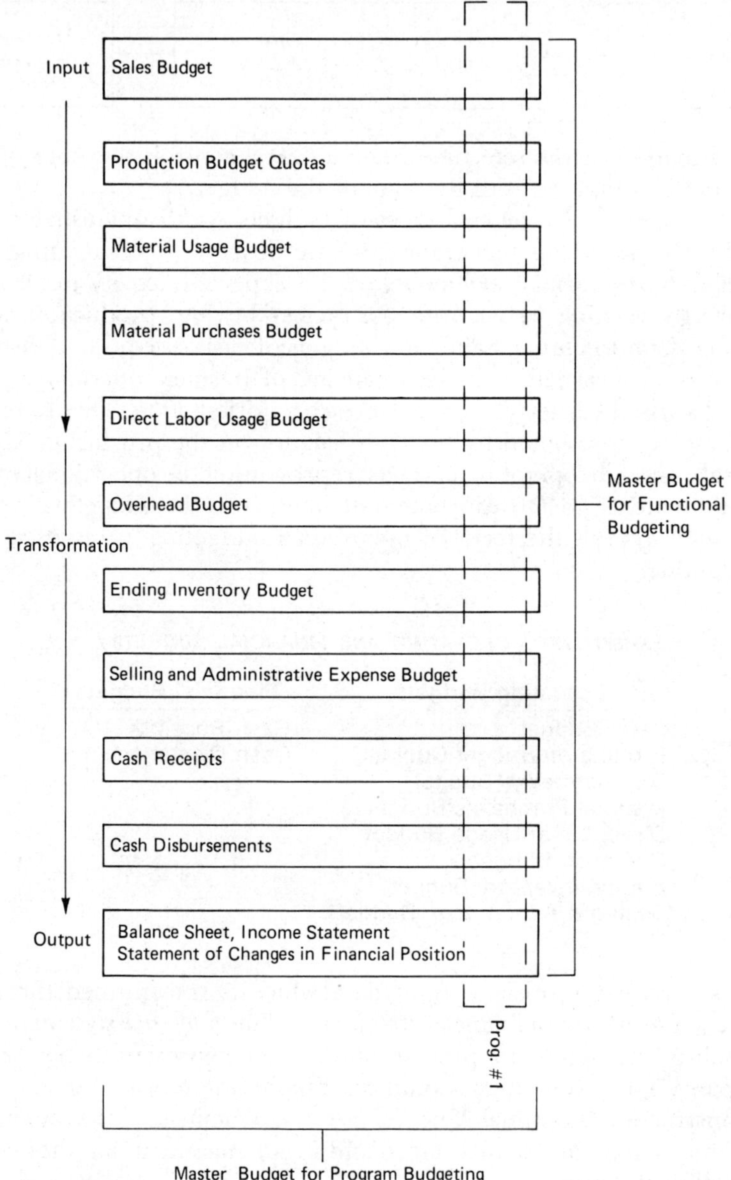

prepare what is referred to as a *master budget* as illustrated in Exhibit 23-8. This budget contains the detailed operating and financial budgets.

Notice that functional budgeting prepares a budget for each discrete aspect of total operating activity. Program budgeting on the other hand identifies the principal sub-goals of the organization and budgets for the program specifically designed to reach that goal. This type of budgeting is now popular in governmental agencies (especially the military), so that potential costs of solving a problem like air pollution, or developing a program to probe distant planets, can be identified in its entirety rather than being lost as *line items* within departmental or functional budgets. The principal problem with this type of budgeting is the possible operating inefficiencies that result when functional areas are budgeted piecemeal per program. For instance, in program budgeting for school districts, each grade level represents a program. The drawback of this otherwise adequate budgeting is that services, such as school busing, become immeshed within many programs. This means that either each grade level must develop its own busing service, or busing must be treated as a separate program. The latter solution is, of course, the only feasible alternative.

Functional budgeting is not operationally oriented. That is, there are no formal budgets for specific tasks or programs and hence no incentive toward immediate and individualized goals. The result, as we have seen in many instances, is a lack of incentive and operational inefficiencies built into the budgets themselves. Nevertheless, few profit-oriented businesses lend themselves to budgeting by programs since their organizational structure is by functions. With this type of structure, and the philosophy associated with functional separatism, functional budgeting is the only reasonable answer.

23.6 A FUNCTIONAL BUDGETING EXAMPLE

In constructing the master budget, one sub-budget builds upon another. In other words, the results of one budget become an integral part of calculating the next. Each builds upon the other until finally sufficient data is prepared to complete the *pro forma* income statement. Notice further that all budgets are static and based upon a planned production level.

Using the operating budgets of Exhibit 23-7 as a guide, the following step priorities are followed in constructing a budget for the year ending December 31, 19—, assuming that the Pratt Corporation produces only three types of television sets:

STEP 1: Our sales forecasts are formalized into a *sales budget:*

	Units	Selling Price	Total Sales
19-inch portable color TV, Model P1	37,000	$340	$12,580,000
21-inch portable color TV, Model P2	22,000	360	7,920,000
21-inch console color TV, Model C1	14,000	580	8,120,000
			$28,620,000

STEP 2: *Production quotas* are based upon the sales budget and planned inventory balances:

	Model P1	Model P2	Model C1
Sales in units (Step 1)	37,000	22,000	14,000
Planned balance in finished inv.	2,000	1,200	600
Planned equivalent units in W-I-P[6]	240	180	110
Total inventory needs	39,240	23,380	14,710
Less: Beginning finished inv.	2,480	1,650	400
Production quotas	36,760	21,730	14,310

[6]Refer to chapter 19 for a discussion of equivalent units of production.

STEP 3: The *material usage budget* is based upon the production quotas of Step 2:

Material Required	Model P1 Per Unit	Model P1 Per Prod. of 36,760	Model P2 Per Unit	Model P2 Per Prod. of 21,730	Model C1 Per Unit	Model C1 Per Prod. of 14,310	Totals Total Usage	Totals Unit Cost	Totals Cost of Usage
#012 copper wire	9.5′	349,220′	13.2′	286,836′	13.2′	188,892′	824,948′	.015	12,374
#3 flux solder	.75 lb.	27,645 lb.	1.10 lb.	23,903 lb.	1.01 lb.	15,741 lb.	67,289 lb.	.12	8,075
Type A lug bolts (etc.)	14	514,640	14	304,220	18	257,580	1,076,440	.03	32,293 (etc.)
									8,420,460

STEP 4: Compute a *materials purchases budget:*

	#012 Copper Wire	#3 Flux Solder	Type A Lug Bolts
Production needs (Step 3)	824,948 ft.	67,289 lb.	1,076,440
Planned balance in inventory	24,000 ft.	2,500 lb.	11,000
Total inventory needs	848,948 ft.	69,789 lb.	1,078,640
Less: Beginning inventory	47,540 ft.	3,100 lb.	8,800
Purchases required	801,408 ft.	66,689 lb.	1,078,640
Price per unit	.015	.12	.03
Cost of purchases	$12,021	$8,003	$32,359

STEP 5: Compute the *direct labor cost* for budgeted production:

	Budgeted Production (Step 2)	Dept. 1 (Wiring) @ $3.50/hr. Direct Labor Hours Per Unit	Dept. 1 Total Hours	Dept. 1 Total Labor Dollars	Dept. 2 (Assembly) @ $2.75/hr. Direct Labor Hours Per Unit	Dept. 2 Total Hours	Dept. 2 Total Labor Dollars	Total Budget in Dollars
Model P1	36,760	8	294,080	1,029,280	6	220,560	606,540	2,468,700
Model P2	21,730	12	260,760	912,660	6	130,380	358,545	2,597,337
Model C1	14,310	12	171,720	601,020	15	214,650	590,288	2,859,610
			726,560	2,542,960		565,590	1,555,373	7,925,640

STEP 6: Compute the *overhead budget* as follows:

	Dept. 1 (Wiring)	Dept. 2 (Assembly)	Total
Variable Costs			
Indirect labor	$ 220,000	$ 197,200	$ 878,500
Depreciation (units-of-production method)	478,800	254,000	1,840,000
Supplies	12,000	21,700	62,000
(etc.)			
Fixed Costs			
Property taxes	7,400	3,200	17,500
Setup	6,100	2,400	12,400
Maintenance	42,310	9,190	62,000
Employee training	18,400	56,300	1,010,000
(etc.)			
Total overhead	$1,743,744	$1,583,652	$6,630,700
Divided by direct labor hrs. (Step 5)	726,560	565,590	
Overhead per direct labor hour	$2.40	$2.80	

STEP 7: Compute the *ending inventory budget* by calculating the budgeted cost per finished unit and multiplying the result by the planned inventory level:

		Model P1		Model P2		Model C1	
	Unit Cost	Units Required	Amount	Units Required	Amount	Units Required	Amount
Material							
#012 copper wire	.015	9.5	.14	13.2	.20	13.2	.20
#3 flux solder	.12	.75	.09	1.1	.13	1.1	.13
(etc.)							
Direct Labor							
Dept. 1 (Wiring)	3.50	8	28.00	12	42.00	12	42.00
Dept. 2 (Assembly)	2.75	6	16.50	6	16.50	15	41.00
(etc.)							
Overhead							
Dept. 1 (Wiring)	2.40	8	19.20	12	28.80	12	28.80
Dept. 2 (Assembly)	2.80	6	16.80	6	16.80	15	42.00
(etc.)							
Unit Cost			$270.00		$310.00		$430.00
Planned inventory level			2,000		1,200		600
Ending finished inventory			$540,000		$372,000		$258,000

Total ending finished inv. = 540,000 + 372,000 + 258,000 = $1,170,000

STEP 8: Compute a *selling and administration expense budget:*

	Territory A	Territory B	Total
Selling Expenses			
Salesmen's compensation	$ 35,000	$ 24,000	$ 120,000
Commissions	102,000	68,000	38,000
Travel	1,800	23,500	92,500
Dealer aids	54,000	13,400	124,000
Convention expenses	14,000	9,000	37,000
Warranty expenses	145,000	96,000	487,300
Advertising	215,000	134,000	986,400
(etc.)			
Total selling expenses	934,600	657,800	$2,748,700
Administrative Expenses			
Executive salaries			$ 211,000
Office salaries			107,000
Office supplies			87,400
Professional services			15,500
Insurance—Office			1,200
(etc.)			
Total administrative			2,320,000
Total selling & admin.			$5,068,700

STEP 9: Finally, we prepare a *pro forma income statement* by summarizing all the operating budgets:

Sales (Step 1)				$28,620,000
Cost of goods sold:				
Finished goods inventory, beginning			$ 890,000	
Work-in-process, beginning		$ 204,520		
Raw materials inventory, beginning (Step 4)*	$1,113,430			
Purchases of raw materials (Step 4)*	8,537,730			
Raw materials available	9,651,160			
Raw materials inventory, ending (step 4)*	1,230,700			
Raw materials used (Step 3)		8,420,460		
Direct labor (Step 5)		7,925,640		
Overhead (Step 6)		6,630,700		
Total work-in-process		23,181,320		
Work-in-process, ending (from Steps 2 & 7)		167,900		
Jobs finished during the year			23,013,420	
Finished goods available for sale			23,903,420	
Finished goods inventory, ending (Step 7)			1,170,000	
Cost of goods sold				22,733,420
Gross profit				5,886,580
Less: Selling & administrative expenses (Step 8)				5,068,700
Net income from operations before income taxes				$ 817,880

*Total figures are not presented in the materials purchases budget.

23.7 ALTERNATIVE BUDGETING PROCESSES

The *construction* of operating budgets is called the *budgeting process*. This process can be approached from three directions as illustrated in Exhibit 23-9. Approaches A, B, and C correspond to the entry of *forecasted* and *analyzed data* in the budgeting process. Forecasted or analyzed data can enter through A as a sales forecast. From there it is used as a basis for constructing a production quota budget, materials budget, inventory budget, labor budget, etc. The budgets are then summarized and reported as *pro forma* financial statements. Entry through B will generally be analyzed data; that is, data which is based upon forecasts, but is modified by existing or proposed *constraints* upon production facilities, inventory levels, time, money, etc. Entry through C can again be either forecasted or analyzed data. In this instance, *pro forma* statement balances will be decided upon first, and from there budgets will be constructed which in total yield these predisposed balances.

EXHIBIT 23-9 APPROACHES TO BUDGET CONSTRUCTION

Sales Forecast | Operating Budgets | *Pro Forma* Statements
A

Sales Forecast | Operating Budgets | *Pro Forma* Statements
B

Sales Forecast | Operating Budgets | *Pro Forma* Statements
C

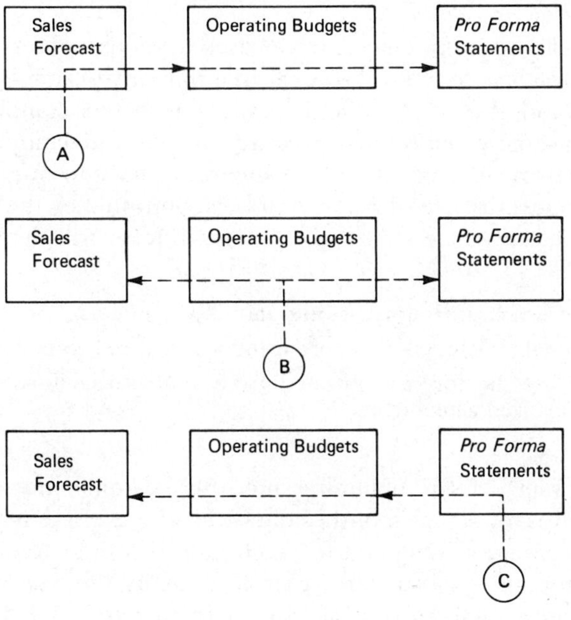

23.8 ANALYSIS IN BUDGET CONSTRUCTION

For all entry points described in Exhibit 23-8, forecasted data must very often be subjected to a *pre-budget analysis*. This intermediary budget stage is illustrated in Exhibit 23-10.

From our diagram, it is apparent that pre-budget analysis is the refinement of forecasted data before it enters the budgeting process. We will examine this refinement as it affects the three approaches to budget construction: (1) analysis of

EXHIBIT 23-10 PRE-BUDGET ANALYSIS

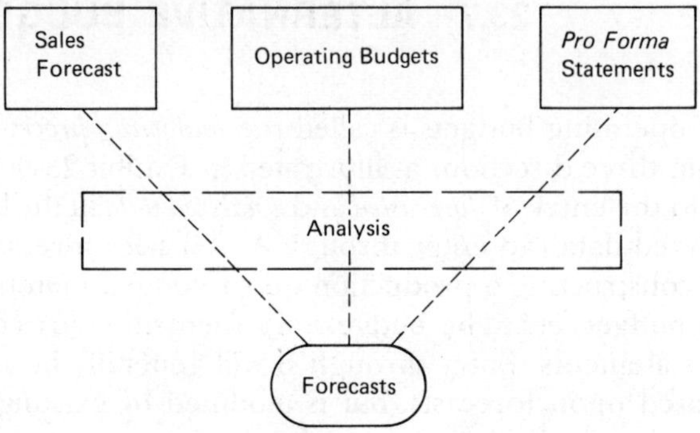

seasonally adjusted input data, (2) analysis of constraining factors, and (3) sensitivity analysis applied to output.

23.9 ANALYSIS OF SEASONALLY ADJUSTED INPUT DATA

The forecasts developed in chapter 22 were based upon past observations, unadjusted for any *seasonal variation.* We know however that in many instances seasonal variation is likely to exist, and thus may adversely affect forecasts computed by structural methods. Since seasonal variation may account for substantial month-to-month movement in sales, such movement should be incorporated into our monthly forecasts. We can do so through the use of *seasonal indexes* computed by the method of *ratio-to-same-year-average* or *ratio-to-moving-average.* These indexes will then be used to:

1. Break-down a yearly forecast into monthly segments.
2. Deseasonalize actual data before using a structured forecasting method.
3. Seasonalize the forecast obtained from a structured forecasting method using deseasonalized actual data.

The first method for obtaining monthly seasonal indexes—ratio-to-same-year-average—compares actual monthly data with the average monthly data for the same year. A percentage is obtained for each month over a number of years. Next, an average percentage is calculated. This average is the seasonal index for the month. The computational process, as illustrated in Exhibit 23-11, shows an index computed from three years of past data. Rather than basing our monthly index on just one year's data, it is thought that an average of indexes for several years will lessen the influence of random movement in data not caused by seasonal factors.

This method contains a potentially serious defect. It does not adjust for any *trend-cyclical movement* of data. That is, if there is a general trend toward increased sales, a comparison of January sales to the yearly average produces a lower percentage than is justified by seasonal factors alone. This is evident because the average sales for the year will be higher with an upward trend in sales, thus producing a lower index. This can be demonstrated by a simple example: suppose each month has exactly the same sales of $100—that is, there is *no* observable seasonal variation. With this set of

EXHIBIT 23-11 SEASONAL INDEXES AS RATIO-TO-SAME-YEAR-AVERAGE

	Actual Monthly Sales (in millions)			Actual Monthly Sales as a % of Average Sales for:			Seasonal Index (average %)
Month	**1969**	**1970**	**1971**	**1969**	**1970**	**1971**	
Jan.	1.8	2.1	2.0	.79	.90	.86	.85
Feb.	1.6	2.0	1.8	.70	.86	.77	.78
Mar.	2.0	2.1	1.9	.87	.90	.81	.86
Apr.	2.2	2.3	2.1	.96	.99	.90	.95
May	2.5	2.5	2.4	1.09	1.08	1.03	1.07
Jun.	2.5	2.6	2.7	1.09	1.12	1.16	1.12
Jul.	2.8	2.7	2.9	1.22	1.16	1.24	1.21
Aug.	2.7	2.5	2.7	1.18	1.08	1.16	1.14
Sept.	2.2	2.1	2.2	.96	.90	.94	.93
Oct.	2.0	1.8	2.2	.87	.77	.94	.86
Nov.	2.4	2.5	2.4	1.05	1.08	1.03	1.05
Dec.	2.8	2.7	2.7	1.22	1.16	1.16	1.18
	27.5	27.9	28.0	12.00	12.00	12.00	12.00

Average for 1969 = 27.5/12 = 2.292
Average for 1970 = 27.9/12 = 2.325
Average for 1971 = 28.0/12 = 2.333

circumstances, the index for any month computed under ratio-to-same-year-average would be 100/100 or 1.0. However, suppose there is an upward trend-cyclical movement of data: 101, 102, 103, . . . , 112. The average for this twelve-month period is 106.5. With this data the index for any month will be higher or lower than 1. Taking February as an example, the index is 102/106.5 or .96. Hence, the ratio-to-same-year-average can produce an inappropriate seasonal index—one which is influenced by upward or downward trends in data.

This problem can be solved by modifying the present method and using an average based upon thirteen months data, with the month in question as the *middle* period. In other words, for each individual month, a new thirteen-month average would be computed and subsequently used to find the percentage relationship. For example, to compute an index for February 1970, we do the following.

1. Compute a monthly average using August 1969 through August 1970:

$$\text{Total} = 2.7 + 2.2 + 2.0 + 2.4 + 2.8 + 2.1 + \textcircled{2.0} + 2.1 + 2.3 + 2.5 + 2.6 + 2.7 + 2.5 = 30.9$$

$$\text{Average} = 30.9/13 = 2.38$$

2. Using 2.38 as the average sales, compute the percentage relationship between February 1970 sales and the average:

$$2.0/2.38 = .84$$

For March 1970, we compute an index from an average using September 1969 through September 1970. In other words, we create consecutive thirteen-month averages using the moving average method.[7] These averages are then compared against the middle month's sales when computing the seasonal index for that month. If the trend-cyclical movement is *approximately linear* within a year (that is, a gradually increasing or decreasing movement throughout the year), this movement is at its average level in the middle month. If our assumption of linearity holds true, we can eliminate the bias of a trend-cyclical movement and isolate only seasonal variation in our index. This can be demonstrated by referring once again to trend influenced data. For example, suppose the following actual data is available for April 19*x*1 through April 19*x*2: 101, 102, 103, . . . , 113. The average for this thirteen-month period is 107 (1,391/13). The seasonal index for the middle month—October—would be 107/107 or 1.0. Clearly, then, the ratio-to-moving-average removes the influence of trends. It does have the drawback, however, of requiring that we compute a new average each time an index is calculated.

An application of seasonal indexes involves the breaking down of our sales forecast for 19*x*1 into monthly budget estimates. By applying each index against the monthly average, as in Exhibit 23-12, we obtain each month's forecast.

EXHIBIT 23-12 COMPUTING MONTHLY BUDGET ESTIMATES FROM A YEARLY FORECAST

Month	Average Monthly Sales (based on yearly sales of 28.6 million)	Index of Seasonal Variation	Monthly Forecast
Jan.	2.385	.85	2.03
Feb.	2.385	.78	1.86
Mar.	2.385	.86	2.05
Apr.	2.385	.95	2.26
May	2.385	1.07	2.55
Jun.	2.385	1.12	2.67
Jul.	2.385	1.21	2.88
Aug.	2.385	1.14	2.72
Sept.	2.385	.93	2.22
Oct.	2.385	.86	2.05
Nov.	2.385	1.05	2.50
Dec.	2.385	1.18	2.81
	28.600	12.00	28.60

Another example is an application to moving average forecasting. With this method actual data used in the average is first *deseasonalized.* Deseasonalized sales are then used in the average to compute October's estimate. In doing so, however, the resulting forecast is itself deseasonalized. Hence, it must be *seasonalized* by using the appropriate index. For example, suppose we use a four-month's moving average for estimating October sales:

[7] Illustrated in chapter 22.

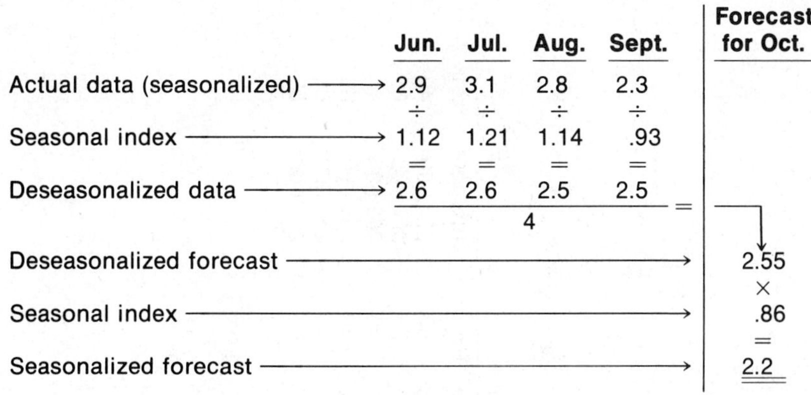

	Jun.	Jul.	Aug.	Sept.	Forecast for Oct.
Actual data (seasonalized) →	2.9	3.1	2.8	2.3	
	÷	÷	÷	÷	
Seasonal index →	1.12	1.21	1.14	.93	
	=	=	=	=	
Deseasonalized data →	2.6	2.6	2.5	2.5	
		4		=	
Deseasonalized forecast →					2.55
					×
Seasonal index →					.86
					=
Seasonalized forecast →					2.2

Had our actual data not been deseasonalized before computing the average, our estimate would have been 2.8 million—a possible error of .6 million. This would have accentuated our failure to consider underlying factors which generate sales revenue, and consequently, our failure to consider the possible variation in sales resulting from seasonal influences.

Seasonal indexes can again be applied to yet another structural forecasting method—correlation analysis. In this instance, before data is correlated it should be deseasonalized. The resulting functional equation will, of course, yield only deseasonalized forecasts. Nevertheless, all we need to do is seasonalize the outcome, as we did with moving average.

23.10 ANALYSIS OF CONSTRAINING FACTORS

With this analysis we are concerned with limitations or constraints on future operations, including such factors as: time, demand, plant capacity, financing, costs, and scheduling. There are two methodologies under which this type of analysis is best exploited—*simulation* and *optimization.* We will examine simulation as a technique and optimization as a group of techniques for solving either zero-sequence problems or network problems.

FORECASTING A RANGE OF OUTCOMES BY SIMULATION

With this method we continuously reevaluate a model until a stable pattern of behavior is discernible. The basis for any simulation is a model—a structural relationship between variables. One generally used business model is the *pro forma* income statement. Presented in basic form, its structure is:

$$P = S \times (U_m \times A) - [V \times (U_m \times A)] - F \qquad (1)$$

where

EXHIBIT 23-13 UNCERTAINTY OF FORECASTED OUTCOMES

	U_m		A		S		V		F	
	Outcome	**Prob.**	**Outcome**	**Prob.**	**Outcome**	**Prob.**	**Outcome**	**Prob.**	**Outcome**	**Prob.**
Most likely	2,800,000	.30	15	.40	8.00	1.00	7.25	.60	260,000	.40
Pessimistic	2,000,000	.05	10	.05			7.40	.05	300,000	.05
Lower quarter	2,300,000	.15	11.75	.05			7.30	.05	282,500	.10
Middle	2,600,000	.20	13.5	.10			7.20	.20	265,000	.35
Upper quarter	2,900,000	.25	15.25	.35			7.10	.05	247,500	.05
Optimistic	3,200,000	.05	17	.05			7.00	.05	230,000	.05

P = profit
S = selling price per unit
U_m = size of market in units
A = market share, percentage of market expected
V = variable cost per unit
F = total fixed cost

Suppose we have made the following forecasts representing the most likely outcomes:

Market Size (U_m) = 2,800,000
Market Share (A) = 15%
Selling Price (S) = \$8.00
Variable Cost (V) = \$7.25
Fixed Cost (F) = \$260,000

With the formula we compute projected profit as:

$$P = 8.00 \times (2{,}800{,}000 \times .15) - [7.25 \times (2{,}800{,}000 \times .15)] - 260{,}000$$
$$P = 8.00 \times 420{,}000 - (7.25 \times 420{,}000) - 260{,}000$$
$$P = \$55{,}000$$

The accuracy of our projected profit is dependent upon the eventual accuracy of our forecasted values. These values, we know, represent the most likely outcome. However, we are aware that variation is possible. Using the five-point estimation scheme presented in chapter 22, we can subjectively measure this variation, as shown by the results in Exhibit 23-13.

From this data we can complete Exhibit 23-14 by calculating the *expected value* of each variable. We do so by multiplying the outcome by its probability.

EXHIBIT 23-14 EXPECTED VALUES

	U_m Expected Value	A Expected Value	S Expected Value	V Expected Value	F Expected Value
Most likely	840,000	6.0000	8.00	4.350	104,000
Pessimistic	100,000	.5000		.370	15,000
Lower quarter	345,000	.5875		.365	28,250
Middle	520,000	1.3500		1.440	92,750
Upper quarter	725,000	5.3375		.355	12,380
Optimistic	160,000	.8500		.350	11,500
	2,690,000	14.6240	8.00	7.190	263,880

We compute our profit again:

$$P = 8.00 \times (2{,}690{,}000 \times .14624) - [7.19 \times (2{,}690{,}000 \times .14624)] - 263{,}880$$
$$P = 8.00 \times 393{,}386 - (7.19 \times 393{,}386) - 263{,}880$$
$$P = \$54{,}763$$

This analysis, while better than simply using the most likely values (mode), is still incomplete since it does not give the decision maker information concerning the uncertainty of the forecasted profit.

The procedure for obtaining this uncertainty is repeated random sampling. A single value is selected at random from each distribution and the forecasted profit is calculated. This process is repeated many times and the resulting profit is added to a frequency distribution in the appropriate interval. The resulting distribution indicates the percentage of trials in which profits fall within specific categories. Exhibit 23-15 summarizes the results.

EXHIBIT 23-15 DISTRIBUTION OF PROFITS RESULTING FROM RANDOM SAMPLING

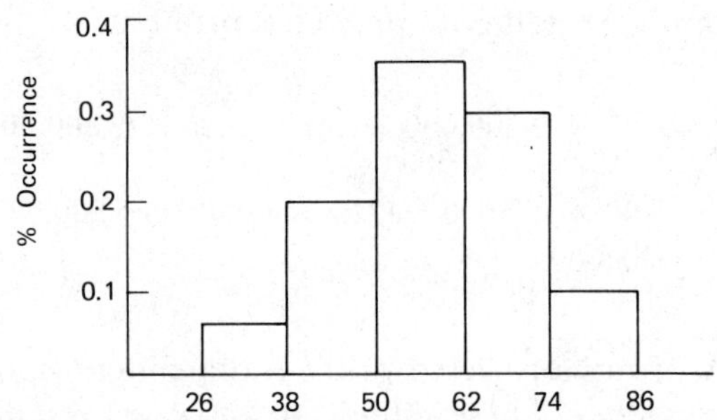

The decision maker is now in a position to evaluate potential profits while examining the possible contingencies or risk.

OPTIMIZATION

The basic process of optimization is presented in Exhibit 23-16.

Notice in this analysis that the criteria for choice are not the prerogatives of the decision maker, but parts of the information system itself. All possible choices are

EXHIBIT 23-16 THE OPTIMIZATION PROCESS

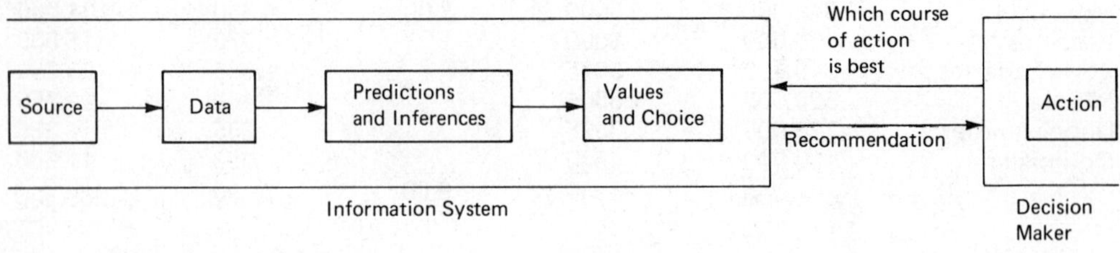

Diagram from Richard O. Mason, Jr., *Basic Concepts for Designing Management Information Systems,* AIS Research Paper #8 (Los Angeles: University of California, 1969), p. 12. Used with permission of the author.

examined and the final selection of the forecast is based upon its relation to all other factors. The value offering the greatest expected return is chosen as the optimizing criterion for the model of interrelated variables.

Zero-Sequence Problems

This group of problems is characterized by an isolated decision, independent of any previous decision and any probability distribution of outcomes resulting from that decision.

OPTIMALITY BY EXPECTED VALUES Demonstrating the usefulness of this technique, we examine an analysis of probable demand as it affects (1) budgeted production of a manufacturing firm, and (2) opening and closing times of a service business.

EXAMPLE 1: BUDGETING FOR PRODUCTION QUOTAS The owner of a small sandwich shop must decide on how many sandwiches to produce each day. He estimates it will cost him 18¢ per sandwich, and each sandwich may then be sold for 40¢. However, if the sandwich is not sold on the day it is made, there is a chance it can be sold the next day for 25¢. After the second day it must be thrown away.

The owner's experience with sandwiches leads him to formulate the following probable demand:

For New Sandwiches		For Day-Old Sandwiches	
Demand Per Day	**Probability**	**Demand Per Day**	**Probability**
less than 15	.00	1	.05
15	.10	2	.25
16	.20	3	.30
17	.45	4	.30
18	.15	5	.10
19	.10	6 or more	.00
20 or more	.00		

To decide on the best production, we must compare the expected value of each production possibility. First, however, we must compute the expected values for each possible number of leftover sandwiches and then, using these expected values, determine the expected value for each production possibility.

Expected Profit From Day-Old Sandwiches:

C.V. = conditional profit
E.V. = expected profit

		Leftover Possibilities									
Demand Per Day	**Probability**	**1**		**2**		**3**		**4**		**5**	
		C.V.	**E.V.**	**C.V.**	**E.V.**	**C.V.**	**E.V.**	**C.V.**	**E.V.**	**C.V.**	**E.V.**
1	.05	.07	.0035	−.11	−.0055	−.29	−.0145	−.47	−.0235	−.65	−.0325
2	.25	.07	.0175	.14	.0350	−.04	−.0100	−.22	−.0550	−.40	−.1000
3	.30	.07	.0210	.14	.0420	.21	.0630	.03	.0090	−.15	−.0450
4	.30	.07	.0210	.14	.0420	.21	.0630	.28	.0840	.10	.0300
5	.10	.07	.0070	.14	.0140	.21	.0210	.28	.0280	.35	.0350
Expected Value			.07		.1275		.1225		.0425		−.1125

For the next table, we compute the conditional value as the revenue from the old and new sandwiches. For instance, with a demand for sixteen and a production of eighteen, we add the expected value of two leftover sandwiches (.1275) to the revenue from selling sixteen new sandwiches (3.5200) and obtain the conditional value of 3.6475.

Expected Profit From Production of New Sandwiches:

Demand Per Day	Probability	15 C.V.	15 E.V.	16 C.V.	16 E.V.	17 C.V.	17 E.V.	18 C.V.	18 E.V.	19 C.V.	19 E.V.	20 C.V.	20 E.V.
15	.10	3.30	.3300	3.37	.3370	3.4275	.3428	3.4225	.3423	3.3425	.3343	3.1875	.3186
16	.20	3.30	.6600	3.52	.7040	3.5900	.7180	3.6475	.7295	3.6425	.7285	3.5625	.7125
17	.45	3.30	1.4850	3.52	1.5840	3.7400	1.6830	3.8100	1.7145	3.8675	1.7404	3.8625	1.7381
18	.15	3.30	.4950	3.52	.5280	3.7400	.5610	3.9600	.5940	4.0300	.6045	4.0875	.6131
19	.10	3.30	.3300	3.52	.3520	3.7400	.3740	3.9600	.3960	4.1800	.4180	4.2500	.4250
Expected Value			3.3000		3.5050		3.6788		3.7763		3.8257		3.8073

The solution is to select the production offering a higher expected profit than any other production. In this case we select a production of nineteen sandwiches, since it promises the highest daily profit over the long run. If the expected value continued to increase for each production selected, it would be necessary to continue examining the expected profit from higher and higher productions until the profit begins to drop off. At this point, the production corresponding to the highest expected value in the range would be selected as the optimizing production.

EXAMPLE 2: DETERMINING OPENING AND CLOSING TIMES Mr. Wash is planning the operation of his car washing facility for next year. He suspects that an adjustment of his opening and closing times might yield a higher profit. Presently, Mr. Wash is operating from 8 A.M. to 5 P.M. and is experiencing the following demand (for simplicity it is assumed that demand always totals in intervals of five):

Cars Per Day	Probability of Occurrence
25	.10
30	.35
35	.20
40	.20
45	.15

Also, he predicts that the following demands can be anticipated during each of the indicated hours:

From 7 A.M.–8 A.M. Cars	Prob.	From 8 A.M.–9 A.M. Cars	Prob.	From 4 P.M.–5 P.M. Cars	Prob.	From 5 P.M.–6 P.M. Cars	Prob.
4	.10	3	.15	2	.10	5	.05
5	.15	4	.25	3	.20	6	.10
6	.25	5	.35	4	.40	7	.35
7	.30	6	.15	5	.30	8	.25
8	.20	7	.10			9	.25

Mr. Wash charges $2.00 per car and 50¢ extra if the car is spray waxed. It has been Mr. Wash's experience that at least 1/2 the total cars each day request spray wax.

The daily operating costs consist of $20.00 in fixed costs per day and 60¢ per car.

From the information, what opening and closing times will produce the greatest profit if an eight-hour working day is used (one hour for lunch, making nine hours total)?

We should approach the solution by first determining the expected profit for an 8-to-5 operation and then the expected profit from each earlier and later time increment. From there, we can add the 7-to-8 increment and subtract the 4-to-5 increment from the 8-to-5 result, and obtain the 7-to-4 expected profit. For the 9-to-6 expected profit, we would add the 5-to-6 increment and subtract the 8-to-9 increment.[8]

First, let us compute the *conditional values* for each possible daily demand and incremental demand.

Cars Per Day	**2**	**3**	**4**	**5**	**6**	**7**	**8**	**9**	**25**	**30**	**35**	**40**	**45**
Rev. from Wash	4.00	6.00	8.00	10.00	12.00	14.00	16.00	18.00	50.00	60.00	70.00	80.00	90.00
Rev. from Wax	.50	.75	1.00	1.25	1.50	1.75	2.00	2.25	6.25	7.50	8.75	10.00	11.25
(Variable Exp.)	1.20	1.80	2.40	3.00	3.60	4.20	4.80	5.40	15.00	18.00	21.00	24.00	27.00
Conditional Value	3.30	4.95	6.60	8.25	9.90	11.55	13.20	14.85	41.25	49.50	57.75	66.00	74.25

1. Expected daily profit for an 8-to-5 operation:

Cars Per Day	**Prob. of Occurrence**	**Conditional Value**	**Expected Value**
25	.10	41.25	4.1250
30	.35	49.50	17.3250
35	.20	57.75	11.5500
40	.20	66.00	13.2000
45	.15	74.25	11.1375
		Expected value	57.3375
		Less: Fixed costs	20.0000
		Expected daily profit	37.3375

2. Expected daily profit for a 7-to-4 operation:

Incremental Daily Profit

Cars in 7–8 Increment	**Prob. of Occurrence**	**Conditional Value**	**Expected Value**
4	.10	6.60	.6600
5	.15	8.25	1.2375
6	.25	9.90	2.4750
7	.30	11.55	3.4650
8	.20	13.20	2.6400
		Expected profit for 7-to-8 increment =	10.4775

[8] Since the unit contribution margin is constant, cost and revenue can be considered irrelevant and a simpler alternative solution can be obtained using *expected cars* rather than expected profit.

Cars in 4–5 Increment	Prob. of Occurrence	C.V.	E.V.
2	.10	3.30	.3300
3	.20	4.95	.9900
4	.40	6.60	2.6400
5	.30	8.25	2.4750
	Expected profit for 4-to-5 increment =		6.4350

Expected daily profit for 8–5 operation	37.3375
Add: Expected daily profit for 7–8 increment	10.4775
	47.8150
Less: Expected daily profit for 4–5 increment	6.4350
Expected daily profit for 7–4 operation	41.3800

3. Expected daily profit for a 9-to-6 operation:

Incremental Daily Profit

Cars in 8–9 Increment	Prob. of Occurrence	C.V.	E.V.
3	.15	4.95	.7425
4	.25	6.60	1.6500
5	.35	8.25	2.8875
6	.15	9.90	1.4850
7	.10	11.55	1.1550
	Expected profit for 8-to-9 increment =		7.9200

Cars in 5–6 Increment	Prob. of Occurrence	C.V.	E.V.
5	.05	8.25	.4125
6	.10	9.90	.9900
7	.35	11.55	4.0425
8	.25	13.20	3.3000
9	.25	14.85	3.7125
	Expected profit for 5-to-6 increment =		12.4575

Expected daily profit for 8–5 operation	37.3375
Add: Expected daily profit for 5–6 increment	12.4575
	49.7950
Less: Expected daily profit for 8–9 increment	7.9200
Expected daily profit for 9–6 operation	41.8750

From the results of this analysis, Mr. Wash should plan to operate from 9 until 6 if he chooses to maximize his daily earnings in the long run.

Further refinements of Example 2 are possible. For instance, if Mr. Wash is only interested in a short-run analysis, he should choose to operate from 7 until 4 based upon the *modal values* of each distribution:

1. Expected daily profit for an 8-to-5 operation:

Modal conditional profit	49.50
Less: Fixed costs	20.00
Expected daily profit	29.50

2. Expected daily profit for a 7-to-4 operation:

Expected daily profit for an 8-to-5 operation	29.50
Add: Modal conditional value for 7-to-8 increment	11.55
	41.05
Less: Modal conditional value for 4-to-5 increment	6.60
Expected daily profit for a 7-to-4 operation	34.45

3. Expected daily profit for a 9-to-6 operation:

Expected daily profit for an 8-to-5 operation	29.50
Add: Modal conditional value for 5-to-6 increment	11.55
	41.05
Less: Modal conditional value for 8-to-9 increment	8.25
Expected daily profit for a 9-to-6 operation	32.80

Additionally, rather than giving a $20 fixed cost figure we could have given a range of possible fixed costs. The same could be said for the variable cost of 60¢ per car. In this case it would have been necessary first to compute an expected value for both fixed and variable costs before proceeding with the solution.

Other Zero-Sequence Techniques

Other common methods employed in solving zero-sequence problems are as follows:

LINEAR AND DYNAMIC PROGRAMMING An equation called an *objective function* is either maximized or minimized. This functional equation relates either the total profit or total cost, respectively, to its component parts—profit per unit or cost per unit. For instance, given the profit equation: $P = 1{,}000X_1 + 1{,}800X_2$, we would attempt to maximize P by selecting the optimal production combination of X_1 and X_2 given any scale-of-plant limitations. These scale-of-plant and other similar limitations are called *constraints.* By expressing the constraints as equations and solving them simultaneously, along with the objective function, the optimal production of both X_1 and X_2 will result.

With linear programming the objective function and all constraints are linear. That is, the cost or profit per unit and available resources are expected to remain constant over the range of production possibilities. With dynamic programming, on the other hand, the objective function and/or the constraints may be nonlinear. That is, the objective function may contain no constants and hence appears as:

$$P = c_iX_1 + c_iX_2 \quad or \quad P = \sum_{i=1}^{2} \sum_{j=1}^{n} c_jX_i$$

Instead of the constants 1,000 and 1,800 per unit, the profit per unit now depends upon the level of chosen production. Contributing factors may include decreased overhead allocation per unit or variable cost reductions because of raw material quantity discounts. Due to the enormous number of possible production combinations, problems of this type generally are not amenable to hand calculation.

Consequently, usually both linear and dynamic programming problems are solved by computer programs.

TRANSPORTATION METHOD AND ASSIGNMENT SOLUTION These methods are a special application of linear programming and have been discussed in chapters 15 and 16.

ECONOMIC ORDER QUANTITY (EOQ) MODELS Inventory is budgeted by considering the following factors:

1. Production needs
2. Planned ending inventory
3. Safety stocks
4. Carrying costs
5. Ordering costs
6. Lead times for placing orders
7. Quantity discounts

These factors were combined in chapter 12 into what was called an *economic order quantity.* This quantity is really a budget figure based on forecasted data. It represents the order size resulting in minimum inventory cost. The trade-off between carrying costs and ordering costs is examined by comparing the resulting total cost from each order size. The order size yielding the minimum cost per unit is selected, and the figures accompanying such selection are then used as budget figures.

Multiple-Sequence or Network Problems

Some operational budgeting has a *task orientation.* That is, a series of *events* culminate in a completed task. The *activity* leading to each event, and the time for completing such activity, is the focus of budgeting. Each event is laid out in sequence and tied together by a *network* of activities, as introduced in chapter 2.

The most popular network technique is PERT/COST (Program Evaluation and Review Technique). This method budgets the *completion time* of each activity by observing the constraint imposed by a fixed completion date. The penalty cost of not finishing on time is compared with the minimized cost of reducing the completion time of individual activities.

The first step in our network analysis is the estimation of completion times for each activity. The most popular method involves a three-point estimation scheme discussed in chapter 22. With this scheme, we give three time estimates – pessimistic, most likely, and optimistic. Using *expected value analysis* (also discussed in chapter 22), we combine these estimates into an *expected completion time.* For instance, suppose we are budgeting for the task shown by the network in Exhibit 23-17. Each event is indicated by a letter, while the activities are indicated by arrows. The expected completion time for each activity is also indicated.

The network in Exhibit 23-17 shows three paths to the completion of the final event:

Path 1: A-B-E-F
Path 2: A-B-D-F
Path 3: A-C-D-F

The expected time for each path is the sum of the expected times for each activity constituting the path:

Path 1: A-B-E-F = 2 + 3 + 3 = 8 days
Path 2: A-B-D-F = 2 + 5 + 6 = 13 days
Path 3: A-C-D-F = 4 + 4 + 6 = 14 days

EXHIBIT 23-17 SIX-EVENT NETWORK

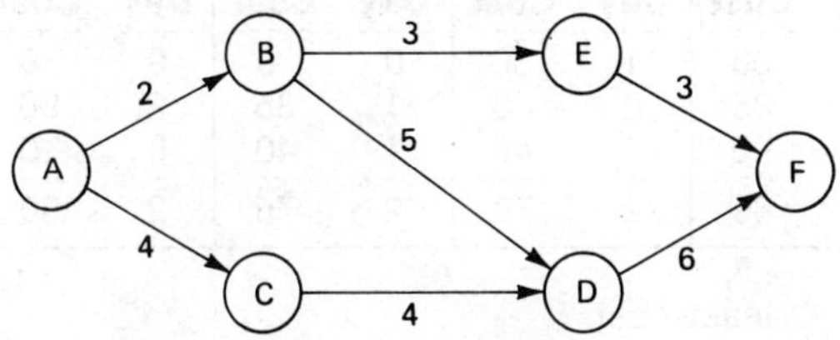

The *critical path* is the one having the highest expected completion time—*Path 3.* It is this path which sets the completion time for the task. In our example, the task cannot be completed before fourteen days unless we somehow reduce the time taken by activities on the critical path.

This reduction is possible by concentrating available resources into a given activity. For instance, working longer shifts, hiring more employees, and subcontracting are all possible ways of reducing expected completion times. By calculating the cost of reducing each activity, we can choose to reduce the time of those activities which, when taken in total, constitute the least-cost alternative.

Suppose the task must be completed in eleven days. In this instance, we must eliminate a *slack* of three days—the difference between the critical path completion time and the scheduled task completion time. This slack is not made up by simply reducing Path 3 by three days, for in doing so Path 2 becomes the *new critical path,* and the expected task completion time is only reduced to thirteen days, not eleven. The new critical path—Path 2—must subsequently be reduced by two days. In this example, the complication appears minor; however, in a task involving hundreds of possible paths, the problem could become enormous.

EXHIBIT 23-18 ADDITIONAL COST TO REDUCE ACTIVITY TIME (CUMULATIVE COSTS)

	Reduce by:					
Activity	**1 Day**	**2 Days**	**3 Days**	**4 Days**	**5 Days**	**6 Days**
A-B	30					
A-C	45	95	120			
B-E	35	80				
B-D	35	90	130	170		
C-D	30	70	145			
D-F	40	85	125	180	235	
E-F	50	110				

Suppose further that Exhibit 23-18 contains the costs of reducing the activities of our six-event network. We hope to reduce our critical path to eleven days by using the least amount of additional resources. We do so by examining the total cost of each possible combination of activity reductions on the critical path and on each potential critical path. Three steps are involved:

STEP 1: Determine the *least-cost combination* of activity reduction for each path whose expected completion time exceeds the scheduled completion time.

Path 2 (reduce by two days)[9]

	1st Trial		2nd Trial		3rd Trial		4th Trial		5th Trial	
Activity	**Day**	**Cost**	**Day**	**Cost**	**Day**	**Cost**	**Day**	**Cost**	**Day**	**Cost**
A-B	1	30	1	30	0	0	0	0	0	0
B-D	1	35	0	0	1	35	2	90	0	0
D-F	0	0	1	40	1	40	0	0	2	85
	2	65	2	70	2	75	2	90	2	85

↖ least-cost combination

Path 3 (reduce by three days)

	1st Trial		2nd Trial		3rd Trial		4th Trial		5th Trial	
Activity	**Day**	**Cost**	**Day**	**Cost**	**Day**	**Cost**	**Day**	**Cost**	**Day**	**Cost**
A–C	1	45	2	95	2	95	1	45	1	45
C–D	1	30	1	30	0	0	0	0	2	70
D–F	1	40	0	0	1	40	2	85	0	0
	3	115	3	125	3	135	3	130	3	115

	6th Trial		7th Trial		8th Trial		9th Trial		10th Trial	
Activity	**Day**	**Cost**	**Day**	**Cost**	**Day**	**Cost**	**Day**	**Cost**	**Day**	**Cost**
A–C	0	0	0	0	3	120	0	0	0	0
C–D	2	70	1	30	0	0	3	145	0	0
D–F	1	40	2	85	0	0	0	0	3	125
	3	110	3	115	3	120	3	145	3	125

↖ least-cost combination

Summarize the activities to be reduced and compute a total:

Activity	Reduced by	Cost
C–D	2 days	70
D–F	1 day	40
A–B	1 day	30
B–D	1 day	35
		175

[9] All activities are necessary to complete the task; therefore, no activity may be reduced to zero. Consequently, a two-day reduction of activity A-B is not a possible combination.

STEP 2: Determine if there are any *common activities.* In this example, D–F is common to Paths 2 and 3. Looking again at our possible activity reduction combinations, for each path with a common activity, select the least-cost combination that contains a reduction in the common activity.

First, look at combinations with a reduction of one day in the common activity, and select the least-cost combinations:

Path 2: select the 2nd trial

Path 3: select the 6th trial

Summarize the activities to be reduced on each path (eliminating the redundancy of the common activity):

Activity	Reduced by	Cost
C–D	2 days	70
A–B	1 day	30
D–F	1 day	40
		140*

**Note:* In those instances where the common activity is not found in all the paths in Step 1 the least-cost combination of those paths without the common activity must be part of the summarization at this point.

Second, look at combinations with a reduction of two days in the common activity, and select the least-cost combinations:

Path 2: select the 5th trial

Path 3: select the 7th trial

Again, summarize the activities to be reduced on each path (eliminating the redundancy of the common activity):

Activity	Reduced by	Cost
C–D	1 day	30
D–F	2 days	85
		115

Third, look at combinations with a reduction of three days in the common activity, and select the least-cost combinations:

Path 2: no trial for three-day reduction

Path 3: select the 10th trial

Again, summarize the activities to be reduced on each path (eliminating the redundancy of the common activity):

Activity	Reduced by	Cost
D–F	3 days	125
		125

Continue the process of selecting combinations until reaching a proposed reduction in the common activity which is unavailable in any trials. At this point, the process stops and the *least-cost* summary of all the tries is chosen. In this example, the second try produced the least cost of $115.

STEP 3: *Compare* the total least cost from Step 1 with the total least cost from Step 2. The *solution* involves a reduction of the common activity D–F:

Activity	Reduce by	Cost
C–D	1 day	30
D–F	2 days	85
		$115

You should understand that this analysis is greatly simplified, since the addition of many more activities and/or longer expected completion times makes hand calculation impractical and computer calculation a necessity. In addition, other factors were purposely left out of our initial discussion:

1. *Reducing expected times by taking resources from one activity and using in another.* For instance, if we reduce activity D-F by three days, Path A-B-D-F will have a slack of one day. This means that, if possible, resources should be diverted from activities A-B and B-D into activity D-F. Also, since Path A-B-E-F now has a slack of three days, a similar diversion should be contemplated.
2. *Calculating the probability of finishing on schedule.* We know that reducing the expected completion time down to the scheduled time only gives us, at best, a 50% probability of completing on schedule. If we consider the expected time to be the mode, and the distribution of possible completion times to be symmetrical, then 50% of the completion times will be higher than our most likely outcome (expected value). Consequently, if we desire a higher probability of finishing on schedule, we must continue attempts at reducing the expected completion time. Finding our *confidence percentage* (that is, our probability of finishing on schedule) involves approximating a standard deviation for the critical path each time expected activity time is reduced. By expressing the difference between the scheduled completion time and our expected completion time as a fraction of the standard deviation, we observe that the probability of finishing on time is the area under the *normal curve* lying to the *left* of this point. The area to the left represents the completion of the task in less time than specified. In other words, this fraction represents the positioning of the scheduled completion time relative to the expected completion time, assuming a normal distribution of possible variation around the expected completion time.

We know from basic statistics that if the variation is normally distributed, the probability of achieving a scheduled completion time can be expressed by the position of the standard deviation relative to the mean time (expected completion time) as shown in Exhibit 23-19 and summarized in the table in Exhibit 23-20. The percentage indicates the area under the normal curve to the left of the indicated point, or, in other words, all those completion times which satisfy the deadline requirement. For example, using the table in Exhibit 23-20, a scheduled completion time which is 1.4 standard deviations above the expected completion time indicates that there is a 92% probability of finishing on schedule.

EXHIBIT 23-19 PROBABILITY OF COMPLETING ON SCHEDULE AS SHOWN BY THE DEVIATION AROUND THE EXPECTED COMPLETION TIME

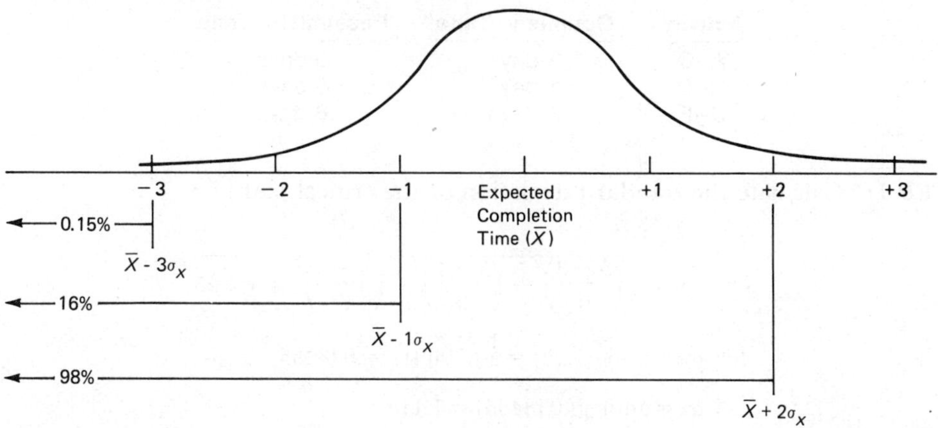

EXHIBIT 23-20 TABLE OF AREAS UNDER THE NORMAL CURVE TO THE LEFT OF SELECTED STANDARD DEVIATIONS

σx	%	σx	%	σx	%	σx	%	σx	%	σx	%
−2.9	00.2	−1.9	03	−0.9	18	0.0	50	1.0	84	2.0	98
−2.8	00.3	−1.8	04	−0.8	21	0.1	54	1.1	86	2.1	98
−2.7	00.3	−1.7	04	−0.7	24	0.2	58	1.2	88	2.2	99
−2.6	00.5	−1.6	05	−0.6	27	0.3	62	1.3	90	2.3	99
−2.5	01	−1.5	07	−0.5	31	0.4	66	1.4	92	2.4	99
−2.4	01	−1.4	08	−0.4	34	0.5	69	1.5	93	2.5	99
−2.3	01	−1.3	10	−0.3	38	0.6	73	1.6	95	2.6	99.5
−2.2	01	−1.2	12	−0.2	42	0.7	76	1.7	96	2.7	99.7
−2.1	02	−1.1	14	−0.1	46	0.8	79	1.8	96	2.8	99.7
−2.0	02	−1.0	16	−0.0	50	0.9	82	1.9	97	2.9	99.8

The standard deviation can be estimated by using the optimistic and pessimistic times of each activity on the critical path. The formula is as follows:[10]

$$\text{(standard deviation) } \sigma x = \sqrt{\sum \left(\frac{t_{pi} - t_{oi}}{6}\right)^2}$$

where

[10]Users of PERT have found that time estimates usually follow a beta distribution. Consequently, because of the weighting scheme for calculating expected activity time, the standard deviation is computed as shown.

t_{pi} = pessimistic time
t_{oi} = optimistic time

Using this formula, and computing the standard deviation for Path 3, we can obtain the probability of finishing on schedule if our expected completion time is left unaltered at fourteen days, and the pessimistic and optimistic times of Exhibit 23-21 are made available.

EXHIBIT 23-21 PESSIMISTIC AND OPTIMISTIC TIMES FOR ACTIVITIES ON THE CRITICAL PATH

Activity	Optimistic Time	Pessimistic Time
A–C	3 days	5 days
C–D	1 day	5 days
D–F	3 days	8 days

STEP 1: Calculate the standard deviation of the critical path:

$$\sigma x = \sqrt{\left(\frac{5-3}{6}\right)^2 + \left(\frac{5-1}{6}\right)^2 + \left(\frac{8-3}{6}\right)^2} = \sqrt{1.25}$$

$$\log \sigma x = \frac{1}{2}\log(1.25) = \frac{1}{2}(.09691) = .048455$$

$$\sigma x = \text{antilog}(.048455) = 1.118$$

STEP 2: Calculate the difference between the scheduled completion time of eleven days and the expected completion time of fourteen days as a percent of the standard deviation:

$$z = (t_s - t_e)/\sigma x$$
$$z = (11 - 14)/1.118 = \underline{\underline{-2.68}}$$

From the table in Exhibit 23-20, we see that a result of −2.7 standard deviations gives us a .3% probability of finishing on schedule, assuming no adjustment of our original critical path expected completion time. In other words, there is a 99.7% probability of taking longer than eleven days to complete the task.[11]

23.11 SENSITIVITY ANALYSIS APPLIED TO OUTPUT

The basic process of sensitivity analysis is presented in Exhibit 23-22.

With this analysis, a basic structure of relationships among variables is assumed to exist. The criteria for choice are the prerogatives of the decision maker, as opposed to optimization, in which the criteria are part of the information system itself. The decision maker inquires "what if" variables assume certain values, "then" what affect will it have on the outcome of the process. In other words, it is an analysis

[11]Alternatively, we could decide on our desired confidence percentage first and then calculate the required task completion time by simply rearranging our formula: $t_e = t_s - z\sigma x$.

EXHIBIT 23-22 SENSITIVITY ANALYSIS

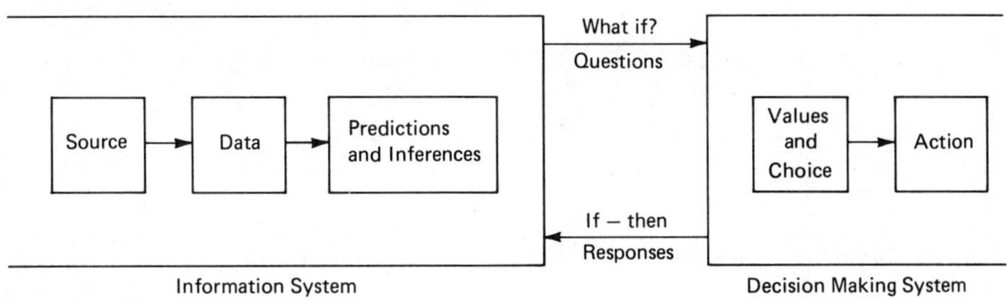

Diagram from: Mason, *Basic Concepts*, p. 8. Used with permission of the author.

to determine the sensitivity of input variables upon selected output variables, and to isolate those having the greatest impact. For instance, using our profit formula from p. 1009 and Exhibit 23-13, let us examine the change in profit resulting when one variable assumes first its pessimistic value and then its optimistic value, while holding all other variables at their most likely values:

Sensitivity to Pessimistic Values

Variable Changed	Profit	Change	Percent
No change	$55,000	0	0
Market size (U_m)	−35,000	−90,000	−163%
Market share (A)	−50,000	−105,000	−191%
Selling price (S)	55,000	0	0
Variable cost (V)	−8,000	−63,000	−115%
Fixed cost (F)	15,000	−40,000	−73%

Sensitivity to Optimistic Values

Variable Changed	Profit	Change	Percent
No change	$ 55,000	0	0
Market size (U_m)	100,000	45,000	82%
Market share (A)	97,000	42,000	76%
Selling price (S)	55,000	0	0
Variable cost (V)	160,000	105,000	191%
Fixed cost (F)	85,000	30,000	35%

The relative variability of each variable can be diagrammed as in Exhibit 23-23. The length of the line indicates the possible spread between the pessimistic and optimistic profit.

Variable cost, market share, and market size appear to be very influential variables. Each may inflict drastic changes in profit if the worst possible outcomes occur. These are the variables which require careful investigation and possibly should be controlled to assure adequate profit.

One large national accounting firm has developed a computerized sensitivity model in which forecasted financial statements can be generated from past financial data.[12] Currently, they are offering this service through interaction with an on-line computer terminal. The client may selectively alter certain input values and observe

[12] Delphi-XX by Arthur Young & Company.

EXHIBIT 23-23 SPREAD BETWEEN PESSIMISTIC AND OPTIMISTIC PROFIT

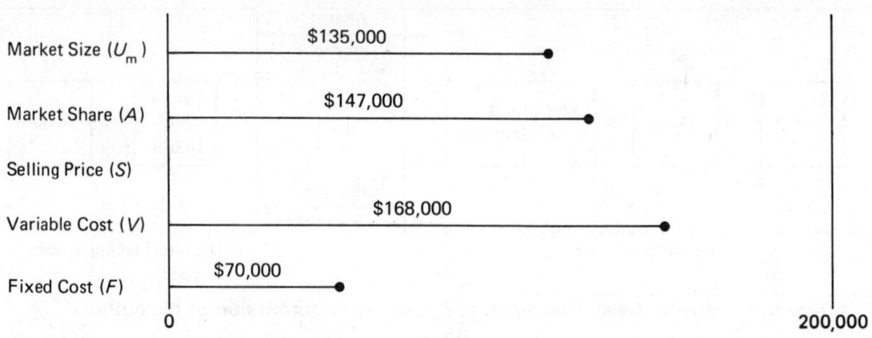

the consequences on the financial statements. Thus he may take note of those variables having significant financial impact and may subsequently plan acceptable solutions.

23.12 SUMMARY

Efficient operation is maintained by using responsibility accounting—the reporting of budget and actual figures via performance reports. These reports contain figures derived from flexible budget formulas.

The budgeting system consists of sales forecasts as inputs and operating budgets representing the transformation into *pro forma* statements. Formal operating budgets can take either of two formats—functional or program. *Functional budgeting* prepares a budget for each discrete aspect of the total operating activity. *Program budgeting* identifies the principle sub-goals of the organization and budgets for the program specifically designed to reach that goal. Both types culminate in the construction of a master operating budget.

The budgeting process describes the entry of forecasted and analyzed data into the budgeting system. Three entry points are used—input, transformation, and output. Before entering, forecasted data must often be subjected to a pre-budget analysis.

Input data, forecasted by a structural method, should be adjusted for seasonal variation. The adjustment is achieved by using seasonal indexes computed by either of two methods—ratio-to-same-year-average or ratio-to-moving-average. These indexes are used to deseasonalize actual data and seasonalize forecasted data.

Another budgetary analysis deals with constraints on future operations, such as demand and plant capacity. Two methodologies are exploited in this analysis—simulation and optimization. Through simulation we formulate a range of outcomes resulting from a business model. With optimization we compare all feasible alternatives and select that alternative offering the greatest expected return relative to all others. Two problem types are handled—zero-sequence and network. Zero-sequence problems are characterized by isolated decisions, as opposed to network problems, which handle decisions whose outcomes are dependent upon a previous decision or a probability distribution of outcomes resulting from that decision. Zero-sequence problems are solved by expected value analysis and network problems by PERT/COST analysis.

The final method of budgetary analysis examines the sensitivity of input variables upon selected output variables and isolates those having the greatest impact.

CHAPTER 23 REFERENCES AND ADDITIONAL READINGS

Alexis, Marcus, and Wilson, Charles Z. *Organizational Decision Making.* Englewood Cliffs, N.J.: Prentice-Hall, Inc., 1967.

Anthony, Robert N. *Planning and Control Systems: A Framework for Analysis.* Cambridge, Mass.: Harvard University Press, 1965.

Bacon, Jeremy. *Managing the Budget Function.* Business Policy Study No. 131. New York: National Industrial Conference Board, 1970.

Bierman, Harold Jr. and others. *Quantitative Analysis for Business Decisions.* Homewood, Ill.: Richard D. Irwin, 1965.

Bradley, Hugh E. "Setting and Controlling Budgets with Regression Analysis." *Management Accounting,* November 1969, pp. 31–34.

Corcoran, A. Wayne. *Mathematical Applications in Accounting.* New York: Harcourt, Brace & World, Inc., 1968.

Corporate Planning Through Simulation. New York: Lybrand, Ross Bros. & Montgomery, n.d.

DeCoster, Don T., and Fertakis, John P. "Budget-Induced Pressure and Its Relationship to Supervisory Behavior." *Journal of Accounting Research,* Autumn 1968, pp. 237–46.

Dopuch, Nicholas, and Birnberg, Jacob G. *Cost Accounting: Accounting Data for Management's Decisions.* New York: Harcourt, Brace & World, Inc., 1969.

Groves, Roger; Manes, Rene; and Sorenson, Robert. "The Application of the Hirsh-Danzig 'Fixed Charge' Algorithm to Profit Planning: A Formal Statement of Product Profitability Analysis." *The Accounting Review,* July 1970, pp. 481–89.

Heckert, J. Brooks, and Willson, James D. *Business Budgeting and Control.* New York: The Ronald Press Company, 1967.

Hitch, Charles J. "Program Budgeting." *Datamation,* September 1967, pp. 37–40.

Horngren, Charles T. *Accounting for Management Control.* Englewood Cliffs, N.J.: Prentice-Hall, Inc., 1970.

———. *Cost Accounting: A Managerial Emphasis.* Englewood Cliffs, N.J.: Prentice-Hall, Inc., 1967.

Ijiri, Yuji. *Management Goals and Accounting for Control.* Skokie, Ill.: Rand McNally Co., 1965.

Ijiri, Y., and Thompson, Gerald L. "Applications of Mathematical Control Theory to Accounting and Budgeting (The Continuous Wheat Trading Model)." *The Accounting Review,* April 1970, pp. 246–58.

Jones, Reginald L., and Trentin, George. *Budgeting: Key to Planning and Control.* New York: American Management Association, Inc., 1966.

Knight, W. D., and Weinwurm, E. H. *Managerial Budgeting.* New York: The Macmillan Company, 1964.

Lev, Baruch. "Testing a Prediction Method for Multivariate Budgets." *Empirical Research in Accounting: Selected Studies 1969,* Supplement to Volume 7 of the *Journal of Accounting Research,* pp. 182.197.

Levin, Richard I., and Kirkpatrick, Charles A. *Planning and Control with PERT/CPM.* New York: McGraw-Hill Book Company, 1966.

Lyden, Fremon J., and Miller, Ernest G. *Planning Programming Budgeting: A Systems Approach to Management.* Chicago: Markham Publishing Company, 1968.

McMillan, Claude, and Gonzalez, Richard F. *Systems Analysis: A Computer Approach to Decision Models.* Homewood, Ill.: Richard D. Irwin, Inc., 1965.

Mastromano, Frank M. "Information Technology Applied to Profit Planning." *Management Accounting,* October 1968, pp. 22–25.

Novick, David. "Long-Range Planning Through Program Budgeting." *Business Horizons,* February 1969, pp. 59–65.

Omlor, John J. "Management Information System for Planning, Forecasting and Budgeting." *Management Accounting,* March 1970, pp. 13–16.

Pryor, LeRoy J. "Simulation: Budgeting for a 'What if. . . .'" *Journal of Accountancy,* November 1970, pp. 59–63.

Rappaport, Alfred. *Information for Decision Making.* Englewood Cliffs, N.J.: Prentice-Hall, Inc., 1970.

Sadowsky, Daniel M. "A Primer in Flexible Budgeting." *Budgeting,* May–June 1967, pp. 18–21.

Schiff, Michael, and Lewin, Arie Y. "Where Traditional Budgeting Fails." *The Financial Executive,* May 1968, pp. 51–62.

Simmons, John K., and Gray, Jack. "An Investigation of the Effect of Differing Accounting Frameworks on the Prediction of Net Income." *The Accounting Review,* October 1969, pp. 757–76.

Sord, B. H., and Welsch, Glen A. *Business Budgeting.* New York: Controllership Foundation, Inc., 1958.

Stedry, A. C. *Budget Control and Cost Behavior.* Englewood Cliffs, N.J.: Prentice-Hall, Inc., 1960.

CHAPTER 23 QUESTIONS, PROBLEMS, AND CASES

23- 1. Distinguish between *fixed* and *flexible* budgeting. If the budgeted level of activity is not attained, explain the inappropriateness of comparing actual performance against a budget based upon anticipated production.

23- 2. Distinguish between *functional* and *program* budgeting. What are the main drawbacks of each?

23- 3. Define or explain the use of the following terms and phrases:
- (a) Performance report
- (b) Variable costs
- (c) Fixed costs
- (d) Controllable variance
- (e) "Relevant range"
- (f) Scale of activity
- (g) Discretionary cost
- (h) Committed cost
- (i) *Pro forma* financial statements
- (j) Master budget
- (k) Line items
- (l) "The budgeting process"
- (m) Seasonal variation

23- 4. Explain the concept of *responsibility accounting.*

23- 5. With fixed budgeting, explain how underproduction could lead to favorable variances.

23- 6. "Instead of formalizing the flexible budget into budgets for each possible production level, a more advantageous expression is a budget formula." What is a budget formula and how is it constructed? "This formula is valid so long as actual production activity falls within a normal or relevant range." Explain why the budget formula is not applicable when actual production falls outside the relevant range.

23- 7. Explain a *discretionary cost* and a *committed cost* as they relate to the concept of controllability.

23- 8. "Direct materials may contain a hundred different items of material, each used in different proportions, each with a different price, and each with a different activity base." How does this fact relate to the problem of constructing budget formulae? On a practical basis, are budgets conceived from formulae based upon diverse activity bases? Why? What activity base is used for budget formulae in a standard cost system?

23- 9. "Budgets are used to control the internal operations of a business, and thus should be expressed in terms most meaningful to persons in charge of operations." Explain what is meant by this statement.

23-10. The ratio-to-same-year-average method of calculating seasonal indexes does not adjust for *trend-cyclical* movement of data. What is a trend-cyclical movement and what effect does it have on indexes produced by this method?

23-11. Give an example illustrating the computation of a seasonal index using the moving average method.

23-12. "Budgets represent an emulated transformation – that is, a duplication of the actual system expected to exist during the budgeting period as well as the *state* of such transformation at discrete time intervals." Explain what is meant by this statement. How is control achieved through the use of budgets?

23-13. Distinguish between *operating* and *financial* budgets. How does the budgeting system output ultimately reveal the focus of each budget? Identify the typical supporting schedules or sub-budgets of each budget.

23-14. Why is functional budgeting referred to as *vertical budgeting* and program budgeting referred to as *horizontal budgeting?*

23-15. "Functional budgeting is not operationally oriented." Explain.

23-16. Distinguish between *seasonalized* and *deseasonalized* data.

23-17. Distinguish between *zero-sequence* and *multiple-sequence* problems.

23-18. The construction of operating budgets can be approached from three directions. The approaches correspond to the entry of *forecasted* and *analyzed data* into the budgeting process. Identify the three approaches and explain what type of data enters through each.

23-19. What are three specific uses of seasonal indexes?

23-20. Explain the procedure for computing a seasonal index using:
(a) Ratio-to-same-year-average
(b) Ratio-to-moving-average

23-21. If the zero-sequence *sandwich shop example* had determined production from a computation using *modal* demand, would the answer have varied? Which analysis do you prefer? Why?

23-22. What is the procedure for calculating a confidence percentage?

23-23. Define the following PERT terms and concepts:
(a) Critical path
(b) Event
(c) Activity
(d) Expected completion time
(e) Slack
(f) Confidence percentage

23-24. What is *sensitivity analysis?* Give an example.

23-25. Explain what is meant by *pre-budget analysis.* Define and explain the use of the following methods of pre-budget analysis.
(a) Seasonal indexes
(b) Simulation
(c) Expected values
(d) Linear programming
(e) Dynamic programming
(f) Economic order quantity
(g) PERT/COST
(h) Sensitivity analysis

23-26. Deseasonalizing data before applying a structured forecasting technique results in a forecast that is itself deseasonalized. Describe the adjustment that must be applied to this value before it becomes an acceptable forecast.

23-27. How do we reduce the critical path time? Why must we compare our final least-cost alternative with the cost of reducing only common activities?

23-28. Identify the parts of the optimization process:

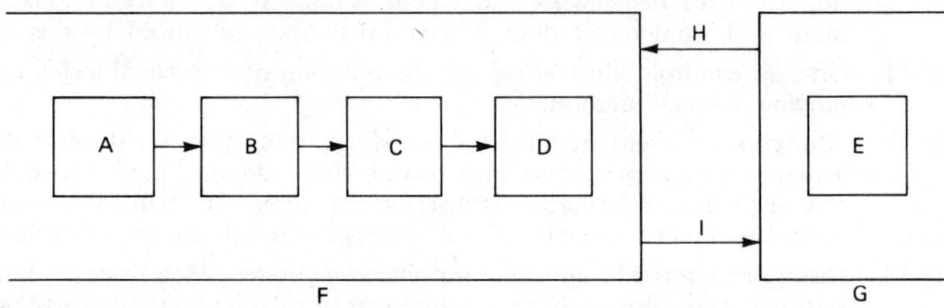

23-29. How is *expected completion time* calculated with PERT/COST analysis?

23-30. Identify the parts of a diagram depicting sensitivity analysis:

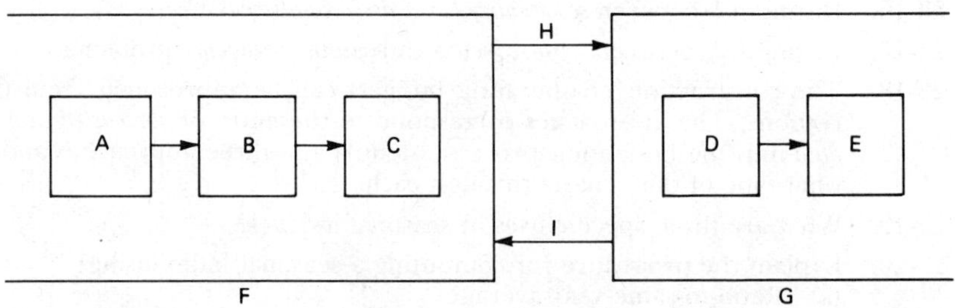

23-31. With sensitivity analysis, the criteria for choice are the prerogative of the decision maker. With optimization the criteria are part of the information system itself. Explain and discuss the significance of this difference.

23-32. What two methodologies are used for analyzing constraining factors?

23-33. "The construction of a *pro forma* income statement using expected values is better than simply using modal values, but is still incomplete since it does not give the decision maker information concerning the uncertainty of the forecasted profit." Explain the procedure for calculating this uncertainty.

23-34. ***EXPECTED VALUE ANALYSIS—SIMULATION*** The Hafter Company used correlation analysis to estimate the basic components of a *pro forma* income statement for 19*x*1:

Market size:	980,000 units
Market share:	28%
Selling price:	$3.40 per unit
Variable cost:	$1.90 per unit
Fixed cost:	$380,000

The Hafter Company is aware that some variation from these estimates is possible. Using the Delphi process, the variation was subjectively measured by a poll of the sales and production staff. The results of the Delphi measurement is as follows:

Values	Market Size		Market Share		Variable Cost		Fixed Cost	
	Outcome	Prob.	Outcome	Prob.	Outcome	Prob.	Outcome	Prob.
Pessimistic	560,000	.05	10	.05	2.05	.05	450,000	.05
Lower quarter	770,000	.10	20	.15	1.90	.35	428,750	.05
Middle value	980,000	.60	30	.25	1.75	.30	407,500	.10
Upper quarter	1,190,000	.20	40	.20	1.60	.25	386,250	.35
Optimistic	1,400,000	.05	50	.05	1.45	.05	365,000	.05
Correlation analysis	980,000	.60	28	.30	1.90	.35	380,000	.40

Required:

(a) Compute the projected profit based on the values obtained from correlation analysis (the modal values).
(b) Compute the projected profit based on the *expected* outcome of each income statement component.
(c) Explain how a simulation analysis can be used to determine the *uncertainty* of the *forecasted profit.*

23-35. ***SEASONAL ADJUSTMENT OF FORECASTS*** From an examination of prior sales records the following seasonal indexes were computed using the ratio-to-same-year-average method:

Month	Seasonal Index
Jan.	1.20
Feb.	1.08
Mar.	1.10
April	.99
May	.86
June	.78
July	.73
Aug.	.85
Sept.	.94
Oct.	1.08
Nov.	1.17
Dec.	1.22

The actual sales data for the last ten months is as follows:

	Month	Actual Sales
19*x*1	Aug.	$343,000
	Sept.	382,000
	Oct.	460,000
	Nov.	478,000
	Dec.	507,000
19*x*2	Jan.	501,000
	Feb.	450,000
	March	435,000
	April	408,000
	May	350,000

Required:

(a) Forecast the sales for June 19x2, using an eight-month moving average:
   (1) Adjusted for seasonal variation.
   (2) Unadjusted for seasonal variation.

(b) Forecast the sales for June 19x2, using a ten-month moving average adjusted for seasonal variation, and assuming that X_1 (current observation) is weighted 30%, X_2 is weighted 20%, and X_3 is weighted 10%.

(c) Forecast the sales for July 19x2, using an eight-month moving average adjusted for seasonal variation, assuming June sales are $338,000.

(d) Forecast the sales for June 19x2, using exponential smoothing adjusted for seasonal variation, assuming the old forecast was $362,000 and the smoothing constant is:
   (1) .25
   (2) .75

(e) Using least squares correlation analysis, determine the first degree polynomial equation that represents the best fit to the:
   (1) Unadjusted historical data.
   (2) Seasonally adjusted data.

(f) Which correlation equation from part (e) provides the most acceptable forecasts. Why?

(g) Using the correlation equation determined from seasonally adjusted data, what is the seasonally adjusted forecast for September 19x2?

23-36. ***SEASONAL INDEXES*** From the sales records of the Marfax Corporation the following monthly sales data has been gathered:

Month	19x1	19x2	19x3
Jan.	$ 87,000	$ 88,500	$ 92,000
Feb.	74,000	76,000	76,500
Mar.	88,000	93,000	94,000
April	89,000	93,500	95,000
May	101,000	108,000	114,000
June	120,000	128,000	135,500
July	122,000	128,500	137,000
Aug.	114,000	121,000	119,000
Sept.	91,000	97,000	96,000
Oct.	82,000	91,000	95,000
Nov.	78,000	81,500	82,000
Dec.	64,000	68,000	74,000

Required:

(a) Compute a seasonal index for each month using the:
   (1) Ratio-to-same-year-average method.
   (2) Moving average method.

(b) If the sales forecast for 19x4 is $1,450,000, compute the monthly budget estimates for 19x4 using the indexes computed from the:
   (1) Ratio-to-same-year-average method.
   (2) Moving average method.

(c) Forecast the sales for January 19x4, using a six-month moving average adjusted for seasonal variation (use the index computed under the moving average method).

23-37. ***ZERO SEQUENCE PROBLEM—EXPECTED VALUE ANALYSIS*** Mr. Tire is the owner of a large retail outlet for a major tire manufacturer. He suspects that an adjustment of opening and closing times might improve profit. Presently, Mr. Tire is operating from 9 A.M. to 6 P.M. and is experiencing the following demand:

Customers Per Day	Probability of Occurrence
50	.05
60	.10
70	.20
80	.25
90	.15
100	.15
110	.10

Also, he predicts that the following demands can be anticipated during each of the indicated hours:

From 9 A.M. to 10 A.M.		From 10 A.M. to 11 A.M.		From 11 A.M. to 12 P.M.	
Customers	Prob.	Customers	Prob.	Customers	Prob.
7	.10	10	.15	12	.15
8	.15	11	.25	13	.40
9	.25	12	.35	14	.35
10	.30	13	.15	15	.10
11	.20	14	.10		

From 6 P.M. to 7 P.M.		From 7 P.M. to 8 P.M.		From 8 P.M. to 9 P.M.	
Customers	Prob.	Customers	Prob.	Customers	Prob.
15	.05	20	.20	18	.10
16	.10	21	.25	19	.15
17	.20	22	.35	20	.25
18	.25	23	.15	21	.30
19	.30	24	.05	22	.15
20	.10			23	.05

Whitewall tires sell for $35 and blackwall tires sell for $30. From Mr. Tire's prior experience at least 75% of his customers buy whitewall tires and at least 50% request a front-end alignment. An alignment job costs $8.50. Further, 60% of his customers buy four tires, while the other 40% buy only two tires.

Each whitewall tire costs Mr. Tire $18 and each blackwall costs $16. Mr. Tire has eight employees. Each employee is paid $3.50 per hour. Mr. Tire is not paid for his time.

Required:

From the information, what opening and closing times will produce the greatest profit if an eight-hour working day is applicable (one hour for lunch, making nine hours total) and the analysis uses:
(a) Modal values
(b) Expected values

23-38. ***ZERO SEQUENCE PROBLEM—EXPECTED VALUE ANALYSIS*** Mr. Taco, a world famous Mexican restaurant, is best known for its tacos and enchiladas. Presently, Mr. Taco is experiencing the following demand for each item (for simplicity it is assumed that demand always totals in intervals of ten):

TACOS		ENCHILADAS	
Demand per day	Probability of Occurrence	Demand per day	Probability of Occurrence
80	.10	140	.30
90	.35	150	.40
100	.20	160	.20
110	.20	170	.10
120	.15		

Mr. Taco figures that each taco costs 10¢ (including the taco shell) while each enchilada costs 14¢. The tacos are sold for 40¢ and the enchiladas for 50¢.

Tacos are prepared when the order is taken. The taco shell, however, must be prepared in advance, at the beginning of the day, since the corn tortillas are hand-made fresh on the premises and immediately fried and formed into the shell. Because of the need to employ special help to make and fry the tortillas, Mr. Taco figures that each taco shell has a cost of 6¢. Although it is this procedure that makes Mr. Taco's tacos so delicious, it is a bit more expensive, for at the end of each day, all leftover taco shells must be discarded.

Because of the lengthy preparation time, enchiladas are prepared at the beginning of each day. All unsold enchiladas are offered for sale the next day through Mr. Taco's take-out window. These day-old enchiladas are sold for 30¢ and experience the following demand (for simplicity it is assumed that demand always totals in intervals of five):

Demand per day	Probability of Occurrence
5	.40
10	.50
15	.10

Any unsold day-old enchiladas are discarded.

Required:

(a) How many taco shells should be produced each day?
(b) How many enchiladas should be produced each day?
(c) If Mr. Taco's kitchen facility is limited, and he can make only a total of 260 items, what combination of taco shells and enchiladas should he make?

23-39. ***FLEXIBLE BUDGETING*** Department A is one of fifteen departments in the plant and is involved in the production of all of the six products manufactured. The department is highly mechanized and as a result its output is measured in direct machine hours. Variable (flexible) budgets are utilized throughout the factory in planning and controlling costs, but here the focus is upon the application of variable budgets only in department A. The following data covering a time span of approximately six months were taken from the various budgets, accounting records and performance reports (only representative items and amounts are utilized here):

On March 15, 1971, the following variable budget was approved for the department; it will be used throughout the 1972 fiscal year which begins July 1, 1971. This variable budget was developed through the cooperative efforts of the department manager, his supervisor, and certain staff members from the budget department.

1972 VARIABLE BUDGET—DEPARTMENT A

Controllable Costs	Fixed Amount Per Month	Variable Rate Per Direct Machine Hour
Employee salaries	$ 9,000	
Indirect wages	18,000	$.07
Indirect materials		.09
Other costs	6,000	.03

On May 5, 1971, the annual sales plan and the production budget were completed. In order to continue preparation of the annual profit plan (which was detailed by month) the production budget was translated to planned activity for each of the factory departments. The planned activity for department A was:

	For the 12 months ending June 30, 1972				
	Year	July	Aug.	Sept.	Etc.
Planned output in direct machine hours	325,000	22,000	25,000	29,000	249,000

On August 31, 1971, the manager of department A was informed that his planned output for September had been revised to 34,000 direct machine hours. He expressed some doubt as to whether this volume could be attained.

At the end of September 1971, the accounting records provided the following actual data for the month for the department:

Actual output in direct machine hours	33,000
Actual controllable costs incurred:	
Employee salaries	$ 9,300
Indirect wages	20,500
Indirect materials	2,850
Other costs	7,510
	$40,160

Required:

The requirements relate primarily to the potential uses of the variable budget for the period March through September 1971.

(a) What activity base is utilized as a measure of volume in the budget for this department? How should one determine the range of the activity base to which the variable rates per direct machine hour are relevant? Explain.

(b) The high-low point method was utilized in developing this variable budget. Using indirect wage costs as an example, illustrate and explain how this method would be applied in determining the fixed and variable components of indirect wage costs for this department. Assume that the high-low budget values for indirect wages are $19,400 at 20,000 direct machine hours and $20,100 at 30,000 direct machine hours.

(c) Explain and illustrate how the variable budget should be utilized:

(1) In budgeting costs when the annual sales plan and production budget are completed (about May 5, 1971, or shortly thereafter).

(2) In budgeting a cost revision based upon a revised production budget (about August 31, 1971, or shortly thereafter).

(3) In preparing a cost performance report for September 1971.

(From the CPA exam.)

23-40. ***SENSITIVITY ANALYSIS*** Using the data in problem 23-34, determine the sensitivity of income statement items upon profit.

(a) Prepare a schedule showing the change in profit resulting when each variable in turn assumes its *pessimistic* value while holding all other variables at their most likely values.

(b) Prepare a schedule showing the change in profit resulting when each variable in turn assumes its *optimistic* value while holding all other variables at their most likely values.

23-41. ***BUDGETING—EXPECTED VALUE ANALYSIS*** Vernon Enterprises designs and manufactures toys. Past experience indicates that the product life cycle of a toy is three years, but there is a substantial sales decline in the final year of a toy's life.

Consumer demand for new toys placed on the market tends to fall into three classes. About 30% of the new toys sell well above expectations, 60% sell as anticipated, and 10% have poor consumer acceptance.

A new toy has been developed. The following sales projections were made by carefully evaluating consumer demand for the new toy:

Consumer Demand for New Toy	Chance of Occurring	Estimated Sales in Year 1	Year 2	Year 3
Above average	30%	$1,200,000	$2,500,000	$600,000
Average	60	700,000	1,700,000	400,000
Below average	10	200,000	900,000	150,000

Variable costs are estimated at 30% of the selling price. Special machinery must be purchased at a cost of $860,000 and will be installed in an unused portion of the factory which Vernon has unsuccessfully been trying to rent to someone for several years at $50,000 per year and has no prospects for future utilization. Fixed expenses (excluding depreciation) of a cash flow nature are estimated at $50,000 per year on the new toy. The new machinery will be depreciated by the sum-of-the-years'-digit method with an estimated salvage value of $110,000 and will be sold at the beginning of the fourth year. Advertising and promotional expenses will be incurred uniformly and will total $100,000 the first year, $150,000 the second year, and $50,000 the third year. These expenses will be deducted as incurred for income tax reporting.

Vernon believes that state and federal income taxes will total 60% of income in the foreseeable future and may be assumed to be paid uniformly over the year income is earned.

Required:

(a) Prepare a schedule computing the probable sales of this new toy in each of the three years, taking into account the probability of above average, average, and below average sales occurring.

(b) Assume that the probable sales computed in (a) are $900,000 in the first year, $1,800,000 in the second year, and $410,000 in the third year. Prepare a schedule computing the probable net income for the new toy in each of the three years of its life.

(c) Prepare a schedule of net cash flows from sales of the new toy for each of the years involved and from disposition of the machinery purchased. Use the sales data given in part (b).

(d) Assuming a minimum desired rate of return of 10%, prepare a schedule of the present value of the net cash flows calculated in (c). In addition to Table B-2 in Appendix B, the following data are relevant:

Year	Present Value of $1.00 Earned Uniformly throughout the Year Discounted at 10%
1	.95
2	.86
3	.78

(Adapted from the CPA exam.)

23-42. ***PRO FORMA INCOME STATEMENT*** Modern Products Corporation, a manufacturer of molded plastic containers, determined in October 1968 that it needed cash to continue operations. The corporation began negotiating for a one-month bank loan of $100,000 which would be discounted at 6% per annum on November 1. In considering the loan the bank requested a projected income statement and a cash budget for the month of November.

The following information is available:

1. Sales were budgeted at 120,000 units per month in October 1968, December 1968, and January 1969, and at 90,000 units in November 1968.

The selling price is $2 per unit. Sales are billed on the 15th and last day of each month on terms of 2/10 net 30. Past experience indicates sales are even throughout the month and 50% of the customers pay the billed amount within the discount period. The remainder pay at the end of thirty days, except for bad debts which average 1/2% of gross sales. On its income statement the corporation deducts from sales the estimated amounts for cash discounts on sales and losses on bad debts.

2. The inventory of finished goods on October 1 was 24,000 units. The finished goods inventory at the end of each month is to be maintained at 20% of sales anticipated for the following month. There is no work-in-process.

3. The inventory of raw materials on October 1 was 22,800 pounds. At the end of each month the raw materials inventory is to be maintained at not less than 40% of production requirements for the following month. Materials are purchased as needed in minimum quantities of 25,000 pounds per shipment. Raw material purchases of each month are paid in the next succeeding month on terms of net thirty days.

4. All salaries and wages are paid on the 15th and last day of each month for the period ending on the date of payment.

5. All manufacturing overhead and selling and administrative expenses are paid on the 10th of the month following the month in which incurred. Selling expenses are 10% of gross sales. Administrative expenses, which include depreciation of $500 per month on office furniture and fixtures, total $33,000 per month.

6. The standard cost of a molded plastic container, based on "normal" production of 100,000 units per month, is as follows:

Materials—1/2 pound	$ .50
Labor	.40
Variable overhead	.20
Fixed overhead	.10
	$1.20

Fixed overhead includes depreciation on factory equipment of $4,000 per month. Over- or under-absorbed overhead is included in cost of sales.

7. The cash balance on November 1 is expected to be $10,000.

Required:

Prepare the following for Modern Products Corporation assuming the bank loan is granted. (Do not consider income taxes.)

(a) Schedules computing inventory budgets by months for:
    (1) Finished goods production in units for October, November, and December.
    (2) Raw material purchases in pounds for October.

(b) A projected income statement for the month of November.

(c) A cash forecast for the month of November showing the opening balance, receipts (itemized by dates of collection), disbursements, and balance at end of month.

(From the CPA exam.)

23-43. ***MULTIPLE SEQUENCE PROBLEM—PERT/COST*** The Task Company is determining budget estimates for the task represented in the following network diagram:

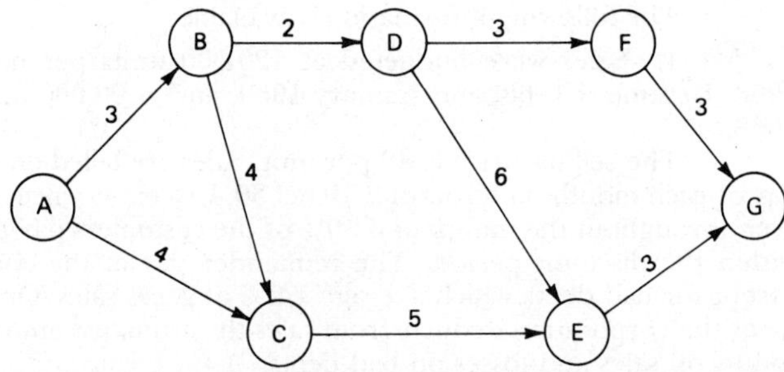

Each event is indicated by the letter, and activities are indicated by arrows. The estimates for *expected completion times* of each activity were obtained from the three-point estimation procedure and are indicated on the network diagram while the pessimistic and optimistic times are as follows (all times are in *days*):

Activity	**A-B**	**A-C**	**B-C**	**B-D**	**C-E**	**D-E**	**D-F**	**E-G**	**F-G**
Pessimistic time	6	6	6	3	8	8	4	5	4
Optimistic time	1	2	1	1	2	3	1	2	1

The costs of reducing activity time are estimated as:

	Reduce by				
Activity	**1 day**	**2 days**	**3 days**	**4 days**	**5 days**
A-B	$25	$45			
A-C	30	50	$65		
B-C	35	60	80		
B-D	40				
C-E	20	40	55	$50	
D-E	10	15	25	40	$60
D-F	40	70			
E-G	30	60			
F-G	35	60			

Required:

(a) Determine which path is *critical.* What is the expected completion time of the critical path?

(b) Determine the *least amount of additional cost* required to complete the task in:

(1) 14 days
(2) 13 days
(3) 12 days

(c) Determine the *probability* of finishing on schedule if the expected completion time is left unaltered at the original estimate and the scheduled completion time is (use Exhibit 23-20):
(1) 14 days
(2) 17 days

23-44. ***BUDGETING*** Demars College has asked your assistance in developing its budget for the coming 1971-72 academic year. You are supplied with the following data for the current year:

1.

	Lower Division (Freshman-Sophomore)	Upper Division (Junior-Senior)
Average number of students per class	25	20
Average salary of faculty member	$10,000	$10,000
Average number of credit hours carried each year per student	33	30
Enrollment including scholarship students	2,500	1,700
Average faculty teaching load in credit hours per year (ten classes of three credit hours)	30	30

For 1971–72 lower division enrollment is expected to increase by 10%, while the upper division's enrollment is expected to remain stable. Faculty salaries will be increased by a standard 5%, and additional merit increases to be awarded to individual faculty members will be $90,750 for the lower division and $85,000 for the upper division.

2. The current budget is $210,000 for operation and maintenance of plant and equipment; this includes $90,000 for salaries and wages. Experience of the past three months suggests that the current budget is realistic, but that expected increases for 1971–72 are 5% in salaries and wages and $9,000 in other expenditures for operation and maintenance of plant and equipment.

3. The budget for the remaining expenditures for 1971–72 is as follows:

Administrative and general	$240,000
Library	160,000
Health and recreation	75,000
Athletics	120,000
Insurance and retirement	265,000
Interest	48,000
Capital outlay	300,000

4. The college expects to award twenty-five tuition-free scholarships to lower-division students and fifteen to upper-division students. Tuition is $22 per credit hour and no other fees are charged.

5. Budgeted revenues for 1971–72 are as follows:

Endowments	$114,000
Net income from auxiliary services	235,000
Athletics	180,000

The college's remaining source of revenue is an annual support campaign held during the spring.

Required:

(a) Prepare a schedule computing for 1971–72 by division:
 (1) The expected enrollment
 (2) The total credit hours to be carried, and
 (3) The number of faculty members needed.

(b) Prepare a schedule computing the budget for faculty salaries by division for 1971–72.

(c) Prepare a schedule computing the tuition revenue budget by division for 1971–72.

(d) Assuming that the faculty salaries budget computed in part (b) was $2,400,000 and that the tuition revenue budget computed in part (c) was $3,000,000, prepare a schedule computing the amount which must be raised during the annual support campaign in order to cover the 1971–72 expenditures budget.

(From the CPA exam.)

CHAPTER

24

CAPITAL BUDGETING

24.1 THE NATURE OF CAPITAL BUDGETING

Capital budgeting is planning for the acquisition of long-lived assets. Capital budgeting is a decision making tool. It is a *process* which allows us to evaluate alternative investment opportunities and select the investment offering the best financial advantage. The decision theory model in chapter 2 is adapted readily to capital budgeting decisions (Exhibit 24-1).

The decision maker begins with the objective of profit maximization. He searches for and ranks alternative assets and makes his choice. The state of nature describes the constraints under which he operates, including the constraints of limited knowledge and resources (i.e., time and money).

Acquisitions resulting from capital budgets have a major financial and operational impact. They involve large expenditures for *durable* long-lived assets. Since the effect of a capital investment is long term and will determine plant scale and operating capabilities for years to come, careful planning is a critical factor if we are to achieve long-run profitability.

Bear in mind that capital budgeting is not the compilation of formal planning documents, but rather the process by which we gather information relevant to the selection of capital investments. The term *capital* is used not in the context of equity, but as a substitute for long-lived or "capital" assets.

EXHIBIT 24-1 ELEMENTS IN THE DECISION PROCESS

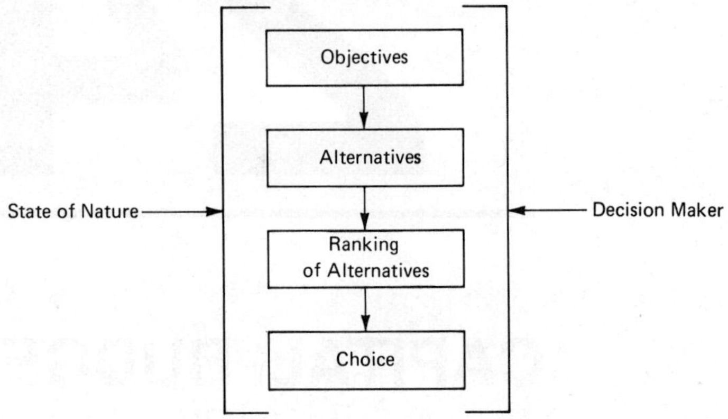

Objectives → Alternatives → Ranking of Alternatives → Choice

State of Nature → [process] ← Decision Maker

FUTURE-DIFFERENTIAL COSTS

All capital budgeting analysis involves fixed-point estimates[1] of future occurrences for each investment opportunity. Estimates are made of future conditions if existing operating assets are maintained, and future conditions if existing assets are altered or replaced. In order to decide on an asset investment we compare the consequences of such investment upon the financial conditions expected to exist under the status quo. If we do nothing—if we make no capital expenditure—the status quo is maintained. If we buy new equipment, the status quo is altered. It is this future-differential change which we measure and use as a criterion for choice. *No other financial information is relevant.*

All costs incurred to date under the status quo are *irreversible*—nothing we can do in the future will change what has occurred already. These *past* or *sunk costs* are *irrelevant.* They are not affected by any new decision. Their only purpose is to serve as a guide for future estimates.

INVESTMENT PERIODS

When we acquire a capital asset, we alter the future financial condition for as long as the asset is retained. In effect, then, we have not purchased a particular asset, but instead acquired the financial consequences for the *period(s)* in which the asset is operational. We make a commitment for a given time period and not for a given asset.

The investment in a capital asset is not made by comparing only the cost of each acceptable machine, but by examining the financial conditions imposed over the period of potential use. The future-differential conditions for each asset are formu-

[1]Refer to chapter 22 for a discussion of fixed-point estimates: single, three-point, and five-point.

lated and compared against each other. If investments are *mutually exclusive,* the investment offering the largest positive differential should be chosen.

This choice criterion carries the assumption that all comparable investments have equal operating lives as shown in Exhibit 24-2.

EXHIBIT 24-2 EQUALITY ASSUMPTION

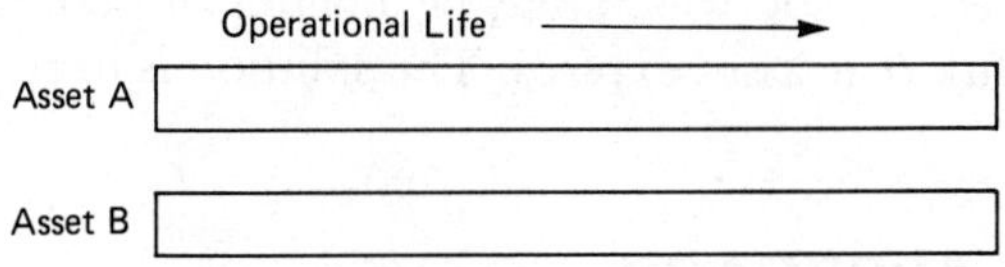

Operational Life →

Asset A

Asset B

This assumption is necessary since we are comparing the future-differential conditions within a fixed operating period. We are comparing two *like investment periods* and not necessarily similar operating assets. Investment lives, however, do not always correspond. In these instances two rules prevail:

RULE 1: If all alternatives have a useful life one-half or less than the useful life of the longest-lived alternative, each of these alternatives should be *recycled.* That is, we assume in each case successive purchases of the same asset, not exceeding the period as determined by the longest-lived asset. The process is illustrated in Exhibit 24-3.

EXHIBIT 24-3 RECYCLING

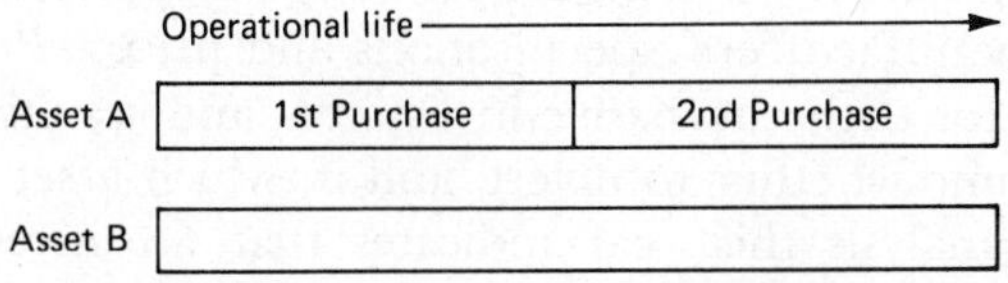

Operational life →

Asset A | 1st Purchase | 2nd Purchase

Asset B

RULE 2: After any possible recycling, all alternatives should be adjusted to the period determined by the shortest-lived asset, by estimating an early retirement. The *truncation* (or shortening) effects of the early retirement are included in the new investment period of the asset affected (Exhibit 24-4).

EXHIBIT 24-4 TRUNCATION

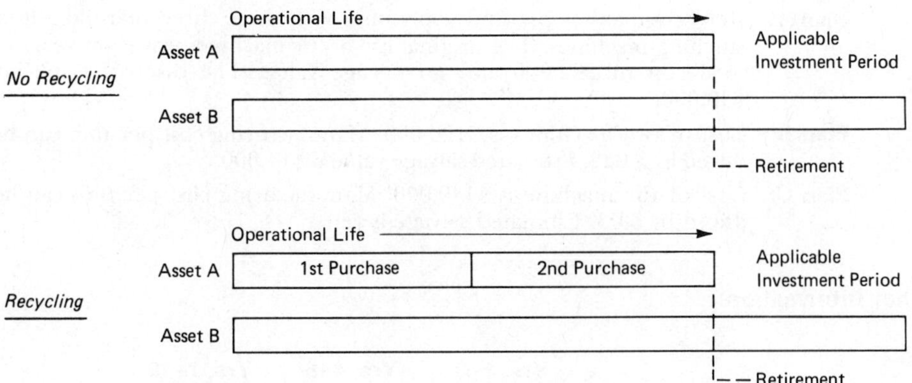

In capital budgeting we provide information bearing directly on future operating capacity. Consequently all alternative capital expenditures are evaluated in terms of their contribution to the financial condition of future operating periods. If different investment periods are used for each alternative, no basis of comparison exists. For instance, how can we compare an asset with a ten-year life and one with a four-year life? The future-differential effects of a ten-year life surely will differ from those of four years. If we compare only the first four years of the ten-year asset, we ignore the latter six-year period which may be a better or poorer investment than any available when the four-year asset expires. The solution is to recycle and/or truncate.

24.2 INCOME FLOW APPROACH

In capital budgeting we must determine the future financial activity of a given period. Often such a representation is in the form of the *pro forma income statement* discussed in chapter 23. Logically, if we wish to determine past financial activity we draw up an income statement. For projected activity we prepare a *pro forma* statement. A method for analyzing capital investment opportunities is the preparation of a series of *pro forma* income statements for each year of the investment period and for each alternative capital expenditure. Using the status quo as a reference, differences in income are computed. These differences are expressed as a return on the respective *incremental investment.* The investment yielding the highest return is the preferred one.

Suppose the Kelly Shoe Manufacturing Company operates from a plant in New York City. Replacement decisions for stitching machines are made on an annual basis by reviewing manufacturers' specifications and prices. *Pro forma* income statements are prepared for each alternative investment and resulting rates of return are compared to determine whether to invest, and in which asset or group of assets to invest. Preliminary analysis this year indicates that *two* investments are possible:

Plan A: *Maintain* the status quo.
Plan B: *Replace* three old machines with two machines having a ten-year life.
Plan C: *Replace* three old machines with one large machine having a seven-year life.

Financial information relating to each plan is as follows:

Plan A: Kelly company is presently operating with three three-year-old automatic stitching machines. The original life of the machines was eight years with a total cost of $92,000 and no salvage value. The disposal value now is $40,000.

Plan B: Cost of two machines is $120,000. Manufacturing cost per unit can be reduced by $.022. Estimated salvage value is $14,000.

Plan C: Cost of the machine is $140,000. Manufacturing cost per unit can be reduced by $.03. Estimated salvage is zero.

Other information:

	Yrs. 1–3	Yrs. 4–6	Yrs. 7–10
Sales in units	1,000,000	1,200,000	1,500,000

Our analysis requires that for each alternative we compute incremental return on investment, using this formula:

$$R = \frac{N_a}{I}$$

where

N_a = average incremental change in net income after taxes
I = incremental investment[2]
R = rate of return

If the return is considered high enough, the new investment is undertaken; if not, Plan A—status quo—is continued.

SOLUTION, STEP 1: Determine the investment period:

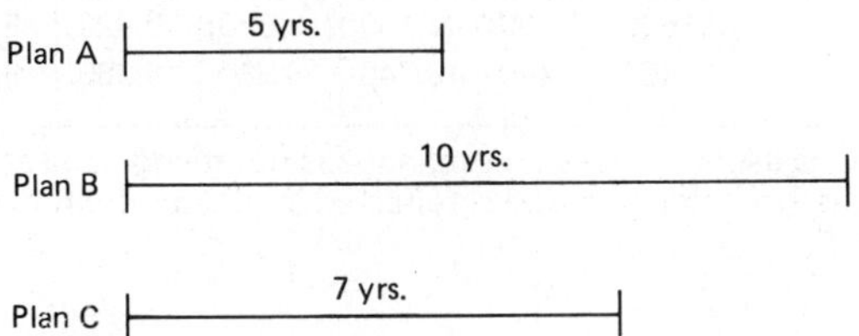

Plan A should be recycled, then all plans should be truncated at seven years:

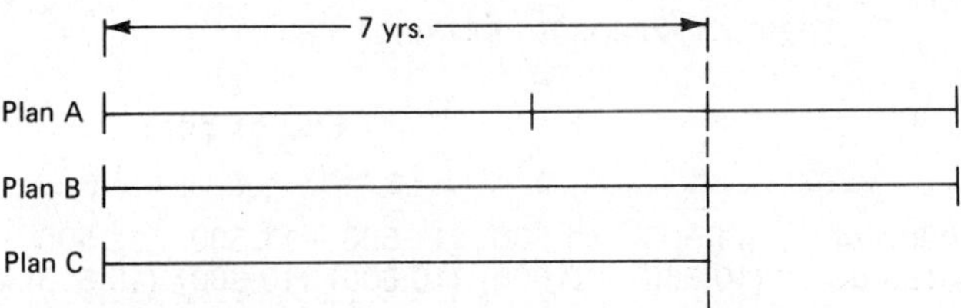

STEP 2: Compute the rate of return (R) for Plans B and C.

Plan B—Refer to Exhibit 24-5. Assume:

1. Straight-line depreciation with provision for salvage value.
2. In seven years the salvage value of the new machine is estimated to be $30,000.
3. Tax rate of 40%.[3]

---

[2]The incremental investment is the difference between the new investment and the *disposal value* of the old investment, plus or minus the tax effect on any gain or loss on the old investment. When there is no old investment, the incremental investment is simply the cost of the new investment.

[3]In this example, and all following examples, one tax rate will be used despite the occurrence of any capital gains or losses. This follows an interpretation of the Internal Revenue Code for *personal property* covered under Section 1245. Under Section 1231, however, a lower tax rate is applicable to any capital gain on *real property*.

Incremental investment $(I) = \$120{,}000 - 40{,}000 - 7{,}000 = \$73{,}000$.[4]
Average incremental change in income $(N_a) = \$76{,}920/7 = \$10{,}989$.

$$R = \frac{10{,}989}{73{,}000}$$

$$R = \underline{\underline{15\%}}$$

EXHIBIT 24-5 INCREMENTAL CHANGE IN INCOME FOR PLAN B

	End of Year							
	1	**2**	**3**	**4**	**5**	**6**	**7**	**Total**
A. Savings in mfg. costs	22,000	22,000	22,000	26,400	26,400	26,400	33,000	178,200
B. Change in deprec.	900	900	900	900	900	(10,600)	(10,600)	(16,700)
C. Loss on disposal of old machines*	(17,500)							(17,500)
D. Loss on premature retirement of new machines							(15,800)	(15,800)
Total before taxes	5,400	22,900	22,900	27,300	27,300	15,800	6,600	128,200
Tax (40%)	(2,160)	(9,160)	(9,160)	(10,920)	(10,920)	(6,320)	(2,640)	(51,280)
Total after taxes	3,240	13,740	13,740	16,380	16,380	9,480	3,960	76,920

*If the income tax method is used, the loss on exchange is not recognized at this point, but is added to the depreciable cost of the new machine and is reflected in greater depreciation charges over the life of the new machines.

Computation of values for Exhibit 24-5:

A. *yrs. 1–3:* $.022 \times 1{,}000{,}000 = \$22{,}000$

yrs. 4–6: $.022 \times 1{,}200{,}000 = \$26{,}400$

yr. 7: $.022 \times 1{,}500{,}000 = \$33{,}000$

B.

	End of Year						
	1	**2**	**3**	**4**	**5**	**6**	**7**
Old deprec.	11,500	11,500	11,500	11,500	11,500	*	*
New deprec.	(10,600)	(10,600)	(10,600)	(10,600)	(10,600)	(10,600)	(10,600)
Change	900	900	900	900	900	(10,600)	(10,600)

*When the status quo is recycled this simply means that the investment continues to operate beyond its depreciable life. We do not show a reinvestment; otherwise a new alternative arises.

Old Deprec. = 92,000/8 = 11,500 per year.

New Deprec. = (120,000 − 14,000)/10 = 10,600 per year.

C. Cost of Old Machines − Accum. Deprec. (3 yrs.) = Book Value.

92,000 − 34,500 = 57,000

Book Value − Salvage = Loss on Disposal.

57,000 − 40,000 = (17,500)

[4]There is a $7,000 reduction in the incremental investment because of the positive cash flow resulting from the tax effect on the $17,500 loss computed in part C of Exhibit 24-5.

D. Cost of New Machines − Accum. Deprec. (7 yrs.) = Book Value.

120,000 − 74,200 = 45,800

Book Value − Salvage = Loss on Disposal.

45,800 − 30,000 = (15,800)

Plan C—Refer to Exhibit 24-6. Assume:

1. Straight-line depreciation with provision for salvage value.
2. Tax rate of 40%.

Incremental investment (I) = \$140,000 − 40,000 − 7,000 = \$93,000.
Average incremental change in income (N_a) = \$85,800/7 = \$12,257.

$$R = \frac{12{,}257}{93{,}000}$$

$$R = \underline{\underline{13\%}}$$

EXHIBIT 24-6 INCREMENTAL CHANGE IN INCOME FOR PLAN C

	End of Year							
	1	**2**	**3**	**4**	**5**	**6**	**7**	**Total**
A. Savings in mfg. costs	30,000	30,000	30,000	36,000	36,000	36,000	45,000	243,000
B. Change in deprec.	(8,500)	(8,500)	(8,500)	(8,500)	(8,500)	(20,000)	(20,000)	(82,500)
C. Loss on disposal of old machines	(17,500)							(17,500)
Total before taxes	4,000	21,500	21,500	27,500	27,500	16,000	25,000	143,000
Tax (40%)	(1,600)	(8,600)	(8,600)	(11,000)	(11,000)	(6,400)	(10,000)	(57,200)
Total after taxes	2,400	12,900	12,900	16,500	16,500	9,600	15,000	85,800

Computation of values for Exhibit 24-6:

A. *yrs. 1–3:* .03 × 1,000,000 = \$30,000

yrs. 4–6: .03 × 1,200,000 = \$36,000

yr. 7: .03 × 1,500,000 = \$45,000

B.

	End of Year						
	1	**2**	**3**	**4**	**5**	**6**	**7**
Old deprec.	11,500	11,500	11,500	11,500	11,500		
New deprec.	(20,000)	(20,000)	(20,000)	(20,000)	(20,000)	(20,000)	(20,000)
Change	(8,500)	(8,500)	(8,500)	(8,500)	(8,500)	(20,000)	(20,000

Old Deprec. = 92,000/8 = 11,500 per year.
New Deprec. = 140,000/7 = 20,000 per year.

C. Cost of Old Machines − Accum. Deprec. (3 yrs.) = Book Value.

92,000 − 11,500 = 57,500

Book Value − Salvage = Loss on Disposal.
57,500 − 40,000 = 17,500

Plan C should be chosen over Plan B, because of its higher incremental return. However, perhaps even Plan C is a poor investment in relation to the firm's concept of an adequate return on investment. This conceptual notion of the adequacy of a return ultimately must rest with the decision maker. Later in this chapter, however, we will show how an adequate rate is conceptualized.

24.3 CASH FLOW APPROACH

An alternative means for evaluating a capital investment opportunity is to examine cash flow rather than income flow. For the *investment period* as a *whole*, the flows should yield *identical totals.* The return on investment, and consequently, the rate of return, will always be higher when using cash flow. This occurs because the *investment* return represented by cash flow does not include the negative cash flow from the incremental investment. With income flow this is not the case, since the incremental investment is represented by depreciation and treated as a reduction in investment return.

Depreciation and gains or losses on disposal cause income flow to be lower than cash flow. As we know, depreciation is essentially an attempt to distribute the investment burden to the periods in which income is earned. As such it actually serves as a distortion of true investment income.

The cash flow calculation is similar to that for income flow. Again, using the status quo as a reference, the differences in cash flow are computed. Incremental cash flow is compared to incremental cash investment and a rate of return is computed as follows:

$$R = \frac{C_a}{I}$$

where

C_a = average incremental change in cash flow after taxes
I = incremental cash investment
R = rate of return

It might be well to establish a rule, at this point, regarding the consequences of taxation. *In a cash flow analysis anything which affects income produces a related cash flow from the income tax effect.* If income increases, more taxes are paid—hence, a *cash outflow.* If income decreases, less taxes are paid—hence, a *cash inflow* (savings). This means that depreciation, while it is not a cash flow, produces cash benefits from the tax effect of the decreased income. Also, the sale of assets produces cash flow effects. For instance, suppose you sell for \$20,000 a machine with a book value of \$18,000. Assuming a tax rate of 40%, an analysis of cash flows shows an \$18,000 cash inflow and an \$800 cash outflow from the tax effect on the \$2,000 gain.

Using our example of the Kelly Shoe Manufacturing Company, an analysis of cash flow is as follows:

Plan B—Refer to Exhibit 24-7:

Incremental cash investment $(I)^5 = \$120,000 - 40,000 - 7,000 = \$73,000$.
Average incremental change in cash flows (C_a) *for periods 1–7:* 149,920/7 = $21,417

$$R = \frac{21,417}{73,000}$$

$$R = \underline{\underline{29.34\%}}$$

EXHIBIT 24-7 INCREMENTAL CHANGE IN CASH FLOW FOR PLAN B

	End of Year								
	0	1	2	3	4	5	6	7	Total
A. Savings in mfg. costs		22,000	22,000	22,000	26,400	26,400	26,400	33,000	178,200
B. *Tax effect* on savings		(8,800)	(8,800)	(8,800)	(10,560)	(10,560)	(10,560)	(13,200)	(71,280)
C. Purchase of new machines	(120,000)								(120,000)
D. *Tax effect* on deprec. change		(360)	(360)	(360)	(360)	(360)	4,240	4,240	6,680
E. Disposal of old machines	40,000								40,000
F. *Tax effect* on disposal loss of $17,500	7,000								7,000
G. Premature retirement of new machines								30,000	30,000
H. *Tax effect* on retirement loss of $15,800								6,320	6,320
Total cash flows	(73,000)	12,840	12,840	12,840	15,480	15,480	20,080	60,360	76,920

Computation of values for Exhibit 24-7:

A. Cash savings:

yrs. 1–3: $.022 \times 1,000,000 = \$22,000$

yrs. 4–6: $.022 \times 1,200,000 = \$26,400$

yr.7: $.022 \times 1,500,000 = \$33,000$

[5]Cash outflows at year 0 (the incremental investment).

B. Cash outflow on increased tax resulting from savings:

yrs. 1–3: 22,000 × 40% = (8,800)

yrs. 4–6: 26,400 × 40% = (10,560)

yr. 7: 33,000 × 40% = (13,200)

C. Cash outflow of $120,000 at the beginning of investment period.

D. Cash flow resulting from tax effect on depreciation change:

	End of Year						
	1	2	3	4	5	6	7
Change in deprec.	900	900	900	900	900	(10,600)	(10,600)
Tax rate	.40	.40	.40	.40	.40	.40	.40
Tax effect	(360)	(360)	(360)	(360)	(360)	4,240	4,240

E. Cash inflow from disposal is $40,000 at the beginning of investment period.

F. Cost of Old Machines − Accum. Deprec. (3 yrs.) = Book Value.

92,000 − 34,500 = (57,500)

Book Value − Salvage = Loss on Disposal.

57,500 − 40,000 = (17,500)

Tax Effect on Loss = (17,500) × 40% = $7,000.

G. Cash inflow from premature retirement is $30,000.

H. Cash inflow resulting from tax effect on retirement loss:

Cost of New Machine − Accum. Deprec. (7 yrs.) = Book Value.

120,000 − 74,200 = 45,800

Book Value − Salvage = Loss on Disposal.

45,800 − 30,000 = (15,800)

Tax Effect on Loss = (15,800) × 40% = $6,320.

Plan C—Refer to Exhibit 24-8:

Incremental cash investment $(I)^6$ = $140,000 − 40,000 − 7,000 = $93,000.
Average incremental change in cash flows (C_a) *for periods 1–7:* 178,800/7 = $25,543

$$R = \frac{25{,}543}{93{,}000}$$

$$R = \underline{\underline{27.47\%}}$$

[6]Cash flows at year 0 (the incremental investment).

EXHIBIT 24-8 INCREMENTAL CHANGE IN CASH FLOW FOR PLAN C

	End of Year								
	0	**1**	**2**	**3**	**4**	**5**	**6**	**7**	**Total**
A. Savings in mfg. costs		30,000	20,000	30,000	36,000	36,000	36,000	45,000	243,000
B. *Tax effect* on savings		(12,000)	(12,000)	(12,000)	(14,400)	(14,400)	(14,400)	(18,000)	(97,200)
C. Purchase of new machine	(140,000)								(140,000)
D. *Tax effect* on deprec. change		3,400	3,400	3,400	3,400	3,400	8,000	8,000	33,000
E. Disposal of old machines	40,000								40,000
F. *Tax effect* on disposal loss of $17,500	7,000								7,000
Total cash flow	(93,000)	21,400	21,400	21,400	25,000	25,000	29,600	35,000	85,800

Computation of values for Exhibit 24-8:

A. Cash savings:

yrs. 1–3: .03 × 1,000,000 = 30,000

yrs. 4–6: .03 × 1,200,000 = 36,000

yr. 7: .03 × 1,500,000 = 45,000

B. Cash outflow on increased tax resulting from savings:

yrs. 1–3: 30,000 × 40% = (12,000)

yrs. 4–6: 36,000 × 40% = (14,400)

yr. 7: 45,000 × 40% = (18,000)

C. Cash outflow of $140,000 resulting from new equipment purchase.

D. Cash flow resulting from tax effect on depreciation change:

	End of Year						
	1	2	3	4	5	6	7
Change in deprec.	(8,500)	(8,500)	(8,500)	(8,500)	(8,500)	(20,000)	(20,000)
Tax rate	.40	.40	.40	.40	.40	.40	.40
Tax effect	3,400	3,400	3.400	3.400	3,400	8,000	8,000

E. Cash inflow from disposal of old machines is $40,000.

F. Cash inflow from tax reduction resulting from loss:

Cost of Old Machines − Accum. Deprec. (3 yrs.) = Book Value.

92,000 − 34,500 = 57,500

Book Value − Salvage = Loss on Disposal.

57,500 − 40,000 = 17,500

Tax Effect on Loss = (17,500) × 40% = $7,000.

24.4 TIME-ADJUSTED RATE OF RETURN

We have seen from the foregoing discussion that an analysis of capital expenditures may be based either on cash flow or income flow. An analysis of cash flow, however, provides a potentially more accurate appraisal since it may be adjusted for the time value of money,[7] whereas strict income flow cannot be adjusted in this manner. Since the present value of money is influenced by *waiting time,* the importance of periodicity of cash flow is too great to ignore. The rate of return should be based upon the present value of all cash flow—it should be a time-adjusted rate. This rate is best explained as being the rate of return that *causes the present value of the net cash inflow to equal exactly the present value of the incremental investment.* For instance, using a simplified example, suppose an investment of $50,000 promises a net cash inflow of $8,000 per year for eight years:

Solution:
Incremental investment = $50,000.
Net cash inflow = $8,000 annuity for eight years

$$50{,}000 = 8{,}000\ (f)$$

where f = some factor that will cause the present value of an $8,000 annuity to exactly equal $50,000.

Solving for f, that factor is:

$$f = 50{,}000/8{,}000 = 6.250$$

We know also that this factor should be the present value of a $1 annuity for eight years at $r\%$ interest:

$$f = \frac{1}{r}\left[1 - \frac{1}{(1+r)^8}\right]$$

Substituting 6.250 for the value of f, we obtain:

$$6.250 = \frac{1}{r}\left[1 - \frac{1}{(1+r)^8}\right]$$

If we solve this equation for r we can obtain the time-adjusted rate of return. Obviously, a simpler way is to look for the factor 6.250 in Table B-4 ("Present Values of a $1 Annuity"—Appendix B) and interpolate to find r:

Look for the factor 6.250 in the eighth row—it falls between the factors for 5% and 6%. Interpolate as follows:

[7]Refer to Appendix B—"Present Value, Future Value, and Annuities."

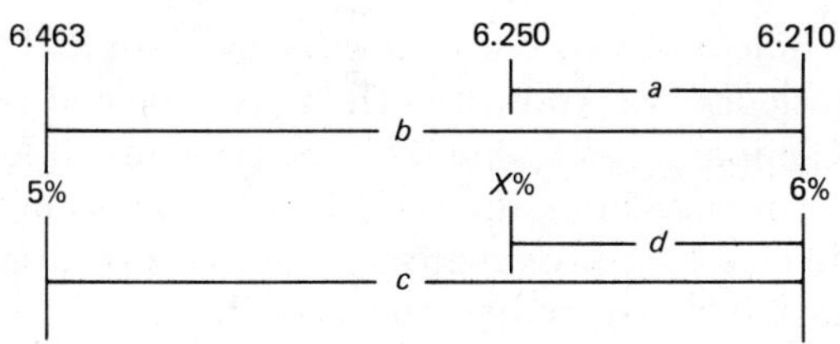

$a = 6.250 - 6.210 = .040$
$b = 6.463 - 6.210 = .253$
$a/b = .040/.253$

$c = 6\% - 5\% = 1\%$
$d = (.040/.252)1\% = .16\%$
$X = 6\% - .16\% = \underline{\underline{5.84\%}}$

Conceptually, a time-adjusted rate of return is superior to our earlier analysis. However, there can be a sizeable burden of calculations caused by *uneven cash flow.* For instance, suppose we set up Plan B for the Kelly Shoe Manufacturing Company.[8]

$$73{,}000 = 12{,}840(f_1) + 12{,}840(f_2) + 12{,}840(f_3) + 15{,}480(f_4) + 15{,}480(f_5) + 20{,}080(f_6) + 60{,}360(f_7)$$

As can be seen, the computations can be formidable. Each factor is different, since each is for a separate year. Consequently, with no way to compute an individual factor value except by trial-and-error, we have to substitute the present value equation for each factor and solve for r:

$$73{,}000 = 12{,}840\left[\frac{1}{(1+r)}\right] + 12{,}840\left[\frac{1}{(1+r)^2}\right] + \cdots + 60{,}360\left[\frac{1}{(1+r)^7}\right]$$

This task is unmanageable. The only solution for a typical analysis involving computation of a time-adjusted rate is *trial-and-error.* To get some bearing on a starting percentage, however, we can use the *unadjusted* rate of return—calculated earlier as $R = C_a/I$—as the upper limit. Our adjusted rate will never exceed this rate. This can be demonstrated by rearranging the equation for the present value of an annuity:

$$P_n = \frac{a}{r}\left[1 - \frac{1}{(1+r)^n}\right] \quad (1)$$

$$P_n = \frac{a}{r} - \frac{a}{r}\left[\frac{1}{(1+r)^n}\right] \quad (2)$$

$$r = \frac{a}{P_n} - \frac{a}{P_n}\left[\frac{1}{(1+r)^n}\right] \quad (3)$$

a is the annuity cash flow and is equivalent to C_a (average cash flow). P_n is equivalent to the incremental investment (I). Therefore:

$$r = \frac{C_a}{I} - \frac{C_a}{I}\left[\frac{1}{(1+r)^n}\right] \quad (4)$$

[8]Cash flows are assumed to occur abruptly at the *end* of each period and not incrementally.

We can see that r (the time-adjusted rate) is always less than C_a/I (the unadjusted rate).

With this knowledge, we know that the time-adjusted rate of return for Plan B of the Kelly Shoe Company is *less than 29.34%.* How much less depends upon the value of n and/or r. If n is very large, the right-hand expression of equation (4) will be very small, hence r will closely approximate C_a/I. If r is very large the same is true. To solve for the time-adjusted rate of return, then, we should arbitrarily pick a rate lower than C_a/I and see how close we come to the true rate.[9] If the rate causes the present value of the net cash inflow to exceed the incremental cash investment, *the rate* chosen *is too low.* We know this, for a higher rate of return would not have required such a high initial investment base to yield the future returns as specified. If the rate causes the present value of the net cash inflow to be *lower* than the incremental cash investment, *the rate* chosen *is too high.* We know this, for a rate higher than the true time-adjusted rate can generate the future returns on a smaller investment base.

Using 10% as our first trial, the equation is set up as:

$$73{,}000 = 12{,}840\left[\frac{1}{1.10}\right] + 12{,}840\left[\frac{1}{1.10^2}\right] + \cdots + 60{,}360\left[\frac{1}{1.10^7}\right]$$

Solving with logarithms, the calculations are:

Year	Present Value of Year	Log	Approx. Antilog
1	12840[1/1.10]	= log 12840 − log 1.10 = 4.06718	11672
2	12840[1/1.10²]	= log 12840 − 2 log 1.10 = 4.02579	10611
3	12840[1/1.10³]	= log 12840 − 3 log 1.10 = 3.98440	9647
4	15480[1/1.10⁴]	= log 15480 − 4 log 1.10 = 4.02421	10573
5	15480[1/1.10⁵]	= log 15480 − 5 log 1.10 = 3.98282	9612
6	20080[1/1.10⁶]	= log 20080 − 6 log 1.10 = 4.05442	11335
7	60360[1/1.10⁷]	= log 60360 − 7 log 1.10 = 4.49102	30976
			94426

Since the present value of the inflow is *higher* than the $73,000 incremental cash investment, the rate used was *too low.* The true rate, then, lies somewhere between 10% and 29.34%. If we find the present value of the net cash inflow at 29.34% we can interpolate to approximate the percentage return for a present value of $73,000 (an amount exactly equal to the incremental investment):

Year	Present Value of Year	Log	Approx. Antilog
1	12840[1/1.2934]	= log 12840 − log 1.2934 = 3.99684	9927
2	12840[1/1.2934²]	= log 12840 − 2 log 1.2934 = 3.88511	7676
3	12840[1/1.2934³]	= log 12840 − 3 log 1.2934 = 3.77338	5934
4	15480[1/1.2934⁴]	= log 15480 − 4 log 1.2934 = 3.74285	5532
5	15480[1/1.2934⁵]	= log 15480 − 5 log 1.2934 = 3.63112	4277
6	20080[1/1.2934⁶]	= log 20080 − 6 log 1.2934 = 3.63238	4192
7	60360[1/1.2934⁷]	= log 60360 − 7 log 1.2934 = 3.99864	9969
			47507

[9]This rate could be based upon an arbitrary assumption that total unadjusted cash flow for Plan B ($149,-920) is received entirely in year 7. The rate of return causing the present value of $149,920 to exactly equal $73,000 will be the low parameter for the trial-and-error procedure. We know this for the future value (in year 7) of the total cash flow is in actuality greater than $149,920, since some cash flows are received earlier in the period. Hence, an amount larger than $149,920 would require a larger rate of return in order to discount to $73,000.

Interpolating, we can now obtain an approximate time-adjusted rate of return for Plan B:

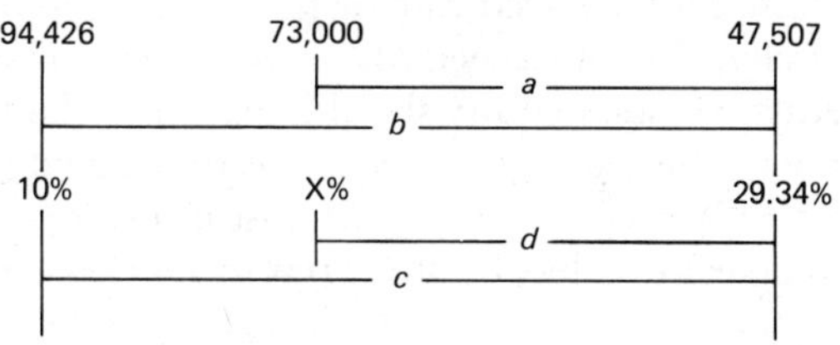

$a = 73{,}000 - 47{,}507 = 25{,}493$
$b = 94{,}426 - 47{,}507 = 46{,}919$
$a/b = 25{,}493/46{,}919$

$c = 29.34\% - 10\% = 19.34\%$
$d = (25{,}493/46{,}919)19.34\% = 10.51\%$
$X = 29.34\% - 10.51\% = \underline{\underline{18.83\%}}$

If we were to check the accuracy of this interpolated rate by finding the present value of the net cash inflow at 18.83%, we would find that our rate is slightly high. Conceptually, we can see why this is so. The *rate of decline* in the *present value* of the inflows decreases as lower and lower rates of return are used. Thus, on our interpolation diagram, the distance *a* is really larger, resulting in a larger distance *d*, and consequently, a lower approximation of *X*%. All of this means, of course, that a *linear* interpolation between our high and low rates will always yield an approximation which is slightly high. Also, the *width of the interpolation interval* will determine the degree of error. In our example, then, since 18.83% is known to be high, and the interpolation interval is rather large, we will use 16% as a trial rate. Again, finding the present value of the net cash inflow, we should obtain an answer close to $73,000:

Year	Present Value of Year		Log	Approx. Antilog
1	$12840[1/1.16]$	$= \log 12840 - \log 1.16$	$= 4.04411$	11069
2	$12840[1/1.16^2]$	$= \log 12840 - 2 \log 1.16$	$= 3.97965$	9542
3	$12840[1/1.16^3]$	$= \log 12840 - 3 \log 1.16$	$= 3.91519$	8226
4	$15480[1/1.16^4]$	$= \log 15480 - 4 \log 1.16$	$= 3.93193$	8549
5	$15480[1/1.16^5]$	$= \log 15480 - 5 \log 1.16$	$= 3.86747$	7370
6	$20080[1/1.16^6]$	$= \log 20080 - 6 \log 1.16$	$= 3.91600$	8241
7	$60360[1/1.16^7]$	$= \log 60360 - 7 \log 1.16$	$= 4.32953$	21357
				74354

This answer is very close. The true time-adjusted rate of return is slightly over 16%.

24.5 MINIMUM DESIRED RATE OF RETURN

The minimum desired rate of return is a rate designated by management to be an acceptable return on capital investments. Time-adjusted rates are computed and compared against the minimum rate. If the time-adjusted rate is lower than our minimum standard, the investment should not take place for we can earn more by investing our capital elsewhere, or by *not borrowing* to finance the investment.

Probably the most frequent conception of a minimum desired rate is the *cost of capital* or *k*. *k* is what it costs the firm to invest using either its own or borrowed capital. This concept of a minimum desired rate of return is based upon the idea that if a capital investment is financed with new equity (loans or sale of stock), or with already existing equity, the return on such equity should not be less than can be earned on old equity. Otherwise the earnings to owners' equity is diluted, and consequently might cause a decline in the firm's market value. The cost of capital, then, is the estimated future earnings (after taxes) divided by the present market value of the company's equity:

$$k = \frac{I}{E}$$

where

k = cost of capital
I = estimated future annual income after taxes
E = market value of equity

Using this formula, assume the cost of capital computations for the Kelly Shoe Company are as follows:

Expected annual net income	$ 81,500
Expected annual interest on debt	8,500
Income before payment of interest	90,000
Income tax (at 40%)	36,000
Expected annual income after taxes (*I*)	$ 54,000
Market value of outstanding debt	$170,000
Market value of owners' equity	280,000
Total market value of equity (*E*)	$450,000

$$k = \frac{54{,}000}{450{,}000}$$

$$k = \underline{\underline{12\%}}$$

Unfortunately, the minimum desired rate of return indicated by this formula is *too low*, and its use as a cut-off criterion could cause an equity dilution in the market value of ownership interest. We know that the equity market value is often not clearly reflected in the marketable *net worth* of a company. When the market value is higher, there is an indication of excess earning power—*unrecorded goodwill*. This situation is shown in Exhibit 24-9.

If unrecorded goodwill exists, the cost of capital will be lower. This could lead to an incorrect investment decision since goodwill (unrecorded or recorded)—as a reflection of excess earning power of the existing asset structure—will be reduced by acceptance of investments having a return which is too low. The preferred computation of minimum desired rate of return, therefore, is to divide the market value of the

EXHIBIT 24-9 UNRECORDED GOODWILL

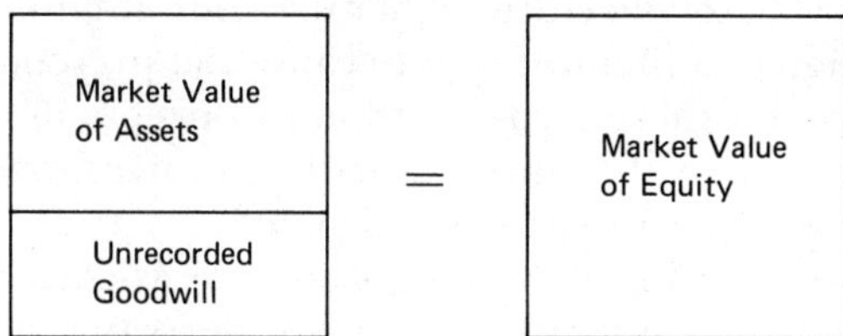

existing assets into the estimated future earnings (after taxes). Using this rate as a minimum we can at least maintain our present return on investment:

$$k = \frac{I}{A}$$

where

$$A = \text{market value of assets}$$

If a goodwill situation exists, the minimum desired rate of return will be higher with our new formula; if not, they will produce identical results. Suppose the market value of Kelly Shoe Company's assets is $420,000. The new computation of a minimum desired rate is:

$$k = \frac{54{,}000}{420{,}000}$$

$$k = \underline{\underline{12.86\%}}$$

The existence of $30,000 unrecorded goodwill (450,000 − 420,000) necessitates the use of a higher cut-off rate in order that such goodwill is not diminished.

This new cost of capital, sometimes called the *weighted average rate,* averages the uncertainty of returns from existing assets. Clearly, this is not necessarily the same uncertainty surrounding any one individual investment opportunity. Also, specific financing arrangements may be available for an investment. In any case, we should be aware that the cost of capital is an average rate and is used as a minimum desired rate of return only if management so chooses.

24.6 NET PRESENT VALUE METHOD

With this method the expected cash flows of a potential investment are discounted to their present values using the company's minimum desired rate of return. The sum of the present value of all cash flows, including the incremental investment, determines the desirability of the investment.[10] If the sum is positive—meaning the present

[10]Present values are used rather than future values or midpoint values because such values can be related to present circumstances and hence are more relevant to the decision making process.

value of cash *inflows* exceed the present value of cash *outflows*—then the investment promises a time-adjusted rate of return higher than our minimum rate. We know this, for it would take a higher minimum rate to cause the present value of cash inflows to exactly equal the present value of cash outflows. Conceptually, the net present value method is less rigorous than the time-adjusted rate of return method, and moreover, a tedious trial-and-error procedure is avoided.

Suppose the Armstrong Publishing Company is considering buying a computer to automate its billing operation, maintain perpetual inventory records, and schedule production runs. The Ace Computer Company has made a computer feasibility study, and as a result, has offered to sell a used Model X22 Computer System for $180,000. The feasibility study and company estimates have produced the following forecasts of expected values:

1. Computer system life of five years.
2. Salvage value of computer system estimated to be $40,000 after five years.
3. Savings per year:

	Yrs. 1–3	Yrs. 4–5
Invoice preparation	$12,000	$12,000
Decreased personnel	32,000	28,000
Improved billing time	7,000	8,000
Improved inventory management	16,000	20,000
Total savings per year	$67,000	$68,000

4. Computer maintenance costs estimated to be $3,600 per year.
5. Income tax rate of 40% for all five years.

Using a minimum desired rate of 12%, and assuming straight-line depreciation, an analysis of this investment opportunity is given in Exhibit 24-10.

EXHIBIT 24-10 AN ANALYSIS OF THE MODEL X22 COMPUTER

	Present Value at 12%	End of Year 1	2	3	4	5
A. Purchase of computer	(180,000)					
B. Deprec. *tax shield*	40,376	11,200	11,200	11,200	11,200	11,200
C. Salvage value of computer	22,680					40,000
D. Savings	242,738	67,000	67,000	67,000	68,000	68,000
E. *Tax effect* on savings	(97,096)	(26,800)	(26,800)	(26,800)	(27,200)	(27,200)
F. Maintenance	(12,978)	(3,600)	(3,600)	(3,600)	(3,600)	(3,600)
G. *Tax effect* on maintenance	5,191	1,440	1,440	1,440	1,440	1,440
Net present value	20,911					

Computation of values for Exhibit 24-10:

A. The *outflow* of $180,000 is already stated at present value.

B. First, compute depreciation:

Step 1: 180,000 − 40,000 (salvage) = \$140,000 (depreciable cost)
Step 2: 140,000/5 yrs. = \$28,000 (depreciation per year)

Second, compute the tax effect (shield) on depreciation:

Step 3: 40% × (28,000) = \$11,200 *cash inflow* per year

Last, compute the present value of an \$11,220 annuity for 5 years at 12%:

Step 4: 11,200 × 3.605 = \$40,376 *inflow*

C. 40,000 × .567 = \$22,680 *inflow.*

D. First, compute present value of the first three years:

67,000 × 2.402 = \$160,934

Next, compute present value of the last two years:

68,000 × (3.605 − 2.402) = 68,000 × 1.203 = \$81,804

Last, find the sum:

\$160,934 + \$81,804 = \$242,738 *inflow* from savings

E. First, compute the present value of the first three years:

\$67,000 × 40% = \$26,800 (tax effect)
\$26,800 × 2.402 = \$64,374 (P.V. of tax effect)

Next, compute the present value of the last two years:

\$68,000 × 40% = \$27,200 (tax effect)
\$27,200 × (3.605 − 2.402) = \$27,200 × 1.203 = \$32,722

Last, find the sum:

\$64,374 + \$32,722 = \$97,096 *outflow* from tax effect on savings

F. (\$3,600) × 3.605 = (12,978) *outflow* for maintenance.

G. \$1,440 × 3.605 = \$5,191 *inflow* from tax effect on maintenance.

The resulting net cash inflow of \$20,911 at present value indicates that the investment is expected to earn more than a 12% minimum desired rate. With this criterion alone we should invest.

Unfortunately, a practical situation would not be quite this simple. There could be competing alternative investments that are *mutually exclusive.*[11] That is, the investment in one alternative precludes investment in the other. Consequently, in addition to deciding whether to invest, the Armstrong Publishing Company would also be deciding upon which alternative investment it should choose. Suppose the Economy Computer Company has also offered the Armstrong Company an investment opportunity. Their offer is for the lease of an E-90 Computer System for \$1,800 per month plus the purchase of necessary input/output equipment. With the E-90 system the following forecasts are applicable:

1. Input/Output equipment life of five years.
2. Purchase prices and estimated salvage of equipment:

[11]Under the net present value method, when mutually exclusive investments have unequal lives, there is an alternative to recycling and/or truncation. For each investment, compute a yearly annuity (at the minimum desired rate) which is equivalent to its net present value. Each equivalent annuity times the present value of a perpetuity of \$1 ($1/r$) will produce the present value of each investment for perpetuity.

	Cost	Salvage
Card reader/punch	$ 14,000	$ 5,000
Printer	38,000	13,000
5 Tape units	85,000	19,000
Total	$137,000	$37,000

3. Savings per year:

	Yrs. 1–3	Yrs. 4–5
Invoice preparation	$11,000	$14,000
Decreased personnel	40,000	40,000
Improved billing time	7,000	8,000
Improved inventory management	15,000	18,000
Total savings per year	$73,000	$80,000

4. Computer maintenance costs of $2,500 per year.
5. Income tax rate of 40% for all five years.

Using the same 12% minimum desired rate, and again assuming straight-line depreciation, the net present value of this alternative is computed in Exhibit 24-11.

EXHIBIT 24-11 AN ANALYSIS OF THE E-90 COMPUTER

	Present Value at 12%	End of Year 1	2	3	4	5
A. Lease of E-90 computer	(77,868)	(21,600)	(21,600)	(21,600)	(21,600)	(21,600)
B. *Tax effect* on lease payments	31,147	8,640	8,640	8,640	8,640	8,640
C. Purchase of I/O equipment	(137,000)					
D. Deprec. *tax shield*	28,840	8,000	8,000	8,000	8,000	8,000
E. Salvage of I/O equipment	20,979					37,000
F. Savings	271,586	73,000	73,000	73,000	80,000	80,000
G. *Tax effect* on savings	(108,634)	(29,200)	(29,200)	(29,200)	(32,000)	(32,000)
H. Maintenance	(9,013)	(2,500)	(2,500)	(2,500)	(2,500)	(2,500)
I. *Tax effect* on maintenance	3,605	1,000	1,000	1,000	1,000	1,000
	23,642					

Computation of values for Exhibit 24-11:

A. $21,600 × 3.605 = $77,868 *outflow* for lease payments.

B. Tax effect = $21,000 × 40% = $8,640.
Present value = $8,640 × 40% = $31,147 *inflow* from tax effect on lease payments.

C. The outflow of $137,000 for I/O equipment is already at present value.

D. First, compute depreciation:

Step 1: 137,000 − 37,000 (salvage) = $100,000 (depreciable cost)

Step 2: 100,000/5 yrs. = $20,000 (annual depreciation)

Second, compute the tax effect (shield) on depreciation:

Step 3: 40% × $20,000 = $8,000 *cash inflow* per year

Last, compute the present value of an $8,000 annuity for 5 years at 12%:

Step 4: $8,000 × 3.605 = $28,840 *inflow*

E. $37,000 × .567 × $20,979 *inflow.*

F. First, compute the present value for first three years:

$73,000 × 2.402 = $175,346

Second, compute present value for last two years:

$80,000 × (3.605 − 2.402) = $80,000 × 1.203 = $96,240

Last, find the sum:

$175,346 + $96,240 = $271,586 *inflow* from savings

G. First, compute present value for first three years:

$29,200 × 2.402 = $70,138

Second, compute present value for last two years:

$32,000 × 1.203 × $38,496

Last, find the sum:

$70,138 + $38,496 = $108,634 *outflow* from tax effect on savings

H. $2,500 × 3.605 = $9,013 *outflow* from maintenance.

I. $1,000 × 3.605 = $3,605 *inflow* from tax effect on maintenance.

Investment in an E-90 computer would also return more than our minimum of 12%. Both offers are acceptable—however, only one can be chosen. With the time-adjusted rate of return method we would simply choose the computer system promising the highest rate of return. With the net present value method it is not as easy to choose between mutually exclusive investments. In this instance, all we know is that both alternatives promise a return higher than 12%. We cannot make the choice on the basis of the excess present value alone, for each alternative requires a different incremental investment. However, considering both elements, we could combine the required incremental investment and the excess present value and determine an index:

$$\text{Excess Present Value Index} = \frac{\text{Excess Present Value}}{\text{Present Value of Incremental Investment}}$$

Using this index as a means for ranking alternatives analyzed with the net present value method, the Armstrong Publishing Company should invest in the E-90 computer system:

X22 COMPUTER SYSTEM:

$$\text{Index} = \frac{20{,}911}{180{,}000} = \underline{\underline{.1162}}$$

E-90 COMPUTER SYSTEM:

$$\text{Index} = \frac{23{,}642}{(77{,}868 - 31{,}147) + 137{,}000} = \underline{\underline{.1287}}$$

24.7 OTHER ASPECTS OF DISCOUNTED CASH FLOW ANALYSIS

The outcome under both of our discounted cash flow methods—time-adjusted rate of return and net present value—can be affected by the choice of depreciation methods and by the way in which an *asset exchange* is handled.

Accelerated depreciation methods produce greater cash flows earlier in the life of an investment, and hence produce larger total present values than straight-line. Using the principle methods of depreciation, Exhibit 24-12 demonstrates the difference in cash flows produced by the tax effect. However, as mentioned in chapter 13, the choice of depreciation methods does not increase or decrease the total amount of depreciation, but it does alter the time flow of depreciation, and hence has a bearing on cash flows resulting from a tax effect.

EXHIBIT 24-12 TAX EFFECT FROM DEPRECIATION

Assume:
- **Asset cost** **$60,000**
- **Salvage** **$6,000**
- **Life** .... **4 years**
- **Tax rate** **40%**
- **Minimum desired rate of return** **10%**

	Present Value	**End of Year 1**	**2**	**3**	**4**
1. Straight-Line	17,118	5,400	5,400	5,400	5,400
2. Double-Declining Balance	10,908	12,000			
	4,956		6,000		
	2,253			3,000	
	410				600
	18,527				
3. Sum-of-the-Years'-Digits	7,854	8,640			
	5,352		6,480		
	3,244			4,320	
	1,475				2,160
	17,925*				

*Alternative calculation using Table B-5 of Appendix B:

P.V. of Deprec. = (60,000 − 6,000) × .830135 = 44,827
P.V. of Tax Effect = 44,827 × 40% = 17,930

Calculation of values for Exhibit 24-12:

1. Straight-line calculations:

$60,000 − $6,000 = $54,000 depreciable cost
$54,000/4 years = $13,500 annual depreciation
$13,500 × 40% = $5,400 tax shield
$5,400 × 3.170 = $17,118

2. Double-declining balance calculations:

$$\text{Deprec. Rate} = (1/4 \text{ yrs.}) \times 2 = 50\%$$

Year	Book Value		Deprec. Rate		Annual Deprec.		Tax Rate		Tax Shield		P.V. Factor		P.V.
1	60,000	×	.50	=	30,000	×	.40	=	12,000	×	.909	=	10,908
2	30,000	×	.50	=	15,000	×	.40	=	6,000	×	.826	=	4,956
3	15,000	×	.50	=	7,500	×	.40	=	3,000	×	.751	=	2,253
4	7,500				1,500[12]	×	.40	=	600	×	.683	=	410

3. Sum-of-the-years'-digits calculations:

$$\text{Fraction Denominator} = n\left[\frac{n+1}{2}\right] = 4\left[\frac{5}{2}\right] = 10$$

Year	Deprec. Cost		Fraction		Annual Deprec.		Tax Rate		Tax Shield		P.V. Factor		P.V.
1	54,000	×	4/10	=	21,600	×	.40	=	8,640	×	.909	=	7,854
2	54,000	×	3/10	=	16,200	×	.40	=	6,480	×	.826	=	5,352
3	54,000	×	2/10	=	10,800	×	.40	=	4,320	×	.751	=	3,244
4	54,000	×	1/10	=	5,400	×	.40	=	2,160	×	.683	=	1,475

Clearly, the choice of depreciation methods will affect the outcome of our discounted cash flow analysis. When examining any one investment opportunity, the depreciation method chosen should be *correct for the circumstances.* That is, it should be the method the company would choose if it already owned the investment. For mutually exclusive alternatives, the same is true. However, for most situations, the analysis would use identical depreciation methods for each investment. Why should the higher rate of return produced by an accelerated depreciation method cause an equal or better investment opportunity to be rejected simply because the analysis used straight-line depreciation? Careful attention should be paid to this point.

Another problem that sometimes arises involves the correct determination of cash flows on an asset exchange. When an exchange is involved, any gain or loss arising from the exchange can either be recognized now or absorbed in the depreciable base of the new asset.[13] For instance, suppose the Newell Company is analyzing an investment opportunity that involves the trade-in of an old machine with a book value of $8,000. The new machine costs $60,000, has a four-year life, and has an estimated salvage of $4,000. The trade-in allowance on the old machine will be $15,000. Assuming a 40% tax rate, a 10% minimum desired rate of return, and straight-line depreciation, the *cash flows* resulting from the exchange are shown in Exhibits 24-13 and 24-14.

When gain or loss is not recognized, the depreciation charges on the new equipment are altered to reflect a spreading of the gain or loss over the life of the new asset. Consequently, when a gain is involved, the non-recognition of this gain produces a larger positive present value then would recognition. Not recognizing an increase in income now results in lower depreciation expense in future periods, and thus spreads the gain over the new investment period. The cash outflow resulting from the increased tax now occurs in later periods. Hence, the present value of these

[12] Book value cannot fall below salvage of $6,000.

[13] On the exchange of similar assets, the IRS will not allow any gain or loss to be recognized on the exchange. The gain or loss must be used to amend the depreciable base of the newly acquired asset.

outflows will be less than if the gain were recognized at the time of exchange. With a loss, the reverse is true. To produce a *greater present value* of cash flows, *losses* should be *recognized on an exchange*, while *gains should not.*

EXHIBIT 24-13 ASSET EXCHANGE WITH RECOGNITION OF GAIN OR LOSS

	P.V. at 10%	End of Year 1	2	3	4
A. Purchase of new machine	(60,000)				
B. Trade-in allowance on old machine	15,000				
C. *Tax effect* on gain	(2,800)				
D. *Tax shield* on deprec.	17,752	5,600	5,600	5,600	5,600
E. Salvage	2,732				4,000
Net present value	(27,316)				

Calculation of values for Exhibit 24-13:

A. Given.

B. Given.

C. \$15,000 − \$8,000 = \$7,000 *gain* on exchange.
\$7,000 × 40% = \$2,800 *outflow* from tax effect on gain.

D. Step 1: \$60,000 − \$4,000 (salvage) = \$56,000 depreciable base.
Step 2: \$56,000/4 years = \$14,000 annual depreciation.
Step 3: \$14,000 × 40% = \$5,600 *inflow* per year from tax effect on depreciation.
Step 4: \$5,600 × 3.170 = \$17,752 *inflow.*

E. \$5,000 × .683 = \$2,732 *inflow* from salvage.

EXHIBIT 24-14 ASSET EXCHANGE WITH NON-RECOGNITION OF GAIN OR LOSS

	P.V. at 10%	End of Year 1	2	3	4
A. Purchase of new machine	(60,000)				
B. Trade-in allowance on old machine	15,000				
C. *Tax shield* on deprec.	15,533	4,900	4,900	4,900	4,900
D. Salvage	2,732				4,000
Net present value	(26,735)				

Calculation of values for Exhibit 24-14:

A. Given.

B. Given.

C. Step 1: \$15,000 − \$8,000 = \$7,000 *gain* on exchange.
Step 2: Cost − Gain − Salvage = depreciable base.
\$60,000 − \$7,000 − \$4,000 = \$49,000
Step 3: \$49,000/4 years = \$12,250 annual depreciation.
Step 4: \$12,250 × 40% = \$4,900 *inflow* per year from tax effect on depreciation.
Step 5: \$4,900 × 3.17 = \$15,533 *inflow.*

D. \$4,000 × .683 = \$2,732 *inflow* from salvage.

24.8 MULTIPLE-SEQUENCE PROBLEMS

So far the purpose of our capital budgeting analysis is to make the one best decision for the investment period—buy machine A, launch a new product, expand our plant by 2,000 sq. ft., etc. There is another type of budgeting analysis, however, involving the *best sequence of decisions* for the investment period. This analysis is facilitated through the use of *decision trees.* With this method, we diagram those decision processes characterized by a sequence of decisions, with each decision being dependent on the previous decision and a probability distribution of outcomes resulting from that previous decision.

There are two techniques for solving decision tree problems—*forward induction* and *backward induction.* With forward induction the result of a decision outcome is expressed as an *annualized expected value.* With backward induction the result of a decision is an outcome expressed as a *probability distribution.* The distribution of each outcome is used to compute a *cumulative expected value* for each decision.

EXHIBIT 24-15 DECISION TREE SHOWING POSSIBLE OUTCOMES FROM EACH DECISION

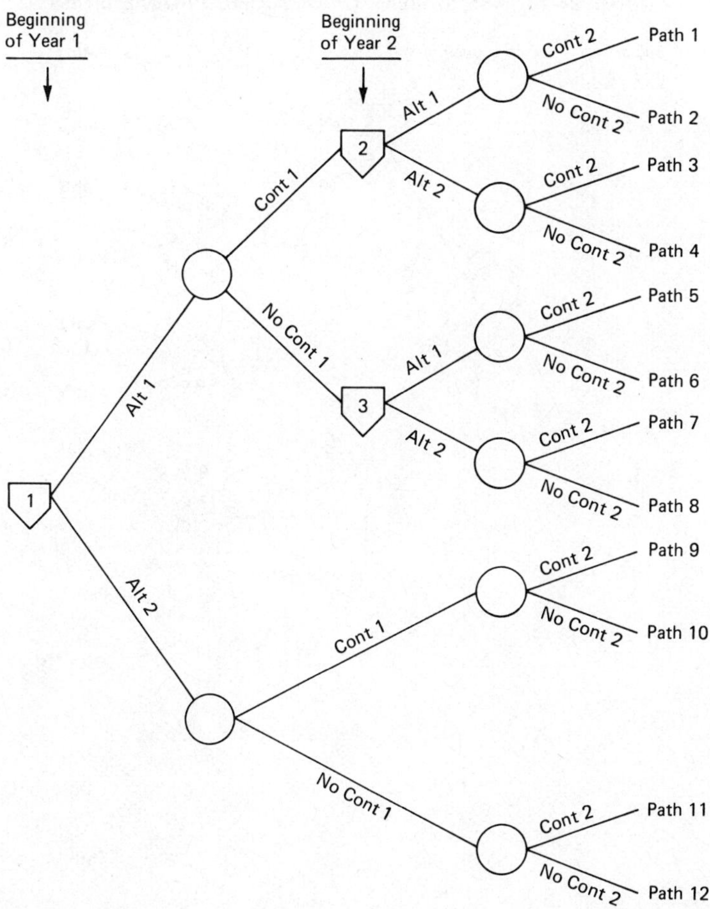

BACKWARD INDUCTION

Suppose the Holly Company must choose between a two-year investment in either alternative 1 or alternative 2. In the first year there is a possibility of obtaining contract 1; in the second, a possibility of obtaining contract 2. Consequently, the decision tree in Exhibit 24-15 shows two possible outcomes for each decision—obtain contract or no contract. The symbol ⬠ represents a decision point and the symbol ○ represents a chance event. Assume the following information is available:

1. The outcome probabilities as assigned in Exhibit 24-16.
2. Present value of incremental cash income is $32,000 for contract 1 and $36,000 for contract 2.
3. Alternative 1 costs $18,000; alternative 2 costs $20,000.
4. Straight-line depreciation; no salvage value; two-year life.
5. 40% tax rate.
6. 12% minimum desired rate of return.
7. The choice of alternative 2 precludes the later choice of alternative 1.
8. Disposal value of alternative 1 after one year is $14,000.

EXHIBIT 24-16 ASSIGNMENT OF OUTCOME PROBABILITIES

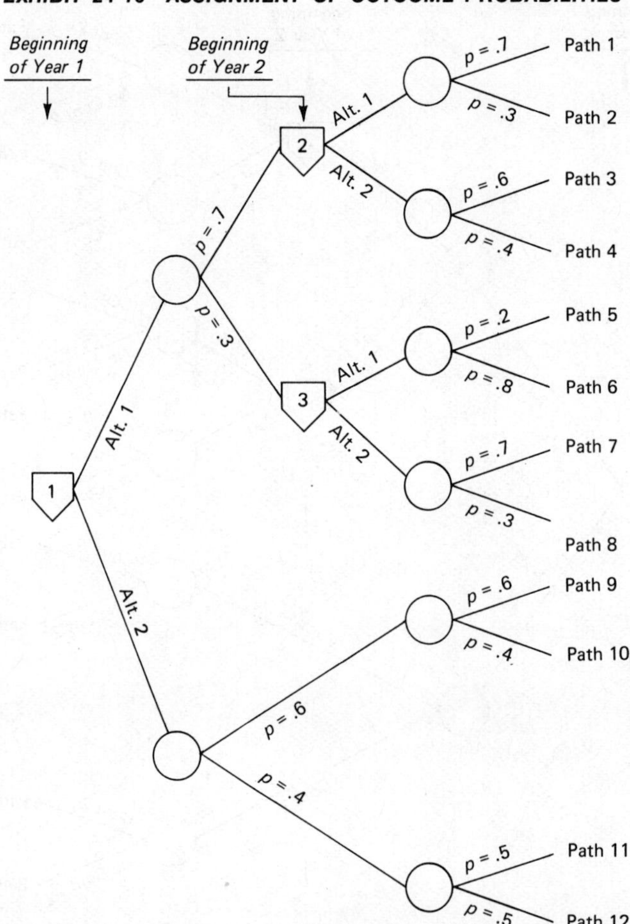

The first stage of the solution requires that we compute the cumulative outcomes for each path:

Depreciation Tax Shield for Alternative 1:

$18,000/2 years = $9,000 annual depreciation
$9,000 × 40% = $3,600 tax shield
Present value 1 year from now: $3,600 × .893 = $3,215
Present value 2 years from now: $3,600 × .797 = $2,869

Depreciation Tax Shield for Alternative 2:

$20,000/2 years = $10,000 annual depreciation
$10,000 × 40% = $3,600 tax shield
Present value 1 year from now: $4,000 × .893 = $3,572
Present value 2 years from now: $4,000 × .797 = $3,188

Purchase of Alternative 2 in Year 2 (and Disposal of Alternative 1):

Disposal of Alternative 1:	$ 14,000	
Purchase of Alternative 2:	(20,000)	
Gain (14,000 − 9,000 accum. deprec.)		
Tax effect on gain: 5,000 × 40%	(2,000)	
Total cash flow	(8,000)	
Present value of cash flow: 8,000 × .893		$(7,144)

Path	Contract 1	Contract 2	Tax Effect on Income	Cost of Alt. 1	Cost of Alt. 2	Depreciation Tax Shield	Cumulative Total
1	32,000	36,000	(27,200)	(18,000)	—	(3,215) + (2,869)	16,716
2	32,000	—	(12,800)	(18,000)	—	(3,215) + (2,869)	(4,884)
3	32,000	37,000	(27,200)	(18,000)	(7,144)	(3,215) + (3,572)	8,869
4	32,000	—	(12,800)	(18,000)	(7,144)	(3,215) + (3,572)	(12,731)
5	—	36,000	(14,400)	(18,000)	—	(3,215) + (2,869)	(2,484)
6	—	—	—	(18,000)	—	(3,215) + (2,869)	(24,084)
7	—	36,000	(14,400)	(18,000)	(7,144)	(3,215) + (3,572)	(10,331)
8	—	—	—	(18,000)	(7,144)	(3,215) + (3,572)	(31,931)
9	32,000	36,000	(27,200)	—	(20,000)	(3,572) + (3,188)	14,040
10	32,000	—	(12,800)	—	(20,000)	(3,572) + (3,188)	(7,560)
11	—	36,000	(14,400)	—	(20,000)	(3,572) + (3,188)	(5,160)
12	—	—	—	—	(20,000)	(3,572) + (3,188)	(26,760)

Using the cumulative totals for each path, we apply backward induction and compute the *cumulative expected cash flow* for all outcomes at each decision point, starting with the last decisions and working back. These cumulative values, as shown in Exhibit 24-17, are computed by finding the expected value of each decision using the probabilities assigned to outcomes. Only the *highest cumulative expected cash flow at each decision node* is considered for further computation. The cumulative expected value computations are as follows:

At Decision Node [2]

Path 1:	.7 × 16,716	=	11,701
Path 2:	.3 × (4,884)	=	(1,465)
			10,236

EXHIBIT 24-17 CUMULATIVE EXPECTED VALUES OF OUTCOMES

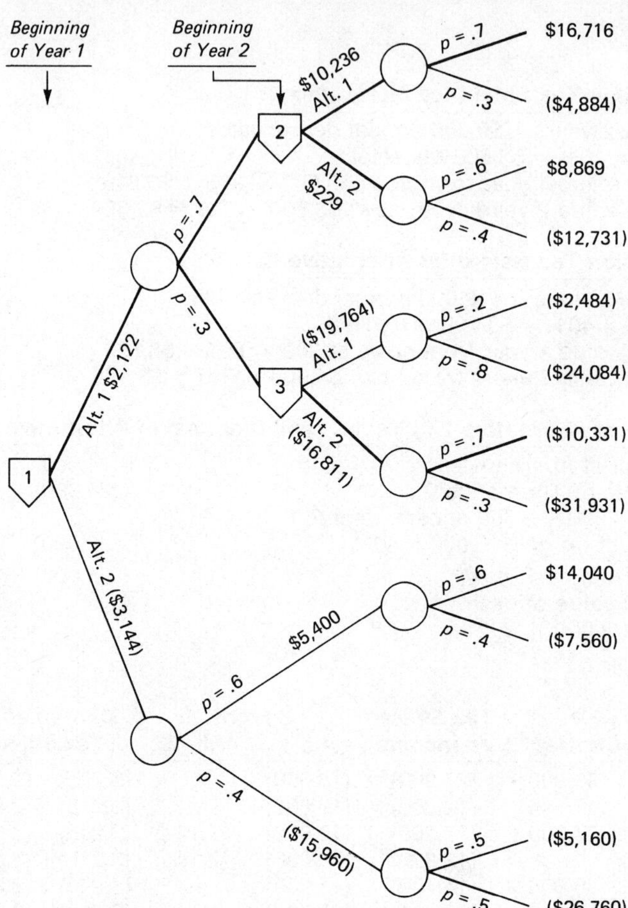

Path 3: .6 × 8.869 =	5,321	
Path 4: .4 × (12,731) =	(5,092)	
	229	Answer: 10,236 > 229

At Decision Node [3]

Path 5: .2 × (2,484) =	(497)	
Path 6: .8 × (24,084) =	(19,267)	
	(19,764)	
Path 7: .7 × (10,331) =	(7,232)	
Path 8: .3 × (31,931) =	(9,579)	
	(16,811)	Answer: (16,811) > (19,764)

At Decision Node [1]

Alternative 1:

Answer at Decision Node 2: 10,236 × .7 =	7,165
Answer at Decision Node 3: (16,811) × .3 =	(5,043)
Cumulative Expected Present Value:	2,122

Alternative 2:

Path 9: .6 × 14,040 =	8,424	
Path 10: .4 × (7,560) =	(3,024)	
	5,400 × .6 =	3,240
Path 11: .5 × (5,160) =	(2,580)	
Path 12: .5 × (26,760) =	(13,380)	
	(15,960) × .4 =	(6,384)
Cumulative Expected Present Value:		(3,144)

From our computations, the best sequence of decisions is shown by the *darkened lines* of Exhibit 24-17:

1. Alternative 1 should be chosen in year 1.
2. Alternative 1 should again be chosen in year 2 if contract 1 is obtained; if not, alternative 2 should be chosen in year 2.

FOREWARD INDUCTION

Suppose the Syverson Company is considering replacing its heavy machinery, now worth $50,000, with new machinery costing $170,000. Labeling the *keep decision* as alternative 1 and the *replace decision* as alternative 2, the possible sequence decisions for a four-year investment period are shown in Exhibit 24-18. The two outer paths represent the same type of decisions as analyzed in earlier discussions—that is, a

EXHIBIT 24-18 DECISION TREE ANALYSIS WITH "EXPECTED VALUE" OUTCOMES

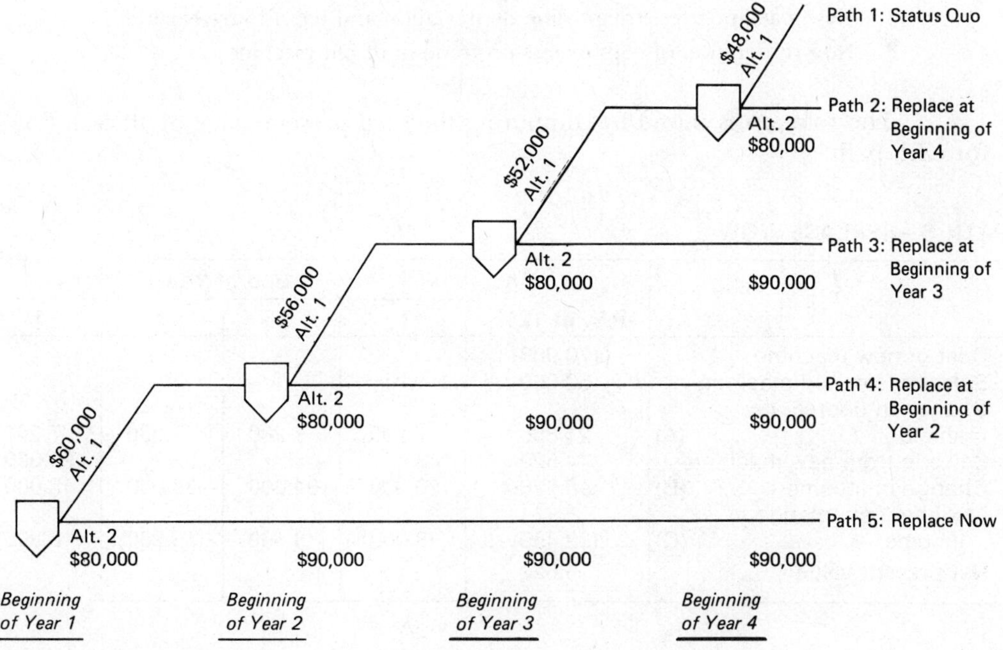

decision either to maintain the status quo (keep the machine for four years) or invest in new machinery now. The remaining paths represent replacement decisions later in the period of analysis. Assume the following information is available:

1.

Beginning of Year	Cost of New Machine*	Value of Old Machine†	Book Value of Old Machine
1	170,000	50,000	46,000
2	173,400	48,000	40,000
3	176,868	46,000	34,000
4	180,405	44,000	28,000

*Cost of new machine increases by 2% per year.
† Value of old machinery declines by $2,000 per year.

2.

	Annual Cash Income			
	1	2	3	4
Alternative 1*	60,000	56,000	52,000	48,000
Alternative 2	80,000	90,000	90,000	90,000

*Income from old machinery will drop off $4,000 per year due to breakdowns, costly labor, etc.

3.

	After Operating:			
	1 yr.	2 yrs.	3 yrs.	4 yrs.
Salvage value or premature retirement value of new machinery	140,000	110,000	80,000	70,000

4. 12% minimum desired rate of return.
5. 40% tax rate.
6. Depreciation on old machine is $6,000 per year.
7. New machine uses straight-line depreciation and has a four-year life.
8. Non-recognition of gain or loss on trade-in of old machine.

The solution is found by computing the total present value of all cash flows for each path:

PATH 5—REPLACE NOW

	P.V. at 12%	End of Year 1	2	3	4
Cost of new machine	(170,000)				
Salvage from old machine	50,000				
Change in deprec. tax shield (A)	21,866	7,200	7,200	7,200	7,200
Salvage from new machine	44,520				70,000
Change in income (B)	98,726	20,000	34,000	38,000	42,000
Tax effect on change in income (C)	(39,490)	(8,000)	(9,600)	(15,200)	(16,800)
Net present value	5,622				

Notes:

A. Gain on trade-in = 50,000 − 46,000 = $4,000
Depreciable base = 170,000 − 4,000 − 70,000[14] = $96,000
Depreciation = 96,000/4 = $24,000 annually
Change in depreciation = 24,000 − 6,000 = $18,000
Tax shield = 18,000 × 40% = $7,200 per year
Present value of tax shield = 7,200 × 3.037 = $21,866

B.
1st yr:	80,000 − 60,000 = 20,000 × .893 =	$17,860
2nd yr:	90,000 − 56,000 = 34,000 × .797 =	27,098
3rd yr:	90,000 − 52,000 = 38,000 × .712 =	27,056
4th yr:	90,000 − 48,000 = 42,000 × .636 =	26,712
		$98,726

C. 98,726 × 40% = ($39,490)

PATH 4—REPLACE AT BEGINNING OF SECOND YEAR

		End of Year			
	P.V. at 12%	1	2	3	4
Cost of new machine	(154,846)	(173,400)			
Salvage from old machine	42,864	48,000			
Change in deprec. tax shield (A)	15,308	0	7,140	7,140	7,140
Salvage from premature retirement of new machine	50,880				80,000
Tax effect from loss on premature retirement (B)	3,523				5,540
Change in income (C)	73,400	0	24,000	38,000	42,000
Tax effect on changed income	(29,360)	0	(9,600)	(15,200)	(16,800)
Net present value	1,769				

Notes:

A. Gain on trade-in = 48,000 − 40,000 = $8,000
Depreciable base = 173,400 − 8,000 − 70,000 = $95,400
Depreciation = 95,400/4 = $23,850 annually
Change in depreciation = 23,850 − 6,000 = $17,850 for last 3 years
Tax shield = 17,850 × 40% = $7,140
Present value of tax shield = 7,140 × (3.037 − .893) = $15,308

B. 3 years depreciation = 23,850 × 3 = $71,550
Book value at trade-in = 165,400[15] − 71,550 = $93,850
Loss on retirement = 93,850 − 80,000 = $13,850
Tax effect = 13,850 × 40% = $5,540
Present value of tax effect = 5,540 × .636 = $3,523

C.
1st yr:	no change = 0 =	0
2nd yr:	80,000 − 56,000 = 24,000 × .797 =	$19,128
3rd yr:	90,000 − 52,000 = 38,000 × .712 =	27,560
4th yr:	90,000 − 48,000 = 42,000 × .636 =	26,712
		$73,400

[14] Salvage at end of four-year life.

[15] The *recorded cost* is $173,400 − $8,000 (gain) = $165,400.

PATH 3—REPLACE AT BEGINNING OF THIRD YEAR

	P.V. at 12%	End of Year 1	2	3	4
Cost of new machine	(140,964)		(176,868)		
Salvage from old machine	36,662		46,000		
Change in deprec. tax shield (A)	9,546	0	0	7,087	7,087
Salvage from premature retirement of new machine	69,960				110,000
Tax effect from loss on premature retirement (B)	1,891				2,974
Change in income (C)	46,648	0	0	28,000	42,000
Tax effect on changed income	(18,659)	0	0	(11,200)	(16,800)
Net present value	5,084				

Notes:

A. Gain of trade-in = 46,000 − 34,000 = \$12,000
Depreciable base = 176,868 − 12,000 − 70,000 = \$94,868
Depreciation = 94,868/4 = \$23,717 annually
Change in depreciation = 23,717 − 6,000 = \$17,717 for last 2 years
Tax shield = \$17,717 × 40% = \$7,087
Present value of tax shield = 7,087 × (3.037 − 1.690) = \$9,546

B. 2 years depreciation = 23,717 × 2 = \$47,434
Book value at trade-in = 164,868[16] − 47,434 = \$117,434
Loss on retirement = 117,434 − 110,000 = \$7,434
Tax effect = 7,434 × 40% = \$2,974
Present value of tax effect = 2,974 × .636 = \$1,891

C. 3rd yr: 80,000 − 52,000 = 28,000 × .712 = \$19,936
4th yr: 90,000 − 48,000 = 42,000 × .636 = 26,712
\$46,648

PATH 2—REPLACE AT BEGINNING OF FOURTH YEAR

	P.V. at 12%	End of Year 1	2	3	4
Cost of new machine	(128,448)			(180,405)	
Salvage from old machine	31,328			44,000	
Change in deprec. tax shield (A)	4,477	0	0	0	7,040
Salvage from premature retirement of new machine	89,040				140,000
Tax effect from loss on premature retirement (B)	205				322
Change in income (C)	20,352				32,000
Tax effect on changed income	(8,141)				(12,800)
Net present value	8,813				

Notes:

A. Gain on trade-in = 44,000 − 28,000 = \$16,000
Depreciable base = 180,405 − 16,000 − 70,000 = \$94,405
Depreciation = 94,405/4 = \$23,601 annually
Change in depreciation = 23,601 − 6,000 = \$17,601

[16] The *recorded cost* is \$176,868 − \$12,000 (gain) = \$164,868.

Tax shield = 17,601 × 40% = $7,040
Present value of tax shield = 7,040 × .636 = $4,477

B. Book value at trade-in = 164,405[17] − 23,601 = $140,804
Loss on retirement = 140,804 − 140,000 = $804
Tax effect on loss = 804 × 40% = $322
Present value of tax effect = 322 × .636 = $205

C. 4th yr: 80,000 − 48,000 = 32,000 × .636 = $20,352

Based upon our decision tree analysis, we should invest in new machinery at the beginning of the fourth year. What this means, of course, is that no investment should take place now despite the fact that an investment now returns more than 12%. It is still the *investment period* we are concerned about, and a decision to invest now is improper when compared with the alternative decision of investing later.

The basic difference, then, between backward induction and forward induction is that with the latter the decision outcome was never in doubt, it was calculated as a long-run result—an annualized expected value. Further decisions were not made upon obtaining or not obtaining a contract, but upon the expected value alone. The use of annualized expected values should yield decisions similar to those obtained by cumulative expected values (obtained through backward induction), but this use will not produce decisions which are responsive to actual outcomes. Backward induction, with the use of probabilities, is the preferable treatment. However, where practical problems are concerned, backward induction, with its many probable outcomes, is a good deal more detailed and cumbersome than using only annualized expected value outcomes of forward induction.

24.9 SUMMARY

Capital budgeting is an analysis that enables us to plan for the acquisition of assets having a significant influence on operating activity. This analysis examines the future differential costs and revenues for each possible investment by estimating future conditions under the status quo and comparing them with estimated future conditions for each new investment.

When investing, we acquire the financial consequences of the period in which the asset is operational. Capital budgeting, then, is essentially a period analysis, not an asset analysis. The investment periods for each alternative should be equal. This is facilitated through recycling and/or truncation.

One method of analysis is to compute a return on investment. This can be based upon either *income flow* or *cash flow.* With cash flow, however, we can adjust for the time value of money and compute a time-adjusted rate of return. The time-adjusted rate is then compared against a minimum desired rate to judge the adequacy of returns.

The minimum desired rate, or *cost of capital,* is what it costs the firm to invest using either its own or borrowed capital. The preferred computation of this rate is the estimated future earnings (after taxes) divided by the market value of existing assets.

Another method of analysis—the net present value method—uses the mini-

[17] The *recorded cost* is $180,405 − $16,000 (gain) = $164,405.

mum desired rate of return to discount future cash flows to the present. For any one investment, if the sum of the present value of cash flows is positive, the investment should be undertaken, for it will earn above the minimum. If there are several competing alternatives, the investment with the highest excess present value index is chosen.

Some aspects of cash flow analysis involve the choice of depreciation methods and the handling of an asset exchange. Accelerated depreciation methods will yield larger present values than straight-line, and asset exchanges can be recorded with or without the recognition of a gain or loss.

A special type of capital budgeting analysis is used when an investment period involves a sequence of decisions. Decision trees are constructed and present values for alternative investments are calculated using either *forward* or *backward induction.*

CHAPTER 24 REFERENCES AND ADDITIONAL READINGS

Anderson, Lesli P., and Miller, Vergil V. "Capital Budgeting: A Modified Approach to Capital Allocation." *Management Accounting,* March 1969, pp. 28–32.

Beechy, Thomas H. "Quasi-Debt Analysis of Financial Leases." *The Accounting Review,* April 1969, pp. 375–88.

Bierman, Harold Jr., and Dyckman, Thomas R. *Managerial Cost Accounting.* New York: The Macmillan Company, 1971.

Bierman, Harold J., and Smidt, Seymour. *The Capital Budgeting Decision.* 2nd ed. New York: The Macmillan Company, 1966.

Binzel, Philip W. "Measurement of Investment Opportunities by the Profitability Index Procedure." *Budgeting,* January–February 1968, pp. 16–19.

Burkert, Ronald L. "Recognizing Inflation in the Capital Budgeting Decision." *Management Accounting,* November 1971, pp. 40–46.

Burton, Richard M., and Holzer, H. Peter. "To Buy or to Make?" *Management Services,* July–August 1968, pp. 26–31.

Christy, George A. *Capital Budgeting: Current Practices and Their Efficiency.* Eugene, Oreg.: University of Oregon Press, 1966.

Dean, Joel. *Capital Budgeting.* New York: Columbia University Press, 1951.

Doney, Lloyd D. "Coping with Uncertainty in the Make or Buy Decision." *Management Accounting,* October 1968, pp. 31–34.

Donis, Jack P. "Unresolved Problems in Capital Budgeting Application." *The Financial Executive,* May 1967, pp. 73–78.

Ferrara, William L. "Capital Budgeting and Financing or Leasing Decisions." *Management Accounting,* July 1968, pp. 55–63.

Financial Analysis Techniques for Equipment Replacement Decision. New York: National Association of Accountants, 1965.

Geiler, Louis. "Analysis of Uncertainty in Capital Expenditures." *Management Accounting,* January 1970, pp. 32–36.

Gilkison, Robert C., and Von Furstenberg, George. "The Use of Regression Analysis to Estimate Accrual of Capital Grants Earned in the Urban Renewal Program." *The Federal Accountant,* December 1968, pp. 21–30.

Greer, Willis R. "Capital Budgeting Analysis with the Timing of Events Uncertain." *The Accounting Review,* January 1970, pp. 103–114.

Gross, Harry. *Make or Buy.* Englewood Cliffs, N.J.: Prentice-Hall, Inc., 1967.

Hammond, J. "Better Decisions with Preference Theory." *Harvard Business Review,* November–December 1967, pp. 123–41.

Hertz, D. "Investment Policies That Pay Off." *Harvard Business Review,* January–February 1968, pp. 96–108.

Hespos, R., and Strassman, P. "Stochastic Decision Trees for the Analysis of Investment Decisions." *Management Science,* August 1965, pp. 244–59.

Hicks, Carl F., and Schmidt, L. Lee Jr. "Post-Auditing and Capital Investment Decisions." *Management Accounting,* August 1971, pp. 24–28, 32.

Hillier, F. S. "The Derivation of Probabilistic Information for the Evaluation of Risky Investments." *Management Science,* April 1963, pp. 443–57.

Hise, Richard T., and Strawser, Robert H. "Application of Capital Budgeting Techniques to Marketing Operations." *MSU Business Topics,* Summer 1970, pp. 69–76.

House, William C. Jr. *Sensitivity Analysis in Making Capital Investment Decisions.* NAA Research Monograph No. 3. New York: National Association of Accountants, 1968.

Jensen, Michael C. "Risk, the Pricing of Capital Assets, and the Evaluation of Investment Portfolios." *Journal of Business,* April 1969, pp. 167–247.

Johnson, Glenn L., and Newton, Sherwood W. "Tax Considerations in Equipment Replacement Decisions." *The Accounting Review,* October 1967, pp. 738–46.

Kolb, Burton A. "Problems and Pitfalls in Capital Budgeting." *Financial Analysts Journal,* November–December 1968, pp. 170–74.

Luneski, Chris. "Continuous Versus Discrete Compounding for Capital Budgeting Decisions." *The Accounting Review,* October 1967, pp. 767–71.

Magee, J. "How to Use Decision Trees in Capital Investment." *Harvard Business Review,* September–October 1964, pp. 79–96.

Mao, James C. T. "Survey of Capital Budgeting: Theory and Practice." *Journal of Finance,* May 1970, pp. 349–60.

Moag, Joseph S., and Lerner, Eugene M. "Capital Budgeting Decisions Under Imperfect Market Conditions—A Systems Framework." *The Journal of Finance,* September 1969, pp. 613–21.

Norgaard, Richard L., and Pettiway, Richard H. "Evaluating Average Ratios Used in Capital Budgeting." *Management Accounting,* December 1966, pp. 16–20.

Parker, R. H. "Discounted Cash Flow in Historical Perspective." *Journal of Accounting Research,* Spring 1968, pp. 58–71.

Querin, G. D. *The Capital Expenditure Decision.* Homewood, Ill.: Richard D. Irwin, Inc., 1967.

Robicheck, Alexander A., and Myers, S. C. *Optimal Financing Decisions.* Englewood Cliffs, N.J.: Prentice-Hall, Inc., 1965.

Robichek, Alexander A.; Ogilvie, Donald G.; and Roach, John D. C. "Capital Budgeting: A Pragmatic Approach." *Financial Executive,* April 1969, pp. 26–38.

Sampson, Anthony A. "Measuring the Rate of Return on Capital." *The Journal of Finance,* March 1969, pp. 61–74.

Schmukler, Nathan. "Capital Mobility and the Investment Decision." *Management Services,* July–August 1967, pp. 13–20.

Vatter, William J. "Continuous Discounting and the Force of Interest." *Management Accounting,* August 1968, pp. 51–54.

CHAPTER 24 QUESTIONS, PROBLEMS, AND CASES

24- 1. Define the following:
(a) Future-differential costs
(b) Status quo
(c) Recycling
(d) Truncation
(e) Time-adjusted rate of return
(f) Minimum desired rate of return
(g) Tax effect
(h) Cost of capital
(i) Mutually exclusive investments

24- 2. "Our investment in an operating asset is not made by comparing only the cost of each acceptable machine, but by examining the financial conditions imposed by each over the period of potential use." Explain the significance of this statement.

24- 3. "For the investment period as a whole, the income flows and cash flows should yield identical totals." Why? What are the advantages of analysis using cash flow over one using income flow? Which yields the higher rate of return? Why?

24- 4. Explain the consequences of taxation on cash flow.

24- 5. When using the time-adjusted rate of return method, what are the difficulties caused by uneven cash flow? What approach is used in handling these difficulties?

24- 6. "The cost of capital computation using market value of equity could lead to an incorrect investment decision, since goodwill—as a reflection of excess earning power of the existing asset structure—will be reduced by acceptance of investments having a return which is too low." Explain the significance of this statement, and its implication for calculating a minimum desired rate of return.

24- 7. If the net present value of an investment is positive, what can we say about the time-adjusted rate of return? Why?

24- 8. "We cannot make the choice among alternatives on the basis of excess present value alone, for each alternative requires a different incremental investment." How is the choice made?

24- 9. What cash flow effects are produced by non-recognition of gain or loss on an exchange of assets? How are the effects different if gain or loss is recognized?

24-10. Explain the basic difference between *forward induction* and *backward induction*. Which is more practical? Why? Explain the computational procedure of backward induction.

24-11. Identify the elements in the decision making process:

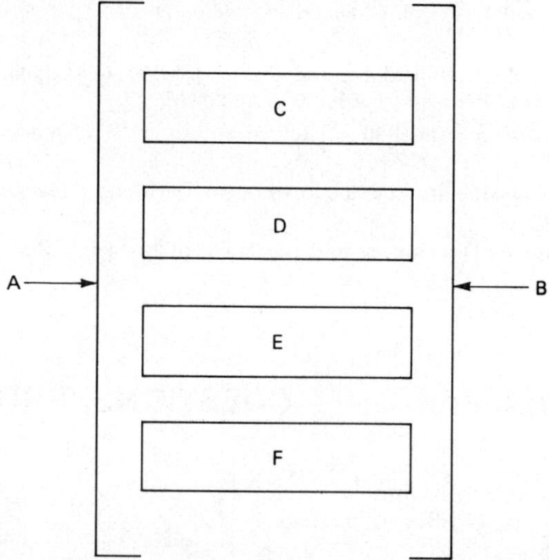

24-12. When making an investment decision, we are only concerned with future financial conditions that differ from the status quo. Discuss.

24-13. Why is it necessary that all alternative investment opportunities have equal lives? When investment lives do not correspond, what are the two rules which apply in this situation?

24-14. How is the incremental investment determined? How is it determined if lease payments are involved and the net present value method is used for analysis?

24-15. When the status quo is recycled, how are the incremental returns of alternative investments calculated?

24-16. "It is depreciation, and any subsequent gains or losses from disposal, that cause income flow to represent a lesser return than cash flow." Explain how this occurs.

24-17. "In a cash flow analysis anything that affects income produces a related cash flow from the tax on the increase or decrease." Explain how this occurs. What does this mean in regard to depreciation?

24-18. Is a *time-adjusted* rate of return potentially more useful than an *unadjusted* rate? Is the time-adjusted rate the *cost of capital?*

24-19. Why is the computation of time-adjusted rate of return so formidable when there are uneven yearly cash flows?

24-20. Demonstrate mathematically that the adjusted rate of return will always be lower than the unadjusted rate.

24-21. How is the interval of investigation determined for a trial-and-error procedure used in the computation of a time-adjusted rate of return? In other words, suggest how the *high* and *low* percentages are calculated.

24-22. In a trial-and-error procedure, if the rate chosen causes the present value of the net cash inflows to exceed the incremental cash investment, the rate chosen is too low. Why?

24-23. With interpolation between a high and low percentage in the trial-and-error method for determining the time-adjusted rate of return, the percentage obtained will always be slightly higher than the true rate. Why is this true?

24-24. Explain the use of a minimum desired rate of return in capital budgeting analysis. What relation does this rate have to the *cost of capital?*

24-25. If the net present value is positive the investment promises a time-adjusted rate of return higher than the minimum desired rate of return. Explain how we can draw this conclusion. Can you think of a circumstance when a net present value analysis can indicate a rate of return higher than the minimum rate yet show a negative net present value?

24-26. "The choice of depreciation methods does not increase or decrease the total amount of depreciation, but it does alter the time flow of depreciation, and hence has a bearing on cash flows resulting from a tax effect." Explain the difference in cash flows resulting from various depreciation methods. How do you determine which method to use in an analysis?

24-27. Define or explain the use of the following terms and phrases in capital budgeting analysis of multiple sequence problems:
(a) Decision trees
(b) Cumulative expected value
(c) Annualized expected value

24-28. ***CASH FLOW ANALYSIS*** The Robinson Company is contemplating the purchase of a machine for $84,000. The machine has a five-year life, a $14,000 salvage value, and will be depreciated using sum-of-the-years'-digits method. In addition to depreciation charges, the machine will produce the following cash flows:
(a) Operating expenses:
Years 1–3: $22,000 per year
Years 4–5: 26,000 per year
(b) The machine will be overhauled at the end of the third year for $8,000.
(c) Insurance premium is $500 per year.
(d) At the end of five years the machine will be sold for $14,000.

Required:

If the minimum desired rate of return is 12% and the tax rate is 40%, what minimum average revenue per year must the machine earn in order to be an acceptable investment?

24-29. ***DETERMINING THE INVESTMENT PERIOD***

(a) Determine the applicable investment period given the following alternative investment opportunities:

Machine A:	13 years
Machine B:	6 years
Machine C:	4 years
Machine D:	5 years

(b) Determine the applicable investment period given the following alternative investment opportunities:

Machine A:	3 years
Machine B:	14 years
Machine C:	16 years

24-30. ***INCOME FLOW APPROACH*** The Hindrickson Milk Products Company is considering the replacement of its conveyor bottling system. Financial information on its present conveyor system is:

Original cost:	$108,000
Original life:	12 years
Remaining life:	2 years
Original estimate of salvage:	0
Disposal value now:	$14,000
Operating cost per bottle:	$.04

Two local contractors have submitted bids to the Hindrickson Company for construction of a new conveyor system. The financial situation for each bid has been estimated as follows:

Bid 1: Cost of Conveyor System: $160,000
Estimated Useful Life: 10 years
Operating cost per bottle: $.03
Estimated Salvage Value:

End of Year

6	7	8	9	10	11	12
$40,000	$32,000	$22,000	$15,000	$8,000	$4,000	$2,000

Bid 2: Cost of Conveyor System: $185,000
Estimated Useful Life: 14 years
Operating cost per bottle: $.025
Estimated Salvage Value:

End of Year

8	9	10	11	12	13	14
$45,000	$34,000	$24,000	$16,000	$10,000	$5,000	$3,000

Other information:

Each conveyor system (including the original) is depreciated using the straight-line method.
Applicable tax rate is 40%.

SALES IN NUMBER OF BOTTLES

Year			
1–4	**5–8**	**9–12**	**13–**
2,000,000	2,200,000	2,300,000	2,400,000

Required:

(a) Prepare schedules detailing the incremental change in income for each bid.
(b) Compute the rate of return for each bid.

24-31. ***CASH FLOW APPROACH—UNADJUSTED*** Use the data from problem 24-30.

Required:

(a) Prepare schedule detailing the incremental change in cash flow for each bid.
(b) Compute the rate of return for each bid.

24-32. ***TIME-ADJUSTED RATE OF RETURN*** Compute the time-adjusted rate of return in each of the following circumstances:
(a) The incremental investment is $120,000 and the annual net cash savings is $26,000.
(b) The incremental investment is $45,000 and the annual net cash savings are:

End of Year				
1	**2**	**3**	**4**	**5**
$10,000	$15,500	$17,200	$14,300	$9,400

24-33. ***CAPITAL BUDGETING ANALYSIS—COMPREHENSIVE PROBLEM*** Consider the following three mutually exclusive investment opportunities:

Plan A A machine costing $700 will be bought. This machine has a useful life of five years (for depreciation purposes) and a disposal value of $100 at the end of five years. This plan, however, requires the machine to be traded in for $250 on a similar machine at the end of four years. The cost of a new machine at this time is expected to be $900 and have an estimated useful life (for depreciation purposes) of only four years. The disposal value of this new machine after four years is expected to be $100. The annual cash operating expenses will amount to $400 in each year the first machine is used and $450 in each year the second machine is used. The sales revenue will be $1,000 per year for each of the eight years.

Plan B A machine costing $1,600 will be bought. This machine has a useful life of eight years (for depreciation purposes) and a disposal value of $160 at the end of eight years. The annual cash operating expenses will amount to $425 and the revenue $1,000. This machine will require an overhaul at the end of the third year costing $200, and at the end of the sixth year costing $100. (Overhauls are expensed in the year of occurrence and are not capitalized.)

Plan C A machine costing $2,000 will be bought. This machine has a useful life of eight years (for depreciation purposes) and a *zero* disposal value at the end of eight years. The annual cash operating expenses amount to $350 and the revenue $1,000.

Assume: Minimum desired rate of return is 8%.
Income tax rate of 40% on ordinary income and capital gains.
Straight-line depreciation is used, and *salvage value* is considered.
In all calculations, maintain two significant digits. Round final answer to nearest dollar.
The sales revenue *should not be excluded* from the analysis because of irrelevancy.

Required:

(a) What is the net present value of Plan A assuming any gain or loss is recognized on the exchange?
(b) What is the net present value of Plan B?
(c) What is the net present value of Plan C?
(d) On the basis of the excess present value index, which is the better investment?
(e) What is the net present value of Plan A assuming any gain or loss is not recognized on the exchange?
(f) Compute the time-adjusted rate of return on Plan C.
(g) What minimum number of service years must the machine in Plan C provide in order to earn a 16% time-adjusted rate of return?
(h) Using Plan A, compute the present value of the tax shield or tax savings resulting from depreciation deductions using sum-of-the-years'-digits depreciation with provision for residual value (both machines use this method). Assume that any gain or loss on the asset exchange in the fourth year is *not recognized.*

24-34. ***CASH FLOW APPROACH—UNADJUSTED*** The Emerson Company is planning to extend its operations and produce a new product—electronic calculators. The electric circuitry can be done by a machine that makes circuit boards, and the cases can be made by a machine that molds plastic into the desired shape. Two bids for each machine have been received:

CIRCUIT BOARD MACHINES

			Disposal Value at End of Year		
	Cost	**Useful Life**	**3**	**4**	**Operating Cost per unit**
Bid # 1	$60,000	3 yrs.	zero	—	$5.50
Bid # 2	80,000	4 yrs.	$8,000	$4,000	6.00

PLASTIC MOLDING MACHINES

			Disposal Value at End of Year				
	Cost	**Useful Life**	**6**	**7**	**8**	**9**	**Operating Cost per unit**
Bid #1	$102,000	9 yrs.	$15,000	$10,000	$7,000	zero	$4.00
Bid #2	96,000	8 yrs.	14,000	8,000	2,000	—	4.20

Other information:

(a) Operating costs per unit do not include materials cost.
(b) The circuit board machines are depreciated using the straight-line method, while the plastic molding machines use sum-of-the-years'-digits depreciation.
(c) The applicable tax rate is 40%.
(d) Each year 8,000 electronic calculators will be produced and sold to wholesalers for $150 each.
(e) The material and labor cost per unit amounts to $142.

Required:

(1) Determine the applicable investment period.
(2) Prepare a schedule of cash flows for each machine.
(3) What is the incremental investment of each circuit board machine?
(4) Which circuit board machine and which plastic molding machine should be purchased in order that together they will maximize the return on incremental investment? What return is this combination expected to earn?

24-35. ***COST OF CAPITAL*** Consider the following financial data for the Douglas Company:

Expected annual interest on debt	$ 12,000
Expected annual future net income	133,000
Market value of outstanding debt	240,000
Market value of owners' equity	360,000
Market value of assets	543,750
Income tax rate	40%

Required:

(a) Determine the cost of capital without regard to unrecorded goodwill.
(b) Determine the cost of capital considering any unrecorded goodwill.

24-36. ***NET PRESENT VALUE METHOD*** A new machine which costs $30,000 will have annual cash operating costs of $76,000 per year. The new machine will have a useful life of five years with an estimated residual value of $1,700.

Assuming a minimum desired rate of return after taxes of 14% and a 40% tax rate on ordinary income and capital gains, answer the following using the net present value technique:

Required: Compute the following:

(a) The after-tax operating costs (net present value).
(b) The tax shield or tax savings resulting from depreciation deductions using sum-of-the-years'-digits depreciation with *no* provision for residual value.
(c) The tax shield resulting from using straight-line depreciation *with* provision for residual value.
(d) The *net* cash inflow at the end of five years *from the sale* of the machine for its estimated residual value, assuming a book value at the end of five years as provided by part (b).
(e) Same as part (d) only with book value as provided by part (c).

24-37. ***NET PRESENT VALUE METHOD*** Consider the following investment opportunities:

Machine A is being offered for $1,000, with an estimated useful life of eight years and a disposal value of $200 at the end of eight years. The annual operating expenses would amount to $50. This machine would require a major overhaul the third year, costing $20, and the sixth year, costing $40.

Machine B is being offered for $500, and will have an estimated useful life of four years and a salvage at the end of four years of $100. The annual operating expenses would amount to $60. This machine will require no major overhauls. The contract would require the purchase at the end of year 4 of another machine under the same conditions described for the first machine.

Assume the following:

Minimum rate of return is 12%.
Income tax rate of 40% on ordinary income and capital gains.
Straight-line depreciation is used and salvage value is considered.

Required:

(a) What is the net present value of machine A?
(b) What is the net present value of machine B?
(c) Using the excess present value index, which machine is the better investment?

24-38. ***NET PRESENT VALUE METHOD*** ABC Co. is contemplating a new product line. If adopted, the new product will be manufactured in a factory currently being used to produce a product that is being dropped because it is losing $10,000 per year. The factory is old and has been fully depreciated. It is expected, however, that the factory has a remaining useful life of five years, which is also the expected life of the new product line. As an alternative the old factory could be sold for $50,000, subject to a capital gain tax rate of 25%.

In addition, equipment necessary to produce the new product would cost $500,000, with an expected resale value of $200,000 at the end of five years. However, for tax purposes the equipment must be depreciated over a ten-year life, using the 200% declining balance method. (Any gain or loss on disposal would be subject to the company's ordinary tax rate of 40%.) The new product line would also require that the company provide additional working capital of $100,000 at the beginning of the project and another $100,000 at the end of two years. Net sales less variable manufacturing expenses would be $100,000 during years 1 and 2, and $200,000 during years 3, 4, and 5. If ABC's minimum acceptable rate of return on investment (after tax) is 10%, should the new product line be adopted?

24-39. ***NET PRESENT VALUE ANALYSIS*** Niebuhr Corporation is beginning its first capital budgeting program and has retained you to assist the budget committee in the evaluation of a project to expand operations, designated as Proposed Expansion Project #12 (PEP #12).

1. The following capital expenditures are under consideration:

$ 300,000	Fire sprinkler system
100,000	Landscaping
600,000	Replacement of old machines
800,000	Projects to expand operations (including PEP #12)
$1,800,000	Total

2. The corporation requires no minimum return on the sprinkler system or the landscaping. However, it expects a minimum return of 6% on all investments to replace old machinery. It also expects investments in expansion projects to yield a return that will exceed the average cost of the capital required to finance the sprinkler system and the landscaping in addition to the expansion projects.

3. Under Proposed Expansion Project #12 a cash investment of $75,000 will be made one year before operations begin. The investment will be depreciated by the sum-of-the-years'-digits method over a three-year period and is expected to have a salvage value of $15,000. Additional financial data for PEP #12 follow:

Time Period	Revenue	Variable Costs	Maintenance, Property Taxes, and Insurance
0–1	$80,000	$35,000	$ 8,000
1–2	95,000	41,000	11,000
2–3	60,000	25,000	12,000

The amount of the investment recovered during each of the three years can be reinvested immediately at a rate of return approximating 15%. Each year's recovery of investment, then, will have been reinvested at 15% for an average of six months at the end of the year.

4. Assume that the corporate income tax rate is 40%.

5. The present values of $1.00 earned uniformly throughout the year and discounted at 15% follow:

Year	Present Value
0–1	$.93
1–2	.80
2–3	.69

Required:

(a) Assume that the cut-off rate for considering expansion projects is 15%. Prepare a schedule calculating the
  (1) Annual cash flows from operations for PEP #12.
  (2) Present value of the net cash flows for PEP #12.

(b) Assume that the average cost of capital is 9%. Prepare a schedule to compute the minimum return (in dollars) required on expansion projects to cover the average cost of capital for financing the sprinkler system and the landscaping in addition to expansion projects. Assume that it is necessary to replace the old machines.

(c) Assume that the minimum return computed in (b) is $150,000. Calculate the cut-off rate on expansion projects.

(Adapted from the CPA exam.)

24-40. ***NET PRESENT VALUE ANALYSIS*** Thorne Transit, Inc., has decided to inaugurate express bus service between its headquarters city and a nearby suburb (one-way fare $.50) and is considering the purchase of either thirty-two or fifty-two passenger buses, on which pertinent estimates are as follows:

	32-Passenger Bus	52-Passenger Bus
Number of each to be purchased	6	4
Useful life	8 years	8 years
Purchase price of each bus (paid on delivery)	$80,000	$110,000
Mileage per gallon	10	7 1/2
Salvage value per bus	$ 6,000	$ 7,000
Drivers' hourly wage	$ 3.50	$ 4.20
Price per gallon of gasoline	$ .30	$ .30
Other annual cash expenses	$ 4,000	$ 3,000

During the four daily rush hours all buses would be in service and are expected to operate at full capacity (state law prohibits standees) in both directions of the route, each bus covering the route twelve times (six round trips) during that period. During the remainder of the sixteen-hour day, 500 passengers would be carried and Thorne would operate only four buses on the route. Part-time drivers would be employed to drive the extra buses during the rush hours. A bus traveling only during rush hours would go 120 miles a day during the 260-day year.

Required:

(a) Prepare a schedule showing the computation of estimated annual revenue of the new route for both alternatives.
(b) Prepare a schedule showing the computation of estimated annual drivers' wages for both alternatives.
(c) Prepare a schedule showing the computation of estimated annual cost of gasoline for both alternatives.
(d) Assuming that a minimum rate of return of 12% before income taxes is desired and that all annual cash flows occur at the end of the year, prepare a schedule showing the computation of the present values of net cash flows for the eight-year period; include the cost of buses and the proceeds from their disposition under both alternatives, but disregard the effect of income taxes.

(Adapted from the CPA exam.)

24-41. ***NET PRESENT VALUE AND TIME-ADJUSTED RATE OF RETURN*** For many years you have prepared John Rich's income tax return on a cash basis and have provided him with tax-planning advice. He has recently inherited $100,000 which will be paid to him about January 1, 1967, when the estate is settled. He is considering the following investments for the $100,000:

1. Lease of a downtown parking lot which is the site of a proposed office building whose construction will begin in January 1977. He would be required to make an advance payment of $90,000 for the lease and to make monthly rental payments of $1,000. In addition he would spend $10,000 for the erection of a shelter which would be completed by the beginning of the lease period, January 1, 1967. The shelter would be depreciated by the straight-line method. Parking revenues are estimated to be $44,000 yearly and annual cash expenses, in addition to the rent, would amount to $8,500.

2. Purchase of an interest in a producing oil well on January 1, 1967, for $100,000. His share of the well's yearly income would be $20,000 less cash expenses of $8,250. The estimated value of his share of the well at the end of ten years is $65,000. The percentage depletion rate applicable to oil wells is 27 1/2%.

The net cash flow after income taxes derived from these alternative investments would be invested at the end of each year in tax-exempt securities offering a 4% return paid in one annual payment at December 31. This annual payment would, in turn, be reinvested in the same kinds of tax-exempt securities.

Taxable income derived from the investment of the $100,000 would be subject to a tax rate of 60%. Long-term capital gains would be taxed at a rate of 25%. The minimum desired rate of return is 14%.

Required:

(a) Prepare a net present value analysis for each investment.
(b) Which investment should be chosen?

24-42. ***MULTIPLE SEQUENCE PROBLEM—FORWARD INDUCTION*** The Foresight Corporation is considering replacing its old computer system for a newer and larger system costing $648,000. Other pertinent financial data is as follows:

(a)

Beginning of Year	Cost of New Computer System	Value of Old System
1	$648,000	$182,000
2	670,000	178,000
3	697,000	174,000
4	725,000	170,000
5	754,000	166,000

(b) Annual cash savings of new machine:

End of Year				
1	2	3	4	5
$120,000	$120,000	$140,000	$160,000	$160,000

(c) Salvage value or premature retirement value of new computer:

After Operating				
1 yr.	2 yrs.	3 yrs.	4 yrs.	5 yrs.
$620,000	$600,000	$590,000	$450,000	$400,000

(d) 14% minimum desired rate of return.
(e) 40% tax rate.
(f) The book value of the old computer is $120,000. The remaining useful life is five years with annual depreciation of $20,000.
(g) New machine uses sum-of-the-years'-digits depreciation and has a five-year life.
(h) Any gains or losses from disposals should be recognized in the period of occurrence.

Required:

Using foreward induction, determine in what year the investment should be undertaken.

24-43. ***MULTIPLE SEQUENCE PROBLEM—BACKWARD INDUCTION*** The Hindsight Company must choose between Plan 1 or Plan 2. In the first year there is a possibility of obtaining contract 1; in the second, a possibility of obtaining contract 2. Other information is as follows:
(a) The outcome probabilities as assigned in the decision tree.
(b) The incremental cash income for contract 1 is $118,000; for contract 2 it is $145,000. Assume cash flow takes place at year-end.
(c) Alternative 1 costs $12,000; alternative 2 costs $16,000.
(d) Straight-line depreciation; no salvage value; two-year life.
(e) Disposal values after one year:
Alternative 1: $8,000
Alternative 2: $7,000
(f) 40% tax rate.
(g) 16% minimum desired rate of return.

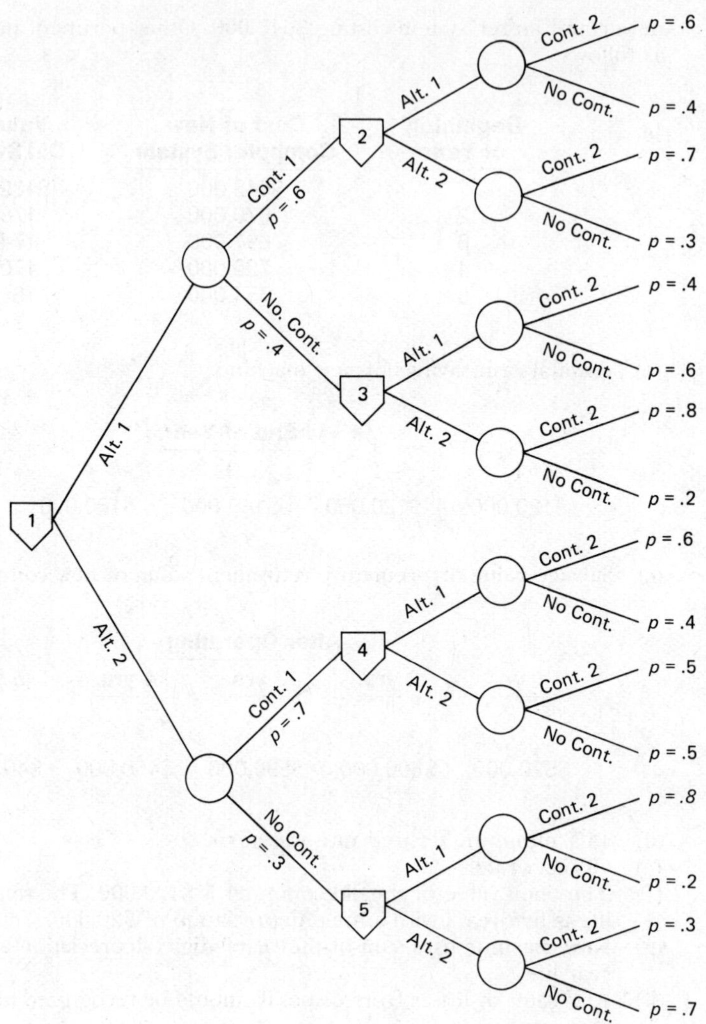

Required:

(1) Using backward induction, determine the cumulative expected value of each alternative at each decision node.

(2) Determine the best sequence of decisions.

CHAPTER

25

LEARNING CURVE ANALYSIS

25.1 THE NATURE OF LEARNING CURVES

Learning curve analysis deals with the phenomenon that as the same task is repeated labor becomes more efficient in the execution of the task. This learning phenomenon is particularly noticeable in industries which are repetitive job-order producers (i.e., aircraft industry). The learning curves for labor in these industries exhibit a regularity in the rate of improvement. It is noted that either of two theorems apply:

THEOREM 1: There is a *constant percentage reduction* in the *cumulative average labor hours* per unit as the *cumulative output doubles.*

THEOREM 2: There is a *constant percentage reduction* in the *marginal average labor hours* per unit as the *cumulative output doubles.*

The learning phenomenon expressed by either theorem can be applied to refine estimates of labor cost and production time. Some of the many applications where such refinement is desirable are:

1. Projection of cash flow timing in capital budgeting
2. Forecasting manpower requirements
3. Rating personnel
4. Scheduling production
5. Negotiating contracts
6. Pricing decisions
7. Sub-contracting at fair prices
8. Setting production goals
9. Calculating military progress payments
10. Make or buy decisions
11. Wage incentive programs
12. Coordination of production and procurement
13. Financial planning
14. Measurement of new employee progress
15. Estimating starting load costs of new products
16. Purchasing of non-standard items
17. Break-even analysis
18. Labor cost control

The formulas developed in our later analysis facilitate all the preceding uses by enabling us to *estimate three types of labor data:*

1. Cumulative *average labor hours* per unit.
2. Marginal average labor hours per unit—labor hours to build a specific unit, sometimes called *unit labor hours.*
3. *Total labor hours* to build a predetermined number of units.

25.2 SELECTING A THEOREM

The *initial lot size* chosen to begin a learning curve analysis and to determine the learning rate is dictated mainly by the manner in which historical labor data is gathered and summarized. For instance in an aircraft industry it may be feasible to keep track of labor hours per airframe assembly, whereas with smaller sub-assemblies this approach may be completely infeasible. Whatever the case, the initial lot should be as small as possible so that learning effects are measurable. Later we will discover that computation time is saved if the initial lot size is one unit.

After the initial lot size is chosen, the applicability of one or the other theorem depends upon our interpretation of historical data. Nevertheless, either theorem provides an acceptable analysis. Data on the effects of learning, however, are computed differently under each theorem. For instance, suppose the constant percentage reduction is 20% as cumulative output doubles. That is, the *learning rate* is 100% − 20%, or 80%. The job will improve at an 80% rate; and further, let us assume the first lot of ten units is produced in 100 hours.

THEOREM 1: *Average labor hour approach*—the average labor hours per unit are 80% of the prior average. Refer to Exhibit 25-1.

EXHIBIT 25-1 DATA SHOWING THEOREM 1 APPLICABILITY

Lot No.	Cum. Output	Marginal Labor Hours	Cum. Labor Hours		Cum. Average Labor Hrs. per Unit	Learning Rate		Marginal Average Labor Hrs. per Unit
1	10		100	100/10	= 10			10
2	20	60	160	160/20	= 8	(10 × 80%)	60/10	= 6.00
3	40	96	256	256/40	= 6.40	(8 × 80%)	96/20	= 4.80
4	80	154	410	410/80	= 5.12	(6.40 × 80%)	154/40	= 3.85
5	160	246	656	656/160	= 4.10	(5.12 × 80%)	246/80	= 3.08
6	320	394	1050	1050/320	= 3.28	(4.10 × 80%)	394/160	= 2.46
7	640	627	1677	1677/640	= 2.62	(3.28 × 80%)	627/320	= 1.96
8	1280	1011	2688	2688/1280	= 2.10	(2.62 × 80%)	1011/640	= 1.58
9	2560	1613	4301	4301/2560	= 1.68	(2.10 × 80%)	1613/1280	= 1.26
10	5120	2560	6861	6861/5120	= 1.34	(1.68 × 80%)	2560/2560	= 1.00

THEOREM 2: *Marginal labor hour approach*—the marginal labor hours per unit are 80% of the prior marginal hours. Refer to Exhibit 25-2.

EXHIBIT 25-2 DATA SHOWING THEOREM 2 APPLICABILITY

Lot No.	Cum. Output	Marginal Labor Hours	Cum. Labor Hours		Cum. Average Labor Hrs. per Unit		Marginal Average Labor Hrs. per Unit	Learning Rate
1	10		100	100/10	= 10		10	
2	20	80	180	180/20	= 9	80/10	= 8	(10.00 × 80%)
3	40	128	308	308/40	= 7.70	128/20	= 6.40	(8.00 × 80%)
4	80	205	513	513/80	= 6.41	205/40	= 5.12	(6.40 × 80%)
5	160	328	841	841/160	= 5.26	328/80	= 4.10	(5.12 × 80%)
6	320	525	1366	1366/320	= 4.27	525/160	= 3.28	(4.10 × 80%)
7	640	838	2204	2204/640	= 3.44	838/320	= 2.62	(3.28 × 80%)
8	1280	1344	3548	3548/1280	= 2.77	1344/640	= 2.10	(2.62 × 80%)
9	2560	2150	5698	5698/2560	= 2.23	2150/1280	= 1.68	(2.10 × 80%)
10	5120	3430	9128	9128/5120	= 1.78	3430/2560	= 1.34	(1.68 × 80%)

This means that given the historical data represented in the cumulative labor hours column of either Exhibit 25-1 or Exhibit 25-2, we establish a *constant learning rate* either between average labor per unit or between marginal labor per unit.

This means of selecting a theorem is not quite complete, however, for we can observe an interesting effect of long-run production experience. The data in Exhibit 25-1, supporting Theorem 1, shows that every time the quantity of production doubles the cumulative average labor hours per unit are reduced by 20%. However, if we compute the percentage reduction in marginal average labor hours per unit for the same data, we find an identical 20% reduction, except for the initial doubling:

Lot	Marginal Average Labor Hours from Exhibit 25-1		Learning Rate
1	10		
2	6.00	=	(10 × 60%)
3	4.80	=	(6.00 × 80%)
4	3.85	=	(4.80 × 80%)
5	3.08	=	(3.85 × 80%)
6	2.46	=	(3.08 × 80%)
7	1.96	=	(2.46 × 80%)
8	1.58	=	(1.96 × 80%)
9	1.26	=	(1.58 × 80%)
10	1.00	=	(1.26 × 80%)

Consequently, after the initial doubling, we observe Theorem 2's applicability with the same data. The conclusion is that historical data supporting Theorem 1 will also support Theorem 2 except in the early production stage.

If we examine Exhibit 25-2, supporting Theorem 2, in which every time the quantity of production doubles the marginal average labor hours per unit are reduced by 20%, we observe the same applicability of Theorem 1, but only after ten lots of production:

Lot	Cumulative Average Labor Hours from Exhibit 25-2		Learning Rate
1	10		
2	9	=	(10 × 90%)
3	7.70	=	(9 × 86%)
4	6.41	=	(7.70 × 83%)
5	5.26	=	(6.41 × 82%)
6	4.27	=	(5.26 × 81%)
7	3.44	=	(4.27 × 80.5%)
8	2.77	=	(3.44 × 80.5%)
9	2.23	=	(2.77 × 80.5%)
10	1.78	=	(2.23 × 80%)

The conclusion, in this instance, is that data supporting Theorem 2 *does not support* Theorem 1 until later production stages.

In all production situations where learning curve analysis is applicable, and after a learning rate is established, *Theorem 2 should always be used.* However, where labor hour projections are most valuable in the very early production stages, we should specifically use the theorem which best explains the learning phenomenon.

When historical data is analyzed, the marginal labor hours per unit will reflect changing conditions and/or errors in record keeping. Consequently it may be difficult to reveal clear evidence of Theorem 2; whereas Theorem 1, because of the "damping effect" produced by the cumulative average, would not be so affected.

25.3 DETERMINING THE LEARNING RATE

One method of finding the learning rate is to construct a table similar to Exhibit 25-1 or 25-2 and compute the percentage change between each successive cumulative average and between each successive marginal average. The theorem with the *constant* percentage change is chosen, and the learning rate will be the complement of the constant percentage (i.e., 100% − 20% = 80%).

Another means involves the use of an equation representing the learning phenomenon. The successive cumulative averages or marginal averages computed from historical data supporting Theorem 1 or Theorem 2 respectively will form an *exponential curve* if plotted against cumulative units or marginal units respectively. Hours per unit will drop rapidly at first, and then more gradually as production increases. For instance, the cumulative average labor hours from Exhibit 25-1 form the curve in Exhibit 25-3.

EXHIBIT 25-3 PLOT OF CUMULATIVE AVERAGE LABOR HOURS

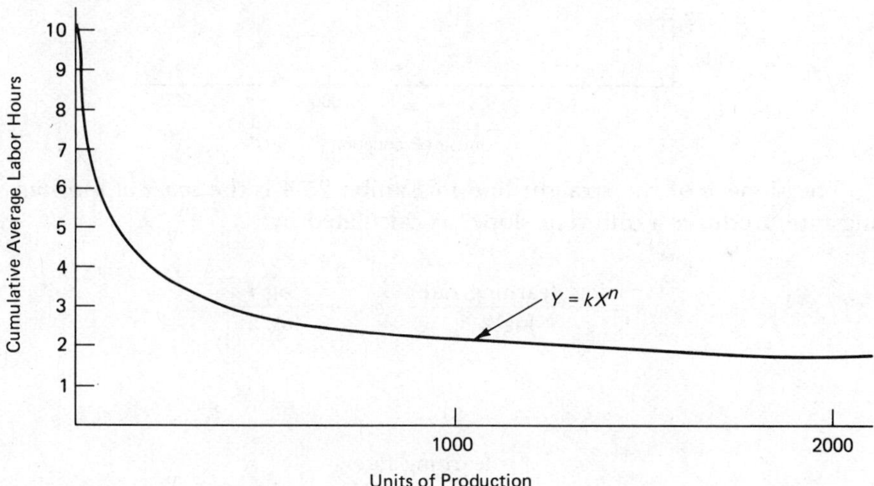

Curves of the shape in Exhibit 25-3 are exponentials and take the equation form:

$$Y = kX^n \tag{1}$$

where

Y_1 = cumulative average labor hours — Theorem 1
Y_2 = marginal average labor hours — Theorem 2
k = labor hours to build the *first unit*
X = any number of completed units
n = index of learning

In logarithmic form, this same learning equation is:[1]

$$\log y = \log k + n \log X \tag{2}$$

Notice in this log form that the equation represents a *straight line* with a *slope of n* and a *Y intercept of k.* Consequently, plotting the data from Exhibit 25-1 or 25-2 on *log-log graph paper* results in a straight-line relationship between the average hours and cumulative production. Exhibit 25-4 represents the logarithmic version of our exponential relationship in Exhibit 25-1.

EXHIBIT 25-4 LOG-LOG PLOT OF CUMULATIVE AVERAGE LABOR HOURS

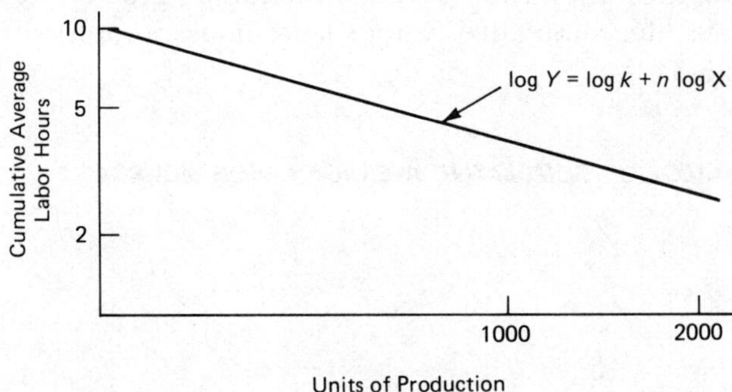

The slope n of the straight line in Exhibit 25-4 is the *index of learning.* Each learning rate produces a different slope, as calculated by:

$$n = \frac{\log \text{(learning rate)}}{\log 2} \quad \textit{or} \quad n = \frac{\log r}{\log 2}$$

where

$$r = \text{learning rate}$$

This equation, showing the relationship between the index of learning and the learning rate, is derived from our basic exponential equation. If the first unit takes k hours to complete, then the cumulative average (or marginal average under Theorem 2) for the second unit is rk. The exponential equation when $X = 2$ is:

$$rk = k2^n \tag{3}$$

Solving this equation for n, we obtain:

$$\log r + \log k = \log k + n \log 2$$
$$\log r = n \log 2$$
$$n = \frac{\log r}{\log 2} \tag{4}$$

[1]Refer to Appendix C (Common Logarithms).

With an 80% learning rate as illustrated in either Exhibit 25-1 or 25-2, the index of learning or the *slope* of our learning curve in Exhibit 25-4 is calculated from equation (4):

$$n = \frac{\log .80}{\log 2}$$

$$n = \frac{9.90309 - 10}{.30103} = \frac{-.09691}{.30103}$$

$$n = -.321928$$

A company's historical data on average hours (either marginal or cumulative) which produces a slope of −.321928 when plotted on log-log graph paper is experiencing an 80% learning rate. Rather than plotting the data, however, the company could use its historical data and solve the learning equation ($Y = kX^n$) for n. After obtaining the value of n, equation (4) could then be solved for r to obtain the corresponding learning rate. To facilitate the conversion from n to r (or *vice versa*), the table in Exhibit 25-5 is constructed using equation (4). With this table, we locate the computed value of n and the corresponding learning rate can be found in the table. Only the n values for learning rates from 65 through 95 are given, as rates outside this range are unlikely. A 95% learning rate is considered *minimum* evidence of learning.

EXHIBIT 25-5 LEARNING INDEXES

Learning Rate (*r*)	Index of Learning (*n*)	Learning Rate (*r*)	Index of Learning (*n*)	Learning Rate (*r*)	Index of Learning (*n*)
95%	−.0740	85%	−.2345	75%	−.4150
94%	−.0893	84%	−.2515	74%	−.4344
93%	−.1047	83%	−.2688	73%	−.4540
92%	−.1203	82%	−.2863	72%	−.4739
91%	−.1361	81%	−.3040	71%	−.4941
90%	−.1520	80%	−.3219	70%	−.5146
89%	−.1681	79%	−.3401	69%	−.5353
88%	−.1844	78%	−.3585	68%	−.5564
87%	−.2009	77%	−.3771	67%	−.5778
86%	−.2176	76%	−.3959	66%	−.5995
				65%	−.6215

Suppose the Kurtig Engineering Company wants to know its learning rate for labor on the Model K-24 jet engine. The company has already produced sixteen of the engines and experienced the following learning behavior:

Total labor hours to build first engine = 940 hours.
Total labor hours to build 16 engines = 8,195 hours.

To find the learning rate we assume that Theorem 1 is applicable and solve for n, when Y_1 = the *cumulative average labor hours*. This is the *safest assumption* to make, for as we demonstrated earlier, any historical data supporting Theorem 1 will also support Theorem 2, whereas the opposite is not true. The learning rate found through this assumption is *applicable to both theorems*. First, we solve the exponential learning equation for n:

$$Y_1 = kX^n$$
$$512 = 940(16)^n$$
$$\log 512 = \log 940 + n \log 16$$
$$n = \frac{\log 512 - \log 940}{\log 16}$$
$$n = \frac{2.70927 - 2.97313}{1.20412}$$
$$n = -.219$$

Next, we look in Exhibit 25-5 for the index $-.219$. The closest index is $-.2176$. The Kurtig Company's learning rate therefore is approximately 86%.

We can check this solution by solving equation (4) for r:

$$n = \frac{\log r}{\log 2}$$
$$\log r = n \log 2$$
$$\log r = -.219(.30103)$$
$$\log r = -.06593 = 9.93407 - 10$$
$$r = \text{antilog}(9.93407 - 10) = .8592 = 86\%$$

The learning curve rate of this and other companies is related directly to the ratio of machine to labor hours. That is, in production situations having a greater proportion of labor activity the opportunities for learning are greater. In production applications where machine hours are three times greater than direct labor hours, the learning rate will be around a slow 90%. In situations where the ratio is one to one the expected learning rate is 85%. Where it is one to three, the rate will most likely be around 80%. There are other important causal factors that also have a direct bearing on the learning rate. Some of these factors are:

1. Inherent susceptability of the operation to learning.
2. Degree that susceptability is exploited.
3. Production labor's training, experience, and skill.
4. The efficiency of ancillary or support activities—material handling, inspection, maintenance, and service.
5. The work environment.
6. Coordination of production by supervisors and managers.
7. Production methodology.
8. Production scheduling.
9. Engineering design of the product.
10. Choice of lot size—affects set-up time, cycle time, storage and handling times.

25.4 DETERMINING THE VALUE OF *k*

The labor hours to build the first unit (k) must be available before the exponential learning equation can be used to solve for values of Y. This information is often available in the accounting records, especially where the unit assembly involves a major effort.

In those instances where records of production lots are maintained, and the initial lot size is greater than one unit, the value of k must be computed. For instance, to construct the values for Exhibit 25-1 using the formula $Y_1 = kX^n$, *we must first find the value of k,* since our initial data is for a lot size of ten. The procedure is as follows:

Use $Y_1 = kX^n$ where:

$Y_1 = 10$ (average hours for first lot)
$k =$ the unknown value
$X = 10$ (number of units in first lot)
$n = -.3219$ (the index for an 80% learning rate)

$$
\begin{aligned}
10 &= k(10)^{-.3219} \\
\log 10 &= \log k - .3219(\log 10) \\
\log k &= \log 10 + .3219(\log 10) \\
\log k &= 1.0000 + .3219(1.0000) \\
\log k &= 1.3219 \\
k &= \text{antilog}(1.3219) = \underline{\underline{20.986 \text{ hours}}}
\end{aligned}
$$

This value of k can now be used in our learning formula to compute the values in Exhibit 25-1. For instance, the cumulative average labor hours (Y_1) for lot 5 (160 cumulative units) is computed as follows:

$$
\begin{aligned}
Y_1 &= kX^n \\
Y_1 &= 20.986(160)^{-.3219} \\
\log Y_1 &= \log 20.986 - .3219(\log 160) \\
\log Y_1 &= 1.3219 - .7095 \\
\log Y_1 &= 0.6124 \\
Y_1 &= \text{antilog}(0.6124) = \underline{\underline{4.10 \text{ hours}}}
\end{aligned}
$$

Since the same data is applicable, the value of k can also be used to compute the marginal averages in Exhibit 25-2. For instance, the marginal average labor hours (Y_2) for lot 8 (1,280 cumulative units) is computed as follows:

$$
\begin{aligned}
Y_2 &= kX^n \\
Y_2 &= 20.986(1280)^{-.3219} \\
\log Y_2 &= \log 20.986 - .3219(\log 1280) \\
\log Y_2 &= 1.3219 - 1.002 \\
\log Y_2 &= 0.3217 \\
Y_2 &= \text{antilog}(0.3217) = \underline{\underline{2.10 \text{ hours}}}
\end{aligned}
$$

In every case where the initial unit is accounted for within a lot, the labor hours to produce this unit must be calculated before learning curve analysis can be applied.

25.5 LEARNING CURVE FORMULAE FOR THEOREM 1

There are three basic formulae—(1) the cumulative average labor hours, (2) the marginal average labor hours, and (3) the total labor hours required to build a predetermined number of units.

FORMULA 1: solves for the *cumulative average labor hours*

$$Y_1 = kX^n \tag{5}$$

where

Y_1 = the cumulative average labor hours for X *number of units*
X = any number of completed units
k = labor hours to build the first unit
n = the index of learning (given in Exhibit 25-5)

An application of this formula can be made from the following data for the Bi-Lab Corporation where:

$X = 30$ units
$k = 96$ hours
$r = 85\%$ learning rate

First, we must find the index n from Exhibit 25-5. It is −.2345. Next, we solve for Y_1:

$$\begin{aligned} Y_1 &= 96(30)^{-.2345} \\ \log Y_1 &= \log 96 - .2345(\log 30) \\ \log Y_1 &= 1.98227 - .2345(1.47712) \\ \log Y_1 &= 1.98227 - .34638 \\ Y_1 &= \text{antilog}(1.63589) = \underline{\underline{43.24 \text{ hours}}} \end{aligned}$$

As a convenience in using this formula, a table could be computed for values of X^n for various learning rates. For instance, the X^n value for a learning rate (r) of 75% and completed units (X) of 8, is as follows:

$$\begin{aligned} \text{"table value"} &= X^n \\ \log(\text{"table value"}) &= -.4150 \log(8) \\ \log(\text{"table value"}) &= -.4150(.90309) \\ \log(\text{"table value"}) &= -.37478 \\ \text{"table value"}^{2} &= \text{antilog}(-.37478) = \frac{1}{2.37} = .4219 \end{aligned}$$

[2] Or antilog(−.37478) = antilog(9.62522 − 10).

EXHIBIT 25-6 VALUES OF X^n

X	r = 70% n = −.5146	r = 75% n = −.4150	r = 80% n = −.3219	r = 85% n = −.2345	r = 90% n = −.1520	X
1	1.0000	1.0000	1.0000	1.0000	1.0000	1
2	.7000	.7501	.7999	.8500	.9000	2
3	.5682	.6338	.7021	.7729	.8462	3
4	.4900	.5625	.6400	.7225	.8100	4
5	.4368	.5128	.5957	.6856	.7830	5
6	.3977	.4754	.5617	.6569	.7616	6
7	.3674	.4459	.5345	.6336	.7440	7
8	.3430	.4219	.5120	.6141	.7290	8
9	.3228	.4018	.4930	.5973	.7161	9
10	.3058	.3846	.4766	.5828	.7047	10
11	.2913	.3697	.4621	.5699	.6946	11
12	.2784	.3566	.4494	.5584	.6854	12
13	.2672	.3449	.4380	.5480	.6771	13
14	.2572	.3345	.4276	.5385	.6696	14
15	.2482	.3250	.4182	.5299	.6626	15
16	.2404	.3164	.4096	.5220	.6561	16
17	.2327	.3086	.4017	.5146	.6501	17
18	.2259	.3013	.3944	.5077	.6445	18
19	.2198	.2947	.3876	.5013	.6392	19
20	.2140	.2884	.3819	.4953	.6342	20
21	.2087	.2827	.3753	.4897	.6295	21
22	.2038	.2773	.3697	.4844	.6251	22
23	.1992	.2722	.3645	.4794	.6209	23
24	.1949	.2674	.3595	.4746	.6169	24
25	.1908	.2629	.3548	.4701	.6131	25
26	.1870	.2587	.3504	.4658	.6094	26
27	.1834	.2547	.3461	.4617	.6059	27
28	.1800	.2509	.3421	.4578	.6026	28
29	.1768	.2472	.3379	.4540	.5994	29
30	.1737	.2438	.3346	.4504	.5963	30
31	.1708	.2405	.3311	.4470	.5934	31
32	.1681	.2373	.3277	.4436	.5905	32
33	.1654	.2343	.3245	.4405	.5878	33
34	.1629	.2314	.3214	.4374	.5851	34
35	.1605	.2282	.3184	.4345	.5825	35
36	.1582	.2260	.3155	.4316	.5800	36
37	.1560	.2235	.3128	.4288	.5776	37
38	.1538	.2210	.3101	.4261	.5753	38
39	.1518	.2186	.3075	.4235	.5730	39
40	.1498	.2163	.3050	.4210	.5708	40
41	.1479	.2141	.3026	.4186	.5687	41
42	.1461	.2120	.3002	.4162	.5666	42
43	.1443	.2100	.2980	.4139	.5646	43
44	.1427	.2080	.2958	.4117	.5626	44
45	.1410	.2061	.2937	.4096	.5607	45
46	.1394	.2042	.2916	.4075	.5588	46
47	.1379	.2024	.2896	.4054	.5570	47
48	.1364	.2006	.2876	.4034	.5552	48
49	.1350	.1989	.2857	.4015	.5535	49
50	.1336	.1972	.2839	.3996	.5518	50

EXHIBIT 25-6 (CONTINUED)

X	r = 70% n = −.5146	r = 75% n = −.4150	r = 80% n = −.3219	r = 85% n = −.2345	r = 90% n = −.1520	X
51	.1322	.1956	.2821	.3977	.5506	51
52	.1309	.1940	.2803	.3959	.5485	52
53	.1296	.1925	.2786	.3943	.5469	53
54	.1284	.1910	.2769	.3928	.5453	54
55	.1272	.1895	.2753	.3909	.5438	55
56	.1260	.1881	.2737	.3891	.5423	56
57	.1249	.1867	.2721	.3875	.5409	57
58	.1237	.1854	.2706	.3859	.5395	58
59	.1227	.1841	.2691	.3843	.5381	59
60	.1216	.1829	.2677	.3828	.5367	60
61	.1206	.1816	.2663	.3813	.5353	61
62	.1196	.1804	.2650	.3799	.5340	62
63	.1186	.1792	.2636	.3785	.5327	63
64	.1176	.1780	.2622	.3771	.5314	64
65	.1167	.1769	.2609	.3757	.5302	65
66	.1158	.1758	.2596	.3744	.5290	66
67	.1149	.1747	.2583	.3731	.5278	67
68	.1140	.1736	.2571	.3718	.5266	68
69	.1132	.1725	.2559	.3705	.5254	69
70	.1123	.1715	.2547	.3692	.5243	70
71	.1115	.1705	.2535	.3680	.5231	71
72	.1107	.1695	.2524	.3668	.5220	72
73	.1099	.1685	.2513	.3656	.5209	73
74	.1092	.1676	.2502	.3645	.5198	74
75	.1084	.1667	.2491	.3633	.5187	75
76	.1077	.1658	.2481	.3622	.5177	76
77	.1070	.1649	.2470	.3611	.5167	77
78	.1063	.1640	.2460	.3600	.5157	78
79	.1056	.1631	.2450	.3589	.5147	79
80	.1049	.1623	.2440	.3579	.5137	80
81	.1042	.1614	.2430	.3568	.5127	81
82	.1035	.1606	.2421	.3558	.5118	82
83	.1029	.1598	.2411	.3548	.5108	83
84	.1023	.1590	.2402	.3538	.5099	84
85	.1017	.1582	.2393	.3528	.5090	85
86	.1010	.1575	.2384	.3518	.5081	86
87	.1004	.1567	.2375	.3509	.5072	87
88	.1001	.1560	.2366	.3500	.5063	88
89	.0993	.1552	.2357	.3490	.5054	89
90	.0987	.1545	.2349	.3481	.5046	90
91	.0982	.1538	.2341	.3472	.5037	91
92	.0976	.1531	.2333	.3463	.5029	92
93	.0970	.1524	.2325	.3454	.5021	93
94	.0965	.1518	.2317	.3446	.5013	94
95	.0960	.1511	.2309	.3437	.5005	95
96	.0955	.1504	.2301	.3429	.4997	96
97	.0950	.1498	.2293	.3420	.4989	97
98	.0945	.1492	.2285	.3412	.4981	98
99	.0940	.1485	.2278	.3404	.4973	99
100	.0935	.1479	.2271	.3396	.4966	100

Similar computations for completed units from 1 through 100, and for learning rates of 70%, 75%, 80%, 85%, and 90%, result in the table in Exhibit 25-6. This table may now be used as a short-cut when computing Y_1 from the formula. For instance, with the Bi-Lab example (85% learning rate) it would be:

$$Y_1 = 96(.4504) = \underline{\underline{43.24 \text{ hours}}}$$

FORMULA 2: solves for the *marginal average labor hours*

$$Y_2 = (n+1)kX^n \quad \text{or} \quad Y_2 = (n+1)Y_1 \tag{6}$$

where

Y_2 = the marginal average labor hours for the Xth unit
all other variables as previously defined

$(n+1)$ is referred to as the *conversion factor.* This conversion factor represents the *ratio* between the marginal average and the cumulative average. As we know, *under Theorem 1,* the cumulative average curve and the marginal average curve have the same slope n when plotted on log-log graph paper—except for the first initial doubling of production. By referring to Exhibit 25-7, we see that *the distance between the two parallel curves is constant* as suggested earlier in data from Exhibits 25-1 and 25-2. Consequently, as the production quantity increases, the ratio of the marginal average to the cumulative average tends to be *constant.* This constant ratio is $(n+1)$. Exhibit 25-8 contains a table of conversion factors $(n+1)$ for various values of r. It may be used as a computational aid in solving formula 2. As an example, suppose we use the same data for the Bi-Lab Corporation and solve for Y_2: First, find the conversion factor $(n+1)$ for 85% from Exhibit 25-8. It is .7655. Next, find the value of X^n from Exhibit 25-6. It is .4504. Now solve for Y_2:

EXHIBIT 25-7 CUMULATIVE AVERAGE AND MARGINAL AVERAGE CURVES UNDER THEOREM 1

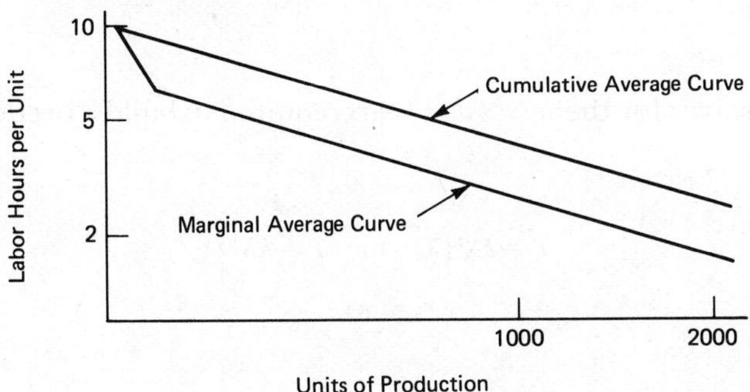

$$Y_2 = (.7655)(96)(.4504)$$
$$Y_2 = \underline{\underline{33.10 \text{ hours}}}$$

Y_2 could be solved the long way without the use of Exhibits 25-6 and 25-8. Find the index of learning for an 85% learning rate from Exhibit 25-5. It is −.2345.

$$\begin{aligned} Y_2 &= (-.2345 + 1)(96)(30)^{-.2345} \\ \log Y_2 &= \log .7655 + \log 96 - .2345 \log 30 \\ \log Y_2 &= 9.88395 - 10 + 1.98227 - .2345(1.47712) \\ \log Y_2 &= 9.88395 - 10 + 1.98227 - .34638 \\ \log Y_2 &= 11.51984 - 10 = 1.51984 \\ Y_2 &= \text{antilog}(1.51984) = \underline{\underline{33.10 \text{ hours}}} \end{aligned}$$

EXHIBIT 25-8 CONVERSION FACTORS (n + 1)

Learning Rate (r)	Conversion Factor (n + 1)	Learning Rate (r)	Conversion Factor (n + 1)	Learning Rate (r)	Conversion Factor (n + 1)
95%	.9260	85%	.7655	75%	.5850
94%	.9107	84%	.7485	74%	.5656
93%	.8953	83%	.7312	73%	.5450
92%	.8797	82%	.7137	72%	.5261
91%	.8639	81%	.6960	71%	.5059
90%	.8480	80%	.6781	70%	.4854
89%	.8319	79%	.6599	69%	.4647
88%	.8156	78%	.6415	68%	.4436
87%	.7991	77%	.6229	67%	.4222
86%	.7824	76%	.6041	66%	.4005
				65%	.3785

FORMULA 3: solves for the *total labor hours* required to build a predetermined number of units

$$T = kX^n(X) \quad \text{or} \quad T = kX^{n+1} \tag{7}$$

where

T = the total labor hours required to build X units

With the same data from Bi-Lab Corporation, we can solve for the total hours to complete thirty units: First, find the value of X^n from Exhibit 25-6. It is .4504.

$$T = (96)(.4504)(30) = \underline{\underline{1{,}297.2 \text{ hours}}}^3$$

[3]This answer should check with our earlier computation of Y_1. Y_1 = 43.24 hours, so the total must be 30 × 43.24 = 1,297.2 hours.

25.6 LEARNING CURVE FORMULAE FOR THEOREM 2

Again, there are three basic formulae—(1) the marginal average labor hours, (2) the total labor hours required to build a predetermined number of units, and (3) the cumulative average labor hours.

FORMULA 1: solves for the *marginal average labor hours*

$$Y_2 = kX^n \tag{8}$$

where all variables are as previously defined.

An application of this formula can be made from the following data for the Missile-Research Corporation where:

$$X = 24 \text{ units}$$
$$k = 482 \text{ hours}$$
$$r = 80\% \text{ learning rate}$$

We can solve the formula with the use of Exhibit 25-6 for values of X^n, or we can compute the result using logarithms. First, the solution using logarithms: Find the index (n) from Exhibit 25-5. It is $-.3219$.

$$\begin{aligned} Y_2 &= 482\ (24)^{-.3219} \\ \log Y_2 &= \log 482 - .3219 \log 24 \\ \log Y_2 &= 2.68305 - .3219\ (1.38021) \\ \log Y_2 &= 2.68305 - .44429 \\ Y_2 &= \text{antilog}\ (2.23876) = \underline{\underline{173.3 \text{ hours}}} \end{aligned}$$

Now, the solution using Exhibit 25-6 for the value of X^n when X is 24 (the value is .3595):

$$\begin{aligned} Y_2 &= (482)\ (.3595) \\ Y_2 &= \underline{\underline{173.3 \text{ hours}}} \end{aligned}$$

FORMULA 2: solves for the *total labor hours* required to build a predetermined number of units

$$T = k\mu \tag{9}$$

where

$$\mu = \text{the cumulative value of } X^n$$

In order to find the total hours under Theorem 2, the marginal averages for each unit, up to and including X, must be added together:

$$T = k(1)^n + k(2)^n + k(3)^n + \cdots + kX^n$$

Factoring out k we get:

$$T = k[(1)^n + (2)^n + (3)^n + \cdots + X^n]$$

The cumulative value of X^n, then, is:

$$\mu = (1)^n + (2)^n + (3)^n + \cdots + X^n \qquad (10)$$

Consequently, the value of μ for any value of X may be found by adding the X^n values in Exhibit 25-6. The table in Exhibit 25-9 is constructed in this manner and the cumulative values μ are given for production of 1 through 100 units. For productions greater than 100, the values of μ can be calculated from equation (10).

With the data for Missile-Research Corporation, the total hours to complete twenty-four units is: Find the value of μ in Exhibit 25-9. It is 11.9550.

$$T = 482\ (11.9550)$$
$$T = 5{,}762.3 \text{ hours}$$

FORMULA 3: solves for the *cumulative average labor hours*[4]

$$Y_1 = \frac{T}{X} \qquad (11)$$

Using the Missile-Research Corporation data, and the *prior computation* of T, the value of Y_1 is:

$$Y_1 = \frac{5{,}762.3}{24}$$
$$Y_1 = \underline{\underline{240.1 \text{ hours}}}$$

For Theorem 2, there are *alternative formulae 2* and *3*. They are:

Cumulative Average Labor Hours:

$$Y_1 = \frac{kX^n}{(n+1)} \quad \text{or} \quad Y_1 = \frac{Y_2}{(n+1)} \qquad (12)$$

Total Labor Hours:

$$T = \frac{kX^n}{(n+1)}(X) \quad \text{or} \quad T = Y_1\,(X) \qquad (13)$$

[4] This formula is also applicable for Theorem 1, *when T is computed under Theorem 1* and X is given.

EXHIBIT 25-9 VALUES OF μ (CUMULATIVE X^n VALUES)

X	r = 70% n = −.5146	r = 75% n = −.4150	r = 80% n = −.3219	r = 85% n = −.2345	r = 90% n = −.1520	X
1	1.0000	1.0000	1.0000	1.0000	1.0000	1
2	1.7000	1.7501	1.7999	1.8500	1.9000	2
3	2.2682	2.3839	2.5020	2.6229	2.7462	3
4	2.7582	2.9464	3.1420	3.3454	3.5562	4
5	3.1950	3.4592	3.7377	4.0310	4.3392	5
6	3.5927	3.9346	4.2994	4.6879	5.1008	6
7	3.9601	4.3805	4.8339	5.3215	5.8448	7
8	4.3031	4.8024	5.3459	5.9356	6.5738	8
9	4.6259	5.2042	5.8389	6.5329	7.2899	9
10	4.9317	5.5888	6.3155	7.1157	7.9946	10
11	5.2230	5.9585	6.7776	7.6856	8.6892	11
12	5.5014	6.3151	7.2270	8.2440	9.3746	12
13	5.7686	6.6600	7.6650	8.7920	10.0517	13
14	6.0258	6.9945	8.0926	9.3305	10.7213	14
15	6.2740	7.3195	8.5108	9.8604	11.3839	15
16	6.5144	7.6359	8.9204	10.3824	12.0400	16
17	6.7471	7.9445	9.3221	10.8970	12.6901	17
18	6.9730	8.2458	9.7165	11.4047	13.3346	18
19	7.1928	8.5405	10.1041	11.9060	13.9738	19
20	7.4068	8.8289	10.4860	12.4013	14.6080	20
21	7.6155	9.1116	10.8613	12.8910	15.2375	21
22	7.8193	9.3889	11.2310	13.3754	15.8626	22
23	8.0185	9.6611	11.5955	13.8548	16.4835	23
24	8.2134	9.9285	11.9550	14.3294	17.1004	24
25	8.4042	10.1914	12.3098	14.7995	17.7135	25
26	8.5912	10.4501	12.6602	15.2653	18.3229	26
27	8.7746	10.7048	13.0063	15.7270	18.9288	27
28	8.9546	10.9557	13.3484	16.1848	19.5314	28
29	9.1314	11.2029	13.6863	16.6388	20.1308	29
30	9.3051	11.4467	14.0209	17.0892	20.7271	30
31	9.4759	11.6872	14.3520	17.5362	21.3205	31
32	9.6440	11.9245	14.6797	17.9798	21.9110	32
33	9.8094	12.1588	15.0042	18.4203	22.4988	33
34	9.9723	12.3902	15.3256	18.8577	23.0839	34
35	10.1328	12.6184	15.6440	19.2922	23.6664	35
36	10.2910	12.8444	15.9595	19.7238	24.2464	36
37	10.4470	13.0679	16.2723	20.1526	24.8240	37
38	10.6008	13.2889	16.5824	20.5787	25.3993	38
39	10.7526	13.5075	16.8899	21.0022	25.9723	39
40	10.9024	13.7238	17.1949	21.4232	26.5431	40
41	11.0503	13.9379	17.4975	21.8418	27.1118	41
42	11.1964	14.1499	17.7977	22.2580	27.6784	42
43	11.3407	14.3599	18.0957	22.6719	28.2430	43
44	11.4834	14.5679	18.3915	23.0836	28.8056	44
45	11.6244	14.7740	18.6852	23.4932	29.3663	45
46	11.7638	14.9782	18.9768	23.9007	29.9251	46
47	11.9017	15.1806	19.2664	24.3061	30.4821	47
48	12.0381	15.3812	19.5540	24.7095	31.0373	48
49	12.1731	15.5801	19.8397	25.1110	31.5908	49
50	12.3067	15.7773	20.1236	25.5106	32.1426	50

EXHIBIT 25-9 (CONTINUED)

X	*r* = 70% *n* = −.5146	*r* = 75% *n* = −.4150	*r* = 80% *n* = −.3219	*r* = 85% *n* = −.2345	*r* = 90% *n* = −.1520	*X*
51	12.4389	15.9729	20.4057	25.9083	32.6932	51
52	12.5698	16.1669	20.6860	26.3042	33.2417	52
53	12.6994	16.3594	20.9646	26.6985	33.7886	53
54	12.8278	16.5504	21.2415	27.0913	34.3339	54
55	12.9550	16.7399	21.5168	27.4822	34.8777	55
56	13.0810	16.9280	21.7905	27.8713	35.4200	56
57	13.2059	17.1147	22.0626	28.2588	35.9609	57
58	13.3296	17.3001	22.3332	28.6447	36.5004	58
59	13.4523	17.4842	22.6032	29.0290	37.0385	59
60	13.5739	17.6671	22.8700	29.4118	37.5752	60
61	13.6945	17.8487	23.1363	29.7931	38.1105	61
62	13.8141	18.0291	23.4013	30.1730	38.6445	62
63	13.9327	18.2083	23.6649	30.5515	39.1772	63
64	14.0503	18.3863	23.9271	30.9286	39.7086	64
65	14.1670	18.5632	24.1880	31.3043	40.2388	65
66	14.2828	18.7390	24.4476	31.6787	40.7678	66
67	14.3977	18.9137	24.7059	32.0518	41.2956	67
68	14.5117	19.0873	24.9630	32.4236	41.8222	68
69	14.6249	19.2598	25.2189	32.7941	42.3476	69
70	14.7372	19.4313	25.4736	33.1633	42.8719	70
71	14.8487	19.6018	25.7271	33.5313	43.3950	71
72	14.9594	19.7713	25.9795	33.8981	43.9170	72
73	15.0693	19.9398	26.2308	34.2637	44.4379	73
74	15.1785	20.1074	26.4810	34.6282	44.9577	74
75	15.2869	20.2741	26.7301	34.9915	45.4764	75
76	15.3946	20.4399	26.9782	35.3537	45.9941	76
77	15.5016	20.6048	27.2252	35.7148	46.5108	77
78	15.6079	20.7688	27.4712	36.0748	47.0265	78
79	15.7135	20.9319	27.7162	36.4337	47.5412	79
80	15.8184	21.0942	27.9602	36.7916	48.0549	80
81	15.9226	21.2556	28.2032	37.1484	48.5676	81
82	16.0261	21.4162	28.4453	37.5042	49.0794	82
83	16.1290	21.5760	28.6864	37.8590	49.5902	83
84	16.2313	21.7350	28.9266	38.2128	50.1001	84
85	16.3330	21.8932	29.1659	38.5656	50.6091	85
86	16.4340	22.0507	29.4043	38.9174	51.1172	86
87	16.5344	22.2074	29.6418	39.2683	51.6244	87
88	16.6345	22.3634	29.8784	39.6183	52.1307	88
89	16.7338	22.5186	30.1141	39.9673	52.6361	89
90	16.8325	22.6731	30.3490	40.3154	53.1407	90
91	16.9307	22.8269	30.5831	40.6626	53.6444	91
92	17.0283	22.9800	30.8164	41.0089	54.1473	92
93	17.1253	23.1324	31.0489	41.3543	54.6494	93
94	17.2218	23.2842	31.2806	41.6989	55.1507	94
95	17.3178	23.4353	31.5115	42.0426	55.6512	95
96	17.4133	23.5857	31.7416	42.3855	56.1509	96
97	17.5083	23.7355	31.9709	42.7275	56.6498	97
98	17.6028	23.8847	32.1994	43.0687	57.1479	98
99	17.6968	24.0332	32.4272	43.4091	57.6452	99
100	17.7903	24.1811	32.6543	43.7487	58.1418	100

These formulae, however, *are only applicable after a long production experience.* This is demonstrated by the analysis in Exhibit 25-2.

Under Theorem 1, the ratio of the marginal average to the cumulative average is *constant* after the first initial doubling of production. This is shown in Exhibit 25-7. Under Theorem 2, however, the ratio is *not constant,* as shown in Exhibit 25-10.

EXHIBIT 25-10 CUMULATIVE AVERAGE AND MARGINAL AVERAGE CURVES UNDER THEOREM 2

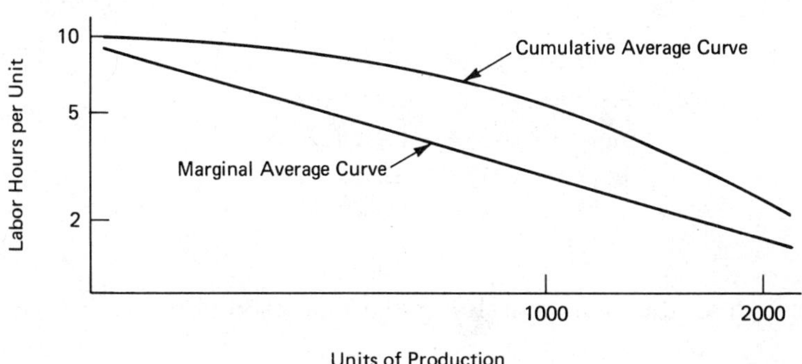

The conversion factor $(n + 1)$ is not applicable until the distance between the curves is constant, or until the curves become parallel. According to data in Exhibit 25-2, this should be after production doubles at least ten times. At this point, the marginal average can be converted to the cumulative average using the alternative formula. Total hours may then be computed easily from the other alternative formula. Once again, however, these alternative formulas are *not applicable, except after long production experience.*

25.7 AN ILLUSTRATION IN THE USE OF LEARNING CURVE ANALYSIS

Consider the following data for the Space Components Company:

1. Theorem 1 applicability.
2. Learning rate = 80%.
3. *First lot* contains fifteen units.
4. *First lot* took 690 hours to complete.
5. Cost data:
   a. Labor = \$8 per hour.
   b. Material = \$50 per unit.
   c. Variable overhead subject to learning effect = \$4 per hour.
   d. Variable overhead *not* subject to learning effect = \$12 per unit.
   e. Fixed overhead = \$100,000 (application rate = \$10 per unit).
6. Sales price per unit = \$592.

QUESTION 1: What will be the total cost to produce 400 units?

First, we must find k (the labor hours to produce the first unit):

$$Y_1 = 690/15 = 46$$
$$X^n = .4182 \text{ (value for 15 units)}$$
$$Y_1 = kX^n$$
$$k = 46/.4182$$
$$k = 109.99 = \underline{\underline{110 \text{ hours}}}$$

Second, find total hours:

$$T = kX^{n+1}$$
$$T = 110(400)^{-.3219+1}$$
$$\log T = \log 110 + .6781 \log 400$$
$$\log T = 2.04139 + .6781\ (2.60206)$$
$$\log T = 2.04139 + 1.76445$$
$$T = \text{antilog } (3.80584) = \underline{\underline{6{,}395 \text{ hours}}}$$

Third, find the total cost for 400 units produced in 6,395 labor hours:

Labor: 6,395 × \$8 =	\$ 51,160
Material: 400 × \$50 =	20,000
Variable overhead subject to learning effect 6,395 × \$4 =	25,580
Variable overhead *not* subject to learning effect 400 × \$12 =	4,800
Fixed overhead allocation 400 × \$10 =	4,000
Total cost for 400 units	\$105,540

QUESTION 2: What will be the cumulative average cost of the 400th unit?

First, find the cumulative average labor hours for the 400th unit. This can be found either of two ways—by dividing the total hours by 400 units or by using the formula for Y_1:

Dividing total hours by 400 units:

$$Y_1 = \frac{T}{X}$$

$$Y_1 = \frac{6395}{400} = 15.98 = \underline{\underline{16 \text{ hours}}}$$

By using the formula for Y_1:

$$k = 110 \text{ hours}$$
$$Y_1 = kX^n$$
$$Y_1 = 110\ (400)^{-.3219}$$
$$\log Y_1 = \log 110 - .3219\ (\log 400)$$
$$\log Y_1 = 2.04139 - .3219\ (2.60206)$$
$$\log Y_1 = 2.04139 - .83760$$
$$Y_1 = \text{antilog } (1.20379) = 15.99 = \underline{\underline{16 \text{ hours}}}$$

Second, find the average cost of the 400th unit:

Labor: 16 × \$8 =	\$128
Material: 1 × \$50 =	50
Variable overhead subject to learning effect 16 × \$4 =	64
Variable overhead *not* subject to learning effect 1 × \$12 =	12
Fixed overhead allocation 1 × \$10	10
Average cost of 400th unit	\$264

QUESTION 3: What will be the unit cost of the 400th unit?

First, find the marginal average hours to produce the 400th unit:

$$k = 110 \text{ hours}$$
$$Y_2 = (n+1)kX^n$$
$$Y_2 = (.6781)\ (110)\ (400)^{-.3219}$$
$$\log Y_2 = \log .6781 + \log 110 - .3219\ (\log 400)$$
$$\log Y_2 = 9.83129{-}10 + 2.04139 - .3219\ (2.60206)$$
$$\log Y_2 = 11.03508{-}10 = 1.03508$$
$$Y_2 = \text{antilog}\ (1.03508) = 10.84 = \underline{\underline{10.8 \text{ hours}}}$$

Second, find the cost of producing the 400th unit:

Labor: 10.8 × \$8 =	\$ 86
Material: 1 × \$50 =	50
Variable overhead subject to learning effect 10.8 × \$4 =	42
Variable overhead *not* subject to learning effect 1 × \$12 =	12
Fixed overhead allocation 1 × \$10 =	10
Cost to produce 400th unit	\$200

QUESTION 4: What is the total cost of producing units 101 through 200?

First, find the total hours to produce units 101 through 200:

$$k = 110 \text{ hours}$$
$$T_{101\text{-}200} = 110(200)^{-.3219+1} - 110(100)^{-.3219+1}$$
$$\log T_{200} = \log 110 + .6781 \log 200$$
$$\log T_{200} = 2.04139 + .6781(2.30103)$$
$$\log T_{200} = 2.04139 + 1.56033$$
$$T_{200} = \text{antilog}(3.60172) = \underline{3{,}997 \text{ hours}}$$
$$\log T_{101} = \log 110 + .6781(\log 100)$$
$$\log T_{101} = 2.04139 + .6781(2.00000)$$
$$\log T_{101} = 2.04139 + 1.35620$$
$$T_{101} = \text{antilog}(3.39759) = \underline{\underline{2{,}498 \text{ hours}}}$$
$$T_{101\text{-}200} = 3{,}997 + 2{,}498 = \underline{\underline{1{,}499 \text{ hours}}}$$

Second, find the total cost of producing units 101 through 200 for 1,499 labor hours:

Labor: 1,499 × \$8 =	\$11,992
Material: 100 × \$50	5,000
Variable overhead subject to learning effect 1,499 × \$4 =	5,996
Variable overhead *not* subject to learning effect 100 × \$12 =	1,200
Fixed overhead allocation 100 × \$10 =	1,000
Total cost of producing units 101 through 200	\$25,188

QUESTION 5: What is the break-even point on an average cost basis?

First, compute the revenue available to cover costs subject to learning effect:

$$\$592 - \$72 = \underline{\underline{\$520}}$$

Second, compute the number of labor hours this excess revenue will support:

$$\$520/\$12 \text{ per hour} = \underline{\underline{43.33}} \text{ hours available per unit}$$

Third, compute the break-even value X:

$$\begin{aligned}
Y_1 &= kX^n \\
43.33 &= 110(X)^{-.3219} \\
\log 43.33 &= \log 110 - .3219 \log X \\
1.63679 &= 2.04139 - .3219 \log X \\
-.40460 &= -.3219 \log X \\
\log X &= \frac{-.40460}{-.3219} = 1.25691 \\
X &= \text{antilog}(1.25691) = 18.07 = \underline{\underline{18 \text{ units}}}
\end{aligned}$$

This answer can also be obtained by computing only the value for X^n and then locating this value in Exhibit 25-6:

$$\begin{aligned}
43.33 &= 110(X)^n \\
X^n &= \frac{43.33}{110} = .3939
\end{aligned}$$

This value falls close to the table value .3944. Consequently, break-even point (X) is approximately eighteen units.

25.8 SUMMARY

Learning curve analysis provides a means for estimating the effects of learning on production. These effects can be explained by either Theorem 1 or Theorem 2. A constant percentage change between the cumulative average labor hours, or between the marginal average labor hours, determines the applicability of either Theorem 1 or Theorem 2, respectively. After the initial doubling of unit production, Theorem 1 applicability to historical data will also support Theorem 2 applicability. The opposite, however, is not true.

The learning rate can be found by a tabular analysis or by finding the index of learning. The index of learning is the slope of the learning equation when represented in logarithmic form. Each learning rate produces a different slope; consequently, the learning rate can be related to the index of learning.

To solve a learning curve problem, the number of labor hours taken to build the first unit must be known. If accounting is maintained by production lots, the first unit hours must be calculated.

There are three basic foumulae for each theorem. These formulae compute (1) the cumulative average labor hours per unit, (2) the marginal average labor hours per unit, and (3) the total labor hours to produce a given output.

CHAPTER 25 REFERENCES AND ADDITIONAL READINGS

Andress, F. J. "The Learning Curve as a Production Tool." *Harvard Business Review,* January–February 1954, pp. 87–97.

Baird, Bruce F. "A Note on the Confusion Surrounding Learning Curves." *Production and Inventory Management,* April 1966, pp. 71–78.

Baloff, N. "The Learning Curve—Some Controversial Issues." *Journal of Industrial Economics,* July 1966, pp. 275–82.

Bierman, Harold Jr., and Dyckman, Thomas R. *Managerial Cost Accounting.* New York: The Macmillan Company, 1971, pp. 81–93.

Billon, S. A. "Industrial Learning Curves and Forecasting." *Management International Review* (Germany), 1966, pp. 65–79.

Broster, E. J. "The Eighty Per Cent Law." *The Accountant* (England), December 28, 1963, pp. 807–9.

Dopuch, Nicholas, and Birnberg, Jacob G. *Cost Accounting: Accounting Data for Management Decisions.* New York: Harcourt, Brace & World, Inc., 1969.

Enrick, Norbert Lloyd. "Productivity Gains with the Learning Curve." *Industrial Management,* April 1971, pp. 9–12.

Hirschmann, W. B. "Profit from the Learning Curve." *Harvard Business Review,* January–February 1964, pp. 125–39.

Holdham, J. H. "Learning Curves—Their Applications in Industry." *Production and Inventory Management,* Fourth Quarter 1970, pp. 40–55.

Jordan, R. B. "Learning How to Use the Learning Curve." *NAA Bulletin,* January 1958, pp. 27–40.

McGarrah, Robert E. *Production and Logistics Management: Text and Cases.* New York: John Wiley & Sons, Inc., 1963.

Summers, Edward L., and Welsch, Glenn A. "How Learning Curve Models Can be Applied to Profit Planning." *Management Services,* March–April 1970, pp. 45–50.

Taylor, M. L. "The Learning Curve—A Basic Cost Projection Tool." *NAA Bulletin,* February 1961, pp. 27–40.

Teichroew, D. *An Introduction to Management Science.* New York: John Wiley & Sons, Inc., 1964, pp. 159–63.

CHAPTER 25 QUESTIONS, PROBLEMS, AND CASES

25- 1. Explain the procedure for selecting the learning curve theorem applicable to a company's historical data.

25- 2. What are some potential uses of learning curve analysis? Is the data necessary for such an analysis available from typical accounting information systems?

25- 3. What are the three types of labor data that can be estimated from learning curve formulae?

25- 4. "The *initial lot size* chosen to begin a learning curve analysis, and to determine the learning rate, is dictated mainly as a result of the manner in which historical labor data is gathered and summarized." However, if the initial lot size is greater than one unit, some preliminary calculation must be done. What preliminary calculation is necessary? Why is it necessary? If the initial lot size is very large, are the learning effects difficult to measure? Why?

25- 5. How can Exhibit 25-6 (Values of X^n) be used to compute the value of k? What is the primary purpose of Exhibit 25-6?

25- 6. Explain the procedure for determining a learning rate from historical data.

25- 7. Why is the computation of "total labor hours" more difficult under Theorem 2 than under Theorem 1? Can the computation be made without the use of Exhibit 25-9 (Values of μ)?

25- 8. Define or explain the use of the following terms and phrases:
(a) Learning rate
(b) Initial lot size (k)
(c) Marginal labor hours
(d) Average labor hours
(e) Exponential curve
(f) Index of learning
(g) Conversion factor

25- 9. "In all production situations where learning curve analysis is applicable, and after a learning rate is established, Theorem 2 should always be used." Explain the meaning of this statement. Is this statement completely true in very early production stages?

25-10. $(n+1)$ is referred to as a *conversion factor.* Why? What does it represent? How is it used? Under which theorem is its use applicable?

25-11. "When historical data is analyzed, the marginal labor hours per unit will inordinately reflect changing conditions and/or errors in record keeping." Why are the marginal labor hours affected so greatly and what implications does this have on determining Theorem 2 applicability to historical data? Is Theorem 1 affected in a similar manner? Why?

25-12. "A 95% learning rate is considered minimum evidence of learning." What is the conceptual justification for this statement?

25-13. The learning rate found through the application of Theorem 2 to historical data is applicable to both theorems. Evaluate this statement.

25-14. How does the ratio of machine to labor hours affect the learning rate?

25-15. "As the production quantity increases, the ratio of the marginal average to the cumulative average tends to be constant." Under which theorem is the phenomenon noticeable? How is this phenomenon translated into a useful relationship for computing learning curve data?

25-16. Why is the formula for the cumulative average labor hours under Theorem 1 the same as the formula for the marginal average labor hours under Theorem 2?

25-17. "In those instances where records of production lots are maintained, and the initial lot size is greater than one unit, the value of k must be computed." Why?

25-18. "Any company's historical data on average hours that produces a slope of −.3219 when plotted on log-log graph paper is experiencing an 80% learning rate." Evaluate this statement.

25-19. Why is Theorem 2 applicable when Theorem 1 is applicable, but not *vice versa?*

25-20. What is the basis for the determination of alternative formulae under Theorem 2 for calculating cumulative average labor hours and total labor hours? When are these alternative formulae applicable?

25-21. Define the *index of learning* and the *rate of learning*. How do they relate to one another? Derive this relationship from the exponential learning equation.

25-22. How are the values of Exhibit 25-5 computed? What do the values mean?

25-23. Name some factors that influence a company's learning rate.

25-24. How is Exhibit 25-6 (Values of X^n) used? How are the values of this table derived?

25-25. ***DETERMINING THEOREM APPLICABILITY*** From an examination of Shellman Company's labor and production records for 19x1 the following data is available:

Lot No.	Cumulative Production in Units	Cumulative Labor Hours
1	16	80
2	32	128
3	64	205
4	128	328
5	256	525
6	512	840
7	1,024	1,343
8	2,048	2,150

Required:

(a) Using log-log graph paper, plot the cumulative average labor hours and the marginal average labor hours as a function of cumulative production.
(b) From the graph, determine which theorem is applicable.
(c) Using the slope of the applicable theorem, determine the learning rate.
(d) Compute the value of k
(e) Calculate the value of Y_1 (for Theorem 1) and Y_2 (for Theorem 2) when the cumulative production is:
(1) 1,024
(2) 1,000
(3) 200
(4) 4,000

25-26. ***DETERMINING THE LEARNING RATE*** The Pulse-Jet Corporation produces highly sophisticated terrain-following guidance radar for the government's advanced fighter aircraft. The company wants to know its learning rate for labor in order to submit a bid for a new contract. To date, the company has produced sixty-two radar units and has experienced the following:
(a) Total labor hours to build first unit was 710 hours.
(b) Total labor hours to build sixty-two radar units was 32,240 hours.

Required:

(1) Assuming Theorem 1 is applicable, determine the learning rate for the Pulse-Jet Corporation's radar units.
(2) Under Theorem 1, determine:
a. The total labor hours to build 100 units.
b. The cumulative average labor hours to build 100 units.
c. The marginal average labor hours to build 100 units.

25-27. ***THEOREM 1 FORMULAE*** The High-Power Corporation experiences a 75% learning rate on the production of electronic calculators.

Required:

For all calculations assume Theorem 1 is applicable.

(a) If the first unit required sixty hours to assemble, compute:
 (1) The cumulative average labor hours to produce seventy units.
 (2) The marginal average labor hours to produce seventy units.
 (3) The total labor hours to produce seventy units.

(b) If the first unit required forty hours to assemble, compute:
 (1) The cumulative average labor hours to produce 1,000 units.
 (2) The marginal average labor hours to produce 1,000 units.
 (3) The total labor hours to produce 1,000 units.

25-28. ***THEOREM 2 FORMULAE*** The Scientific Matrix Corporation experiences an 85% learning rate on the production of tape-controlled drill presses.

Required:

For all calculations assume Theorem 2 is applicable.

(a) If the first unit required 840 hours to assemble, compute:
 (1) The marginal average labor hours to produce twenty machines.
 (2) The cumulative average labor hours to produce twenty machines.
 (3) The total labor hours to produce twenty machines.

(b) If the first unit required 1,020 hours to assemble, compute:
 (1) The marginal average labor hours to produce ninety-five machines.
 (2) The cumulative average labor hours to produce ninety-five machines.
 (3) The total labor hours to produce ninety-five machines.

(c) Using the *alternative formulae* for calculating cumulative average labor hours and total labor hours, rework parts (a) and (b). From your results, what conclusions can you draw concerning the applicability of these alternative formulae?

25-29. ***COMPREHENSIVE PROBLEM—THEOREM 1*** From the financial records of Advanced Technology Corporation the following data is gathered:

(a) The learning phenomenon is best described by Theorem 1.
(b) Learning rate is 85%.
(c) *First lot* contains eight units.
(d) First lot took 1,560 hours to complete.
(e) Cost data:
 (1) Labor = \$6 per hour.
 (2) Material = \$13,500 per unit.
 (3) Variable overhead subject to learning effect = \$4.50 per hour.
 (4) Variable overhead *not* subject to learning effect = \$1,400 per unit.
 (5) Fixed overhead = \$370,000 (application rate \$925 per unit).
(f) Sales price per unit = \$18,000.

Required:

a. Compute the total cost of producing:
 1. 50 units
 2. 80 units
 3. 300 units
b. Compute the cumulative average cost of the:
 1. 50th unit
 2. 80th unit
 3. 300th unit
c. Compute the unit cost of the:
 1. 50th unit
 2. 80th unit
 3. 300th unit

d. Compute the total cost of producing units 50 through 300.
e. Compute the break-even point on an average cost basis.

25-30. ***CALCULATING EXHIBIT VALUES***
(a) Exhibit 25-5: Calculate the learning index for a learning rate of:
  (1) 64%
  (2) 60%
(b) Exhibit 25-8: Calculate the conversion factor for a learning rate of:
  (1) 64%
  (2) 58%
(c) Exhibit 25-6: Calculate the value of X^n for a production of (assume a 80% learning rate):
  (1) 101
  (2) 156
(d) Exhibit 25-6: Calculate the value of μ (the cumulative X^n value) for a production of (assume an 80% learning rate):
  (1) 101
  (2) 102

25-31. ***COMPREHENSIVE PROBLEM – THEOREM 2*** From the financial records of Myers Electronic Corporation the following data is gathered for the production of transistorized stereo receivers:
(a) The learning phenomenon is best described by Theorem 2.
(b) The learning rate is 80%.
(c) *First lot* contains twenty units.
(d) First lot took thirty hours to complete.
(e) Cost data:
  (1) Labor = $5 per hour.
  (2) Material = $60 per unit.
  (3) Variable overhead subject to learning effect = $3.00 per hour.
  (4) Variable overhead *not* subject to learning effect = $20 per unit.
  (5) Fixed overhead = $150,000 (application rate $15 per unit).
(f) Sales price per unit = $280.

Required:

For all production values outside the range of Exhibit 25-9, use the alternative formulae.

a. Compute the total cost of producing:
  1. 100 units
  2. 1,000 units
  3. 8,000 units
b. Compute the cumulative average cost of the:
  1. 100th unit
  2. 1,000th unit
  3. 8,000th unit
c. Compute the unit cost of the:
  1. 100th unit
  2. 1,000th unit
  3. 8,000th unit
d. Compute the total cost of producing units 50 through 8,000.
e. Compute the break-even point on an average cost basis.

25-32. ***COST PROJECTION*** The Mitton Aircraft Company manufactures aircraft and missile parts. The company is beginning production on a second contract for its new advanced wing assembly. The company's experience on the first contract is as follows:

Contract 1 (200 Wing Assemblies)

Labor hours to produce first wing assembly	2,479 hours
Total labor hours	55,000 hours
Direct materials	$600,000
Direct labor	$357,500
Overhead:	
Variable subject to learning	$ 22,000
Variable *not* subject to learning	$100,000
Fixed	$ 40,000

Required:

(a) Determine the learning rate for production of the advanced wing assembly.

(b) Determine the total cost of Contract 1 if it is for a production of (assume Theorem 1 is applicable):
   (1) 150 wing assemblies
   (2) 400 wing assemblies

25-33. ***COST PROJECTION*** The North-West Aircraft Company is a manufacturer of aircraft and missile parts. The company is going into production of a new nose assembly. The project manager has forecasted the following data concerning the new nose assembly:

Material costs per unit	$42
Labor costs per hour	$ 9.30
Projected standard hours per unit	35 hours
Projected hours to complete unit 1	200 hours
Inspection hours: 5% of production hours	
Estimated unit sales price	$600

Required:

The North-West Aircraft Company uses an 80% learning curve in projecting project costs. Based on initial projections, you are to prepare the following estimates concerning this proposed project.

(a) Assuming Theorem 1 is applicable:
   (1) How many hours will it take to finish unit:
      a. No. 25
      b. No. 50
      c. No. 100
   (2) What will be the *average cumulative hours* per unit after:
      a. 25 units
      b. 50 units
      c. 100 units
   (3) Determine the *total* hours to build:
      a. 30 units
      b. 60 units
      c. 90 units
   (4) What will be the *average* hours per unit for units:
      a. 21 through 40
      b. 51 through 70
      c. 81 through 100

(b) Assuming Theorem 2 is applicable, answer questions 1 through 4.

UNIT VII

DESIGN AND ANALYSIS OF ACCOUNTING INFORMATION SYSTEMS

Previous units dealt with an inquiry into the utility of accounting services. The art and science of accounting was defined and extracted into a "body of knowledge" sufficient to build systems responsive to the needs of users. In this unit we deal specifically with design and analysis by examining the structure of automated information systems and the role and function of operational auditing.

In chapter 26 we present a comprehensive overview of essential design features found in automated information systems. The reliance by numerous organizations upon some form of automated accounting makes it imperative that students in accounting understand automated systems.

Ever since the first large-scale commercial computer was born with the introduction of UNIVAC I in 1951, organizations have become increasingly dependent upon the information handling ability of machines. Today, in the United States, there are over 70,000 computers in operation.[1] One estimate raises this total to 200,000 by 1975, and perhaps as many as 350,000 by 1980.[2]

Although computers perform the same accounting tasks as humans, they

[1] "OCR: The Evasive User's Recognition," *Business Automation* 19, no. 1 (January 1972): 14.

[2] Eric A Weiss, ed., *Computer Usage Applications* (New York: McGraw-Hill Book Company, 1970), p. 8.

present a fundamentally unique situation by their profound impact on the characterization of accounting system design. Many contemporary information systems are inextricably tied to the availability and sophistication of data processing equipment.

In chapter 27 we discuss the audit of an accounting information system by focusing on the *attest function* of independent expert observers. Contemporary auditing is a *full service activity.* It consists of two distinct services: an *operational audit* designed to reveal control weaknesses, operating efficiencies, and the effectiveness of operations in meeting their goals; and a *financial audit* designed to reveal the fairness of financial statement figures.

Notoriety surrounding the legal liability of auditors—for their opinions on financial statements—has forced them to rethink their role as independent observers and to adopt more stringent guidelines for the conduct of professional audits. Unfortunately, the outcomes of courtroom battles have left auditors anxious about the propriety of the attest function and have led to unwarranted precaution in the exercise of professional judgment. Over-testing and over-documentation are two precautions that auditors have instituted to compensate for the growing problem of legal liability. Over-auditing, however, has simply worked to further erode public confidence in the "expertness" of auditors and to support legitimate suspicions about the equity of the cost-benefit of the audit function.

To overcome contemporary inadequacies in the investigation of financial statements, the auditor is adopting a scientific approach that supports a more professional image. Interestingly, this scientific approach also supports the extension of operation auditing. The natural extension into "management services" is an outgrowth from the *art* of accounting into the *science* of accounting. The intrusion into management services is the *application* of accounting as a science. It is an extension of expertise—gained by rigorous apprenticeship and study—into the diagnosis of system design weaknesses, omissions, and redundancies. The benefits accruing from such an extension are obvious.

CHAPTER

26

THE DESIGN OF AN AUTOMATED SYSTEM

26.1 SYSTEM FUNCTIONS

System design involves the orderly arrangement of activities geared to the production of information. Structurally, there are five functional components in every formal information system. In Exhibit 26-1 we see that these components are data gathering,

EXHIBIT 26-1 FUNCTIONAL COMPONENTS OF AN INFORMATION SYSTEM

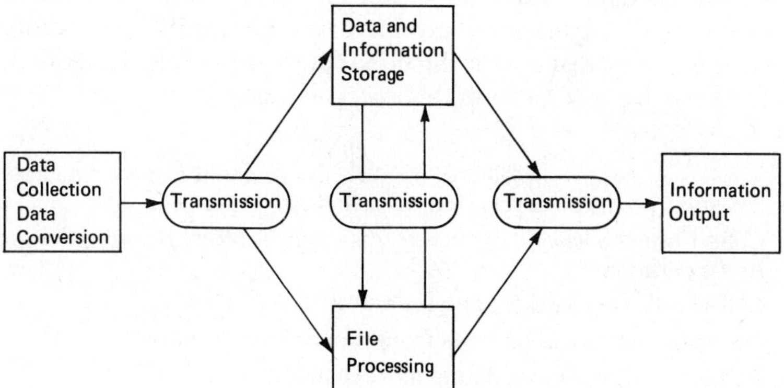

data and information storage, file processing, information output, and message transmission.

26.2 DATA COLLECTION

Data is the symbolic manifestation of an occurrence or experience that can be perceived by a person or machine. Data collection, as shown in Exhibit 26-2, involves the *measurement* of events and objects and *recording* of the measurements.

The first design consideration of any system is to establish the need for information, and the second is to determine what *type of information* can fulfill this need.

EXHIBIT 26-2 DATA COLLECTION

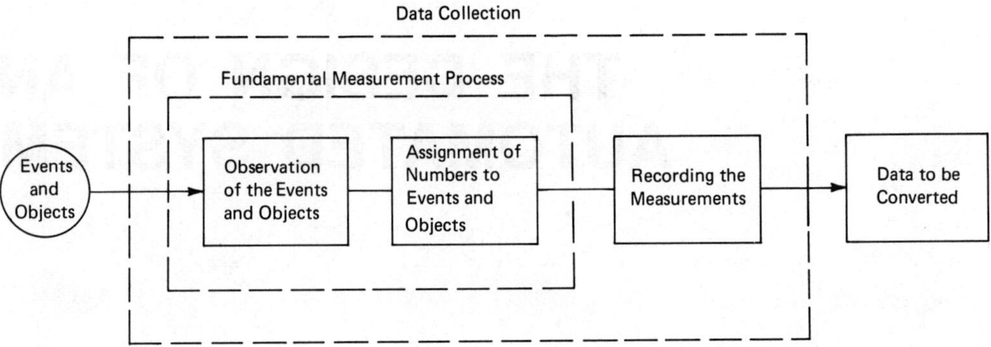

Modified diagram from: "Accounting and Information Systems," *Accounting Review,* Supplement to Volume XLVI, Committee Reports (1971): 309. Used by permission of the American Accounting Association.

In this way we set parameters for the acceptance or rejection of raw data into the system structure. Only that data which supports our specific information needs are admitted. This screening of data is accomplished using *input rules.* The rules may be formal or informal. For an accounting information system, there are seven formalized input rules, as discussed in chapter 3.

Even with these input rules, a typical organization must handle enormous quantities of data. As data volume increases, the collection task places a considerable financial burden on an organization and increases the possibility of errors. The solution is to find some means of data reduction that does not impair the data's information content. There are several ways this is accomplished:

1. Avoid a complete surveillance of the environment. Collect data at a few key observation points or collect only sample data.
2. Collect only *exception data;* that is, data which differs from predetermined or desired conditions.
3. Collect only *variable data* and predict *fixed data.*
4. Use statistical data as raw data from experimental events.
5. Avoid collecting a given datum more than once.

Once data is extracted from the environment and measured, it is recorded on a "transaction document." In a large organization, many man-hours are consumed in the preparation of transaction documents. For this reason, forms design is an important aspect of data collection. Although practical experience is a necessity for learning the subtleties of forms design, a few general guidelines are as follows:

1. Provide precise and distinctive identification of the form.
2. Provide ease in entering and extracting data.
3. Produce multiple copies with the least expense and greatest readability. This will entail the selection of colored paper or colored printing, and reusable or nonreusable carbons (or chemically treated pressure-sensitive paper).
4. Prominently display important data.
5. Coordinate with other forms in positioning of similar or identical data. For instance, the space for signature approval should be in the same relative position on each form.
6. Provide space coordination with the method of entering data—pencil, typewriter, computer printer, etc.
7. Provide a degree of *durability* commensurate with the environmental conditions under which the form is used and commensurate with the instrument or machine used to complete the form.
8. Fit in standard-size filing equipment and envelopes. If folding is necessary, the positioning of folding marks should be part of the design plan.
9. Produce the minimum waste in cutting from standard sizes of mill paper.

Many of the controls over data gathering activity arise directly from adequate forms control. Other controls include separation of duties and a procedure by which authorized personnel must approve events before they are recorded. These controls, like others to follow, are specifically designed to reduce the deleterious effects of system *noise.*[1]

26.3 DATA CONVERSION

Data represented on a transaction document may not be in a convenient form for storage and processing by machines. In this instance, it may be necessary to (1) change from one symbolic representation to another, (2) change recording media, or (3) change the data's physical form. In any case, we must change the data to a form acceptable to the receiving device. This does not necessarily mean that conversion changes data into a form suitable for processing, but only to a form capable of being read by a receiving device.

There are a variety of machines capable of converting *source* transactions documents to a machine-readable medium. A number of these machines and the converted media they produce are listed in Exhibit 26-3. Some machines convert

[1]Charles J. Sippl, *Computer Dictionary and Handbook* (Indianapolis, Ind.: Howard W. Sams & Co., Inc., 1970), p. 207, defines *noise* in these terms: "1. Meaningless extra bits or words that must be ignored or removed from the data at the time the data is used. 2. Errors introduced into data in a system, especially in communication channels. 3. Random variation of one or more characteristics of any entity such as voltage, current, and data. 4. Loosely, any disturbance tending to interfere with the normal operation of a device or system."

EXHIBIT 26-3 CONVERSION MACHINES AND MEDIA

SOURCE DOCUMENT	CONVERTING DEVICE	CONVERTED DOCUMENT
Handwritten or Typewritten Documents	CARD PUNCH OR KEY PUNCH	Punched Cards
Handwritten or Typewritten Documents	PAPER TAPE PUNCH (as an attachment to bookkeeping machines, calculators, adding machines, teletype machines, etc.)	Punched Paper Tape
Handwritten or Typewritten Documents	MAGNETIC TAPE ENCODER	Magnetic Tape Reel
Handwritten or Typewritten Documents	MAGNETIC TAPE CARTRIDGE OR CASSETTE ENCODER	Magnetic Tape Cartridge Magnetic Tape Cassette
Handwritten or Typewritten Documents	MAGNETIC DISK ENCODER	Magnetic Disk
Imprinted Documents	OPTICAL CHARACTER ENSCRIBER	Optical Tape
Handwritten or Typewritten Documents	KEYBOARD CARDWRITER	Plastic Embossed Card
Plastic Embossed Card & Pre-Punched Card	DATA COLLECTION TERMINAL	Punched Cards Magnetic Tape
Bar Code Imprints on Source Documents & Mark Sense Cards	OPTICAL MARK READER (OMR)	Punched Cards Magnetic Tape Paper Tape
Handprinted or Typewritten Documents & Turnaround Documents (airline tickets, credit card invoices, etc.) Adding Machine and Cash Register Tapes	OPTICAL CHARACTER READER (OCR)	Bar Code Imprint on Original Document Punched Cards Magnetic Tape Paper Tape

source documents directly into machine-readable media, while others produce the machine-readable media as a by-product of the original recording.

Once the conversion has been accomplished, the new machine-readable media can be entered into storage or processing through a receiving device. This device makes the necessary transformation into a symbolic representation acceptable to the storage device or processor. Not all receiving devices, however, require machine-readable media. Some can transform data on source documents directly into proper symbolic representation. These machines, or the configuration that must support such machines, are generally very expensive and the cost advantage of eliminating media conversion may be lost.

Additionally, there are other conversion aspects of some importance:

1. Punched cards and paper tape cannot be read by receiving devices fast enough to be compatible with the internal speeds of computers. There is a great disparity of transfer time when compared with magnetic tape. For example, the transfer

rate for punched cards ranges from 400 to 1,600 characters per second, whereas magnetic tape has a typical transfer rate from 15,000 to 350,000 characters per second. Therefore, if a computer is used in the system, it may be necessary to convert a second time into another media, such as magnetic tape. This conversion can again take place through conversion equipment or can be converted as a preliminary processing stage.

2. Selection of a machine-readable media should be based upon cost, durability, storage capacity, reuse, and handling speed.
3. Most Optical Card Readers are designed to read only one type font (type style)—the National Standard OCR-A. There are OCR readers that read a variety of type fonts and hand printing. The price differential, however, is considerable—$36,000 for a single-font machine to above $220,000 for a multiple-font machine.
4. With some conversions no permanent, human-readable records are produced. This obviates their use in some organizations.

After conversion, the data on machine-readable documents must represent the same data as on source documents. Some controls over the conversion process are:

1. *Machine verification of punched cards:* The same source document is used a second time to key data into a card verifier machine. A comparison of this keyed data with the data on the punched card reveals any exceptions. With "electronic" or "buffered" keypunches, the punching and verifying are done on the same machine. On standard keypunches, the verifier is a separate unit. The significance of the buffered keypunch/verifier results from the elimination of error correction steps.
2. *Observing a one-to-one correspondence of source documents and punched cards.*
3. *Data buffering in magnetic tape and disk encoders:* Before data is encoded on magnetic tape or disk, a prescribed number of characters is collected in a temporary storage or buffer. After visually examining the content of the buffer, or re-keying, the machine then encodes the data as a record.
4. *Visual inspection of the printing on punched data cards or inspection of punched card listings.*
5. *Comparison of control totals (document counts, dollar totals, etc.) of source document batches with tabulated totals of punched card batches.*

26.4 DATA AND INFORMATION STORAGE

Fundamentally, three types of data are subject to storage:

1. Source data (transaction data) resulting from a fundamental measurement of an event or object affecting the organization.
2. Data resulting from the processing of source data.
3. Procedural data used as *instructions* for processing source data.

Storage is necessary to facilitate processing and to facilitate inquiry and retrieval of information. Not only must this function preserve the integrity of data, but it must also preserve the relationships among data.

DATA ELEMENTS

Maintaining data integrity and the relationships among data is accomplished by a hierarchical arrangement that provides for a distinction between elementary data and complex data. Exhibit 26-4 shows the conceptual treatment of such an arrangement, while Exhibit 26-5 shows the same arrangement in a more familiar context.

EXHIBIT 26-4 HIERARCHICAL ARRANGEMENT OF DATA

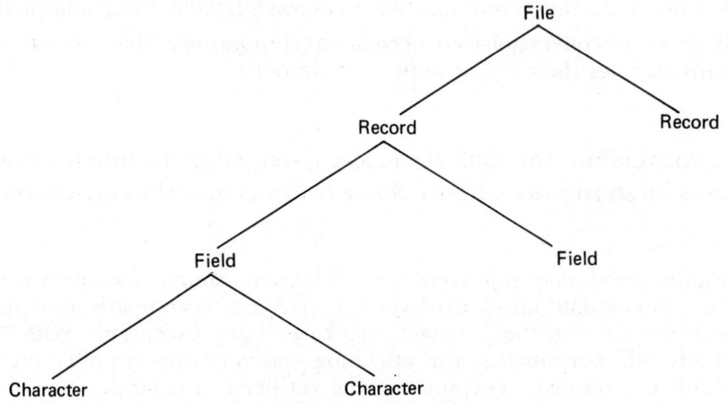

File

Record Record

Field Field

Character Character

EXHIBIT 26-5 RELATIONSHIP BETWEEN CHARACTER, FIELD, RECORD, AND FILE

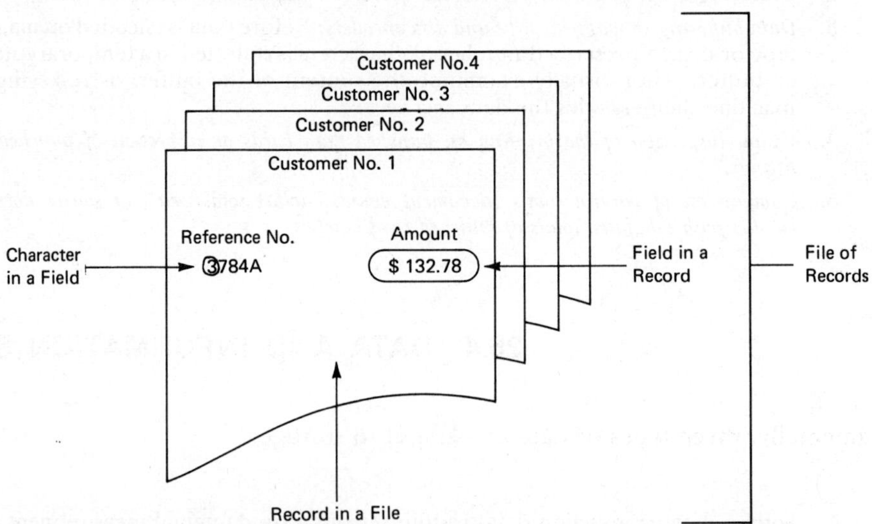

Modified diagram from Gordon B. Davis, *Computer Data Processing* (New York: McGraw-Hill Book Company, 1969), p. 4. Copyright 1969 by McGraw-Hill. Used with permission of McGraw-Hill Book Company.

A *character* is an elementary datum; a *field* is a character or group of characters treated as a unit and conveying a special meaning; a *record* is a group of fields that are related to a specific transaction or processing result; and a *file* is an ordered assembly of logically related records.

DATA MODES

The most elemental data form is a character. The characters that can be used in a given information system are contained in a *character set.* Generally, an information system's character set will contain three categories of characters – *alphabetic, numeric,* and *special.* Some special characters commonly used in message editing and mathematical operations are similar to those found on a standard typewriter keyboard: @ # $, ; ¢ % * (+ = ? /.

Since a field is composed of characters, and since characters are classified by type, a field will assume the *mode* of the characters it contains. For example, if all the characters in a field are numeric, the field is described as numeric. If all are alphabetic, the field is described as alphabetic. All fields, however, may safely be designated as *alphameric* regardless of the characters they contain. Even a numeric or alphabetic field may be described as alphameric. The reverse, however, is not always true. For example, the California License number UNT589 is strictly alphameric since it contains both numeric and alphabetic characters. Also, $1,000 is an alphameric field since it contains special symbols for a comma and dollar sign. The same field, however, written as 1000 could be described as both numeric and alphameric. Whatever the mode of a field, a clear identification of mode is *required* by the receiving device upon entry of source data for storage or processing, and is essential to the understanding of file structure.

FIXED AND VARIABLE FIELDS

When a fixed-length field is in numeric mode, the characters of that field must be *right-justified.* That is, the right-most character or *low-order character* must occupy the extreme right of the field. When a fixed-length field is in alphabetic or alphameric mode, the characters of that field must be *left-justified.* That is, the left-most character or *high-order character* must occupy the extreme left of the field. Exhibit 26-6 shows the placement of the number 2785 in a fixed numeric field of seven positions, while the same number in a fixed alphameric field is shown in Exhibit 26-7.

EXHIBIT 26-6 RIGHT-JUSTIFICATION IN A FIXED NUMERIC FIELD

			2	7	8	5

EXHIBIT 26-7 LEFT-JUSTIFICATION IN A FIXED ALPHAMERIC FIELD

2	7	8	5			

In a fixed numeric field all unused positions will automatically be filled with zeros, whereas in an alphameric field all unused positions are filled with blanks.[2] The positioning of numerals is important in a fixed numeric field since the meaning can

[2] A "blank" is a permissable *special* character.

be altered by misplacement, as shown in Exhibit 26-8. The number 2785 is changed to 278500. In a fixed alphameric field the same misplacement (as shown in Exhibit 26-9) does not result in misinterpretation, since blanks carry no numerical significance.

EXHIBIT 26-8 MISPLACEMENT OF NUMERIC CHARACTERS IN A FIXED FIELD

0	2	7	8	5	0	0

EXHIBIT 26-9 MISPLACEMENT OF NUMERIC CHARACTERS IN AN ALPHAMERIC FIELD

	2	7	8	5		

Although fixed-length fields do create some formating problems, there is a distinctive advantage in their use. Side-by-side fields can easily be distinguished from one another by merely counting the positions of each field. For instance, the two fields in Exhibit 26-10 are easily distinguishable. If a field length varies for each new set of characters, the fields become indistinguishable, as shown in Exhibit 26-11. The distinguishing benefit of fixed-length fields is exchanged for the benefit of *improved storage utilization.* Obviously, variable fields provide more compact storage, but just as obviously, they make data less accessible.

EXHIBIT 26-10 SIDE-BY-SIDE FIXED FIELDS

Check Number							Employee Number						
				2	8	6					7	3	4

EXHIBIT 26-11 SIDE-BY-SIDE VARIABLE FIELDS

2	8	6	7	3	4

In automated storage devices the problem of distinguishing side-by-side variable fields is overcome by using a *field designator* or *flag.* This special symbol sometimes *precedes* the high-order character and sometimes is placed *above* the high-order character, as shown in Exhibit 26-12. In situations where the designator precedes the

EXHIBIT 26-12 PLACEMENT OF FIELD DESIGNATOR

•	2	8	6	•	7	3	4

$\bar{2}$	8	6	$\bar{7}$	3	4

field, it simply becomes the high-order character of the field and for purposes of field interpretation is ignored. In situations where the designator is placed over the high-order character, the designator does not have the status of a separate character.

With handwritten documents or records, fields need not appear side by side. With machine-readable documents, however, fields must be sequential. This enables an internal procedure for locating all the fields that logically belong to a specific record, and for locating one field from another. The low-order position of the record is established, and starting at this position, we locate each field in the record by sequentially *moving toward the high-order position* of the record and locating each field designator in turn. This procedure is shown in Exhibit 26-13.

EXHIBIT 26-13 LOCATING FIELDS IN A RECORD

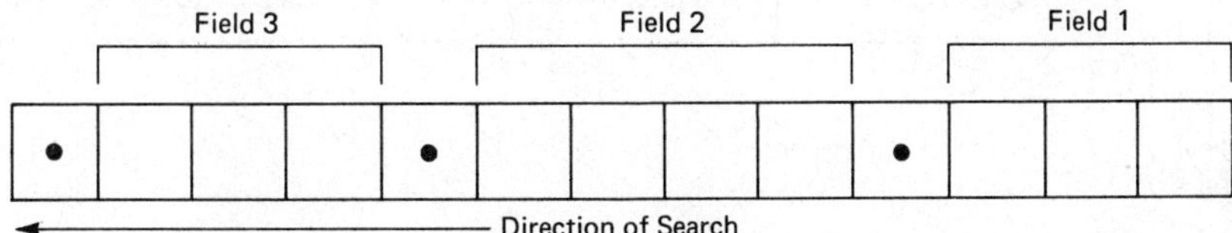

RECORD FORMATING

Records may be separated by *gaps* or *blocked* into groups of records. Gapping (as shown in Exhibit 26-14) is a requirement of some storage media, such as magnetic tape,[3] while in other instances it is employed to provide room for the insertion of new records into a file. Blocking (shown in Exhibit 26-15) is a method for conserving storage space and for increasing record processing time.

EXHIBIT 26-14 RECORD GAPS

Record	Gap	Record	Gap	Record	Gap	Record

EXHIBIT 26-15 BLOCKING OF RECORDS

Record	Record	Record	Record	Gap	Record	Record	Record
Block 1					Block 2		

In order to distinguish one record from another, a *record prefix* or *tag* is attached to the high-order portion of the record. As shown in Exhibit 26-16, this *special field* indicates either the number of characters found in the record, or in the case of fixed-length fields, the number of fields found in the record. If all records of a particular file are the same length, however, the record prefix is not needed.

In the same manner, blocks are distinguished from one another by a *block prefix,* as shown in Exhibit 26-17. This prefix or *special record* indicates the number of records, fields, or characters found in the block. If all blocks of a particular file are

[3]Magnetic tape uses a 3/4-inch record gap as a provision for starting and stopping the tape drive.

EXHIBIT 26-16 RECORD PREFIX

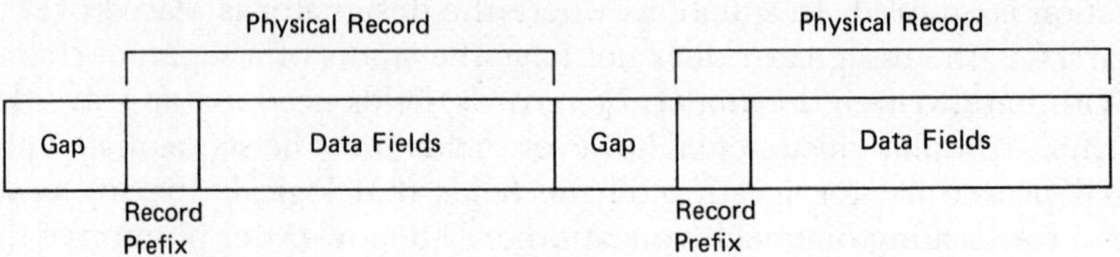

EXHIBIT 26-17 BLOCK PREFIX

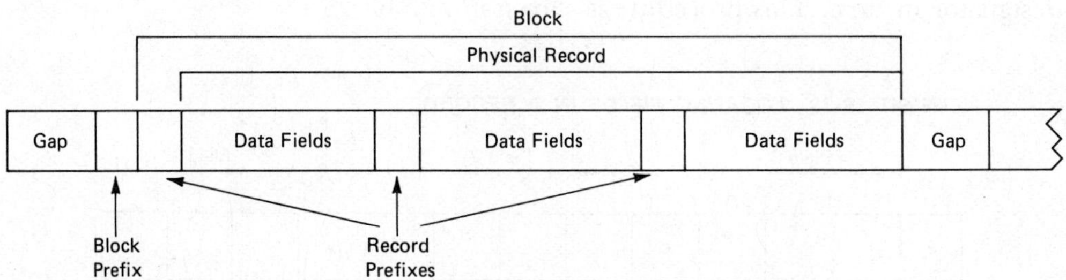

the same length and contain the same number of fixed-length records, the block prefix is not needed.

LOCATION OF RECORDS AND FIELDS

The location of a record in storage is found by using a *record key* or an *address.* A record key is used in sequentially organized files and an address is used in randomly organized files.

EXHIBIT 26-18 RECORD KEY

Customer Number	Customer Name	Credit Rating	Credit Limitation	Account Balance
78420	BENTLEY CORPORATION	B1	20000.00	4670.20

↑ Record Key

A record key is one field of a record specifically designated to identify the record. For example, the customer account number for the Bentley Corporation can be used as an identifier or record key for an accounts receivable record shown in Exhibit 26-18. The customer name—Bentley Corporation—could have been used as the record key; but generally speaking, alphabetic fields should be avoided as record keys for the following reasons:

1. There is a possibility of duplicate names.
2. Location of alphabetic keys is more difficult since they may not be mathematically compared.
3. Use of names will require the record key to be a variable-length field.

To obtain the credit rating, credit limitation, or account balance for the Bentley Corporation, the entire accounts receivable file has to be searched until the record key 78420 is located. This would not be necessary, however, if we knew in advance the specific location of our record in storage. With some storage facilities, this is possible. The specific location is identified by an address.

Random-access files have the capacity to store data in specific storage locations, each with a unique numerical address. Conceptually, this arrangement may be viewed in Exhibit 26-19. Data is stored in a specific cell or series of cells, and is referred to by an address.

EXHIBIT 26-19 ADDRESSING

Addresses	12	13	14	15	16	17
Cells						

In a *primary storage* facility (computer memory), each individual character may be stored in an addressable cell. To locate a complete record, the *high-order character of the record is addressed,* and reading or writing into or out of cells commences until the record prefix is satisfied or until a *record mark* is located. As shown in Exhibit 26-20, this involves reading or writing from the low-order address to the high-order address.

EXHIBIT 26-20 LOCATION OF RECORDS AND FIELDS

Low-Order Address — Reading and Writing Records → — High-Order Address

71	72	73	74	75	76	77	78	79	80	81	82	83
$\overline{2}$	4	3	7	$\overline{N}$	A	M	E	$\overline{A}$	7	8	4	6

High-Order Character — ← Processing of Fields — Low-Order Character

Primary storage is also used as *working storage* for the processing and conversion of records, or more specifically, *data fields.* To locate a specific field, the *low-order character of the field is addressed.* This character and all successively higher characters are included in the field until the *field mark* is encountered. As shown in Exhibit 26-20, this means that a field is located by its high-order address. For example, the field NAME is located at address 78.

Not all random-access storage devices have the capacity to be completely random. That is, some do not have the capacity to store one character per addressable cell. They must store many characters per address in order to make efficient use of storage. For example, disk storage, consisting of a stack of rotating disks, stores data by individual track or by sectors on a track, as shown in Exhibit 26-21. An address (called a *home address*) refers to a disk number, a track number, and a sector number. Conceptually, each data cell holds the characters that can be recorded by the fixed length of track within a disk sector. Since this cell will normally have the capacity

EXHIBIT 26-21 ADDRESSING IN DISK STORAGE

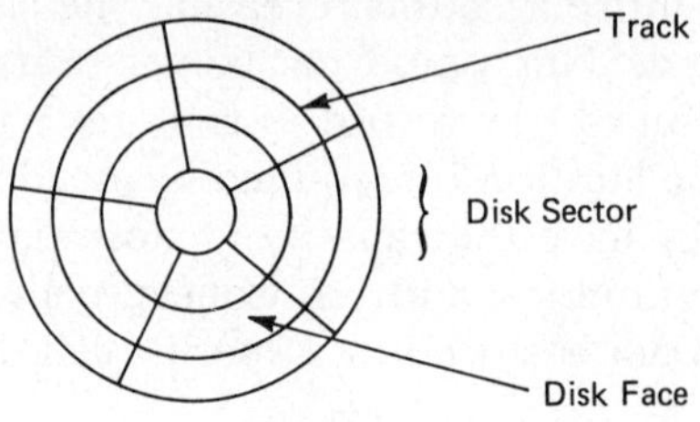

to store several hundred characters, each addressable location must store several records in order to use storage space efficiently. In this circumstance, the location of a specific record in an addressable location requires the use of a record key. That is, a record is located by its address and record key. The file is able to select randomly only groups of records, with individual records being selected sequentially.

CHAINING

Chaining is a method of linking sequential records or blocks that are not stored in consecutively numbered address locations. A chain address located in a special field of the record, or in a special record of the block, indicates the location of the next sequential record or block, respectively. Each successive record or block in turn contains the chain address of the next. If the chain is unbroken, we should be able to trace a closed loop from record to record, or from block to block, as shown in Exhibit 26-22.

EXHIBIT 26-22 ADDRESS CHAINING

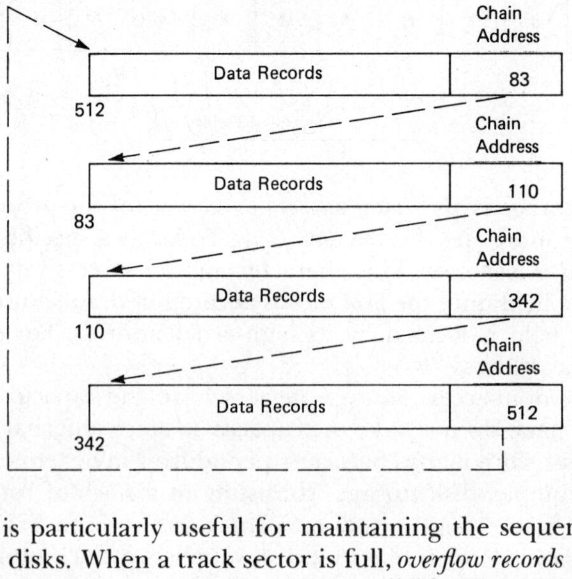

Chain Address
Data Records | 83
512
Chain Address
Data Records | 110
83
Chain Address
Data Records | 342
110
Chain Address
Data Records | 512
342

Chaining is particularly useful for maintaining the sequential order of data records stored on disks. When a track sector is full, *overflow records* are placed on successively higher tracks where record space is available. For example, suppose the loading sequence of records is A1, B1, A2, D1, C1, A3, C2, A4, B2, C3, B3, A5. In a

EXHIBIT 26-23 A CHAINED FILE

Track	Chaining Record	Data Records		
A	B	A1	A2	A3
B	D	B1	A4	B2
C		C1	C2	C3
D		D1	B3	A5

chained file the resulting storage is indicated in Exhibit 26-23, and the following questions and answers explain how records are located:[4]

Q. If looking for an "A" record, where does the search begin?
A. On Track A. Searches always begin with the home track.
Q. If an "A" record is not found on track A, what is the next track searched?
A. Track B. Searches always continue at the track specified in the chaining record.
Q. If the "A" record is not found on track B, what is the next track searched?
A. Track D.
Q. If a "C" record is not found on track C, what is the next track searched?
A. None. The blank chaining record shows that there are no more "C" records.

FILE ORGANIZATION

A file is a group of logically or structurally related records. The arrangement of these records in a file follow three general patterns that are largely dictated by design features of the storage facility.

Sequential Organization

Records are arranged in serially ascending or descending order by record key and/or address location. In other words, a *data string* is produced.

Indexed-Sequential Organization

Records are arranged in serially ascending or descending order by record key and are blocked into major sections. These sections are called *prime storage areas* and are addressable at the first record of the block.

For each prime storage area there is an *overflow area.* When a prime storage area is filled, any additional records are stored in the overflow area and linked to the

[4]Example reprinted by permission from: *Introduction to IBM System/360: Direct Access Storage Devices and Organization Methods* (New York: International Business Machines Corporation, 1969), p. 45. © 1969 by International Business Machines Corporation.

prime area by a chain address. Partitioning storage in this manner allows for the insertion of new records without the necessity of creating a new file.

To find a particular record in storage we must find the address of its prime storage area and then read sequentially within this area until the record key is located. First, we must find the prime storage area containing the record. We can do this by comparing the key of the record with the lowest key of each block. Taking each block in reverse order, we compare to see if the key is higher than or equal to the low key. When the condition is met, the prime storage area has been found. For example, suppose the record key is 1245 and there are seven prime storage areas containing the following records:

Prime Storage Area	Record Keys
1	1–340
2	341–678
3	679–982
4	983–1203
(5)	1204–1486
6	1487–1601
7	1602–1893

The record whose key is 1245 is stored in prime storage area 5. Referring to a special sector of the file called a *file index,* we can locate the address location of any prime storage area.[5] At this address, we can read the block of records serially until the record key 1245 is located.

Random or Direct Organization

Random file organization is possible only in storage facilities utilizing addressing. In these facilities records can be completely randomized—that is, not arranged in sequential order and not located in adjacent storage cells. When this random storage process is employed the record key must be *transformed* into an address. There are several transformation methods available:

KEY SAME AS ADDRESS The record key can be the address of the record. This *requires* that records be *fixed-length* and the keys numeric. This also requires that employee numbers, account numbers, inventory part numbers, etc., be based on the address numbers of storage cells. These numbers, however, may be entirely unsatisfactory as identification numbers, and purging of obsolete records will leave unused storage locations.

The use of a record key as an address in disk storage will require a preliminary calculation. The key divided by the number of records per track will produce a quotient equal to the track address, and a remainder plus one equal to the record number.

[5]Before finding a specific address, it may be necessary to search through several hierarchical indexes. For instance, in a disk file it may be necessary to first search a master index, next a cylinder index, and finally a track index before finding the proper address.

CROSS-REFERENCE INDEX Each record is assigned a specific address and cross-referenced with its key in an index. The index can be used to assign an address to each record before it is stored or can be used to assign addresses in the same manner as with an indexed-sequential file.

RANDOMIZING METHODS Randomizing methods are *indirect addressing* methods that compress a range of record keys into a smaller range of addresses. In many instances, record keys rely on account codes[6] that purposely leave numbering gaps for the insertion of new records. With this situation, direct addressing is uneconomical because there will be too many unused numbers.

Record addresses are calculated from the record keys and records are stored in the calculated addresses. Since the randomizing calculation reduces the record key numbering range, it will sometimes produce the same address for two or more record keys. The record already stored in this address location is called a *home record,* while the records whose keys also randomize to this address are called *synonyms* or overflow records. Instead of being stored in their calculated address, the synonyms will be stored in a special overflow section and *chained* to the calculated address.

In disk storage, synonyms are reduced by randomizing to a track address rather than a record address. An overflow will not occur until the track is full.[7] In other direct-access storage facilities, a *packing factor* may be added to the initial file size.

When selecting a specific randomizing technique, two objectives must be considered:[8]

1. Every possible key in the file must randomize to an address in the allotted range, and
2. The address should be distributed evenly across the range so that there are few synonyms.

The following are just four of a number of techniques for calculating a relative record address:[9]

1. **Prime Number Division:**[10] A record address is calculated as the *remainder* when the record key is divided by the *largest prime number less than the number of file records.* For example, suppose a file has 400 records, and we must obtain an address for the record with a key of 9742:
   a. The largest prime number less than 400 is 397.
   b. Divide 9742 by 397.
   c. The remainder of 214 equals the record address.

[6]Refer to Appendix E, "Account Coding."

[7]Multiple record storage at one address location is sometimes called "bucket storage."

[8]Reprinted by permission from: *Introduction to IBM System/360: Direct Access Storage Devices and Organization Methods,* p. 42. © 1969 by International Business Machines Corporation.

[9]A "relative address" must be added to the starting address of the file to obtain an "absolute address." With disk storage, however, track addresses are noncontiguous and files frequently occupy several nonadjacent areas. In this special circumstance, absolute addresses are much more difficult to obtain.

[10]A prime number is only divisible by itself and by one.

2. **Digit Analysis:** This technique analyzes the evenness in the distribution of keys and uses this evenness to develop addresses. A count is made of the number of times each digit appears in each position of the key. The positions having an evenness in the distribution of digits can be used to obtain an address directly. For example, suppose addresses range from 0 to 999, and analysis of record key positions reveals an evenness in the distribution of digits in the following decreasing order: Positions 2, 7, 4, 3, 1, 6, 5. If the key is 4087344, it will be converted into the three digit address 447. The second, seventh, and fourth positions of the key are used as the address.
3. **Folding:** With this technique the key is split into two or more parts, and the parts are added together to form an address. For example, folding the key 87123 can be accomplished as follows:

$$\text{(two part split) } 87 + 123 = 210$$
$$\text{(four-part split) } 8 + 71 + 2 + 3 = 84$$
$$\text{(split of alternate digits) } 813 + 72 = 885$$

4. **Radix Transformation:** This technique produces an address by *assuming* the key is written in the radix or base indicated by its highest numeric digit, and then transforming the key to the base ten. For example, suppose the key is 5472 and the addresses can range from 0 to 999. The highest digit in the key is 7. This leads us to assume that the key is written in base eight.[11] We can now convert to an address with the formula:

$$A = \Sigma d_i R^{i-1}$$

where

A = the decimal address
i = the digit position to the left of the radix point
d_i = the ith digit
R = the assumed radix of the key

Convert the key 5472 to an address:

$$A = (5 \times 8^3) + (4 \times 8^2) + (7 \times 8^1) + (2 \times 8^0)$$
$$A = 2560 + 256 + 56 + 2$$
$$A = 2874$$

In this example, since the address may not exceed three digits, we must strike the leading digit and leave the address as 874.

TYPES OF FILES

There are five main types of files, identified by their function or use:

Master File

This type of file is used for reference and contains permanent and semi-permanent historical, statistical, and summary data records: for example, general ledger accounts, subsidiary accounts, and special name lists.

[11]If the highest digit is 7, this indicates that eight symbols, 0 through 7, are used in this radix.

Transaction or Detail File

This type of file contains a collection of transaction records used to update or support master file records: for instance, a file of sales invoices.

Report File

This type of file contains special output *information* extracted from master files: for instance, an analysis of territorial sales or an inventory of employee skills.

Document File

This type of file contains complete documents and is part of a document retrieval system. The file media is usually microfilm or paper books and pamphlets.

Document Index File

This type of file contains index records that reference the documents in a document file.

INTEGRATED FILES

In random file organizations, data records belonging to separate master files can be linked together by using *additional chain fields,* as shown in Exhibit 26-24. These new

EXHIBIT 26-24 INTEGRATED FILES

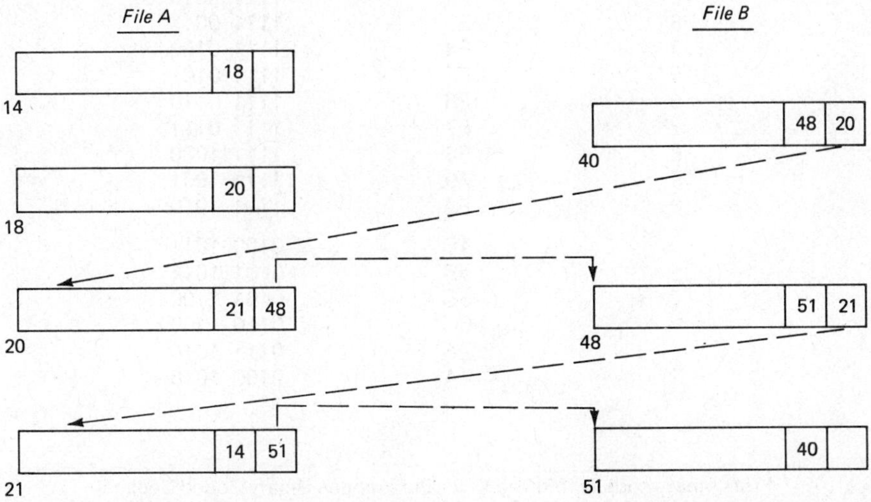

chain addresses allow overlapping data records to be available to several files on a consolidated basis, and hence obviate the need for repeating data records within separate files. Storage space is utilized more efficiently and data records can be members of several chains, each established for a processing application that can span several separate files.

EXHIBIT 26-25 BCD CHARACTER CODES*

CHARACTER	HEXADECIMAL CODE†	BINARY CODE
A	C1	1100 0001
B	C2	1100 0010
C	C3	1100 0011
D	C4	1100 0100
E	C5	1100 0101
F	C6	1100 0110
G	C7	1100 0111
H	C8	1100 1000
I	C9	1100 1001
J	D1	1101 0001
K	D2	1101 0010
L	D3	1101 0011
M	D4	1101 0100
N	D5	1101 0101
O	D6	1101 0110
P	D7	1101 0111
Q	D8	1101 1000
R	D9	1101 1001
S	E2	1110 0010
T	E3	1110 0011
U	E4	1110 0100
V	E5	1110 0101
W	E6	1110 0110
X	E7	1110 0111
Y	E8	1110 1000
Z	E9	1110 1001
1	F1	1111 0001
2	F2	1111 0010
3	F3	1111 0011
4	F4	1111 0100
5	F5	1111 0101
6	F6	1111 0110
7	F7	1111 0111
8	F8	1111 1000
9	F9	1111 1001
0	FA	1111 1010
.	4B	0100 1011
$	5B	0101 1011
*	5C	0101 1100
%	6C	0110 1100
:	7A	0111 1010
?	4A	0100 1010

*This binary code is referred to as an Extended Binary Coded Decimal Interchange code (EBCDIC) since it extended the character set from 64 characters to a possible 256 characters.

†Because the hexadecimal number system requires sixteen symbols, six additional digits, in addition to 0 through 9, must be devised. In most instances, letters are used because of their familarity and ordering property. For a hexadecimal system the complete list of symbols is 0,1,2,3,4,5,6,7,8,9,A,B,C,D,E,F.

DATA REPRESENTATION

Data is represented in manual files as numbers and words on source documents, and in machine-readable files as code. On most file media, each *character* is represented by a column of punched holes (punched cards and paper tape) or by magnetized elements called *bits.* Each character of a character set is coded by a unique configuration of punched holes or by a unique configuration of bits representing binary ones and zeros. These binary bits are recorded on magnetic surfaces as the presence or absence of magnetic spots, or by the direction of the surface's magnetic polarization. Since there are two polarized directions, both binary digits can be represented.

In computer memory all data received for storage is represented in Binary Coded Decimal (BCD).[12] The most popular BCD coding scheme assigns every character in the character set a unique *two-digit hexadecimal* number and then translates each digit into *four binary bits.*[13] Exhibit 26-25 shows a list of characters, their hexadecimal code, and their binary code.

SELECTION OF STORAGE DEVICES

Storage devices are generally classified into three basic groups according to size, speed, and function: (1) primary storage, (2) secondary storage, and (3) peripheral storage. Primary storage is the internal memory of a computer, secondary storage is an on-line auxiliary storage that directly augments the capacity of primary storage, and peripheral storage is a *stand-alone* storage of drawings, abstracts, and texts not subject to processing. Exhibit 26-26 shows some storage devices and some major features of each.

FILE SAFEGUARDS

A number of generally applicable file safeguards are as follows:

1. *Environmental Control:* Files should be protected from extreme temperature and fire and water damage, and from high-voltage magnetic fields.
2. *Security Control:* Adequate security precautions should be exercised for portable files (i.e., magnetic tape and disk packs) and for preventing unauthorized duplication or alteration of files. This latter point is extremely important since computer files can be duplicated or altered, leaving no trace. Special authorization codes or machine keys should be required of those persons accessing files.
3. *Procedural Controls:* The transfer of data *into* storage destroys or erases any data already in that particular location. For this reason, we must be sure that only authorized data enters a file. There are several specific controls that help to minimize the possibility of file destruction through inadvertent data transfer:
   a. *File Protection Ring:* This is a plastic or metal insert ring that prevents accidental data insertion on magnetic tape. Only when the ring is inserted on the tape reel can writing take place.

---

[12] Since computers perform arithmetic in *straight binary,* it is necessary to convert numeric quantities from BCD before any computation and back again to BCD before storing the result.

[13] It takes only four binary positions to represent every possible one-place hexadecimal number.

EXHIBIT 26-26 STORAGE DEVICES

TYPES OF DEVICES	STORAGE MEDIA	FILE ORGANIZATION	HOW DATA IS REPRESENTED	RATE OF TRANSFER TO PRIMARY STORAGE (Characters Per Second)	STORAGE CAPACITY (In Characters)
Primary Storage					
Computer Memory	Magnetic Cores Thin-Film Plated-Wire Magnetic Rods	Random or Sequential	Binary or BCD	Not Applicable	10,000–550,000
Secondary Storage					
Bulk or Mass Core Unit	Magnetic Cores	Random or Sequential	Binary or BCD	250,000–2,000,000	1–8 million
Data Cell Storage	Magnetic Tape Strips Magnetic Cards in Cartridges	Random & Sequential	BCD	55,000–150,000	1–400 million
Fixed Module Disk Storage	Magnetic Disks	Random & Sequential	BCD	156,000	10–700 million
Removable Module Disk Storage	Magnetic Disk Packs	Random & Sequential	BCD	156,000–312,000	3–10 million
Drum Storage	Magnetic Drum	Random & Sequential	BCD	275,000–1,200,000	1–8 million*
Magnetic Tape Storage	Magnetic Tape Reels and Cartridges	Sequential	BCD or Alphameric Code	15,000–350,000†	10–65 million
Peripheral Storage					
Stand-Alone Storage Devices	Microfilm Reels Microfilm Strips Microfilm Chips Aperture Cards Microfiche	Sequential Sequential & Random	Reduced Photographs & High-Resolution Photographs		

*The drum storage capacity of a UNIVAC FASTRAND storage is approximately 33 million characters.

† Only *hypertape units* are capable of achieving transfer rates in excess of 300,000 characters per second.

b. *External Labels:* Portable files should be labeled externally for ease of identification.

c. *Internal Labels:* The beginning of a file can be labeled internally by a special record called a *header label.* This label can be checked to see if the proper file is being referenced. A header label typically used on magnetic tape files is shown in Exhibit 26-27.

EXHIBIT 26-27 MAGNETIC TAPE FILE HEADER LABEL

Record Prefix	Name of File	File I.D. Number	Reel Sequence Number	Creation Date	Purge Date

d. *Interlocks or Boundary Protection:* Interlocks are controls designed to protect the integrity of storage locations by preventing the internal overlap of files. The boundaries must be planned in advance or can be part of the hardware design.[14]

e. *File Library:* There should be a systematic and organized method for physically storing portable files. A log of file usage should be maintained and clear policies should be established for the retention, reuse, and reconditioning of files.

4. *File Reconstruction:* There should be a file retention plan that provides for the reconstruction of files that are inadvertently damaged during processing or have suffered environmental damage. Usually, the procedure involves periodic *dumping* or recopying of master files on portable machine-readable media. These duplicate files, along with intervening transactions data, provide a means for file reconstruction.

When magnetic tape is used, however, no dumps are required. The processing of tape files to produce an updated master file does not destroy the old master file. This feature of magnetic tape files allows an organization to follow the grandfather-father-son scheme of file retention illustrated in Exhibit 26-28. In any one period, the older generation master file and transactions file will always be available in case of the need for reconstruction.

26.5 FILE PROCESSING

As shown in Exhibit 26-29, processing consists of two basic activities: *file manipulation* and *file updating.* File manipulation involves sorting, merging, matching, sequence checking, scanning, and editing of data records. File updating involves the posting of transaction file data or calculated data to selected master file records and fields, and the preparation of report files.

SORTING

Sorting is the arrangement of *data records* into ascending or descending sequence according to record key. Several sorting methods are available:[15]

[14]For instance, as part of the hardware design, the IBM 360 core memory provides boundary protection for blocks of 2048 BCD characters.

[15]Standard sort routines are commonly available with computer installations, and manufacturers usually provide sort-timing tables for estimating the time to sort a given number of records.

EXHIBIT 26-28 GRANDFATHER-FATHER-SON SCHEME OF MAGNETIC TAPE FILE RETENTION

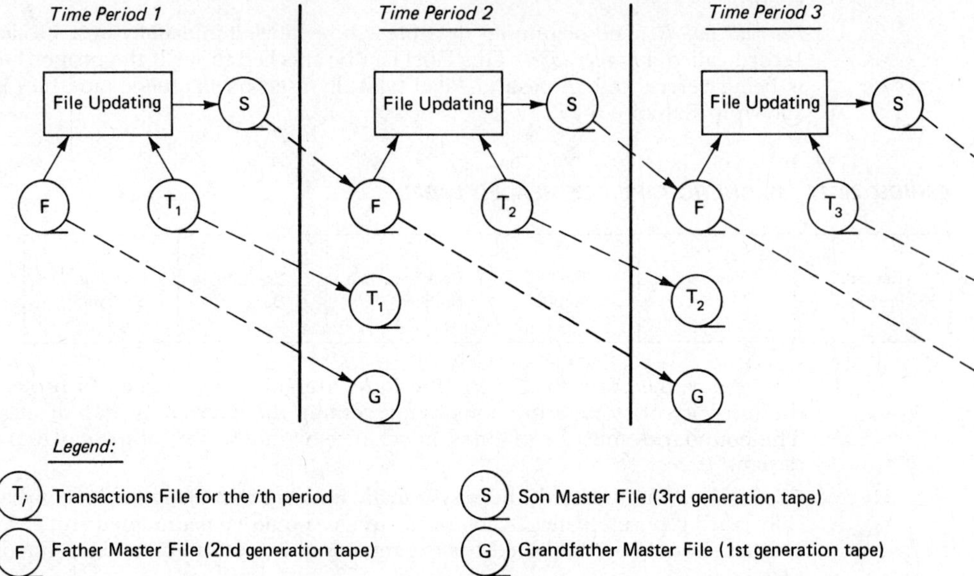

EXHIBIT 26-29 FILE PROCESSING

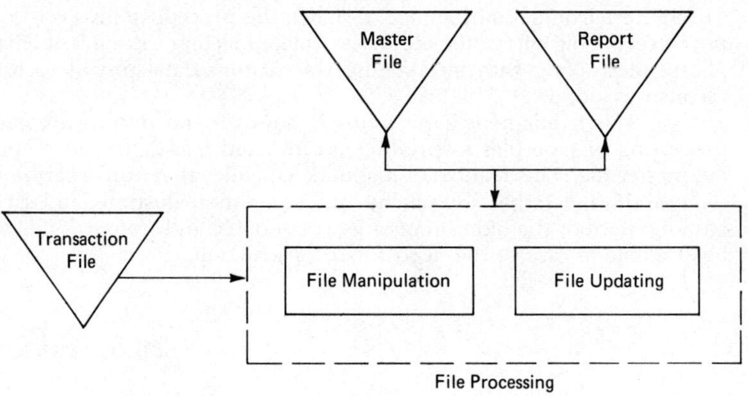

Straight Insertion Sorting

With this method each key is inserted into its proper sequence as each record is read. The file is sequenced one record at a time, with the key of each new record compared successively with the keys in the existing *string* until the proper position is located. For example, Exhibit 26-30 shows how the record keys 20, 92, 43, 17, 29 can be sorted into an ascending sequence. The number of passes required is determined by the number of records to be sequenced.

If the records are in completely random sequence, and are stored on sequential-access media, this method requires a considerable amount of time searching for record positions. The problem can be relieved somewhat by using random-access file media, but even at best this method is cumbersome, with large numbers of records.

EXHIBIT 26-30 STRAIGHT INSERTION SORTING

Record Keys in Original Sequence				
20	92	43	17	29

Passes				
1	2	3	4	5
(20)	20	20	(17)	17
	(92)	(43)	20	20
		92	43	(29)
			92	43
				92

On the average, a record insertion position cannot be located until at least one-half of the sequenced records are searched.

Binary Insertion Sorting

This method provides a more efficient scheme for finding the insertion position of a record. The new record key is compared against the middle value of the existing record string. If the record key is higher, we confine our search to the higher half of the sequence; if it is lower, we confine our attention to the lower half. Of the remaining records, a new middle value is determined, and the elimination procedure is continued. Sequence halves are divided again and again into halves until the insertion position is located. For example, Exhibit 26-31 shows how to locate the insertion position for a record key of 109.

In long record sequences or strings this method considerably reduces the number of compare operations. For instance, if a string of 1,024 records were sequenced using straight insertion, an average of 512 compare operations would be required. The same string, using binary insertion, would require only 9 compare operations.

Extraction Sorting

This method compares the record key of adjacent *record pairs* and successively *extracts* the *lowest* key for an ascending sort and the *highest* key for a descending sort. Extracted records from this first pass form a new string. The procedure is repeated for a number of passes until a pass is unable to improve the sequence. At this point, the file is in order. For example, Exhibit 26-32 shows how the record keys 20, 92, 43, 17, 29 can be sorted into an ascending sequence.

Exchange Sorting

This method sorts a string by initially comparing the key of the *first record* with the key of each record in succession. If the first record is out of order, it is exchanged and the

EXHIBIT 26-31 BINARY INSERTION

Existing Record String	1st Comparison	2nd Comparison	3rd Comparison	4th Comparison	Answer: Insert Between 98 & 112	
5					5	
6					6	
14					14	
18					18	
24					24	
32					32	
54					54	
77	$77 < 109$				77	1st Midpoint
83					83	
98			$98 < 109$		98	3rd Midpoint
					109	
112				$112 > 109$	112	4th Midpoint
123		$123 > 109$			123	2nd Midpoint
125					125	
142					142	
157					157	
168					168	

EXHIBIT 26-32 EXTRACTION SORTING

Original String	20 92 43 17 29
1st Pass	20:92 92:43 92:17 92:29 92
	20 43 17 29 92
2nd Pass	20:43 43:17 43:29 43:92 92
	20 17 29 43 92
3rd Pass	20:17 20:29 29:43 43:92 92
	17 20 29 43 92
Final Pass (no improvement)	17:20 20:29 29:43 43:92 92
Sequenced String	17 20 29 43 92

other record becomes the new first record. The process is continued, always with the new first record, until the pass is complete. At this point, a second pass begins, and now the key of the *second record* is compared with the key of each record in succession. If it is out of order, a new second record emerges and the process continues until the pass is complete. After a number of passes, the file will be ordered. For example, Exhibit 26-33 shows how the record keys 20, 92, 43, 17, 29, can be sorted into an ascending sequence.

This method is very simple, but unfortunately not very practical. Records must be moved too often, and more importantly, since all records should be available simultaneously, a random-access media is desirable.

MERGING

Merging is the process of combining two or more *key ordered strings* into *one key ordered string*. Groups of *two* strings are merged successively until one string remains. If there are any odd strings, they are successively merged with the final string as a group of two. When the original number of strings is some power of two (2, 4, 8, 16, etc.) there will be no odd strings. For example, Exhibit 26-34 shows the merging of eight strings into one, while Exhibit 26-35 shows the merging of seven strings into one.

Groups of two strings are merged into single strings by successively comparing the keys of *only* two records at a time—one from each record string. If the strings are in ascending order, the record with the smallest key is *extracted* and placed on the new string. It is then *replaced* by the next record from the string whose record was extracted. A new comparison is made, and another extraction and replacement

EXHIBIT 26-33 EXCHANGE SORTING

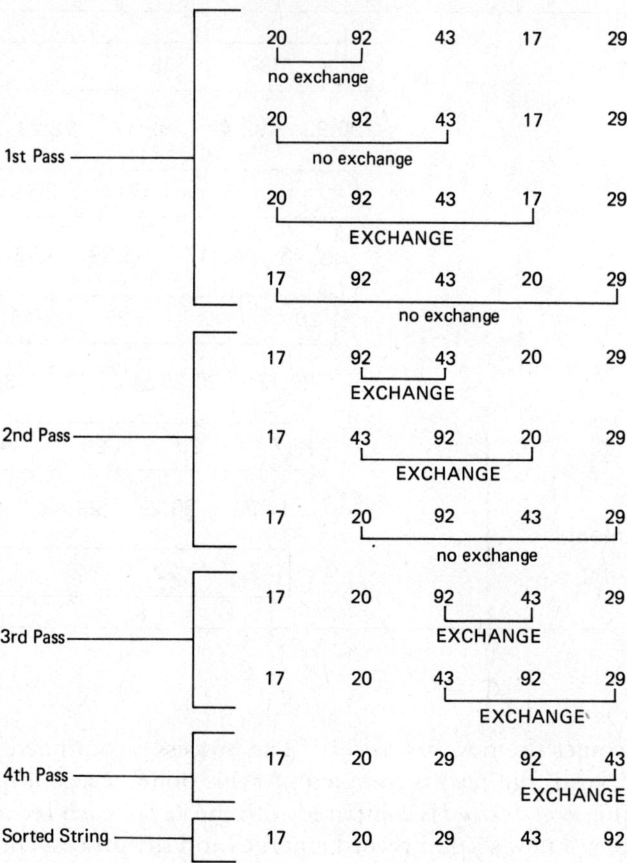

EXHIBIT 26-34 MERGING OF EIGHT STRINGS

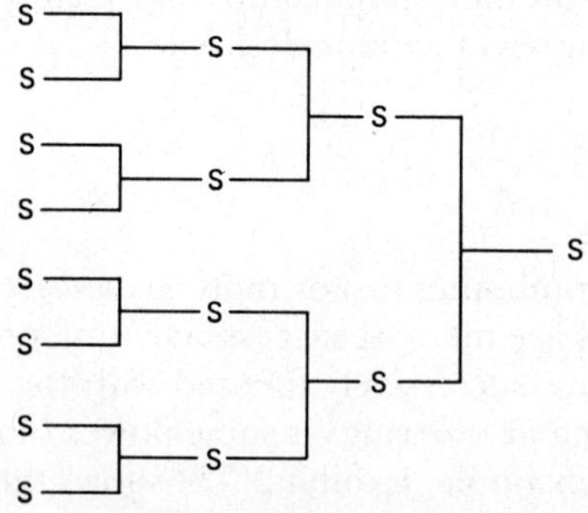

results. The comparison-extraction-replacement cycle is repeated until a new merged string results. For example, suppose the sequenced string 102, 97, 83, 41, 13, is merged with the sequenced string 90, 64, 57, 34, 12. The resulting string is obtained by the procedure shown in Exhibit 26-36.

EXHIBIT 26-35 MERGING OF SEVEN STRINGS

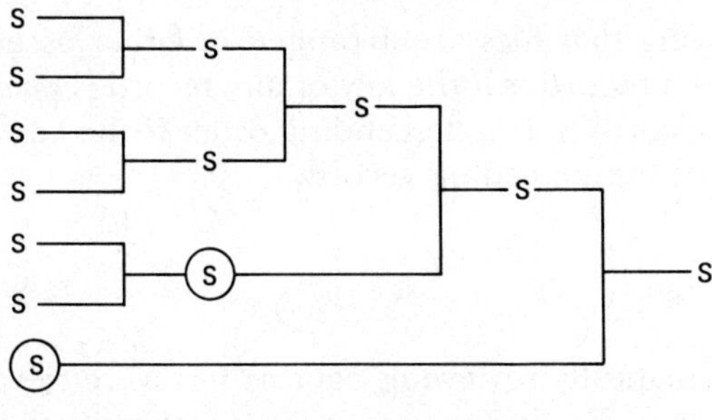

Note: Odd strings are circled.

EXHIBIT 26-36 MERGING OF TWO STRINGS

		MERGED STRING
Start, Compare	13:12	
EXTRACT		12
Replace, Compare	13:34	
EXTRACT		13
Replace, Compare	41:34	
EXTRACT		34
Replace, Compare	41:57	
EXTRACT		41
Replace, Compare	83:57	
EXTRACT		57
Replace, Compare	83:64	
EXTRACT		64
Replace, Compare	83:90	
EXTRACT		83
Replace, Compare	97:90	
EXTRACT		90
Replace, Compare	97:	
EXTRACT		97
Replace, Compare	102:	
EXTRACT		102

OTHER FILE MANIPULATION ACTIVITIES

In addition to sorting and merging, there are four other common activities:

Matching

The determination that two or more files have identical record *sequences,* as determined by a comparison of record keys.

Sequence Checking

A procedure for proving that files are arranged in either ascending or descending order. A file is in ascending order if the key of any record is *equal to or greater than* the key of the preceding record. It is in descending order if the key of any record is *equal to or less than* the key of the preceding record.

Scanning

A procedure for systematically reviewing data strings to retrieve records whose keys meet a particular criterion. For instance, customer records could be scanned to locate all customers in Region A with balances over $1,000. Records meeting these two requirements would be *grouped* into a special string. Another example involves scanning a file of table values. In this instance, the table is searched for a matching *argument.* When found, the corresponding *table function* is retrieved.

Editing

A process for manipulating the text of a file by rearranging or modifying record fields and by deletion and insertion of characters and fields into existing records. For instance, some common editing activities include insertion of dollar signs, page numbers, commas, periods, etc.; increasing the size of a record; deleting redundant data fields or records; the suppression of zeros; correction of errors; modifying a chain address; and changing the sequence of fields in a record.

FILE UPDATING

File updating is the process of posting transaction records to a *master file.* This is accomplished by either of two basic processing methods—*batch processing* or *in-line*

EXHIBIT 26-37 BATCH PROCESSING

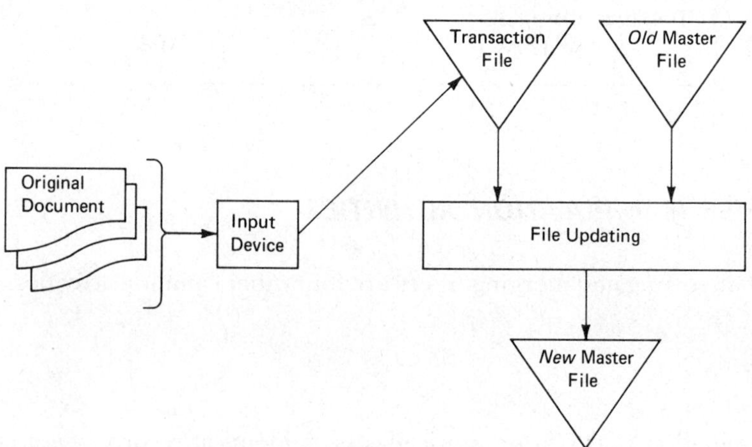

Note: The *original documents* may also be converted documents on such media as punched cards or magnetic disk packs.

processing. As shown in Exhibits 26-37 and 26-38, the methods are distinguished by the way in which input data is received for processing.

With batch processing any incoming *transaction records* are accumulated in batches according to *transaction type.* After a stated time interval, or after a batch reaches a particular size, it enters processing as a *transactions file.* If the master file is in sequential order, however, the transaction file must be sorted in the same sequence before updating is initiated.

EXHIBIT 26-38 IN-LINE PROCESSING

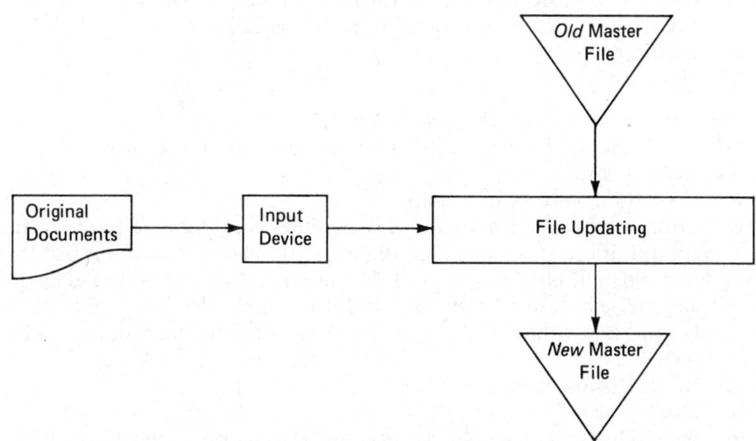

The main disadvantage of batch processing is the delay in updating while batches are accumulated. Nevertheless, it may be the only feasible way of updating master files recorded on sequential-access media, and furthermore, there is a significant control advantage in using batches. *Batch control totals* can be computed from source documents and subsequently used to assure that all transactions are placed in the transactions file, and to assure that all transaction records have been used to update the master file. Batch control totals are normally maintained throughout file manipulation and updating and are stored in a special end-of-file record called a *trailer label.* The control total can take any of three forms:

1. *Financial Totals:* totals of dollar amounts normally added together and normally appearing in financial summaries.
2. *Hash Totals:* totals of document data not usually added. For instance, invoice numbers, dates, etc.
3. *Record Counts:* total of transaction documents processed.

With in-line processing, incoming *transaction records* are processed in the order of their occurrence. No transactions file is created. Transactions are processed on a continuous basis, and without regard to transaction type. These features make in-line processing heavily dependent upon random-access storage facilities.

The main advantages of in-line processing are the elimination of sorting and merging requirements, the smoothing of processing peaks, and the maintenance of up-to-date master files. The disadvantages are the heavy dependence upon random-access storage facilities and the attendant higher cost of hardware dependent file media.

Both updating methods administer controls that are specifically designed to (1) prevent mishandling and resubmittal of input data; (2) validate input records; and (3) assure that master files are properly updated. Some common controls under each grouping are as follows:

1. *Controls to prevent mishandling and resubmittal of input data:*
   a. *Route slips* attached to batch.
   b. Maintaining a *list of batches* received by processing center.
   c. *Perforation* of numbering of forms after processing.
   d. *Color code* for ease of return to proper originator.
   e. *Document counts.*
   f. *Hash totals.*
2. *Controls over the validity of input records:*

   Validity controls signal errors caused by faulty input data. Specifically, they search for:
   a. Invalid characters in a field.
   b. Computational agreement with self-checking digit. A series of mathematical computations performed on digits of a code (e.g. account number) must agree with the self-checking digit if the code is valid. The self-checking digit is usually the last digit of the code. Refer to Appendix E.
   c. Invalid input data, by comparing input account codes against a list of current codes.
   d. Invalid transactions.
   e. Missing data.
   f. A matching data sequence between transactions and master file.
   g. Unreasonable figures. Certain data fields are constrained by upper or lower limits to prevent unreasonable computational outcomes.
3. *Controls to assure that master files are properly updated:*
   a. *Limit* or *reasonableness test* of minimum and maximum constraints on computational outcomes.
   b. *Crossfooting* of output arrays by comparing the sum of the horizontal totals with the sum of the vertical totals.
   c. *Control figures* to assure that all records are processed and that a file is truly updated (financial totals, hash totals, record counts). For a particular account (or for the file as a whole) a control to assure that all transactions are processed is to compare the transaction amount (or total) with the difference between the beginning account balance (or file balance) and the ending account balance (or file balance). This procedure is similar to a bookkeeping machine proof.
   d. *Comparing the record keys* of transaction file records with those of master file records: for instance, the comparison of account numbers or customer names.
   e. Maintenance of a *suspense file* for error messages and unprocessed records caused by out-of-sequence conditions.
   f. *A means to reverse or correct an erroneous entry* of data on a file.
   g. *File labels* to identify proper master file and transactions file:
      (1) *Internal header label* for program identification of proper file.
      (2) *External file label* for proper identification by the machine operator.
   h. *Program test* of proper machine conditions (switch settings).
   i. *Operator instruction books.*
   j. *Program generated messages* for the machine operator.
   k. *Time utilization records.*
   l. *Log of operator accesses* to files via on-line terminals.
   m. *Review of access log* by authorized personnel.

n. *Updated test decks* that check for proper functioning of programmed controls.
o. *Authorization for program modification* with appropriate supporting documentation.

INPUT RECEIVING DEVICES

Exhibit 26-39 contains a list of input receiving devices. With the exception of magnetic tape and disks, the input speed of these devices is extremely slow when compared with the internal operating speed of storage facilities and processor control units. To alleviate this disparity, data synchronizers or *buffers* are used as temporary storage for input data. Data transfer from buffers is more compatible with processing speed. Buffers are not general storage devices, since their memories are only addressable in total.

EXHIBIT 26-39 INPUT RECEIVING DEVICES

DEVICE	FORM IN WHICH DATA RECEIVED
Punched Card Reader	Machine-Readable
Paper Tape Reader	Machine-Readable
Magnetic Ink Reader	Machine- & Man-Readable
Optical Mark Reader	Machine- & Man-Readable
Optical Character Reader	Man-Readable
Magnetic Tape Unit	Machine-Readable
Magnetic Disk Pack	Machine-Readable
Data Collection Terminals	
Light Pen on Cathode Ray Tube	Man-Readable
Badge & Plastic Card Reader	Man-Readable
Keyboard	Man-Readable
Voice-Recognition Devices	Man-Readable
Automatic Data Converters or Digitizers	Man-Readable

The data collection terminals in Exhibit 26-39 facilitate in-line processing in *real-time.* That is, data can be processed continuously with the results of such processing being available soon enough to have an effect on further transactions. These devices are connected on-line to the computer and have free access to all storage areas.[16] The possible magnitude of errors and dishonesty in the use of such devices has prompted special attention to control of on-line terminals. A few of these controls are as follows:

1. Transaction recorded and visible record of input created.
2. Copy of input log kept in locked portion of machine.
3. Terminal device accumulates control totals mechanically.
4. Input is in visible form for visual review.

[16]"On-line systems" is a generic name for systems featuring a direct communication with the *central processing unit* of a computer. No intermediary stages of off-line data conversion are necessary. Translation of input data into machine-readable form, and re-translation into man-readable form, requires no appreciable time lapse.

5. Customer receives record of processing for visual review.
6. Erroneous input will lock machine and only supervisor can release it.
7. Teller must reconcile terminal device input with computer control total and with transaction slips and cash.

26.6 THE CENTRAL PROCESSING UNIT

The central processing unit or CPU performs the necessary arithmetic and logical operations on data, handles file processing, supervises the storage of data, and directs the input of data and the output of information. In short, a good central processing unit is the human brain. On a practical level, however, the human brain has been replaced by a more efficient machine processor.

As diagramed in Exhibit 26-40, the CPU consists of three physical components—a control unit, an arithmetic and logic unit, and a primary storage unit. The arithmetic and logic unit contains the necessary electronic circuitry to perform complex tasks using elementary arithmetic and logic. The control unit directs the operation of the arithmetic and logic unit and controls the internal movement of data.

EXHIBIT 26-40 THE CENTRAL PROCESSING UNIT

Secondary Storage

Data Input

Control Unit

Information Output

Arithmetic and Logic Unit

Primary Storage

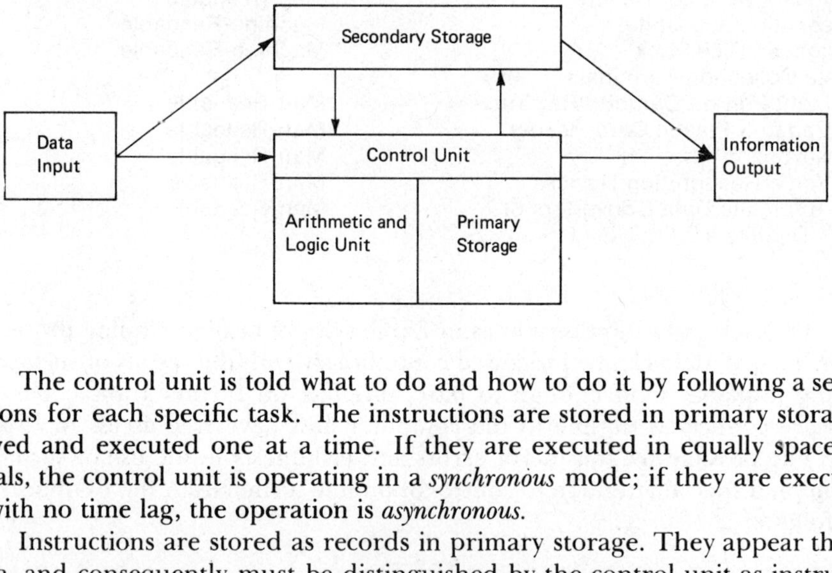

The control unit is told what to do and how to do it by following a set of instructions for each specific task. The instructions are stored in primary storage and retrieved and executed one at a time. If they are executed in equally spaced time intervals, the control unit is operating in a *synchronous* mode; if they are executed in turn with no time lag, the operation is *asynchronous.*

Instructions are stored as records in primary storage. They appear the same as data, and consequently must be distinguished by the control unit as instructions. This means of storing instructions accounts for the power and flexibility of modern computers—they can be instructed to treat another instruction as data, and thus may alter their own operation.

As shown in Exhibit 26-41, an instruction consists of an *operation code* and one or more *operands.* The operation code tells the control unit exactly what action is to be taken. An operand refers to either (1) the *address location* of data that will be needed for the particular instruction, (2) the *address location* of another address, (3) the *code number* of an input/output device or control function, or (4) the *address location* of the

EXHIBIT 26-41 INSTRUCTION FORMATS

Operation Code	Operand Address				Single-Address Instruction
Operation Code	Operand Address	Next Instruction Address	OR	Operation Code / Operand Address / Operand Address	Two-Address Instruction
Operation Code	Operand Address	Operand Address	Next Instruction Address		Three-Address Instruction
Operation Code	Operand Address	Operand Address	Result Address	Next Instruction Address	Four-Address Instruction

Diagram from: *Information Systems: Data Processing and Evaluation* by Gene Dippel and William C. House. Copyright © 1969 by Scott, Foresman and Company. Reprinted by permission of the publisher.

next instruction.[17] If the next instruction address is not part of the instruction format, it will be located in a special *instruction address register* in the control unit.

Every computer has its own instruction format and set of operation codes. In other words, each has a unique *machine language* syntax for writing instructions. A complete set of machine language instructions is called an *object program.* Every object program has a particular function or task orientation.

Writing programs in machine language for each individual task can be very difficult and time-consuming. The problem, however, has a relatively easy conceptual solution. Make up a new language syntax that is easier to use and more closely resembles a human language. It is not necessary for us to invent new computers with new languages, but simply to write a program *in machine language* whose function will be to translate our new syntax into machine language instructions. Such machine language programs are called assemblers and compilers. An *assembly* program translates on a one-for-one basis—*one source language* instruction into *one machine language* instruction. A *compiler* program, on the other hand, translates one source language instruction into *many* machine language instructions. Obviously, then, in a hierarchical relationship, compiler languages are of a higher order and accommodate the use of syntax that is very far removed from a mundane and tedious machine language. Unfortunately, there are two very specific problems that accompany the use of high-order languages: (1) the compiler or assembler requires large amounts of storage space, and (2) the object program that results from translation is often longer and less efficient than if machine language had originally been used.

Exhibit 26-42 shows a list of commonly used compiler languages and their specific uses. Each language is *machine independent.* That is, the same source language program can be used with any computer, providing the computer has the necessary compiler program. The resulting object language programs are not transferable, however, since each computer model will have a different machine language. Never-

[17] If the operand refers to the address of data, this address will indicate the low-order position of a field (the high-order address). If the operand refers to the address of the next instruction, this address will indicate the high-order position of a *record* (the low-order address).

theless, the standardization of compiler languages has made transferability feasible despite machine language differences.

EXHIBIT 26-42 COMPILER LANGUAGES

LANGUAGE	PRINCIPAL USE
FORTRAN	Complex Scientific and Commercial Problems
COBOL	Complex Commercial Problems
ALGOL	Complex Scientific and Numerical Procedures
PL/1	Complex Scientific and Commercial Problems, Information Retrieval, String Manipulation, Data Editing
IPL	Manipulation of Non-Numeric Symbols and List Structures
SLIP	Manipulation of Non-Numeric Symbols and List Structures
LISP	Manipulation of Non-Numeric Symbols and List Structures
COMIT	Manipulation of Non-Numeric Symbols and List Structures
SNOBOL	Manipulation of Non-Numeric Symbols and List Structures
QUIKTRAN	Basic Language for Remote Computing
BASIC	Basic Language for Remote Computing
SIMSCRIPT	Simulation Modeling
GPSS	Simulation Modeling
RPG	Report Writing and File Maintenance
JOVIAL	Time-Sharing Applications, Command and Control Networks
APT	For Automatically Controlled Machine Tools

A program must specify explicitly each step the control unit follows to complete a task. The planning of program logic, and the communication of such logic, is generally accomplished by constructing program flow charts and/or decision tables.

PROGRAM FLOW CHARTS

This method presents program logic by an interconnected set of symbols. It is much the same as *system flowcharting* as explained in Appendix D, except that system flow charts describe *system logic*, whereas *program flowcharting* explains the detailed logic of a particular operation or series of operations. The basic flow chart symbols used in program flowcharting are indicated in Exhibit 26-43.

Symbols are arranged in a flow pattern corresponding to their expected execution sequence. This provides a graphic display of the programming necessary to support a particular processing application. For example, Exhibit 26-44 shows the logical structure of a program for processing a purchase order.

EXHIBIT 26-43 PROGRAM FLOW CHART SYMBOLS

Symbol	*Meaning*
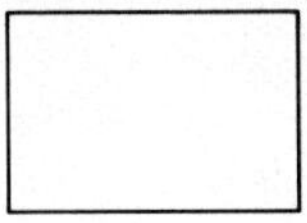	*Processing* involving data manipulation and calculation
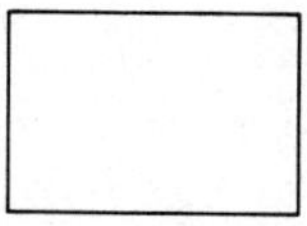	*Predefined Process* that requires no user programming
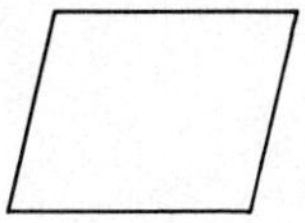	*Input/Output* specification of data entry and exit
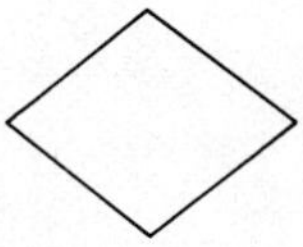	*Decision Point* where program logic may branch to another path
	*Flowline*
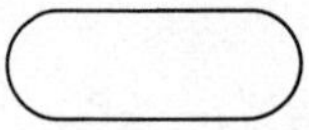	*Terminal* where the program originates or ends
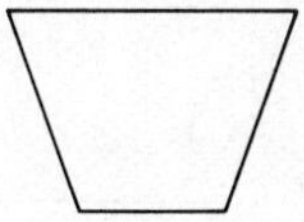	*Manual Operation* not performed by the CPU
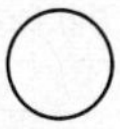	*Connector* for handling a continuation on another page or for handling the junction of several flowlines
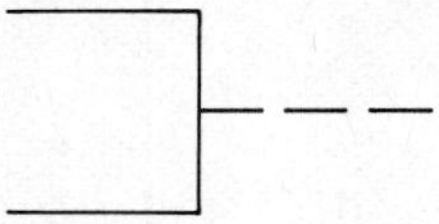	*Annotation* for handling non-programmable comments

DECISION TABLES

This method is a tabular presentation of program logic. It divides the program structure into two categories: *conditions* and *actions.* This division is based upon the logical relationship of cause-and-effect: *if* a set of conditions are met, *then* a set of actions result.

A *set of conditions* is called a *decision rule.* There can be many decision rules for each application and the number is determined by the *feasible combinations* of Yes-No responses to all possible conditions. The theoretical combinations or decision rules is

EXHIBIT 26-44 PROGRAM FLOW CHART OF INVENTORY REORDERING

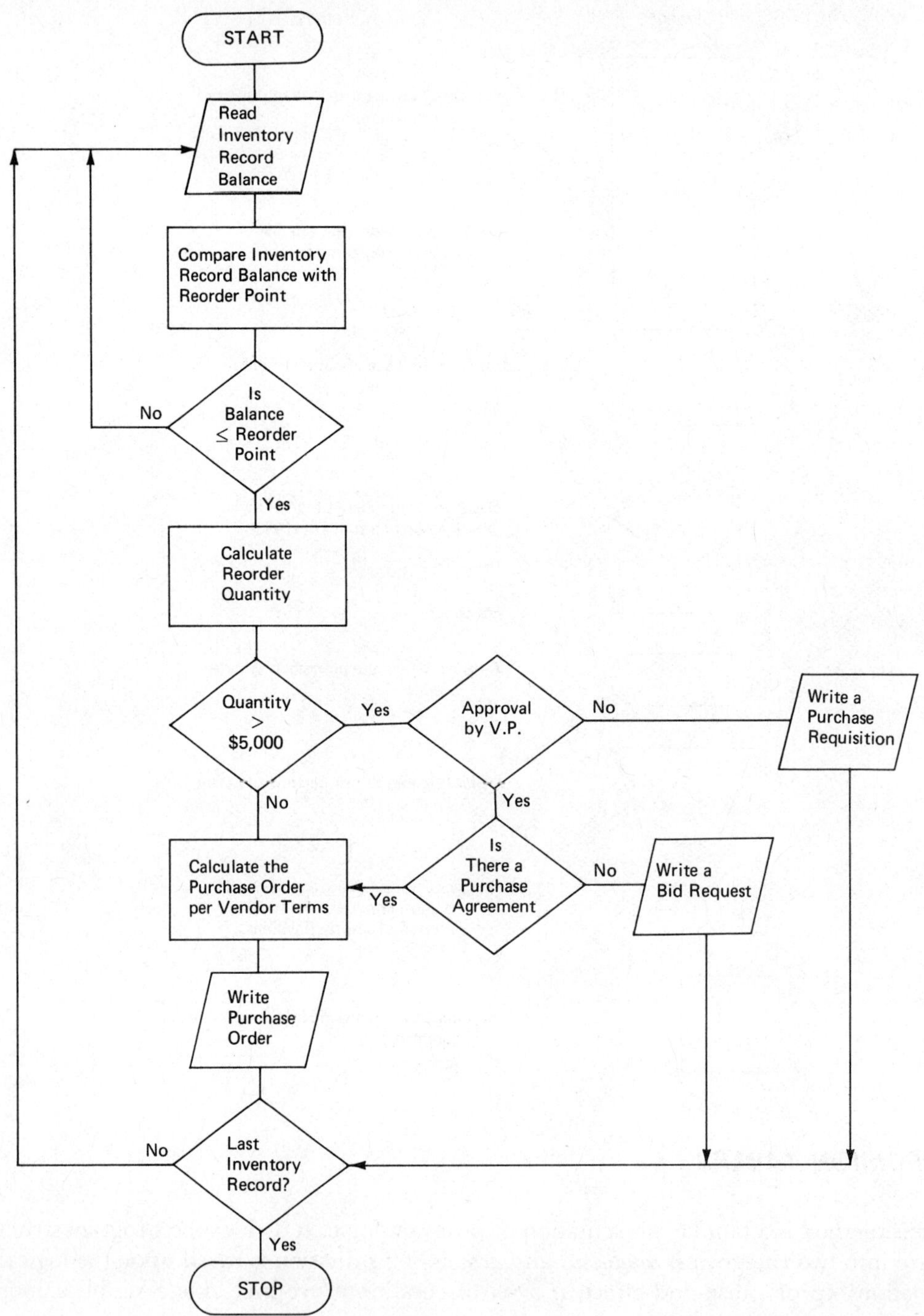

2^n (where n = the number of conditions); however, this number is reduced to include only feasible decision rules by permitting an "Immaterial" response to conditions that may be answered *either* Yes or No.

Suppose the purchase order flow chart example in Exhibit 26-44 is described in decision-table form. From Exhibit 26-45 we can see that the table is physically divided into four quadrants:

1. A *condition stub* that describes each condition in the task.
2. A *condition entry* that gives a YES, NO, or IMMATERIAL answer to a condition.
3. An *action stub* that describes each possible action.
4. An *action entry* that records an X for action taken and a "blank" for no action.

Condition and action entries are indicated for each decision rule. For every condition entry there is a corresponding action entry, but there is not necessarily an equal number of conditions and actions.

The example in Exhibit 26-45 is constructed as a *limited-entry* table. That is, each condition and action statement is entirely contained in the stubs. In an *extended-entry* table, part of the condition and action statements may be contained in the entry quadrants. For example, Exhibit 26-46 shows how the fourth action stub can be extended into the entry quadrant. As can be seen, the advantage of an extended-entry format will be realized in those instances when the operators and operands of a stub statement may vary among decision rules.

Compilers are available that translate data from a decision table directly into machine language instructions. Flow charts, on the other hand, are not amenable to

EXHIBIT 26-45 DECISION TABLE FOR INVENTORY REORDERING

	STUB	ENTRIES					
		Decision Rules					
		1	2	3	4	5	6
CONDITIONS	Inventory Balance ≤ Reorder Point	Y	Y	Y	Y	Y	N
	Request ≥ $5,000	N	Y	Y	Y	Y	I
	Request Covered under Purchase Agreement	I	Y	N	N	Y	I
	Purchase Request Approved by V.P.	I	Y	Y	N	N	I
ACTIONS	Calculate Reorder Quantity	X	X	X	X	X	
	Prepare Purchase Requisition				X	X	
	Negotiate a Purchase Agreement (Bid)			X	X		
	Prepare Purchase Order per Vendor Terms	X	X				

EXHIBIT 26-46 EXTENDED ENTRY FORMAT

	STUB	ENTRIES					
		Decision Rules					
		1	2	3	4	5	6
	Prepare Purchase Order	Per Catalog	Per Purchase Agreement				

direct conversion and must first be coded by hand into a machine-processable language. This feature of decision tables makes subsequent changes in logic quite easy to accomplish when compared with flow charts. Often flow charts have to be extensively redrawn, and machine language programs rewritten, to accommodate changes in logic. With decision tables, however, only a new table entry may be required.

SOFTWARE

Software is a generic name applied to *pre-written* machine language programs and subroutines provided by computer manufacturers and user groups.[18] There are two main categories of software: operating systems and library programs.

Operating Systems

Many computer installations are run automatically by operating systems. These operating systems are groups of machine language programs with the specific task of operating the system with a minimum of human interference. They take care of such tasks as (1) making sure the proper input/output device is activated; (2) making sure that source programs get translated into object programs and that object programs are then executed; (3) housekeeping chores, such as assigning storage location to data and programs, blocking and unblocking records, and creating file labels; (4) supervising job queues according to priority scheduling; (5) maintaining a log of time utilization; (6) detecting and reporting errors and machine malfunctions; and (7) communicating with the operator.

Library Programs

All pre-written programs and subroutines available to the operating system on request are stored in a system-based library and are referred to as library programs.

[18] The existence of large-scale computer systems has promoted the emergence of *user groups* that meet to develop and share common interest programs.

These programs generally fall into three sub-categories: language translators, utility programs, and application routines.

LANGUAGE TRANSLATORS These programs were described earlier as assemblers and compilers. The function of these machine language programs is to translate a symbolic or high-order language program into its machine language equivalent.

UTILITY PROGRAMS These machine language programs are designed for tasks *essential* to normal system functioning. For example, most installations require programs for loading other programs into storage, sorting and merging files, duplicating files, dumping files onto another media, clearing storage, and providing diagnostics for tracing errors.

APPLICATION ROUTINES These machine language *programs* and *subroutines* are designed to perform various service tasks that are common to many users. Some are complete programs and require only input data in a prescribed format, while others are *problem-dependent* and require programming support. Complete programs frequently include such applications as: PERT, Transportation Method, Report Generation,[19] Symmetric Linear Programming, Inventory Simulation, Assembly Line Balancing, Least Squares Regression, Multiple Linear Regression, Billing and Payroll. Subroutines often include such applications as: Random Number Generation, Square Roots, Polynomial Expansions, Matrix Inversion and Addition, Double-Precision Arithmetic, and Double-Precision Sine-Cosine Functions. The distinction between subroutines and complete programs depends upon how they are used. If they take data from another program and then *return* the result, they can be thought of as subroutines. If the results are stored or returned to a different program, they are complete programs.

TIME-SHARING

Time-sharing is a system configuration that allows *many users* to accomplish in-line processing in *real-time.* Frequently, users are in remote locations and share one large computer through special cables or telephone lines. Each user *shares* the available CPU time but operates independently from other users and experiences *no appreciable delay in response time.*

User autonomy, simultaneous operation, and rapid response time place unique requirements on a processor. One means of handling the situation is with *multiprocessing,* in which the system configuration contains two or more independent processors. The processors act on programs independently and have asynchronous access[20] to common files. Another method is *multiprogramming.* A very sophisticated operating system allows two or more independent programs or portions of independent programs to reside in primary storage and to be executed in input/output and calculating segments. While one program is referencing a secondary file or performing input/output operations, the CPU is simultaneously performing the calculation

[19] RPG (Report Program Generator) is a well-known application program or compiler.

[20] Asynchronous access means that file inquiries by different processors can take place one after the other without adhering to a fixed time cycle clock.

requirements of a different program.[21] The CPU time is shared among programs by either switching from one program to another at the end of each calculation segment, or by switching at the end of a fixed time interval.

When a program is completed, it is replaced by another in *the same section of primary storage.* This requires the use of relative addressing in programmed instructions. The operating system will automatically add a *base address* to each relative address to obtain the proper absolute address.

User programs operating in a time-sharing mode should facilitate segmentation. That is, it should be relatively easy for the operating system to break a user program into more convenient segments. In this way, a technique called *paging* can be employed. Each user program is segmented into pages, with each page containing a specified number of instructions. Instead of the CPU handling complete programs, it only handles a page at a time. In this way, multiprogramming can handle individual pages of many user programs. When one page is finished, the next page of the program will be transferred to primary storage and executed. The cycle continues until the complete program is executed.

With many programs or pages residing in primary storage at one time, boundary protection of assigned storage areas is a necessity. Typically, boundary protection is achieved by designating a *storage key* for each block of data and then adding the same memory key to each instruction using this block. Later, an instruction will not be allowed to enter any storage area without a matching memory key.

CPU CONTROLS

With CPU's there are two natural control groupings: hardware and software. Hardware controls are built in by manufacturers and deal with the integrity of internal data transfer. Software controls, in this context, deal exclusively with program safeguards and maintenance.

Hardware Controls

1. *Parity Bit or Redundancy Check:* A control designed to insure the accurate *internal* transfer of characters from one storage location to another. Every character is represented by a coded group of binary bits. An extra *binary bit* or *parity bit* is added to this group so that each character is always represented by an odd number of 1 bits (or even). Computer hardware is designed to check this parity each time a character is moved internally.
2. *Validity Check:* This control determines whether the information represented internally is within the realm of possibility—for instance, is a valid operation called for, is a valid storage address location given, is it a valid combination of magnetic bits, etc.
3. *Interlocks:* Interlocks are security controls designed to protect the integrity of storage locations and to permit operations to occur only at designated times. Interlocks have been discussed earlier as a file storage protection device, and again, in preventing an improper overlapping in time-shared systems.

[21] In this instance, control of input/output is passed from the CPU to a special *data channel* device. After the CPU has activated the channel, it is free to continue other processing. The operation of data channels is explained later under section 26.8, "Message Transmission."

4. *Duplicate Process Check:* This control compares the results of a redundant or complementary action with original results. It checks the accuracy of the original action.
5. *Echo Check:* This control internally verifies the proper activation of a mechanical part. When activated, this mechanism returns a signal to the activating source.

Software Controls

1. Maintenance of flow chart and decision table documentation for all company programs.
2. Retention of the most current program listing for each currently used application.
3. Proper authorization and documentation of all program modifications and minor machine language *patches.*
4. Descriptions of file media contents, format design, and internal labels.
5. Descriptions of input data format.
6. Maintenance of up-to-date test decks for each program. Test deck data should check the workability of major control features and computational algorithms.
7. Maintenance of *complete* computer operator instructions including job set-up requirements, special switch settings, and output routing instructions.
8. Separation of programming duties from machine operation. This includes the restriction of program documentation from machine room operators.
9. Protective storage of programs and program documentation. Protection should be provided against environmental damage and unauthorized program modification.

26.7 INFORMATION OUTPUT

Information has *value* and *usefulness* if it enables an organization to operate effectively in its environment—that is, if it enables the proper decisions to be made at the proper times and satisfies the requirements of regulatory agencies and other interested parties. The attributes of value and usefulness are to a large extent determined by how information is presented—on what display media and in what format.

OUTPUT MEDIA

Exhibit 26-47 contains a list of commonly used output devices. These devices report information on either machine-readable or man-readable media. If output is used in further processing operations, it is reported on a machine-readable media such as punched cards, punched paper tape, magnetic tape, or magnetic disk packs. If output is intended for human use, reports are written on paper media, displayed on cathode ray tubes, or spoken through audio-response units. As a practical matter, however, information is frequently output on machine-readable media and then translated into man-readable form. This procedure helps alleviate the great disparity between the internal operating speed of the CPU and the operating time of output devices producing man-readable media.

Man-readable media are classified as *hard copy* or *soft copy.* Hard copy is

EXHIBIT 26-47 OUTPUT DEVICES

OUTPUT DEVICE	REPORT MEDIA	OPERATING SPEED (In Characters Per Second)
Punched-Card Punch	Machine-Readable	130–650
Paper Tape Punch	Machine-Readable	20–120
Character Printer (Typewriter)	Man-Readable	6–16
Line Printer	Man-Readable	650–2,400
Electrostatic Line Printer	Man-Readable	up to 10,000
Cathode Ray Tube (CRT)	Man-Readable	250–10,000
Audio-Response Unit	Man-Readable	
Graph Plotter (Mechanical or CRT)	Man-Readable	
Magnetic Tape	Machine-Readable	15,000–350,000
Magnetic Disk Packs	Machine-Readable	156,000–312,000

permanent or semipermanent material, while soft copy is visual or audio. Hard copy reports are generally produced on line printers using continuous forms (possibly interleaved with carbon paper). These forms must be *burst* subsequently into individual documents or pages.[22] Soft copy reports are generally produced on cathode ray tubes, and consequently are well suited to graphical and pictorial formats. Soft copy reports generally result from specific inquiry and generally are not standardized or of a routine nature. In many applications, these soft copy reports result from a *conversational* on-line interaction with a time-shared system.

REPORTING FORMATS

There are three common man-readable reporting formats: narrative, graphic, and tabular. Narrative formats arrange characters into a succession of lines forming sentences and paragraphs; graphic formats arrange information comparisons and trends using graphs and charts; and tabular formats arrange groups or classes of information items into separate columns. Whichever format or combination of formats is chosen, however, some special design features should be noted:

1. *Two-Up Printing:* In some instances it will be possible to print more than one report across the form on a line printer. Such printing format will save paper and output time.
2. *Standard Paper Width:* The use of standard paper sizes for reports will reduce paper costs, set-up time, filing, and bindery costs.
3. *Preprinted Titles and Headings:* Preprinting of titles and headings reduces printing time and produces a higher quality report.
4. *Preprinted Form Alignment Mark:* An alignment mark should be used on preprinted forms to enable the machine operator to correctly align the form in the line printer.

[22] Bursting and collating may be done automatically by special machines.

DOCUMENT RETRIEVAL SYSTEM

Some documents are not subject to processing and remain unaltered in storage. These documents are part of a document retrieval system that frequently employs microfilm for storage media. Complete documents or portions of documents are stored intact. They are *classified* by subject matter, given a document number, and *indexed* by key words, heading, titles, or other *descriptors.* Indexes are stored by *document number* or by *descriptor.* When particular information is requested, all those documents with the pertinent descriptors can be retrieved. Either the document file is searched serially until the proper document numbers are found, or documents are located at the address furnished by the index.

REPORT AND DOCUMENT DISSEMINATION

Information must reach the proper user. This means that a clear and unambiguous name should be given to each output report, and specific routing instructions should be given to machine operators. In addition, reports must contain accurate and complete information. This means that each report should be reviewed for reasonableness by checking for:

1. Print quality.
2. Line spacing.
3. Page numbering and headings.
4. Completeness of output reports.
5. Correct number of copies.
6. Agreement of control totals—total produced by processing and total from original input documents.
7. Cross-check with output of related programs.
8. Checking for obvious omissions and errors.
9. Comparisons with physical counts (i.e., inventory counts).

With soft copy reports, control must be provided over on-line output stations. Principally, this will involve the use of key-locked stations and/or user and file security codes.

26.8 MESSAGE TRANSMISSION

The structural components of an information system must be able to communicate with one another. An input device must be able to communicate with a processor, and a processor must be able to communicate with storage and output devices. Communication is achieved with messages sent through transmission channels.

MESSAGE CONSTRUCTION

Messages are converted or *modulated* by a *transmitter* into electrical signals represented conceptually by a sequence of *pulses* and *spaces*. These pulses and spaces travel through a transmission channel and are interpreted or *demodulated* by a *receiver*. In fixed time intervals, a pulse represents a binary 1, and the absence of a pulse represents a binary 0. For example, Exhibit 26-48 shows the representation of an "E" using the EBCDIC code 1100 0101 from Exhibit 26-25.

EXHIBIT 26-48 AN "E" REPRESENTED IN A COMMUNICATION CHANNEL

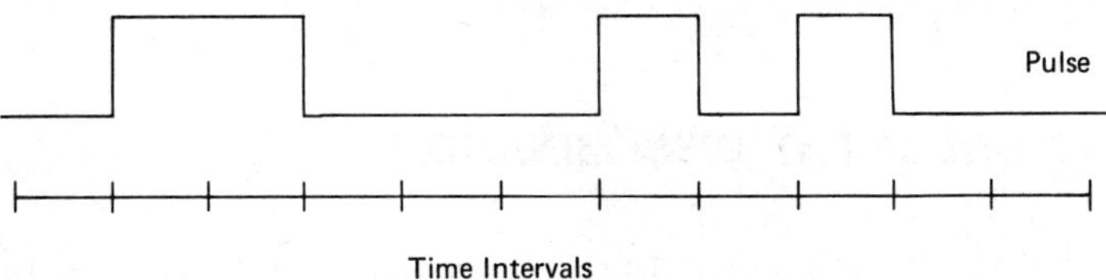

In actuality, pulses are encoded by observing changes in the "state" of an electrical signal. As depicted in Exhibit 26-49, an electrical signal is characterized by its *phase* or wave form duration, by its *amplitude* or signal strength, and by the *frequency* in which a wave form is repeated in a fixed time interval. A pulse or space can be represented by allowing one of these characteristics to change between two values (for binary 1 or 0), while holding the other two characteristics constant. During the

EXHIBIT 26-49 WAVE FORM OF AN ELECTRICAL SIGNAL

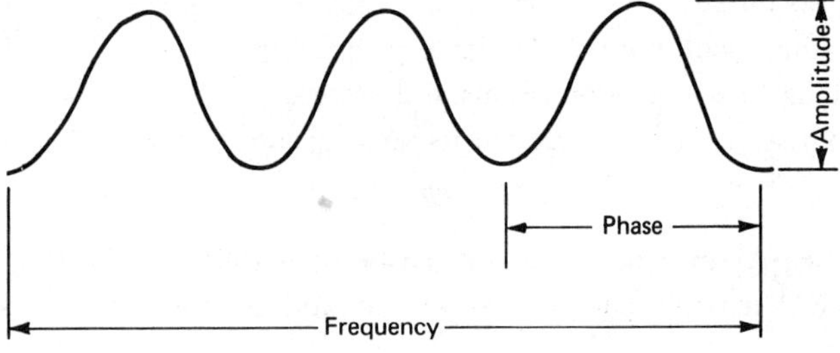

allotted time interval, a receiver can determine the value of the characteristic, and hence determine a pulse or space.

Proper interpretation of coded pulses requires that transmitting and receiving devices be in timing *synchronization.* That is, they must start and stop in unison, and both must maintain identical time intervals. For each message, a synchronizing character or start signal is sent from transmitter to receiver. Once received, a special timing mechanism keeps the receiving device in synchronization with the transmitter.

TRANSMISSION CHANNELS

Message communication between system components is achieved through a configuration of transmission *channels.* A channel controls the movement of data between primary storage and other system components. It acts as a small computer and executes a stored program for the transfer of data into and out of primary storage. All input/output and secondary storage devices are connected to data channels. When the CPU requires a data transfer from one of these devices, it directs the appropriate channel to the location of the first instruction of the desired channel program. The program tells the channel what to do and specifically what storage locations are involved in the data transfer. While the channel is executing the data transfer program, the CPU is free to continue other processing activities. Normally, when the channel finishes the execution of its program, it either *interrupts* the CPU or waits in a queue to be serviced.

EXHIBIT 26-50 SELECTOR AND MULTIPLEXOR CHANNELS

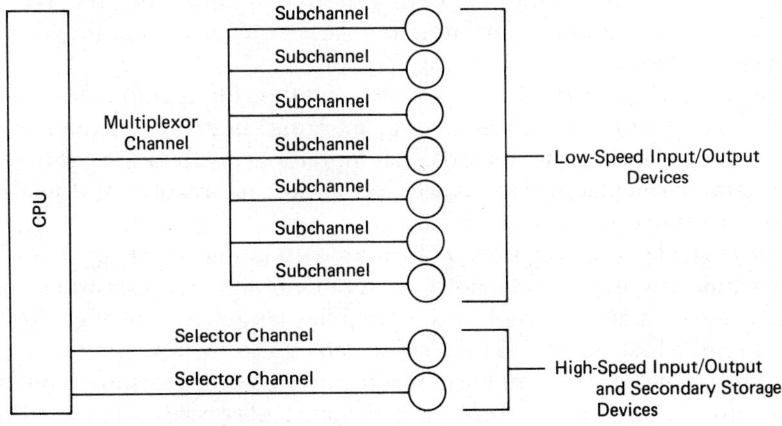

As shown in Exhibit 26-50, a system configuration can employ both *selector* and *multiplexor channels.* This allows a system to be characterized by simultaneous operation of several input/output or secondary storage devices. A selector channel handles high-speed data transfer through *one subchannel,* while a multiplexor channel handles low-speed data transfer through *several subchannels.* For simultaneous operation of high-speed devices, several selector channels are required. With low-speed devices, however, this configuration is too costly. A less expensive alternative uses a multiplexor that divides one channel into many subchannels and shares channel facilities. Since the attached devices are low-speed, the multiplexor is able to service each subchannel fast enough to make it appear that each device has exclusive use of the channel.

High-speed input/output or secondary storage devices can be attached to certain subchannels of a multiplexor. When they are being serviced, however, the multiplexor channel can no longer *interleave* other devices and must operate in a *burst* mode. Individual subchannels are too slow to service a high-speed device. The full channel must be made available, and while it is in operation, the channel must lock out other devices.

26.9 SUMMARY

Design of automated systems centers around five structural components: data input, data and information storage, file processing, information output, and message transmission.

Data input is concerned with the extraction of data from the environment and the subsequent conversion to machine-readable form.

Data and information storage is achieved through a hierarchical arrangement of characters, fields, records, and files. A *character* is the smallest data unit and is represented on machine-readable media as a coded group of bits. A *field* contains one or more characters and a *record* contains one or more fields. A group of logically related records forms a *file*. Fields are located within records by field designators, and records are located within files by record keys and addresses.

The arrangement of records in a file follows three general patterns: sequential, index-sequential, and random. With random organization, the record key is transformed into an address by using either keys equivalent to address numbers, a cross-reference index, or a randomizing method.

File processing consists of two basic activities: file manipulation and file updating. File manipulation involves sorting, merging, matching, sequence checking, scanning, and editing of data records. File updating involves the posting of transaction file data or calculated data to selected master file records and fields, and the preparation of report files.

The central processing unit performs file updating activity by following a program of machine-language instructions. Generally, however, a user will communicate with the processor by using a high-order compiler language. The logic for the user's source program is first described in decision tables and/or flow charts.

Information is output on hard or soft copy, man- or machine-readable media. There are three man-readable reporting formats: narrative, graphic, and tabular.

System components are tied together by a configuration of selector and/or multiplexor data channels. Messages are sent through these channels as coded pulses.

CHAPTER 26 REFERENCES AND ADDITIONAL READINGS

"Accounting and Information Systems." *Accounting Review,* Supplement to Vol. XLVI, Committee Reports (1971): 287–350.

Arnold, Robert R.; Hill, Harold C.; and Nichols, Aylmer V. *Introduction to Data Processing.* New York: John Wiley & Sons, Inc., 1966.

Awad, Elias M. *Business Data Processing.* 2nd ed. Englewood Cliffs, N.J.: Prentice-Hall, Inc., 1968.

Brightman, Richard W.; Luskin, Bernard J.; and Tilton, Theodore. *Data Processing for Decision-Making.* New York: The Macmillan Company, 1971.

Carter, Norman H. *Introduction to Business Data Processing.* Belmont, Calif.: Dickenson Publishing Company, 1968.

Clark, Frank J. *Information Processing.* Pacific Palisades, Calif.: Goodyear Publishing Company, 1970.

Clifton, H. D. *Systems Analysis for Business Data Processing.* Princeton, N.J.: Auerbach Publishers, 1971.

Daniels, Alan, and Yeates, Donald, eds. *Systems Analysis.* Palo Alto, Calif.: Science Research Associates, Inc., 1971.

Davis, Gordon B. *Auditing and EDP.* New York: American Institute of Certified Public Accountants, 1968.

Davis, Gordon B. *Computer Data Processing.* New York: McGraw-Hill Book Company, 1969.

Dippel, Gene, and House, William C. *Information Systems: Data Processing and Evaluation.* Glenview, Ill.: Scott, Foresman and Company, 1969.

Ditri, Arnold E.; Shaw, John C.; and Atkins, William. *Managing The EDP Function.* New York: McGraw-Hill Book Company, 1971.

Farina, Mario V. *Flowcharting.* Englewood Cliffs, N.J.: Prentice-Hall, Inc., 1970.

Fergus, Raymond M. "Good Decision Tables and Their Uses." *Systems & Procedures Journal,* September–October 1968, pp. 18–21.

Germain, Clarence B. *Programming the IBM 360.* Englewood Cliffs, N.J.: Prentice-Hall, Inc., 1967.

Greiman, John D. "How Decision Tables Make EDP Specs Clearer." *Production and Inventory Management,* Fourth Quarter 1969, pp. 7–12.

Gupta, Roger. *Electronic Information Processing.* New York: The Macmillan Company, 1971.

Hartman, W.; Matthes, H.; and Proeme, A. *Management Information Systems Handbook.* New York: McGraw-Hill Book Company, 1968.

Hughes, Marion L.; Shank, Richard M.; and Stein, Minor Svendsen; *Decision Tables.* Wayne, Pa.: Management Development Institute, 1968.

Kelly, Joseph F. *Computerized Management Information Systems.* New York: The Macmillan Company, 1970.

Krauss, Leonard I. *Computer-Based Management Information Systems.* New York: American Management Association, 1970.

Li, David H., ed. *Design and Management of Information Systems.* Palo Alto, Calif.: Science Research Associates, 1972.

McCarthy, E. Jerome; McCarthy, J. A.; and Humes, Durward. *Integrated Data Processing Systems.* New York: John Wiley & Sons, Inc., 1966.

Martin, James. *Design of Real-Time Computer Systems.* Englewood Cliffs, N.J.: Prentice-Hall, Inc., 1967.

Meadow, Charles T. *The Analysis of Information Systems: A Programmer's Introduction to Information Retrieval.* New York: John Wiley & Sons, 1967.

Pierce, J. R. *Symbols, Signals and Noise.* New York: Harper & Row, 1961.

Schriber, Thomas J. *Fundamentals of Flowcharting.* New York: John Wiley & Sons, Inc., 1969.

Shaw, John C., and Atkins, William. *Managing Computer System Projects.* New York: McGraw-Hill Book Company, 1970.

Sippl, Charles J. *Computer Dictionary and Handbook.* Indianapolis, Ind.: Howard W. Sams & Co., Inc., 1966.

Sprowls, R. Clay. *Computers: A Programming Problem Approach.* Rev. ed. New York: Harper & Row, 1968.

Swanson, Robert W. *An Introduction to Business Data Processing and Computer Programming.* Belmont, Calif.: Dickenson Publishing Company, 1967.

Wanous, S. J.; Wanous, E. E.; and Wagner, Gearld E. *Fundamentals of Data Processing.* Cincinnati: South-Western Publishing Company, 1971.

CHAPTER 26 QUESTIONS, PROBLEMS, AND CASES

26- 1. Suggest four ways in which data reduction can be achieved without impairing the information content of data.

26- 2. How is the screening of input data accomplished in an accounting system?

26- 3. Give the possible *source documents* and *converted documents* for each of the following input conversion machines:
(a) Magnetic tape encoder
(b) Optical character enscriber
(c) Data collection terminal
(d) Paper tape punch
(e) Optical character reader

26- 4. "Controls are specifically designed to reduce the deleterious effects of system noise." Explain the meaning of this statement.

26- 5. Why is forms design an important aspect of data collection? List at least six guidelines that should influence forms design.

26- 6. When compared to other conversion media, what is the chief disadvantage in the use of punched cards and punched paper tape?

26- 7. List and explain at least four controls over the data conversion process.

26- 8. "Storage is necessary to facilitate processing and to facilitate inquiry and retrieval of information. Not only must this function preserve the integrity of data, but it must also preserve the relationships between data." Explain the meaning of this statement.

26- 9. Distinguish between a character, field, record, and file.

26-10. Explain the concept of left-justification and right-justification in fixed-length fields.

26-11. How are unused positions treated in a fixed numeric field, as opposed to a fixed alphameric field?

26-12. Despite the formating problems of fixed-length fields, what is the greatest advantage in their use?

26-13. How is the problem of distinguishing side-by-side variable fields overcome?

26-14. Explain and diagram the procedure for locating fields in a record.

26-15. Explain what is meant by record blocking and explain the advantage of its use with magnetic tape file media.

26-16. Explain the conditions under which a block prefix is not needed for blocked records.

26-17. "Chaining is a method of linking sequential records or blocks that are not stored in consecutively numbered address locations." Explain how the method works. Draw a diagram of your explanation.

26-18. Give three reasons why alphabetic fields should be avoided as record keys.

26-19. Compare the addressing of a field with the addressing of a record. What is the address location of the field 482 in the following record?

12	13	14	15	16	17	18	19	20	21	22	23	24	25
$\bar{0}$	0	1	$\bar{4}$	8	2	$\bar{A}$	4	$\bar{5}$	3	1	4	$\bar{6}$	0

26-20. Disk storage is not completely random, it is partially sequential. Explain what is meant by this statement and explain how individual records are located in disk storage.

26-21. Explain the meaning or use of the following terms and phrases:

(a) Transaction document
(b) Character set
(c) Alphameric mode
(d) Left-justified
(e) Field designator
(f) Block prefix
(g) Record key
(h) Address
(i) Primary storage
(j) Overflow records
(k) Data string
(l) Randomizing
(m) Chaining
(n) Home record
(o) "Relative address"
(p) Binary coded decimal
(q) Header label
(r) Trailer label
(s) Buffer
(t) Decision rule

26-22. The arrangement of records in a file is largely dictated by design features of the storage facility itself. Explain what is meant by this statement.

26-23. Random file organization requires the record key to be transformed into an address. How is this accomplished?

26-24. In an index-sequential file, what is the procedure for finding the prime storage area containing a record? How is a *file index* used in the procedure?

26-25. Since a randomizing calculation reduces the record key numbering range, it will sometimes produce the same address for two or more record keys. What are these records called, and how is the situation handled?

26-26. What are the two objectives in selecting a randomizing technique?

26-27. Explain the function or use of each file type:
(a) Master file
(b) Transactions file
(c) Report file
(d) Document file
(e) Document index file

26-28. How are characters represented in machine-readable files?

26-29. Distinguish between primary, secondary, and peripheral storage.

26-30. Complete the following table:

STORAGE DEVICE	STORAGE MEDIA	RATE OF TRANSFER TO PRIMARY STORAGE (characters per second)	STORAGE CAPACITY (in characters)
Data Cell			
Magnetic Tape			
Drum			
Removable Module Disk Pack			
Fixed Module Disk			
Bulk or Mass Core			

26-31. Describe four controls that help minimize the possibility of file destruction through inadvertent data transfer.

26-32. Explain the grandfather-father-son scheme of file retention.

26-33. Explain and discuss the value of each of the following file manipulation activities:
(a) Sorting
(b) Matching
(c) Sequence checking
(d) Scanning
(e) Editing

26-34. Identify and diagram the two basic methods of file updating.

26-35. "Batch control totals can be computed from source documents and subsequently used to assure that all transactions are placed in the transactions file, and to assure that all transaction records have been used to update the master file." Explain how this is accomplished.

26-36. Distinguish between the following control totals:
(a) Financial totals
(b) Hash totals
(c) Record counts

26-37. "The main advantages of in-line processing are the elimination of sorting and merging requirements, the smoothing of processing peaks, and the maintenance of up-to-date master files." Discuss these advantages in relation to the advantages of batch processing.

26-38. What are six processing controls to prevent the mishandling and resubmittal of input data?

26-39. List and discuss seven processing controls to assure that master files are properly updated.

26-40. During processing, input records are validated by searching for specific types of errors. List five such errors.

26-41. Name six controls over the use of on-line terminals.

26-42. Distinguish between *synchronous* and *asynchronous* execution of CPU instructions.

26-43. "Instructions are stored as records in primary storage. They appear the same as data, and consequently, must be distinguished by the control unit as instructions." How does this feature account for the power and flexibility of modern computers?

26-44. In an instruction format, what are the possible referents for an operand?

26-45. Distinguish an *object program* from a *source program.*

26-46. "Writing programs in machine language for each individual task can be very difficult and time-consuming." As an alternative, how is this dilemma handled?

26-47. Distinguish between a compiler language and an assembly language.

26-48. What are two specific problems that accompany the use of high-order languages?

26-49. Explain what is meant by the reference to compilers as *machine independent.*

26-50. Give the principal use of each of the following compiler languages:
(a) COBOL
(b) COMIT
(c) BASIC
(d) SIMSCRIPT
(e) RPG

26-51. Upon what logical relationship is a program structure divided into *conditions* and *actions* when constructing a decision table?

26-52. What are the five basic types of hardware controls found on central processing units? Explain what each type of control is designed to achieve and how such controls operate.

26-53. Distinguish between a *limited-entry* and an *extended-entry* decision table. When is it advantageous to use an extended-entry format?

26-54. What feature of decision tables makes any subsequent changes in logic easier to achieve than with flow charts?

26-55. What are seven tasks of a computer operating system?

26-56. Identify and discuss the three subcategories of library programs. Use specific examples with your explanation.

26-57. Define and explain the use of the following time-sharing terms and phrases:
(a) Multiprocessing
(b) Multiprogramming
(c) Segmentation
(d) Paging
(e) Storage key

26-58. How is boundary protection achieved in a time-shared system?

26-59. List and define five CPU hardware controls and eight software controls.

26-60. Give the range of operating speeds (in characters per second) for each of the following output devices:
(a) Line printer
(b) Cathode ray tube
(c) Magnetic tape
(d) Punched-card punch

26-61. Why is information frequently output on machine-readable media and then translated into man-readable form?

26-62. Distinguish between *hard* and *soft* copy output media.

26-63. Explain how a document retrieval system works.

26-64. When reviewing output reports for reasonableness, what specific features are checked?

26-65. Define and explain the use of the following communication terms and phrases:
(a) Modulation
(b) Demodulation
(c) Phase
(d) Amplitude
(e) Frequency
(f) Pulse
(g) Space
(h) Timing synchronization
(i) Selector channel
(j) Multiplexor channel
(h) Burst mode

26-66. Show the representation of a 9 in a communication channel using an EBCDIC code.

26-67. How are pulses and spaces represented or encoded by an electrical signal?

26-68. "A channel *controls* the movement of data between primary storage and other system components." How is this achieved?

26-69. What problem can arise from the use of a high-speed input/output device on a multiplexor subchannel?

26-70. Distinguish between a *selector* and *multiplexor* data channel.

26-71. ***FIELD STRUCTURE*** Show the proper positioning of the number 18734 in a:

(a) Ten-place fixed numeric field
(b) Eight-place alphameric field
(c) Variable alphameric field

26-72. ***SORTING*** Explain and diagram the procedure for sorting the record keys 48, 34, 72, 16, 52, 63, using:
(a) Straight insertion sorting
(b) Binary insertion sorting
(c) Extraction sorting
(d) Exchange sorting

26-73. ***MERGING***
(a) Diagram the merging of ten strings.
(b) Explain and diagram the procedure for merging the sequenced string 243, 214, 198, 180, 164, 132, 120, with the sequenced string 220, 210, 190, 184, 158, 140, 128.

26-74. ***CONTROL OF AUTOMATED FUNCTIONS*** The following items contain examples of internal control deficiencies observed in a computer data processing system. For each of these conditions or situations, determine and explain the control features or procedures which, if properly utilized, would have been *most* useful in either preventing the error or in ensuring its immediate and prompt correction.
(a) The night operator understood more about programming than anyone realized. Working through the console, he made a change in a payroll program to alter the rate of pay for an accomplice in an operating department. The fraud was discovered accidentally after it had been going on for several months.
(b) A customer payment recorded legibly on the remittance advice as $13.01 was entered into the computer from punched cards as $1,301.00.
(c) A program for the analysis of sales provided questionable results and data processing personnel were unable to explain how the program operated. The programmer who wrote the program no longer works for the company.
(d) Due to an unusual program error which had never happened before, the accounts receivable updating run did not process three transactions. The error was not noted by the operator because he was busy working on a card punch malfunction. There were control totals for the file which were printed out. An examination of the console printout would have disclosed the error.
(e) A new computer program to process accounts payable was unreliable and would not handle the most common exceptions.
(f) A batch of cards was next to the computer waiting for processing. The personnel manager, showing some visitors through the installation, pulled a card from the batch to show the visitors what it looked like. He absent-mindedly put the card into his pocket rather than back into the batch. The missing card was not detected when the batch was processed.
(g) An apparent error in input data describing an inventory item received was referred back to the originating department for correction. A week later the department complained that the inventory in question was incorrect. Data processing could not easily determine whether or not the item had been processed by the computer.
(h) The master inventory file, contained on a removable magnetic disk, was destroyed by a small fire next to the area where it was stored. The company had to take a special complete inventory in order to reestablish the file.
(i) The master file for inventory did not seem right. The file was printed out and many errors were found.

(j) The master payroll file on magnetic tape was inadvertently written on by another processing run.

(k) A weekly payroll check was issued to an hourly employee based on ninety-eight hours worked instead of thirty-eight hours. The time card was slightly illegible and the number looked somewhat like ninety-eight.

(l) In preparing payroll checks the computer omitted 24 of a total of 2,408 checks which should have been processed. The error was not detected until the foremen distributed the checks.

(m) The magnetic tape containing accounts receivable transactions could not be located. A data processing supervisor said that it could have been put among the scratch tapes available for use in processing.

(n) A sales transaction document was coded with an invalid customer account code (seven digits rather than eight). The error was not detected until the updating run when it was found that there was no such account to which the transaction could be posted.

(o) The operator, in mounting the magnetic tape containing the cash receipts for the processing run to update accounts receivable, mounted the receipts tape from the preceding rather than the current day. The error was not detected until after the processing run was completed.

(p) An expense report was prepared by the cost center. One executive questioned one of the amounts and asked for the source documents which support the total. Data processing was not able to routinely provide the documents.

(Adapted from the CPA exam.)

26-75. ***CHAINING*** Suppose the loading sequence of records is E1, G1, D1, D2, G2, F1, G3, E2, G4, H1, D3, E3, F2, H2, E4, H3, E5. When a track is full, overflow records are placed on successively higher tracks where record space is available. If each track layout contains three records plus a chaining record, complete the following file:

Track	Chaining Record	Data Records		
D				
E				
F				
G				
H				
I				

26-76. ***RANDOMIZING METHODS***

(a) *Prime Number Division:*

For a file of 100 records, what is the address of a record with a key of 634?

(b) *Folding:*

What is the address of a record with a key of 731041, if folding involves a split of alternate digits?

(c) *Digit Analysis:*
Suppose addresses can range from 0 to 9999, and an analysis of record key positions reveals an evenness in the distribution of digits in the following decreasing order 3, 4, 1, 7, 2, 5, 6. If the key is 107043, what is the record address?

(d) *Radix Transformation:*
What is the address of a record with a key of 3412 if the addresses can range from 0 to 9999?

26-77. ***INTEGRATED FILES*** Show the integrated file *linkage* between files A and B:

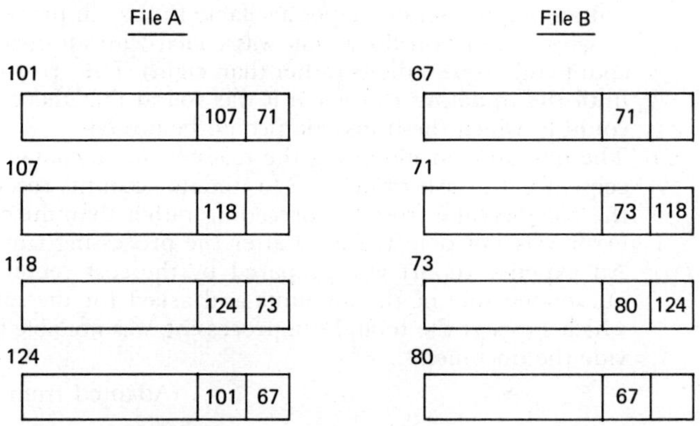

26-78. ***DECISION TABLE AND FLOW CHART*** Prepare (1) a flow chart and (2) a limited-entry decision table based upon the following customer billing procedure of a large department store chain:

(a) On the 25th of each month, determine the balance of each customer account.
(b) Add $1\frac{1}{2}$% interest charge to each account with a balance.
(c) Sort customer credit sales slips.
(d) Calculate *payment due* from each customer based on 10% of outstanding balance plus accumulated interest; or if balance is over $200, calculate *payment due* as 20% of outstanding balance plus accumulated interest.
(e) Prepare customer account statement showing last month's itemized purchases, previous balance, payments received, new outstanding balance plus cumulative interest, and payment due.
(f) If payment is received, credit the customer's account and interest revenue account.
(g) If customer's check is returned nsf (not sufficient funds), debit customer's account and send overdue notice.
(h) If partial payment or no payment by the 10th, send overdue notice.
(i) If payment is thirty days overdue, send a second overdue notice.
(j) If payment is sixty days overdue, send the customer a special statement indicating *total balance* is now due and payable.
(k) If payment is 120 days overdue, refer bill to a collection agent.

CHAPTER

27

FINANCIAL AND OPERATIONAL AUDITING

27.1 THE NATURE OF AUDITING

Auditing is an *independent* or detached appraisal of the effectiveness and reliability of an information system. *Effectiveness* concerns the adequacy of a system to meet its objectives, and *reliability* concerns the adequacy of the financial statements to *present fairly* the financial picture of the firm. The *objectives* of auditing are to:

1. *Attest* to the *fairness* of the financial statements as they purport to represent *financial position* and *results of operations.*
2. Make *recommendations* on system design and operation.

The auditing process involves an independent examination of the entire system as shown in Exhibit 27-1. The audit examination follows an orderly approach. It consists of understanding the system and its controls; testing for the use of controls and the existence of feedback; and substantiating financial statement figures.

In 1963, the American Institute of Certified Public Accountants established

EXHIBIT 27-1 THE AUDITING PROCESS

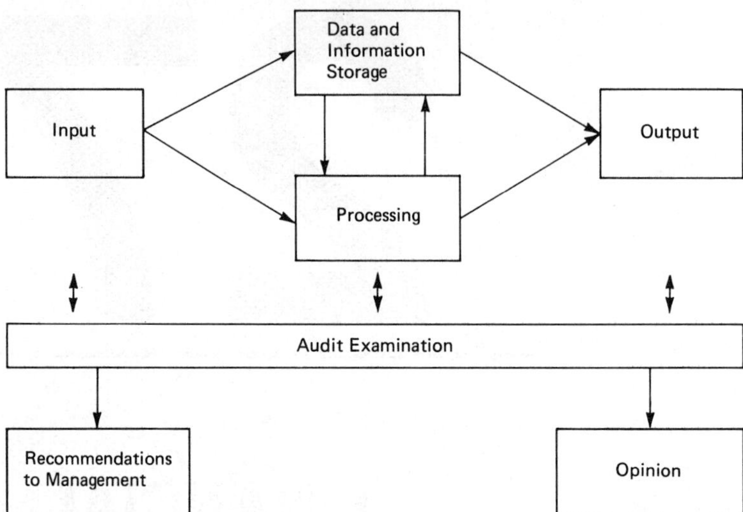

broad guidelines for attesting to the fairness of financial statements. These standards are categorized into three areas:[1]

GENERAL STANDARDS

1. The examination is to be performed by a person or persons having adequate technical training and proficiency as an aduitor.
2. In all matters relating to the assignment an independence in mental attitude is to be maintained by the auditor or auditors.
3. Due professional care is to be exercised in the performance of the examination and the preparation of the report.

STANDARDS OF FIELD WORK

1. The work is to be adequately planned and assistants, if any, are to be properly supervised.
2. There is to be a proper study and evaluation of the existing internal control as a basis for reliance thereon and for the determination of the resultant extent of the tests to which auditing procedures are to be restricted.
3. Sufficient competent evidential matter is to be obtained through inspection, observation, inquiries and confirmations to afford a reasonable basis for an opinion regarding the financial statements under examination.

STANDARDS OF REPORTING

1. The report shall state whether the financial statements are presented in accordance with generally accepted principles of accounting.
2. The report shall state whether such principles have been consistently observed in the current period in relation to the preceding period.

[1] *Auditing Standards and Procedures,* Statement No. 33 (New York: American Institute of Certified Public Accountants, 1963), pp. 15–16.

3. Informative disclosures in the financial statements are to be regarded as reasonably adequate unless otherwise stated in the report.
4. The report shall contain an expression of opinion regarding the financial statements, taken as a whole, or an assertion to the effect that an opinion cannot be expressed. When an over-all opinion cannot be expressed, the reasons therefor should be stated. In all cases where an auditor's name is associated with financial statements the report should contain a clearcut indication of the character of the auditor's examination, if any, and the degree of responsibility he is taking.

Unfortunately, these guidelines are not fully applicable to broad systems-based audits, nor are they applicable to contemporary audit objectives. The primary focus of these standards is toward the present auditor's opinion. We suggest a refocusing of auditing standards to a simpler overall survey approach which is allied to well-known characteristics of scientific observation:

1. The observer approaches the task with an open mind.
2. The observer conducts his observation in a systematic manner.
3. The observer is trained adequately in order to grasp the significance of his observations.
4. The observer is able to synthesize and summarize his findings into meaningful hypotheses which can be tested.

27.2 AUDIT PROCESSES

The objectives of an audit—a management report and an opinion—require that the auditor adhere to certain sequential steps or processes. These processes are based on a deductive methodology as illustrated in Exhibit 27-2.

Audit tasks describe *what* the auditor does. By observing the steps that an auditor takes, we can determine whether or not he has gone about things in a professional manner.

The auditor's role is essentially that of an evaluator. He evaluates controls in order to determine the degree of testing that is needed. He evaluates evidence as to its validity and reliability. He evaluates the degree and mode of disclosures in terms of the law, the client, and the public interest, and in terms of conformance with accounting standards and principles. He evaluates specific items: the collectibility of receivables, the salability of inventory, the probability of liabilities, and so on.

The auditor is not a casual evaluator—he holds himself to be an expert evaluator—which suggests that he is trained and qualified to observe meaningfully, test appropriately, and evaluate correctly.

The auditor is not in the business of setting or evaluating ("second-guessing") management's goals, but he should know what the goals are, the extent to which they have (or are being) met, and he should be familiar with management's reasons for variances. Having this information enables an auditor to evaluate the relevance and effectiveness of planning and control procedures.

It is at the process level where we identify *expertness* or *professionalism.* The steps taken by an archaeologist (establishing the coordinates of a finding, carefully observing and recording important features of the environment, the manner in which

EXHIBIT 27-2 A DEDUCTIVE AUDIT EXAMINATION

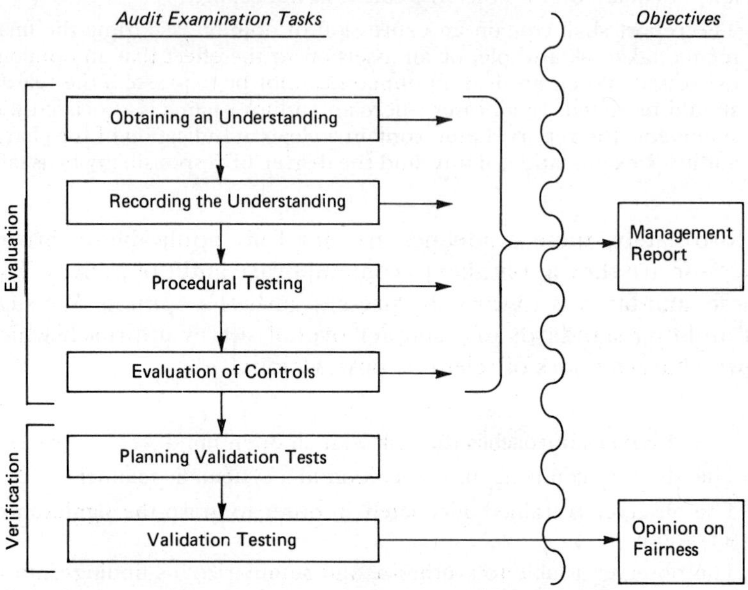

the object is removed, cleaned, stored, etc.), distinguish him as professional in contrast with Sunday-afternoon fossil-hunters, and may also serve to distinguish him from other archaeologists. The essence of auditing is to understand a problem and to conceive its solution systematically.

27.3 THE AUDIT EXAMINATION

The audit examination is performed in *two phases,* as shown in Exhibit 27-3 – *evaluation* and *validation.*

These phases correspond to the grouping of the deductive *audit steps* in Exhibit 27-2. Both phases are necessary to form an opinion on the financial statements; however, only the first is necessary for commenting on system design.

EXHIBIT 27-3 AUDIT PHASES—EVALUATION AND VALIDATION

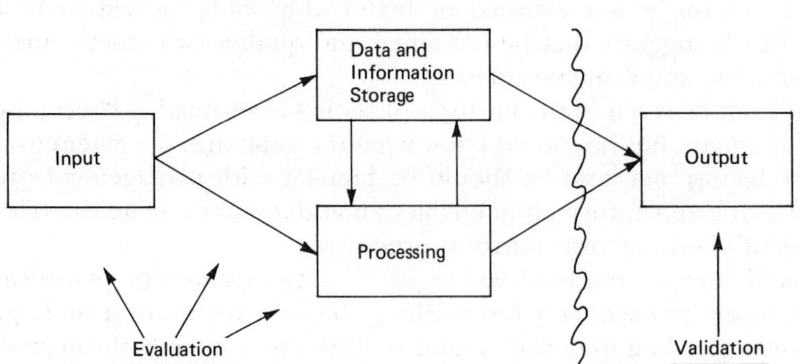

27.4 EVALUATION

This portion of the audit examination consists of four operations:[2]

1. Obtaining an understanding of the firm and its environment.
2. Formalizing that understanding.
3. Testing the understanding.
4. Evaluating controls.

The auditor begins by reading the financial statements for the purpose of obtaining an overall impression—for example:

1. Do the statements describe a very successful business or otherwise?
2. Would the statements lead a user to believe (justifiably) that the firm has moved forward since its last annual report?

These overall impressions should be noted at the outset of the audit and recalled later for comparison with post-audit impressions. Users of financial statements may rely more on the general impression of a set of financial statements than on its detailed figures; hence, the auditor, in playing the role of an informed user, should keep his first impressions in mind as he conducts the audit. As the audit progresses he should increasingly confirm or deny the validity of those impressions vis-à-vis the facts.

Sole reliance on post-audit impressions can be challenged on the grounds that the auditor's impressions at this point are biased by his audit work, and that he is not looking at the statements from the first-hand, limited perspective of the typical user—whose interests he purportedly represents.

At any rate, the auditor should orient his perspective to the business and its operationing environment in order to get a "feel" for the audit situation. He can do so by consulting:

1. Industry manuals
2. Prior audit working papers
3. Annual reports and prospectus of the company
4. SEC reports
5. Correspondence files
6. Tax records
7. Interviews

A more specific and detailed understanding is required for completion of the first audit task. The auditor must familiarize himself with all the *functions* comprising the company's accounting system and identify and evaluate the controls influencing account balances. Some of the most noticeable sources of information are:

[2] *Lybrand Training Program, Staff Training Course I* (New York: Lybrand, Ross Bros. & Montgomery, 1970).

1. Company procedure manuals
2. Plant tours
3. Company flow charts
4. Interviews

The importance of interviews cannot be overemphasized. The auditor relies heavily on interviews of company personnel to gain an understanding of the system. An improper or poorly conceived interview can result in an erroneous understanding, and later in a great deal of wasted time when the auditor attempts to substantiate this understanding. It is important to get accurate information the first time.

The understanding is recorded in a manner that reveals the system cycles, the major transactions that support each, and the functions necessary to complete the transactions. Many auditors prepare operational flow charts or use client prepared flow charts as a means of recording their understanding. In addition, they use flow charts to:[3]

1. Analyze the client's control practices, to identify alternative controls, and to provide preliminary answers to control questionnaires.
2. Serve as a means of communication between the staff man and audit supervisor during the current audit and between auditors on recurring audits.
3. Provide a basis for review of changes in the system from year to year.
4. Enable the auditor to explain weaknesses in the client's controls in the Report to Management.

At this point, the auditor's understanding of the system, as documented by operational flow charts, represents the company's version of how things should be operating, not necessarily how they are operating. The auditor must find out if this system is really the one in operation or whether any part or parts are erroneous. In some instances, the way the company says things are done turns out to be the way they had originally conceived that things should be done, rather than what actually happened.

Procedural testing, viewed in Exhibit 27-4, establishes the correctness of the auditor's recorded understanding. It employs a test of major transactions—*transactions* testing—and a test of financially significant functions—*functional* testing.

EXHIBIT 27-4 PROCEDURAL TESTING

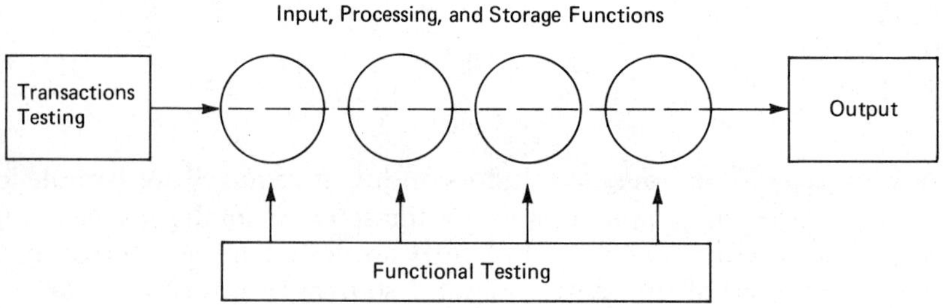

Input, Processing, and Storage Functions

Transactions Testing

Output

Functional Testing

[3]*Lybrand Training Program, Staff Course I, Tab 2* (New York: Lybrand Ross Bros. & Montgomery, 1970), p. 11. Used with permission.

27.5 TRANSACTIONS TESTING

With this testing procedure the auditor selects a few transactions from each *transaction type* (referred to as a finite process in chapter 1) and follows them through to where their identity is lost in the accounts. It is a test of the *existence* of internal control procedures, not a test to establish the extent of compliance. Primarily, then, it is

EXHIBIT 27-5 TRANSACTIONS TESTING OF PURCHASING ACTIVITY

	Transaction 1	Transaction 2	Transaction 3
Voucher Number	2432		
Vendor/Payee	McRuder Co.		
Description	Copper Wire		
Amount of Voucher	$7,824.00		
Account Distribution			
Name	Raw Material		
Number	942		
Purchase Requisition			
Number	R14321		
Approval	✓		
Purchase Order			
Number	0247		
Approval	✓		
Receiver			
Number	048		
Examined for Agreement with Purchase Order	✓		
Signature Noted	✓		
Invoice/Check Request			
Audit Stamp Proper	✓		
Approval Noted	✓		
Examined Supporting Documents/Check Request Only	✓		
Math Verified	✓		
Posted to Voucher Register	✓		
Perforation Noted	✓		
Check			
Number	43412		
Posted to Voucher Register	✓		

a test of the *linkage between functions* necessary to complete a transaction. In addition, it verifies the existence of controls within functions. The number of transactions selected should be sufficient to convince the auditor that linkage is complete and acceptable controls exist. For instance, in testing purchasing activity we could refer to the voucher register and select a few vouchers for each transaction type. From this source we check for a supporting invoice or check request. Next, we check for other supporting documents—purchase requisition, purchase order, receiver, paid check. Exhibit 27-5 shows the auditor's documentation of a sample transactions test. Each check mark indicates that performance of the test was noted. Usually, the detail of the testing is described in footnotes.

27.6 FUNCTIONAL TESTING

Functional testing is an examination of functions (referred to as repetitive processes in chapter 1) considered to have material influence on the eventual financial recording of transaction types. It is a test of the *extent of compliance* to internal control functions found to exist through transactions testing. It is a test of data accumulation within a function. Generally, this testing involves functions not normally tested by transactions testing. Principally, this would include *summarizing or posting functions* and *review of files*. The following are several representative functional tests for the purchasing activities of a typical business:[4]

1. Select a representative sample of paid checks and compare detail with copy of check serving as cash disbursements file.
2. Foot cash disbursements file checks for several days and trace posting to cash control schedule.
3. Foot cash control schedule for one month and trace posting to general ledger.
4. Test foot voucher register and trace posting to general ledger.
5. Select a representative sample batch of vouchers from the files and study each from an operating and an accounting viewpoint, noting the following among other things:
   a. Purchase order: terms with BPA, on bid
complete
approved properly
terms match invoice
   b. Receiver: approved properly
matches invoice
   c. Invoice check requisition: audit stamp proper
approved
supporting documentation proper
accounting distribution proper
perforated
   d. Voucher and check information agrees with cash disbursement file copy of check and is posted to voucher register properly.
6. Select a representative sample of purchase orders filed in the purchasing department and compare with purchase requisition, noting completeness of the requisition and proper approval.

[4]*Lybrand Training Program, Staff Course I, Tab 4,* pp. 9–10. Used with permission.

7. Review accounts payable clerk's file of open P.O., receivers and invoices. Note unusually old items. Review schedule of "received-not-billed" items.

The purpose of both transactions and functional testing is to confirm the auditor's understanding of the system. If this testing reveals exceptions, they must be resolved satisfactorily or the flow charts must be amended. Also, frequent exceptions, even if resolved, may in actuality constitute the rule rather than the exception, and consequently must be so amended on the auditor's system documentation.

27.7 EDP TRANSACTIONS TESTING

Transactions containing computer automated functions can be tested by the following methods:

1. Testing around the computer.
2. Testing through the computer.
3. Use of auditor's computer programs.
4. Comparison of company programs on a recurring basis.
5. Testing with live transactions.

TESTING AROUND THE COMPUTER

With this method, transactions testing is performed in the customary manner because intermediary computer reports provide a complete *audit trail.* That is, sufficient records are provided to allow the auditor to trace any transaction back to an original document and/or forward to an output document (account balances). An illustration of this testing arrangement is shown in Exhibit 27-6. The intermediary reports, produced during the input validation run and used as an audit trail, are special reports, and as such the auditor must usually request the client to produce such reports as part of his normal processing.

No testing of automated functions is required with this method. Sole reliance is placed on the correspondence between input documents and output records, and as such has several disadvantages:[5]

1. Input data may undergo such drastic change during processing that the accountant may have to trace prohibitively large groups of data before comparison with computer printouts and accounts becomes possible.
2. Constant changes may be taking place in the operating instructions such that the samples traced and the results obtained might be applicable only to a limited portion of the data audited.
3. Functions converted to computer application may be so numerous and their volume so large that testing a representative sample may be impracticable in terms of audit time needed.
4. The application of this approach may not have complied with the second standard

[5]David H. Li, *Accounting, Computers, Management Information Systems* (New York: McGraw-Hill Book Company, 1968), p. 298. Used with permission of the author and publisher.

of field work, the proper study and evaluation of the existing internal control as a basis for placing reliance on and determining the extent of tests.

EXHIBIT 27-6 TESTING AROUND THE COMPUTER

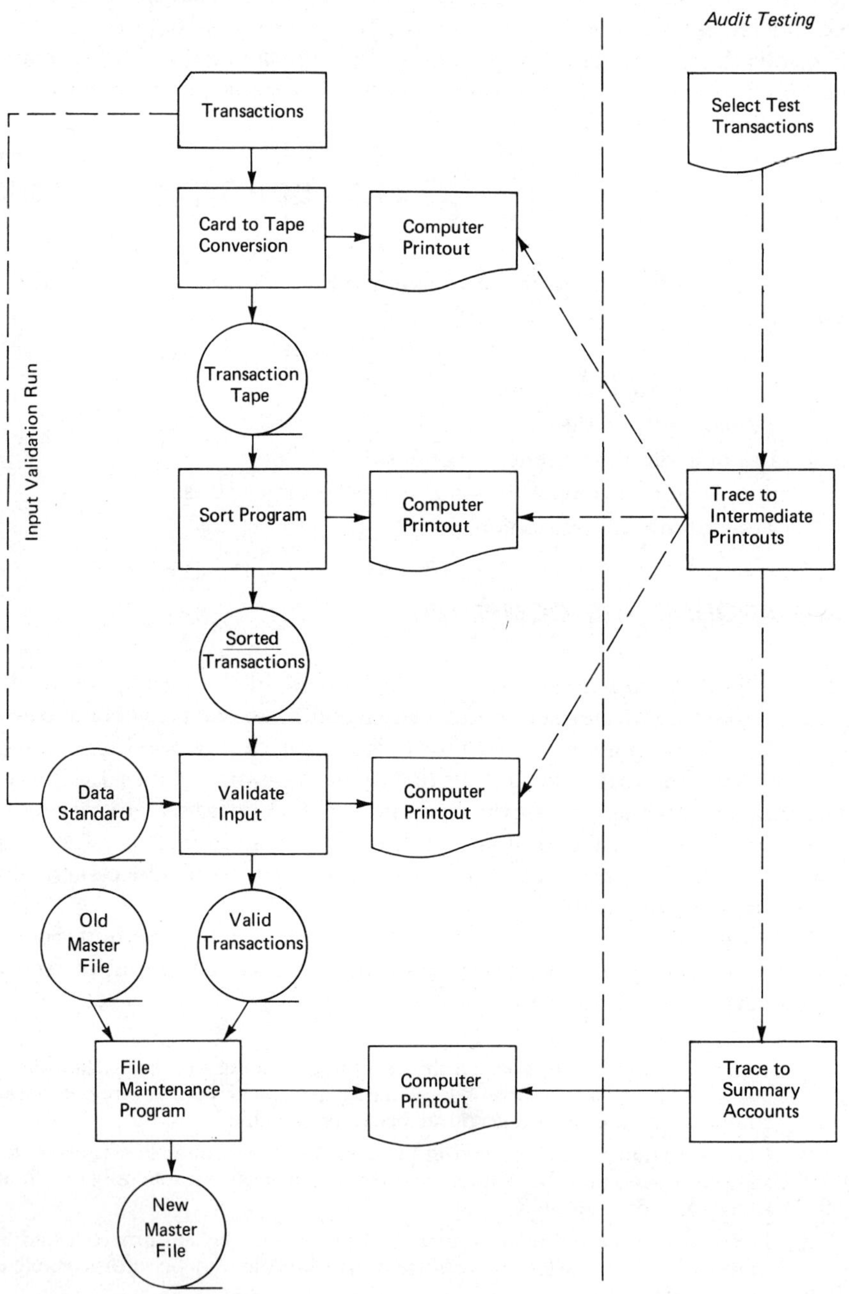

TESTING THROUGH THE COMPUTER

With this method, the auditor tests the company's computerized functions by using *test data.* That is, specifically designed imput data is processed by the company's com-

EXHIBIT 27-7 AUDITING THROUGH THE COMPUTER

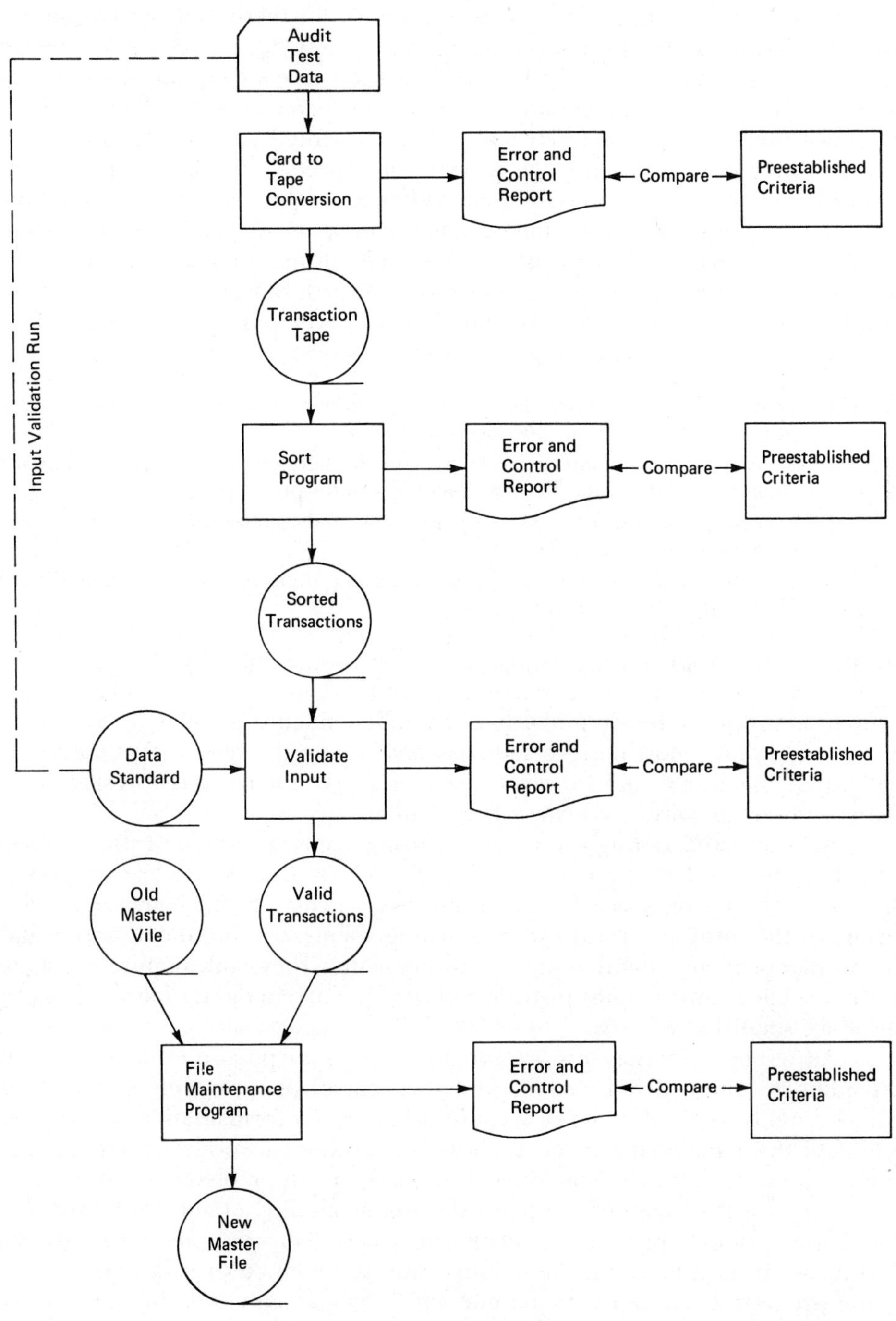

puter programs and the output is compared against predetermined criteria, as illustrated in Exhibit 27-7. Test data has the same format as real data, but purposefully contains erroneous figures. These figures are designed to evoke error reports substantiating the existence of company prescribed controls. An understanding of control functions is obtained from interviews and any detailed computer program documentation. (These are the same controls discussed in chapter 26.) It is this understanding which enables the auditor to test specifically for these controls. For instance, suppose no company employee should exceed a seventy-hour work week. The company has a programmed control which deletes the processing of any incorrect data card and indicates such deletion and reason on an "error listing." The auditor tests this control function by deliberately violating the seventy-hour limitation. If processing is deleted and an error message correctly interprets the violation, the existence and viability of the control is established. Other test data possibilities include deliberate use of an invalid account number, missing data, invalid field combination, out-of-sequence processing against a master file, and so on. Each test data card must contain only one error. In addition, some test data cards must have no errors, so that transaction *linkage* may be tested for completeness to the point of entry into the account balances. Four testing arrangements are possible:[6]

1. Process test transactions along with the client's "live" (actual) transactions and update them on the client's current master file.
2. Process test transactions as in (1), but update them only on a special section of the client's current master file maintained for audit purposes.
3. Process test transactions as a separate run and update them on a copy of the client's current master file.
4. Process test transactions as in (3), but update them only on a simulated master file designed by the public accountant.

Unfortunately, all four testing arrangements have some difficulty. The most potentially hazardous is the first arrangement, whereby company files are altered. This is a definite impropriety for an auditor, as his independence is violated. At any rate, test data recordings must be reversed *immediately* from the files so that correct balances are reestablished and automatic activities are not triggered—for example, inventory orders, invoices, and check preparation.

An alternative testing arrangement, using a special section of the company's master file, still involves a question of independence. It may also lead to poor file utilization by requiring space for recording the outcome of infrequent audit tests. Turning to the third and fourth testing arrangements, we find them more suitable from an independence standpoint, but unfortunately they both require extra computer time. The company must provide copies of its current master file and programs or produce simulated records.

All testing arrangements are for the express purpose of evaluating our understanding of automated functions and the control features they entail. At this point, our aim is not verification of account balances, but formalization of our understanding of the audit environment. With this in mind, we advocate arrangement 3 or a modification which uses a *grandfather file* in place of a duplicated current file.

The test deck method confirms our understanding of automated functions, but it *does not* confirm procedures relating to source data *conversion,* output control, and control of machine room operations. Also, the method provides no assurance that the program being tested is the one which was actually used by the company. Unless the auditor can observe its use, run test data immediately after the company processes real transactions, or devise some other safeguard, the test data method could yield a completely erroneous evaluation.

---

[6]David H. Li. *Accounting, Computers, Management Information Systems,* p. 301. Used with permission of the author and publisher.

AUDITOR'S COMPUTER PROGRAMS

Under this method the auditor uses his own "ad hoc" computer programs. These programs contain what the auditor considers to be acceptable internal control.[7]

Using actual company input data, as in Exhibit 27-8, the results of these programs are compared with the results from programs currently used by the company. If results compare favorably, the auditor can make a judgment as to the adequacy of the company's system. Note that with this method the auditor makes no deliberate attempt to understand the company's automated functions, but accepts or rejects their adequacy by examining output and comparing it with acceptable audit criteria.

Like the test data method this form of testing requires safeguards to assure that the company's program being tested is the version actually used by the company. In addition, the method does not confirm an understanding of input conversion, output control, or machine room operation.

PROGRAM COMPARISON ON RECURRING BASIS

This method requires that the auditor retain a copy of the client's computer program and subsequently compare this program with current programs on each recurring audit. This necessitates that during the first audit, evaluation of computerized functions be obtained by other means, e.g., test decks and review of detailed computer logic. A copy of the program then becomes the basis for future audits. Using the company's original input data, the output and intermediary reports from the auditor's program are compared against actual company output. The procedure is identical to that in Exhibit 27-8, except that the auditor's program is an "audited copy" of the company's program. Any programming changes in the company's current program will be reflected in the comparison process and this information will be used to amend the auditor's understanding of the current system.

Once again, this method requires additional tests to confirm an understanding of input conversion, output control, and machine room operation; also, it requires a method to assure that the program being tested is the version actually used by the company. A particular disadvantage of this method is the possible non-operability of the auditor's program when the company has introduced changes in the computer operating system.[8]

TESTING WITH LIVE TRANSACTIONS

With this method, the auditor observes the actual processing of transactions on an unannounced basis. A few transactions are selected, their processing is observed, and

[7]These computer programs *are not* the *generalized audit programs* frequently used for validation testing (refer to section 27.11). They are specifically written programs used for transactions testing of a particular company.

[8]A computer operating system is a group of programs which enable the computer to run uninterrupted. They take care of such things as scheduling, translations, execution, and automatic monitoring of input/output devices. Slight changes in these programs, particularly in translation or *compiler* programs, can cause previously operable company programs to fail.

transaction and master file tapes are checked for propriety and proper updating. The chief drawbacks of this method are: (1) the need for a statistically reliable sample, and (2) the absence of a deliberate testing for error controls.

While the foregoing methods for transactions testing of automated functions are generally applicable to on-line computer systems as well as batch controlled

EXHIBIT 27-8 TESTING WITH AUDITOR'S COMPUTER PROGRAM

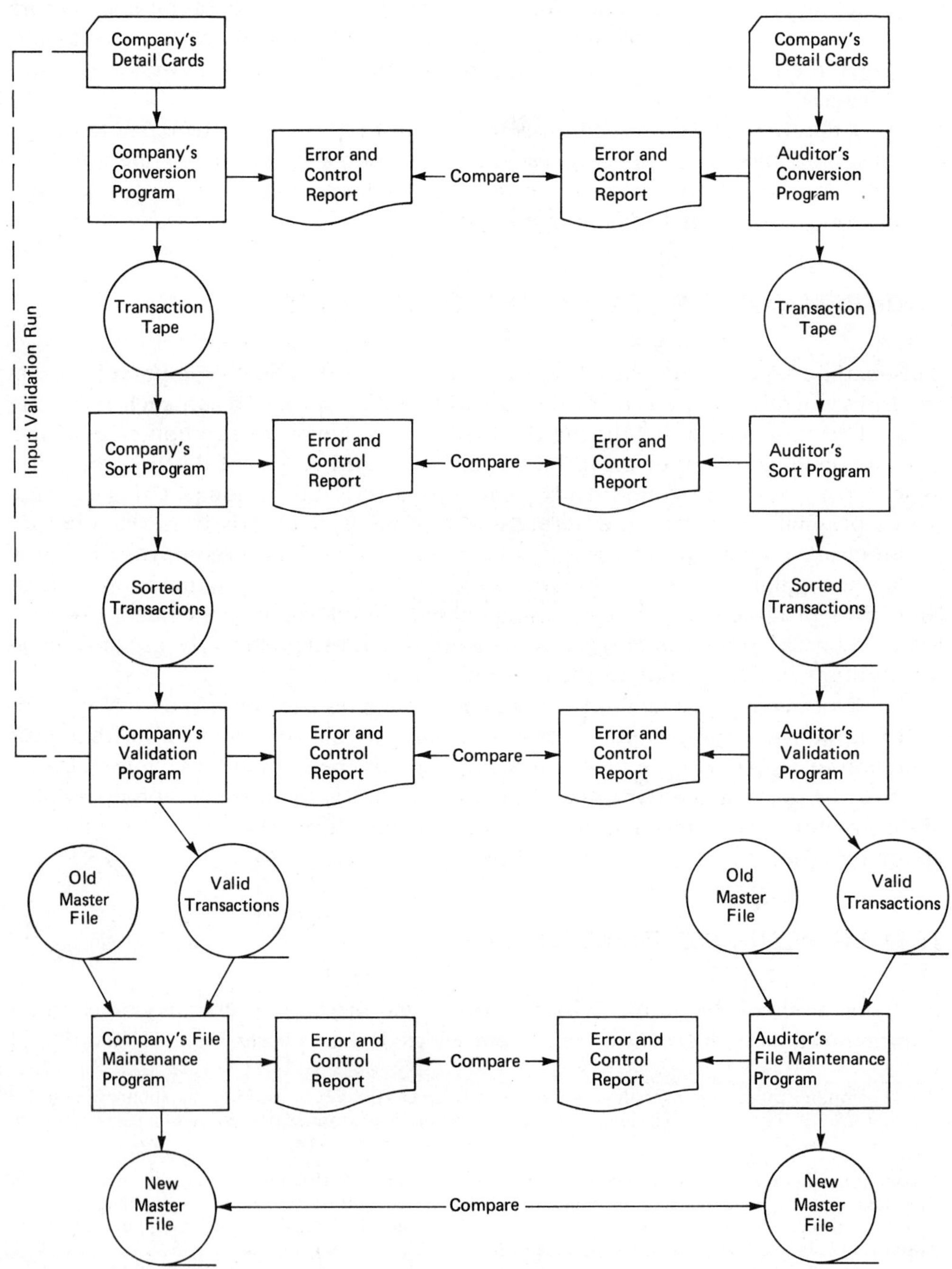

systems, the absence of intermediary processing stages causes some difficulty. Clear *audit trails* are lacking in on-line facilities; consequently, testing arrangements must focus on input-output relationships. The auditor is forced to abandon the first method—testing around the computer—but may use the other four as illustrated in Exhibit 27-9.

EXHIBIT 27-9 AUDITING ON-LINE COMPUTER SYSTEMS

(a) Testing Through the Computer

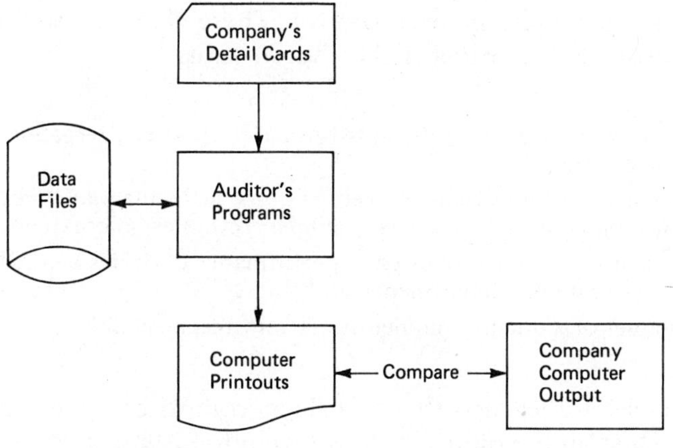

(b) Testing with Auditor's Computer Programs

27.8 FUNCTIONAL TESTING OF EDP-RELATED FUNCTIONS

True functional testing of computerized functions is unnecessary. If transactions testing reveals the *existence* of control functions, it is unnecessary to test for *compliance* (functional testing) because computers will not deviate from prescribed programming (as opposed to humans), and hence system understanding can be confirmed by prima facie evidence alone. In effect, transactions testing fulfills functional testing as well. There are, however, many functions that are non-computerized, but related to the maintenance of computer processing. Some tests of these functions are as follows:[9]

1. Test batch control or alternative procedures.
2. Test method of verifying accuracy of conversion.
3. Trace computer run-controls through one processing cycle.
4. Review reject activity for a selected period, ascertaining that rejects are properly controlled and resubmitted where appropriate.
5. Examine controls over error correction procedures, paying particular attention to corrections to master file records.
6. Ascertain by inquiry of the users of EDP-prepared reports whether they are satisfied with the accuracy of such reports.

27.9 EVALUATION OF CONTROLS

The last stage of the evaluation process is a review of the documented (flow charts) system for adequate internal control. Two types of control are reviewed—operational and accounting. *Operational controls* relate to the efficiency of operating activities, and *accounting controls* relate to the safeguarding of assets and the reliability of financial records. The review of these controls is not necessarily on a yearly basis, but generally follows the plan as flowcharted in Exhibit 27-10.

When reviewing internal control the auditor generally uses a pre-written internal control questionnaire[10] which focuses attention on fundamental characteristics necessary for adequate internal control. These characteristics are outlined by the American Institute of Certified Public Accountants:[11]

1. A plan of organization which provides appropriate segregation of functional responsibilities,
2. A system of authorization and record procedures adequate to provide reasonable accounting control over assets, liabilities, revenues, and expenses,
3. Sound practices to be followed in performance of duties and functions of each of the organizational departments, and
4. Personnel of a quality commensurate with responsibilities.

In chapter 1 we learned that a business comprises three distinguishable yet interrelated systems: an operating (or flow-through) system, a control system, and a feedback (or information) system. This interrelationship is shown in Exhibit 27-11.

The *operating* system denotes what is happening in the firm: a product is made, cash is received and disbursed, inventory is purchased and requisitioned, and so forth. The *control* system serves as a constraint on the operating system—it requires that operations conform to certain standards of quality and integrity.

[9] *Lybrand Training Program, Staff Course I, Tab 9,* p. P–9–6. Used with permission.

[10] Refer to Appendix A of this chapter for some excerpts from a questionnaire for purchasing activity, and to Appendix B for an evaluation of EDP controls.

[11] *Auditing Standards and Procedures,* Statement No. 33, pp. 28–29.

EXHIBIT 27-10 REVIEW OF CONTROLS

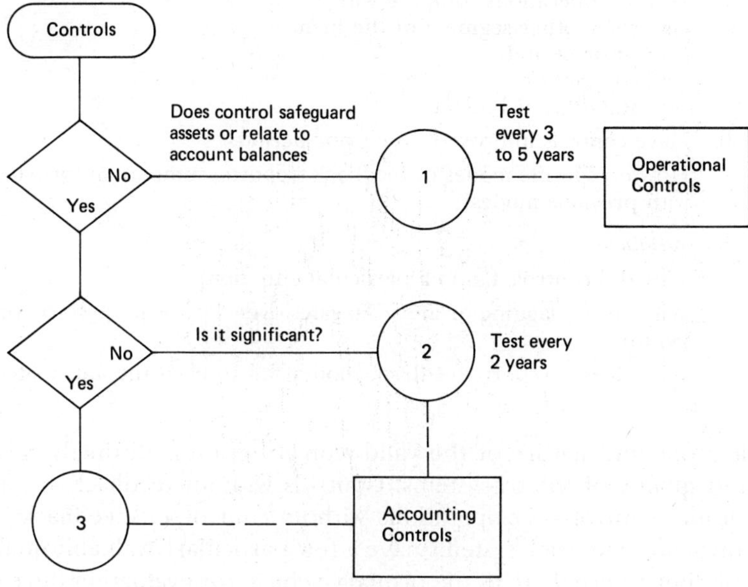

EXHIBIT 27-11 TRI-SYSTEM COMPLEX OF A BUSINESS

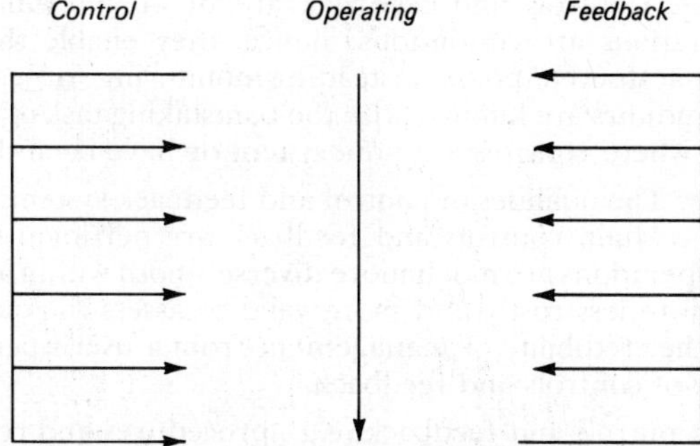

The *feedback* system provides management with information concerning:

1. *Controls:*
   a. What controls have been specified?
   b. To what extent are planned controls actually implemented?
   c. Are controls too lenient or too harsh?
   d. Are out-of-control situations common? How are they handled?
   e. Has feedback on the functioning of controls led to correction or improvement?
2. *Exceptions:*
   a. What items has the control system rejected?
   b. How are exceptional items handled?
   c. With what frequency do certain exceptions occur?

3. *Comparisons:*
   a. How do operations compare with:
      (1) some other segment of the firm,
      (2) prior period,
      (3) competitor,
      (4) standard or budget?
   b. Have controls improved over prior periods?
   c. How do specific modes of feedback (reports) compare in format and content with previous modes?
4. *Interpretations:*
   a. Why did controls fail in a particular situation?
   b. Why are we lagging or ahead in sales over a prior period—or versus a competitor?
   c. Why does a report (feedback mode) fail to elicit the anticipated response?

The scope and nature of the validation program is distinctly related to the existence and quality of the tri-systems. Controls without feedback are as sterile as feedback without controls—or operations without control and feedback.

Control and feedback systems have a few particularly valuable qualities which enable the auditor to use them as the primary vehicle for evaluating the effectiveness of operations:

1. *Intermittency:* Controls and feedback are of an intermittent (periodic) nature, while operations are continuous; hence, they enable the auditor to check on operations at discrete points instead of monitoring (or testing) every transaction. (Veteran auditors are familiar with the painstaking task of reconstructing a stream of activity where controls are nonexistent or have been destroyed.)
2. *Universality:* The qualities of control and feedback systems are relatively universal in nature—certain controls and feedback are pertinent to all organizations. By contrast, operations are much more diverse—both within and between companies. It is therefore less costly and more valid to assess the quality of operations (the extent of the credibility of management from a user's perspective) by examining the quality of controls and feedback.
3. *Specificity:* Controls and feedback (e.g., procedures and reports) are usually more carefully defined and specific than operations, hence the auditor can obtain a clearer picture of operations in less time than is required to analyze operations directly.

The value of control and feedback systems lies in the extent to which they are *used* and not *shelved.* Therefore, the auditor should examine the controls and feedback "in action" versus "on paper." If control and feedback is specified but not used, the evaluation process must be cognizant of their "nonexistence-in-fact."

On the other hand, evidence that even the best controls and feedback are in effect does not mean that further audit activity is unnecessary—but it would serve to reduce detailed audit activity to a minimum level consistent with the requirements of independent evaluation. The extent to which control and feedback can influence audit scope is represented in Exhibit 27-12.

Evaluation of controls and feedback requires that the auditor be familiar with the qualities of "good" control and feedback systems. Hence, his repertoire should include the essentials of (1) management controls, (2) operational controls, (3) account-

EXHIBIT 27-12 RELATION BETWEEN QUALITY OF CONTROL AND AUDIT ENERGY

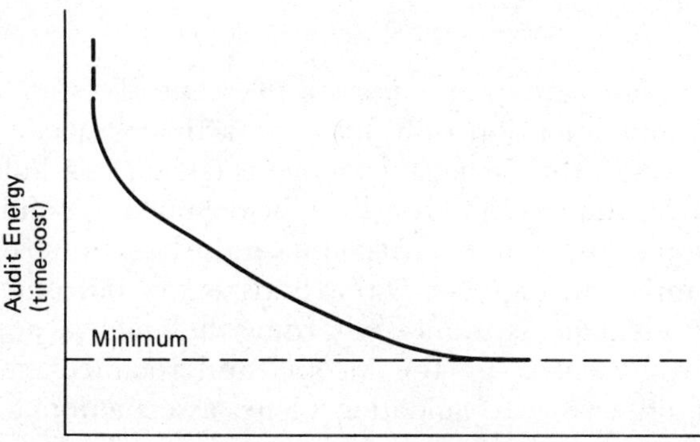

ing controls, and (4) management information systems (information records, reports, and flow).

Upon completing the four tasks of the evaluation phase—obtaining an understanding, recording the understanding, testing the understanding, and evaluation of controls and feedback—the auditor is in a position to make some specific recommendations on system design. At this point, he formulates a management letter. In general the letter should:

1. Contain carefully chosen, concise, and understandable sentences.
2. Indicate internal control weaknesses and the resulting risks.
3. Indicate redundant or needless functions.
4. Point out inefficiencies in operations.
5. Indicate *specific* corrective action.
6. Indicate both immediate and long-range dollar savings resulting from the implementation of design changes, or, if more appropriate, indicate the aggregate amount subject to risk.

The management letter is perhaps the greatest benefit resulting from an audit, for it contains an independent appraisal of system design, and thus enables management continually to assess the best means of reaching company objectives.

27.10 VALIDATION

This audit phase encompasses the planning and execution of tests designed to give reasonable assurance that account balances are properly stated. Part of this assurance rests on the outcome of the evaluation phase and on tests formulated to examine the fairness of estimates, valuations, and judgments made by the company in computing account balances. This latter activity is validation testing or *bona fide* testing.

There are some assumptions underlying the formulation of validation tests:

1. Double-entry bookkeeping inherently produces mathematical accuracy.
2. Management and other company personnel are honest and competent.

3. Detection of fraud and defalcations is not a specific audit purpose.
4. Accounts are interrelated and the substantiation of one may corroborate the validity of another.

These assumptions are used to narrow the scope of testing, and consequently, to confine the auditor's attention only to those activities needed to formulate an opinion on the fairness of the financial statements taken as a whole.

An audit satisfaction as to fairness can be obtained by validation tests emphasizing a substantiation of balance sheet accounts at the beginning and end of the audit period. This substantiation, together with a satisfactory outcome of the evaluation phase, produces an adequate assurance regarding the financial activities in the intervening period as represented by the income and retained earnings statements. Mathematically, we observe that validation of net assets automatically validates net income. Let:

$$I = \text{net income}$$
$$A^n = \text{net assets}$$
$$A = \text{assets}$$
$$L = \text{liabilities}$$

Beginning balance sheet: $A^n_1 = A_1 - L_1$

Ending balance sheet: $A^n_2 = A_2 - L_2$

Income statement: $I = A^n_2 - A^n_1$

or $I = (A_2 - L_2) - (A_1 - L_1)$

With adequate internal control and a reliable accounting system, validation testing excludes a direct examination of income accounts. Only asset and equity accounts are validated. The only possible difficulty lies in improper classification of such accounts on the statement itself. Material misclassification, however, can be sighted by reviewing figures for reasonableness in relation to other components of income and in relation to prior periods' figures.

The focus of validation testing on balance sheet accounts is the optimal solution to a mix of audit time and the degree of assurance obtained. Balance sheet accounts contain the residual effects of multitudinous transactions, as opposed to income accounts, which summarize the total effects. A focus on residual items rather than flow-through items results in a substantial savings of time.[12] Nevertheless there are recognizable hazards of this approach. Understatement of net assets resulting from expensing capitalizable items or from unauthorized diversion of resources are difficult to disclose. Since they result in a conservative financial position, however, the impact of non-disclosure is not serious.

There are a number of audit observations which are necessary in determining the propriety of account balances and in determining acceptable form and clarity of financial statements. These audit observations enter directly into the design of validation tests and serve to focus every facet of testing upon essential questions underlying the formulation of an audit opinion. These audit observations are performed within the overall auditing framework depicted in Exhibit 27-13.

[12] Despite the obvious time savings resulting from a balance sheet approach, some national CPA firms still validate account balances by focusing on income statement accounts.

EXHIBIT 27-13 THE AUDITING FRAMEWORK

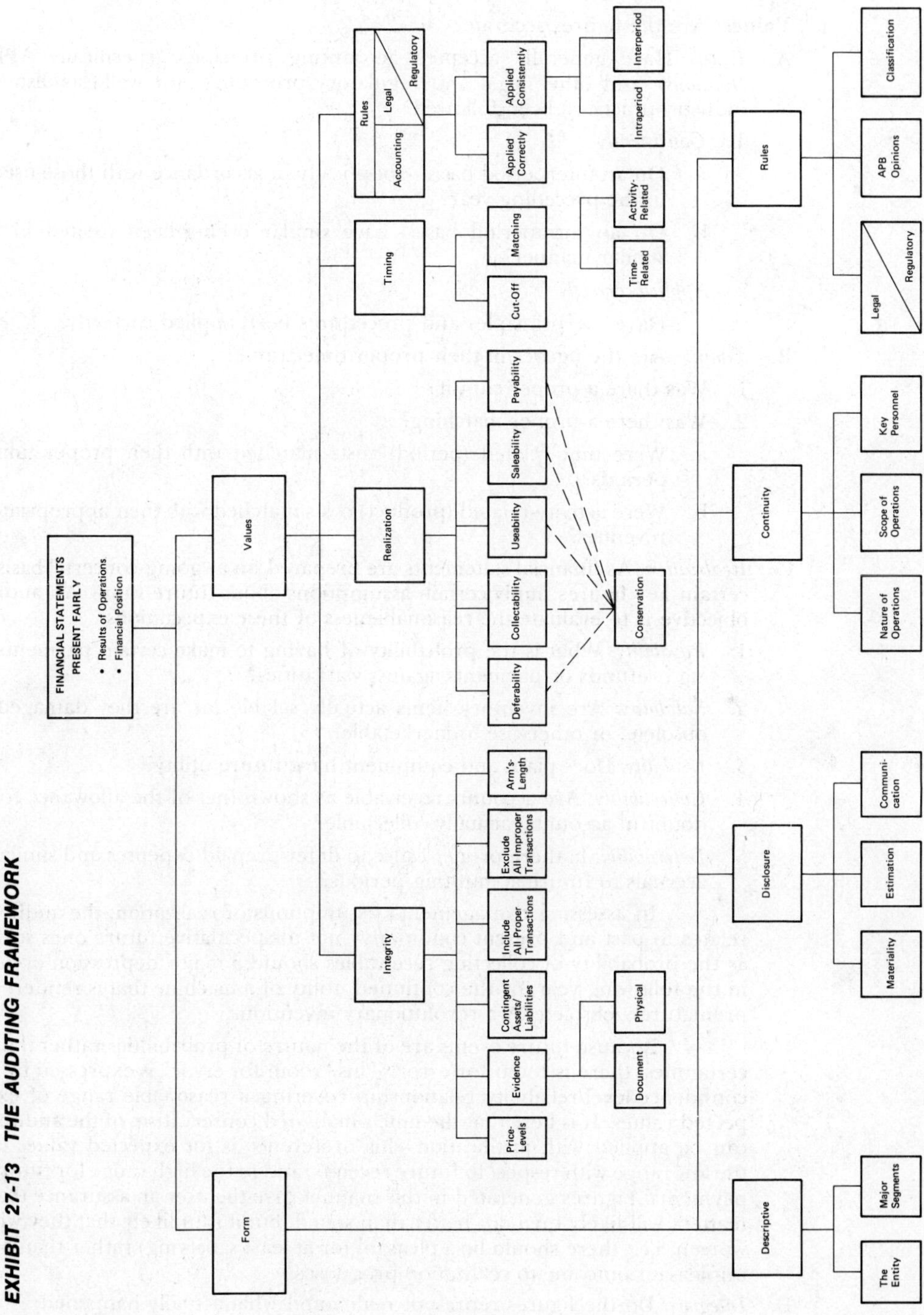

This framework is purposive in that all observations are directed to the fundamental question of fair presentation:

I. **Values:** Are the figures accurate?

  A. *Rules:* Have generally accepted accounting principles (specifically APB *Opinions*), and other legal and regulatory procedures (or well-established industry practices) been followed?

    1. *Consistently*

      a. On an interperiod basis—specifically in accordance with those used in the preceding year?

      b. On an intraperiod basis—have similar events been treated in a similar manner?

    2. *Applied correctly*

      Have the principles and procedures been applied correctly?

  B. *Timing:* Are the figures in their proper time-frame:

    1. Was there a proper cut-off?

    2. Was there a proper matching?

      a. Were time-related (period) costs matched with their proper time periods?

      b. Were activity-related (product) costs matched with their appropriate revenues?

  C. *Realization:* As financial statements are prepared on a "going-concern" basis, certain key figures imply certain assumptions about future value. An audit objective is to evaluate the reasonableness of these expectations.

    1. *Payability:* What is the probability of having to make certain payments, e.g., refunds or payments against warranties?

    2. *Salability:* Are inventory items actually salable, or are they damaged, obsolete, or otherwise unmarketable?

    3. *Usability:* Does plant and equipment have future utility?

    4. *Collectibility:* Are accounts receivable as shown (net of the allowance for doubtful accounts) actually collectable?

    5. *Deferability:* Is there proper cause to defer prepaid expenses and similar accruals to future accounting periods?

  In assessing management's assumptions of realization, the auditor relates to past and present conditions—not to speculative future ones such as the probability of collecting receivables should a major depression occur in the following year, or the continued utility of a machine that is rendered prematurely obsolete by a revolutionary invention.

  Because future events are of the nature of probabilities rather than certainties, there is room for error. This "room for error" is expressed by a confidence-level/reliability relationship covering a reasonable range of expected values. It is here that the much-maligned conservatism of the auditor can be applied with justification—his preference is for expected values in the low range with respect to future receipts, and in the high range for future payments. Figures generated in this manner give the user an assurance that matters will likely turn out better than stated, but it is unlikely that they will worsen, i.e., there should be a pleasant (or at least satisfying) rather than an unpleasant outcome to realization prognoses.

  D. *Integrity:* Do the figures represent reality and what actually happened:

    1. *Arm's-length:* Were sales and other transactions consummated at arm's-length, or do the figures represent certain undisclosed "discounts," "gifts," or "kickbacks"?

2. *Exclude all improper transactions:* Do the figures include transactions that are improper from the viewpoint of generally accepted accounting principles, e.g., "puffing" sales or the cost balance to make things look better, or valuing fixed assets at market value?
3. *Include all proper transactions:* Do the figures represent a complete account of all proper transactions—have all sales been recorded, have all receipts been deposited, and so forth?
4. *Contingent liabilities:* Has the firm honestly disclosed contingent liabilities arising out of past or present transactions, such as pending lawsuits, warranties and guarantees, tax liability arising out of differences between income reported for tax versus financial purposes?
5. *Evidence:* Can the integrity of the financial data be substantiated by independent means:
   a. by direct physical examination,
   b. or by examining the system of documents and records?
6. *Price-levels:* Do the financial statements imply real increases in sales and earnings on the basis of stable or constant dollars in the presence of a changing purchasing power—without some effort to alert the users to the significance of constant versus current dollar reporting?

II. **Presentation:** Are the financial statements in good form and do they communicate with clarity to the average user?

A. *Rules:* Are the various rules and regulations relating to presentation being followed?
   1. *Classification:* Are items in the right place, such as extraordinary gains and loss that should appear in the income statement rather than in the statement of retained earnings?
   2. *APB:* Are disclosure rules of APB *Opinions* being followed, such as "fully diluted" earnings per share?
   3. *Other rules, regulations, and practices:* Are other rules, regulations, and practices with respect to form and presentation being followed?

B. *Continuity:* Do the financial statements reveal any major known changes that may influence realization expectations, such as:
   1. *Nature of operations:* A major switch from one line of business to another?
   2. *Scope of operations:* A major change in the size of operations, such as doubling capacity?
   3. *Key personnel:* Has the top salesman resigned, taking his top customers with him?

While the case may be made that management ought to attempt a prediction as to the consequences of major changes on future financial earnings and position, the auditor's responsibility is limited to seeing that the statements do not imply continuity when major change is already committed. A disclosure of the change is sufficient for the auditor's purposes, while he may encourage the client to go further.

C. *Disclosure:* Is there sufficient disclosure:
   1. *Materiality:* of all facts and figures of a material nature?
   2. *Estimation:* of the rules and degree of estimation used in arriving at certain figures?
   3. *Communication:* of an understandable and unequivocal nature so that the financial statements, and especially their footnotes, communicate with clarity with respect to "the average user"?

D. *Descriptive of Reality:* Do the financial statements in their form and presentation reflect the reality of what the business is all about as:

1. *Economic entity:* An economic entity that has production, buying, and selling cycles?
2. *Major segments:* Are the major economic segments (industries, markets, domestic versus foreign) of the business identified with sufficient clarity to enable the average user to make discriminative judgments about the scope and nature of business operations?

Using these background observations, the auditor validates balance sheet accounts by substantiating a majority of the dollar value in each account tested. This is accomplished by concentrating on high-value items comprising the account balance; in other words, using a *biased sample.* For instance, with accounts receivable the auditor could choose all subsidiary balances over $1,000. This type of selection is not possible where all items comprising the account are of relatively equal value. In this instance, the auditor must rely on *statistical sampling* to provide a measure of fairness. A common technique is *acceptance sampling* where the confidence level is based upon the number of errors found in the sample. Exhibit 27-14 shows the confidence levels

EXHIBIT 27-14 RELATIONSHIP BETWEEN SAMPLE SIZE, ERRORS, AND CONFIDENCE OF DATA

IMPLICATIONS OF ACCEPTING DATA BASED ON THE NUMBER OF ERRORS DISCLOSED BY THE AUDITOR'S TEST CHECKS

Number of items test checked	Number of errors disclosed	Number of times in 100 that the auditor will be justified in deciding that the actual error rate is less than:					Number of items test checked	Number of errors disclosed	Number of times in 100 that the auditor will be justified in deciding that the actual error rate is less than:				
		0.5%	1%	2%	5%	10%			0.5%	1%	2%	5%	10%
25	0	12	22	39	72	92	300	4	2	18	71	100	100
25	1	1	3	9	36	71	300	5	0	8	55	100	100
25	2	0	0	1	13	46	300	6		3	39	99	100
25	3			0	4	24	300	7		1	26	98	100
25	4				1	11	300	8		0	15	96	100
25	5				0	4	300	9			8	93	100
25	6					1	300	10			4	88	100
25	7					0	300	11			2	81	100
							300	12			1	73	100
50	0	22	39	63	92	99	300	13			0	64	100
50	1	3	9	26	71	96	300	14				53	100
50	2	0	1	8	46	87	300	15				43	100
50	3		0	2	24	73							
50	4			0	11	56	400	0	86	98	100	100	100
50	5				4	38	400	1	59	91	100	100	100
50	6				1	24	400	2	32	76	99	100	100
50	7				0	13	400	3	14	57	96	100	100
50	8					7	400	4	5	37	90	100	100
50	9					3	400	5	2	21	81	100	100
50	10					1	400	6	0	11	69	100	100
							400	7		5	55	100	100
100	0	39	63	86	99	100	400	8		2	41	100	100
100	1	9	26	59	96	100	400	9		1	28	99	100
100	2	1	8	32	87	100	400	10		0	18	99	100
100	3	0	2	14	73	99	400	11			11	98	100
100	4		0	5	56	97	400	12			6	96	100
100	5			2	38	93	400	13			3	93	100
100	6			0	24	87	400	14			2	89	100
100	7				13	78	400	15			1	84	100
100	8				7	67	400	16			0	78	100

EXHIBIT 27-14 (CONTINUED)

Number of items test checked	Number of errors disclosed	Number of times in 100 that the auditor will be justified in deciding that the actual error rate is less than:					Number of items test checked	Number of errors disclosed	Number of times in 100 that the auditor will be justified in deciding that the actual error rate is less than:				
		0.5%	1%	2%	5%	10%			0.5%	1%	2%	5%	10%
100	9				3	54	400	17				70	100
100	10				1	42	400	18				62	100
							400	19				53	100
150	0	53	78	95	100	100	400	20				44	100
150	1	17	44	80	100	100							
150	2	4	19	58	98	100	500	0	92	99	100	100	100
150	3	1	7	35	94	100	500	1	71	96	100	100	100
150	4	0	2	18	87	100	500	2	46	87	100	100	100
150	5		0	8	76	100	500	3	24	73	99	100	100
150	6			3	62	99	500	4	11	56	97	100	100
150	7			1	48	98	500	5	4	38	93	100	100
150	8			0	34	96	500	6	1	24	87	100	100
150	9				22	93	500	7	0	13	78	100	100
150	10				14	88	500	8		7	67	100	100
							500	9		3	54	100	100
200	0	63	86	98	100	100	500	10		1	42	100	100
200	1	26	59	91	100	100	500	11		0	30	100	100
200	2	8	32	76	100	100	500	12			21	100	100
200	3	2	14	57	99	100	500	13			14	99	100
200	4	0	5	37	97	100	500	14			8	99	100
200	5		2	21	93	100	500	15			5	98	100
200	6		0	11	87	100	500	16			3	96	100
200	7			5	78	100	500	17			1	94	100
200	8			2	67	100	500	18			1	91	100
200	9			1	54	99	500	19			0	87	100
200	10			0	42	99	500	20				81	100
							500	21				75	100
300	0	78	95	100	100	100	500	22				68	100
300	1	44	80	98	100	100	500	23				61	100
300	2	19	58	94	100	100	500	24				53	100
300	3	7	35	85	100	100	500	25				45	100

SOURCE: Howard F. Stettler, "A Simple Tool to Assist the Auditor in Statistical Interpretation of Test Checks," *The Journal of Accountancy* 97, no. 1 (January 1954):57. Copyright 1954 by the American Institute of Certified Public Accountants, Inc. Used with permission.

(based upon an assumed Poisson distribution) associated with the number of errors disclosed per sample size.

For each application of acceptance sampling, the auditor must use his expert *judgement* and (1) establish his tolerance for any errors found in the sample; (2) establish his degree of confidence in the sample as representative of the population. For example, suppose the auditor wants at least a 70% confidence that no more than 5% of the population is in error. From Exhibit 27-14, a 70% degree of confidence requires a sample size of at least 50, if no more than one error is disclosed. If more than one error is disclosed, the sample size must be increased until a 70% degree of confidence can be obtained. For instance, if five errors are found with a sample of 50, the confidence is only 40%. Consequently, we must sample at least 100 more items (total of 150 items) and find no more errors. If more errors are found, we must continue to increase the sample size until we meet the 70% criterion.

A brief description of validation testing by major account group is as follows:

1. **CASH**

   a. Obtain a *confirmation* of the company cash balance at year-end directly from the bank.
   b. Reconcile bank balance to company prepared bank reconciliation.
   c. Trace the reconciled balance per reconciliation to the general ledger balance.
   d. Examine records for any bank transfers made at year-end.

2. **RECEIVABLES**

   a. Obtain an aged trial balance of accounts receivable.
   b. Select those accounts which together represent a significant portion of the balance, and mail confirmation requests to debitors. These requests can be positive and/or negative. A *positive confirmation* asks for a reply as to whether or not the balance is correct. A *negative confirmation* asks for a reply only if the amount is disputed.
   c. Send second and third requests if necessary.
   d. Instruct company to resolve all reported differences and disputes.

3. **INVENTORY**

   a. Review company's inventory count procedures.
   b. Test count inventory; trace to company inventory tickets; and trace to summary of inventory.
   c. Check footings and extensions on a group of company inventory tickets, and test foot inventory summary.
   d. Review for obsolete inventory.
   e. Examine receiving and shipping cut-offs, and determine whether transactions have been recorded in the proper period.

4. **EQUIPMENT AND PREPAYMENTS**

   a. Request the company to prepare a schedule of additions and disposals.
   b. Prepare a summary schedule of equipment and related accumulated depreciation.[13]
   c. Examine all supporting evidence for additions and disposals per company prepared schedule.
   d. Review leased assets and determine appropriate accounting disclosure.
   e. Review the repair account for unusual fluctuations over the preceding year.
   f. Review the company's book and tax depreciation expense for mathematical accuracy and propriety of methods and asset life.
   g. Tie in totals from supporting schedules into trial balance.
   h. Review the insurance coverage of plant assets.
   i. Review the insurance register for propriety of unexpired amounts.

5. **LIABILITIES**

   a. Trace notes payable and bonds payable balances to supporting documents and/or send confirmations to creditors.

[13]Generally, the auditor's summary schedule for property, plant, and equipment is prepared in a format similar to that prescribed by form 10-K required by the SEC.

b. Obtain trial balance of accounts payable and trace detail to voucher register and total to general ledger. Possibly send confirmations to vendors.
c. If year-end is December 31, examine disbursements in January for possible unrecorded liabilities of December.
d. Examine unpaid invoices and vouchers.
e. Review open purchase order file for significant commitments.
f. Obtain a written statement from the company's attorney about any existing or pending litigation.

27.11 EDP VALIDATION TESTING

When computerized processing ends in machine-readable files, the auditor can utilize the computer in validating account balances. The validation tests are the same as those described for manual auditing, except that the auditor can now perform his operations via computer programs. Scanning, comparing, matching, arithmetic verification, sample selection, account analysis, and confirmation preparation can all be performed automatically. This automated validation testing is illustrated in Exhibit 27-15.

EXHIBIT 27-15 AUDIT PROGRAMS FOR REVIEW OF FILES

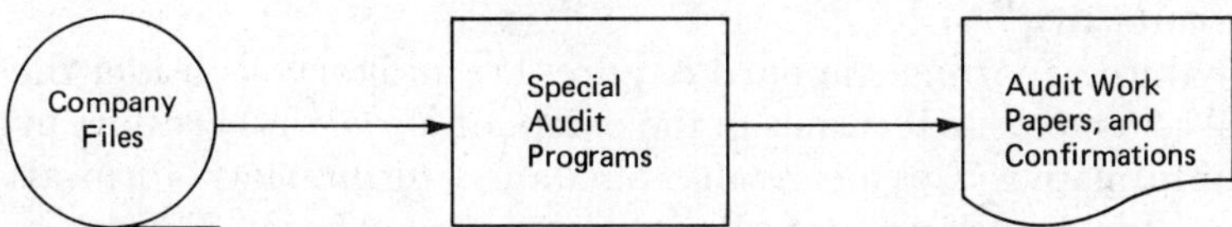

Two schemes are possible: either the auditor can specify his needs and have the company develop the programs, or he can write his own programs. The later scheme is the most popular. All of the larger auditing firms have developed generalized computer audit programs which can be adapted to a variety of account balances as well as to the requirements of diverse companies.[14] By writing in a common computer language (COBOL) the programs can be run on most computer systems. Some applications of generalized programs are:[15]

1. Scanning a 10,000-item perpetual inventory file, printing out all items over $20,000 and every two hundredth item, to test quantity and standard cost. Checking *all* extension and footing of inventory file. Printing out all items with a credit balance.
2. Matching file of cash disbursements in first twenty days of January with accounts payable file at December 31. Printing out all disbursement items that do not match for test of unrecorded liability.
3. Comparing standard cost file at beginning of year with end-of-year cost file. Printing out all standard costs that vary more than 10% for test.

[14] Some of the available generalized audit programs are (1) Audassist, (2) Audex, (3) Audit Thru, (4) Auditall (MARK IV), (5) Audipak, (6) Score, (7) Miracl, (8) Auditape, (9) GRS, (10) Strata, (11) Autronic 16, (12) Cars, and (13) Audit/Management System.

[15] From: John J. O'Donnell, Jr., "EDP and Auditing in Perspective," *Lybrand Journal* 49, no. 3 (1968): 12. Used with permission.

4. Matching cash receipts after year-end with an A/R file to substantiate the collectibility of account receivables at year-end.

27.12 AUDIT OPINIONS

The American Institute of Certified Public Accountants has established rather definitive guidelines or standards for the expression of an audit opinion. All these *Reporting Standards,* as quoted at the beginning of this chapter, call for an expression of *opinion,* not a statement of fact. No financial audit can accomplish any more. The worthiness of an opinion and its influence in financial decisions rests upon the acknowledged expertise of the auditor and the public confidence engendered by his role as an independent and impartial observer.

The first reporting standard requires an evaluation and opinion on the *general acceptance* of company accounting procedures as established by the expert judgment of the auditor and/or by pronouncements of the Accounting Principles Board.

The second reporting standard requires the auditor to report the financial effects of any changes in accounting principles from those used in prior periods. The auditor looks for breaches in consistency from prior periods that in themselves will affect the comparability of financial statements. The reporting requirement applies to changes in accounting procedures resulting from changes in accounting principles. It does not apply to the financial consequences of changes in the underlying conditions of the company.[16]

The third reporting standard requires the auditor to consider the fairness of the financial statements as it relates to the extent of *disclosures* necessary to make them sufficiently informative. This means an evaluation of terminology, form, arrangement, and content of the statements as well as their appended notes. The auditor's opinion on disclosure, however, does not extend to those items whose disclosure would cause subsequent harm to the company, and whose non-disclosure is not misleading to outsiders. Such items include contingency reserves and confidential information about production processes, management, and marketing that could possibly benefit a competitor.

The fourth reporting standard characterizes the degree of responsibility assumed by the auditor for the fairness of a company's financial statements. He can issue a *qualified opinion* when the statements are fairly presented *except* for certain qualifications which by themselves would not negate the fairness of the statements taken as a whole. When they do negate an expression of fairness, the auditor issues an *adverse opinion.* When the scope of his examination is insufficient to form an opinion, he issues either a *disclaimer,* or in limited cases, a *negative assurance.*[17] When the auditor has satisfied himself as to the fairness of the financial statements, and has done so without qualification, he issues an *unqualified* opinion for which the accounting profession has adopted a standard format:[18]

[16]The exception to this general rule is Regulation S-X of the SEC, which requires the auditor to report the financial effects of any change in accounting procedures having a material effect on comparability.

[17]Negative assurances *do not constitute an opinion* on the fairness of the financial statements as a whole, but rather they state that the auditor is unaware of any information which would negate the amounts in question. Usually such assurances have very limited circulation.

[18]*Auditing Standards and Procedures,* Statement no. 33, p. 57.

We have examined the balance sheet of X Company as of June 30, 19__ and related statement(s) of income and retained earnings for the year then ended. Our examination was made in accordance with generally accepted auditing standards, and accordingly included such tests of the accounting records and such other auditing procedures as we considered necessary in the circumstances.

In our opinion, the accompanying balance sheet and statement(s) of income and retained earnings present fairly the financial position of X Company at June 30, 19__, and the results of its operations for the year then ended, in conformity with generally accepted accounting principles applied on a basis consistent with that of the preceding year.

27.13 SUMMARY

The objectives of auditing are twofold: to express an opinion of the fairness of the financial statements taken as a whole, and to make suggestions for improving the accounting system. These objectives are achieved by performing the six audit tasks of obtaining an understanding of the company's accounting system, documenting this understanding, testing the understanding, evaluating the internal control and feedback, deciding upon the tests needed to check the validity of account balances, and performing the tests on account balances. The tasks are summarized into two audit functions—*evaluation* and *validation.* The outcome of evaluation is the management letter on accounting system design, and the outcome of validation is the expression of an opinion on the financial statements.

Testing the understanding of the documented system is called *procedural testing.* One part of this testing involves tracing sample transactions from inception to termination in the accounts, and is thus used as a test of proper linkage of functions. The other part of procedural testing—*functional testing*—checks for compliance and workability of functions having an accounting significance. When EDP functions are involved, procedural testing is accomplished by using test decks or auditor's programs.

From the results of procedural testing, the auditor confirms his understanding of the system and can then evaluate the extent and suitability of internal control functions. Generally, internal control questionnaires are used as an evaluative tool.

The auditor is now in a position to make substantive comments to management on system design, and also to formulate the extent and type of tests necessary to validate account balances.

Validation testing focuses upon residual items in an account balance rather than flow-through items, and is therefore a balance sheet approach. This approach yields substantial time savings and provides a high degree of assurance over both balance sheet and income statements.

The auditor attempts to substantiate a majority of the dollar value in each account tested. This validation activity enables the auditor to formulate an opinion on the financial statements taken as a whole.

CHAPTER 27 APPENDIX A

EXCERPTS FROM AN INTERNAL CONTROL QUESTIONNAIRE FOR PURCHASING ACTIVITY

Yes	No	
		Purchase Orders:
		1. Are purchase orders, including any firm commitments, listed in detail showing vendors' names, quantities, and prices? (Purchase requisitions, *retained copies of purchase orders,* or listings in purchase books or elsewhere, provide a means of controlling both the disposition of purchase orders and the recording of purchases by the use of detailed listings to check against subsequent steps in completing transaction.)
		2. Are such orders under numerical control?
		Receiving Reports:
		3. Are receiving reports listed in detail, showing vendors' names and quantities? (This listing may consist of a materials received book, *copies of receiving reports or purchase orders,* or copies of receipts issued. When necessary, receiving reports should be supplemented by inspection reports.)
		4. Are such reports under numerical control?
		5. Are unmatched receiving reports reviewed periodically? (Internal accounting control over accounts payable requires that open [unmatched] receiving reports be investigated. The receipt of merchandise represented by an unmatched receiving report may indicate an unrecorded liability or the payment of an invoice which has not been properly processed. A delay in matching receiving reports to invoices often results in unreliable inventory accounts.)
		6. On receipt of *vendors' invoices* is a detailed listing made showing: a. Vendor's name? b. Amount of invoice? c. Disposition of invoice? (Control over accounts payable may be established at the time vendors' invoices are received by recording invoices in a register or by maintaining an *invoice file.* Frequently the amounts of such invoices are entered in the accounts as "Unaudited Vouchers.")
		7. Are unprocessed invoices reviewed periodically?
		Processing Invoices and Substitute Documents:
		8. Do invoices, substitute documents or appropriate attachments indicate that the following work has been performed? a. Comparison with purchase orders? b. Comparison with receiving reports? c. Verification of extensions, discounts, and footing? d. Investigation and correction of differences?
		9. Does a responsible person indicate on the invoice, substitute document, or attachments his: a. Approval of the accounting distribution of invoices? b. Approval of the invoices for payment?

Yes	No	
		10. Are processed invoices (vouchers) listed in detail showing names and amounts? (This listing may be made in a purchase journal, a *voucher register,* or in a cash disbursement record.)
		11. Is the total of unpaid items in the voucher register reconciled periodically with the general ledger accounts payable control? (The unpaid items may be indicated in various ways; frequently, paid items are identified by insertion of dates of payment or check numbers.)
		Purchase Orders:
		12. Are purchase order personnel independent of: a. Processing of invoices? b. Cash disbursements functions? c. Receiving functions?
		Receiving Reports:
		13. Are receiving personnel independent of: a. Processing of invoices? b. Cash disbursements functions? c. Purchasing functions?
		Vendors' Invoices:
		14. Is the detailed listing of vendors' invoices prepared by persons independent of: a. Receiving functions? b. Purchasing functions?
		Processing Invoices and Substitute Documents:
		15. Are invoices or substitute documents compared with purchase orders or receiving reports by persons independent of: a. Purchasing functions? b. Receiving functions?
		16. Is the detailed listing of processed invoices (vouchers) prepared by persons independent of: a. Purchasing functions? b. Receiving functions? c. Cash disbursements functions? d. Posting of general ledger accounts?
		17. Are unpaid items in the voucher register compared with the general ledger control by an employee independent of those who: a. Record cash disbursements? b. Process invoices or substitute documents?

SOURCE: Lybrand, Ross Bros. & Montgomery, B-1 Internal Control Questionnaire. Used with permission.

CHAPTER 27 APPENDIX B

EXCERPTS FROM AN EDP INTERNAL CONTROL QUESTIONNAIRE

Yes	No	
		Organizational Controls
		1. Are the functions of systems analysis and computer programming independent of machine operations, so the programmers are not permitted access to the computer equipment during production, *and* computer operators are not given access to program documentation?
		2. Are employees within the systems and data processing areas separated from all duties relating to the initiation of transactions and the initiation of changes to the master files?
		Source/User Controls
		3. Are control totals for transactions predetermined and subsequently reconciled to totals of records and reports produced by the EDP system, by persons independent of the data processing function? For each transaction file the auditor should indicate (by an "X") the control technique used and the name of the data field(s) to which each technique is applied.

Name of File:	Name of Data Field:	Dollar and/or Quantity Totals	Hash Totals	Other Data Field Control Technique (Describe)	File Document /Item or Record Count?

Yes	No	
		4. Similarly, are control totals for master file changes predetermined and subsequently reconciled to master file totals by persons independent of the data processing function? For each master file, the auditor should indicate (by an "X") the control technique used, and the name of the data field(s) to which each technique is applied.

Name of File:	Name of Data Field:	Dollar and/or Quantity Totals	Hash Totals	Other Data Field Control Technique (Describe)	File Document /Item or Record Count?

Yes	No	
		5. Where important changes to master file data (such as pay rates, selling prices) are processed by computer, is a printed register prepared which lists the changes for review by persons independent of the data processing function?

Yes	No	
		6. Are persons independent of the data processing function responsible for seeing that data rejected from the EDP system is reviewed, corrected, and reentered in timely fashion? Describe the procedure.
		Data Conversion Controls 7. Are all data fields which have accounting significance verified by an individual other than the original operator? For each converted file, identify the verification technique used with the name of the data fields verified.
		Documentation Controls 8. Are program changes, including the effective dates of changes, subject to review and approval prior to implementation?
		9. Are machine operations logs maintained for all processing? (Machine logs should include operator identification, run identification, start and stop time, error halts and delays, and details of reruns. The log should include written explanations for all processing errors, reruns, and unusual operator interventions. These machine logs should be examined periodically by a supervisory person, and should be signed off to reflect this review.)

Verification table for item 7:

Name of File:	Name of Data Field:	Mechanical (Re-keyed)	Sight (Proofread)	Other (Describe)

(Columns "Mechanical (Re-keyed)", "Sight (Proofread)" and "Other (Describe)" are under the heading **Verification Technique**.)

SOURCE: Lybrand, Ross Bros. & Montgomery, *Staff Course II,* Module 2—EDP Applications, 1971. Used with permission.

CHAPTER 27 REFERENCES AND ADDITIONAL READINGS

AUDITING STANDARDS, ETHICS, LEGAL LIABILITY, AND GENERAL REFERENCES

Armstrong, Marshall S. "Some Thoughts on Substantial Authoritative Support." *The Journal of Accountancy,* April 1969, pp. 44–50.

Carey, John L., and Doherty, William O. *Ethical Standards of the Accounting Profession.* New York: American Institute of Certified Public Accountants, 1966.

Cerf, Alan R. *Professional Responsibility of Certified Public Accountants.* Palo Alto, Calif.: California Certified Public Accountants Foundation for Education and Research, 1970.

Committee on Auditing Procedure. *Auditing Standards and Procedures.* Statement on Auditing Procedures No. 33. New York: American Institute of Certified Public Accountants, 1963.

Holmes, Arthur W., and Overmyer, Waynes S. *Auditing: Principles and Procedures.* Homewood, Ill.: Richard D. Irwin, Inc., 1971.

Imke, Frank J. "The Future of the Attest Function." *The Journal of Accountancy,* April 1967, pp. 51–58.

Lawrence, Charles. *Auditing Methods.* Belmont, Calif.: Wadsworth Publishing Company, 1967.

Lenhart, Norman J., and Defliese, Philip L. *Montgomery's Auditing.* New York: The Ronald Press Company, 1957.

Mautz, R. K., and Sharaf, Hussein A. *The Philosophy of Auditing.* Sarasota, Fla.: American Accounting Association, 1961.

Meigs, Walter, and Larsen, E. John. *Principles of Auditing.* Homewood, Ill.: Richard D. Irwin, Inc., 1969.

Porter, W. Thomas, and Burton, John C. *Auditing: A Conceptual Approach.* Belmont, Calif.: Wadsworth Publishing Company, 1971.

Stettler, Howard F. *Systems Based Independent Audits.* Englewood Cliffs, N. J.: Prentice-Hall, Inc., 1967.

Willingham, John J., and Carmichael, D. R. *Auditing Concepts and Methods.* New York: McGraw-Hill Book Company, 1971.

AUDITING AND THE COMPUTER

Bates, Robert E. "Auditing the Advanced Computer Systems." *Management Accounting,* June 1970, pp. 34–37.

Boutell, Wayne S. *Auditing with the Computer.* Berkeley, Calif.: University of California Press, 1965.

Brown, Harry L. *EDP for Auditors.* New York: John Wiley & Sons, Inc., 1968.

Davis, Gordon B. *Auditing and EDP.* New York: American Institute of Certified Public Accountants, 1968.

Horwitz, Geoffrey B. "EDP Auditing—The Coming of Age." *Journal of Accountancy,* August 1970, pp. 48–56.

Lewis, William F. "Auditing On-Line Computer Systems." *Journal of Accountancy,* October 1971, pp. 47–52.

Lobel, Jerome. "Auditing in the New Systems Environment." *Journal of Accountancy,* September 1971, pp. 63–67.

Moore, Michael R. "EDP Audits: A Systems Approach." *Internal Auditor,* May–June 1969, pp. 9–25.

Porter, W. Thomas. "Generalized Computer-Audit Programs." *Journal of Accountancy,* January, 1969, pp. 54–62.

Porter, W. Thomas. *Auditing Electronic Systems.* Belmont, Calif.: Wadsworth Publishing Company, 1966.

Stole, Carlton D. "Computer-Based Audits." *Management Adviser,* May–June 1971, pp. 38–43.

Will, H. J. "Computer-Based Auditing." *Canadian Chartered Accountant,* February 1972, pp. 29–34.

Wohl, Gerald, and D'Angelico, Michael. *The Computer in Auditing—The Use of Test Data.* Homewood, Ill.: Richard D. Irwin, Inc., 1968.

STATISTICAL SAMPLING AND OTHER TECHNIQUES

Carmichael, D. R. "Tests of Transactions—Statistical and Otherwise." *Journal of Accountancy,* February 1968, pp. 36–40.

Corbett, P. Graham. "Critical Path for Auditors." *The Accountant* (England), September 13, 1969, pp. 319–25.

Doege, Richard L. "Photogrammetrics in Auditing." *Journal of Accountancy,* April 1972, pp. 60–63.

Kaufman, Stuart F. "Sampling Zero Defects." *Journal of Accountancy,* October 1968, pp. 66–69.

Kirchheimer, Harry W. "Flow Charting—The Modern Method of Evaluating Internal Control and Procedures." *Internal Auditor,* Fall 1967, pp. 46–50.

Professional Development Division, AICPA. *An Auditor's Approach to Statistical Sampling.* Vols. 1–4. New York: American Institute of Certified Public Accountants, 1967.

Sauls, Eugene H. "An Experiment on Nonsampling Errors." *Empirical Research in Accounting: Selected Studies 1970,* Supplement to the Journal of Accounting Research, pp. 157–71.

Stickler, Alan D. "An Appraisal of Flow Charting as an Audit Technique." *Canadian Chartered Accountant*, December 1968, pp. 412–15.

Tracy, John A. "Bayesian Statistical Methods in Auditing." *The Accounting Review*, January 1969, pp. 90–98.

Tracy, John A. "Bayesian Statistical Confidence Intervals for Auditors." *The Journal of Accountancy*, July 1969, pp. 41–47.

Trentin, H. G. "Sampling in Auditing—A Case Study." *Journal of Accountancy*, March 1968, pp. 39–43.

Trueblood, Robert M., and Cyert, Richard M. *Sampling Techniques in Accounting*. Englewood Cliffs, N. J.: Prentice-Hall, Inc., 1957.

Vanasse, Robert W. *Statistical Sampling for Auditing and Accounting Decisions: A Simulation*. New York: McGraw-Hill Book Company, 1968.

OPERATIONAL AUDITING

Boe, Edmund S., and Doppelt, Neil. "Operational Auditing and the Management Letter." *Journal of Accountancy*, August 1, 1971, pp. 80–82.

Buckley, John W. "Operational Audits by Public Accountants." *Abacus* (Australia), December 1966, pp. 159–71.

Cadmus, Bradford. *Operational Auditing Handbook*. New York: The Institute of Internal Auditors, 1964.

Dodwell, Joseph W. "Operational Auditing: A Part of the Basic Audit." *Journal of Accountancy*, June 1966, pp. 31–39.

Morse, Ellsworth H. "Performance and Operational Auditing." *Journal of Accountancy*, June 1971, pp. 41–46.

Norgaard, Corine T. "Extending the Boundaries of the Attest Function." *The Accounting Review*, July 1972, pp. 433–42.

Norgaard, Corine T. "Operational Auditing: A Part of the Control Process." *Management Accounting*, March 1972, pp. 25–28.

Norgaard, Corine T. "The Professional Accountant's View of Operational Auditing." *Journal of Accountancy*, December 1969, pp. 45–48.

Operational Auditing for Management. New York: American Management Association, Inc., 1969.

Shenkir, William G. "A Paradigm for Operational Accounting." *Federal Accountant*, March 1971, pp. 106–111.

CHAPTER 27 QUESTIONS, PROBLEMS, AND CASES

27- 1. Differentiate and briefly explain the six audit tasks.

27- 2. Define *effectiveness* and *reliability* as they relate to the audit of accounting information systems.

27- 3. What are the two broad objectives of auditing? Should these objectives be expanded? What proposals can you suggest?

27- 4. What purposes are served by the attest function of the accountant? Are the benefits of auditing sufficient to justify the effort expended?

27- 5. Define or explain the use of the following terms and phrases:
- (a) Attest function
- (b) Due professional care
- (c) "Audit trail"
- (d) Test deck
- (e) Bona fide testing

27- 6. An audit satisfaction of the fairness of financial statements can be obtained by validation tests emphasizing a substantiation of balance sheet accounts at the beginning and end of the audit period. Explain the rationale behind this balance sheet approach.

27- 7. One of the general standards of auditing as prescribed by the AICPA is that "in all matters relating to the assignment an independence in mental attitude is to be maintained by the auditor or auditors." Explain what is meant by an independence of mental attitude. How is it achieved? How does this independence reflect on the auditor's obligation to the company being audited and to the users of financial statements?

27- 8. One of the standards of field work as prescribed by the AICPA is that "there is to be proper study and evaluation of the existing internal control as a basis for reliance thereon and for the determination of the resultant extent of the tests to which auditing procedures are to be restricted." How does an auditor determine the propriety of his study and evaluation of internal control? On the basis of such study, how does the auditor determine the extent of his validation work?

27- 9. What are the qualities of control and feedback systems that enable the auditor to use them in evaluating the effectiveness of operations? Explain each.

27-10. As a reasonable basis for an opinion on the financial statements, the auditor must obtain sufficient competent evidential matter. What constitutes sufficient competent evidential matter? What documentation and supporting write-up does the auditor prepare for such evidential matter? Is the auditor required to prepare audit working papers and other documentations to give evidence of audit activity? Give reasons for your answer.

27-11. What responsibility does the auditor assume for subsequent financial losses to persons using audited financial statements to make operating or investment decisions?

27-12. What role does the auditor have in helping management set or evaluate goals?

27-13. Explain the function of test data decks when testing through the computer. What are four possible testing arrangements? What are the difficulties of each? Which arrangement is most preferable? Why?

27-14. What are the three broad categories of auditing standards as defined by the AICPA? What are the auditing standards as suggested by a survey approach based on the tenants of scientific observation? Do the standards differ in substance? In what ways?

27-15. "It is at the process level where we identify *expertness* or *professionalism.*" Discuss.

27-16. Explain what the auditor intends to accomplish during the two audit phases—evaluation and validation.

27-17. Explain what factors of *realization* are important to the auditor.

27-18. When auditing EDP systems, is it necessary to perform functional testing? Why?

27-19. Identify five sources that an auditor could consult to orient himself to a business and its operating environment. What are three sources that an auditor may use to familiarize himself with the *functions* comprising a company's accounting system?

27-20. "Many auditors prepare operational flow charts or use client prepared flow charts as a means of recording their understanding." What are some additional uses of flow charts?

27-21. Once the system is flowcharted, the auditor must then find out if this system is really the one in operation or whether any part or parts are erroneous. What is the procedure for making such determination?

27-22. Identify the sequence steps and objectives of a deductive audit examination:

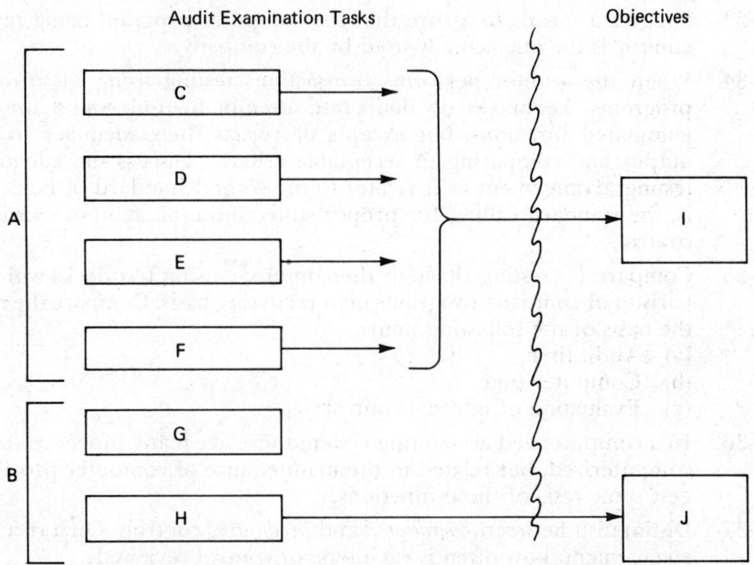

27-23. "Users of financial statements may rely more upon the general impression of a set of financial statements than upon its detailed figures; hence, the auditor, in playing the role of an informed user, should keep his first impressions in mind as he conducts the audit." However, "sole reliance on post-audit impressions can be challenged on the grounds that the auditor's impressions at this point are biased by his audit work, and that he is not looking at the statements from the first-hand limited perspective of the typical user—whose interests he purportedly represents." Evaluate and comment on:
(a) The problem of bias.
(b) The audit opinion regarding detailed financial figures.
(c) The auditor's role as an informed user.

27-24. Transactions testing is a test of the *existence* of internal control procedures, not a test to establish the extent of compliance. Explain the meaning of this statement. How many transactions should be selected for testing?

27-25. Compare transactions and functional testing. What does each testing procedure accomplish?

27-26. Name the five methods of EDP transactions testing. Explain two methods in detail.

27-27. "The auditor's role is essentially that of an evaluator." Explain.

27-28. If procedural testing reveals numerous exceptions, but they are all satisfactorily resolved, should any amendments be made to the auditor's system documentation?

27-29. Transactions testing around the computer places sole reliance on the correspondence between input documents and output records with no testing of automated functions. What are the disadvantages of this testing method?

27-30. When testing the company's computerized functions by a test deck, why do some test data cards contain no intentionally erroneous data?

27-31. From an audit standpoint, what potential compromise is possible when test data is processed along with the client's live data and consequently is recorded on the client's current master file or on a special audit section of the file?

27-32. What audit procedures should be used to evaluate those procedures relating to source data conversion, output control, and control of machine room operations?

27-33. Suggest a means to assure that the computer program being tested by the auditor is the one actually used by the company.

27-34. When the auditor performs transactions testing using his own computer programs, he makes no deliberate attempt to understand the company's automated functions, but excepts or rejects their adequacy by examining output and comparing to acceptable criteria. Discuss the adequacy of this testing arrangement as it relates to the second standard of field work—that is, the standard calling for proper study and evaluation of existing internal control.

27-35. Compare (1) testing through the computer using test decks with (2) a comparison of company programs on a recurring basis. Compare the methods on the basis of the following items:
(a) Audit time
(b) Computer time
(c) Evaluation of internal control

27-36. In a computerized accounting system there are many functions that are noncomputerized, but related to the maintenance of computer processing. Suggest some tests of these functions.

27-37. Distinguish between *operational* and *accounting* controls. On a recurring audit engagement, how often is each type of control reviewed?

27-38. According to the American Institute of Certified Public Accountants, what are the fundamental characteristics of adequate internal control?

27-39. For each of the following areas, describe how the *feedback* system provides management with information:
(a) Control
(b) Exceptions
(c) Comparisons
(d) Interpretations

How is the scope and nature of validation testing related to the existence and quality of an adequate feedback system?

27-40. "Evidence that even the best controls and feedback are in effect does not mean that further audit activity is unnecessary." Discuss.

27-41. "The management letter is perhaps the greatest benefit resulting from an audit, for it contains an independent appraisal of system design, and thus enables management continually to assess the best means of reaching company objectives." In general, what information should the management letter contain?

27-42. What are the assumptions underlying the formulation of validation tests? Why are these assumptions necessary?

27-43. What are the potential hazards of the balance sheet approach to validation testing?

27-44. "There are a number of audit observations which are necessary in determining the propriety of account balances and in determining acceptable form and clarity of financial statements." What are the audit observations that are engendered by the following concepts:
(a) Consistency
(b) Matching
(c) Realization
(d) Integrity
(e) Disclosure
(f) Continuity

27-45. Explain the procedure used for validating balance sheet accounts. Under what circumstances is a biased sample used? Under what circumstances is statistical sampling applicable?

27-46. What are the factors which suggest that statistical sampling has only limited applicability in an audit situation? What is the propriety of auditors using judgmental sampling (biased sample) rather than statistical sampling? Is the use of judgment over statistical assurance a compromise of the third standard of field work calling for sufficient competent evidential matter?

27-47. Briefly describe the validation testing of receivables.

27-48. Distinguish between a *negative* and *positive* confirmation request. Suggest the circumstances under which each may be applicable.

27-49. "When computerized functions process transactions ending in machine-readable files, the auditor can utilize the computer in validating account balances." Describe some tests that the auditor may perform on machine files. Are the validation tests different from those employed in a manual accounting system? What are the two schemes for accomplishing validation testing of machine-readable files? Which scheme is most popular among larger auditing firms? Suggest a reason for its popularity.

27-50. "The worthiness of an opinion, and its influence in financial decisions, rests upon the acknowledged expertise of the auditor and the public confidence engendered by his role as an independent and impartial observer." Discuss the implications of this statement.

27-51. Indicate the degree of responsibility assumed by the auditor for the fairness of a company's financial statements when he issues:
(a) An unqualified opinion
(b) A qualified opinion
(c) An adverse opinion
(d) A disclaimer
(e) A negative assurance

27-52. ***PROCEDURAL AND VALIDATION TESTS*** Your examination of the financial statement of General Department Store, Inc., disclosed the following:

1. The store has 30,000 retail accounts which are billed monthly on a cycle basis. There are twenty billing-cycle divisions of the subsidiary accounts receivable ledger, and accounts are apportioned alphabetically to the divisions.

2. All charge sales tickets, which are pre-numbered, are microfilmed in batches for each day's sales. These sales tickets are then sorted into their respective cycle divisions, and adding machine tapes are prepared to arrive at the total daily sales for each division. The daily totals for the divisions are then combined for comparison with the grand daily total charge sales determined from cash register readings. After the totals are balanced, the daily sales tickets are filed behind the related customer account cards in the respective cycle divisions.

3. Cycle control accounts for each division are maintained by postings of the tapes of daily sales.

4. At the cycle billing date the customers' transactions (sales, remittances, returns, and other adjustments) are posted to the accounts in the individual cycle. The billing machine used automatically accumulates six separate totals: previous balances, purchases, payments, returns, new balances, and overdue balances. After posting, the documents and the customers' statements are microfilmed and then mailed to the customer.

5. Within each division a trial balance of the accounts in the cycle, obtained as a by-product of the posting operation, is compared with the cycle control account.

6. Credit terms for regular accounts require payment within ten days of receipt of the statement. A credit limit of $300 is set for all accounts.

7. Before the statements are mailed they are reviewed to determine which are past due. Accounts are considered past due if the full balance

of the prior month has not been paid. Past due accounts are noted for subsequent collection effort by the credit department.

8. Receipts on account and customer account adjustments are accumulated and posted in a similar manner.

Required:

(a) List the procedural tests and validation tests that you would apply in the audit of the accounts comprising one billing-cycle divison. Confine your audit procedures to the sales tickets and charges to the accounts and to the verification of account balances. Do not discuss the audit of cash receipts or customer account adjustments.

(Adapted from the CPA exam.)

27-53. ***DISCLOSURE AND THE AUDITOR'S OPINION*** Lancaster Electronics produces electronic components for sale to manufacturers of radios, television sets, and phonographic systems. In connection with his examination of Lancaster's financial statements for the year ended December 31, 1970, Don Olds, CPA, completed field work two weeks ago. Mr. Olds now is evaluating the significance of the following items prior to preparing his auditor's report. Except as noted, none of these items have been disclosed in the financial statements or footnotes.

Item 1:

Recently Lancaster interrupted its policy of paying cash dividends quarterly to its stockholders. Dividends were paid regularly through 1969, discontinued for all of 1970 in order to finance equipment for the company's new plant, and resumed in the first quarter of 1971. In the annual report, dividend policy is to be discussed in the president's letter to stockholders.

Item 2:

A ten-year loan agreement, which the company entered into three years ago, provides that dividend payments may not exceed net income earned after taxes subsequent to the date of the agreement. The balance of retained earnings at the date of the loan agreement was $298,000. From that date through December 31, 1970, net income after taxes has totaled $360,000 and cash dividends have totaled $130,000. Based upon this data the staff auditor assigned to this review concluded that there was no retained earnings restriction at December 31, 1970.

Item 3:

The company's new manufacturing plant building, which cost $600,000 and has an estimated life of twenty-five years, is leased from the Sixth National Bank at an annual rental of $100,000. The company is obligated to pay property taxes, insurance, and maintenance. At the conclusion of its ten-year noncancelable lease, the company has the option of purchasing the property for $1. In Lancaster's income statement the rental payment is reported on a separate line.

Item 4:

A major electronics firm has introduced a line of products that will compete directly with Lancaster's primary line, now being produced in the specially designed new plant. Because of manufacturing innovations, the competitor's line will be of comparable quality but priced 50% below Lancaster's line. The competitor announced its new line during the week following completion of field work. Mr. Olds read the announcement in the newspaper and discussed the situation by telephone with Lancaster executives. Lancaster will meet the lower prices, which are high enough to cover variable manufacturing and selling expenses but will permit recovery of only a portion of fixed costs.

Required: For each item (1 to 4) discuss:

(a) Any additional disclosure in the financial statements and footnotes that the CPA should recommend to his client.
(b) The effect of this situation on the CPA's report upon Lancaster's financial statements. For this requirement assume that the client did not make the additional disclosure recommended in part (a).

(From the CPA exam.)

27-54. ***CONSISTENCY—CHANGE IN ACCOUNTING PROCEDURE*** In prior years your client, Noches, Inc., a manufacturing company, has used an accelerated depreciation method for its depreciable assets for both federal income taxes and financial reporting. At the beginning of 1969 the corporation changed to the straight-line method for financial reporting. As a result, depreciation expense for the year was $200,000 less for financial reporting than for income tax reporting, an amount which you consider to be material. The corporation did not use interperiod income tax allocation in 1969. Taxable income for 1969 was $600,000. Assume that the income tax rate was 48% and ignore the tax surcharge and state and local income taxes.

Required:

(a) Financial statement presentation:
    (1) Describe the effect of the accounting change on Noches' 1969 balance sheet, income statement, and statement of changes in financial position. Cite amounts in your answer.
    (2) Explain what disclosure of the accounting change should be made in Noches' 1969 financial statements.
(b) Auditor's report:
    (1) Assuming that the financial statement disclosure is considered to be adequately informative, discuss the effects that the change in depreciation methods should have on the auditor's report.
    (2) Assuming that the financial statement disclosure of the change in depreciation methods is not considered to be adequately informative, discuss the effects on the auditor's report.
    (3) Discuss whether the auditor's report should indicate approval of the change in depreciation methods.
    (4) Discuss the effects on the auditor's report of the failure to use interperiod income tax allocation.

(From the CPA exam.)

27-55. ***VALIDATION TESTING—EDP SYSTEM*** Roger Peters, CPA, has examined the financial statements of the Solt Manufacturing Company for several years and is making preliminary plans for the audit for the year ended June 30, 1972. During this examination Mr. Peters plans to use a set of generalized computer audit programs. Solt's EDP manager has agreed to prepare special tapes of data from company records for the CPA's use with the generalized programs.

The following information is applicable to Mr. Peters' examination of Solt's accounts payable and related procedures:

(a) The formats of pertinent tapes are as follows:

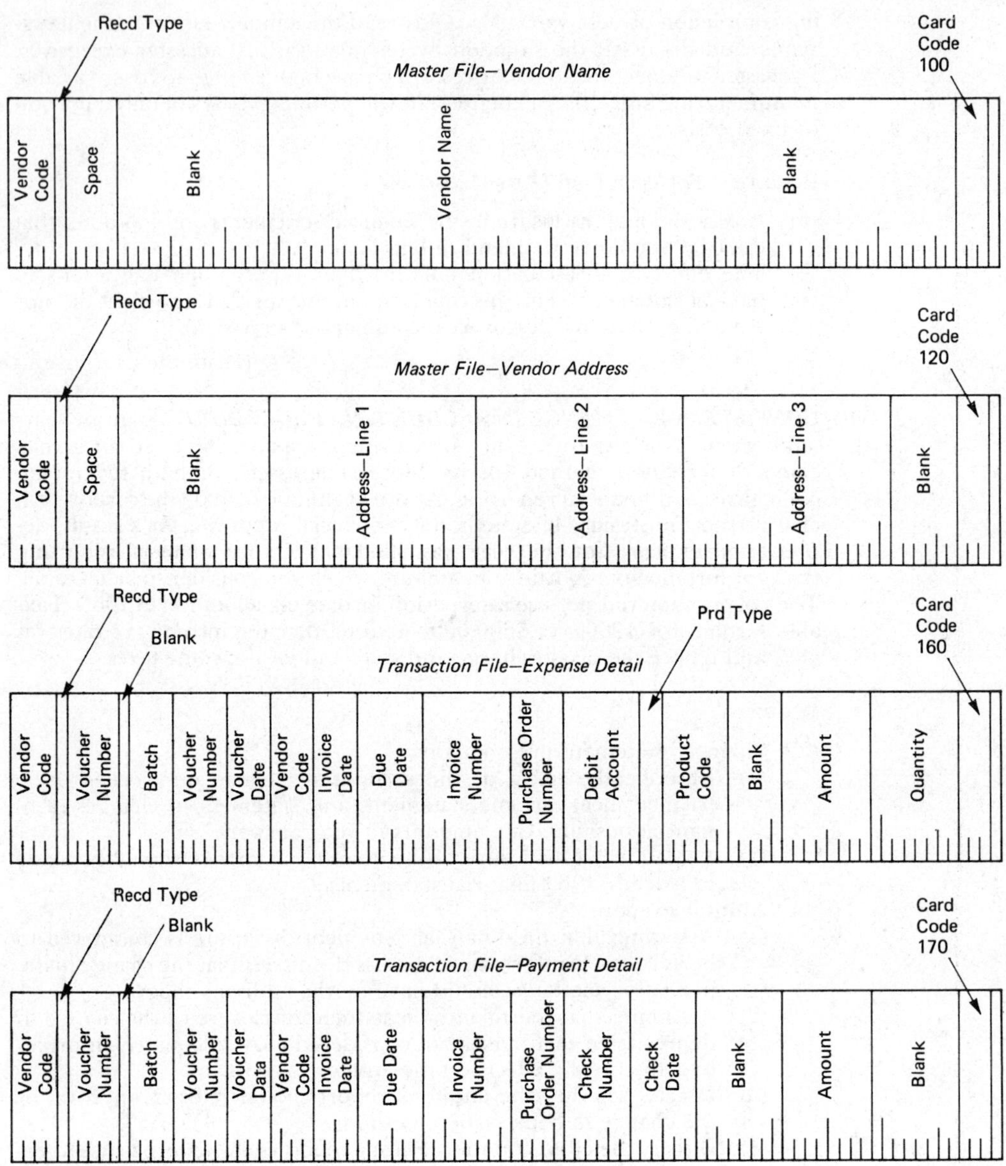

(b) The following monthly runs are prepared:
   (1) Cash disbursements by check number.
   (2) Outstanding payables.
   (3) Purchase journals arranged (a) by account charged and (b) by vendor.

(c) Vouchers and supporting invoices, receiving reports, and purchase order copies are filed by vendor code. Purchase orders and checks are filed numerically.

(d) Company records are maintained on magnetic tapes. All tapes are stored in a restricted area within the computer room. A grandfather-father-son policy is followed for retaining and safeguarding tape files.

Required:

a. By referring to chapter 26;
   1. Explain the grandfather-father-son policy. Describe how files could be reconstructed when this policy is used.
   2. Discuss whether company policies for retaining and safeguarding the tape files provide adequate protection against losses of data.

b. Describe the controls that the CPA should maintain over:
   1. Preparing the special tape.
   2. Processing the special tape with the generalized computer audit programs.

c. Prepare a schedule for the EDP manager outlining the data that should be included on the special tape for the CPA's examination of accounts payable and related procedures. This schedule should show the:
   1. Client tape from which the item should be extracted.
   2. Name of the item of data.

(Adapted from the CPA exam.)

27-56. ***SCHEDULE OF ADJUSTMENTS AND DISCLOSURES*** You have been engaged in an audit of the financial statements of the Hayhurst Company for the year ended March 31, 1971. Field work was completed on May 4, 1971, and you are now preparing a list of potential adjustments and disclosures for the financial statements. To do this, you must evaluate the following points raised in the course of the audit:

1. A review of accounts payable vouchers for April and May 1971 disclosed the following items which were not recorded until April or May and were listed for evaluation as possible unrecorded liabilities:

(a) Voucher 4–07 to Albion Supply Co. for saleable merchandise; f.o.b. destination, shipped March 22, 1971, received March 28; merchandise was included in the physical inventory on March 31—$1,200.

(b) Voucher 4–13 to Skyview Office Management; payment due April 1 for April rental of office space—$450.

(c) Voucher 4–28 to Albion Supply Co. for saleable merchandise; f.o.b. destination, shipped March 26, received April 2; merchandise was not included in physical inventory on March 31—$650.

(d) Voucher 4–81 to Hoosier Equipment Co. for the final payment on a new machine which went into service in late March 1971—$3,450. (Two previous payments of $3,450 each were charged to the property, plant, and equipment account in March.)

(e) Voucher 5–01 to Acme Services for janitorial services in the months of March, April, and May—$1,800.

(f) Voucher 5–06 to Phelps and Cox, Attorneys at Law, for invoice dated May 2 for retainer fee for March and April at $750 per month—$1,500.

2. Cash collections of $144,000 were made during the period April 1 to May 4, 1971, for accounts receivable outstanding as of March 31, 1971.

3. On April 15, 1971, a payment of $17,000 was made to retire currently maturing serial bonds. This amount was recorded on a March accounts payable voucher and included in the balance of accounts payable at March 31, 1971. Serial bonds of $20,000 will mature on April 15, 1972; these have been included among current liabilities for the March 31, 1971, balance sheet.

4. Emory Company, a debtor, filed for bankruptcy on April 5, 1971. Full provision had been made as of March 31, 1971, in estimated uncollectibles for the $2,000 account receivable.

5. As a result of the general economic recovery and a later Easter season, sales of the company's products in April 1971 were $5,500 higher than in April 1970.

6. The company has been informed by the Second National Bank that Gregory Supply Co. failed to pay a $30,000 note due May 1, 1971. Hayhurst had provided an accommodating endorsement for this note. As of May 4, Gregory's financial status was uncertain.

7. The company owes $25,000 on a note payable on demand to the Second National Bank. The note is presented in the March 31, 1971, balance sheet as a current liability, but company officials indicated the note probably would not be called or paid during the year ending March 31, 1972.

8. The company began using an accelerated depreciation method for both income tax and financial reporting on all property additions after April 1, 1971, which meet Internal Revenue Service requirements. Prior to April 1, 1971, only the straight-line method was used.

9. At its April 5, 1971 meeting, the board of directors authorized:

(a) The doubling of plant capacity to be financed by issuing bonds and additional common stock. (Contractual arrangements for a $300,000 building program were concluded on April 26, 1971, and the company plans to expend an additional $400,000 on equipment during the next two years.)

(b) The extension from April 30, 1971, to April 30, 1972, of the maturity date of a $10,000 loan by the company to its president. (The loan has been presented in the balance sheet as a current asset.)

(c) The extension of the company's lease to its primary manufacturing site from its scheduled expiration in 1975 to 1985.

10. March raw materials issue slips of $14,000 were misplaced and not found until after the process costing entries for March had been completed. These slips were then included with the April issues. Raw materials inventory records are maintained on a perpetual basis, and no physical inventory was taken at the end of March. Of the goods manufactured in March using these raw materials, 50% were still in work-in-process and finished goods inventory at March 31, 1971.

11. A $13,000 check for an interbank transfer of company funds was listed in the March 31 bank reconciliations as a deposit in transit to one bank and as an outstanding check to another bank. This check cleared both banks during April.

12. A letter from Phelps and Cox, company attorneys, disclosed the following:

(a) The company is defending itself against a patent infringement suit in which a competitor is seeking $1,000,000 in compensatory damages and an injunction to stop Hayhurst's production and sale of the competing product. The attorneys state in writing that Hayhurst will prevail with no loss to the company. (The $120,000 cost of developing the new product is being written off over a ten-year period ending in fiscal year 1980.)

(b) Legal fees of $6,500 accumulated to March 31, 1971, by Phelps and Cox for defending the patent infringement suit have not been billed to the Hayhurst Company.

(c) The company has been sued for $76,000 by a former executive under an employment contract which had an expiration date of January 1, 1973. The executive's services were terminated on January 1, 1971. The company has offered to settle for $15,000 and expects that this will be accepted by the former executive.

(d) The company has been sued for $200,000 in connection with a personal injury from a February 1969 accident involving one of the company's trucks. The company is fully insured.

(e) An examination of the company's federal income tax returns by revenue agents is in progress for fiscal years 1968, 1969, and 1970. It is believed that all potential deficiencies are fully provided for in the federal income tax liability account.

(f) At March 31, 1971, Phelps and Cox had not been paid the $750 due on the retainer for regular legal services for the month of March.

Unless otherwise noted, no provision has been made for any of the above items in the accounts of the Hayhurst Company to March 31, 1971.

Required:

Prepare a schedule of proposed adjustments and disclosures with the following columnar headings:

(1) Item number
(2) Description
(3) Adjusting journal entries – debit (credit)
  a. Current assets
  b. Other assets
  c. Current liabilities
  d. Other liabilities
  e. Stockholders' equity
  f. Income statement
(4) Footnote disclosure
(5) No further consideration

Complete this schedule of proposed adjustments and disclosures as follows:

(1) If an adjusting journal entry is appropriate, show the effects of this entry in the proper column(s).
(2) If footnote disclosure is advisable, place a check mark in the appropriate column. You should indicate this only if you feel a footnote is necessary for adequate disclosure. Footnote disclosure may be used either as supplementary explanation of an adjustment to the financial statements or when no adjustment is required.
(3) If the item requires no adjusting journal entry or footnote disclosure, place a check mark in the No Further Consideration column.
(4) Formal footnote disclosures and journal entries are not required.

(Adapted from the CPA exam.)

27-57. ***UNRECORDED LIABILITIES*** You were in the final stages of your examination of the financial statements of Ozine Corporation for the year ended December 31, 1967, when you were consulted by the corporation's president, who believes there is no point to your examining the 1968 voucher register and testing data in support of 1968 entries. He stated that: (a) bills pertaining to 1967 which were received too late to be included in the December voucher register were recorded as of the year-end by the corporation by journal entry, (b) the internal auditor made tests after the year-end, and (c) he would furnish you with a letter certifying that there were no unrecorded liabilities.

Required:

(a) Should a CPA's test for unrecorded liabilities be affected by the fact that the client made a journal entry to record 1967 bills which were received late? Explain.
(b) Should a CPA's test for unrecorded liabilities be affected by the fact that a letter is obtained in which a responsible management official certifies that to the best of his knowledge all liabilities have been recorded? Explain.
(c) Should a CPA's test for unrecorded liabilities be eliminated or reduced because of the internal audit tests? Explain.
(d) Assume that the corporation, which handled some government contracts, had no internal auditor but that an auditor for a federal agency

spent three weeks auditing the records and was just completing his work at this time. How would the CPA's unrecorded liability test be affected by the work of the auditor for a federal agency?

(e) What sources in addition to the 1968 voucher register should the CPA consider to locate possible unrecorded liabilities?

(From the CPA exam.)

27-58. ***VALIDATION TESTING*** Terra Land Development Corporation is a closely held family corporation engaged in the business of purchasing large tracts of land, subdividing the tracts, and installing paved streets and utilities. The corporation does not construct buildings for the buyers of the land and does not have any affiliated construction companies. Undeveloped land is usually leased for farming until the corporation is ready to begin developing it.

The corporation finances its land acquisitions by mortgages; the mortgagees require audited financial statements. This is your first audit of the company and you have now begun the examination of the financial statements for the year ended December 31, 1965.

Your preliminary review of the accounts has indicated that the corporation would have had a highly profitable year except that the president and vice president, his son, were reimbursed for exceptionally large travel and entertainment expenses.

Required:

(a) The corporation has three tracts of land in various stages of development. List the validation procedures to be employed in the verification of the physical existence and title to the corporation's three landholdings.

(b) The president of the corporation has asked you if you will prepare a report that will contain only the balance sheet. Before you can reply, he adds that he will remove the income statement from your report before submitting it to the mortgagees if you refuse to prepare a report containing only the balance sheet.

(1) Would generally accepted auditing standards permit the preparation of an auditor's report containing only a balance sheet? Discuss.

(2) What would be your response to the president's threat to remove the income statement from your auditor's report? Discuss.

(Adapted from the CPA exam.)

27-59. ***INTERNAL CONTROL OF CASH—MANAGEMENT LETTER*** Mr. William Green recently acquired the financial controlling interest of Importers and Wholesalers, Inc., importers and distributors of cutlery. In his review of the duties of employees Mr. Green became aware of loose practices in the signing of checks and the operation of the petty cash fund.

You have been engaged as the company's CPA and Mr. Green's first request is that you suggest a system of sound practices for the signing of checks and the operation of the petty cash fund. Mr. Green prefers not to acquire a check-signing machine.

In addition to Mr. Green, who is the company president, the company has twenty employees including four corporate officers. About 200 checks are drawn each month. The petty cash fund has a working balance of about $200 and about $500 is expended by the fund each month.

Required:

Prepare a letter to Mr. Green containing your recommendations for good internal control procedures for:

(a) Signing checks. (Mr. Green is unwilling to be drawn into routine check signing duties. Assume that you decided to recommend two signatures on each check.)

(b) Operation of the petty cash fund. (Where the effect of the control procedure is not evident, give the reason for the procedure.)

(From the CPA exam.)

APPENDIX A

CHART OF ACCOUNTS

The chart of accounts lists general ledger accounts as they appear in financial statements. Following this sequence accounts are numbered systematically, allowing room for additional future items.

The example below illustrates these characteristics using a five-digit numbering system suitable for manual or computerized applications.

BALANCE SHEET

1 xx–xx	Group (assets)
1 11–xx	Major account category (cash)
1 11–10	Explicit account (demand deposit)
2 xx–xx	Liabilities
2 11–xx	Accounts payable
2 11–10	Domestic customers
3 xx–xx	Owners' equity
3 11–xx	Capital stock
3 11–10	Common stock authorized

INCOME STATEMENT

4 xx–xx (and 500)	Gross profit
4 11–xx	Operating income
4 11 10	Sales—Product A
6 xx–xx (and 700)	Operating expenses
6 00–xx	Sales expenses
6 00–10	Supplies
8 xx–xx (and 412)	Non-operating income and expense
8 00–xx	Non-operating expense
8 00–10	Discount allowed
9 xx–xx	Income and franchise taxes
9 00–10	Federal income tax—current year

GENERAL LEDGER CHART OF ACCOUNTS FOR A MANUFACTURING COMPANY

Number	Account Name
111–	Cash on hand and in banks
10	Demand deposits in domestic banks
20	Demand deposits in foreign banks
30	Special bank accounts
40	Cash on hand
50	Petty cash fund
60	Other cash items
112–	Accounts receivable
10	Domestic customers
20	Foreign customers
30	Employees
40	Officers, directors, stockholders
50	Intercompany
60	Accounts receivable factored
113–	Allowance for doubtful accounts
114–	Notes receivable
10	Domestic customers

Number	Account Name
20	Foreign customers
30	Employees
40	Officers, directors, stockholders
50	Intercompany
115–	Marketable securities
10	U.S. government securities
20	State, city, and county securities
30	Affiliated companies
40	Other corporations
50	Miscellaneous
116–	Inventories
10	Materials and supplies
20	Goods in transit
30	Work-in-process
40	Allowance for shrinkage and obsolescence
50	Finished goods
117–	Prepaid Assets
10	Insurance
20	Rent
30	Taxes
118–	Investments
10	U.S. government securities
20	State, city, and county securities
30	Affiliated companies
40	Other corporations
50	Miscellaneous
121–	Land
10	Operating property
20	Future building site
122–	Buildings
10	Manufacturing facilities
20	Administrative facilities
123–	Accumulated depreciation – buildings
10	Manufacturing facilities
20	Administrative facilities
124–	Equipment and machinery
10	Machinery
20	Tools, dies
30	Fixtures
40	Furniture
50	Construction in process
60	Equipment
125–	Accumulated depreciation – equipment and machinery
10	Machinery
20	Tools, dies
30	Fixtures
40	Furniture
50	Construction in process
60	Equipment
126–	Leasehold improvements
10	Manufacturing facilities
20	Administrative facilities
127–	Accumulated depreciation – leasehold improvements
10	Manufacturing facilities
20	Administrative facilities
128–	Automobiles, trucks, and other vehicles
10	Automobiles
20	Trucks
129–	Accumulated depreciation – automobiles, etc.
10	Automobiles
20	Trucks
130–	Intangibles and other assets
10	Patents
20	Organization costs

Number	Account Name
30	Copyrights
40	Franchises
131–	Amortization–intangibles, etc.
10	Patents
20	Organization costs
30	Copyrights
40	Franchises
211–	Accounts payable
10	Domestic suppliers
20	Foreign suppliers
30	Current contracts
40	Union dues
50	Other
212–	Accrued salaries and wages
10	Salaries, administrative
20	Salaries, supervisory
30	Wages, manufacturing
40	Vacation and holiday
50	Accident and health benefits
213–	Accrued payroll taxes
10	Federal withholding
20	F.I.C.A.–employee
30	F.I.C.A.–employer
40	Federal unemployment
50	State disability insurance
60	State unemployment insurance
214–	Accrued other taxes
10	Federal income
20	State franchise
30	State sales and use
40	Real and personal property
50	Licenses
215–	Other current liabilities
10	Accrued interest payable
20	Accrued workmen's compensation
30	Dividends payable
216–	Long-term obligations
10	Notes payable–long-term portion
20	Notes payable–current portion
30	Mortgage payable–long-term portion
40	Mortgage payable–current portion
50	Bonds payable
60	Loans payable–stockholders
217–	Special reserves
311–	Capital stock
10	Common stock authorized
20	Common stock issued at stated value
30	Common stock paid in capital
40	Preferred stock authorized
50	Preferred stock issued
60	Preferred stock paid-in capital
70	Treasury stock
312–	Earned capital
10	Retained earnings
20	Reserve for treasury stock
30	Dividends paid
411–	Operating income
10	Sales–Product A
20	Sales–Product B
30	Sales–Product C
40	Sales allowances–Product A
50	Sales allowances–Product B
60	Sales allowances–Product C
70	Sales discounts taken (lost)

Number	Account Name
80	Miscellaneous income
412–	Non-operating income
10	Interest
20	Rents
30	Dividends
40	Gain (loss) on sale of capital assets
50	Extraordinary gain (loss)
413–	Cost of goods sold
10	Product A
20	Product B
30	Product C
40	Purchase discounts taken (lost)
414–	Variances affecting gross profits—Product A
10	Material prices
20	Direct labor
30	Burden
415–	Variances affecting gross profits—Product B
10	Material prices
20	Direct labor
30	Burden
416–	Variances affecting gross product—Product C
10	Material prices
20	Direct labor
30	Burden
417–	Variances other than cost
10	Sales of waste
20	Defective merchandise allowances
30	Defective merchandise repairs
40	Inventory obsolescence and adjustments
418–	Cost analysis for cost of sales
10	Purchases
20	Labor
30	Transfers
40	Purchase returns
419–	Contra-accounts for 418 and 500 accounts
500–	Production expenses
10	Indirect material
20	Indirect labor
30	Insurance
40	Depreciation
50	Taxes
60	Rent and utilities
70	Freight
80	Printing
90	Research and development
600–	Selling expenses
10	Supplies
20	Salaries
30	Insurance
40	Depreciation
50	Taxes
60	Rent and utilities
70	Postage
80	Advertising
90	Bad debt expense
700–	Administration and general expenses
10	Supplies
20	Salaries
30	Insurance
40	Depreciation
50	Taxes
60	Rent and utilities
70	Postage
80	Contributions

Number	Account Name
90	Service charges
800–	Other expenses
10	Incidental rental expense
20	Interest expense
30	Factor expense
40	Other expenses
900–	Income and franchise taxes
10	Federal income tax, current year
20	Federal income tax, prior years
30	State franchise tax, current year
40	State franchise tax, prior years
50	Foreign income taxes

APPENDIX B

PRESENT VALUE, FUTURE VALUE, AND ANNUITIES

Money has a time value. That is, its value at any moment in time is directly related to the *waiting time* before it is either received or paid out. The value *now* of an amount to be received or paid out in the future is the *present* value. The value in the *future* of an amount to be received or paid out now is the *future value.* Seen on a horizontal scale, the present value is always to the left of a future value. For instance, the present value of $5 (at 4% interest) received six periods from now is $3.95:

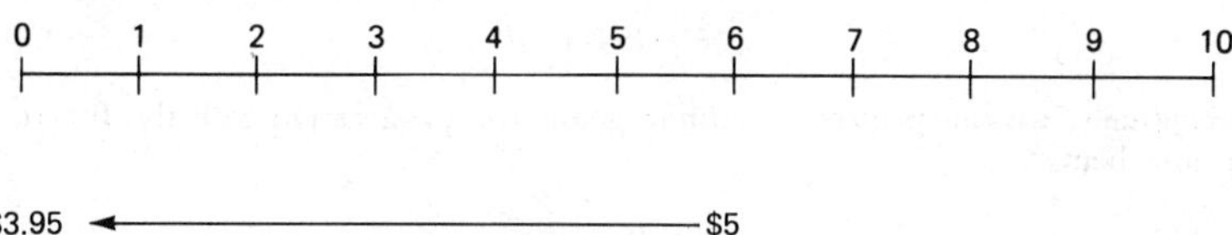

The present value of any future amount could be expressed as a value at any earlier point in time. For instance, the present value at the *end of year 2* of $5 received four periods from this date is $4.27:

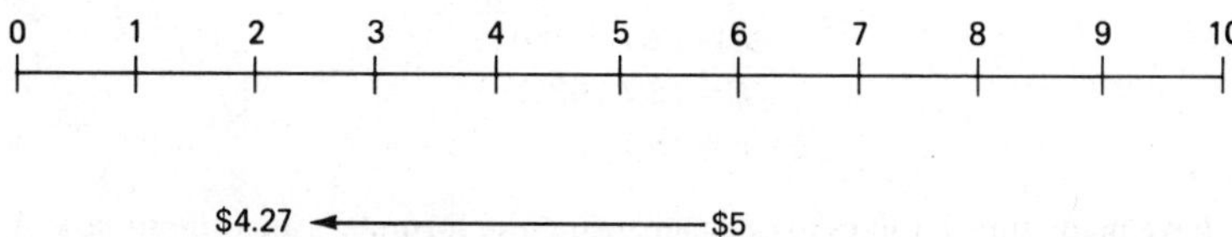

This means, of course, the present value *now* of $4.27 received two periods from now is $3.95. In other words, a future value can be expressed at its present value at any earlier point in time, and thus, this present value can be a future value for any still earlier period:

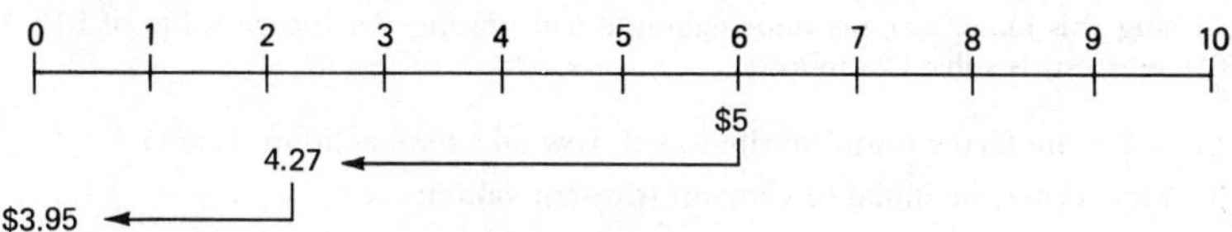

Notice that the future value is always higher than any of its earlier values. If you have to wait six years to receive $5, the present worth of this future receipt is less than $5. We know that $3.95 invested now could accumulate to exactly $5 at an interest rate of 4%. Hence, we should be willing to accept $3.95 now in lieu of receiving $5 six periods from now; or accept $4.27 two years from now in lieu of the future amount.

FUTURE VALUES

The idea or conceptual base behind present value analysis is *compound interest.* That is, an amount invested now accumulates interest from period to period with the investment base each period being the cumulative total. For example, suppose $12 is invested now and earns 6% interest for four periods. The future amount at the end of year 4 is $15.15:

End of Period	**0**	**1**	**2**	**3**	**4**
Old investment base:		12.00	12.72	13.48	14.29
Interest on old base:		.72	.76	.81	.86
New investment base:	12.00	12.72	13.48	14.29	15.15

With this procedure, and using variables in place of actual amounts, we can develop a *general formula* for compound interest:

Suppose

P = initial investment (present value)
r = rate of interest per period
F = future value

Then:

0	1	2	3	4
P	P	$P(1+r)$	$P(1+r)^2$	$P(1+r)^3$
	$r(P)$	$r[P(1+r)]$	$r[P(1+r)^2]$	$r[P(1+r)^3]$
	$P(1+r)$	$P(1+r)^2$	$P(1+r)^3$	$P(1+r)^4$

The future value of P four periods from now at $r\%$ interest is:

$$F = P(1 + r)^4$$

Conceptually, we can project an infinite geometric progression with the future value of P, n periods from now, being:

$$F = P(1 + r)^n$$

Each time we need to formulate a future value, we simply use the formula. Using our \$12 example, the solution is as follows:

$$F = 12(1 + .06)^4$$
$$F = 12(1.2625)$$
$$F = 15.15$$

If we have many future values to calculate, using the formula is an arduous task. A simpler solution is available. Construct a table containing the future values for \$1. Since one dollar is a common money unit, amounts to be taken to the future can simply be treated as many \$1's. In this instance, then, the future value of an amount can be determined by multiplying by the appropriate future value factor from the table.

The factors in Table B-1 are constructed from the future value formula and are based upon \$1 of investment. Using this table, our previous example (calculating the future value of \$12, four periods from now, at 6% interest) is solved as follows:

1. Look for the factor found in the fourth row and sixth column: 1.2625
2. Multiply times the initial investment (present value):

$$F=12(1.2625)$$
$$F=15.15$$

A complete Table B-1 would contain a future value factor for every possible rate of return. However, since such a table would be of impractical size, only a limited number of rates are offered. If needed future value factors are not available in the table, they can be obtained by *linear interpolation.* For example, suppose we wanted the future value of \$16 at the end of five periods at 4.5% interest compounded annually:

1. Find the available future value factors for percentages on both sides of 4.5%

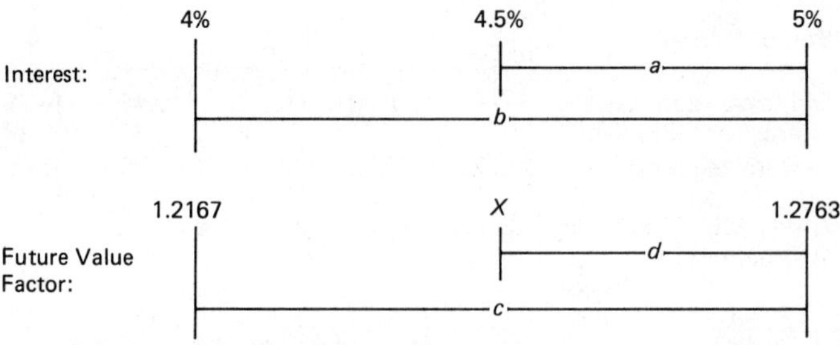

On a scale between 5% and 4%, b represents the total distance. Between 5% and 4.5%, a represents the distance. Consequently, a can be expressed as a fraction of b: a/b. With linear interpolation, this fraction applied against the distance c will yield d. d subtracted from the factor for 5% yields the factor for 4.5%. The answer of 1.2465 is computed as follows:

$$a = 5 - 4.5 = .5 \qquad c = 1.2763 - 1.2167 = .0596$$
$$b = 5 - 4 = 1 \qquad d = 1/2(.0596) = .0298$$
$$a/b = 5/10 = 1/2 \qquad X = 1.2763 - .0298 = \underline{\underline{1.2465}}$$

PRESENT VALUES

The present value of a future amount can be expressed by rearranging our original future value formula:

$$F = P(1 + r)^n$$

$$P = \frac{F}{(1 + r)^n} \quad \text{or} \quad P = F_n(1 + r)^{-n}$$

With this formula we can compute the present value of any amount. For example, the present value of $52 received six years from now at 8% interest is:

$$P = \frac{52}{(1 + .08)^6}$$
$$P = \frac{52}{1.5869}$$
$$P = \$32.77$$

Again, if we have many present value calculations, a table would be helpful. Table B-2 contains the present values of $1. Using this table, the present value of $52 received six years from now at 8% interest is the product of $52 and the appropriate present value factor. In other words, the present value is the sum of the present values of fifty-two separate $1's:

1. Look for the factor found in the sixth row and eighth column: .6302
2. Multiply the future value by this factor:

$$P = 52(.6302)$$
$$P = 32.77$$

Table B-2 is not complete for every possible percentage; hence, linear interpolation should be used whenever factors are unavailable. For example, suppose we use 7.25% interest instead of 8%:

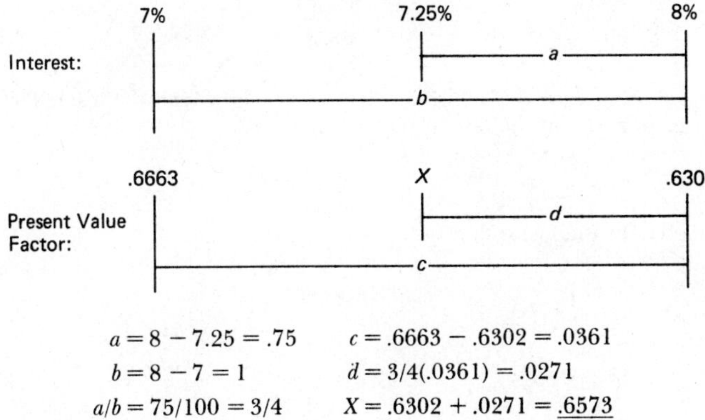

$$a = 8 - 7.25 = .75 \qquad c = .6663 - .6302 = .0361$$
$$b = 8 - 7 = 1 \qquad d = 3/4(.0361) = .0271$$
$$a/b = 75/100 = 3/4 \qquad X = .6302 + .0271 = \underline{\underline{.6573}}$$

The present value factor for 7.25% for six years is ≈ .6573.

COMPREHENSIVE PROBLEM—PRESENT VALUE OF SINGLE PAYMENTS OR RECEIPTS

With the data given, each case is solved for the unknown value:

Case	A	B	C	D
Present value (*P*)	—	$4,172	$620	$1,272
Amount of payment or receipt (*F*)	$510	—	$916	$5,376
Rate (*r*)	7%	8%	—	14%
Time in years (*n*)	5	7	8	—

Case A

Step 1: Locate the factor (f) in Table B-2 for five years at 7%. It is .7130.
Step 2: Multiply the amount of payment (F) by the factor (f) to give P:

$$P = F \times f$$
$$P = \$510 \times .7130$$
$$P = \underline{\underline{\$363.63}}$$

Case B

Step 1: Locate the factor (f) in Table B-2 for seven years at 8%. It is .5835.
Step 2: Divide the present value (P) by the factor (f) to give the future amount (F):

$$P = F \times f$$
$$F = \frac{P}{f}$$
$$F = \frac{\$4,172}{.5835}$$
$$F = \underline{\underline{\$7,149.96}}$$

Case C

Step 1: Solve for the factor (f):

$$P = F \times f$$
$$f = \frac{P}{F}$$
$$f = \frac{\$620}{\$916}$$
$$f = .6768$$

Step 2: Locate the factor .6768 in the eighth row (eight years) of Table B-2. Read the column heading to find the rate of return (r). r is $\underline{\underline{5\%}}$.

Case D

Step 1: Solve for the factor (f):

$$P = F \times f$$
$$f = \frac{P}{F}$$
$$f = \frac{\$1,272}{\$5,376}$$
$$f = .237$$

Step 2: Locate the factor .237 in the 14% column of Table B-2. Read the row heading to find the time (n). The payment or receipt is at the end of eleven years.

ANNUITIES

An annuity is a *fixed* sum of money either paid out or received at the *end of each period* for n successive periods.[1] Calculating the present or future value of an annuity is conceptually the same as calculating the present or future value of many individual amounts and simply adding the results in the present or future.

FUTURE VALUE:

For instance, the *future value of an annuity* for four periods is as follows:

Let a = the amount of the annuity[2]

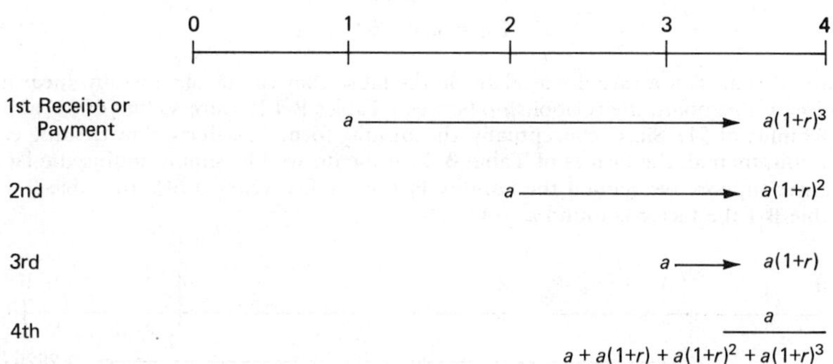

The result is a geometric sequence which we can project into the nth period and obtain a general formula for the future value of an annuity of a:

$$F_n = a + a(1 + r) + a(1 + r)^2 + \cdots + a(1 + r)^{n-1} \quad (1)$$

A simpler form of this general formula is obtained as follows:

Multiply equation (1) by $(1 + r)$:

$$(1 + r)F_n = a(1 + r) + a(1 + r)^2 + a(1 + r)^3 + \cdots + a(1 + r)^n \quad (2)$$

subtract equation (1) from equation (2):

$$(1 + r)F_n - F_n = a(1 + r)^n - a \quad (3)$$

$$F_n(1 + r - 1) = a[(1 + r)^n - 1] \quad (4)$$

$$F_n r = a[(1 + r)^n - 1] \quad (5)$$

$$F_n = \frac{a}{r}[(1 + r)^n - 1] \text{ or } F = A\left[\frac{(1 + r)^n - 1}{r}\right] \quad (6)$$

Using this formula we can obtain the *future value* of any annuity. For example, the future value of an annuity of \$40 for fourteen periods at 6% interest is:

[1] A payment or receipt at the *end* of each period is an *annuity in arrears*, and a payment or receipt at the *beginning* of each period is an *annuity in advance*. All subsequent discussion and table values of this appendix will side with historical convention and assume an annuity in arrears.

[2] Also, $a = A$.

$$F_{14} = \frac{40}{.06}[(1 + .06)^{14} - 1]$$

$$F_{14} = \frac{40}{.06}[2.2609 - 1]$$

$$F_{14} = \$840.60$$

The factors in Table B-3 were computed from the general formula and based on an annuity of \$1. With these factors, then, we can compute future annuity values more easily. For instance, using the same example, the future value of the \$40 is found as follows:

1. Look for the factor found in the fourteenth row and sixth column: 21.0151
2. Multiply the annuity by the factor:

$$F_{14} = 40(21.0151)$$
$$F_{14} = \$840.60$$

Again, if some factors are not available in the table, they can be obtained by linear interpolation.

Notice, at this point, the relationship between Tables B-1 (Future Values of \$1) and B-3 (Future Values of an Annuity of \$1). Since, conceptually, the annuity formula is derived by treating each period as a separate amount, then all the factors of Table B-3 can be derived by simply adding the factors in Table B-1. For instance, suppose we wanted the annuity factor for five years at 6%. In Table B-3 the factor is 5.6371. In Table B-1 the factor is found as follows:

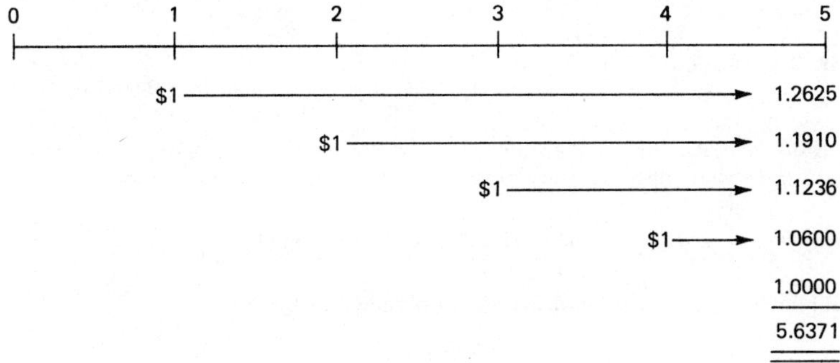

Also, another relationship is apparent. The annuity formula can be solved more easily with the help of Table B-1. The expression $(1 + r)^n$, found in the annuity formula, is the basis for all factors in Table B-1. All we need do, then, is look up the appropriate factor and substitute into the annuity formula, thus greatly simplifying our calculations.

Before leaving the subject of future values, let's examine some variations of annuity problems.

Variation 1: The future value at the *end of eight years* of an annuity of \$15 for four periods at 8% is:

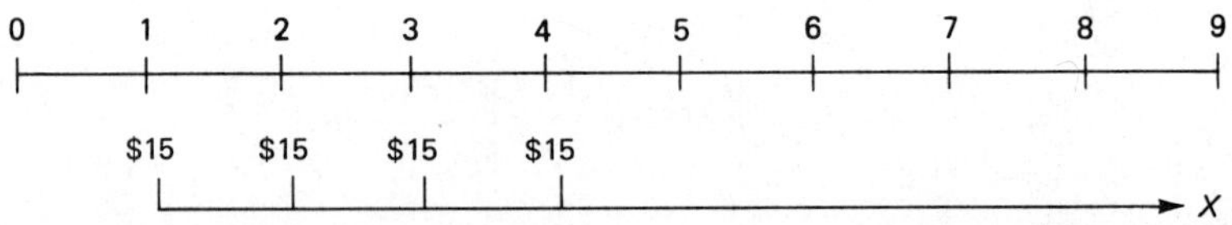

1. Find the future value of the annuity at the end of the fourth period (use Table B-3):

$$F_4 = 15(4.5061)$$
$$F_4 = \$67.5915$$

2. Find the future value of \$67.5915 four years from this date (use Table B-1):

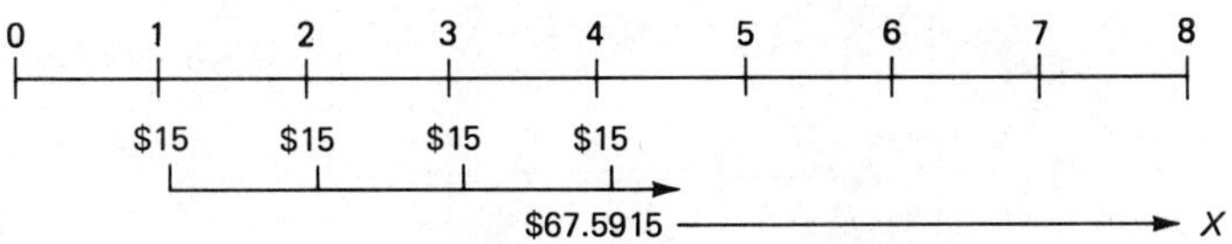

$$F_8 = 67.5915(1.3605)$$
$$F_8 = \$91.96$$

Variation 2: The future value of a four-year annuity of $15 at 8% starting at the end of the fifth year:

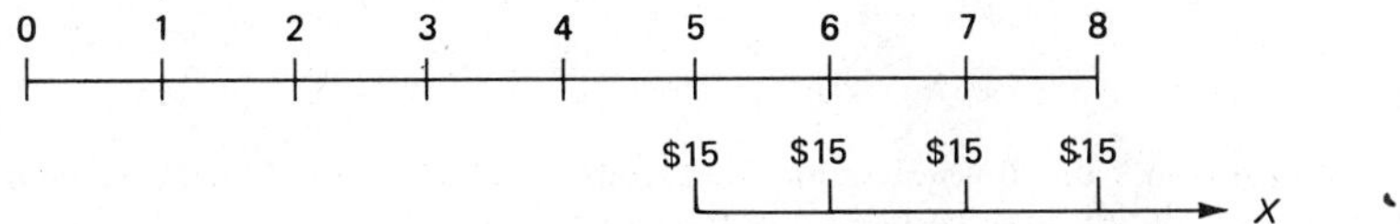

1. Find the future value of a four-year annuity:

$$F_8 = 15(4.5061)$$
$$F_8 = \$67.59$$

PRESENT VALUE:

The conceptual treatment for the *present value of an annuity* is as follows:

	0	1	2	3	4
1st Receipt or Payment	$\frac{a}{(1+r)}$ ←	a			
2nd	$\frac{a}{(1+r)^2}$ ←		a		
3rd	$\frac{a}{(1+r)^3}$ ←			a	
4th	$\frac{a}{(1+r)^4}$ ←				a

$$\frac{a}{(1+r)} + \frac{a}{(1+r)^2} + \frac{a}{(1+r)^3} + \frac{a}{(1+r)^4}$$

Projecting this geometric sequence to the nth period results in a general formula for the present value of an annuity of a:

$$P_n = \frac{a}{(1+r)} + \frac{a}{(1+r)^2} + \cdots + \frac{a}{(1+r)^n} \tag{1}$$

A simpler form of this general formula is obtained as follows:
Multiply equation (1) by $(1+r)$:

$$P_n(1+r) = a + \frac{a}{(1+r)} + \cdots + \frac{a}{(1+r)^{n-1}} \tag{2}$$

subtract equation (1) from equation (2):

$$P_n(1+r) - P_n = a - \frac{a}{(1+r)^n} \tag{3}$$

$$P_n(1+r-1) = a\left[1 - \frac{1}{(1+r)^n}\right] \tag{4}$$

$$P_n r = a\left[1 - \frac{1}{(1+r)^n}\right] \tag{5}$$

$$P_n = \frac{a}{r}\left[1 - \frac{1}{(1+r)^n}\right] \quad \text{or} \quad P_n = A\left[\frac{1-(1+r)^{-n}}{r}\right] \tag{6}$$

With this formula we can obtain the *present value* of any annuity. For example, the present value of an annuity of $70 for eight periods at 10% interest is:

$$P_8 = \frac{70}{.10}\left[1 - \frac{1}{(1+.10)^8}\right]$$

$$P_8 = \frac{70}{.10}[1 - .4665]$$

$$P_8 = \$373.44$$

The factors in Table B-4 were computed from this formula and based on an annuity of $1. With this table, then, the solution to our problem is as follows:

1. Look for the factor found in the eighth row and the 10% column: 5.3349
2. Multiply the annuity by the factor:

$$P_8 = 70(5.3349)$$
$$P_8 = \$373.44$$

Again, if factors are unavailable in the table they can be found by linear interpolation.

From our derivation of an annuity formula, and from the subsequent computation of table values, notice there is a relationship between Tables B-2 (Present Values of $1) and B-4 (Present Values of an Annuity of $1) similar to the relationship between the future value tables. For instance, suppose we wanted the annuity factor for five years at 12%. In Table B-4 the factor is 3.605. From Table B-2 the same factor is found as follows:

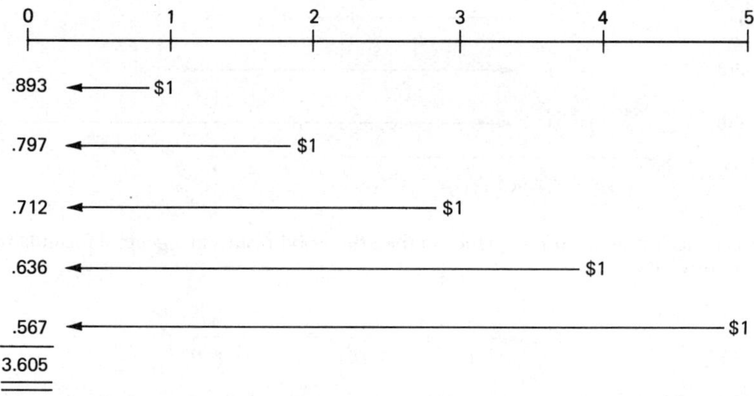

Table B-2 can also be used in conjunction with the annuity formula to simplify calculations. The expression $1/(1+r)^n$, found in the annuity formula, is the basis for all factors in Table B-2. Consequently, the appropriate factor may be substituted into the annuity formula to simplify calculations.

As with future values, an additional insight may be gained from a variation to our standard annuity problem. For example, the present value of an 8% four-year annuity of $38 starting at the end of three years is:

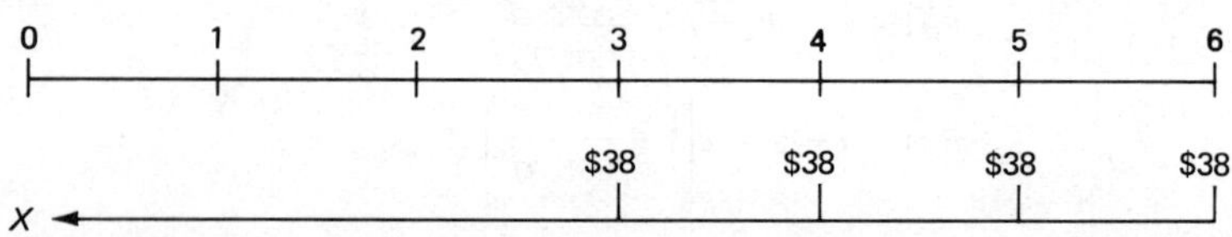

1. Find the present value of the annuity at the beginning of year 3 (end of year 2). Use Table B-4:

$$P_4 = 38(3.312)$$
$$P_4 = \$125.86$$

2. Find the present value of \$125.86 received (or paid out) two years from now (use Table B-2):

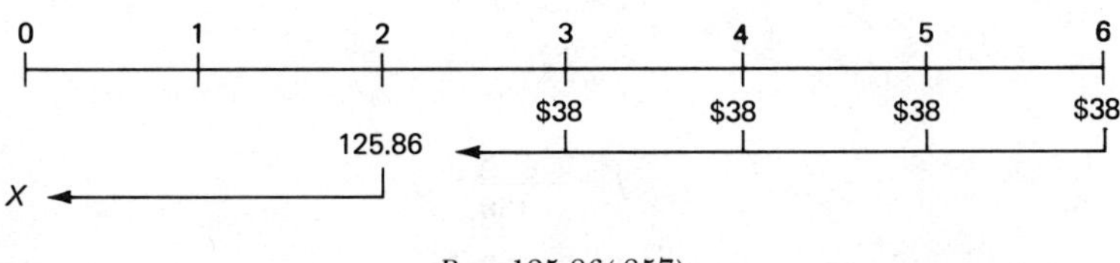

$$P_8 = 125.86(.857)$$
$$P_8 = \$107.86$$

COMPREHENSIVE PROBLEM—PRESENT VALUE OF ANNUITIES

With the data given, each case is solved for the unknown value:

Case	A	B	C	D
Present value (P_n)	—	\$5,170	\$4,676	\$8,978
Amount of annuity (F_n)	\$40	—	\$ 495	\$1,136
Rate (r)	20%	16%	—	8%
Time in years (n)	14	20	16	—

Case A

Step 1: Locate the factor (f) in Table B-4 for fourteen years at 20%. It is 4.6106.
Step 2: Multiply the annuity (F_n) by the factor (f) to give P:

$$P_n = F_n \times f$$
$$P_n = \$40 \times 4.611$$
$$P_n = \underline{\underline{\$184.44}}$$

Case B

Step 1: Locate the factor (f) in Table B-4 for twenty years at 16%. It is 5.929.
Step 2: Divide the present value (P_n) by the factor (f) to give the annuity F_n:

$$P_n = F_n \times f$$
$$F_n = \frac{P_n}{f}$$
$$F_n = \frac{\$5,170}{5.929}$$
$$F_n = \underline{\underline{\$871.99}}$$

Case C

Step 1: Solve for the factor (f):

$$P_n = F_n \times f$$
$$f = \frac{P_n}{F_n}$$
$$f = \frac{\$4,676}{\$495}$$
$$f = 9.4465$$

Step 2: Locate the factor 9.4465 in the sixteenth row (sixteen years) of Table B-4. Read the column heading to find the rate of return (r). r is approximately 7%.

Case D

Step 1: Solve for the factor (f):

$$P_n = F_n \times f$$

$$f = \frac{P_n}{F_n}$$

$$f = \frac{\$8{,}978}{\$1{,}136}$$

$$f = 7.9032$$

Step 2: Locate the factor 7.9032 in the 8% column of Table B-4. Read the row heading to find the time (n). The annuity is for approximately thirteen years.

PRESENT VALUE OF CASH FLOW FROM ACCELERATED DEPRECIATION METHODS

Accelerated depreciation methods produce *uneven* cash flows (from tax effect) over the life of the asset. The standard procedure for calculating the total present value of such flows is to adjust each year's tax effect to the present and obtain a sum. For example, suppose a $3,000 machine is purchased. The machine has a five-year life, no salvage value, and depreciation will be computed using sum-of-the-years'-digits method. The applicable tax rate is 40% and the interest rate is 12%. The present value of the cash flow produced from the tax effect on depreciation is as follows:

$$\text{Fraction denominator} = n\left(\frac{n+1}{2}\right) = 15$$

Year	Fraction		Depreciable Cost		Depreciation		Tax Rate		Tax Effect		P.V. Factor		P.V.
1	5/15	×	$3,000	=	$1000	×	40%	=	$400	×	.893	=	357.2
2	4/15	×	3,000	=	800	×	40%	=	320	×	.797	=	255.0
3	3/15	×	3,000	=	600	×	40%	=	240	×	.712	=	170.9
4	2/15	×	3,000	=	400	×	40%	=	160	×	.636	=	101.6
5	1/15	×	3,000	=	200	×	40%	=	80	×	.567	=	45.4
													930.1

This same calculation can be greatly simplified through the use of tables giving the present value of depreciation charges for $1 of assets depreciated using sum-of-the-years'-digits. Table B-5 is such a table. By using this table, the result of our earlier computation can be obtained more readily:

Present Value of Deprec. Charges = Cost × Table B-5 factor
= 3,000 × .775
= $2,325

Present Value of Tax Effect = P.V. of Deprec. × Tax Rate
= 2,325 × .40
= $930

Table B-6 is a similar table and is used to compute the present value using double-declining balance depreciation. With our same example, both the standard and table methods are as follows:

Standard Method:

Year	Depreciation Rate		Declining Book Value		Depreciation		Tax Rate		Tax Effect		P.V. Factor		P.V.
1	40%	×	$3,000	=	$1,200	×	40%	=	$480	×	.893	=	428.64
2	40%	×	1,800	=	720	×	40%	=	288	×	.797	=	229.54
3	40%	×	1,080	=	432	×	40%	=	172.8	×	.712	=	123.03
4	40%	×	648	=	259.2	×	40%	=	103.68	×	.636	=	65.94
5			388.8	=	388.8*	×	40%	=	155.52	×	.567	=	88.18
													935.33

*Undepreciated cost must be zero at the end of year 5.

Table Method:

Present Value of Deprec. Charges = Cost × Table B-6 factor
= 3,000 × .781
= $2,343

Present Value of Tax Effect = P.V. of Deprec. × Tax Rate
= 2,342.65 × .40
= $937.06

If there had been a salvage value in our example, the depreciable cost (cost less salvage) under sum-of-the-years'-digits method would be multiplied by the table factor. For double-declining balance method, however, the table value would no longer be applicable.

TABLE B-1 FUTURE VALUES OF $1

$$F_n = P(1 + r)^n$$

Periods	2%	2½%	3%	4%	5%	6%	8%	10%
1	1.0200	1.0250	1.0300	1.0400	1.0500	1.0600	1.0800	1.1000
2	1.0404	1.0506	1.0609	1.0816	1.1025	1.1236	1.1664	1.2100
3	1.0612	1.0769	1.0927	1.1249	1.1576	1.1910	1.2597	1.3310
4	1.0824	1.1038	1.1255	1.1699	1.2155	1.2625	1.3605	1.4641
5	1.1041	1.1314	1.1593	1.2167	1.2763	1.3382	1.4693	1.6105
6	1.1262	1.1597	1.1941	1.2653	1.3401	1.4185	1.5869	1.7716
7	1.1487	1.1887	1.2299	1.3159	1.4071	1.5036	1.7138	1.9488
8	1.1717	1.2184	1.2668	1.3686	1.4775	1.5938	1.8509	2.1436
9	1.1951	1.2489	1.3048	1.4233	1.5513	1.6895	1.9990	2.3589
10	1.2190	1.2801	1.3439	1.4802	1.6289	1.7908	2.1589	2.5938
11	1.2434	1.3121	1.3842	1.5395	1.7103	1.8983	2.3316	2.8532
12	1.2682	1.3449	1.4258	1.6010	1.7959	2.0122	2.5182	3.1385
13	1.2936	1.3785	1.4685	1.6651	1.8856	2.1329	2.7196	3.4524
14	1.3195	1.4130	1.5126	1.7317	1.9799	2.2609	2.9372	3.7976
15	1.3459	1.4483	1.5580	1.8009	2.0709	2.3966	3.1722	4.1774
16	1.3728	1.4845	1.6047	1.8730	2.1829	2.5404	3.4259	4.5951
17	1.4002	1.5216	1.6528	1.9479	2.2920	2.6928	3.7000	5.0545
18	1.4282	1.5597	1.7024	2.0258	2.4066	2.8543	3.9960	5.5600
19	1.4568	1.5987	1.7535	2.1068	2.5270	3.0256	4.3157	6.1160
20	1.4859	1.6386	1.8061	2.1911	2.6533	3.2071	4.6610	6.7276
22	1.5460	1.7216	1.9161	2.3699	2.9253	3.6035	5.4365	8.1404
24	1.6084	1.8087	2.0328	2.5633	3.2251	4.0489	6.3412	9.8498
26	1.6734	1.9003	2.1566	2.7725	3.5557	4.5494	7.3964	11.9183
28	1.7410	1.9965	2.2879	2.9987	3.9201	5.1117	8.6271	14.4211
30	1.8114	2.0976	2.4273	3.2434	4.3219	5.7435	10.0627	17.4495
32	1.8845	2.2038	2.5751	3.5081	4.7649	6.4534	11.7371	21.1140
34	1.9607	2.3153	2.7319	3.7943	5.2533	7.2510	13.6901	25.5479
36	2.0399	2.4325	2.8983	4.1039	5.7918	8.1473	15.9682	30.9130
38	2.1223	2.5557	3.0748	4.4388	6.3855	9.1543	18.6253	37.4047
40	2.2080	2.6851	3.2620	4.8010	7.0400	10.2857	21.7245	45.2597
42	2.2972	2.8210	3.4607	5.1928	7.7616	11.5570	25.3395	54.7643
44	2.3901	2.9638	3.6715	5.6165	8.5572	12.9855	29.5560	66.2648
46	2.4866	3.1139	3.8950	6.0748	9.4343	14.5905	34.4741	80.1804
48	2.5871	3.2715	4.1323	6.5705	10.4013	16.3939	40.2106	97.0182
50	2.6916	3.4371	4.3839	7.1067	11.4674	18.4202	46.9016	117.3920
60	3.2810	4.3998	5.8916	10.5196	18.6792	32.9877	101.2571	304.4846

SOURCE: Myron J. Gordon and Gordon Shillinglaw, *Accounting: A Management Approach* (Homewood, Ill.: Richard D. Irwin, Inc., 1964), p. 780. Reprinted with permission.

TABLE B-2 PRESENT VALUES OF $1

$$P = F_n(1 + r)^{-n}$$

Periods (n)	1%	1½%	2%	2½%	3%	3½%	4%	4½%	5%	6%	7%	8%	10%
1	.9901	.9852	.9804	.9756	.9709	.9662	.9615	.9569	.9524	.9434	.9346	.9259	.9091
2	.9803	.9707	.9612	.9518	.9426	.9335	.9246	.9157	.9070	.8900	.8734	.8573	.8264
3	.9706	.9563	.9423	.9286	.9151	.9019	.8890	.8763	.8638	.8396	.8163	.7938	.7513
4	.9610	.9422	.9238	.9060	.8885	.8714	.8548	.8386	.8227	.7921	.7629	.7350	.6830
5	.9515	.9283	.9057	.8839	.8626	.8420	.8219	.8025	.7835	.7473	.7130	.6806	.6209
6	.9420	.9145	.8880	.8623	.8375	.8135	.7903	.7679	.7462	.7050	.6663	.6302	.5645
7	.9327	.9010	.8706	.8413	.8131	.7860	.7599	.7348	.7107	.6651	.6227	.5835	.5132
8	.9235	.8877	.8535	.8207	.7894	.7594	.7307	.7032	.6768	.6274	.5820	.5403	.4665
9	.9143	.8746	.8368	.8007	.7664	.7337	.7026	.6729	.6446	.5919	.5439	.5002	.4241
10	.9053	.8617	.8203	.7812	.7441	.7089	.6756	.6439	.6139	.5584	.5083	.4632	.3855
11	.8963	.8489	.8043	.7621	.7224	.6849	.6496	.6162	.5847	.5268	.4751	.4289	.3505
12	.8874	.8364	.7885	.7436	.7014	.6618	.6246	.5897	.5568	.4970	.4440	.3971	.3186
13	.8787	.8240	.7730	.7254	.6810	.6394	.6006	.5643	.5303	.4688	.4150	.3677	.2897
14	.8700	.8118	.7579	.7077	.6611	.6178	.5775	.5400	.5051	.4423	.3878	.3405	.2633
15	.8613	.7999	.7430	.6905	.6419	.5969	.5553	.5167	.4810	.4173	.3624	.3153	.2394
16	.8528	.7880	.7284	.6736	.6232	.5767	.5339	.4945	.4581	.3936	.3387	.2919	.2176
17	.8444	.7764	.7142	.6572	.6050	.5572	.5134	.4732	.4363	.3714	.3166	.2703	.1978
18	.8360	.7649	.7002	.6412	.5874	.5384	.4936	.4528	.4155	.3503	.2959	.2502	.1799
19	.8277	.7536	.6864	.6255	.5703	.5202	.4746	.4333	.3957	.3305	.2765	.2317	.1635
20	.8195	.7425	.6730	.6103	.5537	.5026	.4564	.4146	.3769	.3118	.2584	.2145	.1486
21	.8114	.7315	.6598	.5954	.5375	.4856	.4388	.3968	.3589	.2942	.2415	.1987	.1351
22	.8034	.7207	.6468	.5809	.5219	.4692	.4220	.3797	.3418	.2775	.2257	.1839	.1228
23	.7954	.7100	.6342	.5667	.5067	.4533	.4057	.3634	.3256	.2618	.2109	.1703	.1117
24	.7876	.6995	.6217	.5529	.4919	.4380	.3901	.3477	.3101	.2470	.1971	.1577	.1051
25	.7798	.6892	.6095	.5394	.4776	.4231	.3751	.3327	.2953	.2330	.1842	.1460	.0923
26	.7720	.6790	.5976	.5262	.4637	.4088	.3607	.3184	.2812	.2198	.1722	.1352	.0839
27	.7644	.6690	.5859	.5134	.4502	.3950	.3468	.3047	.2678	.2074	.1609	.1252	.0763
28	.7568	.6591	.5744	.5009	.4371	.3817	.3335	.2916	.2551	.1956	.1504	.1159	.0693
29	.7493	.6494	.5631	.4887	.4243	.3687	.3207	.2790	.2429	.1846	.1406	.1073	.0630
30	.7419	.6398	.5521	.4767	.4120	.3563	.3083	.2670	.2314	.1741	.1314	.0994	.0573
40	.6717	.5513	.4529	.3724	.3066	.2526	.2083	.1719	.1420	.0972	.0668	.0460	.0221
50	.6080	.4750	.3715	.2909	.2281	.1791	.1407	.1107	.0872	.0543	.0339	.0213	.0085

TABLE B-2 (CONTINUED)

	12%	14%	16%	18%	20%	22%	24%	25%	26%	28%	30%	40%	50%
1	0.893	0.877	0.862	0.847	0.833	0.820	0.806	0.800	0.794	0.781	0.769	0.714	0.667
2	0.797	0.769	0.743	0.718	0.694	0.672	0.650	0.640	0.630	0.610	0.592	0.510	0.444
3	0.712	0.675	0.641	0.609	0.579	0.551	0.524	0.512	0.500	0.477	0.455	0.364	0.296
4	0.636	0.592	0.552	0.516	0.482	0.451	0.423	0.410	0.397	0.373	0.350	0.260	0.198
5	0.567	0.519	0.476	0.437	0.402	0.370	0.341	0.328	0.315	0.291	0.269	0.186	0.132
6	0.507	0.456	0.410	0.370	0.335	0.303	0.275	0.262	0.250	0.227	0.207	0.133	0.088
7	0.452	0.400	0.354	0.314	0.279	0.249	0.222	0.210	0.198	0.178	0.159	0.095	0.059
8	0.404	0.351	0.305	0.266	0.233	0.204	0.179	0.168	0.157	0.139	0.123	0.068	0.039
9	0.361	0.308	0.263	0.225	0.194	0.167	0.144	0.134	0.125	0.108	0.094	0.048	0.026
10	0.322	0.270	0.227	0.191	0.162	0.137	0.116	0.107	0.099	0.085	0.073	0.035	0.017
11	0.287	0.237	0.195	0.162	0.135	0.112	0.094	0.086	0.079	0.066	0.056	0.025	0.012
12	0.257	0.208	0.168	0.137	0.112	0.092	0.076	0.069	0.062	0.052	0.043	0.018	0.008
13	0.229	0.182	0.145	0.116	0.093	0.075	0.061	0.055	0.050	0.040	0.033	0.013	0.005
14	0.205	0.160	0.125	0.099	0.078	0.062	0.049	0.044	0.039	0.032	0.025	0.009	0.003
15	0.183	0.140	0.108	0.084	0.065	0.051	0.040	0.035	0.031	0.025	0.020	0.006	0.002
16	0.163	0.123	0.093	0.071	0.054	0.042	0.032	0.028	0.025	0.019	0.015	0.005	0.002
17	0.146	0.108	0.080	0.060	0.045	0.034	0.026	0.023	0.020	0.015	0.012	0.003	0.001
18	0.130	0.095	0.069	0.051	0.038	0.028	0.021	0.018	0.016	0.012	0.009	0.002	0.001
19	0.116	0.083	0.060	0.043	0.031	0.023	0.017	0.014	0.012	0.009	0.007	0.002	
20	0.104	0.073	0.051	0.037	0.026	0.019	0.014	0.012	0.010	0.007	0.005	0.001	
21	0.093	0.064	0.044	0.031	0.022	0.015	0.011	0.009	0.008	0.006	0.004	0.001	
22	0.083	0.056	0.038	0.026	0.018	0.013	0.009	0.007	0.006	0.004	0.003	0.001	
23	0.074	0.049	0.033	0.022	0.015	0.010	0.007	0.006	0.005	0.003	0.002		
24	0.066	0.043	0.028	0.019	0.013	0.008	0.006	0.005	0.004	0.003	0.002		
25	0.059	0.038	0.024	0.016	0.010	0.007	0.005	0.004	0.003	0.002	0.001		
26	0.053	0.033	0.021	0.014	0.009	0.006	0.004	0.003	0.002	0.002	0.001		
27	0.047	0.029	0.018	0.011	0.007	0.005	0.003	0.002	0.002	0.001	0.001		
28	0.042	0.026	0.016	0.010	0.006	0.004	0.002	0.002	0.002	0.001	0.001		
29	0.037	0.022	0.014	0.008	0.005	0.003	0.002	0.002	0.001	0.001	0.001		
30	0.033	0.020	0.012	0.007	0.004	0.003	0.002	0.001	0.001	0.001			
40	0.011	0.005	0.003	0.001	0.001								
50	0.003	0.001	0.001										

Source: Myron J. Gordon and Gordon Shillinglaw, *Accounting: A Management Approach* (Homewood, Ill.: Richard D. Irwin, Inc., 1964), pp. 782–783. Reprinted with permission.

TABLE B-3 FUTURE VALUES OF AN ANNUITY OF $1 (IN ARREARS)

$$F_n = A\left[\frac{(1+r)^n - 1}{r}\right]$$

Periods	2%	2½%	3%	4%	5%	6%	8%	10%
1	1.0000	1.0000	1.0000	1.0000	1.0000	1.0000	1.0000	1.0000
2	2.0200	2.0250	2.0300	2.0400	2.0500	2.0600	2.0800	2.1000
3	3.0604	3.0756	3.0909	3.1216	3.1525	3.1836	3.2464	3.3100
4	4.1216	4.1525	4.1836	4.2465	4.3101	4.3746	4.5061	4.6410
5	5.2040	5.2563	5.3091	5.4163	5.5256	5.6371	5.8666	6.1051
6	6.3081	6.3877	6.4684	6.6330	6.8019	6.9753	7.3359	7.7156
7	7.4343	7.5474	7.6625	7.8983	8.1420	8.3938	8.9228	9.4872
8	8.5830	8.7361	8.8923	9.2142	9.5491	9.8975	10.6366	11.4360
9	9.7546	9.9545	10.1591	10.5828	11.0266	11.4913	12.4876	13.5796
10	10.9497	11.2034	11.4639	12.0061	12.5779	13.1808	14.4866	15.9376
11	12.1687	12.4835	12.8078	13.4864	14.2068	14.9716	16.6455	18.5314
12	13.4121	13.7956	14.1920	15.0258	15.9171	16.8699	18.9771	21.3846
13	14.6803	15.1404	15.6178	16.6268	17.7130	18.8821	21.4953	24.5231
14	15.9739	16.5190	17.0863	18.2919	19.5986	21.0151	24.2149	27.9755
15	17.2934	17.9319	18.5989	20.0236	21.5786	23.2760	27.1521	31.7731
16	18.6393	19.3802	20.1569	21.8245	23.6575	25.6725	30.3243	35.9503
17	20.0121	20.8647	21.7616	23.6975	25.8404	28.2129	33.7502	40.5456
18	21.4123	22.3863	23.4144	25.6454	28.1324	30.9057	37.4502	45.6001
19	22.8406	23.9460	25.1169	27.6712	30.5390	33.7600	41.4463	51.1601
20	24.2974	25.5447	26.8704	29.7781	33.0660	36.7856	45.7620	57.2761
22	27.2990	28.8629	30.5368	34.2480	38.5052	43.3923	55.4568	71.4041
24	30.4219	32.3490	34.4265	39.0826	44.5020	50.8156	66.7648	88.4989
26	33.6709	36.0117	38.5530	44.3117	51.1135	59.1564	79.9544	109.1835
28	37.0512	39.8598	42.9309	49.9676	58.4026	68.5281	95.3388	134.2119
30	40.5681	43.9027	47.5754	56.0849	66.4388	79.0582	113.2832	164.4962
32	44.2270	48.1503	52.5028	62.7015	75.2988	90.8898	134.2135	201.1402
34	48.0338	52.6129	57.7302	69.8579	85.0670	104.1838	158.6267	245.4796
36	51.9944	57.3014	63.2759	77.5983	95.8363	119.1209	187.1021	299.1302
38	56.1149	62.2273	69.1594	85.9703	107.7095	135.9042	220.3159	364.0475
40	60.4020	67.4026	75.4013	95.0255	120.7998	154.7620	259.0565	442.5974
42	64.8622	72.8398	82.0232	104.8196	135.2318	175.9505	304.2435	537.6428
44	69.5027	78.5523	89.0484	115.4129	151.1430	199.7580	356.9496	652.6478
46	74.3306	84.5540	96.5015	126.8706	168.6852	226.5081	418.4261	791.8039
48	79.3535	90.8596	104.4084	139.2632	188.0254	256.5645	490.1322	960.1827
50	84.5794	97.4843	112.7969	152.6671	209.3480	290.3359	573.7702	1163.9209
60	114.0515	135.9916	163.0534	237.9907	353.5837	533.1282	1253.2133	3034.8470

Note: To convert this table to values of an annuity in advance, take one more period and subtract 1.000.

SOURCE: Myron J. Gordon and Gordon Shillinglaw, *Accounting: A Management Approach* (Homewood, Ill.: Richard D. Irwin, Inc., 1964), p. 781. Reprinted with permission.

TABLE B-4 PRESENT VALUES OF AN ANNUITY OF $1 (IN ARREARS)

$$P_n = A\left[\frac{1-(1+r)^{-n}}{r}\right]$$

Periods (n)	1%	1½%	2%	2½%	3%	3½%	4%	4½%	5%	6%	7%
1......	0.9901	0.9852	0.9804	0.9756	0.9709	0.9662	0.9615	0.9615	0.9524	0.9434	0.9346
2......	1.9704	1.9559	1.9416	1.9274	1.9135	1.8997	1.8861	1.8727	1.8594	1.8334	1.8080
3......	2.9410	2.9122	2.8839	2.8560	2.8286	2.8016	2.7751	2.7490	2.7232	2.6730	2.6243
4......	3.9020	3.8544	3.8077	3.7620	3.7171	3.6731	3.6299	3.5875	3.5460	3.4651	3.3872
5......	4.8534	4.7826	4.7135	4.6458	4.5797	4.5151	4.4518	4.3900	4.3295	4.2124	4.1002
6......	5.7955	5.6972	5.6014	5.5081	5.4172	5.3286	5.2421	5.1579	5.0757	4.9173	4.7665
7......	6.7282	6.5982	6.4720	6.3494	6.2303	6.1145	6.0021	5.8927	5.7864	5.5824	5.3893
8......	7.6517	7.4859	7.3255	7.1701	7.0197	6.8740	6.7327	6.5959	6.4632	6.2098	5.9713
9......	8.5660	8.3605	8.1622	7.9709	7.7861	7.6077	7.4353	7.2688	7.1078	6.8017	6.5152
10......	9.4713	9.2222	8.9826	8.7521	8.5302	8.3166	8.1109	7.9127	7.7217	7.3601	7.0236
11......	10.3676	10.0711	9.7868	9.5142	9.2526	9.0016	8.7605	8.5289	8.3064	7.8869	7.4987
12......	11.2551	10.9075	10.5753	10.2578	9.9540	9.6633	9.3851	9.1186	8.8633	8.3838	7.9427
13......	12.1337	11.7315	11.3484	10.9832	10.6350	10.3027	9.9856	9.6829	9.3936	8.8527	8.3577
14......	13.0037	12.5434	12.1062	11.6909	11.2961	10.9205	10.5631	10.2228	9.8986	9.2950	8.7455
15......	13.8651	13.3432	12.8493	12.3814	11.9379	11.5174	11.1184	10.7395	10.3797	9.7122	9.1079
16......	14.7179	14.1313	13.5777	13.0550	12.5611	12.0941	11.6523	11.2340	10.8378	10.1059	9.4466
17......	15.5623	14.9076	14.2919	13.7122	13.1661	12.6513	12.1657	11.7072	11.2741	10.4773	9.7632
18......	16.3983	15.6726	14.9920	14.3534	13.7535	13.1897	12.6593	12.1600	11.6896	10.8276	10.0591
19......	17.2260	16.4262	15.6785	14.9789	14.3238	13.7098	13.1339	12.5933	12.0853	11.1581	10.3356
20......	18.0456	17.1686	16.3514	15.5892	14.8775	14.2124	13.5903	13.0079	12.4622	11.4699	10.5940
21......	18.8570	17.9001	17.0112	16.1845	15.4150	14.6980	14.0292	13.4047	12.8212	11.7640	10.8355
22......	19.6604	18.6208	17.6580	16.7654	15.9369	15.1671	14.4511	13.7844	13.1630	12.0416	11.0612
23......	20.4558	19.3309	18.2922	17.3321	16.4436	15.6204	14.8568	14.1478	13.4886	12.3034	11.2722
24......	21.2434	10.0304	18.9139	17.8850	16.9355	16.0584	15.2470	14.4955	13.7986	12.5504	11.4693
25......	22.0232	20.7196	19.5235	18.4244	17.4131	16.4815	15.6221	14.8282	14.0939	12.7834	11.6536
26......	22.7952	21.3986	20.1210	18.9506	17.8768	16.8904	15.9828	15.1466	14.3752	13.0032	11.8258
27......	23.5596	22.0676	20.7069	19.4640	18.3270	17.2854	16.3296	15.4513	14.6430	13.2105	11.9867
28......	24.3164	22.7267	21.2813	19.9649	18.7641	17.6670	16.6631	15.7429	14.8981	13.4062	12.1371
29......	25.0658	23.3761	21.8444	20.4535	19.1885	18.0358	16.9837	16.0219	15.1411	13.5907	12.2777
30......	25.8077	24.0158	22.3965	20.9303	19.6004	18.3920	17.2920	16.2889	15.3725	13.7648	12.4090
40......	32.8347	29.9158	27.3555	25.1028	23.1148	21.3551	19.7928	18.4016	17.1591	15.0463	13.3317
50......	39.1961	34.9997	31.4236	28.3623	25.7298	23.4556	21.4822	19.7620	18.2559	15.7619	13.8007

Periods (n)	8%	10%	12%	14%	16%	18%	20%	22%	24%	25%	26%	28%	30%	40%	50%
1......	0.9259	0.9091	0.893	0.877	0.862	0.847	0.833	0.820	0.806	0.800	0.794	0.781	0.769	0.714	0.667
2......	1.7833	1.7355	1.690	1.647	1.605	1.566	1.528	1.492	1.457	1.440	1.424	1.392	1.361	1.224	1.111
3......	2.5771	2.4869	2.402	2.322	2.246	2.174	2.106	2.042	1.981	1.952	1.923	1.868	1.816	1.589	1.407
4......	3.3121	3.1699	3.037	2.914	2.798	2.690	2.589	2.494	2.404	2.362	2.320	2.241	2.166	1.849	1.605
5......	3.9927	3.7908	3.605	3.433	3.274	3.127	2.991	2.864	2.745	2.689	2.635	2.532	2.436	2.035	1.737
6......	4.6229	4.3553	4.111	3.889	3.685	3.498	3.326	3.167	3.020	2.951	2.885	2.759	2.643	2.168	1.824
7......	5.2064	4.8684	4.564	4.288	4.039	3.812	3.605	3.416	3.242	3.161	3.083	2.937	2.802	2.263	1.883
8......	5.7466	5.3349	4.968	4.639	4.344	4.078	3.837	3.619	3.421	3.329	3.241	3.076	2.925	2.331	1.922
9......	6.2469	5.7590	5.328	4.946	4.607	4.303	4.031	3.786	3.566	3.463	3.366	3.184	3.019	2,379	1.948
10......	6.7101	6.1446	5.650	5.216	4.833	4.494	4.192	3.923	3.682	3.571	3.465	3.269	3.092	2.414	1.965
11......	7.1390	6.4951	5.988	5.453	5.029	4.656	4.327	4.035	3.776	3.656	3.544	3.335	3.147	2.438	1.977
12......	7.5361	6.8137	6.194	5.660	5.197	4.793	4.439	4.127	3.851	3.725	3.606	3.387	3.190	2.456	1.985
13......	7.9038	7.1034	6.424	5.842	5.342	4.910	4.533	4.203	3.912	3.780	3.656	3.427	3.223	2.468	1.990
14......	8.2442	7.3667	6.628	6.002	5.468	5.008	4.611	4.265	3.962	3.824	3.695	3.459	3.249	2.477	1.993
15......	8.5595	7.6061	6.811	6.142	5.575	5.092	4.675	4.315	4.001	3.859	3.726	3.483	3.268	2.484	1.995
16......	8.8514	7.8237	6.974	6.265	5.669	5.162	4.730	4.357	4.033	3.887	3.751	3.503	3.283	2.489	1.997
17......	9.1216	8.0216	7.120	6.373	5.749	5.222	4.775	4.391	4.059	3.910	3.771	3.518	3.295	2.492	1.998
18......	9.3719	8.2014	7.250	6.467	5.818	5.273	4.812	4.419	4.080	3.928	3.786	3.529	3.304	2.494	1.999
19......	9.6036	8.3649	7.366	6.550	5.877	5.316	4.844	4.442	4.097	3.942	3.799	3.539	3.311	2.496	1.999
20......	9.8181	8.5136	7.469	6.623	5.929	5.353	4.870	4.460	4.110	3.954	3.808	3.546	3.316	2.497	1.999
21......	10.0168	8.6487	7.562	6.687	5.973	5.384	4.891	4.476	4.121	3.963	3.816	3.551	3.320	2.498	2.000
22......	10.2007	8.7715	7.645	6.743	6.011	5.410	4.909	4.488	4.130	3.970	3.822	3.556	3.323	2.498	2.000
23......	10.3711	8.8832	7.718	6.792	6.044	5.432	4.925	4.499	4.137	3.976	3.827	3.559	3.325	2.499	2.000
24......	10.5288	8.9847	7.784	6.835	6.073	5.451	4.937	4.507	4.143	3.981	3.831	3.562	3.327	2.499	2.000
25......	10.6748	9.0770	7.843	6.873	6.097	5.467	4.948	4.514	4.147	3.985	3.834	3.564	3.329	2.499	2.000
26......	10.8100	9.1609	7.896	6.906	6.118	5.480	4.956	4.520	4.151	3.988	3.837	3.566	3.330	2.500	2.000
27......	10.9352	9.2372	7.943	6.935	6.136	5.492	4.964	4.524	4.154	3.990	3.829	3.567	3.331	2.500	2.000
28......	11.0511	9.3066	7.984	6.961	6.152	5.502	4.970	4.528	4.157	3.992	3.840	3.568	3.331	2.500	2.000
29......	11.1584	9.3696	8.022	6.983	6.166	5.510	4.975	4.531	4.159	3.994	3.841	3.569	3.332	2.500	2.000
30......	11.2578	9.4269	8.055	7.003	6.177	5.517	4.979	4.534	4.160	3.995	3.842	3.569	3.332	2.500	2.000
40......	11.9246	9.7791	8.244	7.105	6.234	5.548	4.997	4.544	4.166	3.999	3.846	3.571	3.333	2.500	2.000
50......	12.2335	9.9148	8.304	7.133	6.246	5.554	4.999	4.545	4.167	4.000	3.846	3.571	3.333	2.500	2.000

Note: To convert this table to values of an annuity in advance, take one less period and add 1.0000.

SOURCE: Myron J. Gordon and Gordon Shillinglaw, *Accounting: A Management Approach* (Homewood, Ill.: Richard D. Irwin, Inc., 1964), pp. 784–785. Reprinted with permission.

TABLE B-5 PRESENT VALUE OF SUM-OF-YEARS' DEPRECIATION*

Years of Useful Life	2%	4%	6%	8%	10%	12%	14%	15%	16%	18%
3	0.968	0.937	0.908	0.881	0.855	0.831	0.808	0.796	0.786	0.765
4	0.961	0.925	0.891	0.860	0.830	0.802	0.776	0.763	0.751	0.728
5	0.955	0.914	0.875	0.839	0.806	0.775	0.746	0.732	0.719	0.694
6	0.949	0.902	0.859	0.820	0.783	0.749	0.718	0.703	0.689	0.662
7	0.943	0.891	0.844	0.801	0.761	0.725	0.692	0.676	0.661	0.633
8	0.937	0.880	0.829	0.782	0.740	0.702	0.667	0.650	0.635	0.605
9	0.931	0.869	0.814	0.765	0.720	0.680	0.643	0.626	0.610	0.580
10	0.925	0.859	0.800	0.748	0.701	0.659	0.621	0.604	0.587	0.556
11	0.919	0.848	0.786	0.731	0.683	0.639	0.600	0.582	0.565	0.534
12	0.913	0.838	0.773	0.715	0.665	0.620	0.581	0.562	0.545	0.513
13	0.907	0.828	0.760	0.700	0.648	0.602	0.562	0.543	0.526	0.494
14	0.902	0.818	0.747	0.685	0.632	0.585	0.544	0.525	0.508	0.476
15	0.896	0.809	0.734	0.671	0.616	0.569	0.527	0.508	0.491	0.459
16	0.891	0.799	0.722	0.657	0.601	0.553	0.511	0.492	0.475	0.443
17	0.885	0.790	0.711	0.644	0.587	0.538	0.496	0.477	0.460	0.428
18	0.880	0.781	0.699	0.631	0.573	0.524	0.482	0.463	0.445	0.413
19	0.874	0.772	0.688	0.618	0.560	0.510	0.468	0.449	0.432	0.400
20	0.869	0.763	0.677	0.606	0.547	0.497	0.455	0.436	0.419	0.387
21	0.863	0.754	0.666	0.594	0.535	0.485	0.443	0.424	0.407	0.376
22	0.858	0.746	0.656	0.583	0.523	0.473	0.431	0.412	0.395	0.364
23	0.853	0.738	0.646	0.572	0.511	0.461	0.419	0.401	0.384	0.354
24	0.848	0.729	0.636	0.561	0.501	0.450	0.409	0.390	0.373	0.344
25	0.843	0.721	0.626	0.551	0.490	0.440	0.398	0.380	0.364	0.334
30	0.818	0.683	0.582	0.504	0.442	0.393	0.353	0.336	0.320	0.293
35	0.794	0.648	0.542	0.463	0.402	0.355	0.317	0.300	0.286	0.260
40	0.771	0.616	0.507	0.428	0.369	0.323	0.287	0.271	0.257	0.233
45	0.749	0.586	0.476	0.397	0.339	0.296	0.261	0.247	0.234	0.212
50	0.728	0.559	0.448	0.370	0.314	0.273	0.240	0.227	0.214	0.194

Years of Useful Life	20%	22%	24%	26%	28%	30%	35%	40%	45%	50%
3	0.745	0.726	0.707	0.690	0.674	0.658	0.621	0.588	0.558	0.531
4	0.706	0.685	0.665	0.646	0.628	0.611	0.572	0.538	0.507	0.479
5	0.670	0.647	0.626	0.606	0.588	0.570	0.530	0.494	0.463	0.435
6	0.637	0.613	0.591	0.571	0.551	0.533	0.492	0.456	0.425	0.398
7	0.606	0.582	0.559	0.538	0.518	0.500	0.458	0.423	0.392	0.366
8	0.578	0.553	0.530	0.508	0.488	0.470	0.429	0.394	0.364	0.338
9	0.552	0.527	0.503	0.482	0.462	0.443	0.402	0.368	0.339	0.313
10	0.528	0.502	0.479	0.457	0.437	0.419	0.378	0.345	0.316	0.292
11	0.506	0.480	0.456	0.435	0.415	0.397	0.357	0.324	0.297	0.273
12	0.485	0.459	0.435	0.414	0.395	0.376	0.338	0.306	0.279	0.257
13	0.465	0.439	0.416	0.395	0.376	0.358	0.320	0.289	0.264	0.242
14	0.447	0.421	0.398	0.377	0.359	0.341	0.304	0.274	0.250	0.229
15	0.430	0.405	0.382	0.361	0.343	0.326	0.290	0.261	0.237	0.217
16	0.414	0.389	0.367	0.346	0.328	0.312	0.277	0.248	0.225	0.206
17	0.400	0.375	0.352	0.333	0.315	0.299	0.264	0.237	0.215	0.196
18	0.386	0.361	0.339	0.320	0.302	0.286	0.253	0.227	0.204	0.187
19	0.373	0.348	0.327	0.308	0.291	0.275	0.243	0.217	0.196	0.179
20	0.360	0.336	0.315	0.297	0.280	0.265	0.233	0.208	0.188	0.171
21	0.349	0.325	0.304	0.286	0.270	0.255	0.224	0.200	0.181	0.165
22	0.338	0.315	0.294	0.276	0.260	0.246	0.216	0.193	0.174	0.158
23	0.327	0.305	0.285	0.267	0.252	0.238	0.209	0.186	0.167	0.152
24	0.318	0.295	0.276	0.259	0.243	0.230	0.201	0.179	0.161	0.147
25	0.308	0.287	0.267	0.250	0.236	0.222	0.195	0.173	0.156	0.142
30	0.269	0.249	0.232	0.216	0.203	0.191	0.167	0.148	0.133	0.120
35	0.238	0.220	0.204	0.190	0.178	0.168	0.146	0.129	0.116	0.105
40	0.213	0.197	0.182	0.170	0.159	0.149	0.129	0.114	0.102	0.093
45	0.193	0.178	0.164	0.153	0.143	0.134	0.116	0.103	0.092	0.083
50	0.176	0.162	0.150	0.139	0.130	0.122	0.106	0.093	0.083	0.075

*The table values are based on the formula $D(n, r) = \sum_{i=1}^{n} \frac{2n(n-i+1)}{n(n+1)(1+r)^i}$.

TABLE B-6 PRESENT VALUE OF DOUBLE DECLINING BALANCE DEPRECIATION*

Years of Useful Life	2%	4%	6%	8%	10%	12%	14%	15%	16%	18%
3	0.972	0.945	0.920	0.896	0.873	0.851	0.831	0.821	0.811	0.792
4	0.964	0.930	0.898	0.868	0.840	0.814	0.789	0.777	0.766	0.744
5	0.956	0.916	0.878	0.843	0.811	0.781	0.753	0.739	0.727	0.702
6	0.948	0.901	0.858	0.819	0.783	0.749	0.718	0.704	0.690	0.663
7	0.941	0.888	0.840	0.796	0.756	0.720	0.687	0.671	0.656	0.628
8	0.934	0.874	0.821	0.774	0.731	0.692	0.657	0.641	0.625	0.596
9	0.926	0.861	0.804	0.753	0.708	0.667	0.630	0.614	0.597	0.567
10	0.919	0.849	0.787	0.733	0.685	0.643	0.605	0.588	0.571	0.541
11	0.907	0.832	0.767	0.711	0.661	0.618	0.579	0.562	0.545	0.514
12	0.905	0.824	0.755	0.696	0.644	0.599	0.559	0.541	0.524	0.493
13	0.898	0.810	0.738	0.676	0.623	0.579	0.538	0.520	0.503	0.472
14	0.891	0.801	0.725	0.661	0.607	0.560	0.520	0.501	0.484	0.453
15	0.882	0.790	0.711	0.644	0.589	0.542	0.501	0.483	0.466	0.435
16	0.878	0.779	0.697	0.630	0.573	0.526	0.485	0.466	0.450	0.419
17	0.871	0.768	0.684	0.615	0.558	0.510	0.469	0.451	0.434	0.404
18	0.865	0.757	0.671	0.601	0.543	0.495	0.454	0.436	0.419	0.389
19	0.858	0.747	0.659	0.587	0.529	0.480	0.440	0.422	0.405	0.376
20	0.852	0.737	0.647	0.574	0.515	0.467	0.427	0.409	0.392	0.363
21	0.846	0.727	0.635	0.562	0.503	0.454	0.414	0.396	0.380	0.352
22	0.839	0.718	0.624	0.550	0.490	0.442	0.402	0.385	0.369	0.341
23	0.833	0.708	0.613	0.538	0.479	0.430	0.391	0.374	0.358	0.330
24	0.827	0.699	0.602	0.527	0.467	0.419	0.380	0.363	0.348	0.320
25	0.821	0.690	0.592	0.516	0.457	0.409	0.370	0.354	0.338	0.311
30	0.792	0.648	0.544	0.468	0.409	0.363	0.327	0.311	0.297	0.272
35	0.765	0.610	0.503	0.427	0.370	0.327	0.293	0.278	0.265	0.242
40	0.739	0.576	0.468	0.393	0.338	0.297	0.265	0.251	0.239	0.218
45	0.715	0.545	0.437	0.364	0.311	0.272	0.242	0.229	0.218	0.198
50	0.692	0.517	0.409	0.338	0.288	0.251	0.223	0.211	0.200	0.182

Years of Useful Life	20%	22%	24%	26%	28%	30%	35%	40%	45%	50%
3	0.774	0.757	0.740	0.725	0.709	0.695	0.661	0.630	0.602	0.576
4	0.723	0.703	0.684	0.666	0.649	0.633	0.596	0.563	0.533	0.506
5	0.679	0.657	0.637	0.617	0.599	0.582	0.543	0.509	0.479	0.452
6	0.638	0.615	0.594	0.574	0.555	0.537	0.497	0.463	0.433	0.406
7	0.603	0.579	0.556	0.536	0.516	0.499	0.459	0.424	0.395	0.369
8	0.570	0.545	0.522	0.501	0.482	0.464	0.425	0.391	0.362	0.338
9	0.540	0.515	0.492	0.472	0.452	0.434	0.395	0.363	0.335	0.311
10	0.513	0.488	0.465	0.444	0.425	0.408	0.370	0.338	0.311	0.288
11	0.487	0.463	0.441	0.420	0.400	0.384	0.346	0.316	0.291	0.269
12	0.466	0.441	0.418	0.398	0.380	0.363	0.327	0.297	0.272	0.252
13	0.444	0.421	0.398	0.378	0.360	0.344	0.308	0.280	0.256	0.236
14	0.426	0.402	0.380	0.360	0.343	0.327	0.293	0.265	0.242	0.223
15	0.408	0.384	0.363	0.344	0.327	0.311	0.278	0.251	0.230	0.211
16	0.392	0.369	0.348	0.329	0.312	0.297	0.265	0.239	0.218	0.201
17	0.377	0.354	0.334	0.315	0.299	0.284	0.253	0.228	0.208	0.191
18	0.363	0.340	0.320	0.303	0.287	0.272	0.242	0.218	0.199	0.182
19	0.350	0.328	0.308	0.291	0.275	0.262	0.232	0.209	0.190	0.174
20	0.338	0.316	0.297	0.280	0.265	0.251	0.223	0.200	0.182	0.167
21	0.327	0.305	0.287	0.270	0.255	0.242	0.215	0.193	0.175	0.160
22	0.316	0.295	0.277	0.261	0.246	0.234	0.207	0.186	0.168	0.154
23	0.306	0.286	0.268	0.252	0.238	0.226	0.199	0.179	0.162	0.148
24	0.297	0.277	0.259	0.244	0.230	0.218	0.193	0.173	0.156	0.143
25	0.288	0.269	0.251	0.236	0.223	0.211	0.186	0.167	0.151	0.138
30	0.251	0.234	0.218	0.205	0.193	0.182	0.160	0.143	0.129	0.118
35	0.223	0.207	0.193	0.180	0.170	0.160	0.140	0.125	0.113	0.103
40	0.200	0.185	0.173	0.161	0.152	0.143	0.125	0.111	0.100	0.091
45	0.182	0.168	0.156	0.146	0.137	0.129	0.113	0.100	0.090	0.082
50	0.167	0.154	0.143	0.133	0.125	0.118	0.103	0.091	0.082	0.074

*The table values are based on the formula: $D(n, r) = \sum_{i=1}^{n} \frac{d_i}{(l + r)^n}$ where $d_i = \begin{cases} (2/n)(l - 2/n)^{i-1} \text{ for } i < K \\ \dfrac{(l - 2/n)^{K-1}}{n + 1 - K} \text{ for } i > K \end{cases}$ and K is the smallest integer $\geq (n/2 + 1)$.

APPENDIX C

COMMON LOGARITHMS

The common logarithm of a number is the exponent to which the base ten is raised to equal the number.[1] For instance, if $10^L = N$, then, L is the logarithm of N; or $L = \log N$. It is this exponential property of logarithms that makes them useful for computation.

Logarithms allow us to perform multiplication by adding logarithms, division by subtracting logarithms, and exponentiation by multiplying logarithms. The computational savings resulting from the use of logarithms only arises, however, because logarithms of numbers are calculated in advance and compiled into tables. If we had to compute the logarithm of each number in a computation, the advantage of using logarithms would be lost. Table C-1 is a table of logarithms for numbers 1 through 1,100.

The logarithms of *integral powers of 10* are integers. For instance, here are some examples:

$$1000 = 10^3 \quad \text{or} \quad \log 1000 = 3$$
$$10 = 10^1 \quad \text{or} \quad \log 10 = 1$$
$$1 = 10^0 \quad \text{or} \quad \log 1 = 0$$
$$.1 = 10^{-1} \quad \text{or} \quad \log .1 = -1$$
$$.001 = 10^{-3} \quad \text{or} \quad \log .001 = -3$$

This means, of course, that the following can be observed about *non-integral powers of 10:*

$$1 < N < 10 \quad \text{or} \quad 0 < \log N < 1$$
$$10 < N < 100 \quad \text{or} \quad 1 < \log N < 2$$

•

•

•

$$.1 < N < 1 \quad \text{or} \quad -1 < \log N < 0$$
$$.01 < N < .1 \quad \text{or} \quad -2 < \log N < -1$$

•

•

•

The logarithms of all these numbers are irrational and are derived by using calculus. Some results are:

$$4 = 10^{.60206} \quad \text{or} \quad \log 4 = .60206$$
$$9 = 10^{.95424} \quad \text{or} \quad \log 9 = .95424$$
$$23 = 10^{1.36173} \quad \text{or} \quad \log 23 = 1.36173$$
$$.23 = 10^{-1.36173} \quad \text{or} \quad \log .23 = -1.36173$$

CHARACTERISTIC AND MANTISSA OF LOGARITHMS

Notice that logarithms in Table C-1 are for numbers expressed in *normalized form.* The logarithm of 9 is read as .95424, and the logarithm of 23 is read as .36173. Our previous calculation, however, indicated the answer for 23 is 1.36173. The logarithm we have read, then, is for 2.3, not 23. In fact all logarithms given in Table C-1 are for numbers from 1 to 10. Any number greater than 10 or less than 1 must be converted to normalized form before a logarithm can be found from the table.

Normalized form merely expresses a number as a product of two numbers. Some examples are: .

---

[1] Another system of logarithms—Natural or Napierian—uses an irrational number (designated as e) for its base. This system is useful for theoretical purposes, but is not as convenient for computations as common logarithms. Hereafter, all reference to logarithms will be understood as common logarithms.

$$12 = 1.2 \times 10^{1}$$
$$124 = 1.24 \times 10^{2}$$
$$26743 = 2.6743 \times 10^{4}$$
$$.434 = 4.34 \times 10^{-1}$$
$$.00434 = 4.34 \times 10^{-3}$$

As can be observed, the decimal point of a number is shifted just to the right of the first nonzero digit counting from the left. The exponent of 10 is the number of places the decimal point is moved. If moved to the right, the exponent is negative; if moved to the left, the exponent is positive. This exponent is the *characteristic* of the logarithm of a number, and incidentally, is itself the logarithm of the integral power of 10 (i.e., $100 = 10^2$ *or* $\log 100 = 2$). For the logarithm of any number the characteristic of the number is added to the logarithm obtained from the table. The logarithm obtained from the table is called the *mantissa.* Mantissas are decimal fractions, but for convenience are printed in the tables without decimal points. Consequently, *none of the leading zeros of a mantissa may be dropped,* otherwise the value will be altered.

Since normalized form represents a number as the product of two factors, the logarithm of such number may be obtained as the *sum* of the logarithm of each factor. For instance:

$$\log 4678 = \log 4.678 + \log 1000$$
$$\log 4678 = .67006 + 3$$

Log 4.678 – the mantissa – is found directly from the table, while log 1000 – the characteristic – being an integral power of 10, is 3 because $10^3 = 1000$. Conceptually, the characteristic is more simply the number of places the decimal point is moved to the left in order to express the number in normalized form.

The mantissa and characteristic of a number are separate. That is, *when a characteristic is negative, it does not mean the mantissa is also negative.* For instance,

$$\log .04678 = .67006 - 2 \neq -1.32994$$
$$\log .04678 = .67006 - 2 = -2.67006$$

A more convenient method of handling this problem is to write *negative characteristics* in an equivalent form as the difference of two positive numbers – one of the numbers being a multiple of 10. For example,

$$-1 = 9 - 10$$
$$-2 = 8 - 10$$
$$-14 = 6 - 20$$

The log of .04678 would now be 8.67006–10.

Demonstrating the use of Table C-1, let's find the logarithm of 6328:

1. Find the entry in row 632 and in column 8. This entry is .80127.
2. Changing 6328 to its normalized form 6.328×10^3 requires moving the decimal point three places to the left, thus the characteristic is 3.
3. The log of 6328 is 3.80127.

The logarithms of some other numbers found in Table C-1 are as follows:

Number	Logarithm	Characteristic	Mantissa
.0783	8.89376–10	−2	.89376
.000843	6.92583–10	−4	.92583
5.6	0.74819	0	.74819
100.4	2.00173	2	.00173

INTERPOLATION TO FIND A LOGARITHM

Table C-1 gives the mantissas for all numbers having no more than four significant digits. If mantissas for larger numbers are desired, they can be obtained through *interpolation* by proportional parts. With this interpolation an increase in a number is thought to cause a proportional increase in its logarithm. For example, suppose we find the logarithm of 7.4326:

1. Find the logarithms for numbers on both sides of 7.4326:

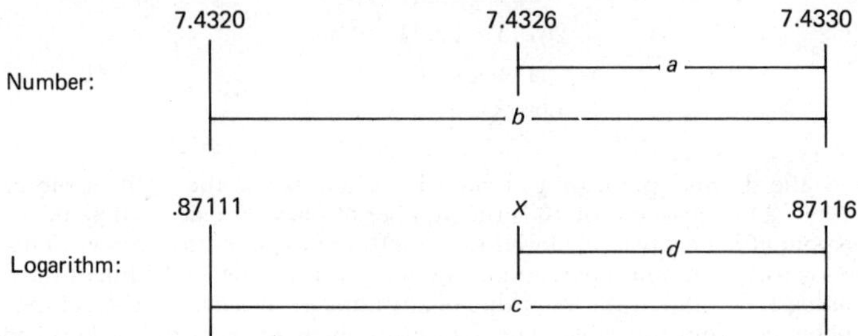

On a scale between 7.4320 and 7.4330, b represents the total distance. Between 7.4320 and 7.4326, a represents the distance. Consequently, a can be expressed as a fraction of b: a/b. With interpolation by proportional parts, this fraction applied against the distance c will yield d. d subtracted from the logarithm of 7.4330 yields the logarithm of 7.4326. The answer .87114 is computed as follows:

$$a = 7.4330 - 7.4326 = .0004 \qquad c = .87116 - .87111 = .00005$$
$$b = 7.4330 - 7.4320 = .0010 \qquad d = 4/10(.00005) = .00002$$
$$a/b = .0004/.0010 = 4/10 \qquad X = .87116 - .00002 = \underline{\underline{.87114}}$$

ANTILOGARITHMS

When computations involve the use of logarithms, the answer will be a logarithm. It will be necessary, then, to find the number corresponding to this logarithm—its *antilogarithm.* Using Table C-1 backwards we can *locate the mantissa* as a table value. Reading outward to the left and top margins, we can locate the sequence of digits representing the number. Next, we position a *decimal point* in the sequence as *determined by the characteristic.* For instance, to find N if $\log N = 2.62767$, we locate the mantissa .62767 in Table C-1. Reading outward to the left and top margins, the number sequence is 4.243. With a characteristic of +2 we locate the decimal point two places to the right of standard position. Therefore, $N = 424.3$.

INTERPOLATION TO FIND AN ANTILOGARITHM

If the antilogarithm of a given mantissa cannot be located in Table C-1, it can be obtained by interpolation. The process is the same as demonstrated for finding logarithms. For example, suppose we locate the antilogarithm of 2.62772:

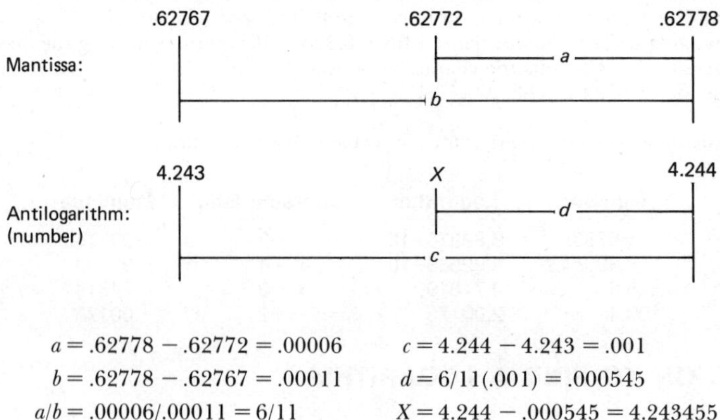

$$a = .62778 - .62772 = .00006 \qquad c = 4.244 - 4.243 = .001$$
$$b = .62778 - .62767 = .00011 \qquad d = 6/11(.001) = .000545$$
$$a/b = .00006/.00011 = 6/11 \qquad X = 4.244 - .000545 = \underline{\underline{4.243455}}$$

Since the logarithm has a characteristic of 2, we locate the decimal point two positions to the right of standard position. The answer, then, is $\underline{\underline{424.3455}}$.

USES OF LOGARITHMS

Use 1: Multiplication

Multiplication of numbers can be accomplished by *adding their corresponding logarithms:*

$$\log uv = \log u + \log v$$

For example, if $A = 768.2 \times 4.876 \times .00701$, the solution by logarithms is as follows:

$$\begin{aligned}
\log A &= \log 768.2 + \log 4.876 + \log .00701 \\
\log A &= 2.88547 + 0.68806 + 7.84572-10 \\
\log A &= 11.41925-10 = 1.41925 \\
A &= \text{antilog}(1.41925) = \underline{\underline{26.2575}}^{*}
\end{aligned}$$

Use 2: Division

Division of numbers can be accomplished by *subtracting their corresponding logarithms:*

$$\log \frac{u}{v} = \log u - \log v$$

For example, if $A = \dfrac{482 \times .072}{5403}$, the solution by logarithms is as follows:

$$\begin{aligned}
\log A &= \log 482 + \log .072 - \log 5403 \\
\log A &= (2.68305) + (8.85733-10) - (3.73263) \\
\log A &= 7.80775-10 \\
A &= \text{antilog}(7.80775-10) = \underline{\underline{.00642314}}
\end{aligned}$$

Use 3: Powers

Raising a number to a power can be accomplished by *multiplying the logarithm of the number by its exponent:*

$$\log u^v = v(\log u)$$

For example, if $A = 471^4$, the solution is as follows:

$$\begin{aligned}
\log A &= 4(\log 471) \\
\log A &= 4(2.67302) \\
\log A &= 10.69208 \\
A &= \text{antilog}(10.69208) = \underline{\underline{49{,}213{,}300{,}000}}
\end{aligned}$$

Use 4: Roots

The root of a number can be found by *dividing the logarithm of the number by the index of the root:*

$$\log \sqrt[v]{u} = \frac{1}{v}(\log u)$$

For example, if $A = \sqrt[6]{7423}$:

$$\begin{aligned}
\log A &= \frac{1}{6}(\log 7423) \\
\log A &= \frac{1}{6}(3.87058) \\
\log A &= .6450967 \\
A &= \text{antilog}(.6450967) = \underline{\underline{4.4164}}
\end{aligned}$$

*Interpolating between 2625 and 2626.

If $A = \sqrt[6]{.0074}$:

$$\log A = \frac{1}{6}(\log .0074)$$

$$\log A = \frac{1}{6}(7.86923-10) = \frac{1}{6}(57.86923-60)^*$$

$$\log A = 9.64487-10$$

$$A = \text{antilog}(9.64487-10) = \underline{\underline{.44144}}$$

The sums and differences of numbers *cannot* be found by the sums and differences of their respective logarithms:

$$\log(u + v) \neq \log u + \log v$$

In computations involving sums and differences, each term is evaluated separately and the results are added or subtracted. For instance, if $A = 47^3 + (115 \times .071)$ the solution is as follows:

$$\begin{aligned} A_1 &= 47^3 \\ \log A_1 &= 3(\log 47) \\ \log A_1 &= 3 \times 1.67210 \\ \log A_1 &= 5.01630 \\ A_1 &= \text{antilog}(5.01630) \\ A_1 &= 103825 \end{aligned}$$

$$\begin{aligned} A_2 &= 115 \times .071 \\ \log A_2 &= \log 115 + \log .071 \\ \log A_2 &= 2.06070 + 8.85126-10 \\ \log A_2 &= 10.91196-10 \\ \log A_2 &= .91196 \\ A_2 &= \text{antilog}(.91196) \\ A_2 &= 8.165 \end{aligned}$$

$$\begin{aligned} A &= A_1 + A_2 \\ A &= 103825 + 8.165 \\ A &= \underline{\underline{103833.165}} \end{aligned}$$

*When dividing a logarithm with a negative characteristic, it should be changed to an equivalent form such that the resulting quotient will contain −10.

TABLE C-1

TABLE I.—Six-place Mantissas

N.	0	1	2	3	4	5	6	7	8	9	D
100	000000	000434	000868	001301	001734	002166	002598	003029	003461	003891	432
1	4321	4751	5181	5609	6038	6466	6894	7321	7748	8174	428
2	8600	9026	9451	9876	010300	010724	011147	011570	011993	012415	424
3	012837	013259	013680	014100	4521	4940	5360	5779	6197	6616	420
4	7033	7451	7868	8284	8700	9116	9532	9947	020361	020775	416
105	021189	021603	022016	022428	022841	023252	023664	024075	4486	4896	412
6	5306	5715	6125	6533	6942	7350	7757	8164	8571	8978	408
7	9384	9789	030195	030600	031004	031408	031812	032216	032619	033021	404
8	033424	033826	4227	4628	5029	5430	5830	6230	6629	7028	400
9	7426	7825	8223	8620	9017	9414	9811	040207	040602	040998	397
110	041393	041787	042182	042576	042969	043362	043755	044148	044540	044932	393
1	5323	5714	6105	6495	6885	7275	7664	8053	8442	8830	390
2	9218	9606	9993	050380	050766	051153	051538	051924	052309	052694	386
3	053078	053463	053846	4230	4613	4996	5378	5760	6142	6524	383
4	6905	7286	7666	8046	8426	8805	9185	9563	9942	060320	379
115	060698	061075	061452	061829	062206	062582	062958	063333	063709	4083	376
6	4458	4832	5206	5580	5953	6326	6699	7071	7443	7815	373
7	8186	8557	8928	9298	9668	070038	070407	070776	071145	071514	370
8	071882	072250	072617	072985	073352	3718	4085	4451	4816	5182	366
9	5547	5912	6276	6640	7004	7368	7731	8094	8457	8819	363
120	079181	079543	079904	080266	080626	080987	081347	081707	082067	082426	360
1	082785	083144	083503	3861	4219	4576	4934	5291	5647	6004	357
2	6360	6716	7071	7426	7781	8136	8490	8845	9198	9552	355
3	9905	090258	090611	090963	091315	091667	092018	092370	092721	093071	352
4	093422	3772	4122	4471	4820	5169	5518	5866	6215	6562	349
125	6910	7257	7604	7951	8298	8644	8990	9335	9681	100026	346
6	100371	100715	101059	101403	101747	102091	102434	102777	103119	3462	343
7	3804	4146	4487	4828	5169	5510	5851	6191	6531	6871	341
8	7210	7549	7888	8227	8565	8903	9241	9579	9916	110253	338
9	110590	110926	111263	111599	111934	112270	112605	112940	113275	3609	335
130	113943	114277	114611	114944	115278	115611	115943	116276	116608	116940	333
1	7271	7603	7934	8265	8595	8926	9256	9586	9915	120245	330
2	120574	120903	121231	121560	121888	122216	122544	122871	123198	3525	328
3	3852	4178	4504	4830	5156	5481	5806	6131	6456	6781	325
4	7105	7429	7753	8076	8399	8722	9045	9368	9690	130012	323
135	130334	130655	130977	131298	131619	131939	132260	132580	132900	3219	321
6	3539	3858	4177	4496	4814	5133	5451	5769	6086	6403	318
7	6721	7037	7354	7671	7987	8303	8618	8934	9249	9564	316
8	9879	140194	140508	140822	141136	141450	141763	142076	142389	142702	314
9	143015	3327	3639	3951	4263	4574	4885	5196	5507	5818	311
140	146128	146438	146748	147058	147367	147676	147985	148294	148603	148911	309
1	9219	9527	9835	150142	150449	150756	151063	151370	151676	151982	307
2	152288	152594	152900	3205	3510	3815	4120	4424	4728	5032	305
3	5336	5640	5943	6246	6549	6852	7154	7457	7759	8061	303
4	8362	8664	8965	9266	9567	9868	160168	160469	160769	161068	301
145	161368	161667	161967	162266	162564	162863	3161	3460	3758	4055	299
6	4353	4650	4947	5244	5541	5838	6134	6430	6726	7022	297
7	7317	7613	7908	8203	8497	8792	9086	9380	9674	9968	295
8	170262	170555	170848	171141	171434	171726	172019	172311	172603	172895	293
9	3186	3478	3769	4060	4351	4641	4932	5222	5512	5802	291
150	176091	176381	176670	176959	177248	177536	177825	178113	178401	178689	289
1	8977	9264	9552	9839	180126	180413	180699	180986	181272	181558	287
2	181844	182129	182415	182700	2985	3270	3555	3839	4123	4407	285
3	4691	4975	5259	5542	5825	6108	6391	6674	6956	7239	283
4	7521	7803	8084	8366	8647	8928	9209	9490	9771	190051	281
155	190332	190612	190892	191171	191451	191730	192010	192289	192567	2846	279
6	3125	3403	3681	3959	4237	4514	4792	5069	5346	5623	278
7	5900	6176	6453	6729	7005	7281	7556	7832	8107	8382	276
8	8657	8932	9206	9481	9755	200029	200303	200577	200850	201124	274
9	201397	201670	201943	202216	202488	2761	3033	3305	3577	3848	272
N.	0	1	2	3	4	5	6	7	8	9	D.

TABLE I.—Six-place Mantissas

N.	0	1	2	3	4	5	6	7	8	9	D.
160	204120	204391	204663	204934	205204	205475	205746	206016	206286	206556	271
1	6826	7096	7365	7634	7904	8173	8441	8710	8979	9247	269
2	9515	9783	210051	210319	210586	210853	211121	211388	211654	211921	267
3	212188	212454	2720	2986	3252	3518	3783	4049	4314	4579	266
4	4844	5109	5373	5638	5902	6166	6430	6694	6957	7221	264
165	7484	7747	8010	8273	8536	8798	9060	9323	9585	9846	262
6	220108	220370	220631	220892	221153	221414	221675	221936	222196	222456	261
7	2716	2976	3236	3496	3755	4015	4274	4533	4792	5051	259
8	5309	5568	5826	6084	6342	6600	6858	7115	7372	7630	258
9	7887	8144	8400	8657	8913	9170	9426	9682	9938	230193	256
170	230449	230704	230960	231215	231470	231724	231979	232234	232488	232742	255
1	2996	3250	3504	3757	4011	4264	4517	4770	5023	5276	253
2	5528	5781	6033	6285	6537	6789	7041	7292	7544	7795	252
3	8046	8297	8548	8799	9049	9299	9550	9800	240050	240300	250
4	240549	240799	241048	241297	241546	241795	242044	242293	2541	2790	249
175	3038	3286	3534	3782	4030	4277	4525	4772	5019	5266	248
6	5513	5759	6006	6252	6499	6745	6991	7237	7482	7728	246
7	7973	8219	8464	8709	8954	9198	9443	9687	9932	250176	245
8	250420	250664	250908	251151	251395	251638	251881	252125	252368	2610	243
9	2853	3096	3338	3580	3822	4064	4306	4548	4790	5031	242
180	255273	255514	255755	255996	256237	256477	256718	256958	257198	257439	241
1	7679	7918	8158	8398	8637	8877	9116	9355	9594	9833	239
2	260071	260310	260548	260787	261025	261263	261501	261739	261976	262214	238
3	2451	2688	2925	3162	3399	3636	3873	4109	4346	4582	237
4	4818	5054	5290	5525	5761	5996	6232	6467	6702	6937	235
185	7172	7406	7641	7875	8110	8344	8578	8812	9046	9279	234
6	9513	9746	9980	270213	270446	270679	270912	271144	271377	271609	233
7	271842	272074	272306	2538	2770	3001	3233	3464	3696	3927	232
8	4158	4389	4620	4850	5081	5311	5542	5772	6002	6232	230
9	6462	6692	6921	7151	7380	7609	7838	8067	8296	8525	229
190	278754	278982	279211	279439	279667	279895	280123	280351	280578	280806	228
1	281033	281261	281488	281715	281942	282169	2396	2622	2849	3075	227
2	3301	3527	3753	3979	4205	4431	4656	4882	5107	5332	226
3	5557	5782	6007	6232	6456	6681	6905	7130	7354	7578	225
4	7802	8026	8249	8473	8696	8920	9143	9366	9589	9812	223
195	290035	290257	290480	290702	290925	291147	291369	291591	291813	292034	222
6	2256	2478	2699	2920	3141	3363	3584	3804	4025	4246	221
7	4466	4687	4907	5127	5347	5567	5787	6007	6226	6446	220
8	6665	6884	7104	7323	7542	7761	7979	8198	8416	8635	219
9	8853	9071	9289	9507	9725	9943	300161	300378	300595	300813	218
200	301030	301247	301464	301681	301898	302114	302331	302547	302764	302980	217
1	3196	3412	3628	3844	4059	4275	4491	4706	4921	5136	216
2	5351	5566	5781	5996	6211	6425	6639	6854	7068	7282	215
3	7496	7710	7924	8137	8351	8564	8778	8991	9204	9417	213
4	9630	9843	310056	310268	310481	310693	310906	311118	311330	311542	212
205	311754	311966	2177	2389	2600	2812	3023	3234	3445	3656	211
6	3867	4078	4289	4499	4710	4920	5130	5340	5551	5760	210
7	5970	6180	6390	6599	6809	7018	7227	7436	7646	7854	209
8	8063	8272	8481	8689	8898	9106	9314	9522	9730	9938	208
9	320146	320354	320562	320769	320977	321184	321391	321598	321805	322012	207
210	322219	322426	322633	322839	323046	323252	323458	323665	323871	324077	206
1	4282	4488	4694	4899	5105	5310	5516	5721	5926	6131	205
2	6336	6541	6745	6950	7155	7359	7563	7767	7972	8176	204
3	8380	8583	8787	8991	9194	9398	9601	9805	330008	330211	203
4	330414	330617	330819	331022	331225	331427	331630	331832	2034	2236	202
215	2438	2640	2842	3044	3246	3447	3649	3850	4051	4253	202
6	4454	4655	4856	5057	5257	5458	5658	5859	6059	6260	201
7	6460	6660	6860	7060	7260	7459	7659	7858	8058	8257	200
8	8456	8656	8855	9054	9253	9451	9650	9849	340047	340246	199
9	340444	340642	340841	341039	341237	341435	341632	341830	2028	2225	198
N.	0	1	2	3	4	5	6	7	8	9	D.

TABLE I.—Six-place Mantissas

N.	0	1	2	3	4	5	6	7	8	9	D.
220	342423	342620	342817	343014	343212	343409	343606	343802	343999	344196	197
1	4392	4589	4785	4981	5178	5374	5570	5766	5962	6157	196
2	6353	6549	6744	6939	7135	7330	7525	7720	7915	8110	195
3	8305	8500	8694	8889	9083	9278	9472	9666	9860	350054	194
4	350248	350442	350636	350829	351023	351216	351410	351603	351796	1989	193
225	2183	2375	2568	2761	2954	3147	3339	3532	3724	3916	193
6	4108	4301	4493	4685	4876	5068	5260	5452	5643	5834	192
7	6026	6217	6408	6599	6790	6981	7172	7363	7554	7744	191
8	7935	8125	8316	8506	8696	8886	9076	9266	9456	9646	190
9	9835	360025	360215	360404	360593	360783	360972	361161	361350	361539	189
230	361728	361917	362105	362294	362482	362671	362859	363048	363236	363424	188
1	3612	3800	3988	4176	4363	4551	4739	4926	5113	5301	188
2	5488	5675	5862	6049	6236	6423	6610	6796	6983	7169	187
3	7356	7542	7729	7915	8101	8287	8473	8659	8845	9030	186
4	9216	9401	9587	9772	9958	370143	370328	370513	370698	370883	185
235	371068	371253	371437	371622	371806	1991	2175	2360	2544	2728	184
6	2912	3096	3280	3464	3647	3831	4015	4198	4382	4565	184
7	4748	4932	5115	5298	5481	5664	5846	6029	6212	6394	183
8	6577	6759	6942	7124	7306	7488	7670	7852	8034	8216	182
9	8398	8580	8761	8943	9124	9306	9487	9668	9849	380030	181
240	380211	380392	380573	380754	380934	381115	381296	381476	381656	381837	181
1	2017	2197	2377	2557	2737	2917	3097	3277	3456	3636	180
2	3815	3995	4174	4353	4533	4712	4891	5070	5249	5428	179
3	5606	5785	5964	6142	6321	6499	6677	6856	7034	7212	178
4	7390	7568	7746	7923	8101	8279	8456	8634	8811	8989	178
245	9166	9343	9520	9698	9875	390051	390228	390405	390582	390759	177
6	390935	391112	391288	391464	391641	1817	1993	2169	2345	2521	176
7	2697	2873	3048	3224	3400	3575	3751	3926	4101	4277	176
8	4452	4627	4802	4977	5152	5326	5501	5676	5850	6025	175
9	6199	6374	6548	6722	6896	7071	7245	7419	7592	7766	174
250	397940	398114	398287	398461	398634	398808	398981	399154	399328	399501	173
1	9674	9847	400020	400192	400365	400538	400711	400883	401056	401228	173
2	401401	401573	1745	1917	2089	2261	2433	2605	2777	2949	172
3	3121	3292	3464	3635	3807	3978	4149	4320	4492	4663	171
4	4834	5005	5176	5346	5517	5688	5858	6029	6199	6370	171
255	6540	6710	6881	7051	7221	7391	7561	7731	7901	8070	170
6	8240	8410	8579	8749	8918	9087	9257	9426	9595	9764	169
7	9933	410102	410271	410440	410609	410777	410964	411114	411283	411451	169
8	411620	1788	1956	2124	2293	2461	2629	2796	2964	3132	168
9	3300	3467	3635	3803	3970	4137	4305	4472	4639	4806	167
260	414973	415140	415307	415474	415641	415808	415974	416141	416308	416474	167
1	6641	6807	6973	7139	7306	7472	7638	7804	7970	8135	166
2	8301	8467	8633	8798	8964	9129	9295	9460	9625	9791	165
3	9956	420121	420286	420451	420616	420781	420945	421110	421275	421439	165
4	421604	1768	1933	2097	2261	2426	2590	2754	2918	3082	164
265	3246	3410	3574	3737	3901	4065	4228	4392	4555	4718	164
6	4882	5045	5208	5371	5534	5697	5860	6023	6186	6349	163
7	6511	6674	6836	6999	7161	7324	7486	7648	7811	7973	162
8	8135	8297	8459	8621	8783	8944	9106	9268	9429	9591	162
9	9752	9914	430075	430236	430398	430559	430720	430881	431042	431203	161
270	431364	431525	431685	431846	432007	432167	432328	432488	432649	432809	161
1	2969	3130	3290	3450	3610	3770	3930	4090	4249	4409	160
2	4569	4729	4888	5048	5207	5367	5526	5685	5844	6004	159
3	6163	6322	6481	6640	6799	6957	7116	7275	7433	7592	159
4	7751	7909	8067	8226	8384	8542	8701	8859	9017	9175	158
275	9333	9491	9648	9806	9964	440122	440279	440437	440594	440752	158
6	440909	441066	441224	441381	441538	1695	1852	2009	2166	2323	157
7	2480	2637	2793	2950	3106	3263	3419	3576	3732	3889	157
8	4045	4201	4357	4513	4669	4825	4981	5137	5293	5449	156
9	5604	5760	5915	6071	6226	6382	6537	6692	6848	7003	155
N.	0	1	2	3	4	5	6	7	8	9	D.

TABLE I.—Six-place Mantissas

N.	0	1	2	3	4	5	6	7	8	9	D.
280	447158	447313	447468	447623	447778	447933	448088	448242	448397	448552	155
1	8706	8861	9015	9170	9324	9478	9633	9787	9941	450095	154
2	450249	450403	450557	450711	450865	451018	451172	451326	451479	1633	154
3	1786	1940	2093	2247	2400	2553	2706	2859	3012	3165	153
4	3318	3471	3624	3777	3930	4082	4235	4387	4540	4692	153
285	4845	4997	5150	5302	5454	5606	5758	5910	6062	6214	152
6	6366	6518	6670	6821	6973	7125	7276	7428	7579	7731	152
7	7882	8033	8184	8336	8487	8638	8789	8940	9091	9242	151
8	9392	9543	9694	9845	9995	460146	460296	460447	460597	460748	151
9	460898	461048	461198	461348	461499	1649	1799	1948	2098	2248	150
290	462398	462548	462697	462847	462997	463146	463296	463445	463594	463744	150
1	3893	4042	4191	4340	4490	4639	4788	4936	5085	5234	149
2	5383	5532	5680	5829	5977	6126	6274	6423	6571	6719	149
3	6868	7016	7164	7312	7460	7608	7756	7904	8052	8200	148
4	8347	8495	8643	8790	8938	9085	9233	9380	9527	9675	148
295	9822	9969	470116	470263	470410	470557	470704	470851	470998	471145	147
6	471292	471438	1585	1732	1878	2025	2171	2318	2464	2610	146
7	2756	2903	3049	3195	3341	3487	3633	3779	3925	4071	146
8	4216	4362	4508	4653	4799	4944	5090	5235	5381	5526	146
9	5671	5816	5962	6107	6252	6397	6542	6687	6832	6976	145
300	477121	477266	477411	477555	477700	477844	477989	478133	478278	478422	145
1	8566	8711	8855	8999	9143	9287	9431	9575	9719	9863	144
2	480007	480151	480294	480438	480582	480725	480869	481012	481156	481299	144
3	1443	1586	1729	1872	2016	2159	2302	2445	2588	2731	143
4	2874	3016	3159	3302	3445	3587	3730	3872	4015	4157	143
305	4300	4442	4585	4727	4869	5011	5153	5295	5437	5579	142
6	5721	5863	6005	6147	6289	6430	6572	6714	6855	6997	142
7	7138	7280	7421	7563	7704	7845	7986	8127	8269	8410	141
8	8551	8692	8833	8974	9114	9255	9396	9537	9677	9818	141
9	9958	490099	490239	490380	490520	490661	490801	490941	491081	491222	140
310	491362	491502	491642	491782	491922	492062	492201	492341	492481	492621	140
1	2760	2900	3040	3179	3319	3458	3597	3737	3876	4015	139
2	4155	4294	4433	4572	4711	4850	4989	5128	5267	5406	139
3	5544	5683	5822	5960	6099	6238	6376	6515	6653	6791	139
4	6930	7068	7206	7344	7483	7621	7759	7897	8035	8173	138
315	8311	8448	8586	8724	8862	8999	9137	9275	9412	9550	138
6	9687	9824	9962	500099	500236	500374	500511	500648	500785	500922	137
7	501059	501196	501333	1470	1607	1744	1880	2017	2154	2291	137
8	2427	2564	2700	2837	2973	3109	3246	3382	3518	3655	136
9	3791	3927	4063	4199	4335	4471	4607	4743	4878	5014	136
320	505150	505286	505421	505557	505693	505828	505964	506099	506234	506370	136
1	6505	6640	6776	6911	7046	7181	7316	7451	7586	7721	135
2	7856	7991	8126	8260	8395	8530	8664	8799	8934	9068	135
3	9203	9337	9471	9606	9740	9874	510009	510143	510277	510411	134
4	510545	510679	510813	510947	511081	511215	1349	1482	1616	1750	134
325	1883	2017	2151	2284	2418	2551	2684	2818	2951	3084	133
6	3218	3351	3484	3617	3750	3883	4016	4149	4282	4415	133
7	4548	4681	4813	4946	5079	5211	5344	5476	5609	5741	133
8	5874	6006	6139	6271	6403	6535	6668	6800	6932	7064	132
9	7196	7328	7460	7592	7724	7855	7987	8119	8251	8382	132
330	518514	518646	518777	518909	519040	519171	519303	519434	519566	519697	131
1	9828	9959	520090	520221	520353	520484	520615	520745	520876	521007	131
2	521138	521269	1400	1530	1661	1792	1922	2053	2183	2314	131
3	2444	2575	2705	2835	2966	3096	3226	3356	3486	3616	130
4	3746	3876	4006	4136	4266	4396	4526	4656	4785	4915	130
335	5045	5174	5304	5434	5563	5693	5822	5951	6081	6210	129
6	6339	6469	6598	6727	6856	6985	7114	7243	7372	7501	129
7	7630	7759	7888	8016	8145	8274	8402	8531	8660	8788	129
8	8917	9045	9174	9302	9430	9559	9687	9815	9943	530072	128
9	530200	530328	530456	530584	530712	530840	530968	531096	531223	1351	128
N.	0	1	2	3	4	5	6	7	8	9	D.

TABLE I.—Six-place Mantissas

N.	0	1	2	3	4	5	6	7	8	9	D.
340	531479	531607	531734	531862	531990	532117	532245	532372	532500	532627	128
1	2754	2882	3009	3136	3264	3391	3518	3645	3772	3899	127
2	4026	4153	4280	4407	4534	4661	4787	4914	5041	5167	127
3	5294	5421	5547	5674	5800	5927	6053	6180	6306	6432	126
4	6558	6685	6811	6937	7063	7189	7315	7441	7567	7693	126
345	7819	7945	8071	8197	8322	8448	8574	8699	8825	8951	126
6	9076	9202	9327	9452	9578	9703	9829	9954	540079	540204	125
7	540329	540455	540580	540705	540830	540955	541080	541205	1330	1454	125
8	1579	1704	1829	1953	2078	2203	2327	2452	2576	2701	125
9	2825	2950	3074	3199	3323	3447	3571	3696	3820	3944	124
350	544068	544192	544316	544440	544564	544688	544812	544936	545060	545183	124
1	5307	5431	5555	5678	5802	5925	6049	6172	6296	6419	124
2	6543	6666	6789	6913	7036	7159	7282	7405	7529	7652	123
3	7775	7898	8021	8144	8267	8389	8512	8635	8758	8881	123
4	9003	9126	9249	9371	9494	9616	9739	9861	9984	550106	123
355	550228	550351	550473	550595	550717	550840	550962	551084	551206	1328	122
6	1450	1572	1694	1816	1938	2060	2181	2303	2425	2547	122
7	2668	2790	2911	3033	3155	3276	3398	3519	3640	3762	121
8	3883	4004	4126	4247	4368	4489	4610	4731	4852	4973	121
9	5094	5215	5336	5457	5578	5699	5820	5940	6061	6182	121
360	556303	556423	556544	556664	556785	556905	557026	557146	557267	557387	120
1	7507	7627	7748	7868	7988	8108	8228	8349	8469	8589	120
2	8709	8829	8948	9068	9188	9308	9428	9548	9667	9787	120
3	9907	560026	560146	560265	560385	560504	560624	560743	560863	560982	119
4	561101	1221	1340	1459	1578	1698	1817	1936	2055	2174	119
365	2293	2412	2531	2650	2769	2887	3006	3125	3244	3362	119
6	3481	3600	3718	3837	3955	4074	4192	4311	4429	4548	119
7	4666	4784	4903	5021	5139	5257	5376	5494	5612	5730	118
8	5848	5966	6084	6202	6320	6437	6555	6673	6791	6909	118
9	7026	7144	7262	7379	7497	7614	7732	7849	7967	8084	118
370	568202	568319	568436	568554	568671	568788	568905	569023	569140	569257	117
1	9374	9491	9608	9725	9842	9959	570076	570193	570309	570426	117
2	570543	570660	570776	570893	571010	571126	1243	1359	1476	1592	117
3	1709	1825	1942	2058	2174	2291	2407	2523	2639	2755	116
4	2872	2988	3104	3220	3336	3452	3568	3684	3800	3915	116
375	4031	4147	4263	4379	4494	4610	4726	4841	4957	5072	116
6	5188	5303	5419	5534	5650	5765	5880	5996	6111	6226	115
7	6341	6457	6572	6687	6802	6917	7032	7147	7262	7377	115
8	7492	7607	7722	7836	7951	8066	8181	8295	8410	8525	115
9	8639	8754	8868	8983	9097	9212	9326	9441	9555	9669	114
380	579784	579898	580012	580126	580241	580355	580469	580583	580697	580811	114
1	580925	581039	1153	1267	1381	1495	1608	1722	1836	1950	114
2	2063	2177	2291	2404	2518	2631	2745	2858	2972	3085	114
3	3199	3312	3426	3539	3652	3765	3879	3992	4105	4218	113
4	4331	4444	4557	4670	4783	4896	5009	5122	5235	5348	113
385	5461	5574	5686	5799	5912	6024	6137	6250	6362	6475	113
6	6587	6700	6812	6925	7037	7149	7262	7374	7486	7599	112
7	7711	7823	7935	8047	8160	8272	8384	8496	8608	8720	112
8	8832	8944	9056	9167	9279	9391	9503	9615	9726	9838	112
9	9950	590061	590173	590284	590396	590507	590619	590730	590842	590953	112
390	591065	591176	591287	591399	591510	591621	591732	591843	591955	592066	111
1	2177	2288	2399	2510	2621	2732	2843	2954	3064	3175	111
2	3286	3397	3508	3618	3729	3840	3950	4061	4171	4282	111
3	4393	4503	4614	4724	4834	4945	5055	5165	5276	5380	110
4	5496	5606	5717	5827	5937	6047	6157	6267	6377	6487	110
395	6597	6707	6817	6927	7037	7146	7256	7366	7476	7586	110
6	7695	7805	7914	8024	8134	8243	8353	8462	8572	8681	110
7	8791	8900	9009	9119	9228	9337	9446	9556	9665	9774	109
8	9883	9992	600101	600210	600319	600428	600537	600646	600755	600864	109
9	600973	601082	1191	1299	1408	1517	1625	1734	1843	1951	109
N.	0	1	2	3	4	5	6	7	8	9	D.

TABLE I.—Six-place Mantissas

N.	0	1	2	3	4	5	6	7	8	9	D.
400	602060	602169	602277	602386	602494	602603	602711	602819	602928	603036	108
1	3144	3253	3361	3469	3577	3686	3794	3902	4010	4118	108
2	4226	4334	4442	4550	4658	4766	4874	4982	5089	5197	108
3	5305	5413	5521	5628	5736	5844	5951	6059	6166	6274	108
4	6381	6489	6596	6704	6811	6919	7026	7133	7241	7348	107
405	7455	7562	7669	7777	7884	7991	8098	8205	8312	8419	107
6	8526	8633	8740	8847	8954	9061	9167	9274	9381	9488	107
7	9594	9701	9808	9914	610021	610128	610234	610341	610447	610554	107
8	610660	610767	610873	610979	1086	1192	1298	1405	1511	1617	106
9	1723	1829	1936	2042	2148	2254	2360	2466	2572	2678	106
410	612784	612890	612996	613102	613207	613313	613419	613525	613630	613736	106
1	3842	3947	4053	4159	4264	4370	4475	4581	4686	4792	106
2	4897	5003	5108	5213	5319	5424	5529	5634	5740	5845	105
3	5950	6055	6160	6265	6370	6476	6581	6686	6790	6895	105
4	7000	7105	7210	7315	7420	7525	7629	7734	7839	7943	105
415	8048	8153	8257	8362	8466	8571	8676	8780	8884	8989	105
6	9093	9198	9302	9406	9511	9615	9719	9824	9928	620032	104
7	620136	620240	620344	620448	620552	620656	620760	620864	620968	1072	104
8	1176	1280	1384	1488	1592	1695	1799	1903	2007	2110	104
9	2214	2318	2421	2525	2628	2732	2835	2939	3042	3146	104
420	623249	623353	623456	623559	623663	623766	623869	623973	624076	624179	103
1	4282	4385	4488	4591	4695	4798	4901	5004	5107	5210	103
2	5312	5415	5518	5621	5724	5827	5929	6032	6135	6238	103
3	6340	6443	6546	6648	6751	6853	6956	7058	7161	7263	103
4	7366	7468	7571	7673	7775	7878	7980	8082	8185	8287	102
425	8389	8491	8593	8695	8797	8900	9002	9104	9206	9308	102
6	9410	9512	9613	9715	9817	9919	630021	630123	630224	630326	102
7	630428	630530	630631	630733	630835	630936	1038	1139	1241	1342	102
8	1444	1545	1647	1748	1849	1951	2052	2153	2255	2356	101
9	2457	2559	2660	2761	2862	2963	3064	3165	3266	3367	101
430	633468	633569	633670	633771	633872	633973	634074	634175	634276	634376	101
1	4477	4578	4679	4779	4880	4981	5081	5182	5283	5383	101
2	5484	5584	5685	5785	5886	5986	6087	6187	6287	6388	100
3	6488	6588	6688	6789	6889	6989	7089	7189	7290	7390	100
4	7490	7590	7690	7790	7890	7990	8090	8190	8290	8389	100
435	8489	8589	8689	8789	8888	8988	9088	9188	9287	9387	100
6	9486	9586	9686	9785	9885	9984	640084	640183	640283	640382	99
7	640481	640581	640680	640779	640879	640978	1077	1177	1276	1375	99
8	1474	1573	1672	1771	1871	1970	2069	2168	2267	2366	99
9	2465	2563	2662	2761	2860	2959	3058	3156	3255	3354	99
440	643453	643551	643650	643749	643847	643946	644044	644143	644242	644340	98
1	4439	4537	4636	4734	4832	4931	5029	5127	5226	5324	98
2	5422	5521	5619	5717	5815	5913	6011	6110	6208	6306	98
3	6404	6502	6600	6698	6796	6894	6992	7089	7187	7285	98
4	7383	7481	7579	7676	7774	7872	7969	8067	8165	8262	98
445	8360	8458	8555	8653	8750	8848	8945	9043	9140	9237	97
6	9335	9432	9530	9627	9724	9821	9919	650016	650113	650210	97
7	650308	650405	650502	650599	650696	650793	650890	0987	1084	1181	97
8	1278	1375	1472	1569	1666	1762	1859	1956	2053	2150	97
9	2246	2343	2440	2536	2633	2730	2826	2923	3019	3116	97
450	653213	653309	653405	653502	653598	653695	653791	653888	653984	654080	96
1	4177	4273	4369	4465	4562	4658	4754	4850	4946	5042	96
2	5138	5235	5331	5427	5523	5619	5715	5810	5906	6002	96
3	6098	6194	6290	6386	6482	6577	6673	6769	6864	6960	96
4	7056	7152	7247	7343	7438	7534	7629	7725	7820	7916	96
455	8011	8107	8202	8298	8393	8488	8584	8679	8774	8870	95
6	8965	9060	9155	9250	9346	9441	9536	9631	9726	9821	95
7	9916	660011	660106	660201	660296	660391	660486	660581	660676	660771	95
8	660865	0960	1055	1150	1245	1339	1434	1529	1623	1718	95
9	1813	1907	2002	2096	2191	2286	2380	2475	2569	2663	95
N.	0	1	2	3	4	5	6	7	8	9	D.

TABLE I.—Six-place Mantissas

N.	0	1	2	3	4	5	6	7	8	9	D.
460	662758	662852	662947	663041	663135	663230	663324	663418	663512	663607	94
1	3701	3795	3889	3983	4078	4172	4266	4360	4454	4548	94
2	4642	4736	4830	4924	5018	5112	5206	5299	5393	5487	94
3	5581	5675	5769	5862	5956	6050	6143	6237	6331	6424	94
4	6518	6612	6705	6799	6892	6986	7079	7173	7266	7360	94
465	7453	7546	7640	7733	7826	7920	8013	8106	8199	8293	93
6	8386	8479	8572	8665	8759	8852	8945	9038	9131	9224	93
7	9317	9410	9503	9596	9689	9782	9875	9967	670060	670153	93
8	670246	670339	670431	670524	670617	670710	670802	670895	0988	1080	93
9	1173	1265	1358	1451	1543	1636	1728	1821	1913	2005	93
470	672098	672190	672283	672375	672467	672560	672652	672744	672836	672929	92
1	3021	3113	3205	3297	3390	3482	3574	3666	3758	3850	92
2	3942	4034	4126	4218	4310	4402	4494	4586	4677	4769	92
3	4861	4953	5045	5137	5228	5320	5412	5503	5595	5687	92
4	5778	5870	5962	6053	6145	6236	6328	6419	6511	6602	92
475	6694	6785	6876	6968	7059	7151	7242	7333	7424	7516	91
6	7607	7698	7789	7881	7972	8063	8154	8245	8336	8427	91
7	8518	8609	8700	8791	8882	8973	9064	9155	9246	9337	91
8	9428	9519	9610	9700	9791	9882	9973	680063	680154	680245	91
9	680336	680426	680517	680607	680698	680789	680879	0970	1060	1151	91
480	681241	681332	681422	681513	681603	681693	681784	681874	681964	682055	90
1	2145	2235	2326	2416	2506	2596	2686	2777	2867	2957	90
2	3047	3137	3227	3317	3407	3497	3587	3677	3767	3857	90
3	3947	4037	4127	4217	4307	4396	4486	4576	4666	4756	90
4	4845	4935	5025	5114	5204	5294	5383	5473	5563	5652	90
485	5742	5831	5921	6010	6100	6189	6279	6368	6458	6547	89
6	6636	6726	6815	6904	6994	7083	7172	7261	7351	7440	89
7	7529	7618	7707	7796	7886	7975	8064	8153	8242	8331	89
8	8420	8509	8598	8687	8776	8865	8953	9042	9131	9220	89
9	9309	9398	9486	9575	9664	9753	9841	9930	690019	690107	89
490	690196	690285	690373	690462	690550	690639	690728	690816	690905	690993	89
1	1081	1170	1258	1347	1435	1524	1612	1700	1789	1877	88
2	1965	2053	2142	2230	2318	2406	2494	2583	2671	2759	88
3	2847	2935	3023	3111	3199	3287	3375	3463	3551	3639	88
4	3727	3815	3903	3991	4078	4166	4254	4342	4430	4517	88
495	4605	4693	4781	4868	4956	5044	5131	5219	5307	5394	88
6	5482	5569	5657	5744	5832	5919	6007	6094	6182	6269	87
7	6356	6444	6531	6618	6706	6793	6880	6968	7055	7142	87
8	7229	7317	7404	7491	7578	7665	7752	7839	7926	8014	87
9	8101	8188	8275	8362	8449	8535	8622	8709	8796	8883	87
500	698970	699057	699144	699231	699317	699404	699491	699578	699664	699751	87
1	9838	9924	700011	700098	700184	700271	700358	700444	700531	700617	87
2	700704	700790	0877	0963	1050	1136	1222	1309	1395	1482	86
3	1568	1654	1741	1827	1913	1999	2086	2172	2258	2344	86
4	2431	2517	2603	2689	2775	2861	2947	3033	3119	3205	86
505	3291	3377	3463	3549	3635	3721	3807	3893	3979	4065	86
6	4151	4236	4322	4408	4494	4579	4665	4751	4837	4922	86
7	5008	5094	5179	5265	5350	5436	5522	5607	5693	5778	86
8	5864	5949	6035	6120	6206	6291	6376	6462	6547	6632	85
9	6718	6803	6888	6974	7059	7144	7229	7315	7400	7485	85
510	707570	707655	707740	707826	707911	707996	708081	708166	708251	708336	85
1	8421	8506	8591	8676	8761	8846	8931	9015	9100	9185	85
2	9270	9355	9440	9524	9609	9694	9779	9863	9948	710033	85
3	710117	710202	710287	710371	710456	710540	710625	710710	710794	0879	85
4	0963	1048	1132	1217	1301	1385	1470	1554	1639	1723	84
515	1807	1892	1976	2060	2144	2229	2313	2397	2481	2566	84
6	2650	2734	2818	2902	2986	3070	3154	3238	3323	3407	84
7	3491	3575	3659	3742	3826	3910	3994	4078	4162	4246	84
8	4330	4414	4497	4581	4665	4749	4833	4916	5000	5084	84
9	5167	5251	5335	5418	5502	5586	5669	5753	5836	5920	84
N.	0	1	2	3	4	5	6	7	8	9	D.

TABLE I.—Six-place Mantissas

N.	0	1	2	3	4	5	6	7	8	9	D.
520	716003	716087	716170	716254	716337	716421	716504	716588	716671	716754	83
1	6838	6921	7004	7088	7171	7254	7338	7421	7504	7587	83
2	7671	7754	7837	7920	8003	8086	8169	8253	8336	8419	83
3	8502	8585	8668	8751	8834	8917	9000	9083	9165	9248	83
4	9331	9414	9497	9580	9663	9745	9828	9911	9994	720077	83
525	720159	720242	720325	720407	720490	720573	720655	720738	720821	0903	83
6	0986	1068	1151	1233	1316	1398	1481	1563	1646	1728	82
7	1811	1893	1975	2058	2140	2222	2305	2387	2469	2552	82
8	2634	2716	2798	2881	2963	3045	3127	3209	3291	3374	82
9	3456	3538	3620	3702	3784	3866	3948	4030	4112	4194	82
530	724276	724358	724440	724522	724604	724685	724767	724849	724931	725013	82
1	5095	5176	5258	5340	5422	5503	5585	5667	5748	5830	82
2	5912	5993	6075	6156	6238	6320	6401	6483	6564	6646	82
3	6727	6809	6890	6972	7053	7134	7216	7297	7379	7460	81
4	7541	7623	7704	7785	7866	7948	8029	8110	8191	8273	81
535	8354	8435	8516	8597	8678	8759	8841	8922	9003	9084	81
6	9165	9246	9327	9408	9489	9570	9651	9732	9813	9893	81
7	9974	730055	730136	730217	730298	730378	730459	730540	730621	730702	81
8	730782	0863	0944	1024	1105	1186	1266	1347	1428	1508	81
9	1589	1669	1750	1830	1911	1991	2072	2152	2233	2313	81
540	732394	732474	732555	732635	732715	732796	732876	732956	733037	733117	80
1	3197	3278	3358	3438	3518	3598	3679	3759	3839	3919	80
2	3999	4079	4160	4240	4320	4400	4480	4560	4640	4720	80
3	4800	4880	4960	5040	5120	5200	5279	5359	5439	5519	80
4	5599	5679	5759	5838	5918	5998	6078	6157	6237	6317	80
545	6397	6476	6556	6635	6715	6795	6874	6954	7034	7113	80
6	7193	7272	7352	7431	7511	7590	7670	7749	7829	7908	79
7	7987	8067	8146	8225	8305	8384	8463	8543	8622	8701	79
8	8781	8860	8939	9018	9097	9177	9256	9335	9414	9493	79
9	9572	9651	9731	9810	9889	9968	740047	740126	740205	740284	79
550	740363	740442	740521	740600	740678	740757	740836	740915	740994	741073	79
1	1152	1230	1309	1388	1467	1546	1624	1703	1782	1860	79
2	1939	2018	2096	2175	2254	2332	2411	2489	2568	2647	79
3	2725	2804	2882	2961	3039	3118	3196	3275	3353	3431	78
4	3510	3588	3667	3745	3823	3902	3980	4058	4136	4215	78
555	4293	4371	4449	4528	4606	4684	4762	4840	4919	4997	78
6	5075	5153	5231	5309	5387	5465	5543	5621	5699	5777	78
7	5855	5933	6011	6089	6167	6245	6323	6401	6479	6556	78
8	6634	6712	6790	6868	6945	7023	7101	7179	7256	7334	78
9	7412	7489	7567	7645	7722	7800	7878	7955	8033	8110	78
560	748188	748266	748343	748421	748498	748576	748653	748731	748808	748885	77
1	8963	9040	9118	9195	9272	9350	9427	9504	9582	9659	77
2	9736	9814	9891	9968	750045	750123	750200	750277	750354	750431	77
3	750508	750586	750663	750740	0817	0894	0971	1048	1125	1202	77
4	1279	1356	1433	1510	1587	1664	1741	1818	1895	1972	77
565	2048	2125	2202	2279	2356	2433	2509	2586	2663	2740	77
6	2816	2893	2970	3047	3123	3200	3277	3353	3430	3506	77
7	3583	3660	3736	3813	3889	3966	4042	4119	4195	4272	77
8	4348	4425	4501	4578	4654	4730	4807	4883	4960	5036	76
9	5112	5189	5265	5341	5417	5494	5570	5646	5722	5799	76
570	755875	755951	756027	756103	756180	756256	756332	756408	756484	756560	76
1	6636	6712	6788	6864	6940	7016	7092	7168	7244	7320	76
2	7396	7472	7548	7624	7700	7775	7851	7927	8003	8079	76
3	8155	8230	8306	8382	8458	8533	8609	8685	8761	8836	76
4	8912	8988	9063	9139	9214	9290	9366	9441	9517	9592	76
575	9668	9743	9819	9894	9970	760045	760121	760196	760272	760347	75
6	760422	760498	760573	760649	760724	0799	0875	0950	1025	1101	75
7	1176	1251	1326	1402	1477	1552	1627	1702	1778	1853	75
8	1928	2003	2078	2153	2228	2303	2378	2453	2529	2604	75
9	2679	2754	2829	2904	2978	3053	3128	3203	3278	3353	75
N.	**0**	**1**	**2**	**3**	**4**	**5**	**6**	**7**	**8**	**9**	**D.**

TABLE I.—Six-place Mantissas

N.	0	1	2	3	4	5	6	7	8	9	D.
580	763428	763503	763578	763653	763727	763802	763877	763952	764027	764101	75
1	4176	4251	4326	4400	4475	4550	4624	4699	4774	4848	75
2	4923	4998	5072	5147	5221	5296	5370	5445	5520	5594	75
3	5669	5743	5818	5892	5966	6041	6115	6190	6264	6338	74
4	6413	6487	6562	6636	6710	6785	6859	6933	7007	7082	74
585	7156	7230	7304	7379	7453	7527	7601	7675	7749	7823	74
6	7898	7972	8046	8120	8194	8268	8342	8416	8490	8564	74
7	8638	8712	8786	8860	8934	9008	9082	9156	9230	9303	74
8	9377	9451	9525	9599	9673	9746	9820	9894	9968	770042	74
9	770115	770189	770263	770336	770410	770484	770557	770631	770705	0778	74
590	770852	770926	770999	771073	771146	771220	771293	771367	771440	771514	74
1	1587	1661	1734	1808	1881	1955	2028	2102	2175	2248	73
2	2322	2395	2468	2542	2615	2688	2762	2835	2908	2981	73
3	3055	3128	3201	3274	3348	3421	3494	3567	3640	3713	73
4	3786	3860	3933	4006	4079	4152	4225	4298	4371	4444	73
595	4517	4590	4663	4736	4809	4882	4955	5028	5100	5173	73
6	5246	5319	5392	5465	5538	5610	5683	5756	5829	5902	73
7	5974	6047	6120	6193	6265	6338	6411	6483	6556	6629	73
8	6701	6774	6846	6919	6992	7064	7137	7209	7282	7354	73
9	7427	7499	7572	7644	7717	7789	7862	7934	8006	8079	72
600	778151	778224	778296	778368	778441	778513	778585	778658	778730	778802	72
1	8874	8947	9019	9091	9163	9236	9308	9380	9452	9524	72
2	9596	9669	9741	9813	9885	9957	780029	780101	780173	780245	72
3	780317	780389	780461	780533	780605	780677	0749	0821	0893	0965	72
4	1037	1109	1181	1253	1324	1396	1468	1540	1612	1684	72
605	1755	1827	1899	1971	2042	2114	2186	2258	2329	2401	72
6	2473	2544	2616	2688	2759	2831	2902	2974	3046	3117	72
7	3189	3260	3332	3403	3475	3546	3618	3689	3761	3832	71
8	3904	3975	4046	4118	4189	4261	4332	4403	4475	4546	71
9	4617	4689	4760	4831	4902	4974	5045	5116	5187	5259	71
610	785330	785401	785472	785543	785615	785686	785757	785828	785899	785970	71
1	6041	6112	6183	6254	6325	6396	6467	6538	6609	6680	71
2	6751	6822	6893	6964	7035	7106	7177	7248	7319	7390	71
3	7460	7531	7602	7673	7744	7815	7885	7956	8027	8098	71
4	8168	8239	8310	8381	8451	8522	8593	8663	8734	8804	71
615	8875	8946	9016	9087	9157	9228	9299	9369	9440	9510	71
6	9581	9651	9722	9792	9863	9933	790004	790074	790144	790215	70
7	790285	790356	790426	790496	790567	790637	0707	0778	0848	0918	70
8	0988	1059	1129	1199	1269	1340	1410	1480	1550	1620	70
9	1691	1761	1831	1901	1971	2041	2111	2181	2252	2322	70
620	792392	792462	792532	792602	792672	792742	792812	792882	792952	793022	70
1	3092	3162	3231	3301	3371	3441	3511	3581	3651	3721	70
2	3790	3860	3930	4000	4070	4139	4209	4279	4349	4418	70
3	4488	4558	4627	4697	4767	4836	4906	4976	5045	5115	70
4	5185	5254	5324	5393	5463	5532	5602	5672	5741	5811	70
625	5880	5949	6019	6088	6158	6227	6297	6366	6436	6505	69
6	6574	6644	6713	6782	6852	6921	6990	7060	7129	7198	69
7	7268	7337	7406	7475	7545	7614	7683	7752	7821	7890	69
8	7960	8029	8098	8167	8236	8305	8374	8443	8513	8582	69
9	8651	8720	8789	8858	8927	8996	9065	9134	9203	9272	69
630	799341	799409	799478	799547	799616	799685	799754	799823	799892	799961	69
1	800029	800098	800167	800236	800305	800373	800442	800511	800580	800648	69
2	0717	0786	0854	0923	0992	1061	1129	1198	1266	1335	69
3	1404	1472	1541	1609	1678	1747	1815	1884	1952	2021	69
4	2089	2158	2226	2295	2363	2432	2500	2568	2637	2705	68
635	2774	2842	2910	2979	3047	3116	3184	3252	3321	3389	68
6	3457	3525	3594	3662	3730	3798	3867	3935	4003	4071	68
7	4139	4208	4276	4344	4412	4480	4548	4616	4685	4753	68
8	4821	4889	4957	5025	5093	5161	5229	5297	5365	5433	68
9	5501	5569	5637	5705	5773	5841	5908	5976	6044	6112	68
N.	0	1	2	3	4	5	6	7	8	9	D.

TABLE I. — Six-place Mantissas

N.	0	1	2	3	4	5	6	7	8	9	D.
640	806180	806248	806316	806384	806451	806519	806587	806655	806723	806790	68
1	6858	6926	6994	7061	7129	7197	7264	7332	7400	7467	68
2	7535	7603	7670	7738	7806	7873	7941	8008	8076	8143	68
3	8211	8279	8346	8414	8481	8549	8616	8684	8751	8818	67
4	8886	8953	9021	9088	9156	9223	9290	9358	9425	9492	67
645	9560	9627	9694	9762	9829	9896	9964	810031	810098	810165	67
6	810233	810300	810367	810434	810501	810569	810636	0703	0770	0837	67
7	0904	0971	1039	1106	1173	1240	1307	1374	1441	1508	67
8	1575	1642	1709	1776	1843	1910	1977	2044	2111	2178	67
9	2245	2312	2379	2445	2512	2579	2646	2713	2780	2847	67
650	812913	812980	813047	813114	813181	813247	813314	813381	813448	813514	67
1	3581	3648	3714	3781	3848	3914	3981	4048	4114	4181	67
2	4248	4314	4381	4447	4514	4581	4647	4714	4780	4847	67
3	4913	4980	5046	5113	5179	5246	5312	5378	5445	5511	66
4	5578	5644	5711	5777	5843	5910	5976	6042	6109	6175	66
655	6241	6308	6374	6440	6506	6573	6639	6705	6771	6838	66
6	6904	6970	7036	7102	7169	7235	7301	7367	7433	7499	66
7	7565	7631	7698	7764	7830	7896	7962	8028	8094	8160	66
8	8226	8292	8358	8424	8490	8556	8622	8688	8754	8820	66
9	8885	8951	9017	9083	9149	9215	9281	9346	9412	9478	66
660	819544	819610	819676	819741	819807	819873	819939	820004	820070	820136	66
1	820201	820267	820333	820399	820464	820530	820595	0661	0727	0792	66
2	0858	0924	0989	1055	1120	1186	1251	1317	1382	1448	66
3	1514	1579	1645	1710	1775	1841	1906	1972	2037	2103	65
4	2168	2233	2299	2364	2430	2495	2560	2626	2691	2756	65
665	2822	2887	2952	3018	3083	3148	3213	3279	3344	3409	65
6	3474	3539	3605	3670	3735	3800	3865	3930	3996	4061	65
7	4126	4191	4256	4321	4386	4451	4516	4581	4646	4711	65
8	4776	4841	4906	4971	5036	5101	5166	5231	5296	5361	65
9	5426	5491	5556	5621	5686	5751	5815	5880	5945	6010	65
670	826075	826140	826204	826269	826334	826399	826464	826528	826593	826658	65
1	6723	6787	6852	6917	6981	7046	7111	7175	7240	7305	65
2	7369	7434	7499	7563	7628	7692	7757	7821	7886	7951	65
3	8015	8080	8144	8209	8273	8338	8402	8467	8531	8595	64
4	8660	8724	8789	8853	8918	8982	9046	9111	9175	9239	64
675	9304	9368	9432	9497	9561	9625	9690	9754	9818	9882	64
6	9947	830011	830075	830139	830204	830268	830332	830396	830460	830525	64
7	830589	0653	0717	0781	0845	0909	0973	1037	1102	1166	64
8	1230	1294	1358	1422	1486	1550	1614	1678	1742	1806	64
9	1870	1934	1998	2062	2126	2189	2253	2317	2381	2445	64
680	832509	832573	832637	832700	832764	832828	832892	832956	833020	833083	64
1	3147	3211	3275	3338	3402	3466	3530	3593	3657	3721	64
2	3784	3848	3912	3975	4039	4103	4166	4230	4294	4357	64
3	4421	4484	4548	4611	4675	4739	4802	4866	4929	4993	64
4	5056	5120	5183	5247	5310	5373	5437	5500	5564	5627	63
685	5691	5754	5817	5881	5944	6007	6071	6134	6197	6261	63
6	6324	6387	6451	6514	6577	6641	6704	6767	6830	6894	63
7	6957	7020	7083	7146	7210	7273	7336	7399	7462	7525	63
8	7588	7652	7715	7778	7841	7904	7967	8030	8093	8156	63
9	8219	8282	8345	8408	8471	8534	8597	8660	8723	8786	63
690	838849	838912	838975	839038	839101	839164	839227	839289	839352	839415	63
1	9478	9541	9604	9667	9729	9792	9855	9918	9981	840043	63
2	840106	840169	840232	840294	840357	840420	840482	840545	840608	0671	63
3	0733	0796	0859	0921	0984	1046	1109	1172	1234	1297	63
4	1359	1422	1485	1547	1610	1672	1735	1797	1860	1922	63
695	1985	2047	2110	2172	2235	2297	2360	2422	2484	2547	62
6	2609	2672	2734	2796	2859	2921	2983	3046	3108	3170	62
7	3233	3295	3357	3420	3482	3544	3606	3669	3731	3793	62
8	3855	3918	3980	4042	4104	4166	4229	4291	4353	4415	62
9	4477	4539	4601	4664	4726	4788	4850	4912	4974	5036	62
N.	0	1	2	3	4	5	6	7	8	9	D.

TABLE I.—Six-place Mantissas

N.	0	1	2	3	4	5	6	7	8	9	D.
700	845098	845160	845222	845284	845346	845408	845470	845532	845594	845656	62
1	5718	5780	5842	5904	5966	6028	6090	6151	6213	6275	62
2	6337	6399	6461	6523	6585	6646	6708	6770	6832	6894	62
3	6955	7017	7079	7141	7202	7264	7326	7388	7449	7511	62
4	7573	7634	7696	7758	7819	7881	7943	8004	8066	8128	62
705	8189	8251	8312	8374	8435	8497	8559	8620	8682	8743	62
6	8805	8866	8928	8989	9051	9112	9174	9235	9297	9358	61
7	9419	9481	9542	9604	9665	9726	9788	9849	9911	9972	61
8	850033	850095	850156	850217	850279	850340	850401	850462	850524	850585	61
9	0646	0707	0769	0830	0891	0952	1014	1075	1136	1197	61
710	851258	851320	851381	851442	851503	851564	851625	851686	851747	851809	61
1	1870	1931	1992	2053	2114	2175	2236	2297	2358	2419	61
2	2480	2541	2602	2663	2724	2785	2846	2907	2968	3029	61
3	3090	3150	3211	3272	3333	3394	3455	3516	3577	3637	61
4	3698	3759	3820	3881	3941	4002	4063	4124	4185	4245	61
715	4306	4367	4428	4488	4549	4610	4670	4731	4792	4852	61
6	4913	4974	5034	5095	5156	5216	5277	5337	5398	5459	61
7	5519	5580	5640	5701	5761	5822	5882	5943	6003	6064	61
8	6124	6185	6245	6306	6366	6427	6487	6548	6608	6668	60
9	6729	6789	6850	6910	6970	7031	7091	7152	7212	7272	60
720	857332	857393	857453	857513	857574	857634	857694	857755	857815	857875	60
1	7935	7995	8056	8116	8176	8236	8297	8357	8417	8477	60
2	8537	8597	8657	8718	8778	8838	8898	8958	9018	9078	60
3	9138	9198	9258	9318	9379	9439	9499	9559	9619	9679	60
4	9739	9799	9859	9918	9978	860038	860098	860158	860218	860278	60
725	860338	860398	860458	860518	860578	0637	0697	0757	0817	0877	60
6	0937	0996	1056	1116	1176	1236	1295	1355	1415	1475	60
7	1534	1594	1654	1714	1773	1833	1893	1952	2012	2072	60
8	2131	2191	2251	2310	2370	2430	2489	2549	2608	2668	60
9	2728	2787	2847	2906	2966	3025	3085	3144	3204	3263	60
730	863323	863382	863442	863501	863561	863620	863680	863739	863799	863858	59
1	3917	3977	4036	4096	4155	4214	4274	4333	4392	4452	59
2	4511	4570	4630	4689	4748	4808	4867	4926	4985	5045	59
3	5104	5163	5222	5282	5341	5400	5459	5519	5578	5637	59
4	5696	5755	5814	5874	5933	5992	6051	6110	6169	6228	59
735	6287	6346	6405	6465	6524	6583	6642	6701	6760	6819	59
6	6878	6937	6996	7055	7114	7173	7232	7291	7350	7409	59
7	7467	7526	7585	7644	7703	7762	7821	7880	7939	7998	59
8	8056	8115	8174	8233	8292	8350	8409	8468	8527	8586	59
9	8644	8703	8762	8821	8879	8938	8997	9056	9114	9173	59
740	869232	869290	869349	869408	869466	869525	869584	869642	869701	869760	59
1	9818	9877	9935	9994	870053	870111	870170	870228	870287	870345	59
2	870404	870462	870521	870579	0638	0696	0755	0813	0872	0930	58
3	0989	1047	1106	1164	1223	1281	1339	1398	1456	1515	58
4	1573	1631	1690	1748	1806	1865	1923	1981	2040	2098	58
745	2156	2215	2273	2331	2389	2448	2506	2564	2622	2681	58
6	2739	2797	2855	2913	2972	3030	3088	3146	3204	3262	58
7	3321	3379	3437	3495	3553	3611	3669	3727	3785	3844	58
8	3902	3960	4018	4076	4134	4192	4250	4308	4366	4424	58
9	4482	4540	4598	4656	4714	4772	4830	4888	4945	5003	58
750	875061	875119	875177	875235	875293	875351	875409	875466	875524	875582	58
1	5640	5698	5756	5813	5871	5929	5987	6045	6102	6160	58
2	6218	6276	6333	6391	6449	6507	6564	6622	6680	6737	58
3	6795	6853	6910	6968	7026	7083	7141	7199	7256	7314	58
4	7371	7429	7487	7544	7602	7659	7717	7774	7832	7889	58
755	7947	8004	8062	8119	8177	8234	8292	8349	8407	8464	57
6	8522	8579	8637	8694	8752	8809	8866	8924	8981	9039	57
7	9096	9153	9211	9268	9325	9383	9440	9497	9555	9612	57
8	9669	9726	9784	9841	9898	9956	880013	880070	880127	880185	57
9	880242	880299	880356	880413	880471	880528	0585	0642	0699	0756	57
N.	0	1	2	3	4	5	6	7	8	9	D.

TABLE I.—Six-place Mantissas

N.	0	1	2	3	4	5	6	7	8	9	D.
760	880814	880871	880928	880985	881042	881099	881156	881213	881271	881328	57
1	1385	1442	1499	1556	1613	1670	1727	1784	1841	1898	57
2	1955	2012	2069	2126	2183	2240	2297	2354	2411	2468	57
3	2525	2581	2638	2695	2752	2809	2866	2923	2980	3037	57
4	3093	3150	3207	3264	3321	3377	3434	3491	3548	3605	57
765	3661	3718	3775	3832	3888	3945	4002	4059	4115	4172	57
6	4229	4285	4342	4399	4455	4512	4569	4625	4682	4739	57
7	4795	4852	4909	4965	5022	5078	5135	5192	5248	5305	57
8	5361	5418	5474	5531	5587	5644	5700	5757	5813	5870	57
9	5926	5983	6039	6096	6152	6209	6265	6321	6378	6434	56
770	886491	886547	886604	886660	886716	886773	886829	886885	886942	886998	56
1	7054	7111	7167	7223	7280	7336	7392	7449	7505	7561	56
2	7617	7674	7730	7786	7842	7898	7955	8011	8067	8123	56
3	8179	8236	8292	8348	8404	8460	8516	8573	8629	8685	56
4	8741	8797	8853	8909	8965	9021	9077	9134	9190	9246	56
775	9302	9358	9414	9470	9526	9582	9638	9694	9750	9806	56
6	9862	9918	9974	890030	890086	890141	890197	890253	890309	890365	56
7	890421	890477	890533	0589	0645	0700	0756	0812	0868	0924	56
8	0980	1035	1091	1147	1203	1259	1314	1370	1426	1482	56
9	1537	1593	1649	1705	1760	1816	1872	1928	1983	2039	56
780	892095	892150	892206	892262	892317	892373	892429	892484	892540	892595	56
1	2651	2707	2762	2818	2873	2929	2985	3040	3096	3151	56
2	3207	3262	3318	3373	3429	3484	3540	3595	3651	3706	56
3	3762	3817	3873	3928	3984	4039	4094	4150	4205	4261	55
4	4316	4371	4427	4482	4538	4593	4648	4704	4759	4814	55
785	4870	4925	4980	5036	5091	5146	5201	5257	5312	5367	55
6	5423	5478	5533	5588	5644	5699	5754	5809	5864	5920	55
7	5975	6030	6085	6140	6195	6251	6306	6361	6416	6471	55
8	6526	6581	6636	6692	6747	6802	6857	6912	6967	7022	55
9	7077	7132	7187	7242	7297	7352	7407	7462	7517	7572	55
790	897627	897682	897737	897792	897847	897902	897957	898012	898067	898122	55
1	8176	8231	8236	8341	8396	8451	8506	8561	8615	8670	55
2	8725	8780	8835	8890	8944	8999	9054	9109	9164	9218	55
3	9273	9328	9383	9437	9492	9547	9602	9656	9711	9766	55
4	9821	9875	9930	9985	900039	900094	900149	900203	900258	900312	55
795	900367	900422	900476	900531	0586	0640	0695	0749	0804	0859	55
6	0913	0968	1022	1077	1131	1186	1240	1295	1349	1404	55
7	1458	1513	1567	1622	1676	1731	1785	1840	1894	1948	54
8	2003	2057	2112	2166	2221	2275	2329	2384	2438	2492	54
9	2547	2601	2655	2710	2764	2818	2873	2927	2981	3036	54
800	903090	903144	903199	903253	903307	903361	903416	903470	903524	903578	54
1	3633	3687	3741	3795	3849	3904	3958	4012	4066	4120	54
2	4174	4229	4283	4337	4391	4445	4499	4553	4607	4661	54
3	4716	4770	4824	4878	4932	4986	5040	5094	5148	5202	54
4	5256	5310	5364	5418	5472	5526	5580	5634	5688	5742	54
805	5796	5850	5904	5958	6012	6066	6119	6173	6227	6281	54
6	6335	6389	6443	6497	6551	6604	6658	6712	6766	6820	54
7	6874	6927	6981	7035	7089	7143	7196	7250	7304	7358	54
8	7411	7465	7519	7573	7626	7680	7734	7787	7841	7895	54
9	7949	8002	8056	8110	8163	8217	8270	8324	8378	8431	54
810	908485	908539	908592	908646	908699	908753	908807	908860	908914	908967	54
1	9021	9074	9128	9181	9235	9289	9342	9396	9449	9503	54
2	9556	9610	9663	9716	9770	9823	9877	9930	9984	910037	53
3	910091	910144	910197	910251	910304	910358	910411	910464	910518	0571	53
4	0624	0678	0731	0784	0838	0891	0944	0998	1051	1104	53
815	1158	1211	1264	1317	1371	1424	1477	1530	1584	1637	53
6	1690	1743	1797	1850	1903	1956	2009	2063	2116	2169	53
7	2222	2275	2328	2381	2435	2488	2541	2594	2647	2700	53
8	2753	2806	2859	2913	2966	3019	3072	3125	3178	3231	53
9	3284	3337	3390	3443	3496	3549	3602	3655	3708	3761	53
N.	0	1	2	3	4	5	6	7	8	9	D.

TABLE I. — Six-place Mantissas

N.	0	1	2	3	4	5	6	7	8	9	D.
820	913814	913867	913920	913973	914026	914079	914132	914184	914237	914290	53
1	4343	4396	4449	4502	4555	4608	4660	4713	4766	4819	53
2	4872	4925	4977	5030	5083	5136	5189	5241	5294	5347	53
3	5400	5453	5505	5558	5611	5664	5716	5769	5822	5875	53
4	5927	5980	6033	6085	6138	6191	6243	6296	6349	6401	53
825	6454	6507	6559	6612	6664	6717	6770	6822	6875	6927	53
6	6980	7033	7085	7138	7190	7243	7295	7348	7400	7453	53
7	7506	7558	7611	7663	7716	7768	7820	7873	7925	7978	52
8	8030	8083	8135	8188	8240	8293	8345	8397	8450	8502	52
9	8555	8607	8659	8712	8764	8816	8869	8921	8973	9026	52
830	919078	919130	919183	919235	919287	919340	919392	919444	919496	919549	52
1	9601	9653	9706	9758	9810	9862	9914	9967	920019	920071	52
2	920123	920176	920228	920280	920332	920384	920436	920489	0541	0593	52
3	0645	0697	0749	0801	0853	0906	0958	1010	1062	1114	52
4	1166	1218	1270	1322	1374	1426	1478	1530	1582	1634	52
835	1686	1738	1790	1842	1894	1946	1998	2050	2102	2154	52
6	2206	2258	2310	2362	2414	2466	2518	2570	2622	2674	52
7	2725	2777	2829	2881	2933	2985	3037	3089	3140	3192	52
8	3244	3296	3348	3399	3451	3503	3555	3607	3658	3710	52
9	3762	3814	3865	3917	3969	4021	4072	4124	4176	4228	52
840	924279	924331	924383	924434	924486	924538	924589	924641	924693	924744	52
1	4796	4848	4899	4951	5003	5054	5106	5157	5209	5261	52
2	5312	5364	5415	5467	5518	5570	5621	5673	5725	5776	52
3	5828	5879	5931	5982	6034	6085	6137	6188	6240	6291	51
4	6342	6394	6445	6497	6548	6600	6651	6702	6754	6805	51
845	6857	6908	6959	7011	7062	7114	7165	7216	7268	7319	51
6	7370	7422	7473	7524	7576	7627	7678	7730	7781	7832	51
7	7883	7935	7986	8037	8088	8140	8191	8242	8293	8345	51
8	8396	8447	8498	8549	8601	8652	8703	8754	8805	8857	51
9	8908	8959	9010	9061	9112	9163	9215	9266	9317	9368	51
850	929419	929470	929521	929572	929623	929674	929725	929776	929827	929879	51
1	9930	9981	930032	930083	930134	930185	930236	930287	930338	930389	51
2	930440	930491	0542	0592	0643	0694	0745	0796	0847	0898	51
3	0949	1000	1051	1102	1153	1204	1254	1305	1356	1407	51
4	1458	1509	1560	1610	1661	1712	1763	1814	1865	1915	51
855	1966	2017	2068	2118	2169	2220	2271	2322	2372	2423	51
6	2474	2524	2575	2626	2677	2727	2778	2829	2879	2930	51
7	2981	3031	3082	3133	3183	3234	3285	3335	3386	3437	51
8	3487	3538	3589	3639	3690	3740	3791	3841	3892	3943	51
9	3993	4044	4094	4145	4195	4246	4296	4347	4397	4448	51
860	934498	934549	934599	934650	934700	934751	934801	934852	934902	934953	50
1	5003	5054	5104	5154	5205	5255	5306	5356	5406	5457	50
2	5507	5558	5608	5658	5709	5759	5809	5860	5910	5960	50
3	6011	6061	6111	6162	6212	6262	6313	6363	6413	6463	50
4	6514	6564	6614	6665	6715	6765	6815	6865	6916	6966	50
865	7016	7066	7117	7167	7217	7267	7317	7367	7418	7468	50
6	7518	7568	7618	7668	7718	7769	7819	7869	7919	7969	50
7	8019	8069	8119	8169	8219	8269	8320	8370	8420	8470	50
8	8520	8570	8620	8670	8720	8770	8820	8870	8920	8970	50
9	9020	9070	9120	9170	9220	9270	9320	9369	9419	9469	50
870	939519	939569	939619	939669	939719	939769	939819	939869	939918	939968	50
1	940018	940068	940118	940168	940218	940267	940317	940367	940417	940467	50
2	0516	0566	0616	0666	0716	0765	0815	0865	0915	0964	50
3	1014	1064	1114	1163	1213	1263	1313	1362	1412	1462	50
4	1511	1561	1611	1660	1710	1760	1809	1859	1909	1958	50
875	2008	2058	2107	2157	2207	2256	2306	2355	2405	2455	50
6	2504	2554	2603	2653	2702	2752	2801	2851	2901	2950	50
7	3000	3049	3099	3148	3198	3247	3297	3346	3396	3445	49
8	3495	3544	3593	3643	3692	3742	3791	3841	3890	3939	49
9	3989	4038	4088	4137	4186	4236	4285	4335	4384	4433	49
N.	0	1	2	3	4	5	6	7	8	9	D.

TABLE I.—Six-place Mantissas

N.	0	1	2	3	4	5	6	7	8	9	D.
880	944483	944532	944581	944631	944680	944729	944779	944828	944877	944927	49
1	4976	5025	5074	5124	5173	5222	5272	5321	5370	5419	49
2	5469	5518	5567	5616	5665	5715	5764	5813	5862	5912	49
3	5961	6010	6059	6108	6157	6207	6256	6305	6354	6403	49
4	6452	6501	6551	6600	6649	6698	6747	6796	6845	6894	49
885	6943	6992	7041	7090	7140	7189	7238	7287	7336	7385	49
6	7434	7483	7532	7581	7630	7679	7728	7777	7826	7875	49
7	7924	7973	8022	8070	8119	8168	8217	8266	8315	8364	49
8	8413	8462	8511	8560	8609	8657	8706	8755	8804	8853	49
9	8902	8951	8999	9048	9097	9146	9195	9244	9292	9341	49
890	949390	949439	949488	949536	949585	949634	949683	949731	949780	949829	49
1	9878	9926	9975	950024	950073	950121	950170	950219	950267	950316	49
2	950365	950414	950462	0511	0560	0608	0657	0706	0754	0803	49
3	0851	0900	0949	0997	1046	1095	1143	1192	1240	1289	49
4	1338	1386	1435	1483	1532	1580	1629	1677	1726	1775	49
895	1823	1872	1920	1969	2017	2066	2114	2163	2211	2260	48
6	2308	2356	2405	2453	2502	2550	2599	2647	2696	2744	48
7	2792	2841	2889	2938	2986	3034	3083	3131	3180	3228	48
8	3276	3325	3373	3421	3470	3518	3566	3615	3663	3711	48
9	3760	3808	3856	3905	3953	4001	4049	4098	4146	4194	48
900	954243	954291	954339	954387	954435	954484	954532	954580	954628	954677	48
1	4725	4773	4821	4869	4918	4966	5014	5062	5110	5158	48
2	5207	5255	5303	5351	5399	5447	5495	5543	5592	5640	48
3	5688	5736	5784	5832	5880	5928	5976	6024	6072	6120	48
4	6168	6216	6265	6313	6361	6409	6457	6505	6553	6601	48
905	6649	6697	6745	6793	6840	6888	6936	6984	7032	7080	48
6	7128	7176	7224	7272	7320	7368	7416	7464	7512	7559	48
7	7607	7655	7703	7751	7799	7847	7894	7942	7990	8038	48
8	8086	8134	8181	8229	8277	8325	8373	8421	8468	8516	48
9	8564	8612	8659	8707	8755	8803	8850	8898	8946	8994	48
910	959041	959089	959137	959185	959232	959280	959328	959375	959423	959471	48
1	9518	9566	9614	9661	9709	9757	9804	9852	9900	9947	48
2	9995	960042	960090	960138	960185	960233	960280	960328	960376	960423	48
3	960471	0518	0566	0613	0661	0709	0756	0804	0851	0899	48
4	0946	0994	1041	1089	1136	1184	1231	1279	1326	1374	48
915	1421	1469	1516	1563	1611	1658	1706	1753	1801	1848	47
6	1895	1943	1990	2038	2085	2132	2180	2227	2275	2322	47
7	2369	2417	2464	2511	2559	2606	2653	2701	2748	2795	47
8	2843	2890	2937	2985	3032	3079	3126	3174	3221	3268	47
9	3316	3363	3410	3457	3504	3552	3599	3646	3693	3741	47
920	963788	963835	963882	963929	963977	964024	964071	964118	964165	964212	47
1	4260	4307	4354	4401	4448	4495	4542	4590	4637	4684	47
2	4731	4778	4825	4872	4919	4966	5013	5061	5108	5155	47
3	5202	5249	5296	5343	5390	5437	5484	5531	5578	5625	47
4	5672	5719	5766	5813	5860	5907	5954	6001	6048	6095	47
925	6142	6189	6236	6283	6329	6376	6423	6470	6517	6564	47
6	6611	6658	6705	6752	6799	6845	6892	6939	6986	7033	47
7	7080	7127	7173	7220	7267	7314	7361	7408	7454	7501	47
8	7548	7595	7642	7688	7735	7782	7829	7875	7922	7969	47
9	8016	8062	8109	8156	8203	8249	8296	8343	8390	8436	47
930	968483	968530	968576	968623	968670	968716	968763	968810	968856	968903	47
1	8950	8996	9043	9090	9136	9183	9229	9276	9323	9369	47
2	9416	9463	9509	9556	9602	9649	9695	9742	9789	9835	47
3	9882	9928	9975	970021	970068	970114	970161	970207	970254	970300	47
4	970347	970393	970440	0486	0533	0579	0626	0672	0719	0765	46
935	0812	0858	0904	0951	0997	1044	1090	1137	1183	1229	46
6	1276	1322	1369	1415	1461	1508	1554	1601	1647	1693	46
7	1740	1786	1832	1879	1925	1971	2018	2064	2110	2157	46
8	2203	2249	2295	2342	2388	2434	2481	2527	2573	2619	46
9	2666	2712	2758	2804	2851	2897	2943	2989	3035	3082	46
N.	0	1	2	3	4	5	6	7	8	9	D.

TABLE I.—Six-place Mantissas

N.	0	1	2	3	4	5	6	7	8	9	D.
940	973128	973174	973220	973266	973313	973359	973405	973451	973497	973543	46
1	3590	3636	3682	3728	3774	3820	3866	3913	3959	4005	46
2	4051	4097	4143	4189	4235	4281	4327	4374	4420	4466	46
3	4512	4558	4604	4650	4696	4742	4788	4834	4880	4926	46
4	4972	5018	5064	5110	5156	5202	5248	5294	5340	5386	46
945	5432	5478	5524	5570	5616	5662	5707	5753	5799	5845	46
6	5891	5937	5983	6029	6075	6121	6167	6212	6258	6304	46
7	6350	6396	6442	6488	6533	6579	6625	6671	6717	6763	46
8	6808	6854	6900	6946	6992	7037	7083	7129	7175	7220	46
9	7266	7312	7358	7403	7449	7495	7541	7586	7632	7678	46
950	977724	977769	977815	977861	977906	977952	977998	978043	978089	978135	46
1	8181	8226	8272	8317	8363	8409	8454	8500	8546	8591	46
2	8637	8683	8728	8774	8819	8865	8911	8956	9002	9047	46
3	9093	9138	9184	9230	9275	9321	9366	9412	9457	9503	46
4	9548	9594	9639	9685	9730	9776	9821	9867	9912	9958	46
955	980003	980049	980094	980140	980185	980231	980276	980322	980367	980412	45
6	0458	0503	0549	0594	0640	0685	0730	0776	0821	0867	45
7	0912	0957	1003	1048	1093	1139	1184	1229	1275	1320	45
8	1366	1411	1456	1501	1547	1592	1637	1683	1728	1773	45
9	1819	1864	1909	1954	2000	2045	2090	2135	2181	2226	45
960	982271	982316	982362	982407	982452	982497	982543	982588	982633	982678	45
1	2723	2769	2814	2859	2904	2949	2994	3040	3085	3130	45
2	3175	3220	3265	3310	3356	3401	3446	3491	3536	3581	45
3	3626	3671	3716	3762	3807	3852	3897	3942	3987	4032	45
4	4077	4122	4167	4212	4257	4302	4347	4392	4437	4482	45
965	4527	4572	4617	4662	4707	4752	4797	4842	4887	4932	45
6	4977	5022	5067	5112	5157	5202	5247	5292	5337	5382	45
7	5426	5471	5516	5561	5606	5651	5696	5741	5786	5830	45
8	5875	5920	5965	6010	6055	6100	6144	6189	6234	6279	45
9	6324	6369	6413	6458	6503	6548	6593	6637	6682	6727	45
970	986772	986817	986861	986906	986951	986996	987040	987085	987130	987175	45
1	7219	7264	7309	7353	7398	7443	7488	7532	7577	7622	45
2	7666	7711	7756	7800	7845	7890	7934	7979	8024	8068	45
3	8113	8157	8202	8247	8291	8336	8381	8425	8470	8514	45
4	8559	8604	8648	8693	8737	8782	8826	8871	8916	8960	45
975	9005	9049	9094	9138	9183	9227	9272	9316	9361	9405	45
6	9450	9494	9539	9583	9628	9672	9717	9761	9806	9850	44
7	9895	9939	9983	990028	990072	990117	990161	990206	990250	990294	44
8	990339	990383	990428	0472	0516	0561	0605	0650	0694	0738	44
9	0783	0827	0871	0916	0960	1004	1049	1093	1137	1182	44
980	991226	991270	991315	991359	991403	991448	991492	991536	991580	991625	44
1	1669	1713	1758	1802	1846	1890	1935	1979	2023	2067	44
2	2111	2156	2200	2244	2288	2333	2377	2421	2465	2509	44
3	2554	2598	2642	2686	2730	2774	2819	2863	2907	2951	44
4	2995	3039	3083	3127	3172	3216	3260	3304	3348	3392	44
985	3436	3480	3524	3568	3613	3657	3701	3745	3789	3833	44
6	3877	3921	3965	4009	4053	4097	4141	4185	4229	4273	44
7	4317	4361	4405	4449	4493	4537	4581	4625	4669	4713	44
8	4757	4801	4845	4889	4933	4977	5021	5065	5108	5152	44
9	5196	5240	5284	5328	5372	5416	5460	5504	5547	5591	44
990	995635	995679	995723	995767	995811	995854	995898	995942	995986	996030	44
1	6074	6117	6161	6205	6249	6293	6337	6380	6424	6468	44
2	6512	6555	6599	6643	6687	6731	6774	6818	6862	6906	44
3	6949	6993	7037	7080	7124	7168	7212	7255	7299	7343	44
4	7386	7430	7474	7517	7561	7605	7648	7692	7736	7779	44
995	7823	7867	7910	7954	7998	8041	8085	8129	8172	8216	44
6	8259	8303	8347	8390	8434	8477	8521	8564	8608	8652	44
7	8695	8739	8782	8826	8869	8913	8956	9000	9043	9087	44
8	9131	9174	9218	9261	9305	9348	9392	9435	9479	9522	44
9	9565	9609	9652	9696	9739	9783	9826	9870	9913	9957	43
N.	0	1	2	3	4	5	6	7	8	9	D.

TABLE II.—Seven-place Mantissas

10000–10509

N.		0	1	2	3	4	5	6	7	8	9	D.
1000	000	0000	0434	0869	1303	1737	2171	2605	3039	3473	3907	434
1001		4341	4775	5208	5642	6076	6510	6943	7377	7810	8244	434
1002		8677	9111	9544	9977	*0411	*0844	*1277	*1710	*2143	*2576	433
1003	001	3009	3442	3875	4308	4741	5174	5607	6039	6472	6905	433
1004		7337	7770	8202	8635	9067	9499	9932	*0364	*0796	*1228	432
1005	002	1661	2093	2525	2957	3389	3821	4253	4685	5116	5548	432
1006		5980	6411	6843	7275	7706	8138	8569	9001	9432	9863	431
1007	003	0295	0726	1157	1588	2019	2451	2882	3313	3744	4174	431
1008		4605	5036	5467	5898	6328	6759	7190	7620	8051	8481	431
1009		8912	9342	9772	*0203	*0633	*1063	*1493	*1924	*2354	*2784	430
1010	004	3214	3644	4074	4504	4933	5363	5793	6223	6652	7082	430
1011		7512	7941	8371	8800	9229	9659	*0088	*0517	*0947	*1376	429
1012	005	1805	2234	2663	3092	3521	3950	4379	4808	5237	5666	429
1013		6094	6523	6952	7380	7809	8238	8666	9094	9523	9951	429
1014	006	0380	0808	1236	1664	2092	2521	2949	3377	3805	4233	428
1015		4660	5088	5516	5944	6372	6799	7227	7655	8082	8510	428
1016		8937	9365	9792	*0219	*0647	*1074	*1501	*1928	*2355	*2782	427
1017	007	3210	3637	4064	4490	4917	5344	5771	6198	6624	7051	427
1018		7478	7904	8331	8757	9184	9610	*0037	*0463	*0889	*1316	426
1019	008	1742	2168	2594	3020	3446	3872	4298	4724	5150	5576	426
1020		6002	6427	6853	7279	7704	8130	8556	8981	9407	9832	426
1021	009	0257	0683	1108	1533	1959	2384	2809	3234	3659	4084	425
1022		4509	4934	5359	5784	6208	6633	7058	7483	7907	8332	425
1023		8756	9181	9605	*0030	*0454	*0878	*1303	*1727	*2151	*2575	424
1024	010	3000	3424	3848	4272	4696	5120	5544	5967	6391	6815	424
1025		7239	7662	8086	8510	8933	9357	9780	*0204	*0627	*1050	424
1026	011	1474	1897	2320	2743	3166	3590	4013	4436	4859	5282	423
1027		5704	6127	6550	6973	7396	7818	8241	8664	9086	9509	423
1028		9931	*0354	*0776	*1198	*1621	*2043	*2465	*2887	*3310	*3732	422
1029	012	4154	4576	4998	5420	5842	6264	6685	7107	7529	7951	422
1030		8372	8794	9215	9637	*0059	*0480	*0901	*1323	*1744	*2165	422
1031	013	2587	3008	3429	3850	4271	4692	5113	5534	5955	6376	421
1032		6797	7218	7639	8059	8480	8901	9321	9742	*0162	*0583	421
1033	014	1003	1424	1844	2264	2685	3105	3525	3945	4365	4785	420
1034		5205	5625	6045	6465	6885	7305	7725	8144	8564	8984	420
1035		9403	9823	*0243	*0662	*1082	*1501	*1920	*2340	*2759	*3178	420
1036	015	3598	4017	4436	4855	5274	5693	6112	6531	6950	7369	419
1037		7788	8206	8625	9044	9462	9881	*0300	*0718	*1137	*1555	419
1038	016	1974	2392	2810	3229	3647	4065	4483	4901	5319	5737	418
1039		6155	6573	6991	7409	7827	8245	8663	9080	9498	9916	418
1040	017	0333	0751	1168	1586	2003	2421	2838	3256	3673	4090	417
1041		4507	4924	5342	5759	6176	6593	7010	7427	7844	8260	417
1042		8677	9094	9511	9927	*0344	*0761	*1177	*1594	*2010	*2427	417
1043	018	2843	3259	3676	4092	4508	4925	5341	5757	6173	6589	416
1044		7005	7421	7837	8253	8669	9084	9500	9916	*0332	*0747	416
1045	019	1163	1578	1994	2410	2825	3240	3656	4071	4486	4902	415
1046		5317	5732	6147	6562	6977	7392	7807	8222	8637	9052	415
1047		9467	9882	*0296	*0711	*1126	*1540	*1955	*2369	*2784	*3198	415
1048	020	3613	4027	4442	4856	5270	5684	6099	6513	6927	7341	414
1049		7755	8169	8583	8997	9411	9824	*0238	*0652	*1066	*1479	414
1050	021	1893	2307	2720	3134	3547	3961	4374	4787	5201	5614	413
N.		0	1	2	3	4	5	6	7	8	9	D.

TABLE II.—Seven-place Mantissas

10500–11009

N.		0	1	2	3	4	5	6	7	8	9	D.
1050	021	1893	2307	2720	3134	3547	3961	4374	4787	5201	5614	413
1051		6027	6440	6854	7267	7680	8093	8506	8919	9332	9745	413
1052	022	0157	0570	0983	1396	1808	2221	2634	3046	3459	3871	413
1053		4284	4696	5109	5521	5933	6345	6758	7170	7582	7994	412
1054		8406	8818	9230	9642	*0054	*0466	*0878	*1289	*1701	*2113	412
1055	023	2525	2936	3348	3759	4171	4582	4994	5405	5817	6228	411
1056		6639	7050	7462	7873	8284	8695	9106	9517	9928	*0339	411
1057	024	0750	1161	1572	1982	2393	2804	3214	3625	4036	4446	411
1058		4857	5267	5678	6088	6498	6909	7319	7729	8139	8549	410
1059		8960	9370	9780	*0190	*0600	*1010	*1419	*1829	*2239	*2649	410
1060	025	3059	3468	3878	4288	4697	5107	5516	5926	6335	6744	410
1061		7154	7563	7972	8382	8791	9200	9609	*0018	*0427	*0836	409
1062	026	1245	1654	2063	2472	2881	3289	3698	4107	4515	4924	409
1063		5333	5741	6150	6558	6967	7375	7783	8192	8600	9008	408
1064		9416	9824	*0233	*0641	*1049	*1457	*1865	*2273	*2680	*3088	408
1065	027	3496	3904	4312	4719	5127	5535	5942	6350	6757	7165	408
1066		7572	7979	8387	8794	9201	9609	*0016	*0423	*0830	*1237	407
1067	028	1644	2051	2458	2865	3272	3679	4086	4492	4899	5306	407
1068		5713	6119	6526	6932	7339	7745	8152	8558	8964	9371	406
1069		9777	*0183	*0590	*0996	*1402	*1808	*2214	*2620	*3026	*3432	406
1070	029	3838	4244	4649	5055	5461	5867	6272	6678	7084	7489	406
1071		7895	8300	8706	9111	9516	9922	*0327	*0732	*1138	*1543	405
1072	030	1948	2353	2758	3163	3568	3973	4378	4783	5188	5592	405
1073		5997	6402	6807	7211	7616	8020	8425	8830	9234	9638	405
1074	031	0043	0447	0851	1256	1660	2064	2468	2872	3277	3681	404
1075		4085	4489	4893	5296	5700	6104	6508	6912	7315	7719	404
1076		8123	8526	8930	9333	9737	*0140	*0544	*0947	*1350	*1754	403
1077	032	2157	2560	2963	3367	3770	4173	4576	4979	5382	5785	403
1078		6188	6590	6993	7396	7799	8201	8604	9007	9409	9812	403
1079	033	0214	0617	1019	1422	1824	2226	2629	3031	3433	3835	402
1080		4238	4640	5042	5444	5846	6248	6650	7052	7453	7855	402
1081		8257	8659	9060	9462	9864	*0265	*0667	*1068	*1470	*1871	402
1082	034	2273	2674	3075	3477	3878	4279	4680	5081	5482	5884	401
1083		6285	6686	7087	7487	7888	8289	8690	9091	9491	9892	401
1084	035	0293	0693	1094	1495	1895	2296	2696	3096	3497	3897	400
1085		4297	4698	5098	5498	5898	6298	6698	7098	7498	7898	400
1086		8298	8698	9098	9498	9898	*0297	*0697	*1097	*1496	*1896	400
1087	036	2295	2695	3094	3494	3893	4293	4692	5091	5491	5890	399
1088		6289	6688	7087	7486	7885	8284	8683	9082	9481	9880	399
1089	037	0279	0678	1076	1475	1874	2272	2671	3070	3468	3867	399
1090		4265	4663	5062	5460	5858	6257	6655	7053	7451	7849	398
1091		8248	8646	9044	9442	9839	*0237	*0635	*1033	*1431	*1829	398
1092	038	2226	2624	3022	3419	3817	4214	4612	5009	5407	5804	398
1093		6202	6599	6996	7393	7791	8188	8585	8982	9379	9776	397
1094	039	0173	0570	0967	1364	1761	2158	2554	2951	3348	3745	397
1095		4141	4538	4934	5331	5727	6124	6520	6917	7313	7709	397
1096		8106	8502	8898	9294	9690	*0086	*0482	*0878	*1274	*1670	396
1097	040	2066	2462	2858	3254	3650	4045	4441	4837	5232	5628	396
1098		6023	6419	6814	7210	7605	8001	8396	8791	9187	9582	395
1099		9977	*0372	*0767	*1162	*1557	*1952	*2347	*2742	*3137	*3532	395
1100	041	3927	4322	4716	5111	5506	5900	6295	6690	7084	7479	395
N.		0	1	2	3	4	5	6	7	8	9	D.

APPENDIX D

SYSTEM FLOWCHARTING

Flow charts are used in accounting systems design and analysis to identify controls, files, documents, and reports. Operations and procedures are described in their actual sequence by continuous flow lines that trace the processing steps of each document. The flow chart symbols typically used for *system flowcharting* are given below, with the meaning and use of each described in the right-hand column.

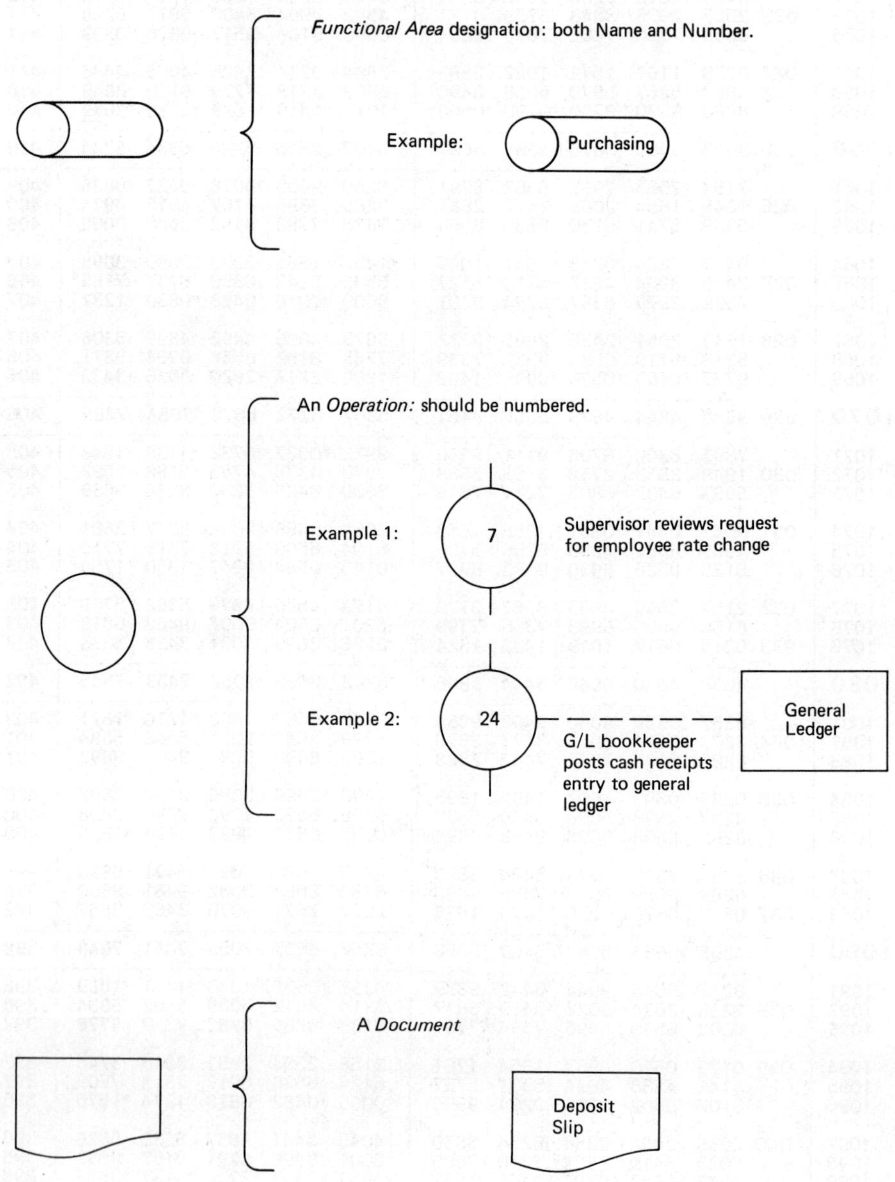

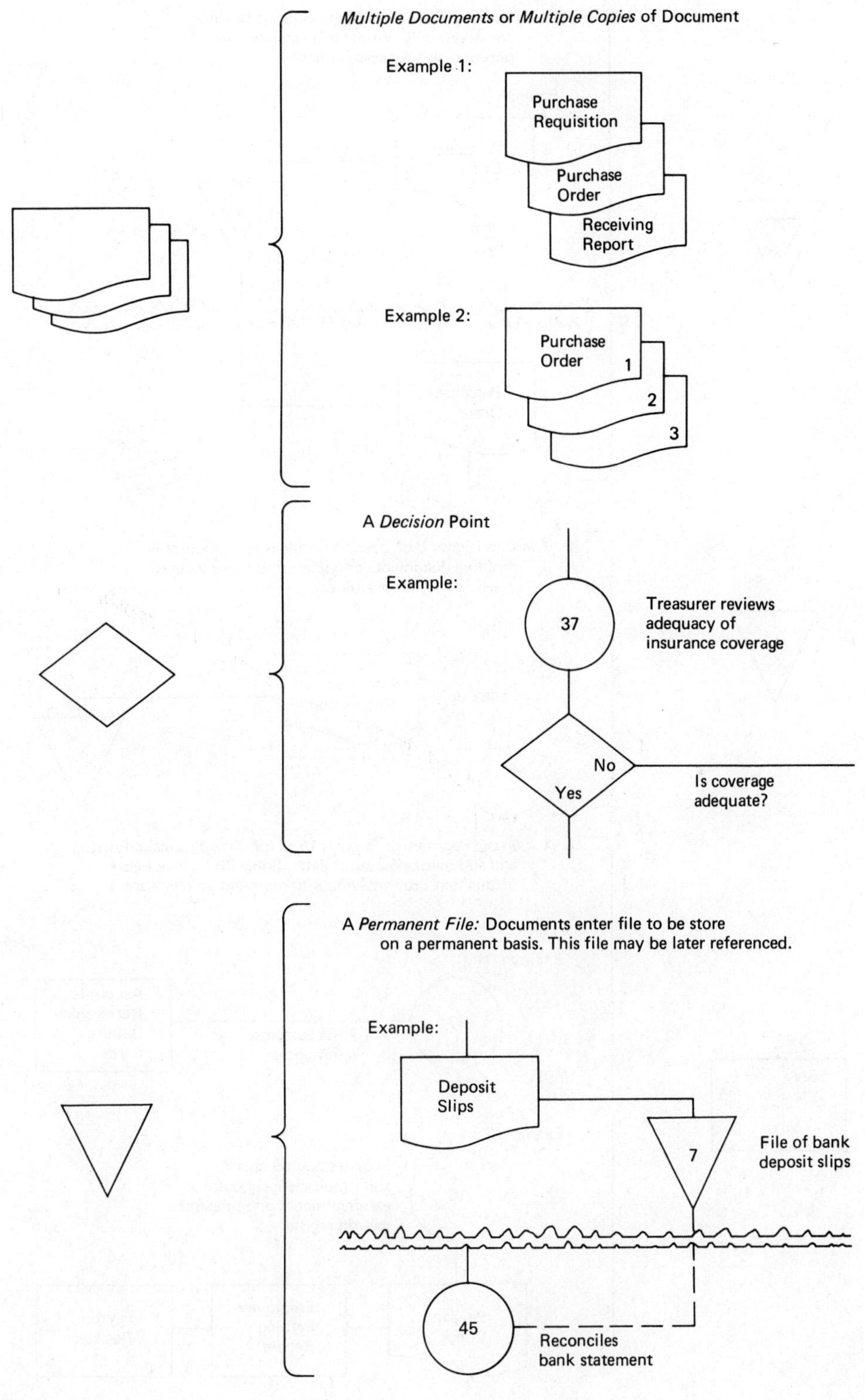

Multiple Documents or *Multiple Copies* of Document
Example 1:
Purchase Requisition
Purchase Order
Receiving Report
Example 2:
Purchase Order
1
2
3
A *Decision* Point
Example:
37
Treasurer reviews adequacy of insurance coverage
No
Yes
Is coverage adequate?
A *Permanent File:* Documents enter file to be store on a permanent basis. This file may be later referenced.
Example:
Deposit Slips
7
File of bank deposit slips
45
Reconciles bank statement

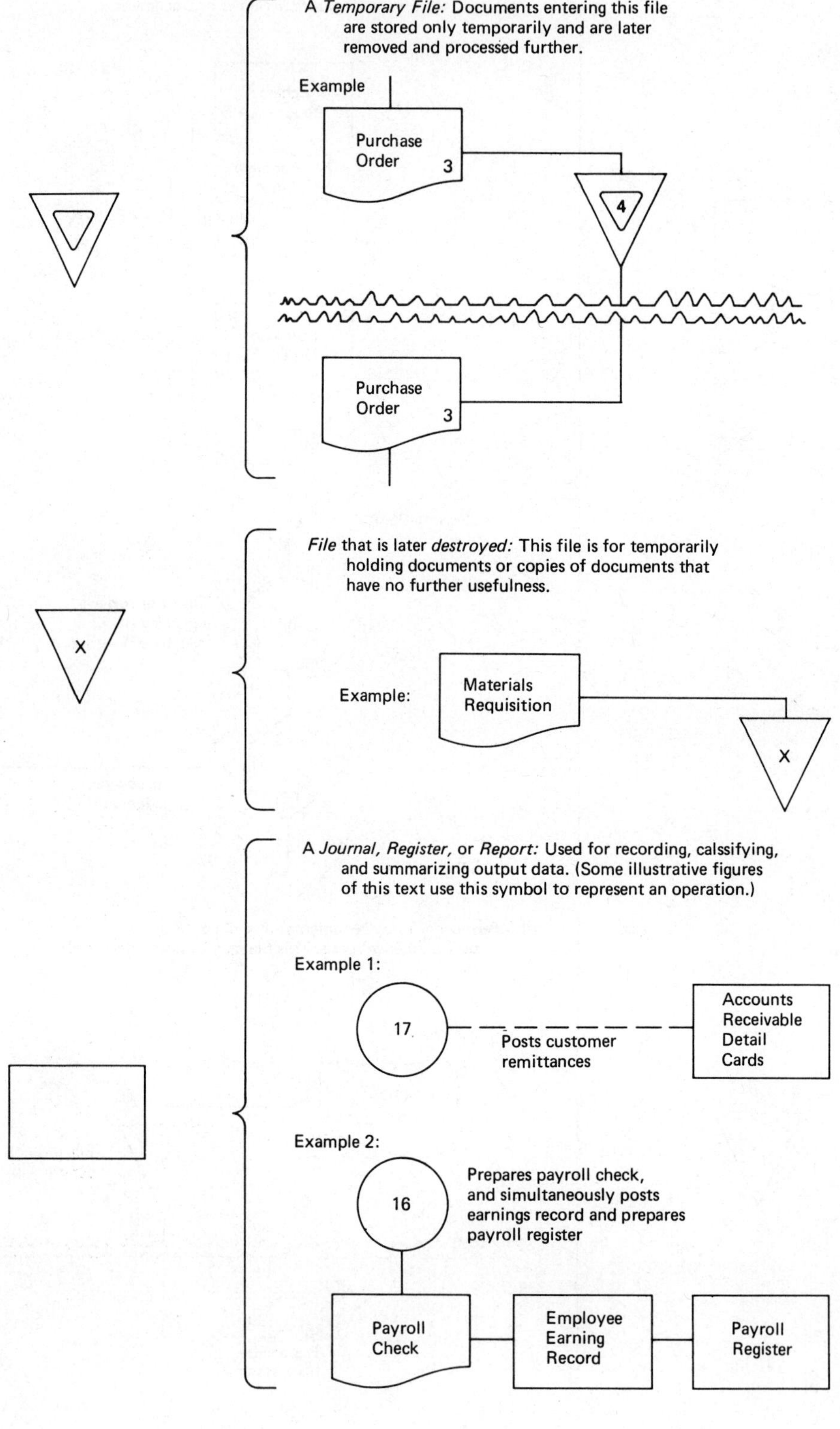
A *Temporary File:* Documents entering this file are stored only temporarily and are later removed and processed further.
Example
Purchase Order 3
4
Purchase Order 3
File that is later *destroyed:* This file is for temporarily holding documents or copies of documents that have no further usefulness.
X
Example:
Materials Requisition
X
A *Journal, Register,* or *Report:* Used for recording, calssifying, and summarizing output data. (Some illustrative figures of this text use this symbol to represent an operation.)
Example 1:
17
Posts customer remittances
Accounts Receivable Detail Cards
Example 2:
16
Prepares payroll check, and simultaneously posts earnings record and prepares payroll register
Payroll Check
Employee Earning Record
Payroll Register

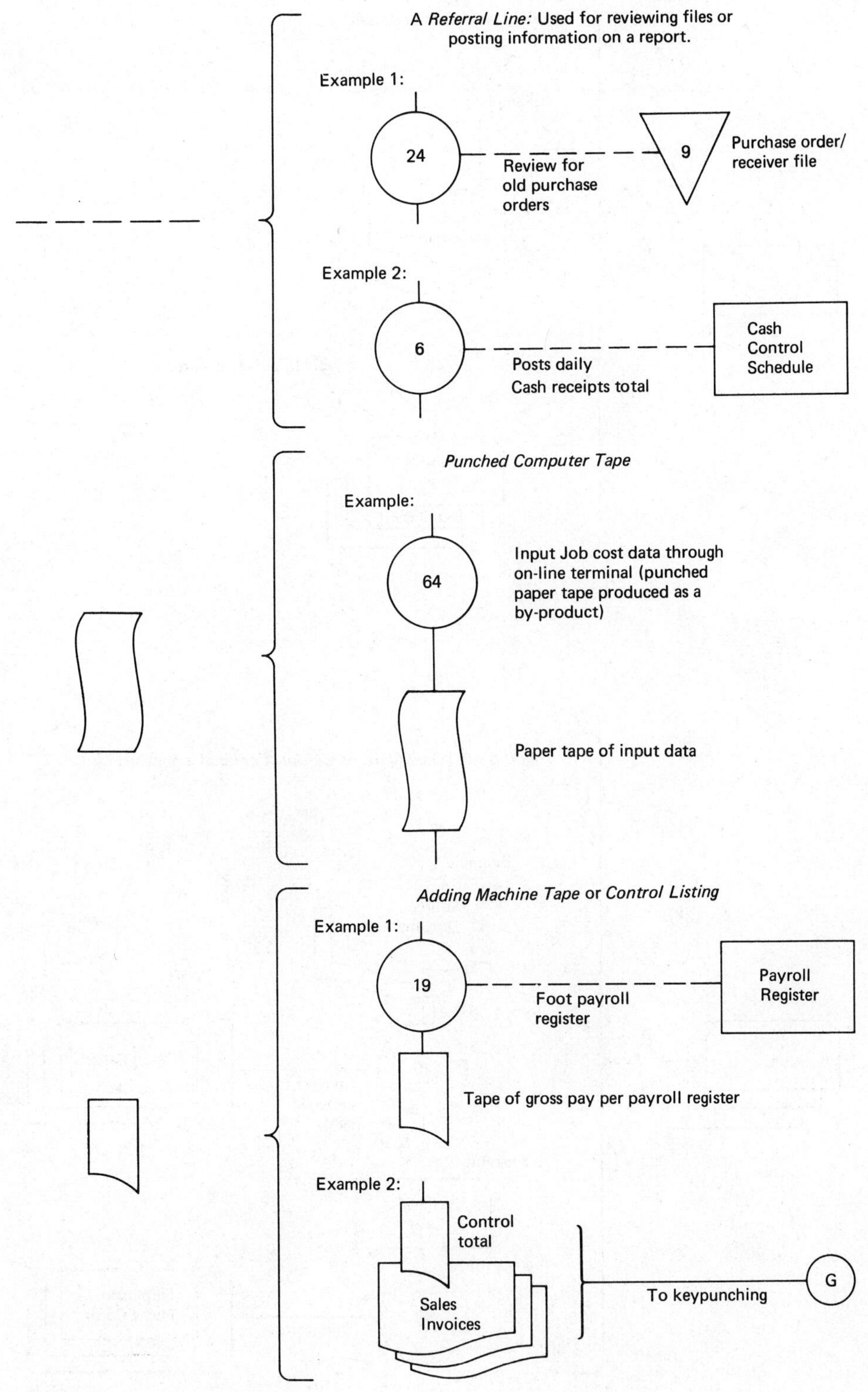
A *Referral Line:* Used for reviewing files or posting information on a report.
Example 1:
24
Review for old purchase orders
9
Purchase order/ receiver file
Example 2:
6
Posts daily Cash receipts total
Cash Control Schedule
Punched Computer Tape
Example:
64
Input Job cost data through on-line terminal (punched paper tape produced as a by-product)
Paper tape of input data
Adding Machine Tape or *Control Listing*
Example 1:
19
Foot payroll register
Payroll Register
Tape of gross pay per payroll register
Example 2:
Control total
Sales Invoices
To keypunching
G

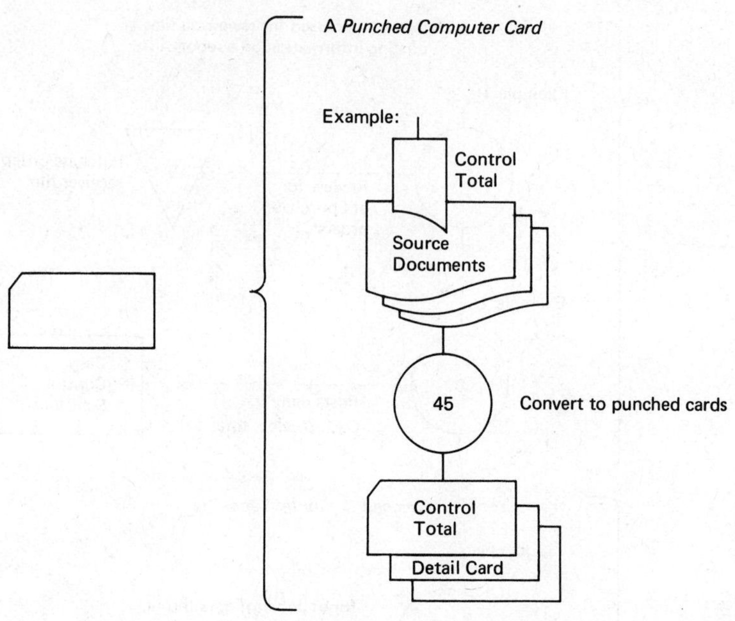
A *Punched Computer Card*
Example:
Control
Total
Source
Documents
45
Convert to punched cards
Control
Total
Detail Card

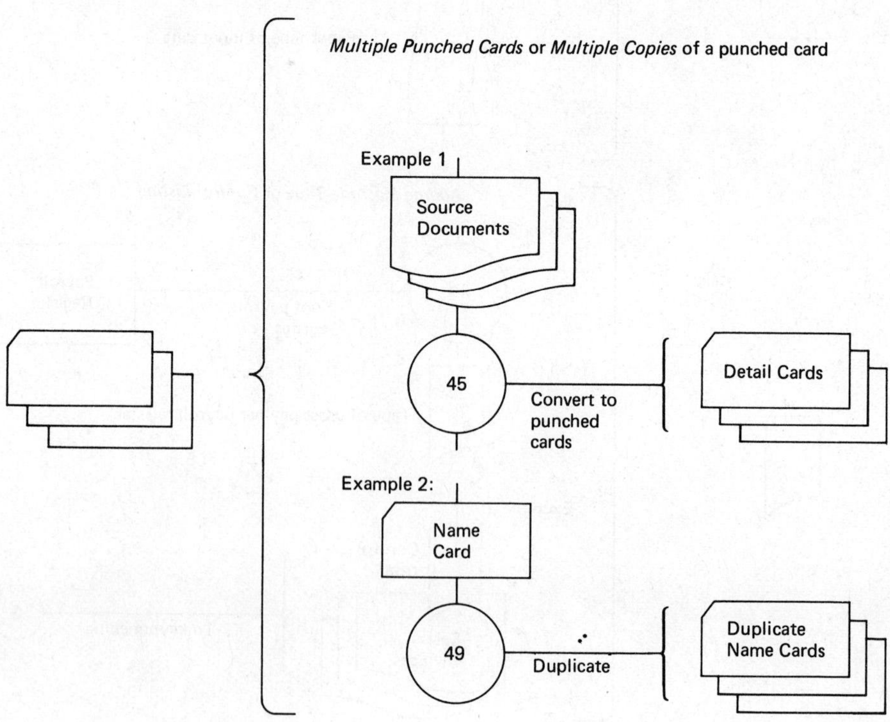
Multiple Punched Cards or *Multiple Copies* of a punched card
Example 1
Source
Documents
45
Convert to
punched
cards
Detail Cards
Example 2:
Name
Card
49
Duplicate
Duplicate
Name Cards

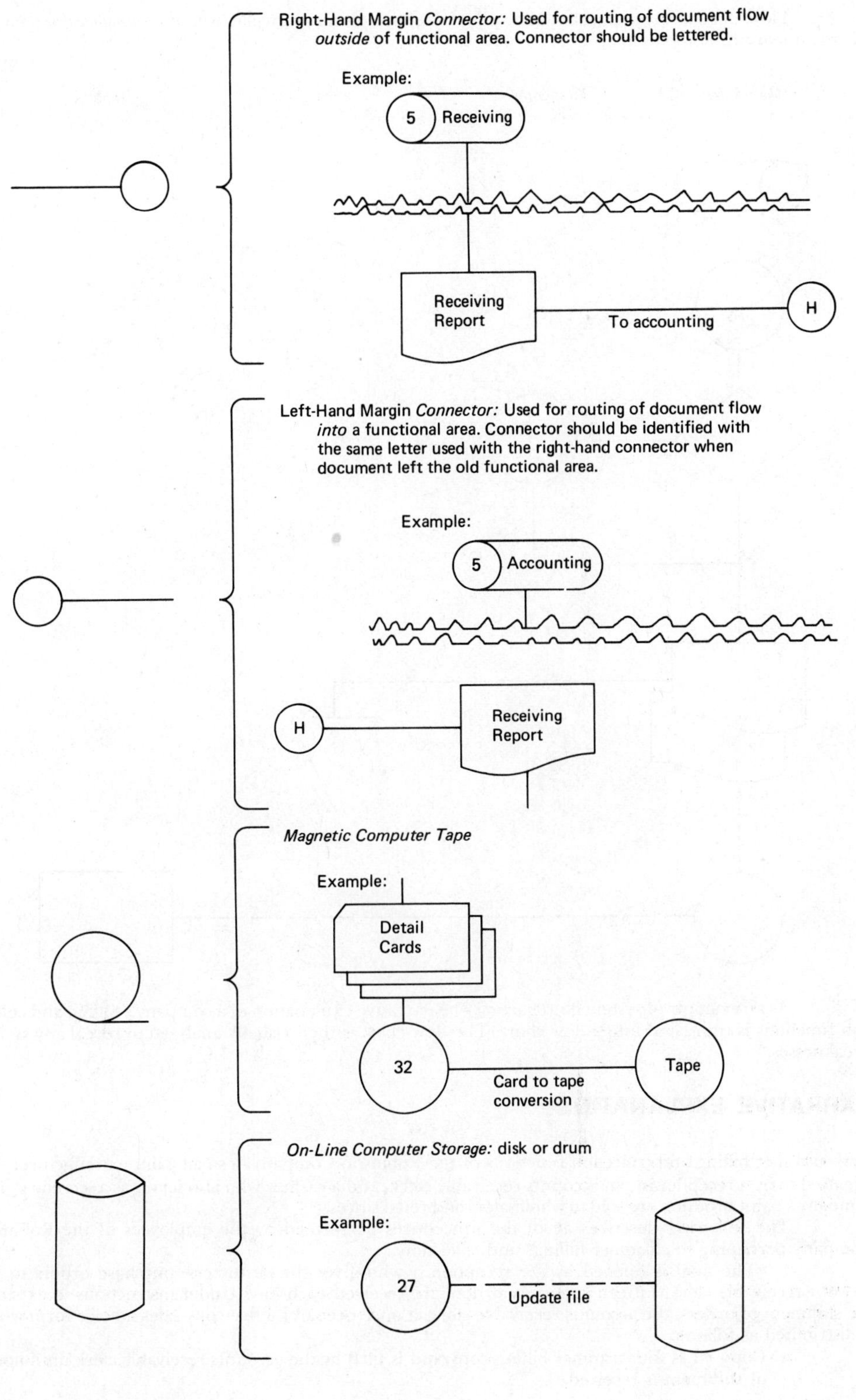
Right-Hand Margin *Connector:* Used for routing of document flow *outside* of functional area. Connector should be lettered.
Example:
5
Receiving
Receiving Report
To accounting
H
Left-Hand Margin *Connector:* Used for routing of document flow *into* a functional area. Connector should be identified with the same letter used with the right-hand connector when document left the old functional area.
Example:
5
Accounting
H
Receiving Report
Magnetic Computer Tape
Example:
Detail Cards
32
Card to tape conversion
Tape
On-Line Computer Storage: disk or drum
Example:
27
Update file

Flow chart information should be maintained in columnar format, with the *main flow line* near the left-hand margin. For example:

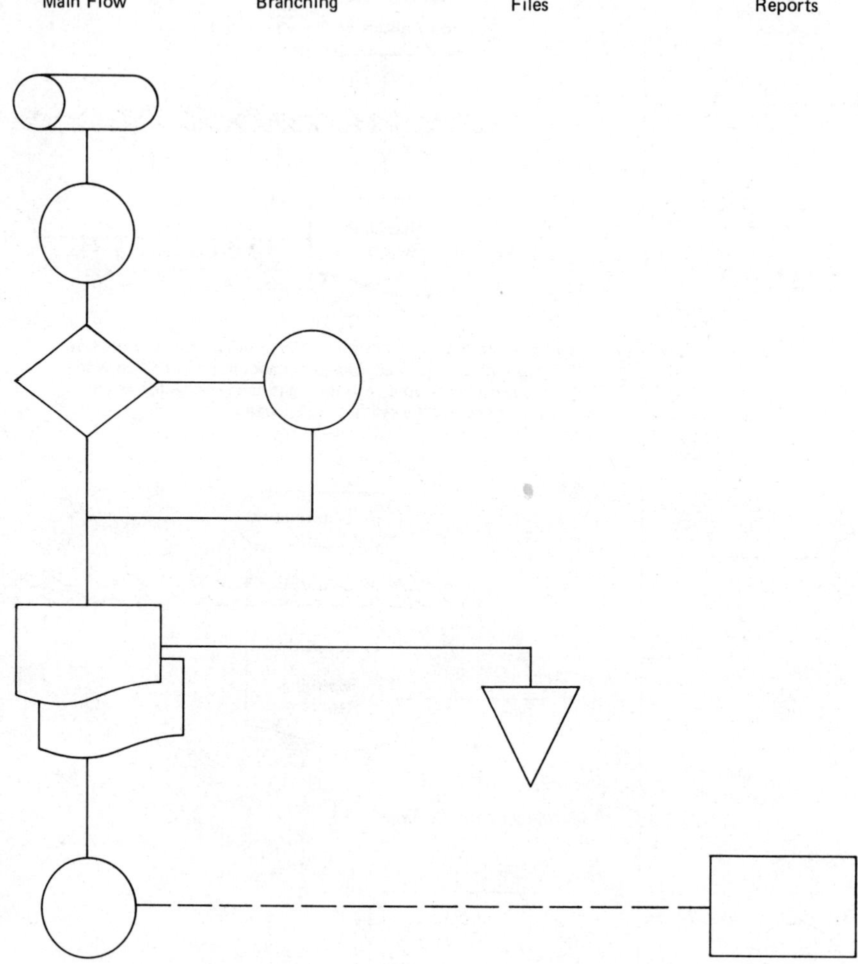

As an example of system flowcharting, the narrative explanation of a company's billing and collection functions is translated into a flow chart. The flow chart is then visually analyzed to reveal any system "weaknesses."

NARRATIVE EXPLANATION[1]

The customer billing and collection functions of the Robinson Company, a small paint manufacturer, are attended to by a receptionist, an accounts receivable clerk, and a cashier who also serves as a secretary. The company's paint products are sold to wholesalers and retail stores.

The following describes all of the procedures performed by the employees of the Robinson Company pertaining to customer billings and collections:

1. The mail is opened by the receptionist who gives the customers' purchase orders to the account receivable clerk. Fifteen to twenty orders are received each day. Under instructions to expedite the shipment of orders, the accounts receivable clerk at once prepares a five-copy sales invoice form which is distributed as follows:
   a. Copy #1 is the customer billing copy and is filed by the accounts receivable clerk until notice of shipment is received.

[1]Adapted from a CPA examination problem.

b. Copy #2 is the accounts receivable department copy and is filed for ultimate posting of the accounts receivable records.
c. Copies #3 and #4 are sent to the shipping department.
d. Copy #5 is sent to the storeroom as authority for release of the goods to the shipping department.

2. After the paint ordered has been moved from the storeroom to the shipping department, the shipping department prepares the bills of lading and labels the cartons. Sales invoice copy #4 is inserted in a carton as a packing slip. After the trucker has picked up the shipment, the customer's copy of the bill of lading and copy #3, on which are noted any undershipments, are returned to the accounts receivable clerk. The company does not "back order" in the event of undershipments; customers are expected to reorder the merchandise. The Robinson Company's copy of the bill of lading is filed by the shipping department.

3. When copy #3 and the customer's copy of the bill of lading are received by the accounts receivable clerk, copies #1 and #2 are completed by numbering them and inserting quantities shipped, unit prices, extensions, discounts, and totals. The accounts receivable clerk then mails copy #1 and the copy of the bill of lading to the customer. Copies #2 and #3 are stapled together.

4. The individual accounts receivable ledger cards are posted by the accounts receivable clerk by a bookkeeping machine procedure whereby the sales register is prepared as a carbon copy of the postings. Postings are made from copy #2, which is then filed, along with staple-attached copy #3, in numerical order. Monthly the general ledger clerk summarizes the sales register for posting to the general ledger accounts.

5. Since the Robinson Company is short of cash, the deposit of receipts is also expedited. The receptionist turns over all mail receipts and related correspondence to the accounts receivable clerk, who examines the checks and determines that the accompanying vouchers or correspondence contains enough detail to permit posting of the accounts. The accounts receivable clerk then endorses the checks and gives them to the cashier, who prepares the daily deposit. No currency is received in the mail and no paint is sold over the counter at the factory.

6. The accounts receivable clerk uses the vouchers or correspondence that accompanied the checks to post the accounts receivable ledger cards. The bookkeeping machine prepares a cash receipts register as a carbon copy of the postings. Monthly the general ledger clerk summarizes the cash receipts register for posting to the general ledger accounts. The accounts receivable clerk also corresponds with customers about unauthorized deductions for discounts, freight or advertising allowances, returns, etc., and prepares the appropriate credit memos. Disputed items of large amount are turned over to the sales manager for settlement. Each month the accounts receivable clerk prepares a trial balance of the open accounts receivable and compares the resultant total with the general ledger control account for accounts receivable.

FLOWCHART EXPLANATION

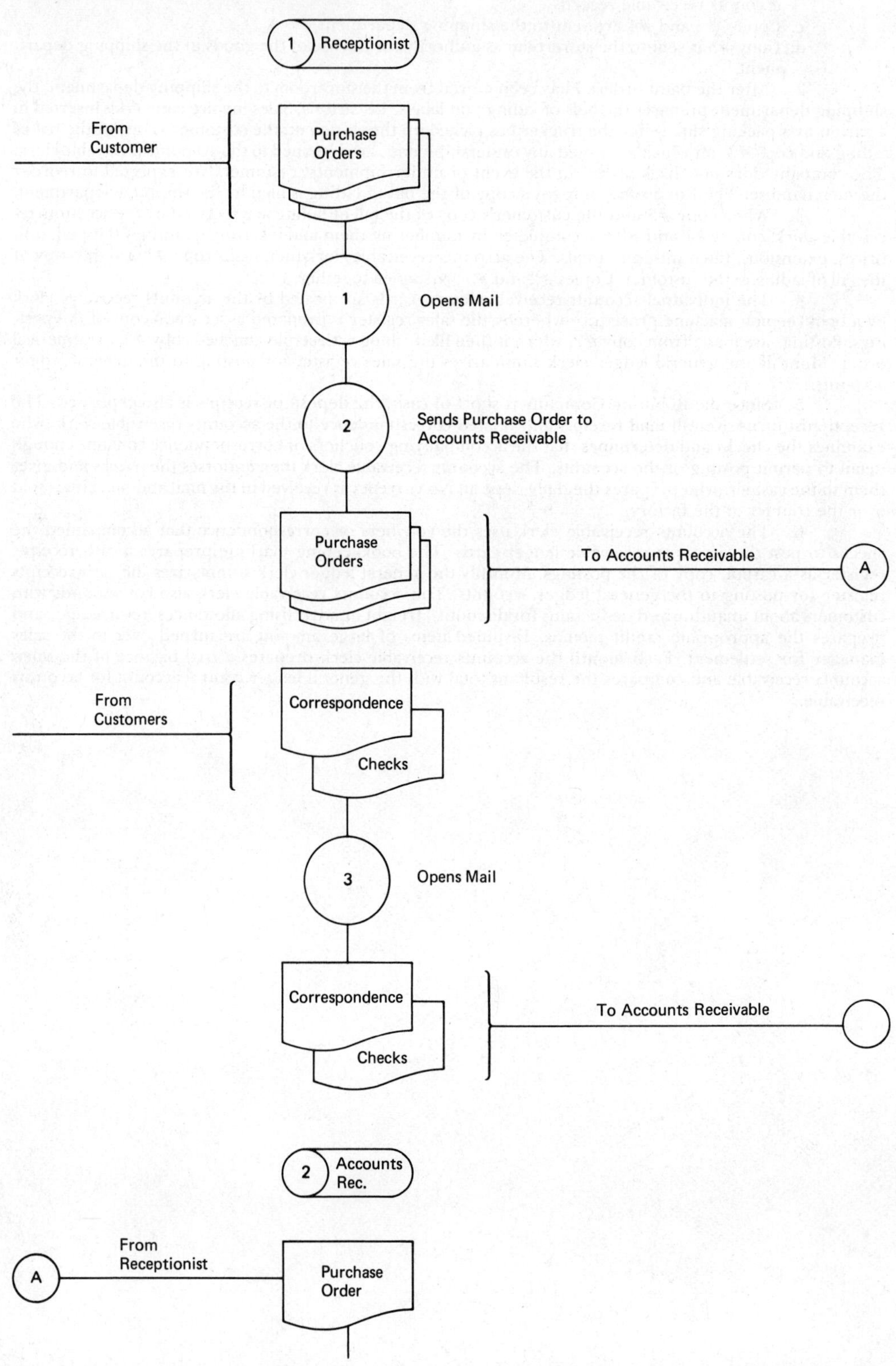

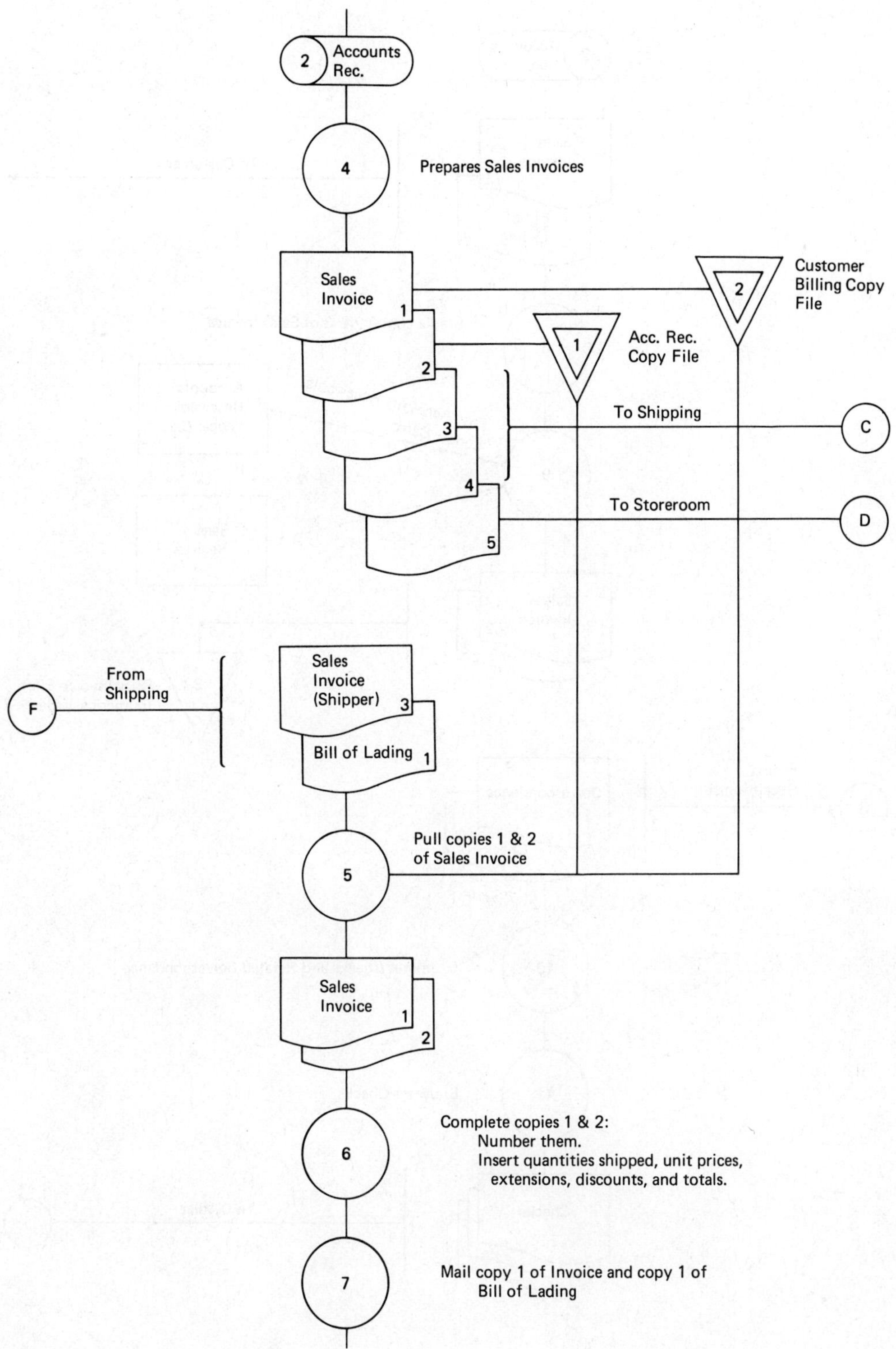

2 Accounts Rec.
4
Prepares Sales Invoices
Sales Invoice
1
2
3
4
5
2
Customer Billing Copy File
1
Acc. Rec. Copy File
To Shipping
C
To Storeroom
D
F
From Shipping
Sales Invoice (Shipper)
3
Bill of Lading
1
Pull copies 1 & 2 of Sales Invoice
5
Sales Invoice
1
2
6
Complete copies 1 & 2:
Number them.
Insert quantities shipped, unit prices, extensions, discounts, and totals.
7
Mail copy 1 of Invoice and copy 1 of Bill of Lading

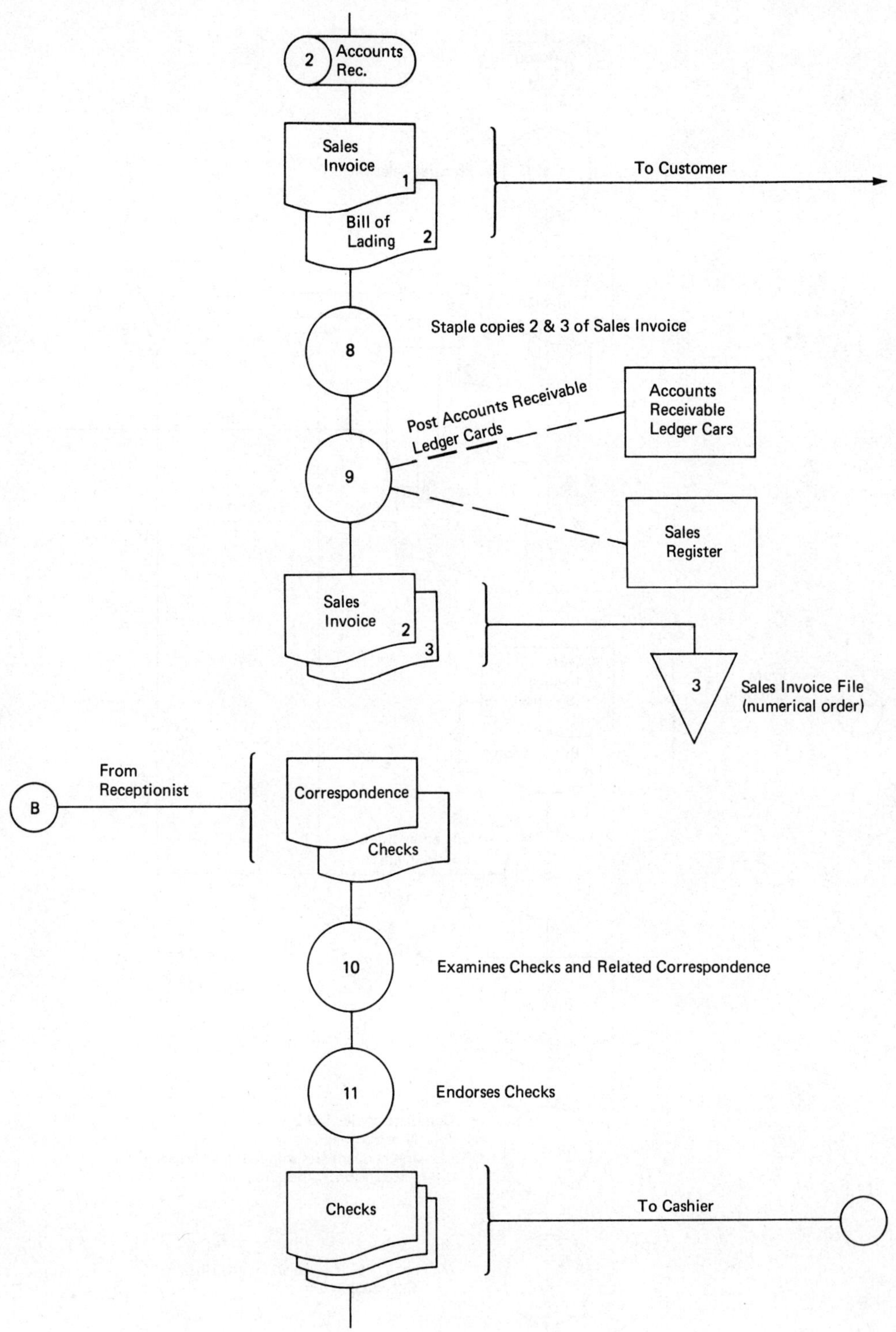
2
Accounts
Rec.
Sales
Invoice
1
Bill of
Lading
2
To Customer
8
Staple copies 2 & 3 of Sales Invoice
Post Accounts Receivable
Ledger Cards
Accounts
Receivable
Ledger Cars
9
Sales
Register
Sales
Invoice
2
3
3
Sales Invoice File
(numerical order)
B
From
Receptionist
Correspondence
Checks
10
Examines Checks and Related Correspondence
11
Endorses Checks
Checks
To Cashier

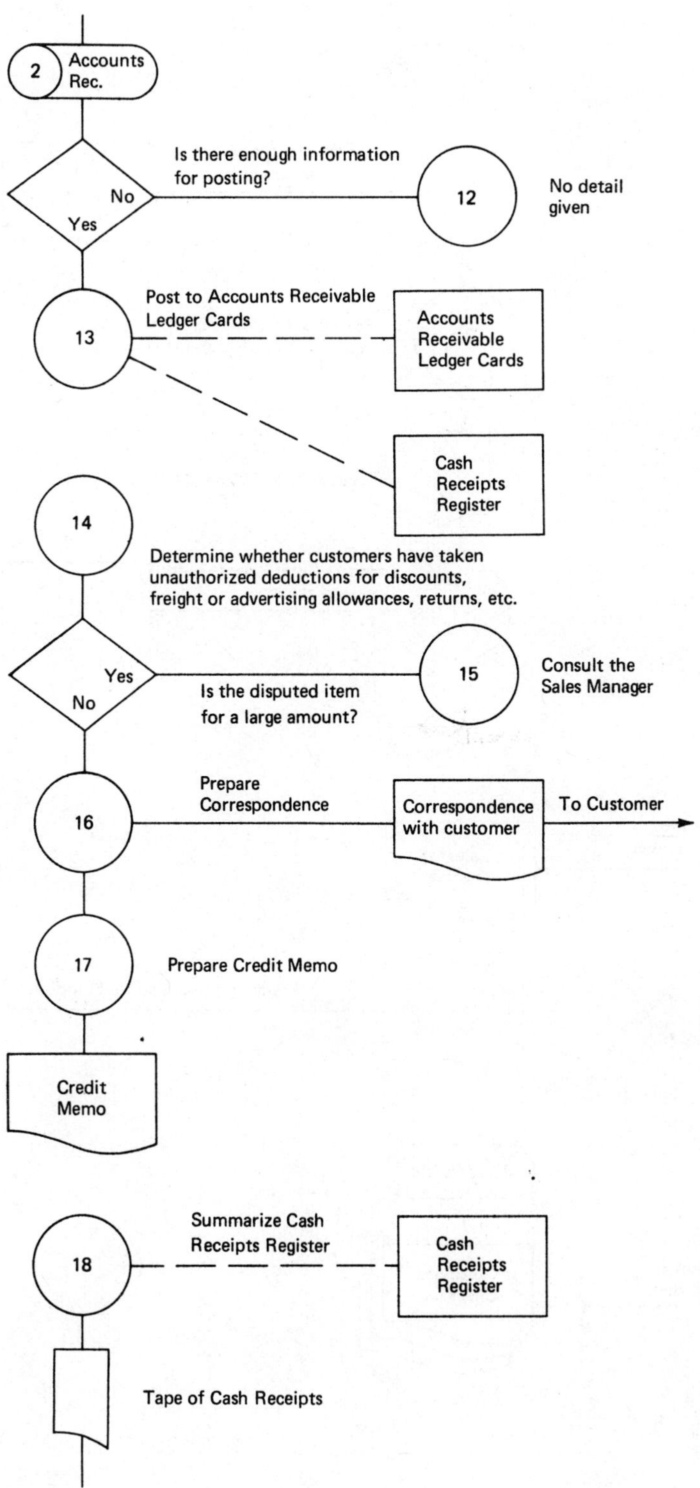
2
Accounts Rec.
Is there enough information for posting?
No
Yes
12
No detail given
13
Post to Accounts Receivable Ledger Cards
Accounts Receivable Ledger Cards
Cash Receipts Register
14
Determine whether customers have taken unauthorized deductions for discounts, freight or advertising allowances, returns, etc.
Yes
No
Is the disputed item for a large amount?
15
Consult the Sales Manager
16
Prepare Correspondence
Correspondence with customer
To Customer
17
Prepare Credit Memo
Credit Memo
18
Summarize Cash Receipts Register
Cash Receipts Register
Tape of Cash Receipts

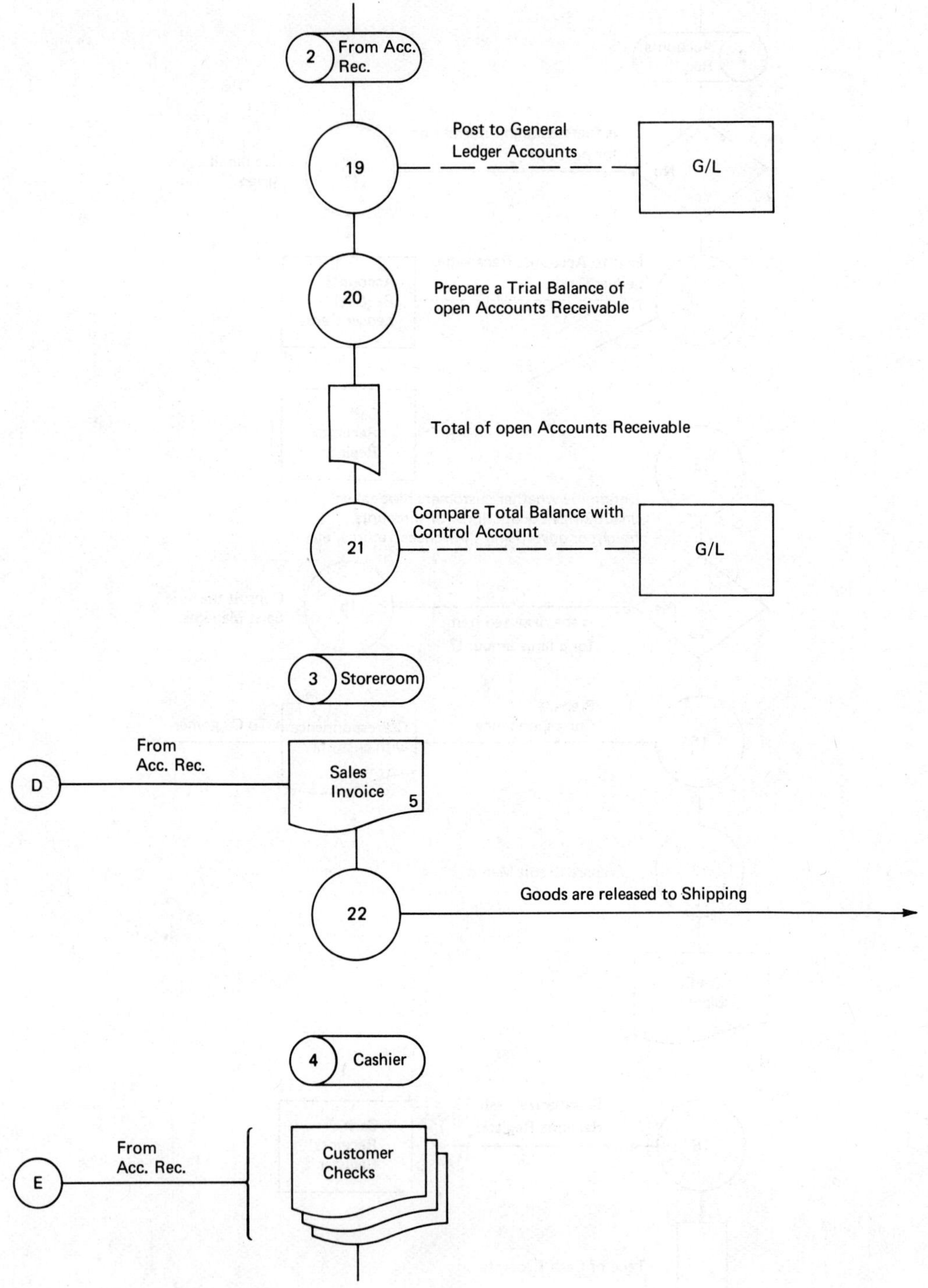
2 From Acc. Rec.
19
Post to General Ledger Accounts
G/L
20
Prepare a Trial Balance of open Accounts Receivable
Total of open Accounts Receivable
21
Compare Total Balance with Control Account
G/L
3 Storeroom
D
From Acc. Rec.
Sales Invoice
5
22
Goods are released to Shipping
4 Cashier
E
From Acc. Rec.
Customer Checks

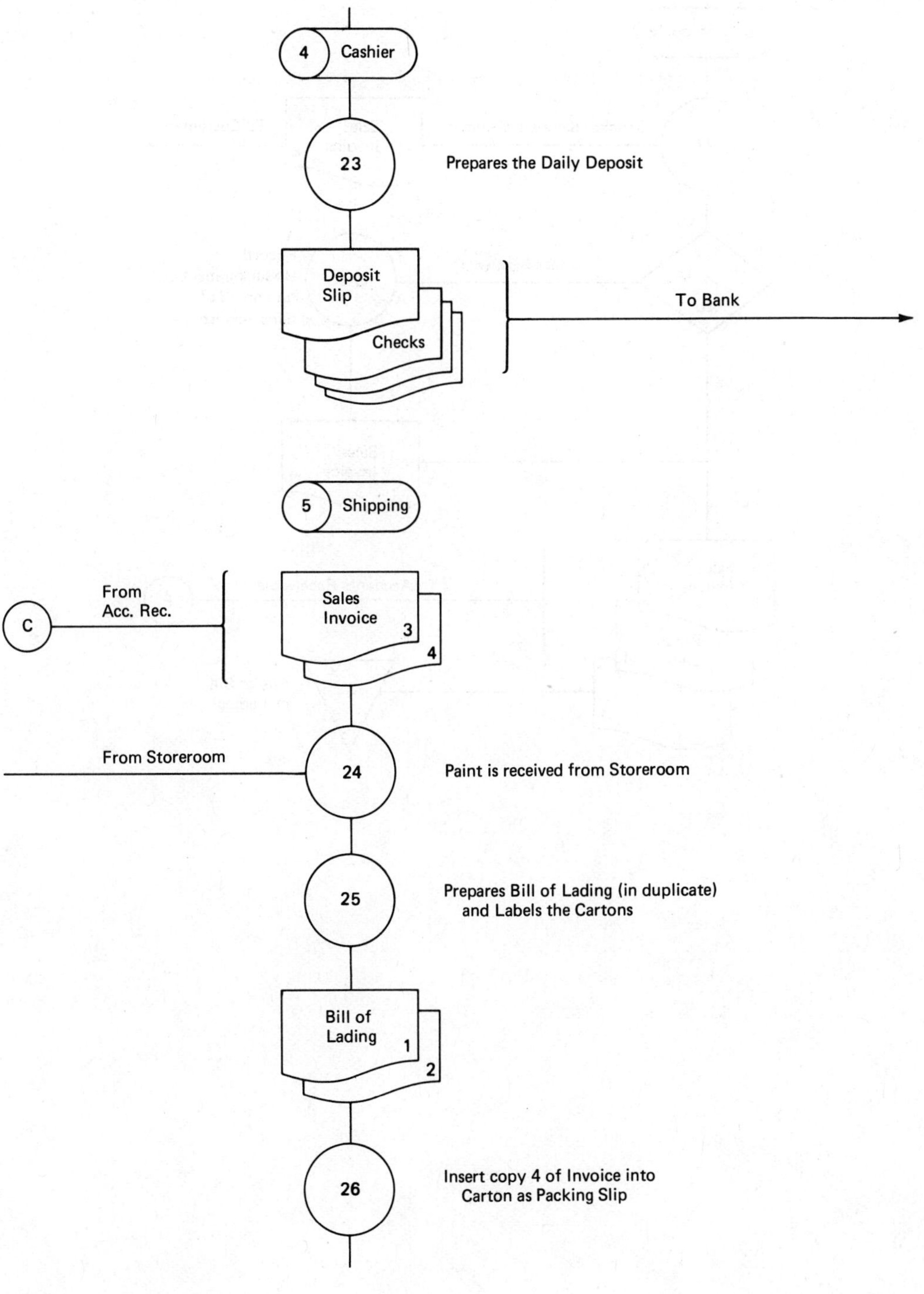
4 Cashier
23
Prepares the Daily Deposit
Deposit Slip
Checks
To Bank
5 Shipping
C
From Acc. Rec.
Sales Invoice
3
4
From Storeroom
24
Paint is received from Storeroom
25
Prepares Bill of Lading (in duplicate) and Labels the Cartons
Bill of Lading
1
2
26
Insert copy 4 of Invoice into Carton as Packing Slip

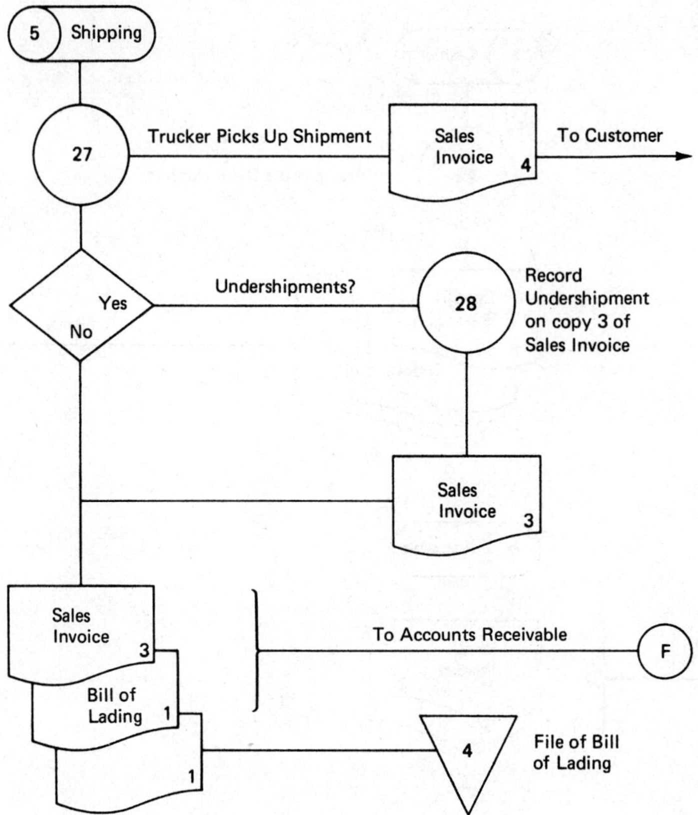
5
Shipping
27
Trucker Picks Up Shipment
Sales Invoice 4
To Customer
Undershipments?
Yes
No
28
Record Undershipment on copy 3 of Sales Invoice
Sales Invoice 3
Sales Invoice 3
Bill of Lading 1
1
To Accounts Receivable
F
4
File of Bill of Lading

SYSTEM WEAKNESSES[2]

The weaknesses of internal control related to customer billings and remittances by the Robinson Company arise in large part from entrusting too many duties to the accounts receivable clerk. Specific weaknesses include the following:

1. The receptionist who opens the mail should prepare a list of the checks received each day, and should stamp each check with an endorsement showing the company's name and the words "For Deposit Only." This listing of receipts and restrictive endorsement of checks should precede the transmission of checks and related documents to the accounts receivable clerk. Each day's list of collections should later be compared with the bank deposit slip and the cash receipts register. These procedures will avoid abstraction of cash and concealment of the theft by improper posting of the customer accounts.

2. The authority to approve deductions by customers for discounts, freight or advertising allowances, returns, etc., should be shifted from the accounts receivable clerk to a responsible person not maintaining customers' accounts or handling cash receipts. At present the accounts receivable clerk could abstract a check and conceal the theft by giving the customer credit for goods returned.

3. The accounts receivable clerk presently prepares sales invoices, has access to cash collections before endorsement, and maintains accounts receivable records. These functions should be separated; otherwise the accounts receivable clerk could deliberately fail to record an invoice and later abstract the customer's check when payment is received.

4. The person who can authorize shipments should not also perform the function of billing the customer. At present the accounts receivable clerk could authorize shipment of goods to himself under a fictitious name, and after shipment, destroy all copies of the invoice rather than recording a receivable. If he did record the receivable he could wipe out the account with an unauthorized credit for a return.

5. Incoices should be reviewed and approved in writing by a person other than the one preparing them. Presently, there is no safeguard against errors by the accounts receivable clerk as to pricing, quantities, discounts, or computations.

6. The monthly trial balance of accounts receivable should be prepared by someone other than the accounts receivable clerk and compared with the general ledger control account. Otherwise, the clerk may conceal a lack of agreement between the subsidiary ledger and the control account to avoid criticism of his work. Underbilling of customers may cause losses to the Robinson Company.

7. All invoices should be serially numbered and all numbers accounted for by a person other than the accounts receivable clerk. At present there is no assurance that all invoices are included in the posting to the control account. Consequently, the accounts receivable clerk is free to hold up invoices to conceal improper shipments or to pave the way to diversion of incoming checks.

8. Apparently Robinson Company does not require approval of a customer's credit before shipment of goods. This weakness may permit sales to customers who cannot or will not pay for the merchandise. Credit approval in writing should be obtained from a credit and collection department before shipment is authorized.

---

[2] Taken from a solution recommended by the AICPA.

APPENDIX E

ACCOUNT CODING

Coding is the *representation* of words or groups of words by numbers and/or symbols. This representation is for the express purpose of providing faster handling, organizing, inputing, storing, and retrieving of data. Some basic considerations for proper coding are:

1. *Expandability:* can the code be expanded without destroying the usefulness and meaning of numbers already assigned, and without the use of secondary codes?
2. *Transcription:* can the code be transcribed easily and with minimum errors?
3. *Decodability:* can the code be deciphered easily?
4. *Security:* can the code be checked for authenticity?
5. *Adaptability:* can the code be easily adapted to machine operations?

STRAIGHT NUMERIC SEQUENCE CODE

This code assigns numbers to data starting with the lowest number and continuing in ascending order. Each new data item is assigned the next open sequence number. For instance, obtain a data list and assign code numbers to the alphabetized or sequenced list:

Alphabetized List:

001 Joseph Albert
002 Samuel Baker
003 Richard Cootes
(etc.)

Sequenced List:

001 6″ Cedar Table Legs
002 8″ Cedar Table Legs
003 12″ Cedar Table Legs
004 24″ Cedar Table Legs
005 6″ Mahogany Table Legs
(etc.)

Disadvantages:

1. Alphabetic sequence (or significant data sequence) cannot be maintained for the addition of new data items.
2. A decoding book is required to decipher the data item represented by the code.

GAPPED NUMERIC SEQUENCE CODE

The objective is to leave enough numbers between data items so that new data can be added constantly, yet maintain the accounts in exact alphabetic and numeric order.

Step 1: Select a gap—say 256.
Step 2: Maintain the gap between the assignment of initial accounts:

1.	Aaron	000–256
2.	Aarons	000–512
3.	Aaronson	000–768

Step 3: A new account is introduced between Aaron and Aarons, say in position 1a:

1.	Aaron, A	000–256
1a.	Aaron, B	?
2.	Aarons	000–512
		768 divided by two = 384

1a, then, is assigned the number 000–384.

Step 4: Add a new account between 1a and 2, say 1b:

1a.	Aaron, B	000–384
1b.	Aaron, C	?
2.	Aarons	000–512
		896 divided by two = 448

1b, then, is assigned the number 000–448.

Disadvantages:

1. File size: 10,000 accounts with a 256 gap would require 2,560,000 numbers or seven digits.
2. Manual errors: filing name cards incorrectly or making an error in computing new numbers.

TELEPHONE MASTER LIST

Numbers are assigned on the basis of listings in the area telephone book on the assumption that the telephone list constitutes a *complete name list.* Under this method, pages and columns in the telephone book are numbered and an account is given a number relative to its position on the page.

Disadvantages:

1. File size may be much more than needed.
2. No provision is made for missing names from unlisted telephone numbers (e.g., in Washington D.C., one-third of all numbers are unlisted).

PARTIAL SEQUENCE CODE

This code is an extension of a straight numeric sequence, except that data items beginning with the same letter are grouped together. Each group of data items is arranged in alphabetic order, with any new names assigned to the next open sequence number.

Step 1: Screen or break down all accounts into small groups using the first two, three, or four letters common to all surnames in the group:

Aa	Am	Ba	Bas
Ad	Anda	Bak	Bea
Al	Andr	Bar	Bec
All	Ar	Barr	Bel

Step 2: Groups should consist of about twenty names. For example, if the file contains 6,000 names, there will be 300 break-downs (6,000 divided by 20).

Step 3: Assign blocks of say 200 numbers to each group. This leaves room to add 180 persons to each group and swell the total file to 60,000 names.

Aa	00-001 – 00-199	Al	00-400 – 00-599
Ad	00-200 – 00-399	All	00-600 – 00-799

Not all sections of the alphabet increase proportionately, however; consequently, certain groups should be assigned a larger block of numbers.

Disadvantages:

Code does not guarantee an exact alphabetic assignment.

COMPLETE SEQUENCE CODE

This coding scheme is similar to a partial sequence, except *gaps* are left between the sequence codes given to the data items on the original list. This enables the list of data items to be maintained in strict alphabetic sequence, by allowing new data items to enter the coding scheme in their correct position. This position is determined by employing the method described for a gapped numeric sequence code.

Step 1: Screen or break down all accounts into small groups using the first two, three, or four letters common to all surnames in the group:

Aa	Am	Ba	Bas
Ad	Anda	Bak	Bea
Al	Andr	Bar	Bec
All	Ar	Barr	Bel

Step 2: A separate page is set up in the codebook for each group. If each page contains 100 data items and a letter designation requires more space, then additional pages are used for that group (e.g., Ba uses pages 10, 11, and 12). The original page assignment is determined by the initial name list, plus possible expansion. With 100 names per page, and 9,000 names (original plus estimated future names), 900 pages will be required. The first three numbers of the code designate the page.

Aa	001–001	–	001–100
Ad	002–001	–	002–100
Al	003–001	–	003–100
All	004–001	–	004–100
Am	005–001	–	006–100
Anda	007–001	–	007–100
(etc.)			

Step 3: Divide the number of original and future names by the number of original names to obtain the *gap* between codes given in the initial name list. For instance, if the future names number 8,000 and the initial names number 1,000, then 9,000 divided by 1,000 gives a gap of 9 spaces between names on the initial list. If the division produces a remainder, the lowest whole number should be used as the gap. The page number together with the assigned *gapped* sequence number constitutes the code.

Baar, Andrew	011–001
Bailey, Joseph	011–010
Baker, Clyde	011–019
Ball, John	011–028
Bamby, William	011–037
Banker, Charles	011–046
(etc.)	

Step 4: New names are assigned a code number according to the gap procedure described for the gapped numeric sequence code.

DIEBOLD ALPHA NUMERIC SYSTEM (DANS)

This coding system maintains true alphabetic access to operational files, is adaptable to any numbering requirements, and eliminates the need for gap calculations or cross-reference files. The method is basically an extension of the gapped numeric sequence code, but it provides a preprinted register sheet with a standard gap of 32 numbers. New numbers, then, can be assigned visually, thus avoiding the problem of manual computational error. There is also an overflow provision so that, out of 1,000 numbers, the 900s are reserved for assigning numbers to overflow accounts.

BLOCK CODE

The block code reserves blocks of numbers in a special *item classification.* Generally, such blocks are portions of a sequence code. For example:

Code	Item	Type
1	8″ Table Legs	Cedar
2	"	Mahogany
3	"	Pine
4	"	Walnut
5	10″ Table Legs	Cedar
6	"	Mahogany
7	"	Pine
8	"	Walnut
(etc.)		

GROUP CLASSIFICATION CODE

This code classifies data items into major and minor groups. The first number of the code represents the major financial statement classification (e.g., asset), the second represents the major account category (e.g., cash), and the third represents the explicit account (e.g., demand deposits). This coding scheme is particularly amenable to machine sorting where the selection of an entire group can be obtained from a one-column sort. A comprehensive example of group classification is contained in Appendix A.

SIGNIFICANT-DIGIT CODE

The significant-digit code provides a visual identification of data items represented. Numeric digits of the code represent such attributes as weight, size, volume, distance, and temperature. For example,

010	10 gallon barrel
020	20 " "
030	30 " "
045	45 " "
410–018	#18 insulated electrical wire
410–016	#16 " " "
410–014	#14 " " "
410–012	#12 " " "

(The number 410 is a group classification code for insulated electrical wire.)

Disadvantages:

Code must be used in conjunction with another code in order to avoid duplication of assigned numbers.

MNEMONIC SYMBOL CODE

This code assigns a series of numbers and letters to identify the data item explicitly. For instance, the code for a brown leather attaché case, measuring 20″ x 14″ x 6″, might be:

ALB20146

where

A = attaché case (item)
L = leather (material)
B = brown (color)
20 = length
14 = width
6 = thickness

Disadvantages:

1. Duplication can easily occur.
2. Code length may vary greatly.

3. Possible misinterpretation of the meaning of side-by-side symbols.
4. Difficulty in adapting to machine use due to length variation and nonuniform mixing of numbers and letters.

VALIDITY CODES

These codes have an express purpose of serving as a means to later check on the validity of coded information. The codes can be either secondary or primary. A check digit can be added as a final digit code, and thus play a secondary coding role, or it can be used to formulate the primary code itself.

SECONDARY VALIDITY CODE

This code is a *final digit code*, and is *strictly a secondary assignment*. Its *meaning* bears no relation to the primary code. The number or numbers added by this code can be used as a special identification, or more frequently, as a *check digit* for determining the authenticity of the primary code.

Disadvantages:

1. May interfere with the correct interpretation of the primary code.
2. May cause the selection and assignment of a primary code to be limited.
3. Adds to the total code length.

Two schemes for instituting a final digit as a check on the validity of a primary code are:

Double-Add-Double Method (D-A-D)

Basic Number 12-436

Step 1: Double 6.................12
Step 2: Add 3 3
Step 3: Double 4................ 8
Step 4: Add 2 2
Step 5: Double 1................ 2
Step 6: Add the *digits:*

$$1 + 2 + 3 + 8 + 2 + 2 = \underline{\underline{18}}$$

Step 7: Subtract 18 from nearest multiple of 10:

$$20 - 18 = \underline{\underline{2}}$$

Step 8: The mathematically computed check digit is 2.
Step 9: The entire code now appears as 12–436–2.
Other examples:

Basic Number	Check Digit	Coded Number
248–711	4	248–711–4
8642	1	8642–1
034–32–612	4	034–32–612–4

Modulus 11 Method

The purpose of this method is to provide a positive check on transpositions of all types.

Step 1: Multiply each digit of the account number by 2, 3, 4, 5, 6, and 7 successively:

Account No.:	1	2	4 –	3	6	2
Multiplier:	7	6	5	4	3	2
	7	12	20	12	18	4

Step 2: Add the resulting numbers:

$$7 + 12 + 20 + 12 + 18 + 4 = \underline{\underline{73}}$$

Step 3: Divide the total by 11:

$$73/11 = \underline{\underline{6}}, \text{ plus a remainder of } \underline{\underline{7}}$$

Step 4: Subtract the remainder of 7 from 11 to find the check digit.
Step 5: The entire code now appears as 124–362–4.

Other examples:

Basic Number	Check Digit	Coded Number
248–711	10	248–711–10
8642	8	8642–8
4823–0122	3	4823–0122–3[1]

PRIMARY VALIDITY CODE

This code is constructed by a scheme which allows the assigned number to later be mathematically checked for authenticity. No additional final digit is required by this code; however, the code itself is determined by the selection of arbitrary intervals and/or gaps. For instance, the following two methods employee a built-in check for determining permissable code numbers.

Constant Remainder Method

Step 1: Select a constant remainder, e.g., 5.
Step 2: Select a constant interval, e.g., 12.
Step 3: Establish a numbering system, e.g.:

00–005 – constant remainder
00–017
00–029
00–041
00–053
00–065
00–077
•
•
•
00–389

Step 4: Divide by constant interval and if constant remainder is the balance, the number is valid; e.g., 389 divided by 12 = 32 and a remainder of 5.

Gap System

The purpose is to leave numbers for future assignment and to place these new numbers in alphabetic position.

Step 1: Select a number gap, e.g., 32, 64, 128, 256, 512, which is divisible by 2.
Step 2: The constant remainder method can be applied to determine all usable numbers for the gap system, e.g., if the gap is 64 it may be multiplied by the constant interval 12 to which the constant remainder of 5 is added to yield the first usable number:

$$64 \times 12 = 768$$
$$\text{Add } 5 \quad +5$$
$$\text{First number} = \underline{\underline{773}}$$

Step 3: The "gap multiple" (64 × 12) is used to determine the next usable numbers:

773
1541
2309
3077
3845

Step 4: Divide by constant interval and if constant remainder is the balance the number is valid; e.g., 3845 divided by 12 = 320 and a remainder of 5.

[1]When the number of digits in a code *exceeds six,* the multiplier sequence repeats itself:

Account No.:	4	8	2	3	0	1	2	2
Multiplier:	3	2	7	6	5	4	3	2

subject index

author index